Brian McFarlane

AN
AUTOBIOGRAPHY
OF
BRITISH CINEMA

as told by the filmmakers and actors who made it

Foreword by Julie Christie

Methuen

The views of the interviewees in *An Autobiography of British Cinema* are not necessarily those of the editor or the publisher.

Published by Methuen 1997

Some material from this edition was previously published
in *Sixty Voices* in 1992 by British Film Institute
An Autobiography of British Cinema first published
in Great Britain in 1997 by Methuen,
Random House, 20 Vauxhall Bridge Road, London SW1V 2SA

Random House Australia (Pty) Limited
20 Alfred Street, Milsons Point, Sydney,
New South Wales 2061, Australia

Random House New Zealand Limited
18 Poland Road, Glenfield
Auckland 10, New Zealand

Random House South Africa (Pty) Limited
Endulini, 5A Jubilee Road, Parktown 2193, South Africa

Random House UK Limited Reg. No. 954009

A CIP catalogue record for this book
is available from the British Library

ISBN 0 413 70520 X

Typeset in Gill Sans and Times
by Deltatype Ltd, Birkinhead
Printed and bound in Great Britain
by Butler & Tanner Ltd, Frome and London

This book is dedicated to
the memory of Lindsay Anderson

Contents

Illustrations

Foreword

Hollywood, with its apparently limitless resources, so often seems to overshadow British cinema. We tend not to value fully what has been produced in this country: British cinema, at its best, is truly distinctive. There is a body of films we can point to and say: 'Those are British films. They could not have come from anywhere else.'

There have been obvious high points of achievement. The crisis of World War II produced some of the most memorable films ever made here (or anywhere else) and the boom in British films continued after the war when people like Michael Powell, David Lean and Carol Reed did some of their best work. Then there were the great days of Ealing comedies and popular successes like the *Carry On* films and the Hammer horror series.

I think I came into films at a very exciting time, which is the sort of thing that becomes clear in hindsight. My first films were part of the tradition of British comedy and it was only later I realised how skilful some of those players were. It was a time when British cinema was changing, when a new realism and class awareness was making itself felt, and I was lucky to be in some of the films that helped to produce those changes. It is true that the industry has suffered some terrible crises since then, but I think there have been encouraging signs since the 1980s of new life at work in British cinema.

Brian McFarlane's book is called *An Autobiography of British Cinema* because it is the story as remembered by those who made the films. We hear about – and from – key filmmakers and about the films that made history in one way or other. The book also gives us an insight into the less well-known aspects of British cinema: into the work of those behind the camera (directors, of course, and producers, but also art directors, editors, writers, music directors, cameramen) and some of those who were involved in the industrial side. We hear not just about the big films known to everyone, but also the less well-known, the ones that filled out the programme in the days of the double bill, about films decried by critics at the time but which now seem fascinating as products of their time.

Over-all, we get a story of fifty or more years of filmmaking, with all the ups and downs of this very volatile industry. I am glad to be able to write a Foreword to a book which is in many ways long overdue.

Introduction

This book is a story of British cinema told by those who made it. Hence, 'Autobiography'. It is *not* an encyclopedia, exhaustive and all-embracing; it is *not* a conventional survey; and it is *not* a critical appraisal. Above all, the subtitle means what it says: the book offers a range of interlocking first-person accounts – sometimes complementary, sometimes contradictory – of more than fifty years of British cinema, centred on the period 1930 to 1980. These were decades which saw both peaks and declines.

Britain's is a very rich, complex cinema, both for the films themselves *and* for their relation to the social reality which produces them and of which they offer no doubt distorting reflections. Yet, there is still a curious sense of its being inadequately known and mapped. Imperial Britain may have colonised much of the world in its heyday, but British cinema never achieved anything like the effect of Hollywood in the 'colonising of our imagination'. Discussion about it has suffered from that reckless auteurism which picks out alpine heights (Powell, Lean, Reed) and, in doing so, obscures a good deal of attractive and revealing work in the foothills, let alone on the plains.

British cinema nevertheless has its own distinctiveness: there are obviously major periods (for example, World War II and just after), major studios (Ealing, London Films and others), and key filmmakers and films, and some of these have been canvassed in various ways. What is missing from existing accounts, though, is a sense of what it was like to be part of a prolific industry – or rather, to quote Roy Boulting in a recent interview, to be taking part in a process of 'creation on the scale of industry'. This *Autobiography* seeks to give a sense of this from the point of view of those who worked in British cinema, who in varying degrees saw its strengths and weaknesses, and saw that both were essentially British. They recognised the difficulties of sustaining an indigenous industry in the face of the dominance of American money and the extraordinary appeal of American cinema. They realised that the British theatrical and literary heritage for decades left its cinema in the shade. They are alert to these and many other matters of continuing importance in the struggle to assume anything like a national identity in a commercially viable cinema.

From this book, I hope a sort of verbal mosaic will emerge, offering a range of insights, not from critical outsiders who have different perceptions to offer, but from those whose knowledge, partial as it must always be, is drawn from within. If you actually worked at Pinewood or Merton Park Studios or were directed by Anthony Asquith or acted with Dirk Bogarde or Margaret Lockwood or edited for Hitchcock, you might be expected to have insights that are necessarily denied to the critic or theorist. Put together, for instance, what director John Schlesinger, actor Julie Christie and costume designer Julie Harris have to say about *Darling* and you may get a new angle on that archetypal '60s film. One would expect a diversity of views from those behind the camera, from those in front of it and from those responsible for selling the finished product. Consider, for instance, the range of opinions about working for Michael Powell or on key films such as *In Which We Serve*. For readers browsing in the book, the Index will help them to find evidence of such diversity in relation to films, filmmakers, and studios, to experiences with services film units during World War II, to Hollywood and its influence on British cinema, and to recurring matters of legislation and finance, such as 'quota quickies' and the Eady levy.

*

The idiosyncratic English novelist, Ivy Compton-

Burnett, once spoke about how books grow out of other books. The genesis of *An Autobiography of British Cinema* is in two other books. First, in 1989 I began the co-authoring of a book called *New Australian Cinema: Sources and Parallels in American and British Film* (1992), in which my brief was to compare Australian cinema of the 1970s and '80s with the British cinema heyday of the 1930s and '40s. This led me to interview about thirty survivors of that rich period of British film. They gave me far more – and far more interesting – information than I felt should be relegated to footnotes in an academic text, and it occurred to me that this material might well be fascinating to a wider audience. So, after two further visits to England (and British cinema has essentially been 'English' cinema; most of the major studios were/are within easy distance of London), I had more than doubled the number of interviews. The British Film Institute then published these as *Sixty Voices* (1992).

This new book contains about 186 entries: the earlier sixty interviews reappear, several of them in considerably extended form; I have added about eighty new interviews; and the remainder are entries on key figures who either have died or were unavailable for interview, drawing as far as possible on their own quoted words on aspects of their work, in order to maintain the idea of 'autobiography'.

A number of principles were at work in determining which voices would be chosen for interview and therefore to speak for and about British cinema, but availability had to override every other consideration. Some people one would like very much to have talked to eluded all one's attempts to track them down. Several replied very courteously that they didn't enjoy talking about the past, or that (in two cases) though they loved acting, they made it a rule never to try to talk about it, and such preferences had to be respected. Some, too, in these days of international filmmaking, were too busy dashing from continent to continent. In some cases, potential difficulties were overcome by interviews conducted on the telephone, on audio-cassette or by letter, but the overwhelming majority were the result of face-to-face encounters.

The key criterion was to choose people to represent various sides of the industry, and at different periods – not only its creative personnel (directors, producers, writers, actors and a range of other behind-camera collaborators), but also figures prominent from an industry point of view (agents, a studio head, Rank's managing director). I wanted to include those who could speak for British film-making at its various levels of achievement – and it becomes clear that we are talking of a very hierarchically organised and perceived industry or art form. Also, there are very obvious highpoints from which British cinema gained immediate and lasting prestige: one thinks, for instance, of the literary strain of the immediate post-war boom period, typified by such films as *Great Expectations* and *Hamlet*; or of the New Wave of social realism ushered in at the end of the '50s by *Room at the Top* and lasting through to the early '60s. It was instructive to talk to those who, like Lindsay Anderson or Karel Reisz, were prepared to speculate about these large movements in British cinema. There were those who had very successful and long careers working in the mainstream (the team of Ralph Thomas and Betty Box, for instance) and those who have elected to work as independents (say, Peter Greenaway or Sally Potter). Then there were those who had worked hard on small budgets and tight schedules to make entertaining second features, or 'B' films, from the '40s to the '60s (Robert Baker's account of Tempean Films is an example), and those who, like Pat Jackson or Ken Annakin, cut their teeth on wartime documentary and whose subsequent careers were influenced by this. There were those who admired and sometimes worked in Hollywood and those who stood opposed to what they saw as its tinsel values. And there are many examples of people whose careers have been pursued in the theatre and television, as well as on the big screen. I wanted all these and other voices to make themselves heard in this autobiographical mosaic. If your favourite star is missing and a filmmaker you haven't heard of is included, the reason is probably to do with this urge to suggest what a complex and many-stranded story it is that is being told. The autobiography of British cinema is not to be told by its stars alone, crucially influential though they are in shaping our perception of it; what we see up on the screen is the end product, and to love that is, for many of us, to be interested in how it came to be so.

A large number of the participants in British cinema, past and present, were willing to be interviewed, and they were extraordinarily frank, obliging, and co-operative. I operated on the basis that, whatever they said in interview, they would have the final say over what got published, and I think this produced a freer discussion. This is not, then, oral history in its purist form, but it does mean that what is printed has been offered in every case to the interviewees to amend, so that they would be willing to stand by remarks attributed to them. Where they have had second thoughts about something they have said, it has seemed only fair to them to print the revisions.

Very often I was struck by the modesty of the interviewees in appraising their achievements; maybe fiercer egos would have engendered a tougher industry. I was also impressed by the sense of camaraderie that kept bitchy comments at bay, though I did like the editing principle of one actor who, when I said I'd sent the transcript for her vetting, replied, 'I'll cut out anything nasty I've said about other people – unless it's true!' Regretfully, in the interests of avoiding litigation, I've had to cut out some remarks which were preceded by the instruction, 'Turn off that machine and I'll tell you something really interesting.'

The fifty-odd entries interspersed with the interviews were similarly chosen as representative of their periods, of certain key tendencies in British cinema, of their importance to the industry, and/or of popular taste. In choosing them, I suspect that inevitably some element of personal preference has crept in, despite conscientious efforts to suppress this. However, I was guided above all by the need to plug gaps left by the interviews, either because they were individually important figures or because of the range of their references. For instance, it seemed important to represent the prolific 1930s, many of whose exponents are no longer with us, by such icons as Gracie Fields and filmmakers such as Victor Saville and Alexander Korda. The influential documentary strain in British filmmaking is represented by John Grierson and Humphrey Jennings. In later decades, there are pieces on such stars as Sean Connery and Michael Caine who, after their beginnings in British cinema of the '60s, went on to international, largely Hollywood-based careers. (The lure of Hollywood is, of course, a recurring motif in the story of British cinema.) These brief career sketches are not primarily critical assessments; that would be at odds with the spirit of the book. I have tried to make the entries under their names reflect a consensual view of their places in British cinema history, and to make them derive from the published utterances of the persons concerned. In tracking down these utterances, I have drawn on such sources as biographies and autobiographies, popular magazines and critical journals, television interviews and newspaper reporting. The

sources are in each case given in footnotes in the belief that they may be useful to future researchers.

My brief Afterword mentions those who, having made some mark now, seem likely to be key shapers of the future. I have chosen them as representative of certain strains in contemporary British cinema. Should this book be updated, I hope the people referred to in the Afterword, and the others they stand for, will be the subjects of full-scale interviews.

There are no doubt other 'autobiographies' of British cinema that await the telling; I look forward to them, especially if they cut across, or throw new light on, the 'evidence' offered here. My own pleasure in British cinema is such that I want to see it fully chronicled. Increasingly though, I feel there is no such thing as the *full* story: it is certainly not to be confined in an account of Great Works: there is only a multiplicity of facts and perceptions and recollections, from which patterns may be seen to emerge.

*

In an undertaking of this size, it must be clear that thanks are due to a great many people. First, and most obviously to the interviewees themselves. Without their co-operation, the book would not have been possible. Some, for instance, helped by establishing a chain of introductions which led me from one fruitful encounter to another. I am very grateful for the care they took in attending to the details of the transcripts to ensure these reflected what they intended.

Second, I must thank Sam Oliphant, Eleni Goimil and, especially, my daughter Sophie, all in Australia, for their heroic work in the preparation of a hefty manuscript. Third, various staff of the British Film Institute, London, notably Philip Dodd, Ed Buscombe, John Atkinson and Dawn King in BFI Publishing, the staff of the Stills Department at the BFI and the staff of the BFI Archive and Viewing Services (including Elaine Burrows and Bryony Dixon) have been helpful over several years. Fourth, the staff of the Australian Film Institute Library, Melbourne, especially Carol Abbott and Aysen Mustafa, constantly gave me assistance well beyond the call of duty.

I must thank, too, the Australian Government's Research Council for a grant which enabled me to conduct the interviews and research which provide the basis for the book, and Monash University

Department of English which gave me the leave and support to pursue the project. I am also very grateful to members of the BECTU (Broadcasting Entertainment Cinematograph and Theatre Union) History Project for their help in providing me with valuable contacts.

In Michael Earley, of Methuen, I have had an exemplary publisher. He made a number of suggestions I was happy to act upon and disagreed with me just enough for me to realise that he was thinking seriously about the entire venture. I should also like to acknowledge my indebtedness to the meticulous copy-editing of Liz Hornby and to Desk Editor, Helena Beynon for her care on the final manuscript.

To the Melbourne office of Reed Books, especially Julie Pinkham and Fran Berry, I owe thanks for their initial encouragement of the proposal and for presenting it to the right people.

Finally, I must thank my family for bearing with the more or less obsessive activity the book has entailed over several years. My wife Geraldine, particularly, has my love and my main thanks for her support and forbearance in the face of various sorts of domestic neglect during the long gestation that has attended the birth of this book.

Brian McFarlane
Melbourne, 1996

Note on the filmographies

Films are listed under the person's main contribution, for example: **Director**. Where other functions are credited in addition to, or instead of, the main contribution, these are noted. For example, '(& pr)', in a director's filmography indicates that he or she also produced the film; '(pr)' means producer only.

The following abbreviations are used:

adpt	adapter
ass	assistant
assoc	associate
auth	author of original story
cam op	camera operator
des	designer
dir	director
ed	editor
exec	executive
narr	narrator
ph	cinematographer (lighting cameraman, chief photographer or director of photography)
pr	producer
sc	scriptwriter
sup	supervising
uncr	uncredited

Dates in the filmographies are British release dates; interviewees may refer to the year in which they were working on the film.

John Addison

b. 1920

Composer: *Fame is the Spur* (1947), *The Guinea Pig* (1948), *Seven Days to Noon* (1950), *Pool of London, High Treason* (1951), *Brandy for the Parson, Hour of 13*, *Operation Hurricane* (1952), *The Man Between, Time Bomb*, *The Queen's Colours, The Red Beret* (1953), *The 'Maggie', The Black Knight, End of the Road, Make Me an Offer, One Good Turn* (1954), *That Lady, Touch and Go*, *Highways of Tomorrow, Josephine and Men, Cockleshell Heroes* (1955), *Private's Progress, Reach for the Sky, It's Great to be Young, Three Men in a Boat* (1956), *The Shiralee, Barnacle Bill, Lucky Jim* (1957), *I Was Monty's Double* (1958), *Carlton-Browne of the FO, Look Back in Anger* (1959), *School for Scoundrels, The Entertainer, The French Mistress* (1960), *His and Hers, A Taste of Honey* (1961), *Go to Blazes, The Loneliness of the Long Distance Runner* (1962), *Tom Jones, Girl in the Headlines* (1963), *Girl with Green Eyes, Guns at Batasi, The Uncle, The Peaches* (1964), *The Amorous Adventures of Moll Flanders, The Loved One, I was Happy Here* (1965), *A Fine Madness, Torn Curtain, The Honey Pot* (1966), *Smashing Time* (1967), *The Charge of the Light Brigade* (1968), *Start the Revolution Without Me, Country Dance, Hamlet* (1969), *Mr Forbush and the Penguins* (1971), *Sleuth* (1972), *The Concert* (short), *Luther* (1973), *Dead Cert, Back of Beyond* (1974), *Ride a Wild Pony* (1975), *Swashbuckler, The Seven-per-cent Solution, Joseph Andrews* (1976), *A Bridge Too Far* (1977), *Death in Canaan, Bastard* (1978), *The Pilot* (1979), *Highpoint* (1980), *Charles & Diana: A Royal Love Story* (1982), *Strange Invaders* (1983), *The Ultimate Solution of Grace Quigley* (1984), *Code Name: Emerald* (1985), *Mr Boogedy* (1986), *Bride of Boogedy* (1987)
* Short film.

As well as the seventy-odd film scores John Addison has composed, and almost always conducted, he has also been enormously productive in composing for the concert hall and the theatre. For the latter, he has written music for many notable productions of both classic and modern plays, including, for example, the *Hamlet* which opened the National Theatre and Ionesco's *The Chairs* at the Royal Court. In the history of British film music, he is the great survivor, his versatility no less remarkable than his musicianship. He worked his way through the studio system of the 1950s, assisted (as many have been) by the Boulting brothers, then adapted readily to the demands of the new realism of the early '60s, working often with Tony Richardson. His work contributes to a wide range of film genres and has been at the service of notable directors from both sides of the Atlantic. *Interview date: November 1995*

What were the chief emphases of your training at the Royal College of Music? Was composition for the cinema an element of this training?

At the Royal College of Music there were no courses specifically for film composing. I studied theory and orchestration with the composer Gordon Jacob, who was a strong influence and to whom I owe a great deal. When I first went to the College, my first subject was piano and my second study was oboe. However, my studies were interrupted by World War II after my first year at the RCM, and I didn't resume until the war ended six years later when I went back for a further three years, but I gave up the piano studies, switched from oboe to clarinet and my principal study was in fact Composition with Dr Jacob.

The Instrumental studies that I did were invaluable from the point of view of simply being involved with some of the finest instrumentalists in the country as teachers, even though I never went on to earn a living as an instrumentalist myself. I got the ARCM Degree (that's Associate of the Royal College of Music) and I also won the Sullivan Prize for Composition.

When I finished as a student, I began doing some teaching at the RCM. However, the opportunity to be involved in composing film music was entirely through Roy Boulting, whom I'd met in the Army and who had a sort of hunch that I might be good at film music. He started by giving me small jobs to do in the studios. I did also go to a couple of recordings with Gordon Jacob when he was doing a film at one time.

Am I right in thinking that, apart from composing for films and television, you have also composed for plays and ballets? Do you find one medium more demanding, more stimulating than the others?

You're right about my having written music for the theatre; however, unlike most young composers who started in the theatre and progressed, if that's the word, later into films, my first paid jobs were writing film music for the Boulting brothers who, after I did the score for *Seven Days to Noon*, put me under a yearly contract, with their company Charter Films. This was a pretty light-hearted document because by this time Roy Boulting had become a great personal friend.

My work in the theatre started later through Tony Richardson, who had heard some of my film music and evidently liked it and asked me to write the score for John Osborne's play *The Entertainer*, which starred Laurence Olivier and which involved me in the English Stage Company at the Royal Court Theatre, for whom I did a number of plays. I had also been commissioned to write a score for a ballet, *Carte Blanche*, by the Sadler's Wells ballet company.

At this time (and perhaps ever since), in London it was possible to compose music for films and theatre and continue to write concert music, and after leaving the RCM as a student I was fortunate in getting commissions from the BBC and also from some very good instrumentalists to write works for them. I was also taken on by a music publisher and in time I progressed to Oxford University Press, which of course I was very thrilled about, because they published Walton and Vaughan Williams and other very well-known composers.

Does writing for films make very different demands on a composer?

Between films, the theatre and the concert hall, obviously composing concert music is the most personal. It can also be fairly lonely but films and theatre are collaborative, so if you don't like working with other people it's better to stay away from them. In films you're mainly involved with the director, who is the leader of the team; in theatre you're involved with the actors as well as the director, and I enjoy the differences between these various experiences and it gives one pleasant variety in one's work.

You may well be the most prolific of all music directors in British cinema. This was really due to the Boultings?

It was entirely through Roy Boulting of the Boulting brothers. The first complete score I did for them was *Seven Days to Noon*, but before that I did one or two small jobs, including writing the school song for *The Guinea Pig*, a school story which starred a young Richard Attenborough.

How do you conceive of the music director's function? Do you think of it as an adjunct to the visual images, reinforcing them, or can it ever work to provide a conflict with the images?

A composer's score for a film is one of many elements on the soundtrack and is, by its very nature, an adjunct to the visual images. In many instances it reinforces what is happening on the screen and in others it provides a counterpoint. Its most powerful effect is on the emotions of the audience and it can influence the audience's reaction to an actor's performance. If the mood of the music is wrong it can actually do damage to a scene.

Do you, on the other hand, believe in the idea of the film music's having an independent life of its own? What do you think of soundtrack recordings? Of concerts of film music? Have you frequently performed your own work before live audiences?

When I'm writing a score all I think about is the film. That's the *raison d'être* for the music; however, there are people who like to be reminded of a film by listening to its soundtrack album or by concert performances of the score. I have conducted film scores at pop concerts with American symphony orchestras, and, if there is an audience for these concerts, there's no harm in playing the music live. Since I write chamber and orchestral music intended for the concert hall, there isn't a tremendous need on my part to hear my film-oriented music played on its own, but if others like to hear it that's fine by me.

When and how would you first become involved in a film's production?

As a rule, in Hollywood the composer gets involved when the editing of the film is nearly completed, but in the 1950s and '60s in England, especially when I was working with Tony Richardson, I would have discussions about the style of the score much earlier, sometimes before the shooting had started. Moreover, I was asked to visit the unit on location for discussions with Tony and I was able to absorb the atmosphere of what was going on. I would also advise on any source music that had to be recorded while I was there. Occasionally I was even roped in to appear in a scene; for instance, in *A Taste of Honey* I was the accompanist on camera for Dora Bryan singing a vaudeville song in a pub scene.

Which personnel would you have most to do with? What sorts of matters would you discuss?

Obviously, the director is the key person with whom I worked; however, on the technical side, the music editor is crucial, since he attends my spotting sessions with the director and afterwards provides timing sheets giving the timings of all the action and dialogue in every music cue. The music editor is also with me at the recording sessions and prepares the music tracks we have recorded for all the dubbing sessions. Naturally I would have discussions with the recording engineer before the recording sessions. However, I should add that in my early days there were no music editors, the job didn't exist in England, although it was common in Hollywood. The timing sheets were prepared by the assistant to the film editor in those days.

Were you regularly on the set or location? Did you do most of your work at home or in the studio?

I composed the score at home and visited studios for meetings with the director or producer at the screenings of the picture, including the spotting sessions with the director, at which the exact footage and timing in minutes and seconds where each music cue starts and ends is decided.

Sometimes you not only composed the film's score but conducted the orchestra which played it for the soundtrack. Did you prefer this double function?

My first three or four films were conducted by Muir Mathieson at Denham Studios or by Ernest Irving at Ealing. Ever since then I've conducted all of my films myself and very much enjoy doing so.

You've worked for many of the most famous directors. However, two names stand out: the Boulting brothers, for whom you scored eight films, and Tony Richardson, for whom you did about a dozen. I'd be very interested in anything you could tell me about how you worked with each.

I think I've said enough about my work with Tony Richardson. The Boulting brothers were highly intelligent and cultivated and I learnt a great deal from Roy on my first film, *Seven Days to Noon*; he had a lot of good ideas and guided me along the way.

You won the Oscar for your *Tom Jones* score. How far do you think this affected your career? Do you also recall working on a famously unseen Richardson film, *Dead Cert*?

Regarding *Tom Jones*, I don't know if it helped my career but it certainly did no harm! I couldn't attend the Academy Awards show in Hollywood because my wife was expecting to give birth to our son in London that night! I still lived in England at that time. Regarding *Dead Cert*, I think it was released in England but not elsewhere.

Did you find that some directors had much firmer ideas than others about what they wanted in the way of a musical score? What were your experiences of working with, say, Hitchcock, Mankiewicz, Desmond Davis, Richard Attenborough, or the Ealing director Michael Truman?

Yes, I worked with a variety of directors. Bernard Herrmann was hired to do Hitchcock's *Torn Curtain*, but, as you probably know, they had a row at the scoring stage. Bernie was fired and I was then engaged to take over. I found Hitchcock very nice to work for. He knew what he wanted and he was very knowledgeable.

I first worked with Joe Mankiewicz on *The Honey Pot*; he liked the composer to come up with ideas and then he would comment on them. We got on well together and Joe liked what I'd done. Unfortunately the film was unsuccessful at the box-office, and most directors would have found that a good enough reason for not employing me in their next film, but Joe was no ordinary director, and, when he subsequently decided to make a film of *Sleuth*, he immediately asked me to do the score. That was a nice thing for me particularly because I received an Oscar nomination for it, and in addition the music over the main titles, which I called 'Overture', has become quite popular in a full 'symphonic' version that I made.

Joe had felt that the score for *Sleuth* should have a 1930s feel about it, but after studying the film I came to the conclusion that, since there were 1930s records played from time to time on the gramophone in the novelist's country home where all the action took place, those records would take care of the 1930s aspect of the film. In the musical ideas I came up with, I included, for instance, a harpsichord, which of course had nothing particularly to do with the 1930s. When I played some of the musical ideas to him on the piano, he accepted them and could evidently hear how they might work; and he had no hang-ups about having to stick with the idea that he'd thought of first.

Richard Attenborough is very musical and enormously supportive. We had long discussions about the music for *A Bridge Too Far* and the approach we worked out was that, in the battle scenes, we would have no music because we wanted those scenes to be as realistic as possible. So we saved up the music for the emotional reactions of different characters and military units in the film. I played him the main themes on the piano before the recordings, and as far as I remember I didn't have to alter a note. The music departments in Los Angeles tend to think this is a bad policy, because so often the director can't imagine how what you're playing on the piano will sound like on the orchestra. However, in my case, I've always liked to have sessions at the piano with a director and the main thing I get from it is through asking questions and getting the director's response.

I don't remember any details of working with Mike Truman, it's such a long time ago now, but I do know that he was very pleasant and that I enjoyed working with him. At Ealing studios, the director and producer worked together as a two-man team and there was also a lot of discussion between different pairs of directors and producers about each other's films, so it did have a rather nice family feeling there.

I was lucky to work with some very intelligent and gifted directors, who were often inspiring and never in any way destructive to anything I was trying to do.

Quite a number of the films you scored were based on novels or plays. Did it seem valuable to you to go back to these sources or would you wait until you saw the rushes before you began your work?

In general, the most important thing to react to is what is on the screen; whether that turns out to be the same as what was intended by the screenplay really is neither here nor there when it comes to writing the music. But obviously there have been some cases, such as a famous novel, when there's no harm in reading the original. In the case of the film of *The Entertainer* I'd previously done the music for the play and so naturally I used a lot of that. In the case of *Sleuth*, I'd seen the play before I ever dreamt there would be a film of it or that I'd be asked to do the music for it. Once again the key was the director – it's always good to try and find out what the director's vision is of how his film should turn out and what it is trying to say.

You've worked in virtually every film genre: did you have any preferences?

Writing music for movies makes you versatile and you need to be. Every film is a new challenge and that is what makes it interesting.

Which studios did you work at? Which ones had the best facilities as far as you were concerned?

In England I worked at Pinewood and at Shepperton Studios, and in the very early days at Denham, amongst others. In Hollywood my first experience was working at Disney and I worked for Universal many times, also at Warner Brothers and at MGM; in other words, at a lot of them. In Hollywood the studios could afford to do more to help the composer than was possible in England. For instance, the studios provided considerable numbers of copyists who could get the score copied very efficiently and very quickly. In England, one had only one or two people to do the whole thing. One had one's preferences about recording studios, and that was mostly to do with the particular recording engineer.

How much control did you have over the performers and performance of your scores?

The orchestral musicians are booked by a contractor and you will ask the contractor for any particular people you especially want to have. Otherwise, if they know their job, they will give you the best within the budget, and of course the budget is a key thing.

What were some of the major problems a music director might run into? Do you recall any films as being especially difficult to work on?

You've probably noticed I don't use the expression 'music director': I'm a composer who conducts his own scores. I'm also responsible for the music as a whole, but what I am essentially is a composer. I don't suppose any artistic project can be without difficulties of some kind. All that matters is how the work turns out in the end.

Were you ever under contract to studios, to companies? If not, how did you come by so much film work?

Apart from that early contract with the Boulting brothers, I've never been under contract to a studio or a company. What I did come by very early on was an agent. I was with London Management in all my English days and when I went to America in 1975 I got myself an American agent.

Who do you think of as some of the other great names in British film music?

Of course there are many such, and one could perhaps start with William Walton and Vaughan Williams.

Having worked in both Britain and the US, what differences would you note between the functioning of the music director in the two filmmaking countries?

There was a difference in the atmosphere between London and Los Angeles, but the job is of course exactly the same. In Los Angeles, success is measured in terms of receipts at the box office; in London, perhaps artistic merit counts for a bit more than in LA. There, the big studios have music departments, who do everything they can to help the composer do his job; in England, there isn't a big organisation, but in a way the composer is in a more individual and simple situation in which it may be easier to experiment and to work very closely with the directors.

What are some of the movies on which you've been most satisfied with your work?

I'm tempted not to answer! However, I *can* tell you that when I've been asked to talk about my film music to university students and the like, the ones I've chosen have been *Tom Jones*, *A Bridge Too Far* and *Sleuth*. Not long ago I saw Tony Richardson's film *The Charge of the Light Brigade* and I must say I was quite pleased with the music then. His first two films, *A Taste of Honey* and *The Loneliness of the Long Distance Runner*, also gave me some very nice opportunities. Likewise some of the Boulting brothers' comedies such as *Carlton-Browne of the FO*, *Private's Progress* and even *Lucky Jim*.

Jean Anderson

b. 1908

Actor: **The Mark of Cain* (1947), *The Romantic Age*, *Elizabeth of Ladymead* (1940), *The Franchise Affair* (1950), *Out of True*, *Life in Her Hands*, *White Corsridors* (1951), *The Brave Don't Cry* (1952), *The Kidnappers*, *Johnny on the Run* (1953), *The Dark Stairway*, *Lease of Life* (1954), *The Secret Tent*, *A Town Like Alice* (1956), *Heart of a Child*, *Robbery Under Arms*, *Lucky Jim*, *The Barretts of Wimpole Street* (1957), *Solomon and Sheba*, *SOS Pacific* (1959), *Spare the Rod* (1961), *The Inspector*, *The Waltz of the Toreadors* (1962), *The Silent Playground*, *The Three Lives of Thomasina* (1963), *Half a Sixpence* (1967), *Country Dance*, *Run a Crooked Mile* (1969), *The Night Digger* (1971), *The Lady Vanishes* (1979), *Screamtime* (1983), *Madame Sousatzka* (1988), *Leon the Pig Farmer* (1993)
* Scenes deleted from final print.

One of the incontestable strengths of British cinema in the 1940s and '50s was the range of character players who could be counted on to stamp their scenes with authority in even the most anodyne enterprises. Jean Anderson, tall, eloquent of face and voice, has an honourable place among their ranks. She is in fact such a striking presence, especially in the films she made for Philip Leacock and Jack Lee, that it comes as a surprise to find she has not made as many films as one had supposed. Usually cast in austerely kindly roles, most notably in *The Kidnappers*, her own favourite, she has a quality of stillness that compels attention. Very adept at sympathetic professionals, she could nevertheless be convincingly sinister (as in the dire remake of *The Lady Vanishes*), or bossy (as the parishioner in *Lease of Life*), and, at least once, in *Lucky Jim*, she showed fine flair for comedy.

Interview date: July 1990

When you came to feature films in the late '40s, did you have to make many adjustments in technique, after being on the stage since 1929?

I learnt that through working in documentaries for the Ministry of Information during the war, under excellent directors like Phil Leacock. It's a matter of learning not to project to an audience, and of being more relaxed, with less facial expression; you learn that in close-up your *eyes* can tell it.

That work led later to my being in four films for Phil, one of which was *Out of True*, England's answer to *The Snake Pit*. I enjoyed it enormously. Then there was *Life in Her Hands*, in which I had to go through the entire process of teaching Kathleen Byron what a nurse did when a baby was being born! Then I had a small part in *The Brave Don't Cry*, about a Scottish mining disaster; the actors were almost all Glasgow citizens and of course I have a Scottish background. It was through that small part that I got *The Kidnappers*, which was the most marvellous part for me, without a surplus word of dialogue. That film – and *A Town Like Alice* – I can still watch and forget it's me up there.

Those films established a certain image of you as the wise, understanding, if somewhat astringent type. Is it good for an actress to have an image?

I think so; I've been very lucky in that way. Some producers see me as a warm, sympathetic character and some see me as very dominating. Probably my biggest success as far as the public goes was a

television series called *The Brothers*, in which I played a pretty dominating matriarch. My mail at the time was pretty equally divided between those who thought she was a wonderful woman whose wretched boys didn't understand her and the others who thought she was 'just like my mother-in-law'!

You worked with several veteran Hollywood directors . . .

Yes, I liked King Vidor enormously but he couldn't cope with Gina Lollobrigida in *Solomon and Sheba*; he would argue very nicely with her but she made her own rules and he had no luck at all. If you were taller than she, you must not be level with her; and she always liked walking into close-up at the end of a scene so that I, even as her friend, must never have an arm left in frame for her close-up! It was a very unhappy film; there was a dreadful hiatus after Tyrone Power died, before we got Yul Brynner, and Tyrone was so loved by everyone. King Vidor was a great director though.

George Sidney was really the wrong director for Tommy Steele, who had been playing his *Half a Sixpence* role in the theatre for quite a few years, and it was difficult for him to cut it down for film. He got no help at all from George Sidney, who was really only interested in building up the dance routines.

Then there was Sidney Franklin, who made both the original and the remake of *The Barretts of Wimpole Street*. I never thought I would get that part, which was played originally by tiny Una O'Connor, who used to go about as if she was on roller skates, which got big laughs. I went to the interview expecting so much *not* to get the part that I was completely relaxed and laughing. I even said, 'I'm not going to do that business of pretending I'm on roller skates!' and Sidney Franklin assured me that was all right. But it was not a happy film. I had always thought of Jennifer Jones as being what I call an '*actress* star'; when we came to work, however, she needed to be told every thought that went through her head; she was terribly 'starry' and nervous. I played Wilson, her companion, and to her I was just a piece of furniture. She never spoke to me, but Virginia McKenna [Henrietta] was lovely; I made two films with her and she is a wonderful actress.

How did you feel about the wholesale importation of American actors into British films in the '50s?

You were always rather thrilled to play with them because in those days we thought Hollywood was 'it'. When we were making *The Kidnappers* at Pinewood, there was a big American-financed film also being made at the time, called *The Million Pound Note* with Gregory Peck. That was one of my high spots because I had the dressing room next to him and used to see him lying on his chaise longue with his guitar. There we were, a tiny budget film with that wonderful Scottish actor Duncan Macrae, the two children, Adrienne Corri and myself, and the other film had every star in London playing small parts. The irony was that our film was a big success and *The Million Pound Note* wasn't.

Did you enjoy working at Ealing on *Lease of Life* with Robert Donat?

I was thrilled to be in one of the last Ealing films. I had worked with Robert in the theatre in the '30s, at the famous Festival Theatre, Cambridge, but I hadn't seen much of him since then until *Lease of Life*. He was a very sick man: you would be asked to rehearse a scene with him in his car; so we would do a few lines and then he would have a coughing fit. He would apologise and you would go back again later. The one funny thing about that film was that, as a very 'county' lady, I had a dog; then they said, 'We've decided you're not going to have the dog but we're giving you Edie Martin instead.' She was about five feet nothing and we did look very funny, with her always sort of peering up at me!

Do you remember *The Mark of Cain*, your very first film?

I can remember having to take Sally Gray in charge as a wardress and going through her bag. She was supposed to have murdered her husband. I was excited at my first film coming on in the West End and the posters going up; there was my photograph, even for this tiny part, so I went to see the film and my scene had been cut! But I do remember Brian Desmond Hurst who directed it; he was a great character.

Do you remember working with Herbert Wilcox and Anna Neagle?

Yes, they were extremely nice and courteous to work with. That was the first time I ever had a stand-in. I was playing a very 'refeened' lady help. My very first line when I was handing out the plates and things was after Anna asked what time would I be going; I had to reply, 'I have a slow puncture in my front' – it brought the house down.

And do you recall working with Pat Jackson in *White Corridors*?

Yes, I loved it. I think I had worked with him earlier in documentaries. I played the casualty sister in that, a good little part. I saw the film again recently and thought how good it was; it has such reality about it. Pat was a very good director and such a nice man.

***A Town Like Alice* concentrates, unlike most British war films, more on women than men. Was it a happy experience?**

Oh yes it was, very. Renee Houston hated being made to look awful in it but I thought she was wonderful. For three days we were wading in a stagnant lake in Burnham Beeches, carrying heavy stretchers with babies and about six heavy rifles on them. We were in bare feet in water. They did long tracking shots with the camera, very difficult shots to get, and it took ages to do them. It was very cold and they had a bottle of rum for us, to bring the circulation back occasionally. Marie Lohr fell, poor thing. She was very old and so was Nora Nicholson; I was the youngest of that lot. Once, there was a very heavy white frost and Nora had to kneel down in this frost and say the Lord's Prayer, even though she was an old lady then. Of course, we were in rags, with bare arms, legs and feet.

Another night the cold was so awful, and all the extras playing Australian soldiers were lined up to watch this scene in which Peter Finch gets crucified. (I loved working with him, by the way.) As we women walked past this line of extras you could hear their teeth rattling. They had to stand close together to prop each other up, so as not to show how much they were shaking. But we all survived it, and I maintain that all that discomfort in fact helped the film. Once, I recall, they sprayed us, in freezing weather, with ice-cold glycerine for sweat!

You were also in *Lucky Jim* at about this time. It seems to have been a troubled production.

Yes, it was. Charles Crichton started directing it for the Boultings, and he had a great reputation. He had engaged me in a great comic part and he wanted to be very true to the book. We all knew exactly what we wanted – a sophisticated light comedy. We started shooting, with Hugh Griffiths playing my husband, and we turned up at the end of the first week's shooting to find that the Boultings had taken over the production and they wanted it as a *tour de force* for Ian Carmichael. It was made broader than had originally been envisaged. It has some very funny things in it, all the same, including a scene where I had to ride one of those motorised bicycles and Terry-Thomas had to ride a Vespa scooter.

You finished the '50s with what sounds like a rather hectic melodrama, called *SOS Pacific* ...

That was my first really international film. It had French, German, British and American stars, lovely Pier Angeli and an excellent director in Guy Green. We made that in the Canary Islands. Dickie Attenborough nearly died on it. We had a seaplane in the film, from which we had to be rescued in rafts. There was a question of whether they could shoot this stunt because there was a very rough sea that day. They waited and waited and then decided to have a go. I think Dickie was in the small boat that the camera was on; I can't quite remember what happened but he came ashore absolutely unconscious. He was shot off to hospital to be revived. His character actually was killed by a shark in the film, which went over the top in the end, unfortunately, because a lot of the drama was quite exciting. Everybody adored Pier Angeli, who was so beautiful; and Dickie in fact brought her back to England for *The Angry Silence*.

What is your favourite amongst your films?

Oh, *The Kidnappers* still, and *A Town Like Alice*.

Lindsay Anderson

1923–1994

Director: *Meet the Pioneers (1948), *Idlers that Work (1949), *Three Installations, *Wakefield Express (1952), *Thursday's Children, *O Dreamland (1953), *Trunk Conveyor (1954), *Green and Pleasant Land, *The Children Upstairs, *A Hundred Thousand Children, *Henry, *Foot and Mouth, *£20 a Ton, *Energy First (1955), *Every Day Except Christmas (1957), *The March to Aldermaston (co-dir) (1957), This Sporting Life (1963), *The White Bus, *The Singing Lesson / RAZ, DWA, TRZY (1967), If ... (1968), O Lucky Man! (1973), In Celebration (1974), Britannia Hospital (1982), The Whales of August (1987)
*Short film.

Lindsay Anderson managed to make no more than six feature films in thirty years. If he had begun making feature films in the studio years, he would have probably churned out a feature a year. As it is, there is no junk in his work: *This Sporting Life* is a masterpiece, an epic of the emotional life unlike anything else in

British cinema; *If . . .* still speaks to young audiences nearly thirty years later, and, with *O Lucky Man!* and *Britannia Hospital*, deals swingeing blows at an Establishment which Anderson never ceased to regard as anachronistic and obstructive; and *The Whales of August* is a beautiful elegy to two great actresses. He was of course often busy in the theatre, where he produced classics as well as ground-breaking new plays; he also acted from time to time (as in *Chariots of Fire*); he was the author of two books, *Making a Film: The Story of* Secret People and *About John Ford*, and a reviewer of acidulous elegance. He may have had a satirist's cauterising wit, but his work is also marked by concern for understanding human relationship, for the emotional as well as for the social forces that inhibit its free development. By any standards, he is a major figure in British cinema, both as a practitioner and as one of its most trenchant commentators.

Interview dates: June 1982, May 1984, September 1989, and July 1994

Does it seem to you that the '40s and, to a lesser extent, the '50s constituted a sort of boom in the British cinema industry?

I think the '40s definitely did, because of the war, which obviously gave a great fillip to British production and introduced into British feature films some elements of reality which weren't very noticeable in the '30s. The Ealing pictures today are pretty stagey, really, but in terms of theme they did bring some middle-class reality into cinema. I would simply say that during the '40s it was chiefly due to the need for wartime entertainment. But I would have thought the '50s was a period of stagnation.

There was a sort of prestige boom after the war. I remember an article in *Vogue*, written by the very nice film critic of the *New Statesman*, William Whitebait, which was called 'The Ascending Spiral': this was the time of Lean, Powell and Pressburger, the short period of Carol Reed's wonderful ascendancy, which would be late '40s and early '50s. But somehow that all disintegrated. My remembrance of the '50s is of a period of dullness and of failure to grasp the opportunity that was given when American films were not allowed to be imported. There was a deliberate attempt, then, by the Rank Organisation and Sydney Box, to fill the void, which they failed to do. I suppose I am so accustomed to thinking it was the *end* of the '50s that reawakened interest in British cinema through the introduction of new writers, actors and new

class themes. However, I suppose you're right in saying that British cinema kept chugging along; but I wouldn't have thought it was a period of much excitement or fertility. My impression is of a 'hack' period.

By the mid '50s, there is a flatness about it, with the repetition of winning formulas with the freshness gone out of them.

This does very much correspond to the state of English society in the '50s, which was stagnant. What had to happen was the 'mini-revolution' or whatever you care to call it, at the end of the '50s, when things – however superficially – did change. But I think of the '50s as a long period of marking time, as it was in the theatre as well. It was a sort of 'West End' period when anything innovatory was in terms of poetic drama: TS Eliot, Christopher Fry.

Would you say British cinema has been limited by being too literary, too closely tied to the theatre, and too class-bound?

I'm not sure I mind so much about its being literary or connected with the theatre, because I think perhaps that is the British style. I remember it struck me ages ago in an editorial in *Sight and Sound*, a very characteristic editorial by Penelope Houston, saying, 'Why can't we produce a Godard?' And *Time Out* will say, 'Why can't we produce a Samuel Fuller?' And the truth is that the personality of the British cinema is not that of Godard or of Fuller. I think it has had a personality of its own; it is connected with acting that can be very good. Now, whether that means the English can't make films, I don't know; but I'm sometimes tempted to think it does. We certainly don't seem to have produced writers for films.

One of the problems is that the cinema in Britain has always been so bedevilled by the disastrous economic situation that it has probably never had the opportunity to develop. Government intervention has always been crucial for the survival of the British cinema – in whatever form that intervention may take. The British cinema has needed protection against the American cinema. A variety of protective measures have been tried – Eady money, the quota system and so on; generally they didn't work well but to some degree they *did* work.

I do become very conscious of the fact that the whole problem of British cinema is intimately connected with the decline of Britain, so it becomes part of a big historic analysis, and the economics of it are part of that. But the other part of it is the British lack of vitality. We *are* going downhill; we are a *passé* country, a *passé* culture. The class thing is obviously central to it. To me, what is interesting is that the English really like their class system, although there are always people who *don't* like it and try to fight against it. As a result of British films being middle-class, they didn't attract a very large popular audience. A popular audience in this country has always preferred American pictures, which have seemed to them to be classless (although they're not).

I suppose at the end of the '50s we were attacking the class system – not because we were being political, but because we were bored with the middle classes and we took on material which reflected this. In my case it was *This Sporting Life* by David Storey, who is a writer from the working class. He has always written from his background; he is a very personal writer. I suspect you will never radically change the class system in Britain, and this *must* affect our theatre and cinema.

You and your colleagues, notably Karel Reisz and Tony Richardson, were clearly at odds with mainstream British cinema of the 1950s. What did you see as some of its major deficiencies?

I think one of the worst things was this restriction in terms of class: the subjects were almost invariably middle-class and the characters were middle-class, and this very much restricted the range of British cinema. Going with that middle-class quality

was a lack of emotion and dynamic, a certain politeness which we didn't warm to and which made us, back in those days of the late '40s and early '50s, prefer American films.

And, of course, on the critical level, you would have to also include Gavin Lambert. When we brought the critical journal *Sequence* from Oxford to London, I got Gavin to write for it and to be an editor. So *Sequence* in its classic period became Peter Ericsson, Gavin Lambert and myself. Gavin was always a staunch contributor to and editor of *Sequence*, until he was invited to go to the British Film Institute by Denis Forman and he took over *Sight and Sound*.

How did the Free Cinema films mean to be different from the mainstream, in sociological terms?

Well, they didn't. It is important to realise what people always get wrong: they think of Free Cinema as being a deliberate and conscious movement. The truth was that, at that time, Tony Richardson and Karel Reisz had worked on *Momma Don't Allow*, which was financed by the Film Institute Production Fund or whatever it was called then. Lorenza Mazzetti from Italy had shot a film which was originally known as *The Glass Marble* and Lorenza was left to edit it by herself; she couldn't do that and, when I saw the material, I said we must do something with it. I agreed to take it on, complete the editing and produce the final shooting of *Together*, which was a title I had thought of when leafing through Walt Whitman's poems. And I had on my shelf *O Dreamland*, which had been there for some years and which nobody had ever seen.

When we talked about it – Karel, Lorenza, myself and Tony – we came to the conclusion that we really should start a movement purely to attract critics and journalists, to get our films reviewed, and if we did invent a movement we should try to get booking for a season into the National Film Theatre. Karel was Programme Manager of the NFT and we managed to do that. Our aim was to get press coverage, and of course we had to concoct a manifesto – which we did, although not entirely cynically. We *did* all feel the same, that mainstream British cinema was unadventurous, class-bound and uninteresting.

The first season of Free Cinema was in 1956 and it comprised *O Dreamland*, *Momma Don't Allow* and *Together*. It was really our aim only to show those films in one programme; it wasn't our aim to start a series of programmes, but what happened was that Lionel Rogosin turned up in London with his film, *On the Bowery*. We thought a way to help him to try and get a booking for his film was to concoct a second Free Cinema programme. We got together a programme of, I think, Georges Franju's *Le Sang des Bêtes* and maybe another film, and *On the Bowery*, and we called that Free Cinema 2. That's how the programmes started and we thought we would do some more. It was a way of showing our own films and, when I made *Every Day Except Christmas* for the Ford Motor Company, we concocted a programme about Britain. Then we showed the first New Wave films from France and a programme of films from Poland. Then Karel had *We Are the Lambeth Boys*, which I think was the last Free Cinema programme.

It was essentially a pragmatic series for a purpose. It wasn't a movement with a kind of conscious theoretical attack on British cinema; that may have been in our consciousness but it wasn't invented for that purpose. We wanted to get into filmmaking but the barriers were very great at that time and we didn't succeed. That is the reason why, after the last Free Cinema programme, I directed plays at the Royal Court, where I was invited by Tony Richardson. One of these was a play called, I think, *The Disciplines of War*. I said I'd do it but I suggested we change the title to *The Long and the Short and the Tall*.

Jack Clayton, who did *Room at the Top* at this time, had a quite different background.

Yes, he had worked as assistant director and so on for the Woolf brothers, after Korda. The first film he made was a Wolf Mankowitz story, *The Bespoke Overcoat*, and he did that successfully (it was a forty- or fifty-minute film), which led to the opportunity to direct *Room at the Top*. But he wasn't part of our group at all, although the novel *Room at the Top* was from the new generation of novelists who were doing working-class subjects.

The interesting thing is that *Room at the Top* was, in theme, very much like a Warner Brothers film of seven or eight years before, like a John Garfield picture. But it was new in England; the British cinema had never acknowledged the existence of a working class and never openly acknowledged, apart from in the films with Gracie Fields and George Formby, the existence of a Britain north of the Trent. Northern society was, as far as the cinema went, material for comedy or servants.

People speak of the New Wave of social realist films as a coherent movement, whereas you really all came from quite different approaches.

What really happened, starting in, say, 1956, was the beginning of the English Stage Company at the Royal Court and the production of *Look Back in Anger*; at the same time there were a number of novels written by northern, working-class writers: a play like *A Taste of Honey* by Shelagh Delaney, who came from Manchester; Alan Sillitoe, who wrote *Saturday Night and Sunday Morning*; David Storey, whose novel *This Sporting Life* came out in 1960, and John Braine. In that way there was quite a strong cultural and social movement in this country, not directly coming out of the cinema.

The cinema was really influenced by the Royal Court Theatre, and the single most influential film was probably *Saturday Night and Sunday Morning*, which Tony Richardson and John Osborne's company Woodfall produced and got Karel Reisz to direct. It found an appreciative audience and, of course, appreciative critics. *Saturday Night and Sunday Morning* was a very pronounced box-office hit, probably because it had a strong sense of anarchic comedy.

Would you agree that, although superficially your film *This Sporting Life* shares the social realist ethic, it really goes beyond that?

I think it does have an emotional and poetic quality. I think the resemblances between all of those films are pronounced, so that the critics tend to lump them all together. But they have to remember that it's not just me in the film; it was also David Storey, who was a very different writer from, say, Alan Sillitoe. The same can be said of David Mercer, who had quite different characteristics that led to *Morgan*, which is not in the least like *Look Back in Anger*.

Can you tell me about the setting up of *This Sporting Life*?

At that stage Tony Richardson wanted to sponsor films, to create a group of films and filmmakers, and he said I should do a film for Woodfall. I read about *This Sporting Life* when it came out and ordered a copy. I must have been one of the first people to read it. When I had read it I took it to Tony and said it might make a good film for Woodfall.

I honestly don't remember very well my immediate reaction to the book. I know I got it wrong, thinking it was more of a social subject than it was. In fact it is more of an emotional subject, but of course the whole social question comes into it very strongly. Tony Richardson read the book and later said to me he didn't think it would be good for me. It was only later I discovered that Tony had then bid for the rights of *This Sporting Life* and tried to buy them from David Storey for himself to make.

Anyway, since people were now looking out for working-class subjects and new directors after *Saturday Night and Sunday Morning*, the Rank Organisation bought *This Sporting Life*. I think it was bought for Joe Losey to make with Stanley Baker, who wanted to play the part. The Rank Organisation passed it on to Julian Wintle of Independent Artists, and Julian Wintle had told Stanley Baker he could play the part but he (Julian) would not make another film with Joe Losey (with whom he had made *Blind Date*). As an honourable man, Stanley declined to do the film.

Then Julian Wintle went to Karel Reisz, who had made *Saturday Night and Sunday Morning*, and asked him to direct it. Karel said he didn't want to direct the film, he wanted the experience of production. Karel then came to me to ask if it was OK for him to put me up to direct *This Sporting Life* and he would produce it. I said he could try. Greatly to my surprise, Karel came back a few days later and told me Independent had agreed. So we made it.

It must have been the most challenging thing that Independent Artists ever did.

To be honest, I don't know if they regarded it as such. There is a tendency to look at the film in the light of the past. I think they definitely had the feeling that, with Karel producing it, he could take over if I failed. So they felt safe. I don't think Julian Wintle ever actually interfered with production but he did put in Albert Fennell, as a sort of associate producer, who initiated Karel into the mysteries of production, so he did work on the film and we all got on very well.

First of all, Karel and I and David Storey worked on the script and that really wasn't very successful, because, although Karel and I are – and have always been – great friends, we are not temperamentally alike. I was rather intimidated by Karel at that stage and I think David had a completely false idea of the script. He wanted it to be a creative experience, like writing the novel, rather than adapting the novel for film. I think it was his idea originally that Richard Harris would be right to play the part, but Richard complained about the script not being a script of the novel but something new, and didn't want to do it.

When I told David Storey this, he said Richard was quite right and he got down to rewriting the script, turning it back into very much a script of the

book. The structure of the film is very much the structure of the novel, including those flashbacks. I think the film as it stands is quite noticeably an adaptation of the novel, and Richard Harris was originally responsible for pushing it back that way.

Richard was in *Mutiny on the Bounty* and when we had sent him the script we didn't hear any more from him. Karel and I telephoned him and in the end I asked if I should come and talk to him in Tahiti. I did go, and that is where Richard criticised the script as not being the novel we had originally sent him. That was when David started rewriting the script. I don't know how long after that it was before we started shooting, but Richard had to do retakes for *Mutiny on the Bounty* and we had to wait for him. Karel and I were paid some microscopic sum for waiting, because there was no point in starting until Richard was available.

Was Rachel Roberts your first choice for Mrs Hammond?

No, there was a lot of discussion about that. Karel was very keen on casting Rachel because she had been in *Saturday Night and Sunday Morning*, but I had originally thought that she was too impulsive and passionate a temperament. In that way I was, in theory, right because Mrs Hammond in the book was not really like Rachel.

Rachel herself was rather apprehensive about it, particularly because she had just got together with Rex Harrison and he had forbidden her to do *This Sporting Life*. There was a period when Rachel backed out and I tested about four other people, but realised that nobody was as good as Rachel, and Rachel herself eventually felt that she had to do the film. She really wanted to make it and so we signed her for Mrs Hammond.

She gives a wonderful impression of a woman with powerful feelings buttoned down.

Well, I think this is why it worked. It was necessary for the actress to have that strength of temperament and to suppress it; Mrs Hammond in the film does have that strength of suppressed emotion, which was very important.

The football ground footage even now still looks dangerously violent.

It may be because we filmed with the Wakefield Trinity team and about five or six actors did take part in the game (we didn't have stand-ins). Richard himself had played rugby football when young, so it wasn't anything new to him. He was strongly physical. I think it was his greatest part. Richard was tremendously ambitious; he was also in many ways unconfident, which made him a difficult actor to handle, but ideally cast.

There was a strong influence from the Royal Court on the film. The casting director, Miriam Brickman had been casting director at the Royal Court and I'd worked with her. Then she had left the Court and begun casting films. I think she had cast John Schlesinger's *A Kind of Loving* before casting *This Sporting Life* and she worked on the film very much as we worked in the theatre. She knew a lot of actors, who had probably not worked much in film. Everyone looks absolutely right in the film.

Did you ever expect it to be a big commercial success, given the downbeat nature of its ending?

I didn't think I was taking a commercial risk with the ending. This was the advantage of coming from the Royal Court, where that kind of box-office success was never a consideration. I did feel – and said – that the title was not a good popular title but we could never think of another one so it remained.

There was never a question of changing the story's end. I don't think it was a great success commercially, and of course the Rank Organisation had no idea how to handle it and John Davis thought the film was horrid, sordid, disgusting. He made an announcement after that that the Rank Organisation was going to make family films, which, from a box-office point of view, was disastrous.

What happened to the proposed trilogy of which The White Bus was to form a part?

It was made under the title of *Red, White and Zero*. Karel Reisz was to be one of the three directors but he made *A Suitable Case for Treatment* as a feature film which became *Morgan*; the three directors who in the end made *Red, White and Zero* were Peter Brook, Tony Richardson and myself. Originally this was to be a picture from stories by Shelagh Delaney – this was Oscar's [Lewenstein] conception – but I made *The White Bus* first. In fact Peter Brook and Tony Richardson came to see it before they made their films, and they were so struck by the original nature of the script that they decided to abandon their stories and invent something new. Peter Brook made a film called *Ride of the Valkyries* with Zero Mostel, and Tony Richardson made a film called *Red and Blue*, which was to have been with Jeanne Moreau until she was cited by Vanessa Redgrave in her divorce from Tony. Amazingly enough, Vanessa took on the part

even though she was suing Tony for divorce. It was shown briefly at the Paris Cinémathèque but it was never released – and anyway, what do you do with a fifty-minute film? United Artists couldn't do anything with *Red, White and Zero*. They split it up and tried to show it as single short films, but it was a failure. However, I never had the feeling that it had been a waste of time making *The White Bus* because I thought it was a very good film. It was based on an autobiographical story by Shelagh Delaney, who did the screenplay as well.

Did you run into difficulties setting up the production of If . . .?

Oh yes, of course. I worked with David Sherwin on the script of *If . . .*, which was a development of a treatment he had written with a friend and schoolfellow of his, John Howard. It had been called *Crusaders* and was sent to me quite out of the blue by Seth Holt, who had rung me up and asked if I would consider directing a film with him as producer. I said I'd be very happy to, because one always wanted a producer, so he sent me the script.

At first I said I couldn't do it, then I was persuaded to work with David Sherwin and we did work on it, producing another script, still called *Crusaders*. We were in Wardour Street one day and Albert Finney was cutting his film *Charlie Bubbles*. I said we were trying to do something with our script and he suggested we take it to Michael Medwin, who ran his company with him. I showed the script to Michael, who immediately liked it. So he took it on, but, of course, they couldn't get anybody in Britain to finance it. No production company would risk it and it was only by the merest chance that Charlie Bluhdorn of Paramount finally agreed to do it. That was a period when American companies were financing British productions quite considerably, which they gave up after a time; that is a totally American picture financially – although *creatively* it is a British picture.

Were the schools you used, including your own, amenable to being used as locations?

They were very co-operative, really. Mind you, I don't think any of them took films all that seriously and I think that I was also a bit dishonest, certainly as regards Cheltenham, in playing down the anarchic, critical side of the script. But I don't know that they would have been bothered anyway, though it isn't a flattering picture of English education. At any rate, it isn't a sentimental one, not at all like *Goodbye Mr Chips*. In some ways, it is a very un-British film.

How exact a metaphor for British life did you find the education system at that stage?

I think this was instinctive; it wasn't a worked-out intellectual concept. I suppose it seemed to me absolutely obvious, the idea of there being two distinct streams of British education which help to perpetuate the class system. There is a system which is open to parents who are prepared to pay for their children's education, and certainly what they get out of that system is power, positions of power in society. And of course, it is very characteristic of the conservatism of this country that no government, whether Conservative or Labour, has ever wanted radically to change the education system.

Does the film's ending, in your view, suggest that there is really no hope for revolutionary acts in Britain?

You may say that's what it says to you, but I didn't intellectualise about it and I think that the end of the film is emotional and instinctive. One can rationalise about it afterwards – I mean, is it an optimistic or a pessimistic film? I don't know, that's for you to decide. It is interesting that when it was first shown, particularly in the West End, audiences would applaud at the end of the film.

The boys were emotional rebels; they weren't rebelling against a system. They aren't young Marxists at all. In fact, I think the only place where the film got a really hostile reception was in Germany with an audience of young Marxists: they objected strongly to the film because it didn't have an optimistic ending. But in this country I would say *If . . .* was just a bit too difficult for a popular audience to understand.

Michael Medwin was also your producer on your next film, *O Lucky Man!*. What do you look for in a producer?

Someone who'll get the money and organise the production. It is always nice to have a producer who is sympathetic and will make sympathetic or intelligent comments as far as the creative side of filmmaking is concerned. But I've never worked with a producer to whom I *had* to listen, it wouldn't work. I have never wanted to be a producer myself, I am not an entrepreneur, I'm afraid. It's unfortunate, because I think film directors need to be entrepreneurs if they are going to survive, which is probably why I haven't really survived – or have I? I don't know. I suppose I have, but only on my own terms.

Were you deliberately aiming at a kind of Brechtian revue-like effect in *O Lucky Man!*?

I think you're perfectly justified in talking about Brecht, and perhaps the use of titles, which there are in *If . . .*; also the way in which *O Lucky Man!* is structured is quite deliberately following in the footsteps of Brecht, who wanted people to think rather than just feel.

Of course this is also true of *If . . .* – the fact that we shot certain sequences in monochrome. It is, incidentally, quite untrue to say (as it always is said) that it was because we didn't have enough money to shoot it all in colour: that's absurd. It really arose because the cameraman, who came from Czechoslovakia and whom I'd met there, was scared of shooting in the chapel in Cheltenham without either more lamps or taking more time. We talked endlessly about it and finally I decided to shoot it in black and white; it was a practical step. Having decided that, I then thought that there would have to be regular black-and-white sequences throughout the picture. That seemed to echo the Brechtian style of thought, of making people realise that they were watching a film. So really all of these things followed out of one another rather than its being a single or artistic decision.

***O Lucky Man!* uses other distancing devices, such as actors turning up in several parts.**

This is quite true, and many of these decisions were made simply instinctively. I think this is what a lot of people, particularly critics, find so difficult to understand because they're so used to rationalising. You might say that the whole use of music in *O Lucky Man!* is a – perhaps not 'distancing', that sounds too intellectual or conscious – but . . . It had always been my hope that, even if that 'distancing' effect resulted from the style of *O Lucky Man!*, I had made a picaresque film exactly so that audiences would never quite know what was going to happen next.

I think it was amazing that the film was ever made! I can't imagine it being made now. It was just part of the freedom that was around then. Plus the fact that Malcolm McDowell was regarded by Warner Brothers as being a potential star, having been a big success in *A Clockwork Orange*, so they were prepared to go ahead with *O Lucky Man!* Of course it is not as expensive a film as it looks. In those days British films were comparatively inexpensive for Hollywood studios.

How did Warner Brothers go about selling the film, as it didn't fit any of the genre categories?

They didn't go about selling it. They were rather

inept at publicity, didn't know how to do it. We were fortunate in having Mike Kaplan, who had been working in publicity for Stanley Kubrick, which is how he got to know Malcolm McDowell. He came in to help on *O Lucky Man!* and to a great extent was the agent in getting its release and publicity.

All your films have wonderful acting performances, none more so perhaps than *In Celebration*. Do you, in general, like working with actors?

Yes, indeed, I do like working with actors and to that degree I enjoy working in the theatre. With *In Celebration* we were very fortunate in having exactly the cast that we had used at the Royal Court Theatre. I don't think we needed to make much modification of their theatrical performances when we came to make the film. Maybe when working on it you unconsciously tone it down, but I think a good actor instinctively acts to the camera, just as on stage at the Royal Court he will instinctively act to the audience. Of course Alan Bates and Bill Owen were experienced film actors in any case.

Do you put your actors through a lot of rehearsal?

I have always rehearsed, although sometimes not very much, depending on the subject. I didn't in *If . . .* because I didn't want the young actors to become self-conscious. In general I believe in rehearsing because actors on the whole like it. I've never been the kind of director who just goes in blindly.

***In Celebration* is very fluid. Was it shot in a studio?**

Yes, at Elstree. We did a couple of days on location, that's all. The director of photography was Nick Bush and we didn't get on particularly well, but that was the way we were making it. I think that, from the beginning, the American Film Theatre was designed to film plays that had been produced in the theatre and take them from the stage production. We filmed it in about four or five weeks. People expected us to take the play and film it like a television play but we didn't do it that way. It was done like a film.

It has been suggested that *Britannia Hospital* was unpopular because it coincided with an upsurge of patriotic feeling associated with the Falklands War.

I think this is quite untrue. There was a certain amount of typical media publicity about the Falklands, but my guess is that *Britannia Hospital* was too continuously satirical and probably a bit beyond its audience. It was rather sophisticated, not like a *Carry On* film, and, as a result, the audience didn't respond very strongly to it. I don't think it had anything to do with an upsurge of patriotism. It could be said that we used the incompetently-run hospital as an image of the nation, I suppose, but I don't think the audience was going to grab that particularly. I think it was just too much for them – and possibly a bit too jaundiced. It is certainly more of a pessimistic film than an optimist one. Nobody gets off lightly, it satirises everything, Left as much as Right. If I were doing it again today I don't think I would want to change the focus.

Do you see *If . . .*, *O Lucky Man!* and *Britannia Hospital* as a kind of state-of-the-nation trilogy?

They can only loosely be described as a 'trilogy'; it would be far too limiting – and misleading – to regard them as a 'state-of-the-nation' trilogy. In every case, I would hope, they transcend their local significance to make much more general comment on the human situation – and most particularly the situation of man in society . . . One has to start somewhere, and naturally I start with my British circumstances. The ambition is for the films to grow imaginatively, so that they transcend locality.

With a cast of some of the world's most famous pros in *The Whales of August*, how much and what kind of direction would you have given people like Lillian Gish, Bette Davis and Ann Sothern?

The same sort of direction you would give to anyone. You work together towards a truthful performance. It's the kind of question one can't really answer. It was not so much to do with them being experienced as with them being difficult at taking direction. Someone like Ann Sothern, for instance, is a very good actress and she was quite happy to take direction, as was Lillian. It was Bette who was rather difficult, but that was Bette. Unfortunately Bette was an incredibly difficult personality and temperament. She was destructive, as well as *self*-destructive. She needed to fight. I think one can be a great star and a great actress as she was, without being a monster, but she couldn't. She had turned it down when she read the play, but she agreed quite easily three or four years later when she read the film script. Generally though, I think the better the actor, the more he or she will appreciate intelligent and sympathetic direction.

We did the whole film on Cliff Island off

Portland, Maine, in Casco Bay outside Portland. We were very, very lucky and I think Mike Flash was an excellent cameraman for it. I was lucky that Mike, whom I'd met in Britain shooting *Britannia Hospital* (his first feature film), emigrated and he now lives in Connecticut, so he was available to shoot *The Whales of August*. Again, I was lucky that we made *Glory Glory* [television mini-series] together in Toronto.

How did that come your way?

Home Box Office wanted to do it but I think they were scared of the subject. It was originally to have been directed by the writer but then HBO wouldn't approve that; they wanted the producer to get hold of a director who was 'unexpected', not just a routine television director and also not a totally inexperienced director like the writer. Somehow the script was sent to me from my agent in Hollywood; I read it and, very unusually, I liked it. It was pretty abrasive about evangelical religion in the US but it

went extremely well and it was very well received. It was enjoyable to do but very, very hard work. It was a three-hour film and we did it in thirty-five days, which is fast. I couldn't have done it without Mike shooting it.

Why have you not made anything in the last five years?

It isn't that I haven't had certain scripts I've wanted to do, but nobody has wanted to back a film directed by me. Perhaps it is because I have allowed myself to acquire a reputation for being 'difficult', or for not being particularly 'box-office'. Nothing is happening with the *If . . . 2* project and nothing will. Maybe I've done myself a damage by continuing to do theatre, which has probably weakened the impetus of my film career.

Do you think producers think of you as primarily a stage director who does an occasional film?

I don't think people think of me at all.

Rona Anderson

b. 1926

Actor: *Sleeping Car to Trieste* (1948), *Floodtide, Poet's Pub, Torment* (1949), *The 20 Questions Murder Mystery, Her Favourite Husband* (1950), *Home to Danger, Scrooge* (1951), *Whispering Smith Hits London, Circumstantial Evidence* (1952), *Noose for a Lady, Black 13* (1953), *Double Exposure, The Black Rider* (1954), *Shadow of a Man, Little Red Monkey,* *The Flaw, A Time to Kill, Stock Car* (1955), *Soho Incident, The Hide-Out* (1956), *The Solitary Child, Man with a Gun* (1958), *The Bay of San Michel* (1963), *Devils of Darkness* (1964), *River Rivals, Interlude* (scenes cut) (1967), *The Prime of Miss Jean Brodie* (1969)

Engagingly modest about her screen career, Rona Anderson was undoubtedly one of the most attractive leading ladies of the British supporting feature film industry of the '40s and '50s. She brought a fresh prettiness and vivacity to many a 'B' heroine, embarking on ill-advised enterprises either to clear the name of, or otherwise assist, her reporter or detective boyfriend (John Bentley, say, or Paul Carpenter). Her husband, the late actor Gordon Jackson, advised taking whatever came along: a steady stream of 'Mary or Joan' roles did come, and she was a popular face on the first half of the double bill. As Derek de Marney's jittery girl-friend in her début, in *Sleeping Car to Trieste*, and as an Italian gangster's moll in *Her Favourite Husband*, she showed a rarely exploited talent for comedy. For one who saw acting as an enjoyable job, it must be said that she was also always enjoyable company.

Interview date: July 1994

How did you get into films?

For some reason – I suppose I had become a bit known as a result of my willingness to come tearing down from Scotland to London to do screen tests for films like *They Were Sisters* – the director John Paddy Carstairs and producer George Brown came to see me in a matinée. Perhaps they had seen the tests I'd done for Alexander Korda for the part of Flora MacDonald. Anyway, they came up to Glasgow and offered me the part in *Sleeping Car to Trieste*.

I did enjoy doing it; it was a film full of nice little cameo performances. Paddy Carstairs liked me a great deal, although I was so naïve at the time I barely recognised this. I remember my asking him on the set, 'If I do anything wrong, could you just give me a wee poke?' I was so prim and proper I had no idea what I'd said, but it became a byword! I was always playing prim girls later on, always called Mary or Joan. Actually I spent my entire time during the film with my eyes wide open because I thought the one rule about being in films was 'Don't blink'! But I enjoyed the whole experience enormously. I wasn't at all nervous then – I became a lot more nervous later on but not then. Paddy Carstairs had a good way of relaxing you and I think he had a very good way with actors generally.

Jean Kent didn't like Carstairs's direction much, but remembered she'd enjoyed meeting you.

Jean had a real toughness, a real strength, and I liked her. We really got to know each other in Rome on *Her Favourite Husband* later: she was great fun and I liked her enormously. Anyway, I enjoyed *Sleeping Car to Trieste* very much indeed and Derrick de Marney, with whom I played most of my scenes, was very nice and very helpful. He drove me every day out to Denham, where the film was being made. The studios at Denham were absolutely huge.

You then made two films for Frederick and Donald Wilson, director and producer. Any recollections of them and of their company, Aquila? Were they brothers?

They weren't related at all. Freddy had always been a cutter and the first film I did with him, *Floodtide*, was his first film as a director. It was made on the Independent Frame system, which was absolutely dreadful. I think it may still be in use at Pinewood for back projection filming, but it was not liked by actors. I think the first film they did using the Independent Frame system was *Warning to Wantons*, which Donald Wilson also directed. But, as actors, all your action was in pictures down the page of the script. The house in *Floodtide* was a set, I think, but the rest was just backdrops, back projection against which we were acting. This was very tricky for lighting. I'm not sure of the technicalities, but I suppose it had to be lit from behind and this created problems for lighting the actors from the front. Whatever the system was, it made for very static performances. I guess they thought it would save time and money, especially on set-building and not using locations. I think there were only about half a dozen films made on Independent Frame at the time: Gordon [Jackson] was in one called *Stop Press Girl*; then he and I were both in *Floodtide*; and *Poet's Pub*, which I was in.

I wasn't really very pleased with *Floodtide*. One review said, 'There were flaccid performances from Gordon Jackson and Rona Anderson,' so we raced to the dictionary to see what that might mean and it wasn't very complimentary. I just lacked naturalness, but Gordon didn't. There was too much 'Cocktail, Daddy?' in the dialogue, but there were some good things. Jimmy Logan, a Scottish stand-up comedian, had a naturalness that couldn't be spoiled by this particular kind of production method. It was also Elizabeth Sellars' first film. I remember she had very striking eyes.

Freddy Wilson was a nice man and so was Donald, and they ran Aquila under the Rank banner. I suppose *Floodtide* was one of their better efforts, though I can't say I'm very pleased with it.

Poet's Pub was adapted from the Eric Linklater novel *Private Angelo* in the same year.

I don't remember anything about Eric Linklater but I did think that *Poet's Pub* was a sweet film. Above all, I had the great joy of meeting Joyce Grenfell. We used to lunch together with James Robertson Justice, and he and Joyce Grenfell used to talk constantly about Bach at lunch. I think the film was done at Pinewood and a lot of it was done in the grounds. Certainly there was no location work but there used to be a road with a ford on it at Pinewood, and a film with a road that has a ford on it usually means it was shot at Pinewood. There was some work on *Poet's Pub* done on Independent Frame, but not as much as was done on *Floodtide*, as I recall.

I also remember *Poet's Pub* because it was the film on which I met Barbara Murray, who has been a close friend ever since. She was another of the Rank 'young ladies' at the time, along with myself and Lana Morris.

Did you and Gordon not do another film together until you made *The Prime of Miss Jean Brodie* in 1968?

Yes, that's true, and it was really only a gimmick. I was only in *Jean Brodie* because Gordon was in it and because Maggie Smith and Robert Stephens were also married. I think they thought it would be a good gimmick to have another married couple in it.

You had ten very busy years from then on, making two or more films a year. How did you come by this work? Was it largely a matter of contract?

No, I was under contract with Rank earlier on but through the '50s it was really a matter of distributors. Mine turned out to be a name that was OK for 'B' pictures. I don't really remember those films very well. I got married in 1951 and I just went about it as a job of work after that. Most of those films were made in about three weeks and I enjoyed the work; it was relaxing and friendly. I think I got paid about £100 a week – I was cheap, and that's probably why they used me. There was an industry going then; there was a bit of continuity, though I think really I came in at the end of it. After my contract with Rank finished, it was just a matter of parts coming my way and my taking them.

You worked for a variety of production companies – Renown, Hammer, Aquila, Beaconsfield, Merton Park. Did it make much difference to you where the films were made or by which company?

No, it didn't make the slightest difference which company was making them. I didn't really care, either, which studio they were made at. I think maybe Walton Studios, where I did a film for Charles Saunders, was probably the crappiest of all; it was certainly a bit naff after Pinewood and Denham and Shepperton. It seemed to be in a sort of siding in a suburb, stuck in amongst a whole lot of houses. But really, it hardly mattered where the film was made, once you were inside the studio.

What distinctions did you find between making main and supporting features: for example, were the supporting films filmed much faster?

There wasn't much sense of difference between the 'A' and 'B' films once you actually got on the floor. It didn't seem very different in the studios, but I suppose there were differences. 'B' films were mostly cops and robbers, weren't they? You never thought them as good as the major films being made elsewhere. And I'm sure they cut the costs; for instance, I think they cut costs a great deal on lighting. They didn't go in for very elaborate lighting set-ups and they didn't need to. And of course, they didn't have huge sets. They were filmed fast; usually in about three weeks.

I'd be grateful for any recollections of some of the directors you worked with. Take John Guillermin first.

I was in his very first film, *Torment*. There was Dermot Walsh and John Bentley and me. What I remember about it was that at one point I was meant to be pushing a wardrobe; he didn't think I was making enough effort, so he filled it up with things. I said, 'John, I'm an actress. I can *act* greater pressure, I don't need to have it terribly heavy!' I don't remember much more about him but of course he went on to do great things later on, and in Hollywood too.

What about Ken Hughes?

He went on to big things too, but he didn't take me with him! You know, I think if you did second features it didn't really do you much good. It looked as if you hadn't made it. I don't think people thought of you for major films if you went in for doing those 'B' films and agents didn't really look after you at all.

I remember doing *Little Red Monkey*, for Ken, because its theme song was popular at the time. And I remember the American, Richard Conte, starred in it and he was quite a big name at the box office in those days.

You did two for Terence Fisher, later of Hammer fame: *Home to Danger* in 1951 and *The Flaw* in 1955.

I don't remember anything about *The Flaw* but I do remember *Home to Danger* because Guy Rolfe was in that. He was a strange, very saturnine man who used to play *vingt-et-un* for money – and always used to win – while we were sitting around on the set. I was rather dubious about him, but one day, I had a scene where I had to ride a horse – and I fancied myself riding a horse – but the thing went out of control. I couldn't make it stop and I had a terror of being dragged along with my feet in the stirrups, so I took my feet out of the stirrups and thought, I'll just fall off. The next thing I knew, I was lying in the mud and who should be picking me up and wrapping me in his camel-hair coat but Guy Rolfe, so I changed my opinion of him after that.

What about Wolf Rilla, for whom you made *Noose for a Lady*, *The Black Rider*, and *Stock Car*?

Oh yes, I remember doing *Stock Car* for him with that nice Canadian actor, Paul Carpenter. Wolf always liked to rehearse. Most film directors – and most film actors – don't want to rehearse. I wouldn't mind if I were doing a film now, but in those days I didn't want to. They would just line you all up to establish various technical things, and then rehearse a bit after that. Paul Carpenter didn't want to rehearse at all, and Dennis Price, who was in *Noose for a Lady*, especially didn't. Wolf was a very intense man, the son of Walter Rilla, the actor. He was rather intellectually inclined. He made some very successful first features, like *A Pattern of Islands* [aka *Pacific Destiny*], which Gordon was in. He writes books now, and runs a hotel in the south of France.

One director I hope you remember is Lance Comfort. You did two films for him, one he produced (*Home to Danger*) and one he directed (*Devils of Darkness*).

I don't remember Lance much in relation to *Home to Danger*, which was directed by Terence Fisher, but I remember *Devils of Darkness*. I went into Wardour Street and Lance explained the film to me at great length. I sat there listening and thinking, this seems like a good big part for me. Then I got sent the script and I realised that Lance had given me this enormously long account of a part that was all going to be over in the first ten minutes of the film, that Tracey Reed had the lead, and I was to be killed by a vampire! I was amazed to get the script and realise how little there was to this part but Lance was a lovely, sweet man and I liked working for him.

As far as I was concerned I was just a jobbing actor: I learned my lines, went in and did my stuff, and came home. I always just said yes to everything; I never turned anything down. Gordon used to say that this might be the last job we were offered, and of course the jobs kept on coming.

Brian Desmond Hurst's *Scrooge* was a charming version of Dickens, I think. What do you recall of working with Hurst, Alastair Sim, George Cole, etc?

I was Alice, the young woman whom Scrooge nearly married, so all of my scenes were with George Cole, who played Scrooge as a young man. I have to tell you, I was never directed by Brian Desmond Hurst; Alastair Sim directed the scenes between George Cole and me. I think George was a sort of protégé of Alastair's. Alastair was a very nice man. I agree with you that it's a charming film, I liked it very much.

What do you regard as the highlights of your career?

I don't think I had any, did I? I was quite pleased with *The Bay of San Michel* and I liked *Her Favourite Husband*, in which I played Stellina, the gangster's moll. That made a nice change from 'Mary' and 'Joan' and of course, the film was made in Rome so that was a treat as well. Also, I think farce is quite difficult to do on film and it came off, up to a point. It was a nice change for me and it was certainly my favourite role.

Daniel Angel

b. 1911

Producer: *Dancing Thru (1946), *All the King's Horses, *The King's Music (1947), Murder At the Windmill (1949), Miss Pilgrim's Progress, The Body Said No! (1950), Mr Drake's Duck, Another Man's Poison (1951), Women of Twilight (1952), Cosh Boy, Albert RN (1953), The Sea Shall Not Have Them (1954), Escapade (1955), Reach for the Sky (1956), Seven Thunders (1957), Carve her Name With Pride, The Sheriff of Fractured Jaw (1958), We Joined the Navy (1962), West 11 (1963), King and Country (1964), The Romantic Englishwoman (1975) *Short film.

B ritish cinema has not been rich in powerful producers, but the name of Daniel Angel was one of the most respected in the two decades after the war. He is now most frequently associated with three directors: Val Guest, who made a series of light comedies for him; Lewis Gilbert, for whom he produced some enormously popular war films, including *Reach for the Sky* and *Carve Her Name With Pride*, which both won awards; and Joseph Losey, with whom he made a different sort of war film, the sombre *King and Country*, and *The Romantic Englishwoman*. Angel, from other people's comments, seems to have been the sort of producer who was highly skilled at providing financial and industrial support for the filmmaker, at the same time having a creative interest in the enterprise. *Interview date: September 1992*

Is the producer's primary function dealing with the financing of the production?

Oh yes, he has a hundred-per-cent responsibility for that. The producer has got to find the finance; he's got to arrange the distribution, because, normally, there's no point in producing a film if it's not going to be distributed. To my mind it's very clear what the difference between the director and the producer is. The director does everything on the floor, whereas the producer has over-all approval of everything – including casting, script and any alterations it may need, and so on.

Would you want a guarantee of distribution before you began shooting?

Today I would, yes, though it was different when I started. A producer now puts up a certain amount of his own money to get the script off the ground. We're talking of a feature film and this is very expensive. Then he goes to a distributor, and the first thing he'll ask is, 'Who's in it?' because films are not easy to sell now, unless there are names in them. And, of course, there are not many British names.

Did being a producer satisfy you creatively?

Yes. I was always involved in creative discussions with the director. I went into films because of the necessity to earn a living at the end of the war. I started making documentaries, I made two or three of those. The first was *All the King's Horses*, a half-hour film about King George VI's racehorses and ceremonial horses. When I finished it, I got someone to write a commentary, which I then had to shoot and add to the film.

Was there anything in your background to incline you to this?

Yes, there was. I worked for the family firm, called Maurice Angel, a leading theatrical costumier in Shaftesbury Avenue. As a result, I came to see almost every West End show, which the family firm would have dressed.

The earliest commercial credit I have found for you is a short revue film called *Dancing Thru*, directed by Victor Gover.

Yes, actually that was the first film I ever made – it was just after the war. It was distributed by a firm called Pioneer Exclusives, based in Golders Green. It got mainstream distribution as a half-hour short. I did it before *All the King's Horses*, which was my second film.

As I understand it the next four features you did were all with Val Guest as director . . .

Yes. After I made *All the King's Horses*, I made my first feature film, which was *Murder at the Windmill*, with Val Guest. My father-in-law, Vivian Van Damm, owned the Windmill Theatre, and we made up a story up there and I cast it. We had quite a strong cast – Jon Pertwee, Jimmy Edwards, Diana Decker, dear old Garry Marsh. I really just don't remember how my association with Val began. He was a very nice man and it was a good, harmonious working relationship. He's still alive and lives in America. He's married to an American actress called Yolande Donlan, who was the star of three of the films we did together [*Miss Pilgrim's Progress*, *The Body Said No!*, *Mr Drake's Duck*]. She was over here in the '40s in a West End play called *Born Yesterday*.

Val wrote and directed the films and I looked after the rest. They were all Angel Productions, and I always used to say that I was the first producer who started at the top, though I hadn't had any training and had to pick it all up as I went along.

You did four films with Val Guest, then five with Lewis Gilbert. Did it make much difference to your producer's function who your director was?

Oh yes. Lewis Gilbert, who I started, came into my office one day and said, 'I'd like to make a film for you.' He did a couple of early ones for me, then of course later we did *Reach for the Sky* together. Lewis's films were in a different class from those early ones of Val's. Lewis went on after *Reach for the Sky* to make big films and he also wrote a lot of his scripts, with his sidekick, Vernon Harris.

What was your experience of working with Hollywood directors, such as Irving Rapper, who did *Another Man's Poison* for you?

I'll tell you how I got Irving Rapper. I went to Hollywood to get Bette Davis. She wasn't all that keen to come, so I said to her, 'You can bring your own director over,' and she said, 'There's a man called Irving Rapper I like,' so he came over to direct the film. Not that she took much notice of him. She was a cow! But, you know, she was very talented, *very* talented, and her husband [Gary Merrill] was a very nice man.

From what one gathers, it sounds as if the British stars would never have behaved like Bette Davis . . .

They didn't know *how* to behave like this. You have to remember that Hollywood was founded on sex, though it was said that Bette Davis was the only female star who hadn't slept her way to becoming a star. But Irving Rapper couldn't handle her at all. She was a very dominating character and at that time she was on her way down, but she was an interesting woman just the same.

You had another Hollywood director, Raoul Walsh, on *The Sheriff of Fractured Jaw* . . .

Right. He was one of the greatest in Hollywood. He was a lovely man. He was a great personality and easy to work with from a producer's point of view. He'd made some wonderful Hollywood pictures.

Did you like *The Sheriff of Fractured Jaw* with Jayne Mansfield?

At the time, yes. I must say she was charming. You know, my wife always said that, below the waist, she had this marvellous figure, but, front-on above the waist, she was a monstrosity. She was a very nice woman and I liked her husband, Mickey Hargitay, too. I don't want any of my artistes to give me presents, and there's a lot of that goes on and it doesn't mean anything, but whenever Jayne came to London she brought me a gift.

***The Sheriff of Fractured Jaw* must be almost the only British Western. Where did you film it?**

All the exteriors were done in Spain. You can

always find somewhere there that will pass for America. Kenneth More and Jayne Mansfield were a good team. He started at the Windmill, you know.

You made several films with him as star. What do you think was the secret of his considerable popularity?

He did that wonderful film with Vivien Leigh, *The Deep Blue Sea*, and then I was about to make *Reach for the Sky*, with Richard Burton. Well, Burton went to Spain to make a film, and my wife said to me, 'Kenneth More *is* Douglas Bader.' And so he was! He was a good actor, but, looking back, I don't think he was all that versatile, and he wasn't physically a very attractive man. He couldn't play love scenes. He was more of a playboy type. He *was* Douglas Bader! Bader wasn't a technical adviser, but I suppose Kenny More modelled himself physically on Bader.

My favourite part in the film was the scenes in the hospital where he's trying to learn to walk again, with Dorothy Alison as the nurse. I took an awful lot of trouble with that, because I've been in hospital myself, on and off since the war, and I'd seen a lot of that sort of thing. It was a very touching performance from Dorothy Alison, who seemed to sum up so much in a few moments.

Another girl who was in it was Beverly Brooks, later Viscountess Rothermere. She was under contract to the Rank Organisation and she played Bader's girlfriend early in the film.

A couple of your earlier films – *Women of Twilight* and *Cosh Boy* – seem to have been co-productions with Romulus Films.

That was through Jimmy Woolf, who was a very talented man. He had these two stories and we made the films with the idea of showing them in cinemas together on the one programme. They turned out better than we'd expected and we showed them separately. Jimmy said, 'If you like these we can co-finance them and Romulus will distribute them,' and they turned out more successful than we'd thought they would be.

***Women of Twilight* has a strong cast of British character players ...**

Yes, Freda Jackson, René Ray – and Laurence Harvey, a bloody good actor, who was a friend of Jimmy Woolf's. He was really under contract to Romulus.

You made four war films with Lewis Gilbert as director. Why do you think there were so many war films made in Britain ten years after the war had ended?

I've no idea. It may be that there were very few women stars, and in general a war film is easier to make than, say, a love story. You don't have to worry so much about the dialogue; you just keep the action going. But really there was just a shortage of women stars at that time. There was Virginia [McKenna] of course, and she was a very, very good actress. We had her in *Carve Her Name With Pride*. But British films have never been strong on love stories and the sex element.

Perhaps, too, the war just produced good stories?

This is the point. Take *Reach for the Sky*, for example. When we screened it again recently for some charity performance, I said to someone there, 'It's very easy to have a successful film if you have a good story.' And how many good stories are there? Very often producers have to make a film whether they have a good story or not.

Were they difficult films to make, *Reach for the Sky* and *Carve Her Name With Pride*, both huge successes with the public?

They were *all* difficult at the time. Starting at the top as producer didn't make it any easier. I liked working with Lewis Gilbert, though; he's a very nice, modest, talented man.

You'd done two earlier war films with him, hadn't you – *Albert RN* and *The Sea Shall Not Have Them* ...

Yes. *Albert RN* was based on a stage play by Guy Morgan, and it was a true story.

They are very strongly cast films. Were they expensive to make in their time?

No. They were very cheap. A lot of the people in them became stars afterwards, but weren't expensive at the time. I think *Albert RN* cost about £75,000. *Reach for the Sky* only cost £365,000 – made today, it would cost about nine million.

Did you as producer individually engage those actors, or were they under contracts?

Michael Redgrave was individually engaged. Dirk Bogarde, was under contract to the Rank Organisation, so I got him through Rank's Olive Dodds, who was in charge of their contract players. I'd give her the script and if she approved it she'd pass it on. Dirk's a charming man, very nice indeed, and he'd be happy to be loaned out if he liked the script.

Did you spend much time at the studios during shooting?

I used to go down to the studios in the afternoons. Twickenham and Pinewood were the two I worked at most, I think. I did one at Elstree, but I didn't enjoy that so much. The boss of Elstree, or rather of ABPC [Associated British Picture Corporation] was Robert Clark, a man who, it was said, left £84 million; he was a Scot, a very nice man, very kind, but very careful with the money.

How did you come to be involved in *King and Country*?

Well, I knew Joe Losey, and when I got hold of this script from the play *Hamp*, I got on the phone to Joe. He was going to do something for Rank. Anyway, we had Dirk Bogarde, who was anxious to do it, and we did it in black-and-white, and on a small budget. It wasn't very popular at the time, but since then it's become a classic.

To go back to earlier British cinema, would you agree that the '40s and '50s constituted a sort of 'boom' period?

Oh yes, they were. The trouble today is that no one wants to make films. They're too expensive. And whatever they say about John Davis [Rank's Managing Director], he *did* make it possible for people to make films, whereas, today, it's terribly expensive to set up a film for those who do want to make them. When I started over forty years ago, when I was just out of the war, it was comparatively easy – if I had a script, I'd ring up Val Guest,

we'd talk about it, and, if we both liked it, we'd go ahead.

Why do you think it has been so difficult for British films to be successful in mainstream American distribution?

Partly, I think, because we didn't sell our stars properly; it cost too much money. We had the talent here. But nobody over here had the money, or the flair in spending it, except Korda.

Someone has made the criticism that British films were too middle-class to appeal widely in America.

They *were* middle-class. They also didn't like showing sex in the movies and of course Hollywood is founded on sex. It developed a star system based on sex appeal – think of people like Marilyn Monroe and Ava Gardner. Over the years, Hollywood spent fortunes promoting the stars. And, also, for many *English* actors, the stage was their first love. Britain had wonderful character actors. It *always* did, and a lot of the good character actors went to America.

Another thing that made British films difficult for America in those times was the accents and these meant the stars were often a bloody big bore. We've never really produced stars – someone like Guinness is more of a character actor.

Ken Annakin

b. 1914

Director: *The Sixteen Tasks of Maintaining Vehicles, *We Serve (1942?), *Cooks, *London (1942), *A Ride with Uncle Joe (1943), *Black Diamonds, *The New Crop, *Combined Cadets (1944), *A Farm in the Fens, *Crop Rotation, *Make Fruitful the Land, *Pacific Thrust, *Three Cadets (1945), *We of the West Riding, *It Began on the Clyde, *English Criminal Justice (1946), *Turn It Out, Holiday Camp, Broken Journey (1947), Here Come the Huggetts, Miranda, Quartet ('The Colonel's Lady') (1948), Vote for Huggett, Landfall, The Huggetts Abroad (1949), Trio ('The Verger' and 'Mr Knowall'), Double Confession (1950), Hotel Sahara (1951), The Planter's Wife, The Story of Robin Hood and his Merrie Men (1952), The Sword and the Rose (1953), The Seekers, You Know What Sailors

Are (1954), *Value for Money* (1955), *Loser Takes All, Three Men in a Boat* (1956), *Across the Bridge* (1957), *Nor the Moon by Night* (1958), *Third Man on the Mountain* (1959), *Swiss Family Robinson* (1960), *A Very Important Person, The Hellions* (1961), *Crooks Anonymous, The Fast Lady, The Longest Day* (co-dir) (1962), *The Informers* (1963), *Those Magnificent Men in Their Flying Machines, The*

Battle of the Bulge (1965), *The Long Duel* (& pr) (1966), *The Biggest Bundle of Them All* (1967), *Those Daring Young Men in Their Jaunty Jalopies* (& co-sc, pr) (1969), *Call of the Wild* (1972), *Paper Tiger* (1974), *The Fifth Musketeer* (1977), *Cheaper to Keep Her* (1980), *The Pirate Movie* (1982), *Pippi Longstocking* (& sc, co-pr) (1986)
* Documentary short film.

In many ways Ken Annakin's busy, nearly fifty-year-long career follows a classic pattern for British directors. Invalided out of the RAF, he quickly became involved with documentary filmmaking, like so many of his contemporaries, before embarking on feature films. His first batch of features was made for Gainsborough Studios, under the regime of Sydney Box, and included such typical Gainsborough product as the 'Huggett' films and the Somerset Maugham compendia. To *Holiday Camp*, which introduced the Huggetts, he brought some of the feeling for ordinary lives he had acquired in the documentary field. In the 1950s he began a very successful association with Walt Disney, for whom he made four popular films. His '50s output also features outpost-of-Empire films (*The Planter's Wife*, *The Seekers*, *Nor the Moon by Night*) and several light comedies (including the inventive *Hotel Sahara*), before he moved on to the international phase of his prolific career. In spite of the big box-office successes of such large-scale enterprises as *Those Magnificent Men in Their Flying Machines*, which he handled with assurance, it is nice to know that he would like best to be remembered for 'The Colonel's Lady', one of the *Quartet* stories, and for *Across the Bridge*, a taut adaptation from Graham Greene, two very accomplished pieces about which he feels strongly.
Interview date: June 1990

One source claims that you began in films as an assistant cameraman and that you were also assistant director to Carol Reed.

That's true. After I was injured in the Liverpool blitz, the RAF switched me from being a flight mechanic into the Film Unit, and I worked on films for the Ministry of Information and the British Council, and on Army and RAF training films. The switch to being an assistant director came about when I was working as camera operator on *We Serve*, a recruiting film for women in the Army that was being directed by Carol Reed, with important actresses like Flora Robson working for £5 per day.

Finally, one day Carol said, 'I think you should switch over to our side,' meaning into directing. Maybe he thought I wasn't very good with a Mitchell camera! At any rate, I switched to being his assistant and after that I directed quite a lot of documentary and training films.

You were very busy between 1942 and 1946, making documentaries and shorts. How did you get in to feature films?

I became attached to Verity Films run by Sydney Box, who opened many doors for me. Just before the war finished, Sydney had made the very successful picture, *The Seventh Veil*, and was given the job of running Gainsborough Pictures. He said to me, 'You ought to be making features, Ken, because you've got a good story mind and visual sense. Try and get one picture to make which shows that you can handle actors as well as documentary people.' I was lucky in that I got a picture called *British Criminal Justice*, which really explained the British system of law and gave me a wonderful break.

Sydney kept his promise and gave me *Holiday Camp* to direct. I was dying to get into feature films but I was a typical documentary guy and *Holiday Camp* taught me a lot about fictional movies – like the need for humour and good women's roles.

Whose brainchild was *Holiday Camp*? There are no fewer than six writers credited to it.

Godfrey Winn was the first writer engaged for it. He was a popular magazine writer, and he and I went to Butlin's holiday camp at Filey to see what really happened and to devise a story. I think he put together a very good story but then Sydney and Muriel Box, who were both writers, decided we should add certain elements, like the Heath Murder character played by Dennis Price; that was news then, so Muriel worked it into the story. I remember a round-table conference with Ted Willis (a working-class writer from the Unity Theatre), Peter Rogers (who later wrote the *Carry On* pictures), Mabel Constanduros (who was a popular writer of very funny, working-class plays): all came together to add their ideas. Godfrey wasn't terribly happy about it because he thought he was going to have a single screen credit, but it was a great popular success, partly perhaps because I had come from documentary and British cinema at that time was very artificial.

The Huggetts absolutely caught the spirit and feeling that existed after the war. Whilst waiting for the invasion, troops were always being lectured on equality and how, when they came home, England would be the country where everybody had equal opportunities. People didn't want more fairy stories; they wanted something in which they could recognise themselves. Being of lower-middle-class origins myself, I felt at home with these people who were having a fine holiday in a very cheap place which provided wonderful entertainment. I think I caught the spirit of the holiday camps and we had a very warm, natural cast. Kathleen Harrison was a wonderful, working-class actress; Jack Warner was a very amiable type whom people loved to watch; Flora Robson was a great theatre actress with a gift for pathos, and her story with Esmond Knight, as

the blind radio commentator, was very touching; and Hazel Court, my first 'star', is still a friend here in LA. I'm not embarrassed about *Holiday Camp* today, although the later Huggett films don't hold up so well.

I must say, too, that *Miranda*, my third feature, also holds up well today. My favourite scene in *Miranda* is the one where Glynis Johns gives Margaret Rutherford the pearls. Maggie was wonderful when we were shooting that scene. She was a complete original, she had no technique at all that she admitted to. I recall telling her to do that funny little flutter of her lips as she came into close-up, and she said, 'I don't do any fluttering of my lips!' You had to shoot until you caught what you wanted from her. What she did have was an original zany quality and you felt she was a very strong, loving person you'd like around.

What do you remember about filming *Broken Journey*?

When we finished *Holiday Camp*, Sydney Box came up with a fascinating story of a plane crash in the Alps. He had engaged Bob Westerby to write it and he told me to go to France, find a crashed aeroplane and a location to shoot it! So I went to France and was lucky to find an old Dakota that had crashed. I then found a plateau just under Mont Blanc, at Les Huches, and discussed with the man who owned the téléférique how we could cut up this plane and get it up the mountain. I went home, polished the script with Bob Westerby, cast it with Sydney and was back in France four weeks later for location shooting, using doubles. I found a wonderful climber and stills photographer in Chamonix; he was able to go up and photograph on glaciers, where normal cameramen couldn't work, and he made a second unit for me.

When I came back to England we shot for forty-odd days in the studio – in summer, using a lot of back projection. We had Phyllis Calvert, a natural screen actress, Margot Grahame, a bit stagey but a very funny woman all the same, and also Francis L Sullivan, Guy Rolfe and Mary Hinton in the cast.

Gainsborough was a very important studio making twenty-eight pictures a year under Sydney, so he could get almost anyone he wanted. It was a happy experience working for the Box family: Sydney was an inspiring boss, and Betty Box supervised all the production at Islington, where I made *Miranda*.

The films from the Somerset Maugham stories hold up very well. Was it difficult to get big-name stars to play in a third or a

quarter of a film?

Not really; they all loved the idea of working on a Maugham story because he was recognised as one of the best story tellers of that era. 'The Colonel's Lady' from *Quartet* is one of the best pictures I ever made, and is touching though not sentimental. Nora Swinburne was great as the writer of a novel about 'a secret love' and Cecil Parker was superb as her county-squire husband. 'Mr Knowall', in *Trio*, was also a very good story. That's the one with Nigel Patrick. 'The Verger' was a good character study, with Kathleen Harrison and James Hayter. But I would like to be remembered for 'The Colonel's Lady' of all my British films, and for *Across the Bridge*, which I made in 1957.

The importation of American stars was common in the '50s: you had Yvonne de Carlo in *Hotel Sahara*, one of my favourites among your films.

I like it too; it ran for years in Germany because it was the first to show that many Germans were human beings serving just like other soldiers. The idea for *Hotel Sahara* came from George Brown, the producer, and it was one of the best pictures he ever made. The screenplay was written by George himself and Patrick Kirwan. The witty stuff came from Kirwan but George had a great feel for it because he had been with the Desert Rats.

Yvonne was charming to work with even though she wasn't the greatest of actresses. Getting a scene in the can was terribly difficult with the cast I had. All Ustinov needed was *one* rehearsal; you knew you had to shoot by the third rehearsal, otherwise he would start playing the scene like ten other actors, mimicking them because he was bored. But Yvonne was a girl who had been taught to do things step by step, so I had to do private rehearsals with her and keep Peter out of the way, in order to get her performing equally well. Despite its desert exteriors, the film was made entirely at Pinewood.

Starting in 1952, you made the first of four films for Disney. How developed was the Disney set-up in England at that time?

It was not developed at all; he just had Carmen Dillon designing everything and Guy Green working for him as a cameraman. Apart from that there was no real set-up. *Robin Hood* was a great lesson to me because Guy had been on the picture a long time before I came on, and he and Carmen had designed practically every set-up and they'd all been approved by Walt in Hollywood! With the second movie I directed, *The Sword and the Rose*, I

was in from the beginning and every set-up was *my* design. I learnt a tremendous amount on these two productions so that, by the time I made *Swiss Family Robinson*, Walt and I were on a completely friendly, equal basis and it was a joy creating with him.

By that time, there was a true Disney Organisation in England. We made *Robin Hood* and *The Sword and the Rose* at Denham; *Third Man on the Mountain* mainly in Switzerland, with the small amount of studio work done at Pinewood. *Swiss Family Robinson* was made entirely on location in Tobago and a studio I built there out of corrugated iron sheets. We had terrible sound because torrential storms battered on the tin roof, so I had to spend twenty-eight days at Pinewood post-synching the entire film.

You made three 'outpost-of-Empire' films in the '50s: *The Planter's Wife. The Seekers* and *Nor the Moon by Night*. Why do you think there were suddenly so many of these films?

Because a few of us wanted to go on location in interesting places, I guess! I know I did *The Seekers* because I wanted to go back to New Zealand. It wasn't a great script; it was George Brown again, and he had a playwright called Bill Fairchild write the script, which was only so-so from the first. We did our best with it during shooting, but the premise and the casting were ridiculous. The part in the opening reel about the creation of the Maori world was all right; the rest was junk. We took only Jack Hawkins, Laya Raki and Noel Purcell to New Zealand because George was very tight with the money; it was a fourteen-day continuous shoot and the shop steward caused us to miss the geyser blowing because the tea wagon hadn't arrived for the morning break! I stayed behind with the cameraman and we did a lot of 'doubling' ourselves.

Of the three films you mentioned, I am quite proud of *The Planter's Wife*. For that I went to Malaya but it was too dangerous to take actors there, so most of it was shot in Ceylon, the rest in Pinewood.

I shouldn't really have accepted *Nor the Moon by Night*, but I wanted to see South Africa! The film I really wanted to do was *The Singer Not the Song*, which was eventually made by Roy Baker, with Dirk Bogarde. In Natal we had all kinds of disasters: Belinda Lee tried to commit suicide by cutting her wrists; Patrick McGoohan turned his car over three times and had concussion; one day there was only me and a snake available to work! We were filming in the 'Valley of a Thousand Hills', where all the trouble is now between the Zulus and Mandela's ANC. In 1958 it was a marvellous place to work and I met my wife Pauline there. That was a plus, but the picture was a mediocre hotch-potch.

You were associated with some well-known British producers throughout the '50s – Peter Rogers, John Stafford and Jack Clayton. What sort of relationship did you have with your producers?

With John Stafford I had a marvellous relationship; with George Brown a good relationship until he became very mean in New Zealand. Clayton wasn't really a producer but the production controller on *Three Men in a Boat*. He was very envious of me because he wanted to direct! You expect a producer to back you through thick and thin, and to try to help you obtain the best picture possible. I hate a weak producer who allows stars to behave in a way which is against the interests of the picture, or who doesn't fight for the extra finance you need to achieve what you and he set out to do. I have done several pictures, as we all have, during which you get fed up with the producer and decide to produce yourself. It doesn't work, because you are wearing two different hats. The way I have solved the dilemma on the last few pictures is to have my wife as either associate producer or, if possible, producer. She can be quite tough on running the picture but her interests are *identical* with mine.

You made two films based on novels by Graham Greene – *Loser Takes All* and *Across the Bridge*. What attracted you to these projects?

Across the Bridge was a very classy picture, and very non-British! I took stills of locations in Texas and Mexico, then we staged the whole movie in Spain. I'm very proud of that picture. John Stafford found the short story and he engaged a young writer, Guy Elmes, to expand it. The movie is really half a Graham Greene story (the part from when he has crossed the bridge) and Guy 'manufactured' the story that leads to the bridge. So it was based on Greene's moral attitude and Schaffer's [Rod Steiger] new character, and it worked marvellously.

I wanted to make *Loser Takes All* because, in its moral attitude to wealth, it was different. It was a satirical comedy which Graham Greene wrote to work off his spleen against Sir Alexander Korda for having messed up his life over a period of years. Robert Morley played the Korda role brilliantly; unfortunately, the head of British Lion insisted that Rossano Brazzi play the role of Bertrand. Brazzi had made a hit in David Lean's *Summertime* but he was completely wrong casting because Bertrand was a very English chap. The basic concept of Graham Greene's story is the opposite of what normal people want; everyone wants to win money and everyone admires someone who has a system that wins in a casino. Nobody could understand it when Glynis Johns said she would prefer an honest student's love, rather than her husband's now he is rich! I spent a lot of time with Graham Greene, and now that I write screenplays myself I still think very much of Graham and his credo.

Renee Asherson

b. 1920

Actor: *The Way Ahead* (1944), *Henry V, The Way to the Stars* (1945), *Caesar and Cleopatra* (1946), *Once a Jolly Swagman* (1948), *The Small Back Room* (1949), *The Cure for Love* (1950), *Pool of London*,

The Magic Box (1951), *Malta Story* (1953), *Time Is My Enemy* (1954), *The Day the Earth Caught Fire* (1961), *Rasputin the Mad Monk* (1965), *The* *Smashing Bird I Used To Know* (1969), *Theatre of Blood* (1973), *A Man Called Intrepid* (1979)

To be directed in your first three films by Carol Reed, Laurence Olivier and Anthony Asquith was as good a start as a British actress could expect in the 1940s. Even if the roles were small, Renee Asherson began in good company, and as Olivier's Princess Katherine in *Henry V* she is entirely charming, securing her niche in 1940s British cinema. Her English-lesson scene with Ivy St Helier as her lady-in-waiting is one of the film's most perfectly judged. She was a convincing working-girl heroine in *Once a Jolly Swagman* and in Ealing's *Pool of London*, and she held her own in the broad comedy of *The Cure for Love*, in which she was directed by, and co-starred with, her husband, Robert Donat. It says something for the quiet authority of her playing in the latter that one remembers her against the stiff competition of such noted comic players as Dora Bryan and Gladys Henson, as well as the dominant star presence of Donat himself. After the '40s, she rarely had another worthwhile film role, though television offered many better opportunities from 1955 onwards, most notably in Jack Clayton's *Memento Mori* in 1992, and, as she says, the stage remained her first allegiance.

Interview date: June 1990

Was your stage training valuable to you when you went into films?

There were things you had to unlearn, but the first film I did was *Henry V* and I was with an actor directing, so I was lucky. Larry Olivier saw me when I was at the Mercury, doing a revival of *The Mask of Virtue*, the play in which Vivien Leigh had made her name. Apparently they came to see the play and then asked me to do a test for *Henry V* – I didn't even know Larry was filming it. Larry also asked Janet Burnell, who was playing my mother, to test for the Queen, and we both got the parts. It had been intended that Vivien should play the Princess but, after *Gone With the Wind*, her agents didn't think it was a big enough part for her.

Those scenes you have with Ivy St Helier are charming.

Yes, and she was lovely to be with. She was as nervous as me because neither of us had done any filming, except that she had done the film *Bitter Sweet* in the '30s, because she was a Coward actress.

Did you have a lot of rehearsal for those court scenes?

I went through the wooing scene with Larry on that extraordinary set and he told me to go to a teacher called Alice Gachet who taught French drama at RADA and go through the scenes with her. So I did, and I then got hold of a Frenchman who had a beautiful Parisian accent. I would go through my scene with him, working on the French accent and listening to every intonation. He said that when he saw the film I sounded like a Russian speaking French! I did *The Way Ahead* whilst I was waiting to retake the wooing scene. Larry wanted to retake the wooing scene, not, he said, because of me, but because he didn't like himself in it. It was an immensely demanding thing to direct and play at the same time; he had never directed a film and everyone was slightly sceptical, especially that marvellous cameraman, Bob Krasker, who used to look through his viewfinder, shake his head and say, 'No no no!' But Larry fought all the way and as a result he didn't altogether like himself when he saw the wooing scene. When he showed me the black-and-white rushes I absolutely hated seeing myself, it was such a shock! The film was made in colour, with the only colour camera in the country at that time, but the rushes were in black-and-white. It was done in a very stylised way, with sloping floors and strange perspective, taken from a medieval Book of Hours – the Duc de Berri's, I think – which makes it much less dated than it would otherwise be. The French court scenes are done with a comic edge which gives them a weird charm, whereas, in Kenneth Branagh's, these are totally realistic like the whole film.

You had a small part in *The Way Ahead* released before *Henry V*.

My part *was* tiny but, as you say, I really started at the top with my first two films being for Laurence Olivier and Carol Reed! I played Mary Jerrold's daughter and I remember she was an enchanting person. I can't remember much about Carol Reed as a director because I was so scared; I just did what he told me as far as I could.

Following your trend of working with top directors, you next made *The Way to the Stars* for Anthony Asquith. Did you have a good agent getting you these roles?

I got an agent for the first time just before I did *Henry V*. Perhaps because of *Henry V* my name got around a bit. I didn't know Anthony Asquith at all so I don't know how I came to get that part. I was very scared in that film too, because I was up against the real 'film thing' and Asquith, like Carol Reed, was a complete film man. I suddenly became aware of the cameras and all the technicalities and I was rather at sea, whereas in *Henry V* I was in a sort of dream and it didn't matter whether there were cameras or not.

I understand Anthony Asquith was a very gentle director of actors.

Oh yes, a very charming man. I wasn't scared of him, it was just the medium that suddenly became unfamiliar. I came to understand more about filming after a few more films, but I never, except at the beginning, did any films on end and with long enough parts to get really used to the medium. So it has always eluded me and I would love to get a grasp of it and really feel at home. I would like to have grasped more the very naturalistic level at which you must play; I *did* do it, but I never *knew* whether I did! I never had a part long enough to get totally relaxed in it.

What do you remember of making *Caesar

and Cleopatra*?

Just before *Henry V* came out, this extraordinary man Gabriel Pascal asked to see the rushes and he then wanted me to be in *Caesar and Cleopatra*. Meanwhile, Larry had asked me to go with him to the Old Vic and I had of course said yes. Because I was so ignorant of theatre matters, this American agent [Al Parker] had unbeknown to me tied me up to Pascal for first call for half a year, in anticipation of doing *Caesar and Cleopatra*. Had I been less frightened of everybody, I would have gone straight to Larry, who probably would have got me out of it. But I didn't dare approach him, so I found myself trapped. When I finally came to my scene I was so furious with Pascal that I burst into tears and wasted feet of Technicolor before I could do the scene! It was a very tense, emotional affair and they had a lot of high-powered personalities together in it.

Pascal was an extraordinary character – half-genius, half-conman, I think. He had the most marvellous cast, of course: Claude Rains was wonderful as Caesar. I only had one scene with Vivien and was with her very little. I was staggered at the sets and Oliver Messel's costumes – they were beautiful. Still, in spite of the outstanding cast and everything, it looks like a sort of stage thing. I think it is because Pascal was no film director. He was heavy-handed and there were tensions, many frustrations because of him, and people weren't pulling together.

Did you enjoy playing the nice, ordinary girl who saved Dirk Bogarde from himself in *Once a Jolly Swagman*?

Yes, I liked the film, because there were very nice people in it. Dirk was very tense as far as I can remember and I'm tense too. But I can't honestly remember much of it. All my stuff was done on the set although some of the rest was done in London on the dirt-track race circuit.

I was surprised to see you in the small role of the ATS corporal at the end of *The Small Back Room*, after playing important roles.

I think I just hadn't been offered much else at the time. Powell and Pressburger had such a name at the time, my agent probably felt I should take the part. It was shot on a beach somewhere in Dorset. Powell had a reputation for being slightly alarming to actors, but I don't think my part was big enough for that to worry me. He was more concerned with the leading lady, Kathleen Byron, an unusual person, with a very interesting face. I found David Farrar very nice too; I can't remember much about the film otherwise, but he and Kathleen were very good in it.

Having already played Millie in *The Cure for Love* on stage, did you have to make many adjustments for your screen performance?

It was rather nice to do a film of something you knew a lot about, but of course there were some scenes which hadn't existed in the play. It was co-scripted by Walter Greenwood and my husband Robert Donat, who were great friends. I played a Cockney evacuee, billeted on Marjorie Rhodes. It was very broad comedy at times but also very warm and human, I think. Walter really seemed to understand about working-class lives, particularly in the North. Marjorie had also been in the play, as had Thora Hird, who played Mrs Dorbell. I enjoyed playing that sort of comedy: I wasn't actually dispensing the broad comedy but was in humorous situations.

You made your only film at Ealing, *Pool of London*, in 1951. How did you find Ealing as a place to work?

It had rather a nice atmosphere, as I remember. Its people seemed to stay there forever, which helped this, and it seemed much less formal and claustrophobic than places like Denham, where you tended to feel trapped. I haven't seen *Pool of London* for ages, can't even remember what it was about. I did a lot of my work on location near the docks; I remember Michael Relph and Basil Dearden, who made it, but not vividly. I have just worked again with Leslie Phillips, my boyfriend in it, for the first time since then, in a TV pilot for a series, *Life After Death*.

Why did you make so few films after that? Was the '50s not a good decade for women in British films?

Perhaps that was it. I just seemed to do almost no films, I seemed to drop out of it. It wasn't a conscious decision to turn films down, just that I wasn't offered many. I did *The Malta Story* in 1954, directed by Brian Desmond Hurst, and spent a hard-working week on location in Malta. Alec Guinness was there but I never actually met him; my part was totally separate from his. Most of my work was with Anthony Steel.

Were you under any sort of contract?

I was offered a contract soon after *Henry V* by the Rank Organisation, but Larry said I shouldn't tie myself up. In England, they tended to use their contract players most of the time. I could have gone to Rank and probably been sent to the Charm School; and I was once asked to go to Hollywood but didn't because I was doing something on stage with Robert and it would have been too difficult to dash off to Hollywood then.

Anthony Asquith

1902–1968

Director: *Shooting Stars* (with AV Bramble), *Underground* (1928), *The Runaway Princess* (1929), *A Cottage on Dartmoor* (1930), *Tell England* (1931), *Dance, Pretty Lady, Marry Me* (co-sc) (1932), *The Lucky Number, Youth Will Be Served* (1933), *Unfinished Symphony* (co-dir) (1934), *Moscow Nights, *The Story of Papworth: The Village of Hope* (1936), *Pygmalion* (co-dir) (1938), *French Without Tears, *Guide Dogs for the Blind* (1939), *Freedom Radio, Quiet Wedding, *Channel Incident* (1940), *Cottage to Let, *Rush Hour* (1941), *Uncensored* (1942), *We Dive at Dawn, The Demi-Paradise, *Welcome to Britain* (1943), *Fanny by Gaslight, *Two Fathers* (1944), *The Way to the Stars* (1945), *While the Sun Shines* (1946), *The Winslow Boy* (1948), *The Woman in Question, World Without Shadow* (1950), *The Browning Version* (1951), *The Importance of Being Earnest* (1952), *The Net, The*

Final Test (1953), *The Young Lovers, Carrington VC* (1954), **On Such a Night* (1955), *Orders to Kill* (1958), *The Doctor's Dilemma, Libel* (1959), *The Millionairess, Zero* (1960), *Two Living, One Dead* (1961), *Guns of Darkness* (1962), *An Evening with the Royal Ballet, The VIPs* (1963), *The Yellow Rolls-Royce* (1964)
*Short film.

'I will only say that every work of art, even where more than one mind has gone to its shaping, ultimately bears the imprint of a single personality,' wrote Anthony Asquith in 1951.[1] The comment is suggestive in relation to a director whose 'imprint' – discreet, graceful, humane – usually made itself felt in collaboration with other major figures. For instance, he directed half a dozen plays and/or screenplays by Terence Rattigan and three by Bernard Shaw, refusing the lure of flashy camera work to make them more 'cinematic'. Writing of a scene in *The Browning Version* in which the schoolmaster reveals 'a glimpse of the pathetic, disappointed, vulnerable human being', Asquith insists that 'what makes it a film scene is, firstly, the extreme intimacy which the camera establishes between actor and audience.'[2] He was in fact much more articulate about his filmmaking procedures than many directors, as his writings suggest; he was also highly conscious of what film could do.

Asquith's career began in the silent days, when, in 1928, he scored a notable success with *Shooting Stars* (co-directed by AV Bramble). A decade later he was still concerned that 'the arrival of the talking film . . . not only killed the silent film but at first, at any rate, failed to substitute anything positive for it . . . there seems no impulse to explore and exploit this medium as there was in the later days of silent film.'[3] A superficial view might be that his own films were heavily dependent on dialogue, and often dialogue of a highly literary kind. However, throughout his films, there are moments of real visual flair when the camera is plainly doing the story-telling, most often unobtrusively, but sometimes in a virtuoso sequence such as that in *Tell England* in which the mother's wide-eyed face comes into the foreground oblivious of her friend's chatter. (Was David Lean 'quoting' from this fifteen years later in *Brief Encounter*?) Asquith modestly wrote of Fay Compton, who played the mother, 'Miss Compton made her own opportunities,'[4] but the director's imagination is very clearly at work.

And there is no questioning the quality of the performances he elicited from his actors, who all speak of him with warm admiration. 'Often he encouraged us to rehearse by ourselves and accepted what we produced without a change. (If it was right!),' wrote Paul Massie, star of *Orders to Kill*.[5] There are not only the obvious triumphs like Michael Redgrave's schoolmaster in *The Browning Version*, Wendy Hiller's Eliza Dolittle in *Pygmalion* ('For some reason or another . . . Shaw liked my phrase "she came up the stairs like a sleepwalker", and he wrote the Ambassador's Ball scene for us,' Asquith recalled later)[6] or Edith Evans's Lady Bracknell, caught forever on film like a fly in amber. As well one thinks of Cedric Hardwicke as the epitome of middle-class decency as the accused boy's father in *The Winslow Boy*; Margaretta Scott as the cold-hearted Alicia in *Fanny by Gaslight*; Douglass Montgomery and Rosamund John as American flier and English widow quietly creating a friendship in *The Way to the Stars*; and many others.

As early as *Tell England*, he was accused of being a class-bound director, because his heroes spoke in public-school accents. He replied: 'Doe and Ray were educated at a public school and, therefore, they speak as public schoolboys do speak.'[7] His own background was, of course, upper-class; he nevertheless was venerated by the Association of Cine-Technicians, from whose journal the opening quotation comes. He was its president for thirty-one years, and his devotion to its cause was legendary.

1 *The Cine-Technician*, July–August 1951, p 54
2 *Films and Filming*, February 1959, p 13
3 *Sight and Sound*, Spring 1938, p 5
4 *Film Weekly*, 7 November 1931, p 9
5 *Films and Filming*, February 1958, p 28
6 *Films and Filming*, October 1963, p 14
7 *Film Weekly*, 7 November 1931, p 9

Richard Attenborough (Lord Attenborough)

b. 1923

Actor: *In Which We Serve* (1942), *Schweik's New Adventures, The Hundred Pound Window* (1943), *Journey Together* (1945), *A Matter of Life and Death, School for Secrets* (1946), *The Man Within, Dancing with Crime, Brighton Rock* (1947), *London Belongs to Me, The Guinea Pig* (1948), *The Lost People, Boys in Brown* (1949), *Morning Departure* (1950), *Hell Is Sold Out, The Magic Box* (1951), *The Gift Horse, Father's Doing Fine* (1952), *Eight O'Clock Walk* (1954), *The Ship that Died of Shame* (1955), *Private's Progress, The Baby and the Battleship* (1956), *Brothers-in-Law, The Scamp* (1957), *Dunkirk, The Man Upstairs, Sea of Sand* (1958), *Danger Within, I'm All Right Jack, Jetstorm, SOS Pacific* (1959), *The Angry Silence, The League of Gentlemen* (1960), *Only Two Can Play, All Night Long, The Dock Brief* (1962), *The Great Escape* (1963), *Seance on a Wet Afternoon, The Third Street, Guns at Batasi* (1964), *The Flight of the Phoenix* (1965), *The Sand Pebbles* (1966), *Dr Dolittle* (1967), *The Bliss of Mrs Blossom, Only When I Larf* (1968), *David Copperfield, The Magic Christian* (1969), *The Last Grenade, Loot, 10 Rillington Place, A Severed Head* (1970), *And Then There Were None* (1974), *Conduct Unbecoming, Rosebud, Brannigan* (1975), *The Human Factor* (1979), *Jurassic Park* (1993), *Miracle on 34th Street* (1994), *Lost World* (1997)

Producer and/or Director: *The Angry Silence* (co-pr) (1960), *Whistle Down The Wind* (1961), *The L-Shaped Room* (1962), *Seance on a Wet Afternoon* (1964), *Oh! What a Lovely War* (1969), *Young Winston* (1972), *A Bridge Too Far* (1977), *Magic* (1978), *Gandhi* (1982), *A Chorus Line* (1985), *Cry Freedom* (1987), *Chaplin* (1992), *Shadowlands* (1994), *In Love and War* (1997)

Few names have been so tenaciously associated with the survival of British cinema as that of Richard Attenborough. In the last two decades he has concentrated on making a series of large-scale films, among which *Gandhi* was a multi-award-winning success, both commercially and with the critics. His films as director (or producer-director) have been ambitious, often showing that sense of social concern which he sees as so important a responsibility of the filmmaker. During the 1940s and '50s, he appeared in over thirty films but expresses dissatisfaction with many of his film roles, in which he began to feel himself typed. Nevertheless, there are some remarkable performances in this period, dating from his memorable bit role as the frightened seaman in *In Which We Serve*. His cold-eyed killer in *Brighton Rock* is one of the most chilling performances in British cinema of the '40s and accounts for much of the film's power to disturb some fifty years later. As the weak, flashy Percy Boone in *London Belongs to Me*, the schoolboy used for social experiment in *The Guinea Pig*, the profiteering ex-serviceman in *The Ship that Died of Shame*, and the workman sent to Coventry in *The Angry Silence*, he created a gallery of sharply drawn characters that suggest a wider range than he may himself allow. He has always been willing to take risks as an actor and became one of that rare species, the character star.

Interview date: October 1989

How did you come to make your film début in *In Which We Serve*?

I went to RADA in 1941 on a scholarship and that year acted in Eugene O'Neill's *Ah, Wilderness!* in a little repertory on the periphery of London, where I was seen by the American agent, Al Parker. He heard that Noël Coward was looking for new faces for his ship's crew in *In Which We Serve*, which was about the Mountbatten story of the war in the Mediterranean, and he got me an audition. I had a screen test as well, and as a result Coward cast me as the young stoker. I might say that if you coughed you missed me, but getting to know Noël was the great thing. He was the most influential and supportive figure in my early life.

Your association with the Boultings seems crucial too . . .

Yes. When I was in Flying Training Command, I was seconded to the Royal Air Force Film Unit under the direct command of John Boulting, and played in a film called *Journey Together*, which Terry Rattigan wrote and John directed. It was his first film and people like George Cole, David Tomlinson and Bessie Love were in it. But a miracle occurred for me in that the Air Force flew Edward G Robinson over from Los Angeles. I came to know him very well and he granted me a vision of *film* acting which I had never encountered before.

Having been noticed at once in *In Which We Serve*, throughout the '40s you had a series of interesting parts. Was someone guiding your career at this time?

Nobody was *guiding*. I was still under contract to Al Parker, who was a mentor in some measure, but the person who really took me under his wing was John Boulting – John *and* Roy. Roy was in the Army and John was in the Air Force as I was, so my association with John was closer. John became not only my instructor in many ways (he had a wonderful, wonderful gift for dealing with actors),

but also my closest friend. He lent us the money to get married, and he was a most extraordinary, courageous, remarkable man. He served in the International Brigade in Spain. It was John who first talked to me about Thomas Paine, about whom I want to make my next movie. I shall dedicate it to John as it belongs to him, really. Well, after *Journey Together*, John and Roy said, 'We'd like you, if we come out and go into production, to go under contract to us.' This was during '44 or '45. In *A Matter of Life and Death*, I only say two words. It happened because I was engaged to Sheila [Sim], and she had done *A Canterbury Tale* for Mickey Powell. I came home on forty-eight hours' leave and Sheila had to go down to see Mickey, so I went down with her in my uniform. Mickey said, 'How long are you here for?' and I said, 'Forty-eight hours.' He said, 'Just enough time to do a part for me,' and that's how I played in *A Matter of Life and Death*.

I came out of the Air Force in '46 and played in *The Man Within* by virtue of Sydney Box seeing *Journey Together*. It was the first colour movie at Shepherd's Bush. I remember we constantly had to stop. The heat required for colour in those days was so intense that we would be in the middle of a scene and the sprinklers would go off. We all wore bright orange make-up. It seems like another world now. It was a very bad film, I think, but it was marvellous to play with Michael Redgrave, who was a sweet man and a lovely actor.

Your Pinkie in *Brighton Rock* is one of the most vivid performances in '40s British cinema. How do you regard it now?

I haven't seen it for a very long time. I don't think it would have been anything like as good, whatever quality it does have, if it had not been for John. It was an advantage and a disadvantage, having played it in the theatre. I already had quite firm characterisation concepts, and, although it meant I was familiar with the character and didn't therefore have to do a great deal of additional thought and research, nevertheless it was conceived in theatrical terms. John forced me into transferring it into the cinema. It was a very bold film and, when you think of that sort of sociological subject matter and the truth of its settings, it was very remarkable in 1946.

How difficult was the filming in Brighton? I gather a lot of it was done on location.

Very. Oh, there was a lot of opposition because it was casting shame upon the comfortable seaside town of Brighton and so on. But that was all dealt with. We had to use a caption saying, 'Of course Brighton is not like this today.'

There are some overhead shots of Alan Wheatley being chased through the back streets. Were there major logistic problems in location filming in those days?

Well, fortunately, the camera was not a difficulty, Alan was relatively unknown, and an awful lot was 'stolen'. By 'stolen', we mean putting a camera where people don't know about it, so that you place your actor into a perfectly normal circumstance. You don't stage it at all. I made a film a long time later called *Seance on a Wet Afternoon* for which we shot an enormous amount of it 'stolen' in Leicester Square, and other parts of London. The camera would be hidden in a house somewhere and I would simply get off the bus at the appointed place.

Brighton Rock **has a joint writing credit for Terence Rattigan and Graham Greene. They seem improbable collaborators.**

Absolutely. What happened was that John [Boulting], who worked with Terry on *Journey Together*, asked him to do the screenplay. When it was finished John took it to Graham, who had major reservations about it, so he did a rewrite of Terry's version. Graham had had very little film-writing experience at that time, so the credit became a joint one. They never worked together; it wasn't a co-operative effort. But Graham was very complimentary about the film. He sent me a copy of *Brighton Rock* in which he wrote, 'For my perfect Pinkie'. I treasure it almost as much as anything I've ever had.

What differences did you find between the stage and screen versions of your performance as Pinkie?

Oh, inevitably in the theatre the degree of subtlety of characterisation, of ambivalence of

attitude, is just not possible, particularly when the piece has to move at such a great pace. John used to make me go through and work out every reaction and thought that would occur to that person in a particular situation. He would then say, 'Now Dick, we've got all this worked out, in terms of this reaction to what Rose said or whatever. Now, those thoughts will go through your mind *infinitely* faster than you can possibly *consciously* convey them. But they have to *be* there and if I shoot it right, I will find those on the screen for you.' He taught me that there was no such thing in cinema acting as a short cut.

Some critics greeted it as a splendid example of realism; others talked about a dilution of Greene's novel. What do you think?

There *is* a dilution, firstly from containing a very complex and sophisticated novel within an accepted screen length of one hour thirty, or forty. Again, the question of sophisticated thought and argument was difficult to spend sufficient time on. So you did dilute in a way: you simplified. And there were moments, particularly at the end ... Graham still didn't like the end of the movie, but I thought it was a very skilful end; that was Terry [Rattigan]. What people don't remember – and I don't know whether they were contemporary views or not – is how much courage there was in making that movie at all in 1946.

You followed *Brighton Rock* **with several films that now look as if they're addressing themselves to a range of social problems:** *The Guinea Pig*, *The Lost People*, **and** *Boys in Brown*. **Did they seem to you significant at the time?**

The Guinea Pig seemed very significant, but again that was John and Roy. Roy directed and John produced for Charter Films. They were highly socially conscious and aware. Therefore the statement made in Warren Chetham-Strode's play was the thing that excited them in moving it on to the screen. For the others I cannot claim any motivation of social awareness, although I come from parents who were *constantly* consciously aware of social problems and the environment in general, and our place in it. Throughout my life, things which had that particular feeling, in any sense, appealed to me perhaps more. But I cannot claim for *Boys in Brown*, *Lost People* and so on, that those were the reasons; unlike *10 Rillington Place*, for instance, which I did for very specific reasons.

Did you feel *The Guinea Pig* **was consciously**

directed against the class system as such?

Without question. I'm not sure how passionate Warren was but the reason John and Roy wanted to do the picture was their active opposition to the class system. It was an *attack* on the class system; if they had thought it was merely a palliative, they wouldn't have made it. There was a condescension towards the 'lower classes' that manifested itself in some measure in the sort of work we did. I mean, you've only to look at some of the wartime pictures.

You were extremely busy throughout the '50s, over twenty films by my count. How satisfied were you with the kinds of films being made?

I don't think many were satisfied, and I certainly was not satisfied with my own participation. The industry seemed indigenously immensely secure and, what with the Rank Organisation, with what was the old ABPC corporation and eventually British Lion, the great Two Cities (the prestige company under Filippo Del Giudice), the Korda pictures, it *seemed* that we were on a bandwagon which was really rolling quite happily. A number of us who placed aesthetic considerations high on our agenda were concerned that the fundamental quality of much of what we were doing was in question, and that the wrong priorities were being addressed. Commercial success, presentation and promotion were everything, while the actual kernel of the thing was very often not what it ought to be. This resulted, as far as I was concerned, in a dissatisfaction with the degree to which I was typecast. It seemed to us that the same old movies, in some form re-dressed, re-shaped, were being churned out. There were very few people challenging the subject matter or the form in which pictures were made, so that, rather like typecasting, you went on making the kind of movie which had a history of success.

You did at least three films in the '50s that, in one way or the other, break out of that: *The Ship that Died of Shame*. *I'm All Right Jack* and *The Angry Silence*. What do you think of them, in retrospect?

The Ship that Died of Shame came from Ealing and I think Mickey Balcon, withal conforming to the Ealing comedies which, God knows, were very remarkable in the history of British cinema, nevertheless ventured every now and again into other territory. Mickey had an urge to move out of the genre which he had been largely responsible for creating. That was the urge that led to *The Ship that Died of Shame*. *I'm All Right Jack* was very much

an expression of the Boultings' disillusioned, radical views. That and *Private's Progress* and *Carlton-Browne of the FO* were very much John and Roy's style. These were attacks on institutions, whether of the left or right, with a satirical capability which was unique to them in many ways.

The Angry Silence was a different matter. It arose for the reasons that I was just talking about, not only as far as I was personally concerned, but I was desperately distressed at the direction in which British cinema was starting to go in the mid to late '50s. It was down a blind alley. It was in fact becoming dominated in large measure by the requirement of Eagle-Lion and others to find markets in the US. That involved making concessions and bringing over usually (I am afraid) fading American stars to supposedly bolster a marquee value in the United States and, as I said, playing the same old stuff over and over again. I decided quite consciously to give up acting for a time. I went to Al Parker, my agent, and I talked with my wife: I would eventually persuade somebody to allow me to play not only parts of my own age but to venture outside. Whatever I did, I would not go on playing these baby-faced young *ingénues*.

After that decision, I found the story, which had been written by Michael Craig and his brother Richard Gregson. I persuaded Bryan Forbes to write the screenplay and I set about trying to make it. I went to everybody except the Boultings. I was determined not to go back into the nest, as it were, but nobody would give me a penny. 'Dealing with a social subject in this way will empty the cinemas. Nobody would be interested. Anyway, who the hell are you? You're an actor, actors have no brains, etc, etc . . .'

Finally, in absolute despair, I had to go to British Lion – to the Boultings, Launder and Gilliat, and two remarkable people, Lord Arnold Goodman and Sir Max Rayne (now Lord Rayne). They had a board meeting and said they thought the script was marvellous, the subject courageous, but that the budget, which was £142,000, was out of the question. However, if I could make it for £100,000 they would back it. So Bryan went back and started to cut out this and reduce that, and I remember very clearly ringing him and saying, 'Forbsie, this is a bleeding disaster. If we cut the picture now – it's a small picture anyway – we are going to reduce the whole drama, the whole concept, the set-up. We cannot do this. What we have to do is to do it for nothing. We've got to persuade everybody – the costumiers, the lawyers, the accountants, the musicians, the actors, the cameraman – to come in for absolute scale salary; I'll get 70 to 80 per cent of the picture in profit terms and we'll divide it proportionately to their true salaries.' Anyway, the concept was accepted and I set about persuading everybody.

Two and a half weeks before the picture started shooting, I still couldn't persuade any actor to play the part of Tom for nothing. After keeping us waiting for weeks, Kenny More eventually said no. So I played in *The Angry Silence* because I couldn't get anybody else to do it. It was lucky for me, because it permitted me to do something that had the contemporary social awareness I wanted so desperately. *The Angry Silence* changed, for what it's worth, my acting career. It was perhaps the best thing Guy Green ever did, I think, and it had wonderful performances. Pier Angeli gives a devastating performance in it, and Bernard Lee . . . what a wonderful actor that man was. It really was, I think, a beautifully made movie.

Would you agree that the '40s and '50s constitute a boom period in British cinema, numerically and aesthetically?

Oh yes, absolutely. It was the period when we were most capable of creating pieces of work which demonstrated our social and aesthetic awareness. There was essentially indigenous subject matter, there were views and convictions which were tenable amongst quite a large number of people. There was a conviction, led by Uncle Arthur [Rank]. He knew bugger-all about films, but the quality and standard and pride in British cinema which Arthur demonstrated was very remarkable, and if you add to that the underrated Del [Guidice], who with his Two Cities Films worked within the Rank Organisation, and then add Korda and Mickey [Balcon] – not ABPC, that was a dreadful place, it created nothing in terms of a feeling of commitment – but the others really meant something so that you had Arthur putting huge sums into the dual circuit at that time, Odeon and Gaumont, you had Pinewood and Denham – marvellous studios, the best in the country.

There was a feeling altogether that cinema merited major national attention and resultant pride. It was the only time. Of course it happens in America too, when you get a studio head who has sufficient faith in those who are actually doing the job to grant them the degree of autonomy which is a prerequisite for any decent piece of work. Arthur, who had no knowledge at all, was prepared to be persuaded by Earl St John or by Del or by Mickey or whoever it was, that such and such a person was worth backing and that's how it happened.

Is it true that when John Davis became his lieutenant these halcyon days gradually came to an end?

Well, yes. JD does have a terrible name although I have a story in his favour which I'll tell you in a moment, if I may. JD came in for the right reasons. He was fascinated by film but believed it could be administered and run like any other business. What he never appreciated was that there is no such thing as a prototype in cinema, and if you attempt to use a prototype you destroy the innovation and artistic integrity of what you are about to produce. JD started to look to Independent Frame, to anything that would reduce cost, and he did so, not out of a disrespect for cinema, but out of a passionate belief that only by making it that much more financially viable would it survive. And of course everything that he said was pretty well wrong.

But, you see, this tough man also had extraordinary moments of understanding. I went to him with *Gandhi*. I went to ask him for some money for a screenplay. I'd got a screenplay which I had financed myself, and I needed more money to go on to a new version. I went in to see him up that great marble staircase that used to be at Rank's South Street offices and there he was behind this *huge* desk.

'Why do you want to make this bloody film?' he said. 'What do you mean, a wonderful story? Who's interested? Nobody knows a thing about India. A ridiculous old man with his sheet and his bean bowl. I'm not interested. You wouldn't get me in the cinema to see it. Why do you think *I* should back it?' And I said, 'Well, John, you are the principal figure of the British film industry. Who else would I go to? I'm not going to get the money from anybody else. I don't want to go to the Americans.' 'Well, Dick,' he said, 'I'll tell you this. Over the years you made a lot of money for the Rank Organisation in the pictures you have played in, and if you really want to go into production and to direct, which is something that may well be a good move – I don't know how efficient you are, you were certainly efficient in terms of *Angry Silence*, which I understand came in under budget – then I think it would be inappropriate if we didn't back you.'

And he opened the door and said, 'How much do you want?' And I said, 'Well £5,000 would be wonderful.' He said, 'OK, here you are, £5,000. That's yours and it's a gift, because you'll never get the film made and there's no way in which anybody will go and see it if you do get it made. However, if you *do* get it made, I want the money back, with interest. If you don't make it, forget it.'

What is your attitude to the way in which the Government has intervened in the film industry in Britain?

There has been, in my opinion, only one minister who – no, two in fact, but one very evidently so – who has ever actually taken on board the value, artistically, socially, commercially, of British cinema, and that's Harold Wilson. Harold set up the Eady Fund and created a possible banking situation for British cinema. British cinema has in large measure moved from what was called the Board of Trade; it's now called the DTI (Department of Trade and Industry). Now it wobbles between the DTI, the Home Office, the Foreign Office and, indeed, the Arts and Libraries and Education offices. In other words, there are about five different ministries which in some way or another deal with the cinema in the UK. The result is that on each of those individual agendas, cinema – if it can be seen at all – is likely to be far down at the bottom. We are in this ridiculous position of being spread so thin over so many ministries that we have no muscle whatsoever.

The only other person who ever did anything was Geoffrey Howe at the time of *Chariots of Fire* and *Gandhi*, when we were doing quite well in terms of capital allowances. 'Capital allowances' means that you may set your production costs against your over-all company accounts long before you know precisely when the film is going to be shown, what the returns will be, etc. You may claim immediately on that investment in fiscal terms. I remember going to Geoffrey when he was Chancellor, and his very clearly saying, 'Look, I don't favour capital allowances for everything, but I do see that it would cripple the film industry to lose them at a stroke and I will reduce them slowly over a period of five, six or seven years.'

When he left, Nigel Lawson came in and said, as he was perfectly entitled to, 'I'm not having any exceptions, capital allowances are out.' Within three months the whole of the funding of British cinema from the City disappeared. It was the most heartbreaking blow. Now it's a one-off deal every time, and the really cruel thing is that we are not going out with begging bowls. What we are asking is that the country *values* its film industry. We are still thought of as a crude imitation of the theatre here.

George Baker

b. 1929

Actor: *The Intruder* (1953), *The Ship that Died of Shame, The Dam Busters, The Woman for Joe* (1955), *The Feminine Touch, The Extra Day, A Hill in Korea* (1956), *These Dangerous Years, No Time for Tears* (1957), *The Moonraker, Tread Softly Stranger* (1958), *Lancelot And Guinevere* (1963), *The Finest Hours* (narr) (1964), *The Curse of the Fly* (1965), *Mister Ten Percent* (1967), *On Her Majesty's Secret Service, Goodbye Mr Chips, Justine* (1969), *The Executioner* (1970), *A Warm December* (1972), *The Spy Who Loved Me* (1977), *The Thirty-Nine Steps* (1978), *North Sea Hijack* (1979), *Hopscotch, A Nightingale Sang in Berkeley Square* (1980), *For Queen and Country* (1988)

As television's Inspector Wexford in the Ruth Rendell mysteries, George Baker has enjoyed a whole new surge of popularity. His film career began as a handsome young leading man in the 1950s, when, like several others such as Michael Craig and Dirk Bogarde, he was under contract to unimaginative studio bosses who simply pushed him through film after film. Most of these films, whether for his parent company, Associated British Pictures, or on loan-out to Rank, required him to make bricks from the straw of conventional heroes. However, on several occasions he was luckier than this: in Ealing's *The Ship that Died of Shame*, in ABPC's charming swashbuckler *The Moonraker*, and as a Yorkshireman on the run in *Tread Softly Stranger*, he showed some of that effortless authority he would later bring to character work on stage, screen and television. *Interview date: June 1994*

How did you come to make your first film, Guy Hamilton's very interesting *The Intruder*?

Oh yes, *The Intruder* ... By this time I'd done quite a bit of acting in rep and so on, and was at the Haymarket – I think it was 1953 – in a production of *Aren't We All?* with Ronnie Squire, Marjorie Fielding and Marie Lohr, who became my theatrical grandmother. Guy came to see the play and afterwards he asked to meet me. He offered me a part in *The Intruder* and from that I got *The Dam Busters*. And *The Dam Busters* gave me the seven-year contract with Associated British Pictures.

You have a small, telling scene at a mess table in *The Intruder*. I think it is a neglected film; what did you think about it?

I loved it. But I have other reasons for loving it, because Jack Hawkins was wonderful to me. I remember my first entrance into the film. They were standing, he, Dennis Price, Nicholas Phipps and others at the bar, and he was colonel of the regiment. I had to do a long walk, and say to him, 'The CO wants something or other done,' – I can't remember the line now, obviously. I started this long walk, on my very first day at a film studio, and I thought, 'I can't bear this, this is terrible': I couldn't remember what I had to say! Jack must have seen it in my eyes, and he suddenly said, 'Oh, George, I'm terribly sorry,' and he turned to Guy Hamilton and said, 'Guy, what do you think I should do on such-and-such?' Well, he just became a hero forever. He certainly saved my bacon.

It's one of a few films, like your next one, *The Ship that Died of Shame*, which seemed to offer a critique of life in post-war England. Is that how they felt to you at the time?

Certainly *The Intruder* did. Somehow we'd left the soldier muddled and alone in peacetime. I mean, there's historical precedent for it: the soldier comes back and nothing is done for him. Certainly I think *The Intruder* had that. I don't think *The Ship that Died of Shame* was so much of a case, because I think that [Basil] Dearden was doing a different thing. The Attenborough character was quite determined to make good and be a spiv and would have been a spiv anyway. I do think my character was left to drift in *The Ship that Died of Shame*. But was that his own fault or is that society's fault? Or the fault of his wife being killed? That's a life circumstance rather than what I think was the case in *The Intruder*, where it was the fault of society that let the soldier down. There was an awful lot of people wandering about who were unable to find their place again, soldiers who felt they couldn't go back and say, 'Well, I have to start again and I have to be an office boy and I have to tough it through.'

How far in a film like *The Intruder* is the class system really to blame?

Well, I think that it has gone quite the other way now. The class that used to be depicted in films – the middle or the upper-middle class – is no longer used because we say it doesn't reflect British life now. You're quite right, though, and our society does need another look at it, because it is still the most class-ridden society in the world and we should be exploring what those classes are still doing to each other.

It seems to me some actors are absolutely tied to certain levels, including an excellent actor like Bill Owen in *The Ship that Died of Shame*.

He is a wonderful actor and, of course, still going very strong. One of the nice things about my gift (whatever it is) is that I have a very good ear for accents. So I can play myself or a Cockney, Yorkshiremen, Irishmen, Scotsmen – and have done so, even in their own countries, if you know what I mean. It is a *very* valuable gift. With Wexford in the Ruth Rendell mysteries on television, I took the Hampshire accent, because an awful lot of senior policemen do speak like that. But I can do the toff, and that's great fun.

You did two films at Ealing in the '50s, *The Ship that Died of Shame* and *The Feminine Touch*. What do you recall of working there?

It was wonderful. It felt as though I was working at the National Theatre. Pinewood was obviously a film factory; ABPC, and then MGM and Denham, had the Americans in, but when you were working at Ealing you really felt that you were working in *British* films. It really had that 'cottage industry' feel. Michael Balcon, of course, was totally accessible; he was always there and came on to the set. Dave Frampton and Wilton and all those make-up boys had been there forever, and everyone was drinking over at the Red Lion. Going over to chat with Sandy Mackendrick, Charles Frend, Charlie Crichton and all the actors at lunchtimes was a joy.

Were you under contract to Ealing?

Not to Ealing, no. I was under contract to ABPC and they let me out to Ealing. To their advantage, no doubt. I think it would have been different if I hadn't needed, for family reasons, to have that sort of security for those five or six years that I was with ABPC. I was loaned out to Ian Dalrymple on *A Hill in Korea*; I was then loaned out for *The Woman for Joe* to Pinewood and to Ealing for *The Ship that Died of Shame* and *The Feminine Touch*. I actually worked for ABPC very little; I did *No Time For Tears* and *The Moonraker* there, that was all.

What do you remember of *The Feminine Touch*, directed by Pat Jackson?

I remember *The Feminine Touch* because I loved working with Pat, who had had a remarkable career making documentaries. At that time I might have liked to have a little more direction but it wasn't in Pat's nature to give it, although he did help. There are some directors who can give you an awful lot of help; there are others who, just by their aura, by

making a space for you to work in, give you almost more help because you feel totally confident that you can try something and, if it's wrong, they'll say so. So this giving of direction – 'Do this and then do that' – is a very young director's idea of what they should be doing.

One person in *The Feminine Touch* I wanted to ask you about was Diana Wynyard, one of whose last films it must have been.

I got to know Diana very well and loved working with her; she was, indeed, a marvellous actress. They didn't use her enough in films, it was the old English snobbery. The films didn't like to use theatre people because they thought they over-acted, and the theatre people looked down on film actors because they thought they under-acted. Utter nonsense, but it prevailed then.

***A Hill in Korea* is one of the few films dealing with the Korean war. What do you remember of it, of your role as a national service lieutenant?**

I'd done my national service in Hong Kong and I was a lieutenant in the Royal Tank Regiment. I helped Anthony Squire to write the script and Julian Amyes was a great friend, and I think that we really were trying to be as authentic as possible about war. And of course, Harry Andrews had been a major in the Artillery. Harry knew about war and we'd all had experience with our national service, so we all *knew*. It was still new enough for all of us, except perhaps for people like Michael Caine and Harry Landis, who were younger. I actually gave Michael Caine his first line! I said, 'You can't bring this actor all the way over from England to Portugal and not give him something to say.' So I suggested we have him sitting down reading a book of poetry, to give him a bit of character, and that's what we did. And there was Robert Shaw, being as truculent and difficult as ever – not on the set, but he was just a wild and ambitious man who had to beat everybody.

You did two films in 1957 for Herbert Wilcox. *These Dangerous Years* and, with Anna Neagle, *No Time for Tears*. What do you think was the secret of her enduring popularity?

She was an immensely hard worker; she was very pretty; and she was actually not half as bad an actress as people thought. If she hadn't had to work for Herbert all the time, she would have been a much better actress. She could have got tougher, but Herbert's image of her was all floating in powder blue. If you think of her in *Spring in Park Lane*, it's a lovely comedy performance. But Wilcox, who genuinely adored her, saw her as Queen Victoria. One would be sitting talking to this intelligent woman and he would answer for her, before she could open her mouth. In the end, of course, Herbert lost touch with what the public wanted, with the reality of what he could possibly do. *These Dangerous Years* wasn't a good film. Herbert was trying to break away, you see. They'd all gone for Frankie Vaughan and this was a Liverpool film with a message about how tough it is in the Dingle. It wasn't attractive to a lot of people because it wasn't well enough made. The script was by Jack Trevor Story and he and Herbert had no meeting-ground whatever.

You worked with Sylvia Syms on *No Time for Tears* and also *The Moonraker*. I think she is now one of the great character actresses.

Yes, she is. A highly intelligent woman, very sharp, and I like her enormously. I enjoyed making *The Moonraker* very much and I actually wrote quite a lot of it. A couple of the love scenes with Sylvia were entirely my work. We have been friends ever since and the film is always popular on television. David Macdonald, who directed it, was unfortunately a bit of a lush, and it was almost his last film. When we got the script he went through it with us, saying, 'Here you don't "walk" across the room – you either "jump" or "swing" across but you don't "walk". And this twelve lines of dialogue is absolutely useless, we can cut it down to a few words.' He did this all the way through, so it's absolutely an action film.

During the '50s you worked for several directors of whom not much is written: George More O'Ferrall, William Fairchild, Cyril Frankel and Gordon Parry. What recollections have you of them?

George More O'Ferrall is dead now and he had a very short film career – his nickname used to be 'More and More Awful'. I'll tell you how sensitive he was. In *The Woman for Joe* there was a very difficult scene where I had to pick up Jimmy Karoubi, the midget, and throw him against a caravan. Just as I was about to throw him, someone in the studio made a noise and More O'Ferrall blew his top. He yelled, 'Will you be silent! Isn't it enough that the little man's deformed?!'

William Fairchild was really a writer and he went back to writing after he directed a couple of films. He wasn't a bad director but he was a *very* good writer. Absolutely everybody was in that film I did with him, *The Extra Day*, including Richard Basehart. Basehart was quite a drawcard then because he

had done *Fourteen Hours* and he'd just done – or been about to do – *Moby Dick* as Ishmael. We did an awful lot of bringing over Americans to do British films; that was when the industry had started to decline and those people were really doing 'B' pictures. I did one myself, for Don Sharp, who did some very good films like *Bear Island*. We did *The Curse of the Fly* with Brian Donlevy, who was way past his prime, and couldn't handle it at all, and was having trouble with his lines, although at sixty-six he looked pretty good. He'd had great success with the *Quatermass* films about ten years before.

Cyril Frankel is an extraordinary man. Why he wanted to direct, I really don't know. He was rich enough not to have to work, but he directed about four or five quite good films. I think he had an idea about what theatre and films meant to him and it actually had nothing to do with the reality of what theatre and film were about.

Gordon Parry was a throwback, really. I liked Gordon and I think *Tread Softly Stranger* was quite a good little film. It was the first time in films that I was allowed to use an accent – I played it with a Yorkshire accent, if you remember. In a way, it helped me to step out of the mould. This was the moment when the casting people in various media changed their minds about me – that I wasn't just the pretty doctor, I could actually act. Gordon was always very civilised and urbane; he was one of those people who went into the industry as a tea-boy and had moved quietly through it as though it were an office job, doing it perfectly well.

I admired Diana Dors [co-star] very much.

You're quite right to. She was a wonderful actress and she and I were great chums. She had a strange private life, a positive genius for choosing the wrong husbands, but a tremendous actress. She really started to show them when she made *Yield to the Night*. She did play up that platinum blonde image, of course, because she saw that as the way to make money.

Were you pleased with the range of roles you were offered in the '50s?

No, I wasn't in a position to pick and choose. One of the terrible things about the ABPC contract was that they would just send me a script and say, 'You will do this,' which isn't quite the best way to run a career. That was the reason I walked out and went into theatre. Robert Clark was very cross with me for breaking my contract and he blackballed me so that I didn't work in films again for years. When the New Wave started to come in with Lindsay Anderson and others in about 1958, I was classed as being among the 'old fellows'. The new directors didn't want to know the people who had been around the studios for years. It was a long, hard fight back, through the theatre and the Old Vic.

Did you enjoy the remake of *The Thirty-Nine Steps* and did you enjoy Buchan?

I reread Buchan at about that time, just for the fun of it, and I found him a very strange man. I do admire *The Thirty-Nine Steps* but I don't think I admire John Buchan very much. It is a good film, though I'm sorry they went a bit over the top with

Big Ben. It was fun to do, working with Ronald Pickup and John Mills. They did a bit of location work in Scotland but I did all my stuff here in London, at Walton Studio. I was so busy in the theatre and also on television that I didn't do much cinema work after then. I was also writing radio and television plays, and I've done a lot of adaptations of the Ruth Rendell 'Wexford' series. If a cinema director rang me up and asked me to do something I was delighted, but I really wasn't looking for film work by then.

Robert S Baker

b. 1916

Producer (with Monty Berman, unless otherwise noted):*The Way from Germany (1946), A Date with a Dream (& co-sc) (1948), Melody Club (1949), No Trace, Blackout (& dir) (1950), The Quiet Woman (1951), 13 East Street (& dir), The Frightened Man, The Lost Hours, The Voice of Merrill (1952), The Steel Key (& dir), Recoil, Love in Pawn, Three Steps to the Gallows, Black Orchid, Deadly Nightshade (1953), Escape by Night, Double Exposure, The Embezzler, Delayed Action (1954), Impulse (& co-auth), The Gilded Cage, Tiger by the Tail, The Reluctant Bride, Windfall, No Smoking, Barbados Quest (1955), Passport to Treason (& dir), Breakaway, Bond of Fear (1956), Hour of Decision, Stranger in Town, Professor Tim (& sc), High Terrace (1957), Stormy Crossing, The Trollenberg Terror, Sally's Irish Rogue, Blind Spot (& co-auth), Blood of the Vampire, Sea of Sand (1958), Jack the Ripper (& dir, co-ph), Home is the Hero (1959), The Siege of Sidney Street (& dir, ph), Boyd's Shop, Flesh and the Fiends (1960), The Hellfire Club (& dir), The Secret of Monte Cristo (& dir) (1961), What a Carve Up! (1962), Cross Plot (1969)

*Documentary

The British 'B' film has had an almost uniformly bad press, when, that is, it has had any press at all. Some of this obloquy derives no doubt from the infamous 'quota quickies' of the 1930s, when films were made to satisfy legislation relating to the exhibition of British films and with no thought at all for quality. But some of it is the result of ignorance: the British supporting feature of the late '40s and the '50s is now virtually unknown, unlike its Hollywood counterpart, which often attracted critical attention and 'sleeper' or cult status. There is, however, a considerable number of British second features of this prolific period which deserve to be known for their unpretentious excellence, and it is a striking fact that a good many of these were made by Robert Baker and Monty Berman's company, Tempean. They produced over thirty of these films in the '50s. At their best, as in *The Quiet Woman, Impulse* and *The Embezzler*, they depend on character as much as action, though the latter is staged with a lively efficiency that rivals the Americans'. Even lesser ones like *No Trace* and *13 East Street* are never less than fast-moving, entertaining and well played by an engaging repertory of actors. Baker later went on to make 'A' films, including the unusual *The Siege of Sidney Street* (as well as much polished television); but anyone can make an 'A' film, whereas it took real ingenuity to make so many nifty 'B's. This is intended as a long overdue salute to the work of the Baker and Berman enterprise.

Interview date: August 1995

As I understand it, you and Monty Berman set up Tempean Films in 1948.

I met Monty Berman in the Army Film Unit in the desert and we decided that when we got out of the Army we were going to make our own pictures. We were demobbed at roughly the same time and we begged, borrowed and stole to get finance together to make a picture called *A Date with a Dream*, directed by a man called Dickie Leeman who was at one time in vaudeville. Monty was a very competent cameraman; he had worked with people like Michael Powell as a camera operator and he was extremely good. We jointly produced and he invariably photographed the films. He's still about today but he's now involved in selling pictures.

You are sometimes listed as co-producer and less often as director. Which function did you prefer?

The producing function is a chore, whereas the directing function is creative and more fun. A director is in command of the operation on the floor while the producer has to deal with contracts and all sorts of office work to get the thing going. A director is free of that so that he can worry about the picture itself; he doesn't have to worry about finance and so on. I was a hands-on producer. Usually, as co-producers, Monty would look after the contracts and the financial aspects of putting a film together, and I would tend to look after developing the script. We would jointly cast the film but I was more on the creative side; he was

more on the financial side until we went on the floor, when he would photograph it. The divided responsibility worked out very well; we complemented each other.

Having watched around a hundred and fifty British supporting films, I think Tempean's were the most entertaining.

They were, for the money spent on them, good value. What we used to do – an innovation at the time – was to shoot in natural locations. The fact was that with our budget we couldn't afford to build the sets that the films required. This has now become the norm but we made a hell of a lot of films on location back then.

Was *The Quiet Woman* actually filmed in the Romney Marshes?

Yes, we went down to Winchelsea, although a lot of it was also done in the studio. I think it was shot in about three weeks, a week of which we spent in the Romney Marshes.

Were there any difficulties about location shooting?

In those days we didn't have the lightweight equipment that we do today – lightweight lamps, for instance. All the gear was very heavy and the cameras were very big; they had to be on dollies, for which you needed tracks. The lamps were the big old-fashioned kind they used in the studios, so that meant you needed a big crew of electricians to cart them around. We probably needed about double the crew they would use today. So it was cumbersome, but the idea of shooting on location gave another dimension to the picture, which was good. But Britain has never been geared to location shooting like America has. You had to get police permission and there were all sorts of problems. During a middle-of-the-night shoot sometimes, people would object to it and try to stop it, so we had problems but somehow or another we managed to sort them out. This country's very backward as far as offering filmmaking facilities is concerned; it's more obstructive than anything.

Would it have been a director's or producer's decision, to shoot on location?

Basically all decisions made on our pictures were producers' decisions, because we had to keep a tight control on the budgets. If you let directors make decisions they tend to make rather expensive ones! They were told what they had to do and they did it.

How much would the average supporting feature cost then?

Anything from about £12,000 to £20,000. Costs crept up later and I think the most expensive co-feature we made (apart from the colour ones) was about £25,000. The actors would have been the most expensive component, and then studio costs. I would say about a quarter of the cost was usually actors; the studio costs and sets would also have occupied about a quarter of the budget.

Were the budgets meagre enough to be frustrating?

One had to be a realist. We were making films for a certain market: they were either second features or co-features. If they were co-features (that is, a split bill) you could spend more money on them, whereas there was only an allocation that was granted for the second feature, so you were very conscious of the budget all the time. You had to make decisions that you didn't always want to but, in some respects, a shortage of money can be a creative thing, because if you couldn't afford to do something a certain way, you would have to find another way of doing it – and very often it was better than the original way.

Was it comparatively easy to get a film career going in Britain in the late '40s and '50s?

No, I don't think it was any easier than it is today. There weren't film schools going at the time, so it was a question of who you knew and being in the right place at the right time – a lot of luck. There was no problem setting up the company; the only problem was getting the money to make the picture. Both Monty and I had just come out of the Army and we had a little money; my father backed me, he borrowed some money and between us we raised money through friends and relatives. We didn't go to a distributor to get a deal to make the film and get bank discount and so forth; we had to find the money ourselves and we managed to do it. We got distribution for *A Date with a Dream* through Grand National. That started the ball rolling; we showed it to a company called Eros who wanted to make second features. They liked the picture and decided to finance us on our next pictures, so we then had a distribution deal with them. We were coming in on budget with presentable pictures and they were happy with them. We must have made twenty to thirty pictures with Eros.

Would they be sold to distributors for a flat fee rather than a percentage?

Usually, yes. In those days you could sell a feature to a house and make an allocation for the second feature. An allocation was usually a flat fee although sometimes it was a small percentage of the house take. There was no fixed rule.

Was it discouraging to know that, however good your film might be, you were only going to get a flat fee as a rule?

It *was* discouraging to a certain extent. On the other hand, it provided work and got us moving. We weren't so interested in making a fortune in those days; we were just keen to make pictures. At that time the second-feature industry was thriving, providing you could make them at the price.

How much critical coverage would you get?

You'd get it from trade magazines like *Cinema* and *Kine Weekly* which would review all pictures made; the exhibitors would look at the reviews and tend to favour good reviews when they were booking second features.

Critics in the quality papers rarely seemed to comment on supporting films. Was it hard to get a better-than-average supporting film noticed?

It was really, because the main feature was always the attraction. Lots of people wouldn't even bother to see the supporting feature; they'd come in half way through just to see the feature film. The second feature was the 'poor relation' of a show. Later on they developed co-features, in which they would have two medium-sized pictures making up the show instead of one big one and one small one. Some of our films were co-features and they were usually eighty to ninety minutes in length while the supporting pictures were usually about seventy to seventy-five minutes. It wasn't solely a matter of length, though; it was a matter of quality. We made some pictures on a very modest budget – for instance, *The Voice of Merrill* with Valerie Hobson. That was made for about £25,000 but it turned out so well that they said they couldn't release it as a second feature. It went out as a co-feature instead.

How would the public distinguish between the two?

They wouldn't as a rule. The billing would have something to do with it; when it comes to putting up the fliers, two co-features would be equally prominent. One might be on one half of the poster and the second one on the other half, but they would both be the same size. When it came to second features, the main feature would occupy about eighty per cent of the poster and the second feature would be about twenty per cent. Also, when we did a deal with an American and we would have an American star, we tended to make those as co-features.

There is a steady stream of American actors in your films – Mark Stevens, Scott Brady, Mary Castle, Larry Parks, Dale Robertson, Forrest Tucker. Were you aiming for US distribution?

Yes, we decided with our distribution that we would make co-features and, in order to do that, we had to have a bigger name in the picture, to enable it to stand as a co-feature. These people were established in America, consequently all their films were shown over there and they were known names to the public here as well. I wouldn't say the films got *wide* American distribution, but they certainly got a much bigger distribution than they would have done if they'd had totally unknowns in them. The American names you mentioned weren't big stars but they were known and recognised by the American public, so they helped to sell the pictures in America.

Would you arrange to employ American actors through a Hollywood agent?

No, we worked through a man named Bob Goldstein who was involved for many years as a casting director for Universal Pictures. Then he came over here and established a co-production organisation. He was able to get quite big names; we would make a deal together whereby he would supply the actor and a certain amount of the finance and we would supply the rest. The American actors were more expensive because you had to pay for their air fare or boat fare and their hotel and living expenses. And you handled them a little differently, but we never had any real problems with actors.

We found that the American actors were extremely efficient. They understood the camera; they'd had very good training; they would ask the cameraman what lens he was using and they would know how to play to that lens. The American actors are trained in the art of filmmaking. They didn't have stage backgrounds so often, but they knew the camera and consequently their performances were always very, very smooth. In that way, they gave a lift to British co-features – plus the different accent helped to make the picture more universal. I remember one occasion when we were making *The Lost Hours* with Mark Stevens, directed by David Macdonald; there was a scene being filmed in an underground car park and he had to drive a car fast down the ramp and stop at a certain point. If he didn't stop at that point we would have got reflections of the lights in the windscreen, so he had to stop within six inches of a certain point, get out, go to another point and hit a certain mark. He did this on the first take and I said, 'That was bloody efficient of you.' He said, 'In Hollywood, unless we can do that we don't get work.'

How did you get on with Larry Parks on *Tiger by the Tail*? Sadly, he was pushed out of America by McCarthy.

Yes, for 'un-American activities'. When the McCarthy thing started he couldn't get work. That's why we got him. He was a little edgy at times; he didn't get on very well with Connie Smith on a personal basis, although they played together all right. He was a little bit 'Hollywoody' but it's understandable, he was under a lot of pressure at the time. He was very good, though, a good actor.

I'd be interested to know at which studios your films were made, and anything about the production conditions. You made quite a few at Alliance Studios.

Yes, we used Alliance quite a lot. They had several studios, one in Hammersmith and one in Southall, owned by a man named Shipman. They weren't as efficient as Pinewood as far as facilities go, or Denham, or Shepperton. They were smaller, there was less space to operate in, and the workshops were smaller. You had to plan everything a bit more carefully because you couldn't bring things out of thin air in the way you could at Pinewood; they hadn't the facilities to do it. Conditions weren't very luxurious; the offices were very dingy and probably cleaned only about once a year but, apart from that, it didn't affect the filmmaking. Once you got on the stage, whether you were at Pinewood or at Southall made no difference.

Is the number of camera set-ups a way of saving money if you have a modest budget?

I suppose on the average day we would shoot about twenty set-ups. You had to shoot about four to five minutes' screen time a day in those days, in order to make a seventy-five-minute film in three weeks. On the co-features we'd spend four weeks, occasionally five, so you could work at a slightly slower pace. Your canvas was bigger so it was a little more difficult to make. But the number of camera set-ups would really be determined by the director, who would plan his day to make it as simple for himself as he possibly could. In other words, he would shoot out of continuity to avoid having to change a set-up; he might want to start a scene from a certain angle and finish it at that same angle, so he would shoot those two sequences together and shoot the other bits and pieces later. It made it more difficult in a way, because you had to keep in your mind exactly how each section was; but in most cases you would rehearse the entire scene so that the actors knew what the whole general pattern was. It saves time, doing it that way. It takes about twenty minutes to get a set-up going – to light it, do all the measurements and get the camera in position – so the less movement you make with your camera, the better.

Your films had very strong casts: how were these arrived at? Did Tempean have people under contract?

We did at one time but not for very long. We had Michael Craig under contract for about a year, then I think we sold his contract to Rank. We also had a Canadian girl, Dianne Foster, for a while. She went back to Canada and I don't know what happened to her after that.

What about all those excellent people who recur in your films – John Horsley, Michael Balfour, Dora Bryan, Thora Hird, Arthur Lowe, etc?

They were what you would call our repertory company. We knew them and if a suitable part came up for one of them, we would give it to them. John Horsley, for instance, played in a lot of our pictures; we liked his style, he was easy to work with, he was flexible, so we tended to use him. Probably we weren't as adventurous as we might have been, but then we never had casting directors in those days. Michael Balfour was a chum of ours, so whenever we could find work for him we gave it to him. We knew they were reliable so we tended to use them again. I suppose a lot of actors must have had good,

steady careers in second features/co-features in the '50s and '60s, and some of them are still around today.

It was sometimes very effective, putting those people together with American stars. One I'm thinking of is *Impulse* with Arthur Kennedy: it's like an American *film noir*.

Yes, I was very keen on American *film noir* and quite a few of our pictures tended to be that kind of thing. *Impulse* was one and Arthur Kennedy was a remarkable actor, an in-depth actor, who got very much into the character. I also made a film with him in Ireland, called *Home is the Hero*, which was based on an Irish play. I thought he and Constance Smith worked very well together in *Impulse*.

I wondered if you'd had an American film called *Pitfall* in mind when you made *Impulse*.

Probably, because I used to see all those American *noir* films. Certainly *Impulse* is similar to it in many respects. There was another *film noir*, made by Fritz Lang, called *Woman in the Window*, which was the same kind of thing – a woman luring a husband away from his wife.

I'm also struck by some of the directors' names that recur in Tempean productions, above all John Gilling, but also others like Charles Saunders and Henry Cass.

I suppose John Gilling was the director we had most contact with. He used to write his own scripts – he was a writer who directed, basically. He was very good and very conscientious; a little bit tough with the actors on the set, but he maintained discipline and turned out some very good pictures.

Henry Cass made quite a few pictures for us. I first saw his work in a film called *The Glass Mountain*, which impressed me, and I thought we must somehow use him.

Charles Saunders made only a couple of pictures for us: a comedy called *Love in Pawn*, and *Black Orchid*.

Charles Saunders seems to have been a very efficient director.

Yes. As an editor, he always knew exactly how he was going to shoot a picture because he knew exactly how he was going to cut it. Being an editor is probably the best training for a director. We made *Black Orchid* for Kenilworth, the Shipman company. It was a very cheap picture, made in three weeks for about £10,000.

Most of Tempean's second features are crime films. Did this reflect your preference, or was it a matter of response to market

demand?

Market demand, I would say. A thriller is always acceptable. It's very difficult to make a soft romance as a second feature, it needs something harder. I don't know why. The public appetite was in favour of thrillers rather than comedies, but you could make a comedy or a thriller – anything in between was very dubious!

Maybe audiences wanted the big romance to be conducted by major stars.

Yes, I think that's the answer. With a murder there's something to interest you, whether it's a question of whodunit, or someone's life in jeopardy, or someone on the run from the law or from the villains. It's easy to hook an audience with a thriller, not so easy to hook them on a romantic plot. It was demand, basically. Thrillers were easier to sell and therefore easier to set up.

What kind of distribution arrangements did you have – with Eros, sometimes RFD or RKO?

Most of our films were made through Eros, with whom we had a long-standing relationship. They were happy with us and we were happy with them. We made a couple of films for RKO, the first of which was *Barbados Quest*, I think. Then we formed a company with a man named Joe Vegoda, who was sales director of RKO at that time, and a man named Emmett Dalton, who was Sam Goldwyn's British representative over here. We formed a company called CIPA. Emmett Dalton was a well-known Irishman, a colleague of Michael Collins, as a matter of fact, during the Irish Troubles, and he was endeavouring to start a film industry in Ireland. He was responsible for building Ardmore Studios. So we made a few films with the Abbey Players in Ireland, including *Professor Tim*, *Boyd's Shop*, *Sally's Irish Rogue* and a few other films, which were all released through RKO. They all did well in Ireland. Rank RFD distributed *Sea of Sand*; that was the only film we did for them.

From the late '50s you went on to make what are clearly 'A' films – *Sea of Sand*, *The Siege of Sidney Street*, *The Hellfire Club*. How would you describe some of the major differences between producing 'A' films and supporting films?

The main difference was that you had more money to spend, consequently you could have more time to make the film. We'd make an 'A' picture in five or six weeks as opposed to three or four weeks.

Did you make a conscious decision to go into 'A' film production?

Yes. One of the reasons was that Joe Vegoda had left RKO and formed his own distribution company called Regal Films International with another man called Michael Green, who was a foreign sales representative. We worked with Regal Films, making a number of bigger pictures. We made five or six with them, some in colour and some in black-and-white. The others, apart from the three you mentioned, were *Jack the Ripper*, *The Flesh and the Fiends* and *What a Carve Up!*

***The Siege of Sidney Street* is a very strange and interesting story. It reminded me of Joseph Conrad's *The Secret Agent*, also about foreign anarchists in London.**

It's a true story, in fact – embellished, of course. We filmed it in Ireland, actually, because we wanted 1911 in England but Ireland looked more like it! We found a street in Dublin which was physically very much like Sidney Street; it had the same housing and there were very few television aerials or other modern things around, so we didn't have to alter the street very much. Sidney Street itself is in the East End of London. We had Donald Sinden playing a straight part, and Kieron Moore (who is Irish). We made quite a few films with him. We had Peter Wyngarde playing the main role and we imported a French actress called Nicole Berger.

I must say I regard your 'B' films as being the smartest made in Britain. I admire the spirit behind Group 3 but I don't admire the films much.

Well, they were a little arty-farty. We were more commercial and I suppose very much influenced by American pictures, particularly of the genre we were discussing earlier. American films in those days were always very fast-playing and we tended to emulate them, trying to make them as American as possible, basically. Our pictures had to have a drive to them.

They seem less dated than some of the bigger, more ambitious films of the time. Is *The Quiet Woman* one that you particularly like?

No, oddly enough, I'm rather surprised you chose that one. It was a departure for us, a kind of romantic drama. Some of the technical things weren't well done in it, as I remember – the back projection that we used at Hammersmith Studios wasn't really first-class. It didn't have the technical qualities that pleased us but we were stuck with it at the studios and just had to use it. The boat stuff at the end involved quite a lot of back projection. It worried me because it was technically imperfect, and we tried to make our films as technically right as possible. We'd have shot it on location if we could have, but we didn't have the money. It wasn't in good balance with the foreground. It turned out looking like twilight but it wasn't meant to be! But Jane Hylton was a good actress, with a quality of stillness. Now you mention the film, I recall the part of the barmaid was to be played by Diana Dors instead of Dora Bryan. We shot one day with Diana and she and the director (John Gilling) didn't get on; he was a bit abrasive to her, so the next day she was 'ill' and couldn't work. We had to bring in Dora instead.

I liked her too in *13 East Street*, in which she plays a gossipping middle-class neighbour.

I directed that one, actually. Patrick Holt and Sandra Dorne married later, after making the film together. Michael Balfour was in it also, and Sonia Holm as Patrick Holt's wife.

The one you mentioned earlier, *The Voice of Merrill* with Valerie Hobson, was really almost an 'A' picture, wasn't it?

It was, yes. It became an 'A' picture, as a matter of fact. It wasn't a very expensive film to make but the distributors felt it was too good to go out as a second feature. Valerie thinks she has killed her husband, even though she hasn't, and she dies. The unwritten law at the time was that you have to pay for your crimes, you see. She's run over at the end, in the climax, as she's running to meet her lover.

***The Frightened Man* is an interesting film.**

We actually made the film under the title *Rosselli and Son* and the distributors didn't like the title, so it was changed to *The Frightened Man*. I was pleased with it, particularly with the actor who played Rosselli, Charles Victor. He's a lovely actor, one of those English supporting actors who today would make a fortune. He was absolutely first-class. It was an original screenplay by John Gilling, not based on a play or anything. All our stuff was original, really, because we couldn't afford to pay for the rights of an existing novel or play. The only exception, based on a thing called *The Ghoul*, was *What a Carve Up!* – and so loosely based I don't know why we bothered. That was a more expensive film anyway.

***Deadly Nightshade*, with Emrys Jones playing a convict, presumably had some location shooting.**

Yes, most of the action took place in one cottage. That was made for about £10,000. It's notable for

having Joan Hickson in it, who went on to such success on television as Miss Marple. Of course, these people were the bread and butter of the British film industry for years and years – people like Raymond Huntley, who made a career of playing unpleasant bank managers and the like. He was a wonderful character actor. John Le Mesurier was another, a great actor.

***Double Exposure* seems to me to be a very typical, fast-moving thriller.**

Yes, with John Bentley and Rona Anderson. She sees someone pushed out of a window by Alexander Gauge (a wonderful character, almost our Sydney Greenstreet). Rona Anderson goes off in pursuit of some villain to Winchester or somewhere, but I can't remember where we photographed it. Certainly it would have been within easy distance of London because we could never have afforded to take a unit away and pay hotel expenses. We invariably chose locations we could motor out to and be back by night-time. Some would get there themselves by their own car; others would go from the studio in a coach with the crew.

What about *The Embezzler*, which benefited very much from Charles Victor's work?

Yes, Charles Victor was just a damn fine actor; and there were Michael Craig, Avice Landone and Peggy Mount too. And the girl was played by Zena Marshall. It wasn't really a thriller, more a character study, as you suggest. There was a play called *The Man Who Played God* years ago and that's really what it was. Again, that was a Gilling picture. It's more like a play than a film, really. You rely entirely on your characters to carry the story through, rather than the situation. It's 'the man who played God' idea; the Henry Cass film with Alec Guinness, *Last Holiday*, is similar in that respect. It's an idea that's very attractive for a cheap picture because the requirements are very small in terms of sets. What you do need is good actors and a good director.

British films always seem to me to have relied a lot more on dialogue than American films do, and perhaps less on action.

Americans will cut out dialogue if they possibly can, relying on the action. In England we tend to use six words when two would do. Americans *indicate* things, they're much better at it. Cinema is a visual medium and should be as visual as possible, whereas over here the stage background tends to be pinned to our drama.

You then did a great deal of television after

the '60s. Was this your preference or simply the way things were going?

It was the way things were going. It was fairly obvious that with the advent of television, the second feature was doomed. Television began to make inroads in the cinema because people were staying at home to watch television. That meant that cinema had to fight back and the only way to do that was to make exciting things like Cinemascope and big-screen epics that couldn't be done on television. Consequently they made longer pictures and the need for second features just faded. It was fairly obvious to us that the kinds of films we were making were on the decline.

Roy Ward Baker

b. 1916

Director: *The October Man* (1947), *The Weaker Sex* (1948), *Paper Orchid, Morning Departure* (1949), *Highly Dangerous* (1950), *The House in the Square* (1951), *Night without Sleep, Don't Bother to Knock* (1952), *Inferno* (1953), *Passage Home* (1955), *Jacqueline, Tiger in the Smoke* (1956), *The One That Got Away* (1957), *A Night to Remember* (1958), *The Singer Not the Song* (1960), *Flame in the Streets, The Valiant* (1961), *Two Left Feet* (1963), *Quatermass and the Pit, The Anniversary* (1967), *Moon Zero Two* (1969), *Vampire Lovers* (1970), *Dr Jekyll and Sister Hyde* (1971), *Asylum* (1972), *And Now the Screaming Starts, Vault of Horror* (1973), *The Legend of the Seven Gold Vampires* (1974), *The Monster Club* (1980)

A man who has made two striking *films noirs* and one of the best 3-D films (*Inferno*), sunk the *Titanic*, grappled with 'Quatermass', and presented Bette Davis as a one-eyed monster would seem to have had a richly varied career. Roy Ward Baker is not in any doubt about the obligation of films, in whatever genre, to be enjoyable; and casting one's eyes over his 1940s and '50s credits, one finds that he has made several of the most enjoyable films of the period, though 'enjoyable' seems too bland a word for the tensions of, say, *The October Man*, or the genuinely chilling first two-thirds of *Tiger in the Smoke*, or the impressive staging of the *Titanic* disaster in *A Night to Remember*, or the very lively war escape thriller, *The One That Got Away*, or the submarine drama, *Morning Departure*, which brought him to the attention of Hollywood. Roy Ward Baker's British films are characterised by well-chosen casts performing with clarity and conviction, by a no-nonsense approach to storytelling, and by their propensity to be oddly unnerving, possibly partly the result of the camera techniques he speaks of. *Interview date: June 1991*

You made some of the most enjoyable British films of the '40s and '50s. Do you regard this sort of viewer-pleasure as a top priority?

I don't think there's any other reason for making a film. There's no point in making films in a vacuum or for your twelve friends in Hampstead or wherever. I am not saying I would do anything to please an audience; I try to provoke them, to poke them in the eye occasionally. Of course, the ordinary working director's life is such that you do a lot of pictures simply because they are on offer. You never have perfect freedom of choice.

Were you occupied with filmmaking during the war?

Yes, I had about three years in the Infantry, then a message was sent around that anyone who had experience in making films should send their names into the War Office, which I did, because I'd been at Gainsborough in various capacities before the war. I was taken on as a production manager with the Army Kinematograph Service, which was part of the Royal Army Ordnance Corps. After about six weeks a film came up and there was nobody to direct it, so I proposed myself. It was eight reels of what we would now call 'urban guerrilla warfare' – how to clear a street. I shot it in Battersea, which had been very heavily bombed by that time, so I had the most magnificent set – all absolutely genuine! I went on to make straightforward instructional films, like 'how to handle a 25-pounder gun', and so on.

One day I met Eric Ambler at an Army church parade. Ultimately he became the executive producer for the Army Film Unit, so that I came to work with him quite a lot. We became very close friends and, when we could see that the war was going to be over very soon, we began to think about what we were going to do. Eric had already had several of his books filmed and Del Guidice from Two Cities (really part of the Rank Organisation) wanted him to write a script and produce it as soon as the war was over, and Eric asked me to direct it. That's how *The October Man* came about.

The character played by John Mills is a typical Roy Ward Baker protagonist – a man pushed to the edge to see how he might react.

That has always intrigued me, because most people lead comparatively ordinary lives and don't come up against enormous crises. One of the most interesting things to me about *Morning Departure* was when they all get bottled up in that submarine and the question was how they would react to facing death.

We had a very fine cast in *The October Man*, most of whom were not under contract. It was only later, when the Rank Organisation moved into production properly instead of doing it through Two Cities, that they started to build up a catalogue of star names. Catherine Lacey was superb as the landlady, wasn't she? She is one of those actresses who never gave a bad performance, it just wasn't in her to do so.

***Morning Departure* is an adaptation of a play, by Kenneth Woollard. Did William Fairchild's adaptation alter it very much?**

In general, he kept very close to the original but, of course, in the play the rescue operation all had to be done with frantic telephone calls, whereas we could actually show it. It was really more suited to the cinema than the theatre. That downbeat ending of the four men dying was in the play also, they didn't get them up.

I was very proud of that film and still am. It was an immense success in its day and that's how I came to go to Hollywood in 1952, because the Americans had seen that film. It's probably become a bit dated now, but, even now, in any service there is a pretty rigid distinction between the officers and the other ranks. Under stress it does break down in a sense, although even at the end of the film, the two officers are still officers and the two others are still the other ranks. They are never on a classless level, although they are on an *equal* level in that they know they are all going to die at any moment.

You worked again with Eric Ambler on *Highly Dangerous* and *A Night to Remember*. Did you find him a particularly sympathetic collaborator?

Oh yes. We developed a long-lasting friendship and, of course, one thing about Eric is that he presents you with a script which is beautifully finished in every detail. *Highly Dangerous* wasn't a very successful picture. I think Margaret Lockwood wanted to play a modern woman and this character was a scientist, to do with germ warfare. It was actually Eric Ambler's first or second book, although the book had a different title and its main character was a man; Eric changed it to a woman to make it more interesting. It was a good idea although I don't think I did it very well.

Dane Clark, your leading man, seemed a sort of poor man's John Garfield. What do you think of that practice of importing American stars throughout the 1950s?

It was all part of a fatal delusion that we could distribute our pictures in America, and it started in the 1920s. The answer is that there is no *need* for British pictures there. Most of the successful British pictures, like *Chariots of Fire*, have not been directed at America anyway. In making that film, I don't think anyone for one moment considered the American distribution, but David Puttnam, being the brilliant salesman he is, did it anyway and they loved it.

What was your experience of working with Tyrone Power and Ann Blyth in *The House in the Square*?

They were both absolutely marvellous. Tyrone Power was one of the nicest men I've ever met, and really super-professional. I learned quite a lot from him. He was amenable, a perfect gent. Ann Blyth was fine; she was actually more of a singer. She played rather a misty character, not entirely real, and I thought she did it very well. That was an American picture made here for 20th-Century-Fox.

You worked with the great cameraman, Georges Périnal, on that film and you worked with other great cameramen, such as Geoffrey Unsworth. What have you, as a director, looked for and valued in a cameraman?

You must have the top cameraman, it's vital. It even affects the editing. If you have a slipshod cameraman you will find that when you cut some of the sequences they don't seem to fit properly, because the lighting has gone awry, or he has changed his mind in the middle of a scene. I've been very fortunate in that respect. Geoff Unsworth was a bosom friend, a really charming man. He developed his reputation very strongly because he was extraordinarily good at photographing women. Very few British cameramen had bothered to do that well. The quality I value most in a cameraman is being *simpatico* with the story, the characters and the atmosphere. There is a great deal in being a good lighting man.

When you returned from Hollywood in the mid '50s, did you then work for the Rank Organisation for four to five years on films like *Jacqueline*, *Passage Home* and *Tiger in the Smoke*?

Yes, those are all Rank films made at Pinewood. It was about seven years actually, from 1953 or 1954 to about 1961.

What recollections have you of working with Peter Finch in *Passage Home*?

Oh, very good, he was a genuine actor. Probably rather more a theatre actor than a cinema actor, even though he was very successful in films and did some wonderful things, particularly later in America. I liked him, of course; he was a wonderful sort of con-man – you know, he had about three different life stories he would tell you, all completely different and hilariously funny. I really don't know what the truth was and one didn't care, he was such great fun and a very, very good actor. It was a marvellous cast, I remember: Diane Cilento was in it and Pat McGoohan; I think Tony Steel was under contract to Rank and Michael Craig may have been, but the others weren't.

Would you agree that *Tiger in the Smoke*, from Margery Allingham's novel, is a genuinely scary thriller?

I think it never really worked because its dénouement depends on the revelation of a wonderful treasure in Brittany – the writing and description, incidentally, was very detailed about what the place should be like – and of course I could never find a place that remotely resembled it. So when they open the box and the treasure is just a plaster statue of the Madonna, it just wasn't good enough, not striking or thrilling enough.

Anthony Pelissier did the basic screenplay adaptation and about half the script, then he went off to direct some television thing and Leslie Parkyn, the producer, and I more or less had to complete the script ourselves. I'm not sure we did a very good job. We had a marvellous cast and the atmosphere was all there, with Geoffrey Unsworth on camera, and strangely enough this was the first film where some of the critics began to take me seriously. Suddenly I found myself getting a slightly fancy reputation, which I thought was rather nice. I don't know why that film did it, though. The major flaw was Tony Wright – he was wrongly cast; it should have been Stanley Baker or Jack Hawkins, someone you could really be frightened of.

The one trick I had in *Tiger in the Smoke* was that

I decided to shoot the whole picture on a baby crane and the camera is in fact always moving, it's never absolutely still. I did it to produce a feeling of unrest; nobody ever commented on it and I think I should have been a bit bolder. Or perhaps it was one of those subliminal effects. It was all shot at Pinewood except for some location work at Liverpool Street station and in Brittany. I got a certain amount of criticism about Donald Sinden and Muriel Pavlow because they were so immaculate and middle-class. I wouldn't play them like that now but I think it was right at that time.

Among the many British war films of the 1950s, *The One That Got Away* suddenly stands out. Where did you find the story?

I had a friend who ran a bookshop in Piccadilly and one day he said he had two books for me; one was *The One That Got Away* and the other was *A Night to Remember*. I read them both over the weekend.

The One That Got Away was an essay in total realism. There was a lot of opposition to my making it; I was heavily criticised for making a German into a hero. I said it wasn't making him a hero, it was simply because he was the only man who had ever escaped. I was determined to make it, for two reasons. Firstly, it was a marvellous chase story, like a Western in some ways. Secondly, I'd got sick to death of the propaganda pictures during the war, and after the war they went on making the Nazis either beer-swilling krauts or homosexual Prussians. So I thought something should be said to show the Germans for the very resourceful and determined people they can be.

I decided that the main character was in a way a villain/hero, and, since everyone in Europe reads from left to right, throughout the movie I always had him going from right to left and everyone else going from left to right. That was another thing that nobody noticed; but I hoped it worked unconsciously to differentiate him from the others.

Then there was a tremendous fuss about who would play the main part. Originally the studio refused to have a German but I insisted. Luckily, just at that time there was a luncheon at Pinewood to entertain a lot of Rank's European representatives, including our man in Hamburg. I asked him if he could help me. He phoned me as soon as he got back to Germany and I went over there. As soon as I clapped eyes on Hardy Kruger I knew he was it. We got on very well and it was one of the best experiences with an actor I've ever had.

The Canadian sequences were mostly shot in Sweden and partly on the stage we built. It was very arduous; it went over schedule; everyone was worried. I had another marvellous cameraman called Eric Cross; it was the only time I worked with him. He was a documentary man and an exterior man – Julian Wintle brought him into the film, and he was absolutely right. Eric was a rock; he simply wouldn't shoot unless it was right and, of course, the end result was superb.

You next filmed the other book, *A Night to Remember*. Did you have a special feeling about the *Titanic* as a subject?

Oh yes, the whole purpose of making the film was to show a society which had persuaded itself into a view that you could make a ship which could never be sunk. It turned out that William Macquitty was going to produce and you couldn't have a better man than that. He was emotionally involved because he is an Ulsterman and the ship was built at the Ulster shipyards. He remembers being held in his father's arm, as a very small child, to see the *Titanic* as it went down the river. We built half of the deck on the back lot of Pinewood. It needed a lot of organising and planning, but luckily Alex Vetchinsky was the art director – I'd known him since I first went to work at Gainsborough and had worked with him many times.

You could say the people who believed the ship to be invulnerable were a bunch of arrogant fools, but it's no good caricaturing them. There *are* one or two people caricatured in the picture – like the aristocrats played by Patrick Waddington and Harriette Johns – but you see, those sorts of people *were* caricatures even in their own lives.

Michael Goodliffe was in *The One That Got Away* and several of my pictures after that; he was a great favourite of mine. Laurence Naismith was also in several things I did, as were Sam Kydd, Victor Maddern and quite a few others. Those were reliable people and they fitted in so easily and so well.

I have not seen your film *The Singer Not the Song*, which has acquired an extraordinary cult reputation. Why, do you think?

I hated it, it broke my heart. It put me completely out of kilter for years afterwards, it was a disaster. I'm told it's a cult picture and quite probably in countries with large Catholic communities it has some special reference. I should never have made it. I actually turned it down once and said if they really wanted to make the picture they should get the great

Spanish/Mexican director Luis Buñuel to do it. I fought it off for over twelve months but the Rank Organisation pressured me to make it. I can't think why they wanted the damned thing. It wasn't a good book, it was the old phoney story of a little girl falling in love with a priest and it's been done so many times. It has not been financially unsuccessful, and if I go to France I have a much bigger reputation there than I do here – principally for that film and for *Quatermass and the Pit*, which they loved. But as far as I'm concerned it just gives me the horrors. Anyway, it's all a long time ago and many much pleasanter things have happened to me since.

Sir Michael Balcon

1896–1977

Rather than attempt a filmography for Michael Balcon, it seems more appropriate to list the key positions he held. His function in British cinema is essentially that of a **chief executive**, a studio head, rather than a producer in the creative sense of the word.

1921 Victory Motion Pictures – co-founded with Victor Saville.
1924 Gainsborough Pictures – co-founded with Graham Cutts. In charge of production there for Gaumont-British from 1931.
1936 MGM-British – director of production.
1937 Ealing Studios – director and chief of production.
1959 Bryanston Films – founder.
1964 British Lion – chairman.

Some of the films he produced for Gainsborough are: *The Pleasure Garden* (1925), *The Mountain Eagle, The Lodger* (1926), *Woman to Woman* (1929), *Rome Express* (1932), *The Good Companions, I was a Spy* (1933), *Man of Aran, Evergreen, Little Friend* (1934), *First a Girl, The Thirty-Nine Steps* (1935), *Tudor Rose* (1936)
His name appears as producer on most Ealing films of the period of his incumbency, but one needs to check the name of the associate producer to discover who actually performed the producer's function on an individual Ealing film.

'Can we ever build up a real British film industry?'[1] asks Michael Balcon in his 1969 autobiography. No one could accuse him of not having made his contribution to this tricky enterprise. In an industry which threw up few moguls (Rank and Korda are the only others that come to mind), Balcon emerges as a somewhat headmasterly figure, a benevolent dictator, in the accounts one receives of his leadership at Ealing. In the twelve years he presided over Gainsborough Pictures, he notably produced some of Hitchcock's most charming entertainments. He then had two frustrating years in charge of production at MGM-British, from which he escaped to Ealing, where he spent 'the most rewarding years in my personal career, and perhaps one of the most fruitful periods in the history of British film production.'[2]

Balcon was always concerned to establish a recognisable British industry, believing 'that a film, to be international, must be thoroughly national in the first instance.'[3] While at Gainsborough, however, as well as making such wholly indigenous works as the Jessie Matthews musicals, Balcon also imported American stars and made films with an eye consciously on the US market. He nevertheless bewailed the loss of British talent to America, later claiming that '. . . before the war a debilitating effect was had upon British films by the fact that it was generally the British technician's and the British actor's ambition to go to Hollywood as the Mecca of filmmaking.'[4]

The plaque he had erected at Ealing when the studio was sold in 1955 said: 'Here during a quarter of a century many films were made projecting Britain and the British character.'[5] What most people associate with the studio is 'Ealing comedy'. This term derives from a batch of comedies ushered in by *Hue and Cry* in 1947 and followed famously by *Passport to Pimlico, Kind Hearts and Coronets, Whisky Galore!* and *The Lavender Hill Mob*. They are really more heterogeneous than the 'Ealing comedy' label suggests: they are variously gentle or dry, sunny or black, whimsical or tough. 'Our theory of comedy . . . is ludicrously simple,' wrote Balcon. 'We take a character, or a group of characters, and let them run up against either an untenable situation or an insoluble problem. The audience hopes they will get out of it, and they usually do: the comedy lies in *how* they do it.'[6]

He goes on to say that 'comedy at Ealing usually starts with an original filmic idea rather than a best-selling book',[7] and certainly among the charms of

the films is their quirky freshness and originality, their cinematic inventiveness. (Compare them with some of the stiffly theatrical comedies whose production Balcon oversaw at Gainsborough in the '30s.) Elsewhere, he wrote that 'film producers *want* good authors to work for them and with them . . . provided they are prepared to acquire . . . an understanding of films and a skill in writing for them.'[8] And it's true that Ealing films avoid debilitating literariness. But Ealing offered more than comedy, and its war films (e.g., *San Demetrio, London*) and its post-war dramas (e.g., *Mandy*) were much praised for their realism. In their way, they also 'projected Britain and the British character'. In its representations of courage, fortitude and consensual effort, the Ealing ethos was characterised by a low-key realism which was the legacy of 'the men who kept realism going on the screen':[9] by these 'men', he meant the documentary filmmakers he praised in a lecture he gave to the Film Workers' Association in 1943.

The worst that could be said of Balcon's achievement is that it was sometimes too suburbanly cosy; against this it may be said that he brought a new naturalness into British feature films.

1 Michael Balcon, *Michael Balcon presents . . . A Lifetime of Films*, Hutchinson, London, 1969, p 217
2 Balcon, p 184
3 Balcon, p 61
4 'The British film during the war', in *The Penguin Film Review 1*, Penguin, Harmondsworth, 1946, p 73
5 Balcon, p 185
6 'The secret of Ealing comedy' in Campbell Dixon (ed), *International Film Annual No 1*, John Calder, London, 1957, p 62
7 'The secret of Ealing comedy', p 62
8 'An author in the studio', *Films and Filming*, July 1957, pp 7 and 34
9 'Realism or tinsel?' in M Danischewsky (ed), *Michael Balcon's Twenty-Five Years in Films*, World Film Publications, London, 1947, p 70

Vincent Ball

b. 1924

Actor: *The Blue Lagoon* (as stunt double), *A Warning to Wantons, The Interrupted Journey, Stop Press Girl* (1949), *Come Dance With Me* (1950), *Talk of a Million, London Entertains, Encore* (1951), *The Drayton Case* (1953), *The Dark Stairway, Dangerous Voyage, Devil's Harbour, The Black Rider* (1954), *John and Julie, The Blue Peter, The Big Fish, Stolen Time* (1955), *The Baby and the Battleship, A Town Like Alice, Secret of the Forest, Reach for the Sky* (1956), *Face in the Night, Robbery Under Arms* (1957), *Blood of the Vampire, Sea of Sand* (1958), *Danger Within, Summer of the Seventeenth Doll* (1959), *Dentist in the Chair, Identity Unknown, Feet of Clay, Dead Lucky* (1960), *Nearly a Nasty Accident, Very Important Person, Highway to Battle, The Middle Course, A Matter of WHO* (1961), *Carry On Cruising* (1962), *Echo of Diana, Mouse on the Moon* (1963), *Follow That Camel* (1967), *Where Eagles Dare* (1968), *Oh! What a Lovely War* (1969), *Not Tonight Darling* (1971), *Clinic Xclusive* (1972), *Death Cheaters* (1976), *The Irishman* (1978), *Alison's Birthday* (1979), *Time Lapse, Breaker Morant* (1980), *Deadline* (1981), *Phar Lap* (1983), *Flight into Hell, Butterfly Island* (1985), *Call Me Mr Brown* (1986), *The Year My Voice Broke* (1987), *Turtle Beach* (1990), *Love in Limbo* (1993), *Frauds, Sirens, Muriel's Wedding* (1994), *Paradise Road* (1997)

Vincent Ball's career in 1950s British cinema is instructive about what was available to a working actor at the time. As a man with family responsibilities, he took what came along, including a television series which was more lucrative than most film work. He had ample experience of the 'B' films of British cinema of the period, films of a kind that virtually disappeared in the '60s, as the nature of exhibition altered and as television took up some of the 'B' film genres. Ball worked with the legendary Danzigers; who regularly made films in three weeks and less, and with prolific directors such as Montgomery Tully and Wolf Rilla. Threading their way through these films was a steady line of 'A' films, such as two films he made with director Jack Lee, *A Town Like Alice* and *Robbery Under Arms*, two war films, Guy Green's *Sea of Sand* and Don Chaffey's *Danger Within*, and Richard Attenborough's *Oh! What a Lovely War*. A likeable, convincing actor always, his work has gained authority in recent years when he has appeared in Australian films and television.

Interview date: October 1991

Did you really begin as a stunt double, as one reference says?

Yes. One day I read in a Sydney paper that they were looking for someone for the original *Blue Lagoon* [1948], with Jean Simmons. So I sent some photographs showing off my muscles to the Rank Organisation at Pinewood. About three weeks later I got a reply saying I would be considered for the part if I should ever be over that way. Six months later, via a Swedish cargo boat, I arrived in England and took my very tatty letter to Pinewood, where the man who had written it, Dennis Van Thal, apologised for the fact that they had already finished the film, having been to Fiji and back again. Then he asked if I could swim and explained that Donald Houston couldn't; so they offered me £10 a day to do the underwater swimming sequences in the big studio tank. My first job was wrestling rubber octopuses in the tank at Pinewood. That's my body you see in *Blue Lagoon*. I remember Frank Launder saying, 'Vince, old boy, try to keep your face away from the camera, there's a good chap.'

After about eighteen months I won a scholarship to RADA, where I spent about two terms. Then I had a day off and went to audition for a film, *Talk of a Million*, with Jack Warner and Barbara Mullen, directed by John Paddy Carstairs. I did the test playing an Irishman with a couple of chaps from the Abbey Theatre and eventually got the part. RADA gave me a term off to do it. I also had bits in *Stop Press Girl*, and *Interrupted Journey*, which starred Valerie Hobson.

You made a number of supporting or 'B' pictures during the '50s.

Yes, do you remember the Danziger brothers? They used to make films every ten days and I'd go from one film set to another; we made most of them at Elstree. If I finished one film at Friday lunchtime, I'd walk to another set and start the next one that afternoon, changing my jacket or whatever for the new character. I made about ten of them and can't even remember their names. It was good experience but the trouble was that you also got the tag of 'B' picture actor.

I remember Danziger used to do four-minute takes, which was very demanding on the actors. Half the time you didn't have time to learn the dialogue. Doing a Danziger was really the end of the line, but I had a wife and kids and a mortgage to pay. You would play a lead for ten days and get your money – in cash, which was most unusual. The films were made on a shoestring, with minimum crews.

I remember once finishing a film for Montgomery Tully and he pulled out another script, saying, 'Now, what about this one? I haven't read it yet'! While we were chatting, some new wallpaper was slapped up on the set and the furniture was moved around a bit, then we started off again! At least they knew they had an assured outlet for their films because it was the time when cinemas showed double features.

Around this time, there was *Dangerous Voyage*, directed by Vernon Sewell, for whom I did at least two films. He had a yacht called the *Gelert* and we sailed on it to France to shoot part of the film. Vernon didn't have permission to shoot there so he'd conceal the camera under his mac and film me walking into a police station or whatever. We lived on the yacht, supposedly on holiday but sneakily making a film, shooting from the back of a van or through windows.

I remember, too, doing a couple of films for Wolf Rilla – *The Black Rider* in 1954, and *The Blue Peter*, in Wales, with Kieron Moore and Greta Gynt. That was quite a big deal, we were in Wales for six or seven weeks' filming.

You were also on television a lot, weren't you?

Yes, I had my own programme, junior television on ATV, which I did for four years, telling stories about the Australian bush hospital at Wee Waa in NSW, reading Banjo Patterson and talking about the brumbies and so on. When Lew Grade offered me a contract at £100 a week, I took it.

Later I wanted to get out of the ATV job and Bob Baker rang me up to ask if I'd like to go to North Africa to make *Sea of Sand*, so I said, 'Yes, please!' I made *Sea of Sand* with Dickie Attenborough, who asked me what I planned to do next. He was to do a film called *Danger Within* for Don Chaffey, and when I got back to London I was called to see Don and found I had a part in the film, which was very nice of Dickie.

Where were those two war films made?

Sea of Sand was made in Tripoli in North Africa. I think we had six of the worst old army trucks in North Africa; half the time they were being towed past the cameras, even though they'd had new engines fitted. But it was probably one of the best locations I've ever been on, staying at the Imperial Hotel by the sea. It was pretty rough filming in the desert but we played poker, drank a lot of beer, and swam.

Danger Within was set in Italy but made in England; a camp was built out near Gerrards Cross and we shot it there. I've made six or seven films for Don Chaffey, particularly here in Australia. We became mates and I think he would just find parts for me – although I'm sure he wouldn't have if he didn't think I could do the job.

What was your experience of working with Donald Wolfit in *Blood of the Vampire*?

Oh, marvellous. He would drag Victor Maddern and me into his room, lie on the bed and talk about the theatre for hours. It was fascinating. He was very grand, very much *Sir* Donald, but he treated us well. Henry Cass was called in at the last moment to direct the film; I don't think he'd even read the script when he arrived on the first day. In one scene there were glass jars containing entrails and bits of human bodies, supposedly. Of course, they'd been to the butcher's shop for hearts, kidneys and livers. Now, imagine all that under the hot lights after two or three days!

Was the '50s a good time to be getting a career going in British films?

It was good for me when I started doing 'A' pictures like *A Town Like Alice*. An actor is never secure, though. The only time I felt secure was when I had the ATV contract. I left RADA in 1951 and you could say I've been semi-retired ever since! Still, in the '50s everybody was making films. Elstree, Shepperton, Pinewood were doing the big 'A' features and the small studios like Wimbledon and Merton Park were making second features, so there was a lot of work around. If you'd done a stint in rep and had a decent agent, you could get work.

How did you come to be in the two Jack Lee films? Was it because you were Australian?

After *A Town Like Alice*, Joe Janni told me I'd got the job because after RADA I'd understudied Michael Denison and Ronnie Lewis in a play called *The Bad Samaritan*, by Willy Douglas-Home. In that play was Virginia McKenna, with whom I'd been very friendly; when they sent the script of *A Town Like Alice* to Ginny (whom I used to call 'my English rose', she's a lovely lady and a wonderful actress), she agreed to do it and suggested I would be ideal for the part of Ben. I got a call from my agent to go to see Jack Lee and Joe Janni at Heathrow Airport; they were on their way to Australia to do location shots for *A Town Like Alice*, and Joe offered me the part of Ben.

A Town Like Alice was all done with back projection against the 'jungles' of Pinewood. It was so cold and drizzling with rain, we used to have to sip brandy to keep ourselves warm. And while I was at Pinewood I changed uniforms and nipped across to another studio and did one scene for *Reach for the Sky*, playing Muriel Pavlow's brother or cousin.

Then Peter Finch gave Jack Lee the book *Robbery Under Arms*, suggesting he and I could play the Marsden boys. When Jack decided to make the film, John Davis, Rank's Managing Director, insisted that contract artistes be used for the leads. I was offered the much smaller part of the brother of one of the girls and said I'd do it if we were going to film in Australia. Joe Janni said we wouldn't be and, when I said I didn't want to do it in that case, I didn't hear from him for a couple of weeks. Then he asked me to lunch at Pinewood with himself, Jack Lee and Finch, and Joe asked why wouldn't I be in the film for old times' sake and I agreed.

After they had been in Adelaide for a couple of weeks I got a call to join them. I finally flew there (after two weeks in Sydney) and was given a hotel room and a big car, until I was told to join the unit at Wulpina Farm. Ultimately, I was filmed saying one line. I had been away ten or eleven weeks, being paid all the time, and when I returned I shot my scenes at Pinewood. It was great working with Peter Finch and after the filming we knocked around together for about four or five years. He was very generous – never had any cigarettes or any money, but he would take twenty people to Casa Pepe in the Fulham Road for dinner and just sign for it.

How did you get involved in making *Summer of the Seventeenth Doll*?

John Mills asked if I would coach his daughter Juliet in an Aussie accent, because she was going to test for the part of Bubba. I offered to do the test with her, playing Johnny Dowd, believing that part had been cast. As it happened, I was working on the day of Juliet's test and couldn't make it. Then John asked if I would give him a hand with *his* script. So we worked all morning, had lunch, and that night I got a message from my agent. He'd received a telegram from Hollywood which said, 'Availability Vincent Ball, Johnny Dowd, January, Australia'. He explained it meant they wanted me for the part. They asked for a clip of film of me and I suggested they get a copy of *A Town Like Alice*. They got a copy in New York somewhere and the next day I was offered the part of Johnny Dowd. When Burt Lancaster dropped out the budget went right down. We shot it all around Sydney, didn't go to Queensland at all. They changed the ending, of course, made it into a nice Hollywood-type ending.

Alan Bates

b. 1934

Actor: *Three on a Gas Ring, The Entertainer (1960), Whistle Down the Wind (1961), A Kind of Loving (1962), The Running Man, The Caretaker, Nothing but the Best (1963), Zorba the Greek (1964), *Insh'Allah (voice only) (1965), Georgy Girl, King of Hearts (1966), The Fixer, Far From the Madding Crowd (1967), Women in Love (1969), The Go-Between, A Day in the Death of Joe Egg (1970), *Second Best (1972), Impossible Object, Butley (1973), In Celebration (1974), Royal Flash (1975), An Unmarried Woman (1977), The Rose (1978), Nijinsky (1979), Quartet (1981), The Return of the Soldier, The Wicked Lady, Britannia Hospital (1982), Duet for One (1986), A Prayer for the Dying, We Think the World of You (1987), Force Majeure (1989), Docteur M, Hamlet, Mister Frost (1990), Secret Friends (1992), Silent Tongue (1994), The Grotesque (1996)
* Short film.

Of all the bright young acting talents who suddenly brought new life to British films in the early '60s, none has lasted so well or remained so persistently a *British* star. He has outlasted, say, Albert Finney or Tom Courtenay or Richard Harris, in the sense of working steadily in major films (as well as much notable stage and television work); and unlike Michael Caine or Sean Connery, for example, he hasn't had to make a lot of international kitsch to keep working. It was his articulate compassion that makes his performance in *A Kind of Loving* as the young man caught in an unpromising marriage so affecting and memorable. It is greatly to his credit that he makes an unflashy character such as the bemused young Englishman abroad in *Zorba the Greek* more interesting than Anthony Quinn's bravura display or that he more than holds his own as solid, loyal Gabriel Oak in *Far from the Madding Crowd* against the more obviously eye-catching work from Terence Stamp and Peter Finch. From at least a dozen expert performances, I choose three more examples: he is an iconoclastic Birkin, broken by a conventional Ursula in *Women in Love*; his Guy Burgess, that other *Englishman Abroad* (for television), is magisterially witty and painful; and he offers a very moving study in polite bewilderment in *The Return of the Soldier*. His work is central to any study of British cinema of the last three decades.
Interview date: November 1995

After notable successes on the stage – *Long Day's Journey into Night*, for instance, and several at the Royal Court – how did you come to make the transition from stage to screen?

I didn't regard it really as a transition. I was asked to be in a film called *Whistle Down the Wind* and also in *The Entertainer*. I did *The Entertainer* first and Tony Richardson was the director of that and John Osborne was the author, and I had been in *Look Back in Anger* in the theatre. They began in the theatre and then they formed a film company and this happened at the time when there was a renaissance in British films, and I just found myself in both media quite naturally. It was just a very lucky piece of timing.

***The Entertainer* looks interesting now as a combination of hot new talents like Tony Richardson, Albert Finney, yourself, and established people like Laurence Olivier, Brenda de Banzie, Roger Livesey. Was there any sense of a couple of generations of actors at work together?**

I suppose there was, although, particularly with Olivier, I think he was seeking out something new with *The Entertainer*; he had sought out the new dramatists and had made a very conscious effort to place himself at the forefront of all that. But apart from that sort of conscious choice on his part, I think everyone merged pretty well. He did too, but we were just conscious that he had chosen to do something specifically of the day, as it were, rather a break from his classical mould.

So there wasn't a sense of new young people being in great awe of him?

I think in every generation there's a certain amount of, not awe exactly, but that sort of awareness of other people's achievements. It's a natural sort of rollover, an evolution, people moving into other people's positions.

Were you aware, at the time, of major changes going on in the nature of British films?

I think things are slightly clearer when you look back at them, but there was a conscious feeling that we had found something, or at least those who wrote and produced it touched on something, that people wanted to change: a change of scene, a change of orientation, a change of focus on what films were about. Style and people were more experimental and more daring, and there was the spirit to back these films, which sadly has gone for the moment. It was a very good moment, a very

good time, and we were aware of it. We were aware of it as a change, as a difference. There was a new concentration on the social issues of the day, the underprivileged; there was no arena untouched, every area of life began to be explored.

Did you have a good agent at the time or was it just a matter of getting to be known?

No, I think I was in the right place at the right time and I just got into the right things. I was in the Royal Court Theatre and that's where a lot of it sprang from; that and Joan Littlewood's theatre at Stratford East were the two theatres that seemed to spawn this whole new energy.

What do you remember about filming Bryan Forbes's charming parable. *Whistle Down the Wind*? I'd be fascinated to know anything you remember about, say, the location work, or working with the children.

I was more aware that it was my first major part than anything. The children really were the star of the film, or, if not the star, the *focus* of the film, and the character I played became *their* focus and that's why it was such a good part. It was very naturalistically shot, it was done with a very conscious realism. I looked at it again a few years ago and it seemed absolutely a Biblical parallel. It's not just a windy children's tale; it does tell of treachery, of the Judas character, of the whole area of credibility and faith. It's quite a strong film and I think it stands up very well.

What do you remember about those children, who were not actors at all?

There were the two, her [Hayley Mills'] brother and sister, I remember of course. I believe the little girl is no longer with us, I believe she died at some point in her adulthood. I don't think the boy Alan Barnes ever acted again; he was just a natural at that moment. He was a sort of person you thought might go on to be a comedic actor of some distinction if he'd wanted to, but he didn't. I think he ended up as a chemist somewhere. He just had this little burst of glory as a boy. He was a great character.

And what do you remember about the location filming?

I'd been in that area before; the Midlands is where I came from. I filmed there later in *A Kind of Loving* in the same sort of areas – rural, quite tough farmland. One of the great things of filming is to act in location, in the elements, you know; it's quite an exciting way to work.

Do you prefer it to studio work?

Yes I do, yes. Studios are OK but there's an unreality there and I much prefer to be on location.

Of all those New Wave films that came out of the period, *A Kind of Loving* still seems perhaps the warmest and most sympathetic. How do you feel about it now?

I think that's quite a likely way to look at it now: it had a lot of human understanding, a lot of awareness of young people's problems and their blindness and the whole pot-luck chance of life. It was very well understood, it was a beautiful book, very gentle, almost a lyrical book in a kind of raw way, which I think John [Schlesinger] captured on screen. It wasn't brutal; it was absolutely life as it was lived; it wasn't about exceptional folk, it was really about everyday people and their struggles.

Did you feel that even the monstrous mother Thora Hird plays is entirely believable, that she never becomes a caricature, however hideous she is?

No, I think it's a rather great performance. It's wonderfully naturally funny and terrific at the same time – a blinkered and prejudiced and dominating woman. There are such people.

How did you respond to the character of Vic Brown and his plight? Did you see him as a victim?

I just accepted him for what he was. He seemed in one way to understand himself very well and at the same time not to be able to do anything about it. I think it's a quite unusual scene when he goes back home to his mother. Unusual in the sense that his mother does not take his side, she takes the side of the girl he's married and that's quite unusual. Mothers usually can see no wrong in their sons but this woman thought, no, he took a step and he must follow it through, and he must deal with the woman he's married.

What became of June Ritchie, who seemed so perfectly right as Ingrid?

June is a very fine actress who is now married quite happily, and works from time to time. I've worked with her since a couple of times and she's done some marvellous work when she feels like it. She doesn't chase her career with great ambition, but she was very fine.

Your three 1963 releases each seem to me interesting for different reasons. First, *The Running Man*. How did you find working with Carol Reed, who really belongs to a previous generation?

I was just very lucky to have worked with him and I'm sorry the film wasn't a bigger success. He was the most subtle and sensitive director, one of the best I've ever worked with, and I'm very glad that I crossed paths with him once. He was a great gentleman and he made three of the greatest British films that have ever been made: I mean *Fallen Idol*, *Odd Man Out* and *The Third Man* – unparalleled, really. Brilliant films, as good as you can get. I was a very young actor but I felt his incredible generosity of spirit, which I'm afraid a lot of directors just don't have.

How did this generosity of spirit come over in the kind of direction he gave you?

Just in the understanding of your particular situation, who you were at the time. Whether you were young and inexperienced, or experienced, he would respond accordingly to the actor who was in front of him. He wouldn't expect more or less than what their own experience had brought them to. He listened to you and if he wanted more or less than you were giving he would just guide you towards it extremely gently, without making you feel at all inadequate. He was quite a marvellous man, I think.

And what about *The Caretaker*?

The Caretaker was a deliberate translation of the play to film. It seemed to have enormous filming possibilities and it is an excellent film, perhaps somewhat exclusive in some ways, although the play was hugely popular. It was done out of pure love of the piece and to record it and make sure the people could see the cast that had done it, with one exception, absolutely from scratch. Peter Wood-thorpe played it in the London theatre and Robert Shaw took it over in New York and for the film.

And *Nothing but the Best*, which I haven't seen now for a while?

That was just a social comedy of the sixties. It was written by a very witty writer, Freddie Raphael. It was a home-grown, home-based film about society at that moment and it's still great fun today – a bit dated, but fun. Not dated actually, but a sort of pictorial essay of its time and it's quite witty. It was a great favourite of mine.

It still looks like one of the few films that tackles class head-on.

It does, absolutely. It's the *Room at the Top* area, isn't it? It's the young man who sees his way through crime and a completely immoral attitude, but who sees what ticks and what makes the people tick, and finds someone to teach him and to break all the class barriers. Absolutely, yes, it's class comedy.

Do you know what Lindsay Anderson thought of this? He was always criticising

British films for being too middle-class.

That was Lindsay's *bête noire*; he couldn't stand anything that smacked of the middle class. But I think they do have their agonies as well, they have their tragedies, they're not just non-people.

Had you read Kazantzakis's novel *Zorba the Greek* before you filmed it?

No, I hadn't. It's a great piece and it was a great stroke of luck to be in it. It seemed like a wild idea to do it, but it turned into one of the most famous films I ever made. It's a classic, wonderful piece.

My sympathies are always with the Englishman as opposed to the Greek, full of the life force, and I wondered how you felt about that English character you played.

I had sympathy with him, of course, but he's rather an extreme product. But then there are such people in English society – indeed in every society, though I think sometimes they're often thought of as being particularly English: closed, locked-up, longing to break out. And one has sympathy for him for those reasons, of course. But Zorba is meant to be the great romantic free character that we all want to be. They're extremes, both of them.

I don't really want to be like Zorba at all. and it makes an interesting tension for me as I watch the film.

I don't know why; maybe he's completely self-loving and self-orientated; he's not really concerned with anyone else. He's got huge momentary generosity to other people, but it's all really rather motivated by who he is, isn't it?

You did another film version of a great novel at the end of the decade, *Woman in Love*, which still seems the best film ever made from a Lawrence novel and one of the best British films ever. How do you rate it?

I rate it like that too. I thought it was extraordinary when I read the book; I thought, why are we attempting this? It's too complex; it's too dense. But Ken Russell somehow understood what to take from that book to make it work on the screen and the film has a wonderful understanding of the book. I think it was slightly excessive here and there but, apart from that, the whole thing was a wonderful reflection of the spirit of the book.

The thing that seems most daring about it isn't, say, the nude scenes, but how much discussion there is in it. I wondered what you thought about the film on this level.

The discussions were cut down to an accessible state, I think. I think Lawrence *is* accessible, I don't think he's obscure. He's symbolic, but I think it's so basic, what he is actually talking about, that it comes through quite clearly. It's based greatly on the physical – the sensual attitude to the physical presence, if you like. I think people are immediately drawn to try and understand themselves through the sensual. He seems to be able to touch on things that most people are perhaps obsessed with, or at least concerned with. And those fundamental basic relationships between men and women, between women and women and between men and men: he understood them all.

The film caused some censorship uproar at the time. Was the nudity a worrying thing for filming, especially the famous wrestling scene?

We knew that it was a very unusual step to take. It was written and directed with great skill – it did just catch that area in which Lawrence was expressing that feeling of friendship and frustration through a sort of sense of combat, through the physical – it's the animal in us, in a way. Whatever sexual overtone it has is not actually stressed and it's not even probably meant to be. I've always regarded it as a sort of sensual expression of friendship rather than a sexual one.

You did another film from a famous book, which is *Far from the Madding Crowd*, on which you worked with Julie Christie and John Schlesinger. Did you have a specially good rapport with those people?

Yes, I did. I worked with Julie four times. She's a completely ego-free actress, an intelligent woman who is utterly concerned with the meaning of what she's doing, rather than the effect; and John is someone I've always had an absolute rapport with, so that was a very, very happy time. We were doing something we all understood and we could talk freely with one another about it; there were no barriers between us. I've always had this ease with those two people.

John Schlesinger told me that you at first wanted to play Sergeant Troy.

Yes, I did at the time, because I felt about the part I played that I'd been in that area before. Gabriel's a wonderful part but I felt that it wasn't a challenge for me, that's all.

The next film I want to mention is another triumph based on a novel, Joseph Losey's *The Go-Between*. Do you think sex and class and their interconnection are really the main elements of British film narratives?

I think very often that's true. I can't go on about it much more than that, but that is a fact, I think.

How do you think Losey, an American, responded to the extreme Englishness of this story?

I think he was fascinated by that. I think it was one of his key observer interests. I think he loved exploring that. And I think sometimes it comes better from someone who is not born into it, because they can really see it. He lived here long enough to see and understand it. He hadn't just arrived in England, he'd really lived amongst it, but could see it very clearly. So I think perhaps that's why it's so well brought out.

What do you remember about filming it?

I only did the last six weeks; they'd done most of the filming before I came into it – not quite, but, yes, my part was all shot towards the end of the film. The thing I mostly remember about the filming was that my children were about to be born, so I was rather preoccupied! I was down in Norfolk for my scenes.

What do you think about the transposing of plays to the screen which you did: *Butley* and Lindsay's version of *In Celebration* in the '70s?

I think it's very good to record them, to put them there, and sometimes they worked for our country. I think there is something to do with language which is essentially theatre, whereas screen is image and visual and, finally, the fewer words very often the better on the screen. The theatre can stand as many as you like. You can put words on screen, it can work; we've touched on this with the Lawrence thing; but there is a fundamental difference between them, and something truly filmic needs economy of language.

***In Celebration* really worked as a film.**

That was something to do with Lindsay's particular attitude to it. He seemed to be able to bridge it with that film almost better than anyone I know. You have to really be able to understand that difference and he, I think, somehow lightened it. He was able to bring a highly cinematic flair to that.

There's a very strange film, *The Shout*, which I find more or less impenetrable and I wondered what you thought it was about.

It was quite a daring piece, from a short story by Robert Graves, about an Aboriginal, and the old concept of the use of sound as a sort of element with which to kill. It's a quite extreme idea to write a film about, but it is a fact that sound is often used in violence and in war as a sort of killer instrument. It worked in its own way, I think, and it had a strange kind of artistic success.

I particularly liked *The Return of the Soldier*, which I thought was a very underrated film.

It *was* an underrated film but there was one thing that it missed: it should have had a voice-over because the book was written in the first person. The first person was the Ann-Margret character, who is a seemingly very sweet woman, the victim cousin who's in love, long-suffering, but in her head she's quite a bitch. If you don't get the voice-over, you don't get the bitch: all you get is a very sweet woman. It lacked edge because of that. I think if it had had that it would have been much more successful.

How did you respond to those three leading ladies, who are all quite brilliant in their different ways?

Absolutely. I thought Julie was at her best, I think Glenda [Jackson] was terrific in her part and Ann-Margret was wonderful, and I wish for her sake it had just had her voice-over. I mean, she really resented Glenda's character; while being seemingly sweet to her, she absolutely resented her and that wasn't fair.

What were your impressions of Zeffirelli as a director, after working on *Hamlet*?

He first gives you a wonderful arena, he's a brilliant designer, and he gives you a platform second to none. He knows how to dress you, to put you in the right atmosphere, get the right effect, and he creates a sort of pitch, an emotional pitch. He then leaves you alone, he absolutely sets you up and lets you free. It's quite an interesting way of doing it.

Is that really the kind of direction you like?

I do, in a way. He trusts you to work on it yourself and to bring your own self to the part. I think it's sort of danger; I think some people aren't used to that. Artistes do need more help than that but it depends who you are and at what point you are in your experience.

Honor Blackman

b. 1926

Actor: *Fame is the Spur* (1947), *Daughter of Dark-ness, Quartet* ('The Alien Corn') (1948), *A Boy, a Girl and a Bike, Conspirator, Diamond City* (1949), *So Long at the Fair* (1950), *Green Grow the Rushes, The Man in the Moon* (1951), *The Rainbow Jacket, The Delavine Affair, Outsiders, Diplomatic Passport* (1954), *The Glass Cage* (1955), *Breakaway* (1956), *Suspended Alibi, You Pay Your Money, Account Ren-dered, Danger List* (1957), *A Night to Remember, The Square Peg* (1958), *A Matter of WHO* (1961), *Serena* (1962), *Jason and the Argonauts* (1963), *Goldfinger* (1964), *Life at the Top, The Secret of My Success* (1965), *Moment to Moment* (1966), *A Twist of Sand* (1967), *Shalako, Twinky, The Last Roman* (1968), *The Last Grenade, The Virgin and the Gypsy* (1970), *Something Big* (1971), *Fright* (1972), *Lola* (1973), *To the Devil a Daughter* (1976), *The Age of Innocence* (1977), *The Cat and the Canary* (1978), *The Secret Adversary* (1986)

It was her television role of Cathy Gale in the 1960s cult success, *The Avengers*, which decisively rescued Honor Blackman from the thornless English rose syndrome to which her early experiences with the Rank Organisation had consigned her. In hindsight, it is instructive to see her working away conscientiously to give life to the pallid heroines of *A Boy, a Girl and a Bike* and *Diamond City*, in both of which she gets her man but Diana Dors gets the good lines. Agreeable as she is in them, those films offer virtually no pointer to the kinds of wit and sharpness she would display in her post-*Avengers* career, notably as Pussy Galore in *Goldfinger*. Sadly, of course, by that time the British film industry was winding down and she was often left making bricks with limp straw, as she does in *To the Devil a Daughter*, in which her sheer professionalism imposes a sense of personality on a character so thinly written as to be almost non-existent. When she *does* get a chance to behave badly in a film, as in *Shalako* or *The Virgin and the Gypsy*, she is very enjoyable company indeed.

Interview date: August 1995

Your first film, *Fame is the Spur,* **was for the Boulting brothers ...**

Yes, I nearly got killed in it, because there's a shot where I'm marching with my boyfriend in the Peterloo marches and the dragoons are charging us, the marchers. One of them runs me through with a sabre and as I fall his horse rears. They wanted a shot under the horse's legs of me falling. I was wearing a great long wig, and, when I fell dead, the horse's hooves came down and they were actually on my hair. I heard the director say 'Cut!' but, as I was totally inexperienced, I lay very still just in case it wasn't over and of course they all thought the horse had gone through my head. Both John and Roy came rushing up and when I heard them call my name I finally opened my eyes, realising they had cut. Boy, were they relieved!

Your first major role was in Lance Comfort's *Daughter of Darkness*. What do you remember about him and making that strange film?

I just remember Lance being very round and cuddly and sweet. To me it was absolute heaven because I'd never been anywhere under my own steam, and to go all the way to Cornwall on location was wonderful. I remember going to rushes and seeing Siobhan McKenna fingering Maxwell Reed's chest, saying, 'You have a very deep chest.' I thought it was so terribly exciting. I don't know why she did that film because she was an actress of enormous standing in Ireland. I don't think I even saw the film at the time. I think I did most, if not all, of it in Cornwall.

Of your next five films, four were made for Gainsborough. What sort of contract were you under?

I have a vague idea it was supposed to be a ten-year contract but it only lasted for two because our film business only lasted that long. I was put into films that Margaret Lockwood or someone else had turned down. My contract was with Rank and everybody keeps putting me in the Charm School but I was never there. I'd been in two West End plays by the time I went under contract, and, whereas people in the Charm School earned £10 a week, I earned £100 a week then.

Your four Gainsborough films did give you some variety. What do you remember of *A Boy, a Girl and a Bike*, an attractive film?

I can remember things like Diana Dors making all that noise at six-thirty in the morning in the make-up room! We were on location for six months – the money they wasted then! We sat there waiting for a cloud the shape of a figure eight, you know what I mean? Maybe that's why I've never been keen on the bicycle since; I was saddle-sore by the end of it, I must say, but Dors was such fun. There were so many good character actors in that film – Thora Hird, Leslie Dwyer and Cyril Chamberlain, Tony Newley – it was just amazing.

How did you come to do the part of Joyce in *Conspirator* with the two Hollywood Taylors, Robert and Elizabeth?

I was loaned by Rank and I suppose they must have made money on it. That was one of the most horrific films I've ever made. The director, Victor Saville, was a bastard. Though English, he'd just come back from Hollywood, where he'd been during the war. It was his first film in Britain since the 1930s. He was hated by the crew, a lot of whom had served, and someone actually did drop a lamp which just missed him – unfortunately. It was one of those films on which the director has to have a whipping boy. I was it. He couldn't whip Elizabeth Taylor or Robert Taylor, who were big stars, and Willy Hyde-White wouldn't notice if you tried to whip him anyway, so I was it. There must have been a difference between the professionalism of Elizabeth Taylor and me, because she'd been filming for most of her life. She and Robert Taylor were perfectly professional, although neither of them was inspired.

***Green Grow the Rushes* has two points of interest: first, it was made by ACT Films; second, it had the young Richard Burton in it. Do you recall anything of ACT Films, which was run by the Technicians' Union?**

I only remember being conscious of the budget, which I hadn't been before. They certainly didn't hang about. I don't remember anything else about it being an ACT film; that didn't matter to me. Of importance to me were what was my contract, how much was I being paid, who was in it, did I like it, and so on. That's another film that was full of wonderful character actors – Roger Livesey, Geoffrey Keen, and Vida Hope, who married the director.

As to Richard Burton, I have to say I didn't take to him very much because he was pretty arrogant and often drunk. I remember that they asked us to go and give out prizes at a church hall or something silly, to publicise the film, and he made such a fuss about it. He was a serious actor, he didn't want to do trivial stuff like publicity. It was ironic when you think he lived the rest of his life on publicity! He was a fine actor but he practically chucked it in Hollywood.

In the '50s you made a number of supporting features, with names like *Diplomatic Passport*, *The Delavine Affair* and *The Glass Cage*. What was your experience of making these sorts of pictures, compared with the 'A' films you'd been doing?

A great difference, because you had to find your own clothes to begin with. The facilities weren't as good and things were much more rushed. You weren't employed unless they knew you were a pro, as speed was of the essence. I did them for the money. They worked one to an absolute frazzle – one used to be called for seven in the morning and work sometimes until eleven at night. They would do a close-up sometimes at nine-thirty or ten at night. How could you do good work at night when you'd been up at five-thirty in the morning? Finally we got a twelve-hour day and they had to pay for overtime. I would much rather have played in 'A' films but I wasn't offered them and in truth so few were being made. All I wanted to do was earn some money. The reason I did lots of 'B' films in the '50s was that my then husband and I emigrated to Canada in 1951 at the end of the Rank contract, and I was out of the swim for eighteen months and had lost my place on the ladder by the time I returned. But like most actors, I relied on an agent; I would be sent to see a producer and either get the part or not.

In *Suspended Alibi* and *Account Rendered*, you were the 'nice girl', whereas Naomi Chance and Ursula Howells were the respective 'bad lots'. How did you feel about this?

I thought the heroine was the thing to be. It wasn't until I'd done it for years that I thought, 'This is so boring, and look at that lovely scene *she's* got!' Just before *The Avengers* came along I had started to play a few people who weren't very nice, and that was lovely. But when you look like I did, a natural blonde, people always think of you as the 'nice girl'. They don't see you being a bitch or killing your husband.

You were suddenly back to doing 'A' pictures, such as *A Night to Remember* in 1958 with John Merivale.

Yes, I do remember that lovely director, Roy Baker. It was technically very difficult, though – jumping into boats and being on a tank in the studio. I remember thinking, 'I don't know if I'll be very good with these children because I'm a bit young to have had them.' I know I was very brave in it, but John Merivale was braver because he went down with the ship.

How did you come to be Norman Wisdom's leading lady in what I see as his best film, *The Square Peg*?

I don't know if Wizzy asked for me, perhaps he did. I enjoyed it, in any case. I must say I don't find

him hysterically funny on the screen but in person he makes me fall about. I remember John Paddy Carstairs, who directed that, was just lovely. He was the first director I'd ever known who used to play music on the set to keep everybody jolly – and he was always jolly himself, I never knew him bad-tempered.

Was it your television success as Cathy Gale in *The Avengers* that led to your role as Pussy Galore in *Goldfinger*?

Yes, I'm always very immodest about this. People ask me how I got the part and I say it was because there wasn't anybody else! I mean, I was very hot, I was doing judo in the series, and, since I was *so* popular and had the same sort of qualities in *The Avengers* as might be required in *Goldfinger*, I got the part. It was a tremendous boost for my film career, because Bond films had the highest profile of any films at that time. There was so much promotion, so much publicity – and it was one of the best Bond films anyway. I was probably the only strong leading lady in them. The other day my agent rang and said the *Daily Express* wanted my comment as I had been voted the best Bond girl of all the films. I said, 'Well, naturally!' I mean, most of them were bimbo types while mine was a real character.

There seems to be a hint of lesbianism about her.

Yes, well, it's in the book. She starts off as a lesbian but the moment she falls for James Bond she decides to become a heterosexual, which is wonderful! Ian Fleming didn't go in for profundities, did he? The only little edge we were allowed to keep in the film, more or less as our own private joke, was that she called all her pilots Joe or whatever – androgynous sort of names.

Was it physically a very arduous film to make?

No. To me it was wonderful because I was doing judo on the cement in *The Avengers* and when we came to do it in the film they built up so many bales of hay, asking me if that would be all right. They didn't want to kill me, you see, because of money. I thought it was a piece of cake!

***Life at the Top* is one of the few sequels which doesn't seem like a let-down to me. How did you feel about it?**

I was so unhappy on that picture, I don't know. Jimmy Woolf produced it and he and Larry Harvey mocked Ted Kotcheff, the director, a lot. It was very messy. Ted was a good director but he wasn't allowed to be, on that. I haven't seen the film so I don't know how it holds up. Larry wasn't difficult to work with, though. He was always very waspish but we got on very well. I didn't have much contact with Jean Simmons because I was the 'other woman' and we didn't have scenes together.

Shalako looks like a Western. Where was it made?

In Spain. It was almost the worst film I've ever made, from the point of view of pleasure. Eddie Dmytryk had just come off the 'black list' so he had a lot to prove and was tense. Eric Sykes was going through a terribly deaf period. Brigitte Bardot they didn't dare leave alone in case she committed suicide. Stephen Boyd was going through a religious conversion and used to come in each morning saying 'Peace' instead of 'Good morning'. Jack Hawkins, who played my husband, had recently had an operation for cancer of the larynx and had this hole in his throat covered by a medallion and we were terrified of sand getting into it. He couldn't speak and therefore mouthed his lines silently. In one scene we were supposed to have a row in which one tops the other; now, it's very difficult to have a row with somebody who's not speaking! I re-did it when we dubbed it – Charles Gray, I think it was, who dubbed for Jack. I can't tell you what that film was like!

You can't beat a scheming adultress in a film to catch the eye!

I liked the part very much because it's much more fun playing somebody who's horrid. But shoving the diamonds down my throat was awful – those two Red Indians didn't understand what rehearsal meant and they did everything for real.

The Virgin and the Gypsy still seems to me one of the most intelligent films made from a DH Lawrence novel.

Yes, I liked that very much and I liked Christopher Miles, the director. My character was so progressive for that time, and one really did feel horribly out of it, felt that everyone disapproved of one. It was a very good film and lovely actors in it, really great. I remember Christopher used to practically beat Joanna Shimkus to make her work, and she never seemed to get upset. I realised later that he was very clever, because he knew it was the only way to get her going. It was made around Matlock in Derbyshire, in the right sort of area. I don't know that we had any studio work; we shot some of it in a house up there on location. I certainly know that the lake or pond we had to jump into was up to here in mud, it was really lovely! And the entire neighbourhood suddenly found themselves by the side of the lake, strangely enough.

What was your experience of working with that fabulous cast in The Cat and the Canary – Wendy Hiller, Beatrix Lehmann, Wilfred Hyde-White, all those people?

Willy Hyde-White! He never read the whole script, he only read his bit! Anyway, in The Cat and the Canary Willy played the dead man in a flashback. Oh, the number of my fans who like that picture! They must like me playing a lesbian, I think. I was 'room mates' with Olivia Hussey in the picture and she seemed to be on cloud nine all the way through. I had to give her a massage or something, didn't I? Yes, my fans liked it very much. The director had come from directing soft-porn movies and he was out of his skull. By the time Edward Fox joined us we'd all given up, because Metzger didn't know A from a bull's foot and we were all hysterical. Edward came and rehearsed the first scene and there was a lot of giggling – which I strongly disapprove of, but you've no idea what it was like working with that director. Edward cracked us all over the knuckles and got us working. Metzger hadn't the most basic idea of how to shoot a film. For example, he wouldn't shoot a master, he'd shoot close-ups and then hope to put a master on the end of it. It wasn't fun because you felt you were in the hands of a lunatic – and you were!

It must seem very difficult to maintain a movie career in Britain nowadays.

Yes, and who has? No, you've got to go to the other side and even then, there's a limited life for you because of who you are, your accent and everything. And of course, there is fierce competition over there and English people don't survive all that well in that atmosphere anyway. Over here, if you didn't work in theatre and television you'd die. But, thankfully, I love theatre and TV and get a lot of work in them.

Sir Dirk Bogarde

b. 1921

Actor: *Come on George* (1939), *Dancing with Crime* (1947), *Esther Waters, Quartet* ('The Alien Corn'), *Once a Jolly Swagman* (1948), *Dear Mr Prohack, Boys in Brown* (1949), *The Blue Lamp, So Long at the Fair, The Woman in Question* (1950), *Blackmailed* (1951), *Penny Princess, Hunted, The Gentle Gunman* (1952), *Appointment in London, Desperate Moment* (1953), *They Who Dare, Doctor in the House, The Sleeping Tiger, For Better, For Worse, The Sea Shall Not Have Them* (1954), *Simba, Doctor at Sea, Cast a Dark Shadow* (1955), *The Spanish Gardener* (1956), *Ill Met By Moonlight, Doctor at Large, Campbell's Kingdom* (1957), *A Tale of Two Cities, The Wind Cannot Read* (1958), *The Doctor's Dilemma, Libel* (1959), *Song Without End, The Angel Wore Red, The Singer Not the Song* (1960), *Victim* (1961), *We Joined the Navy* (guest role), *HMS Defiant, The Password is Courage, The Mind Benders* (1962), *I Could Go On Singing, Doctor in Distress, Hot Enough for June, The Servant* (1963), *King and Country, The High Bright Sun* (1964), *Darling* (1965), *Modesty Blaise, *The Epic That Never Was* (1966), *Accident, Our Mother's House* (1967), *Sebastian, The Fixer* (1968), *The Damned, Justine, Oh! What A Lovely War* (1969), *Death in Venice* (1970), *The Serpent* (1972), *The Night Porter* (1973), *Permission to Kill* (1975), *A Bridge Too Far, Providence* (1977), *Despair* (1978), **The Patricia Neal Story* (1981), *These Foolish Things / Daddy Nostalgie* (1990)
* Made for television, some cinema release.

Though he would not care for the appellation, Dirk Bogarde was almost certainly the most popular British film star of the 1950s. During the 1960s and after, he devoted himself increasingly to more obviously taxing roles, especially in the films of Joseph Losey and Luchino Visconti, and won a new reputation as one of the world's most authoritative film actors. But this should not cloud his achievement in the '50s; true, there are no doubt more complex demands made by roles such as Barrett in *The Servant* or Aschenbach in *Death in Venice*, but the days at Gainsborough and Pinewood have their rewards as well. Apart from two bit parts, he began as a star and has stayed one for nearly fifty years. In the early films, he shows a striking intensity as the sensitive pianist in 'The Alien Corn' sequence of *Quartet*, offers a vivid contrast to the homely Ealing virtues as the vicious thug in *The Blue Lamp*, is a convincingly romantic hero in *So Long at the Fair* and a sympathetic fugitive in *Hunted*. Among the many felicities of *Doctor in the House*, his likeable Simon Sparrow provides a crucial, credible centre, and it is this film which began his long and successful association

with the team of Ralph Thomas and Betty Box over the next decade. His playing of the homosexual barrister in *Victim* in 1961 seems, with hindsight, to have been a decisive step away from the 'idol of the Odeon' roles and towards the mature triumphs of the ensuing decades. His performance as the dying father in Tavernier's *These Foolish Things* (*Daddy Nostalgie*) was an eloquent swansong to a remarkable acting career.
Interview date: July 1990

How did you get into *Dancing with Crime* in 1947?

By the grace of God, after the war I got into an actors' reunion thing when you had the chance to be in a half-hour play once a month, to which agents and managements would come. I played Jesus Christ in my demob suit, and from there I got an 'overnight star' job in the theatre, in *Power Without Glory*. But £5 a week really wasn't enough to live on, so a friend told me to see someone else who was sympathetic to actors who had been in the war. I was given a job in *Dancing with Crime*, in which I had to be a policeman. My uniform didn't fit so they pinned it up in the front and you only ever saw the back of my head. I came back on the bus that afternoon with twenty quid, whereas my take-home pay from the theatre (which was much harder work to do) was only five pounds.

You then starred in *Esther Waters* and have remained a star ever since. How do you feel about being a 'star'?

I dislike it now. It's a word that belonged to another period. I had been a serious actor in the theatre, and there was a terrible snobbery about film actors, film stars. It didn't require anything except that the girls had to be pretty and have good tits; and if a guy was OK-looking they could get him to do anything. But there *is* something called 'star quality'; you have to have 'watchability'.

What sorts of contracts were you under up until the end of the '50s?

I signed my contract with Rank in February 1947 – it's burned into my head. It was for £3,000 a year, with a modest annual increase, for a minimum of three films a year and they had the contractual right to dump me every July. I said I would agree to those terms if I could go back to the theatre at least once every two years if I got something I wanted to do. They agreed but I didn't realise I had to add the time off to the end of the contract; in the end I was not seven years with Rank but seventeen and had to

buy myself out for £10,000. My only choice was that, out of every four films submitted, I had to do three.

***Esther Waters* and *Once a Jolly Swagman* were both made for Ian Dalrymple's Wessex Films. What do you remember of this unit?**

I liked Ian. He was an erudite and intelligent man and a man I could talk to. I would never have signed a contract unless it had been for him. Then I found out he was under the umbrella of Rank and Rank in those days were what they are now: businessmen who didn't know anything about making movies, so they employed people who did and gave them the chance to do it. The whole system broke up in the early '50s and it failed because Wessex didn't know how to handle it.

Esther Waters must have cost a fortune; I mean, my costumes were made by a Savile Row tailor and I was an unknown creature! Since then I've been working in films for peanuts so I can see the difference. *Esther Waters* was a gloomy movie but then I was a gloomy subject and I wasn't capable of carrying it. My co-star, Kathleen Ryan, at the end of the film, gave me a silver brandy flask which I still have, saying 'To hell with Esther Waters!'

You had a range of roles in *Esther Waters*, *Once A Jolly Swagman*, *Quartet* and *Boys in Brown*. What did you learn from them?

Nothing, except never to do it again – that is, not do what the directors were telling me to do. I think *Quartet* was my second film and I remember being so disheartened by the fact that I had done *Esther Waters* and ahead of me were two terrible roles with which I wasn't going to be able to do anything. One was the motorcycle rider in *Swagman* and the other was in an Arnold Bennett story called *Dear Mr Prohack*. So I went to Sydney Box, then head of Gainsborough studios, and pleaded to be allowed to be in *Quartet* before the other movies came out, because if I hadn't done that I would have been sacked. Sydney Box was kind enough to let me be in it; I think he was rather overcome by this crawling amateur pleading with him! But I knew I could work in the part of a sensitive pianist, whereas the rest of the stuff I was totally wrong for.

Was it *The Blue Lamp* that established you as a major British film star?

Yes, no question of that. I'd worked with the director Basil Dearden before – on the stage. When he got *The Blue Lamp* he wasn't sure I could do it, but it did work. It was the first of what we would call today *cinéma vérité*: the first true, on-location, movie we had ever made. I think they built the policeman's flat but everything else was done in Paddington Green police station and the White City dog-racing track. I had never in my life before had to act outdoors but then I realised this was how to do it. Some of it was done in the sleazier parts at the back of Regent's Canal, which has mostly been pulled down now as it was nearly all bombed stuff.

The whole of the chase at the end of the film was shot during a greyhound derby at White City and nobody was told that we were shooting a movie. It was a crowd of 30,000 and I had to run through it; some people were taking a razor at me! My clothes were torn to shreds. When Jimmy [Hanley] and I had to run across an electric railway track at one point, all we were told was that we hadn't been given permission because it was too dangerous. We had to cross the live tracks and I only remember the faces of the train drivers coming out of the tunnel and seeing a man and a policeman in uniform, standing between the tracks. We never got any danger money in those days! There was a very good actor in it called Pat Doonan, who eventually killed himself. He would have been one of the great British character actors.

What are your recollections of working with Anthony Asquith, first in *The Woman in Question*?

He didn't want me at all in *The Woman in Question*, I think he wanted William Holden, but he was forced by Rank to use a contract artiste. I was one, and Susan Shaw and Jean Kent were also. I don't think he really enjoyed working with me then, but we went on to work together later and we became very close. We did try to do one film together which was aborted, a film about Lawrence of Arabia. Asquith and Terence Rattigan were working on the story of Lawrence from his youth at Cambridge right through until his death. I wasn't anything like Lawrence but they had detected in me the kind of sensitivity they needed for this part; a

blond wig was made and we were going out to do this wonderful script. I had tremendous help from Geoffrey Woolley, whose father was *The Times*' correspondent during Lawrence's campaigns during the First World War. Geoffrey gave me all his father's personal correspondence between himself and Lawrence, which has never been published.

For some reason, we were never told why, ten days before we were due to shoot on a huge BP petrol compound in the desert (which King Feisal had given permission for us to use), Rank pulled the plug. It destroyed Asquith and it practically destroyed me. Rattigan then turned what remained of his work into a play called *Ross*. So there we all were, the whole team, and Asquith felt we couldn't just lose everything, so he said we must find an alternative within the next ten days. The only thing we could find ready to go was a script, adapted from Shaw's *The Doctor's Dilemma*, and a lot of the people who were to have been in *Lawrence* were employed in that, and Leslie Caron joined us. It was a very good film; one of the definitive Shaw productions I have seen. But nobody went to see it. They all thought it was a *Doctor in the House* sequel, sat through the first ten minutes with all that discussion going on and then they walked out. It *is* all argument and audiences have a very short attention span.

I liked *Libel* very much and I wonder what you think of it.

I haven't seen it but I think it was a load of shit. *The Doctor's Dilemma* was a success for Metro in America and they asked us to do something else straight away, because we still had the studio space, the whole crew, Bob Krasker lighting, everyone who had been employed for *Lawrence*. The only thing they could come up with was *Libel*, for which they were in the process of working on the script. We got Olivia de Havilland, Robert Morley came back, and we just went tramping on. It was certainly melodrama; we knew it was and we hammed it up to the elbows. We had to do something because of the failure of *The Doctor's Dilemma*, and *Libel* was quite a success.

Speaking of full-blooded melodrama, can we go back to *So Long at the Fair*?

I didn't like it but I had to do it, and, at that point, I was very much in love with Jean Simmons. Rank thought it was a great idea to encourage their two juvenile stars and we were given this film which was supposed to launch our engagement. Unfortunately, by the time the film was finished Jean had fallen in love with Stewart Granger, thereby ruining the publicity effort.

The story of *So Long at the Fair* is perfectly true; it was all right and the kids went to see it because Jean and I were pretty; and it was the first time I had the chance to use my own voice rather than an Irish or a Cockney one. It was also my first association with Betty Box as a producer.

What were the special strengths of the Betty Box–Ralph Thomas team?

They knew just what the public at that point wanted. We were just coming out of the doldrums of post-war austerity and audiences wanted to laugh, to be 'taken out of themselves', to see things that were glamorous. I did four or five of those *Doctor* films and Betty in particular fought for me to be in them, although the studio didn't want me. I had been noted by critics but I hadn't become the major star Rank had hoped I'd be. Betty and Ralph had seen me in a couple of plays and realised that I could play comedy. The studio believed I could only play spivs and Cockneys, but Betty and Ralph put me in tweeds and let me speak in my own voice, and the rest was history.

Doctor in the House was such a runaway success, I think, basically because it was a ragbag of all the old doctor jokes which everyone in hospitals knows, real student jokes, cleverly strung together by Richard Gordon [author]. Betty and Ralph had the script rewritten by Nicholas Phipps; I changed my character's name to Simon Sparrow because I thought it was funnier, and so it stayed. The one stipulation I made was that I had to be a *real* doctor; I would do things that were funny, but would never instigate anything funny. We had two doctors always on the set; if any of us had to perform an operation or some medical procedure, there was always someone there to explain exactly how to do it. I wouldn't put a stethoscope to a body until I knew exactly how it was done and what I would have said. It was very strictly controlled, but it was also an enormously happy film to make.

You were in a couple of the more serious Box–Thomas films, including *A Tale of Two Cities* Did you feel Sydney Carton was a very good part?

Yes, we all thought we were doing something unusual. We saw the Ronald Colman version and we knew that was what we had to lick. I don't know why, but ours didn't work. It was the best I could do at the time; I chose Dorothy Tutin for Lucie Manette and we had very good stage actors – Cecil

Parker, Christopher Lee before he became a monster. But then Betty and Ralph made one capital error, which was not to make it in colour. If it had been in colour, people would still watch it today.

Did you steep yourself in Dickens for the film?

No, I knew about Sydney Carton from school; I didn't sit there sweating my arse off reading it. Tibby [TEB] Clarke's scenario was excellent, in that it typified the essence of the book so I didn't have to read the book itself. I have involuntarily read books of which I have then made movies; I read *The Singer Not the Song* long before the movie, which was a travesty of what it should have been. So was *The Spanish Gardener*, which was a perfectly straightforward novel by AJ Cronin which was also ruined as a movie. Some of it's quite good, I suppose, but I saw it and was heartbroken because it just wasn't true.

How did you find working in that with the boy Jon Whiteley, with whom you'd worked in *Hunted*?

He was five-and-a-half when I first worked with him and we were together for three months. He and I were almost the only two in it and I was with him all the time; I actually tried to adopt him because we became so devoted. All that we did together was extemporary, we just invented it. We didn't have much rehearsal; I hate rehearsals unless it's something technically complicated, such as in *The Servant*, where I had something like forty-one camera changes to make while laying and unlaying a dinner table. Then I do want to know exactly where my props are so it all happens on cue. I always insist on a technical rehearsal, when no emotion is happening, just saying the lines. The crew have to know what you are doing and sound has to know that you may turn your head as you say a line, but you don't put the guns in until the red light is on.

Did you find Michael Powell a good director of actors when you made *Ill Met By Moonlight*?

That's a very difficult question. He was wonderful but he was a real bastard! But I have discovered that the great directors do not direct; or you don't think they're directing. They leave it to you to get on with it and, if you're wrong, they will have a few words with you, saying something like, 'Do you have a reason for doing that?' And if you have a reason, they will very often agree to try it your way. Visconti never told me anything on *Death in Venice*

– he took it on board that I had known what I was asked to do. It is only fussy directors, and not very good ones, who give you all those instructions.

Powell and I became the closest friends. He was very bitter about his reputation until the last few years of his life; *Peeping Tom* really killed his career and it nearly killed me too, because I turned it down. I didn't mind being controversial, but I would *not* play a child molester or anyone with really warped sensuality.

I very much liked *Cast a Dark Shadow*, in which you played an unusually unwholesome hero.

The unwholesomeness of the hero was what was fun about it. The film was a failure, though. It was the first time I had come under another star's name – Margaret Lockwood's – and it just died, which was a pity because it was a very good movie and I had persuaded Maggie to do it. I remember being on tour in Cardiff with a play and I saw a poster for *Cast a Dark Shadow* and it had 'Dirk Bogarde in *Cast a Dark Shadow*' and, at the very bottom, 'with Margaret Lockwood'. They altered the billing order because they saw it was dying and that, astoundingly, her name had killed it, though it was probably her best performance ever.

I have never seen *The Singer Not the Song* but it has acquired a cult reputation.

Yes, especially in Europe, in France and Germany. It is about a young Mexican bandit who, with his gang, holds a small Mexican town to ransom. Then a young Canadian priest on his first mission comes in to try and disarm the situation; the bandit falls in love with him and that was basically the story. It was such a terrible script and they put John Mills in as the priest when it should have been someone like Paul Newman, as he was in those days. I should have been in blue jeans and a beat-up old jacket, driving an old Chevy, and there I was in black leather and riding a white horse – I did the whole thing for camp and nobody had any idea what was happening! Mylène Demongeot played the girl who was in love with the priest and who then kind of fell for me – you know, a berserk three-hander.

***Victim* was really the first commercial film to deal openly with homosexuality. What do you recall now of how you all approached it?**

It was the first time a man had said he was in love with another man on the screen. It was not in the script, I wrote that bit. The script was intended for another actor; he turned it down because he said, if he played this part, it would prejudice his chances

of a knighthood. Basil Dearden called me on Christmas Eve and told me he was in a jam. Now, Michael Relph and Dearden had made some controversial films, including *Sapphire* and *A Life for Ruth*; and this was the one they were going to do about homosexuality. I said to my father I thought I would do this movie because I had always wanted to make a fuss in the movies, and this one was about homosexuality. My father's response was, 'Dear boy, don't do it, it's so boring because we get it on television all the time in documentaries. Do something interesting like *The Mayor of Casterbridge*'! Then he said, 'Remember that your mother lives in a very small village and it is rather difficult with the neighbours.'

So I went back to Basil and agreed to do the film on condition that we put in a scene at the end in which the man says to his wife that, yes, he did love a boy. We then couldn't find anyone to play the wife; until Sylvia Syms, bless her dear little heart, finally said, 'No problem, it's a wonderful part and I'd love to play it,' which she did.

Janet Green had written the script and very kindly agreed to allow me to write that one little scene. Originally it was to have ended with us all going off to the Old Bailey, with nobody having said a word; all that happened was a photograph was shown of me in a car with some young man. It was total rubbish, so we put in the extra scene and it went off like a humdinger. It was a commercial success because, in a way we hadn't anticipated, it touched upon something that affected a lot of people. Women wrote in their hundreds, all these tragic letters saying '*That*'s what was wrong with my husband/brother/father' and they hadn't known. I was applauded in England for my 'great courage'.

In 1954 you made a film for Joseph Losey called *Sleeping Tiger*: how difficult was it for Losey in England, working under a pseudonym?

It was totally impossible for him. He got out of America just in time, before he was shopped and put in prison. He worked for a while in Italy, then he came over here with Carl Foreman. He and Carl got together and got hold of a crummy script written by another McCarthy throw-out whose name I can't remember, and they tried to get it made. Joe's only chance was if he could get a star name to play the boy in the film. I had already made three films that year and was knackered; there was no money available, and so I didn't want to do it. However, the woman in charge of contract actors at Rank,

Olive Dodds, felt it might lead to something very important for me. So I agreed to meet Mr Losey and he ran *The Prowler* for me. I saw about twenty-four minutes of it and then told him I'd do the film.

So I joined forces with Joe; Alexis Smith came over from America and she was shattered when she arrived at my house to see Joe sitting there; she had thought the director's name was Vic Hanbury, which was Joe's pseudonym. She was very concerned at making the film with him, given the charges of 'un-American activities' against him, but she stayed – and stayed my friend ever since, a wonderful woman. So we made the film and it was a success; Joe made a lot of money. He was hounded around England by Ginger Rogers and her mother, who were in London at the time, making a film with Stanley Baker. Joe and I didn't work together then for about ten years, although I got him a contract at Rank, which he just about forgave me for, finally!

***The Servant* is still one of the most engrossing films of the 1960s. What did you find impressive about working with Losey?**

It's what I said to you earlier: working with Joe is the way I have worked with all great directors. He would say, 'I don't know what you can do,' and I'd say, 'All right, I'll think of something,' and do it. *The Servant* was wonderful for a stage actor because of the long, long takes – you had a whole magazine of time to do your thing. Sometimes, working with other directors in England, you were very lucky if you could say, 'We got eighty seconds of film for a day's work.' With Joe you got ten minutes, so it was possible to make a film in five weeks. *The Servant* took six weeks to make and Joe was ill for two of them.

There was a lot of very elaborate setting up for it, of course. That film was the only time the dolly-pusher has been given a main credit. There is one scene with Wendy Craig and myself, when I let her in the front door and we go around the drawing room and then into the kitchen, where I fill up the jar with some flowers, then back into the drawing room; I think there were something like forty different camera angles and he never got them wrong. And the lighting was incredible – we took all day but it didn't matter. We would rehearse for about three hours in the morning and the lighting man would say, 'I can't do it,' and Joe would say, 'Yes you can.' Then he would disappear and we wouldn't see each other again until five o'clock in the afternoon, and then we would shoot the whole thing in an hour. Douglas Slocombe [director of photography], in tears on the last day of shooting, said this was the first time he had been able to put into practice all the things he had learned, and he was never so happy in his life. What's more, he got the Oscar. There was no elaborate set; it was simply the house, an actual house in Chelsea, and Joe uses the house as the metaphor all the way through.

I took over the direction while Joe was in hospital for two weeks. He staggered back early, with a nurse, and picked up. He did not re-shoot anything I had shot, which was what we had hoped. He gave me minute instructions, by telephone, on every set-up. We knew The Money wanted to close us down and grab the insurance. We saved them from doing that. All the companies hated Joe and me because they swore that audiences, seeing our names, left the theatre knowing we were 'art house'. No wonder we finally gave in after five films together!

Did it seem to you that the film was a metaphor for what was happening in British society at the time?

No, it never occurred to me, I just thought it was a great camp joke. I still think it's a very black comedy. It's very disturbing and complex as you say, if you think about it, but it is still a marvellous film which doesn't date. It was a brilliantly written script by Harold Pinter and it was the first script he ever wrote for the movies. When I first read it I didn't know what the hell it was about. I had agreed to go in as co-producer with Joe on it when he first found the book ten years before. It was originally planned that I would play Tony, the nice young man, but then I found the boy, James Fox, here on television. I was too old by that time to play the young man, so I said to Joe we should get Ralph Richardson for the servant. Joe said we couldn't afford it, so that's how I came to play the servant.

The only criticism I would make of the film is that the orgy seems a bit tame by orgy standards today.

Well, when we did that it was the first time we had understood what was happening with LSD parties. Joe and I knew they were taking place, particularly around Chelsea, but the audiences and the critics didn't know. They expected an orgy to involve people screwing each other and they simply didn't understand at the time that it was people going off into space under the influence of an hallucinatory drug – perhaps doing unspeakable things to the boy, but . . . Since then, the critics have reconsidered it in light of their understanding of drugs, but then they didn't understand it. Nowadays LSD comes on sugar cubes but in those days you had it from 'a little man in Jermyn Street' – that's one of the clues that Barrett uses. Harold knew about it all, of course, and that's what the young man was being given by his hairdresser in Jermyn Street.

The extraordinary thing was that once we had finished the film, nobody would touch it so it was put on the shelf for a year. It was actually on the shelf at Warner Brothers' studios in London. I have a very good friend called Arthur Abeles, an American who, at that time, was the European representative for booking films for Warners; he had a movie on at Warners in Leicester Square which was fading and he knew it couldn't hold up. He had a fortnight's gap to fill. He asked to look at some stuff Warners had stocked away and, by the grace of God, one of the things he looked at was *The Servant*. He saw the first two reels and said, 'We're sitting on a masterpiece, for Christ's sake!' He put it on for a fortnight and it ran for seven months, yet the studio had wanted to kill it. Equally so, they wanted to kill another film Joe and I made, *King and Country*. We never made a single film they wanted! And of course, they loathed *Accident*. I never understood how Joe, an American, knew about English university life and mores so well.

How did you come to make *Death in Venice* and *The Damned* for Visconti?

I was out of work in England because suddenly the chocks were away and English cinema was collapsing, and there was no work. My last job had been in 1966 with Jack Clayton in a film called *Our Mother's House* and that was a failure. I was getting very windy and didn't quite know where I was going next. The only offer I had in a year was for a voice-over in a commercial for the timber industry. Then I was offered $25,000 to make a commercial, which I had never done before, in Rome for an American company; all it meant was that I had to run up and down the Spanish Steps in Rome, twice, in a pair of what were called Foster Grant sunshades. At the top of the steps two women turn to each other and say, 'Wasn't that Dirk Bog*arde* I saw in those Foster Grant sunshades?' and that was the end of it.

It was printed in the local Rome papers that I was in town, filming on the Spanish Steps. Visconti read the paper, saw I was in town, dropped off a script for *The Damned* at my hotel and asked if I would like to read it. That was that. I have never seen the cut version although I saw the original version, which was four and a half hours.

Visconti was enormously interested in what was going on between the characters in his films. I am often asked about the differences between Losey and Visconti, being the two people who have given me my biggest opportunities, and I always say that Losey was the king as far as I was concerned – and Visconti was the emperor. And he is. He is above everybody else – every single detail was incredible. He checked bowls of roses, he checked everything, but he never told you how to do anything.

Would you agree that, as far as British cinema is concerned, the '40s and '50s constitute a boom period?

Certainly the early '40s were of vast importance for Britain because we were at war; that's when Powell, Pressburger, Dearden and a number of others began to surface and Ealing came out with modest-budget films. The moment the war was over, we lost our way a little. It went on for a couple of years, I suppose. We had *Odd Man Out, The Man in the White Suit*, and a number of others but, by the early '50s, we were smug and complacent and we lost the track. There was still an industry, of course, and some of the best technicians ever. Pinewood was a fantastic place to be in because every old craftsman who had ever been a carpenter or plasterer or whatever was somewhere in those warrens of buildings behind the studios, still practising their craft and making staircases, cornices, pilasters. It was a lovely studio. The great restaurant was the smoking room of the *Mauritania*, and the front door was a huge fireplace from a great house in Derbyshire. Yes, we had an industry from about 1939 through the '40s, then it began to slacken off at the turn of the decade. I think it began to crack apart as soon as I came in! Since 1966 I have only worked in Europe and with European directors. I am glad that I was fortunate enough to be in before the gate closed; at least I was able to work with some of the best doing their best.

Roy Boulting

b. 1913

Director: *The Landlady, *Ripe Earth, *Seeing Stars, Consider Your Verdict (1938), Trunk Crime, Inquest (1939), Pastor Hall (1940), *Dawn Guard, Thunder Rock (1942), *Desert Victory (1943), *Tunisian Victory (co-dir) (1944), *Burma Victory (1945), Fame is the Spur (1947), The Guinea Pig (1948), Singlehanded, High Treason (1951), Seagulls over Sorrento (1954), Josephine and Men (1955), Run for the Sun (1956), Brothers-in-Law (1957), Happy is the Bride (1958), Carlton-Browne of the FO (1959), Suspect (1960), A French Mistress (1960), The Family Way (1966), Twisted Nerve (1968), There's a Girl in My Soup (1970), Soft Beds, Hard Battles (1973), The Last Word (1979)
*Documentary or short film.

R oy Boulting and his twin brother, John, formed one of those director–producer teams which thrived in British cinema during the 1940s and '50s. Like their friends, Sidney Gilliat and Frank Launder, they regularly interchanged roles, so that for a good deal of the period it is possible to think of 'the Boulting brothers' as a unit. In fact, Roy's directorial career is the longer and more varied of the two. He began with short films before the war and made two distinguished feature films, *Pastor Hall* and *Thunder Rock*, in the early years of the war, before his involvement with three major wartime documentaries. In the post-war years, there were socially committed dramas (*Fame is the Spur*, *The Guinea Pig*), several films for American companies, and then, in the latter half of the '50s, a string of very popular satirical comedies which took swipes at the Army, the Law, the Unions, the Church and the Civil Service. These films made excellent use of what came to seem like a Boulting repertory company, including Ian Carmichael, Richard Attenborough, Terry-Thomas and others. Whether in comedy or drama, the Boulting films typically exhibit a vein of social commitment which gives coherence and weight to their output. One awaits with impatience the publication of Roy Boulting's memoirs.

Interview date: October 1989

How did you and your brother go about setting up Charter Films?

When John came back from the war in Spain, I proposed that he join me in setting up a film company of our own. War would be coming to England soon enough, so let's get started before that happened. In six years he'd lifted himself from office boy in Wardour Street to one of Ace Films's principal salesmen: he knew his way around Wardour Street. In the office, he'd be boss: on the floor, the last word would be mine. But I couldn't do it on my own – so, what did he say? And that was the start of Charter Film Productions.

How do you account for its extraordinarily long life as a production company?

I'd say it was probably due to the speed with which we learned to avoid repeating the mistakes of the beginner. Our first film – of hideous memory – was titled *The Landlady*, and we learnt several lessons from it. Lesson One: Read and assess any script you are offered, alone, apart and without assistance. Never allow an author to act it out for you: he may be a better actor than he is a writer! Lesson Two: Never permit a technician to alter your judgement of how a scene should be played unless he can provide good and convincing reason. He *may* know something you don't and, later, wish you had! Lesson Three: Never allow the prospect of profit to determine a creative decision.

As we absorbed into our filmmaking philosophy these and other lessons learned in the tough school of experience, so were the Boulting brothers credited with a reputation of being a couple of 'toffee-nosed' bastards, arrogant, opinionated, inflexible, difficult. That the films we chose to make, despite opposing advice, should, mostly, prove successful only served to baffle and exacerbate. The longevity of Charter Films, then, may be attributed to lessons learned and acted on; a readiness to stand or fall by our own judgement; a measure of talent; and a hell of a lot of good luck!

After the disaster of our first film and the sale of two one-reel documentaries, we made a film called *Consider Your Verdict*, based on a BBC playlet by Laurence Housman. In contrast to the frustrations of *The Landlady*, all moved forward as if on oiled wheels. It opened at London's first art house, the Academy, in support of a sombre but magnificent French film, *Quai des Brumes*, and ran there for over six months before playing across the country on the Odeon circuit. The critics lauded the film with a generosity that even we felt was excessive.

Although only a supporting feature, it was to earn at the box office more than ten times its cost. And that is how the Boulting brothers and Charter Films started fifty years of filmmaking.

You sometimes made films for other companies. Were these one-off deals?

In 1945, when we emerged from the services, there was little in Charter's financial kitty. Largely due to their cinemas, Rank and ABPC had enjoyed five prosperous war years, and both were now into production. Two Cities was just one of the production companies taken over by Rank. The head man was a volatile, extravagant but engaging Italian, Filippo Del Giudice. He invited us to make *Fame is the Spur* for him. Despite a splendid cast – Michael Redgrave, Rosamund John, Bernard Miles, etc – a sixteen-week schedule, and an exorbitant cost (over which, unhappily, we had little control), the film proved a disappointment. It received a mixed press – and died at the box office. That was in 1946.

At the end of '40s I directed *High Treason* for Paul Soskin's Conqueror Films, also a Rank-controlled company. Soskin's first approach came with a 'thriller' titled 'First Spy, Second Front'. I pointed out that the war was over, that a more topical 'thriller' could be taken from the headlines of any newspaper any day of the week. He solemnly picked up a morning daily. I, with equal solemnity, seized on a headline. He agreed. And, together with Frank Harvey, I went away and wrote the screenplay of *High Treason* – not, by the way, our title. Cast with then largely unknowns, of its genre it was a pretty good example.

John and I had learned that freedom from interference in choosing and making a film only comes when you have a financial stake in it. For this reason alone, from time to time, I would stagger off to Hollywood, with John's agreement, to make a film. Whatever I earned went into Charter Films. It bought us time, independence and finance sufficient to invest in the films we wanted to make. They were brought to me – *Singlehanded* by 20th-Century-Fox, *Seagulls over Sorrento* by MGM, *Run for the Sun* by RKO – in the early '50s. If not subjects I would have chosen myself, I do not regard the results as, in any way, dishonourable; and the experience was both illuminating and valuable.

Happy is the Bride came towards the end of the '50s. We were already tied to British Lion. It was brought by my old associate, Paul Soskin, and the NFFC [National Film Finance Corporation], who had an investment in the project. Lion wanted me to do it, and it was a great success.

Once you settled with British Lion in the late '50s, you seemed more or less to stay put. Was that a way of stabilising the distribution of your films?

No, it had nothing to do with stabilising our distribution: it was a response to the increasing pressure the two great combines – Rank and ABPC – were exerting on film production, distribution and exhibition. Between them they controlled the three largest cinema circuits. Now, to get a decent return on investment, the independent filmmaker had to be sure of a booking on one or other of the major circuits. As a consequence, the two combines always had first choice of the new films, whether made in Hollywood or in England. The independent cinema owner was gravely disadvantaged: he could only exhibit a film after it had already been widely shown by one of the combines.

To further intensify their attack on competition, Rank and ABPC had devised a system by which the major American distributors of Hollywood's output 'voluntarily' became what was called 'tied suppliers': that is, they dealt either with one or the other of the combines, but not both. MGM and Warner Brothers, for example, were pledged to ABPC; Universal and Columbia to Rank. Inevitably, too, most of the supine heads of British distribution companies followed their American colleagues into 'voluntary' bondage.

This was the scene when, in 1958, David Kingsley, erstwhile Managing Director of the Government's NFFC, asked John and me to join him on the board of British Lion Films. Lion made and distributed films, and owned and operated Shepperton Studios. Alas, it owned no cinema circuits. Acquired by Alexander Korda at the end of the war, it was already in deep trouble towards the end of the '40s. The Labour Government viewed the growing power of the two combines with a justifiably jaundiced eye. Korda, pressing Harold Wilson, then President of the Board of Trade, for assistance, pointed out that Lion was the only independent force, of any size, still operating. Wilson responded by obtaining £5 million from the Treasury to aid British production. Administered by the NFFC, £3.5 million of this found its way to Korda's company.

Wilson also introduced a levy (the brainchild of Sir Wilfred Eady at the Treasury) on cinema admission tickets. This went to the filmmaker in direct proportion to the public popularity of his film. A side-effect of this latter measure was an increase in the number of films made in England by Hollywood.

Together, Wilson's measures provided a shot in the arm for filmland's inhabitants. But, only briefly. The scene was still one of contraction. Too much power remained in too few hands. Cinema admissions continued to fall. Cinema closures continued to increase. And, above all, in the '50s, millions became infected with television fever. By 1956, the taxpayers' money had vanished. Government auditors now drew two firm lines beneath the figures in the ledger: the loss was written off.

Was that the end of Korda's dealings with British Lion?

Alexander Korda bowed silently from the scene as David Kingsley, vacating his chair at NFFC headquarters in Soho Square, advanced to the rescue. In the existing state of near-monopoly, he saw the continuance of an independent British Lion as of prime importance. He persuaded a reluctant Government to provide a fresh injection of capital. With a meagre £600,000 granted, Kingsley marched off to the banks, resolved to secure a line of credit for £3 million against British Lion's assets: the film library and Shepperton Studios. Again, his negotiating skills were rewarded: a new British Lion rose like a phoenix.

Through 1957 and into '58, Kingsley soldiered on. Films were made. Many flopped. Box-office success was elusive. Equally worrying, his financial projections pointed to a drying-up of the line of credit some time in '59. It was then that Kingsley came up with a revolutionary idea. His own particular talents were actuarial, financial. Why not co-opt the creative talents of filmmakers? – make them responsible for taking the production decisions? At Rank and ABPC, down-to-earth, hard-fisted money-men arrogated to themselves the right to decide those films made, those rejected. But they had a safety net: the playing time commanded from their own circuits. Without this, survival would have been unlikely. When Rank, on occasion, seized by a sort of *folie de grandeur*, ventured to embark on a large-scale production, the results were, almost invariably, melancholy, the losses horrific.

It was, no doubt, with such thoughts in mind that Kingsley turned to John and myself in 1958 with his invitation to join the board of British Lion. He was, I remember, very frank. He didn't want us, he told us, just for the films we'd be making at Shepperton and contributing to the distribution arm. He needed people who could guide and advise the board on filmmaking, the talent to be encouraged, the scripts that should be made into films. 'The company is still in a loss situation,' he said. 'The taxpayers' £600,000 gives it just one more chance, but it's the banks' line of credit that has made a production programme possible. However, if you do take the job on, you'll get a stake in the equity – you'll become part-owners – and if, between us, we manage to pull the company around – and I believe we can – then that stake might be worth more than a bob or two – ultimately.'

Now, ours had always been a two-man operation. We had fought for, and largely achieved, complete creative freedom. To what extent would answering to a board inhibit that? So the issue was simple: our freedom, or a battle to help save and promote British Lion as an independent 'third force' in its unequal struggle with the Rank–ABPC cartel? Could we, whose voices had for long been raised in protest – to Parliament, the press, on radio and television – now stand by merely to watch as the combines administered the last rites? The answer was obvious; we phoned David Kingsley to say, in effect: 'Let battle commence!'

What other filmmakers were involved?

A little later, a further filmmaking team – Frank Launder and Sidney Gilliat – brought additional production muscle to the board of British Lion. Starting as writers – Alfred Hitchcock's early success, *The Lady Vanishes*, was written by them – towards the end of the war they had decided to write for themselves, alternating, as we did, the roles of director and producer. With the films that followed – *Millions Like Us*, *Green for Danger*, *State Secret*, *The Happiest Days of Your Lives*, *inter alia* – they had as proud a record of success as any filmmakers could wish for. Between 1958 and 1961 the company, from being a great loss-making enterprise, was turned around and became, within two years, a profit company. In 1964 our having done that was enough for the Government to say, 'Whilst they're doing well, let's sell it off.' But that wasn't the end, because British Lion by that time had become a kind of flagship for the independent filmmakers, and they rallied round to help us resist the idea of a Government sale. Innumerable offers for the company came from all sorts of people, some with no experience at all in films. Finally, a consortium was put together with other filmmakers and we bought the company ourselves.

Once you settled into British Lion, did you need Rank or ABPC as exhibitor?

Good heavens, no! – the board's watchword was 'Independence'. We would have regarded such a

step as being a betrayal of the mandate we held. Our insistence on a freedom to deal with both combines, to argue the best terms for each film on its merits, didn't, of course, enhance our popularity. But if *we* were vulnerable, there were also limits to the powers the monopolists could exercise with impunity. We did not hesitate to focus the attention of Parliament and the media on the less attractive restraints the combines attempted to impose. In the '60s, films were referred to the Monopolies Commission. This obliged both to be on their best behaviour for quite a time. That, and the popularity of so many of Lion's films at the box-office, safeguarded our ability to resist their desire to gobble us up!

To go back to the war years, what attracted you to filming Robert Ardrey's play, *Thunder Rock*?

It seemed then that it justified everything that was being fought for. There we were; France had collapsed; all our allies were powerless. Today, I think it's very hard to convey to people just how perilous the time and the scene was then. Ardrey had written this play, which was put on in '38 in New York and had failed lamentably, and was then put on in this country. John and I saw it and we felt this play could explain – to America in particular – what time and history required of them. The British Ministry of Information felt as we did, that it should be made, and in 1941, Sam Eckman, who was the head of MGM in this country, said he wanted to finance the film. I was in the Army and John was in the RAF, and we were taken out of the services for six months to make *Thunder Rock*.

It's full of fascinating, fluid movement between present and past, between reality and fantasy . . .

Yes, it is. I remember talking with Mutz Greenbaum [aka Max Greene], the most brilliant and versatile lighting cameraman I have ever worked with, and saying, 'This is a film about the past that has to be related to the present – that's its purpose. But when dealing with characters from the past, I don't want them to be "film ghosts", double-exposure figures. I want the past to be as present and as solid as the figures of today. But, in some way, odd – strange, unnatural.' And we sat throughout the day discussing this.

Suddenly I heard a voice: 'Roy! I am thinking, I am thinking now of many years ago in Germany. We are lighting a film with the same problem: the characters are ghosts but must look real. So I tell the producers, then you must build the set at an angle, tilt it, the camera too, so that on the screen all will be normal, the set appear level. But it is the characters who will seem strange. As they move, they are the ones who are tilted in response to gravity, their bodies real, their movements strange, ghostlike.' What a bloody marvellous idea, I thought – and how simple! 'Good,' I told him, 'then we'll have a go.' The towering lighthouse interior was built at an angle of 120 degrees. Literally and metaphorically it worked like a dream – testimony to Mutz Greenbaum's brilliance as a lighting cameraman. That was the visual secret of *Thunder Rock*.

How influential were your wartime documentaries in opening up post-war opportunities to you?

Honestly, I doubt that many people thought about 'post-war opportunities' in those days. About coming through with one's skin intact, perhaps. But I did get a kick out of the making of *Desert Victory*. It happened quite by chance. Just returned to the Army from 'civvy street' on the completion of *Thunder Rock*, I was up in the War Office one day, seeking information on something or other, when I encountered a Major Woolley, who couldn't help me with the information I sought, but revealed that *his* job was to keep a day-by-day diary on the course of the war in the Middle East. What I didn't know at the time was that Major Sir Leonard Woolley happened to be the most distinguished British archaeologist of the age, and knew that area like the back of his hand.

The British Eighth Army had recently been driven back over the Egyptian border by Rommel, and was now dug in at El Alamein, awaiting a further onslaught. Quietly and graphically, he outlined the implications should Rommel once again smash through our defences: Egypt would be lost; all the oil riches of the area, on which our industries at home depended, would fall to his hand; and, with virtually nothing there to impede them, the Germans would be in a position to drive up into the Crimea and join with von Paulus's army about to drive down from the north. As he told it, the battle, when it came – whether resulting in victory or defeat – would determine the whole course of the war.

I returned to AFU [Army Film Unit] headquarters at Pinewood Studios, knowing what I had to do. And there *was* a battle. It commenced on the night of 25 October 1942 and ended ten days later on the morning of 5 November with Rommel's Afrika Korps in full retreat, their Italian allies gladly surrendering in their thousands. During those ten days, Major David Macdonald's front-line cameramen had been sending back nearly a million feet of film recording the first victory of British arms on land since the start of the war. At Pinewood, the AFU was in a state of frenetic activity. Three reels outlining the background and prelude to the battle had already been cut. I had written and shot a reconstruction of the night of 25 October to intercut with actual scenes of the thousand-gun barrage with which it opened.

A short time later, after a rapturous response from the Secretary of State and others at the War Office, *Desert Victory* opened at the Odeon, Leicester Square, to a cheering audience, and a glowing press on the following morning. My old friend, David Macdonald, sent back from the desert by General Montgomery to see that justice was done to the feats of the Eighth Army – and, perhaps, himself – was promoted Lieutenant Colonel overnight, and flew off to the States the next day to promote its future there. In America, the film triumphed again. *Desert Victory* was awarded an Oscar as the documentary film of the year. And I looked like being pegged down at Pinewood for the duration.

After the war, what sort of impulses led you to *Fame is the Spur* and *The Guinea Pig*?

As peace broke out, I think we held, with many others, a belief that, after all people had endured, it must result in a more just and equitable society. That this sentiment was felt by the overwhelming majority had already been reflected in the landslide Labour vote at the first post-war Elections. *Fame is the Spur* was a cautionary tale, however, that warned of the dangers to which the political idealist is vulnerable on achieving power; the difficulty facing every politician elevated to Government when trying to reconcile the original 'dream' with the harsher imperatives involved in 'trying to get things done' and the subtle seductions offered by society to someone who has become a public figure.

Howard Spring's central character, Hamer Radshaw, who rises from poverty to Prime Minister, was clearly inspired by the fate of the late Ramsay MacDonald. Played immaculately, I think, by Michael Redgrave, he emerges as a sad, rather than unsympathetic, character, reluctant to face his gradual abandonment of early principles, but doing so briefly, when his dying wife, played by Rosamund John, gently reminds him of his early ideals. However, after five years of death, destruction and austerity, it was far too grim for an audience now seeking escapism and peace. It flopped.

The Guinea Pig, on the other hand, though with strong political overtones and serious purpose, was a huge success. It was adapted from an entertaining, if untidy, play written by Warren Chetham-Strode. It also provided Richard Attenborough – who had just played for us in Graham Greene's *Brighton Rock* as the young, malevolent boy gangster, Pinkie – with an opportunity to demonstrate his versatility in the role of a working-class boy of fourteen, sent to a posh English public school. Just twenty-four when the film started shooting, he brought it off triumphantly, although many were deeply sceptical at the outset.

Chetham-Strode's play was sparked by educational recommendations to the Government in the Fleming Report, which urged that bright scholars, no matter what their background or financial circumstances, should be admitted to the advantages of a public school education. John and I found the play's basic situation intriguing, contemporary, exciting. We bought the play and invited the author to work on the adaptation to film.

I felt a weakness in the play was the dialogue and characterisation of those, particularly the boy's parents, who were 'working-class'. The words they spoke, their response to the situation, didn't ring absolutely true. Without knowing it, Chetham, as author, had patronised his characters, the boy's father – an ex-Sergeant Major – and mother, in a paternalistic fashion that neither would have accepted or allowed. So I turned to my ex-neighbour and friend, Bernard Miles, and asked him to come and work on the screenplay with the author. It was hardly a meeting of minds. Nor a marriage of convenience, with each recognising the other's strengths. The solution came when I took over three offices in a row with interconnecting doors. Warren I placed on one flank, Bernard on the other. Working independently, as each completed the draft of a scene it would be brought in and placed on my desk. I took what I thought was good from both – and much was – although the merging of two such opposing talents and viewpoints proved far from easy, and for the first time in my career, I took a writer's credit on the screen! Strangely enough, no seams showed in the finished work, which says much for the basic worth of the original play.

What do you recall of another unlikely-sounding screenplay collaboration – Graham Greene and Terence Rattigan on *Brighton Rock*?

Greene and Rattigan! Chalk and cheese, would you say? But the joint screen credit was determined, not so much by a collaboration, as by a prior contract. *Brighton Rock* had been purchased jointly by Anatole de Grunwald (who would produce), Anthony Asquith (direct) and Terence Rattigan (to adapt and write a screenplay). It was hardly their cup of tea: the undertones of Graham's highly idiosyncratic Catholicism eluded Terry, while the gentle, cultivated 'Puffin' Asquith found the brutal milieu, the savage action, extremely uncongenial. Finally, defeated, they gave up on the subject. Those hardier roughnecks, the brothers Boulting, arriving on the scene, acquired the film rights from them.

A condition of the sale was screen recognition of Rattigan's aborted script. Having read it, we wrote it off and decided to turn to the author himself. Graham was somewhat unsure but, pressed, agreed to have a go. What he eventually came up with may have been a trifle 'rough' as a final screenplay; but it was all that we had hoped for, containing, as it did, the distilled essence of a story that was pure 'film' from beginning to end. John, whose second feature film this would be as director, was delighted.

In Brighton, in search of location backgrounds, I traipsed up and down the Palace Pier and across the pebble beaches; discovered the dramatic web of narrow lanes between clock-tower and sea front; scoured the sleazy area around Brighton's Kemp Town; found those pubs the race gangs had haunted on the eve of a meeting; and trudged up on to the Downs to take pictures of the racetrack and the sites where, with razors and knives at the ready, the 'Nottingham Lads', battling with the 'Brighton Boys', brought notoriety and shame to Brighton. At the end of a month, I sat down to incorporate all this detailed research into Graham's screenplay.

Two weeks later, the final work had been broken down loosely into shots. I returned to London and handed over the blueprint – the shooting script – to brother John. With casting complete, he took the film to the floor – and handled a quite sensitive subject in a quite masterly fashion. Generously, no objection was raised to Terry's name appearing up on the screen credits; but adaptation and writing glory were, in truth, entirely Graham Greene's.

These films of yours seem unusually realistic in the context of British cinema of the time.

I think that from the very beginning of our filmmaking, John and I sought to convey, in subject, or technique, or both, a feeling for the truth. We shied away from the trite escapism to which pre-war British films had been wedded. War itself had brought liberation and a national identity to the British film for the first time in its history. We didn't want to lose that. Even when, in the middle '50s, we turned a satirical and jaundiced eye on the pillar institutions of the Establishment – the Army, Law, Foreign Office, City of London and Trades Unions and, finally, the Church – we were not abandoning our role as critical commentators on society, we were merely demonstrating that it is possible to be extremely serious without being solemn.

I'm All Right Jack seems deeply sceptical about most aspects of post-war England. I can't think of another film which gives it in the neck to so many different kinds of people.

Yes, that's absolutely true. Both John and I at the time felt the idea that one particular part of society should be held guilty and responsible for the failures of society at large, and that some other area should be free of blame, was ridiculous. We felt that all areas of society shared some common blame, and this is what we had to address ourselves to. I do remember that both John and I, at that time, felt we could see the terrible inadequacy of all those accepted beliefs within society. Such arrogance! I think the film still works because it's still relevant, still true. Of course, it was Peter Sellers' madman that took off. And, you know, those malapropisms were written out of our own experience. There was a man who in fact used these words, they were part of the truth of the scene. He wasn't a caricature.

How successful do you believe the British industry has been in establishing (a) a studio system and (b) a star system?

There has never been a studio system here since after the war when Rank and ABPC sought to establish that kind of Hollywood image. I don't think either a studio system or a star system is important to developing a sturdy film industry. I think the idea of an actor or actress grabbing attention *is* important and we should seek to hold this, but that is what film is all about – to understand that somebody has star qualities. If we can keep them within this country, that is worth doing.

The Boultings seemed to establish almost a repertory company in the late '50s with Dennis Price, Ian Carmichael, Richard Attenborough and many others. Was this a conscious policy?

Yes it was. They were actors and actresses that we respected greatly – Ian Carmichael, Terry-Thomas, Irene Handl, Kenneth Griffith, etc. There was this great body of talent and they all wanted to act in film. And we loved them, admired their talent and wanted to use it. It all happened in the '50s and '60s.

Were you ever aware of difficulties with theatre-trained actors adjusting to film?

From time to time, less so today. Our most vivid encounter on this subject was when John and I, aged twenty-three, decided to cast Sir Seymour Hicks, aged seventy-one, as a German general of World War I vintage in *Pastor Hall*. Now Seymour belonged to the old school of theatre, was by repute 'difficult', and used to having his own way. So, you can imagine, I approached him with suggestions very gingerly indeed. I thought things were going pretty well until the very last scene of the day, when perhaps age and fatigue combined to produce an explosion: he wanted to know why I employed him since I wouldn't allow him to act! A moment's thought and then I suggested that he play the scene exactly as he wished. He brightened up at that; but I went on to ask if he would indulge me, and film it again, playing it this time in the way I thought more effective. His doubts returned. 'Look, Sir Seymour,' I said. 'We'll see both takes in tomorrow morning's rushes. Whichever one you judge to be the best, I promise to use in the finished film.'

At eight-thirty the next morning, Seymour came and sat himself down in a theatre packed with the film crew. We ran the rushes. Eventually, the disputed scene came on. As Seymour, looking magnificent, hammed it up, first there came titters and then outright laughter. The *second* take restored the situation. Seymour – doing nothing, as he thought – held the unit in pin-drop silence, so moving did they find his performance, and they gave him a round of applause.

Later Bernard Miles had a scene with Seymour, and I said certain things with which Bernard didn't agree at all. At the end of the day Bernard came to me and told me Seymour had said to him, 'Bernard, don't argue with the boy – he *knows*! Mind you, it isn't acting, of course.'

Dallas Bower

b. 1907

Sound recordist: *Under the Greenwood Tree (1929), Such is the Law, Suspense (1930), Other People's Sins (1931) and many 'quota quickies'*

Associate producer: *Escape Me Never (1935),*

As You Like It (1936), Henry V (1944)

Director: *The Path of Glory (1934), Alice in Wonderland (1950), The Second Mrs Tanqueray (1952), Doorway to Suspicion (1957), Fire One (1957)*

Though much has been written about Laurence Olivier's *Henry V*, and notice how quickly – and carelessly – one attributes it to its star and director, there is relatively little to read about the man who may be said to have initiated the whole project. Dallas Bower has had a varied career in film, radio and television which ought to be more widely known. He was indeed one of the pioneers of television drama and he had considerable experience in directing Shakespeare, including *The Taming of the Shrew*, with Margaretta Scott and Austin Trevor, *The Tempest*, with John Abbott and Peggy Ashcroft, and a production of *Julius Caesar* in modern dress. He had, as well, been associated with Paul Czinner's 1936 version of *As You Like It*, so that, when he came to promote the cause of the famous 1944 film of *Henry V*, he was no newcomer to filming Shakespeare. His own memoirs, when complete, will add importantly to the filming of the great World War II success: he gives enough information here to make us wish for more. *Interview date: October 1992*

Did you actually start as a sound recordist in British films from 1929?

Yes, I was invited to go to British International Pictures by the RCA representatives in the UK, to become a recordist, largely because of my radio experience. Eighteen months later, I moved to Cricklewood, where I found myself working very closely with Thorold Dickinson, who was then a freelance editor, and due to his good offices, I did a lot of work for the original London Film Society as a voluntary editor.

Then you went on to direct *Path of Glory* with Maurice Evans and Valerie Hobson in 1934?

Yes. Inevitably while I was at Cricklewood as a sound recordist I did a number of 'quota quickies' and there was an interesting character called Reginald Smith who ran a concern called Producers' Distributing Company. He had decided that he would make some quota films for Metro and set himself up at the Riverside Studios, which in those days consisted of a tyre depot, one large silent and one small sound stage. He asked me if I would like to direct a film there. This was an opportunity I hadn't expected to come so quickly. So I agreed and he gave me choice of subject. I chose *Path of Glory*, which was a highly successful radio play written by an amateur, L du Garde Peach, a doctor of medicine. I found that the film copyright was available although I wanted some extra scenes.

It was quite an expansion on the original radio play and I cast it in a way I thought was interesting. Felix Aylmer played the lead; I had two very distinguished, elderly character actors, Athole Stewart and Harvey Braban. I was terrified of Athole, who was very imposing, a fine actor and also a very good stage director in his own right. He came to me one day, apologising if he seemed to be interfering, but with a suggestion for the casting of the part of the young girl. At the time he was playing in *Conversation Piece* with Heather Thatcher and a young woman was understudying her. She came to see me and it was Valerie Hobson. I thought, 'This is it!', did some tests and that was that.

Then Stewart asked me who was to play the juvenile lead and suggested Maurice Evans. I was sure he wouldn't be interested as he had an immensely successful career playing Hamlet, but Athole assured me Evans would be grateful for the opportunity. So Maurice did indeed play the lead, for which he was paid a very modest sum. The film, a bitter but funny satire, was good to do and in a way quite ambitious.

You then became associated with Paul Czinner on *Escape Me Never* and *As You Like*

When I was recording at Elstree, such silent films as BIP had in hand at the time they decided to issue with musical accompaniment as cinemas became more and more wired for sound. On one occasion Dr Paul Czinner came to BIP to record the music for a sound film he'd directed. Very little was known about the film other than that it had been made in Cornwall with Pola Negri and was called *Street of Lost Souls*. Czinner had of course been associated with Elizabeth Bergner, who was even then something of a myth in her own lifetime. (Eventually they married.) So I got to know him.

After I made *Path of Glory* there was an inevitable gap and my wife wrote a note to Czinner, knowing that he and Bergner were about to make *Escape Me Never*, asking if I could be of any help to him. Czinner responded instantly and took me on as his personal assistant and I was delighted. I learned

a great deal from him. After *Escape Me Never* we went on to make *As You Like It* and both those films had pretty high-powered teams, inasmuch as David Lean edited both of them, and I was responsible for bringing in William Walton for the music of a small ballet Czinner wanted for *Escape Me Never*. That was Walton's first connection with film music and he did the most marvellous job so that we had him do the music for *As You Like It*. Périnal photographed *Escape Me Never* and we brought in Sadler's Wells for the ballet in both films. We had Lazare Meerson doing the decoration and Alexander Trauner was his assistant. Both had worked previously for René Clair and Marcel Carné.

Were you then Director of BBC Television from 1936 to 1939?

I was the first Producer-Director. There were two of us – Stephen Thomas, who was a stage director, and myself from the cinema. I produced and directed the first programme (2 November 1936) on both systems, Baird and EMI.

Is it true that you prepared a television script of *Henry V* in the late '30s which was shelved when war broke out?

Yes. I did a TV script after Munich with a view to the possibility of Ralph Richardson's playing Henry V but I put it to one side. After I left the Army to go to the Ministry of Information as Executive Producer for the Films Division, I thought in terms of making it into a film script, which I did. That was the basis of the script which was used for the Olivier film.

Was the MoI sympathetic to the idea of *Henry V*?

Well, Kenneth Clark was, very much so. He tried valiantly to secure public money for film production but the only public money ever put into a film by the MoI was for *49th Parallel*. Then Clark was 'shot upstairs' and the division was taken over by Jack Beddington, an advertising man whose only experience of filmmaking came when he set up a small film unit for the Shell Organisation, by whom he was employed. He wasn't a very popular figure, not sympathetic to filmmakers as he knew nothing about films other than the sort of documentary that advertised Shell petrol. He succeeded in casting Noël Coward into Malet Street with the script of *In Which We Serve* behind him. If Coward hadn't had access to Mountbatten, *In Which We Serve* would never have been made. Much the same thing would have happened to me, except that Filippo Del

Giudice, who had set up the Two Cities production company, was released from the Isle of Man, where he had been interned, and set up *Henry V* at my instigation. It was my script that he bought and finally used. By then I had left the MoI; I didn't get on with Beddington and thought I would be called back to the Army – I still held my commission – but they thought I was better doing radio for BBC sound, so I did two large-scale pieces for them. Then this opportunity arose to make *Henry V* so I threw my bonnet over the mill and resigned from the BBC.

At what point did you become involved with Olivier?

Larry knew very little about my previous work on Shakespeare productions for television. I had done the Garrick version of *The Taming of the Shrew*, *Julius Caesar* in modern dress and *The Tempest* with the Sibelius score. My first encounter with Olivier was during a radio production of the MacNeice script of *Columbus* with the Walton score. That was a wartime effort, the 450th anniversary of the discovery of America. I had met him on the set of *As You Like It* but that was all; he didn't know until later that we had employed Walton to do the score. In fact, when we were setting up *Henry V* I had some difficulty in selling Walton to Olivier. Larry had completely forgotten everything about *As You Like It*. He hated working on it, didn't like Bergner or Czinner. In due course I got my own way and, afterwards, he was more than handsome in admitting that Walton's contribution was enormous. I went to Del Giudice and suggested we do the film and he agreed. Del put up financial backing for it, quite independent of the Rank Organisation, but by the time we were in work he could see clearly that his own resources weren't adequate. At that time Rank thought very highly of Del Giudice and he took over the financing of Two Cities. That is really how the film was completed.

I would like to make clear that if it hadn't been for John Betjeman – who had been film critic for the London *Evening Standard* for some years and who had left the Scenario Department of the Films Division of the MoI (again largely because he couldn't get on with Beddington) – we would never have been able to make the Agincourt sequences that we made near Dublin. Betjeman was the press attaché to our High Commissioner in Dublin and was *persona grata* with the Irish Government, hence we were able to do the Agincourt scenes at Powerscourt near Dublin. He also knew Lord Powerscourt and knew he would be pleased to have us work in his domain at Inneskerry.

Larry had brought in his own people inasmuch as he'd worked with Roger Furse and wanted him to design the production and he wanted Alan Dent to contribute to the scenario – and Alan indeed did. It was Alan's idea that we should open and close in the Globe Theatre. I thought it was a first-rate strategy.

The one thing that was a little disturbing was that Larry didn't really want anyone to disturb his performance of Henry that he'd done somewhere in the theatre. I was going to direct it, you see. I stayed a weekend with him at Gerrards Cross, where he'd taken Coward's house, and he said, 'I want you to produce the film.' I asked why, and he more or less said he'd never seen anything I had directed for the cinema. As I'd resigned from the BBC, I was in a pretty difficult situation, so I asked what he wanted. Did he want to direct it himself? Yes, he did. Then suddenly his nerve went – he wasn't at all happy about this and he asked all sorts of directors, including William Wyler, Carol Reed and David Lean – and they all said no. Terence Young was brought into it but the MoI simply refused to release him from the Tank Corps, largely through Ralph Nunn May, Deputy Director of the Films Division. Ralph was an estimable man in all ways and *Henry V* would probably never have been made without him. We managed to cast most of the actors without having to request their release from the forces.

For the technicians – we wanted Périnal to photograph, of course, and he would have been only too pleased to come. He checked the long-shot interiors, even though Robert Krasker has the credit. Krasker had been Périnal's operator for years and practically knew how he thought. But Korda wouldn't release Périnal to us. In fact we had enormous opposition all round and some of them were pretty disagreeable about it, too. Anyway, Robert Krasker was excellent. The film was Renee Asherson's first screen appearance. Larry and I discovered her in a play at the Palmers Green repertory theatre. We also tested and cast Janet Burnell (in the same play) as her mother. We wanted Vivien Leigh but Selznick would not have considered releasing her for such a small role. He had her under long-term contract and wouldn't give an inch.

As associate producer on *Henry V*, were you involved in all the matters of casting?

Oh yes, very much so. One of the things I pride

myself on having been adamant about was this: I discovered that Larry had never seen George Robey's Falstaff and was astonished. Robey had been absolutely marvellous and so we had him in the film. He was pretty frail but coped beautifully.

I remember one night Larry and I went to the Haymarket to pick up Vivien, who was playing in *The Doctor's Dilemma*; John Gielgud was playing Dudebat, and by this time it had become known that we were going to make *Henry V*. To my astonishment Gielgud turned to me and said he hoped I would let him play the King of France, it was an excellent part! He also asked why didn't I ask Edith Evans to play Mistress Quickly? Hugh Beaumont had both of them under contract, however, and wouldn't release them. Harcourt Williams was wonderful as the King but, let's face it, Gielgud and Evans were stars and we wanted to make this a star affair in the interests of everyone concerned.

I do think Larry might have been not quite so all-embracing as to the credits he took for himself but he may have been pressured. But I did produce the thing, there is no question of it. The reaction of the film profession was that nobody, let alone a first-time filmmaker, could have produced, directed *and* played the leading part. He set up a measure of disbelief, as it were. I was on the set all the time – never left the place. And I brought in Laurence Evans, the high-powered international agent as he became, as assistant production manager, and very glad I was to do so. Subsequently Larry and Ralph both invited me to replace Tyrone Guthrie when he left the Old Vic, which was a very handsome gesture on both their parts. Del Giudice very naturally told Larry he would release me if Larry would give him his next two films, but Larry wasn't prepared to do that and I wasn't willing to engage in that sort of horse-trading. Furthermore I didn't want to go into the theatre, I wanted to stay in films.

But – referring to *Henry V* again – I think Larry did a very silly thing by not saying to people that he wanted to preserve his own performance and simply wanted a technician. Nonetheless, I was impressed with his performance as a director. He had, after all, worked with some good directors, and he had an excellent technician in Reginald Beck (the editor) at his elbow as well. And he did know a lot about Shakespeare. He was inclined to show everyone how he wanted their parts done – not being dictatorial, just giving a little cameo, and the actors would, of course, do what they had been asked to do. We were able to get all the people we wanted,

fortunately. Either because they were too old or because of health reasons they were not in the services, they were all available.

Did you see the film as having a valuable morale-building, propaganda element? What do you think of the way the French court is presented in this respect?

That's why I set it up. I was, after all, at the Ministry of Information and that's more or less what Kenneth Clark had hoped the Films Division would do – make films with propaganda value. I don't think we had any problem with the French court business – Vichy was on everyone's mind and to all intents and purposes that was what the French court was meant to represent.

Had you expected the film to be such a popular success?

Yes, I never doubted it, quite frankly. It attracted mass audiences from the time of its opening. One of the things we were rather careful about – and we had nothing but full support from Rank – was that we had Roger Furse design the advertising for both the London buses and Underground station posters, and of course they looked wonderful: people had never seen anything like that on a bus before. That was Larry's doing. It upset the distributors in the biggest possible way, put their noses right out of joint. Anyway, we had said that it was to be road-shown rather than put on general release, that is to say played with an interval between the afternoon and evening shows rather than in continuous sessions. It worked very well.

After the night of the première, Rank said to me he felt I hadn't been given proper credit, which was handsome of him. It made seven per cent profit even here and of course it made a fortune in America, although neither Larry nor I made a penny out of it. Two Cities bought the script and Larry and I simply earned our fees. The point that's important to make is that there are two people who have never been given enough credit for making the film possible – Filippo Del Guidice and Arthur Rank.

Was *The Second Mrs Tanqueray* made on the Independent Frame system?

No, nothing to do with it. It was made as a result of an independent producer called Roger Proudlock wanting to make a film with me. I suggested we do a period piece and said I would like to do Pinero's play, which was very popular and well crafted. So Roger bought the film rights. Pinero had died a widower with no family and had left his royalties to the Garrick Club, so the £2,000 that we paid went straight to the Garrick's trading account, to its delight. I decided to do the film as if I were doing a live television play. I rehearsed it at the Adelphi Theatre, where we did one week's preliminary work, then another week with all four camera crews and the two sound crews in the old Stoll rehearsal rooms atop the Stoll Theatre in Kingsway. Then I went into Riverside and shot the film in eight days. That worked rather well. We brought it in for just under £25,000. Pamela Brown's performance was quite superb. We had a very good cast, very distinguished. It was made for a company called Vandyke and distributed by Associated British.

I made *Alice in Wonderland* in English and there was a French version. There was an American-Russian puppeteer called Lou Bunin who found himself in France with a group of extremely politically left-wing people; he persuaded UGC, which was the company operating in France with

French public money, to make *Alice in Wonderland*, which has always been very popular in France. My agents at the time were MCA and one day Bunin went into their offices in London and said he wanted a British director for the project. Robin Fox produced the *International Motion Pictures Almanac*, giving my credentials, and suggested me, so I found myself in France. It got itself into the most appalling tangle, an absolute nightmare. The sterling requirements were very difficult to obtain because of the exchange controls at the time. People like Felix Aylmer, Ernest Milton, Stephen Murray were in it; Pamela Brown was wonderful as the Queen of Hearts; with eminent people like Joyce Grenfell and Peter Bull simply playing voices of the puppets. It was in AnscoColour, which fades quickly, and I gather that the Museum of Modern Art in New York is now re-establishing the colour frame by frame.

Betty Box

b. 1920

Producer: *The Upturned Glass* (co-pr), *Dear Murderer, When the Bough Breaks* (1947), *Miranda, The Blind Goddess, Here Come the Huggetts* (1948), *Vote for Huggett, Marry Me, It's Not Cricket, The Huggetts Abroad* (1949), *So Long at the Fair, The Clouded Yellow* (1950), *Appointment With Venus* (1951), *The Venetian Bird* (1952), *A Day to Remember* (1953), *Doctor in the House, Mad About Men* (1954), *Doctor at Sea* (1955), *Checkpoint, The Iron Petticoat* (1956), *Doctor at Large, Campbell's Kingdom* (1957), *A Tale of Two Cities, The Wind Cannot Read* (1958), *The Thirty-Nine Steps, Upstairs and Downstairs* (1959), *Conspiracy of Hearts, Doctor in Love* (1960), *No Love For Johnnie, No, My Darling Daughter* (1961), *A Pair of Briefs, The Wild and The Willing* (1962), *Hot Enough For June, Doctor in Distress* (1963), *The High Bright Sun* (1964), *Deadlier than the Male, Doctor in Clover* (1966), *Nobody Runs Forever* (1968), *Some Girls Do* (1969), *Doctor in Trouble* (1970), *Percy* (1971), *It's a 2'6" Above the Ground World / The Love Ban* (1972), *Percy's Progress* (1974)

In *Odd Man Out: James Mason*, Sheridan Morley quotes Mason as saying of Betty Box: '. . . she sailed with her tide and became the most sensible and hardworking producer in the British industry, where she remained one of its few survivors.'

She is modest about her own 'creative' capacities and prefers to stress the producer's housekeeping role. Her films came in on schedule and budget. Furthermore, she knew what the public wanted and, in over thirty films made in collaboration with the director Ralph Thomas, the public, generally speaking, proved her right. After cutting her teeth on over two hundred training and propaganda films during World War II, as assistant to her brother Sydney Box, she then moved with him to Gainsborough. Here she made a string of popular films, including the Huggett family series, and, still in her twenties, she was in charge of production at Gainsborough's Islington studios. It was she who saw the potential of *Doctor in the House* and, once settled on a secure run of box-office successes, held out to make more problematic enterprises such as *No Love for Johnnie*. It may be that what the British cinema really needs today is a producer with her shrewd, no-nonsense approach to the task.
Interview date: September 1989

Was your first film work as assistant to your brother [Sydney Box] during the war?

Yes. I came into the business in early '42 when my brother was making a lot of documentary and propaganda films for the War Office and the Ministry of Information, training films for the Army, and films for the British Council which went all over the world. He had about ten film units covering all these various subjects. I was the dogsbody who made the tea and fetched the rushes from the station, went to the laboratories, and eventually learned how to do the budgets, and I suppose, in three years from '42 until '45, I did about ten years' hard work. I was very lucky indeed to be given that chance to learn, and I'd never be able to do all that again now, because of the trade unions!

Then towards the end of the war the only entertainment films made were supposed to be films that aided the war effort. Sydney, who always wanted to make feature films, seized the opportunity to make things like *The Flemish Farm*, which were of help to the war effort. When the war ended, he said to me, 'I'm going into feature films now and I'd like you to come with me.' I was very anxious to learn and very quickly did, because of the background he'd already given me on documentaries.

After his enormous success with *The Seventh Veil*, he was making two follow-ups when J Arthur Rank asked him to take over Gainsborough. Partly because of British quota and partly because there were people coming back from the war wanting their jobs back, he went on to make about twenty films a year, for two years at Shepherd's Bush; and I took over Islington, both of which belonged at that time to Gainsborough Pictures. I made a dozen or so films at these studios, before Gainsborough closed down and we all joined Rank's major operation at Pinewood studios.

How did you view the producer's function?

As a producer I had to find the subjects, the director, and someone to write the script; to cast it and to see it right through to delivery into the cinemas. I watched all the costs and made sure the money I'd been allocated was sufficient. I didn't overstep the budget and I was a very good housekeeper in that way. Had I had, perhaps, more faith in my creative ability, I might have decided occasionally to risk spending a little more. But I just felt that I had to present, to the people who trusted me, a good product for the money they gave me. So, really, I think the answer to your question is a producer has to tie together the best creative ability, produce the best artistic effort he can, for the money at his disposal. And maybe it was an unfair advantage I took, but I always found it a bonus rather than a disability being a woman film producer!

Is *Dear Murderer* the first film on which you're credited as a producer?

Just before that, I finished off the last picture that Sydney had financed and organised at Riverside

Studios, where we made *The Seventh Veil*. It was a film called *The Upturned Glass*, and he said to me, 'I promised Arthur Rank I'll take over Gainsborough and make all those films. Therefore you've got to do *Upturned Glass* for me.' And I said, 'I can't produce it.' He insisted I could and, if I remember rightly, I was given an Associate Producer credit with James Mason on that. Then I went on to Islington and did *Dear Murderer*, a run-of-the-mill detective story. I remember that my present husband, Peter Rogers, worked on the script and that it was not an easy one to do.

Eric Portman and Jack Warner were both very special in their own way – Eric Portman was one of the best actors I ever worked with – but he and Jack Warner didn't get on very well together. They were always fluffing and we would get to Take 20. I'd say to Arthur Crabtree, 'Oh, for goodness' sake, break the scene up.' There were great pages of dialogue in those days and Arthur as a cameraman hadn't quite got the director's finesse. I had to more or less force him to break the scene up into smaller pieces.

How did you find working at Gainsborough? It seems absolutely central to '40s British cinema.

Yes it was, but I worked at the poor man's studio at Islington. Shepherd's Bush, which is now the BBC, had five stages and every facility you could want, because it was built as a film studio, but Islington had only two stages, one on top of the other, both very small. On the top stage, where we obviously had to do half the work, everything had to be taken up in a very antiquated lift. You couldn't get a bus up there, or a car beyond a certain size, and it was a very difficult studio to work in. But we managed; we made our films on time. It was my job to ensure that the studio was always working, that the technicians and the craftsmen got paid every week, and that I had a film ready to go the day I finished the previous one, which, I think, very few producers have to do nowadays. But it was great fun to do it; I was young, and most of the technicians were relatively young, so we got through it.

The worst of all was the winter of 1947, when we had not only the coldest winter I think we've ever had, but power cuts the whole time. I had to hire a generator from a fairground to provide electricity to go on shooting, else we would have had to stop. We all froze, but we carried on. I remember we were working with Patricia Roc and Rosamund John and Bill Owen on *When the Bough Breaks*, and they were wearing summer clothes – poor Pat Roc in little cotton dresses. But nobody grumbled and we finished the film.

Gainsborough closed down when Rank finally took over the whole set-up; and I moved to Pinewood Studio when Sydney moved over from Shepherd's Bush. It was at Pinewood that I made my last film under that Rank contract deal I had at Gainsborough; it was *So Long at the Fair*, when I first met Dirk Bogarde. I loved working with him and Jean Simmons. It was made partly in France on location and here at Pinewood.

Did you spend the rest of your career here at Pinewood?

I worked from Pinewood from 1949 to '79, but a lot of that time I was on location. I remember being in France in 1948, I think, and going to a restaurant in a little village up above Cannes, and there was a French film unit there making a film on location. I watched them and, as I had my lunch, I listened to them talking and I thought, 'This is what is I've missed in shooting film. I've always been stuck in a studio.' From then on my aim was to shoot as much film as I could outside, because I reckoned you got so much more screen value for the same amount of money. So from then I made between thirty and forty films at Pinewood studios and most of them were made abroad, and I think I got much bigger-looking films by shooting outside.

Did you find your range of opportunities at Pinewood satisfying?

I never had an enormously inflated idea of my own importance and ability. I always thought I was very lucky to be able to say to Rank, 'I like this idea for a story, can I buy it? Can I make it with this or that star?' and they nearly always said yes. Very often they would say to me, 'The most successful film you've made for us so far was *Doctor in the House*. You can make that one which we're not a hundred-per-cent sure about if you will also make another *Doctor*.' So I had to make a *Doctor* every year or two. Well, there are only so many jokes about doctors and so many situations you can put them into and I felt, although the public didn't seem to show it, that they were getting repetitive. When I made *Conspiracy of Hearts*, which I rather like, they didn't want me to make it and they said, 'It's religion, it's nuns, it's wartime, who wants to know? Tell you what, make us another *Doctor* and you can do it!' And the interesting thing was that that year in the UK the three top box-office films were the *Doctor* film, *Conspiracy of Hearts* and a *Carry On*.

You had an enduring association at Pinewood with the director, Ralph Thomas. How did it begin?

It started at Islington when I did *Miranda*, one of my happiest films. Rank said to me, 'We've got a new man just out of the Army and he's going to do all the trailers. His name is Ralph Thomas.' I said, 'Right, I can show him the film Thursday.' So Ralph came down; I'd never met him before, but he was obviously very knowledgeable about film, and I discovered that, as a very young man, he had worked in films as a clapper-boy and then an assistant cameraman and an editor. He was very wise about the way the story worked and he was very helpful. I didn't see him again until I did my next film, which I think was *So Long at the Fair*, and he came to do the trailer for that, and again I found him artistically very helpful.

When I came to make my first independent film, which was *The Clouded Yellow*, I teamed up with him to direct it. By that time he had directed a couple of films for my brother. We were both fairly new to the game but were keen and knew what we were doing. He was a very hard worker, very clever artistically, and my sort of technician, and eventually we formed our own little company together and that's why it says A Betty Box–Ralph Thomas Production on our films.

Within the Rank Organisation and made at Pinewood?

That's right, and Rank fully financed us. I bought *Doctor in the House* on my way back from a provincial film-showing in Cardiff. I bought the book from a bookstall and read it on the train coming back. I thought it would make a good film and rang the publishers from Victoria Station and was told who the agent was. The agent said, 'Oh, I sold it six months ago, to ABPC,' and told me that ABPC's option expired in a couple of weeks. So I said, 'Don't say a word when it expires and I'll buy it.' And of course they didn't make it and I bought it. ABPC said to me when I bought the option, 'You'll never be able to make a film, it's just a string of anecdotes.' And even Sydney agreed with them. But I said, 'I think I know how to do it. I take my four students through the three or four years of their training as medical students and make that the story.' I was very lucky because I got a wonderful man called Nicholas Phipps who wrote the script. There wasn't a great deal of the book in it, except for the characters. The main idea really wasn't in the book. When we showed it to the press, Leonard

Mosley, who was the *Express* critic, said to me, 'You know, you've got a winner here.' In six weeks in the Odeon Leicester Square, it more or less paid for itself. I think it was the youthful gaiety of it that made it so popular, and it was something everybody knows about – doctors, hospitals, illness. We had people write from hospitals all over England saying, 'Thank God you've shown hospitals as being places with some humour!'

You had a marvellous cast . . .

I wanted Robert Morley to play the surgeon, so I rang up his agent and she said, 'I'm afraid he's £15,000.' Well, I couldn't pay that; then I remembered dear old Jimmy Justice and I thought, he can do it! He doesn't have to do very much except be himself, so we got him for £1,500. The day I started shooting, I was running the first day's rushes, when I got a call from Earl St John to say, 'Betty, I've just come back from the board meeting, they're very worried about *Doctor in the House*. They don't like doing hospital films, films about illness. Your budget's £100,000 – can you cut it down?' I said, 'I don't know how, I'm paying Dirk what you pay him under his Rank contract, which is too much for my budget. And I've got Kay Kendall on her Rank deal, but I'll do my best.'

I made it for, I think, £97,000. I never told Ralph that they were moaning about the £100,000. Of course they took much more than that in six weeks. We had a very good quartet in Dirk, Donald Sinden, Donald Houston and Kenneth More. I did that poster with Guinness, you know, 'GUINNESS IS GOOD FOR YOU, as good as a *Doctor in the House*', with all four of them at the bar drinking their Guinness. Guinness put that poster up all over the UK. That was worth a fortune in free publicity – just luck.

Among your more serious films was *No Love for Johnnie*, which seems to me a courageous film – and a cynical one.

I'm not a political animal although I'm more so now than I was then. Then I wasn't interested in the least. I'm still very surprised that Rank let me do it, that they didn't tell us, 'We don't want to be involved with sort that of thing,' because they were very politically conservative as an organisation. Perhaps they liked the Peter Finch character being so corrupt because, after all, he *was* left-wing! I must say I liked it very much. I was very sad that Wilfred Fienburgh, who wrote it, was dead before we made it. Driving home from the House of Commons one night he crashed his car. It wasn't financially as successful as a lot of films I've made but I enjoyed making it very much. I loved working with Peter Finch. He was drunk some of the time, and not always very easy, but I was just very fond of him. Ralph and I both knew how to work with him.

You made a lot of films with Dirk Bogarde, whom I've always regarded highly. What was your experience of working with him?

Well I found him very . . . what's the word? He *gave* a lot, almost too much. But he had great integrity, artistically. He decided what he felt he should give in a part and he did his best to give that, though he really wasn't suited to some of the films I did with him. Ralph had a clear idea of what he wanted and Dirk didn't always agree, but they respected each other's opinions.

I've recently seen him again in your version of *A Tale of Two Cities*. Why did you do it in black-and-white?

That was Ralph's and my fault. We saw one or two French films around that time, like *Gervaise*, and I remember thinking they were wonderful films and they were in black-and-white, and I thought, I can't see *Tale of Two Cities* in colour. Looking back, I realise what an idiot I was. At that time Rank would have said OK if I'd told them I wanted to make it in purple. What we didn't realise was that very soon we were going to depend quite a lot on television sales. And they paid nothing for black-and-white. So we dropped £100,000 straight away, which in those days was a lot of money. We shot in Bourges in central France for four or five weeks, and it poured with rain the whole bloody time. It was fated from beginning to end. It was unbearably hot until the day we started shooting, and then the heavens opened. All the costumes were wet and everything was muddy and sets fell down in the street. But of course Dirk was very good indeed, and he was certainly handsome!

Muriel Box

1905–1991

Co-screenwriter (with Sydney Box): *Alibi Inn* (1935), *29 Acacia Avenue, The Seventh Veil* (1945), *The Years Between, Daybreak, A Girl in a Million* (1946), *The Man Within, The Brothers, When the Bough Breaks, Dear Murderer, Holiday Camp* (1947), *Easy Money, Good Time Girl, The Blind Goddess, Here Come the Huggetts, Portrait from Life* (1948), *Christopher Columbus* (1949).

Director: **The Happy Family* (1952), **Street Corner* (1953), *To Dorothy a Son, The Beachcomber, Simon and Laura* (1955), *Eyewitness* (1956), **The Passionate Stranger* (1957), **The Truth About Women, Subway in the Sky, This Other Eden* (1959), **Too Young to Love* (1960), *The Piper's Tune* (1962), *Rattle of a Simple Man* (1964)
* Co-screenwriter with Sydney Box.

It was not easy for a woman to be a director in British films in the 1950s and Muriel Box was virtually the only regular, mainstream practitioner. She had had a long experience in filmmaking – as continuity girl, screenwriter and co-producer with her husband Sydney – before directing her first film, *The Happy Family*. Thereafter, she worked steadily throughout the decade, often using the formulas of popular genres to foreground her interest in women's lives. *Street Corner*, for instance, was conceived as a female reply to *The Blue Lamp*. Her best film is probably *Simon and Laura*, adapted from Alan Melville's successful West End play, satirising various aspects of television, which was becoming a major threat to cinema by the mid-'50s. *The Passionate Stranger* is a well-cast romantic comedy; *To Dorothy a Son* and *Rattle of a Simple Man* were broader comedies adapted from stage successes; *The Beachcomber* is derived from a Maugham short story; and *Eyewitness* is a neat thriller largely set in a hospital. They are business-like films from a woman who knew the business better than most. *Interview date: October 1989*

Before starting to direct, you had a very busy career as screenwriter and producer. Did you always want to direct?

Yes, I actually started to direct in 1950, as a freelance. I never dreamed I would be allowed to direct; the position of women in films was very precarious at the time. Hardly any woman had achieved the position of director on a film – it was unheard of – and I felt I was very lucky to be offered the chance. I had been for a long time a continuity girl, which is a matter of assisting the director to cut his film. I knew the business backwards from about 1925, ages before I was the script director at Gainsborough.

When Sydney Box founded his motion picture company in 1939, I believe it produced propaganda and training films . . .

Yes, Sydney started the company and it flourished. He was very much in touch with the Government and they knew that he was a very efficient producer. The films were all paid for by the Government, although you never got the money until months after the films had been made. I remember one film was called *Road Safety for Children* and my husband said I should write and direct it. All the scripts had to be passed in embryo form. Sydney took my script up to Elton, the Minister for Information, who said it was very good but he couldn't come at the idea of a woman director, so we had to find another director in a hurry. Ken Annakin was chosen to do it; he was young and fresh although he only knew a tenth of what I did about films then. But women had to take

second place.

According to my count, you and Mr Box co-authored twenty-two screenplays, including *The Seventh Veil* in 1945.

Yes, we got the Oscar for that – there it is over there. It's quite heavy! I used to do the over-all plot, then Sydney would start work on it and 'diddy it up' wherever he could. Then I'd have another go at the script, then he'd do a further one; it would usually go through five or six stages. We were starting to produce then; the first one we did was *29 Acacia Avenue*.

You had an enormous success with *The Seventh Veil*.

It was that which propelled us into Gainsborough Studios. The idea for the film came simply enough. Sydney was doing one of the propaganda films for the Army or the RAF, and he was at lunch with people connected with it. One of them was a doctor who tended the shell-shocked prisoners and very badly injured men, and he mentioned that he used narcosis; the patients were put under a drug and were then questioned and examined while they were unconscious; in this way the doctors could find out things the patient himself didn't know, and they could gradually form an opinion about his case. The doctor said they had achieved some wonderful cures with men who had been badly shell-shocked. I said later it would be a wonderful idea for a film, if you had an artist who had some terrible accident and was crippled with a psychosis like that. Sydney told me to write it and we would start work on it!

The first draft was very rough, just a few pages,

and we gradually developed it. We got hold of a psychiatrist, who knew about the technique, to come to the studio to demonstrate it to everyone there. I am still stunned by the film's success! It opened in Leicester Square and we were astounded to see queues all around the cinema. It was the first film about psychiatry, so perhaps it was the originality which attracted people. It was a good story, too.

Perhaps there was something comforting about the notion of a film which suggests solutions to problems.

Yes, whenever a woman tries to commit suicide, as she did, you know there is something terribly wrong with her, and the Herbert Lom character was able to go back over her childhood and find out how it all built up from that.

Was it an easy film to cast and make?

We got nice people, the ones we wanted. The terrible constriction was the war being on, bombs falling while we were shooting and water dripping through the roof where it had been damaged by bombs. The rationing of clothes was another problem – to dress Ann Todd well enough to suit the part – and I hadn't enough coupons for the clothes. I went around the second-hand shops to find what I needed. Up until the last minute I had no frock for the scene where she wears a débutante gown in Venice. She was very particular about her clothes and she was right to be, because she had good taste. I finally found the dress she wore in the film and sent it to the costume designer to get her approval. I shut myself in the lavatory rather than face Ann in case she rejected the dress! I was so astonished – and relieved – when she was delighted with it! Ann was only difficult because she wanted the right thing for the part.

This was followed by two further collaborations with the director Compton Bennett, *Daybreak* and *The Years Between*. What sort of director was he?

He never went out after publicity. If he had any publicity it was what accrued to him from his directing of other films. Really, Sydney got more credit for directing *The Seventh Veil* than Compton did. He went to America and directed *The Forsyte Saga* but after that he got a bad deal over there, and eventually his contract was cancelled. I think it was more that we had chosen the right people for the right parts, so that it was made for him.

You were associated with several other directors in the '40s including David Macdonald (*Good Time Girl*, *Christopher Columbus*

and others). What do you recall of him?

Christopher Columbus was a calamity but we couldn't avoid it happening. We were pressed into making it, didn't want to do it at all. The script had been paid for by Gainsborough Pictures, and when we got there in 1945 they asked us to make it. I got in one or two other authors to help us work on it, but it was doomed from the start. The whole unit went out to the Caribbean with the *Santa Maria* and they were sailing the ship around, and they lost it! Later it caught fire! You wouldn't believe the things that happened on that film. There was trouble with the artistes, everything. The first rehearsal we called was for a preliminary run-through of the script, to give the artistes an idea of the film as a whole. We called the whole cast to the Dorchester but Fredric March, who was Columbus, didn't turn up, nor did Mrs March [Florence Eldredge], who was playing Isabella! We waited an hour or more, then I sent off the first assistant to find them. Freddie was very apologetic but said he couldn't possibly come until their contract was signed. Of course people in England knew that, if Arthur Rank was financing the film, he would never break his word, that was enough. But it wasn't the same for Freddie; he had too much experience of broken words in Hollywood.

Arthur was very generous, and also very frank about things when he disagreed with you. For instance, *Acacia Avenue* was tried out and was a great success, it got laughs all the way through. However, Arthur didn't like it because he didn't approve of the Dinah Sheridan/Jimmy Hanley couple trying to sleep together. He thought it would be a bad example for young people, and said he would prefer to put it on the shelf; he would pay us for our work anyway. Sydney and I argued that the cast and the director would be very upset at being shelved, but Arthur was adamant. It was eventually released after two years, but not by Arthur. Fortunately it did very well, because we had all our money in it. Arthur was an extraordinarily nice man, very honest. His high moral stance was very rare! He had a good grasp of the importance of stars, but he was really a stranger in a strange land as far as films were concerned.

None of the big epic films made in Britain at that time was really popular. Were these not the kinds of films at which Britain was best?

I think it was probably a combination of dud scripts and the fact that they didn't ring a bell. The one that cost us most money was *The Bad Lord Byron*. That was meticulously researched and several authors worked on it; Dennis Price was very good as Byron, but people didn't go for it. I could understand the academics wanting something more literary, but you couldn't have more of that if you wanted mass audiences. I thought it was a reasonable saga of his life, and was very disappointed because we worked like stink on it. [Muriel Box has no credit on this film.]

How do you feel about *Good Time Girl*? Were you forced to have that very moral frame to the story?

We felt we had to justify the story in some way because at that time the girls were really going haywire over the Americans. I worked very hard on the script, and went round to homes for delinquent girls to make it realistic. After it was filmed, the censor got his hands on it and he was an absolute bastard! He objected to certain scenes in it, including the one where the girls in the home – Jean Kent and Jill Balcon – had a fight. Yet you couldn't have the horrid things that had to go into the film without showing what the girl's plight was. It was dreadful to have cut it about as they did. I was pleased with Jean Kent's performance, and it was a very good cast all round. Again, that was David Macdonald, who I liked – a good, sympathetic director.

You directed your first film, *The Happy Family*, for London Independent.

That was just a cover name for our independent producing company. When we had left Rank at Pinewood, Sydney wanted to start up on his own and he wanted me to direct. We operated out of any studio where we could get space. *The Happy Family* was from a West End play. It got very good reviews in America, much better than here. George Cole was in it, as a very young man. We were always terribly insistent on getting the cast right.

Was your next film, *Street Corner*, meant as a kind of female answer to *The Blue Lamp*?

Yes, I thought *The Blue Lamp* had had too long a run for its money because it never mentioned women and how they co-operated in doing police work. It was about time women had a chance to show what they did do, and it was specifically designed to show their work. It was a mixture of documentary and crime story.

How difficult was it for a woman to operate as a director in the '50s?

Terribly difficult. They were prejudiced against you from the very start. I went to my agent,

Christopher Mann, and told him I had made several films and got good notices. I had always wanted to make a film in Hollywood and asked Chris to put me up, as director, to any of the Hollywood producers who came over here – as they often did at that time. He sighed deeply and said, 'Muriel, I wish I could tell you different but, if I mention the name of a woman as a director, they just turn away and look out of the window.' That was absolutely true. There were only two in Hollywood – Dorothy Arzner and Ida Lupino. They elbowed you out. Even with my last film (*Rattle of a Simple Man*), for which Sydney had got me the contract, they were still worried about the director. This was three weeks after we had booked the studio space. One of the officials at ABPC said they hadn't used a woman director before and were chary of it. They would prefer not to go ahead with the film if Sydney insisted on my directing.

The stage–screen relationship is closer in Britain than in America. Has the British stage tradition worked against the cinema's interests?

I think they more or less worked hand-in-glove. For instance, with *Simon and Laura* I had seen Ian Carmichael do the part on stage and I thought he would be wonderful in the film, so I insisted on having him even though Rank didn't want him. They wanted a more established 'star' name. I knew the cast I wanted – Kay Kendall, Peter Finch and Thora Hird. Normally the casting is left to the director but Rank had no hesitation in saying if they disagreed with you. But, with Ian Carmichael, I really dug in my heels because I knew he would be excellent in the part.

You directed some very diverse stars in your next few films. What you recall about working with Ralph Richardson and Margaret Leighton in *The Passionate Stranger*; Laurence Harvey in *The Truth About Women*; and Van Johnson and Hildegarde Neff in *Subway in the Sky*?

I could tell you heaps of stories! We got Ralph Richardson by the skin of our teeth. Sydney took him the script and he read it and liked it, except for the ending; he typed out some ideas for a different ending but I didn't like them. I had worked on the script for months and didn't think Ralph's ending was as good as our own. Now, Ralph was easy about whether he did the film or not, and we only had a few days left before filming was due to start. Ralph was still very keen on his idea, so I said the only way out was to shoot alternative scenes for the two endings and somehow cut them together. We set out doing the film, knowing that I had to do the alternative scenes on different days; Ralph was unaware that we were shooting alternative endings. We didn't dare tell him that! Margaret Leighton was in on it; she was splendid and she knew Ralph!

The Truth About Women was the most difficult film I ever made, and Laurence Harvey was the most difficult artiste. I don't know whether his stardom had gone to his head, or whether he was just like that. It was a lovely cast, too, considering the money we spent. The film was reasonably successful but the Rank group wasn't behind us as they should have been. The publicity people knew that I was doing a comedy and they expected belly laughs, but it wasn't like that; it was ironical, pure satire really. It was mainly to show up the situation of women that I agreed to make the film at all.

Van Johnson was a very charming man, but Hildegarde Neff was a pain in the neck. She was the first artiste who ever refused to take a direction I gave on the floor. I asked her to do another take because she hadn't done the first one correctly, a reaction shot to Van Johnson. I had to cajole her to do the shot the way I wanted, and as we shot it I could see she was determined to do the complete opposite. Eventually I had to cut around her, which was very hard.

As a director, what has interested you most in your career? Is it the directing of the actors?

That is by far the most important thing, I believe – and the honest and right interpretation of the story. The director's job is to ensure that the best artistes interpret the script as best they can; you have to be clear about what your team are giving you. They come to the director and say, 'This is how I see it,' and if you don't see it the same way you have to tell them. I never had any trouble with the units at all, never, as a woman. With artistes sometimes, yes, and certainly with the distributors, although not always.

John Brabourne (Lord Brabourne)

b. 1924

Producer: *Harry Black* (1958), *Sink the Bismarck!* (1960), *HMS Defiant* (1962), *Othello* (1965), *The Mikado* (1967), *Romeo and Juliet, Up the Junction* (1968), *The Dance of Death* (1969), *The Tales of Beatrix Potter* (1971), *Murder on the Orient Express* (1974), *'Copter Kids* (1976), *Death on the Nile* (1978), *Stories from a Flying Trunk* (1979), *The Mirror Crack'd* (1980), *Evil under the Sun* (1982), *A Passage To India* (1984), *Little Dorrit* (1988)

The producing team of John Brabourne and Richard Goodwin has been responsible for some of the most civilised entertainments offered by the British cinema in the last three decades. Brabourne also co-produced *Up the Junction* and *Romeo and Juliet* with Sir Anthony Havelock-Allan; it is tempting to see a line of descent from the prestige days of Cineguild, of which Havelock-Allan was a prime mover and which also produced some very superior adaptations of literary works. *Romeo and Juliet* may well have been the first Shakespeare to tap a really

large, youthful audience; it chimed absolutely with the rebellious '60s. As well, the Agatha Christie adaptations, especially the first two, are films of wit and charm, and *Little Dorrit* is on any counts a film of great daring. Brabourne's entrepreneurial skills have been crucial to creating some major successes for British cinema.
Interview date: July 1994

In what capacity did you enter films in the late '40s?

My first job was as a production assistant, a non-union job. The industry was a hundred-percent unionised then, of course, and it was difficult to get into it. I went to see Alexander Korda, having been introduced to him by my father-in-law, and he put me in touch with Ian Dalrymple. Ian later set up his own company, called Wessex, and gave me a job on the escape story, *The Wooden Horse*. It was the first of its sort, and a great success. I stayed with him as a production assistant on his next couple of pictures. Then the union got on to me and I decided I was really serious about continuing to work in films, so I got a union card.

I then left Ian Dalrymple, and went with Herbert Wilcox on *The Lady with the Lamp* (as location manager) and then *Trent's Last Case*, *Derby Day* and others, including one or two very bad films, like *Laughing Anne*. I also worked on the Highland film, *Trouble in the Glen*, with Orson Welles in a kilt! It certainly had curiosity value. I learned a lot working with Herbert, who knew a great deal about what the public wanted and how the industry worked. I stayed with him for several years, in the midst of which I also worked temporarily on *Reach for the Sky*.

I worked as associate producer for Danny Angel on *The Seven Thunders* (with James Robertson Justice, in Marseilles). This film was important to my life for two reasons: first, because I was associate producer; second, because I brought on to it someone with whom I was associated when I worked with Ian Dalrymple, called Richard Goodwin (this was in about 1954, I think). I had been very impressed by him and from then on, in every step I took, Richard (who was ten years younger than me) came with me. Our last film was *Little Dorrit* in 1988, so we worked together for over thirty years, which in this business is very rare.

Harry Black was my first film as a producer. I had quite a lot of connections with India as my father, who had been Governor of Bombay, was Viceroy for a short time and my father-in-law (Lord Mountbatten)

was the last Viceroy. I wanted to make a film about India, and then found *Harry Black*. I took on Richard Goodwin as location manager. He had been born in India, and although he was only twenty-three, he had such a way with people that I knew he could do the job. He built the camp, found the tiger and did all those things; he was absolutely invaluable to me on the film.

Your next film, *Sink the Bismarck!*, was a change of pace . . .

Sink the Bismarck! is one of those extraordinary films that people go on watching. That was in 1960 and I've been getting a cheque every six months since it was made! It was one of those films which just goes on running and everyone likes it.

You did the next film with Lewis Gilbert also, *HMS Defiant*.

Yes, we got on very well: he's an extremely good director and it's a shame we couldn't do more films together. Unfortunately *HMS Defiant* was too tough for those days, particularly for women.

What about the Argentine director, Hugo Fregonese?

I met him on *The Seven Thunders* and formed such a good friendship and working relationship with him that I asked him to direct *Harry Black*. He was also acceptable to 20th-Century-Fox, who had to approve the director. In dealing with a young producer like me, as financiers, they wanted to be sure the director was efficient and knew his job. More important to distribution considerations were the actors and we had Stewart Granger, Anthony Steel and Barbara Rush, who were all big at the time.

There's one rather odd '50s film we've missed – *The Stranger's Hand*.

That was a fascinating experience for me because we made it all in Venice and I was co-production manager with an Italian who spoke no English at all – we communicated in French. Mario Soldati was the director, and Graham Greene wrote the script. It was a film I always liked very much and Greene worked on it so hard, he really believed in it. I got to know him very well, and wouldn't have missed the experience for anything.

When did you set up Mersham Productions?

That was when I made *Harry Black*. All of my films have been for Mersham but not necessarily under that name. In those days you were able to buy loss companies, so I would buy one when I was about to make a film. As I was very lucky with my early films being successful, it was a good way to get your money out because, if you had bought a loss, you didn't pay any tax until the loss was worked out.

How do you distinguish between production assistant, associate producer and co-producer?

'Production assistant' was just a name to get me on the set. It is literally a runner, which is what I was at the beginning. After that I was assistant director (on *Trouble in the Glen*) and location manager; I also worked in the cutting room. I then became a production manager on several films including *The Stranger's Hand*; and that involves all the financial matters. Then I became associate producer on *Seven Thunders* before I became a producer. All of those jobs are scaling up; there is a hierarchy involved.

Are you a 'creative' producer rather than someone who sits in the office?

Yes, and very involved with the directors. I set out to become a director myself but changed my mind. The things that interested me were: the story, which is number one for me; the script is certainly number two; and the third really important factor is the editing. I found that, although I liked to work with actors, I didn't really have a feeling for directing. Richard Goodwin has written a very interesting book in which he says that the director makes the film but the producer *gets it made*. That is a very important distinction and it was what I liked to do. I did like being around the studio but, at certain times, I relied tremendously on Richard. On *A Passage to India*, for example, he was invaluable, particularly in the relationship with David Lean. While I wasn't always on the set I nonetheless had to see that the thing got made, and Richard acted as what is called today a line producer, though he is much more than that. He and I became partners and did everything jointly. He was the best person I've met anywhere for being on the floor and overseeing things there.

You are co-producers on the four Agatha Christie adaptations.

That's right. Another crucial one, though, is *Romeo and Juliet*, directed by Franco Zeffirelli. There, Richard was actually production manager but we made him associate producer, because he did such a wonderful job on the set. Tony Havelock-Allan, of whom I'm very fond, was co-producer on that and also on *Up the Junction*.

I don't think people realise that *Romeo and Juliet* was one of the most successful films ever made. It cost £1 million to make and was a most enormous success. On its first release, it grossed $17 million, which, in those days, was unheard-of. It was a film about youthful rebellion and that was what made it so successful. I felt the play had been ruined for me by seeing people in it who were much too old for the parts. It occurred to me that this was really a modern play, a ballad of youth. So Tony and I talked to Zeffirelli and when we said that, he said, 'We must make this.' The censors were worried about the fact that these two youngsters were sleeping together, so I spoke to them and said, 'We are surprised to hear you are worried about this – you do realise that they're married, don't you?' 'What?!' they said. By an incredible fluke I had formed a great relationship with Charlie Bluhdorn, then the President of Paramount. He personally agreed to finance the picture, which is how it got made.

When I was making *Murder on the Orient Express* and EMI Films were wondering how to distribute it in the United States, I went to see Charlie again and mentioned that we were looking for an American distributor, and he suggested that Paramount might be interested. Then he said, 'The *Orient Express* runs through Vienna, doesn't it? I used to work in Vienna, in a café there . . . I want to handle this film!' That was a totally British picture, shot over here, financed by EMI Films (all British money), and in those days it grossed something like $50 million. At that time it was the most successful wholly British film ever made. But it was Paramount who financed and distributed *Romeo and Juliet* and they also helped finance *Death on the Nile* because *Murder on the Orient Express* had been so successful.

Zeffirelli had made a great success of *The Taming of the Shrew* just before *Romeo and Juliet*. In fact, Elizabeth Taylor and Richard Burton were still working together in Italy and they came on to our set, so that I got to know them both quite well. That's one reason we got Elizabeth for *The Mirror Crack'd*. Zeffirelli's greatest successes have been with his Shakespearian films. These are very cinematic, untheatrical films of Shakespeare, and, while I may be biased, I still think *Romeo and Juliet* is his best – and so does he!

How did you come to make *The Tales of Beatrix Potter*?

That's another film I'm very proud of. It was

absolutely unique. It was made for £250,000 and I have never worked with such professional people as the ballet company [members of the Royal Ballet]. They were absolutely dedicated. We were in Rome, very nearly finished shooting *Romeo and Juliet*, when one day Richard said there were some things he wanted to talk to me about. One was that he was going to get married again – to Christine Edzard, who was our set dresser and had done a brilliant job. Then he said they wanted to make a ballet film of the tales of Beatrix Potter. I said it was a wonderful idea but who was going to finance it? He said, 'Oh, you'll fix that!' He hadn't produced a picture at this stage, but this was his and Christine's idea, jointly. They made all the costumes in their own house and we used my production company. Christine brought in that fantastic man, Rotislav Doboujinsky, who did the masks. It was all their conception, their idea, so I got behind it and pushed it but I thought it only fair that Richard should have the Producer credit. Although Christine didn't get credit as Director [Reginald Mills does], we couldn't have made it at all without her. She shares the credit for the screenplay, however. As a ballet picture it is quite different from *The Red Shoes* – it doesn't have one single word of dialogue.

We were extremely lucky that Bryan Forbes was the head of production at EMI, when we came to make *The Tales of Beatrix Potter*. He thought it was a terrific idea and he was in a position to say they would put up the money, as it was such a small budget. He was really supportive over the Beatrix Potter film, just as Nat Cohen later made such a difference to getting the Agatha Christie films made. He was head of production at EMI Films at the time we were making the Agatha Christie ones. He was very supportive and always saw that we got the money for the first two. This continued when budgets kept on going up because of all the stars we were using.

Why do you think those Agatha Christie films were so popular?

That is what Richard and I asked ourselves. Christie herself hated the films made from her novels up to that time, except for *Witness for the Prosecution*, and her agent kept telling me that he didn't think we had a chance. I told him how we wanted to do *Murder on the Orient Express*, and he said, 'Why don't you take her out to lunch?' So I did. I explained our ideas to her and then mentioned *The Tales of Beatrix Potter* and she said, 'Good Lord! That's something I really like!' From then on she was interested in what we wanted to do and that's how we got the rights.

Then we got Sidney Lumet to direct and that was really a coup. He had recently made some very successful films, including *Dog Day Afternoon*, and his name, along with Albert Finney's, suddenly made everybody want to be in it. I think the next person we got was Sean Connery and it grew from there. What's more, everyone except Sean Connery (who got a special deal) was on a flat fee. But a flat fee for everyone else – that's how we did it within budget, which was $1.4 million altogether! Mind you, it was a long time ago but, even so, it was very cheap. It made millions. And Tony Walton, who was also a great friend, was very important to the film in doing the production and costume design.

How did you find Bette Davis on *Death on the Nile*?

A great experience, it really was. I went to meet her at the airport, which apparently shocked and surprised her, and on the way back to the car I said, 'It is wonderful of you to come over here to do this film.' She drew herself up and said, 'You see, I'm not used to coming on location. Locations used to come to me!'

You produced David Lean's last film, *A Passage to India*. What do you recall of setting up that production?

That's a long story. When I was making *Harry Black* I was at the airport on Boxing Day morning in 1958 and bought a copy of *A Passage to India*. As I was reading it I thought, I'm making the wrong film, this is the one I want to make! I went to see E M Forster and had quite a lot of correspondence with him. He didn't want films made from his books, but he had liked *Harry Black* very much and I'd got him to the position where he said he thought I might get the right people together and so he agreed. Then he died without putting his agreement in writing. His great friend [E. R. Leach] was Master at King's College, Cambridge, who were his literary executors; he was very nice over the years, but wouldn't agree. Then he left and Bernard Williams became Master and he was a great movie fan. He agreed to let us make a film based on Forster's work.

Richard Goodwin and I decided that the one person who could probably make a success of the film was David Lean, who hadn't made a film for fourteen years. I rang him at the Berkeley Hotel and when he picked up the phone the first thing he said was, 'What happened in the caves?' He had already heard on the grapevine that I'd got the rights and he told me he, too, had been trying to get them since 1958. He agreed to meet us and, when he didn't like the script, we suggested he write it himself. So he did. Santha Rama Rau wrote the first draft and she got a credit for it because she had done a lot of work on it.

Having got David Lean, I thought it would be easy from then on, but we had a dreadful time. I went to see Paramount and Barry Diller, who was President at that time, said no, it was too risky. Then Warner Brothers thought of doing it but ultimately said no. It was eventually financed by Thorn EMI Films in this country and in America, for the first time, Home Box Office put in a lot of money, and Columbia took the US theatrical distribution rights. This was set up by John Heyman. It got eleven Academy Award nominations but only won two. Perhaps there had been too many British film winners in previous years!

Was *Little Dorrit* a very demanding project to put together?

It was Christine Edzard Goodwin's idea. She directed it and wrote the script. Richard asked me if I'd join with him this time and I agreed, so we co-produced it. We were able to get the money through Thorn EMI. But it was a really sad story because, although it is a brilliant piece of work, theatrically it wasn't a great success. On television and video, though, it is a fantastic hit. Christine did the costumes, the lot – a marvellous film. It was the last film I co-produced with Richard.

You were a member of the Prime Minister's Working Party on Films in 1975. What do you feel about the British Government's intervention in the film industry?

The interventions have been disastrous lately. The Labour Governments, particularly under Harold Wilson, were supportive. What Wilson did then (actually Sir Wilfred Eady's idea) was to create a means of circulating money through the industry without taking government money, and it kept the industry alive. That ended when the Thatcher Government took away all its support in the '80s. What the British Government did was to take away all support, all the props. There is no film industry in Britain at the moment; producers in this country are making films that the international market doesn't want.

In February 1996, Lord Brabourne added:

I think the situation has changed since we spoke, and that films are indeed being made for the international market in this country. Further, the situation may change, as far as support for the industry is concerned, if there is a change of Government in the next year or two.

Kevin Brownlow

b. 1938

Editor: *The White Bus* (1965), *Red and Blue* (1966), *The Charge of the Light Brigade* (1967) and many documentaries 1958–65

Co-director, co-producer and co-screenwriter (with Andrew Mollo): *It Happened Here* (1964), *Winstanley* (1975)

Director-editor of documentaries: *Ascot – A Race Against Time* (1960), *Nine Dalmuir West* (1966), *Abel Gance: The Charm of Dynamite* (1968)

Kevin Brownlow is Britain's leading film historian, his books including landmark studies of silent film: *The Parade's Gone By* (1968), *The War, the West, and the Wilderness* (1978) and *Behind the Mask of Innocence* (1990); and a biography of David Lean (1996). His historical research, marked by rigour and affection for his subjects, has also led to the production, with David Gill, of the highly regarded television series *Hollywood* (Thames Television, 1980) and *Cinema Europe: The Other Hollywood* (BBC2, 1995), to series on Chaplin and Keaton, and above all the magisterially restored version of Abel Gance's *Napoléon*, a labour of love extending over more than twenty years. He has also made what is arguably the best British historical film: *Winstanley* (1975), which recreates the failure of the Leveller and Digger movements during the Civil War and which dazzles the eye with its black-and-white imagery while it engrosses the mind and heart with the passion and intelligence of its narrative. That he has not been able to make another feature film since is perhaps the blackest mark one could register against recent British film history. And speaking of British film history, would some enterprising person empower Brownlow to make a full study of it to parallel his *Hollywood* and *Cinema Europe* series? *Interview date: September 1992*

How did you come to make *It Happened Here*?

I took a job as office boy in 1955 at World Wide Pictures, which was a documentary company. The first job I was given was to take some film cans to Humphreys Laboratories. While I was doing that a black Citroën suddenly screeched to a halt beside me and two men jumped out, ran into the shop and yelled back at the driver . . . I thought, 'Gosh, this is like a Gestapo raid. I wonder what would happen if . . .?' I was seventeen at the time and I decided I couldn't wait; I thought I was going to be the second Orson Welles. I wanted to prove it could be done, so I chose the most difficult scene – a big rally in Trafalgar Square. I financed it myself on 16mm with the £4 10s I earned each week, so it could only be shot at infrequent weekends. I staged a Nazi rally in Trafalgar Square and did one or two other things that got a bit of notice in the press, and quite a lot of interest resulted.

The film got more and more elaborate and still nobody was financing it. I had joined forces with Andrew Mollo, even younger than I was, who was already, in this period, a historian and who really knew the Third Reich. To cut a long story short, he

went into the film industry proper, into features. I had gone into the cutting rooms by this time but on documentaries. The picture Andrew went in on was *Saturday Night and Sunday Morning*. He was only a runner but he met Tony Richardson. After a few more productions he told Richardson what we were doing. Richardson asked how much it would cost to do it on 35mm and Andrew said, 'About £3,000.' Richardson said if we could do it for that he would back us. So we squeezed the budget as tight as we could, eventually going about a hundred per cent over. However, we did make *It Happened Here* on 35mm for £7,000, blowing up the 16mm we had already shot. It was released by United Artists and nearly thirty years later I'm still trying to get the rights back.

We had to do absolutely everything, except the processing, and it was so much fun that it gave us the feeling we didn't really want to work in an industry where you could only do one job. If we thought up a new scene, we could just do it as the film progressed. One thing we avoided like the plague – which was terribly self-destructive – was to write the script. Had we written the script much earlier on, we could have seen what the problems were. We put that off because it would have meant showing people our intentions, and that would have revealed our limitations. Eventually, we did write one, but we wasted a lot of time.

When the film came out, it received some very enthusiastic and some very condemnatory notices. We had proved we could at least make a film, but nobody wanted to employ us, because we hadn't proved we could make films which made money. *It Happened Here* had been appallingly handled by United Artists, so, despite having a quite high-powered agent, all we were offered was second-unit work. Andrew started a company called Historical Research Ltd and became a technical adviser on big films like *Doctor Zhivago*. I cut *The Charge of the Light Brigade* in the 1960s, then we tried to get another film together. Since nobody wanted to give us a job as professional directors, we decided to do it ourselves and not make any compromises. You can imagine how uncommercial it was, because we decided to make an absolutely accurate historical film with no concessions to entertainment.

Did you feel that *Winstanley* was not so much an historical film as a political film?

It's supposed to be both but it was a sincere attempt to recreate that period as closely as possible, without having to bring in melodrama and without having to alter the facts. It didn't work – nobody was interested in seeing it.

The only print I've seen was fairly aged, but it looked absolutely superb.

It was supposed to have the look of the silent films, particularly those of Dreyer, those deep blacks and so on. We tried very hard on that. It got a release here at The Other Cinema, and something very interesting happened which I've never known before or since. The owner of The Other Cinema, Nick Hart-Williams, said, 'Tell you what, we'll put it on with a whole lot of other films as well – the films that influenced it, the films you reacted against.' The irony is that the one film I really couldn't bear, which did exactly the opposite of what we were trying to do, was *Witchfinder General*: that is now a cult favourite. The films that influenced us included *The Parson's Widow* (1920), by Dreyer, which I loved, and *Chronicles of the Grey House* (1923). There must be something in me that goes straight back to the seventeenth century, because I found it so congenial.

One thing that comes over very strongly in *Winstanley* is the sheer physical arduousness of life. Was this one of the things you were aiming at?

Absolutely, and *we* had to endure it, of course, working in all the seasons – rain, heatwave and even in the teeth of a gale. But it was an attempt to make a film about an aspect of English history which is always ignored. There are films about all the great figures of history, but the lives of ordinary people have very seldom been looked at.

Did it get any kind of release after the showing at The Other Cinema?

Not any commercial release, no, although it's always being borrowed by film societies. It was bought for television but never shown. In fact one BBC executive told me he disliked it intensely. Our distributor in Australia was Bruce Beresford, who liked it, to my delight. He ran the BFI Production Board, before Mamoun Hassan, who took over in the early 1970s. It was Mamoun who did more than anyone to get *Winstanley* made.

Winstanley has a most pessimistic conclusion. Do you think this was a factor in its not being popular?

It Happened Here also had a pessimistic conclusion – I *like* pessimistic conclusions! In this case we presented it exactly as it happened. That's when the army and the landowners arrived and smashed the commune, so there was no possibility of an optimistic conclusion. After all, the monarchy was brought back in the 1660s. The chance that England had in 1649 was thrown away.

It's a very sobering film. You can't have expected to reach the audiences of *The Sound of Music*, surely?

No, but I hoped it would do better than it did in terms of reaching people. I hoped there would have been slightly more interest in what happened in the past in our own country. In modern films, people do take much more care over the visual look and even the authenticity of films. In Attenborough's Chaplin film, the chronology's all over the place but they have taken a great deal of care over the look of it. Certainly as far as British films go, the standard of accuracy of historical films of that period was excruciating. Even British war films – made shortly after the event – could be wildly inaccurate and nobody seemed to care about the standard of reconstruction.

Even some people who are quite serious about cinema would perhaps be more concerned about structure and story.

Well, you see, when I started *It Happened Here* I didn't care. What I wanted to make was an exciting melodrama about German-occupied England. But when I met Andrew he poured scorn on what I had done. He said, 'You have to be more authentic.' And I discovered, through him, that people, from Erich von Stroheim on, did care and did get it right – and what a difference when you saw it, when it was right.

However, when that was over there were even fewer offers than before, the only one being connected with the other aspect of my life. Jeremy Isaacs made a programme for Thames Television called *The World at War* which I wish to God I had worked on, because I think it was magnificent. To follow it up he decided to do one on immigration, which David Gill worked on, and then he decided he wanted to do the history of Hollywood. So I was asked if I wanted to do it. I thought no, I don't want to go into television, it would be awful. He said, 'Well, it *is* an ulcer-producing activity.' The meeting ended and I was out on the street when I collapsed suddenly. It turned out I had appendicitis and was carted off to hospital.

Eventually my wife persuaded me I should do the series. They asked me if I wanted somebody to work with and they teamed me with David Gill. As an artist, my father had always talked about his great hero, Eric Gill, the calligrapher/sculptor/artist, and David turned out to be his nephew. I decided the best thing to do was to show him lots and lots of silent films, but somehow I felt I wasn't getting through to him. He just wasn't responding, and I was worried. I thought maybe this was the end, nobody really cared much about them any more. But in fact David was tremendously affected, we became partners and we have stuck together for twenty years, doing these documentaries on silent film history, and restoring and reviving them with live orchestra for a new generation.

Andrew went off to do art direction: he did *Dance with a Stranger* and *Pascali's Island* and he's now doing a *Sharpe*, a Napoleonic Wars TV series in Russia. To my regret we've never worked together since *Winstanley*, simply because the damned thing didn't make money and didn't establish itself . . .

You've worked outside the mainstream of British cinema. If you had been working in that period of greater productivity, would you have been tempted to be a commercial director?

Yes, we did try and in fact there was a period when we were hired to do a film for Bryan Forbes's outfit at Elstree. Mercifully, we were fired from the film before a frame was shot. It was called *The Breaking of Bumbo*. We had a classic battle with the producer over casting. The producer was the son of David O Selznick and the grandson of Louis B Mayer, so you could see at once we would not get on very well. We had chosen a young actor to play the lead and the producer didn't want him; he wanted Richard Warwick, who is actually in it. We were so angry that, like fools, we confronted Selznick and you do not behave like that in the film business. He got rid of us. The young man's name was Christopher Cazenove. Richard Warwick was a perfectly good actor but not right for the part, whereas Cazenove was absolutely spot-on. The film was finally directed by Andrew Sinclair, who wrote the book on which it was based. It was never released, although it has been shown on BBC 2.

Who are the filmmakers you do admire in mainstream British cinema?

I now realise what it takes to be a director – it takes real talent to produce mediocrity, it really does! It takes much more talent to make a masterpiece, but it takes an awful lot just to make an ordinary film. Just to get it done. Everything is stacked up against you, so in principle I admire all directors unreservedly, because they have a hell of a job and I don't know how they do it. That's because I had a tough job on the pictures I made, I suppose. But in British cinema, there are the obvious ones – Alfred Hitchcock, David Lean, Carol Reed, Asquith to a degree before he got into his polished Rolls-Royce period – an awfully nice man though. Victor Saville is remarkable. I saw a film called *Hindle Wakes* directed by him and Maurice Elvey in 1928 and it has some astonishingly mobile camerawork in the fairground scenes, the roller-coaster stuff, which is terrific. It has a lot going for it; the only drawback is that they fudged the sets. They do real location shooting in the cotton factory, which is mesmerising, but the ordinary terraced houses they put up in the studio – it's heartbreaking. The British love to get inside a studio – even Carol Reed loved to. Again, it's my puritan nature. I can't bear exterior sets in the studio, it really hurts.

The 1940s and 1950s now look like a boom in the British film industry. Would you agree?

Yes, but again I still say the mid-'60s was the time when the British cinema began to produce a series of pictures of which you didn't have to be ashamed. I suppose *Saturday Night and Sunday Morning* is a bit earlier – 1960, wasn't it? The one I love, which was unconnected with all that, is *The Innocents*. I would agree with you as to the best of the 1940s films, *Fallen Idol* and so on. On the other hand, the average run of 1940s British films were British in a way that makes one's flesh creep – middle-class actors trying to play Cockneys. It wasn't until Ken Loach came along that you actually heard a whole variation of genuine Cockney accents on the screen, as strident as they really are. When *Poor Cow* came out, I remember thinking, 'My God! At last!' We'd never heard people talking in authentic Cockney accents. Before that they always gave people *Pygmalion* Cockney: 'Cor, strike a light, Guv.'

Lindsay Anderson always says that class is at the basis of why British cinema has not gained a wider international audience.

It seems to me that, in the early days, to practise a craft like photography, the British allowed the working-class and lower-middle-class people to handle the mechanics, saying, 'Go away and play with this but don't bother us.' And they became the professional photographers and gained a fantastic reputation for craftsmanship. Photography was all the domain of the lower class. Then when films came in they didn't quite know how to cope with this, so they went to the same people, 'uneducated' people. But you do need a bit more education to cope with adapting books, so occasionally they would allow a middle-class person to be a scenario editor or something. It wasn't until late in the 1920s that people like Anthony Asquith and Ivor Montagu began to come in – upper-class men, most of whom were extremely left-wing. Then you get someone like Alfred Hitchcock, a genuine south London lower-middle-class genius, and where he learned it all from I don't know. It seems to be from the Germans and the Americans he worked with at Famous Players, Islington.

What do you think of that smart-alec comment by Truffaut that the terms 'British' and 'cinema' are incompatible?

I think it's terribly funny; but you can't help thinking he's got a point. On the other hand, we have produced some of the most famous filmmakers imaginable, if you think from Chaplin through Hitchcock. They might have been working in America, but imagine if we'd had them all here in the right sort of environment, we would have had the most astounding film industry anywhere. But as soon as you poked your head above the parapet and showed any sort of talent, you emigrated. People like Basil Rathbone, Clive Brook, Ronald Colman, all left. In the English defence, it must be said that the Americans made sure our films didn't get decent distribution. When you see even a minor American picture, it's working on a different plane from so many English pictures. Take some of those early American films with people like James Cagney, for instance – the speed, the wisecracks, the sheer energy (and energy is very important) which is not encouraged in British pictures.

How crucial do you think a studio and a star system are to commercial cinema?

Much as I hate to admit it, I think they were very important. The ruthlessness of the studio system was very valuable, because they could follow failures up very quickly with successes and keep people working. On the other hand, when I made a commercial failure like *Winstanley* I never worked again as a feature director, and that's wasteful.

Dora Bryan

b. 1923

Actor: *Odd Man Out* (1947), *The Fallen Idol, No Room at the Inn* (1948), *Once Upon a Dream, Now Barabbas, Adam and Evelyne, Don't Ever Leave Me, The Interrupted Journey* (1949), *The Blue Lamp, The Cure for Love, No Trace, Something in the City* (1950), *Files from Scotland Yard, The Quiet Woman, Circle of Danger, Scarlet Thread, High Treason, No Highway, Lady Godiva Rides Again* (1951), *Whispering Smith Hits London, 13 East Street, The Gift Horse, Time Gentlemen Please!, Mother Riley Meets the Vampire, Made in Heaven, The Ringer, Women of Twilight, Miss Robin Hood* (1952), *Street Corner, The Fake, The Intruder* (1953), *You Know What Sailors Are, Fast And Loose, The Crowded Day, Mad About Men, Harmony Lane* (1954), *As Long As They're Happy, See How They Run, You Lucky People, Cockleshell Heroes* (1955), *The Green Man, Child in the House* (1956), *The Man Who Wouldn't*

Talk, Carry On Sergeant, Hello London (1958), Operation Bullshine, Desert Mice (1959), Follow That Horse!, The Night We Got the Bird (1960), A Taste of Honey (1961), The Great St Trinian's Train *Robbery, The Sandwich Man (1966), Two a Penny (1967), Hands of the Ripper (1971), Up the Front (1972), Screamtime (1983), Apartment Zero (1989)*

Although Dora Bryan engagingly claims not to remember half of the fifty-five films she has made, it is safe to say that no film-goer of the 1950s has ever forgotten her face or voice. Perhaps it is not surprising that the titles of the films often elude her: by her own account, she was rarely sent a script before turning up to do her day's shooting and she would learn her part in the make-up room. She played tarts with hearts of gold, conniving hussies, 'refeened' receptionists, vicious trollops, and a range of characters called Mavis or Maisie or Winnie or Glad or Pearl. In a few minutes' screen time, she could transmute dross into pure gold. Her approach to her career was to take what came along: she was – and still is – always busy on the stage, and film was really the icing on the cake. Nevertheless, apart from many two-minute delights, she did have more substantial roles in *The Fallen Idol*, *The Cure for Love* (in which she is irresistibly spiteful), as Glad, the warmhearted barmaid in the dull war film, *The Gift Horse*, as Gladys (again!), the Sultan's knitting wife, in *You Know What Sailors Are*, and above all as the ageing tartish Helen in *A Taste of Honey* ('Every wrinkle tells a dirty story'), for which she won a BAFTA award.

Interview date: July 1990

You seem to have mastered a great range of regional accents. Did you make a specialty of this?

No, but when I was making all those films in the '40s and '50s the parts were always written for little Cockney girls. I was living in London and I can pick up accents, so although I was born in Lancashire I found that a Cockney accent came more naturally to me than my own. In fact, when I came to do *Cure for Love* with Robert Donat and had to use a Lancashire accent, I felt a bit phoney; I never had that broad an accent, so I felt as if I were making fun of my upbringing, almost. I felt more comfortable doing a Cockney accent. I did do a 'refeened' accent in some films but people knew it was a pseudo-lady talking like that; for instance, in *The Great St Trinian's Train Robbery*, the refined lady I played sounded so 'fraffly genteel' I felt she would lapse into broad Cockney at any moment.

You made your screen debut with a small part in *Odd Man Out* ...

Yes, Carol Reed saw me in *Peace in Our Time*, in which Noël Coward had written a part for me, and gave me a nice little bit in *Odd Man Out*. It wasn't a speaking part but it was a telling little part of a young blonde girl in a telephone box. My next film was *Fallen Idol*, again for Carol – a much better part.

For many, *The Fallen Idol* really fixed you in their minds.

This was the first real filming I did. I have very strong recollections of it; I know I had to get up terribly early to get to the studio by seven o'clock for make-up. I lived in Piccadilly in those days and, having done a show at night, I was always terrified I wouldn't wake up. I used to have two alarm clocks set for five o'clock. No hired cars or anything, I used to get to Denham by public transport. On my first day I had on high-heeled shoes, a little red suit and a plastic mac. At that hour of the morning, of course, there was no one about to ask where the studios were, so there I was, walking through fields of snow in the depths of winter. I got there late, it was a quarter to eight; nobody could care less, of course, but I was so keen to be good on my first day.

I had no script, didn't have any idea what sort of part I was playing until Carol Reed met me on the set and explained the story to me. He told me the sort of feeling he wanted and said there were a few lines of dialogue, but that I could say whatever I wanted if I didn't like them. I asked him what I would wear and he said, 'Oh, just what you've got on,' and I was horrified to think I was playing a prostitute in my own clothes!

Carol was a very gentle director, lovely. I don't recall much about the little boy except that they had a bit of trouble with him; over the weekend his mother had his hair cut. Can you imagine what that did to the continuity?! I did my bit of filming all on one half-day. It was very quick, concentrated filming.

Did you reach a stage where you could pick and choose your parts?

No, I just took whatever came along. That's been my motto always – do everything you can, don't get choosy! It's amazing with some of the things you are offered, you think there isn't much to it and it turns out to be the best thing you've done. That's happened to me a few times, such as doing Mistress Quickly in *The Merry Wives of Windsor* [Open Air Theatre, Regent's Park, 1984]; I thought I'd have a crack at Shakespeare and I was so happy when I pulled it off.

You seem to me to have been a female version of Raymond Huntley in that you were instantly recognisable when you came on ...

Oddly enough, the lady who used to clean for me also cleaned for Raymond Huntley; she used to say to me, 'Ooh, you've not done any filming this week, Miss Bryan – Mr Huntley has, he's had two days down at Pinewood and he got £100 a day!' She used to go through his papers!

Did it worry you after this that you were often confined to small cameo roles?

Oh no. To me, my job was in the theatre anyway, so this was all extra, a bit of fun, a day's work for £100, which was a lot of money then. Anyway, nobody asked me to do any more major film work; if they had I would have done, because if they wanted you badly enough they would allow for the fact that you had to be at the theatre in the evenings.

You had a much bigger part in Robert Donat's *The Cure for Love*.

Yes, that was a long part and it took a lot of work, because Robert was ill a lot of the time and we'd sometimes hang around all day and he couldn't work. So that took us six months. I was in *Traveller's Joy* in the theatre at the time. Yvonne Arnaud got very cross about it because I was filming every day, and I had to get to the studio at seven o'clock every day in case Robert was all right. He chose me for the part; I wasn't tested, although Diana Dors was. I think they were a bit wary of me because I was working in the theatre as well and it was to be a long part in the film, but they didn't allow for my stamina!

What was your view of Robert Donat, as either a director or an actor?

As a director, I don't know. I really haven't had the experience of a director helping me with a role, apart from Carol Reed telling me to 'think it'. I liked Robert as a man and Gladys Henson, who played my mother, was wonderful; we got on so well and shared the same sense of humour.

Did it matter much to you who was directing?

No, not at all. I didn't even care what the script was, it was just getting down to the studio and meeting fresh faces again. Half the time you would get to the studio without even having seen the script. In my case the parts were never long enough to worry about, I could learn them while I was being made up! It was always a big surprise if I went to see the film, because usually I would have no idea what it was all about.

You have what amounts to a starring role as Gladys, the Sultan's wife, in *You Know What Sailors Are*. Was it fun to do?

That was a good part and I looked nice. There were other films going on at the same time and the people working in them couldn't wait to get on to our set, because it was all glamorous girls around a swimming pool. Akim Tamiroff was in it, a lovely man, and dear Shirley Eaton, too. I enjoyed that film; there was a very nice atmosphere. All I had to do was sit there, knitting or something, surrounded by my husband's concubines. But I didn't seek it out, it would have come through my agent.

What do you remember of playing a mermaid in *Mad About Men*?

I remember nearly drowning in it, because of the tail. It was at Shepperton and I can remember being wheeled down a corridor in a bath chair with the tail on. They had an enormous tank which was supposed to be the sea, with all the fish swimming around in it. All the fish were dead by the end of the day because Glynis Johns insisted on the tank water being so hot that the fish just gave up and died. When they put me in the water, the tail went up because it was buoyant, and I went down. It was very nasty, splashing around in the bottom of the tank. They fished me out eventually, by which time Glynis had gone back to her dressing room (in her bath chair) very fast. So they sent for Dunlop, who had made the tails, and I was sent home 'suffering from shock'. After that they put weights in the tails and we got used to them.

In 1958, you sang 'That Deadly Species the Male' in one of the most peculiar British films I know, *Hello London*, directed by Sidney Smith and starring Sonja Henie. Whose idea was this oddity?

I don't remember. What did I do? I can remember going to the studio and seeing the ice on one of the stages, and the ice was black. I did meet Sonja Henie and I recall she had a tiny body and rather a big face, and she wore a navy blue dress with white Peter Pan collar and cuffs, like a little girl. Other than that I don't remember a thing about it. Oh yes, she had oxygen tanks in her dressing room!

After a few more services comedies, such as *Desert Mice*, you had in *A Taste of Honey* what is perhaps the best role of your film career. How did you come by this?

About those services comedies, Basil Dearden

directed *Desert Mice* (and *The Blue Lamp*); I think he felt actors got in the way of his films! He was nice to me because I didn't give him any trouble, but generally I don't think he liked actors very much. *A Taste of Honey* was certainly my best film role – *and* I had a script! Helen was really *in* the film, not just a cameo. I've no idea how I came by the role but thank goodness Tony Richardson chose me. Although perhaps I shouldn't say 'thank goodness' because I didn't do many films after that. I enjoyed doing that part very much but I didn't realise the film would be such a success. It was filmed at Salford in Manchester and also in a big attic over two garages in London. The seafront stuff was all shot at Salford Docks. I saw the film again last year and loved it. And it's interesting to see a film in black-and-white now, after everything being in colour for so long; it adds something to it, gives it something of a documentary look. Tony Richardson gave a lot of direction to Rita Tushingham but it was her first film. With me, I think he cast me to be as he sees me. It's funny that, having won a BAFTA award for the film, no one asked me to do any films for such a long time.

You did a couple of thrillers – *Hands of the Ripper* for Hammer was one.

Yes, that was a nice part. I played a medium and I ended up being stabbed through the stomach, then I was hung on the door for a little while.

Kathleen Byron

b. 1922

Actor: *The Young Mr Pitt* (1941), *The Silver Fleet* (1943), *A Matter of Life and Death* (1946), *Black Narcissus* (1947), *The Small Back Room* (1948), *Madness of the Heart* (1949), *The Reluctant Widow, Prelude to Fame* (1950), *Tom Brown's Schooldays, Scarlet Thread, Life in her Hands, Hell is Sold Out,* *Four Days, The House in the Square* (1951), *My Death is a Mockery, The Gambler and the Lady* (1952), *Young Bess, Star of My Night* (1953), *The Night of the Full Moon, Profile, Secret Venture* (1954), *Handcuffs London* (1955), *Hand in Hand* (1960), *Night of the Eagle* (1962), *Hammerhead*

(1968), *Wolfshead: The Legend Of Robin Hood* (1969), *Private Road, Twins of Evil* (1971), *Nothing but the Night* (1972), *Craze* (1973), *The Abdication* (1974), *One of our Dinosaurs is Missing* (1975), *The Elephant Man* (1980), *Emma* (1995)

Representation of the erotic was never the strong point of British cinema, but there is a moment in *Black Narcissus* which, forty-odd years later, still seems remarkable in that respect. Kathleen Byron as Sister Ruth, in a Himalayan convent, mad with lust for the District Commissioner, suddenly appears out of her nun's habit, in a low-cut dress, applying lipstick to her mysteriously beautiful face. It remains a brilliant study in suppressed sexuality suddenly asserting itself and it is to the undying discredit of British cinema that it never gave her another comparably exciting role. She might, with half a chance, have been a great melodramatic heroine: she had wit, intelligence, sensuality and a flamboyant streak that she often used to salvage inferior roles. However, to be grateful for what we got, there is a clutch of films for Michael Powell which she rightly sees as the high point of her film career; and *Prelude to Fame* gave her some scope as a selfish obsessive manipulating a small boy's life. Though wickedness or madness possibly brought out the best in her, she was also a more interesting than usual straight lead in *The Small Back Room* and *Life in Her Hands*, both of which she imbues with individuality and appealing sympathy. The screen has wasted her talents appallingly in the last two decades.
Interview date: June 1990

How did you come to make your film début in Carol Reed's *The Young Mr Pitt*?

While I was still at the Old Vic Drama School, I came up to London to try to find an agent; I met John Gliddon, who was Deborah Kerr's agent, and he sent me to see the people who were doing *The Young Mr Pitt*. They gave me a part and after that I used to go around saying, 'I had two lines opposite Robert Donat!' I did very little after that because of the war and I was working for Censorship.

Your next four films were all made by Michael Powell. Would you agree that these gave you your most exciting opportunities?

Oh yes, one wasn't aware of it at the time, but I remember, when I was offered *Black Narcissus*, Michael Powell sent me a telegram saying, 'We're offering you the part of Sister Ruth; the trouble is, you'll never get such a good part again'! He had a very caustic way of talking. He was more or less right, though – it's still my favourite role.

Though *The Silver Fleet* was technically direc-ted by Vernon Sewell, how involved was Michael Powell as producer?

I suppose Michael did watch everything that went on but Vernon was there, he *did* direct us, and he was very kind and helpful; I was terrified, up to a point, and he was very encouraging, which was good because when I came to work with Michael you really had to be able to hold your own. I didn't think Micky was a great director of actors; I thought he used to put people down and upset them. It was only later, looking back at the way he directed, that I realised he was determined to get something from you and didn't mind how he did it. All he wanted was the best for that particular scene. At the time, I always used to fight with him. He wanted me to overstate the madness in *Black Narcissus* and I used to argue with him that the character didn't *know* she was mad. For one scene I argued with him about what I wanted to do and he walked off the set, saying to Jack Cardiff that I would tell him what I wanted; so I did. Jack set it all up and called Michael back to the set and he just said, 'Shoot it.' Afterwards he said, 'It wasn't what I wanted but it was very good.' I was lucky starting with Vernon Sewell; I think if I'd started off with Michael I would have come unstuck.

Did you feel *A Matter of Life and Death* was angled towards cementing Anglo-American relations?

I thought we were trying to be friends with all nations – particularly in that big courtroom scene with the jury lining up. I think Micky was trying to do a United Nations thing in it, seeking friendship between other nations besides the Americans and the British. The sets were fantastic; poor Kim Hunter had to run up that staircase, which was the most horrifying thing; there seemed to be miles of it. Michael was very good in his direction of those huge crowds and he was lovely to his technical crew.

I think your performance as the neurotic Sister Ruth in *Black Narcissus* is one of the most remarkable in British films. How do you feel about it now?

I saw it quite recently and I was quite convinced, even by myself, but a hell of a lot of it was the photography, and the music was fantastic, almost like a ballet. I didn't realise when I was stalking Deborah that there would be all that music to it. Although I had read the part, I didn't realise until I started doing it that it had such strength and power. I wanted to go into a convent to prepare for the part, but Michael said, 'Oh no, we haven't got time for all that nonsense!' I thought she was quite sane really, just doing a lot of thinking inwards. I think she *is* a bit touched by the time she takes off the habit and gets into the red dress to visit Mr Dean [David Farrar] in the bungalow. She's planning her escape. I think that's the beginning of the real switch to madness, which could have been avoided if he had been at all sympathetic, but he just sent her back.

What do you recall of working with Deborah Kerr and David Farrar?

Deborah, who was a very big star, was absolutely charming throughout, and as helpful as possible. It was only my third film and the previous ones had been tiny parts, and she used to whisper to me, 'Don't argue with him, just say, "Oh, what a marvellous idea!" and then do exactly what you want to.' She was very shrewd! Later on I met other leading ladies who were not so sweet! David Farrar lives near Durban now. He told me about ten years ago, when I was out there in *Separate Tables*, that he simply gave up his career once they started offering him parts as uncles or fathers of the leading ladies. It's a shame, he was a

very strong actor and he had a very rugged approach. Again, I wasn't impressed at the time by what he was doing; it's only now that I can watch him and think what a marvellous performance he gave.

How much latitude did Michael Powell give you in creating your own performance?

He expected you to have a feeling about it all and he wasn't going to tamper with that very much; but visually, it had to be the way he wanted it. I remember a shot in *Black Narcissus* where I say about Mr Dean to Deborah Kerr, 'All the same, I notice you're very fond of seeing him,' or something like that; it could have been said several ways, but Michael wanted me to say it right across the table, in a quite grotesque position, almost as if suddenly the devil had popped out. I didn't think it was necessary but that was how he wanted it done. I must say that after him I could cope with *any* director!

It must have been a shock to your system to have an almost conventional leading-lady role in your next film, *The Small Back Room*.

Yes. I nearly lost that part because of the censorship – you couldn't have two people living together and that was the whole thrust of the story, that he wouldn't marry her because he was not happy with himself. They had offered me the part and sent me the script; then I discovered the couple were to be engaged. I argued against it and sent Micky a letter saying I thought he had buggered up the whole story! Then I thought, 'What have I done?!' But they thought about it and agreed I was right.

I also remember on *The Small Back Room* that Micky said I was to wear those Dior 'New Look' clothes, with yards and yards of material in the skirts. I argued with Micky, saying that the film was set in wartime and we just couldn't get the material then; but Micky wanted me to look glamorous, so he said, 'If they remember that you wore the "New Look" during the film, then you've failed as an actress'! I enjoyed playing that un-neurotic character because I thought she had a nice lot of strength and quality. That and the *Black Narcissus* part were two wonderful roles and such a contrast.

You were 'wicked' again with Margaret Lockwood in *Madness of the Heart* . . .

I got a bit fed up with those 'mad, bad and dangerous-to-know' parts. I was a very nasty and dangerous character in *Madness of the Heart*. I did enjoy it, although the film was hard work because we did a lot of swimming around in a tank in the studio at Denham. I got jaundice from it. I didn't actually do the riding sequences in the South of France; they had a young boy with a wig on doing them. Margaret Lockwood wasn't very easy to work with. I know from other people that she can be very charming and sweet but I'm afraid our relationship was never very easy or cordial. Desmond Dickinson was the cameraman on *Madness of the Heart* and he said to me one day, 'You're only allowed close-ups in profile or if your face is distorted in anger – but we're getting round it!' Margaret had a great deal of power then and she certainly influenced which takes or prints could be used.

Did you ever feel anyone was looking after your career in films?

Not really. I owed a great deal to John Gliddon at the start of my career; he used to push for me but, later, of course, by the time I was in my thirties, when nothing much was happening, I had children anyway. I was asked to do a film for MGM; my agent sent me a script, which was for *Young Bess*, and I called him back saying it looked all right. He said it should be quite fun for me, going over to Hollywood, whereas I had thought it was to be made in the MGM studios in England. I was pregnant at the time but I went to Hollywood anyway, not telling anyone that I *was* pregnant. MGM were pleased with the way the film was going and they wanted to write scenes in for me with Charles Laughton; they thought I was very odd when I said that wasn't a good idea and that I wanted to get home! I might not have liked working there forever because I found it very unreal, but the time I spent there was very pleasant.

Do you remember a director I admire, Fergus McDonell, for whom you made *Prelude to Fame*?

I did like him, although he was very subdued. He was quite correct in everything he wanted done, never gave you a false move. We were doing it all on the Independent Frame technique, in which you had to make everything you did coincide with scenes of the opera house in Rome behind you, or going along in the car – terribly technical, and it didn't last. It was quite a difficult film to do. McDonell spent a lot of time with the little boy and with the musical side of it; he was quite musically knowledgeable, I think. He was very careful, and yet never very inspiring. My part was very unsympathetic, I recall; I haven't seen the film for a long time. It was based on an Aldous Huxley story ['Young Archimedes'] and my character was a bit cobbled together; she was a rich, selfish woman and yet she had to have some motivation because she wanted success – for herself, not for the boy particularly.

You made a lot of films at this time, including six in 1951. What sort of choice did you have over your parts then?

I think I tended to take what was offered. Some of them were quite good parts. Lewis Gilbert directed *The Scarlet Thread* with Laurence Harvey, who was impossible even then. If he hadn't got the camera on him he wouldn't bother to act. I do remember Philip Leacock, who directed *Life in Her Hands*, he was very charming. It was made on a shoestring; it was more or less a documentary made by the Crown Film Unit to recruit nurses. I actually got Paul Dupuis to come in and sing on it, as we were quite friendly at that time. Oh, and I had to learn to drive for that film – just so that I could crash into an ambulance.

What do you recall of the independent film, *Private Road*, for Barney Platt-Mills?

That was extraordinary. The script wasn't written when they were casting it and we were improvising a lot of the time while we were filming. It was quite an interesting way to work – not knowing quite who you were supposed to be or what you were doing. I think they ultimately did try to get a bit of script written; the young man, Bruce Robinson, loved working that way but the girl, Susan Penhaligon, didn't enjoy it any more than I did. Barney Platt-Mills was very laid back; we wouldn't start shooting until he felt 'in the mood', that sort of thing. It was an experience!

Michael Caine

b. 1933

Actor: A Hill in Korea (1956), How to Murder a Rich Uncle (1957), Blind Spot, The Two-Headed Spy, The Key, Passport to Shame (1958), Foxhole in Cairo, The Bulldog Breed (1960), The Day the Earth Caught Fire (1961), Solo for Sparrow, The Wrong Arm of the Law (1962), Zulu (1963), The Ipcress File (1965), Alfie, The Wrong Box, Gambit, Funeral in Berlin, Hurry Sundown (1966), Billion Dollar Brain, Woman Times Seven, Deadfall (1967), Play Dirty, The Magus (1968), The Italian Job, Battle of Britain, Too Late The Hero (1969), The Last Valley, Get Carter (1970), Kidnapped, Zee and Co (1971), Pulp, Sleuth (1972), The Black Windmill, The Marseilles Contract (1974), The Wilby Conspiracy, The Romantic Englishwoman, Peeper, The Man Who Would Be King (1975), The Silver Bears, The Eagle Has Lan-ded, A Bridge Too Far, Harry and Walter Go to New York (1976), Beyond the Poseidon Adventure (1977), California Suite, Ashanti (1978), The Swarm, The Island (1979), Dressed to Kill (1980), The Hand, Escape to Victory (1981), Deathtrap (1982), Educating Rita, The Honorary Consul, The Jigsaw Man (1983), Blame It On Rio, Water, The Holcroft Covenant (1984), Hannah and Her Sisters, Sweet Liberty, Half Moon Street, Mona Lisa, The Fourth Protocol (1986), The Whistle Blower, Jaws – The Revenge, Surrender (1987), Dirty Rotten Scoundrels, Without a Clue (1988), Mr Destiny, A Shock to the System (1990), Bullseye! (1991), Noises Off, Blue Ice (1992), A Muppet Christmas Carol (voice only) (1993), On Deadly Ground (1994), Blood and Wine (1996), Curtain Call (1997), The Shadow Run (1998)

'I've come to America to try to be a really big international star with a big following here in America,'[1] said Michael Caine with customary frankness in 1980. And, of course, through films good and bad, he has succeeded, though he was really well under way by 1980. A decade earlier he had complained (hyperbolically), 'I've never got good reviews for anything in England,'[2] and claimed later that 'You can't get anything done in Britain because it's top-heavy with bureaucracy.'[3] In 1977, he protested, 'I love my country and I want to live in it, but I have no intention of standing by and watching everything I've worked for taken away [i.e. by taxation].'[4]

He reached British stardom in the '60s, after some years in rep, television and tiny roles in films. 'Everyone in my crowd seemed go be coming into prominence. I was the last one to make it.'[5] He was first noticed in Zulu, cast – despite his well-known Cockney background – by director Cy Endfield, who 'was convinced my face was that of an English aristocrat . . . This was based on my "horsey" face, longish blond hair, and I was somewhat slimmer then.'[6]

The other aspect of his private life widely reported by the tabloids was his carefree sexual adventuring, and it was the womanising title role in Lewis Gilbert's Alfie that clinched his ascent. He recalls reading the script: 'It began: "Alfie turns to the camera and says: 'Never mind about the titles'" – and it was at that point I thought, the guy has an idea of film.'[7] He attributes much of the film's success to the audience's 'identification' of Alfie with himself: 'You had playing the leading part an actor whose private life was a bit of a symbol of that.'[8] And years later he said, 'I made Alfie in 1966 and he still won't lie down.'[9]

Nearly twenty years later, he worked again for Gilbert in Educating Rita and says, 'That was when I stopped worrying about the leading man's image.

The film taught me I could act anything on the screen and make it real.'[10] And so, many would claim, he can. Look at the record. For every misfire like *Blame It On Rio* ('just a romantic comedy in a lush place'[11]), there are two or three others where he appears, like many great film stars, to be doing very little but with absolute conviction. A selection of such titles includes: *The Ipcress File*, introducing bespectacled gastronome-cum-intelligence man, Harry Palmer, to films; *The Wrong Box* ('an antidote to *Alfie* . . . That picture was so English it went well everywhere except in Britain'[12]); the inventive thriller, *The Italian Job*, with its dazzling car chase; *Sleuth* ('People thought I'd be over-awed . . . but Larry [Olivier] hadn't done a full-length role for ten years'[13]); Huston's *The Man Who Would Be King* ('It's a marvellous role for me. Humour, a good change of pace, a real gift'[14]), working with his coeval, Sean Connery; *California Suite*, as Maggie Smith's homosexual husband; and *Hannah and Her Sisters*, for which he won a best supporting actor's Oscar.

It's an impressive list and, though he is now very critical of the British film industry, it can claim some of his best work. He has, as he says, been willing to go out on a limb, as some of these roles suggest. His career bears out this statement of 1985: 'I'm a completely committed movie actor . . . and Britain doesn't produce many of them . . . I think the subtlety of film acting is wonderful.'[15]

1 Marjorie Rosen, 'The man who would be Caine', *Film Comment*, July–August 1980, p 21
2 David Austen, 'Playing dirty', *Films and Filming*, April 1967, p 7
3 Rosen, p 21
4 Anne Billson, *My Name is Michael Caine*, Muller, London, 1991, p 116
5 William Hall, *Raising Caine*, Sidgwick & Jackson, London, 1981, p 97
6 Austen, p 7
7 Hall, p 114
8 David Austen, 'Making it or breaking it', *Films and Filming*, May 1969, p 16
9 Elaine Gallagher, *Candidly Caine*, Chivers Press, Bath, 1990, p 106
10 David Lewin, *The Sun* (Melbourne), 12 March 1987
11 *Screen International*, 15 October 1983, p 18
12 Hall, p 127
13 Hall, p 158
14 Billson, p 106
15 *Films and Filming*, January 1985, p 28

Phyllis Calvert

b. 1915

Actor: *Discord, Anne One Hundred* (1933), *Two Days to Live* (1939), *They Came By Night, Let George Do It, Charley's Big-Hearted Aunt, Neutral Port* (1940), *Inspector Hornleigh Goes To It, Kipps* (1941), *The Young Mr Pitt, Uncensored* (1942), *The Man in Grey* (1943), *Fanny by Gaslight, 2000 Women, Madonna of the Seven Moons* (1944), *They were Sisters* (1945), *Men of Two Worlds, The Magic Bow* (1946), *The Root of All Evil, Time Out of Mind* (1947), *My Own True Love, Broken Journey* (1948), *The Golden Madonna, Appointment with Danger* (1949), *The Woman with No Name* (& co-pr) (1950), *Mr Denning Drives North* (1951), *Mandy* (1952), *The Net* (1953), *It's Never Too Late, Child in the House* (1956), *Indiscreet, A Lady Mislaid, The Young and the Guilty* (1958), *Oscar Wilde* (1960), *Battle of the Villa Fiorita* (1965), *Twisted Nerve* (1968), *Oh! What a Lovely War* (1969), *The Walking Stick* (1970)

Phyllis Calvert had already made ten films before she became a household name in the 1943 period romance *The Man in Grey*. Along with her co-stars, Margaret Lockwood, James Mason and Stewart Granger, she became identified with the Gainsborough melodramas that enjoyed so remarkable a success in the mid-1940s. Phyllis Calvert was usually cast in the 'good girl', 'English rose' mould, and it says much for the intelligence of her playing that she held her own in these roles and made them interesting. She made the most of the showy role of the schizophrenic heroine of *Madonna of the Seven Moons*, was sympathetic and believable as *Fanny by Gaslight* for Asquith, and made good use of Launder and Gilliat's dialogue in *2000 Women*. All three of these were released in 1944, the peak of her Gainsborough period. She had perhaps her best role in Alexander Mackendrick's *Mandy*, in which she showed a tough-minded understanding as the mother of the deaf and dumb child; and in 1958, in *Indiscreet*, as Ingrid Bergman's sister, she played the first of a series of incisive character roles – on screen, stage and television.

Interview date: October 1989

Your career seems to divide into pre-Gainsborough, high Gainsborough and post-Gainsborough, with a sidetrack to Hollywood ...

I think that's a marvellous idea but I always think that my Gainsborough days were war days and, of course, the war did break up one's life. Oh, Gainsborough was wonderful – I don't say all their films were wonderful, but they made *Kipps*, they made *The Young Mr Pitt*, all the Launder and Gilliat pictures. The ones that made money were the ones we were in – *The Man in Grey*, *The Wicked Lady* ...

In the early stages of your career you worked with a number of notable comics, including George Formby in *Let George Do It*. What do you recall of this?

Well, I was learning my craft. The parts weren't all that terrific but I loved doing comedy and I made friends of Richard Murdoch and Arthur Askey. George Formby was protected by Beryl, so I didn't really get to know him. He was a strange creature, he seemed to be quite brainless but he was a brilliant technician. In one number he was singing and undressing at the same time, getting into pyjamas, cleaning his teeth, getting into bed and putting the light out on the last bar of the song. He never deviated; he was absolute perfection. It's hard to believe now but he was the highest paid entertainer in his day.

In 1941 you co-starred with Michael Redgrave and Diana Wynyard in *Kipps* for Carol Reed. Did this feel suddenly like the big-time?

I have never felt like that in my whole life. I did my job and that's it. Originally for *Kipps* I was cast for the Diana Wynyard part [Helen] and Margaret Lockwood was going to play the maid. I went to have my clothes fitted, all these beautiful clothes that Cecil Beaton had designed for Helen Walsingham, when they told me Margaret didn't want to play the maid's part and they'd got Diana as Helen and I was to play the maid. I burst into tears. Everybody in that film was playing a character who was acting a part – they were trying to get on in society, or trying to be a different person – the only 'real' person in it was Anne, the maid, and that is how I got such good notices! As for Carol, he didn't give a lot of advice but he encouraged one to be courageous. If it didn't work he would say no, try it such and such way, but half the time your courage was your creativity.

You worked for him again in 1942 in *The Young Mr Pitt*.

Yes, he was under contract to the same company. They cut a lot of me out of the film eventually. They put me in as a love interest, but there wasn't really any of that. But I had played the Cockney maid in

Kipps, so they wanted to use me again, though Robert Donat, who had seen the clippings from *Kipps*, had said I was completely the wrong person to play a duchess. One day I was standing outside the studios waiting for my car and he walked out. I had never met him. He looked me up and down and went back into the studio. He went straight to Maurice Ostrer and said, 'I've just seen the girl I want to play the part!' The film was propaganda, really. It was during the war and they made it to keep the spirits up.

Your period of intense Gainsborough activity began with *The Man in Grey* in 1943. Did it make household names of you, Stewart Granger, Margaret Lockwood and James Mason?

Margaret was already a household name but it certainly did that for the rest of us. *The Man in Grey* was also the first Gainsborough film to make a great deal of money. Don't forget it was wartime and people wanted films to make them forget the war. I suppose it happened at just the right moment. It is the only film that has had two West End premières. It had one première, got terrible notices, went through the provinces and made so much money that it had to come back to London.

How far were Leslie Arliss as director and Ted Black as producer responsible for its success?

Arliss, not at all. We all said we would never work with Leslie again and I never did, although the other three did. He was a lazy director; he had got a wonderful job there and he just sat back ... Ted Black was the one who would watch it, cut it, and know exactly what the audience would take. I don't say he wanted to do really good films, but he knew where the money was and he made all those escapist films during the war.

Was there a lot of care devoted to costumes, settings, historical period?

Tremendous, yes. Elizabeth Haffenden was the main costumier and she was very clever. She did a great deal of historical research on the costumes all the time, and of course we had Cecil Beaton – you couldn't get higher than that! He did *Kipps* and *The Young Mr Pitt*; Elizabeth did *The Man in Grey*. Don't forget, I was an antiquarian bookseller and I had a tremendous collection of costume books, which we made use of when we did *Fanny by Gaslight*.

Was the modern 'frame' story at the auction to permit a happy ending?

It was in the original book; I suppose they wanted the family to go on, to feel that all wasn't lost. We can put up with sad things when there isn't a war on but it is difficult to be entertained during a war by seeing something sad. You needed something that had a beginning, a middle and a happy ending and that's what they did. They weren't great films but they filled a gap at that time.

This was the first of a number of 'good girl' roles for you. Did you yearn for wickedness, or were you just as happy making a career out of goodness?

I was *not*! I was under contract for seven years and at the end of those seven years, it took me *ten* years in the London theatre to prove that I wasn't just the girl that all the troops wanted to marry, that I could act. I played all sorts of rather vicious parts after that but it took me ten years to get rid of that image, which had stuck to me like Araldite. I do think it is much more difficult to establish a really charming, nice person than a wicked one – and make it real.

Do you feel films like *Fanny by Gaslight* and *Madonna of the Seven Moons* showed goodness as finally triumphant but also allowed audiences to experience the thrill of wickedness along the way?

Oh yes indeed, although of course there wasn't the sort of sexual permissiveness there is today. At that time you couldn't have two people on a bed together unless their feet were on the ground! But in *Madonna of the Seven Moons* we got away with it by having a very dark room, with the two heads on the pillow – there was just a light on our faces made by the cigarettes we were smoking. You couldn't see the foot of the bed, it was too dark. Sex wasn't talked about in those days; it was there, implied, we all knew it happened.

Whose idea was the final image of you with the cross and the rose?

I think that was our director, Arthur Crabtree. If that film had been made today, you would have seen the rape, the passion on the bed, but *then* it had to be imagined. Arthur was a very good cinematographer, but there weren't enough directors, and so people who were scriptwriters or were behind camera were suddenly made directors, and they had no idea about actors at all. It wasn't that Crabtree was an unsatisfactory director, just that we found ourselves *very* satisfactory – we did it ourselves. But the fact that he had been a lighting cameraman was wonderful for us, because he knew exactly how to photograph us.

1944 was a big Gainsborough year for you, with *Fanny by Gaslight*, *2000 Women* and *Madonna*. I admire *Fanny* most of these films . . .

Yes, I do too. I'm not very good at watching my old films but I did watch that. It was a little slow but it holds together even nowadays, I think, and it was a fascinating story. I adored 'Puffin' [Anthony] Asquith, but I think he reached his peak some years before *Fanny*. Remember *Pygmalion*? But then, maybe he was like me and had to earn a living, so he did the films he was asked to do. Of course the director OKs everything, décor and so on. It was a marvellous cast, and Wilfred Lawson was my favourite actor, I loved working with him. It's lovely to work with someone you have admired. In my young days I had great heroes but when you work with them they are just ordinary people. But Wilfred Lawson never lost his magic.

They *were Sisters* would, I suppose, have been rather insultingly called 'a women's film' at the time but it had a powerful performance from James Mason. Very dangerous and destructive.

Oh yes, and this has come out so much into the open lately but all those things were suppressed then. Now you never stop reading that people are bashed about. Yes, it was a very good performance. Dulcie Gray was very good too – a very underrated actress, I always thought.

After making several films with Launder and Gilliat as screenwriters, you were directed by Gilliat in *2000 Women*. How did you find him as a director?

I loved Frank and Sidney; we were tremendous buddies *before* I did *2000 Women*. They asked me to play the nun who falls in love with the airman, and I said I just couldn't do that. That broke up our friendship. Pat Roc played the part I was originally cast for. From then on I didn't see much of them – they didn't like me turning down a part they had written for me, which I can understand. I enjoyed playing Freda Thompson, though. It was a great film to work on, except that Renee Houston and Flora Robson didn't get on at all. And Thora Hird – and her little girl, Janette Scott – was in it too. Thora told me she didn't know how to keep Janette off the stage and I told her not to try, it was a talent that ought to be encouraged. And there was Betty Jardine, who died in childbirth. She was a great young character actress in those days, very clever indeed.

Men of Two Worlds **must have seemed a change of pace to you. Was Thorold Dickinson notably different from the other directors you had worked for?**

I loved him. I enjoyed being in the film enormously but one thing that worried me was that all my clothes were so beautifully pressed and that didn't seem right if I was supposed to be in the jungle; but they told me I would have had all sorts of people doing those things for me. It was all rather tricky because we had American negroes and African negroes who used to have great fights on the set. They spent a year in Africa doing the exteriors, although I didn't go, then a year in the studios after that. It was the most expensive film ever made in England at the time, £2 million or something. It was a Government-sponsored film and it was to show what we were trying to do in Africa, trying to get people out of the villages and into the big towns so they would have education and health. And of course we were fighting the witch-doctors. It was done with very high-minded notions. I didn't know Thorold very well but he coped with the situation marvellously. Thorold was very good with the coloured actors. He left the rest of us to our own devices pretty much.

Someone has summarised the Paganini life story, *The Magic Bow*, as 'Violinist's childhood sweetheart lets him wed French aristocrat'. What do you think of it?

I tried to get out of it, it was the *last* thing I wanted to do. I rang Granger up and asked him if he thought we should do it. I didn't want to do it, it was absurd – I made more laughs out of that film than any other, and the way Granger played the violin! He had the leader of the London Philharmonic bowing and someone else doing the fingering, and he had a little man standing underneath . . .

Maggie [Lockwood] was cast in it too and we both went along to see Rank himself on Park Lane. There was a long onyx table in the room and he was sitting at the end of it, a very big man. We came in through the door and Margaret went around one side of the table, and I went to the other. Then he stood up and said, 'I hear you've coom ter talk about more brass.' Mostly, he was absolutely charming. He was very nice, until I signed a contract with America and he turned my picture to the wall. He admitted that in *Time* magazine.

You made a film for Independent Film Producers, directed by Ladislas Vajda, called *The Woman with No Name*, with the young Richard Burton . . .

At the time he couldn't act for nuts! I had just seen him do *The Lady's Not For Burning* and thought he would do for this part, so I cast him (I was co-producer). He told me he had saved some money and had just taken out a mortgage on a house. It had three floors; he had the middle flat and he intended to let the upper and lower flats. He said, 'I will never have to work again!' That's sweet, isn't it?

How did you find working at Ealing again (in *Mandy*) for the first time since 1940?

Well, you were talking about directors, and there was a perfect director of actors, Alexander Mackendrick. Sandy was the first person who let me cry naturally. In the early days if you were to cry, you had to have tears streaming down your face but no frowning or looking ugly. He was a wonderful director. Then he went to America. I think *Mandy* was a very moving film. Sandy Mackendrick really was sensitive to actors. He was the first man who had directed me since Carol Reed. There was a long time in between!

When you worked with Ingrid Bergman and Cary Grant in Stanley Donen's *Indiscreet*, had you made a conscious decision to play character parts?

I was very lucky as far as character parts go: *Mandy* was my first break; my second was theatrical, when Wendy Hiller came out of *Crown Matrimonial* and I went in to play Queen Mary. Those two gave me the entrée into character parts, which is difficult, because they always expect you to go on being glamorous. But I liked the part in *Indiscreet* very much.

Ian Carmichael

b. 1920

Actor: *Bond Street* (1948), *Trottie True, Dear Mr Prohack* (1949), *Ghost Ship, Time Gentlemen Please* (1952), *Meet Mr Lucifer* (1953), *Betrayed* (1954), *The Colditz Story, Storm Over the Nile, Simon and Laura* (1955), *Private's Progress, The Big Money* (1956), *Brothers-in-Law, Lucky Jim* (1957), *Happy is the Bride* (1958), *Left, Right and Centre, I'm All Right Jack* (1959), *School for Scoundrels, Light Up the Sky* (1960), *Double Bunk* (1961), *The Amorous Prawn* (1962), *Heavens Above!, Hide and Seek* (1963), *The Case of the '44s* (1964), *Smashing Time* (1967), *The Magnificent Seven Deadly Sins* (1971), *From Beyond the Grave* (1973), *The Lady Vanishes* (1979), *Diamond Skulls* (1989), *The Great Kandinsky* (1996)

For about five years, Ian Carmichael was one of the 'hottest' stars in British films. He came in towards the end of the British cinema's most prolific period, but between 1955 and 1960 he established himself securely in the popular imagination. His image was essentially that of slightly bumbling innocent abroad in a corrupt world, but he combined this with a capacity to play the romantic element convincingly. As a result, he was indisputably a leading man rather than a character comedian and

British films have always been richer in the latter than the former. It was Muriel Box's persistence in casting him in *Simon and Laura* that initiated the series of slightly frazzled young men on whom he worked skilful variations over the next few years. However, it is with the Boulting brothers that his name is inextricably linked – as the relatively sane centre of their satires on various British institutions. Stanley Windrush, the character introduced in *Private's Progress* ('Feeling a little fragile, sir,' he confided to his sergeant), made him a major British star, and he repeated the role three years later in *I'm All Right Jack*. The 'silly ass' strain is less apparent in *Lucky Jim*, and *Happy is the Bride* gives him a more or less straight romantic lead; he adapts well to their different demands. Semi-retired, he still appears occasionally, most recently in *The Great Kandinsky*.
Interview date: September 1989

At the start of your film career, you had unbilled roles in three late '40s films. Do you remember these parts and how you got them?

Through my agent. They were bit parts, one-day parts, and I felt a little lost. I remember I was on location in Camden Town for *Trottie True*. The director was Brian Desmond Hurst and the cameraman asked me at one point, 'What are you doing here?' and I said, 'Well, the director's just told me I've got to do so and so, but in this bit of script they sent me I do something else,' and Hurst heard this, turned round, and absolutely snapped my head off with, 'Will you bloody well learn to do as you're told?' I never looked favourably on Brian Desmond Hurst from that day onwards.

You were in *Meet Mr Lucifer* (1953) and *Simon and Laura* (1955), which satirise television. Did '50s British cinema respond well to the threat of television?

I think they were terribly frightened of it for a long while. Front office was very reluctant – if they had contract players, like Associated British or Rank – to let them appear on television, fearing it would do them infinite harm. It took a long time for them to realise they could start selling their old movies to television. I don't think the film industry took television into serious consideration. As for *Simon and Laura*, I've done that in three different media. I did the stage play, then Muriel Box was directing the film for Rank. She had a hell of a battle with them, because she wanted me to play my original part in the movie, but they said, 'We must have a name that means something in the cinema.'

On the stage the stars were Roland Culver and Coral Browne, whose names would have meant nothing at provincial cinema box offices. So, in the film, there were Kay Kendall and Peter Finch and myself and Muriel Pavlow. Muriel Box fought for me and I was the only one from the theatre who went into the movie. Then, a few years later, when I repeated it on television I moved up one, and played Simon. I did some television direction for the BBC in the early days, and I had enough experience to know that, in many ways, the technical aspects of *Simon and Laura* were incorrect. It has hardly ever been shown again, and I wondered if it was because it was all old-hat now, technically, in regard to television.

In 1954 you made your only American film, *Betrayed*, with Clark Gable and Lana Turner. Did you find notable differences between American and British film production methods and attitudes?

Again, it was the star system. I had a very good part in *Betrayed*, a tip-top light comedy juvenile role written by Ronnie – now Sir Ronald – Millar. But it was an American company (MGM), it had an American director, with very big American stars, and I never got a look in. They never did the reverse shots, I had no close-up, and they gradually whittled my part down. I remember vividly my only scene with Lana Turner. She was ill in bed in hospital, and I went in to take her some flowers. I was standing at the end of the bed talking to her and it was either over my shoulder or close on Lana Turner. This was my experience with a Hollywood company.

You made several films in rapid succession. Were you being carefully groomed?

No, I wasn't. I think I got parts purely as a result of my name coming to the fore a bit in the theatre, as with *Simon and Laura*. Then came the Boulting brothers, and that was an entirely different matter. They'd got two subjects: *Private's Progress* and *Brothers-in-Law*, and they wanted a man to play both parts. I'd just done *Simon and Laura* on the stage. I thought that, once I'd got out of revue and into a play (it was my first for a long while), there might be a chance for me getting into the cinema, because casting directors in those days didn't look upon revue performers as actors. Then suddenly I got these two parts from the Boultings and I told them what I just told you. They said, 'You're quite wrong, dear boy, we gave you the part because we saw you do that undressing-on-the-beach sketch in a revue and we knew we wanted you, but we couldn't remember your bloody name.'

Did you find noticeable differences between the methods of the two?

Yes, but, if I praise one more than the other, it is trying to compare two splendid directors. I found with the Boultings that many actors who worked for them usually *preferred* the one they worked for first always; but they were *liked* by everybody. It was John who first directed me, in *Private's Progress*, and when you're inexperienced in the cinema you really want all the help you can get from the director and John gave me that. I found him very sympathetic and tactful. He could bring out a performance without ever raising his voice. But this is not to say that Roy isn't very good too. In those days they used to take turns to direct and produce, because they both enjoyed being on the floor. You always talk of the Boultings as a team, as 'the Boulting brothers'. There was never any kind of conflict between them.

How influential was the Stanley Windrush character in your career?

Enormously. It was the big break for me, into national – as distinct from West End theatre – recognition. As soon as I read it, I thought, 'God, this is a funny part,' and I fancied myself playing comedy. It was a bit overshadowed five years later when I did *I'm All Right Jack*, because I was repeating a performance. We all were, with the exception of Peter Sellers, who was brought in new and fresh. He was given a tremendous part and he did it brilliantly.

It's perhaps one of the most cynical British

films. What, if anything, is it in favour of, do you feel?

I think they would like to feel they were exposing the frailties of both sides in industry, but I don't think there's any doubt that the unions were a bigger target than management. There was such opportunity, they provided such material with their pomposity and follies. It was about time somebody took them down a peg and the Boultings did it. But they didn't neglect also having a go at management. It still works because it is still topical.

You also made *Lucky Jim* for the Boultings. It seems to me entertaining, though in a different way from the novel.

There was trouble with *Lucky Jim*. I don't think I named names in my book [*Will the Real Ian Carmichael* . . . , 1979], and I would hate to do so now, but a triumvirate got hold of the rights to *Lucky Jim* – the late Patrick Campbell, who was a journalist, his then lady friend, who eventually married him, and the director I prefer not to name. They'd got this script and they asked me to play Jim. I had a contract with the Boultings for five movies; I could do what I wanted between these movies, but they had been marvellous to me and I admired their experience, so I naturally asked them about this. I think they'd like to have done it, though they didn't like the script terribly much. Anyway, the first fortnight we were in one set – the big quadrangle in the university – and it was on the large stage at MGM, and I personally found the director intimidating. Whereas the Boultings whispered in my ear, he was apt to stand behind the camera and shout, which I didn't like very much. This production company worked through British Lion, who were distributors, and by now the Boultings were on the board of British Lion, and they were not happy with the daily rushes. After two weeks they, i.e. British Lion, who had the power to do so, sacked the three of them, including the director, and on the following Monday morning John Boulting took over. It was a ten-week schedule, of which two had gone. Now John was hamstrung inasmuch as we were already in production on the floor and he had to accept largely the existing script. The Boultings always believed you should start with a script and work to it. So John was stuck with that script, and then the next day, when he came on, there was terrible trouble with an actor called Hugh Griffiths, who hadn't liked the changeover and who was a pal of the original director. Generally speaking it was a bloody mess.

At the end of it all, not a bad movie came out, which was lucky, but it was a bit of a hybrid. For my part, I'd done two greenhorns, two innocents abroad, and was most anxious not to do a third. I did want to try and give Jim at least a bit of backbone and John helped me. If the over-all product still looked as if it was in the same mould, as I suspect it did a bit, that is because there *was* a similarity in script and he was a man against authority, really.

I wondered what you recalled about working with the great Robert Hamer, in *School for Scoundrels.*

He was very, very unhappy really, because he had just been taken off the bottle. One was aware all the way through that he was nursed along by the producer, an American called Hal Chester, who used to pick him up every morning, bring him to the studio, and take him home every night to make sure he *went* straight home. He managed to last for about eight weeks. Then, when I came down for a night shoot in London, he was absolutely sloshed. The producer sent him home and himself directed that night's work and brought in a new director to finish the film, a man called Cyril Frankel, who never actually got a credit. In the weeks I did with Hamer, I felt the *effect* of his alcoholism was on him – he was beyond his best powers.

In your last film for the Boultings, *Heavens Above!,* **yours is a guest appearance. Did you do it as a favour to them?**

Entirely. They rang up my agent and Roy said – they were excellent salesmen, the Boultings – 'You know this is John's major opus, he spent ages on this. It is so sad that we can't find a big part for Ian

in it, but there's one small part he *could* play. I wonder if he would like to,' and told me what it was [the new vicar who replaces Sellers at the end]. They were very fair, they paid me very well for doing it. I did it as a favour, because I owed them so much and I wanted to be in the movie.

Did you find satisfying film roles hard to come by in the '60s?

Very much so. I was very 'hot' in the '50s and the early '60s, and I seemed to be first choice for anything that was funny, but I had such a high standard as a result of the Boulting pictures that I didn't want to make inferior movies. Like so many actors, I kept saying, 'Will somebody please find me a nice Cary Grant-type part. Can I please have a *North by Northwest?*' And they never came, and by the mid '60s, with the New Wave that came, that sort rather dropped off. When a film called *Hide and Seek* came along, I was sure this was going to be it. It was produced by Hal Chester, who'd done *School for Scoundrels*, and it had a superb script. However, it turned into a chaotic mess, with Chester breathing down the neck of the director, Cy Endfield, and it ran weeks over schedule. It was an enormous disappointment for me – I don't think my one chance of a 'gear-change' even got a London showing or press show.

Would you say the later '50s were the key part of your career?

Oh yes, I saw only five or six years of it, but I think the happiest five or six years of my whole career. There *was* a studio system, there *were* contract artistes. I was in on the tail-end of that, and as an actor I was terribly happy, working the hours I liked and doing something I loved.

Maurice Carter

b. 1913

Set designer, art director, or production designer: *Bees in Paradise, Miss London Ltd, Dear Octopus, The Man in Grey* (1943), *Give us the Moon* (1944), *Jassy, The Root of all Evil, Good Time*

Girl (1947), *The Bad Lord Byron, Snowbound* (1948), *Christopher Columbus, The Astonished Heart, Mr Drake's Duck, Trio* (1949), *I Believe In You* (1951), *Made in Heaven* (1952), *Desperate Moment, A Day to Remember, Top of the Form, Always a Bride* (1953), *The Seekers* (1954), *A Woman for Joe, To Paris with Love* (1955), *The Spanish Gardener* (1956), *Campbell's Kingdom, Doctor at Large* (1957), *The Wind Cannot Read, Violent Playground, The Square Peg, The Thirty-Nine Steps* (1958), *Upstairs and Downstairs, Follow a Star* (1959) *Doctor in Love,*

Double Bunk (1960), *The Boy Who Stole a Million, No Love for Johnnie, No My Darling Daughter, In the Doghouse* (1961), *It's Trad Dad, A Pair of Briefs, Lancelot and Guinevere* (1962), *Two Left Feet* (1963), *Becket, The Beauty Jungle, Guns at Batsai* (1964), *Battle of Britain, Anne of the Thousand Days* (1969), *10 Rillington Place* (1970) *All Coppers Are* ... (1972),* *The Land That Time Forgot* (1974), * *The People That Time Forgot* (1977)
* Co-screenwriter, uncredited.

'Carter has a great appreciation and understanding of art and this and his pen and watercolour technique should take him a long way.' So wrote Edward Carrick in his 1948 study *Art and Design in the British Film*, and it proved an accurate prediction, in that Maurice Carter went on to design ever more demanding feature films and was twice nominated for Oscars – for his work on *Becket* and *Anne of the Thousand Days*. In fact his career covers over forty years of British cinema history, during which time he worked at most studios and saw major changes in the nature of production design. He had first-hand experience of working with such other masters of his field as Alfred Junge and Alex Vetchinsky, and is articulate about the challenges of Technicolor and other improved camera techniques for his craft. He is responsible for having made good films better (e.g., *Good Time Girl*) and bad films such as *Bad Lord Byron* and *Christopher Columbus* at least worth looking at when they weren't worth listening to. British cinema has a fine tradition of production design and Maurice Carter is one of those who helped to shape it.
Interview date: June 1994

You are listed on the credits sometimes as Art Director, sometimes Production Designer, or Set Design. Does it make a difference?

When I first started in the business, both here and in America the accepted term was generally Art Director. Then they formed a guild of art directors in England; John Bryan and others sat down and decided that their assistants should be promoted to the title of Art Director and they would take the title of Production Designer. They felt they had become much more involved in the construction of the film and probably 'designer' was a more cover-all title. They were always involved in supervising the building of sets, but they became involved in costume and various other art aspects of the film

like the storyboard. I think 'Set Design' is now a somewhat old-fashioned term.

The earliest credit I could find for you was on *Bees in Paradise*.

My first picture was actually *Tudor Rose*. I came to the studios halfway through it. Then we did a whole series of the old Will Hay comedy films, but nobody used to get credits then except the art director. They were very sparing on credits in those days! *Bees in Paradise* was the first credited film I ever did. I knew Val Guest, the director, fairly well because he'd been a gag writer at Islington [one of the Gainsborough studios], and knew I was then an up-and-coming art director. I worked there with Alex Vetchinsky, who used to give me a lot of licence; I was virtually doing art direction work although not getting credits.

You did a lot of work for Gainsborough throughout the '40s. Did you have a contract there with Gaumont-British?

No, I didn't have a contract until much later in life, with the Rank Organisation. It didn't feel insecure because it was then an entirely different business. Islington was like a repertory company. Everybody sort of mucked in, except for the electricians, who were already unionised, so you daren't touch a light. But everything else, except cables and so on, you moved, with our dear old director Marcel Varnel (who directed most of the Will Hay films) squawking at us. There was no time limit as to when you finished the day. In our case, it would be Jack Cox, the cameraman, who would say he'd had enough and he'd send his assistant up to get his hat and coat. I didn't really approve of the trade-union activity when it began to dominate the business, because it made it very difficult to operate. Of course we [art directors] felt the impact of trade unionism more than anyone else because our responsibility was to get the set there and get all the furniture on. I suppose we and the production manager were the people who used to suffer, because you'd have guys saying they were knocking off for supper, or they wanted an extra hour's pay because it had been dusty that day, and so on. I think we are all grateful for the limitation on hours and not having to be in the position of accepting the director arbitrarily saying we were going on until eleven o'clock that night, after a full day's work.

Not having a contract, would you therefore have been out of work between films?

I just went from one film to another because that's how the studio was run. If there was a week's break in between, they paid me just the same, but at that time budgets were very low and they would have cried their eyes out if the studios had been idle for a week, with the overheads going on. No, they just made one picture after another, using two stages. Islington was an incredible place; every piece made in the shop had to be moved up in a lift because it was on several floors, so you had to think in terms of making each piece to fit the size of the lift.

Did you work at Lime Grove as well as at Islington?

Yes, because in the later '30s I was varying between art director and assistant. For instance, I went with Alfred Junge as his assistant to do a Jessie Matthews picture, *Climbing High*. I was hauled backwards and forwards between the two studios.

In the '40s you were working on some of the most expensive of the Gainsborough films, like *Jassy* and *The Bad Lord Byron*. Were they mostly done at Lime Grove?

Yes, they were. The facilities at Lime Grove were very good. Islington had only a tiny little backyard for storage, otherwise we had to leave things out in the street. When we were shooting *Bank Holiday*, for instance, we wanted sand for a beach. We couldn't put it on the stage initially, so the lorries came and tipped it into the street. It was an embarrassment but that's the sort of limitation we had at Islington, in a building only adapted as a studio from an old power house.

Would you take part in early discussions with the director and the writers?

Not at Islington, but much later on at Pinewood I did. I got involved quite early on for the films I made for Sydney Box, and from then on I was fairly much involved, particularly for all the pictures I made for Tony Darnborough, the Somerset Maugham pictures, and later in most of the major pictures I did.

Who else would have been involved in those early discussions?

The director, the costume designer, and sometimes the director of photography, although usually they came in very late, because they would be working on other productions. The cameraman was probably one of the last people engaged. Because I was preparing the sets before the start of production, I would be involved for quite a long time. For instance, I worked on *The Battle of Britain* for six or eight months before shooting commenced. The most pleasant part of my work, the design, research and location-hunting, took place well before production began.

Films like *Jassy* and *Good Time Girl* have most impressive sets. When you were designing, would you specify that something ought to be made of wood, or plaster or whatever?

Yes, I would specify the materials, together with the construction manager. Set-making has always been a big part of a film's budget but it goes in phases. Later on, with films like *Becket* and *Anne of the Thousand Days*, we had really heavy, carefully-treated plaster and gave detail much more attention, because by this time cameras had so much improved that it became a necessity. As camera definition improved, we gradually improved the quality of the sets. It was very rough in my early days because the camera just couldn't comprehend it.

Good Time Girl has a very impressive look over a wide range of settings. Were you pleased with your work as set designer on that?

Yes, reasonably. It was not the most inspiring subject as to settings but working with David Macdonald was always fun, and I had enjoyed the making of *Snowbound* with him. Once Sydney and Muriel Box came to the studio, they had a large hand with the scripts. For instance, on *Christopher Columbus* we had the original script, which I thought was pretty good, and they decided to rewrite it. So one weekend I went up to their house to help where I could. They divided the script into four parts and they each wrote a part in separate rooms, shouting between two terrace doors to each other. It was all rewritten that way.

Finally the film ran out of money because the budget was inadequate, in building the ships, mainly. One of the ships was burnt to the waterline because one of the nightwatchmen didn't quite understand wooden boats and made a fire on deck to cook his supper! It was the *Pinta* that was lost. It was essential to show, at some point, all three ships together, but sadly now there was no money left in the kitty, not even enough to make an optical. All we could do was to add the silhouette of the *Pinta* on a back projection plate of the other two, with a cardboard cut out suitably moved in the projector beam. I loved doing the sets for it, though. Apart from the ships themselves, most of the money probably went on the Spanish Court, in settings and costumes.

Did the studio have a great stock of furniture of various periods?

No, Lime Grove never kept a big property stock, it was all hired in. Denham did have a big stock, though. It was the set dresser's and the buyer's job to go out and hire all the furniture at Lime Grove. I would do sketches of the set and illustrate the sort of thing I wanted and, as time went on, I became more and more detailed. It saved talking!

Which personnel did you tend to have most contact with?

Apart from my assistant and set dresser, I suppose I worked pretty closely with the director of photography – and the costume department, of course, because the worst thing was to get a clash between costume and set.

Elizabeth Haffenden was in charge of costume at Gainsborough for quite a long time.

Did you have much contact with her?

Yes, Liz would ask what sort of colours I was thinking of for the main part of the set and she'd say, 'That's what I had in mind for the costume,' so we'd come to a suitable compromise. I can't ever remember us getting into a clash of any sort, we always compromised. Later, when Liz Haffenden and Joan Bridges collaborated as technical advisers, then I had a bit of a problem and life became more complicated. Joan Bridges came over with Natalie Kalmus and they were teamed as the Technicolor experts. I'm afraid that we clashed somewhat, as Natalie was a little overbearing, a bit difficult to deal with. I had direct dealings with her as I had to show her all the colours I was using. We'd have a fabric for a chair, for instance, and she'd say, 'Oh no, that's too red,' because of the great colour exaggeration of Technicolor. We don't have that problem any more, of course, but originally if you wanted to show an orange on a table, you had to paint it like a lemon as the gain on the red register was enormous. The Americans didn't seem to get hold of colour restraint as quickly as we did, we had much more subtle colour. We got hold of it particularly through John Bryan. He had come from Denham and they had really got down to working with the Technicolor process there, and he was wonderful. John really made most of his sets basically grey, with just a slight emphasis of colour coming in where required.

You worked with some very distinguished directors of photography: Arthur Crabtree. Geoffrey Unsworth and Douglas Slocombe. Did it make much difference to you who was the cameraman?

The main thing always is the light source – the direction of light and how the set was to be lit. John Bryan liked to put ceilings on his sets and I rather tended to follow him. That was where I came into a big battle on *Becket* and *Anne of the Thousand Days*. I was building Tudor sets, a period when ceilings rarely exceeded eight or nine feet high, so the sets obviously needed ceilings to be seen. You couldn't shoot the length of a palace room without having a ceiling but the producer, Hal Wallis, insisted on no ceilings because he reckoned it slowed up shooting as they would have to be lit with reflectors and so forth. On this, I collided head-on during the making of those pictures, but he had to give way to me in the end. I couldn't build a set that went up ten or twenty feet high, it just looked absurd; but the battle continued, set by set by set.

As you can imagine, he was a pretty dogmatic man and John Bryan came into collision with him as well, in similar points on *Becket*. (John was production designer and I was art director.) When John had stonework to do, for instance, and needed dyes mixed for it, he wouldn't paint it; he would have the plasterers mix dyes into it as it was cast, because he believed that you could not obtain the effect by surface paint. He felt stone had a life of its own in depth. Finally, the plaster was wire-brushed when it came out of the cast, to obtain the porous quality of real stone. It was important because it showed on the screen.

I think *Jassy* was your first colour film. Did it make any difference to you whether you were working in black-and-white or colour?

Oh yes, it's much more laborious to work in colour. You have all the painters working for you and you have to watch each man on the set, watch what he's using and go with him when he mixes it up in the bin. You couldn't just say, 'Use Number Two Grey,' it wasn't possible. You had to watch the colours being mixed and guide it step by step. It was more exciting, of course. I mean, people think in colour – at least I do, I've never thought in black-and-white. But it was never pure white because the light would 'bounce' off it.

Would you have to know a good deal about fabrics and how they were going to photograph, too, as part of your work?

Yes. There was a big difference between using wool and artificial fabrics, for example. Wool fabrics usually gave fairly true colour to the Technicolor process, whilst artificial fabrics – certainly things like nylon – and even cotton looked very different than as seen by the eye. So you had to know about how much colour error the fabric would give on screen. It was much more difficult than designing for the stage. Now, of course, the latest colour processes present colours almost as you see them. But with three-strip there was so much variation because the laboratory could print it just about any way they liked – they could vary it and you wouldn't know whether it was you or the labs at fault when you saw the rushes.

You worked quite often with the same directors. How much did you count on directors to give you information about the sorts of sets they wanted?

It mattered a lot who the director was, but I'm afraid you usually had to tell *them* what they required. They only had the script to go by. I often had to get in touch with the writers and ask about the nature of this or that character – was he an old-school-tie man? Had he been in business? and so on. It was important to know, because how can you build a room and dress it unless you know what the man's interests were, the things he was likely to be involved in? On the whole the writers were more helpful to me than the directors. The director is interested in how the action takes place; if he had a definite idea he would tell you, but normally you would put down a plan of the set with sketches and tell *him* how *you* saw the characters moving within it for various scenes.

You obviously had close associations with John Bryan, Andrew Mazzei, Vetchinsky and Alfred Junge. I'd be interested in any recollections you have of them.

My first art director, Alex Vetchinsky ('Vetch'), was a wonderful character; a sweet man. I don't quite know how he did his designs for films because he never made a sketch. He'd draw on the back of an envelope for me, or a page torn out of *Homes and Gardens*, and that was as much instruction as I got. He was very happy for me when I moved up to become an art director myself. What he had, firstly, was great knowledge of set-building: when he had your idea he could see how to build it into a form that was very easily shootable; he would work out how to leave out the whole side of a set with a foreground piece of masking. He had a very good perception of shooting and he could put it over to a director – except when he came to Hitchcock, because, as you can imagine, Hitchcock took little instruction from anybody! We worked for Hitchcock on *The Lady Vanishes*, a phenomenal film, and we were trying to pack this huge station and train by building in perspective in a tiny studio which was only ninety feet long.

Andy Mazzei was lovely, a very quiet man and a good designer, very efficient. There was a team of us at Lime Grove – Andy, John Bryan, Wally Merton, myself – all working at the same time on alternate pictures. John Bryan had come from working with Korda at Shepperton and he came over to Islington to art-direct *Dear Octopus*; I was his assistant on that and our long association went on from there.

Then I worked with Alfred Junge during that time of moving between Lime Grove and Islington. Junge was a German, very dogmatic but a wonderful art director and he did brilliant sketches, so you had no lack of information, you just reproduced the sketch. He had a clause in his contract that he would set the long shot, the major establishing shot of the set, and with the cameraman he would also light it. He was virtually a lighting man himself and it was a very dominant, positive form of lighting he had learnt in the old UFA studios in Berlin. Art direction in England was basically German, and that's how it ties up with Alfred Junge. At that time we had numbers of Germans, in special effects especially, and used a process called the Schufftan process. Then Korda, who was the dominant importer of crews from his old studios in Berlin, brought in Andreyev and people like that – importantly, Ferdie Bellan. Ferdie was a man who seldom gets recognition but he dominated in the background of films. He was mainly a sketch artist, he did sketches for Andreyev and many other art directors and he was also a great scenic painter. That's where he actually started. He worked mainly pre-war, during the '30s, at Denham and later at Shepperton. It was this German influence from which we all took our cues. The same with the colour restraint, it all came from that basic German influence; the lighting, too, with that Expressionist look about it.

How did you like working at Pinewood?

Pinewood was a fine studio; it had every facility and none of the restrictions I had been used to working with. They had a whole department for special effects – and when you think that 'special effects' at Lime Grove was one little man called Guido Garibaldi, confined to one little room . . . He was a great technician on opticals, the first special effects optical man I had come across. But he blew himself up eventually; he was very hot on explosives (literally) and one day he was packing French letters with explosives which would be thrown into the water and explode on contact. He was mixing up these explosives when he sneezed – and it blew the roof off his little room! He was left standing there in the remains of his underwear.

At Pinewood they had things like a great store of doors and windows – you could choose just what you wanted. There were whole set-pieces you could choose from. The most dreadful thing in an art director's life is meeting the budget; it's such a transient thing, something you can't really get hold of. We used to sit down at Pinewood and set a budget for a film; they would ask you, 'How much do you need for the ballroom?' when you hadn't even drawn it yet, and if you went a bit over the budget you got a good old stripping down. You

wouldn't get the next picture – that was the penalty. I did eventually get a contract with Rank but, if you went over budget consistently, they would simply not renew your contract.

On the whole did you have a good experience working with the Rank Organisation at Pinewood?

Yes, I think so. It was the first time I'd had a contract so I knew where I was going to be for a couple of years (the contracts used to run for about two years). I had some very unfortunate dealings with John Davis, though. My very favourite producer of all, and one of the most talented producers I ever met, was Tony Darnborough and Davis absolutely demeaned him. He didn't actually fire him but he got him into a position where he had to resign. Davis was an accountant and that was the doom of the studio. It was very difficult, having to be penny-pinching with the sets, and it became harder and harder – this business of being accountant-dominated at all times.

A lot of those Pinewood films involved location work. Would you have gone on location?

Oh yes, always, because there was often a lot of construction work to be done on location and sites to be chosen. Very seldom was the location accepted as it was. For *Campbell's Kingdom*, for instance, we had to build the dam in the Italian Dolomites. The worst thing I had to do up there was to build a lift, a cable-car which had to be capable of carrying a lorry. It wasn't possible to fake it, they had to be on it and a lot of shooting was done from it. They took terrible risks by overloading it, although I'd built it as best I could with Italian labour – and in the snow, working in the most bitter cold.

You worked quite a lot in the horror/fantasy/science fiction genre late in your career.

Yes, I've always been very interested in special effects. At Islington we were in the early days of back projection and we had a great projectionist called Alf Davies. He and I worked hard on back projection. We had enormous problems in those days because, with arc lighting for the projector, you always had a hot spot. We did a lot of work with trains, for instance, on the Will Hay pictures and we had to work out how to link the foreground piece of train with the perspective of the actual train on the plate, how to get them to work together. If someone was hanging out of a train, you had to build the piece of train he was hanging on and then join that exactly with what was on the back projection plate. We would work it out on a drawing board and provide a diagram of camera angle and lens for the people who were going out to shoot the plates. You had to tell them exactly where the camera was to be – how high, how far off the centre-line of the track, and so on. I gradually became more and more involved in that sort of work, was eventually involved in the large business of getting front projection to work on films like *Battle of Britain*. That was an enormous job; the travelling alone was stressful. We had about seven sites in England and three in Spain, where building was going on, but of course I did have three other art directors working with me in different areas. Just building all those dummy aircraft was an enormous task in itself, especially the ones that had to be burned. We had to build the inside construction as they actually were, because when you burned the skin off all was revealed. We had lawn-mower engines in them on the ground, to turn the propellers. We actually had only three or four real flying Spitfires going at one time; all the rest were activated dummies.

You mentioned storyboarding before. Did you like this process and were you very much involved with it?

Yes, I liked it very much, I often did my own storyboards if I had time. Directors liked them too. It was very much in the interests of economy; you could just point to a storyboard and say, 'That's what we're doing.' That's why Hitchcock was so good. He drew them himself for every shot, for the cameraman and everyone else.

Julie Christie
b. 1941

Actor: *Crooks Anonymous* (1962), *The Fast Lady, Billy Liar* (1963), *Young Cassidy* (1964), *Darling, Dr Zhivago* (1965), *Fahrenheit 451* (1966), *Far from the Madding Crowd,* *Tonite Let's All Make Love In London* (1967), *Petulia* (1968), *In Search of Gregory* (1970), *The Go-Between, McCabe and Mrs Miller* (1971), *Don't Look Now* (1973), *Shampoo* (1974), *Nashville* (1975), *The Demon Seed* (1977), *Heaven Can Wait* (1978), *Memoirs of a Survivor,* *The Animals Film* (1981), *The Return of the Soldier, Les Quarantièmes Rugissants* (1982), *Heat and Dust* (1983), *The Gold Diggers* (1984), *Miss Mary, Power* (1986), *Agent Orange: Policy of Poison* (1987), *Mémoire Tatouée* (1988), *Fools of Fortune* (1990), *Short Step* (1991), *The Railway Station Man* (1992), *Dragonheart, Hamlet* (1996), *Afterglow* (1997)
* Documentary.

When Julie Christie swung into the High Street of Billy Liar's grey northern town, she brought not merely a challenge to Billy's fantasy-dominated life but as well a whole new kind of high-spirited, open sensuality into British films. It was a time when many new breezes were blowing through the often musty corridors of British cinema of the time, with social realism as the dominant strain. Julie Christie, having made her debut in an amusing traditional comedy, *Crooks Anonymous*, almost missed this 'new wave', but found herself in demand for many of the most prized women's roles throughout the rest of the decade. She worked twice more for John Schlesinger, winning an Oscar for that archetypal '60s film *Darling*, and for Truffaut, Richard Lester and David Lean, lighting up the elephantine *Dr Zhivago* when she is on the screen, and becoming an international star in the process. She matured rapidly as an actress, and gave three remarkable performances in short order in Losey's *The Go-Between*, Altman's *McCabe and Mrs Miller* (very affecting as the tough Cockney madame out west) and Roeg's alarming *Don't Look Now*. In later decades, she chose many of her films for their ideological slant, and returned triumphantly to the stage in Pinter's *Old Times* in 1995. *Interview date: July 1994*

Did the 1960s seem like a great time to be embarking on a film career?

I suppose the only way to know that is in retrospect. Perhaps one thing that made it better than it was before was that women were allowed to look natural: they didn't have to have their hair permanently fixed and make-up all over their face all the time no matter what daredevil adventures they were up to. I did actually make a couple of comedy films early on and it drove me mad, all that doing your hair up and wearing make-up and posh clothes, no matter what was happening, with people keeping you looking like a china doll. I couldn't have borne that, if that was what filmmaking had had to be. Suddenly naturalism – or realism – came in, just as it had in Italy in the neo-realist cinema after the war, and I was lucky to be part of that. It was also the subjects of the films and the way we were allowed to behave. Suddenly we were able to challenge audiences to accept us – which they did, because it was the right time, for whatever reason. That, I suppose, made it a good time to come into film as opposed to earlier.

Also I think the '50s was a very, very bad time for women in films. I don't think the '60s were necessarily very much better in terms of their status, but at least women were allowed to be rebellious creatures, they weren't necessarily either madonna or whore as they had been in the '50s. I would say that women's lot in film is improving – not the middle-aged woman's but the *ingénue*'s lot is improving. There is a sexual objectification of women in films at present which, to me, is reminiscent of the '50s, but I don't think women are expected to be submissive in films now.

Having trained for theatre at the Central School of Speech and Drama, did you find this a useful background for film acting?

I wasn't in the least interested in film acting, in fact I rather looked down on it. The films were an inferior way of expressing your art and the Central School had nothing to do with film at all. I can't remember any of the process of learning or unlearning specific techniques for the cameras; all I can remember is that awful business of having my hair done and so forth, which I couldn't stand. And there was the business of photographers and being taken to parties, none of which was on the cards for me, because all I wanted was to get on to the stage and be an actress. It wasn't until I made *Billy Liar* that at last nobody gave a hoot about what I looked like. That was outside the system, and the people who made those films felt themselves to be outside the system and they didn't approve of that kind of fabrication of stars at all.

How did you come to be in the two Ken Annakin comedies, *Crooks Anonymous* and *The Fast Lady* which, though conventional, are quite attractive and good-natured films of their kind?

When I emerged from drama school I think I was considered especially good-looking, and people were always on the lookout for the good-looking girls, just as they are with models today. I think it was purely on looks. Ken Annakin was very kind to me but we were on different wavelengths. I was crazy on French film and, if I was to be in a film, I wanted it to be a *Nouvelle Vague* film. Instead, there I was in a bikini, my hair piled up on top of my head and wearing a hundred pounds of lipstick. If I were doing those films now, of course, I would quite enjoy them; I would look on them as pieces of entertainment and do my job as best I could. Then, it was intellectual snobbism; I was very young and young people are apt to be snobs of one kind or another. Those two films were quite high-class entertainment with very skilled people in them, like Stanley Baxter and the wonderful Leslie Phillips.

Did you find such people instructive to work with?

No, I didn't find them instructive at all – I was far too snobby for that! I thought I was much too good for them, you know, and didn't talk to anybody. I'd go roaring away from the studio on a motorbike every evening, thinking I was just the last word in nonconventionality! I was in that sort of state and I wasn't learning anything from anybody.

For many people, including me, when you swung down that drab northern street in *Billy Liar*, you seemed to announce a new spirit in British films. How did you feel about the part of Liz?

I can't remember much about the actual part because other factors were much more dominant. One was that at last I was in a New Wave film, an English equivalent to the French stuff, so that I was realising my ambition to be in class (in this case *working*-class!) films, something that aspired to be a reaction against the status quo, which is what I wanted to do most of all because I thought myself a rebel. The other thing I remember was absolute terror, because I hadn't a clue what I was supposed to be doing from beginning to end, although John Schlesinger was very good to me.

Did you share Liz's approach to life?

I can't say I did. Despite the fact I thought of myself as a rebel, I was very shy, and Liz wasn't shy. She was also of a very different class from me, so that when she got lifts from lorry drivers she had the confidence of equality, whereas I would have been absolutely paralysed by my awful middle-classness and unable to say anything at all. In a way it was her class that gave her her strength and I didn't have that class.

Do you think it's a major disappointment that Billy hasn't the nerve to go off with her?

No, not really. When you read a script you understand the aspirations of the film and what you are contributing to, the shape of it, and I was contributing to something the shape of which had to end the way it did. The outcome was very much the point of the film, I think. For all his fantasising,

Billy is trapped; he is as conservative as anyone else. I wouldn't agree with John, however, that the ending was triumphant; I think it is a successful ending because it is a truthful one.

You did three major films in the '60s for John Schlesinger, plus the television version of *Separate Tables* in the '80s. What did you like about working with him?

It wasn't so much that we had a good working relationship as that John was so terribly kind and a very dear person. I have a great fondness for him and we understand each other. After *Darling* I think we both understood a lot about each other's weaknesses and faults and that bound us together. It wasn't until I did *Separate Tables* that I was able to relax and really appreciate John as a director. Beforehand I was terrified of the whole acting business, but in *Separate Tables* his skills as a director of actors really struck me – and they worked, because I think I gave a good performance. Some people might say that, considering my unresponsive attitude, his skill with actors was manifest from my first film with him!

What kind of direction did he give?

He gives a lot of direction – he is an actor's director – as opposed to Joe Losey, who doesn't give much direction. Of course John was an actor himself; he knows what he wants and he is jolly well going to get it. He is watching you all the time and, if it's going well, he lets you get on with it. If it's not going well, he is with you and altering it for you.

***Darling* won a number of Oscars, including yours for Best Actress. It seems to me a key film of the '60s. How do you feel about it today?**

I think it is a film of its time. I'd call it very good source material for the '60s. I think it needs a bit more time before I could judge it on a 'forever' basis, but that sharp, slick dialogue grates a bit now. It's a bit too slick, not naturalistic, so I think one would have to wait a bit longer to see it as a product on its own and whether it holds up as a period piece.

I can't think of another film in which the protagonist is such a silly, selfish, superficial character as Diana Scott. Was it a difficult role to play, to keep her interesting?

It wasn't difficult for me, I think it was probably the easiest part I've done! I *was* pretty silly, selfish and superficial then, if I'm not now! I understood a lot of what that silly girl was going through. I did despise that vacuous, empty-headed part of her, although one should never despise one's character, but I was reading a lot of highbrow books and being an intellectual snob at the time. But the rest – all that ruthless selfishness and superficiality – I understood very well indeed.

What was your experience of working with your two notable and very diverse co-stars, Dirk Bogarde and Laurence Harvey?

I must stress that fear was the experience which dominated my work in films, then and for a long time afterwards. I never had confidence in myself as an actress because I hadn't quite learned it through. I was put much too early into too big parts and I wasn't prepared for them, didn't have the grounding. So my main feeling was that people were being kind to me because I was so terrified. Certainly they were both very kind to me.

Laurence Harvey was leading a very sophisticated life then, very jet-setty, so I didn't have much to do with him. He worked terribly hard too: during most of the filming of *Darling* he was also working in a play at night and he had to have B-12 injections in his bum to keep him going. I remember being terribly impressed by that because I was knackered just doing the film, whereas he was working on the film all day, then working in a play half the night and probably going off to party after that. Anyway, I liked him very much indeed, even though we said hardly more than a few words to each other.

Dirk was a darling and still is; he's a very special and dear man and I was very lucky to be working with him. What a treasure for an inexperienced, frightened young girl, to have this terribly experienced, kind person acting right opposite! And of course he is the most wonderful actor to act with – he gives you everything when you work with him, so that you're transported into the situation. He holds nothing back and he's there.

Your third Schlesinger film was *Far from the Madding Crowd*, from the Thomas Hardy novel. Did you find it useful to go back to the original text?

Well, at that time I was not only selfish and superficial but also lazy, I think. I don't remember doing proper work on those things. I think I just walked in and assumed I would be directed through them. I wish I had done more preparation because I don't think I was very good in that. I am about to do a small part in a medieval thing and I am simply immersing myself in medieval history, none of which will be of the slightest use and nobody will know any of this stuff except me, but it is essential

to get a backing for my character. I didn't do that then and I should have studied the Hardy book with a fine toothcomb. I have done since and I understand it so much better than I did then, I'm afraid. I certainly read it at the time but not with attention: I didn't explore it or investigate its detail like a historian, which I should have done. I now know that the original book is the best thing you could possibly have because you are being led, told what you feel by the author. It's marvellous – you can't make those mistakes, you have beautiful stage direction. Screenplays don't tell you what you feel or why you feel it; all that is extra work, whereas if you have a book with all the signposts up, it's an enormous help.

Far from the Madding Crowd was shot in Dorset, a most beautiful place and very important to my life. I lived in a little cottage and I remember driving to work very early each morning, seeing the dew in the trees – and lots of dead animals on the roads, too, because it was early and they hadn't been cleaned up yet. How fast motorists travel on country lanes! Apart from that, it was a wonderful experience, after which I decided I was going to live in the country.

Peter Finch was the most wonderful actor I've ever worked with, almost. What an actor! First of all, I admired Peter on screen, I just couldn't keep my eyes off him. It wasn't that he was the most wonderful person to work with but that he was one of the best *actors* I've ever worked with. I think his work is so complex, dense, original and heartfelt, I could watch him forever. The other quality Peter had as a screen actor was his charisma and that is sometimes missing in such a good actor. It was a privilege to work with him, thrilling. And in the part of that awful man, the pain – oh, he was lovely!

Throughout the '60s you were stunningly photographed by Denys Coop in *Billy Liar*, Freddie Young in *Dr Zhivago*, Nicolas Roeg in *Fahrenheit 451*, *Petulia* and *Far from the Madding Crowd*. How important was the cameraman to you and did you become technically expert?

Never! That's what I mean about being lazy – what an opportunity to miss! I really rejected the idea of beauty, which is such a shame; all the lighting just drove me potty. I just didn't appreciate the power it gave me as an actress. I think I resented the attention and the skill that was lavished on me in that area. I wish I had taken that opportunity to learn, because it's a wonderful skill and art. I admire lighting and camera people so much now, but I'm ashamed to say the cameraman didn't matter to me then, apart from as a chap, of course, which they always were, like Nicolas Roeg, with whom I got on terribly well.

Dr Zhivago seems to have had an interminable shooting schedule. How long were you in Spain?

A year, I think. That was another thing which changed my life, but nothing to do with the film. Or perhaps the film took a year and I was out there for a good part of it, mostly in Madrid. We did the studio work in Madrid too – no air conditioning and one-hundred-degree heat, in fur coats!

In making the film, were you aware of how beautiful it was going to look?

Oh no, I was so removed from all that stuff and so much more interested in something else all the time. You know, 'The grass is always greener in French film, or Italian film . . .' I was annoyed by all the money, the cost and the grandiosity of it all, although I'm an admirer of David Lean's earlier work.

How did you find him as a director?

He was very paternalistic, that's for sure. If at that time I had developed any feminist ideas, there would have been a lot of problems. Fortunately, I hadn't. I loved his paternalism, just loved it; it reassured me because once again I was so scared. He was very reassuring. He had the power, he knew what he wanted and I have always been delighted to deliver to people what they want me to deliver. I suppose you could call me a bit passive in that way, though I'm not so much like that now. My joy was in trying to do what the director wanted me to do, and if he was going to tell me exactly what that was, then it was fine by me. So David fathered and mothered me through that role. He is a good director of actors – he had to be. What people didn't like, I think, was that he perhaps imposed his will on them too much, because he was extremely authoritarian and some people dislike that. Fortunately, I didn't mind it at all.

You appeared in three of the best films of the early '70s – The Go-Between, the American film McCabe and Mrs Miller, and Don't Look Now. Did you feel you were getting a very satisfying range of roles at this time?

Yes, I think by that time I had managed to look outside myself and become aware that I was very lucky in realising certain ambitions. I've not been interested in roles, I'm interested in the director and I don't think that will change now. I am absolutely a believer in the *auteur* and I am convinced that the director is the only thing that really matters, that he or she will make or break the film. To do those three films gave me a great deal of pleasure because I was working with three directors whom I very much admired and respected.

Were you in a position by then to exercise choice in the roles you took?

Whether or not I was in a position to, I'm pig-headed enough to have always done it. I've turned down some wonderful things and with it turned down an enormous amount of money. I sometimes think I have been too pig-headed in turning things down, because you can't build in that way. If I did it all again I might be cleverer in accepting things, but I have always thought, 'I'm better than this, this is rubbish, and I'm not going to do it.'

Of those three women you played, Marian Maudsley, Mrs Miller and Laura Baxter, which did you find the most interesting and sympathetic?

It's very confusing because all of these things obviously become involved with your personal life as well, and that was a precious time in my life. Making *Don't Look Now* was a combination of Venice, Nic [Roeg] and Donald [Sutherland] and my own family of friends from England who stayed with me a lot. It was a very happy, creative and atmospheric time, very precious. The same is true of *McCabe and Mrs Miller* because working with Robert Altman is such a treat, such a fabulous experience. He treats everyone as a collaborator, so that makes it immediately fun and not too serious. There's no great responsibility about some vision you have to perform, you are just a collaborator in this great adventure. He uses all sorts of people's ideas, slams them in and improvises; he uses all the skills anybody has. He is a very good director of actors, apart from being a very exciting creator. That is one of my favourite films, I love it. I think it's very romantic indeed. There is a strange, intangible atmosphere that captures you; it's almost like an opium dream.

Did you ever think of Marian in The Go-Between as having something in common with Diana Scott? That is, great surface charm and beauty but capable of real selfishness and cruelty.

Now that you say it, I think you're probably right. I think Marian is a bit smarter than Diana and she would probably have handled her life a bit better. Another part I played like that was in *The Return of the Soldier*. But you're right, Marian was quite ruthless and incapable of thinking of anyone but herself. She would have been like her mother.

What are your recollections of Margaret Leighton, who played the mother?

I have very little recollection of anything to do with that film. Once again, the location mattered to me most of all. It was a brilliant location in Norfolk and its effect on me was all to do with my own private life. The house itself wasn't anything special, although Carmen Dillon and Geoffrey Fisher did wonderful work to make it photograph so well. But it was the countryside that was so ravishing.

Unlike many British film, that one really confronts the class issue head on. Did you feel that was important about it?

I don't know whether I felt it then. I have been quite late in coming to class-consciousness, so I probably wasn't aware of it then. Now, I appreciate that very much about the film; I think it is a wonderfully caustic view of this cruel system. As you say, though, it's a very fair-minded film because Alan's [Bates] character is as cruel as anyone else. The finesse, the cultivation and the civility of that life was so exquisite, yet those people exhibited such dirty, piggy emotions and behaviour.

Except Trimingham. Edward Fox gives a beautiful and moving performance of the wounded lord. That's what I meant also about the film's fairness: to make a character like that emerge so sympathetically seemed to me important to the balance of the film.

Yes, that's your mixture of Hartley, Pinter and Losey – not a bad trio, really! – very compassionate and intelligent, none of them was didactic.

You have done a lot of filming in America: have you enjoyed it, and do you find it very different from making films in Britain?

I've filmed everywhere – Italy, France and many other places. One of the things that struck me as different in America is their positive discrimination policy, so you've always got women and people from minority groups on the crew, and I think that's terribly important. I wish we had positive discrimination in filmmaking here, because women are having such a hard time in the British film industry.

How do you feel about *The Return of the Soldier*, which seems to me an underrated film?

I liked it very much indeed. I think it is the best film that Alan Bridges has made, it's excellent. Some people felt it was too slow but I think there is very little wrong with it and I don't find it boring. People aren't interested in characters that low-key and complex, or perhaps they'd just had enough of those 'heritage' films.

By that time I was working properly and I certainly went back to Rebecca West's novel. As to my character, Kitty, when you're playing a part you can't judge the person, you don't see her selfishness. What you feel is Kitty's needs, her fear and terror and desires which overwhelm her, and she's not strong enough to deal with them in a humane way. She is so weak that she has to react in that appalling, bullying way, so what you feel is the pain of her weakness.

How did you find working with your co-stars, Glenda Jackson and Ann-Margret?

I did it because I wanted to work with Glenda, although, as it turned out, I worked with her hardly at all. But I loved working with Ann-Margret, she is a marvellous actress; I admire her very much and I was most impressed by her. She is a very private person and I really couldn't say how she worked, but I think she's got a very intelligent instinct.

What do you recall of filming *Heat and Dust*?

I was born in India so it was another wonderful life experience to go back. It was a very emotional film for me because my mother died during the filming and I had been so looking forward to going back and telling her all about it. I suppose it was a little bit like the story of the film – this person going back – so it was all very intermingled. But I adored working in India, it was heaven: I enjoyed the part, I loved the casualness of Jim and Ismail's [Ivory and Merchant's] way of working, and it was a total pleasure.

In the '80s and afterwards, you seem to have been much influenced by political and social matters in your choice of roles.

I saw the world through a political spectrum from before the '80s; I think I could call myself a political person, so I had no option when it came to choosing roles.

What do you look for in helping you to decide to take a role?

I think it's what I *don't* want to do rather than what I do want to do. There's a hell of a lot of negative stuff that comes along. You would like to do everything that comes your way because, firstly, you retain your power as an actress – you get better as you practise it more – and of course, secondly, you make some money. So it is very difficult to keep saying no. But a lot of work comes along that, to me, is simply contributing to the misinformation that permeates so much of life, whether it is to do with women's roles, racial, environmental or emotional stuff. I think a lot of films, especially American ones, are based on untruthful premises and some of them are extraordinarily sentimental – and I hate that because I think that is simply untruth. So there is a lot of stuff I just don't do for those reasons. Most of them I would call exploitative in one way or another. I have come to the conclusion that films can't often change things, but I think *The Animals Film*, which I did in the early '80s, certainly changed things, albeit at a minuscule level. But I know that people saw it and changed their habits. All you can do is make more people aware of the realities, and I think it is difficult for a film to do that; but it can certainly compound people's prejudices.

Do you think the idea of 'stars' is important to a film industry?

It seems to be incredibly important, doesn't it? I think that stars serve a purpose in a world without religion. I came to this conclusion when I was in America. People used to go potty when they saw me in the streets of New York: they used to scream, run at me and pull at me – I wasn't a real human being. And I got so furious! I got angry at the lack of intelligence that could treat a person as if they were not actually flesh and blood. So I worked out for myself this theory that stars were like religious icons: we weren't real and it was stupid to pretend that we were. People were just projecting their unhappiness, their longings, their desires on to us as though we were something magical – totems, really, rather than icons. However, I do detest this celebrity cult which has gone beyond that. I don't do interviews now because it's got to a point where the interviewers themselves are so caught up in this whole celebrity business. I don't want to have my life, words and thoughts interpreted through the views of someone who is completely incapable of understanding them.

Jack Clayton
1921–1995

Assistant director, production manager or editor: *Men are not God, Wings of the Morning, Conquest of the Air* (1936), *Under the Red Robe, Over the Moon* (1937) *The Divorce of Lady X, Prison Bars* (1938), *Q Planes, Spy in Black* (1939), *The Thief of Baghdad* (1940), *Major Barbara, Atlantic Ferry* (1941), *An Ideal Husband, While the Sun Shines* (1947), *Bond Street* (1948)

Assistant producer, producer or co-producer: *Queen of Spades* (1948), *Flesh and Blood* (1951), *Moulin Rouge* (1952), *Beat the Devil* (1953), *The Good Die Young* (1954), *I Am a Camera* (1955), *Dry Rot, Sailor Beware!, Three Men in a Boat* (1956), *The Story of Esther Costello* (1957), *The Whole Truth* (1958)

Director: **Naples Is A Battlefield* (1946), **The Bespoke Overcoat* (1955), *Room at the Top* (1959), *The Innocents* (& pr) (1961), *The Pumpkin Eater* (1964), *Our Mother's House* (& pr) (1967), *The Great Gatsby* (1974), *Something Wicked This Way Comes* (1983), *The Lonely Passion of Judith Hearne* (1987), *Memento Mori* (for television) (1992)
* Documentary or short film.

A glance at Jack Clayton's credits (and his cutting-room contributions are not listed here) reveals the range of his experience in British films – and his patience in making his way towards his goal of directing feature films. He had cut his teeth on a wide variety of British genres before the Woolf brothers gave him his chance to direct the award-winning short, *The Bespoke Overcoat* in 1955, but several more years would pass before his feature début with *Room at the Top*. On many counts, this is a landmark in the history of British cinema: it is a film which takes working-class aspirations seriously; it is set in the North, far from the Technicolored South of middle-class comedy; and it addressed the matter of sexual passion with a candour that was quite new to British films. Its bleak, grainy look, in Freddie Francis's black-and-white images, its streetscapes and its hillside idyll, were much copied in the next five years – but not by Clayton. He never repeated himself, and, though his work was sadly curtailed by the stroke he suffered in the late '70s, there are some very notable achievements: from the ambiguous ghost story, *The Innocents*, adapted from Henry James, to the fine film version of Brian Moore's *The Lonely Passion of Judith Hearne* and the delectable television film, *Memento Mori*, from Muriel Spark's cryptic novel about the approach of death.

Interview date: October 1992

Did you really enter films at the age of fifteen as third assistant director at London Films?

Yes, it's true, but it is a very fancy name. In America it means a 'gofer', who's like a callboy in the theatre. I went into the cutting rooms immediately after having done three films as an assistant director, as I wanted to have editing experience. Then I think I was promoted to second assistant before the war, and, when the war came, I went into the RAF. I was a rear gunner on the bombers and fortunately, after about five months of it, and because of my previous experience in films, I was drafted in to the RAF Film Unit.

What do you remember of your first post-war work on *An Ideal Husband* with that starry cast, and Georges Périnal, and all those distinguished people?

Georges was the wonderful cameraman who worked on most of Alex's [Korda] films. I came out of the war as a first assistant to a wonderful director called 'Puffin' Asquith, who was actually responsible for starting the ACT, the union here. After that I was supposed to become first assistant on *An Ideal Husband*, but, for various reasons which I did not know, I was promoted to production manager, and I did it. The first assistant really creates the atmosphere on the floor for the director, making everything work. A production manager is much more office-bound and is concerned with the production as a whole.

You had several dealings with producer Anatole de Grunwald, one of those recurring names in British cinema. What reminiscences do you have of him on such films as *Flesh and Blood*, *Queen of Spades* and *Bond Street*?

He had produced the first film I did with Asquith after the war. It was an awful film called *While the Sun Shines*, written by Terence Rattigan. I think it was on *Queen of Spades* that I was promoted to associate producer. Now you're going to ask me what *he* does, and I'll tell you. Usually you only have an associate producer when the producer is not really doing his job. A producer, first of all, finds the money, is responsible for the cast, and that is under the instructions, or should be, of the director. It's a high-class production manager, really. And I was delighted to become a friend of Thorold

Dickinson who directed it, and it's an extremely good film; one reel of it is as good as anything you could ever see. *I* thought his main talent was teaching and I learnt a lot from him.

In 1951 you became an associate producer for Romulus Films with the Woolf brothers and stayed there throughout the decade. Did you have a very harmonious relationship with them?

Yes. It all started because, I think, they financed one of the de Grunwald films – *Flesh and Blood*, I think – and they asked me to join them for *Moulin Rouge* with John Huston. That was a wonderful experience, and I made another film with John, *Beat the Devil*. Although it's got a sort of cult following in New York, I think that's an awful film. But, it was fun to make and it also had an interesting connection with Truman Capote, who wrote the script of it. Later, when I became a director, he wrote the script for *The Innocents*.

I was about eight years with the Woolf brothers, Romulus, doing something that I really didn't want to do. I really wanted to be a director, and, because I was rather good at being a producer, which really means just organisation, I got stuck with that. I don't regret those years; I did at the time, but looking back I don't, because I had great experiences with John Huston. It came to a moment when Huston offered me the chance to be his producer for his next four films, and it was an enormous decision to make because I adored working with him. At the same time, I suddenly thought to myself, 'You're supposed to be trying to be a director.' So I said no, and then I asked John and Jimmy Woolf to let me do a little short [*The Bespoke Overcoat*], which, after a lot of arguments, I was allowed to do on condition that I would continue there for two years. I was lucky to get all sorts of awards for it, and what was also quite unusual was that almost all the press, who don't usually write about shorts, this time did. Anyway, that's how I started a future. Next I had to serve Romulus and John Woolf for two years, on films like *Dry Rot* and *Sailor Beware!* and *Three Men in a Boat*, and then came *Room at the Top*.

Room at the Top **is a landmark film in Britain. At what stage did you become associated with it?**

I think from the very beginning. The Woolfs were interested in the book, and they asked me if I would like to direct it, and I said yes.

And were the Woolf brothers themselves very conspicuous around the making of the film?

No. John was really more interested in, and took his attitude about films from, the financial side. He very seldom interfered in anything artistic. Jimmy had the good sense to do much the same but always be there if you needed any help.

Was Laurence Harvey your first choice?

Yes, but also because I'd worked with him, and he was part of Romulus. I knew him well. He was in *Three Men in a Boat* and so on. I was very happy with the choice of him. It was really such a wonderful part for him.

Was he easy to work with?

Lovely. All sorts of people talk about actors, about how difficult they are and about the problems you have with them. I've never in my experience had a problem with any actor or actress. When they are artistic, or have the tendency to be an artist, you have to expect some sort of leaning towards not doing exactly what they're supposed to do.

You had a brilliant cast in *Room at the Top*. What do you recall of some of those people like Donald Wolfit, Ambrosine Philpotts, Raymond Huntley, Hermione Baddeley?

The most interesting is Donald. Now, he was supposed to be absolute murder for any director and even for other actors because he was his own producer on the stage. He was absolutely like a lamb. I was so nervous. I sat next to him and said, 'Excuse me, Sir Donald,' and he said, 'Forget the Sir, just call me Donald.' I think his performance in *Room at the Top* is probably better than anything he had ever done before. But you must realise that I've always, throughout my career, been lucky with casting directors. Now, that was Romulus's casting director called Jenia Reisser, who's an absolutely wonderful person. She was responsible for all the small parts in it. A casting director's job is to produce a number of actors or actresses for a given part for the director to interview or read, but the ultimate choice, of course, is mine. Nevertheless, I didn't even know half of them, and many of them were new to the screen . . . Richard Pasco, Delena Kidd, Mary Peach and so on. There were some old ones too, like Raymond Huntley and May Hallatt in tiny parts.

How closely were you involved with Neil Paterson during the writing of the screenplay?

Quite close. I always get involved in the script with the writer, because I have never done a film where I've seen a script that I wholly liked or didn't want to change. A director should work with the writer.

The film has got a very convincing bleak, grey, North Country look. How much of this do you attribute to Freddie Francis?

A lot. I think we shot it when it was very cold actually, which helped. The idea was for it to be the first really natural film made in England and I instructed everybody accordingly, but what comes on the screen is totally Freddie's. We shot it in Bradford; I chose the locations. After its success, almost everybody offered me what they called 'kitchen sink' films. And, of course, I turned them all down because I felt I didn't want to do it again.

What do you remember about audience response to the finished film?

We had a sneak showing in the East End of London, and it certainly turned me off ever having a sneak in future. The audience . . .! Over the titles there were fireworks being let off in the bottom of the stalls. I sat next to two lovely old landladies, who continued throughout the whole film to have a conversation about their own life. And the preview cards! The first card that I opened, and I've got it still today, said, 'It stinks.' From that moment on, I have never done a sneak preview.

Were you surprised when it got all those Oscar nominations?

Yes. I was even more surprised that everybody thought it was so original, and, another thing, that it was so sexy. I wasn't aware of it being sexy. All that sort of glamour went over my head, I didn't know what they were talking about. The idea of casting Simone Signoret came from Jimmy Woolf and I immediately loved it. And I don't think that anyone else was thought of.

Was the film a big success in the US?

Oh, yes. It was the first English film to be on a large circuit. Prior to that, we'd been on art-house circuits. This was a full-blooded mainstream release.

You've rationed yourself very rigorously in the films since. Is this because you do not move on a film until it's something you really want to do? Or was it hard in England to get the films made that you wanted?

I think both. I've always wanted to have total control, as a director, of everything, including the editing. About a third of the choices that I've turned down were because they didn't want me to have that right, and I'm a slow person. Until I get over my last film, I can't think of anything else.

Your next feature film, The Innocents, was a very unexpected film to be making after Room at the Top. What drew you to this?

I don't know. I always loved certain stories that I know from my reading years, which were my teens, and Turn of the Screw was one of them.

You really captured the ambiguity. Did you think of the whole thing as being a figment of the governess's imagination?

I've been asked that question so many times, and I've still got no replies ready. Life is not as straightforward as that. If it was, we would be different people and we wouldn't be discussing this. I just love a film that, at the end, lets you take it either way.

Just as the novel does. What about directing the children? Was this at all a problem?

I think that directing children – and I've been fortunate in having chosen the right children – is really an enormous conceit of the director. Because you really are responsible for their performance. You have to – I suppose the word is – hypnotise them into something. I'm not saying anything about the ability of the children, but, for instance, those children had no idea of the story. I wouldn't allow them to read the story. They had their lines the day before the scene was to be shot. I didn't want to alarm them. I think it was my way of being careful about children. I didn't want them to get the idea of what it was really about in case, as it could easily with a sensitive child, it gave them nightmares. Neither of them saw it at the time.

Your films always seem to me to be very much actors' films in the end. Is working with actors perhaps your major interest in directing?

I think the whole voyage of making a film is like a big package. I'm fascinated by all of it.

Not all directors are associated with such terrific performances from actors. In The Pumpkin Eater you have James Mason, Peter Finch, Maggie Smith, Cedric Hardwicke, Anne Bancroft all giving wonderful performances.

Perhaps the reason is because I love actors and a lot of directors don't, but it's not all that simple. Every actor has to be directed according to his personality. So, you can't say I do this or that; they're all different. I obviously choose them very carefully, and I know that they're right for the part before they even start. And a lot of them do need a little assistance . . . maybe two or three words is enough. For instance, Anne Bancroft in the scene with the psychiatrist. I said to her just before the start, 'Pretend your mouth is very dry,' and it worked. It was that sort of silly little thing that makes a good performance.

I guess everyone remembers vividly the scene in Harrods. Was that difficult to shoot?

No, it was actually done in Harrods, on two Sundays I think. All those wonderful food halls are still there.

***Our Mother's House* is the only one of your films that I've not seen. What drew you to this novel by Julian Gloag?**

I think somebody gave it to me, possibly my friend the Canadian novelist, Mordecai Richler, and just asked me to read it. I was fascinated by it and, again, it's about a family of children. It's well worth seeing.

What was your experience in working with Dirk Bogarde, who seems to me a great film actor?

He was wonderful. He's had such a long and varied career and I really got him at his best. Let's say, at the start of his best. He had just made, I think, a film by Joe Losey, but it hadn't come out yet. He was just wonderful, and his career spanned so many years and so many different things. I think his best was, of course, *Death in Venice*, which is one of my favourite films.

***The Great Gatsby* was the only film you had released in the 1970s. I just wondered what you saw as the essence of the novel? What excited you about it?**

It's another one of the novels that I've always cared about, having read it during my reading period in my teens. I just love the idea of the whole thing. It is almost word for word from the book. I know that because I rewrote the script after I wasn't happy with it. I think, first of all, Fitzgerald's a brilliant writer (which is obvious) and I just like the ideal at the heart of it. One of the reasons why I was even tempted to do it was because it is about snobbery and I felt, knowing a little bit about the Americans, they're even more snobbish than we are. I felt very capable of doing it, because I understood that perfectly. The film was shot at Newport, New York, and Pinewood Studios and locations in England, I think about fifty-fifty between America and England. I shot in almost all those wonderful palaces in Newport, you know. Bits of them all appear throughout.

How did you come to work for the Disney organisation on *Something Wicked This Way Comes*?

It was an enormous mistake. I had so many problems with it. After I had a stroke in 1977, which left me without any speech of any kind, I had to relearn how to speak, like a child, and I was fortunate that it worked. It was because of that that there was such a long break from *Gatsby* to *Something Wicked* – ten years. It was too soon for me, after the stroke.

For decades, it seems, someone was always going to film *The Lonely Passion of Judith Hearne*, one of my favourite modern novels.

Well, I'd been trying to make it for twenty years. It was just sheer luck. Every time that I had the opportunity to make it, the book was always out on somebody else's option. Brian Moore, the author, told me that that was his alimony, that when the option wasn't out, he knew that there was no more money coming! Then, suddenly by chance, my agent said to me on the phone, 'I've got a script here that you may not be interested in but it's called, a funny title, oh something about lonely . . .'. I couldn't believe it, so I made it then.

Wendy Hiller at one stage had been going to play Judith Hearne but she was very happy to end up playing Aunty.

That is obviously true. John Huston wanted to make it with Katharine Hepburn. Deborah Kerr was another one that I once heard of. I'm more than happy with Maggie Smith.

In the last shot the camera pulls up as she and Bob Hoskins are driving away. Did you want, deliberately, to leave it ambiguous about their future?

It's such a bleak ending, I mean the idea of it. The truth of it is so bleak that I just wanted to leave it with anybody's idea as to whether she recovers. Obviously the chances are that she will be back there in six months.

When you came to *Memento Mori*, was it hard to get those remarkable people together?

No. I think perhaps it was the film I enjoyed most. Mainly because of the ability to cast such wonderful artistes in roles according to their age. You knew, for them, a lot of them, it might be their last role. They all knew each other and they were so happy to be in it.

George Cole

b. 1925

Actor: *Cottage to Let* (1941), *Those Kids From Town* (1942), *The Demi-Paradise*, **Fiddling Fuel* (1943), *Henry V*, *Journey Together* (1945), *My Brother's Keeper*, *Quartet* (1948), *The Spider and the Fly* (1949), *Morning Departure*, *†The Happiest Days of Your Life*, *Gone To Earth* (1950), *Flesh and Blood*, *Laughter in Paradise*, *Scrooge*, *Lady Godiva Rides Again* (1951), *The Happy Family*, *Who Goes There?*, *Top Secret* (1952), *Will Any Gentleman?*, *The Intruder*, *Our Girl Friday*, *The Clue of the Missing Ape* (1953), *†An Inspector Calls*, *The Belles of St Trinian's*, *Happy Ever After* (1954), *A Prize of Gold*, *Where There's a Will*, *The Constant Husband*, *The Adventures of Quentin Durward* (1955), *It's a Wonderful World*, *The Green Man*, *The Weapon* (1956), *Blue Murder at St Trinian's* (1957), *Too Many Crooks* (1958), *Don't Panic Chaps*, *The Bridal Path* (1959), *The Pure Hell of St Trinian's* (1960), *Dr Syn Alias The Scarecrow*, *Cleopatra* (1963), *One Way Pendulum* (1964), *The Legend of Young Dick Turpin* (1965), *The Great St Trinian's Train Robbery* (1966), *The Green Shoes* (1968), *The Vampire Lovers* (1970), *Fright* (1971), *Take Me High* (1973), *The Blue Bird* (1976), *Mary Reilly* (1996)

* Short film.

† Unbilled.

From cheeky resourceful Cockney kid to awkward or inhibited young man to St Trinian's 'Flash Harry' to television's sensationally successful Arthur Daley, George Cole has hurdled the decades with effortless ease. He was immediately noticed as the Cockney evacuee in Asquith's *Cottage to Let*, repeating his stage role in his first film and holding his own with some distinguished talents, including Alastair Sim, who was to be a continuing influence in his career. Briefly moving as the boy in Olivier's *Henry V*, he played a string of sharply differentiated young misfits throughout the late '40s and early '50s. In doing so, he showed himself equally adept in comedy (as the timid bank clerk in *Laughter in Paradise*) or drama (as the obsessive kite flyer in an episode of *Quartet*). In fact the St Trinian's role, starting in 1954, really obscures by its popularity the range of his film work during these busy decades just as the cult success of Arthur Daley in the '80s, a marvellously detailed study in incorrigible deviousness, has probably obscured for many people the fact that this was preceded by nearly forty years of the most solid kind of film success.

Interview date: June 1990

You are one of the few child actors who went on to a successful adult career. How did you come in to acting?

It's a terrible story really, one which I would be careful not to tell my children if any of them were planning to go on the stage. I left school at the age of fourteen, on a Friday; during the evenings I used to sell newspapers around the streets, and, on that particular Friday night, I looked through the London evening newspapers I had been selling and in one of them there was an advertisement for a boy, wanted for a big musical in London. I went up to the West End the next morning and, although I didn't get the part, I got the understudy's job, and I never went home again. People say what wonderful parents I must have had, to let me do it. I sometimes think they must have been bloody awful parents, not to have come after me!

Did Anthony Asquith choose you to play the Cockney boy in *Cottage to Let* as a result of seeing you play the part on the stage?

Yes, I think so. It was my first play as well as my first film; and I was a Cockney so there wasn't a problem there. The idea of going on the stage, being a rude little boy and being paid for it and having people clap you for it – I don't think I took in what it was all about.

What do you recall of working with Laurence Olivier in *The Demi-Paradise* and in *Henry V*?

I don't recall very much of *The Demi-Paradise*, except being terribly in awe of Olivier; but *Henry V* was a wonderful experience. Olivier's direction was extremely detailed; I wasn't aware of what being directed was all about when I did *Cottage to Let*. Olivier would play everybody's part, showing you what he wanted done with a scene, but he never played it anything like you were going to play it. I did tell one journalist that I was rather hurt Kenneth Branagh hadn't called me back for my original part [i.e., the Boy!]. I had one line that was cut by the censor (which shows what censorship was like in those days); one character had a Frenchman down on his knees and he called me in as his interpreter. He said, 'Tell him I'll ferret him, I'll fur him, I'll ferk him,' and then I had to say, 'I dunno the French for "ferk"'!

Did you ever have coaching from Alastair Sim, as one source suggests?

Not really. I did *Cottage to Let* with him as a play and while we were playing at Wyndham's Theatre the London Blitz started, which closed all the theatres. Alastair thought that my mother and I should get out of town to avoid the bombing and he found a place for us, very near to where he and his wife lived. Well, my mother couldn't stand the country so she came back to London, and we (that is, Alastair and all the cast) took *Cottage to Let* around all the Army camps. I then did about six plays and three or four films with him and, although I can't say he actually coached me, you can't work with someone like that without learning something. He was a most wonderful comedy actor, with incredible timing. He was also extremely generous with other actors, provided they were pulling their weight. He once said to me during a scene from *The Green Man*, 'If that's all you're going to do, then I'll just have to take over the scene.' I realised then I hadn't really looked at the scene and wasn't doing nearly as much as I could with it.

Your post-war films seem to present you as a shy, awkward young man, as in 'The Kite' episode in *Quartet* and in *My Brother's Keeper*. Was it helpful to have an image established in that way?

I think I did develop that image but I doubt if you can think like that until you *are* established and can then afford to turn things down, whereas then I just took what came along. I think the young man in *Quartet* wasn't so much shy as a bit nervy and introverted. Sadly, they couldn't use Maugham's ending, again because of the censor. In the original story he went to gaol – and kept going back – for refusing to pay his wife maintenance. It didn't have a happy ending.

What do you recall of some very distinctive directors you worked with at the end of the 1940s – Robert Hamer, Roy Baker and Michael Powell?

I recall little of Robert Hamer other than that he was very nice. The film was *The Spider and the Fly*, in which I really consider I played Eric Portman's walking stick; it was a dreadful part. I think the drink was beginning to undermine Hamer by that time.

Roy Baker is astonishing: in 1948 we made *Morning Departure* and the year before last he did the *Minder* special! For *Morning Departure* I had a very good part in the original script, the important aspect of my character being that he was a Jew; the money for the film finally came from Jewish businessmen, who didn't like the others behaving towards this character as they did. Now, Dickie Attenborough's hatred of me in that film was originally to have been because I was Jewish, so you're left wondering why he hates me. It was a pity to have altered the film script in that way because it would have set up a very interesting situation; there was no anti-Semitic feeling while the submarine was all right; it was only when it was in trouble that the conflict was to arise – either he goes or the Jew goes. It was an interesting film, though, in showing the breaking down of class barriers towards the end; there *has* been a considerable breaking down of those barriers, as in the introduction of regional and working-class accents on television.

As for working with Michael Powell, I didn't like him at all. He was fine to me but he would reduce actresses to tears; he even tried with Jennifer Jones. He tortured one particular actress, kept making her do retakes which were totally unnecessary. He was more interested in the visual aspects of a film than in the actors and he was often horrid to them. I am a great admirer of his work but I didn't like that side of him.

You worked often with the team of Launder and Gilliat. What were the special pleasures of working with them?

They always had a good script, although terrible money. If Alastair was in the film, it was even worse money because he got most of it! They were wonderful people to work with; Sidney Gilliat was very much the intellectual director and Frank was the down-to-earth one. Sidney always produced Frank's films and vice versa. When you were doing a film with Frank, Sidney would go mad because, at the end of every take, Frank would say, 'That was lovely, just do another one,' Sidney would say, 'Well, if it was so lovely, why are we doing another one?' It was just a habit Frank couldn't get out of.

Between the films each directed I think there was probably a difference in subject matter; I don't say that Frank couldn't direct one of Sidney's scripts or vice versa: either of them could have directed the St Trinian's films but it was always Frank. *Green for Danger* was another Alastair film and *that* was a Sidney Gilliat film. What I'm saying is that I don't think Sidney *would* have directed a St Trinian's film; I think I'm right in saying Frank directed all of them. Frank directed a film called *Lady Godiva Rides Again* – that could have been Sidney but it was more suited to Frank. *Green for Danger* couldn't have been Frank, it had to be Sidney, and *Gilbert and Sullivan* was another which had to be Sidney's. I think Frank enjoyed the broader comedy.

What do you think was the key to the success of the St Trinian's films?

Basically I think the first one, *The Belles of St Trinian's*, was the best, with Alastair as the headmistress and as the brother. They did have wonderful casts and were great fun to make. The scripts were not as good by about the third or fourth film; they did another one about five years ago which I couldn't do it because I was in *Minder*. It was awful – X-rated, topless girls – they had ruined the whole idea. The early ones had a real understanding of farce and I would say the script was the most important thing about them. But it was all there, in Ronald Searle's cartoons. That character of Flash Harry was in the cartoons. Ronald Searle has him coming around the wall at an angle that is physically impossible to do – worse than forty-five degrees.

You made several films for Mario Zampi. Would you agree that for an Italian he had a remarkable grasp of British comedy?

Oh yes, wonderful, but I think he had the knack of finding the right scriptwriter. Jack Davis and Michael Pertwee wrote those scripts for *Laughter in Paradise, Top Secret, Happy Ever After* and *Too Many Crooks*, Pertwee was first-rate; he wrote practically all of Mario's films. Those were very good comedies and Zampi was very nice to work with. In those days, of course, most films were 'family' films, and they had a good audience.

I recently saw *Will Any Gentleman?* again and found it very fresh and funny. How do you rate it among your films?

I enjoyed doing it; it was a contract film for ABC. I had certain disagreements with them because they wanted me to play it rather like the man who had created the part, Robertson Hare, and I wouldn't do that. I think I was fairly arrogant as a youthful actor, digging my heels in and very blinkered about my attitude. I can remember some terrible rows about them wanting me to copy someone else's performance.

How did you feel about the steady stream of Hollywood actors pouring into Britain all through the '50s?

I think we had feelings about it, but we can't have had very *much* feeling because the only way the film was going to get distribution was if it had American stars. One was grateful that these films were being made. One who became a close friend was Dick Widmark – I did *Prize of Gold* with him. Admittedly some of the people who came over here to make films weren't huge stars but, in the case of someone like Tom Conway, these were people who made 'B' pictures and the picture would only get distribution if it had an American name in it. The whole thing would be sold as a package – you would have an Yvonne de Carlo film and with it a Tom Conway film, as a package. Yvonne wasn't a particularly good actress I don't think, but she was fun. She got good direction here and got better parts than in America.

I am struck by the way you keep adapting to each period. How much of it was chance and how much clever calculation?

People think you plan things and you like to think you do, which is absolute rubbish because you don't. I do feel I have become aware, about three times in my career, that it has been time to change direction. There was the *Life of Bliss* character, a young bachelor; then there was St Trinian's, which couldn't be more different. One change I did make very consciously was when I was offered the television series, *A Man of our Times*, in 1966; I had been playing a man of twenty-five for forty-two years and suddenly here was my first opportunity to play a middle-aged man, which I did. Of course, as soon as you make a success of playing a forty-year-old, everything you get from then on is a forty- or forty-five-year-old. That went on for quite a while and then came *Minder*, where I suddenly went from forty to whatever Arthur's age is (he says he's the same age as Paul Newman) and suddenly you're into your fifties, which is very nice.

Sidney Cole

b. 1908

Editor: *Freedom of the Seas, Mr Cinders (1934), Royal Cavalcade* (co-ed), *Dance Band, Midshipman Easy (1935), Lonely Road (1936), High Command (1937), *Spanish ABC* (co-dir, co-ed), *Behind the Spanish Lines* (co-dir, co-ed) (1938), *Roads Across Britain* (dir), *Gaslight (1940), Pimpernel Smith* (sup ed) (1941), *The First of the Few* (tech adviser) (1942), *Nine Men* (sup ed), *The Bells Go Down* (sup ed), *Undercover* (sup ed), *Went the Day Well?, San Demetrio, London* (sup ed) (1943), *Halfway House* (sup ed), *For Those in Peril* (sup ed), *They Came to a City* (assoc pr, co-sc) (1944), *Dead of Night* (assoc pr) (1947), *Against the Wind* (assoc pr), *Scott of the Antarctic* (assoc pr) (1948), *Train of Events* (co-dir) (1949), *The Magnet* (assoc pr) (1950), *The Man in the White Suit* (assoc pr) (1951), *Secret People* (pr) (1952), *The Angel Who Pawned Her Harp* (pr, co-sc), *North Sea Bus* (sc) (1954), *Escapade* (assoc pr) (1955), *Sword of Sherwood Forest* (co-pr) (1960) *The Kitchen* (pr, sc) (1961)
* Documentary.

S idney Cole was a key member of the Ealing family during its most productive years (1942–52). He had been an editor at several studios during the 1930s, and in 1938 he went to Spain, with Thorold Dickinson and others, to make documentaries. His Leftish sympathies, which he traces back to his time at the London School of Economics, made this work important to him, and no doubt helped him to find Ealing a sympathetic home when he returned there in 1942, after editing Dickinson's

Gaslight and Leslie Howard's *Pimpernel Smith*. His most frequent Ealing collaborators were the Basil Dearden–Michael Relph team, Charles Frend and Charles Crichton, and his role varied. He was sometimes supervising editor, often associate or co-associate producer; he was also co-author of at least one screenplay (*They Came to a City*) and directed the most characteristically Ealing episode of the portmanteau film, *Train of Events*. From 1935 onwards he was active in the Association of Cinema [*later* and Television] Technicians, and was on the board of its production company, ACT Films.

Interview date: June 1990

Did the documentary work you did in Spain during the Civil War have any connection with the Grierson-dominated documentary movement in Britain in the '30s?

Not really. I had worked with Grierson in the early days and I knew him, not only in the context of the documentary film movement but also on the Council of the Film Society. But, except in the most general terms, those Spanish films didn't have any connection with Grierson.

What do you recall of two films you edited in 1940 – Thorold Dickinson's *Gaslight* and Leslie Howard's *Pimpernel Smith*?

They are very, very different. Of course I knew Thorold very well from Spain and *Gaslight* was a great pleasure to work on. I was very nervous when I started to edit it. I showed Thorold the first sequence I'd cut, which was the prologue of the film; Thorold looked at it and said, 'Well, that wasn't quite what I had intended,' so I apologised. He ran it again and then said, 'Oh, I see what you've done.' He had had a chronological sequence in mind and I had cut it purely on a visual basis of increasing and accelerating action, so that it had a mounting rhythm in terms of what was happening and was not related to chronology or the topography of the house. Thorold made a few small suggestions and that totally restored my confidence. What happens with directors who are also editors is that they like to have a good editor with them because they shoot material that can *be* edited. *Pimpernel Smith* was the first film Leslie Howard had directed and he had great style as an actor which came over in the way he directed; but he safeguarded himself by asking me (as supervising editor) to be on the studio floor all the time during shooting so that he could ask me questions or I could tell him if I thought I needed another shot. I found when I was

editing it that Leslie's style – as an actor and as a director – more or less dictated the way I edited it.

What do you regard as the editor's essential contribution?

An editor can help to make a good film even better; he can make a mediocre film look reasonably good, but there is very little he can do about a film which is absolutely terrible anyhow! I think the editor is very important, either in carrying out to its maximum possibility the director's intention, or in rescuing things that, for various reasons, haven't quite come off. In my youth as an editor, there was a surprising number of directors who desperately needed a good editor to try and do something with the material they had shot.

On what basis did you rejoin Ealing in 1942?

I went in as a supervising editor, when there were a number of young editors who needed guidance. At Ealing we always had several films going at the one time and it was the fashion to have a supervising editor then. Film terminology is always difficult but, for instance on *Pimpernel Smith*, it could be said that I was the editor and the so-called editor was an assembly cutter or assembly editor. It's a little unfair to him but what happened on that film was that, as supervising editor, I spent a lot of time actually on the studio floor with Leslie; the editor would make the first assembly of a sequence and then I would look at it and make suggestions, then he would make any changes I had suggested. At a later stage I would take a reel myself and alternate, then we would look at it together; we would then switch things around as necessary. In short, I made sure that I worked physically on every reel, although the editor had done the preliminary putting-together, in most cases, of that particular sequence. Michael Balcon wanted a supervising editor and I was known in the industry, so he asked me in.

Leslie was starting *The First of the Few* about the Spitfires when he discovered I had gone to Ealing; he told Balcon he wanted me on his film, so that in my first year at Ealing I was working both on *The First of the Few* and at Ealing.

During your time at Ealing you are variously described as editor, producer, director, and co-author. Do you have any preference among these roles?

Not really. On the whole we were very co-operative at Ealing, which was part of the pleasure of working there. I worked on one very well-known film called *Dead of Night*, which started with Charles Frend and myself deciding we would like to make an anthology film on the works of writer MR James, ghost stories which were very chilling and frightening. Then we decided the stories weren't as visual as we had thought when viewed in film terms. Everybody got interested in the idea and we had very interesting script discussions; it finally evolved into what it is and involved practically the entire studio – except, oddly enough, Charles Frend, who was by then involved in making another subject. We shot it with two units and shot in parallel; there was a kind of friendly rivalry between the two units. When the film was put together I wasn't specifically the supervising editor; I was one of the associate producers who had a lot to do with the editing. That's why it is difficult to answer your question because, as associate producer or producer, I feel one of the most important things is to be there all through the editing process, including the dubbing stage, to the final print. So I suppose I would have to say I like being a producer, because then I am involved in the scripting and in the editing as well, even if I am not billed as scriptwriter or editor.

A lot of Ealing films have your name or that of Michael Relph as associate producer. Did that mean that technically Michael Balcon was producer?

Yes, that's correct. Michael never wanted to take the title of executive producer; I think that was partly because in the early days he didn't get credited and when he was totally in charge he wanted the credit as producer. In many cases films were made because a producer and a director went to him and told him what they would like to do; if it was a novel or a play he would buy it. He would then want to approve, or himself suggest, the top

casting and he would see the rushes every day. Beyond that he didn't interfere – not at all in the editing. He backed his judgement of us by letting us get on with the job.

Another name which crops up in your earlier years is that of Sergei Nolbandov, director of *Undercover*, now perhaps the least remembered name in the Ealing canon. Was he out of touch with the wartime spirit of Ealing?

Yes, he was a bit. I don't know much about Sergei but he was a nice chap. One of the early films I did there was *Undercover* – an extraordinary film about Yugoslavia. The main character was someone called Mikhailovich, who at that time was supposedly heading the Yugoslav Resistance to the Germans; when the film was nearly finished the previous British ambassador to Yugoslavia came down to see it and said it would never do because our aid was then going to Tito. The aid which had been going to Mikhailovich had in fact been used to fight Tito. It was a rather old-fashioned film and didn't fit in with the way the younger directors were working.

Of course, the big influence at Ealing in those days was Cavalcanti. He not only had a feature background, which he had before he went into documentary, but he also gave documentary a great sense of style. One of the first things I did at Ealing was to edit his *Went the Day Well?*, which has stood up remarkably over the years and was regarded enormously highly in the United States. He knew how to shoot to be edited, therefore we were very much in tune as to how the film should be put together.

You were associate producer on *They Came to a City*, which seems a most daringly uncommercial venture. How did it come about?

This was in the immediate post-war period and there was a great deal of feeling around that, now the war had ended, there was going to be a new world opening up. Priestley always had his ear to the ground and he wrote the play, which was quite successful. It used the same cast as that which ultimately appeared in the film. I saw the play and, being a socialist, I thought it was extremely interesting and captured the mood of the moment. I went to Balcon and suggested making a film of the play. Priestley was very well known as a screenwriter as well as a playwright, and several of his books and plays had been turned into films by the studio, so Balcon agreed and we made it, very cheaply. I've no idea how it fared commercially.

You worked on four films for Charles Frend, *San Demetrio, London*, *Joanna Godden*, *Scott of the Antarctic* and *The Magnet*. Did you have a particularly sympathetic working relationship with him?

Yes. Somehow we gravitated together. We found we agreed on a great number of things and that's how we came to work together quite often. *Scott of the Antarctic* took us about two years altogether; both Charles and I had boyhood memories of the Antarctic expedition and we both felt it had epic quality, so we went to Balcon and told him we wanted to make the film. It was one of the biggest productions Ealing had tackled at the time. We got a great deal of co-operation from the Polar Research Institute at Cambridge, from Professor Debenham, who had actually been on the expedition. We did a great deal of research as to where we needed to shoot and we found that for some purposes we needed to shoot at the Aletsch Glacier in Switzerland, running down from the Jungfrau; and for other things we went just north-west of Bergen in Norway, to the place where Scott himself actually went to try out his motor-sledges before he decided not to take them. So we really had a tough time with the picture because it was very cold on location and occasionally the cameras would stop turning.

Joanna Godden was also made almost entirely on location, which really became something of an Ealing tradition. That's where Cavalcanti and Harry Watt, myself to some extent, and Charles Crichton had a considerable influence.

You worked with Crichton twice – *For Those In Peril* as supervising editor and *Against the Wind* as associate producer.

For *Against the Wind* we needed a French girl to play one of the parts. We went to Paris and saw a film with Simone Signoret, after which we met her in the bar of the Hôtel George V. She was the only leading actress whom Michael Balcon agreed to cast without having seen or met her, because we phoned him with such enthusiasm from Paris. A very debated piece of casting was that we persuaded Jack Warner to be in it; there is a very good scene in which Simone Signoret, as the radio operator with a group of Resistance fighters, is listening to London and gets the news that there is a traitor in the group, who is Jack Warner. She turns to Jack, who is sitting there quite calmly, and she shoots him. It was a tremendous shock to audiences, Jack Warner being so much loved by them.

Your one directorial assignment was the 'Engine Driver' sequence in *Train of Events*; it seems to me the most characteristically 'Ealing' sequence of the four stories.

It probably is, because of its being down-to-earth, about working-class people and shot on location. We thought we'd try to do a 'portmanteau' type of film; the stories aren't connected, of course, as they were in *Dead of Night*, where it all gels together and becomes quite frightening.

How did you find working with Alexander Mackendrick at the end of your time there?

The film was *The Man in the White Suit*. Unlike with most other directors I worked with, I had some clashes with Sandy; however, they were fruitful clashes. *The Man in the White Suit* was so full of meaning that all sorts of small things became debatable in it. We had long discussions about the attitude of union representatives, for instance. I remember Sandy saying it was probably one of the most important films he had been connected with. Some of my friends criticised the film for the way it portrayed union attitudes but I thought Mackendrick was right in the way he approached it, because the Alec Guinness character is an innocent, a naïve person and an idealist who doesn't realise any of the social implications of what he is doing.

Ealing was like a repertory company of actors, wasn't it?

Yes it was, and it was successful in creating stars with whom audiences fell in love. I always remember travelling on a train and two young girls were reading the *Evening Standard*. One of them scanned the cinema listings and said to her friend, 'Oh, a Googie Withers film! I must go and see it!' And I thought, 'Well, Ealing did that.' Googie was remarkable, very strong.

What recollections do you have of the setting up of ACT Films?

This company was set up by the film technicians' union, the Association of Cinematograph Technicians, in the early '50s. It was a time when many technicians were unemployed, and even one-off film jobs were getting scarce. The ACT's executive committee set up the film company to help alleviate this situation. Apart from buying a few hundred pounds of shares, the union did not have anything directly to do with the running of the company, though its board of directors included some members of the executive committee, such as myself. The purpose was to give employment and the films produced were mainly low-budget second features, with the crews receiving union basic rates, with occasionally a film on a slightly more ambitious scale. One such was *The Man Upstairs* in 1958, starring Richard Attenborough, who had made a great impact on British films since his success in *Brighton Rock*. I produced *The Kitchen*, from Arnold Wesker's play, for ACT Films in 1962. Anthony Asquith, who had done the ACT itself great service already by becoming its President, and thereby bringing the prestige of his reputation as a director to that office, made *The Final Test* for ACT Films. This encouraged other directors to work for it too.

If you were asked what you saw as the highlight of your career, do you have something which stands out for you?

I like to think back on certain films such as *Dead of Night*, *The Man in the White Suit* and *Scott of the Antarctic*, but I think looking back can become rather self-indulgent. Most of my films I like to remember but, most of all, I like to remember that I have been very fortunate in having spent my working life in a sphere which I enjoyed and always wanted to work in.

Lance Comfort

1908–1967

Director: **Throughbreds* (1934), **My Friend the Dog*, **Toddlers and a Pup* (1938?), **Sandy Steps Out* (1938), **Laddie's Day Out*, **Judy Buys a Horse* (1939), *Hatter's Castle*, *Penn of Pennsylvania* (1941), *Those Kids from Town*, *Squadron Leader X* (1942), *Escape to Danger*, *When We Are Married*, *Old Mother Riley Detective* (1943), *Hotel Reserve* (co-dir) (1944), *Great Day* (1945), *Bedelia* (1946), *Temptation Harbour* (1947), *Daughter of Darkness* (1948), *Silent Dust* (1949), *Portrait Of Clare* (1950), *The Girl on the Pier*, *The Genie* (1953), *Bang! You're Dead*, *Eight O'Clock Walk* (1954), *The Man in the Road* (1956), *Face in the Night*, *The Man from Tangier*, *At the Stroke of Nine* (1957), *The Ugly Duckling*, *Make Mine a Million* (1959), *The Breaking Point*, *Rag Doll*, *Pit of Darkness*, *The Painted Smile* (1961), *The Break*, *Tomorrow at Ten* (1962), *Touch of Death*, *Live It Up*, *Blind Corner* (1963), *Devils Of Darkness* (1964), *Be My Guest* (1965)
* Short film.

The name of Lance Comfort may not now be well known to the readers of this book. It is included here for two reasons: first, on the evidence of the films, he is shamefully neglected; and, second, he stands for all those other unsung talents whose craftsmanship in the service of British cinema deserves more recognition. Such names include: Lawrence Huntington (director of lively thrillers such as *Night Boat to Dublin* and the impressively sombre school-based drama, *Mr Perrin and Mr Traill*); Lewis Allen (one minor masterpiece, *So Evil My Love*, which enshrines Ann Todd's best work as a missionary turned murder-

ess); David Macdonald (for his zestful pre-war comedy, *This Man is News*, his wartime documentaries, and the post-war cautionary tale, *Good Time Girl*); and Charles Frank, who, at very least, orchestrated some remarkable talents in one of British cinema's rare Gothic romances, *Uncle Silas*. There are plenty of others, who made films of more than passing interest – Fergus McDonell, Bernard Knowles, Brian Desmond Hurst and so on. The time is ripe for their reappraisal.

Of all these directors, Lance Comfort has the strongest claim in the form of a substantial body of work in several genres and stretching over several decades. It is not possible to draw on his own published words here, because, like most of those listed above, he was not given to interview – or given the opportunity. On the basis of talking to those who worked *with* him, including actors such as Margaret Johnston, Rona Anderson, Harry Fowler, Nanette Newman, Honor Blackman and Dermot Walsh, he seems to have been uniformly liked as a director who respected his actors sufficiently to give them room to breathe in shaping their characterisations. Deborah Kerr, who starred twice for him, thought him 'underrated'. Let's change that.

After a long apprenticeship from 1925 to 1940, when he worked as a sound recordist, trick cameraman, editor and director of shorts, he made a very striking features début in 1941 with *Hatter's Castle*, a rare British excursion into full-blooded melodrama. This adaptation from AJ Cronin's novel is devoid of gentility: it is robustly conceived in plot terms (a pregnant daughter is literally driven out into the snow, an idolised son kills himself rather than endure the wrath of his father, the hatter of the title); its cast – Deborah Kerr, James Mason, Beatrice Varley and, above all, the mad-eyed Robert Newton – enters superbly into the spirit of the enterprise; and Mutz Greenbaum/Max Greene's lustrous black-and-white images strikingly abet Comfort's story-telling skills.

These skills – including a capacity to get a story moving swiftly and suggestively from its opening images, and the ability to hold several strands of plot in concurrent development – and his capacity to draw performances of high nervous intensity from his players stood Comfort in good stead to the end of his career. In the '40s he made a string of highly atmospheric 'A' films: the utterly charming regional comedy, *When We Are Married*, from JB Priestley's play; *Great Day*, with its compassionate and abrasive picture of village life; a wicked-woman thriller, *Bedelia*; the moody Georges Simenon adaptation, *Temptation Harbour*, with Newton again, this time effectively restrained; and *Daughter of Darkness*, unique perhaps in '40s British cinema in having a murderous nymphomaniac as its protagonist – and making us sympathise with her.

After the '40s, his work is largely confined to 'B' films, but it should be noted that some of these are first-class: *Touch of Death* executes swiftly and unpretentiously a plot based on crime and the spread of dangerous contamination; *Eight O'Clock Walk* riskily combines courtroom thriller and child molestation; and, best of all, *Tomorrow at Ten* is a teasing, suspenseful kidnap melodrama.

What his body of films, and their reception, suggest to us is that melodrama, unless upholstered in period trappings, was not a favoured British mode at the time: now, when its basis in class and gender is more generally understood, and the mode cleared from critical obloquy, Comfort's achievement may get the attention it deserves.

Sean Connery

b. 1930

Actor: *No Road Back, Time Lock, Action of the Tiger, Hell Drivers* (1957), *Another Time, Another Place* (1958), *Darby O'Gill and the Little People, Tarzan's Greatest Adventure* (1959), *The Frightened City, On the Fiddle* (1961), *The Longest Day, Dr No* (1962), *From Russia With Love* (1963), *Goldfinger,* *Marnie, Woman of Straw* (1964), *Thunderball, The Hill* (1965), *A Fine Madness* (1966), *You Only Live Twice* (1967), *Shalako* (1968), *The Molly Maguires, The Red Tent* (1970), *The Anderson Tapes, Diamonds are Forever* (1971), *The Offence* (1973), *Zardoz, Murder on the Orient Express* (1974), *Ran-*

som, *The Wind and the Lion*, *The Man Who Would Be King* (1975), *Robin and Marion*, *The Next Man* (1976), *A Bridge Too Far* (1977), *Meteor*, *The First Great Train Robbery*, *Cuba* (1979), *Outland*, *Time Bandits* (1981), *The Man with the Deadly Lens*, *Five Days One Summer* (1982), *Sword of the Valiant*, *Never Say Never Again* (1983), *The Highlander*, *The Name of the Rose* (1986), *The Untouchables* (1987), *The Presidio*, *Indiana Jones and the Last Crusade*, *Family Business* (1989), *The Hunt for Red October*, *The Russia House* (1990), *Robin Hood: Prince of Thieves*, *Highlander II – The Quickening* (1991), *Medicine Man* (1992), *Rising Sun*, *Wrestling Ernest Hemingway* (1993), *A Good Man in Africa* (1994), *Just Cause*, *First Knight* (1995), *The Rock*, *Dragonheart* (1996), *A Life Less Ordinary* (1997)

'Sean Connery is James Bond': thus ran the publicity when *Dr No* burst on to delighted box offices all round the world in 1962. Ironically, Bond's creator, Ian Fleming, didn't want Connery for the role: Connery recalls that 'he was a terrible snob, but a very entertaining man. I don't think he approved of me terribly.'[1] Nevertheless, Connery made the part his own as none of his successors has been able to do. He claims that 'it took some time to hit the right sort of humour,'[2] but he indubitably found it and his capacity to combine the cool and the self-mocking contributed enormously to the spoof element of the films. By his own admission, 'I look for humour in whatever I'm doing,'[3] and part of the graceful ageing lies in a humorous willing-ness to try different things – like Indiana Jones's father – and not to take himself too seriously.

Bond made him a world name though it made him feel that 'nobody wants to be pigeonholed to the extent that they only do this or only do that.'[4] Early on, in fact, he felt '. . . it was a bit of a joke around town that I was chosen for Bond. The character is not really me at all.'[5] He had told producer Cubby Broccoli, with whom he had a prickly and eventually litigious relationship, 'You either take me as I am or not at all.'[6] The hard edge to the handsome face and body, formidable in the action stuff and in the bedroom alike, meant he would have trouble leaving the image behind, however often he might say, 'I don't want to be Bond all the time.'[7]

Pre-Bond, Connery escaped from a poor Edin-burgh working-class background, first to the Navy and later the stage and then a handful of British movies, in which he typically played low-life thugs. The training as working-class villains (e.g., in *The Frightened City*) no doubt feeds into the ferocity one often detects in *his* Bond but not in Roger Moore's smoother incarnation.

Post-Bond, he has simply become one of the best film actors in the world. Among his British-based films, three will do to represent his range. *The Hill*, first of several for Sidney Lumet ('. . . a fine director who creates a team'[8]), gave him the part of a prisoner brutally punished in a British military stockade. 'The idea was to make an ensemble movie, and we made it,'[9] and he had the pleasure of 'the time to prepare . . . to find out if we were all on the same track.'[10] He worked for Lumet again as an obsessive cop wearing down a child molester in the gripping drama, *The Offence*, a film Connery believes explores 'areas that people just don't get to in films as a rule.'[11] Richard Lester's *Robin and Marion* (technically a US film, but with an all-British cast), in which he played Robin as 'a guy who was ageing, and at the end of a myth,'[12] is perhaps his most moving work on film, even if it failed in the States, where, he says, 'They can't take the idea that a hero might be over the hill and falling apart.'[13]

His Oscar for Best Supporting Actor for *The Untouchables* deserves to be seen as a tribute to his whole career. He has become a riveting actor, even in bad films – and they would have been worse without him.

1 Chris Peachment, 'Breaking the Bond', *Time Out*, 28 January – 4 February 1987, p 21
2 Peachment, p 15
3 Ben Fong-Torres, 'Connery. Sean Connery.', *American Film*, May 1989, p 32
4 John H Richardson, 'Straight talk', *Premiere*, February 1992, p 66
5 'A secretive person – Sean Connery interviewed by Gordon Gow', *Films and Filming*, March 1974, p 14
6 Michael Feeney Callen, *Sean Connery: The Untouchable Hero* (first published 1983), Virgin Books, London, 1993, p 108
7 Callen, p 127
8 'A secretive person', p 17
9 Callen, p 146
10 Callen, p 143
11 'A secretive person', p 17
12 Fong-Torres, p 80
13 Peachment, p 21

Tom Courtenay

b. 1937

Actor: *The Loneliness of the Long Distance Runner*, *Private Potter* (1962), *Billy Liar* (1963), *King and Country*, *Operation Crossbow* (1964), *Doctor Zhivago*, *King Rat* (1965), *The Night of the Generals* (1966), *The Day the Fish Came Out* (1967), *A Dandy in Aspic*, *Otley* (1968), *Catch Me a Spy*, *One Day in the Life of Ivan Denisovich* (1971), *The Dresser* (1983), *Happy New Year*, *Leonard Part 6* (1987), *Let Him Have It*, *The Last Butterfly/Cri du Papillon/Posledni Motyl* (1991), *The Boy from Mercury* (1997)

'I never did anything about my stardom, it never meant anything to me,'[1] said Tom Courtenay in 1995, and his erratic film career bears this out. Briefly in the '60s, his pinched, hungry features and the chip-on-the-shoulder attitude he projected so eloquently marked him a star of the new British wave of social realism, but the wave had broken by the end of the decade. 'I'm not sure that being a movie star appeals to many English actors,'[2] he was reported as saying.

Tony Richardson never had any doubts about casting him as the working-class Borstal athlete who thumbs his nose at the Establishment in *The Loneliness of the Long Distance Runner*. The tight anger, the cultural and actual poverty, and the odd anarchic outbursts, were limned with an accuracy of repressed feeling and taunting resentment which perhaps no other English actor could have matched. 'I was next in line at Woodfall,'[3] he remembered. Next, that is, after Albert Finney, who also brought a whiff of the north (though from the other side of the Pennines, Lancashire) to British films; Courtenay went on to say, 'We both have the same problem, overcoming the flat harsh speech of the North.' Luckily, the latter was almost an asset in the '60s.

Finney had created *Billy Liar* on stage, but Courtenay made the part his own in John Schlesinger's film, as the fantasising clerk in an undertaker's office in a dreary northern town. He later said, 'I thought I looked a bit raw in some of it,'[4] but most reviewers would have disagreed. In 1961, he had said in an interview, 'Take all this thing now about working-class actors and writers: it's simply a release of certain talents from that class.'[5] *Billy Liar* gave him a valuable chance to extend his range in the fantasy sequences which remove Billy from his working-class ambience.

A brutally frank account would suggest that he never had more than two or three further roles of comparable interest, though he did his most moving work in Joseph Losey's *King and Country*, as a young World War I private who walks away from combat and is tried and executed. Twenty years later, after more than a decade away from the screen, he was flexible, funny and touching as *The Dresser* to Finney's touring tragedian. In between, like most others, he is swamped by the production values in *Dr Zhivago* (a turning point in his view of filmmaking: 'We were all sitting in a horrible hotel in Spain waiting for snow . . . In six months, I did only three weeks' work';[6] did *A Dandy in Aspic*, *The Night of the Generals* – but 'found it very unsatisfying to do these bigger films with more money';[7] made a couple of modish, mildly enjoyable pieces, *Otley* and *Catch Me a Spy*, for Dick Clement; and was appropriately harrowed – and harrowing – in *One Day in the Life of Ivan Denisovich*.

'I would be quite happy if *Denisovich* was my swansong,'[8] he said after this. In view of *The Dresser*, at least, we may be glad it wasn't. 'Perhaps I should have done one or two more films earlier and not lost touch quite as I did . . .' he said in 1995, but 'I didn't like the parts I had and I just *longed* to work in the theatre, and so that's what I did.'[9]

1 *Empire*, November 1995, p 52
2 *Films in Review*, February 1984, p 105
3 *Films in Review*, p 101
4 *Films in Review*, p 102
5 *Daily Express*, 2 November 1961, quoted in Alexander Walker, *Hollywood, England* (first published 1974), Harrap, London 1986, p 127
6 *Films in Review*, p 102
7 *Empire*, November 1995, p 92
8 *Films and Filming*, January 1983, p 43
9 *Empire*, November 1995, p 52

Michael Craig

b. 1928

Actor: *Passport to Pimlico* (extra) (1948), *Malta Story* (1953), *The Love Lottery, Svengali, The Embezzler, Forbidden Cargo* (1954), *Passage Home, Handcuffs, London* (1955), *The Black Tent, Eyewitness, Yield to the Night, House of Secrets* (1956), *High Tide at Noon, Campbell's Kingdom* (1957), *The Silent Enemy, Nor the Moon by Night, Sea of Sand* (1958), *Life in Emergency Ward 10, Sapphire, Upstairs and Downstairs* (1959), *The Angry Silence, Cone of Silence, Doctor in Love* (1960), *Payroll, No, My Darling Daughter* (1961), *A Pair of Briefs, The Mysterious Island, Life for Ruth, The Iron Maiden* (1962), *The Captive City, The Stolen Hours* (1963), *Life at the Top, Sandra* (1965), *Modesty Blaise* (1966), *Star!* (1968), *Twinky, The Royal Hunt of the Sun, Country Dance* (1969), *A Town Called Bastard* (1971), *Vault of Horror* (1973), *Inn of the Damned, Ride a Wild Pony* (1975), *The Irishman* (1978), *Turkey Shoot* (1982), *Stanley* (1983), *Hot Resort* (1985), *Appointment with Death* (1988)

Considering that Michael Craig's screen career began to gather momentum just as British films were beginning to lose theirs (i.e., in the mid-1950s), he managed to run up an impressive number of credits in the decade that followed. The last of the Rank contract artists, he made about twenty films between 1956 and 1966. Though he grew tired of the handsome young professional men he was always being called on to play, he brought to these often bland leading roles an easy charm and authority. Along with his brother Richard Gregson, Richard Attenborough, Bryan Forbes and Guy Green, he was one of the driving forces behind *The Angry Silence*, a film he saw as offering him a distinct break from the roles in which he had become a star. Unfortunately for him, as he points out, he had acquired the wrong sort of image to be acceptable to the new wave of realist directors who came along at the end of the '50s. Despite his modest and articulate disclaimers about his career, he was never less than a convincing screen presence, and in the

1978 Australian film, *The Irishman*, he gave a fine character performance in the title role.

Interview date: October 1988

You became a film star after several years on stage. How did you get your first break in films?

The Rank Organisation and indeed ABPC [Associated British Picture Corporation] during the '50s ran these studio programmes they hoped were a carbon copy of the American system, whereby they had a stable of young people under contract. The Rank Organisation scouts came to see a play I was in at the Oxford Playhouse and I was offered a seven-year contract, in the summer of '54. That sounds OK but there was an option at the end of every year, which was on their side. They could drop you if they wished. That's how I got started at Rank: I signed in August or September and about a week later I found myself playing a part in a picture they were doing with Finch and Diane Cilento, *Passage Home*, about a ship and its crew. Then I got my first lead in *House of Secrets*, a sort of James Bond thing. A huge part, with various leading ladies, love scenes and fights, and all that idiot stuff. Some of it was filmed in Paris, I remember. Thirty quid a week I was getting.

Did the '50s seem to you a good time for a budding film star in Britain? Did you have a sense of a sturdy industry?

It depended on how naïve you were. Television was just coming into real significance as a competitor to the film business, and Rank believed that competition could be beaten by making good family entertainment. However you define that, the end product was bland and dated and hadn't very much to say. I did five films at Pinewood which are exactly the same: the same writers, same directors, producers, camera team, actors. In one I'd be a doctor, in another I'd be an architect, whatever. Same jokes. Same character people. Well, there's a limited life for that kind of product. Anyway, after a series of rows over one thing or other, the lively talent went off and did independent production. The same sort of thing was happening at ABPC and the studio idea was breaking down. When I first was under contract in '54, there were forty-odd people under contract to Rank; when I finished in '61 there was me and Dirk Bogarde, who I think had a different kind of deal.

Was anyone looking after your career in the '50s?

No. For example, when I did *The Angry Silence*, which I'd also written, so I had a big stake and interest in the whole project, they first of all refused to let me do it, because it wasn't the kind of character they said they had been grooming me to play, which was the upmarket, upper-class juvenile lead. This chap was a bit of a wide-boy, a layabout with Cockney accent and so on. And weak. I had the most terrible bloody row about that. Finally I did it because I said, 'I'll go to the press, you know,' and it would have looked a bit daft if they'd stopped me.

How did you get the roles you had then?

The studio did it. If a picture came into Pinewood the pressure would be on – a lot of them were Rank pictures anyway – and the producers and directors would be persuaded, if possible, to use Rank contract people. The reason I lasted all that time, and was quite well known (though I don't think my being in a picture ever specifically sold a ticket, even in England), was that they would loan you out, under the terms of contract, and I did several pictures for other people, Romulus, ABPC, Fox, whatever. And their loan-out price on you would be your year's salary, so in my third year, when I did a picture for Romulus, I was getting £4,000 a year, and the cost to Romulus was £4,000 for me. Rank was then clear. They'd got their money back on me and I went on to do another three pictures for them that year, so they had me in three pictures for nothing. If I was loaned out again, as I was in another couple of years, we would split the overage.

Yours looks like a typical '50s career in the kinds of films you were in. War stories, colonial adventures, frivolous romantic comedies, and so on. How did you feel about this at the time?

It was very difficult. Take the reason *The Angry Silence* got made. I was doing a war picture in '58 or '59 called *Sea of Sand*, with Dickie Attenborough. The director was Guy Green, whom I'd worked with in *House of Secrets*, and we were having lunch just before we went off to Libya to make the film, and I said, 'Honestly, Guy, I think it's pathetic. Here we are more than ten years after the war has finished, and we're still making pictures about it. Why aren't we making pictures about what's happening now?' 'Such as?' he said. I said, 'Well, when I was in rep in York, a chap there had refused to join a strike, because it wasn't a union-called strike, it was a wildcat strike, and he'd been sent to Coventry, not just him, but his family too, and it'd gone on for a year or more and he finally gassed himself. He couldn't take it any more.' It must have stuck in my head and I said, 'That's the sort of thing we should be making movies about.' He said, 'Why don't you? Have you written any of that?'

Then, by coincidence, Dickie had just formed a company with Bryan Forbes called Beaver, and they were looking for a subject. I spoke to Dickie about it when we were on location out in the desert, and he said, 'Get me your script.' So when I got back, I bashed it out with my brother [Richard Gregson]. First draft, story outline and first script. And Dickie by this time, with Guy Green again, coincidentally, had gone off to make a picture called *SOS Pacific*, in which they met Pier Angeli. She was so engaged by the script of *The Angry Silence* that she asked Dickie if she could be in it, playing his wife. Now it hadn't been written for an Italian, obviously, and we couldn't have afforded to pay Pier Angeli her sort of money, but she really wanted to do it. Then Bryan did the shooting script and that's how it got made. We all did it for nothing – £1,000 each, against a percentage, which still owes me a few pounds.

Did you have much choice in the roles you played in these war films or romantic comedies?

Technically, you had none. You had to play as cast. I was suspended once and had one of my first big rows. It was over a picture called *The Gypsy and the Gentleman*. Keith Michell played the part they wanted me to do. And Pat McGoohan played a gypsy, and Melinda Mercouri played his sister. It was directed by Joe Losey; now, I knew Joe's reputation and he wanted me to do it. I read it and I thought the part was awful, and the gypsy was a far better part, but that was the part that Pat was under contract to do. So I told Olive Dodds I didn't want to do it and she said, 'Well, go and have dinner with Joe Losey, who'd like to talk to you about it.' So I did. If he'd said, 'Look, it's a piece of junk, but I think we can do something good with it,' I'd have said OK, but he tried to tell me that it was a good script. And I'm listening to this man and I thought, how could you possibly have stood up against

McCarthy and you're giving me this. If he'd been honest with me, I'd have done it, but people are very seldom honest with actors. So I said no and was suspended.

Then somebody asked for me for an outside picture. I was taken off suspension and loaned out to somebody else. And they added on the suspended time, you see. You didn't get paid, you weren't allowed to work for anybody else. And the time that you were on suspension, which could be as long as the picture that you'd turned down was shooting, was added on to your contract, but not at the end rate for that year, whichever year it was. It was autocratic to a degree.

Then there's a really odd one among your '60s films. *The Royal Hunt of the Sun*, which I don't think was commercially successful.

No, it wasn't. That's the one I met Phil Yorden on. Phil had been out there in Spain, through the Samuel Bronson days, he'd been a writer for Bronson and I think he was the producer on *The Battle of the Bulge* that Bob Shaw was in. He was very fond of Bob. He had the rights to do *Royal Hunt of the Sun* from the play and it was to have been done in whatever huge wide-screen thing that *The Battle of the Bulge* was done in. Then for some reason the budget was cut by two-thirds and so, instead of their going to Peru and doing it all on a big scale, it was all reduced and ends up a rather small-scale picture. Chris Plummer played Atahualpa and Bob Shaw was Pizarro. My character was the king's representative, and Phil liked me and built my part up a bit. But it was too much chat, we ended up just shooting the play really, on a set in a studio in Madrid.

You then did *Doctor in Love*. Did you simply have to do this?

Well, Dirk had decided he didn't want to do any more 'Doctors', though he later went back to them. *Doctor in Love* was really nothing to do with me but it was the top money-making film in England that year. It was quite fun, you know, and anyway, I didn't have any choice about it.

To an outsider, what looked like your more serious roles were in films like *Sapphire*, *The Angry Silence* and *Life for Ruth* in the early '60s. What do you recall about these?

I made *Angry Silence* because I knew what I wanted to do. I certainly wasn't going on playing those architects or doctors. But it wasn't very easy. In fact, most actors don't have much option, you do what you get offered. There have never been bundles of scripts coming through my letter-boxes. I've never been out of work much, but that's partly because I've done what came along. In the '60s, I worked for Visconti, Joe Losey and Bob Wise, three of the most successful directors ever, but the pictures I did with them probably were their least successful films. Now that's the luck of the draw. But, I liked *Sapphire*. That was Basil Dearden and Michael Relph, at Pinewood, where they had a sort of independent status because of their track record from Ealing, they had a certain amount of autonomy. And *Life for Ruth* was made by them as well. There was the same writer too, Janet Green. I *did* choose to do *Life for Ruth* because my contract with Rank was finished then. It was, I think, in '61 and I was under contract to Columbia for two years. Basil knew what kind of picture he wanted to make, and Michael was a very good producer. I remember Basil talking to me once on *Life for Ruth*, which was quite a hard picture to do. I said, 'I'm a bit worried about this,' and he said, 'Michael, old chap, you are the actor, we pay you to know how to do these things. I would no more expect to tell you how to play this scene than I would expect you to tell me how to direct.'

What do you recall of some of those other directors you worked for?

Guy Green was a friend of mine; he taught me a lot about lighting as he began as a cinematographer, and won an Oscar as David Lean's cameraman on *Great Expectations*. As for Joe Losey, I thought he was a pretentious, very overrated director. I did a picture for him called *Modesty Blaise* and I found him no help. Ralph Thomas was enormously supported by Betty Box, who was a very good producer, and I think most of Ralph's pictures were done with Betty. They were a team for years, that whole Box–Rogers–Thomas clan, and Muriel Box, who was Betty's sister-in-law, directed me in *Eyewitness*.

What do you remember of Philip Leacock's *High Tide at Noon*?

Phil was in favour then because he'd made a very successful and charming picture called *The Kidnappers*, which was set in Nova Scotia, like *High Tide*. It had the same writer, Neil Paterson. There were a lot of problems with it, because we didn't go to Canada; we shot it down in the West Country. Also,

Betta St John, an American dancer in *South Pacific* at Drury Lane, was cast as the girl in it, and what she hadn't told them was that she was four months pregnant. By the time we finished shooting the picture she couldn't be shot below the shoulders. There were a lot of problems with that. Flora Robson and Pat McGoohan were in it, but I don't remember much about it except that it was about lobster fishermen, and the last line, 'The bugs [vernacular for lobsters] are crawling.' There must be a happier line than this to bring down a curtain.

What about *The Silent Enemy*, directed by William Fairchild?

Yes, he wrote the script too. It was nearly all shot in Gibraltar and Malta. All of the water stuff was. It was about a real person, 'Buster' Crabb, who foiled the Italians who had this flotilla of midget submarines that were banging off all these ships in the harbour just across the bay from Gibraltar. I loved working with Larry Harvey in it; he was a wonderful bloke. Always got a bad press because he bated them, he used to send them up, and they couldn't stand it. He was one of the wittiest and most relaxed people you ever met, but as soon as he got in front of a camera he became all stiff and started to 'act'. I never admired him as an actor. He was OK as Joe Lampton, but the part carried him rather. He was his own man, Larry. The crew always loved him, you can always tell from that. He lived this wonderful sort of elegant lifestyle, even on location, which used to annoy people, but I thought it was very funny.

From the mid '60s you appeared in a number of films that seemed much more consciously aimed at international markets. Was this a conscious decision on your part?

No, it's just the way it happened. There were fewer pictures around and I found that I couldn't get cast by the new directors. They'd seen enough of me. I'd had seven years of Rank pictures and I consciously tried to break that image by going back into acting at Stratford and doing plays and so on. I never worked for any of those directors, Schlesinger or Jack Clayton or Lindsay Anderson, either in a movie or on stage, which I regret, but they didn't want me, so I did what there was to do. They wanted Albert Finney or Tom Courtenay. They wanted a different type, a different look.

▲ The Private Life of Henry VIII *1933*   ▼ Evergreen *1934*

▲ Sing As We Go *1934* ▼ The Thirty-Nine Steps *1935*

▲ Fires Were Started *1943*   ▼ Fanny by Gaslight *1944*

▲ Henry V *1945* ▼ Brief Encounter *1945*

Charles Crichton

b. 1910

Assistant editor, editor or co-editor: *Men of Tomorrow* (1932), *Cash, The Private Life of Henry VIII, The Girl from Maxim's* (1933), *Sanders of the River* (1935), *Things to Come* (1936), *Twenty-One Days, The Elephant Boy* (1937), *Prison without Bars* (1938), *The Thief of Baghdad, Old Bill and Son* (1940), **The Young Veterans, *Yellow Caesar, *Guests of Honour, *Find, Fix and Strike* (1941), *The Big Blockade, *Greek Testament* (1942), *Nine Men* (1943)

Associate producer: *Nine Men* (1943)

Director: *For Those in Peril* (1944), *Painted Boats, Dead of Night* (1945), *Hue and Cry* (1947), *Against the Wind, Another Shore* (1948), *Train of Events* (1949), *Dance Hall* (1950), *The Lavender Hill Mob* (1951), *Hunted* (1952), *The Titfield Thunderbolt* (1953), *The Love Lottery, The Divided Heart* (1954), *The Man in the Sky* (1957), *Floods of Fear, Law and Disorder* (1958), *The Battle of the Sexes* (1959), *The Boy Who Stole a Million* (1960), *The Third Secret* (1964), *He Who Rides a Tiger* (1965), *A Fish Called Wanda* (1988)

* Documentary or short film.

Neither as drily satirical as Alexander Mackendrick nor as mordant as Robert Hamer, Charles Crichton is perhaps more responsible than either of the others for the affection in which the idea of 'Ealing comedy' is held. As he points out, the genre was far less homogeneous than popular memory would have it. His own major contributions to it were *Hue and Cry*, which set the ball rolling and which still looks fresh and inventive, and *The Lavender Hill Mob*, that archetypal Ealing celebration of English eccentricity and little-man-triumphant (more or less). He had his failures with such films as *Another Shore* and the tired prettiness of *The Titfield Thunderbolt*; but, as well as the comedy triumphs, there are real pleasures to be had from the unusual war film, *Against the Wind*, and *The Divided Heart*, the poignant story of a child who becomes a battleground in post-war Europe. By his own admission, Crichton was not drawn to the abrasive or the violent, but, within the range he elected, he showed again in the 1988 hit *A Fish Called Wanda* why his achievement is so fondly remembered.

Interview date: October 1992

You were involved as assistant editor or co-editor on some of the most important London Films productions of the '30s. Did this come about because you'd met Zoltan Korda?

Yes it did, and because I worked for Zolly it followed that I also worked for Alex [Alexander Korda]. I dearly loved them both and Vincent [Korda] as well. But at the beginning, Alex was, to me, a remote and formidable figure. When I became one of the editors on *Things to Come*, I showed him a rough cut of a sequence showing London under attack from the air. (This was before the war.) The sequence was full of violence, gunfire, bombs, people running for their lives ... Alex said, 'Charlie, you have made a bloody mess of this. It should be that everyone is standing there worried, waiting because they know something is going to happen, and you haven't put that in the cut at all.' And I said, 'But the director didn't shoot such a scene.' So he said, 'You are a bloody fool, Charlie! You take the bits before he has said "Action!" and you take the bits after he has said "Cut!" and you put them all together and you make a marvellous sequence. What's wrong with you?' From the moment I was called a bloody fool, I knew that my job was safe! I was a member of the Korda team. But what was more important was that I was beginning to learn that a script is not the Bible, it is not a blueprint which must be followed precisely, word for word, to the very last detail.

Did you start at Ealing with the editing of Alberto Cavalcanti's *The Young Veterans*?

I was obviously going to be called up for the Army and, while I was waiting, I edited some propaganda films for Cavalcanti, such as *Young Veterans* and *Yellow Caesar*. Then, because I became involved in propaganda, I *wasn't* called up. So I worked with Cav, who was the real guru of Ealing Studios. 'Sir Mick' [Balcon] was a lovely man and loved films, but he hadn't a clue about how to make them. His instinct was more for the box office and how to lay out a programme for the studio. Cavalcanti was the one who had the inspirational effect on us all. These so-called documentaries which Cav made weren't really documentaries at all. He would assemble masses of material from many sources – newsreels, libraries, etc . . . and then completely re-edit them to put over a point which had never been intended by the originators of the material. *Young Veterans*, for example, was about 'the boys' returning from the disaster of Dunkirk

and rebuilding a new and formidable Army. Somehow or other, Cav managed to use shots of French troops skiing in the Alps to put over his point. Another lesson for me: film is a highly malleable medium.

How did you come to be a director?

Well, in those days it never crossed my mind that I might direct. Suddenly I heard that my assistant in the cutting room had been elevated to that noble position! 'What about me?' Mick said, 'Why not? All right, go off and do something.' There was a brief delay while I edited *The Big Blockade* for Charles Frend. Charlie was a good pal of mine, but on this picture we had terrible rows and were on the verge of being deadly enemies – until the pub opened across the road. The Red Lion was a spot where we all gathered in the evening and discussed the day's work, each other's scripts, rough cuts, future projects and so on. Many problems were sorted out over a pint of beer or a tot of whisky.

How did you come to direct your first feature, *For Those in Peril*?

Not a feature film. In those days, there was always a film of about fifty-five minutes long to support the main feature. This one was about the Air–Sea Rescue boats which lay along the length of our southern coast and went charging across the sea, defying enemy interference, to rescue aircraft crews who had been forced to ditch it in the Channel. It was written by TEB Clarke – Tibby, as he was called – who later became instrumental in creating the legend of Ealing comedy.

What was the purpose behind *Painted Boats*, your next film for Ealing?

It is hard to believe that a picture which was largely about the history of the English canal system could, at the time of war, have in any way encouraged the people of Britain. But the war was clearly coming to an end and we wanted people to believe, as we believed, that when peace did come it wouldn't be like 1918, with the soldiers all coming back and no work for them. We were trying to say there was a future. I don't remember much more than that, except that when the doodlebugs were exploding all over London we were peacefully making this gentle, moving picture some sixty miles away in the heart of Buckinghamshire. The main character was played by a total amateur, Bill Blewitt, a postman from Cornwall with a strong Cornish accent. In spite of his accent, he would sit in a canalside pub and beguile visitors for hours with stories of his childhood working on the barges, 'man and boy', year after year, ever since, supposedly, he'd first opened his eyes to see his mother straining at the tiller of the barge.

What do you recall of your involvement in *Dead of Night*?

Well, as you know, *Dead of Night* was what was called a portmanteau film. It was made of five separate ghost stories, four of them grisly creepy, but the fifth, the one I directed, pure comedy written by my old friend, Tibby Clarke. This was the first time I had worked with experienced professional actors and I was scared stiff of them even though they were those most helpful of gentlemen, Basil Radford and Naunton Wayne. On the first day of shooting, I was trying to slow up Basil's performance, trying to make him express every single thought which might lie behind each line of dialogue and hitting it on the head with a hammer. Basil very politely said, 'I don't think it will work that way. I will try, but it won't be funny.' He was dead right. The rushes were awful. We reshot the scene Basil's way and it was very funny indeed. I'd learnt another lesson. Cast with care and then trust the instincts of your artistes.

Would you say your next film. *Hue and Cry*, established your particular niche at Ealing?

I'm not sure what you mean by 'particular niche'. It certainly established me as a comedy director and I am still very proud of it. It was fresh and original. This is how it all came about: one day the producer Henry Cornelius (when you see 'associate producer' on an Ealing film, it means 'producer') said, 'Wouldn't it be marvellous to see shots of hundreds of young kids charging through the bombed ruins of London?' Tibby Clarke overheard the remark, took it up and invented an impressive story which would have its climax in these rushing hordes which Cornelius had imagined. Tibby, Cornelius and I worked closely together on the screenplay. That was the admirable practice at Ealing in those days.

This was, some would say, the film which ushered in the whole idea of Ealing comedy.

I think it broke away from traditional film comedy, which relied heavily on dialogue and slapstick. But if *Hue and Cry* had not been made, Robert Hamer would still have given us *Kind Hearts and Coronets* and Sandy Mackendrick would have made *The Man in the White Suit* and *The Ladykillers*. *Kind Hearts* and *The Ladykillers* were black comedies. *The Man in the White Suit* had a serious theme behind it. I do not think *Hue and Cry* was the first of a genre.

To me the one thing they all have in common is their way of homing in on certain ideas of Englishness – like the legendary English love of the eccentric, etc. They couldn't have been made in any other country.

There was a time when the Rank Organisation went mid-Atlantic, which really meant they were trying to tailor their films to American tastes and styles. That's all very well, but let the USA make its own kind of films and let us make ours. The most successful of our pictures in America have been essentially British and American audiences have enjoyed them because of that.

Did you enjoy working at Ealing more than anywhere else?

Ealing was a snug nursery where one was surrounded by talented playmates and supervised by a tolerant headmaster – Sir Michael Balcon. Well, he was not *all* that tolerant. We were each expected to make one picture a year, or else! Outside, it was very much colder, more daunting, but once a script had been financed and a unit gathered together, things were not all that very much different from Ealing.

Gordon Jackson told me about how you came in on *Whisky Galore!* to help Sandy Mackendrick.

It seems funny to say 'help Sandy', but what happened was very simple. It was Sandy's and Danischewsky's first picture, and they had an inexperienced editor. There came a time when the resulting mishmash (caused by editing) convinced Balcon the film should be issued as a second feature. I had had nothing to do with the subject, though I had read the script (and wanted to direct it), and could not believe that such a decision should be made. Balcon told me to look at the version as it stood. I did. I said (as an ex-editor), 'This is a cutting-room mishmash.' Balcon said; 'OK, recut it.' Which I did, checking up with Sandy all the time. The final result was the brilliant picture which Sandy and Danischewsky had envisaged in the first place.

Considering what a much-loved character actor Jack Warner was, it seems daring to have twice cast him as a villain – first as the chief crook in *Hue and Cry* and later as the traitor in *Against the Wind*. How did audiences react to this?

Good question. *Against the Wind* was a very serious picture which dealt with the training of agents who were being parachuted into enemy territory. One of the main characters was a double agent, a traitor, but a man of great charm. Who could be better to play this, we thought, than Jack Warner? He accepted the role, then suddenly, one week before shooting, he foresaw danger. He wanted to withdraw, but it was too late. He played the villain and the result was disastrous; the audience would not believe that their beloved Jack was a two-faced sewer rat. It destroyed their belief. In *Hue and Cry* his villainy was a joke. The picture was pure fantasy. Jack could do what he liked.

I thought *Against the Wind* was an exciting and interesting piece, very unlike other Ealing war films.

Simone Signoret was wonderful in it, of course, and so was Gordon Jackson. Simone was then at the top of her form and very beautiful. Gordon was an innocent twenty-year-old. We were preparing to shoot a love scene between the two of them. Simone came to me in an unusually worried state of mind. 'So we kiss,' she said, 'and what will Gordon's reaction be, how will he respond? . . . All right, leave it to me.' I left it to her. We shot the scene. Gordon's reaction was ecstatic. Afterwards he came to me, eyes bulging from his head. 'Charlie, why didn't you warn me? I went to kiss her and before I knew it her tongue was halfway down my throat!'

Ealing often made films focusing on a group of people. This was true of your film, *Dance Hall*. Was it difficult following the threads of each character and keeping the audience's interest?

Yes, very difficult. Diana Morgan did a most creative job in writing the script. It was a film I didn't particularly wish to make, in the first place, but Balcon called me into his office and we had one of those conversations: 'I'm not putting pressure on you, Charlie, but if you don't . . .' Once we had got the research started behind the project, I found myself deeply involved – with the people who went to dance halls once a week, the different types of bands, a world which has now disappeared. The film was shown on television some years ago and critics were interested in it as a sort of documentary of the '50s.

For many people, your next film, *The Lavender Hill Mob*, is perhaps the most fondly remembered of all the Ealing comedies.

Strange, because it started off as a serious thriller! Tibby had been asked to write a sequel to his crime story, *The Blue Lamp*, but instead came up with this comedy idea. As you know, the story concerned two respectable and ageing gentlemen, the one a bank-teller, the other a purveyor of gew-gaws and trinkets, who managed to purloin a hundredweight or two of gold ingots from the bank. These they melted down and turned them into toy miniatures of the Eiffel Tower and whisked them abroad under the very noses of the police and customs officials. The original script then followed the adventures of these gew-gaws as they passed into different hands.

Michael Truman (associate producer) pointed out that the audience would not care less about the Eiffel Towers or about any new characters who became involved with them. They would want to know what happened to the architects of this imaginative crime. So the three of us sat down and hammered out a new storyline, with Tibby, of course, doing most of the hammering. We were very lucky with the casting. Stanley Holloway and Alec Guinness worked wonderfully together. Their styles were completely different but they made a perfect duet.

The film you made with Dirk Bogarde – *Hunted* – seems like an Ealing project but it isn't.

The producer of *Hunted* was Julian Wintle of the Rank Organisation. He approached Jack Whittingham (also from Ealing) and me with his script and Balcon was willing to subcontract us if we so wished. The picture was due to start in four weeks' time and we were given one week to make up our minds. The script was terrible. The idea behind it was possible. Within six days Jack had come up with a stunning idea about how to solve the story's problems. Within another three weeks we had a shooting script. I had actually started shooting before the wee boy who was central to the story was actually found. We had, of course, tested dozens of children and not been happy. Then one week after we had started, we heard Jon Whiteley reciting 'The Owl and the Pussycat' on radio, and that was that. He got the part. I don't think Dirk Bogarde had been enthusiastic about playing the lead in the film. He was sick of playing what he called a 'mackintosh boy'. But when he started to work with Jon Whiteley, something happened and the result was two perfect performances, and, I think, a moving film.

***The Titfield Thunderbolt* was your first use of colour. Did you enjoy this?**

I don't think colour necessarily adds a great deal to most films, but *The Titfield Thunderbolt* just required it, to do justice to the ancient and gaily painted engine and the rural scenery. Douglas Slocombe was the cameraman, and, if the picture was not entirely satisfying, at least his work gave one something lyrical to look at.

The Divided Heart is still a touching film. Was Jack Whittingham's screenplay based on fact?

Absolutely, except that there were three trials of the case, which we compressed into one. We interviewed all of the people concerned in that sad story, the German foster-parents, who had adopted the child in the belief that he was a war orphan, the boy himself, who had thought he was a German and did not know that he had Slovenian parents. His real father had been shot as a member of the Resistance. When his mother was released from Auschwitz, she had no idea what had happened to her child. The relationship between the boy and his foster-parents had been very warm indeed, and I cannot judge whether it was right or wrong to bring the whole affair out into the open instead. Certainly it was a very tragic moment when the boy was removed from the care of those he had loved as if they had been his real mother and father.

Were you with Ealing until it finished? Two of your later films – The Battle of the Sexes and Law and Disorder – seem like Ealing projects but were not.

I left two or three years before Balcon announced to an astonished world that the studio was to be sold. I do not feel that the pictures you mention were quite the success they should have been.

Maybe they lacked the Ealing ambience. But I do think the performance of Peter Sellers in *The Battle of the Sexes* was about the best thing he ever did. Mr Martin, the ancient retainer of a long-established company, which was being shaken to its roots by a 'new broom', was a part with every opportunity for overplaying, but Peter didn't take the bait.

How did you come to make the hugely successful *A Fish Called Wanda*?

John Cleese and I had known each other for many years. We had often worked together for Video Arts, the very successful company which he had been instrumental in founding to make serious training films for business people – in comedy. In 1983, he started to explain to me an idea he had for a feature film in which he would play a barrister – just that. In 1987, we made *A Fish Called Wanda*. Of course, we didn't spend the intervening years just slogging away at the script, we did other things in between, but those four years gave time for John's original idea to mature naturally, unhurried by the pressure of time. And during those years, John approached the artistes he wanted: Jamie Lee Curtis, Michael Palin and Kevin Kline. He told them our basic story and listened to any ideas or suggestions they had to make. Finally, in 1987, we had a week of rehearsals in front of the basic unit and then a gap of two weeks in which to incorporate any new ideas which had been thrown up and to polish the script. I think this is the ideal way to work, with everybody contributing their special talents and feeling they are part of the film.

Peter Cushing

1913–1994

Actor: *The Man in the Iron Mask, A Chump at Oxford* (1939), *Vigil in the Night, Laddie, *Dreams* (1940), *They Dare Not Love, Your Hidden Master, *We All Help, *The New Teacher, *Safety First* (1941), *Women in War* (1942), **It Might Be You* (1947), *Hamlet* (1948), *Moulin Rouge* (1953), *The Black Knight* (1954), *The End of the Affair* (1955), *Alexander the Great, Magic Fire, Time Without Pity*

(1956), *The Curse of Frankenstein, The Abominable Snowman, Violent Playground* (1957), *Dracula, The Revenge of Frankenstein* (1958), *John Paul Jones, The Hound of the Baskervilles, The Mummy* (1959), *The Flesh and the Fiends, Cone of Silence, The Brides of Dracula, Sword of Sherwood Forest, Suspect* (1960), *Fury at Smuggler's Bay, The Hellfire Club, The Naked Edge, Cash on Demand* (1961), *Captain Clegg, The Man Who Finally Died, The Devil's Agent* (1962), *The Evil of Frankenstein, The Gorgon, Dr Terror's House of Horrors* (1964), *She, Dr Who and the Daleks, The Skull* (1965), *Island of Terror, Daleks Invasion Earth AD 2150* (1966), *Frankenstein Created Woman, Some May Live, Night of the Big Heat, Torture Garden, Caves of Steel, The Mummy's Shroud* (narr only) (1967), *Blood Beast Terror, Corruption* (1968), *Frankenstein Must Be Destroyed, Doctors Wear Scarlet, Scream and Scream Again, One More Time* (1969), *The House That Dripped Blood, The Vampire Lovers, I, Monster, Incense for the Damned* (1970), *Twins of Evil* (1971), *Tales from the Crypt, Dracula AD 1972, Nothing but the Night, Fear in the Night, Dr Phibes Rises Again, Asylum, The Creeping Flesh, Bride of Fengriffen, Horror Express* (1972), *Frankenstein and the Monster from Hell, The Satanic Rites of Dracula, And Now the Screaming Starts, From Beyond the Grave* (1973), *The Beast Must Die, The Legend of the Seven Golden Vampires, Madhouse, Legend of the Werewolf, Shatter, Tender Dracula* (1974), *Death Corps, The Ghoul* (1975), *The Devil's Men, At the Earth's Core, Trial by Combat* (1976), *The Uncanny, Star Wars, Die Standarte* (1977), *Hitler's Son, Touch of the Sun, *The Detour* (narr only) (1978), *Arabian Adventure* (1979), *Monster Island* (1980), *Black Jack* (1981), *House of the Long Shadows, Sword of the Valiant* (1982), *Top Secret!* (1984), *Biggles* (1986)
* Short film.

'It's funny, isn't it? The public want the same thing over and over again.'[1] So, in 1971, Peter Cushing mused about the extraordinary success story of the Hammer horror series, of which his multiple incarnations of Dr Frankenstein and Van Helsing in the Dracula films were so crucial a component. His chiselled features, refined, even ascetic, speech and bearing are by now so firmly associated with these mythic figures that it requires an effort of will – or research – to complete the picture of his career.

In fact, and improbably, he began in pre-war Hollywood. 'James Whale was at that time directing *The Man in the Iron Mask*, in which Louis Hayward played the twins ... and the director was looking for someone to play opposite him in this split-screen process,'[2] and he followed this with several roles in Hollywood. Post-war in England, Olivier cast him as Osric in the film of *Hamlet*, and he then toured Australasia with the Olivier company. Throughout the early '50s, he worked in the theatre, and television, notably in *1984*, as a man locked in a cell with rats: 'I came out of it with a quite mistaken reputation for horror';[3] and there was an odd selection of films, including *Moulin Rouge*, Losey's *Time Without Pity* and *The End of the Affair*, in which he gave the film's best performance as the cuckolded husband of Deborah Kerr, in an adaptation of Graham Greene's novel.

'*The Curse of Frankenstein* in 1957 ... was my first appearance as that enterprising individual ... It proved to be an enormous box-office success, and six more of this anti-hero's adventures were made by the same company over a period of fifteen years.'[4] In 1973, he said, 'Frankenstein ... has perhaps become a little more ruthless, but basically he remains the same though the way in which these scripts are written is bound to reflect current attitudes to some extent.'[5] Cushing doesn't go on to develop this interesting idea, but has clearly thought a good deal about the role, elsewhere considering: 'I think Frankenstein is basically right. We must experiment in every way we can and push forward the boundaries of our knowledge and understanding.'[6] Playfully, he notes, '... now Dr Barnard has caught up. He hasn't gone quite as far as me, because I have transplanted brains. Not very successfully, I admit, but we've all got to start somewhere.'[7]

That last comment is from the John Player Lecture, given at the National Film Theatre in London, suggesting the *réclame* which Hammer came to enjoy. Cushing remembers that: 'Hammer films were slated in some quarters when they were first shown, but are now preserved as classics of their kind.'[8] As well as the Frankenstein films, he also 'had the good fortune to appear in several Dracula pictures made by Hammer, in which my dear friend Christopher Lee was quite magnificent as the Count. They became known as Hammer-Horror Films, but we both prefer the title Fantasy Films ...'[9]

Both Cushing and the tall, elegant, mesmeric Lee became inextricably linked in the public mind with

Hammer, especially with director Terence Fisher, who began his career on Rank's Highbury Studios 'B' picture programme and directed a number of pre-horror Hammers before hitting pay-dirt in 1957. Lee went to Hollywood in search of different roles (e.g., *Airport '77*) but Fisher stayed with horror until the end of his career, acquiring popularity and cult status in the process.

Cushing's work, though dominated by the horror mode, is by no means restricted to it. In his autobiography, he recalls the things he 'learnt to do in the line of duty', naming such varied films as *The Skull* (he learnt snooker), *She* ('I had to ride a camel'), *Cone of Silence* (it 'dealt with civil aviation, and I had to learn how to control an aeroplane'), and 'I rode at my peril in many films, among them ... *The Black Knight* and *Fury at Smuggler's Bay*.'[10] Stylishly dedicated as he is in, say, Fisher's *The Brides of Dracula* or John Hough's *Twins of Evil*, his most incisive performance in my view is as a thin-lipped bank manager, under dreadful strain, in Quentin Lawrence's *Cash on Demand*, possibly the best 'B' film ever made in Britain.

1 David Castell, 'Professor Van Helsing is alive and well and living in the King's Road, SW3' in *Films Illustrated*, December 1971, p 6
2 John Player Lecture, National Film Theatre, London, extracted in *Films Illustrated*, October 1973, p 150
3 Castell, p 6
4 Peter Cushing, *Past Forgetting: Memoirs of the Hammer Years*, Weidenfeld & Nicolson, London, 1988, p 13
5 Allen Eyles *et al* (eds), *The House of Horror: The Story of Hammer Films*, Lorrimer Publishing, London, 1973, p 20
6 Castell, p 8
7 John Player Lecture
8 Cushing, *Past Forgetting*, p 75
9 Cushing's foreword to Richard Dalby (ed), *Vampire Stories*, Michael O'Mara Books, London, 1992, p vii
10 Cushing, *Past Forgetting*, pp 41 and 43

Sir John Davis

1906–1993

One of the names most closely associated with the Rank Organisation during the 1940s and, particularly, the '50s was that of John Davis. He had early turned to accountancy 'because it taught general management', and he became involved with Oscar Deutsch, having responsibility for keeping the records and management accounting in good order. Eventually he became Managing Director for Deutsch's Odeon Cinemas chain, which was bought by Rank after Deutsch's death. In the late '40s, Davis worked closely with Rank in devising strategies to remedy financial difficulties. These made him a sometimes unpopular figure in the eyes of creative personnel who queried his policies. However, Davis insists that he never interfered with creative decisions, and makes clear that his first loyalty was always to J Arthur Rank, whom he greatly admired. His knowledge of the British film industry, from a managerial point of view, is unique and would repay further documentation.

Interview date: July 1990

Your name is always associated with the Rank Organisation. When did you and Mr Rank, as he was then, meet and in what circumstances?

The Dorchester Hotel in London has a big reception area and I was told to go there to meet Arthur Rank; I was standing on one side of the vestibule and he was standing on the other side; I was wondering to myself who that was and thinking I wouldn't like to cross swords with him because he looked a very austere person. It turned out to be Mr Rank and that was in March 1938. I found out in later years that he wasn't austere at all. I had worked as accountant to Oscar Deutsch in the 1930s and later became Managing Director of his Odeon Cinemas chain. Arthur Rank became associated with Oscar Deutsch only twelve or eighteen months before Deutsch's death and it was agreed in principle that when Oscar died his estate would sell his interest to Arthur Rank. When Arthur realised how important film was in the life of a nation, and that the American film industry had largely a stranglehold throughout the world, he decided to take them on, to show the British way of life as compared with the American. He wasn't anti-American at all, though.

What would you say to an account I've read somewhere that yours and Mr Rank's qualities were complementary – that is, his unbridled optimism was complemented by your more cautious approach?

Our relationship was complementary for a much deeper reason: he believed in the things I could do and I believed in him. I have never known such a fine man, whose attitude towards life applied to everything he did. He was undoubtedly a happy man himself. He was a man of great vision as far as the film industry was concerned; one of the problems was that many of the people whom he trusted completely to make films didn't share this vision. On the one hand, you had those who thought the only things you could make were so-called 'English films' – small comedies and the like; and on the other hand, there were people wanting to make international pictures – neither of which was the answer to the question. When he got to grips with the film industry, he realised the importance of supplying his people with the latest equipment; he relied on them to produce the actual film. He was not a picture-maker and never tried to be, although he enjoyed films, and that was my situation too.

In box-office – and artistic – terms, British

cinema reached a peak in the mid '40s. How difficult was it to arrange overseas distribution, especially in the US, even for the best of such films?

It was my responsibility at that time to go out and acquire cinemas all around the world or make distribution arrangements, so that these films could be shown. It was particularly difficult in America but that's a another subject, it's very complicated. You must have international markets. Because of the strength of the American industry, if one is to compete with them one must have a strong foreign market as well as a domestic one, if the producing country has only a limited population. You couldn't include the Commonwealth countries in that context. I had to go to Canada, where the circuit was dominated by an American corporation (the name of which doesn't matter), and they were trying to block any foreign film of any sort from coming in.

With hindsight, the '40s and '50s seem a sort of boom period in British cinema. Is that how it seemed to you in your managerial position?

The question you raise is difficult to answer briefly. At the end of World War II, this country was, for all practical purposes, bankrupt, and certainly insofar as the US dollar was concerned. The Government was looking for ways to save dollar payments to the American companies. At that time Arthur Rank and I were in America and were told by the American industry that the British Government intended to bring in legislation which would restrict the flow of dollars to America. At that time the Americans thought incorrectly that Arthur Rank was sponsored by the British Government. We were trying to negotiate with the Americans to arrange for British films to be shown in the United States with the support of their industry. They told us that they would support any scheme which conserved dollars, *provided it was voluntary* and not by legislation. They were afraid that, if it was by legislation, other countries also short of dollars would follow the same road. Arthur agreed to send me back with a message to the Chancellor of the Exchequer. I spent a whole day sitting outside the Cabinet Office and was not seen by anyone until the end of the day, when I was told that the problem was settled. Consequently, I could not convey to the Government that they would get voluntary support from America if they produced a scheme which would control sending dollars to America.

In a nutshell, the Government intended to impose

legally an *ad valorem* duty on all foreign films imported, basically American. The *ad valorem* duty was to be calculated by estimating what a film would earn, and this had to be deposited with the British authorities before the film could be released to the public. This, of course, would involve large sums of money, which the Americans either didn't have or were not prepared to put up. Sir Stafford Cripps and Mr [Harold] Wilson came to see Arthur, at which meeting I was present, saying that the country desperately needed his help to provide British films to replace the American films whose import would be restricted. Needless to say, Arthur agreed to support them. We were told we 'would be taken care of' when the *ad valorem* arrangement came to an end. We stepped up film production (in retrospect, beyond the capacity of the creative people), and ultimately incurred a loss of some £20 million.

The problem was further complicated by international politics. At the end of World War II the Americans were very generous in providing Marshall Aid to help restore Europe's economies and industries. Many Americans thought that we, the British, should only receive Marshall Aid if we were allowing films into this country, with the Americans having the right to remit dollars to pay for them. The outcome was that the Americans sent over one of their top people to negotiate a deal with the British Government, which cancelled the *ad valorem* duty, without, as far as I know, consulting any members of the British industry as to the effects of doing so. The fact was that a large backlog of American films, many of them great box-office attractions, flooded into the British market without any restriction, which explains the disaster with which we at Rank were faced. We had to work our way out of the problem without any help from the Government, but fortunately the National Provincial [now National Westminster] Bank gave us a lot of help, which enabled Rank over a period of time to pay off the bank with slow recovery.

Do you think the whole concept foundered because the British public always wanted to see American films anyway and because it was impossible for the British film industry to fill in the gap with production?

It really goes deeper than that. The real question was that the British Government could not afford the dollars that the importation of American films incurred; they produced a lot of money and we (i.e., the British film industry) could not afford to pay the dollars back to America, because we were desperately short of hard currency, particularly dollars, at the end of the war. As to whether we could fill the gap with British-made films, Arthur Rank was pressed very hard to do his best, which he did. Some films were good, some were not, and that created the problem.

When you were appointed Managing Director of the Rank Organisation, it had just suffered a loss of about £8 million. How did you go about reversing this trend?

The effect of the *ad valorem* duty and the promises which were made to slowly bring back American films meant, in round figures, we lost £20 million towards the end of the '40s. The broad issue was either to reverse that trend or go bust. In order to do that I had to make myself very unpopular to start with, by cutting every penny of expenditure that could be saved and selling everything that wasn't directly needed by the Organisation for it to continue.

What was your attitude to those independent production companies that operated under the Rank umbrella, for example Cineguild, The Archers, and so on?

They were independent units which approached Rank for the projects they wanted to make. They were indeed ideal filmmaking conditions and this was the great thing about Arthur Rank: he was convinced this was the way films ought to be made, and I think it was right. But the producers didn't play their cards very well and some took Arthur's approach as a sign of weakness, whereas it was giving them adequate facilities and opportunities to be creative. That set-up had essentially dwindled away by the early '50s; by then much of the film production was at Pinewood, which had by then become the best-equipped studio in Europe. Arthur Rank's approach was always 'I will give you the tools; you make the product.' It was very attractive to filmmakers – or should have been.

What do you recall of the American, Earl St John, whose name appears as Executive Producer on virtually all Pinewood films?

He came over to this country during the First World War as an American soldier and stayed here. Arthur and I appointed him Executive Producer and he was jolly good. As Executive Producer, his function was to produce films – to get together the units to make them. He was both a creative influence and a facilitator, with a grasp of the technical side of making films, and he understood the creative atmosphere.

I gather budgets were meant to be kept modest. If producers wanted to do something more extravagant, how would they persuade you?

They would use the subject matter and whether or not we could get a partner to come in – say, an American or European distributor. There was never a general limit on budgets, though. We tried to work with budgets which were realistic and then expected producers to keep to them. We would consider each project, the marketing people would express their views as to its potential. They would have looked back at another film of a similar type to see what it had done and attempted to measure the potential of a new film against its performance – whether a particular director had a good track record, things

like that. If the budget of a film was higher than we thought would enable it to recover its cost, we suggested to the producer he should get an American distributor, or maybe a European, to participate in the cost of the film.

How much time did you spend in the actual studios?

When you're running a large organisation you can't divide your time that way; it's all intermixed. I spent a lot of time at Pinewood, of course. I didn't want to exercise any influence over the kinds of films we made. Arthur Rank and I had one intention only and that was to make what today we would call 'clean' films which would be successful at the box office.

Basil Dearden
1911–1970

Director: *The Black Sheep of Whitehall (1941), *The Goose Steps Out (1942), *My Learned Friend, The Halfway House, The Bells Go Down (1943), They Came to a City (1944), *Dead of Night (1945), The Captive Heart (1946), Frieda (1947), Saraband for Dead Lovers (1948), *Train of Events, The Blue Lamp (1949), Pool of London, Cage of Gold (1950), *I Believe In You (1951), The Gentle Gunman (1952), *The Square Ring (1953), The Rainbow Jacket (1954), *The Ship that Died of Shame, *Out of the Clouds (1955), *Who Done It?, The Green Man (uncr) (1956), The Violent Playground, The Smallest Show on Earth (1957), Sapphire, The League of Gentlemen, Desert Mice (1959), *Man in the Moon (1960), Victim, The Secret Partner, *All Night Long (1961), Life for Ruth (1962), A Place To Go, The Mind Benders (1963), Woman of Straw (1964), Masquerade (1965), Khartoum (1966), Only When I Larf, The Assassination Bureau (1968), *The Man Who Haunted Himself (1970)

Producer: Davy (1957), Rockets Galore (1958)
* Co-directed.

'A ... struggle between material problems and matters of taste and intention faces the film director, who must be the driving force behind the industrial machine,'[1] wrote Basil Dearden in 1948. In the over forty films he made before his death in a car accident in 1970, critics sometimes argued that

his 'intention', often reformist in nature, achieved a somewhat muted realisation because of a 'taste' too blandly liberal. However, in dealing with 'material problems', with actually getting films made, he and his long-time associate, producer Michael Relph, made more than their share of intelligent, smartly paced entertainments, offering evidence for Dearden's dictum: 'Inspiration can be disciplined and organised.'[2]

By Relph's account in this book, they were not prepared, as some Ealing directors were, to wait for just the right subject. They wanted to work and they did, acquiring – somewhat unfairly – a reputation as Ealing's journeyman team. Further, it could be argued that they outlived Ealing more successfully than their colleagues.

The range of Dearden's credits is striking. He began at Ealing by co-directing three Will Hay comedies; there are fantasy/morality dramas in *They Came to a City* and *The Halfway House*; an episode in the famous horror film, *Dead of Night*; and a well-made all-out melodrama, *Cage of Gold*, which in fact says as much about the Ealing ethos, especially in relation to its wariness about sexuality, as the more famous comedies and realist dramas. *The Captive Heart* is a moving prisoner-of-war story (Dearden recalled filming in Germany: 'It was with something of the feeling of pioneers that we embarked upon the prospect of making the first peacetime film in Germany'[3]); *The Ship that Died of Shame*, a metaphorical losing-the-peace drama, gathers resonance with the years; and the heist comedy, *The League of Gentlemen*, surveys the peacetime doldrums with a cynical eye. ('It's a very good script. Not quite right, but very good. ... You'd better come and see me then. Talk about it,'[4] is how its author, Bryan Forbes, recalls Dearden's approach to him.) Underestimated at the time is the sumptuous period melodrama, *Saraband for Dead Lovers*, set at the court of the Elector of Hanover, who became George I of Great Britain and Ireland. It was produced according to a strict storyboard process, not always welcomed by directors.

Alexander Mackendrick, sketch artist for the process, recalled: 'I stood at the elbow of Basil Dearden; and he, on a set-plan, said, "I want a shot from here," and I'd say, "Well, if you want it like that, *this* will be in the foreground; do you want it like this?" And he'd say, "No, bigger" or "Further away", or "I want it to pan over here".'[5] The tiny recollection just hints at Dearden's careful craftsmanship.

It is for the 'social problem films' that he is best known: for *Frieda*, dramatising the plight of a German war bride in an English middle-class town (Dearden went to Sweden to cast the title role and tested Mai Zetterling: '... twenty-three, blonde, attractive and regarded as one of Sweden's foremost actresses'[6]); for that influential study of police in conflict with post-war delinquency, *The Blue Lamp*, which made Dirk Bogarde's name ('I need a weedy type . . . and you're a Rank contract artist,'[7] Dearden told him); for *Sapphire*, which tackled racial prejudice; for *Victim*, the first mainstream treatment of homosexuality; and, perhaps most impressive of all, *Life for Ruth*, which deals with religious fundamentalism. All these films use a melodramatic framework to accommodate a concern for social reform.

1 *Saraband for Dead Lovers – The Film and its Production*, Convoy, London, 1948, p 65. No author or editor given
2 *Saraband*, p 67
3 *The Cine-Technician*, January–February 1946, p 3
4 Bryan Forbes, *Notes for a Life*, Collins, London, 1974, p 291
5 Philip Kemp, *Lethal Innocence: The Cinema of Alexander Mackendrick*, Methuen, London, 1991, p 18
6 Basil Dearden, 'Tomorrow's Garbos want to come to Britain', *Picturegoer*, 20 September 1946, p 10
7 Dirk Bogarde, *Snakes and Ladders*, Chatto & Windus, London, 1978, p 129

Dame Judi Dench

b. 1934

Actor: *The Third Secret* (1964), *A Study in Terror,* *He Who Rides the Tiger, Four in the Morning*

(1965), *A Midsummer Night's Dream* (1968), *Luther* (1973), *Dead Cert* (1974), *Wetherby, A Room with a View, The Angelic Conversation* (voice only) (1985), *84 Charing Cross Road* (1986), *A Handful of Dust* (1987), *Henry V* (1989), *Jack and Sarah* (1994), *GoldenEye* (1995), *Hamlet* (1996), *Mrs Brown, Tomorrow Never Dies* (1997)

Much as she dislikes the whole filmmaking process (especially in winter), Judi Dench has become a consummate screen actress. She is the archetypal British actress who, stage-trained, retains her allegiance to the theatre, in which she has enjoyed an extraordinary run of successes in both modern and classic plays. She is very articulate about why the theatre remains more satisfying for her than the screen and she also distinguishes between working for the large and small screens. Some British stage actors have never seemed wholly comfortable on the screen, but Judi Dench is not one of them. Above all, she seems to understand when to appear to be doing nothing, to know how to reduce the scale of her performance to the demands of the screen's intimacy. As a result, we have a handful (not nearly enough) of beautifully realised characters: the reserved, utterly ordinary wife in *84 Charing Cross Road*; a heartbreaking Mistress Quickly in Kenneth Branagh's *Henry V*; the interfering mother in *Jack and Sarah*; and two somewhat more florid cameos in *A Room with a View* and *A Handful of Dust*. Set these beside her stage work in Chekhov, Shakespeare *et al.* (as director as well as actor) and the wide-ranging television roles, and it is easy to believe she can do anything. *Interview date: July 1994*

Why did you wait so long to make your first film, in 1964? Was it because you were simply so busy on the stage from 1957?

It's because filming doesn't come naturally to me, it isn't easy for me, and I don't enjoy it very much. I admire great film actors very much indeed because filming is so imperfectly to do with us. It is never necessarily the best performance you give which is chosen for the film; it's really to do with something else, and you can't perfect it. It is always the day after filming that I find the way I would like to do it. It isn't like the theatre where you can go on and on, perfecting and honing something. It is a one-off, really – and a matter of luck – and talent, of course, but I don't have that for films.

As a stage-trained actress, did you regard the theatre as offering more interesting opportunities?

For me, it's the way I want to work, especially in repertory, because you play perhaps six performances and then have four or five days off, then do another four or six performances. It's like coming back to a first night each time and, in that interim you have off, you are able to look back at things and assess them so that there is a chance to rethink and work at a performance. There is a chance, in the end, that you might get somewhere near what you imagine you could do with the part. That opportunity doesn't exist in film, not for me at any rate.

Two of your very early films were for the veteran Ealing director, Charles Crichton – *The Third Secret* and *He Who Rides the Tiger*. How did you find his direction?

Oh, he was enchanting. The very first film I ever did was with him and I was extremely frightened. I said to the runner who came to get me and show me to my room, 'Is he frightening? Will I like him?' and he said, 'Oh no, he's not at all intimidating and you'll probably like him very much.' It wasn't until four or five days later that I found out I'd been talking to his son! But I find direction in films totally different from the theatre. It is really somebody telling you on the day what they want you to do. You don't build up to it, you don't work it out; you just slot in very quickly with another performance – without consideration, it seems to me. I don't mean to knock it quite as much as I seem to be doing, but you do have to be very much able to make decisions instantly in filming, whereas I need time to get to know the actors I'm with and to adjust to their performances. With films, I feel that you are cast if you look like a certain sort of person. In the theatre, I know that in an hour and a half I can get myself up in such a way as to persuade people that I am a five-foot-nine Nordic blonde, or whatever. With film directors, they need to see you looking like the character, so there is very little you can do, in fact.

What do you recall of an interesting-sounding film for director Anthony Simmons, *Four in the Morning*?

It was *cinéma vérité*, shot in black-and-white. It had Norman Rodway who played my husband, and Ann Lynn, Joe Melia and Brian Phelan. It was fascinating to do; it was improvised around a kind of skeleton on which we built the film. We rehearsed it and improvised it, so that it was more like performing in the theatre. There were three separate stories and they were done in sequence, then the film intercut them. It won the Critics' Award at Cannes.

You played Titania in Peter Hall's 1968 film of *A Midsummer Night's Dream*. Was this a film version of a production you'd been in?

That's what it was going to be, and I had the most wonderful Lila de Nobile costume. We did the play for a whole season at Stratford and Peter wanted to film it. Then, when they found that we were at Compton Verney in November, these costumes looked very incongruous, so gradually my costume got whittled away until it was just leaves, really, at the end. I've never seen the film but I don't think it bore any relation to the stage production finally.

To jump twenty-odd years, you then played the very best Mistress Quickly I have ever seen, in Kenneth Branagh's *Henry V*. How did you come to be associated with that?

Because I had directed Ken in my first production, *Much Ado About Nothing*, for Renaissance, and we had worked together in *Ghosts* for television. It was a very happy collaboration and it went very well. Then I directed *Look Back in Anger* for Renaissance, then *Henry V*. I was asked to be in the film of *Much Ado* also, but I couldn't do it because

of other engagements. Mistress Quickly is a wonderful part, certainly.

Branagh's treatment of *Henry V* was interesting, with those inserts from *Henry IV, Parts I and II*; it makes Henry a more interesting character, I think.

That's right, so you see all those memories. It's always better to do the *Henry IV* plays first, followed by *Henry V*, in the theatre anyway. You see this young boy growing up and being a kind of wastrel, a boy about town with his mates, and suddenly having to assume so much authority.

Were your scenes as Mistress Quickly shot in sequence? I thought that, as it was Shakespeare, you might have had very firm views on that.

More or less, I think. My scenes were all shot in the studio at Shepperton. I don't like not shooting in sequence, but it is something you have to settle for in filming. I don't like the whole process of filming anyway, but it makes it easier if you rehearse it, and it is also easier if you film in sequence.

***Luther* was photographed by Freddie Young, the Oscar-winning cameraman, and directed by another great cameraman, Guy Green. Were you aware of their vast filmmaking experience at work on the film?**

I do remember Freddie well, but I can't say I became sensitive to cameramen, absolutely not. Guy Green was a friend, although I don't remember how I met him.

Your only other '70s film is an absolute mystery to me – Tony Richardson's *Dead Cert*.

So it should be, and it should jolly well stay so! It's based on a Dick Francis novel. It was terrible, appalling. We were all down at Findon and we had a wonderful time doing it in Josh Gifford's racing stable and at Aintree, but it wasn't a good film and was never released. Scott Anthony played the lead, and Michael [Williams] was also in it. It encourages me a lot to hear that it's disappeared!

How different did you find doing television work from filmmaking – for instance, doing a sitcom such as *A Fine Romance*, how do you react to having a studio audience?

Having a studio audience is very difficult, and doing a situation comedy is the most difficult thing of all, I think. People denigrate them but, my goodness, they are terribly hard to do. It is like the discipline of weekly rep except that you only get one go at it, in front of an audience. On television you have to hit it bang on the nail, on that one night.

You did six films in the 1980s and I thought at last you were beginning to take your film career seriously. How did you come by those films – did your agent seek them out?

No, my agent doesn't seek them out because he knows I don't like asking people if I can do their films. I prefer to wait and see if they come to me. I would never move for a film, never – isn't it awful!

One of these was *The Angelic Conversation* ...

Oh yes, *The Angelic Conversation*! That was when Derek Jarman asked me to read Shakespearian sonnets. So I sat in a studio doing the sonnets and I thought 'How wonderful!' I couldn't think of anything I'd like better. When I'd done them, Derek asked me if I'd like to see what they were going behind, and he showed me the film of young boys picking up shells and pouring water over each other. I was completely riveted. Derek was a very inventive man.

Was *Henry V* the last film you have done?

No, I did one just the other day! It's called *Jack and Sarah*, directed by Tim Sullivan, and it has Richard E Grant, Ian McKellen, Eileen Atkins, David Swift, Imogen Stubbs and Kate Hardy. I'm Richard Grant's mother. And I'm going to be in the new James Bond film.

You played Ian Holm's bitchy wife in *Wetherby* (as in *The Browning Version*) and a less nasty wife to him in *Mr and Mrs Edgehill* for television. Is he an actor with whom you feel a special rapport?

Yes, because we were at Stratford together and have done a lot of things together over a long time. I admire him tremendously, so it was terrific to work together. We have a shorthand between us and we know that we work in the same way.

Wetherby is a strange and disturbing film. How did you react to it and its author/director David Hare?

I rang up David and said I wanted to know two things. First, what was it about, and, secondly, how did I get to Lavender Gardens the following morning for the first reading? He said, 'Just get to Lavender Gardens!' and he never told me what the film was about. I kept saying, 'Wouldn't there be blood all over the wall?' and he would say, 'No, not necessarily.' It drove me mad. There were all kinds of logical issues and I was told to shut up about them, so I just did it and had a very nice time up in Yorkshire with all my mates. There is always something a bit unnerving about David's writing,

but if I ask him what's going on, he just bursts out laughing, so I leave it alone.

***A Room with a View* was a huge popular success. Why do you think it took off in that way?**

I've never seen it, so I don't know. Florence was lovely, of course, and it's a wonderful love story. I did enjoy doing the part, because Maggie Smith and I were old friends from 1958. We both arrived in Florence on the same day and neither of us had any of our family with us, so we would spend all day together filming and then go out to dinner together, catching up on our Old Vic days. But I didn't enjoy working with James Ivory. I didn't feel that I was on his wavelength and I didn't feel that he wanted me in the film, I have to say that. I remember doing that scene in the middle of the square where she goes mad and attacks the man selling postcards; James went to see the rushes and told me afterwards that everyone had laughed at it, they'd thought it was very funny. 'Well done,' he said to me. I thought perhaps we'd turned the corner, but, when I came to post-sync the film, that scene was missing. When I asked why, he told me that Helena Bonham Carter hadn't been feeling up to it that day, so he'd cut the whole sequence. I don't know if that was the real reason he cut it – I just don't know.

As far as I know, *84 Charing Cross Road* has been done in every medium except on ice.

Strangely enough, Michael and I were asked to do the stage production of it. After we'd read it we sent it back, saying, 'It'll never work on stage, but it would make a wonderful recital evening.' Then of course it did go on the stage and it worked very well. The character I played in the film wasn't in it originally, it was invented for the film. I had read the book and loved it, but I did feel a bit intrusive in the film. That was one of my films that I did go to see and, on seeing it, I didn't feel that my part was quite so intrusive as I had imagined.

It's another of the 'ordinary housewife' parts you do so well, with a nice edge to it. You make it look as if you are doing nothing.

That's a lovely compliment. They are very confined, quiet, respectable people living in the suburbs of London. They don't have rows and they don't raise their voices because the people next door might hear, so they are terribly difficult to project.

There was an actor in the film with whom you've worked several times – Maurice Denham.

I don't think I had a scene with him, no. I know

Maurice terribly well, because he played my father in *Talking to a Stranger* and he is in fact very like my father, very close to him. He is an adorable man.

Did you like the contrast provided by the showier part of Robert Graves's predatory mum in *A Handful of Dust*?

I don't remember much about that except wearing a very good hat. I never saw it. I do remember the director, though, Charles Sturridge; he directed *Brideshead Revisited* very beautifully.

Did British cinema seem to you not to offer many opportunities, or do you really just not want to do filming work?

Perhaps I am a bit eccentric, in that I don't mind doing a film in summer but I don't want to do one during the winter – not when I have to get up at half past four in the morning and make that long journey. When I get to the studio I don't understand what they ask me to do, and at the end of the day I'm upset because I haven't done it very well – and the next day it's too late. So if I can't do a film, I always breathe a sigh of relief!

Well, I'm going straight out to find your agent to tell him to find more films for you.

It's no use. He'll only say to you, in his very English way, 'My dear sir, she just won't do them.'

Maurice Denham

b. 1909

Actor: *Home and School, Daybreak (1946), Fame is the Spur, The Peaceful Years, The Man Within, They Made Me a Fugitive, Take My Life, The Upturned Glass, Holiday Camp, Jassy, Captain Boycott, The End of the River, Dear Murderer (scenes cut) (1947), Easy Money, Blanche Fury, Escape, Miranda, Oliver Twist, My Brother's Keeper, London Belongs to Me, The Blind Goddess, Here Come the Huggetts, Quartet, Look Before You Love (1948), The Bad Lord Byron, It's Not Cricket, The Blue Lagoon, Once Upon a Dream, Poet's Pub, A Boy, a Girl and a Bike, Traveller's Joy, Landfall, Scrapbook For 1933 (voice only), The Spider and the Fly, Don't Ever Leave Me, Madness of the Heart (1949), No Highway (1951), The Net, Time Bomb, Street Corner, (narr) *Prince Philip (1953), Eight O'Clock Walk, The Million Pound Note, The Purple Plain, Carrington VC, Animal Farm (voice only) (1954), Doctor at Sea, Simon and Laura (1955), 23 Paces to Baker Street, Checkpoint (1956), Night of the Demon, Barnacle Bill, Campbell's Kingdom (1957), Man with a Dog, The Captain's Table (1958), Our Man in Havana, Sink the Bismarck!, Two Way Stretch, Ali and The Camel (camel's voice only) (1960), The Greengage Summer, Invasion Quartet, The Mark, The Last Rhino (1961), HMS Defiant (1962), The Set-Up, The King's Breakfast, Paranoic, The Very Edge (1963), Downfall, The Seventh Dawn, The Uncle, Hysteria (1964), The Legend of Young Dick Turpin, Those Magnificent Men in Their Flying Machines, The Alphabet Murders, The Nanny, The Heroes of Telemark, Operation Crossbow, The Night Caller (1965), After the Fox (1966), Torture Garden, The Long Duel, Danger Route (1967), Attack on the Iron Coast, Negatives (1968), A Touch of Love, Some Girls Do, Midas Run (1969), The Best House in London, The Virgin and the Gypsy, Countess Dracula (1970), Sunday Bloody Sunday, Nicholas and Alexandra (1971), The Day of The Jackal, Luther (1973), Shout at the Devil (1976), Julia (1977), The Chain (1985), 84 Charing Cross Road (1986), Tears in the Rain (1988), The Last Journey of Robert Rylands (1996)
* Short film.

With over a hundred films to his credit, as well as an enormous amount of radio, television and theatre work, Maurice Denham has, for fifty years, been one of Britain's busiest and most affectionately regarded character actors. His voice first became famous on radio in *ITMA* and *Much Binding in the Marsh*; then in the post-war '40s he played one vivid 'character' after another. My personal favourites are as the yokel policeman in *Poet's Pub* and the mad Nazi in *It's Not Cricket*, one of the most unjustly neglected of British comedies. But, funny as he could be, he was also perfectly convincing as the dignified Major in *Blanche Fury* or the child molester in Lance Comfort's tense *Eight O'Clock Walk* or the shifty, unshaven Dawson in Muriel Box's *Street Corner*. The bottom may have been falling out of the film industry in Britain but Denham seems not to have noticed this: throughout the '60s, '70s and '80s, he went on filming at the same rate, for screens large or small, giving some of his finest performances, in such films as *The Virgin and the Gypsy* (as the appalling vicar), *Sunday Bloody Sunday*, and Jack Clayton's telemovie, *Memento Mori*, with its superlative cast of Britain's senior citizens of the film world.

Interview date: June 1994

After your début in *Daybreak*, you made about thirty-five films between 1946 and 1950. Were you getting all these parts through a contract or an agent?

I was with the same agent for almost fifty years and just changed agents recently because he was giving up, while I'm still ploughing on. I did *Much Binding in the Marsh* on radio and it was a terrific hit; it was front-page news when we were doing a new series. That gave me something of a reputation, so I was inclined to get films because I had a reputation on radio. I didn't have any contract at that stage; it was just one film to another. I used to go to the studio every morning and go to sleep in the chair while I was being made up. One morning during the making of *The Bad Lord Byron*, I woke up in the chair expecting to see myself in a great set of whiskers; instead I had an immaculate little moustache and a toupee! 'What's this?' I said. 'This is all wrong.' 'No, no,' they said, 'they've changed the schedules. You're working on another film.' It was like a repertory company of actors who'd turn up every morning in case one of their scenes was being done.

I remember *Traveller's Joy*, with Googie Withers and John McCallum, and Dora Bryan as a Danish maid who could only say, 'Yak, yak!' I played some sort of flashy shyster. I'll never forget that film because Googie and I had a scene where we were drinking cocktails; we had to stop shooting the scene halfway through one evening, then we picked it up again the next morning, still drinking these cocktails. About an hour later, both of us suddenly turned green and rushed out. The cocktail shaker had not been washed overnight and it's lucky we weren't poisoned.

Much of your work then was for Gainsborough. Were you working at both Lime Grove and Islington?

Yes. *Miranda* was done at Islington, as was *Dear Murderer* (which I was cut out of). Sydney Box would have four or five films shooting at the same time. I also did some films for other people during that time, including Cavalcanti's *They Made Me a Fugitive*, which was done at Riverside. Cavalcanti was a great name and I was very excited to work with him, although it was terribly difficult to understand what he said. We had great fun making it, nonetheless.

There didn't seem to be the tension about filmmaking that there is now. I mean, I can remember playing Major Fraser in *Blanche Fury* with Valerie Hobson and Stewart Granger; there was a big ball scene which lasted about three minutes on the screen, but it took about five days to shoot by the time it was all set up. Now it would have to be done in half a day. That's a very good-looking film. Major Fraser was quite a big part but I also did some dubbing for the film. The butler was played by a very old actor [Townsend Whitling], who looked wonderful but proved to be incomprehensible on the soundtrack, so I was asked to dub his voice. There is one scene between me and him, where I am talking as Major Fraser in my normal voice, then he answers and it's still me, talking in my 'old man's' voice. Suddenly there is a shout off-camera, 'Fire!' – and that's me as well! For the ballroom scene, the pillars of the set only went up a certain height; the rest of it – cornices, ceilings and so on – was painted on a large piece of glass fitted in front of the camera and that took days to set up. It might have been simpler to build a full-height set but the studio didn't have the height they needed. In that scene, I wore a suit that was made for me by Huntsman's, the best tailors in London at the time. It was an immaculate tailcoat and so on, all for about a minute and a half's appearance. Valerie was very good in the witness box in the court scene, I remember. It was made by Cineguild, of which Tony Havelock-Allan, David Lean and John Bryan were members. It was a very classy company.

You were involved in several other Cineguild productions, including _Take My Life_.

Yes, in _Take My Life_ I played the Counsel for the Defence opposite Francis L Sullivan as the Prosecuting Counsel – a magnificent man. I learned a lot from that film. When I got this part, I went and sat in various courts as an observer – and for hours nothing seems to happen. It's the most undramatic thing you can imagine. I thought I had to do something to make it a bit interesting but the director, Ronald Neame, took me right down again.

Did it make much difference to you, as an actor, which companies you were working for?

Not at all, because one had a standard of pay and the good thing about it was that it was mostly daily rates. It wasn't very much, about £12 or £15 a day, but that was a lot of money in those days. You could get a three-course meal for one and sixpence. It gradually built up the more films you did and the better you became known, so that you moved higher up in the billing. Of course, my agent would look after all that sort of thing for me, including the billing.

Your voice must have been very well known too. In those early films you often played small but highly individual characters, such as that yokel policeman in _Poet's Pub_.

That's right, with the bicycle! They shot it on that new system they had, Independent Frame. It didn't worry me at all but it worried the technicians no end, with the vast pieces of machinery they had to have for bringing in the side of a house and taking it out again. The studio spent thousands of pounds on it and they only did about half a dozen films using the method. I was in a curious position with that part because I had done all sorts of voices and accents on radio; now, in films, unless you were someone like Richard Wattis and a definite 'type', you could be left out of a cast because all the others were playing 'themselves'.

You played a craven vicar in _Once Upon a Dream_.

Oh yes, with the vegetable competition. I remember I had to hand someone a huge great marrow and say, 'If you want my advice, you'll take that home and _stuff_ it!'

What do you recall of working with any of those Gainsborough directors, such as Bernard Knowles on _Jassy_, _The Man Within_ and _Easy Money_.

The trouble is, they were just directors to me, part of the film, so it's difficult to know if they were extremely good or not. It very much depended on the part and what help they could give you, or if they accepted what you offered – and, in those smaller early parts, one just did it. The director would give you your moves but that was about it. Later on, for the bigger parts, motivation came into it and it was very much a question of working things out with the directors. Ronnie Neame, for instance, was an extremely good director. Of course, when you say 'he was a good director', it's probably because he put up with your suggestions and let you do what you wanted to do!

It's curious, you know, that even directors with whom you've worked many times cannot see you as anyone else but you. I'm thinking of _HMS Defiant_ with Dirk Bogarde and Alec Guinness, for example, in which I played the drunken doctor. Prior to the filming they asked me to go down and play Alec Guinness's part while they were trying to cast the young man's part (which Dirk Bogarde eventually got); so I used to play Alec's part in scenes while they filmed with various candidates – Michael Caine was one. I'd read the script, of course, so I said to Lewis Gilbert that I wanted to play the old doctor but he didn't think I was rough enough. So the next time I had to go down there I didn't shave for four days beforehand; Lewis Gilbert looked at me and said, 'Good God! Yes, you *could* play it!' It was a good part, I enjoyed that.

You did several films for him: *The Greengage Summer*, *Sink the Bismarck!* **and** *The Seventh Dawn*.

He's a very nice bloke indeed. He would seek me out, I suppose, because we worked well together and that's a lucky thing that can happen. If a director likes you he will put you in most of his films, if you're suitable. The last film I made with Lewis was *The Seventh Dawn*. We went out to Kuala Lumpur for it. I was killed in the car and the camera was put into the car; I had this special vest with exploding devices in it and on the windscreen. I went off in the car on my own, started the camera, and off I drove, out of their sights and minds up this road. There was a certain point where I had to swerve the car and push a button so the explosives all went off, blood would go everywhere and I'd 'collapse' over the wheel before I stopped the car. Then I drove back and told Lewis I thought it had gone all right.

Another director for whom you made quite a lot of films was Ken Annakin, starting with *Holiday Camp*, **then** *Miranda*, *Landfall* **and** *Here Come the Huggetts*.

I played a doctor in *Holiday Camp* and I think I was on screen for about a minute and a half, diagnosing someone [Jeanette Tregarthen] as being pregnant. I was happy to work with Ken again, he's a most competent director. Later I made *The Long Duel* for him, playing the Governor. I didn't go out to India for it, though; my part was all done in the studios.

I did have some good locations at various times – Florence for *Checkpoint*, and Ceylon for *The Purple Plain* with Gregory Peck. I got a nomination for Best Actor for that. It was a wonderful part, the best part I've ever had in a movie. It was directed by the American, Robert Parrish, and it was a curious experience. For the first week we were in Ceylon, it simply poured with rain, no shooting could be done and we sat playing poker all day and night.

A pair of films you made at this time which particularly interest me are *My Brother's Keeper* **and as the mad Nazi Otto Fisch in** *It's Not Cricket*, **the only two films directed by the editor, Alfred Roome. Did he or Roy Rich**

actually do more of the direction?

Roy Rich was a very ebullient character, particularly on *It's Not Cricket*, and I suggested that I play Fisch in all sorts of mad disguises. I think Roy was very much the dominant partner although he didn't actually run things on the stage. Alfred would do all the talking but Roy was behind the scenes, backing him up. *My Brother's Keeper* was one of the Gainsborough films that got bad notices. They were entertainment for the masses, really, though *My Brother's Keeper* was probably better than that. I saw *It's Not Cricket* again quite recently and it's quite fun, but what we suffered in that bloody car, driving through the tent and so on without being able to see anything! Then driving through that great lake and finding all the Highland cattle in it – we were right under water! The ending was very naughty, actually. I ended up becoming Basil Radford and Naunton Wayne's secretary, and at the end I spoke one of my catch-phrases from *Much Binding in the Marsh*: 'Oh I say, I am a fool!'

You worked a lot for Ralph Thomas, including his first film *Once Upon a Dream*, **followed by** *Doctor at Sea* **and** *Checkpoint*. **He seems to have been a very efficient director.**

Yes, he was. *Doctor at Sea* was with Brigitte Bardot, of course. She was lovely. She was seventeen and she came on the set in a rather low-cut jersey with a little crucifix at the neck, and very short pants indeed. Everyone from all the other studio stages just came rushing to see her. Her English was delightful, too. I was standing at the bar at lunch one day when she came up to me, and I said, 'You're not looking very happy today,' and she said, 'I am so sad, my little dog I have to leave in Paris.' I asked how old her little dog was, and she said, 'He is half past one'! It was a good film and Betty Box producer was such a nice woman, very well-organised. I never saw Ralph or her angry or worried.

You've acted with almost everybody, it seems. Who are some of the actors you've found most rewarding to work with?

Gregory Peck was one. He has a great interest in Shakespeare; we used to sit in the jungle together while we were waiting for our scenes, and we'd quote Shakespeare at each other as much as we could. Some of the old character actors I worked with I didn't like very much, but it was probably jealousy that they'd got better parts than I had! I was always happy to stay just 'under the title', though. Once you go 'over the title' you have to hang on to that status and turn down anything that isn't appropriate to maintaining it. There is a terrible strain on these leading actors, in that they've got to carry the film. This was true of Peter Sellers, with whom I did *Two-Way Stretch*.

You almost never made a 'B' picture, other than one called *The Set-Up*. What do you remember about working at Merton Park?

Merton Park was a tiny little studio run by Jack Greenwood. They were really slap-bang films, rushed through as quickly as possible. If there was the slightest pause on the stage, with people not doing anything, Jack would be down from his office where he had television sets linked to cameras on each of the stages, wanting to know why we weren't working. Gerald Glaister, who directed it, is a big producer of TV series now. I did do another 'B' picture called *Downfall*, directed by John Moxey. He was delightful but we were all working under terrific stress. Those 'B' films were done very cheaply. You just got through them, took the money and ran.

You had some excellent parts in the '70s and after, including *Sunday, Bloody Sunday*. How do you rate it?

John Schlesinger was delightful to work with. I had a very good scene with Peggy Ashcroft in *Sunday, Bloody Sunday*, sitting at the table and licking the cream-bowl. John was always able to keep the whole thing underplayed down to nothing. As to rating films, *The Purple Plain* was certainly a highlight and *Doctor at Sea* was a bit of a romp. I also had a nice part in *84 Charing Cross Road*, as Mr Martin, the oldest employee in the firm. I was talking to Hugh Whitemore, the writer, one day and I said, 'At my age I always have a death scene, but I haven't got one in this.' 'Never mind,' he said, 'we'll write you one.' So he did, a lovely scene with Anthony Hopkins in the hospital.

Do you have the slightest intention of ever retiring?

Oh no, never! I live on my own now and it's a joy to wake up in the morning knowing I'm going to be working with other people.

Michael Denison
b. 1915

and Dulcie Gray
b. 1919

Michael Denison, actor: *Tilly of Bloomsbury* (1940), *Hungry Hill* (1947), *My Brother Jonathan, Blind Goddess* (1948), *The Glass Mountain, Landfall* (1949), *The Franchise Affair, The Magic Box* (1951), *The Tall Headlines, Angels One Five, The Importance of Being Earnest* (1952), *There was a Young Lady* (1953), *Contraband Spain* (1955), *The Truth About Women* (1958), *Faces in the Dark* (1960), *Dark River* (1990), *Shadowlands* (1994)

Dulcie Gray, actor: *Banana Ridge* (1941), *2000 Women, Victory Wedding* (short), *Madonna of the Seven Moons* (1944), *A Place of One's Own, They Were Sisters* (1945), *Wanted for Murder, The Years Between* (1946), *A Man About the House, Mine Own Executioner* (1947), *My Brother Jonathan* (1948), *The Glass Mountain* (1949), *The Franchise Affair* (1951), *Angels One Five* (1952), *There Was a Young Lady* (1953), *A Man Could Get Killed* (1965)

Dulcie Gray had already given several fine screen performances before Michael Denison returned to Britain after war service and, by lucky chance, found himself starring in Harold French's *My Brother Jonathan*, in which his wife had already been cast. Denison became an overnight film star in what proved to be the year's most popular film, which initiated a series of co-starring films for him and Dulcie Gray, including two for Lawrence Huntington (*The Franchise Affair* and *There Was a Young Lady*). Dulcie Gray emerges very well from her time with Gainsborough: her servant in Bernard Knowles's charming 'ghost' film, *A Place of One's Own*, is refreshingly free from stereotype, and she makes a genuinely moving figure of Charlotte, the gentle wife driven to alcohol and suicide by her brutal husband (James Mason) in *They Were Sisters*. Michael Denison was delighted to be in Anthony Asquith's elegant film version of *The Importance of Being Earnest*, in which he had exactly the right touch as the dandy Algernon, making the most of some of Wilde's best epigrams. Together the Denisons scored popular successes in the romantic melodrama, *The Glass Mountain*, and the war drama, *Angels One Five*. Working on film, stage, radio and television, they have had two of the busiest careers of any British actors.

Interview date: October 1989

Are you pleased with the balance you've achieved among stage, screen and television?

DG: Yes, I think so. I would rather have done more classical stuff but it didn't come my way for various reasons. I enjoy all the media, so I think I've been extraordinarily lucky to have been a part of all of them. I think Michael loves straight theatre even more than I do; I certainly think it is the cradle of all acting, but of course some things are the same in all media. You are working on the truth of the character that you're portraying, and it is really the kind of projection that is the basic difference: in the theatre you have to *think* towards the dress circle, whereas in television, and even more so in films, you have to think as though the camera is very close to you, so of course you don't project so broadly. I remember James Mason telling me I must never forget that, in close-up on film, my face would probably be eight feet high, so that was already enlarging my performance; I didn't have to go any further than that. I believe it is easier to make the transition from stage to film than the other way about, unless one is obstinately going to say, 'This is trash – the theahtah is the great thing and I can't possibly . . .' and all that stuff.

A lot of notable British films have been written by playwrights and novelists. Do you think the British cinema of the '40s and '50s is really a very literary cinema in some ways?

DG: Yes, I think so, especially the Ealing comedies. Gainsborough, which was my kind of stuff, was rather lowbrow, but it was very 'film-y', full of *story*. The best of the Gainsborough films, even if they were called 'weepies' or 'women's films', had *stories* to tell – and the public loved them!

MD: It's interesting what you say about a literary cinema. In my comparatively brief cinema experience, I think every film I did except perhaps one was based on novels. *The Importance of Being Earnest* was based on a play, of course. *The Glass Mountain* was somebody's brainchild and was purely cinematic from that point of view. But *My Brother Jonathan*, *The Franchise Affair*, *Hungry Hill*, *Landfall*, were all based on novels. I think that meant there was a good narrative skeleton to those films.

What sort of association did you have with the Rank Organisation?

MD: Very little. But I admired the way Rank

tried to establish a deal for British films to be properly distributed in America. His talks were very successful and he was on his way home when the Government – Stafford Cripps was the Minister involved – put an embargo on American films coming into Britain. The Americans thought Rank had taken them for a ride when it was really the Government's doing. Dulcie was with Gainsborough before it became associated with Rank, then she went to Korda and I was with Associated British.

Korda seems to have been the one great entrepreneur.

DG: He was a one-off. He was a quite extraordinary man. I had decided not to sign with him for various reasons, and I went to see him to tell him so – and signed within ten minutes! He had enormous charm and a very kind, piercing logic, and I was very happy with him. The thing about our contracts was that they were one-sided. We couldn't opt out once we had signed, but they could sack us at any time, or at least on a yearly basis. Your seven-year contract was actually one year guaranteed and six options on their side.

MD: This didn't worry me because I had emerged from the Army – to be signed for a seven-year contract, which the press people described as a £55,000 contract! That was the aggregate which I would be paid if I lasted the full seven years. In fact I was being paid £25 a week in the first year but, in comparison with Army pay, I went from penury to what I thought was being pretty well off!

DG: In my first year at Gainsborough, for several little pictures I earned £600. My contract was with Gainsborough Studios, but they were thrilled if they could loan you and make money out of you. That is how they lost Audrey Hepburn years later: Michael and I had seen Audrey at Ciro's, dancing with six other girls, and she was outstanding. We took Robert Lennard, the casting director of Associated British, to see her. They were about to do a remake of *The Good Companions* with Michael and myself and couldn't find a girl to play the Jessie Matthews part. We urged them to use Audrey, whom they had put under contract. But the film was made without her (and us) and, within six months, Audrey was making *Roman Holiday*. She was loaned out, which they were thrilled about, and was lost to British films.

Mr Denison, apart from *Tilly of Bloomsbury* in 1940, you played one supporting role in *Hungry Hill* before being given the title role in *My Brother Jonathan*. Did this seem like an awesome responsibility at the time?

MD: It seemed very exciting, after six years in the Army. About halfway through my Army career, I was coming back from Northern Ireland on forty-eight hours' leave. I rang Dulcie to tell her and she said, 'Oh well, I'll cancel the film test then.' I told her not to and went along with her instead. They hadn't provided a man to play the scene with the girls being tested so, rather than have someone stand there reading from a script, it was an advantage to have me, as an actor, do it. It was a love scene, a typically British love scene! So I did the scene, albeit with my back to the camera, with Dulcie and the other girls. Three years elapsed while I was in the Army, when Dulcie was approached to do *My Brother Jonathan*. It was hanging fire rather and Dulcie enquired of the casting director, Robert Lennard, what was going on. He said they were trying to find an unknown to play the long leading part. He asked her if she recalled the young man who had played opposite her in the film test she had done three years earlier. She replied of course, that I was her husband and was at home, just back from the Middle East. As a result of that I was tested, got the part and a long-term contract with ABPC. I was loaned for *Hungry Hill*, because they took quite a long time to decide whether to take the risk of giving me Jonathan.

What do you think of the notion that *My Brother Jonathan* is really an allegory of the rise of the National Health system in post-war Britain?

MD: I think all I felt was that it was a bloody good part to play. It was, of course, written well before the war; whether the makers thought they were catching a mood or not I honestly wouldn't know.

DG: But Francis Brett Young was definitely on that side – that's what he would have wanted.

MD: Yes, it was strongly autobiographical; he had been a GP fighting abuses in medical care in the West Midlands as a young man, but that was pre-World War I period. Of course, considerable works in the literary field will have messages for all time, even though they are rooted in their period.

My Brother Jonathan was the first film you made together. Were you promoted after that as a team, or did you seek work together?

MD: We have always enjoyed working together, but Dulcie's already strong film reputation meant that I was riding in on that, which was very good for me after having been away for so long. They cashed in on the team idea with *The Glass Mountain* and then, for various reasons, it didn't last. I think I contributed to that because, having been away from the theatre for a long time, I was very grateful to films for persuading *theatre* managers to employ me. I think the studios looked for opportunities to co-star us, and publicity sold us as the cosiest couple unhung, all that his-and-hers stuff with the thatched cottage in Essex. I did one film on my own, a terrible thing called *The Tall Headlines*, in which I played twin brothers, one of whom was a maniac.

Of your films together, which one do you think gave you the best opportunities?

MD: I don't know. We became rather fond of *The Franchise Affair*, which was not as good as the novel but, then, the novel was particularly good. It had a marvellous cast, including one of Kenneth More's first appearances on celluloid as a garage mechanic.

The director was Lawrence Huntington, with whom you both did several films. What is your recollection of him?

MD: I think of him with great affection. He was a very funny man and splendid with actors.

DG: We were very fond of him. He knew what he wanted from you, but seemed relaxed, friendly and easy-going. He was very much underrated, as I think a lot of directors were.

Do you remember *Faces in the Dark*, which has this plot synopsis in *The British Film Catalogue*: 'Man helps mistress drive her blind husband mad by moving his house from Cornwall to France'? It's based on a story by the authors of *Vertigo*.

MD: Best forgotten! I remember nearly meeting my end because I very properly drove my car off the road into a lake, where I was to drown. It was actually a gravel pit, and the arrangements for the car to sink were rather too effective! I just managed to get out of it and they put a dummy in instead. I did three pictures with Mai Zetterling – that one, *The Tall Headlines* and *The Truth About Women*. I admired Mai a great deal, it's a pity that at least my first two with her were rather claptrappy.

You starred in Anthony Asquith's film of *The Importance of Being Earnest*. What do you think was his aim in making the film as he did?

MD: I think he felt that it was essentially a theatrical piece, and that is why he 'topped and

tailed' it, with the curtain going up on a glamorous first-night audience and all that. Virtually the only changes he made – apart from some cuts, I suppose – were putting in the railway journeys, Algy going Bunburying, and then Lady Bracknell coming on the train too. They were going to have me ride down Piccadilly in the morning – I come on first in riding breeches, you remember – but they called that off when they realised the confusion it would have caused.

I loved Asquith as a director. He was an interpreter and that is how I like my directors to be. I like them to know the script and the subject. He obviously loved the play, loved the wit and the shape of it, and loved the characters. He was completely in tune with the subject and, indeed, with the players. He didn't guide us much, in my recollection. I remember the first day's shooting – that long bit with the cigarette case – and we filmed it in quite large chunks, which was different from the normal method of filming. There are lots of quite long takes in it, not a lot of elaborate cutting.

The play is a masterpiece of artificiality, which on screen must pose real problems.

MD: I think it goes back to what I said. It is a masterpiece and, provided it is faithfully done, it will continue to speak.

DG: I think it was because of its artificiality that Puffin [Asquith] left it as a theatrical piece.

MD: I think my only hope of screen immortality is due to the fact of Edith's [Evans] presence in the film. We once did a television version of it with Martita Hunt, who was a wonderful actress, but she was so determined not to do the handbag bit as Edith had done it that she whispered it, which was legitimate but wrong. It was like playing a major chord pianissimo.

Was it a harmonious film to make?

MD: It was very happy. I think one of the important tasks of a director is a public relations exercise, and Puffin was admirable at that. I don't think any of that company was going to be awkward. Darling old Margaret Rutherford was an eccentric, but she was a most lovable person. The cameraman was an absolute ace, can't recall his name [Desmond Dickinson].

One of your last films was *The Truth About Women*, directed by Muriel Box, produced by Sydney Box and, I think co-written by both. What was your experience of working with them?

MD: That was the only time I worked with them;

they were very nice to me and I thought the film was directed very efficiently. I enjoyed it very much. I had not been a fan of Laurence Harvey in his early days – largely on the disgraceful grounds of the way he dressed and wore his hair. This was when he had just arrived as a contract artist at ABPC. So, I was asked to do this film with him and initially didn't want to, but I made myself do it and told myself to enjoy it. He welcomed me on a location shot in the early morning by saying, 'How lovely to see you, we are going to have a marvellous lunch so we can really get to know each other.' He charmed the birds off the trees, and we became enormous friends and that is my principal recollection of the film – the joy of working with Larry Harvey.

Miss Gray, did you feel those '40s Gainsborough films gave you a good start?

DG: They didn't quite know what to do with me. I was taken on there on the strength of my stage performance in *Brighton Rock*. I think they had decided I was 'a stage actress' and they had made up their minds about me. I was sacked after *They Were Sisters* – it was the most extraordinary day. I woke up to find that James Agate, the top *theatre* critic, had done a notice of the film and said what a tremendous performance I had given. Then I was rung up to be told the Ostrer brothers wanted to see me. I went by bus but on wings as well – and they sacked me on the grounds that they didn't want that sort of reality in films! The notion of Charlotte taking to drink, yes, but they didn't want me to look so plain; they wanted her to look pretty in her agony, which I thought was absurd. She was, after all, taking drugs and alcohol and she was suicidal. It didn't seem to me she would have had her hair done just before she committed suicide. I was stunned, particularly in view of the superb notice which I had just received. I went home and burst into tears. Then the phone rang and it was Eric Portman. He asked me to be his leading lady in *Wanted for Murder*, so in next to no time I was working with him, for the first time with co-star status. He was a darling to work with – a fine actor and very funny.

What do you recall of working with James Mason?

DG: There is a very strange strain among critics in England: they don't like success. I remember James saying that one of the reasons he went to Hollywood was because he knew he'd be rubbished every time he did anything here. Once he went to America he was accepted as the marvellous film actor he was. I don't mean to be unkind but, while being immensely lovable and endearing, James wasn't very funny – unlike practically every other actor. James was, in a way, dull; he was kind of 'sturdy'. But put him into a film and he was inventive and amusing. There was a marvellous moment in *They Were Sisters* when he was talking to me and decided to look at his teeth in a mirror. It was a bit of business he put in himself, and it was so wonderfully cruel, when my character was in agony and pain and needing his help, and that was his reaction to it. It had nothing to do with the script. The moment James was in a play or a film he had this amazing invention, often a cruelly comic invention, that welled up inside him. He was immensely helpful, easy going, just what one dreams of in a co-actor. Another person for whom I had a huge affection was Margaret Lockwood, who sadly became a total recluse in later years.

You made *A Place of One's Own* with her and for former cameraman Bernard Knowles.

DG: I enjoyed doing it very much. I think the powers-that-be may have been a little shocked at my playing the 'below-stairs' character without turning it into a caricature.

Did you enjoy working with Arthur Crabtree, another former cameraman?

DG: Yes, very much. You see, they did know about their cameras, which was great for actors. There was a revolution going on at Gainsborough all the time – every cameraman wanted to be a director, and quite often was. I loved working there, being so fond of Maggie and James, and I was having a quite glamorous start. But it never felt terribly secure and, of course, I was there in its last days.

The Boxes came to Gainsborough after I had left. I did do a film for them, however, with Valerie Hobson, called *The Years Between*. That was directed by Compton Bennett; he was very good too. Those directors weren't greatly inspired, except perhaps Lawrence Huntington, but they were marvellously efficient – they knew it all. When I was doing *They Were Sisters*, I had to come down the stairs crying; I had to do several takes for various reasons, and I finally did one when I wasn't actually crying, and they said, 'That's it!' I said to Arthur Crabtree how sorry I was, that it was the only time I hadn't actually been crying, and why was he going to use that particular take? He showed me eleven rushes and in some of them I hadn't actually hit my light, so all my crying went for nothing; the one they chose had me perfectly lit.

You made two starring films in 1947 before *My Brother Jonathan*. What do you remember about working with Leslie Arliss in the first of these, *A Man About the House*?

DG: He was under estimated, I think, because he did *The Man in Grey* and that was his style, and he was being rubbished by critics all the time. He helped very much indeed on the characterisations. He was shrewd, very kind and absolutely on one's side, and he had a very firm, clear vision of Maggie Johnston and me. It is my great regret that that film wasn't in colour, it was so beautifully photographed. It was all shot on location in Amalfi and Positano. It was decided to hold the opening at Eastbourne, I think, and there was a huge motorcade with a star in every limousine. The film was an absolute flop and Leslie saw at once why it had failed with the audience. He decided which scenes were failing and he was absolutely right; he cut those scenes and the film was then a great success.

It was also Dame Lillian Braithwaite's last film, wasn't it?

DG: Yes. She was doing *Arsenic and Old Lace* at the time, with Mary Jerrold at the Duchess, and she came down to do a few days with Felix Aylmer. I was deeply shocked because she was an old woman and a great star, yet they didn't have a chair for her. I tried to arrange one for her; they said they hadn't got any more, so I said she must have mine. After the film was over I received the most enormous basket of flowers, with a note saying, 'I noticed, dear. From an autumn actress to a spring one, with love.' I realise now that this is part of the difficulty of growing old: that the parts are fewer and you are very lucky to be able to keep going at all.

Did you see the second of those starring films, *Mine Own Executioner*, as a serious film about psychiatry, or as a romantic thriller?

DG: I didn't really see it as either. I played an awful lot of put-upon wives in those days! I really don't see things from the outside when I get a part; my main concern is to try and be that woman. I found her rather upsetting to play; she needn't have been so awfully inadequate. She was so in awe of her husband that I had to invent a background for her to be able to play her. Why does she put up with his having all these affairs? I think she knew she was inadequate but it wasn't ever explained, because he was rather cruel to her even though he was going through trouble himself. In that film poor Kieron Moore was totally miscast. He was a splendid actor in *Man About the House*.

How did you feel about having an American star such as Burgess Meredith, because there was no special reason for his character to be American?

DG: The special reason was that Paulette [Goddard] had come across to do *An Ideal Husband*! That's why he came over; their marriage was on the rocks and finished immediately afterwards. I don't think British actors resented him doing that major part, though. Korda had a very special standing with us all; he was the greatest entrepreneur of that time, so in our eyes he could do no wrong.

I liked Anthony Kimmins as a director; he was a very positive man. He loved the script and seemed to like us too. I was lucky in that I got on very well with all my directors. It's easier that way! I knew I wasn't Arthur Crabtree's type, but then I knew I was a misfit in Gainsborough.

People such as Kieron Moore looked as if they were being groomed for big things but never really reached the top of British screen stardom – also people like Margaret Johnston, Christine Norden, Barbara White. Why, do you think?

DG: Kieron was miscast twice, and that killed him – in *Mine Own Executioner*, and very miscast as Vronsky opposite Vivien [Leigh] in *Anna Karenina*. He could have done splendidly had he been cast right; he was a complicated man. Margaret: I think I pass. Barbara: wildly pretty, very clever and rather self-effacing. Perhaps she just retired into marriage with Kieron. I can't understand why she wasn't promoted. I don't know how good Christine was, how much range she had; I didn't get to know her well, simply because they were either using her or me and we hardly ever met.

Did you simply find fewer congenial opportunities in films by the mid '50s?

DG: Oh, our film industry more or less packed up. I think the heart went out of British pictures, and it wasn't a dream factory any more. I am immensely grateful for the opportunities I had and I enjoyed myself very much indeed.

Thorold Dickinson

1903–1984

Director: *The High Command* (1937), **Spanish ABC* (co-dir, co-ed), **Behind Spanish Lines* (co-dir, co-ed) (1938), *The Arsenal Stadium Mystery* (1939), *Gaslight*, **Westward Ho!*, **Yesterday Is Over Your Shoulder* (1940), *The Prime Minister* (1941), *Next of Kin* (1942), *Men of Two Worlds* (1946), *The Queen of Spades* (1949), *Secret People* (1951), **The Red Ground* (1953), *Hill 24 Doesn't Answer* (1955)
* Short or documentary film.

'It's terribly difficult to direct a film you don't want to make … That's why I've made so few.'[1] Considering that Thorold Dickinson was working in the boom time of British cinema, his output *is* meagre: only nine feature films in seventeen years. Yet, he remains an important British director, articulate about his films and cinema in general, and this no doubt helps to account for his appointment as the first Professor of Film in Britain, at the University of London.

Throughout the early '30s, he was busy editing such films as the Gracie Fields hit, *Sing As We Go*. He made his feature début in 1937, with *The High Command*, a drama of adultery and murder in a West Africa fortress. He took a small unit on location, 'so our production was enriched by invaluable shots and a great deal of authentic detail.'[2] Following this, Dickinson and others went to Spain, where he and Sidney Cole co-directed two films on aspects of the Spanish Civil War. Dickinson later said these were 'not documentary films but news reports: any eloquence depended on the immediacy of the images captured at the moment.'[3] Dickinson's liberal, leftist, but by no means doctrinaire sentiments are also felt in his support for the Association of Cinema Technicians, which, he said, was 'trying to be not so much a trade union but a sort of association of craftsmen, a professional body.'[4]

In 1939, he made the enjoyable thriller, *The Arsenal Stadium Mystery*; with the famous team in person alongside Leslie Banks and other actors: 'it was an absolute muddle,'[5] he recalled. During the war, there were *Gaslight*; *The Prime Minister*, a somewhat turgid biography of Disraeli, made on a low budget ('When in doubt we made it a night scene,'[6] he claimed); and, for Ealing, *Next of Kin*. This began as an instructional film on the need for security, but was very effectively extended through a fictional plot. Dickinson described it as 'an attempt to take this most unpopular element in the Army, the Security Police, and make its work understandable.'[7]

Of his 1946 release, *Men of Two Worlds*, he wrote: 'It was to be a realistic drama, not a spectacle of conquest nor yet a documentary film, but an intimate dramatic study of the two races [British and African] working side by side …'[8] It is a sincere, if laboured, study of attempts to overcome the evil influence of witch-doctors. 'But what was interesting [to him – and us] were the insights into the English in Africa.'[9]

His two masterworks both came to him by default, and are both costume pieces. *Gaslight* is a handsome, suspenseful Victorian melodrama of the woman-in-peril genre: 'I wanted a precise film not merely in composition of shots but in continuity of shots.'[10] *The Queen of Spades* is based on Pushkin's tale of a man who sells his soul for the secret of success at cards. Dickinson took over from Rodney Ackland, of whose work on the film he said, '. . . do you know, it has the most extraordinary effect? It isn't like a British film at all.'[11] The final result is, indeed, one of the most stylish and atmospheric films ever made in Britain.

After *Secret People*, about the filming of which Lindsay Anderson wrote a book,[12] Dickinson made a film about the new state of Israel, *Hill 24 Doesn't Answer*, then left feature filmmaking for good.

1 Lindsay Anderson, *Making a Film – The story of 'Secret People'*, George Allen & Unwin, London, 1952, p 84
2 'Mad dogs and location units', *The Cine-Technician*, June –July 1937, pp 56 and 57
3 'Experiences of the Spanish Civil War' in *The History Journal of Film, Radio and Television*, Vol 4, No 2, p 189
4 *Film Dope*, January 1977, p 7
5 *Film Dope*, p 8
6 Ronald Hayman, *John Gielgud*, Heinemann, London, 1971, p 131
7 *Film Dope*, p 10
8 'Shooting in the tropics is NO fun', *Picturegoer*, 11 November 1944, p 8
9 *Film Dope*, p 13
10 Jeffrey Richards, *Thorold Dickinson: The Man and His Films*, Croom Helm, London, 1986, p 69
11 Rodney Ackland, *The Celluloid Mistress*, Allan Wingate, London, 1954, p 210
12 See note 1

Carmen Dillon

b. 1908

Set designer, art director, or production designer: The £5 Man (1937), The Claydon Treasure Mystery, Father O' Nine, The Last Barricade, Murder in the Family (1938), French Without Tears (1939), Quiet Wedding (1941), Secret Mission (1942), The Gentle Sex, The Demi-Paradise (1943), Henry V (1944), The Way to the Stars (1945), School for Secrets, Carnival (1946), White Cradle Inn (1947), Vice-Versa, Hamlet (1948), Woman Hater, Cardboard Cavalier (1949), The Woman in Question, The Rocking Horse Winner, The Browning Version (1950), The Reluctant Widow (1951), The Importance of Being Earnest, The Story of Robin Hood (1952), The Sword and the Rose (1953), Doctor in the House (1954), Simon and Laura, Rob Roy: The Highland Rogue, Doctor at Sea (1955), Richard III, The Iron Petticoat (1956), Miracle in Soho, The Prince and the Showgirl (1957), A Tale of Two Cities (1958), Sapphire (1959), Carry on Constable, Please Turn Over, Kidnapped, Make Mine Mink, Watch Your Stern (1960), Raising the Wind, The Naked Edge (1961), Carry On Cruising, Twice Around the Daffodils, The Iron Maiden (1962), The Chalk Garden (1964), Battle of the Villa Fiorita (1965), Sky West and Crooked (1966), Accident (1967), Dandy in Aspic (1968), Otley, Sinful Davy (1969), The Rise and Rise of Michael Rimmer (1970), The Go-Between, Catch Me a Spy (1971), Lady Caroline Lamb (1972), Bequest to a Nation (1973), Butley (1974), The Omen (1976), Julia (1977)

For several decades, Carmen Dillon was the doyenne of British production designers. It is probably true to say that she made her name essentially with two directors: Anthony Asquith and Laurence Olivier. For Asquith, she designed seven films, including *The Importance of Being Earnest*, his first colour film and a triumph of high artificiality, its décor permitting no breath of the outside world, but she was equally at home in the black-and-white realities of the airfield life of *The Way to the Stars* and the claustrophobia of the public school in *The Browning Version*. For Olivier, she worked with Paul Sheriff on *Henry V* and with Roger Furse on *Hamlet* and *Richard III*. Through the prolific '50s and '60s, she extended her range in several *Carry On* films, but disliked the Disney Organisation's storyboarding habits and was dissatisfied with her work on *A Tale of Two Cities*. Then came two major successes for Joseph Losey: *Accident* and *The Go-Between*, in which she is substantially responsible for our belief in the worlds of, respectively, academe and the English country house. She retired in 1977, leaving a body of work the equal of anyone in her field, on either side of the Atlantic.

Interview date: June 1994

I understand that you trained as an architect before coming into films. How did you come to make the change to set designer?

I always wanted to know what's going on, and my family were always interested in what was happening in the cinema. We all got quite soft about films, really. And I certainly think I found my architectural training a help when I came to be a production designer. When I was quite young and trying to get into films, they were very against having women in films at all. I just drifted in, I think, and, for a long time, I was the only female art director in the country. My mother was delighted, though, that I was going into films in some capacity. That was really quite progressive of her to be encouraging me to go into films in the 1930s.

The earliest credits I have found for you were for a group of films you designed for Fox-British at Wembley. Was *The £5 Man* first?

I started there at Wembley. That's right. I remember *The £5 Man* for Al Parker but I think I did *The Claydon Treasure Mystery* before that and *Father O' Nine*, directed by Roy Kellino. It was exciting to work with Roy Kellino; he talked well, and was very entertaining.

I think you made five films for Fox-British at Wembley. You would have been designing the sets for those films?

Yes. I was called an art director. I don't think there was much difference between set designer and art director. It depended on how people felt about it, but usually they let me have the credit I wanted.

They were quite easy about that as a rule. In later years, I was called production designer.

Was *French Without Tears* an important film for you?

Oh yes. That was directed by 'Puffin' [Anthony] Asquith, my great friend. He was lovely to work with and talk to. I was very pleased and proud to have met him. He made you think you were doing your work for *him*, very nice. He had lovely manners, and of course the film was a very big success for everyone.

You did several films for him, including *Quiet Wedding*, *The Demi-Paradise*, *The Woman in Question* and *The Browning Version*.

Yes, I was pleased with them all. *The Browning Version* was a very good film, I thought. They were a varied collection but the Asquith films were all very English. He was a splendid person – and so was his mother. They lived in Bedford Square in London. He was very active in the union [the ACT – Association of Cinematograph Technicians] as well, but he wasn't aggressive at all; he wasn't a nuisance.

When you were working for him, would you be involved in early discussions about the film?

Yes, very probably. First of all I would read the 'treatment' – a rough outline of the story – and then try to imagine the kind of settings and do some rough sketches. But Puffin was so good at not offending you in any way that you would do anything for him, and you always felt you were doing what you wanted to anyway. You always had a lot of talks with the director to be sure you both had the same ideas about the look and mood of the film. Then the draughtsman would make the working drawings and the sets would be based on these.

Your first five films for Asquith were in black-and-white. Then you did *The Importance of Being Earnest* for him in colour. Did it make any difference to your work if the film was in colour?

Oh yes, it was lovely to get into the feeling of colour. It was a challenge and also a relief, as there was much more scope for experiment. I enjoy seeing black-and-white now, though, and in later years, as materials improved, it became easier to make black-and-white films look more distinctive.

Do you remember the costume designer Beatrice Dawson on *The Importance of Being Earnest* and did you work closely with her?

We did, yes, and we had fun together. We would discuss the colours to a certain extent. I was grateful she was around because she was a very interesting and creative person.

Do you remember any other costume designers you had a lot to do with?

I remember Julie Harris. I liked her very much and we worked on several films together. *Simon and Laura* and *Miracle in Soho* are two we were on together – and *The Chalk Garden*.

You did the three Shakespeare films for Olivier – *Henry V, Hamlet* and *Richard III*. That must have been exciting.

He was a lovely person, beautiful to look at, although he could be very tough. In *Henry V*, it was my idea to do it in that way, with the French Court looking so unrealistic. We worked for hours and hours late in the evening; we'd go down from the studio and try to work it all out. It was very exciting, very bold and daring. I wasn't responsible for the Globe Theatre beginning, I don't know who came up with that. Larry was very good to work with because he was always very keen and excited about things. He was lovely on *Henry V*, never trying. I also did *Hamlet* and *Richard III* with him – I thought *Richard III* in particular was wonderful. I worked with Roger Furse on both *Hamlet* and *Richard III*. We didn't really work on separate things, we did little patches together: it was a real partnership.

You then worked with the Disney organisation.

I didn't enjoy that. I think they made an awful mess and they're still doing it. I hardly met Walt Disney. They were very keen on having a storyboard and that was very trying. You had to pin down every shot for every scene; it was good for you as a discipline, but it wasn't a way I enjoyed working.

You seem to have been busy all the time!

I don't remember having or wanting holidays. I didn't think of having any free time, though I had some nasty patches in hospital, but I got over it. I was never really out of work, because those were busy days in British films.

You even did a couple of the *Carry On* films.

Yes, I did *Carry On Constable* and *Carry On Cruising* and I enjoyed those. I liked working with all those people, Peter Rogers and Gerald Thomas and so on. Those films were such fun to do! And so was *Doctor in the House*, where we had to be as true to life as possible. Betty Box produced that and I very much liked working with her too.

You also worked for her and Ralph Thomas on *A Tale of Two Cities*.

Yes, but it was a rotten film, very poor, I'm ashamed of my work on it. TEB Clarke did the script and it wasn't his cup of tea. Perhaps it should have been made in colour, but it wasn't good. They lost a lot of money about it, it was bad luck. Betty is such a competent, capable woman, so nice.

Do you have recollections of particular studios where you worked?

In the early days, in the '40s, I worked mostly at Denham on films like *The Demi-Paradise*, but Pinewood was always the best. It had the best facilities, and physically it was very good. We got mixed up with the war quite a bit but Pinewood was set in a beautiful piece of country and one felt rather part of it. They are still working there now. I liked Denham, but Pinewood always had the best feeling, and some of my best friends worked there too.

You worked for Joseph Losey on two remarkable films, *Accident* and *The Go-Between*. Did you find him an interesting man to work for?

Very much so. He was a funny chap, very nice and very good to work with. We went out looking for something that would be suitable for *The Go-Between* and we looked for several months until we found that country house, in Norfolk. It was rather run down, I remember, and we had a lot to do on it to make it look rather grand. A lot of the filming was actually done at the house although we did some studio work too. I had to copy bits of the house to be reproduced in the studio shots. The cameraman was Geoff Unsworth, who was a very good person for that job – very nice to work with and very quiet. Not all the cameramen were so nice to work with!

As a set designer you would be dependent on the cameraman to some extent, for your work to look good?

Yes, I suppose so, but I always liked the carpenters best of all. I worked quite closely with them and I also got on with them very well. They used to prefabricate the framework for the sets in the workshops, then put the separate pieces together in the studio. They had to be flexible and I always found the carpenters and painters were very good in this way.

Do you remember other famous cameramen like Robert Krasker and Desmond Dickinson?

Desmond, yes. I worked with him on *The Importance of Being Earnest* and other films too. He was wonderful, so alive. I didn't get on so well with Jack Cardiff, though. Then there was Bernard Knowles, who later became a director. He wasn't such a good director but he was a great cameraman. I also worked with Arthur Ibbetson on *The Chalk Garden*. The location work was shot quite near here

[Hove], in the Downs. Dame Edith Evans was lovely, very fine – a privilege to work with her.

Did you have very much to do with the actors?

Quite often. I like actors. Some of them took a great interest in the sets and others just zoomed through. A lot liked to interfere – they'd say this or that wasn't right, but the director would have the last say.

Are there any actors you remember with particular affection?

Oh, Larry of course. I did all the Shakespeare films with him and several others too – like *The Prince and the Showgirl*, the one he did with Marilyn Monroe.

Your career looks wonderful on paper. Does it seem that way to you?

No. I think I was just very lucky sometimes. But I never wished I had stayed as an architect. People always say I must have met such interesting people but that's not always the case. Some of the people I liked very much were actors, some were not; some one just got rather bored with. But I always enjoyed my job, on the whole.

Robert Donat

1905–1958

Actor: *Men of Tomorrow, That Night in London* (1932), *The Private Life of Henry VIII, Cash* (1933), *The Count of Monte Cristo* (1934), *The Thirty-Nine Steps, The Ghost Goes West* (1935), *Knight Without Armour* (1937), *The Citadel* (1938), *Goodbye Mr Chips* (1939), *The Young Mr Pitt* (1942), *The New Lot, The Adventures of Tartu* (1943), *Perfect Stran-* gers (1945), *Captain Boycott, *The British – Are They Artistic?* (1947), *The Winslow Boy* (1948), *The Cure for Love* (1950), *The Magic Box* (1951), **Royal Heritage* (narr) (1952), *Lease of Life* (1954), **The Stained Glass At Fairford* (voice only) (1956), *The Inn of the Sixth Happiness* (1958)
* Short film.

'One of the reasons why so few actors are successful both on the stage and on the screen is that too many film actors look upon filming as a rather boring, well-paid job. Their performances in front of the camera, if also rather boring, are not quite so much of a joke.'[1] This is Robert Donat in 1940 on the sore subject of British stage–screen relations. At first impressed only by the fact that 'film actors made *lots of money*,'[2] Donat rapidly assumed ascendancy in 1930s British cinema, with reviewer CA Lejeune writing after his performance as Richard Hannay in *The Thirty-Nine Steps*: 'For the first time on our screens we have a British equivalent of Clark Gable or Ronald Colman playing in a purely national idiom.'[3] He became indisputably a great *film* actor.

Donat is probably not much known to younger cinephiles, but his reputation is secure. After two minor films, he was 'launched', along with several other rising players, including Merle Oberon, by Alexander Korda's hugely successful *The Private Life of Henry VIII,* in which he played a dashing courtier dangerously involved with the king's current wife. He was dashing again in *The Count of Monte Cristo*; in fact he said later: 'The chief thing in my mind was that I must appear dashing. I distinctly remember in *The Count of Monte Cristo* pulling my shoulders back and trying to look handsome.'[4] Which he did, in the best film version of the Alexandre Dumas classic.

Throughout the '30s, despite a continuing commitment to the stage and a constant battle with ill-health ('just about the worst asthmatic I have ever seen,'[5] his physician said at this time), he had the best range of roles offered to a young film actor in Britain. He played both the young laird and his ghostly ancestor in *The Ghost Goes West*, in which American character actor Eugene Pallette 'taught [him] more about filmcraft than any other screen actor.'[6] He is a charming and athletic hero in *The Thirty-Nine Steps*, enthusing that he and Hitchcock 'understood each other so perfectly in the making of that film,'[7] and in *Knight Without Armour*: 'No real acting opportunities for me and little or no drama,'[8] but it is a lively adventure of post-revolutionary Russia. Two of MGM's finest pre-war British films, *The Citadel* and *Goodbye Mr Chips*, gave him still

better chances: first, as a crusading doctor who nearly loses his ideals; and, second, as the most fondly remembered schoolmaster in British fiction. As the gentle, skilfully ageing Chips, he won his Oscar against strong competition. 'As soon as I put the moustache on, I felt the part, even if I did look like a great Airedale come out of a puddle,'[9] he wrote.

He never again had such a run, but all his later films have their riches. He played the title role in *The Young Mr Pitt*, finding it 'a most stimulating experience to work with Carol [Reed]',[10] the director; he and Deborah Kerr teamed attractively in Korda's wartime romance, *Perfect Strangers*; his imposing presence and resonant voice compel attention as the defence counsel in *The Winslow Boy*; and he directed himself in a film version of his stage success, *The Cure for Love*. He was very touching in *Lease of Life*, as a clergyman 'who preaches a sensational sermon in the cathedral after learning that he has only a short time to live,'[11] and, finally, as the Mandarin in *The Inn of the Sixth Happiness*, leaving Ingrid Bergman and the film-going world with: 'We shall not see each other again, I think. Farewell.'

1 *Picturegoer and Film Weekly*, 23 March 1940, p 11
2 *Picturegoer*, 24 February 1951, p 9
3 The *Observer*, 9 June 1935
4 *Film Weekly*, 7 January 1939, p 9
5 JC Trewin, *Robert Donat*, Heinemann, London, 1968, p 89
6 *Film Weekly*, 7 December 1935, p 9
7 *Film Weekly*, 6 March 1937, p 7
8 Trewin, p 90
9 Trewin, p 106
10 *Picturegoer*, 10 March 1951, p 8
11 Trewin, p 222

Diana Dors

1931–1984

Actor: *The Shop at Sly Corner* (1946), *Holiday Camp, Dancing with Crime* (1947), *Oliver Twist, Good Time Girl, My Sister and I, Penny and the Pownall Case, Here Come the Huggetts* (1948), *Diamond City, The Calendar, Vote for Huggett, It's Not Cricket, A Boy, a Girl and a Bike* (1949), *Dance Hall* (1950), *Lady Godiva Rides Again, Worm's Eye View* (1951), *The Last Page, My Wife's Lodger, The Weak and the Wicked, Is Your Honeymoon Really Necessary?* (1952), *It's a Grand Life, The Great Game* (1953), *The Saint's Return / The Saint's Girl Friday, A Kid for Two Farthings* (1954), *Value for Money, An Alligator Named Daisy, Miss Tulip Stays the Night, As Long As They're Happy* (1955), *Yield to the Night, The Unholy Wife, I Married a Woman* (1956), *The Long Haul, The Love Specialist / La Ragazza Del Palio* (1957), *Tread Softly Stranger* (1958), *Passport to Shame* (1959), *Scent of Mystery* (1960), *On the Double, The Big Bankroll, King of the Roaring Twenties* (1961), *Mrs Gibbons' Boys* (1962), *West Eleven* (1963), *Allez France!* (1964), *The Sandwich Man* (1966), *Berserk, Danger Route* (1967), *Hammerhead* (1968), *Baby Love* (1969), *There's a Girl in My Soup* (1970), *Deep End, Hannie Caulder, The Pied Piper of Hamelin* (1971), *Every Afternoon, The Amazing Mr Blunden* (1972), *Steptoe and Son Ride Again, Theatre of Blood, Nothing but the Night* (1973), *Craze, Bedtime with Rosie, The Amorous Milkman, Swedish Wildcats, Three For All* (1974), *From Beyond the Grave* (1975), *Confessions of a Driving Instructor* (1976), *The Groove Room, Adventures of a Private Eye* (1977), *The Galaxy Affair, The Plank* (1979), *Dr Jekyll and Mr Hyde* (1980), *Steaming* (1984)

'They made me a Good Time Girl'[1] is the title of an article by Diana Dors in which she intelligently – and generously – appraises the British star-building procedures of the late '40s. 'Let me tell you about the life of a Rank contract star ... my contract started at £10 a week ... A completely unknown player would be foolish to pass up a contract, but one with some experience and a good agent might, with the right breaks, do much better for herself.'

She did do 'much better' for herself when she left Rank in 1950, landing roles in Carol Reed's *A Kid for Two Farthings* (1954), which was 'the big breakthrough for me as far as being taken more seriously,'[2] and two prison dramas for J Lee-Thompson, *The Weak and the Wicked* and *Yield to the Night*. And of course, she went on to do several remarkable character roles before her untimely death from cancer, in such films as *Baby Love* (1969), *Deep End* (1971) and *The Amazing Mr Blunden* (1972, playing what she described as 'an evil, gin-swigging old tart of 60'[3]), and she brought a note of real warmth to her final role, as Violet in Joseph Losey's *Steaming*.

However, one doesn't need to think only of her best films to see why she was so engaging. Even in the Rank contract days, when she was described as a 'miniature Mae West',[4] she was good-humoured and sexy, in such films as *Dancing with Crime* (as a nightclub 'hostess'), *Penny and the Pownall Case*, a Rank comic-strip 'B' film, and Alfred Roome's often hilarious *It's Not Cricket*; and she was a fleeting but memorable Charlotte in David Lean's *Oliver Twist*. If you want to see how likeable Dors can be, watch her in a couple of more or less inane Technicolored '50s comedies – *Value for Money* and *An Alligator Named Daisy*. She loses the hero in each case, as her flamboyant sort always did; but she is infinitely more diverting than the putative – and aseptic – heroine in either.

Part of her problem was that 'once one had given a promising performance, there was no rapid follow-up, as there is in Hollywood . . .'[5] Rank cast her ludicrously in *Diamond City*: 'At seventeen, I was trying to play a hardbitten belle of about thirty. I saw it on television a couple of years ago and I looked like a little girl dressed up in her mother's clothes.'[6] As well, the British film industry was curiously unable to deal with the frankly sexual: 'I don't think they [directors] know quite what to do with sex,' but 'I might as well cash in on my sex while I've got it. It can't last forever, can it?'[7] And a third problem was she always seemed obdurately working-class in a cinema whose narratives reflected middle-class values.

Yield to the Night (1956) was her big chance and she played the convicted murderess earnestly and touchingly. In her memoirs, *For Adults Only*, she recalls how: 'The Rank Organisation had been offered the script first but they had turned it down, so Associated British Pictures bought it, and it was probably just as well, for . . . they [Rank] would *never* have cast me.'[8] Too true.

1 *Picturegoer*, 7 October 1950, p 8
2 *Films and Filming*, July 1984, p 12
3 *Films and Filming*, February 1973, p 26
4 *Picturegoer*, 9 July 1949, p 5
5 *Picturegoer*, 7 October 1950, p 9
6 *Films and Filming*, July 1984, p 12
7 *Films and Filming*, January 1963, p 23
8 Diana Dors, *For Adults Only*, WH Allen & Co Ltd, London, 1978, p 251

David Farrar

1908–1995

Actor: *Return of a Stranger, Head Over Heels, Silver Top* (1937), *Sexton Blake and the Hooded Terror, A Royal Divorce* (1938), *Danny Boy, Penn of Pennsylvania, Sheepdog of the Hills* (1941), *Suspected Person, Went The Day Well?* (1942), *The Dark Tower, The Night Invader, They Met in the Dark, Headline, The Hundred Pound Window* (1943), *For Those in Peril, Meet Sexton Blake* (1944), *The World Owes Me a Living, The Echo Murders* (1945), *The Trojan Brothers, Lisbon Story* (1946), *Black Narcissus, Frieda* (1947), *The Small Back Room, Mr Perrin and Mr Traill* (1948), *Diamond City* (1949), *Gone to Earth, Cage of Gold* (1950), *The Late Edwina Black, Night Without Stars, The Golden Horde* (1951), *Duel in the Jungle, Lilacs in the Spring, The Black Shield of Falworth* (1954), *The Sea Chase, Pearl of the South Pacific, Escape to Burma* (1955), *Lost* (1956), *Woman and the Hunter* (1957), *I Accuse!, Son of Robin Hood* (1958), *John Paul Jones, Watusi, Solomon and Sheba* (1959), *Middle of Nowhere, Beat Girl, The Webster Boy, The 300 Spartans* (1960)

Like Kathleen Byron, with whom he twice – memorably – co-starred, David Farrar's finest hours in British cinema were in the films he made for Michael Powell, and *Black Narcissus* provided him with a major turning-point in his career. As the caustic, insolent Mr Dean, the British agent deputed to keep an eye on the Himalayan convent, his scenes with Byron and

Deborah Kerr carried a sensual charge rare in British cinema at the time, and this was followed by two further striking roles for Powell: as the lame bomb-disposal expert in *The Small Back Room* and as the swaggering squire in *Gone to Earth*. These opportunities came after a decade of – mostly – second features, in which he established himself as a strongly masculine presence of a kind British cinema needed. The vein of sensitivity that was sometimes allowed to surface in these films worked well with the easy strength that was his hallmark, and resulted in fine performances in Basil Dearden's *Frieda* and Lawrence Huntington's gripping version of *Mr Perrin and Mr Traill*, as well as in the Powell films. It was a pity he elected to retire in 1960, when he might so well have found a niche in the new social realist films of the early '60s.
Interview date: December 1990

Were you already established on the stage before you entered films?

I don't know about 'established' but my wife and I did a repertoire, of mainly costume plays, with some success before films tempted me somewhere about the middle 1930s. A chap called Victor Hanbury, then head of RKO Radio Pictures in Britain, came to my dressing-room and offered me a small part in a film they were making at Shepperton Studios. Then followed a long apprenticeship of small parts in big films and big parts in small films until the outbreak of war put a stop to all this. When I saw myself on the screen for the first time, I realised I had no idea at all of film-acting technique, which really wants naturalness or 'underplaying'. And, of course, on the screen, they can shoot a scene a dozen times and it's a miracle if your best performance coincides with the occasion when everything else is right – camera, lighting, sound and so on.

What sort of film roles were you offered at this time, when war broke out?

There were some I prefer to forget, but I was certainly pleased when I got an offer to play the lead in *Sheepdog of the Hills*, even if my co-star *was* a sheepdog and he had the title role. But it was a lovely acting part, with everything in it I could wish – lots of pathetic blind stuff (I played a vicar who'd lost his sight) and noble self-sacrifice at the end; and I enjoyed the two months' location in Devonshire. Then in 1942 I got my Army call-up papers and was about to be sent to a camp in Paignton, when Warner's were just starting a film called *The Night*

Invader in which I'd already been signed to play the lead. Perhaps it was felt I was more useful providing entertainment than in soldiering, for the producers got the War Office to request me to return my call-up papers.

***Went the Day Well?* still seems a very interesting film. What do you remember about it and the director, Cavalcanti?**

I thought it was a bad title because I doubt if many knew where the quotation came from, but it was a good film and Cavalcanti was a charming person who spoke English with a strong Brazilian accent. It was an Ealing film, with a lot of location work, including some at Henley, where we worked with a regular Army company. I played a Nazi posing as a British officer. My fan mail suggested that, though they were impressed with what they described as a fine 'acting' performance, they almost invariably disliked my playing a brutalised part like this.

After several films for Warner's, you were back at Ealing for *Headline*.

I enjoyed that, it was a thriller with a good script and set in the newspaper world I knew from my own journalism days. Before *Headline* was finished I was already contracted to make *For Those in Peril* for Ealing. Ealing had distributed *Headline* but we actually made the film at Hammersmith Studios; but *For Those in Peril* was really an Ealing production and it turned out to be a great film which got marvellous notices from all the critics. It was about the Air–Sea Rescue service, which did wonderful work during the war. I had a fine part as the tough skipper of the launch and we shot this in the Channel under actual combat conditions. Charlie Crichton, who directed it and was something of a sailor, used to like watching us go green in a rough sea. Unhappily, it turned out that the film was not booked to go into any West End cinema. Perhaps it was because of its awkward length (it was only sixty-seven minutes long), too short for a West End first feature, though it was booked throughout the provinces. I felt I'd given my best film performance to date, but there were no cables from Hollywood! Perhaps if it had been padded by a further thirty minutes and had a feminine interest introduced, it might have been a success at the box-office as well as with the critics.

What do you recall of the three films you made for British National at this time – *The World Owes Me a Living*, *The Trojan Brothers*, and *Lisbon Story*?

I made *The World Owes Me a Living* at Elstree, where I was very happy working. It was from a novel by John Llewellyn Rhys, a young author who was killed during the war, and it was about the growth of aviation between the two world wars. We spent weeks on location doing the flying sequences and I very much liked playing opposite Judy Campbell, who was a grand actress and a lovable person. The director was an unusually inventive man, Vernon Sewell, the first that I had known to lay tracks for continual shooting of up to several minutes.

The other two films you mentioned had to wait till I got back to London after a tour with ENSA of camps and gun-sites in a play called *Jeannie*. *The Trojan Brothers* was taken from a novel by Pamela Hansford Johnson. It had a powerful subject – the fatal attraction for a worthless woman of a Cockney called Sid, who is driven mad by her heartlessness and finally strangles her. I was all for playing the film 'as per book' but the producers wouldn't let me strangle my leading lady and changed it to a happy ending, despite my protests. However, I treasure a letter from Miss Johnson which finished by saying, 'I liked your Sid better than mine.' The ABC circuit snapped it up and it was very popular and financially successful, but as it didn't get a West End showing it didn't add an inch to my stature. However, I had the great pleasure of working with Bobby Howes in it: we played a horse act, with me as the forelegs and Bobby as the hindlegs, which led him to say, 'I feel such an arse!' Patricia Burke was my leading lady in both that and *Lisbon Story*. It

took hours to get her hairdo right, leading to jokes about Burke and Hare. *Lisbon Story* had a long run on the London stage, but the film had a new story about my escapades as an intelligence officer. Pat and Richard Tauber and others added some charming and attractive songs and the film filled two West End cinemas.

Would you agree that your career entered a new phase with *Black Narcissus*?

Yes. The producer and director was, of course, Michael Powell. I was about to sign a Hollywood contract with Universal-International to play Grieg in *The Song of Norway*, when the phone rang and I was asked if I would like to read the script of Mr Powell's next picture. It was *Black Narcissus*, and when I read it it seemed like too good an opportunity to be true. I had a meeting with Powell and Emeric Pressburger, his scripting partner; there was a period of anxious waiting, then I was asked if I would test for the part of Mr Dean. It seemed a long time afterwards that Micky told me, 'The part is yours,' and I never even signed a contract till long after the film was finished.

I can honestly say that every day of shooting was an exciting adventure, mainly due to Micky's creative ideas. The whole thing was an outstanding, fully satisfying artistic creation. People could scarcely believe that the whole film was shot in the studio, with profiles and smokescreens against the skyline to give the effect of the dizzy height of the Himalayas. In some of the 'snow scenes', Sabu and I were wearing bearskin coats in the middle of a heatwave!

You made two further films for Powell and Pressburger – *The Small Back Room* (1948) and *Gone to Earth* (1950). Do you regard these three films as the highlight of your career?

Artistically yes, though I would also include my Ealing films, *Frieda*, with Mai Zetterling, and *Cage of Gold*, with Jean Simmons; and my journeys to Hollywood constituted another sort of highlight – money and glamour and the star treatment as only Hollywood can do it. I was still working on *Mr Perrin and Mr Traill* when Micky was ready to start *The Small Back Room* early in 1948. We shot the location scenes first, in Dorset, where we did the bomb-defusing sequence which many critics thought one of the most thrilling things ever seen on the screen. It was a long and difficult sequence, most of it shot at about 5 am in early March with, as I remember, a biting east wind coming in off the sea. And the artificial foot I wore to play the part of

Sammy Rice was so uncomfortable that I couldn't help limping anyway. But it was a great part and worth all the discomfort in the end, and once again we had excellent notices.

What of those two films you finished before *The Small Back Room* – *Frieda* and *Mr Perrin and Mr Traill*?

Frieda was made for Ealing Studios, with some location work in Oxford. It actually opened to great success in New York when I was there to publicise *Black Narcissus* for the Rank Organisation. Their premières were on two consecutive nights. *Frieda* was a good film and had wonderful notices in both Britain and the States. I attended its premières in London, New York and Stockholm. Before I did *Mr Perrin and Mr Traill*, I was unemployed for eight months because of one deal falling through for me to star in a film version of *Precious Bane* and because of The Archers [Powell and Pressburger's production company] and my not seeing eye to eye on the character they wanted me to play in *The Red Shoes*, but, as under my contract I had to be paid for a film anyway, I agreed to do *Mr Perrin and Mr Traill*, which didn't turn out too badly and was very popular, though I was never mad about it.

Did you like playing the raffish, 'glamorous' cad as opposed to James Donald's character with the sterling 'Ealing' virtues in *Cage of Gold*?

Funny you should ask that. Michael Balcon wanted me to play the 'good guy' but it stood out a mile that the 'baddie' was much more exciting, and I had quite a job to talk him into it.

After a busy time in Hollywood and several more British films in the '50s, you had three films released in 1960 – *Beat Girl*, *The Webster Boy* and *The 300 Spartans* – and then retired. Why did you stop so young, when you were just over fifty?

People find it a mystery. I'd played leading roles in about fifty films and might have been getting a bit blasé with all the artificiality – I'd just finished a flamboyant role as Xerxes for 20th-Century-Fox in *300 Spartans*, which played for seven months in London's West End. I always felt the ideal was to get to the top, stay at the top and get out at the top. The time coincided with some problems, not least the death of my agent, Haddon Mason of Film-rights, who had been my manager for twenty-five years, leaving me feeling a bit lost. I was tired of the hassles and battles, and conceit might have come into it – I'd always been the upstanding young leading man and I was afraid of parts being hinted at for uncles or the girl's father instead of the lover! I just felt 'the Hell with it all', and walked out into the sunset.

Dame Gracie Fields

1898–1979

Actor: *Sally in our Alley* (1931), *Looking on the Bright Side* (1932), *This Week of Grace* (1933), *Love, Life & Laughter*, *Sing As We Go* (1934), *Look Up and Laugh* (1935), *Queen of Hearts* (1936), *The Show Goes On* (1937), *We're Going to be Rich*, *Keep Smiling* (1938), *Shipyard Sally* (1939), *Holy Matrimony* (1943), *Stage Door Canteen* (1944), *Molly and Me*, *Paris Underground* (1945)

'It's slow, awful slow ... It's not so much the work as the waits.'[1] This was Gracie Fields's reaction to making her first film, *Sally in our Alley*. She also said of this experience, 'None of us knew anything about film making and the chaos of those first few weeks is something I shall never forget.'[2] She never greatly enjoyed the processes of filmmaking, and was critical of all her British films except

Sally: the rest were just 'stitched around'[3] her, she said, with some truth. Nevertheless, for several years in the mid-1930s she was the most popular film star in Britain.

Born above a fish-and-chip shop in Rochdale, Lancashire, in 1898, eighty years later she opened a theatre there bearing her name, and was made a DBE. In class-bound Britain, her rise was phenomenal: from music hall, to Ealing and Hollywood, the London Palladium and to semi-retirement on Capri. She won the admiration of millions, from royalty down, and seems never to have lost the common touch, her philosophy remaining simple. 'There is no secret about how I get my laughs. Life provides all the laughs I want ... When I want gags for my films, I take them from the raw material of human nature and from the everyday things of this workaday world,'[4] she explained. 'I'm ordinary,' she warned her fans, 'don't raise me up too high.'[5] The music hall warmth infused the personality on- and off-screen: 'I belong to the music hall. I feel at home here ... giving the folks a bit of a song and a laugh.'[6]

The optimistic titles of her films tell almost all: *Looking on the Bright Side*, *Sing As We Go* (its title song is like a Depression anthem), *Look Up and Laugh* and *Keep Smiling*. Pleasantly homely to look at, invincibly positive, nobody's fool and with a reliable antenna for the phoney, she dragged these sometimes creaky vehicles into major popularity – and made a fortune. She is also able to deal with a dash of sentiment in situation or song, but claimed, 'I just can't help introducing a few vocal gymnastics to show how easy it is to guy the saddest song.'[7]

Of the British films, *Sing As We Go* is generally regarded as the best. Here, she plays an unemployed mill-girl who gets various jobs in Blackpool, loses the hero, and finally, to the title tune, leads fellow workers back to the re-opened mill. Like *Shipyard Sally*, in which she sang 'Wish Me Luck', it is not one of those which 'were built around a few songs, and ... weren't what I'd really call good.'[8] Under the guidance of her second husband, director Monty Banks, 'a skilled and experienced director',[9] she grew to 'dread' films less. She disliked her first American-backed film, *We're Going to be Rich*, finally made in Britain: 'I thought we were going to get something fancier like, so that we could show American audiences what I can do.'[10] However, it was her 1943 Hollywood film, *Holy Matrimony*, which gave her most pleasure: '... the words were rich, it was a *real* story.'[11]

She lost favour when she went to live in America during the war, to prevent her Italian husband's internment, but by the time she died she had long been forgiven. I suspect the young know nothing about her; that is their loss.

1 *Film Weekly*, 18 April 1931, p 10
2 Gracie Fields, *Sing As We Go: The Autobiography of Gracie Fields* (first published 1960), Chivers Press, Bath, 1981, p 109
3 Rachael Low, *Film Making in 1930s Britain*, George Allen & Unwin, London, 1985, p 170
4 *Film Weekly*, 13 October 1933, p 7
5 Joan Moules, *Our Gracie*, Robert Hale, London, 1983, p 82
6 *Focus on Films*, August 1979, p 28
7 *Film Weekly*, 13 October 1933, p 7
8 Moules, p 53
9 Fields, *Sing As We Go*, p 152
10 David Shipman, *The Great Movie Stars: The Golden Years*, Hamlyn, London, 1970, p 192
11 Moules, p 53

Peter Finch

1916–1977

Actor: *The Magic Shoes* (unreleased) (1935), *Dad and Dave Come to Town* (1938), *Mr Chedworth* *Steps Out* (1939), *The Power and the Glory* (1941), *Another Threshold*, *While There's Still Time*

(1942), *South West Pacific (1943), *Jungle Patrol, The Rats of Tobruk (1944), Red Sky at Morning (1945), A Son Is Born (1946), *Primitive Peoples (1947), Train of Events (1949), The Miniver Story, The Wooden Horse (1950), The Story of Robin Hood and his Merrie Men (1952), The Heart of The Matter, The Story of Gilbert and Sullivan (1953), Elephant Walk, Make Me An Offer!, Father Brown (1954), Josephine and Men, Passage Home, Simon and Laura, The Dark Avenger (1955), A Town Like Alice, The Battle of the River Plate (1956), Robbery Under Arms, Windom's Way, The Shiralee (1957), Operation Amsterdam (1958), The Nun's Story, Kidnapped (1959), The Sins of Rachel Cade, The Trials of Oscar Wilde, The Day (pr only) (1960), No Love for Johnnie (1961), I Thank a Fool, In the Cool of the Day (1962), Girl with Green Eyes (1963), The Pumpkin Eater, First Men in the Moon (1964), Judith, The Flight of the Phoenix (1965), 10.30pm Summer (1966), Far from the Madding Crowd (1967), The Legend of Lylah Clare (1968), La Tenda Rossa / The Red Tent, The Greatest Mother of Them All (1969), Sunday Bloody Sunday, Something to Hide (1971), England Made Me, Lost Horizon (1972), Bequest to the Nation (1973), The Abdication (1974), Network, Raid on Entebbe (1976)
* Documentary.

'I do not believe that with a fictional character you can force yourself too far away from yourself. There has to be some of you in it,'[1] said Peter Finch in 1958. This feasible theory about screen acting nevertheless tends to elide the huge differences between the characters Finch undertook with distinction. There is, for instance, little common ground between the shallow, opportunist politician in No Love for Johnnie and the tragic Wilde in The Trials of Oscar Wilde, perhaps his two subtlest performances. More than many British actors, and like Connery and Caine, he understood the screen's love of small effects: 'I like a performance to be as simple as possible ... I like it [cinema] better than the theatre because the place where an audience can see an actor's thoughts is in his eyes.'[2]

Born in England, he had begun filmmaking in Australia in the '30s and came back to England in the late '40s, after being seen on the Australian stage by Olivier, who cast him opposite Edith Evans in Daphne Laureola. But, Finch claims, 'Balcon took the first risk on me in England,'[3] and, at Harry Watt's instigation, cast him as a murderer in Train of Events. He made the best of what came his way in the often uninspired British cinema of the '50s. There was little to be done with The Dark Avenger, Operation Amsterdam or Robbery Under Arms ('Off we all went at half-cock with a half-baked project rushed in and out of the oven because that was the chef's orders'[4]), all tired action films. However, though he complained of Simon and Laura, 'I feel all these camera angles cramping my style ... I become totally strained and awkward,'[5] he and Kay Kendall made a sparkling comedy team; he gave his own favourite performance in the Australian-set Ealing film, The Shiralee ('I knew the character from my early bumming-about period'[6]); and he brought dignity and pathos to the role of the German captain in Michael Powell's dull war film, The Battle of the River Plate ('I think he was a great man ... I feel very deeply the loss of this man dying alone in his hotel room'[7]).

Though he made films in Hollywood, he remained very much a British star. When he first went there in 1953 for studio work on Elephant Walk, he wrote: 'You can't help enjoying it – if you have a regard for the technical excellence that is routine to a Hollywood studio.'[8] His later American films are largely forgettable – and forgotten (The Sins of Rachel Cade, the grotesque Lost Horizon, and, undeservedly, Robert Aldrich's The Legend of Lylah Clare). Even his Oscar-winning Hollywood role in Network, despite his admiration for Paddy Chayevsky's 'devastating attack on the whole way of life,'[9] is floridly overwrought, by comparison with his best work in British films.

'When I approach a part I have a process of unconscious absorption into the character ... I do not make meticulous notes on the script or work out exterior business.'[10] The ten or twelve British films on which his acting – as opposed to the tedious 'roistering' – reputation rests give evidence for the efficacy of this approach. They include: Girl with Green Eyes (as middle-aged novelist); The Pumpkin Eater (unfaithful husband to too-fecund wife); Far from the Madding Crowd (Hardy's obsessed gentleman-farmer to the life); and Sunday Bloody Sunday (Jewish homosexual doctor). These films enshrine a major talent, displayed with precision and compassion.

1 *Films and Filming*, September 1958, p 7
2 *Films and Filming*, August 1970, p 7
3 *Films and Filming*, August 1970, p 6
4 Trader Faulkner, *Finchie*, Angus & Robertson, 1979, p 187
5 Faulkner, p 176
6 *Films and Filming*, August 1970, p 7
7 Faulkner, p 179
8 *Picturegoer*, 5 May 1956, p 9
9 *Australian Women's Weekly*, January 1977, p 7
10 Elaine Dundy, *Finch, Bloody Finch*, Michael Joseph, London, 1980, p 245

Albert Finney

b. 1936

Actor: *The Entertainer, Saturday Night and Sunday Morning* (1960), *Tom Jones, The Victors* (1963), *Night Must Fall* (1964), *Two for the Road* (1966), *The Picasso Summer, Charlie Bubbles* (1967), *Scrooge* (1970), *Gumshoe* (1971), *Alpha Beta* (1972), *Murder on the Orient Express* (1974), *The Duellists* (1977), *Loophole* (1980), *Shoot the Moon, Looker, Wolfen, Annie* (1981), *The Dresser* (1983), *Under the Volcano* (1984), *Orphans* (1987), *Miller's Crossing* (1990), *Playboys, Rich in Love* (1992), *The Browning Version* (1994), *A Man of No Importance* (1995), *The Run of the Country* (1996), *Washington Square* (1997)

'My job is acting, and that is why I hate interviews or lectures, explaining myself to an audience,'[1] said Albert Finney in 1961. Over thirty years later, he courteously refused me an interview saying, 'I am so interested in the Present that I have no wish to discuss the Past.'[2] Finney has kept on acting, in one medium or another, in many major roles, for over thirty years, without ever showing much interest in being a 'star', and commanding wide respect rather than a mass following.

His film career began with a brief scene in *The Entertainer* ('a pre-credits sequence not even in the play, a living screen test,'[3] he said years later), but the film that made his name was Karel Reisz's *Saturday Night and Sunday Morning*, the most commercially successful of the new wave of social realist films in the early '60s. Finney played – memorably – Arthur Seaton, a lathe worker determined not to 'let the bastards grind you down'. '. . . about the scenes where I was working at the lathe, I felt almost like a sculptor – working a real lathe, with real metal, and working it myself.'[4] However, at least partly because of its sexual candour (Arthur beds a workmate's wife), '. . . it was only an art-house movie in the States, my big breakthrough there was *Tom Jones*.'[5]

Tom Jones, directed by Tony Richardson, key figure in the influential Woodfall production company, brought Fielding's picaresque novel to the screen in an irresistible mixture of physical realism and cinematic tricks. The title role could have opened up a career for Finney as a dashing romantic actor (though he thought Tom too 'passive' and 'reactive' a character, according to Richardson,[6] but he chose instead to follow much less predictable paths. 'I'm not the romantic type . . . I'm a bit like the late, great Peter Sellers, only happy in character roles,'[7] he said in 1982.

This insistence on character, rather than the business of stardom, is borne out by the films. He was a psychopathic killer in *Night Must Fall*; the eponymous miser in the musical *Scrooge*; a Liverpool bingo-caller obsessed with Bogart in *Gumshoe*; a heavy-jowled and unrecognisable Hercule Poirot in *Murder on the Orient Express*; and a flamboyant

Wolfit-inspired touring actor in *The Dresser*. A romantic lead in *Two for the Road* found him short of the easy charm the film needed.

He was critical of the class limitations of the British stage and screen in the early '60s: 'Usually, in the theatre and the cinema, you get a middle-class style of acting, which means that when people are playing a working-class character they send it up, they don't act it.'[8] His own work showed a real capacity, as an actor, for representing a proletarian energy.

With Michael Medwin, he formed a production company, Memorial, which produced such films as *If . . .*, *Gumshoe*, and *O Lucky Man*. 'If Michael Medwin and I could produce a picture like *If . . .*

every year I would be happy, never mind the acting lark,'[9] he claims. That would be a pity: a film as recent as *The Browning Version* shows undimmed mastery of the 'acting lark'.

1 *Sight and Sound*, Spring 1961, p 61
2 Letter to Brian McFarlane, February 1994
3 *Time Out*, 4–11 November 1987, p 21
4 *Sight and Sound*, p 61
5 *Time Out*, p 21
6 Tony Richardson, *Long-Distance Runner*, Faber & Faber, London, 1993, p 129
7 *Screen International*, 3 April 1982, p 24
8 *Sight and Sound*, p 102
9 *Screen International*, p 24

Bryan Forbes

b. 1926

Actor: *The Tired Men* (short) (1943), *The Small Back Room*, *All Over the Town*, *Dear Mr Prohack* (1949), *The Wooden Horse* (1950), *Green Grow the Rushes* (1951), *The World in his Arms* (1952), *Appointment in London*, *Sea Devils*, *Wheel of Fate* (1953), *The Million Pound Note*, *An Inspector Calls*, *Up To His Neck* (1954), *The Colditz Story*, *Passage Home*, *Last Man to Hang*, *The Quatermass Xperiment* (1955), *Now and Forever*, *The Extra Day*, *It's Great to be Young*, *The Baby and the Battleship*, *Satellite in the Sky* (1956), *Quatermass II* (1957), *The Key*, *I Was Monty's Double* (1958), *Yesterday's Enemy* (1959), *The League of Gentlemen* (1960), *The Guns of Navarone* (1961), *A Shot in the Dark* (1964), *The Restless Natives* (cameo) (1985)

Screenwriter/producer/director: *The Red Beret* (uncr sc) (1953), *Hell Below Zero* (uncr sc) (1954), *The Black Knight* (co-sc), *Cockleshell Heroes* (co-sc)(1955), *The Baby and the Battleship* (co-sc), *The Black Tent* (co-sc), *House of Secrets* (co-sc)(1956), *I Was Monty's Double* (sc)(1958), *The Captain's Table* (co-sc) (1959), *Man in the Moon* (sc), *The Angry Silence* (sc), *The League of Gentlemen* (sc)(1960), *Whistle Down the Wind* (dir)(1961), *Only Two Can Play* (sc), *Station Six Sahara* (sc), *The L-Shaped Room* (dir, sc)(1962), *Of Human Bondage* (sc), *The High Bright Sun* (sc), *Seance on a Wet Afternoon* (dir, sc, co-pr)(1964), *King Rat* (dir, sc)(1965), *The Wrong Box* (dir, pr) *The Whisperers* (dir, sc)(1966), *Deadfall* (dir, sc)(1967), *The Madwoman of Chaillot* (dir)(1974), *The Slipper and the Rose* (dir, sc)(1976), *International Velvet* (dir, pr, sc) *Sunday Lovers* (dir)(1980), *Better Late Than Never* (dir)(1982), *The Naked Face* (dir, sc)(1984), *The Endless Game* (dir, sc)(1988), *Chaplin* (co-sc) (1993), *Forever England* (1997)

Bryan Forbes, as actor, director, producer and screenwriter, has maintained one of the busiest careers in the British film industry, and in the last two decades he has emerged as an author of distinction. He began in the late 1940s when there was plenty of work for a versatile character actor, taking whatever was offered and giving individuality to roles large and small. He was especially memorable as the unhappy girl's seducer in *An Inspector Calls*, and he worked with some of the most prolific directors of the period, from Michael Powell in 1949 *(The Small Back Room)* to Basil Dearden in 1960 *(The League of Gentlemen*, for which he also wrote the sharply ironic screenplay). Since 1960, he has been influentially involved as director of a number of distinctive realist films (e.g., *Whistle Down the Wind* and *The Whisperers*) and, with Richard Attenborough, as co-founder of Beaver Films, set up initially to produce *The Angry Silence*. From 1969 to 1971, as Head of Production at EMI's Elstree Studios (now demolished), he made a valiant but ultimately frustrated attempt to retain a British industry, but, sadly, was not supported. He has shown himself persistently willing to try his arm in demanding ventures.

Interview date: October 1989

Was it a good time to get an acting career going in British cinema in the late '40s and '50s?

Yes, it was very easy really. I went literally from film to film, because the film industry was booming. The Rank Organisation particularly had made a concerted effort. Old Lord Rank, who was much abused, I think wrongly, poured millions in to try and make a British film industry and to break into the American market. Rank and ABPC, to a lesser extent, and other periphery studios, were pouring them out. There must have been well over a hundred films a year made, because we still had 'B' films, of which I made some.

Rank had a lot of people under contract, myself included. The first big role I ever had was in *All Over the Town*, which was made for Wessex Films, an offshoot of Rank under Ian Dalrymple, who was a very gentle man, probably to his own disadvantage. I was never a star, I was a feature player. You got work through being *in* work, because I was also working in the theatre at the same time. They had to shoot around you on matinée days. If you were on location, of course, and the film was shot down at Lyme Regis like *All Over the Town*, obviously I wouldn't have got the job if I'd have been in a play. But if you were in a play and you were at Pinewood

or Elstree they would let you off in time to get back to the theatre. It provided the British film industry with this enormous reservoir of talent which they could tap. People often, Americans especially, say, 'How did you manage to get Ralph Richardson to play such a small role?' British actors tend, even enormously exalted actors, if they aren't doing anything else and they like the part, not to count the words, whereas American stars tend to feel a bit too proud to accept anything other than a major role.

Did any of your early films give you special satisfaction?

I suppose my best role was in Guy Hamilton's film of the Priestley play, *An Inspector Calls*. Though I was never a star, I had some interesting roles, in *The Wooden Horse* for instance. I originally had an eight-week contract and we arrived out in Lüneburg Heath – shortly after the war, it was '48 – and although there must have been five hundred disused prisoner-of-war camps of one description or another, this being the film industry, they cleared fifty acres of Lüneburg Heath and built a totally new one, so we hung about for six weeks with nothing happening and the script being rewritten. Then we shot for about two weeks. Because the negative came back to England to be developed, we didn't see the rushes very early and there were all these shots of Leo Genn, David Tomlinson, Tony Steel and me, and the rest of the high-ranking RAF officers were cast with displaced persons. So you panned past Leo Genn and me and everybody else, and suddenly saw Mongolian wing commanders with flat noses and fake moustaches which looked totally ludicrous. The producers saw this, junked the whole lot, and ordered a reshoot. So my eight-week contract became fourteen months!

I'd be interested in recollections of working with such directors as Philip Leacock. Guy Hamilton, Ronald Neame, Roy Baker, or Carol Reed.

Carol is the one who stands out for me. I liked the others and I got on with them all, but can't remember that one got a lot of direction. They assumed, when they cast you, that you knew your job. They certainly knew theirs; they were all marvellous technicians. But Carol, for whom I did *The Key*, was my mentor, somebody I admired extravagantly, and I'm sure he influenced my own work when I became a director. Once an actor himself, he understood actors very well. He wasn't a showy director, and when I got the chance to direct I went to Carol and said, 'Is there a secret? Can you give me any tips?' He said, 'Yes, never humiliate an actor and never cut until he's exited frame.' Two very good rules. Film isn't a theatrical medium. I think what you need is a visual eye and a great deal of sympathy with actors. It's very lonely out there in front of the camera; the actor has nobody he can feel any response from except the director. Really, I think the director has to have the feeling, the *taste*, and he's got to set the style of the movie.

How did you find those American stars who were always being brought over to Britain in the '50s?

I suppose the one I worked with most was Alan Ladd, a monosyllabic and very withdrawn character. Not that he was rude, just very withdrawn and, I think, very unhappy. I worked on three of his: *The Black Knight*, *The Red Beret*, *Hell Below Zero*. That's how my screenwriting career started, with Irving Allen and Cubby Broccoli. The first credit of any note I had was *Cockleshell Heroes*, for José Ferrer, whom I didn't get on with terribly well.

What did you feel about the preponderance of war films still being made throughout the 1950s?

I think it was inevitable. The war was so long and so hard and we suffered four years of nothing but reverses, that I think it was only natural afterwards to use that material to say, as it were, 'Listen, we've won, you know.' And a lot of the prisoner-of-war stories were quite extraordinary: *Colditz*, and *The Captive Heart*, and the conception of *The Wooden Horse* and the way they executed it, were good stories in anybody's book. I think it's not unnatural that people want to pat themselves on the back when they've come through a long war, which in the UK involved all the civilians, don't forget. People just wanted to say, 'Jesus, we came through it.'

What did you think of the 'new wave' of British cinema that came in the late '50s?

The revolution started with Osborne. I think I was never a star because I was in the wrong class, as it were, and, in my day, people like Tom Courtenay wouldn't have carried a spear, because you had to have a rather plummy accent. I was once turned down for a part in *The Cruel Sea* – nice letter saying 'Can't cast you because we've decided you're not officer material'! Then suddenly, after Osborne had written *Look Back in Anger*, a few others were writing not for the old-school-ties sort of accent, but for the provincial accents, for Albert Finney in *Saturday Night and Sunday Morning*, and Rachel Roberts. Suddenly you didn't have to have a BBC announcer's voice; you could write a hero who wasn't six feet tall, and get him cast. You could do films which showed a much more realistic picture. I think it came out of a 'new wave' of younger directors, younger writers.

I turned the class thing around in *The League of Gentlemen*. I took the epitome of British stiff-upper-lip acting – and I mean this not in a derogatory sense because I think Jack Hawkins was a considerable actor – and turned it on its head. I made him a cashiered officer who was a crook and everything he said in my screenplay was a reverse of what you'd expect. I'll give you an example. There was a scene between him and 'Paddy' [Nigel] Patrick when they go to Jack's house, and Basil Dearden, with my screenplay, deliberately shot an oil painting of a woman about three times, so that it registered, and finally Paddy says, 'Is that your wife?' Jack says, 'Yes,' and Patrick says, 'Is she dead?', since he appears to be living alone. Now, normally in a British film Jack would have said, 'Yes, I'm terribly sorry, she died in childbirth,' instead of which I made him say, 'No, I'm sorry to say the bitch is still going strong,' which is very minor but a revelation.

Do you think the middle-classness of '40s

and '50s British cinema helps to account for its not acquiring the mass audience of the average American film?

Yes, but as well we didn't really use the country. I mean we still built Bond Street on Stage 4. It wasn't until about the time of *The Angry Silence* that, instead of building a bit of a factory at Pinewood, we went to Ipswich and went into a factory. We shot actual sound. When I made *Whistle Down the Wind*, we went up to Manchester and shot on a real farm, in a real barn. That was my first film as a director. I think there are some films which *have* to be made in studios and it's a great shame that studios are closed because we'll always need them.

There was another great mistake, too, where the money started to go wrong and where they lost their shirt, and that was when they tried to make a mid-Atlantic product, so it was neither fish nor fowl. In war films, they would import, for example, Alan Ladd as a quasi-British soldier with Canadian flashes on his uniform, or – as in *Cockleshell Heroes* – make José Ferrer a Royal Marine officer. It was all faintly ludicrous and didn't work. The French cinema at its best remains uniquely French, and our best British films have only succeeded when they remain indigenous. When we try to capture the vital American market, we design a horse and end up with a camel.

What is your attitude to the ways in which the Government or its instrumentalities have intervened in British cinema?

Well, I think in direct ways they could help us and don't. You get very little co-operation in shooting in London, for example; in fact, you're actively discouraged. When I was shooting *Seance on a Wet Afternoon* I was arrested. Some ridiculous by-law says you can't put a tripod on a pavement. However, the Eady plan undoubtedly helped us and I was sorry to see that go. The Americans helped to wreck the Eady plan because the moment it was introduced, there were back-door routes so that Americans came here, financed films through British companies, because they weren't allowed by law to be American companies, and these companies of course got the Eady money which, in return, went back to the American financiers, instead of flowing back into the industry. Most people took the Eady money and ran. But Allied Film Makers and Beaver Films used the money to go back into business. Nowadays, to make a British film industry, you want a minimum of £100 million injected into it.

No governments are really interested in cinema. Wilson pretended to be, and took credit for it when he was Minister of Trade, but I think it was a gesture in political terms rather than in favour of the British film industry. Nobody since has been interested at all.

The Angry Silence still seems to me a very important British film. What attracted you to it, and what was the nature of your involvement?

Well, Dickie Attenborough, Pier Angeli and Guy Green came together on a film and, while they were out in the desert somewhere, they were all fairly fed up with the way their careers were going, saying, 'We're going down a cul-de-sac. OK, we're getting work, but where's it going?' Just at that time my wife Nanette [Newman] said to me, 'Look, there's a marvellous story here you should write about – a railwayman who'd been sent to Coventry, and eventually, after three years of nobody talking to him, he committed suicide.' I was dickering with that idea when they all returned from location, having talked it over, and Michael Craig and Richard Gregson came up with a famous story of a man who was sent to Coventry, a different story from mine. So we said, 'Let's not fight, let's not make two films, let's join forces.'

I was attracted to the story and I wanted to make it very tough and not the usual thing with the British workman as if he were always the salt of the earth. I felt there were two sides to the thing: Dickie and I were much attacked by the unions. It was black-listed by the miners' union, we had threatening letters sent to us, and to this day some people have never forgiven us, but I felt I was just as hard on management. I made management seem absolutely crass, because it didn't see what was coming. The whole philosophy of the film is that if you can't be different you are nothing. It's a plea for the individual. He supports the strike in the first instance, then thinks it's gone stupid, which so many of the strikes in those days did. I mean, we were in anarchy in the film industry as a result. It was the beginning of a partnership between Dickie and myself which resulted ultimately also in Allied Film Makers.

That was a second company you formed?

Yes, that was, I thought, a very innovative idea which came with the blessing of John Davis. We went to him and said, 'Listen, we're not really getting a fair share because the distributor takes the cream. We'll make films and we want to form a distribution company as well. We're the people who supply the product, it's wrong to be excluded.' And he said, 'Well, put your money where your mouth is and whatever you can raise I'll multiply it by five and we'll give you a differential on the distribution of $2\frac{1}{2}\%$.' That is $2\frac{1}{2}\%$ off the top, which is the important piece of money. And so we all put in £20,000 each, I think, and raised £100,000 and he made it up to half a million. We made *The League of Gentlemen* and *Whistle Down the Wind*, both of which were enormously successful in their own time.

Did *The Angry Silence* actually make any money?

It still makes money. It cost £98,000 and I think, to the last accounting period, it had probably made about £200,000 profit. Now that's not vast, it's not *Indiana Jones*. *The League of Gentlemen* cost about £172,000 and made probably £300,000 or £400,000 profit. If you more than double your initial cost, it can't be bad in business terms.

The idea of having Pier Angeli as Tom's Italian wife is interesting in that working-class setting.

Again, this was a move away from having some rather mousy English little housewife, which would have been the norm. I think it was the first time working-class dialogue had been actually colloquial as opposed to a sort of pastiche written by somebody who actually wasn't, like me, working-class, trying to emulate working-class dialogue.

Do you think the '40s and '50s were a boom period in the Britain film industry?

Yes, I mean cinema-going was a habit, and the habit grew substantially during the war when it was basically the only form of entertainment. In those days a British film could get its money back within this country, and that's another reason why the British film industry did boom. Today, if you don't make it in America, you can never ever hope to get your money back in most cases.

George Formby

1904–1961

Actor: *By the Shortest of Heads* (1915), *Boots, Boots* (1934), *Off the Dole, No Limit* (1935), *Keep Your Seats, Please* (1936), *Keep Fit, Feather Your Nest* (1937), *It's in the Air, I See Ice!* (1938), *Trouble Brewing, Come on George!* (1939), *Spare a Copper, Let George Do It* (1940), *Turned Out Nice Again, South American George* (1941), *Much Too Shy* (1942), *Get Cracking, Bell-Bottom George* (1943), *He Snoops to Conquer* (1944), *I Didn't Do It* (1945), *George in Civvy Street* (1946)

'I wasn't very good, but I had something the public seemed to want.'[1] Whatever he had, there is no question that the vast British movie-going public *did* want George Formby for about ten years, from the mid '30s to the mid '40s. Son of a famous comedian, Formby began to appear in the music halls in the '20s, but it was the movies that made him. 'Until these pictures my success was mostly in the North and the Midlands. I did play the London halls but nobody noticed me. Then if I flopped nobody noticed me. Now it's much more difficult,'[2] he said in 1937.

'Ah'm just an ordinary Lancashire lad. Ah suppose you'd call me a pup of Wigan Pier.'[3] Despite his huge success, as he became one of Britain's highest-paid entertainers, the toothy, ukulele-strumming comedian never lost his regional affiliations. He took to driving Rolls-Royces, but on screen he retained the 'gormless' *persona* that made him so popular. Like Norman Wisdom twenty years on, but without Wisdom's penchant for pathos, George is one of life's incompetents. The odds are always against him: he loves a pretty middle-class girl, but some smooth bounder has her in thrall; he wants to excel (at boxing, motor-bike racing, in the Navy, as a jockey) despite his ineptitude; he is easily deceived, but at core incorruptible. In spite of the obstacles placed in his way, he always ends by justifying his catch phrase: 'It's turned out nice again, hasn't it?' There is nothing threatening about Formby, no element of the smart alec.

The films, naïve enough in their narratives, are nevertheless made with unpretentious skill, and rare sightings today confirm the lively fun to be had from such pieces as *Trouble Brewing*. Inevitably George achieves his goal, by luck rather than design, outwits the villain, and (improbably) wins the girl. Many a young English actress has had to fulfil the hurdle requirement of co-starring with George: the roll-call includes Florence Desmond, Kay Walsh, Coral Browne, Phyllis Calvert ('He appeared quite brainless,'[4] she reflected as she spoke admiringly of his meticulous timing), Linden Travers, Dinah Sheridan and Googie Withers. The latter had a longer-than-usual embrace with George in a vat of beer in *Trouble Brewing* and recalls him saying, 'Ee! if only Beryl knew!'[5] Beryl was Formby's formidable wife and manager who vetted

his leading ladies and timed the rare kisses. 'The public built up a certain picture of us and I had no wish to spoil the illusion,'[6] he told the press when he remarried shortly after Beryl's death: the marriage had been difficult for years because of her drinking.

'I make up most of my own tunes for the ukulele songs ... They sound all right, but I don't know anything about music.'[7] Despite this, Formby's songs, often laced with sexual innuendo, especially of phallic aspiration, were a crucial part of the success formula of the movies. He claimed that 'I always felt they came to a stop whenever I had to play the uke.'[8] The public clearly didn't share his concern and the songs were a key element in his box-office success. Formby's films lost favour after the war.

1 David Shipman, *The Great Movie Stars*, revised edn, Angus & Robertson, London, 1979, p 217
2 *Film Weekly*, 4 December 1937, p 17
3 John Fisher, *George Formby*, Woburn-Futura, London, 1975, p 14
4 Interview with Brian McFarlane, 1989
5 Interview with Brian McFarlane, 1990
6 Fisher, p 45
7 *Film Weekly*, p 17
8 Fisher, p 47

Harry Fowler

b. 1926

Actor: *Those Kids from Town, Salute John Citizen, Went the Day Well?* (1942), *Get Cracking, The Demi-Paradise* (1943), *Give Us the Moon, Don't Take It To Heart, Champagne Charlie* (1944), *Painted Boats* (1945), *Hue and Cry* (1947), *Trouble in the Air, A Piece of Cake* (1948), *For Them That Trespass, Now Barabbas Was a Robber ...* (1949),

Once a Sinner, She Shall Have Murder, Trio, Dance Hall (1950), *Scarlet Thread, There is Another Sun, The Dark Man, Madame Louise, *Introducing the New Worker, High Treason* (1951), *Angels One Five, At Home with the Hardwickes* (six short films in the British Movietonews series), *I Believe in You, The Pickwick Papers, The Last Page* (1952), *Top of* the Form, A Day to Remember (1953), Don't Blame the Stork!, Conflict of Wings, Up To His Neck (1954), Stock Car, The Blue Peter (1955), Fire Maidens from Outer Space, Behind the Headlines, Home and Away (1956), Town on Trial, Lucky Jim, Booby Trap, The Birthday Present, West of Suez (1957), Soapbox Derby, The Supreme Secret, I Was Monty's Double, The Diplomatic Corpse (1958), Idol on Parade, The Heart of a Man, The Dawn Killer, Don't Panic Chaps! (1959), Tomorrow at Ten, The Golliwog, The Longest Day, Lawrence of Arabia, Flight from Singapore, Crooks Anonymous (1962), Clash by Night, Just for Fun, Ladies Who Do (1963), 70 Deadly Pills (1964), Life at the Top, Joey Boy, The Nanny, Doctor in Clover (1965), Secrets of a Windmill Girl (1966), Two By Two (1968), Start the Revolution Without Me (1970), The Prince and the Pauper (1977), High Rise Donkey (1979), Sir Henry at Rawlinson End (1980), The Little World of Don Camillo (1981), Fanny Hill (1983), Big Deal (1986), Body Contact (1987), Chicago Joe and the Showgirl (1990)

* Documentary.

Harry Fowler's extraordinarily prolific career is a testimony to one who believed in taking every opportunity that offered, aware of the limitations imposed on a Cockney actor in British cinema. Since most British films, certainly in the '40s and '50s, were largely middle-class affairs, he often found himself relegated to stereotyped cameo roles. However, he always managed to imbue these with a lively individuality and, when given the chance of something more substantial, he showed himself more than equal to the occasion. Ealing gave him his best roles in such films as *Champagne Charlie*, *I Believe in You*, and, above all, as the leader of a bunch of Cockney schoolboys which routs a gang of crooks in *Hue and Cry*. He was also a notable Sam Weller in *The Pickwick Papers*, and threading its way through the many supporting films he made was a steady trickle of 'A' films such as *High Treason*, *Lucky Jim*, and *Lawrence of Arabia*.

Interview date: June 1991

You are described as having been a newsboy and as having worked in radio before coming into films ...

Yes, I began my working life in 1941 selling newspapers in London's West End and I used to sell them in clubs which were frequented by actors and BBC producers. One of them was the producer of *In Town Tonight*, a very popular interview programme. He asked me if I'd be prepared to relate my vicissitudes (his exact words to a near-illiterate newspaper boy!). So I asked how much I'd get for it and he said two guineas. Considering I was earning eight shillings a week, I agreed! I was interviewed on a Saturday night by a man called Roy Rich, and at that time somebody was casting a picture about British evacuees; they had already cast a boy called George Cole and were looking for another one.

They heard this broadcast, contacted the BBC immediately, and within two days I was doing a film test on the set at Elstree. Again, my first question was 'How much do you get for this?' and they said '£5 a day.' There was no way I was going to fail that film test and that's how it all began. The film was *Those Kids from Town*, starring Jeanne de Casalis, who was very helpful to me, and Bernard Miles's wife, Josephine Wilson, played the kind lady who took in the evacuees.

Do you recall anything of the director, Lance Comfort?

Yes, Lance was the epitome of what I, as a thirteen-year-old Cockney, saw as 'a posh gent'. A nice man but my memories of him aren't all that bright, since I knew nothing about film directing then. Years later, at the end of his career, I made

Tomorrow at Ten for him, with John Gregson and Robert Shaw – a cops-and-robbers thing.

You played twice with George Cole. What do you recall of working with him?

George had a professional approach to acting, whereas I was raw as could be. I didn't meet him on *The Demi-Paradise*, which had Laurence Olivier playing a Russian. His leading lady was Penelope Dudley Ward, a lovely woman, and, again, everyone struck me as being very 'posh'. I was told I should take elocution lessons but that would have defeated the purpose – I was cast by these men because they heard a genuine Cockney voice. Certain directors would say to me, 'Don't pronounce it like that, say "aren't", not "ain't".' Otherwise, they said, they wouldn't get the American market because they wouldn't understand broad Cockney. Firstly, they weren't getting the American market anyway, and, secondly, I was brought up on a series of films about the East Side kids where I couldn't understand a word they said. That didn't stop me going to see them, though! I think it was a legacy of the theatre; it was undoubtedly middle-class and most of my roles throughout my working life, certainly up until the '60s, had me as the obligatory Cockney, just as you had the obligatory 'negro' in American films. Cockneys and working-class characters were never allowed any intellectual horizons, whereas America and France were making pictures with working-class people as heroes. My idol was Jimmy Cagney, but there were no Jimmy Cagney pictures made here, so I had no aspirations regarding roles.

As soon as I finished my ten days on the first film I went straight into another picture called *Salute John Citizen* for Maurice Elvey, simply because I happened to be on the next set at British National studios. The more I appeared, the more obvious it was that I was the 'real McCoy', and there were enough people about who wanted the genuine article to keep me busy. I had an agent but I don't think he had to *look* for parts. Sometimes I might only have a few lines but, once you build up a good track record, that's the way it is.

How did you find working for Ealing, starting with Cavalcanti's *Went the Day Well*?

Ealing was like a university for me. Cavalcanti was an engima: as a South American he could not have been expected to have a great knowledge of English life, yet he was chosen to direct *Went the Day Well?* But they couldn't have chosen anybody better, because often outsiders will see more,

because they are inquisitive. *Champagne Charlie* was a perfect example of what I mean: it was about British music halls in the last century, strictly an English subject, but I don't think anybody could have made it as well as Cavalcanti. Tommy Trinder was one of the stars (Stanley Holloway was the other) and he was a very down-to-earth Cockney from the music halls. Betty Warren was in it too, a lovely lady and very helpful to me.

You are well remembered for Charles Crichton's *Hue and Cry*. How did you come to do this?

By the end of 1944 I was nearly eighteen and, the war still being on, I was called up. I went into the Air Force and at that time Tibby Clark was writing a script about a gang of kids, with me in mind. The film industry at that time had a very good liaison with the Board of Trade, so that I was temporarily released from the Air Force to make *Hue and Cry*. Part of its classic status is that it has actual film of London as it was in the immediate post-war years, when the bomb sites were still evident. The climax takes place on a bomb site adjacent to Cannon Street station, which today is a massive skyscraper. Charles Crichton was a great technician as far as film directing was concerned, but equally important was the producer Henry Cornelius, who was outstanding with the kids, taking their inhibitions out of them so that they gave great performances. And Alastair Sim must be one of the great film actors of all time. He had that underlying sinister quality, but he was a kind, lovely man at the same time. I think that was the first time Jack Warner played the villain and he loved it. I remember Jack telling me: 'Never turn down anything, because every time you appear on that screen it's an advert; to be a character actor at eighteen is worth being; stars come and go but as a character actor you'll work until you're ninety.'

What do you recall about Crichton's semi-documentary, *Painted Boats*?

We made it in a very picturesque part of Northamptonshire, a place called Stoke Bruerne, a major junction on the Grand Union Canal. I think the Board of Trade wanted to show the kind of work the canal boats were doing, lugging steel, coal and wood up and down the canals as part of the war effort. It's worth seeing again now because, outside of myself and an actor called Bill Blewitt (who in fact wasn't an actor but a Cornwall postman, and Ealing took him under its wing), the rest of the cast were actually talking in plum-in-the-mouth English, which doesn't really fit for a bargee.

You were back at Ealing in 1952 for *I Believe in You*, Basil Dearden's film about probation officers. What did you feel about its approach to its subject?

Sewell Stokes wrote the book and I met him. As part of preparing for the role I actually stayed in a Borstal at Rochester for two nights; that was an experience, to say the least. I met people who were in there for all kinds of things, including capital crimes. It could have been a very dour sort of film but for Cecil Parker, who was a marvellous man. It was all shot on bomb sites, rain-laden cobblestone streets at night, and in the depressing atmosphere of the court. Ursula Howells gave a great performance as the inebriate society girl, and I think it was good to have got that into the film, to show that the probation officers were not only dealing with lower-class delinquents. As for Celia Johnson, a marvellous lady! Had you met her in a supermarket, you'd think, 'She's probably a vicar's wife.' It was great to watch her working, to see the transition from this ordinary lady to this great actress. She had a wonderful face and eyes, yet she used them modestly, you never saw her over-act. She was a theatre actress who took the screen by the horns.

Throughout the '50s you did a mixture of 'A' films and supporting films; what were some of the obvious differences between the two?

There was much more time taken over an 'A' film; to light a shot for an 'A' film could take two hours, whereas to light a 'B' film they'd give you the script and a candle! I know I sometimes gave better performances in 'B' pictures, often because the parts were bigger and meatier, but the pay was fifty per cent less than for a smaller part in an 'A' picture. You were pampered on 'A' pictures; sometimes you even got a canvas chair with your name on it! The 'B' picture lark was a marvellous game; the sheer speed of making them before the money ran out made for very good work in some cases.

You made three 'B' films for Lewis Gilbert, *Once a Sinner*, *Scarlet Thread* and *There is Another Sun*.

Yes, Lewis undoubtedly learned his trade on those, all three of them are good films. He was a working-class boy himself, and another of those gentle, kindly directors. *Scarlet Thread* was a good film and Kathleen Byron was marvellous in it; Lewis adored her and he was right to, she was a wonderful actress whose potential was never fully realised. Lewis could see it but he didn't have the power then that he achieved later.

What recollections have you of several directors you worked for who are not much heard of today – John Paddy Carstairs, Wolf Rilla and Vernon Sewell?

Paddy Carstairs was a frustrated actor, if ever I saw one. The one thing you never did when you were working for him was look at him, because he was doing your role behind the camera – very disconcerting! If you were to draw a caricature for *Punch* of 'the film director', it would be him. He was the right man for the job, doing those cheerful comedies.

I always thought Wolf Rilla was kidding! He was always very self-conscious in the part. *Stock Car* didn't need directing, it was more a montage of library footage about these battered old cars smashing into each other. Wolf interspersed it with shots of unrecognisable actors in goggles and helmets, sitting in the cabins of these cars and saying trite dialogue.

I did *Home and Away*, with Jack Warner and Kathleen Harrison, for Vernon, who went from film to film but didn't make a great impact on the industry. Montgomery Tully was another, although he was getting on and in failing health by the time I worked for him in *Clash by Night*. I spent the first two weeks of that picture handcuffed to Terry Longden, which was agonising for both of us. It wasn't a bad little picture at all; Tully did a good job on it.

To return to 'A' territory, you played Sam Weller in Noel Langley's *Pickwick Papers*; was it a role you really enjoyed?

Yes, very much. I'd like to do it again because I think I could give a better performance than that. However, it was a great prestige picture which got a Golden Bear Award in Moscow. The part of Sam Weller, like the Gravedigger in *Hamlet*, is one of those great philosophical comedy roles. One of the joys of the film was that you were working with the *crème de la crème*. Every part was played by somebody who was talented to their fingertips, like Hermione Gingold and Hermione Baddeley, and I was actually going to work with George Robey, whom I only knew from cigarette cards. Noel wasn't a film director really, although he wrote some great things; it would have been a different film if directed by David Lean, who had done those early Dickens films. I later worked for him on *Lawrence of Arabia*; the entire cast and crew respected and admired him as the maestro.

Edward Fox

b. 1937

Actor: *The Mind Benders* (1962), *This Sporting Life* (1963), *Morgan – A Suitable Case for Treatment, Life at the Top, The Frozen Dead, The Jokers* (1966), *I'll Never Forget What's 'is Name, The Long Duel, The Naked Runner* (1967), *The Breaking of Bumbo* (1968), *Battle of Britain, Oh! What a Lovely War, Skullduggery* (1969), *The Go-Between* (1970), *The Day of the Jackal, A Doll's House* (1973), *Galileo* (1974), *The Squeeze, A Bridge Too Far, The Duellists* (1977), *The Big Sleep, Survival Run, Force Ten from Navarone, The Cat and The Canary, Soldier of Orange* (1978), *The Mirror Crack'd* (1980), *Gandhi* (1982), *Never Say Never Again, The Dresser* (1983), *The Shooting Party, The Bounty* (1984), *Wild Geese 2* (1985), *Return to the River Kwai* (1989), *Robin Hood* (1991), *A Feast at Midnight* (1994), *A Month by the Lake* (1995)

When I first interviewed Edward Fox in 1981, I wrote that, unlike many of his contemporaries, he 'has remained that rarity – a British film star'. A rarity, that is, since the 1960s, at least. Maybe it has to do with his quintessentially English *persona*, which he can inflect to emphasise charm, cruelty, integrity or cynicism, as the role demands. It was probably his BAFTA award-winning performance in *The Go-Between*, as the aristocratic Lord Trimingham, played with precision and a generosity important to the film's balance, that established this *persona*. Since then, he has played a mixture of leading roles, such as in *The Day of the Jackal*, and very striking character parts in such films as Losey's version of *A Doll's House* (a notably sympathetic Krogstad), *The Dresser* (his soured-off touring company actor is perhaps the film's most sharply realised portrayal), and as the dangerously competitive pheasant-shooting aristocrat in *The Shooting Party*, Alan Bridges' undervalued elegy to Edwardian England. Some of his best chances have come on television (*Portrait of a Lady*; above all as Harthouse in *Hard Times*); in whatever medium, he is, at best, a mesmeric performer, and one wishes there were a steady film industry to showcase such a strong talent.

Interview dates: June 1981 and July 1994

After a few very small roles, what do you recall of making two films for Michael Winner in the 1960s – *The Jokers* and *I'll Never Forget What's 'is Name*?

They were both fun and *The Jokers*, I think, was probably very good. They were Michael at his vivacious best. They were lucky jobs to get and very enjoyable. They were very much films of their time; and I think they were very good *at* that time. I haven't seen *I'll Never Forget What's 'is Name* for years but I think it is one of Michael's best. He was really sparkling in those days.

After a few more brief roles in films like *The Long Duel* and *Oh! What a Lovely War*, you suddenly made your mark as Lord Trimingham in Joseph Losey's *The Go-Between*. How did this come about?

I remember *The Long Duel*; I appeared in a Mess scene. *The Go-Between* came about because my father was Joe Losey's agent; he was doing some very late business on a film with Joe one night and I was with him. He said to Joe he should have a look at a television programme I was in, one of the Somerset Maugham stories for the BBC, called *Olive*, with Eileen Atkins. Joe looked at it and gave me the part of Lord Trimingham on the strength of it.

Did you see it as vital that Trimingham should be at least as interesting and attractive as the Alan Bates character?

Yes, in a different sort of way. Trimingham had been wounded in the Boer War; he was a great landowner and a great aristocrat, in the best sense. That's how I saw him. It is one of my best filmmaking experiences ever and offered enormous opportunities for an actor. Many people, and all the technicians, turned down work waiting for the moment when this would be made – and it was on and off again until the last moment. They all went to work with such a will and devotion to Joe, and to the subject. Looking back on it now, and I think I felt the same at the time, it was a great privilege to have been part of that film.

Did you feel it gave an accurate account of the British class scene?

It wasn't a bad account. The levels of society were important: Trimingham definitely was an aristocrat, and Margaret Leighton and Michael Gough's characters were more of the *nouveau riche* than of the landed gentry. They chose a marvellous location but the gardens didn't really look right. The garden of a house like that would have been much

grander; it was in fact very run-down and they just patched it together. There was no money to make the film, really, and, given that condition, I think they did terribly well. And Margaret Leighton's performance . . . my God, it's wonderful. Alan Bates is marvellous and Julie Christie is very, very good. It has an excellent cast and Dominic Guard is a very good leading boy.

I'm surprised you say there was little money to make the film because it has a very stylish look about it.

The design was in the hands of the brilliant Carmen Dillon; she knew how to make a silk purse out of a sow's ear. She was trained, skilled and extremely talented. They can't do that now; they all need a lot of money before they can get anywhere, whereas Carmen could do it out of nothing. The whole film was shot on location in that house, which was falling to pieces, and Carmen somehow made it all look right. She is one of the greats in her department.

You did two further films for Joseph Losey, *A Doll's House* and *Galileo*. What was it like to work with him?

Anything Joe offered I would do because he was a master. He was very good, very generous with actors, and, if he liked you, he was never dogmatic. He allowed you to find what you could do. He expected the best, but unless you were seriously in trouble he wouldn't do anything, except let you produce what you could do, which is very rare. It's difficult to describe: he wanted what he wanted from it, but he let you do it your way. You want guidance, of course; very often you are completely on the wrong track in a role, in which case you need to be yanked off that and put on to the right one. You've then got to know how to accept that, too, and understand what's required. If you can provide basically what is required for the part, a director is usually grateful to you for that. If you can't, he'll wonder why he employed you in the first place. He has a 'right' to expect good acting from an actor. And the older one gets, the more sureness one places in one's own conception.

I liked your sympathetic Krogstad in *A Doll's House*. Did you see him as one of life's victims but still capable of real feeling?

I think it's how Ibsen wrote him. In the sequence after the angry scene with the doll wife, he explains his position to the other woman. Ibsen doesn't paint him as a villain but as an oppressed man who shows considerable unpleasantness because of fighting for his job. He's not innately malevolent, This film stresses this, by showing him with his children. I remember having good times with David Warner and especially Trevor Howard in Norway, but it was all a bit turned upside-down because Jane Fonda was not an easy kettle of fish; she was heavily into politics and Women's Lib at the time, and that was colouring her work.

How did you find Fred Zinnemann to work with on *The Day of the Jackal*?

It was a wonderful experience working with Fred. He teaches everyone who is on the unit – actors, technicians alike. He is very like the general who doesn't sit at HQ, but who is out there doing the bravest deeds with the soldiers. And, of course, his over-all conception of how to do something, and his demand upon you, the actor, to show, within a short space of time, many things quickly: that is very exacting but extremely exhilarating. And, I would add, it makes the spectacle rich for the audience.

After working with these notable veterans, what were your impressions of Ridley Scott, in his striking début film *The Duellists*?

I can't remember much about the film except that it was a very agreeable time and Ridley was an interesting filmmaker even then, though, at that stage, his style of filmmaking seemed to rely heavily on extreme assault on its audience. However, he was very pleasant and we had a happy time in the Dordogne. It was a very good Conrad story, although I'm not sure the screenplay is terribly good; if anything, the film suffers from its storytelling, I think. It's probably difficult to do because it's wonderfully done – *mountingly* done – by Conrad in the book.

If you are working in a film based on an adaptation, is it normally a good idea to go back to the original text?

It can't do any harm. But very often there's no point in taking it too seriously because it may run counter to the film's intentions. If you go back to it in order just to try to find something that will be useful, then it's worth doing. It's no good going back to it and then saying this scene should be done like this, because the filmmaker usually has another idea. It can be confusing.

You made a couple of very big-scale films for Richard Attenborough, *A Bridge Too Far* and *Gandhi*. Is it important for the British film industry every now and then to embark on enterprises as huge as those?

Yes, it is. I think both films do great credit to Richard, and that's putting it mildly. He has developed this ability to make a 'big' film that way. I think *Oh! What a Lovely War* is probably a marvellous film, too. *A Bridge Too Far* is full of richnesses. How well it hangs together as a whole I don't know, but it is a remarkable film all the same. For me it was the part that really mattered in *A Bridge Too Far*. General Sir Brian Horrocks was alive then and he took a great interest; he was very helpful to me in the depiction of his *persona* and his work in that part of the campaign and the war. It was a *serious* film. The whole thing involved masses of Allied troops stationed in England, trained to the hilt and ready to do the job, but, because of certain circumstances which either went wrong or were misinterpreted, the whole thing was a disaster in terms of loss of human life and miscalculation.

Do you remember any of the logistics of that film or of *Gandhi*?

There were huge crowds of extras, certainly, although not so much for me. There were reasonably big set-pieces in *A Bridge Too Far* but not masses. There is a huge one in *Gandhi*, yes. Richard is wonderful with crowds, indeed, but mainly the work involved in all that belongs to the assistant director. The getting together of those crowd scenes in *Gandhi* was absolutely prodigious work by a first assistant director. The director expresses his wishes and it is up to his assistants to effect those wishes, yet those people are hardly thought about, in terms of public recognition.

How did you feel about the 1978 remake of the famous thriller. *The Big Sleep*?

I had admired the novel, although it's not exactly my cup of tea. Playing a gangster was a change of pace for me – that was Michael Winner offering me a job again, which was nice. Bob Mitchum was great fun to be with. He's a very, very fine actor. Unfortunately I didn't meet James Stewart; we didn't have any scenes together.

Michael Winner seems to have a way of getting together the people he wants.

He does, yes. He offers you a job and he's scrupulously professional about what it involves for the actor. He brings it in on time, everything works, and you never have any hanging about. He does exactly what he says he will do. He employs you because he expects you to arrive being able to do immediately what he needs, without too much fuss. He's paying you a lot of money to do it, after all.

You made three films for Guy Hamilton:

Battle of Britain. Force Ten from Navarone and *The Mirror Crack'd*. **I have always relied upon him to provide craftsmanlike entertainment ...**

He's very, very agreeable to work with and terribly nice to his actors. Guy's is a very close-knit, well-thought-out, well-planned way of filmmaking and it doesn't try to pretend to be what it isn't. If it is an action adventure, it is just a very good action adventure. But Guy is very appreciative of an actor being able to supply a little more than maybe the part gives on paper. What Guy doesn't know about it all isn't worth knowing. He was Carol Reed's assistant on *The Third Man* and much of what is up there on the screen is due to Guy. The public generally don't know what the first assistant does and it's right that they don't, but the truth is that they are people of great ability. I think Guy is a master craftsman and a prodigious talent.

Did you become a technically knowledgeable film actor?

No, I'm not nearly knowledgeable enough. It doesn't interest me frightfully, I must admit, although I suspect that, if you do interest yourself in it a bit, it is fascinating. However, I'd rather leave it to the cameraman. If you have a camera on you with a very long lens, you only need a director to say, 'We're very big on you here,' and you know what to do immediately.

I particularly liked your performance as the embittered actor in *The Dresser*. Did you?

I did like it, yes. I thought it was comically amusing and the whole thing was a happy experience. We made it at Bradford, at a theatre which has now been restored as the Alhambra, although it was then derelict. It was the kind of early Victorian theatre which was perfect for the environment of the film.

You keep turning up in great casts, as in *The Shooting Party*: what recollections have you of working with James Mason?

It was great fun. James took over because Paul Scofield, who was originally playing the part, had an accident. James was wonderful and I don't think he was feeling too well, and he didn't live very long after that. I remember during a few scenes with him, watching him work in front of the camera and being so full of admiration for his ability – just his technique and his knowledge of how to perform and behave for the camera. He was one of the great screen actors.

Was *The Bounty* a very demanding film to make?

Not really, no, not for me. My scenes all took place in a courtroom and I didn't go to Tahiti. I don't like going on locations, they're hell. It's understandable for people to think that they are jolly places to be and very often they are, but you're not there to have a jolly time.

You've worked with major American stars including Robert Mitchum, Elizabeth Taylor, Rock Hudson and Mel Gibson. Have you detected any differences in their approaches?

They are very commanding in their knowledge of how to act for films, because they do it much more than we do. It's much more of a staple diet for the Americans, so they perfect it. They have a considerable tradition of filmmaking and someone like Mitchum is just completely professional. He does what's needed in the very best way. While he looks as though he's doing nothing, he is in fact doing a hell of a lot.

Did you ever feel you were being built up by studios or producers?

No, never. I'm quite sure I never have been. Possibly an integral part of the success of the Rank Organisation was the star system, which comprised a great range of performers from the great artistes to the prettiest showgirls. However, there hasn't in my time been the infrastructure to promote that as a worthwhile thing, because there hasn't really been a film business of any standing. We've had studios but they've never operated in the way that the American studios did. They have essentially been just places where films got made, in ad hoc situations. I don't think there has ever been anything vaguely like MGM, for instance, in Britain. Back in the days of Ealing comedies and the Boulting brothers, of course, they were making films on a star-system basis, but, since I began making films, it has been completely different. I don't think there is now a regularly functioning English film studio. No, we don't have any moguls or a studio system any more.

James Fox

b. 1939

Actor. As William Fox: *The Miniver Story, The Magnet* (1950)   **As James Fox:** *The Loneliness of the Long Distance Runner* (1962), *Tamahine, The Servant* (1963), *Those Magnificent Men in Their Flying Machines, King Rat* (1965), *The Chase* (1966), *Thoroughly Modern Millie* (1967), *Duffy* (1968), *Arabella, Isadora* (1969), *Performance* (1970), *No Longer Alone* (Religious Film) (1978), *Runners, Greystoke* (1983), *A Passage to India* (1984), *Absolute Beginners* (1985), *The Whistle Blower, High Season, Comrades* (1986), *Boys in the Island, Farewell to the King, She's Been Away* (1989), *The Russia House* (1990), *Afraid of the Dark* (1991), *Hostage, As You Like It, Patriot Games* (1992), *The Remains of the Day* (1993), *Heart of Darkness* (1994), *Never Ever* (1996), *Anna Karenina* (1997), *The Shadow Run* (1998)

Not many actors could take almost a decade off from commercial filmmaking and expect to return to a position, in its own way, as notable as his earlier stardom. And yet, that is what James Fox has achieved. He actually began as a child actor (called William Fox) in the days of the British studio system, and came back, having trained as an actor in the meantime, to play some eye-catching roles throughout the '60s. His performance as the supine upper-class Tony in Losey's *The Servant* is as remarkable as Dirk Bogarde's as his sinisterly opportunist manservant: between them, they mount as telling a critique of the British class system as the cinema has offered. Thirty years later, James Fox played – brilliantly – another aristocrat nannied into idiocy by his butler in *The Remains of the Day*. These are the two films which link the halves of his career. He seems natural casting for these roles, and for other patrician types he has played in *Patriot Games*, *The Whistle Blower* and Bill Douglas's wonderful *Comrades*. However, his range, before and after his retirement in the '70s, has always been wider than this suggests. He was a charming comedian/romantic hero in *Those Magnificent Men . . .* and *Thoroughly Modern Millie*, a convincingly vicious gangster in *Performance* and a troubled liberal in *A Passage to India*. In short, he has made the transition from clever young leading man to character player of effortless authority.

Interview date: June 1994

How did you come to be a child actor in British films, starting with *The Miniver Story* in 1950?

My father was an agent working with MCA [Music Corporation of America] in the post-war period. He knew Kay Brown, who was casting at MGM at the time; he may have read a script, I never got the details exactly, but he took Edward and me to meet Hank Potter, the director. I don't really know whether my father wanted to get us launched as actors, or what. Anyway, Hank Potter liked both of us; he would have offered it to Edward, who didn't want it, so it was offered to me and I took to it like a duck to water. At MGM, of course, I had the experience almost of working in the Hollywood studio system. It was a real, functioning studio in those days; Greer Garson and Walter Pidgeon were huge stars and there was a full American complement there. That part of Boreham Wood was the seat of MGM operations for a long time.

At Ealing, you had the central role in *The Magnet*. What was it like to work at this most famous English studio?

We did at least half of it on location in Liverpool, but I remember Ealing as a wonderful, small, suburban studio with masses of atmosphere, all the sound stages being filled and at the height of its creativity, with Balcon in change. Charles Frend, who directed our film, lived over the road. I was very young but my impression was that there was a lot happening, and I was terribly excited to be working there. Our film was quite successful; it was written by TEB Clarke, who had been a very well-known writer at the studio. It was a great experience. As an eleven-year-old, I had a huge crush on Kay Walsh, who played my mother. She was fabulous to me and I stayed with her in London. I think the performance of hers which really stands out for me is in *Oliver Twist*, in which she is fantastic.

How did you come to get the part in *The Loneliness of the Long Distance Runner*?

My father must have known Tony Richardson (not that my father was pushing me towards an acting career), but I didn't know him at the time because I remember him interviewing me for the part. I had been in a job in advertising for about a year and a half and I chucked that in to do that four-day part. I heard that they were looking for a public-school type so I went along to the auditions. It's an important small part and it was well shot. I think everyone who worked on it with Tony knew it was a special experience.

Tony was following the French New Wave then and he would take his cameras out with the great Walter Lassally. It was a very good filming atmosphere, totally different from anything that had belonged to the studio system in Britain. My scenes were shot in two or three days, all on location a few miles south of London, on very cold February days; also in the woods with a back-of-camera car and running shots, and crowd shots. Then there were dressing-room shots for me in that derelict Borstal-type building.

What attracted you to *The Servant*?

I think it was pure instinct. I just responded to it as a fine piece of film writing, and of course Joseph Losey had a big reputation and I was extremely impressed on meeting him. I was dazzled at the thought of playing such an important part with relatively little experience. I was in it with Sarah Miles, who was then my girlfriend and who was quite brilliant; and Dirk Bogarde was an extremely supportive and well-known star. All the elements – Douglas Slocombe [director of photography] and such people – were sensational; but chiefly, I think, it was that the script, the theme, the subject matter were terrific. It has always been assumed that I walked into the part because I was right for it, which is true, but for me it was a great acting challenge and a very satisfying experience.

What do you think of the notion that the film is really a metaphor for a collapsing class system?

I'm sure that was Joe's paradigm; I'm sure he'd come in as an American and seen the post-war British malaise, and I'm sure that he and Harold Pinter went to work on that, with that perspective. It was a wonderful parable for his purposes, far more than just a story of decadence and degeneracy. It had a very strong political theme.

Why do you think Barrett was able to take over and why was Tony so vulnerable?

He likes being served, therefore he becomes a willing victim. If you like being served and the person who supplies that then chooses to misuse his control because of your need, then … He is spineless because he has no desire to resist it, there isn't anything else for which he has any ambition. There is that wonderful scene where he is talking to the Wendy Craig character about building cities in Brazil and clearing the jungle, yet you know full well he will never do anything about it. It still has a sort of frightening connection with the British entrepreneurial robber-baron spirit, with grabbing, making money and exploiting. With a little more push he might actually have joined our modern buccaneers down there and done it!

Was the unusual stress on long takes, Losey's brilliant gliding tracking shots, a particular challenge for you as a young actor?

No, I don't think so, it was all part of the fun and fascination of filming, which I've always loved. The more complicated the better, and the more exciting in a way. It was certainly complicated. Joe was one of those directors (and I imagine Hitchcock and Welles would be others) who really believed that, if you could sustain a take, not just for the sake of it but because it was right, there is a tension, a drama and reality in there that film loves. It *is* more demanding, yes. But I think actors get rather bored with just close-up, medium shot, master shot.

You could hardly have had a greater contrast with *The Servant* in your next role in *Those Magnificent Men in Their Flying Machines*. Was that fun to do?

That really was great fun. I think it's an excellent film and it was lovely to do a big-scale comedy in contrast to *The Servant*. Big screen, big dollars, big international co-production. It felt very much different from making *The Servant*, but fortunately I think I'd had just enough experience not to be disappointed with the razzamatazz by comparison with *The Servant*. It was just fun in its own way. And it was a delight to rub shoulders with the great comedians and international stars: the spirit of comradeship in the circus was fantastic! Red Skelton – you know, a *giant* Hollywood star! And Sam Wanamaker is in it, and Flora Robson, Tony Hancock, almost everyone you can think of. Of course, they had wonderful words from Jack Davies, and I think Ken [Annakin] was a terrific 'general', but there was such talent, I'm sure most of them managed it themselves. It was a superb treat, but we were quite proud of it because it was strongly British-based and also quite strongly British in character.

And yet Sarah Miles goes off with Stuart Whitman in the end, to our surprise.

Yes, the Americans always get the girl, don't they? I remember the whole idea of who gets the girl was absolutely dominant in the thinking. In fact, the interviews I had afterwards always related to how I didn't get the girl and he did. It was also useful for selling it in America! The whole idea of

'getting the girl' is a tremendous movie convention which I wasn't aware of until then, because in the Losey school everyone's pretty nasty anyway and no one gets anything except what they deserve!

Your next three films were all American-made: *King Rat*, *The Chase* and *Thoroughly Modern Millie*. Why was *King Rat* made in America?

I don't know. They had the weather, of course. Also, I think James Woolf, the producer, had a deal and he wanted to make a Hollywood picture. There may be an even simpler reason: he had a house in California and he wanted to spend some time there. He loved entertaining the Brits and anybody else.

You were securely established as a leading man by this time. How important were agents to you in getting parts, or were you under any contracts?

No contracts, I was completely independent. 20th-Century-Fox had talked to me about a three-picture contract after *Flying Machines* but my father (who was my agent) managed to talk them out of it. Columbia also wanted a contract but I think he talked them out of that as well. It was the age when they wanted to sign you up, but he always wriggled me loose somehow.

You made a film that seems absolutely to belong to the time when London was meant to be 'swinging'. How did you feel about *Duffy* then – and now?

It's a pity it didn't come off. It does belong to *Time* magazine's idea of 'swinging London' but it didn't convey well enough what it was all about. It was awfully hard on Bob Parrish. We were all raving and off the wall ourselves, and we didn't give poor Bob a good time. The film just didn't work. The cast really had more fun than the audience did. It's a great lesson. It's the work that matters and this was an amateurish effort, a waste of a really good director.

The last two films you made before you retired from the screen for over a decade gave you very different roles. What do you recall of working with director Karel Reisz in *Isadora*? Was Gordon Craig a rewarding role?

I don't think I was quite up to it, so I've never cherished very fond memories of it. It wasn't a brilliantly written role, I don't think any of the male roles were; I think it was *her* film. I don't think it really did us justice, by trying to take all the lovers and say something about them. Karel is a terrific director, though, and I'm only judging it from a very subjective angle. It's one of those films that was an enormous financial drain on the resources of Universal; it was the end of the love relationship between Hollywood and swinging London in the '60s. My personal life was quite up in the air, too. It's a pretty well-known anecdote, but during the film (a sixteen-week shoot) we were given eight weeks off; I was invited to South America to the film festival as a British actor and it happened to coincide with the Carnival in the spring, and I was so fed up with the film that I took up an invitation to get involved in a jungle expedition. I broke my contract because the script had (to my mind) a not very significant little sequence in Italy, where Isadora is dancing among the columns and Craig is sketching her. I didn't think it worth coming back from South America for that, so I just chucked it in. I think Karel has forgiven me now, but it wasn't a good moment in my career.

Playing the gangster Chas Devlin in *Performance* must have been a major change of pace.

I read the script, which had been written for Mick Jagger and myself, and I thought it was wonderful. As far as I was concerned it was a very challenging role.

What do you think it was about, essentially?

I don't think there's an answer to that. I don't think it is about any one theme as such. The themes of identity, of violence, of performance, of ambiguous sexuality, of death: all those themes are there. I suppose the film works because it has a very powerful mood and momentum, and it is so arresting and so well performed that it has always stayed in the minds of the generation who were first exposed to it. But I don't think anyone has ever given a very good answer as to what it's about. Perhaps the point of Nic [Roeg] is that he doesn't *want* to be pinned down?

How did you find working with Mick Jagger?

I think there is an element of *The Servant* again in that this person, Devlin, isn't without purpose and yet, according to the Mick Jagger character, he is without a centre. The Jagger character is trying to explore who Chas is, so that he can say, 'I know who you are, because I am that character as well and I want to take you from being a villainous operator for this ludicrous gang, and I want you to find out who you really are.' The way in which Chas is deprived of his macho securities in their home makes it quite clear that that is what it's about at that point. Mick is good at that menace and

attractiveness, he was perfect for the role. So many pop singers just don't seem to be as interested in the drama, so mostly he didn't want to relate very closely to me as an actor. However, he was a most important presence, crucial to the whole film.

Since returning to the screen in 1983, you've worked very steadily.

It's been difficult to find all the wonderful parts that I did in the '60s, and now I am trying to find my niche as a middle-aged actor. I've had to work much more in the '80s because one has more responsibilities, but it's sad there haven't been more British films made recently.

You made two films for Goldcrest – *Runners* in 1983 and *Absolute Beginners* in 1985. Did you have any sense of its imminent collapse?

Those two films are perfect examples. They virtually blamed *Absolute Beginners* for the collapse of Goldcrest. It was an $8 million film, not very good, and it deserved to go down the toilet, but I can't imagine how it sank a major production company. Although it was a musical, it wasn't that big a deal. I think other people blame *Revolution* for Goldcrest's collapse.

Why do you think the British film industry runs into such terrible trouble?

It's an interesting question. I don't think there are people with much to say here at the moment. It would be quite charming if they had some skill and they could just delight you with nothing. There is a crisis in the country which is reflected in its impotence to get on with it, in my view. I have managed to work quite steadily though, even working with David Lean in the '80s – a high point in my acting career. So I feel absolutely thrilled. In the '90s I've worked with Merchant–Ivory [*The Remains of the Day*] and I've worked with Fred Schepisi on a very British subject, *The Russia House*, and I count that sort of work as a privilege.

How did you come to play Fielding in *A Passage to India*?

That was just a great stroke of good fortune. David Lean had his eye on someone else and he didn't want to see me. Then he had dinner with that person and it didn't work out; he was then more amenable to seeing me. I was banging on his door almost, because I'd read the book and thought it was an excellent piece of casting if he saw it my way – and he did! In fact he went one better, because he changed me into his idea of Fielding rather than just taking my own conception of the role. It was a happy coincidence that I managed to get to him at the right moment.

Some see him as the greatest director they ever worked with, others say they don't think he liked actors. What is your view?

I belong to the first category but agree with the comment of the second. Generally, I don't think he liked actors, although when he spoke about Charles Laughton, Peter O'Toole, or Jack Hawkins I knew that he loved *some* actors. You can't get such good performances out of actors unless something is happening besides waves of negativity coming at them! But he *was* difficult; he *was* intolerant of actors. In a way, they just served his purposes and his grand design. There was a kind of authority about David that was absolutely unavoidable. He is, to my mind, the greatest film director our country has produced.

Did he give you much direction?

Yes, a lot, and not always in a very nice way. He was quite irritable; he could have got better work out of me, but what he created was so wonderful that you didn't mind. As far as I'm concerned he was great, because he not only directed beautifully but he also had the essential thing that any director must have: he had something to say, an artistic point of view.

Were you pleased with the way he changed the ending of the novel?

No, and I'd love to know why he changed it. I think what interested David in the end was Aziz the doctor – bitter and yet sentimental about Mrs Moore and Miss Quested – whereas Forster isn't interested in that. He is only interested in the irreconcilable nature of this relationship and in Imperialism and its failure to connect with the Third World. David got excited about mountains too, then we lost the snow and he got really bogged down at Shrinigar. I remember him sitting down on that boat with a frown on his face and he was absolutely foul to us. He was fiddling with the background all the time and he didn't know what to do.

I very much admired your next film, *Comrades*.

I like it very much too. I think it is such a good film but it just disappeared here after the première. Now that was a British film that came out of something and had an idea, a viewpoint. I didn't know about Tolpuddle, but I think it is wonderful that we learn about these appalling injustices in the history of Australian settlement and so forth. I loved its viewpoint and its humanity.

Have you felt a bit trapped in playing various lords and governors, or do you feel that versatility is overrated for film actors?

It probably is. All I know is that you can tell a good role when you get one, and it might be a colonel or it might be a gangster. You look for those roles and hope for the person to cast you right. That's what an actor depends on – a good role and a director who understands what you can do.

The last film I've seen you in is as the dopey, well-meaning Fascist, Lord Darlington in *The Remains of the Day*.

That seems like a fair description of the character as the film conceived it! I was selected to play that role by Harold Pinter, which goes right back to *The Servant*. Harold wrote the original script, which I read and which was to have been shot, then it was rewritten by Ruth Jhabvala. He no doubt saw me as moving on from Tony in *The Servant*, who was a dopey but *non*-well-meaning Fascist! Funnily enough, the main character in both films is a butler. Perhaps the British film industry isn't dead, if it can produce such a good film as that.

Freddie Francis

b. 1917

Camera operator: *The Macomber Affair, Mine Own Executioner, Night Beat* (1947), *The Small Back Room* (1948), *The Golden Salamander* (1949), *Gone to Earth* (1950), *The Tales of Hoffman, Outcast Of The Islands, Angels One Five* (1951), *Twenty-Four Hours of a Woman's Life, Moulin Rouge* (1952), *Rough Shoot, Twice Upon a Time, Beat the Devil* (1953), *Knave of Hearts, Beau Brummell* (1954), *The Sorcerer's Apprentice* (1955), *Dry Rot* (2nd-unit ph), *Moby Dick* (2nd-unit ph) (1956)

Director of photography: *A Hill in Korea* (1956), *The Scamp, Time Without Pity* (1957), *Next to No Time, Virgin Island, Battle of the Sexes* (1958), *Room at the Top* (1959), *Never Take Sweets from a Stranger, Sons and Lovers, Saturday*

Night and Sunday Morning (1960), The Horse-masters, The Innocents (1961), Night Must Fall (1964), The Elephant Man (1980), The French Lieutenant's Woman (1981), Memed My Hawk (1983), The Jigsaw Man (1984), Code Name: Emerald, Dune (1985), Clara's Heart (1988), Glory, Her Alibi (1989), Cape Fear, The Man in the Moon (1991), School Ties (1992), Princess Caraboo (1994), Rainbow (1995)

Director: Two and Two Make Six, Day of the Triffids (uncr), Vengeance (1962), Paranoiac, Nightmare (1963), The Evil of Frankenstein, Hysteria, Dr Terror's House of Horrors, Traitor's Gate (1964), The Skull (1965), Psychopath (1966), The Deadly Bees, They Came From Beyond Space, Torture Garden (1967), Dracula Has Risen from the Grave (1968), The Intrepid Mr Twigg (short), Mumsy, Nanny, Sonny And Girly (1969), Trog (1970), Gebissen Wird Nur Nachts-Happening der Vampire (1971), Tales from the Crypt, The Creeping Flesh (1972), Craze, Tales That Witness Madness (1973), Son of Dracula, Legend of the Werewolf (1974), The Ghoul (1975), Golden Rendezvous (uncr) (1977), The Doctor and the Devils (1985), Dark Tower (uncr) (1987)

Sixty-odd years ago, Freddie Francis began as a clapper-loader in British films. Twenty-five years later, he won his first Oscar as director of photography on *Sons and Lovers* (1960), and twenty-nine years after that his second for the US film, *Glory* (1989). Along the way, after a dozen years as camera operator for some of the major directors of photography in British cinema, he photographed some of the best-looking films ever made in Britain. The glorious black-and-white imagery of Jack Clayton's *The Innocents* (Francis's own favourite among his work); the New Wave grainy verisimilitude of his northern townscapes for *Room at the Top* and *Saturday Night and Sunday Morning*; the harshly poetic realisation of the underside of Victorian life in *The Elephant Man*; and the vivid contrast of the Victorian and present-day sequences of *The French Lieutenant's Woman*: these are more than enough for a substantial reputation to rest on. As well, there is his imaginative work as the director of a series of low-budget horror films, which achieve a visual and thematic subtlety that transcends the basic material.
Interview date: September 1992

I found it difficult to get credits for you until the war. What did you do until that time?

In those days the titles of the films didn't really matter. The quota films, for instance, used to be shown to the cleaners at the Plaza cinema before it opened in the mornings, in order to fulfil the quota! Paddy Carstairs did a lot of those films, as did Harold French. I was just about to become a camera operator when Hitler started all that nonsense; before that I'd been a clapper-boy and a focus-puller, just odd bits of operating at a studio called BIP [British International Pictures].

And after the war, in which you'd had useful experience in the Army Kinema Corporation ...

Within three weeks of getting out of the Army I was asked to go to Kenya and do the location work for a film that Korda's brother Zoltan was doing, *The Macomber Affair*. After that I came back and stayed with Korda for some time. Through Korda I then joined Micky Powell and did several pictures for him. By the time Micky finished with Korda, I think I was probably with John Huston. I became very close to John and, eventually, when we were doing *Moby Dick*, he let me do all the second unit stuff, all the model stuff and half of his first unit stuff as well, which nearly killed me. Immediately after that I did my first film as a cinematographer, *A Hill in Korea*. I was put under contract by Ian Dalrymple of Wessex Films halfway through *A Hill in Korea*, but not for very long, however, because the company was dissolved.

What do you recall of working on the Michael Powell films, *The Small Back Room*, *Gone to Earth* and *The Tales of Hoffman*?

I adored Michael. I know all his faults. I became the resident operator at Worton Hall, which was Korda's second studio and where *The Small Back Room* was made. Michael loved bullying people because he wanted them to bully him back; I've seen him have artistes in tears, but if you kicked back it was all right. We used to have the most fantastic rows, but I always got the last word. I remember the only time he managed to get the last word and he was desperate to get it in. It was on *The Elusive Pimpernel*; he couldn't think of what to say, then he suddenly stormed off the set, saying, 'You know what'll happen to you? You'll end up directing cheap comedies!' But I consider that he and Huston taught me more about film than anybody else. Micky taught me how to enjoy films, because for him they were all a great adventure. He was a brilliantly visual director, unlike many others.

Did your job as camera operator and later as director of photography vary much from one director to another?

No. I suppose I'm arrogant but I don't want to do a film for anybody who doesn't want me to do it more than anyone else in the world. I don't mean that every director who is doing a film ought to have me – not at all; but they really have to want me or else I don't do that film. I don't want to be a hired hand, I want to be a collaborator on the movie. Nowadays I'm in a position to be able to do that, but in those days operators weren't considered very highly. However, I was determined even then that I was going to be a collaborator; so as far as I was concerned I was the assistant or collaborator of the cameraman, and I was always very close to the director. When I was operating for Chris Challis or Ossie Morris, they would talk to the director to establish what he wanted; I would get on with lining up the shot, which gave the DP [director of photography] time to get on with the lighting. This is the way I do it now.

How did you get your chance to be director of photography on *A Hill in Korea*?

It all stems from the fact that I established myself as a different sort of operator, as a co-operative person. A couple of people were impressed by seeing me working – one of whom had been an associate producer on a couple of pictures and the other had been second unit director on some pictures I'd done. One was John Palmer, the other was Tony Squires. They recommended me highly to Ian Dalrymple and that's how it started. We actually shot all the exteriors in Portugal, although a lot of it was done in the studio. One of the problems was that some of the studio sets necessitated having painted backing (which you couldn't do nowadays, because there are no backing artists left). We had a wonderful guy called Basil Manning, who could draw a backing about two feet from your head and make it look like Portugal or Korea. I insisted on Basil being on the picture because he was wonderful; he had done all the backing painting for the tank on *Moby Dick*.

Did any films stand out as ones you were especially happy with?

I always say that I've never been a hundred per cent happy with the films I've photographed, but I've always been happy with those I've directed, for the simple reason that those I've directed have been pretty low-budget and have transcended the scripts. Perhaps I know too much about photographing films; you tend to try something and it almost, but not quite, comes off. I suppose the nearest to one I was completely happy with was *The Innocents*, perhaps because I was young, and, although we were forced to shoot it in a way we didn't want to, it worked out well from my point of view. It is one film which was actually designed for CinemaScope and I was very happy with it.

I've known Jack Clayton for many years and when we were doing *The Innocents* he was very disappointed to discover we had to do it in CinemaScope because 20th-Century were financing it. So I decided to have some special filters made up for the camera, so that we could bring the edges in and take them out as we wanted to. That big garden set was actually built in the studio and I had one side of each of the trees painted silver, so that it was brighter than the other. We did various things like that. In those days, there were focus limitations; we didn't have CinemaScope lenses so we used ordinary lenses with a CinemaScope attachment; for that reason you couldn't get people closer than a certain distance and we got over that by stopping the lens and using enormous amounts of light. Or I would sometimes call in a trolley of enamel paint and paint filters to use for a particular shot. It was quite revolutionary in some ways.

When you did *Room at the Top* it looked different from any other black-and-white British film. Did you aim at that grainy, greyish look?

Everything I did was aiming for the look I got; that is why I say *The Innocents* is the one I'm happiest with. As to *Room at the Top*, I was the darling of the kitchen sink in those days. One of the first things I did up in Nottingham was decide to shoot it in dull light, instead of waiting for the sun as everyone else did. That was the key to the whole thing, because everything then had to look dull. Most things I do are deliberate. The Woolf brothers actually wanted to throw me off the picture because they thought I was doing it wrong. Larry Harvey was very fond of his looks; Jack and I decided we should make him look working-class, and there was a scene in a railway station where we decided that Simone Signoret should look like a woman who has been away for a dirty weekend. Larry was not happy with the way he was made to look throughout the picture, and after the dailies of the railway station scene, he obviously said to Simone that she had looked terrible. Then Larry went to Jimmy Woolf, who was a close friend of his, and Jimmy told Jack Clayton that he wanted him to throw me off the picture. Jack refused, saying that if I left the picture, he would too, so I was saved. When I next saw Jimmy, he was forced to congratulate me because I'd just won an Oscar for *Sons and Lovers*!

What was it like working on *Sons and Lovers* with Jack Cardiff, himself already an Oscar-winning director of photography?

It was very easy, because Jack had never photographed a black-and-white picture. He came up as a cameraman through Technicolor, having started with a series of travelogues. So there was no difficulty in working with him. He wanted me to do the film in a style similar to *Room at the Top*. He was fascinated by that picture, which is why he had Heather Sears in the movie.

Is Wendy Hiller a cameraman's dream? I have always thought of hers as one of the great faces in cinema.

Don't forget, I first worked with Wendy when I was a clapper-boy when she was doing *Pygmalion* at Pinewood! I next worked with her on *Sons and Lovers* and she was absolutely lovely – she radiates anyway, whatever you do with her photographic-

ally. There were about twenty-five years between those two films, then another twenty before I worked with her again on *The Elephant Man*. She would never care what she looked like, within reason; she would know that she transcends everything you do.

Most of the camera work on *Saturday Night and Sunday Morning* is very straightforward, so that the virtuoso stuff, like the fair rides, stands out by comparison. Did you and Karel Reisz work this out together?

I had just done a film for Harry Saltzman, who was producing *Saturday Night and Sunday Morning* and who wanted me to do the film because he needed someone who he thought could help Karel Reisz along. I knew how Karel wanted to direct the picture and therefore it would be wrong to photograph it in any way other than documentary, so it was straightforward. The fairground stuff looked after itself. It was spectacular not so much from a compositional as from a lighting point of view.

Whose decision was it to film *The Elephant Man* in black-and-white?

It was a commercial decision. Mel Brooks was financing the film and I think they wanted to make it as cheaply as possible – in those days it was cheaper to film in black-and-white. I'm glad, because it was the right decision but it was a financial rather than an artistic one. I've got this harebrained idea that if you make a film about that period in colour, people don't believe it because there wasn't colour film in those days. Of course, I'm so old that I was almost around in those days! And I was around in London, in the poorer parts, so I have a pretty good idea of what those places should have looked like.

When you were doing *The French Lieutenant's Woman* were you aiming at distinctly different qualities of lighting between the 1860s story and the modern story?

Yes, but without making it too outrageous. It was very easy to do. A guy who had been my camera assistant had invented a little piece of equipment called the Liteflex; and I humbly say that, although the Liteflex has been taken up by Arriflex and is now called the Varicon, I'm sure I'm the only person in the world who knows how to use it! It's a piece of equipment with which you can control the contrast. In the old days there used to be a lot of films made where they would fog the film before they put it into the camera, by running the film past a small light which created a fogging effect. The effect was very similar to what we did on *Moulin Rouge* and *Moby Dick*. I've never fogged film in that way, though, because if you fog it and then store it for any period of time, you're never quite sure what the effect will be on the finished film. But the Liteflex was something that Gerry Turpin, a very successful cameraman, came up with. He was asked to do *Young Winston* and Dickie Attenborough said he'd like it to look like the *London Illustrated News*, which has a sort of sepia tone to all its pictures. Gerry tried all sorts of experiments, and finally he invented this piece of equipment which goes on the front of the camera and has a little light at the top, above the camera glass. It enables you to put a slight colour on to the camera glass, and it worked fine for *Young Winston* so I suggested we use it for *The French Lieutenant's Woman*. I didn't use any strange colours, just that fogged effect.

Is being a cameraman a good training for a director?

I don't think training is necessary for a director, really. I mean, it is usual to have some training, but I've worked with a number of people who have just gone into it and been extremely good. Working as a cameraman in the UK didn't pay much – more than a dustman, but not much – so that if you wanted to live reasonably well you had to work all the time. Now, I can pick and choose, but then you had to keep on working and it meant working with some very dull directors sometimes. So once I'd got the Oscar for *Sons and Lovers*, people started asking me to direct films and I thought, 'Why not?' Obviously I wanted to direct (everybody in this business wants to direct, no matter who they are) but it was a financial thing as well.

When you became a director you worked almost exclusively on horror films. What drew you to this genre?

When I started as a director, the first film I did was a disaster. In those days, in order to get a film made, you had to have a completion guarantee so that people would accept you. A lovely man called Monja Danischewsky asked me to direct *Two and Two Make Six*; I said the script needed changes and he said that was all right, to go ahead. Had I had any sense I would have refused to do it then, but, having got permission of the completion guarantors that I could direct the movie, I felt it was impossible to back out then. It was a disaster.

After that, I got in with Hammer as Tony Hinds who ran Hammer was a dear friend. I started off

doing one film with them and it was a lot of fun, so I did another, then another, and before I knew it I was right into horror films. By that stage anybody in the world would back me to do a horror film and, because I liked making movies, I just went on and on until another dear friend, Leon Clore (who has just died), found a story he wanted me to do, called *All Neat in Black Stockings*. Certainly there was a vogue for horror films at the time I was making them, but I got a bit bored with them.

They are all interesting, though, not quite like many other Hammer films. They all seem somewhat subdued.

Probably because I can't take them seriously. I suppose I was always looking for something else in them. I remember trying to put a love story into one of them and Hammer cut it out. The real thing that turned me off them was that I became a sort of cult figure; I used to go to all those horror festivals, which I hated. I'd start talking about directors I admired, like William Wyler, and those people didn't know who I was talking about. So I'd start talking about the really good horror films by people like Tod Browning, and they still didn't know who I was talking about. At the time I decided to get out, suddenly along came David Lynch and Jonathan Sanger. We got on very well together and did *Elephant Man*, and the next I knew I was off on the old DP career again, which by this time was fairly lucrative, especially in America.

***The Doctor and the Devils* has a fascinating credit of 'Screenplay by Ronald Harwood, based on an original screenplay by Dylan Thomas'. What can you tell me about this?**

This was something we'd had for a long time. Eventually the guys who owned it got it set up with Mel Brooks. It was a screenplay by Dylan Thomas, based on the Burke and Hare [grave-robbers] theme; it had never been made but had been published as a book. Suddenly Mel wanted Ron Harwood to do a rewrite – which was needed anyway – because he had just been nominated for an Oscar. Mel bullied Ron to do what he wanted, which was to turn it into an out-and-out horror script. The original screenplay by Thomas had been beautifully written but the rewrite was somewhat less so. Day by day I was pushing more of the Dylan Thomas stuff back in during shooting. A lot of the ending was cut, the stuff between Timothy Dalton and Sian Phillips about science versus morality.

Would you give much detailed direction to people like Peter Cushing and Christopher

Lee, or just let them get on with it?

I suppose one would give Chris more detail than one would Peter. I think Peter is absolutely wonderful – there is not an actor in this world who can speak rubbish like Peter and make it sound real. I remember a film called *The Creeping Flesh*; there was a two-page scene where Peter just talked about 'When this body gets wet, it . . .' and I thought it was utter rubbish, that nobody could possibly take it seriously. Then when we were shooting it, I found myself believing every word!

Do you want to work in Britain again?

I don't think there is such a thing as a British film industry any more, not to interest me at any rate. I know that sounds very selfish but, having said that, if that were Karel Reisz or Jack Clayton on the phone now, saying, 'I'm doing a little movie . . .', then I'd do it.

Harold French

b. 1900

Actor: *Hypocrites* (1923), *East Lynne on the Western Front, The Officers' Mess, Jealousy* (1931), *The Callbox Mystery, A Safe Proposition, When London Sleeps, Tight Corner* (1932), *Yes, Madam, Night of the Garter, The Umbrella, I Adore You, Mannequin* (1933), *Faces, Murder at the Inn, How's Chances?* (1934), *Radio Pirates, The Girl in the Crowd, A Fire Has Been Arranged* (1935), *Two on a Doorstep* (1937)

Director: *Dead Men are Dangerous, Cavalier of the Streets* (1939), *House of the Arrow* (1940), *Jeannie, Major Barbara* (co-dir, uncr) *(1941)*, *Secret Mission, Unpublished Story, The Day Will Dawn* (1942), *Our Film* (short), *Dear Octopus* (1943), *English Without Tears, Mr Emmanuel* (1944), *Quiet Weekend* (1946), *White Cradle Inn* (& co-sc) (1947), *The Blind Goddess, Quartet* ('The Alien Corn'), *My Brother Jonathan* (1948), *Adam and Evelyne* (& pr) (1949), *The Dancing Years, Trio* ('Sanatorium') *(1950)*, *Encore* ('Gigolo and Gigolette') (1951), *The Man Who Watched Trains Go By* (& sc) (1952), *Isn't Life Wonderful?, The Hour of 13, Rob Roy: The Highland Rogue* (1953), *Forbidden Cargo* (1954), *The Man Who Loved Redheads* (1955)

The films Harold French directed are, above all, 'actors' films' and in his modest account of his career he would claim to have been essentially an actor's director. When one considers the quality of the performances he elicited, this claim is amply borne out: Barbara Mullen in *Jeannie*, Wendy Hiller in *Major Barbara*, Felix Aylmer in *Mr Emmanuel*, Dirk Bogarde in *Quartet*, Michael Denison in *My Brother Jonathan* and Claude Rains in *The Man Who Watched Trains Go By*. If there is no obviously great film among his credits, there is, equally, no film that is less than entertaining and a number of them have real charm and sharp, compassionate observation. Surviving the hazards (along with David Lean) of putting *Major Barbara* together under Gabriel Pascal's ostensible direction, French then made a trio of lively war films before hitting his stride with *Dear Octopus*. All French's work in the Somerset Maugham films is distinguished, especially perhaps in the Raymond Huntley–Betty Ann Davies vignette in *Trio*. He doesn't care for his last film, *The Man Who Loved Redheads*, but he and Gladys Cooper ensure that its last few minutes provide a fitting swansong.

Interview date: July 1990

After acting in a lot of films, were you really wanting to direct by the late '30s?

Yes, I was. I directed a lot of plays, too, including *French Without Tears*, which was Rex Harrison's first big success; then I was doing *Major Barbara* and the chap we had in it wasn't very good, so I persuaded Gabby [Gabriel] Pascal to play Rex. I co-directed quite a lot of that with David Lean; Pascal knew nothing at all about directing and in the end he paid me quite a lot of money *not* to have my name mentioned as a director of it. Gabby hadn't the slightest idea – I mean, sometimes he would look through a viewfinder the wrong way around! But he had the money and he had the ear of George Bernard Shaw, which he got for £1!

I think Shaw was amused – and bemused – by Pascal. I only met Shaw once, when he came to the set at Denham. I asked him about the character of Undershaft – whether he was honest, merely a money man, or whether he had any integrity at all, and Shaw replied, 'I haven't the slightest idea, but he is amusing.' I ended up shooting the first quarter of the film, then Gabby wanted to be producer, director, the whole caboodle. So I told him I was fed up and David Lean shot the rest of it himself, about three-quarters of it I suppose. Gabby took a lot of credit but it was David mostly.

Was *Jeannie* the film that established you as a director?

Yes it did; that was after *Major Barbara*. The producer, Marcel Hellman, was very generous to me and he forced me through into a major picture; I don't think the distributors wanted me, they wanted someone well known. It made a star of Barbara Mullen, who was terribly good, though we thought she would have become a bigger star. Bernard Knowles was the cameraman; I valued his co-operation. If I got in a muddle in a crowd scene, he always knew how to move the camera. We also had Anatole de Grunwald and Roland Pertwee as the writers, so we had a very well-credentialed film.

You made three war films in 1942 with Bernard Knowles as cameraman – *Secret Mission, Unpublished Story* and *The Day Will Dawn*. Did you value that sort of continuity?

Yes, because I believed in teamwork. It was very difficult to make pictures at that time, because we had so little equipment. We didn't have zoom lenses or anything like they have nowadays. I made a picture called *Dear Octopus* with a lot of people sitting around a table; we didn't have a crane, so the carpenters built a structure in the middle with the camera stuck up on top of it, and we turned the camera around.

Dear Octopus is a charming film. Were you pleased with it?

Yes, I'd liked the play and thought I could make a picture of it and I think I did some of it well. When you think about it, *Jeannie* was a success because Jeannie was Cinderella. And there's a touch of that about the Maggie Lockwood character in *Dear Octopus* – the secretary who marries the son of the house. I remember Celia Johnson in *Dear Octopus*, of course. She could read the dictionary to me and I'd blub if she wanted me to. She played one very moving scene with the children around her; it was quite a long scene and I decided to do it in one shot because of the children. We rehearsed it, then I shot it in one take and printed it. By this time Celia's tears were rolling down her face. I told her she had been marvellous to get into the mood so quickly. She said, 'I'll tell you honestly, I do want to catch the three forty-five bus and I knew damn well if I'd dried you'd do it again, so I put the lot into it!' It was quite true, she wanted to get back to Henley before the rain started!

It was a lovely film to make, a very harmonious cast and I loved working with Mike Wilding – and Roly Culver too, who was in many of my pictures. I was delighted to get away from making war films, to make something light and frothy. It was just what the public wanted. Of course, Margaret Lockwood was the big star at that time and she was charming to work with.

You went on to make *English Without Tears*, which reunited you with Terence Rattigan. Did you find him especially congenial to work with?

Oh yes, we were enormous friends until his death. But as for *English Without Tears*, that was a bit of wickedness on Tolly de Grunwald's part because it wasn't good and made no real sense. Tolly, who was a lovely old villain, had found a backer and he persuaded Terry to lend his name to it and of course Terry, who was then in the Air Force, needed the money. By the time we were shooting, I knew it wasn't Terry's dialogue. Penelope Dudley Ward was in it and she had a lovely comedy sense with a very light touch.

In 1944 you made *Mr Emmanuel*, which seemed an unusual film for you. Was it a personal choice?

Yes it was, I thought it was a very good story. Louis Golding was quite a big name as a novelist then, and a very nice man. It was a rare starring role for Felix Aylmer. He came to audition for it and, while I admired him as an actor, I told him I felt the part needed a Jewish actor. He said, 'But I *am* a Jew!' and I had no idea, nor, I think, did many other people. He did it very well, I thought. It made a lot of money on the art-house circuit in America; the Americans were very sympathetic towards the exiled Jew at that time.

After a two-year gap you directed *Quiet Weekend*. Were you sought out by the producer?

By Warwick Ward, yes. I did two or three pictures with him. I don't know why I did it – the money, I should think. I must confess I wasn't ever really dedicated: I got by and I worked hard while I was doing it, but I think I might have been a better director had I been more choosy. *Quiet Weekend* is pleasant enough in its silly way. We had some good actors – Marjorie Fielding and Frank Cellier and so on – who'd been in the play. Glynis Johns was in the play, too, but her part was played in the film by a charming young actress called Barbara White, who just disappeared shortly after.

You then made two films with very British actresses, Madeleine Carroll at the end of her career in *White Cradle Inn* and Claire Bloom in her first film. *The Blind Goddess*.

White Cradle Inn was my original story and I also co-authored the screenplay and directed it. We made it at Hounslow Studios and on location in Switzerland, where filming had to stop because the money had run out. I didn't mind as long as they paid the actors, which they did; I didn't get all my money from that one. I got on well with Madeleine Carroll but I didn't think she was a very good actress, frankly. I don't think Ian Hunter was terribly good either – a bit stolid. It would have been a better picture with a stronger man. But Michael Rennie was marvellous in it, I thought. I liked that film because I thought it had a lot of atmosphere, because I used Swiss actors quite a lot. Having been an actor myself, I could encourage actors and help them; I think I was 'an actor's director' more than anything else.

I'd forgotten *The Blind Goddess*. Claire Bloom's role was a secondary one but she stood out in it; I thought she was going to be a star. I chose her personally when she auditioned for the part. I don't think the film was successful but it got Claire noticed.

The next film you made was a very big box-office success – *My Brother Jonathan*. What do you recall of that?

It made more money than any other picture made in England that year. It was a great success and it made Michael Denison a star. I didn't actually choose him, although I approved of him. It had a good story once again. I had read the novel, and I believe in staying as close as I can to a novel when I adapt it for the screen. One film I liked which you haven't mentioned was *Adam and Evelyne*, which I produced and directed for Two Cities. At that stage I could pick and choose and I really liked that one. I became producer because Paul Soskin, who was to have produced it, didn't like the fact that I had employed an actor called Edwin Styles for the part of the valet; I thought he was quite good and he got on well with Jimmy [Stewart] Granger in his first comedy role. Paul said he wanted to go back to America, and would I take over as producer? I didn't mind but I told him I knew nothing about money. So each day I used to get a list of expenses which I would put in a desk and lose. But I did enjoy that film and I adored working with Jean Simmons, a lovely actress.

Did you enjoy doing segments of the Somerset Maugham films *Quartet*, *Trio* and *Encore*?

Oh, very much indeed. I particularly liked doing 'Sanatorium' in *Trio* although, again, I don't think I did it as well as I should have done. I should have been more honest about the disease than I was; I was concentrating on the romance too much. I should have made them more ill. When I saw it again some time afterwards it didn't suggest to me a nursing home. I should have done it as a background thing, them looking at their handkerchieves to see if there was blood on them – that's the sort of thing Lean would have done. The part with Raymond Huntley and Betty Ann Davies as husband and wife together was marvellous though. So was Michael Rennie – Guy Rolfe was originally cast for the part but he was dropped when, sadly, he actually came down with consumption like the character in the film.

I did 'Gigolo and Gigolette' for the *Encore* film. A stunt man dressed up as a girl did the dangerous dive sequence and I did it as a very long shot from the top of a ladder. We shot it all at Pinewood and I went to France just for a few wild shots. There's a good little scene with a couple of old troupers backstage – Mary Merrall and a lovely European actor, I forget his name [Charles Goldner].

Your last film is one of my favourites of the '50s – *The Man Who Loved Redheads* – and then you suddenly stopped making films.

Oh, I didn't like that – I didn't enjoy making it or seeing it. I got on all right with Moira [Shearer] but I didn't think she was quite strong enough. I felt we were under-cast. You couldn't meet a nicer man than the leading man, John Justin, but I really wanted Kenneth More. But it wasn't a very good play [Terence Rattigan's *Who is Sylvia?*], and Terry did the screenplay as well. Of course, Gladys Cooper steals the whole thing in the last ten minutes. She wasn't a film actress very often, in Britain at least, so she just said, 'I'm in your hands, tell me what to do.'

I quarrelled with Korda about it. I had a clause in my contract with him that he wasn't to come on the set, but he did come a few times and suggested very old-fashioned ideas. His days as a great producer were pretty much over by then and he was tired.

Sir John Gielgud
b. 1904

Actor: *Who Is the Man?* (1924), *The Clue of the New Pin* (1929), *Insult* (1932), *The Good Companions* (1933), **Full Fathom Five* (voice only) (1934), *The Secret Agent* (1936), **Hamlet* (1939), *The Prime Minister*, **An Airman's Letter to His Mother* (1941), **Unfinished Journey* (1943), **Shakespeare's Country* (1944), **A Diary for Timothy* (1946), *Julius Caesar* (1953), *Romeo and Juliet* (narr) *(1954)*, *Richard III* (1955), *Around the World in Eighty Days*, *The Barretts of Wimpole Street* (1956), *Saint Joan* (1957), **The Immortal Land* (narr) (1958), *Becket*, *Hamlet* (voice only) (1964), *The Loved One* (1965), *Chimes at Midnight* (1966), *Sebastian*, *Assignment to Kill*, *To Die in Madrid*, *October Revolution* (narr) (1967), *The Charge of the Light Brigade*, *The Shoes of the Fisherman* (1968), *Oh! What a Lovely War* (1969), *Eagle in a Cage* (1970), *Lost Horizon* (1972), *Eleven Harrowhouse*, *Gold*, *Murder on the Orient Express*, *Galileo* (1974), *Aces High*, *Joseph Andrews* (1976), *A Portrait of the Artist as a Young Man*, *Providence* (1977), *Murder by Decree*, *Caligula* (1978), *The Conductor*, *Omar Mukhtar*, *The Human Factor* (1979), *The Elephant Man*, *The Formula*, *Priest of Love* (1980), *Arthur*, *Sphinx*, *The Lion of the Desert*, *Chariots of Fire* (1981), *Gandhi*, *The Vatican Pimpernel*, *Invitation to a Wedding* (1982), *The Wicked Lady* (1983), *Scandalous*, *The Shooting Party* (1984), *Time After Time*

(1985), *The Whistle Blower* (1986), *Barbebleu, Barbebleu* (1987), *Appointment with Death, Arthur 2: On The Rocks* (1988), *Getting It Right* (1989), *Strike It Rich* (1990), *Prospero's Books* (1991), *Shining Through, The Power of One* (1992), *First Knight* (1994), *Haunted* (1995), *Hamlet, The Portrait of a Lady, Shine, Looking for Richard, Dragonheart, The Leopard Son* (voice only) (1996), *The Quest for Camelot* (voice only) (1998)
* Documentary or short film.

The list of Sir John Gielgud's films alone is enough to provoke wonder at the sheer prolificity of his career. But, as everyone knows, he has also conducted a stage career of unparalleled longevity and distinction and racked up a notable list of television credits. Of all the great British acting knights, perhaps none has stretched himself so daringly over the three media and over so many decades. As far as film is concerned, he may have begun in 1924, but he seems to have regarded it merely as a sidelight to a coruscating theatrical career until the 1960s. Since then, one remarkable performance has followed another; even in very bad films, such as *Lost Horizon*, one could be sure of at least some stylish screen-time from him. Even in his earlier films there are real pleasures, in the engaging Inigo Jolifant in *The Good Companions*, in the choleric, barely suppressed incestuous display of father Barrett in *The Barretts of Wimpole Street*, and in the '50s Shakespearian roles, Cassius in Mankiewicz's *Julius Caesar* and Clarence in Olivier's *Richard III*. Since then, there have been two more towering achievements in filmed Shakespeare: Henry IV, chilled with disappointment and approaching death in Welles's *Chimes at Midnight*, and the distillation of a lifetime's preoccupation with Prospero in Peter Greenaway's magical *Prospero's Books*. And in 1977 he gave a mesmeric centre to two very different enterprises: to Alain Resnais's *Providence* and, with no more than ten minutes' running time, to Joseph Strick's *A Portrait of the Artist as a Young Man*. On screen in the last thirty years or so, it seems that he can do anything, to which his most famous stage character might have replied, 'Seems? ... I know not seems.'

Interview date: July 1994

In the early days, had you seriously wanted to be in films?

No, I think we all rather looked down on the films in those days, the 1920s. A lot of stage actors did do films but they didn't talk about them a great deal. Although it was better paid than the theatre, people thought of it as a sideline, and British films weren't very well established then. I came of a theatrical family and had a lot of success in the late '20s and '30s, so I didn't really need to do films. But then [Alexander] Korda approached me about doing a film of *Hamlet*; I rather tossed my head and said I didn't think Shakespeare was any good on films. I had seen *A Midsummer Night's Dream* from Hollywood and hated it. I was also approached to play Romeo opposite Norma Shearer but I didn't do it. I think people thought then I wasn't interested in doing films, so I didn't get any more offers.

When working on the screen, do you miss the stimulus of an audience?

Yes, but what is most bewildering is the hours of waiting about and the lack of continuity. There never seemed to be any proper sense of sequence. I soon began to see, when I did do some films, that the director had a tremendous say in what was done. I was very self-conscious and rather vain, and felt that I was very much used as a kind of sounding-board for the ladies who were the stars. Two films I did were *The Good Companions* and *Secret Agent*, one with Jessie Matthews (who was a big star in those days) and the other with Madeleine Carroll, and they got all the camera's attention while I had the back of my head photographed, feeding them the lines.

I had done the part in *The Good Companions* on the stage for about nine months and I did the screen version rather reluctantly, but I was quite pleased with it and they were all very nice to me. I seem to remember, though, I was very angry when it came on at the cinema in the Haymarket, next to the Criterion Theatre where I was starring in a play, *Musical Chairs*, and they hadn't even got my name on the movie bill. I had enough vanity to be cross about that.

What about working with Hitchcock on *The Secret Agent*?

He rather seduced me into playing in *Secret Agent* because I had just had a success as Hamlet, and he told me this was to be a 'modern-dress *Hamlet*'. I read the book from which it was taken and thought mine would come out as the leading part, but he then cast Peter Lorre and Robert Young as well, and I was somewhat eclipsed by the other people in the film. Peter Lorre was a great scene-stealer. He had all sorts of tricks, like adding an extra line when it came to the take, or he'd move an inch and I'd realise I had been upstaged by a very clever actor. He was very nice to me but he was a bit crazy, always having a fix on the roof and not being available when he was wanted – he was a morphine addict – so he was rather difficult to manage, but he was awfully good in the film. He had to have his hair curled every day and was very resentful of having to come in so early.

Madeleine Carroll was charming and we got on very well. She was a big star in those days but Hitchcock was beastly to her. He was a very coarse man, fond of making dirty jokes all the time. But he kept the place alive, he was very vivacious. He picked my brains for actors because he wanted to have some people who were not well known on the screen. I remember I suggested Michel Saint-Denis, who played the old cab-driver, and I also suggested Mrs Max Beerbohm (an American actress called Florence Kahn), who played Percy Marmont's wife in the film. They were both my idea and Hitchcock jumped at them.

Did you become technically knowledgeable about screen techniques?

I began to learn a little bit about how to manage things when I went to Hollywood in 1950 to do *Julius Caesar* and watched James Mason very carefully. I was enormously impressed and he became a great friend. I found he was so cunning and skilful at managing close-ups, showing his thoughts in his face without grimacing as I always used to do, and working out what was effective to do on the screen.

How did you find the Hollywood approach to Shakespeare during *Julius Caesar*?

I was very careful not to appear to be showing off, the British actor telling them how to play Shakespeare. But I got on very well with Mankie-wicz, the director, and also with John Houseman, the producer. We rehearsed for three weeks in the set, which was an enormous advantage, almost like rehearsing a play on the stage. I had played Cassius in the play the year before at Stratford, so I felt very familiar with it.

Do you, in fact, like much rehearsal for filming? Some actors don't care for rehearsal at all except for technical things.

I think it depends what the director wants and what the scenes are like. Sometimes there is a very short scene and you can do it better, more spontane-ously, without very much rehearsal. But I think it is rather embarrassing to be thrown into a scene with someone whom you don't know at all. In the theatre you have a few weeks to get used to the other people and they to you. I think it is partly laziness that makes some directors reluctant to rehearse, but it is very important to get the hang of a scene and to do it a number of ways to try to develop it. Of course it is difficult to rehearse something for three or four hours which is to be only a few short minutes on screen.

When you came to do *Richard III* for Olivier, did you notice any particular differ-ences in the way the British went about filming Shakespeare?

No, I don't think so, but I was tremendously impressed by Olivier because he absolutely was at his peak. He had played the part with great success on the stage; he had a lot of his old friends around – Roger Furse (in charge of scenery), Carmen Dillon, Sir Cedric Hardwicke, Sir Ralph Richardson and myself – so he was in great form and very confident, so it all went very smoothly. I was only there for about ten days but it was a wonderful time.

I wasn't very pleased with it, though, when it came out in America. Larry rang me very sweetly and said, 'I'm awfully sorry, but they say I've got to cut your prison scene practically out,' which as you can imagine I wasn't very pleased about. I think the full version exists and is still shown now. I hadn't played Clarence before, and I'd always wanted to, so I was rather cross at my part being cut.

You didn't make many films in the '50s but I thought you were very striking in *The Barretts of Wimpole Street.*

Oh, I thought that was awful. We had terrible rows during filming. Jennifer Jones was very difficult: she couldn't bear dogs and we had different ones every day, running like mice everywhere, and she hated them. The best performance was Virginia McKenna's [as Elizabeth Barrett's sister Henrietta]; she stole the picture, in my opinion. I didn't think I could touch Laughton as old Barrett. The man who directed it, Sidney Franklin, had made the earlier film with Norma Shearer and Laughton and Freddy March, and we were very much aware that he wasn't happy with all of us. David Selznick, who was married to Jennifer Jones, sent for me before we began filming and said, 'Don't listen to anything the director says, don't take any notice of him at all,' which I thought was a rather bad beginning!

What do you say to my view that *Chimes at Midnight* **is one of the very greatest Shakespearian films?**

I thought a lot of it was awfully good but the trouble was, as it usually was with Orson, that he hadn't enough money, people were always letting him down and he was trying to finish two other films at the same time. He owed money everywhere and he only had us for a week each. I was there for a week, Margaret Rutherford was there for another week, and we never met each other at all. None of us ever saw Orson made up as Falstaff – he did all his scenes at the end, after we'd all gone. It was done in the most haphazard way, but I became devoted to him. I thought his was a very good version of the 'Henry' plays. I thought he'd been very cunning and very clever. He knew them very

well, was very good on the verse, and gave me some valuable hints on what I did with the part. I was always sorry I never worked with him again.

He had the most awful trouble over the money during *Chimes at Midnight*. We had an actor called Andrew Faulds playing one of the parts [as Westmoreland], and he was a member of British Equity; one day Orson's manager came to us and asked if we would accept our hotel bills instead of money for that week, and Faulds said he wouldn't have it because of Equity and so on. It was also fearfully cold; we were in a huge old building in the hills above Barcelona, shooting in a wonderful, decayed castle which had been a prison at one time; there was no glass in the windows, there were stone floors and it was freezingly cold. I was standing around in only a dressing gown and a pair of tights, so Orson sent over little nips of brandy for us to warm ourselves. He was generous and sweet to me and I really did become devoted to him.

One of the great film excitements for me, in recent years, has been Peter Greenaway's *Prospero's Books.* **How did you feel about playing Prospero in that context?**

I suggested it to him actually, and was amazed when he jumped at it and sent me a script and we spent about three weeks talking about it. I had done a little bit for him in a film of *Dante's Inferno*, which is how I met him. I had already admired his previous work enormously, and we got on frightfully well. When he sent me the script I was amazed at its imagination and scope. I never criticised it after that, even when I saw it. It is a marvellous piece of pictorial work. He certainly gave me my head completely and was extraordinarily generous and helpful. There are things that upset me in all of his films, but he is so challenging and such a painterly director, enormously cinematic. I was a bit upset by all the Ariels running around and those girls who danced so much all the time; I thought there were things in it that were too crowded, the screen was too full, and that it would have been much better, towards the end, to have become simpler. But it is not really for me to say that, because he had the idea so firmly in his head and the script was so completely planned out; he sent me every script rewrite, and every scene we shot was completely planned and composed.

The few times I did interfere were when he wanted me to do something I felt was too technical and I said so, and he immediately modified it. I felt he was such an original and remarkable man that there was no use picking at his work, I would rather accept it all. He kept to the play. I have done four different *Tempest*s on the stage with different directors each with different ideas, especially about the last act, and I had to adapt my own imagination to try to follow what they wanted. Those great parts in Shakespeare can be played so differently, and Prospero has always been a favourite of mine.

Two of my favourites among your film roles were both released in 1977: *Portrait of the Artist as a Young Man* and *Providence*. What attracted you to the film version of James Joyce's novel?

I'd never read the novel before. What annoyed me about it was that I learned the whole thing, a tremendous speech – a monologue of about seventeen or eighteen minutes – and it was cut by the editors to about five minutes, after I had worked so hard to memorise it. It was probably the most difficult thing I'd had to do in my whole life; it had taken me about two months to learn and it was cut to pieces. I thought it seemed to come out rather well but I was awfully disappointed by the final version, which had been cut and cut and cut.

I'm glad you liked *Providence* because that and *Brideshead Revisited* are the only two screen performances that I'm fairly proud of. I found that Peter Greenaway is an enormous fan of Resnais and told me that he wouldn't meet him because he admired him so much, which I thought was rather charming! I met [screenwriter] David Mercer only once – he came down here with Resnais to lunch. Resnais speaks very little English but he then had an English-speaking wife, which was a help. Considering that he spoke so little English, I was staggered that he managed to be so enthusiastic about most of the script with all that slang and scatology in it. The moment I read it I was absolutely fascinated by it.

· We were filming in Limoges in terrible weather; the only fine days were Sundays, when we didn't work; all the other days it poured with rain. I remember a garden scene which I had thought was so splendid, when I was actually shivering in a Palm Beach suit while everyone else was in parkas and overcoats. That's the way it always is in films. But it was a wonderful experience and I adored working with Resnais. It certainly isn't everybody's cup of tea, any more than *Prospero's Books* is, but it's nice to have been connected with these two rather *avant garde* things.

You won an Oscar for *Arthur*. How enjoyable was making that?

That was very nice because I got on splendidly with Dudley Moore and Liza Minnelli. And Steve Gordon, the director, was a most delightful man. It was tragic that he died immediately after finishing the film, dropped dead in the street. It was very hard work in a grilling New York heatwave, but I had a great time because I could see it was a good part and they were all so generous to me.

You and Lindsay Anderson have some very telling scenes together in *Chariots of Fire*. Where did you actually film those?

At Eton College. It was terribly difficult because the planes go over all the time. We filmed in the beautiful library there, and it took about a week to do; ordinarily it would only take two days but the planes would go over every five minutes. I rather liked those scenes and I was very amused to act with Lindsay, having been directed by him [on stage, in *Home*] a year or so before. We were both very self-conscious about it for the first day or so. He's a dear man. I was very much struck by Ian Charleson, who had been a young actor at the National, and I was most upset when he died. And Ian Holm was so good too.

You must have worked at most of the British studios in your time and I wonder if you had any favourites amongst them?

No, I never know whether I'm in Denham or Shepperton or where. I remember doing Disraeli in *The Prime Minister*, a terrible film, during the Blitz, for Thorold Dickinson. We had almost finished filming when the studio was bombed, and I had a terrible time because I had long speeches to spout in the House of Lords; all the extras were wanting to get home before the blackout started – and I kept drying up! All the extras were furious. It was a very bad script which had been turned down by a lot of people in Hollywood, so they sent it over to England and someone offered it to me. I rather wanted to play Disraeli, which I thought a very effective character (I had seen Arliss in his film, of course, and had been impressed). It was all very quickly and carelessly done, but Thorold was a charming man to work with, though it was a hectic time with the Blitz going on. We had a tiny little set which was all faked because there was no money. It was filmed at Shepperton, I think.

How do you rate two very different roles which you played in the '80s – Sir Leonard Darwin in *Plenty* and the environmental protectionist Cornelius Cardew in *The Shooting Party*, two films I admire?

I saw a bit of *The Shooting Party* again last night and couldn't think why I had had such good notices for it because I didn't think I was particularly good, but I loved doing it because I was so happy to see James [Mason] again. It was a wonderful last part for him. On the first day of *The Shooting Party*, there were terrible goings-on. Paul Scofield was playing James's part; three of the actors got into an old carriage and the footboard under the driver broke. The horses got loose and the whole carriage was dragged across a huge field and into a fence. Paul broke his leg, I think, and Robert Hardy and the other man were very nearly badly hurt. I had just finished doing ten days of my scenes, in which the part of the lord didn't appear, and I thought, now that Paul couldn't play his part, perhaps they'd offer it to me, but then I heard they were going to have James. James (who unbeknown to me had a heart

problem) was being flown by helicopter from Switzerland where he was finishing *Dr Fischer and the Bomb*, a part which, oddly enough, I had also rather had my eye on.

As for the part in *Plenty*, I hadn't seen the play but I read the script and thought the scenes were awfully good, and I was enormously impressed by Meryl Streep, who I thought gave a brilliant performance. We filmed it in a very poky little house in Holland Park. It was dreadfully uncomfortable, in a small room with all the cameramen and doubles and so on, but there she was every morning at nine o'clock, in full evening dress, playing a very emotional scene and playing it better every day, I thought. I got on marvellously with her and I admired her very much; and I thought Fred Schepisi was an excellent director of actors.

Lewis Gilbert
b. 1920

Director: *Sailors Do Care (1944), *The Ten-Year Plan (1945), *Arctic Harvest, *Under One Roof (1946), *Fishing Grounds of the World, The Little Ballerina (1947), Marry Me (co-sc only) (1949), Once a Sinner (1950), There Is Another Sun, It's a Small World, Scarlet Thread (1951), Emergency Call (& co-sc), Cosh Boy (& co-sc), Time Gentlemen Please (1952), Johnny on the Run (& pr), Albert RN (1953), The Good Die Young (& co-sc), The Sea Shall Not Have Them (& co-sc) (1954), Cast a Dark Shadow (1955), Reach for the Sky (& co-sc), The Admirable Crichton (1956), A Cry from the Streets, Carve Her Name With Pride (& co-sc), (1958), Ferry to Hong Kong (& co-sc) (1959), Sink the Bismarck!, Light Up the Sky (& co-sc) (1960), The Greengage Summer (1961), HMS Defiant (1962), The Seventh Dawn (1964), Alfie (& pr) (1966), You Only Live Twice (1967), The Adventurers (& pr, co-sc) (1970), Friends (& pr, auth) (1971), Operation Daybreak (1975), Seven Nights in Japan (& pr) (1976), The Spy Who Loved Me (1977), Moonraker (1979), Educating Rita (& pr) (1983), Not Quite Jerusalem (& pr) (1984), Shirley Valentine (& pr) (1989), Stepping Out (& pr) (1991), Haunted (1995)
* Documentary.

Lewis Gilbert is a survivor, a fact he attributes to his never having been under contract and therefore free – and as it has turned out, able – to do what he wants. After experience as a child actor in the 1930s, he cut his teeth as a director on

documentaries and ten second features before his first 'A' film, *Albert RN*, in 1953. Since then he has worked successfully in a number of genres, with an emphasis on war subjects in the '50s. With *Reach for the Sky* and *Carve Her Name With Pride*, two celebrations of wartime courage, he scored popular success. Gilbert seems less a director who imposes a strong personal stamp than one who makes a shrewd assessment of the material at hand and approaches it with a craftsman's eye to making it viable entertainment. Two of his early films, the village comedy, *Time Gentlemen Please*, and the thriller, *Cast a Dark Shadow*, hold up remarkably well for just such reasons.
Interview date: July 1990

Your first feature film, after wartime and post-war documentary experience, was the children's film, *The Little Ballerina* in 1947. Did you enjoy working with children?

Yes. They had just started to make films for children and they wanted feature films. I had a background of feature films as well as documentary experience, so that's how I came to do one of the earliest children's films, under the aegis of Mary Field, with whom I'd worked at Gaumont-British. The film had a very good cast – people like Martita Hunt and George Carney – and because of my feature-film background I knew these people and was able to ask them to be in it. The budget was almost nothing so they would have been doing it as a favour, really.

I suppose your real directorial career begins in 1950 with *Once a Sinner*.

Yes, with Pat Kirkwood – it's sad that her career foundered, because she was very good. In those days, in order to get established you had to start at what I call 'Poverty Row' filmmaking; I mean, we were making films in those days for about £15,000. They were all good experience, even though they were pretty trite stuff, which hopefully someone would spot and give you something better to do. I never had an agent in my life – I think I got *Once a Sinner* because the producer, John Argyle, had seen *The Little Ballerina*; he approached me and asked if I would like to do his film. It's very difficult for someone today to break in because there isn't that kind of cheap film to cut your teeth on; you're not allowed to fail now, it's all or nothing.

I recently saw *Time Gentlemen Please* again . . .

That was made for the company run by Grierson and John Baxter, called Group 3, with Michael Balcon in the background. They raised money so that new directors, new cameramen and writers could get a chance at making films, a very laudable idea. It had a very strong cast – people like Hermione Baddeley and Raymond Lovell, whom I'd worked with before. We would only have paid them something like £25 a day but that was pretty good money when you think that the average working man's wage was about £6 or £7 a week. A lot of them would be working in the theatre at the same time.

Hermione Gingold was playing a prostitute in *Cosh Boy*; she was middle-aged by then and she was wearing a dreadful wig for the part. I was doing night shooting with her the night my son was born; we left the studio at about five o'clock in the morning and I gave her a lift because her car hadn't arrived. I suddenly thought to myself, here I am on the night my son is born, driving along with someone who looks like a dreadful old prostitute – if anyone sees me I'll be shot to ribbons!

With *Albert RN* you clearly entered the 'A' film category. Where did you come across that story?

It was a play but it was clearly a much better film subject than a theatre piece. We built the camp out on Headingley Heath, a whole POW camp with barbed wire and so on. I think it gives you some insight into the economics of film, because that film, which had Jack Warner, Anthony Steel and a lot of other stars, cost £80,000 at a time when something like twenty million people a week went to the cinema. Now it would take four or five million pounds to make a film like that and there are only about two million people going to the cinema each week. You couldn't get your money back in England on a film like *Albert RN* today, although we did when it was made.

By this point, you'd established what appear to have been two important working relationships – with producer Daniel Angel and screenwriter Vernon Harris.

That's right, yes. Vernon Harris, who died only a couple of months ago, worked with me in some way on almost every film I did over nearly forty years. In those early days, we very often did the complete screenplay together. Vernon's real strength was as a · script editor. We would lay out the scenario together and we would then usually depend upon a dialogue writer to supply the dialogue.

Daniel Angel was more on the financial side, raising the money and so on. Usually, with the bigger films like *Reach for the Sky* and *Albert RN*, he bought them himself. I bought *Carve Her Name With Pride* myself but I brought Daniel in because he always called on me. It was a good partnership but after six films, which were all successful, you want to go your own way. Then I did a couple of films with Ian Dalrymple, whom I liked very much, as producer. But they were always *my* films. By the time I left Angel, I had learned a hell of a lot about film finance, and so I really went my own way after that. Sometimes, as with *A Cry from the Streets*, which was a very successful film, Ian owned the book and I went to him and said I would like to do it; but I raised the finance for it. So I am very much involved in the business side of making films and I think that's why I've survived, because I'm not dependent on anyone in that sense.

Did you come to make *Cast a Dark Shadow* because you were attracted by Janet Green's play, *Murder Mistaken*?

Yes, I had seen it in the theatre; I was doing *The Sea Shall Not Have Them* at the time and I mentioned it to Dirk Bogarde, who knew the play. I think Janet Green had in fact asked him to do the play but he wasn't doing plays at that time; Derek Farr did it. It was a very interesting plot, very claustrophobic. I think it was the best thing Margaret Lockwood did, she was great in the film. It was reasonably successful but by then Margaret had been in several really bad films and her name on a picture was rather counter-productive. It was a great shame because she could have started a whole new career as a character actress after *Cast a Dark Shadow*. Dirk is still one of my absolutely favourite actors, he is a lovely man to work with and a marvellous actor – now a marvellous writer as well.

War films tend to dominate '50s British cinema. Why, do you think?

After the war Britain was a very tired nation, worn out by five or six years of war, and this was a kind of ego boost, a nostalgia for a time when they were great, because they were rapidly overtaken economically by other countries, particularly by Japan and West Germany, whom they had just defeated. I chose my war films because they were great stories – *Reach for the Sky* in particular. It was extremely successful in the English-speaking countries but, oddly enough, the Rank Organisation was unable to get anywhere with it in the US; they had thought to use its success as a vehicle for setting up their own distribution network in the US but it didn't work. Yet, when I did *Sink the Bismarck!* a few years later, it was very successful in America; it's very difficult to ascertain why one film succeeds and another doesn't. We had a very interesting experience recently: it was the fiftieth anniversary of the Battle of Britain and they chose *Reach for the Sky* to show at a one-night première in aid of the war charity of the RAF; and it was a sell-out night. They ran the film, which was thirty-five years old, and it was like a time warp. I sat there, not having seen the film myself for about thirty years, and it was a really strange experience. All the young faces coming up on the screen, people who are now old men. Muriel Pavlow was there and I saw her again for the first time since making the film. Beverly Brooks [who played Bader's early girlfriend] was also there, married now to Viscount Rothermere.

Did you have a lot to do with Douglas Bader when you were making *Reach for the Sky*?

Oh yes, and was he difficult! He was difficult in the sense of wanting himself to be depicted in a certain way. He knew I was in the RAF and, when we couldn't get anyone to adapt the book, he said I should do it. So I did and then, when he read the script, he said I had made a terrible hash of it because I'd cut out a lot of his friends. I pointed out that the book contained hundreds of names and I had to cut it down or else the film would run for three days. He said, 'That's your problem. If you don't get my friends in, I won't double for the film,' because he was going to double for Kenneth More in long shots. I explained to him that that wouldn't stop the film being made; I said that we could undoubtedly find someone with a disability similar to his – which we did. In fact a number of his friends had helped me with the script, although we didn't tell Douglas that. Douglas wasn't in the film at all.

He was an incredible man, for all that. He was the only man who had ever walked without sticks with that sort of disability. The film was really as much about the triumph over adversity as it was a war film. Kenneth More hadn't been my first choice for the part. The first choice was Richard Burton, who wanted to do it until he was offered *Alexander the Great* at three or four times the salary, so he chose that. Laurence Olivier actually told Kenneth More that the only person who could play it was Bader himself, but Kenny was adamant he could do it.

***Carve Her Name With Pride* is a very grim story. How much licence did you and Vernon Harris feel you could take with a story like that?**

We didn't take much licence with it. One night we invited to dinner RJ Minney, who had written *Time Gentlemen Please*. He told us the story of Violette Szabo and we thought what a wonderful film it would make, so he sent me his proof copy of the book and I bought it. Virginia McKenna really wasn't the right type for it but she was under contract to Rank and they wanted to use her. Ideally it should have been someone like Diana Dors, who was much rougher, because Violette was a Cockney who had lived in Brixton, a very poor area of London. In fact Virginia was wonderful in the film and she got several awards for it. She had Odette [Churchill] as an adviser on *Carve Her Name With Pride*, which was very useful, especially as, having already had a film made about her life, she understood a bit about filmmaking. Some of the dialogue we fictionalised, of course, but most of the story of the film is quite true, including the fact that

Violette did speak perfect French because she used to spend every summer in France with her French grandmother. A lot of the film was set in France but in fact we shot it all in England around the Pinewood area.

When you adapted *The Admirable Crichton*, did you study the original closely?

No, we made it as a vehicle for Kenny More who was a very big star. I would say it was freely adapted from the Barrie play to suit Kenny, and it was a very successful film. I don't think you owe total allegiance to the original text because you are, in a sense, making something that is very different. I was very fond of Kenny as an actor, although he wasn't particularly versatile. What he could do, he did very well. His strengths were his ability to portray charm; basically he was the officer returning from the war and he was superb in that role. The minute that kind of role went out of existence, he began to go down as a box-office star. In something like *The Greengage Summer*, he was somehow too normal, it didn't quite work; that's a role Dirk should have played because you could well imagine a girl of fifteen or sixteen falling in love with Dirk.

Speaking of *Crichton*, I think that until the late '50s British cinema often seemed uncritically middle-class and snobbish.

I think that's true, and I think it changed for two reasons: one was the censorship, which changed, and second was the advent of *Look Back in Anger* in the theatre, which showed that working people could have lives of their own, not just come in to say, 'Dinner is served.' I suppose the cinema reflects its own time and working-class people just didn't 'exist' in the West End or the cinema prior to then.

Sidney Gilliat

1908–1994

Screenwriter, often in collaboration with Frank Launder: *Rome Express* (1932), *Facing the Music, Falling for You, Orders is Orders, Friday the Thirteenth* (1933), *Jack Ahoy, Chu-Chin-Chow, My Heart is Calling* (1934), *Bulldog Jack, King of the Damned* (1935), *Twelve Good Men, The Man Who Changed His Mind, Seven Sinners, Strangers on Honeymoon* (1936), *Take My Tip, A Yank at Oxford* (1937), *Strange Boarders, The Lady Vanishes, The Gaunt Stranger* (1938), *Ask a Policeman, Jamaica Inn, Inspector Hornleigh on Holiday* (1939), *They Came By Night, Night Train to Munich, Girl in the News* (1940), *Kipps, *Mr Proudfoot Shows a Light, *From the Four Corners* (1941), *Unpublished Story, The Young Mr Pitt, *Partners in Crime* (1942), *I See a Dark Stranger* (1946), *The Belles of St Trinian's*

(1954), *Geordie, The Green Man* (1955), *Blue Murder at St Trinian's* (1957), *The Pure Hell of St Trinian's* (1960)

Director (producer usually Launder): *Millions Like Us* (co-dir, co-sc) (1943), *Waterloo Road* (& co-sc) (1944), *The Rake's Progress* (& co-sc) (1945), *I See a Dark Stranger* (& co-sc), *Green for Danger* (& co-sc) (1946), *London Belongs to Me* (& co-pr, co-sc) (1948), *State Secret* (& co-pr, sc) (1950), *The Story of Gilbert and Sullivan* (& co-pr, co-sc) (1953), *The Constant Husband* (& co-pr, co-sc) (1954), *Fortune is a Woman* (& co-pr, co-sc) (1957), *Left, Right and Centre* (& co-pr, co-sc) (1959), *Only Two Can Play* (1961), *The Great St Trinian's Train Robbery* (co-dir, auth) (1966), *Endless Night* (& sc) (1972)

* Short film.

British cinema never developed as confidently as Hollywood did the studio system geared to turning out a steady supply of 'product'. What it did have were producer–director teams of remarkable longevity: for example, Basil Dearden and Michael Relph, Betty Box and Ralph Thomas, the Boulting brothers – and Launder and Gilliat. These two, after a varied apprenticeship in the '30s, became associated with a level of civilised entertainment in the decades that followed. After co-directing *Millions Like Us*, one characteristically produced when the other directed. On the whole Launder as director favoured the broader comedy (e.g., the St Trinian's series) while Gilliat preferred, say, *The Constant Husband* or *Only Two Can Play*. Arguably, Gilliat's finest hour was in the '40s when he directed and co-wrote an unbroken run of successes from *Waterloo Road* to *State Secret*. All those films are informed by a wry tolerance and warmth, as well as an irrepressible and sometimes quirky humour.

Interview date: October 1992

What follows is only the first half of the interview planned with Sidney Gilliat. Because of travelling difficulties, it was conducted by phone in 1992 and the idea was for Sidney Gilliat to complete it on tape. Unfortunately, he became ill very shortly after and the interview remained uncompleted when he died two years later.

You did all sorts of things in your films of the late 1920s/early '30s. Were you simply determined to get into films and were happy to do whatever presented itself?

I feel ashamed in answering that. Though I had got interested in films, I was really a failed scholar, who left the university without a degree and went into journalism. Occasionally, I got tickets from the *Evening Standard* film critic, Walter Mycroft, a hunchback dwarf, who had tried hard to rise above his handicap. I was a sub-editor, when I came back one night from seeing a film and found Mycroft having coffee with my father. I'd seen *The Iron Horse* before John Ford was canonised, and remembered Mycroft had rather panned it, so I adjusted my opinion. Mycroft told my father that I should go into films. He then got a job at Shepherd's Bush and I got in as a sort of appendage. Gareth Gundrey, who gave David Lean his first chance, asked me if I could do a synopsis for him, and I did a lot of review copies of synopses for the *Times*. Then Mycroft invited me to a press day at Elstree to celebrate a new contract for Alfred Hitchcock, who was shooting *The Farmer's Wife*. Mycroft got landed with me again in the scenario department, which was really non-existent, and both the nature and salary of my job were unknown.

Anyway, from New Year's Day 1928, I was employed as Mycroft's assistant at £2 10s per week, checking unsolicited manuscripts, which I would then take to the lady in charge of the scenario department. One I remember was a story that later became Harry Lachman's *Weekend Wives*, with Estelle Brody; I also provided some titles for this silent film. Elstree was then full of eminent Germans and *very* eminent Americans. I was told to do a chapter-by-chapter synopsis of Hardy's *Under the Greenwood Tree* [which was in fact Frank Launder's first script] and I remember a mid-November shooting in a wood meant to be in midsummer, and I was fired for drawing attention to this. I was also responsible for costuming all the character people and fell foul of Marguerite Allan, who blamed me, wrongly, for the failure of her costumes to arrive.

You are credited on Walter Forde's excellent *Rome Express*. What did you do?

I was put to work by Clifford Grey, a lyric writer and not experienced as a writer for films. He is credited with the story, but in fact I did provide some of the material. On *Facing the Music*, the idea of the prima donna wearing her own jewels and deliberately attracting crooks from Covent Garden was mine. But Stanley Lupino claimed to have thought of the idea in his bath and Clifford Grey hadn't protected my rights.

Was *Seven Sinners* the first film on which you and Frank Launder shared a screenwriter's credit?

Yes, though we'd both been on the credits of a film before that [*Facing the Music*, 1933]. *Seven Sinners* had been made as a silent called *The Wrecker*, with a German director, who'd wrecked a South Western Railway train for it. Frank and I saw *The Wrecker* and rewrote L du Garde Peach's screenplay as *Seven Sinners*. We started with a disappearing body, then had to think up a solution. The first two reels were easy, then we were just making it up as we went along. We would each write a sequence separately, then exchange notes and rewrite it.

What do you recall of your dealings with Hitchcock on *The Lady Vanishes*?

Hitchcock had nothing to do with it initially [it was intended for the American director Roy William Neill]. Ted Black had purchased the book [Ethel Lina White's *The Wheel Spins*], probably through Frank Launder. I was still freelancing at Gainsborough and I was commissioned to do it. I got as far as inventing Charters and Caldicott [played by Basil Radford and Naunton Wayne] on my own, then Frank was freed by Ted Black and

joined me. A second unit had been sent to Yugoslavia to shoot exteriors, and there was a real balls-up on location and the company was ordered out and there was still no film on the shelf. Hitch had just finished all but one of his contract films, Gainsborough was in decline, and, according to Frank, the Ostrer brothers suggested they settle Hitchcock's contract. Black objected, and £20,000 was added to the budget because of Hitch and the status of his name. I was working at Metro by this time but worked in the evenings with Frank. Hitch did work very closely to the screenplay, which he had read to him. He had a photographic memory and could visualise the whole thing in his head. I think he found the actual shooting boring. The journalist Jympson Harmon asked him how he'd thought of Charters and Caldicott and Hitch claimed full credit for them, and wouldn't make any kind of retraction when the reviews for *The Lady Vanishes* picked up his remark.

The next prominent director you worked with was Carol Reed on *The Girl in the News*, *Night Train to Munich*, *Kipps* and *The Young Mr Pitt*. How did his methods compare with Hitchcock's?

He seemed to me an interpreter rather than a creator; he followed the screenplay quite closely rather than bringing forth original ideas of his own. I felt he was not at all interested in *Girl in the News*, which I think was a pallid job. The chief obstacle was Carol's stage background – he couldn't really believe in the screenwriter. He needed close collaboration with a writer, which he later had on *The Third Man* with Graham Greene, but Frank and I didn't fulfil his ideas as a screenwriter, whereas Lord Castlerosse did. I didn't feel Carol had any discrimination about dialogue when he accepted Castlerosse's terrible high-flown stuff, but he [Reed] was again and again a young man in search of his father.

How did you come to make the Ministry of Information shorts?

They were commissioned by John Betjeman and we just gave our services. We did two or three of them, like *Partners in Crime*.

Did you consciously aim at a documentary influence in *Millions Like Us*, your first feature film as directors?

Millions Like Us began as commissioned work, but the Films Division of the MoI recommended it as a fiction and we did it for half our Gainsborough salaries. It was consciously aimed at the working girl who had been uprooted. We were *not* responsible for the terrible assault on Beethoven over the final titles: we wanted to achieve our effects indirectly, as in the scene where a welfare officer opens a door and asks for a glass of water and you guess that something serious has happened inside. The film had reservations about the classes working together and you sense this in the scenes between Anne Crawford and Eric Portman – at the end, there's a sense of 'wait and see' about them.

Anne Crawford was brought in to replace Sheila Bell, a lovely girl with a sad story. Eric Portman didn't want to play in the film and went to Halifax and got drunk, but was threatened by Ted Black and ended by being co-operative with us. It was very demanding, being both writers and directors on the film, and the Ostrers thought the whole project ludicrous. Ted Black didn't get on with Maurice and Bill Ostrer, who wanted to take creative credit.

You and Mr Launder didn't co-direct again for over twenty years . . .

Co-directing didn't work. Frank was very easy with actors, whereas I was very diffident. I was always at the back and he was at the front.

Were you pleased with your follow-up film, *Waterloo Road*?

I was taken off *Waterloo Road* before it was finished. Production was stopped when I still had some exteriors to shoot. When it was finally finished and Ted Black had gone, the Ostrers put the film at the end of the dubbing schedule. However, Earl St John, who was then in charge of Odeon cinemas, liked the look of it and intervened and got the dubbing done.

Whose idea was it to use the Alastair Sim character as a commentator?

Val Valentine [author of the story] invented the character of the sixpenny doctor, and I made him into a commentator, which I think proved a bit of a mess. The whole film derived from Val's experience of being caught in a heavy raid and going down into an Underground station, where he saw material for stories. The flashback to the Blitz while the war was still on seems strange today, but the fact was at the time there had been no Blitz for over a year.

What do you remember of the famous fight between Stewart Granger and John Mills?

The fight was not outlined in the script. It was worked out with a boxer and then rehearsed. It got a lot of publicity.

How constrained by censorship were you on *The Rake's Progress*?

It wasn't a matter of British censorship, as such. Mrs Rank took violently against *Waterloo Road* and thought *The Rake's Progress* was terribly immoral. The Methodists ganged up, and when it went to America Joe Breen's office [of the Production Code] condemned it and this influenced Rank. I said we'd devise a way of meeting their points, and that we'd prepare one version for the US and another for the rest of the world. There was opposition to the Griffith Jones character being 'fool enough' to take her [his wife, played by Jean Kent] back after her affair with Rex Harrison: this was seen as condoning adultery. There was also criticism of the ending, as if it were my own views rather than those of the character. I felt his death 'suited' him.

You had a number of the same collaborators on your '40s films, including Wilkie Cooper as cinematographer. Was this a matter of choice?

Up to a point, but in Wilkie's case I ought to have given him more guidance about style on *The Rake's Progress*. I think he found his own style on *Green for Danger*.

I thought *Green for Danger* was much more exciting than Christianna Brand's novel – how did you feel about it?

The Rank story department had bought it at considerable expense and sent a very praising account of it, though they hadn't at first recommended it. Rank wanted us to cast Robert Morley as the detective and it was designed for him from the beginning, but he was appearing in *The First Gentleman* on the stage and was unavailable and that's how we came to have Alastair Sim as the detective. It was very carefully cast and, as you suggested, I thought it was a good idea to have Rosamund John cast against type as the murderess. We did it at Pinewood just after the war and they had sets built for every stage of the film in the most ruinously expensive way.

Those interested in a detailed account of the post-'40s career of Sidney Gilliat and his long partnership with Frank Launder are recommended to Geoff Brown's admirable study, Launder and Gilliat, *BFI Publishing, London, 1977.*

Marius Goring

b. 1912

Actor: *Rembrandt, The Amateur Gentleman* (1936), *Dead Men Tell No Tales, Consider Your Verdict* (1938), *The Spy in Black, Flying Fifty-Five* (1939), *Pastor Hall, The Case of the Frightened Lady* (1940), *The Big Blockade* (1941), *The Night Invader* (1943), *The Story of Lilli Marlene* (1944), *Night Boat to Dublin, A Matter of Life and Death* (1946), *Take My Life* (1947), *The Red Shoes, Mr Perrin and Mr Traill* (1948), *Odette, Highly Dangerous* (1950), *Circle of Danger, Pandora and the Flying Dutchman, The Magic Box* (1951), *So Little Time, Nachts auf den Strassen, The Man Who Watched Trains Go By, Rough Shoot* (1952), *The Mirror and Markheim* (voice only) (1953), *Break in the Circle, The Adventures of Quentin Durwood, The Barefoot Contessa* (1955), *Ill Met By Moonlight* (1957), *The Truth about Women, The Moonraker, Family Doctor, Son of Robin Hood, I Was Monty's Double* (1958), *Whirlpool, The Angry Hills, The Treasure of San Teresa, Desert Mice* (1959), *Beyond the Curtain, The Unstoppable Man, Exodus* (1960), *The Inspector, The Devil's Daffodil, The Devil's Agent* (1962), *The Crooked Road* (1964), *Up from the Beach* (1965), *The 25th Hour* (1967), *Girl on a Motorcycle, Subterfuge* (1968), *First Love* (1970), *Zeppelin* (1971), *The Girl in the Yellow Dress* (1978), *Strike It Rich* (1990)

Marius Goring was so often to be found playing sinister foreigners that it comes as a surprise to find that he is wholly English. In his very long career in films, dating back to the 1930s, when he was not playing Nazi officers he was often seen as neurotic or ambiguously decadent characters. On the rare occasions when he played what might have been seen as more obviously 'leading man' roles, he still invested them with a memorable suggestion of strangeness. He rightly regards the films he made for Michael Powell – especially *A Matter of Life and Death* and *The Red Shoes* – as the highlight of his screen career, but he was also memorable in Lawrence Huntington's *Mr Perrin and Mr Traill*: only in his mid-thirties at the time, he suggested a lifetime of disappointment and frustration. He was extremely busy throughout the '50s, the while maintaining an almost unbroken commitment to the stage.
Interview date: June 1990

As well as doing broadcasts for the BBC's European and World Service during the war, did you also make a number of films, including Roy Boulting's *Pastor Hall*?

In fact no, that was made before the war broke out, although it wasn't released until about 1940. The Chamberlain Government wouldn't allow it to be released. It was about the German concentration camps and, although it was completely true, it wasn't considered a good idea to insult the Germans! If Churchill had been in power he would have said 'Nonsense! Show it everywhere!'

You have made about sixty films for the cinema. Do you have any personal favourites?

Oh yes. I made a film in 1939 with Michael Powell, *The Spy in Black*, but I was unable to make many films during the war because of my broadcasting and other commitments. After the European war came to an end, Powell and Pressburger came up with *A Matter of Life and Death* and offered me a marvellous part. I made four pictures in all for them; I think those films were in a totally different category from any others I've done. They were such a delight to work with, and so inventive, and they gave actors great scope.

But back to *The Spy in Black* – there was a book that came out before the 1914–18 war, *The Riddle of the Sands* by Erskine Childers; it presented an imaginary invasion of Britain which could happen should there be a war with Germany. Powell took the proposition and decided to make a film about a submarine coming into northern Scottish waters and blowing up British warships. The amazing thing was that, although the film was pure fiction, the war had only been on for about three weeks when a German submarine did in fact come in and blow up one of our ships.

Did Powell give his actors a lot of guidance?

No, he really left things up to the appropriate people. At least, he always gave the impression that they were doing it all and he was just checking up on what was going on. With me, as an actor, Powell would simply let me get on with it. I wrote an obituary for him when he died, because a lot of people wrote that he was horrible to actors, whereas I thought he was marvellous. There was a scene in *The Red Shoes* where I, as the composer, halt the orchestra, without permission from the conductor, because I think they aren't playing my music properly. Michael told me about this scene one morning and said we would shoot it that afternoon. I asked him what was going to happen during the scene and he said, 'Oh, I thought you'd tell me that'! Then he looked at his watch and said, 'You've got half an hour; fix it up yourself with the orchestra. You'd better hurry up'! I remembered that Sir Thomas Beecham was rehearsing in the building that day, so I went in to listen. Beecham was very witty and his musicians loved him. At one point he stopped the orchestra and asked the first cello if he had a B or a B flat in a particular bar; the cellist replied that he had a B flat and Beecham said, 'Yes, it does make quite a difference, doesn't it?' The orchestra laughed, so I wrote all that down and showed it to Powell. He thought it was fine and so that's what we shot.

How much in evidence around the studio was Pressburger at this time?

He was certainly in evidence; he did all the scripting, although sometimes Powell would make his own contribution as well. Pressburger also did quite a lot on the business side of things; what he never did at all was to direct. As time went on, he felt he would like to direct a film on his own and it was that which really broke them up. They never worked together again and it didn't do Pressburger any good, because he couldn't direct – and *Peeping Tom*, of course, finished Powell. It's a great movie but we were all so shocked by it then.

Perhaps no British director has quite had Powell's extraordinary visual sense. How much was this the work of Jack Cardiff?

Well, Powell always said Cardiff was the greatest cameraman in the world and he did such things with colour – I wouldn't say people *can't* do it today, but it never seems as good as what Cardiff did. The whole technique – such as in *A Matter of Life and Death*, with the idea of having a mixture of black-and-white and colour – was so good. In fact, I had a line in that film which was originally, 'One is so starved for colour up there,' and during a run-through I said, 'One is so starved for Technicolor up there,' and Powell said, 'That's good, leave it in.' So that was my contribution.

I understand *The Red Shoes* was a big breakthrough for British films in the USA, although Rank thought it wouldn't succeed there.

Yes, it was very successful, but Rank simply thought the picture was awful. He said, 'Nobody is going to go and see this nonsense,' which shows you that he really didn't know anything about film. He even decided he wasn't going to finish the picture, and so Powell asked Alexander Korda to bail him out, and he finished the picture financially and arranged the distribution. It still had Rank's name on it but, being still convinced that nobody would go to see it, Rank didn't even give it a première showing in England. Then a filmhouse in New York picked it up and it played there for a year. In the course of that year, people suddenly realised what they were seeing and, after two or three years, the money came pouring in.

What do you recall of the other Powell–Pressburger film you made, *Ill Met By Moonlight*?

It's not in quite the same class as the others. We were going to make the whole thing in Crete, so we went out there, but it was a very bad time because the good wartime relationship between the British and Greek governments had passed completely. All the cameras and materials we had taken out to Crete were stolen, so Micky Powell said it was useless trying to film there and we shot it in the South of France instead. Micky had lived there as a boy and knew it well, so he was able to choose locations which no one could tell weren't actually Greece.

I greatly admire your performance as the increasingly deranged schoolmaster in *Mr Perrin and Mr Traill*. What did you think of Lawrence Huntington as a director?

I got on very well with him but he just seemed to disappear, I don't know what happened to him. He understood actors very well and, above all, he had a great sense of humour. I don't remember much about the film other than that Lawrence and I had a very enjoyable time together making it. The man who produced it was a German refugee, Alexander Galperson; he knew my work from the theatre and it was his idea that I should play the part – as a change, because most of the time I was playing Nazi officers when I wasn't working for Powell. When I was asked to do the film I read Hugh Walpole's novel first, then agreed to do the part.

In 1951 you made two films with American directors and stars: Jacques Tourneur's *Circle of Danger* with Ray Milland and Albert Lewin's *Pandora and the Flying Dutchman* with Ava Gardner. Did you find their working methods different from what you'd been used to?

No, basically it was just the same. I loved working with Jacques Tourneur, but *Circle of Danger* was one of those odd pictures that I haven't seen since it was first made. I think I played something sinister.

Pandora and the Flying Dutchman was made at Pinewood and Lewin was a very remarkable man: he had been a professor of English and somehow he got a job as a sort of permanent producer with MGM. He had a deal whereby he was allowed to direct one picture every two or three years, and, apart from that, he was just supposed to give advice. James Mason was in *Pandora* and I had known him since I started at the Old Vic. His one ambition had always been to get into films in America – an ambition I didn't share. I wanted to stay in England and also I had never envisaged myself as a film actor, preferring the theatre. As for Ava, she was totally delightful, we had great fun together. There was none of the 'great star' about her, she was absolutely natural.

She was very good in the next movie we did together, *The Barefoot Contessa*, which we made in Italy. Joe Mankiewicz, the director, was an inspiring man to work with, a very good actor's director, and some of the dialogue he gave us was extraordinary. He seemed to fade out just like Powell and Pressburger.

You had almost a conventional romantic lead in a film called *So Little Time*, directed by Compton Bennett.

It was a touching little film, yes, my favourite apart from the Powell films. The story originally happened in Poland but it was changed to Belgium for the film. I played a Nazi officer who falls in love with Maria Schell, who was beautiful and extremely good. It was too soon after the war and people still thought that every German was a horror. It was probably the first picture after the war that dared to suggest all Germans weren't 'Nazi swine' but its timing was wrong; a year later and it would have been all right.

Were the '40s and '50s a good time to be pursuing a film career in Britain, given how busy you were?

Oh yes, from the late '40s. It was a period of immense vitality, invention and drive which came from the big leaders of the film industry in those days. I had a contract with Rank during that time, until he decided to throw the business up. I can't say I think much of my later films. I have done some television work I've enjoyed – for example, *The Old Men at the Zoo* – much more than most of my films.

Stewart Granger

1913–1993

Actor: *A Southern Maid* (1933), *Over the Garden Wall, Give Her a Ring* (1934), *Mademoiselle Docteur, So This is London* (1937), *Convoy* (1940), *Secret Mission* (1942), *Thursday's Child, The Lamp Still Burns, The Man in Grey* (1943), *Fanny by Gaslight, Love Story, Madonna of the Seven Moons* (1944), *Waterloo Road* (1945), *Caravan, Caesar and Cleopatra, The Magic Bow* (1946), *Captain Boycott* (1947), *Blanche Fury, Saraband for Dead Lovers, Woman Hater, Adam and Evelyne* (1948), *King Solomon's Mines* (1950), *The Light Touch, Soldiers Three* (1951), *The Wild North, Scaramouche, The Prisoner of Zenda* (1952), *Young Bess, Salome* (1953), *All the Brothers were Valiant, Beau Brummell* (1954), *Green Fire, Moonfleet, Footsteps in the Fog* (1955), *Bhowani Junction, The Last Hunt* (1956), *Gun Glory, The Little Hut* (1957), *The Whole Truth, Harry Black* (1958), *North to Alaska* (1960), *The Secret Partner, The Swordsman of Siena* (1961), *Commando, La Congiura Dei Dieci, Sodom and Gomorrah* (1962), *The Shortest Day, The Legion's Lost Patrol* (1963), *The Crooked Road, Frontier Hellcat/Among Vultures, The Secret Invasion* (1964), *Rampage at Apache Wells, Old Shatterhand* (1965), *Red Dragon, Target for Killing, Requiem for a Secret Agent* (1966), *The Trygon Factor, The Last Safari* (1967), *The Wild Geese, Hell Hunters* (1978)

Stewart Granger became a household name in British films after co-starring with Phyllis Calvert, Margaret Lockwood and James Mason in *The Man in Grey*. He was a dashing hero in a string of subsequent melodramas made for Gainsborough Studios, though he would prefer to have had the meatier, more villainous roles that often fell to Mason's lot. Though he does not value these films, he was a very important ingredient in their success. Nevertheless, his best performances in British films, in roles that gave him more scope, were either in different vein (e.g., as the spiv-like Ted Purvis in Sidney Gilliat's *Waterloo Road*), or at other studios (e.g., *Saraband for Dead Lovers* at Ealing, *Blanche Fury* for Cineguild, and the attractive comedy, *Adam and Evelyne*, for Two Cities). Hollywood capitalised on his flair for costume drama and action adventure and he was solidly successful in these genres throughout the 1950s.
Interview date: June 1991

As far as I can tell, your fifty-year career in films began with work as an extra in 1933. How did this come about?

I started training to be a doctor. But, since the training was long and I was not such a dedicated fellow, I gave that up and went to work for a firm that made tickets and ticket punches for the buses. After a quarrel with them, I left. A friend asked me whether I had a car and a decent wardrobe – and on that basis I became a film extra at a guinea a day. Then I had to go to the doctor with a cut finger and met his wife, Susan Richmond, who taught at the Webber-Douglas School of Dramatic Art. My grandfather had been an actor and she asked, why didn't I apply for a scholarship?

How valuable did you find such training when you came to films?

One to one-and-a-half years at acting school is valuable, but not to learn to act. They teach you techniques such as how to walk through a door, picking up the telephone and drinking a cup of tea. Technical things like the use of make-up or how to learn dialogue. But to act, you have to *do* it. I learned acting in the reps. The audience teaches you – particularly timing. You have to have an innate sense to act.

Your screen career really got started when you were invalided out of the war ...

Yes. In fact, I did films like *Convoy* and *Secret Mission* while I was still 'Grade E' – that is, in the process of being invalided out, but not quite out. John Clements told me there was a part going in *Convoy* and that's how I came to be in that with him and Clive Brook.

The cinema world is not easy. It is full of envy from little people – heads of studios, for example, who hate people for their attractiveness. I don't regret my film career, but medicine would have had more dignity. Actors are shackled to others. I was always fighting with people. I was resented because I was liked by the press. But it was boring being an actor – at least confined to the swashbuckling hero, as I was for most of the time, playing characters like Beau Brummell or Scaramouche, that weren't based in history but were just tailored to fit my image.

But my career in the USA was better for me than my English one – for example my role in *King Solomon's Mines*. After that, I was offered *Quo Vadis* but I refused to sign the contract, so it was offered to Robert Taylor instead. My divorce ruined me and sent me out of the USA. I went to Europe, where I paid no tax, but ruined my career in lousy films. My last real film was *The Last Safari*, which was the worst film ever made in Africa! I was not a dedicated actor. I have recently gone back to the theatre after forty years, playing in *The Circle* with Rex Harrison and Glynis Johns on Broadway. It got good notices and ran for six months – then two months on the road.

What do you remember about *The Man in Grey*?

I got a call from Gainsborough Studios while I was doing a play [*Rebecca*], and they sent me a script. Robert Donat had suggested that they should try me. I knew if I got the part in *A Man in Grey* it would make me a star. I tested, and was given the part straight away, before the tests were ready to view. I went on doing the play at the same time. I was just out of the Army, where I had learned to speak my mind. My battalion had been wiped out – I felt guilt for surviving and for making films during the bombing.

How happy were you with those Gainsborough melodramas – *Fanny by Gaslight*, *Madonna of the Seven Moons*, etc?

I didn't like *Fanny* and *Madonna* – they both had drippy characters. At least *Fanny* was directed by Anthony Asquith, who was a sweet man. I would have liked to play the villains in these films – someone with character, with balls. James Mason was luckier than me – he played the villains and later got into character parts. I had an OK villain's part in a bad film, *All the Brothers Were Valiant*, in America, but I was generally cast as the hero because I had good looks and a good voice, and I could wear costumes. But so can most English actors because they come out of a theatrical tradition, the greater part of which calls for this ability to wear period costume. And at Gainsborough we were lucky to have Liz Haffenden, who was a wonderful designer, to do our costumes. I was lucky again in this respect at MGM in Hollywood.

Certainly Asquith was much the best of those directors I worked with at Gainsborough. I mean [Arthur] Crabtree and [Bernard] Knowles, both sweet men, were really cameramen, and Leslie Arliss was a writer. Apart from Asquith, I really had a bunch of bloody awful directors at Gainsborough. And, you know, they were terrible films – *Caravan*, *Madonna of the Seven Moons*, and so on. My alibi for doing them was that it was wartime and they provided the escapism that people needed.

Were you pleased with the change offered by Sidney Gilliat's *Waterloo Road*?

Waterloo Road was made in ten days, while I was also making *Love Story*. Well, you had the set, the clothes, the dialogue, so you just got in and did it. It was just hard work. Gainsborough was bombed while we were making *Love Story*, which, as I say in my book [*Sparks Fly Upwards*], was a load of crap – and a smash hit! But *Waterloo Road* was better than that and the famous fight was well done. It was difficult because I was a heavyweight boxer and Johnnie Mills was a good bit lighter than I was. Anyway, we had a pro to help us with telegraphing the punches and so forth and it ended up looking realistic.

What do you recall of filming two later lavish costume melodramas in Britain – Blanche Fury and Saraband for Dead Lovers?

Blanche Fury was a silly story, too grim and melodramatic, but it's a wonderful-looking film. It was photographed by Guy Green [and Geoffrey Unsworth], who did David Lean's Dickens films. I enjoyed working with Valerie Hobson, a lovely woman, but the film didn't work.

Saraband was a sweet film though, and it's one I'm quite proud of. But, whereas Gainsborough loved stars, Ealing didn't like them; the production was the star. *Saraband* was their first big colour film. I said I would do it, but I wanted Marlene Dietrich, whom I loved, for Clara. I felt I couldn't be brutal to Flora Robson. Flora was a great actress, but she'd never been beautiful and it was hard to be cruel to a woman who was never beautiful. That's why I wanted Dietrich for the part. The opening sequence was planned in great detail. Françoise Rosay wanted to rehearse . . . but in the end this wasn't used. You see, Koenigsmark, whom I played, was introduced as penniless, and this was cut out because it involved Jewish moneylenders.

The director Harold French was pleased with Adam and Evelyne. How do you feel about it?

The storyline of *Adam and Evelyne* was mine – I worked on an idea based on the old silent film, *Daddy Long-Legs*, and when I had the outline completed, I contacted the writer Noel Langley to collaborate with me. I wrote it for Jean Simmons, and it was a very good vehicle for her. It was a sweet film, a charming light comedy.

How did you come to go to Hollywood for King Solomon's Mines?

I was bitter because I made no money in the movie industry in Britain and was highly taxed there. So I went to America, where the tax was a bit better. But acting was hard work for little reward. I did all my own stunts in *Scaramouche*, some of them quite dangerous – and got dysentery when filming in Africa!

Were you pleased with the way MGM went about building you up as an international star?

MGM certainly did not build me up. After *King Solomon's Mines* I made *Soldiers Three*, a cheap film. They ruined my career. I made them do *Scaramouche*. *Solomon* was a cheap film to make. They didn't realise what they had. It only cost a million dollars. They had nature, animals, mountains, Africa . . . and they suddenly realised they had a smash hit. My best film, for them, was *Young Bess* – for the costumes, the cast, the story.

Was it very different from working in England?

Hollywood was more professional than British studios. The studio staff loved stars, the English resented stars. It was the technicians who counted there; English crews were bolshie. The plug was pulled on the dot of 6pm. They killed the British film industry – the electricians, the carpenters, and so on. In the USA and in Europe the crew were on your side. They loved stars because stars provided them with work. I liked those crews as fellows. In England left-wing shop stewards dominated. They hindered not helped. In USA the crews were efficient, well trained . . . they wanted the film to be a success. I was too forthright in England and ruined my career there. James Mason too.

What do you recall of the fuss about Beau Brummell, the film you returned to England for in 1954?

Prince Philip told me that the joke about the royals – George III, to be exact – was the Queen's favourite bit. Everyone had said what a tasteless choice it was for the Royal Command Performance.

How did you find working with Fritz Lang on Moonfleet?

I hated working with Fritz Lang – he was a Kraut and it was a bloody awful film. I wanted to produce and act it in Cornwall and made them buy the book. MGM turned it into a big colour film. *Moonfleet* was not Lang's type of film – it is a romantic child's film. It wasn't a bad part.

How do you feel now about the British cinema of your period?

Early British films are embarrassing. The war brought out the best of British cinema: the Powells, the Leans, the Carol Reeds. But the Labour Government didn't take off the tax after the war and the industry was stifled.

I am not proud of my British films. I had no choice of films, I was always under contract. I was a good costume actor, but I shortened my career because I made the wrong choices. I missed *Quo Vadis* and *Ben Hur* and I had the physique for them.

Guy Green

b. 1913

Assistant camera operator or camera operator: *Song of the Plough, Breakers Ahead* (1933), *Radio Parade of 1935* (1934), *Abdul the Damned, I Give My Heart, The Immortal Swan* (1935), *The Tenth Man* (1936), *Glamorous Night, Our Fighting Navy* (1937), *Yellow Sands* (1938), *Hi Gang!, Pimpernel Smith* (1941), *In Which We Serve, One of Our Aircraft is Missing* (1942), *Escape to Danger* (1943), *This Happy Breed* (1944)

Director of photography: *The Way Ahead* (1944), *The Way to the Stars, Carnival* (1945), *Great Expectations* (1946), *Take My Life* (1947), *Blanche Fury, Oliver Twist* (1948), *Adam and Evelyne, The Passionate Friends* (1949), *Madeleine* (1950), *Captain Horatio Hornblower, Night Without Stars* (1951), *The Hour of 13, The Story of Robin Hood, The Beggar's Opera* (1952), *Decameron Nights, Rob Roy: The Highland Rogue, For Better For Worse* (1953), *Souls in Conflict* (1954), *I am a Camera, The Dark Avenger* (1955)

Director: *River Beat* (1954), *Portrait of Alison, Lost* (1955), *House of Secrets* (1956), *Sea of Sand, The Snorkel* (1958), *SOS Pacific, The Angry Silence* (1959), *The Mark* (1961), *Diamond Head, Light in the Piazza* (1962), *A Patch of Blue* (& sc) (1965), *Pretty Polly* (1967), *The Magus* (1968), *A Walk in the Spring Rain* (1970), *Luther* (1973), *Once Is Not Enough* (1974), *The Devil's Advocate* (1977)

Guy Green was certainly one of the finest black-and-white cameramen in the world, and the peak of his achievement was his work for Cineguild in the late '40s, on such films as *Great Expectations* and *Oliver Twist*. In Cineguild's *Blanche Fury*, he also photographed one of the most handsome Technicolor films. He clearly knew how to light distinctive faces, such as Ann Todd's, to maximum effect; broadly, he knew how lighting worked collaboratively with actors and settings to *create* meaning. See, in this respect, the opening sequences of the two Dickens films. As a director, without rivalling his record as a cameraman, he did entertaining work in a number of genres. There are: a very neat thriller, *Lost*, about a kidnapped baby; a taut frightened-woman melodrama, *The Snorkel*; several polished Hollywood star vehicles, one of the most successful being *A Patch of Blue*, which received five Academy Award nominations; and, best of all, the then-controversial drama, *The Angry Silence* (accused of union-bashing, but really a story of individual difference), and *The Mark*, which broached the subject of child molestation.
Interview date: September 1992

Many English directors seem to have begun as cameramen. Did you always want to be a director?

No, I always wanted to be a cameraman! I was very satisfied with being a cameraman, until the break-up of Cineguild, when the Rank finances weren't working and they gave up their really serious operation. Eagle-Lion distribution didn't do so well in America and the funds weren't forthcoming, so Cineguild split up. I was working with David Lean and that was a marvellous experience. I then became a freelance cameraman, working with lots of other directors but never with the same satisfaction that I had with David. Ultimately, I thought I might as well have a go at directing myself.

Was being a cameraman a good preparation for directing?

I think it is an excellent preparation because you then have no fear of the mechanics of it. A camera can be terrifying to someone who doesn't know about where to put it or what lens to use. A lot of directors have come from the acting side and they know nothing about it. They can be marvellous of course, like George Cukor, but I should think having that technical background under your belt would be a help.

You were the camera operator on several prestigious films during the war, like *Pimpernel Smith*, *In Which We Serve*, *One of Our Aircraft is Missing* and *This Happy Breed*. What do you recall of those?

I first met David Lean on *One of Our Aircraft is Missing*; Micky Powell was the director and Ronald Neame was photographer. Then I went on to work on *In Which We Serve*, which was David's first directorial effort, with Noël Coward and Ronnie again as director of photography. I was camera operator. I then did *This Happy Breed* and *Escape to Danger* (directed by Lance Comfort and photographed by Mutz Greenbaum) as camera operator. I remember Lance Comfort was very keen on directing with a wide-angle lens, a 28 or something like that.

My first picture as director of photography was *The Way Ahead*, directed by Carol Reed. There was a good deal of luck attached to that. At the time I was operating for Ronnie and David on *This Happy Breed*, and Carol Reed was preparing *The Way Ahead*. We were all having lunch one day at Denham Studios, when Carol drifted by and said to David, 'I'm stuck, I can't find a cameraman.' David very nicely said, 'Why don't you use Guy?' Carol said, 'Do you think he can do it?', to which David replied, 'Of course he can do it.' So there I was as DoP for Carol Reed.

How far did the semi-documentary technique of *The Way Ahead* influence your strategies as DoP?

I think documentary techniques would influence the director more than they would the cameraman. I remember we went down to the training ground at Aldershot and put the actors in the training squad with the sergeant major; they went through the whole bit. Then we went off to North Africa (dear old Stanley Haynes was in charge of that job until Carol joined us). That was a great experience; we were looked after by the Scots Guards while we were there. I'll never forget Raymond Huntley on that film, he was marvellous.

What did you do as second-unit cameraman on *The Way to the Stars*?

I was responsible for the flying stuff, the stuff at the aerodrome. Derek Williams was the cameraman in charge, he did the interiors, etc.

I'd like to know anything you recall about your Oscar-winning work on *Great Expectations*.

It's done me an awful lot of good, really. People often deride the Oscars, but when you have one you become important! It is still respected. The film was a wonderful experience, with John Bryan as set designer and David as director. It was a great opportunity to do interesting work – and be given time to do it. I was a bit involved in early discussions with John and David about the 'look' of the film, but not to any great extent. I went through that process with the two Disney films we did here [*Robin Hood* and *Rob Roy*]; we went to great lengths to create storyboards and to discuss the set-ups with the producer. I don't like doing that, though, I think it gets you constipated! It becomes mechanical, somehow. I do my own storyboards, of course, but not with a committee.

Were the early scenes, with Pip on the marshes, all done on location?

Not much of them; a few shots like Pip running along the edge of the marshes were exterior. But all the important shots – like the church and the graveyard – were all done on the stage, as were the shots when Pip first comes in contact with the convict. And the early morning when he takes the pork pie, with the cows, that was studio. There was some exterior work near the end where they're trying to save Magwitch, but the sequence with the paddle wheel was done in the tank at Pinewood Studios. Finlay Currie himself was actually in the water for some of it, rather than a stuntman.

Did you work closely with Jack Harris, the editor?

You see, David was a marvellous editor anyway. The famous scene where the little boy gets up from the grave and starts to run off when he's grabbed by the convict was well thought out. David engineered it by the cuts he was going to do, and when we went to the preview he said to me, 'Let's see if this works.' And it did! It was the first time I had seen that trick done and the audience nearly came out of their seats!

Did you have quite clear ideas on how you wanted to light the various, very different settings – like Miss Havisham's house?

It was largely dictated by light sources, by where the light was meant to be really coming from. I tried to follow that religiously. One example is when Estella comes to meet Pip when they are children; she has a candle and she takes him through the house and up the stairs. It took me a whole day to arrange the lighting of that. It was a tracking shot and I tried to imitate what a candle would do all the way along. I did it by rehearsing a squad of electricians with dimmers and so on. It was great fun to do and I was allowed to take my time to do it. I can't remember whether we used a crane or not. Yes, it was a wonderful experience – and so was *Oliver Twist*. I have a feeling that my work on *Oliver* was a little more sophisticated, in fact, than on *Great Expectations*.

***Oliver Twist* is a beautiful film to look at; some of the photography is almost romantic, such as that opening scene with Oliver's mother struggling along the hill to the workhouse. How much was this your wish?**

I thought it was a bit better job than *Great Expectations*; I think the photography was a little more subtle. It's funny you mention that scene and the word 'romantic'. It was almost the first day's shooting; I had set up a very elaborate series of cloud glasses in the roof of the studio that moved in front of arcs, in order to get this idea of the clouds coming across the moonlit hillside. There was a lamp in the foreground in order to throw shadows

on the mother. I was quite pleased at the end of the rushes, but David turned to me with a scowl and said, 'We're going to have to redo all this.' I asked why, because I had thought it was rather good. He said, 'It's too romantic. I want it rougher and harder.' So we had to go back and redo the whole thing! What the director wants is what happens; we're all instruments of getting his idea across. I think his point was that, at the beginning of the story, where the woman is in labour, it shouldn't look romantic.

In between those two films, you shared the photography credit with Geoffrey Unsworth on *Blanche Fury*. What did the shared credit mean in practice?

Not much; he did very little. He did some snow scenes at the big house, but I did all of the interiors. I'm quite pleased with the film, which was my first colour film. People told me you had to have lots of light with Technicolor but I didn't like so much light, so I treated it more or less the same way as I would a black-and-white picture except that, of course, I had to use a bit more light. However, I still kept the same sort of contrast that I liked. People said if I did that the shadows would all go red, but they didn't. Technically it was a marvellous job and I think it looked bloody good! John Bryan, again, did the set design. I suppose it's a bit of a melodrama and at the time an 'unhappy' ending wasn't very popular. It was the only time an outside director (Marc Allegret) came in for a Cineguild film.

You shot two films which David Lean made with his then wife, Ann Todd, *The Passionate Friends* and *Madeleine*. Did you find her easy to light, because she looks very beautiful in them?

I don't say it was particularly easy but I found the kind of light that suited her and, contrary to my usual practice of sticking to the realistic look, I would fit the lighting of the set around the lights that suited her. That made David happy and it made her happy. She functioned very well in the same sort of light that Marlene Dietrich did, that kind of right-height light above head level, at about forty-five degrees, more or less front. It was not very realistic, but it worked.

The Passionate Friends had a strange history. Ronnie Neame started as director of the film and for some reason David took over as director and Ronnie produced it; it stemmed out of some indecision about the script, I think, which influenced the whole production.

As a cameraman, did you have a preference for intimate sequences or big set-pieces?

I prefer intimate scenes and I like interiors, where you have control over them. It is much more interesting working in a studio than on location.

Are some actors easier to photograph than others, in your experience?

I've thought about that and it's interesting. One of the easiest actors I've ever had to photograph was Gregory Peck, and it didn't matter where you put the light on him, he'd look good. One thing it has to do with is having a very small nose; big noses are a problem because they cast shadows.

Your first film as director, *River Beat*, is praised as a superior supporting film. It's the kind of modest film no director would have the chance to start on any more.

No, that's right. Its producer was Victor Hanbury, but what led to me being involved was a man called Julian Wintle, who had some association with the group that made these second features. He was a producer at Pinewood and he was also a partner in Insignia, the production company. They used to bring over American stars and put a small picture together with a low budget and so many days' shooting. I was given that picture to see how I coped with directing.

Any film is a tremendous gamble, so I think I was lucky to be able to cut my teeth on a small film, make my mistakes and not carry a huge load of responsibility. The American stars' names were well-enough known to guarantee some sort of American distribution. Phyllis Kirk was an up-and-coming actress who never became a major star, but she was a very bright, nice girl, whom I was lucky to have. I suppose today's equivalent of that film would be a television 'movie of the week' for a new director. I remember the film had to run seventy minutes, or something, and the script was about ten minutes short of what I needed, so I filled in with this chase down the river, the police chasing someone in a boat.

What sort of working relationships did you have with the well-known cameramen on your '50s films: Wilkie Cooper, Harry Waxman, Arthur Ibbetson and Douglas Slocombe?

It always makes a difference who the cameraman is, but it depends who you can get, of course. Wilkie did a couple of pictures for me, mostly exteriors,

and it worked well; they were very good. Dougie did *The Mark* and Arthur did *The Angry Silence*. Arthur used to be my assistant at one time. They were all more than competent, so the relationship was largely a matter of your personalities; I got on very well with all of them. Harry was a dear man; he and an art director called Vetchinsky on *House of Secrets* were a funny pair.

You made one of the better '50s war films, *Sea of Sand*. Why do you suppose there were so many war films made a decade after the war?

You may remember films like *Journey's End* which became very popular ten years after the end of the First World War. Robert Westerby wrote the script of *Sea of Sand* and I enjoyed it. They wanted to shoot it in the studio with a pile of sand, but I said I didn't think I could do that, so we shot it in Libya at a time when the king still held sway.

It was while we were making *Sea of Sand* that Michael Craig and Richard Attenborough and I talked about making *The Angry Silence*, which Michael wrote for himself. Eventually Dickie got it going through the Boultings for British Lion, but on the condition that Dickie played the lead – to which Michael gave in very gracefully. (I don't believe Michael ever got enough credit for that film.) British Lion wouldn't pay us any money for *The Angry Silence* but we were all so keen on it and it was very good for all of us. It's a little dated now, but it is superbly acted.

There were a lot of techniques in it that were new: the transitions from one scene to another, for instance. There is a scene with Dickie in his young son's bedroom, when the boy has been told that his father is a scab; we cut to a close-up of Dick being shocked by this, then pull back from the close-up and he is in the canteen, reacting to all the noises around him. There are no mechanical devices, just a straight cut, and people weren't used to that kind of thing in those days. We did another nice sequence of a newspaper landing on someone's desk; they look at it and then you pull back from the insert and find you are somewhere else. There were quite a number of those kinds of things in it that were new and rather neat.

It always seems a master stroke to me to have Pier Angeli as the wife; it emphasises Tom Curtis's apartness.

Yes, that was good fortune. We had done a pretty indifferent picture called *SOS Pacific* and it was the same set-up, bringing in a name from America. It was shot in the Canary Islands and Pier was in it; she was very good and we all liked her very much, so we discussed how we could bring her in to *The Angry Silence*. We decided it didn't matter that she was Italian, and she was wonderful in it.

There was a lot of fuss from the unions about the film, threatening to ban it, even though they'd not seen it. I don't think I'd feel any different today about the issues it raised; those issues still remain – a man's right not to be pushed around because other people don't agree with him – and it is as much about that as it is about unions.

You did three melodramas at about this time, including *The Snorkel*, which I particularly liked.

Yes, I liked *The Snorkel* too. It didn't exactly set the Thames on fire but I thought it rather neat. It was Jimmy Sangster's script. Peter van Eyck was perhaps not a big enough star to carry it but he was good; Mandy Miller was perhaps a bit too old for it.

Your next film was *The Mark*. Did you seek that one out?

I was offered it, read the script and said I'd do it without question. I loved the script, which was by Sidney Buchman, who became a dear friend of mine. He had been a scriptwriter for Frank Capra for a number of years but he was one of Hollywood's 'undesirables'. The newspapers were fairly rough with the film. The *Daily Express* came out with this stuff about 'Father of two supports child molesting' – the 'father of two' being me. That was in their first edition but they pulled it out of the later editions. They made some rather nasty comments about it but I think it's a warm, human picture. It didn't run into any censorship problems, in spite of the press.

From 1962 on, from *Diamond Head*, most of your films were American productions. Was this a matter of choice?

Well, that's where the jobs were. And the Americans were still ready to put up the money for a movie they wanted to do. It was a case of 'We're going to make this movie: do you want to direct it?' 'Yes.' 'OK, you start Monday.' There is nothing like that now, not even in America.

Peter Greenaway

b. 1942

Director (cinema films only): *A Walk Through H, *Vertical Features Remake (1978), The Falls (1980), The Draughtsman's Contract (1982), A Zed and Two Noughts (1986), The Belly of an Architect (1987), Drowning by Numbers (1988), The*

Cook, the Thief, his Wife and her Lover (1989), Prospero's Books (1991), The Baby of Macon (1993), Stairs 1 Geneva (doc) (1995), The Pillow Book (1996), Lumière and Company (1997)
* Short film.

One of the most remarkable aspects of Peter Greenaway's career is simply that he has been able to keep making films which seem to offer no concession to the usual demands of popular cinema. He has been fortunate in having a producer who is uncommonly gifted in raising finance from all over the place, and that he is able to make films for modest budgets in a climate of obscene expenditure. However, 'industrial' reasons such as these can't account for the continued popularity of films which, by the standards of the mainstream, are esoteric in the extreme. We are talking about films which deliberately confound genre expectations (*The Draughtsman's Contract*), play games with numbers and other sign systems (*Drowning by Numbers, Prospero's Books*), explore the phenomenon of twinship (*A Zed and Two Noughts*), invoke Jacobean revenge tragedy (*The Cook, the Thief, his Wife and her Lover*) and the medieval miracle play (*The Baby of Macon*), and, in general, which shock and disorient without offering anywhere for the mind or the eye to rest. It is art-house popularity, of course, but a very substantial one, and it is heartening evidence that filmgoers are ready to think if required to do so.

Interview dates: January 1990 and July 1994

You make art-house films that everyone wants to see. There seems to be an anomaly there.

I wish I could totally believe in that statement because we have just made a movie called *The Baby of Macon* which has pushed the patience and the provocation level so far that fewer and fewer people are going to see it. However, I would certainly stand by the film and believe that in some senses it is the most complete film I've made – and there are still sufficient numbers of people around, I hope, who want to see it and producers and financiers who are interested in what I do. So, with some optimism, we have two more films in the pipeline.

Over the last decade you have been able to film steadily, and with commercial success, though you don't set out to woo the public.

I think we ought to be careful about 'commercial success' though, because after all it's been quite modest. For me, the success has been the continuity. I think we've made at least one film about every fourteen months for the last fifteen years, so on the whole that's not too bad and we've now made fifty films, including all the television and the other experimental work, not just the feature films. We've made seven feature films and I've just come back from Hong Kong where we are about to prepare the eighth.

How did you come to make the transition from being an artist to being a filmmaker?

I still don't really feel that I'm a filmmaker. I certainly make films, but I still think that my primary discipline has much more to do with

painting, the aesthetics and the vocabulary of painting, and I certainly feel happier talking about painting than I do about cinema. I think the first hundred years have been a sort of prologue which has been very much illustrative of other art forms – literature, theatre and painting. I still believe that most cinema is either a form of recorded drama, which is probably better expressed in the theatre, or some form of illustrated novel, which is probably better as literature. So there is a way in which all filmmakers are operating in an eclectic, mongrel medium.

Yet it is narrative which has made it famous.

I think that cinema took the wrong turning, in much the same way as Roman Catholicism took the wrong turning when it adopted Virgin Birth – unnecessary, and now we are stuck with it. And people believe that cinema should be a narrative medium. I suppose the Lumières just got away with it by making statements about the visual world rather than going into complex narratives, but I think, from Griffith onward, the die was cast. I say that because I come from painting and I believe that the best means of visual expression is not to tell stories but to make some form of singular visual statement about the world and all that is in it. Of course, film travels through time and therefore must involve sequence, but sequence is not necessarily narrative. So I think you'll find, not only with the feature films but also the more experimental television work I've been involved with, that they are, in some senses, very much concerned with the idea of sequential activity but not necessarily particularly obsessed with the contemporary idea of the narrative psychodrama – the big psychological narrative of cause and effect, in which I am not, on the whole, particularly interested.

Were you surprised at the commercial success of *The Draughtsman's Contract*? It seemed to me like a very original mixture of Restoration and Jacobean genres and Agatha Christie.

It was a surprise to our financiers, our producers, our actors and certainly to me. I'd made some fifteen films before that and in some senses I thought I was making yet another of those slightly obsessive, numerically conscious, self-consciously artificial films like all the others. But I think for me it came at the right time. I agree with your comments about the Restoration, Jacobean and Christie elements. But I do remember a very irate *Daily Telegraph* critic saying it was absolutely impossible to combine Restoration tragedy and Restoration comedy – but English critics tend to be purist. When *Prospero's Books*, a version of *The Tempest*, came out, many said there was much too much Greenaway in it and not enough Shakespeare; I have always had a problematic relationship with English critics.

Did you like that kind of country-house, murder-mystery element about it?

It comes from a long tradition, certainly throughout twentieth-century English fiction. The traditional vocabulary itself makes it attractive, but I deliberately disturbed the situation. It is a characteristic of detective drama to have a coda where the detective and the witnesses get together to discuss what happened; I didn't permit that to happen, I leave a question mark at the end, but I think the circumstances of the detective genre are satisfied. I suppose the nearest parallel to the solution would be *Murder on the Orient Express*, where everybody is responsible.

Were you also aware that you were bombarding your audience in a way that it wasn't used to?

Perhaps I've always done that. Trained as a painter, having an academic turn of mind, being scholastic by inclination, I am interested in the multi-layered work. *The Draughtsman's Contract*, although it can be appreciated as an Agatha Christie story, and although it's a deliberately artificial historical drama (people wear over-elaborate costumes, speak very artificial dialogue), it can also, if

you permit it, debate fruit symbolism at the end of the seventeenth century; discuss the relationships between late seventeenth-century Catholics and Protestants *vis-à-vis* their servants; consider architecture inside the seventeenth-century house being a mirror to the gardens; compare the garden as seen by French Catholics and German and Dutch Protestants. If you aren't interested in the layers of enriching material, you need not let them interfere with your more orthodox enjoyments.

I've always loved British cinema, but I wouldn't call it a cinema of ideas.

I've always looked toward the European continent for cinematic excitement; one couldn't look to America for a cinema of ideas. Americans tell good stories extremely well, they are great professionals, but on the whole they tend to stay away from multiple-meaning projects; they are interested in a literal, straightforward narrative; they are not particularly excited by ideas of English irony; nor are they very interested, generally, in metaphor.

I suppose I have taken all these sorts of concepts very much from nineteenth-century literature, early twentieth-century theatre, middle-twentieth-century European cinema. When I first started thinking seriously about cinema, Europe was full of the most extraordinary 'ideas' people – post-*Nouvelle Vague*, all the middle-period Italians – by and large that doesn't exist any more. I came of age to be influenced by the English '60s generation, which experienced a great sense of freedom, a sense that anything was possible. I suppose, like many of my generation, I was receptive, eclectic in some senses, trying to use all this information and refashion it.

How do you account for your continued capacity to go on setting up films? Do you rely a lot on your producer, Kees Kesander, for this?

The Draughtsman's Contract was funded by the British Film Institute, and produced by Peter Sainsbury, who has now settled in Australia. *The Belly of an Architect* had an English producer. But a great many projects since those films have been produced by Kees Kesander, who has, for the last ten years, provided the essential balance and foil; he is very capable of financing difficult projects. Every credit for the continuity must go to him.

You also seem to have been involved in intricate co-production deals with several production companies, including Film Four.

Well, the budgets are small. Each movie was made for between one and two million pounds –

even the last one, *The Baby of Macon*, which looks pretty luscious, has come in at £2 million and *Prospero's Books*, which has some rather extraordinary actors in it, cost about the same. Kees Kesander has the ability to take small sums of money from lots of disparate sources, so that nobody is desperately out of pocket if the film doesn't succeed. Every movie we've made has recovered its costs – in most cases recovered its costs before we turned the film in the camera, because most of the financing was to do with pre-production deals of one sort or another. Nobody is getting rich, but we're OK with the finance brokers for the present.

In my view, *A Zed and Two Noughts* and *Drowning by Numbers* are your two most difficult – even bizarre – films. How do you feel about them?

A Zed and Two Noughts is the one film I would like to make again, for one thing because it was so outrageously ambitious. There are three films there, all struggling to be synthesised with one another – a film about the world as an ark and our responsibility to the animal kingdom, which, I suppose, is an ecological treatise; there is the film, which I suppose is much more abstract, of the idea of twoness, which rests upon the notion that we are all born as twins and, if we don't manage to come out of the womb with our twin, we spend the rest of our lives searching for the lost partner, and in the end most of us have to make do with a stranger. The third film is more academic, about the Dutch painter Vermeer. Godard suggested that Vermeer was the first true cinematographer – even though we're talking about the 1650s. Vermeer is the first true arch-realist in terms of European painting and he certainly used a camera obscura, working in Delft about the time when the first lenses were being ground. For me, cinema begins with Vermeer, which may sound bizarre in some senses because he was dealing with still images, but he was concerned with the real world photographically-seen and getting everything studiously correct whilst encapsulating and perfecting a metaphysical and moral subjectivity. If you look at a Vermeer reproduced in black-and-white, it can look like a Cartier-Bresson photograph. Godard suggested that Vermeer was valid as a cinematographer because of his interest in light, and the frozen moment – and these two characteristics are a definition of cinema.

How did you see the use of numbers 1 to 100 in *Drowning by Numbers* as unifying the film?

I've always been suspicious of narrative in cinema; constructed narrative is primarily a characteristic of literature. I've often tried to use what I've learned from painting and in the 1960s and '70s a great many people felt antagonistic – and why not? – towards the Hollywood narrative tradition, which is basically organised as a star system, enslaved to telling stories, a vehicle which supports formula psycho-narrative, and therefore is an actor's kingdom. Two of the things that many filmmakers, certainly in Europe and North America, were concerned about were, firstly, to see if it was possible to make a non-narrative cinema, to acknowledge sequence certainly, but to abjure or minimise narrative; and, secondly, to try and limit the vested-interest traditions of the star system.

To a certain extent, for me the second of those problems is ameliorated by the fact that most actors in this country have a status relative to their training in the theatre, essentially as excellent craftsmen. The first of the problems interests me more, which is to say that if you are prepared to throw narrative away you have to find some other system to hold things together. I've used the alphabet, numerical systems, colour-coding, scientific theory, ideas about counting and numerology, and elaborate cabala-like systems which are certainly part and parcel of a long painting history and tradition. But also, on a simplistic level, in *Drowning by Numbers*, although I've acknowledged the narrative, there is a simple number count that relates to a notion of fatalism. If narrative in this film indicates free choice, then the number indicates boundaries, the edge that cannot be overstepped.

What would you say to the idea that *The Belly of an Architect* is your most humanly accessible film so far?

I understand why that question was asked and in part would agree. I think people are seduced, however, by the fact that we have an American actor behaving in a very conventional, psycho-dramatic narrative which, now that Hollywood movies rule the world, is very familiar. It is, of course, a way in to the layering of ideas of the film through the engaging personality of Brian Dennehy. I wanted to portray a large, naïve, bewildered but sympathetic American, and I think we found the right, highly intuitive actor, Hollywood-trained. Most of the actors I've worked with in an English context have tended to be much more cautious perhaps, but much more experienced in some peculiar way to do with the artifice of the cinema, which is what I am interested in.

Do you give your actors much direction?

Well, I say, 'The camera's not going to look at you if you go over there and, if you look out of that window, forget it, you won't be seen.' I'm often creating a classic theatre-proscenium situation. For me, acting circumstances are often determined by the organisation of cinematic pictorial space – an allegiance to painting. Actors often require different sorts of encouragement. The very experienced ones like Helen Mirren read the script, understand what's wanted and off they go. Perhaps some of the younger ones do need a degree of cajoling and organising, maybe some over-telling. What's extremely important is the casting and that is my responsibility. I've made some bad mistakes, of course.

How did you feel *The Cook, the Thief, his Wife and her Lover* compares, in narrative difficulty, with your earlier films?

This is still very much a Greenaway film: the same sort of metaphorical language, the same sort of exterior characteristics, which make you feel you're always only watching a film. It's not a slice of life, not a window on the world; it is an artefact, artificially constructed. But what has happened is that I have allowed a much stronger emotional use of the content in terms of the melodrama, the acting, the violence and the sexual passion. I have allowed these to well up through the other concerns to make a film which a lot of people have found contacts them in the traditional Hollywood fashion. It's also an angry film. The 1980s political situation that existed in Britain was one of such extreme self-interest and greed, and there is a way in which *The Cook, the Thief* is a parody of a consumer society, personified in the Thief, Albert Spica. He has no redeeming features, and is consumed by self-interest and greed.

There is a contrast between, on the one hand, the sheer beauties of music, colour, lighting and composition, and, on the other, the ferocious ugliness of much of the story.

There is a medieval-like feeling in *The Cook, the Thief, his Wife and her Lover* of a rotten, worm-infested body which is covered in a gloss of elaborate clothing, smart manners, expensive tastes, food excesses, as though there is an attempt to try and hide the horror, the despair, the sense of violence and lust that's contained only just underneath. The title itself indicates a Chaucerian medi-

eval parable or fable, as does the very moral ending. And the four characters are set up to be easily representative of certain vices and certain virtues. There's also the way in which colour-coding is used to draw attention to the artificiality of the subject. The film opens with curtains and closes with curtains, as if saying, 'You are about to watch a performance – watch out for the artifices, the performances, the tricks and treats.' I would like to feel *The Cook, the Thief* is very much in the European tradition, which relates to Buñuel and Pasolini, of films which try deliberately, and I hope not merely sensationally, to be provocative, in order to stir up sensibilities about areas which need to be aired.

My personal favourite is *Prospero's Books* but it made me think we shouldn't expect to get everything from a film in one viewing.

Cecil B de Mille once said that, if you don't get everything in one viewing, the film's a failure. That has to be nonsense. It is essential that we read poetry and listen to music many times in order to get all the meanings and possibilities. So why can't we imagine a cinema which will allow us repeated viewings, getting something new from a film each time we see it?

There is a great deal of sheer visual wizardry in the film. How far is this the work of your director of photography, Sacha Vierny?

Sacha, my cinematographer, is my most important collaborator. I'm told the average Hollywood photographer would need two days and a large lighting budget for some of the scenes in *Prospero's Books*; Sacha, however, does it extremely economically and very quickly, which is important because we're only allowed about eight weeks' shooting. He is very modest and retiring, and would certainly shun any sort of noisy public celebration. He puts an enormous amount of imagination and excitement into his work, but quietly. In *Prospero's Books*, I hope we have begun to put one toe into the huge ocean of all the possibilities of a new cinema. *The Tempest* is built around Prospero but it is a fable; it makes no attempt at all to try and organise a cause-and-effect psychodrama narrative. We tried to make a correspondence between Shakespeare as the man, Prospero as the fiction and Gielgud as the actor, to make them one person, and construct an illumination of the Shakespearian text through this composite.

It does, however, continually push one back to the play. Did you want it to do that?

The Tempest is a great classic text and full of infinite meanings that a conventional rendering often underplays. I admire the play enormously and have done so since I was obliged to study it as an adolescent; it has haunted me ever since. Gielgud himself has played the part four times in his long life and he wanted to do it on film. We came together over a television series of another great classic, *Dante's Inferno*. It was a golden opportunity to make my favourite Shakespeare play along with a great actor who wished to put his own personal interpretation of the character on celluloid. I think Gielgud, in making the film, was acknowledging a good performance from himself. For me the Gielgud performance was a still centre around which everything revolves. I think there is every legitimacy in the original text to allow us to do that. Just as it was Shakespeare's swansong, so it was virtually Gielgud's goodbye to the theatre, to the theatricality of putting on costumes and make-up, all the sawdust and tinsel. So there were lots of interesting correspondences which we tried to milk very hard in that film.

As to the actual compositional technique, it was conceived initially as three films in one, using the ideas of background, foreground and middle ground – or, if you take painting, of landscape, portrait and still life. Cinema is very bad at simultaneity of action – you can't do two things at once in cinema very successfully. Simultaneity of action is done very well in painting, particularly medieval painting, and it is very common in the theatre, and I wanted to see if it could be possible at all in the cinema. It was also made as it is in response to the huge number of ideas that are rushing through the original Shakespearian text, which is working on so many different levels. I think that in *Prospero's Books* we have managed to achieve possibly fifty per cent of the ideas contained in this extraordinary work written in 1611, nearly four hundred years ago and still valid.

There is a marvellously affecting moment in *Prospero's Books* where it is as though Prospero suddenly has an access of forgiveness – it takes place on some stairs that suddenly appear outside the portico. Did you think it a crucial moment?

The moment of reconciliation. Perhaps Shakespeare, as a playwright and as a man, felt it necessary to make some sort of ending deeply relevant to himself, as he was about to give up the theatre and retire to Stratford, to tie all the loose ends together, to reconcile and bring all the disparate parts together. Perhaps for him it was a very autobiographical gesture.

Did John Gielgud, as an already famous Prospero, have any qualms about appearing in so idiosyncratic a reading of the text?

We were working together on the television version of *Dante's Inferno*, when he first expressed interest in the possibility of us working together on a version of *The Tempest*. I produced the first four or five scenes of *The Tempest*, in all their multiple detail, very quickly and sent them off to him. I thought, 'If he doesn't like this, I don't want to make the film without him, so we ought not to waste his time or mine.' However, he was ecstatic about it and he telephoned me virtually the same evening, having read those scenes very rapidly, to express his enthusiasm.

Did you conceive of Caliban as some kind of primal force? He looks different from anybody else in the film.

A single disturbing line in the play reports that Caliban attempted to rape Miranda, making him a dangerous, sexually problematic character. The dancer, Michael Clark, has always had a high profile for sexual danger. He is a brilliant dancer and I always wanted to work with him to see what would happen in terms of a filmic performance. Caliban is given some of the most beautiful lines in the play. He is not all ugliness, nor is he Satan incarnate. Innumerable stage performances of Caliban have made him into an animal grotesque or a victim of colonialism, and I don't think that necessarily serves the role in total.

Did you have difficulties with the play as a text?

There are two things about *The Tempest* with which I had some anxieties. One was that the only female character, Miranda, is treated in that way which we object to so much in contemporary cinema. She is the catalyst for male behaviour; she is there to provide an emotional and sexual lure for Ferdinand; in some ways, she is merely a mouthpiece to forward dynastic ambition. I had difficulty with that because there is always a considerable concern that the females in my films should be important protagonists, on an equal dramatic, organising level with their male counterparts; yet here we have a woman who fulfils the tedious stereotype of being an object rather than a subject.

The second problem I had was the notion that Shakespeare, through Prospero, apparently wishes to condone the idea of destroying books and destroying knowledge. It actually says in the play that the books were drowned, but we employed combustion on the water surface as well, as if to remind people about the destruction of knowledge through the burning of books, which has been so dramatic an event in this century – the Nazis burning books; the Ku Klux Klan burning books; in Bradford, England, not so long ago, Salman Rushdie's *Satanic Verses* being burned in the street by Islamic fundamentalists. My intention was to suggest that, if we are indeed going to destroy knowledge, we'd better be pretty certain about the huge responsibility of doing so. Better still, don't burn books. It is the way to iconoclasm.

There is a prodigious amount of nudity on display in this film and I wondered what point you wanted to make with that.

In general terms, in this and in other films, I wanted to stress we're all physical, we come in all shapes and sizes, in all physical guises; there is a way that I believe our physicality should be represented. The nude is the core image of Western painting, can it be the core image of Western cinema? Again, I suppose, it is in opposition to that phenomenon of Hollywood cinema where, if anyone takes their clothes off, they are probably female and probably aged between sixteen and thirty – sexual and sexist stereotyping again. A scholar who had accumulated a large amount of knowledge – as Prospero surely must and as Shakespeare surely must – would, in a visual sense, have taken much of it from the classical pictorial imagination, through Ovid and the Renaissance scholars (*The Tempest* was written in 1611), and I wanted, as it were, to repopulate the island on which Prospero had arrived through the characters of his mental universe. It would have been a classical Humanist universe, and in the classical ideal people don't wear clothes, which avoids fashion, and theoretically is timeless. So we presented the human body in some naked form, as a nod towards the Garden of Eden on a paradisal island seen through classical-world eyes.

Where did the idea for *The Baby of Macon* come from, and where did you film it?

The film was shot in Germany and Holland. We had considerable finance from West Germany, and with film finance you are often obliged to spend the money where it is given, so we shot half the film in a studio we fashioned from an ice-skating rink just outside Cologne, in Troyesdorf in Westphalia. The origin of the film's intention was to debate child exploitation in several interconnected ways. It has been a common journalistic subject now, debated and argued in Western newspapers and media but always hedged about with prurience and some hysteria.

The initial impetus for *The Baby of Macon* was the infamous Benetton poster. You may remember the excitement about five or six years ago about the poster, in which a newborn child was presented as an advertisement for a clothing manufacturer, on thirty-metre-wide hoardings throughout Europe. The furore was so great in England that all the images had to be taken down. I was curious about the sensitivities that the poster generated, not the presentation of this image, which, after all, only represents an event we all can claim as our own, that most of us have witnessed as parents, whose significance can be fascinating, in an overpopulated world that still considers innocence valuable.

There is no debate about sexual exploitation of children in this film, but there is a way in which the child is debated on, as a possible phenomenon for self-advancement. The Church uses him in order to sell miracles, the family use him in order to better their position, so that the innocent child becomes a shuttlecock in a war between the individual and the Church. I suppose it is related historically to the Nativity – the child is exploited for purposes to satisfy Roman Catholic theology and Roman Catholic imagery; we have seen constant images of the Christ-child for two thousand years in European iconography in one form or another. I wanted to explore this iconography and repeat it, homage it, indicate where it had come from, what its associations were with real life. I was interested in the miracle play. I also wanted to talk about the art form of the Baroque (both with a capital 'B' and a small 'b'), because I think the seventeenth century was the first time that art was used as full-scale propaganda for the suspension of disbelief. The cinema demands a great suspension of disbelief, and uses everything that it can – costume, colour, sound, music, light, illusion – it would use incense if it could – it uses everything that the seventeenth-century Baroque used. In the case of the Baroque, it was used for the suspension of disbelief as regards faith, unreason, the Roman Catholic supremacy, whereas cinema today uses the suspension of disbelief in the propaganda of capitalism, tidy solutions to all problems, especially if the solution can be associated with notions of well-being related to money; financial well-being is intimately linked to spiritual wellbeing.

I have envisaged a trilogy of baroque movies. *Prospero's Books* is about the uses and abuses of knowledge; *The Baby of Macon* is about uses and abuses of religion; and the third – 'Augsbergenfeldt', which I hope to make very soon – is to be about the uses and abuses of the power to wage war, to seek a military solution to problems.

In the meantime, our more regular financiers, which tend to be Central European television, suggest that we ought to do something else first to allow some breathing-space, from the excesses that were expressed in *The Baby of Macon* and will continue in the third film of the trilogy. So we are off to China and Hong Kong to make a film which I

hope will fill that gap. It is called *The Pillow Book* and the cast is entirely Japanese and Chinese. It is very much about the tradition of text and calligraphy. One of the fascinations for me about *Prospero's Books* was the act of Shakespeare writing his play. There is a great tradition of calligraphy in the Orient that is still very much alive – the physical act of writing a text is still relevant. To me there are two areas of human experience which can always offer satisfaction: one is the delights of the flesh; the other is literature. I want to bring these two things, flesh and literature, together and the central figure of this film is a woman who likes her lovers to write on her body.

Graham Greene

1904–1991

Screenwriter: *Twenty-One Days* (co-sc), *The Future's in the Air* (short, commentary) *(1937)*, *The New Britain* (short, commentary) *(1940)*, **Brighton Rock* (co-sc) *(1947)*, **The Fallen Idol (1948)*, **The Third Man (1949)*, *Saint Joan (1957)*, **Our Man in Havana (1959)*, **The Comedians (1967)*

Other films adapted from his work: *Orient Express (1934)*, *The Green Cockatoo (1937)*, *This Gun For Hire*, *Went the Day Well? (1942)*, *The*

Ministry of Fear (1944), *Confidential Agent (1945)*, *The Man Within*, *The Fugitive (1947)*, *The Heart of the Matter*, *The Stranger's Hand* (co-pr) *(1953)*, *The End of the Affair (1955)*, *Across the Bridge*, *Short Cut to Hell (1957)*, *The Quiet American (1958)*, *England Made Me*, *Travels with My Aunt (1972)*, *The Human Factor (1980)*, *The Honorary Consul (1983)*

* From his own novel or story.

'I have somehow in the last years lost all my interest in films and I don't think I have seen one for the last nearly ten years,'[1] Graham Greene wrote in 1990 after correspondence in which he had earlier expressed himself 'ready' to give me an interview about his work in British cinema. As one commentator has noted: 'The movies have played a large part in Greene's life, perhaps a larger one than they have in the life of any other writer of his . . . stature.'[2]

His involvement was tripartite. First, as a critic: from 1935 to 1941, he wrote some of the most trenchant reviews in English, taking films seriously

in a way not common then. 'What I object to is the idea that it is the *critic's* business to assist films to fulfil a social function. The critic's business should be confined to the art,'[3] he wrote in 1936. He did not discern a lot of 'art' in British films of the 1930s, but praised the performances in *Rome Express*, the Crazy Gang's *The Frozen Limits*, which seemed to him 'the funniest English picture yet produced,'[4] and Carol Reed's *The Stars Look Down*; he was severe on 'country-house acting' and other affectations of gentility and inhibition. He reviewed films first for *The Spectator*, then for the short-lived *Night and Day*, which folded after Greene was accused of 'a gross outrage' on Shirley Temple in his review of *Wee Willie Winkie*. In the view of the prosecuting counsel, 'it was one of the most horrible libels that one could well imagine.'[5]

Second, as an adapted author, Greene can have few twentieth-century rivals: almost all of his novels have been brought to the screen. In a lecture at the National Film Theatre in London in 1984, he said, 'What I do find is that the American adaptations have been outstandingly bad,'[6] no doubt having in mind such botchings as John Ford's *The Fugitive* (based on *The Power and the Glory*), though it is not clear exactly what he means by 'bad' – as films, adaptations, or both. However, apart from those on which he worked himself, the English adaptations do not fare much better. *The Man Within* ('shockingly bad,'[7] Greene said), *The End of the Affair* (Van Johnson as a tormented Greene hero??), *Travels with My Aunt* (starring a mannered Maggie Smith), *The Human Factor* and *The Honorary Consul* are all miscalculations in varying degrees. On the other hand, George More O'Ferrall's *The Heart of the Matter*, Ken Annakin's *Across the Bridge* and Peter Duffell's *England Made Me* have a whiff of the master's famously seedy, angst-ridden world.

Third, and this is where his real importance for British cinema lies, he worked on the screenplays of several major films based on his own, perhaps significantly minor, works. 'From film-reviewing it was only a small step to script-writing,'[8] he later claimed. On *Brighton Rock*, he shared the credit with Terence Rattigan, but actually took over from him (see interviews with Richard Attenborough and Roy Boulting on this matter). Greene praised the film's ending, less harsh than the novel's, finding it clever in the way it allowed 'anyone who wanted a happy ending to feel they had had a happy ending.'[9] His collaboration with Alexander Korda (to whom he had given a hard time as a reviewer) and Carol Reed first produced *The Fallen Idol*, derived from Greene's novella, 'The Basement Room', dealing with a child's disillusionment with the adult world. Though Greene thought *The Fallen Idol* was 'a meaningless title for the original story,'[10] it became for him 'my favourite screen work because it is more a writer's film than a director's. *The Third Man* ... is mostly action with only sketched characters. It was fun doing, but there is more of the writer in *The Fallen Idol*.'[11] It is interesting to note that the famous ending to *The Third Man*, when Alida Valli walks straight past Joseph Cotten and

into film history, was not Greene's idea: 'One of the few major disputes between Carol Reed and myself concerned the ending, and he was proved triumphantly right. I held the view that an entertainment of this kind was too light an affair to carry the weight of an unhappy ending ... I had not given enough credit to the mastery of Reed's direction.'[12] When one thinks of the highest peaks of British filmmaking, these are two films that at once come to mind, as much for Greene's as for Reed's contribution.

Greene hovers magisterially over the literature –film connections in British cinema, and he sums up what he felt as the influence of the cinema on his work in these words: 'When I describe a scene ... I capture it with the moving eye of the cine-camera rather than with the photographer's eye – which leaves it frozen. In this precise domain I think the cinema has influenced me.'[13]

*

If Greene is the major literary figure associated with the British screen, there are others who should also be noted in the context of their writing for it. British cinema in the 1940s was much enriched by the screenplays of Noël Coward (most notably *In Which We Serve* and *Brief Encounter*, out of true as actor and writer in *The Astonished Heart*) and Terence Rattigan, whose harmonious relationship with Anthony Asquith produced such civilised entertainments as *Quiet Wedding*, *The Way to the Stars*, *The Winslow Boy* and *The Browning Version*, all happily marrying film and literature. Among novelists, Nigel Balchin wrote screenplays for *Fame is the Spur*, *Mine Own Executioner* (based on his own novel) and *The Man Who Never Was*; and Eric Ambler was responsible for *The October Man* and *A Night to Remember* (both for Roy Ward Baker), *The Passionate Friends*, *The Cruel Sea*, and many others. A generation later, the novelist Ruth Prawer Jhabvala is the continuing collaborator of the Merchant–Ivory team, most recently on *Howard's End* and *The Remains of the Day*; and the playwright Harold Pinter has contributed intelligent, edgy screenplays to such films as *The Servant*, *Accident* and *The Go-Between*, all for Joseph Losey, who claimed that he and Pinter shared interests in 'observation of characters, a very acute awareness of class dynamics and contradictions.'[14] The association of novelists and dramatists with particular directors has been a recurring and fruitful strain in British cinema, on the whole much more so than has been the case in Hollywood, where famous novelists wept drunkenly over their idle typewriters.

1 Letter to Brian McFarlane, 14 May 1990
2 Jack Edmund Nolan, 'Graham Greene's movies', *Films in Review*, January 1964, p 23
3 'Is it criticism?', *Sight and Sound*, Autumn 1936, p 64
4 Graham Greene, *The Pleasure Dome*, Secker & Warburg, London, 1972, p 232
5 David Parkinson (ed), *The Graham Greene Film Reader: Mornings in the Dark*, Carcanet, Manchester, 1993, p 450. An account of the trial is given here.
6 The *Guardian*, reprinted in the *Sydney Morning Herald*, 8 September 1984, p 40
7 Parkinson, p 549
8 Introduction to Greene, *The Pleasure Dome*, p 2
9 Quentin Falk, *Travels in Greeneland*, Quartet Books, London, 1984, p 63
10 Nicholas Wapshott, *The Man Between: A Biography of Carol Reed*, Chatto & Windus, London, 1990, p 197
11 Parkinson, p 525
12 Graham Greene, *Ways of Escape*, Bodley Head, London, 1980, p 124
13 David Thomson, 'Greene in the dark', *Film Comment*, July–August 1991, p 19
14 Michel Ciment, *Conversations with Losey*, Methuen, London, 1985, p 242

Joan Greenwood
1921–1987

Actor: *John Smith Wakes Up* (1940), *My Wife's Family, He Found a Star* (1941), *The Gentle Sex* (1943), *They Knew Mr Knight, Latin Quarter* (1945), *A Girl in a Million* (1946), *The Man Within, The October Man, The White Unicorn* (1947), *Saraband For Dead Lovers* (1948), *The Bad Lord Byron, Whisky Galore!, Kind Hearts and Coronets* (1949), *Mr Peek-A-Boo* (1950), *Flesh and Blood, Young Wives' Tale, The Man in the White Suit, The Importance of Being Earnest* (1951), *Knave of Hearts, Father Brown* (1954), *Moonfleet* (1955), *Stage Struck* (1958), *Horse on Holiday* (voice only) (1959), *Mysterious Island* (1961), *The Amorous Prawn* (1962), *Tom Jones* (1963), *The Moon-Spinners* (1964), *Girl Stroke Boy* (1971), *The Uncanny, The Hound of the Baskervilles* (1977), *The Water Babies* (1978), *Little Dorrit* (1987)

'My films have all been unhappy ones, and I'm longing to do a comedy for a change,'[1] said Joan Greenwood in 1948, in what seems to have been her only interview. Happily for this most delectable of British stars, within little more than a year Ealing would have assuaged this longing with key roles in two of the sharpest comedies ever made in Britain, Alexander Mackendrick's *Whisky Galore!* and Robert Hamer's *Kind Hearts and Coronets*. It seems scarcely feasible that these two dazzlers were both released in June 1949 – or that Greenwood could have been so distinctively herself *and* so disparately convincing as she is in them.

Established as a West End actress, she had been in films since 1940, looking younger than her age

and claiming that 'it was beginning to have an awful effect of arrested development on me.'[2] She was the spoilt mummy's girl in Leslie Howard's *The First of the Few*, co-starred in Vernon Sewell's long-unseen Gothic, *Latin Quarter*, and was given her first comedy chance by Sydney Box as a literally dumb wife in *A Girl in a Million*. She suffered in *The White Unicorn* ('. . . she was poor and Margaret Lockwood was rich but they still had the same problems underneath'[3] – essentially the script, that is) and as the tragic Sophie Dorothea in *Saraband for Dead Lovers*.

But for dedicated Greenwood-watchers – and for a few years their name was surely legion – the key roles are the drily beguiling Peggy in *Whisky*

Galore!, the irresistibly minxish Sibella in *Kind Hearts*, the industrialist's daughter in *The Man in the White Suit*, set to deflect Alec Guinness from his purpose ('What could *I* do?' she asks disingenuously), Lady Warren in Hamer's *Father Brown*, and a perfect Gwendolen, Lady Bracknell's daughter to the life, in Asquith's *The Importance of Being Earnest*. Critics overuse words like 'delicious', but it is utterly true of her. 'I asked for bread-and-butter and you have given me *cake*,' she intones in tragic reprimand to Dorothy Tutin's Cecily in *Earnest*. Years later, Tutin recalled being later asked to play Gwendolen and saying, 'I can't do it; all I can hear is Joan Greenwood.'[4]

Her speaking of dialogue, as if 'she dimly suspected some hidden menace in it which she can't quite identify;'[5] the husky voice which is both seductive and iron-purposed; her way of 'always remaining serenely still except for the occasional flutter of her tiny hands'[6] – one can try to catalogue the qualities but not catch the uniqueness.

A happy marriage to actor André Morell seems to have extinguished the never-powerful flame of her ambition, but just before she died she gave a commanding character study as the hero's invalid mother in Christine Edzard's *Little Dorrit*. Her performance incited respect for itself and a poignant nostalgia for the exquisite precisions of earlier decades.

1 John K Newnham, 'Peter Pan grows up', *Picturegoer*, 3 January 1948, p 6
2 Newnham, p 6
3 David Shipman, *The Great Movie Stars: The International Years*, Angus & Robertson, London, 1972, p 196
4 Interview with Brian McFarlane, London 1994
5 Karel Reisz, quoted in *Sight and Sound*, Spring 1956, p 191
6 Elaine Dundy, *Finch, Bloody Finch* (first published 1980), Magnum, London, 1981, p 194

Richard Gregson

b. 1930

Few people have as comprehensive a view of British cinema during a crucial period of transition – from the mid '50s to the end of the '60s – as Richard Gregson. Though he has also filled the role of **producer** (*Downhill Racer*, in Hollywood) and **screenwriter** (he is co-author of the original story and screenplay for *The Angry Silence*), it is above all in his function of **agent** that he has acquired an insider's understanding of the workings of the industry. Beginning with a literary agency in the late '50s, he went on to become one of the most influential film and television agents in the exciting '60s. During that decade he represented such key figures as director John Schlesinger, producer Joe Janni, writer Frederic Raphael and actor Alan Bates. His knowledge of the cultural and economic ups and downs of what now seems like the last gasp of an active British film industry (even if, as he points out, it was largely funded by American opportunism) is probably unrivalled. Properly, he should make it the subject of a book rather than the interview material recorded here.

Interview dates: September 1989 and June 1994

How did you first become involved in the film business?

I started work for an agency called David Higham Associates. That came about because one of its directors, Paul Scott, who later became very famous for *The Raj Quartet*, came into the bookshop in Westminster where I was working and asked the owner if he knew someone who knew anything about the movie business. The owner pointed to me; I was interviewed and got a job with Higham. I worked there, opening a film and television department, for about eighteen months. That was in about 1958 or '59. My brother Michael [Craig] was already established as an actor, so I at least knew something about the industry.

Then I was headhunted, as it were, by a firm called John Redway & Associates. Redway at that time was one of the top agents; he had mostly acting clients but some directing clients, too. They were very successful and wanted to open a literary side, so they chose me. They also brought in Gareth Wigan, from MCA, and we then became the literary department. About eighteen months after that, we broke away from Redway's because we found them to be not that interested in the literary side. We formed our own agency, Gregson and Wigan, in 1961.

From then on Gareth and I operated as an independent agency up until about 1967/68, when we sold the agency to the Grade Organisation, which was bought by EMI six weeks later. For approximately seven years (1961–67), Gareth and I were able to develop an international agency. We had an office in New York and we spent a great deal of time in California, and began to take on American clients. When the Grade Organisation bought our agency they also bought three other agencies, which were merged together into an agency called London International. In 1968 London International opened its own office in Los Angeles and I was the head of that office.

What areas of the film industry did you represent as an agent?

I represented writers, directors and producers principally, but I also personally represented three actors – Alan Bates, Robert Redford and Natalie Wood. My main concern was with writers, directors and producers. For instance, I represented Freddie Raphael, Keith Waterhouse and Willis Hall, John Schlesinger, Bryan Forbes, Joe Janni, Ted Kotcheff (who started as a television director), David Deutsch the producer, among others. Later, with London International, there was a huge acting side.

Does an agent find work for clients, or does he essentially arrange terms after having been approached?

Well, you do both, but a good agent should be able to find work for his clients. The thing about an agent is that people come to you, so that you know what's going on. You talk to producers about projects they have: do they need a director or a writer? are they looking for something, a book, or whatever? Sometimes people would ring you up and ask if so-and-so were available. You might say *he*'s not available but have you thought of so-and-so? In a way you are a sort of clearing-house. Once you'd got the fish on the line, you'd negotiate a deal. That was one aspect. Then, when you had a team, such as Freddie, John and Joe, when they were doing *Far from the Madding Crowd*, I set up the deal with MGM and negotiated the terms and the distribution contract for the whole film.

What do you think have been some of the powerful agencies? How do they acquire this power?

Christopher Mann ran a very powerful agency. He represented David Lean. Then there was MCA, which became London Artists and is now part of ICM – that was Laurie Evans, Olive Harding and all that group. There was Robin Fox at London Management, who were quite powerful, and Fraser & Dunlop. Now, Peters, Fraser & Dunlop is very big. Your power as an agent always comes from your clients. The more powerful the people you represent, the greater access you have, because everybody wants to talk to you. The other side of that is that, if you are representing powerful people, then it becomes a much tougher job because they expect more, the deals become more complicated, the pressures are greater, and the client, ego-wise, has always got something to be unhappy about if he chooses. Basically, I think actors tend to talk a lot about what they would really like to do; but the fact is that an actor is someone for hire. Whatever they *want* to do, if someone offers them £1 million to do a part, their attention will be drawn to that and they will leave whatever it is they would like to do until later.

What about agents like Herbert de Leon, Al Parker and others?

Al Parker was a pre-war type of agent. Those guys were perfectly fine but it was all very easygoing compared with today, even though I'm sure some of them were very tough. Herbert de Leon I didn't know very well, but he represented a lot of good actors such as Margaret Lockwood. Olive Harding, a wonderful woman, represented Julie Christie; if you did that in the '60s it was like representing Princess Diana – it gave you tremendous power, tremendous access.

The '60s was a great period because it was a period of experimentation; there was a huge amount of money *and* talent around; there were all these stars and writers and new material always coming in. We don't have today the powerful actors that we had then. There were Albert Finney, Richard Harris, Robert Shaw, Peter O'Toole, Tom Courtenay, Julie Christie, Vanessa Redgrave, David Warner – a lot of really powerful people, and the directors to move them – Karel [Reisz], Lindsay [Anderson], Richard [Lester], John [Schlesinger]. It was a fantastically exciting time to be here and everyone was working. I was a full-time agent for about ten years and of course that was the best time to be doing it, because all the American companies were over here and there was a tremendous spate of British production, a lot of which was financed by American companies. There was a kind of passion to make movies with English writers, directors, actors: they were the vogue. The Americans thought the English writers, directors and actors had all the answers. But they had pulled their money out of Britain by about 1969/70. Some time around then, there was a big stock-market crash which resulted in a tremendous rearranging of people's priorities. And, because of the new mood prevailing in the States – and because very few of the smaller, English movies made any money – the boom of US investment in English films came to an end.

Those very prestigious films of the early '60s – *A Kind of Loving*, *Billy Liar*, *This Sporting Life* – did they travel well in America?

No, they didn't. I represented both *A Kind of Loving* – its writers, director and producer – and *Billy Liar*, and I also represented *Darling*. *Darling* was really the only one to become successful in America – oddly enough, more successful there than it was in Britain. It had a touch of both art-house and mainstream distribution in America. What happened with it was quite curious. It cost about £300,000 to make, as far as I remember; it had reasonable notices when it opened here, and it had some curiosity value because nothing quite like it had been done here before. Then, because Julie Christie was so hot as a result of that film, it became a sort of 'special' movie and it was bought by Joe Levine – for US $900,000, I think.

The reason Anglo-Amalgamated were so anxious to sell it was that Nat Cohen had put up the whole £300,000, which was quite a lot of money then and it was a really big exposure for him, but it hadn't grossed more than about £250,000 in Britain. Nat was very anxious to get out, so when Joe Levine came along with a fat cheque, he was very happy to take the money and make a profit. I don't know whether Nat ever saw any money out of the American distribution, but, Joe Levine being Joe Levine, he publicised the hell out of it. When it hit America there was tremendous curiosity about the film – the 'swinging '60s' and all that sort of stuff. Then Freddie Raphael won an Oscar for the writing, Julie won one and I think John won one [nomination] also, as did Julie Harris for costume design, and it became a comparative hit.

You have a writing credit on *The Angry Silence*. What was your involvement in this?

The Angry Silence grew out of Richard Attenborough's and my brother Michael Craig's dissatisfaction with playing in umpteen war films, wanting to do something different. Michael wrote to me from Tripoli, where he was on location for *Sea of Sand*, and asked me to research a situation about a man being sent to Coventry because of his refusal to join a wildcat strike. When he came back from Tripoli, we gave the research data and a treatment to Attenborough and Bryan Forbes. Then we wrote a first-draft script. Bryan did a polish on it and we made it for £99,000. This was the time of *Room at the Top* but, because *The Angry Silence* was an original rather than coming from a successful novel, there was a question mark over it. It also had the misfortune to be around at the same time as *I'm All Right Jack*, which was the other side of the coin. A comedy is always easier to sell.

Michael and I worked on *The Angry Silence* in 1958, I think it was, and it was shortly after that I became an agent. I was already an agent by the time it opened. My main side was always the business side, though, and, as I said, the '60s was a terrific time for British films. There were Nat Cohen's Anglo-Amalgamated films; also, British Lion films were successful at this time. I don't think many of the Rank films or the ABPC films of the '60s made very much. All the main money was coming from United Artists, Columbia – and Fox, who had a huge presence over here. They were in Soho Square where they are now. There was a guy called Elmo Williams, who used to edit for Zanuck, and he was put in charge of production here. In about the mid-'60s they were making probably eight or ten movies annually over here, which they usually made at Rank or on location.

United Artists were also a very big presence; they backed Woodfall, as you will know. The Boulting brothers and Launder and Gilliat were still operating out of British Lion, so there was a lot of action. But in the end, the people who had the money were the Americans. They would put up two, three or four hundred thousand pounds for a movie and wouldn't see anything back on some of them. If one studied a list of all the movies that were made over here in the '60s, one would be shocked to find that some of them have hardly ever been seen and most lost money. After all, you could make only so many movies about 'swinging London'.

While Britain never had a Hollywood-style studio system or star system, it did have a curious preponderance of producer–director teams. Has this ever struck you?

It's certainly true that there were a lot of them, but whether there were more than in America, I don't know. If you talk to John Schlesinger, Joe Janni or Frederic Raphael, who made about five movies together, they will tell you that, whatever the pain of it was, they had some fun as well. They were all very idiosyncratic characters, who would scream at each other, but it was fun because it was about making movies together. Whenever you have people who are really keen about making movies, people like Powell and Pressburger, Launder and Gilliat, or Dearden and Relph, and you can find a way to work together, then that's perfect. But if you have someone who has, as his main interest making a deal and raising money, then it is unlikely that they will have the same kind of emotional involvement as a director will have. Therefore the director

has taken over that side of the producing function to a large extent, and the producer has become simply a money man. The *producer* producers, like Joe Janni or David Puttnam, are very few and far between. Joe Janni in the '60s, or Richard Attenborough when he was producing with Bryan Forbes, loved the movies. I represented Bryan during *Whistle Down the Wind* (written by Keith Waterhouse and Willis Hall, whom I also represented), and there was a great love affair with the idea of making a good movie, on the part of everyone involved. I think that if you've ever had a good relationship in a partnership, such as I had with Gareth in the agency, when that ends, for whatever reason, you never do replace that person. It's a kind of serendipity that you come together and find that ability to work together and complement each other and, if you can't replace that, then you don't do it any more. In my view, the movie is rarely as good if the producer is also the director, though I know there are exceptions.

You mentioned the word 'ego' . . . In fact I wonder if British cinema needed more powerful, driving egos than were available to it.

In terms of ego, I think the British directors and producers probably stand up as high as anybody. I think perhaps it's less true of actors, though, because we have never really had here the same kind of movie-star power that exists in America. We don't have Robert Redford or Bruce Willis, we don't have people like that. I don't think British movie stars have been movie stars in the way that Hollywood movie stars are. The acid test in Hollywood has always been whether an actor can 'open' a picture. By that I mean an exhibitor will say, 'If you can get so-and-so, we will open the picture in however-many movie houses.' Julie Christie could open a picture; Sean Connery could; Michael Caine maybe. There never have been that many people who can do it, but that's what they really call movie stars. The reason that actresses don't have the same power as actors do in America is that most of the movies that can be 'opened' are action movies.

How good do you think British cinema has been in creating stars?

It seems to me, the British are just very bad at playing themselves. They are wonderful character actors but they are very self-conscious about playing themselves as leading men. The Americans, whatever else they bring to the craft, play who they are. Look at Humphrey Bogart or John Wayne. For some curious reason, whether to do with our upbringing or whatever, British actors are inhibited from being themselves and therefore very few, unless they went to America (like Ronald Colman and Cary Grant), could manage it. It has nothing to do with acting; it has to do with a kind of ability to believe in being who you are – to trust your presence.

I think probably British women have been better at it than men. Think of Jean Simmons, Deborah Kerr and Audrey Hepburn, who have notably gone to Hollywood, but they also had some film career here and they retained their 'Englishness'; you could never mistake them for anything but English. It is hard to think of the equivalent number of male actors of whom one could say the same. Yes, Stewart Granger, and of course James Mason, although Mason was really a character actor, not a leading man in the sense that Robert Redford is a leading man. Put most of our leading actors into leading parts and a self-consciousness develops.

Perhaps it's something to do with the parts, but I don't think so. My brother, Michael [Craig], was limited by the parts he was given when he was under contract to Rank in the '50s and '60s, but in movies like *The Irishman* and *Sea of Sand* he was brilliant, because he had more of a 'character' to play and he didn't have to play himself. But I think it was also true of other handsome British leading men. Michael Caine is probably the only one here who – although he is really a character actor – in the right part, can carry the leading-man role; for instance, take *Educating Rita*, in which he was brilliant. He could really *be* that person. You don't feel with Michael Caine that he is looking over his shoulder; it is that apparent effortlessness, that feeling of liking the camera and not being afraid of it, not being self-conscious. It must be something in our British character.

What do you think happened to British cinema in the '50s? Do you think it simply ran out of ideas?

I think it was class, wasn't it? If you look at all those early and mid-'50s movies they were all middle-class pictures. Basically they didn't make pictures about real working-class people. What happened with films and also books and theatre from *Room at the Top* onwards was that suddenly you had an absolute cascade of working-class people – oddly enough, mostly from the North – who wrote books and plays, and actors. It was unheard of in the movie business. On television all the announcers spoke with that BBC accent, and in all those films which were made by Rank and, to a large extent, by ABPC, even in the war films, the working-class people were represented by plastic cut-outs. Suddenly all these new films came in a period of about four years; it was absolutely magic. It seemed that the working-class people believed in themselves and decided to tell their own story as it really was – rougher, nastier, earthier, whatever it was.

Yet one of the ironies is that many of the directors were distinctly middle-class, public-school, Oxbridge-educated people.

They certainly were – men like Lindsay Anderson, Tony Richardson, John Schlesinger, all those guys were very much that. They had come from a middle-class culture (the BBC and so on) and made documentaries, Free Cinema, that kind of thing, and all that was run by middle-class people. But you could be a working-class writer if you had the talent, and the writers had to come first. It was later on that the working-class directors, people like Ken Loach, followed the writers and actors.

Would it be true to say that Rank was a kind of benign tycoon?

The truth of the matter is that Rank himself had absolutely nothing to do with it. He put John Davis in to run it, and the American Earl St John was Head of Production – he was a yes man, really, but very nice. He was a kind of buffer between Davis and everyone else. John Davis insisted on certain films being made and others not being made. My belief is that he was very much to blame for the decline in British cinema in the '50s, because he insisted on making those awful middle-class pictures that had no meaning for anyone, because somehow he couldn't come to terms with the fact that the vast majority of people in this country were lower-middle-class and working-class people. So all those boring tales like *Campbell's Kingdom* had nothing to do with real life. If you are clever enough, as Korda and Balcon were, you can get away with it, but Davis wasn't. It was very square entertainment and people wanted a change from it.

Would you say British cinema didn't cope well with the advent of television?

In my opinion it wasn't so much that British cinema couldn't cope with television; it was because, for whatever reasons, television usurped the cinema. Television was getting better and more varied, so in order to get people out of their houses and into the movies, you had to come up with something which was pretty interesting. We have a population of something like fifty or sixty million and we don't have a very large cinema audience. When you think that a movie like *The Angry Silence*, which cost £99,000 to make, didn't make a profit in England with all the controversy that surrounded it, or that a movie like *Darling*, with Julie Christie and all the publicity it received, didn't make a profit here, then you understand that there were very, very few people who were able to make profit on an English-based movie. In order to make the sort of movies that historically we've made, you need to have a sufficient number of blockbusters every year, with money coming back here to fund an industry, and we've never had it.

John Grierson

1898–1972

Though he was crucially involved in making many films, John Grierson's name appears on few of them. Instead of a filmography, what follows is a list of some of his key centres of activity and positions held:

1926 Research takes him to Hollywood.
1928 Returns to Britain as Assistant Film Officer of the Empire Marketing Board; commissioning of his film *Drifters*.
1930 Formation of the Empire Marketing Board Film Unit, with Grierson as head.
1933 EMBFU incorporated in the GPO Film Unit, joined by the Brazilian documentarist Alberto Cavalcanti in 1934.
1938 Co-founder of the Film Centre.
1939 Commissioner of the National Film Board of Canada.
1946 *Grierson on Documentary* (edited by Forsyth Hardy) published.
1947 To UNESCO in Paris, as Director of Mass Communications and Public Information.
1950 Executive Producer for British feature-film-making company, Group 3.
1957 Joined Scottish Television.

'Of course *Moana*, being a visual account of events in the daily life of a Polynesian youth, has documentary value.'[1] In this 1926 comment by Grierson, the word 'documentary' entered our critical language, and since then no one has been more tenaciously associated with the documentary form. Grierson was notably articulate – and outspoken – about what he and his colleagues were up to. 'I have no great interest in films as such ... I look on the cinema as a pulpit, and use it as a propagandist,'[2] he said in 1933.

The documentary movement of the 1930s seems to have flourished quite separately from mainstream British filmmaking of the decade. In his final interview, in 1972, he said, 'Remember documentary was developed on the thought that it was not there necessarily for entertainment. Occasionally it has been in the entertainment business but only incidentally.'[3] This remark is echoed in the last article he wrote, in which he claimed the documentarists had 'some ambitions in the field of entertainment but only in so far as it had duties to audiences and a need for circulation.'[4]

This suspicion of (most) commercial cinema ran alongside a deep distrust for individual, fictional stories. '... We must feel that we are looking at the fate of man,'[5] he said: his interest is in 'man' rather than 'men', the individuals who propel fictional narratives. He always saw film as having an instructional purpose: '... opinion has to be created wherever matters urgently involving the national will are concerned; so a certain number of films inevitably are there to do things to people.'[6] However, this teaching function, this idea of the cinema 'as the servant of public purposes,'[7] is not to be achieved at the expense of the poetic, and by 1950 he feared that 'the deep aspects of public relations, the quality of revelation, are missing . . . In the film sense, we are desperately short of poems and symphonies.'[8] The only film he solo-directed, *Drifters*, a study of North Sea herring-fishermen, embodies the strains of the work he oversaw: poetic documentaries such as *Song of Ceylon* (1934) and *Night Mail* (1936) (the latter draws on WH Auden's verse and Benjamin Britten's music) and more didactic, socially committed but aesthetically less adventurous pieces such as *Housing Problems* (1935) and *Aero-Engine* (1933).

Grierson is a strange, complex figure – part-academic, part-Old Testament prophet ('I derive my authority from Moses'[9]), poet *manqué* – often to be found castigating other filmmakers, loyal to his own colleagues. 'I think we represented the top of Britain . . . We all worked together . . . They didn't put their names on pictures,'[10] he said forty years later of the 1930s documentary movement. However, nurtured in silents, he embraced sound ('it has the same power over reality as the camera had before it'[11]), just as later, nurtured in the cinema, he welcomed television. The feature films he was involved in with Group 3 are, for the most part, well intentioned but bland (Philip Leacock's *The Brave Don't Cry* is the major exception); his real monument remains with the 1930s work and the influence it exerted on wartime and postwar British feature-filmmaking.

1 Paul Rotha, *Documentary Diary*, Hill & Wang, New York, 1973, p xv
2 *Sight and Sound*, Winter 1933–34, p 119
3 *Film Quarterly*, Fall 1972, p 26
4 Ernest Betts, *The Film Business*, George Allen & Unwin, London, 1973, p 318
5 *Take One*, January–February 1970, p 17
6 *Sight and Sound*, July 1950, p 203
7 *Films and Filming*, December 1973, p 11
8 *Sight and Sound*, July 1950, p 203
9 *Take One*, p 19
10 *Film Quarterly*, pp 24, 28–9
11 *Sight and Sound*, Autumn 1934, p 101

Kenneth Griffith

b. 1921

Actor: Channel Incident, The Farmer's Wife (1940), The Black Sheep of Whitehall, Love on the Dole, Hard Steel (1941), The Shop at Sly Corner (1946), Fame is the Spur (1947), Bond Street (1948), Forbidden, Blue Scar, Helter Skelter (1949), Waterfront (1950), High Treason (1951), The Starfish (1952), The Green Buddha, 36 Hours (1954), Track the Man Down, 1984, The Prisoner (1955), Private's Progress, The Baby and the Battleship, Tiger in the Smoke (1956), Brothers-in-Law, Lucky Jim, Blue Murder at St Trinian's (1957), The Naked Truth, A Night to Remember, The Two-Headed Spy, Chain of Events, The Man Upstairs (1958), Tiger Bay, Libel, I'm All Right Jack, Carlton-Browne of the FO, Expresso Bongo (1959), Suspect, Circus of Horrors, A French Mistress, Snowball (1960), Rag Doll, The Frightened City, Payroll (1961), Only Two Can Play, The Painted Smile, We Joined the Navy (1962), Heavens Above! (1963), Rotten to the Core (1965), The Whisperers (1966), The Bobo, Great Catherine (1967), Decline and Fall, The Lion in Winter (1968), The Assassination Bureau, The Gamblers (1969), Revenge (1971), The House in Nightmare Park (1973), S*P*Y*S, Callan (1974), Sky Riders (1976), Why Shoot the Teacher? (1977), The Wild Geese (1978), The Sea Wolves (1980), Who Dares Wins (1982), Four Weddings and a Funeral (1994), The Englishman Who Went Up a Hill But Came Down a Mountain (1995)

Two delightful roles in popular recent films – as a belligerent wedding guest in *Four Weddings and a Funeral* and as the Reverend Jones, who adjusts his views on the Sabbath in the interests of the common cause in *The Englishman Who ...* – offer further evidence that Kenneth Griffith's perception of career-as-survival is holding good for him. As, indeed, it now has for fifty years. There have been bad patches, of course: in the '50s he was involved in some very undistinguished 'B' films. In the main, though, his long filmography shows him to have been very busy and in good company since he first impressed filmgoers with his particular brand of opportunist villainy in *The Shop at Sly Corner*, in which he repeated his successful stage role. As he says, the Boultings gave him some of his best chances, tapping a comic vein in his screen persona, in such films as *Private's Progress* and *I'm All Right Jack*. Whatever the part, and this has remained true, he has managed to stamp it with the authority of insight and long experience: this is as true of major television performances, like those as Roger Casement or Raskolnikov, as it is of fleeting cameo roles in a dozen films.
Interview date: October 1992

Was your first film (before you were twenty) a Ministry of Information short, *Channel Incident*?

I had acted on the screen before that. The very first acting I did was when Rank, a staunch Methodist, started making religious films. They were made in some enormous tin shed, as I remember, directed by a man known as Captain Norman Walker. I acted for him when I was about sixteen and worked for him later, in the 1940s, in *Hard Steel*. Walker was very quiet, very professional, and I liked him a great deal. I saw *Hard Steel* on television recently; when you're seventy, as I am, and you see yourself on the screen as you were at age sixteen or seventeen, you look hard to see how well you did it. I knew I was in *Hard Steel* but couldn't remember what I did in it. In fact I had quite a colourful role in it, and I looked at this boy and thought it was an intelligent, perceptive performance. I wasn't in films for a long time after that, because of the war. Unlike some actors, I had nothing to do with filming during the war. I think I am a survivor and I don't claim that I haven't used a certain amount of cunning to survive, even in the war. I was invalided out while the war was still on and they were desperate for actors, so it was easy to get started again.

Was it a lucky break getting the part of the extremely nasty blackmailer, Archie Fellowes, in *The Shop at Sly Corner* for George King?

When people have a piece of bad luck it can become good luck if you follow it through. In my opinion, the greatest man of the theatre in my time was Tyrone Guthrie. He asked me to take over Alec Guinness's roles for the Old Vic in a very famous season, and I said I'd just got married (for the first time) and needed to make more money. I had been offered the play of *The Shop at Sly Corner*, so I turned down Mercutio to play Archie Fellowes at the St Martin's Theatre in London. I had a big success in it and was the only one of the stage cast who went into the film – and it was a very good film.

Its director, George King, was a great character: a tall, goodlooking chap, and a man-about-town. He was quite a humorous, charming filmmaker-businessman and very nice to me. A good director, yes: that is, someone who selects an actor who can do the job and waits for him to do it, with a minimum of interference. George King certainly wouldn't tell me, or Oscar Homolka (who was a great actor), what to do or not to do.

People commiserated with me when they heard I was to work with Oscar Homolka; they said he was ruthless, selfish, and that I wouldn't stand a chance. He was rather intolerant after his experiences in the great classical plays. In those days, when the camera was off the leading actor for close-ups and there were reverse shots on the other actor – which I was in this case – the second assistant or someone would read the lines while the leading actor returned to his dressing room. I had done one day's work with Oscar and the second director made to do this when Oscar said, 'Give me the script!' Then he put the script aside and *acted* with me, because he thought, to his surprise, that I was a serious actor with ability.

Did this role influence the villainous character parts you were offered?

Unfortunately it did give me that kind of image, yes, because the idea that an actor could become different people was barely accepted. The great breakthrough came with Alec Guinness and my dear friend Peter Sellers. But it is almost impossible for really creative actors – sometimes called 'character actors', which is an unfortunate expression – to become stars. I remember a conversation I had with Anatole de Grunwald, who was one of our more sophisticated film producers; after *The Shop at Sly Corner* he said to me, 'Kenneth, can you do for me exactly what you did for George King?' That was on a film called *Bond Street*; it was virtually a repetition of what I had done: in both cases the situation was me blackmailing an old man, and involved his daughter. As I said yes to Grunwald, I remember thinking, 'How can I make it different?' I hit upon one key in it which allowed me to make it different – although great pains had been taken to make it the same. In *Sly Corner*, Fellowes says to the old man, 'I want £1,000 and I want it now' (with a Cockney accent). In *Bond Street* I said to the old man, 'Would £100 be too much?', which was very funny, and that was the key to make them different. But of course the writing and the quality of the parts degenerated and I was trapped in them, until Roy Boulting broke that mould finally by asking me to play some comedy.

You did eleven films for the Boultings. What do you think were their great strengths as filmmakers?

Their place in British cinema should be higher. They had great intelligence, and that's unusual; great energy for creating film; a great sense of satirical humour; they got at big issues through humour in *I'm All Right Jack*, which was a devastating criticism of both British Labour and British Capitalism. For the first time, the statement was made of the truth about Britain and its extraordinary and appalling decline, from both sides. It would have saved us a lot of trouble if the nation had paid attention to that film. The Boultings would nudge us into these things, myself and people like Irene Handl and Raymond Huntley.

They were identical twins but Roy was my particular friend and is my close friend to this day. I don't think any of us can survive without impresarios – those who decide that you have something to give and take steps to make sure you do it. There haven't been many of them in British cinema, except Balcon, of course, and Korda in that old, grand way, and the Boultings.

Did it seem to be a good time, in the late '40s and '50s, to be getting a career going in British films? You seemed to be working non-stop.

It's always been a battle to survive, even for me who have worked very consistently. I had quite formidable domestic responsibilities, and I wasn't a very good hustler, but it was a matter of getting films to pay the bills. I was never under contract; I was offered one by ABPC and Korda but I declined. I had agents, although sometimes I wonder if such a thing as a 'good' agent exists. People ask for you, or they say, 'Wouldn't Griffith be right for that?' Thank God one didn't hear the reply! I did as many as seven or eight roles a year, some of them fairly substantial and some only a few days' work.

What do you remember of Jill Craigie, one of Britain's few women directors. on *Blue Scar*? Were you attracted to the Welsh setting?

I was offered the job and Jill Craigie had as her partner William MacQuitty, who was a remarkable character. I think probably the money I would earn on a film like that would be less that I would earn normally, but it meant going back to Wales; it was a very serious film, and Jill Craigie is a very intelligent, remarkable woman. I met some Welsh actors, whom I remember with affection, and it was a nice job, worthwhile too.

Your next film was *Waterfront* for Michael Anderson, in which again you were spectacularly nasty, with Richard Burton as the nice guy.

Yes, Burton was 'walking out' with the good sister [Avis Scott] and I was walking out with the naughty sister, played by Susan Shaw. Robert Newton played the father, and even then Robert was already well into alcohol. He lived in a sort of fantasy world, which was alarming; but when he had to do his acting, he was very remarkable. I remember him meeting me one morning at the studio and saying, 'I'm having an affair with a lady wrestler!' I used to sit with him at lunchtime in the grand baronial hall at Pinewood, along with all the important producers and accountants with all that essential shit going on. One day they were all being very respectable and you could see Robert moving. He suddenly said, 'I've got the twinges! *I've got the twinges!!*' and everyone got deeper into their soup. Then he took up a great bread basket and swished it around, and people were trying to pretend it wasn't happening! Kathleen Harrison played his wife – she was a nice Cockney, a clever actress – and she would say, 'Come along now, Robert, sit down and behave yourself,' and he'd listen to her. He also took the relationship in the film, between me and Susan Shaw, literally: he'd say to me off camera, 'I know that you're not really a bad fellow,' and that sort of thing. Michael Anderson was overruled by the producer, Paul Soskin, who was a curious character, Romanian or Hungarian [born Kerch, south Russia]; he wouldn't take on the job of directing but he took the film over, and it was acutely embarrassing.

My relationship with Richard Burton is very interesting: that was the first time we'd met and he was rather stand-offish. I've always avoided that bonhomie with fellow Welshmen, that sort of club. He was extremely handsome, one of the most beautiful young men I've ever seen. I had reason to believe that twice when I had been cast in a film, he had me removed before the film started. I wasn't under contract in either case but in one, *Where Eagles Dare* I think, I had been cast before he had, and he had the muscle to nominate someone he would prefer to play the part. But that's not the end of the story. You have to be philosophical about such things, even though it meant I would lose a lot of money I could ill afford to, but I never discussed

it with him. The director Andrew McLaglen came into the dressing-room when I was acting in *Cause Célèbre* and told me that he was making a film called *The Wild Geese*, with a difficult role, a brave gay, and wanted me to do it. Would I agree to the producer Euan Lloyd buying me out of my contract with the play? I said I'd be very grateful because I dreaded going on stage every night. Then he mentioned they'd already cast Richard Burton and I said they might have a problem, because for some reason he'd had me removed from two films. They said no, I was quite wrong, because when he was asked to do the film he had asked who was playing the character Whitty. When he was told they were hoping to get me, he said, 'Good, good! He won't be afraid to do it.' So we were on the film together, on the Zimbabwean–Transvaal border; after lunch one day, suddenly I became aware that Burton had got up and was walking straight towards me. He stood over me and said, 'Kenneth, when I was a young actor I was in awe of your talent,' and then he turned and walked away. He stopped after four or five paces, turned around and said, 'And of course, I still am,' and then walked off.

In the '50s, there was a steady stream of American imports, who I presume were brought in to bolster distribution in America.

Yes, they did second features, didn't they? I did a lot of those. They were mostly old hands, of course, from Hollywood, and not doing as well as they had. Of course, Katharine Hepburn in *The Lion in Winter* is a quite different case: that was a fine, substantial film with great talent in it. I did feel very dissatisfied with one of those second features, *36 Hours*, which I did with Dan Duryea. It's a film I'd only watch if I disciplined myself!

Are there any film parts you look back on with particular pleasure?

I suppose *The Shop at Sly Corner*; I think I gave a better performance in *Bond Street*. And yes, *Only Two Can Play*. And I rather enjoyed speaking up for my gay friends in *The Wild Geese*.

Val Guest

b. 1911

Screenwriter (or co-screenwriter) only: *The Maid of the Mountains, Innocents of Chicago* (1932), *No Monkey Business* (1935), *Good Morning Boys, Public Nuisance No. 1, All In* (1936), *Okay for Sound* (1937), *Oh Mr Porter, Alf's Button Afloat, Convict 99, Hey, Hey, USA!* (1938), *The Frozen Limits, Old Bones of the River* (1939), *Band Waggon, Ask a Policeman, Charley's (Bighearted) Aunt, Gasbags* (1940), *Inspector Hornleigh Goes To It, Hi Gang!, I Thank You* (1941), *Back Room Boy* (1942), *London Town* (1946), *Paper Orchid* (1949), *Happy Go-Lovely* (1951)

Director (with other functions noted): **The Nose Has It* (1942), *Miss London Ltd* (& co-sc) (1943), *Give Us The Moon* (& sc), *Bees in Paradise* (& co-sc) (1944), *I'll Be Your Sweetheart* (& co-sc) (1945), *Just William's Luck* (& co-sc) (1947), *William Comes to Town* (& co-sc) (1948), *Murder at the Windmill* (& sc) (1949), *Miss Pilgrim's Progress* (& sc), *The Body Said No!* (& sc) (1950), *Mr Drake's Duck* (& sc) (1951), *Penny Princess* (& pr, sc) (1952), *Life with the Lyons* (& sc), *The Runaway Bus* (& pr, sc), *Men of Sherwood Forest, Dance Little Lady* (& sc) (1954), *They Can't Hang Me* (& sc), *Break in the Circle* (& uncr co-sc), *The Lyons in Paris* (& sc), *The Quatermass Xperiment* (& co-sc) (1955), *The Weapon, It's A Wonderful World* (& sc) (1956), *Carry On Admiral* (& co-sc), *Quatermass II* (& co-sc), *The Abominable Snowman* (1957), *Camp on Blood Island* (& co-sc), *Up the Creek* (& uncr co-sc), *Further Up the Creek* (& co-sc) (1958), *Life is a Circus* (& sc), *Yesterday's Enemy, Expresso Bongo* (& pr) (1959), *Hell is a City* (& sc) (1960), *The Full Treatment* (& pr, co-sc), *The Day the Earth Caught Fire* (& pr, co-sc) (1961), *Jigsaw* (& pr, sc) (1962), *80,000 Suspects* (& pr, sc) (1963), *The Beauty Jungle* (& pr, co-sc) (1964), *Where the Spies Are* (& pr, co-sc) (1965), *Casino Royale* (co-dir), *Assignment K* (& co-sc) (1967), *When Dinosaurs Ruled The Earth* (& sc), *Tomorrow* (& sc) (1970), *Au Pair Girls* (& co-sc) (1972), *Confessions of a Window Cleaner* (1974), *The Diamond Mercenaries* (1975), *The Shillingbury Blowers, Dangerous Davies – The Last Detective* (& sc) (1980), *The Boys in Blue* (& sc) (1983)

Remakes of *The Day the Earth Caught Fire, The Quatermass Xperiment* and *Expresso Bongo* are now (1996) in either pre-production or planning stages.

* Short film

It seems unlikely that there will ever again be directors like Val Guest, in terms of sheer output and range. After writing numerous screenplays throughout the 1930s for most of the popular comedians of the day, he then began a forty-year career as director in 1942. He has worked in virtually every popular genre – comedies, musicals, war films, thrillers, science fiction, costume adventures, and so on – and in this respect he resembled, perhaps more than anyone else in British films, the Hollywood directors of the studio years, with their craftsmanlike energy. At their best, Guest's genre films, such as the urban

thriller, *Hell is a City*, exhibit a fine, unpretentious realism and there is vigour and inventiveness in his science-fiction works. There are also several engaging comedies starring his wife Yolande Donlan, and a whole string of other lively entertainments. 'Lively entertainment' is what, one feels, Val Guest was always aiming at – and very often provided.
Interview date: July 1990

When you became a director, more often than not you were also the author or co-author of the screenplay. Was this the arrangement you favoured?

Yes, in fact, in all the films I have made as a director, there are only two I haven't written as well. I started as a writer-director at Gainsborough and I always felt I would rather do the writing myself so that, if it went wrong, there was only me to blame. And of course I'd had a wonderful, chaotic time in the '30s writing for all those great comics like Will Hay and the Crazy Gang. And I also produced quite a few of my films. Yolande and I started our own company and every now and then I had a specific subject which I liked, so I would do it for our company. It gave you control and made you think a little harder; you learned to wear different hats for different departments. It wasn't that difficult, because, as writer, I knew exactly what I wanted to see on that screen.

How did you come to start your directing career at Gainsborough?

The start of my career as a director is a little strange. Although I had done some second-unit stuff for Marcel Varnel, from whom I learned a great deal, I hadn't really been a director as such. I received a request, through the studio, that the Ministry of Information would like me to write a short picture about sneezing – 'sneezes spread diseases and so stops the ammunition'. I found out they had sent it to six other writers first but all their stuff had been turned down and finally they sent it to me. I put on an Academy Award performance, saying, 'How dare they send it to me seventh?!' and I refused to do it unless, if what I wrote was accepted, they allowed me to direct it. So they agreed to this and that was my first job as a director.

It was put on at the Odeon cinema in Leicester Square with a Rita Hayworth/Victor Mature musical, *My Gal Sal*. That was lucky for me because the musical got terrible notices and two critics said that the best thing on the bill was the MoI short about

sneezing [*The Nose Has It*]. I had done this with [Arthur] Askey, having written it for him. That's really how I got my Gainsborough contract to write and direct.

Was Gainsborough a good studio to work for in the '30s and 40s?

Gainsborough was a great studio to work for. There was a lot of work and we went from one picture to another, from one type to another, and it had a 'happy family' atmosphere. I would think Gainsborough was as near as dammit to a solidly based studio system, because there was real continuity. In a different style, Ealing also had a continuity and a studio-based system. I think it helps a film industry enormously to have two or three units that are continually turning out product.

Between 1949 and 1952 you made four more sophisticated comedies with Yolande Donlan, the American stage star you married. Did you enjoy this change of pace?

Yolande was a sophisticated player and I wrote the films – *Miss Pilgrim's Progress*, etc, – for her. I must say that once you get into a line of pictures that have been successful, nobody wants you to leave that particular genre. Many times I wanted to get away from broad comedy to do a thriller or something, but nobody wanted to know about that. So, being able to do pictures of more sophistication, with something of a story to them, helped me to break through and I did enjoy the change of pace.

Mr Drake's Duck is something of a perennial favourite in England; they bring it out every Christmas. The idea of the duck laying the uranium egg came from a very short BBC playlet by a man called Ian Messiter. It had nothing whatever to do with the story of the film, it was just the *idea* which I bought from him.

Did you have control over matters of casting? Players like Reginald Beckwith, Anthony Oliver and Wilfred Hyde-White crop up again and again in your films.

I had, I would say, eighty-per-cent control but the

final control came from the American distribution company, which insisted on a star name and put forward its preferences as to stars. The players you mention were part of my film rep company; I used to write parts for them in every film I made. I kept a whole lot of them going for quite a long time – Sid James was one of my 'rep' people, as were Leo McKern, AE Matthews and certainly Wilfred Hyde-White. Tony Beckwith was actually a partner in Yolande's and my film company and also one of our closest friends.

Someone recently remarked that you are, of all British directors, the one who made genre films with as much flair and energy as Hollywood did. What do you feel about such an assessment?

I'm thrilled that somebody said that of me. I always tried, once I got away from that comedy kick, to make every film I did which had any sort of thrill content or serious content as much *cinéma vérité* as I could. I tried very hard in all the pictures that I made to give a certain reality. I did make a lot of different genres. We had a wonderful success with *The Day the Earth Caught Fire*; now, after that, what do you do? So, for my next I did a very small film called *Jigsaw*, a police thriller which I still think is one of my better films. I can't say I have a preference for one particular genre. I like doing comedy, but I would rather do something more serious, particularly a thriller of some kind if it was a good one.

You were immensely busy throughout the '40s and '50s. Was it a good time to be a director in Britain?

Yes, I was busy and it was a good time to be directing. I was lucky to be around then because I met up with Jimmy and Michael Carreras and they asked me to join the Hammer fold. I joined up with Bebe and Ben Lyon to make *The Lyons in Paris*, which started me off, and I did about thirteen or fourteen pictures with Hammer all told, one of which was *The Quatermass Xperiment*. I had done about three pictures for Hammer at one point and I was going away to Tangier on holidays when Anthony Hinds (the producer of *Quatermass*) asked me to read some scripts based on the television series. I took the scripts with me and more or less forgot about them. I wasn't too interested in science fiction. Once I'd read them I couldn't wait to do a film of them.

What do you recall of your work with other famous comics in the '50s – Ben Lyon and Bebe Daniels, Peter Sellers, Frankie Howerd and others?

Ben and Bebe were very close friends of ours and we spent a lot of time with them. Bebe was the brains of the family and she used to write all their television and radio scripts. Lovely people to work with. As for Sellers, I had decided he should be put into a starring role in *Up the Creek*, but I had a terrible job selling him to the people at Wardour Street because no one had heard much of him other than as a radio comic. I finally had to go to my old friend Jimmy Carreras, who pointed out that Hammer didn't do comedies but that, if I really wanted to do this one, they would back me as long as I had someone well known alongside Sellers. I suggested David Tomlinson and Jimmy OKed that. It was a big hit; it made Hammer a lot of money and Sellers went on to great things. He was also a great chum of ours but he made his life a hell.

I saw Frankie Howerd in a revue at the Palladium; afterwards I told him I'd love to put him into a film. He said he would only do a film if it was a mystery/thriller, so that if the comedy was no good, at least the thriller would be. I talked to Margaret Rutherford, a great fan of Frankie's, and asked if she would co-star with him, which she was happy to do. So I wrote the story, *The Runaway Bus*, for him and her. Frankie would only sign his contract on condition he didn't get top billing, because he didn't want to be blamed for anything, so Maggie had top billing. After the first day's rushes Maggie came to me and said she refused to take top billing over Frankie, so that was that!

What seem to me two of your finest films come right at the end of the decade – *Expresso Bongo* and *Hell is a City*. Do you rate these highly among your work?

Yes, both are very much favourites of mine. If I had to pick favourites I would say *Yesterday's Enemy*, *Hell is a City*, *The Day the Earth Caught Fire*, *Jigsaw* and *Expresso Bongo*, of all my films. With *Expresso Bongo* we had a terrible job getting people to agree to do it; I had seen it on the stage and it was Yolande who said we should film it. Paul Scofield was very good but he wasn't enough of a *film* name. Originally someone had thought of Peter Sellers to play that part on screen, but nobody really wanted to know about that either. Finally they accepted Larry Harvey, so that's how it happened. I thought he did very well in that, an extremely good job. Again, most of the cast were part of my repertory company – Eric Pohlman, Barry Lowe, and so on. And of course, Yolande.

***Expresso Bongo* was your first collaboration with Wolf Mankowitz. Did his having written the book for the play make writing the screenplay easier?**

I found we worked very well together and I admired enormously his turn of phrase, his wit, his bite, and so we joined up; at various times in my film career subjects have come up about which I've thought, 'Wolf would be great to work with on this,' and I have pulled him in and we've done it together. His having written the book for the play didn't make writing the screenplay easier, because there were a lot of things in the play that we couldn't use on the screen or decided not to; for instance, the second half of the play all took place in the South of France and I thought that was all very musical comedy, so we had to bring it to London and make it take place at the Dorchester, in the Oliver Messel Suite, the balcony and the terrace. Wolf understood that you had to undo various things from the stage version and strengthen various other things for the film, but it didn't make it any easier to write the screenplay.

***Hell is a City* carries a caption thanking the Manchester police force. Did you have any problems filming in Manchester? Were you aiming at something like a thriller with documentary touches?**

Manchester Police were wonderful; they gave us everything we wanted, all the help in the world – after they had checked me out! They had checked out that I had made a picture done in Brighton with the police, who'd said I was all right. We didn't really have any problems filming in Manchester; the police roped off streets, even loaned us a lot of their men. It was a tough film to make, in that it was all on location, but we didn't have any trouble. I wanted to give it a newsreel quality. I tried desperately to get the quality of realism about the streets and houses and crowds. I was aiming for documentary touches. The strident music I thought was wonderful; it was written by Stanley Black, who had written a lot of music for me and who is brilliant on film scores.

Would you agree with me that the '40s and '50s was a 'boom' time in British cinema? What do you think were its great strengths and weaknesses in this period?

Yes, I agree it was a boom period. Its great strengths were that Britain was beginning to find its feet, knowing that it could get a world market if it tried hard enough, so everyone tried that little bit harder. It's a terrible thing to say, but I think the unions were the weakness. They put up so many barriers, one way and another, that eventually they drove all the American companies out of Britain; they also made life very difficult when you had a small, shoestring budget to make a movie.

Sir Alec Guinness
b. 1914

Actor: *Evensong* (1936), *Great Expectations* (1946), *Oliver Twist* (1948), *Kind Hearts and Coronets, A Run for Your Money* (1949), *Last Holiday, The Mudlark* (1950), *The Lavender Hill Mob, The Man in the White Suit* (1951), *The Card* (1952), *The Captain's Paradise, The Malta Story* (1953), *Father Brown, To Paris with Love* (1954), *The Prisoner, The Ladykillers* (1955), *The Swan* (1956), *Barnacle Bill, The Bridge on the River Kwai* (1957), *The Scapegoat* (1958), *The Horse's Mouth, Our Man in Havana* (1959), *Tunes of Glory* (1960), *A Majority of One* (1961), *HMS Defiant, Lawrence of Arabia* (1962), *The Fall of the Roman Empire, Situation Hopeless But Not Serious* (1964), *Doctor Zhivago, Hotel Paradiso, The Quiller Memorandum* (1966), *The Comedians* (1967), *Cromwell, Scrooge* (1970), *Brother Sun, Sister Moon* (1972), *Hitler: The Last Ten Days* (1973), *Murder By Death* (1976), *Star*

Wars (1977), *The Empire Strikes Back, Raise the Titanic!, Little Lord Fauntleroy* (1980), *Lovesick* (1983), *A Passage to India* (1984), *Little Dorrit* (1987), *A Handful of Dust* (1988), *Kafka* (1992), *A Foreign Field* (1993), *Mute Witness* (guest) (1995), *Star Wars – Episode IV, A New Hope* (1997)

Alec Guinness claims that he has never felt happy playing parts too like himself, and perhaps this accounts for his having been, since his early thirties, one of the screen's great character stars. One thinks of his Fagin in *Oliver Twist*, the larcenous bank clerk in *The Lavender Hill Mob*, the unctuous and incompetent criminal in *The Ladykillers*, the obsessed Colonel Nicholson in *The Bridge on the River Kwai*, and the boisterous and boorish Jock in *Tunes of Glory*, to choose but five variously memorable roles from the '40s and '50s alone. In this period, he is perhaps most closely associated with that remarkable run of Ealing comedies, beginning with his virtuoso appearances in *Kind Hearts and Coronets*, and he makes some interesting discriminations among the Ealing directors. As well as nearly fifty films, he has also done a great deal of remarkable work on stage and television.

Interview date: October 1989

After appearing as an extra in Victor Saville's *Evensong* in 1936, you made no further film until 1946. Did you feel it important to establish yourself on the stage first?

The stage was my prime interest then. I had no ambition to be a film actor and a screen career seemed unlikely to come my way. I'd done an adaptation of *Great Expectations* before the war and this had been seen by David Lean and Ronald Neame. I went into the Navy during the war, and when I came out they were preparing their film of *Great Expectations*. They remembered my performance on the stage and asked me if I'd go into their film as Herbert Pocket. I'd thought of film as a much greater mystery than the theatre and I felt a need to begin in films with a character I knew something about.

You came into British cinema at its absolute peak. Did your involvement with Cineguild and David Lean and Ronald Neame seem exciting at the time?

Cineguild [a semi-independent production company under the Rank umbrella] certainly seemed to make very stylish and entertaining films. David Lean and Ronald Neame's films seemed a breath of fresh air in the British film scene. In the films of *Great Expectations* and *Oliver Twist*, they surmounted the difficulties of telling those long, complex stories in about two hours each. I think they achieved a great success in telling them so swiftly and stylishly.

To jump forty years, what differences did you feel in filming *Little Dorrit* for Christine Edzard?

One of the main changes is that people have got used to very long entertainments. They feel they're serving the cause of culture if they're sitting on their arses for hours at a stretch. However, with *Little Dorrit*, you knew you were in for some sort of marathon. There was real interest in feeling the difference between a film where you could luxuriate in the leisureliness of the atmosphere, as compared with the tightness of David Lean's storytelling.

***Great Expectations* was perhaps the first of the great post-war international successes for British films. How would you account for these?**

Well, British films at that time *were* a bit classy.

Not just the Dickens films, but Lean's other film of the period, *Brief Encounter*, was also a great success. I mean, an artistic success here and in America, even if not a huge box-office success. There was a sense of a breakthrough into something new. And one mustn't forget the work of Carol Reed.

Valerie Hobson thought David Lean was not a great director of actors at this point but that he'd been very lucky in his casting of the Dickens films. Would you agree?

I think they simply cast the films as well as their budgets would permit. They were just concerned to get the best and most suitable people available. And, of course, with Dickens, it helps if you can get actors who do the larger-than-life stuff well, and I think Lean had a lot of people like that.

What did you make of the fact that *Oliver Twist*, in which you starred as Fagin, was initially banned in the US on grounds of 'anti-Semitism'?

I wasn't aware of *Oliver Twist*'s being banned in the States. But I do remember being at a large party in New York when a sort of doyen of the critics said to me, 'I'd rather give my child a dose of prussic acid than let her see this film.' In Austria, a Russian military audience walked out in bulk in protest against *Oliver Twist* as an anti-Semitic film, which is ironic when you reflect on their bad record for anti-Semitism. Rank wanted Fagin played as a straight character; he wasn't interested in the descriptions in the book or in the original illustrations. I wanted to copy the illustrations and as far as I know my interpretation caused no disturbance in the UK. We all fell over backwards so that the film shouldn't be thought of as anti-Semitic. The word 'Jew' isn't used in the film.

My own chief personal recollection of playing Fagin was the business of the make-up. I had to be at the studio (Pinewood) by 6.30am every day because the make-up took three hours to apply, and filming would start about 9.00 or 9.30.

Apart from Cineguild, your other crucial film connection of the '40s (and '50s) was with Ealing. What was it like to work there?

I suppose you could say it had a cosy atmosphere in many ways. It was smallish, modestly and pleasantly run, and it turned out good things. Balcon had a bunch of young directors who were seen as up-and-coming, and they were always consulting with each other. There were innumerable meetings when a new film was mooted. The Ealing films were tasteful, perhaps in some ways too much so. Their posters were something quite new, much more elegant than film posters usually were and some people didn't care for this. Now, of course, they're collectors' items.

***Kind Hearts and Coronets* still seems the blackest and funniest of the Ealing comedies. What attracted you to it most?**

The script reached me in France where I was on holiday. I read two pages and burst out laughing. I'd been offered two parts (I mean, to play both). I read this extremely stylish script, and sent off a telegram asking if I could play all eight of these characters the [D'Ascoyne family] if they hadn't already been cast. Well, the director and others were intrigued by the idea and that's how it came about. I think it was a great example of *comédie noire*.

You described its director, Robert Hamer, in your autobiography [*Blessings in Disguise*] as your 'very good friend' who 'spoke the same language'. What did you feel were his special qualities as a director?

Hamer was a man of great sensitivity and wit, and he had a fine sense of style, though he was not, perhaps, a very brilliant technical director. He disliked close-ups, he liked distancing things, and he was very good and appreciative with actors. He could see what actors were trying to do and he encouraged them in the working out of their own performances. He was a very intelligent man and I was very fond of him.

Am I right in thinking that the 'one rather awful' and 'one quite dreadful' films you did for him were, respectively. *The Scapegoat* and *To Paris With Love*?

There was a lot of script trouble on *The Scapegoat*, and they brought in Gore Vidal and Kenneth Tynan, others perhaps, to try to fix it up. Hamer was certainly a bit unreliable by this time, but in the final cutting they chopped the story around and made utter nonsense of it. It was a good story at first but it had nothing to do with Daphne du Maurier's conception. The Bette Davis character should have been much more austere to make sense of the plot. She spat our her lines and she, or someone else, insisted on her being all 'flounced up' instead of the severe, hard woman she should have been.

As for *To Paris With Love*, it was a case of a totally wrong director. The original American script for it wasn't bad and I hoped that Hamer would make it sharper, more European. However, he had a miserable drink problem by this time, and, really, the film needed someone brasher, some more extrovert person to deal with it.

In 1951 you made two of Ealing's flagship comedies, *The Lavender Hill Mob* and *The Man in the White Suit*. What do you think was the secret of their success?

Perhaps there was something liberating in the idea that everything is going to be all right, that there's a chance for ordinary people to break out. I suppose they're intelligent nonsense. I think *The Man in the White Suit* is an absolutely terrific film. It's very sad that Sandy [Alexander] Mackendrick gave up and went to Hollywood. He was always intelligent, always had something to say. Now *The Man in the White Suit* is a minor classic, but I remember the headline in the *Observer* (I think) at the time: 'Ignoble film'. It had been quite misinterpreted by the critic who'd expected nothing but joyful laughter. *The Lavender Hill Mob* is a very good-natured film with a well-told story. Charlie Crichton had a very good eye for cutting and a feeling for the idea of getting away from drab reality into a world of fancy.

What distinctions do you make among the Ealing directors?

Hamer had an amused, cynical view of things; Mackendrick was an enthusiast, who took a strong political line; I never got to know Crichton well; [Charles] Frend was a chum: he was always very worried, a charming man but not all that good a director. I did *Barnacle Bill* for Frend, out of friendship for him (not usually a good idea in film), and it was a mistake. I would have been happy to do it as a diatribe against the sloppiness of British life, not just as a jolly comedy which is how it emerged.

I wonder what you remember of *Last Holiday*, *The Card* and *The Captain's Paradise*, three engaging, non-Ealing films of the period.

Priestley's script for *Last Holiday* was very good in a simple, straightforward way, but the film was not very well directed. It was efficient enough and the final effect was quite pleasing, but it could have had more punch. It turns up on TV quite often and I'm interested in how films like it, from this period, are often much more appreciated than they were at the time.

I never felt I was the right actor to play Dendry in *The Card*. They should have had someone more obviously tougher. I think I treated it too lightly and I have never been happy playing parts too like myself.

The Captain's Paradise had a nice script and was very enjoyable to make, especially the experience of working with Celia Johnson, and I also enjoyed working with Tony Kimmins, who was a very easy-going director. Rex Harrison told me that the part had originally been offered to him and I'm sure he would have been more suitable. Yvonne de Carlo was cast to boost the American sales, I suppose.

Is *Bridge on the River Kwai* an early example of the internationalisation of British films?

I suppose so, considering that Sam Spiegel was its producer. The original script was ridiculous, with elephant charges and girls screaming round in the jungle. When David Lean arrived, with a new screenwriter, it became a very different thing. I saw Nicholson as an effective part, without ever really believing in the character. However, it paid off: it was a huge success and I got an Oscar for it, though I don't think it made an enormous difference to my career.

I admire your performance as Jock Sinclair in *Tunes of Glory*. How do you regard it?

As it turned out, I was very pleased with it. Initially, I'd been offered the John Mills character, but I made the wild suggestion that I should play the hard-drinking, hard-swearing man. The impossible appeals to me more than the obvious. I thought it was a very good script, with excellent dialogue and character.

What are your impressions of working with Carol Reed on *Our Man in Havana*? How involved was Graham Greene?

As I remember, Graham Greene was around for some of the time in Cuba. But I didn't enjoy doing the film very much. I didn't get on awfully well with Carol Reed. When you arrived on the set, you found everything had been worked out in finest detail. Also I thought there was a big tactical error in the Cuban boy-and-girl romance and there was a lot of strange angling of the camera. The story wasn't told in the simple way it should have been. I like to find something in a part that I can contribute each day and I felt Reed was inclined to over-direct. He rather threw me when he said early on, 'We don't want any of your character acting.' I felt my concept of the character – not filmed – was closer to Greene's. I never liked playing myself. It's important for me to get some hook to hang my character on. I want to know what I should look like. If I'm frustrated in this, I worry that I won't get to know what's inside. I'm a practical man as far as my work is concerned.

How would you respond to criticisms that British cinema has been too literary, too class-

bound, too tied to the theatre?

It certainly has been too literary but I must say that it is refreshing to read a script that is well-written. As for its being too tied to the theatre, there have been films of stage successes in the past which led to a great deal of staginess on film. But I do think there was a break away from this during the time of Reed and Lean, who'd seek to tell a story more visually. I think the theatre connection often made British films seem very talkative. About the 'class-bound' criticism, I'd say one gets just as weary of seeing working-class types on the screen as one did of upper-class ones. In the time you're talking about, films were about people who *did* have servants, who were often comic when they weren't pathetic. In terms of changes in film, there was a whole batch of socially refreshing films at the end of the '50s.

Greta Gynt

b. 1916

Actor: *Sangen Till Henne* (1934), *Boys will be Girls, The Last Curtain* (1937), *Sexton Blake and the Hooded Terror, The Last Barricade* (1938), *Too Dangerous to Live, Dark Eyes of London, She Couldn't Say No, The Arsenal Stadium Mystery, The Middle Watch* (1939), *Two for Danger, Bulldog Sees It Through, Room for Two, Crooks' Tour* (1940), *The Common Touch* (1941), *It's That Man Again, Tomorrow We Live* (1942), *Mr Emmanuel* (1944), *London Town, Take My Life* (1946), *Dear Murderer, Easy Money* (1947), *The Calendar, Mr Perrin and Mr Traill* (1948), *Shadow of the Eagle* (1950), *I'll Get You For This, Soldiers Three* (1951), *Whispering Smith Hits London, I'm a Stranger, The Ringer* (1952), *Three Steps in the Dark, The Last Moment* (1953), *Forbidden Cargo, Devil's Point* (1954), *See How They Run, The Blue Peter, Dead On Time, Born for Trouble* (1955), *Keep It Clean, My Wife's Family, Fortune is a Woman* (1956), *Morning Call* (1958), *The Witness, The Crowning Touch* (1959), *Bluebeard's Ten Honeymoons* (1960), *The Runaway* (1964)

Greta Gynt brought a touch of Hollywood-style glamour to British films for a brief spell in the '40s. The problem was that British cinema really didn't know what to do with glamour, any more than it did with the cheerful sexuality of Diana Dors. Critics who went overboard for, say, Celia Johnson in a dreadful hat were unlikely to be disposed to wax lyrical over a slinky blonde (it's a shock to find she was not one of nature's blondes) singing 'Shady Lady Spiv', as Gynt did in an enjoyably forgettable Gainsborough portmanteau film, *Easy Money*. Further, the British public generally preferred its wicked ladies in period cleavage, whereas she was resolutely modern as she betrayed Eric Portman in *Dear Murderer*. The more one thinks of Greta Gynt, though, the more she seems a key figure in post-war British cinema, hedonistic and insolently sensual; a slimmer, female version of Raymond Lovell, inevitably corrupt in a cravat, and Gynt's opposite number in *The Calendar*. Hollywood, which didn't need her as much as Britain did, misused her bizarrely; she made some utter stinkers at home, most memorably *London Town*; but her best work – in Harold French's *Mr Emmanuel*, Ronald Neame's *Take My Life* and Arthur Crabtree's *Dear Murderer* – confirms her as a genuine star presence. The '50s was no time for women in British cinema, but even then the old stylishness could bring life to minor enterprises.

Interview date: October 1992

Did you ever feel your glamorous image limited the roles you were offered?

It got in my way. I came from Norway originally, when I was about nineteen. I got myself an agent, Christopher Mann – whom I married. My hair is naturally jet black and Christopher said if I wanted to play spies for the rest of my life that was OK (I looked a Mata Hari type with the black hair and high Norwegian cheekbones). But if I didn't want to do that I would have to dye my hair blonde, so that is how it started. He had discovered Madeleine Carroll and he based me on her (she had been dark originally, too).

Was *The Last Curtain*, directed by David Macdonald, produced by Anthony Havelock-Allan, your first film as Greta Gynt?

I can't recall. The first film I did here was with Lesley Fuller [*Boys will be Girls*]. I was also in *She Couldn't Say No* at Elstree with Googie Withers, Cecil Parker and Tommy Trinder. I did make an awful lot of 'B' pictures to start off with, before I got my seven-year contract with Rank. I remember doing a Sexton Blake film with George Curzon. *Sexton Blake and the Hooded Terror* was directed by George King and I worked often for him in those days. I did masses of television shorts with him, and *Two For Danger* in 1940.

Do you recall making *The Arsenal Stadium Mystery*, directed by Thorold Dickinson?

I can't remember much about him, but I was only too happy to be in it. It was made at Denham, I know, and Esmond Knight was in it – and the entire Arsenal football team. It wasn't an expensive film. It was photographed by Desmond Dickinson; Guy Green was another cameraman I remember, on *Take My Life*. Ronnie Neame was another cameraman-turned-director with whom I worked: he directed *Take My Life*.

Did it matter much to you, as an actress, who the cameraman was?

Oh yes, you had your favourites; you knew that if you were to be photographed by this one or that one you would look more beautiful than you'd ever looked in your life! With some other cameramen, all the shadows went in the wrong places. I wish I had found out more about it.

You made two films in the early 1940s for John Baxter, *Crooks' Tour* and *The Common Touch*. Do you have any recollection of him?

I remember I sang and danced in *The Common Touch*, with Carroll Gibbons playing the piano. It was done by some film company run by Lou Jackson – British National, probably. I also sang in *Crooks' Tour* as a cabaret artiste, but it wasn't my voice. The only time they used my own voice was in *Easy Money*, and EMI have released it on record. The song I sang, 'Shady Lady Spiv', was written by Vivian Ellis. It's a pity Britain didn't make more musicals because I could have done them.

I did *London Town*, of course, that famous disaster. There were people like Sonnie Hale, Kay Kendall and Petula Clark in it, and the famous stage comedian Sid Field, whose work just didn't come over on the screen without the audience laughter. Those people would have been funny on the stage, in a music hall, but they didn't work on the screen. They spent an absolute fortune on it. I don't think the American, Wesley Ruggles, was a good director for a musical; he had made his name as a director of big Westerns. Dear Kay Kendall was so beautiful and they tried to make her into a Hollywood-star type, but she couldn't dance. (If only I could have had that part!) They just didn't know what to do with Kay until those few years before she died, when she was married to Rex Harrison. But what a personality! As for *London Town*, the costumes were bad, the designers were bad.

You starred as Elsie Silver in Harold French's *Mr Emmanuel* with Felix Aylmer.

Yes, what's happened to that film? I've tried and tried to find a copy of it and no one seems to know where it is. I knew the writer of *Mr Emmanuel*, Louis Golding; he wanted to do more films with me in them as the Elsie Silver character, but it never happened. It was one of the best parts I ever had. Walter Rilla played the German, and his son Wolf, who was a director, runs a hotel now. I did *The Blue Peter* for him in Wales.

There was an amazing roll call of people in those films.

Yes, when I look back I can hardly believe I'm still here! I remember making films with people like Tommy Trinder, Martita Hunt and Bela Lugosi. I think my most demanding dramatic role was in *Take My Life*. But, in a way, I think drama is much easier than comedy; comedy is very difficult to play because of the timing. I recall the climax in the moving train – it was all done in the studio, though, no location work whatsoever. The writer, Winston Graham, was a very good woman's writer.

After that I made *Dear Murderer* with Eric Portman. It was the first film Betty Box produced completely on her own. The director was another former cameraman, Arthur Crabtree, a very placid man. He wasn't a strong director, though. About a year later, somebody tried to do the same thing in reality. It said in the papers that this man had tried to copy *Dear Murderer* in how to kill his wife.

Were you under contract?

Yes, to the Rank Organisation and I was absolutely delighted by that. I went over to Hollywood in about 1947 when the 'New Look' came in. I was making it good then, but I thought I'd go to Hollywood and I was put under personal contract to Robert Siodmak, for whom I did a test. It was a six-year contract with Universal-International. In the meantime I had met the father of my son and I thought, 'My family are in Norway, my boyfriend is in England – I can't stay here.' So I came back to England with a six-year contract. John Davis was a very hard nut to crack, and when I came back he didn't want to know. I couldn't work because I was still under contract to Universal-International. I just had to wait and wait until they agreed to let me go.

Then I was offered a film with Valentina Cortesa and Richard Greene, made in Venice. It was called *Shadow of the Eagle*. I remember David Lewin ringing up and asking what it felt like to 'play second fiddle to Valentina Cortesa'. I didn't know what he meant. Then he said, 'Well, you're not starring in it, are you?'

I've heard that it had a very troubled production history.

We all went over to Rome and Margot Grahame was going to play in it; suddenly Binnie Barnes's husband [Mike Frankovitch] said no to her for some reason, and she was replaced with Binnie Barnes. It may have been that Margot had put on too much weight. I remember we were all terribly upset about the whole thing. It was a costume drama and they made two versions of it, one in English and one in Italian. So there were Italian actors, and Hugh French, Richard Greene, and so on. I couldn't work out what was going on and the American director said not to worry, just to say the English lines. I thought it was odd that I had come to do one film and here I was doing two.

In the late 1940s you made one popular film after another. You made *Easy Money* for another ex-cameraman, Bernard Knowles. Do you remember anything of that?

Not much, no, other than singing 'Shady Lady Spiv'. I just went and did a job and enjoyed every moment of it. It was made at Lime Grove. There were four different stories. The last one, to do with the orchestra, had Raymond Lovell in it. There is a little man [Edward Rigby] who has only to clash the cymbals at the end of the recital; while he was waiting for his moment, he was doing the football pools; the conductor suddenly stopped the orchestra and asked him his name. The little man replied, 'Ball, sir.' The conductor replied, 'How very singular!' and I was always surprised that the censor let that through!

One of my favourite British films of the period is *Mr Perrin and Mr Traill*, directed by Lawrence Huntington. Do you recall working for him?

I was completely miscast as the school matron, but it was a good film. The make-up people told me to wear my hair flowing down and it was so wrong for the part. I should have looked the way I do now, with my hair up. Huntington was good with actors, though; his daughter Sheila was one of the 'dozen and one' showgirls in *London Town*.

You finally went to Hollywood after that

and made *Soldiers Three*. **How did that come about?**

Soldiers Three – I thought, 'At last it's happened.' I went to New York and was put into an exquisite luxury apartment at the Plaza, but I had no idea when I was to go to Hollywood. Then suddenly I was told to leave for Los Angeles in two days' time. An MGM representative phoned me to say they wanted me on the set in a couple of days, and said he hoped I was up on my lines, and I replied, 'Do you think I've come four thousand miles to fluff?!' It was a very small part, one of those voluptuous blondes which I'm not. I don't know how the part was offered to me. I went into the make-up room and there was Sidney Guilaroff and the people doing the costumes, and they said they had to 'do a shape on me'. They told me to sit in a barber's chair and strip to my waist, then they put plaster of Paris all over me because, they said, 'Honey, we gotta build you up.' I've never been so unhappy in my life. Why cast me, for God's sake? Diana Dors would have been marvellous!

When you came back you in fact made several films with Hollywood stars and directors: with George Raft and Coleen Gray on *I'll Get You For This* (directed by Joseph Newman), and Arlene Dahl on *Fortune is a Woman*. Were these importations good for British films?

George Raft was enchanting, so nice to me. I was married by this time and nothing happened, but the *Hollywood Reporter* carried an item which said, 'George has found a Raft in Greta Gynt.' Most of the American actors they brought over were past their prime, and some of them were very much quickie 'B' movies. I did *Fortune is a Woman* when I was going through a divorce, and I stopped after that. Arlene Dahl was dull. I had a good part in it, though, and I remember the notices saying that the cameo parts played by Bernard Miles and myself had made the film. Most of those people were beyond it by the time they came over here. Even George Raft was really beyond it by then.

Did you enjoy doing the remake of *The Ringer* in the early '50s?

Yes, I did enjoy doing that; I was pregnant with my son at the time. It was the first film directed by Guy Hamilton, who had worked as Carol Reed's assistant, and Mai Zetterling and Denholm Elliott were in it too. That was my first film which was thoroughly rehearsed just like a play; we rehearsed for about three weeks in every set, so that when it came to the original shooting we knew exactly what to do in each scene.

There were very few good parts for women in the 1950s British cinema.

Yes, the only one who went on doing well at that time was Anna Neagle. Herbert Wilcox was there behind her and he saw the potential of what she could do. We don't all have a Wilcox behind us. The only time when I felt as if someone was looking after my career was for a short period with the Rank Organisation. Mr Rank kept an eye out on everyone who was under contract. I remember going to him one day after I'd been under contract for about two years. I was unhappy because I hadn't worked for so long and he said, 'Miss Gynt, do you think we'd have you under contract if we didn't want you to go into the right part for you?' He was a very nice man, very religious. We were never allowed to drink, of course – we had to use a straw and pretend it was lemonade!

For the rest of the time I was just put into this or that by an agent, until I didn't know who I was, and I also had a husband at the time who pointed out that he had to work for six months to earn what I earned in a couple of weeks. So I just took one film after another, and my name just went down and down.

What did you do when you stopped filming?

I was married to my late husband for twenty-five years and in that time all I did was maybe a couple of television things. Then I went on tour in *The Country Wife* with Julia Foster. After that I gave the whole thing up. I don't think I'd like to work again. I loved the stage. I didn't have a clue about film technique, so I had to rely on good directors. I remember an early director who told me to forget everything I'd learned at drama school! I'd never *been* to drama school, just picked it up as I went along. Acting for the screen did mean a whole lot of new techniques, and it was also very, very boring. You sat around for hours and hours. As a stage actress you have to learn how to breathe, how to throw your voice right into the gallery, whereas on the screen you have to play it way down. The camera picks up on the merest flicker of an eyebrow. You have to be just absolutely normal and natural on the screen.

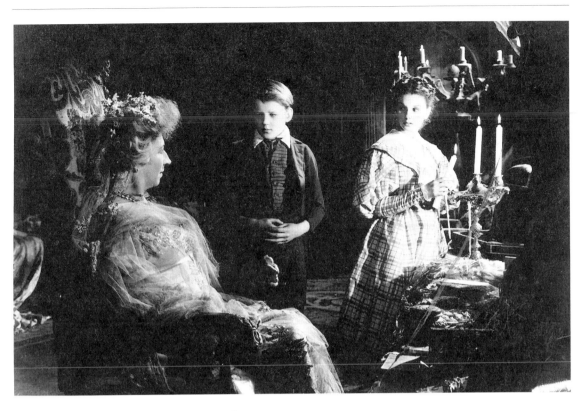

▲ Great Expectations *1946*   ▼ They Made Me a Fugitive *1947*

▲ No Orchids for Miss Blandish *1948*   ▼ The Red Shoes *1948*

▲ Saraband for Dead Lovers *1948*   ▼ Whisky Galore! *1949*

▲ Genevieve *1953*   ▼ The Kidnappers *1953*

Robert Hamer

1911–1963

Editor: *Vessel of Wrath, St Martin's Lane* (co-ed) (1938), *Jamaica Inn* (1939), **La Cause Commune* (& sc), **French Communiqué* (& sc) (1940), **Mastery at Sea* (& sc), *Turned Out Nice Again* (uncr ed), *Ships With Wings, The Foreman Went to France* (1941), *My Learned Friend* (1943)

Director: *Fiddlers Three* (uncr co-dir), *San Demetrio, London* (uncr co-dir & assoc pr) (1944), *Dead of Night* (co-dir), *Pink String and Sealing Wax* (1945), *It Always Rains On Sunday, The Loves of Joanna Godden* (uncr co-dir) (1947), *Kind Hearts and Coronets, The Spider and the Fly* (1949), *His Excellency* (1951), *The Long Memory* (1952) *To Paris With Love, Father Brown* (1954), *The Scapegoat* (1958), *School for Scoundrels* (1959)
* Documentary.

'**P**eople think they have some right to be happy, and are doubly unhappy when they are not . . . ,'[1] wrote Hamer in the screenplay for the unproduced *For Each the Other*. Hamer's own life, studded with several brilliant achievements, cannot, over-all, have been happy. 'My dearest girl, one of the things you don't know about me is my infinite capacity for consuming alcohol. I've a theory I was born several hundred drinks under par, so I'm always catching up,'[2] he tells the writer Pamela Wilcox (daughter of Herbert Wilcox) early in their relationship which ends so sadly. For, as everyone knows, Hamer died of his alcoholism, in which he seems to have sought escape from whatever personal demons drove him.

He began at Denham in 1938, where he had 'the inestimable good fortune to be put to work for Erich Pommer,'[3] as cutting-room assistant for London Films, before fetching up at Ealing two years later, as one of Balcon's bright young Oxbridge men. Early work on several films led to his being rewarded with the direction of 'The Haunted Mirror' episode of *Dead of Night*, followed by *Pink String and Sealing Wax*, in which he 'enjoyed the melodrama but never felt happy with the domestic charm.'[4] This may explain why the domesticity seems so thin and constricting compared with the pub world presided over by the great Googie Withers.

Ten years after the release of *Kind Hearts and Coronets*, Hamer lamented, 'That picture has become a sort of yardstick for everything else I've done. Friends . . . look at my other films and say, "good, brilliant, superb" but not, of course, so "good, brilliant, superb" as *Kind Hearts and Coronets*.'[5] It *is*, nevertheless, a high point in his career and in British film comedy. In 1952 he wrote of what he had seen of its possibilities: 'Firstly, that of making a film not noticeably similar to any previously made in the English language. Secondly, that of using this English language, which I love, in a more varied and, to me, more interesting way than I had previously had the chance of doing in a film. Thirdly, that of making a picture which paid no regard whatever to established, although not practised, moral conventions.'[6]

But, if *Kind Hearts* is a masterpiece, it is not an isolated peak. *It Always Rains On Sunday* has a continental sense of place and realism about relationships. *The Spider and the Fly* is a fine exemplification of what he said he'd like to do if given a free hand: 'Broadly, I would like to make a film about Crime . . . an examination . . . of the respective virtues and faults of the criminal, of the Police, of prosecuting Counsel, of defending Counsel . . .'[7] *Father Brown* has some of this interest; so does *The Long Memory*, which, though a little turgid, draws fine performances from John Mills and from John

McCallum, who praised Hamer as 'a perfectionist who knew more about acting for films than any other director I know.'[8]

Inevitably, perhaps, he clashed with Balcon and left Ealing, where his vision was always too dark for comfort, though he said in 1951: 'We are given complete liberty to follow our personal directions.'[9] Of the rest, *To Paris With Love* is a disaster, full of stereotypical British responses to naughty Paris; *The Scapegoat* has its moments but nothing to thread them together; and he collapsed while making *School for Scoundrels*, of which he said he wanted 'to make a widely understood comedy'[10] from Stephen Potter's books.

Balcon was no doubt right to say Hamer 'was engaged on a process of self-destruction,'[11] but, oh, the pity of it – and the loss.

1 *Film Comment*, May–June 1995, p 78
2 Pamela Wilcox, *Between Hell and Charing Cross*, George Allen & Unwin, London, 1977, p 74. The name Hamer is never mentioned but there is no doubt to whom she refers.
3 *Sight and Sound*, October–December, 1951, p 74
4 *Sight and Sound*, October–December 1951, p 75
5 *Films and Filming*, July 1959, p 27
6 Roger Manvell and RK Neilson Baxter (eds), *The Cinema 1952*, Penguin, 1952, p 52
7 *Sight and Sound*, Spring 1959, p 62
8 John McCallum, *Life with Googie*, Heinemann, London, 1979, p 8
9 *Films in 1951*, BFI, p 9
10 *Films and Filming*, p 27
11 Michael Balcon, *A Lifetime of Films*, Hutchinson, London, 1969, p 163

Guy Hamilton

b. 1922

Director: *The Ringer* (1952), *The Intruder* (1953), *An Inspector Calls* (1954), *The Colditz Story* (1955), *Charley Moon* (1956), *Manuela* (1957), *The Devil's Disciple, A Touch of Larceny* (1959), *The Best Of Enemies* (1961), *The Party's Over* (1963), *Man in the Middle, Goldfinger* (1964), *Funeral in Berlin* (1966), *The Battle of Britain* (1968), *Diamonds Are Forever* (1971), *Live and Let Die* (1973), *The Man with the Golden Gun* (1974), *Force Ten from Navarone* (1978), *The Mirror Crack'd* (1980), *Evil under the Sun* (1982), *Remo Williams: The Adventure Begins* (1985), *Try This On For Size* (& co-sc) (1989)

Unlike many British directors of the period, Guy Hamilton was never a screenwriter, or cameraman, or editor, before turning to direction. He had always wanted to direct and, along the way to achieving this goal in 1952, he became the most sought-after assistant director in the business. When he did begin to direct, he turned out a string of highly entertaining, carefully crafted films in a range of popular genres. His first, *The Ringer*, derived from Edgar Wallace, showed a great deal of unpretentiously deployed craftsmanship and makes excellent use of a strong cast. He had three varied successes with his next films: *The Intruder*, an intelligent version of Robin Maugham's novel of postwar malaise; *An Inspector Calls*, which gave new life to Priestley's morality play; and the very popular POW film, *The Colditz Story*. And *Manuela* is an erotic melodrama of a kind unusual in British cinema, with a remarkable performance from Trevor Howard as the obsessed sea captain. In the best of Guy Hamilton's films, there is a real gift for narrative and an unobtrusive sophistication at work in its display.

Interview date: July 1990

You made some of the most entertaining British films of the 1950s. How did you arrive at that phase of your career?

When I came out of the Navy in one piece, I knew what I wanted to do. I became a third and then a second assistant director, having been lucky enough to work for Carol Reed, who really was my 'father' as a director. I learned a lot from him, working on films such as *The Fallen Idol* and *The Third Man* and for John Huston on *The African Queen* – a wonderful training. I also learned a lot from *bad* directors. The trick I discovered was not to be an assistant director but to be the director's *assistant*. There are certain things the director is not interested in doing and you have to cover for those, while watching very carefully for the things he passionately cares about. In this way you become very valuable to him because you sense his needs. Some of the films I did as assistant director were Launder and Gilliat's *State Secret*, Tony Kimmins's *Mine Own Executioner* and Jean Negulesco's *Britannia Mews* (as well she might!).

The problem then was to become a director because there were plenty of directors but not many good assistants. I was under contract to Alexander Korda, a remarkable man, a combination then of British Lion and London Films, but we were taking much too long to make pictures. I said to Korda I could make a picture in three weeks; there was a series of 'B' pictures being made and that was how I got my first break as a director. My first film, *The Ringer*, took three weeks for rehearsal and shooting.

You had a continuing association with producer Ivan Foxwell.

I got my chance as a director making 'B' pictures but I was looking to make an 'A' picture; I was lucky enough to come across Ivan, who had been in the Army and had had a very similar career to my own, beforehand. He didn't want to direct and I didn't want to produce, so we made an excellent combination. We took the idea for *The Intruder* to Korda and that was my start. It was a happy experience for both Ivan and myself. We decided to team up again and I had wanted to do *The Colditz Story*, having always been intrigued by POWs and their escape attempts. Ivan had a real knowledge of pictures – I like a hands-on producer – and was willing for us to work closely together.

The Ringer was your first feature film as a director, for which you were contracted to London Films, I believe?

That's right. Carol Reed was very instrumental in helping me. He said, 'Don't make the picture you want to make; make a comedy thriller. You'll miss some of the thrills, some of the laughs, but with a bit of luck there'll be something left.' So he suggested I make Edgar Wallace's *The Ringer*, which was all on one set and could be done in two weeks. It had been made before as *The Gaunt Stranger*. Our version was a 'B' picture so it went out as bottom of the bill on a double feature; as such it was successful.

Your next two films were also adaptations – The Intruder from Robin Maugham's novel Line on Ginger, and An Inspector Calls from Priestley's play. How do you approach the business of adaptation?

The Intruder was a script brought to me in more or less a 'go' situation, subject to Jack Hawkins's agreeing to my being the director. There were a lot of pressures about 'My goodness, Jack, how could you work with Guy, he's just a new director and you're a big star,' and so on. I offered to step aside but I had lunch with Jack one day and it turned out the problem was a small one, to do with the homosexual overtones in the original novel, which had been removed from the script. Maugham and his partner, John Hunter, had concocted the screenplay, and structurally there wasn't much of it we had to change.

My next picture I didn't really want to do because I'd discovered *Dial M for Murder* as a play on television and I wanted to do it, but it was ultimately sold to Hitchcock. As a contract director, I had to do the Priestley play instead. I was happy doing it; I had a nice cast and it was fun doing vintage Priestley. I was left very much alone because AD Peters and Norman Collins were not hands-on producers. There's something about that play that undoubtedly works. I considered myself as really the handmaiden of Priestley, for whom I had an admiration, and I tried to be honest to his play. The girl played by Jane Wenham doesn't actually appear in the play; she's just talked about.

The very opposite to that from the point of view of adaptation was *A Touch of Larceny* – a thriller which was written very seriously and which I thought was utter rubbish but, turned around, terribly funny. I asked Ivan if I could make it as a comedy; he saw the point and off we went, working with Roger MacDougall, who was a lovely writer. In that case we had little respect for the novel. I adored working with Vera Miles on that, a very underrated actress. Again I had a very strong cast – James Mason, George Sanders, Harry Andrews, and so on. Of that period, it is definitely my favourite film.

The Intruder is one of a small group of films which seemed to be reappraising post-war British life. Did you see it in that way?

It came not so long after we were all demobbed and I felt very much at ease with all the characters, because I'd met them all in one form or another during the war. Lindsay Anderson came up to me not long after the film was released, and said, 'You've let the side down.' He meant that the burglar rejoined the Establishment when he really should have turned on the Colonel.

You then did The Colditz Story. Unlike many British directors of the period, you didn't make many war films. Was this your choice?

Yes. After *The Colditz Story*, which was my personal baby, I felt a bit too closely involved myself. I had too much admiration for certain things and I hated a lot of war films, which seemed to me too facile and not dealing in any way with the truth, so I steered well clear of them. Eric Portman and John Mills were the backbone of the film, all the rest were basically new boys. It was Lionel Jeffries's first film and Ian Carmichael wasn't a well-known screen actor then.

Was the business with the geranium a sort

of quotation from *La Grande Illusion*? Or the first meeting between the opposing officers?**

As a small boy I had been greatly smitten with *La Grande Illusion* and I think you can't avoid recalling things you've admired, but I was really more influenced by Pat Reid, who was in Colditz and wrote the book the film was based on. I also enjoyed doing those scenes in Polish and French because, having already explained to the audience beforehand that a Polish soldier is to be court-martialled, then doing the scene in Polish without subtitles, I think it works very well as a touch of realism.

But the real importance of *The Colditz Story*, apart from its being a big success, was that it was essentially comedy about something that, up until that point, you could not make fun of – POWs. I was absolutely determined to show that Colditz was exceptional *and* could be very funny – and it worked.

How did your collaboration on the screenplay, with William Douglas-Home and Ivan Foxwell, work?

Essentially, Ivan and I supplied the structure and Willy, who was a playwright, supplied the dialogue. He had been a distinguished officer himself and had a fine, dry humour; he had been in an officers' camp and was able to supply the right humour and the right dialogue.

How would you react to my idea that Trevor Howard in Manuela gives the best performance in a Guy Hamilton film?

That's for other people to judge. It was a very personal film. Ivan and I were at the height of our powers, very cocky, and I enjoyed working in black-and-white, I enjoyed Trevor, I enjoyed the whole thing. It was my first taste of real melodrama. I think the film is unusually direct (for a British film) about the destructive power of sexuality; until then sex in British films had mostly been very well behaved. *Manuela*'s a very French film in mood, I think, probably influenced a little by all the films I'd seen in my childhood in France (and shouldn't have seen, because of my age). It rather shook the critics and the public, it was fairly strong meat and had the censors right on edge. Otto Heller was the cameraman I chose because I always liked his black-and-white work. I pushed him a little bit but then gave him a free hand and he did a lovely job.

How was your next film, The Devil's Disciple, set up?

Sandy Mackendrick had just made that marvellous picture, *Sweet Smell of Success* for Hecht-Hill-

Lancaster in the US, and they'd come over to make *The Devil's Disciple* with Sandy directing. The grosses of *Sweet Smell of Success* were very disappointing and Burt Lancaster and Kirk Douglas started to niggle, so they fired Sandy, who had been shooting for about three weeks. MCA, who were my agents, told me they wanted me to take over. I refused to take over from Sandy and was given a stern lecture to the effect that I would never be a serious director until I had worked with some international stars. Someone would have to direct the picture so it might as well be me, so, in the event, I did it. The terrifying thing was that I found it so easy to be a 'traffic cop' with no 'gut' in the project. I'd never done it before and won't do it again. All you can do is follow the blueprint.

How did I find working with such 'heady' talents? Both made love to me and I could see straight away that whichever way I came down I was going to make an enemy for life. So I said, 'Don't ask me, fellows, because if it was my picture, Kirk would be playing Burt's part and vice versa.' There was a stunned silence and for the rest of the day they were in corners, looking through the script at the other's part! That kept them apart and off my back for the rest of the picture.

Eva le Gallienne was in it and she'd only made two or three pictures. She was a very distinguished lady, and I don't think she terribly approved of these two clowns, who were not my favourite people at that time (and I'm sure they said the same of me). Burt I found irritating because he'd say things like, 'What did George Bern*ard* Shaw mean in this scene? I think we're missing some of the kinetic values,' and he'd go on and on. Then you'd pick him up and say, 'Burt, I think we're losing some of the kinetic values,' and he'd say, 'Ah shit, kid, it's only a *movie!*'

How did you become involved with the four Bond films? What are their rewards for a director?

I had been offered the first Bond film, *Dr No*, but couldn't leave Jamaica for personal reasons, so was delighted when subsequently I had a chance to direct *Goldfinger*. I'd enjoyed the previous two films, but felt there was a real danger of Bond becoming Superman; consequently there would be no suspense in whatever predicaments were dreamt up for him. So we concentrated on the villains; Bond is only as good as his villains. The most fun in later pictures was thinking up 'snake pit' situations – Bond on a small island, surrounded by crocodiles, locked in a coffin and being cremated, etc – and sweating away for weeks trying to rescue him. Tom Mankiewicz [son of Joseph] and I still have some wonderful 'snake pits' but could never use them because we failed ignominiously to find satisfactory escapes.

You direct a Bond movie with an insane sense of power. What other picture is there where the audience, world-wide, knows the characters, knows the ground rules, thus enabling you to say, 'Children, of all ages, don't ask too many questions, leave your brains under the seat and come for a glorious ride.' I believe you can go on making Bonds forever because they contain the basic elements of cinema: adventure, suspense, laughs, excitement, pretty girls . . . as long as the people making them don't get lazy and repetitive – a danger in the past, but the recent team have all pulled together and come up with the splendid *GoldenEye*.

Susan Hampshire

b. 1942

Actor: *The Woman in the Hall* (1947), *Idol on Parade, Upstairs and Downstairs, Expresso Bongo* (1959), *During One Night, The Long Shadow* (1961), *Night Must Fall, The Three Lives of Thomasina, Wonderful Life* (1964), *Paris in August* (1965), *The Fighting Prince of Donegal* (1966), *The Trygon Factor* (1967), *The Violent Enemy, Monte Carlo or Bust!, David Copperfield* (1969), *Time for Loving, Baffled!, Malpertius, Living Free, Roses Rouges et Piments Verts* (US 1975: *The Lonely Woman*), *Neither the Sea nor the Sand* (1972), *Bang!* (1976)

Susan Hampshire is probably right to say that she would have had a more prolific film career if she'd started ten years earlier. On the other hand, she might now be remembered in the way that those other Susans, Stephen and Beaumont, are: that is, hardly at all. She would have been put into a string of anodyne romantic comedies and feeble thrillers and she would have missed the brilliant opportunities that television gave her in *The Forsyte Saga*, *The Pallisers* and *Vanity Fair*. Certainly her type was not in vogue in the early '60s during the ascendancy of the new social realist films, though she worked for one of its chief exponents, Karel Reisz, in his psychological reshaping of *Night Must Fall*. Despite the prettiness which might have consigned her to the 'wallpaper' parts she so candidly speaks of, she nevertheless managed a wider range of films than is at first apparent: she serves her material well in the Cliff Richard musical, *Wonderful Life*; is an engaging witch for Disney in *Thomasina*; makes the most of some bitchy moments in the crime thriller, *The Trygon Factor*; takes over where Virginia McKenna left off in *Living Free*; and is properly sweet as Agnes in Delbert Mann's *David Copperfield*. It would be interesting to see her get a go at well-written, mature-age part to match her obvious self-knowledge. She is the author of *Susan's Story* (1982), in which she records her struggles with dyslexia.
Interview date: July 1994

How did you come to be in Jack Lee's *Woman in the Hall* when you were about seven?

I was on the Underground with my mother and a lady sitting opposite us told us that they were testing children who would look like Jean Simmons as a child, for a film. She said that I looked suitable and asked my mother if I'd like to test. My mother said yes, they sent us all the details, and my mother sat up all night sewing me a nightie to wear for the test. She made me learn my lines, I did the test and got the part. That really gave me a taste of what it was like and the joy of working in that ambience.

What were your experiences of working for Sidney Furie, a lively figure of the early '60s, on the Cliff Richard musical *Wonderful Life* and on *During One Night*?

During One Night was a fairly pleasurable experience. It was a 'B' movie, made very quickly, in about two-and-a-half or three weeks, and of course I was very inexperienced. It was very exciting to make because it involved long, five-minute takes with no cutaways. But I wasn't up to it, because I was too frightened and I don't think a director can work with a frightened actress. Anyway, it was a much more enjoyable experience than doing the Sidney Furie musical and I felt it was my chance to make my way in serious cinema.

When I did the Cliff Richard musical, I had just finished playing Marian Dangerfield in *The Ginger Man* at the Royal Court Theatre opposite Nicol Williamson and I was catapulted from drama, which I desperately wanted to get into, back into a very popular-image musical. To a certain extent, I didn't really fit in off the set; secondly, I didn't have a particularly good part, although it was the lead. However, there was a great sequence where we did the history of the movies; and I had a tremendous opportunity – dancing, singing, acting and imitating people such as Shirley Temple, Garbo, etc – but nobody knows that it's me! People kind of overlooked that excellent part of the film. I can only say that the film was a very good learning experience and turned out to be very successful with the public. But sadly, I never got into really good movies, ever.

I think that's a modest account of your career. Would you say that television offered you better opportunities?

Yes, much better, and I suppose that if there was such a thing as being a star, to a certain extent I became a television queen at that stage. But certainly there was more prestige attached to doing a film than a television series.

What did you think of your 1964 release, *Night Must Fall*, the remake by Karel Reisz?

First of all, it was a great opportunity to work with Karel and with Albert Finney, but I didn't have the confidence and, according to Laurence Olivier, ninety per cent of any acting is believing in yourself, then the audience believe in you. Therefore I used to go to the set each day, worried out of my mind, having lain awake all night and not prepared. The most important thing to come out of it was Albert Finney teaching me that homework is the most vital part of the job. Albert taught me to go on to the set with a true knowledge of your character, knowing your lines extremely well (I used to learn my lines, but not to the extent of having that relaxed knowledge of the part). So, although I felt I had let down Karel and Albert in that film, the good thing was that I came out of it stronger and I was happy to have had that learning experience. Both Karel and Albert were very supportive, too. Karel was wonderful, although – rightly – very demanding. If your expression didn't come from total truth he was not happy.

When you do a film based on a novel or a play like *Night Must Fall*, do you make a point of going back to the original text, or is that confusing?

On that I stuck with the screenplay because my role was very different from the original text; but, with any of those long classic books that have been serialised for television, I have referred to the book throughout. I've virtually gone back to the book in the dressing-room between takes. A long television serial is going to remain much closer to the book than a two-hour film is, and that, of course, is the great luxury in that you have perhaps twenty-four hours in which to develop a character.

Your next films were with the Disney Organisation: *The Three Lives of Thomasina* and *The Fighting Prince of Donegal*. Many people recall Disney as a very efficient organisation: did you feel that?

They were very efficient, yes. They were also very powerful. I met Walt Disney himself a couple of times and he was just wonderful to everyone who worked for him. He genuinely seemed to regard them all as a big family, he ensured that you were protected. I should have been working in the '40s and '50s, really, I would have had a better working life. But I started in the '60s when, if you didn't have a North Country or a Cockney accent, or if you hadn't been nude several times, or if there wasn't something strikingly non-middle-class about you, you faced a lot of prejudice. I was seen as an actress who was not easily accepted because of her middle-class background and the way she sounded. The Disney films tended to reinforce that perception of me, so therefore I was fighting the Disney image instead of going along with it.

In fact, if I had accepted any of the contracts I was offered at the time – one with MGM when I was doing *Night Must Fall*, one with Disney, or the one I was offered with Fox, all great contracts with a lot of money and all offering the opportunity of doing a film every year – I might have had a more prolific film career, albeit not necessarily a better one. But Albert Finney advised me not to get locked up in any of those deals; I became so anxious to hang on to quality of life and I didn't particularly want to go to America, so I refused the other two as well. It would have been quite a nice working life for me, in fact, if I hadn't been so frightened of being cast to type.

On *The Fighting Prince* the cameraman was Arthur Ibbetson. How important was the cameraman to you, as an actress? Did you become technically knowledgeable?

In those days (it's different now), there was a very important relationship with the cameraman or with the make-up man. You start your day with the make-up man and, if you can't come to terms with your own face or you don't agree with what he's doing, well, you're in trouble. There was a make-up artist, John O'Gorman, who made you feel great because he understood your face, so that you went out in front of the camera feeling and looking good. I've always worried about my face, I've always had bags under my eyes, I probably plucked my eyebrows wrongly; so basically I went in front of the camera feeling terrible before we began.

I did become technically knowledgeable, yes, totally. I know exactly what I need. I know that if the light's too high then my bags show; I know that if I have a cross-light my nose-to-mouth lines become too strong, with too many contours. I need a flat light two feet above me and a dinky for my eyes, all pretty well coming from the same direction or maybe one foot to the right. I also knew about my face. I wasn't half as desperate about it in films, though, as I used to be on television. All those cameramen in films made a great effort to make it either atmospheric or in keeping with the film, and they succeeded.

I'd be interested in any recollections you have of working with Stewart Granger, a major British star of the '40s, in *The Trygon Factor*.

I would call that another 'B' picture. Very often I did films because of tax demands. Working with Stewart Granger? In general it is a lot easier to work with women than with men, in the theatre and in films or television. I think that in order to be particularly good at his job, there has to be a strong feminine streak in a male actor, a streak of jealousy so that, if the make-up man comes and powders my nose, he wonders why *his* nose hasn't been powdered too. After all, he wants to look great too. That in itself produces some inexplicable thing in the ego of the man, which many actresses I've spoken to all find that they come across. A lot of actresses are so strong that they override the man, but I tend to worry that I've upset him and so I try to do what he wants. I'm accommodating, if you like.

We had a very interesting director in that film, Cyril Frankel, and I think it was one of the best acting performances I've ever given. The character was a strong girl who wanted to kill her sister or something, and I know I wore a red wig. All I can say is that I surprised myself in the way that I got on with it.

***Monte Carlo or Bust!* was, I take it, a follow-up to *Those Magnificent Men in Their Flying Machines*. Did you enjoy that sort of comedy?**

I did, yes, and I felt that, with all the technical difficulties, the make-up problems and so forth, it was still a happy working experience, and the director, Ken Annakin, certainly knew his onions.

How did you feel about doing *Living Free* as a sequel to the hugely popular *Born Free*?

I think I was really pleased because it was my introduction to conservation; but of course, one never realises how difficult a sequel is. Even if it turns out to be as good as the original, it's never going to be quite so successful.

Where did you make it?

In Africa [Kenya], at Lake Naivasha. When the wind came everything was covered in dust and there I was, trying to feed a six-months-old baby. You would get up at crack of dawn, go to make-up, drive an hour and a half to the shooting location and not get back until very late, but nonetheless it was a fantastically interesting experience.

It was a dry heat; working with the lions was incredibly challenging, and the great thing was that we had a guy who had only a pair of leather gloves and a rope to handle them. We never gave the animals any dope or tranquillisers, except once when the lion was supposed to be dying. I was made to lie on a camp bed with a lion; I was asked to chase a lion who had my hat. The trainer thought out ways to make the lions do the things he wanted. They weren't circus lions either: their parents may have been in captivity, but they were young, wild lions who weren't tamed at all. They had just lived in a safari park or somewhere. I wouldn't do it again, I must say. I wouldn't risk my life again, I think it was unnecessary bravery.

By the late '60s you had had enormous success as Fleur in *The Forsyte Saga* for television. It surely gave you a more interesting part than most of your films, in that there is a bit of the bitch about Fleur, she's quite tough.

Yes, that's why I felt I was better in *The Trygon Factor*, because those nothing parts come out as nothing. At least the witch in *Thomasina* had a bit of spark to her, but a lot of the parts I'd had were just wallpaper against which other people could do their thing. I fought like a tiger on *The Pallisers* too. I had done it on *The Forsyte Saga* because I had the knowledge of the book on my side; if there is something that makes a great novel work and you feel it is an important part of your character, then you fight for it. I would go back to the book and insist that certain scenes that were vital to the character be included. I refused to be part of the wallpaper.

I'm in my fifties now and the lucky thing is that it doesn't matter what I look like, so I feel ready for whatever turns up.

Peter Handford

b. 1919

Sound recordist: *Under Capricorn, Black Magic, Night and the City* (1949), *Lilacs in the Spring, Beggar's Opera, Hobson's Choice* (1954), *Summer Madness, Crest of the Wave, King's Rhapsody* (1955), *Private's Progress, My Teenage Daughter, Dry Rot, Three Men in a Boat* (1956), *Saint Joan, Happy is the Bride* (1957), *The Key, Room at the Top* (1958), *Left, Right and Centre* (1959), *Sons and Lovers, The Entertainer, Saturday Night and Sunday Morning* (1960), *Mysterious Island* (1961), *Billy Liar, Tom Jones* (1963), *The Pumpkin Eater* (1964), *Darling* (1965), *Morgan, Mademoiselle, Charge of the Light Brigade* (1966), *Charlie Bubbles, The White Bus* (1967), *Oh! What a Lovely War, The Railway Children* (1970), *The Go-Between* (1971), *Frenzy* (1972), *Hitler: The Last Ten Days, A Doll's House, From Beyond the Grave* (1973), *Murder on the Orient Express, Akenfield* (1974), *The Romantic Englishwoman* (1975), *Joseph Andrews* (1976), *Holocaust 2000* (1977), *Absolution* (1978), *The Lady Vanishes* (1979), *Heaven's Gate* (prologue) (1980), *Finders Keepers* (1983), *Steaming* (1984), *Out of Africa* (1985), *Hope and Glory* (1987), *Gorillas in the Mist, Dangerous Liaisons* (1988), *White Hunter, Black Heart, Havana* (1990)

In the last decade of his career, Peter Handford worked on large international productions, winning an Oscar for his work as sound recordist on Sydney Pollack's *Out of Africa*. He worked again with Pollack on *Havana*, for Clint Eastwood on *White Hunter, Black Heart*, for Michael Apted on *Gorillas in the Mist*, and for Stephen Frears on *Dangerous Liaisons*, winning world-wide recognition for his contribution to major films. In the history of British cinema sound recording, his is the name that recurs most commonly on quality films. He is regularly associated with the social realist films, beginning with *Room at the Top*, which were the critical favourites from the end of the '50s: they include half a dozen for Tony Richardson, *Saturday Night and Sunday Morning* for Karel Reisz, and several for John Schlesinger, as well as a good deal of rather different work for Joseph Losey. Handford is very articulate about the function of the sound recordist, and in his career of over fifty years (he started at Denham before the war) he has seen important changes in his field.
Interview date: July 1994

Did you do any kind of formal training to become a sound recordist?

There was no such thing then. Many of the early sound recordists came from occupations such as the Merchant Navy, because they had been wireless operators and knew the electronics side of it. Today, the film schools offer training in the basic principles of cinematography but I don't think you can train sound recordists. Technical knowledge, yes, because we have to understand the working of our equipment and its limitations. Until the late '70s, the crew was usually five people, including a maintenance engineer who would put problems right. Now, with a crew of three at most, you normally have two machines so that, if something goes wrong, you just change over to the other machine and get the first one fixed. But in the early days it was nothing to hold up production however long it took to put things right.

So far as the technique of recording is concerned, however, I don't believe you can teach it. I think you have to learn by experience and you have to have a real interest in what you're doing – even more so than in cinematography. Sound recording is more abstract than photography and it's a very difficult thing to teach. You can teach such things as what you must do to avoid problems in editing – overlapping dialogue between two actors, for instance, when one is in frame and the other isn't. And you have to realise the necessity of using playback for music. But beyond that, most people learn by experience.

Which personnel would you have most to do with, apart from the director? The music director?

Yes, usually. Certainly with Tony Richardson's Woodfall films I had a lot to do with the musical director. There is often a very difficult decision to be made about when to use music and when to use effects. The two don't usually go together very well and it can be heart-breaking for a sound recordist who has done a lot of useful, interesting and appropriate sound effects to find that none of them is used because the composer has written music which is considered to be better.

You are an expert on trains and train sounds, I believe.

Yes, that's true. I often supply train sounds for films. *Julia* was one case in point, where I was asked by the director to 'compose' the sounds of a train which was supposed to travel from France to Berlin, but which in fact was all shot in France and used the same engine the whole time. Fred Zinnemann wanted me to make a distinction between the different countries through which the train was supposed to be travelling. I wasn't the sound recordist on *Julia* and I didn't get a credit. Sometimes I do, but not in that situation.

What other personnel, apart from your own team, would you have dealings with?

After the picture is finished (or before it's finished, if you're lucky), there will be a sound editor and it's very important to be in contact with him. The relationship with the lighting cameraman [director of photography nowadays] and the camera operator is most important, because their co-operation is absolutely essential in deciding how and where it will be possible to place microphones in any given set-up. During a production I always make extensive notes, which are handed over at the end of the film to the sound editor, about all the different sound-effects tracks, alternative-dialogue tracks, wild tracks or anything like that. Whenever possible I try to go to the mixing but it's not easy, because often it is six months or more after the end of shooting and I might be on another film by then. I mean the mixing of all the various dialogue, effects and music tracks – the final mix, which is a very complicated process that can take five or six weeks. Unfortunately it is not my responsibility to ensure how all of that is done. The mixing (or dubbing) is done in theatres attached to the studios or independent theatres owned by such organisations as Todd A-O in America, or Twickenham Studios in England.

Were you ever under contract to studios or companies, or did you always negotiate your rates with each new film?

I have been a freelance since 1954. Prior to that I was under contract to Herbert Wilcox for a long time. Before that I was under contract to MGM, which was a catastrophe, because they didn't make any films. Well, they made some in the early '50s, and one or two independent productions for which the studio facilities were rented. It was on one of those independent productions, *Under Capricorn*, that I first worked with Alfred Hitchcock, when I was assigned to do the sound recording for that production.

I also met Herbert Wilcox when I was assigned to work on a production which he made at MGM studios. He told me that he would be delighted if it ever became possible for me to work for him permanently. I found out that MGM were in fact hiring me out to other people (such as to 20th-Century-Fox for *Night and the City*) and charging a great deal more money than I was paid. In between those jobs I would have to go to Boreham Wood every day from 8.30 until 6 pm and do nothing, which was totally demoralising. I told MGM I was tired of this arrangement, that they should either give me some proper work to do or let me go. They had the option to renew my contract although *I* had no option (it was one-sided, as all contracts were), and they were supposed to deliver, by registered post on a certain date, their exercise of the option. They didn't do that, so after a week I consulted a solicitor, who told me I had grounds to leave.

When I told MGM I was leaving, they said I couldn't because I was under contract. I pointed out they'd broken the terms and all hell broke loose! I had already made sure there was a job for me with Herbert Wilcox, because it was unusual for a producer in those days to have all his technical people under contract. However, there was a job for me and he was a most wonderful employer, a marvellous man, and a pleasure to work with. He too used to let me out to other producers from time to time, but in compensation he paid his whole crew all the time, whether they were working or not.

Once you became freelance, how did you come by work?

It was just word-of-mouth. I always had as much work as I wanted and I never wanted to be tied at all. After Herbert Wilcox went bankrupt (after *The Beggar's Opera*) he had to release us all and British Lion at Shepperton Studios, where Herbert had worked most of the time, asked me to come and work for them. I did that for a short time and, as with all film companies, one just did whatever work was going whether the film was any good or not.

What was a typical day's work for you on a film?

It depended whether you were working in the studio or on location. Studio work was very routine, with not much opportunity to be innovative. That's an exaggeration, of course, but it wasn't nearly as interesting as working on location. On location you would have to improvise. There would be problems to overcome; for instance, there is a generator for the lights but where do you put the generator so that it can't be heard? You have to be very diplomatic and not cause great fuss or hold-ups. There can be traffic going past or aeroplanes flying overhead and you have to decide whether, for instance, it is possible to get a usable soundtrack or whether it

will have to be post-synchronised. If you have problems during a take, you can tell the director you need a 'wild' track. Provided you do that immediately after he has chosen the final take, you'll find, with experienced actors, that it will match more often than not. It will have to be cut into sync, of course, but it's much better than going to a post-sync theatre because the actors are used to doing the scene and they have each other to play off. I read the script through in advance and refer to it if necessary, but the worst thing you can do is to sit with the script in front of you during filming. You shouldn't know the dialogue in advance. Sometimes the director or the continuity girl will ask, 'Did they say this or that, because it's in the script?', to which I can say, 'I don't know if it's in the script or not. All I can tell you is the dialogue was unintelligible.' If you like, I am the litmus test for clarity of dialogue, which the audience will hear only once.

Has sound recording become a great deal more sophisticated?

No, I don't think it is nearly as polished as it used to be. The whole method of making pictures has changed. The first things that came in were the crab dolly and the zoom lens; those are the two things that made sound recording more difficult, because previously everything was fixed. The camera was on tracks, you knew exactly where it was going to be in relation to the actors and with a fixed lens you knew where the actors were in relation to the frame. With a zoom lens, anything can happen.

There has been a lot of modernising of equipment, certainly. That changed things a lot because there were no such things as radio microphones until about the early'70s. I have just been doing a documentary about Joseph Losey and I was asked about *The Go-Between*. They wanted to know how, without radio mikes, I got all the voices at the cricket match and I explained that we had to run out cables. We had to have microphones all over the place connected by cables, which was very difficult because the cables as well as the mikes had to be hidden. I remember one marvellous occasion during a tracking shot, when we'd hidden a microphone under a clump of grass. Julie Christie walked past and plucked a piece of grass – and it happened to be the bit under which we'd hidden the microphone, so up it came!

What do you recall of John Schlesinger, for whom you did *Billy Liar* and *Darling*?

He was very interested in sound, fascinated, because he is also very interested in music. On *Billy*

Liar we used to spend hours after shooting finished each day, going out and recording local people. I used to go out and set up a little scene, which I'd record. A lot of it was never used, but now and again John would find a line he liked and it would go into the film. We had to create two different worlds, effectively, for that film and that meant making a lot of decisions about different approaches.

You worked on *Saturday Night and Sunday Morning* and *Morgan* for Karel Reisz, another of the New Wave directors.

I liked Karel very much. *Saturday Night and Sunday Morning* was his first feature and he relied on his crew a lot, myself, the cameraman and the editor. He *used* us, which is a wonderful way to work. It's the best way to work, in fact, because you feel that you're achieving something. The same applied to Tony Richardson and Joe Losey. I did *Joseph Andrews*, *The Entertainer*, *The Charge of the Light Brigade*, *Mademoiselle* (in France, with Jeanne Moreau, and made without any music) for Tony Richardson. I also did a lot of work on *A Taste of Honey*, although I couldn't do the whole film. I did all the soundtracks after shooting; we did a lot of soundtracks in Manchester and the musical director, John Addison, and I did a lot of children's songs and things like that. Those soundtracks were very important to capture the atmosphere of the north of England. I also did the immensely successful *Tom Jones* for Tony and the Woodfall company. After making *The Entertainer*, Tony never worked in a studio, in Britain, again. *Tom Jones*, for instance, was made entirely on location. Tony liked the freedom of working on location and didn't want to be tied to a studio.

It was an exciting time in British films, starting with *Room at the Top*. I was involved in that, too, working with Jack Clayton. At last we got away from the studios, using real locations and real people. It was wonderful, like a breath of fresh air. There had been nothing like it before, nothing which tackled notions of class and so on, in the way that it did. It was a very exciting time in my career. It involved a marriage of drama and documentary, if you like. This was true for both sound recording and cinematography.

Losey was not that kind of director, though, was he?

He was very stimulating to work for, again because he *used* his crew. For instance, on *The Go-Between* he said, 'I want you to send me a memo about what you think the soundtrack of this film should be,' what sounds there would have been at the turn of the century (apart from the music). In fact we first of all mixed *The Go-Between* without any background music other than music which was intrinsic to the film. We used entirely natural sounds, which Tony Richardson had already done in *Mademoiselle*. We showed the picture to the EMI distributors, who were horrified by the soundtrack and told Joe they couldn't accept a film without background music, all films had to have a musical score.

It was then suggested a suitable musical score could include variations on Gilbert & Sullivan's 'Take a Pair of Sparkling Eyes', which is sung in the film. Joe said that, if he had to have music, that was the very last thing he would choose, but the 'audience' insisted that there must be music. EMI could make such demands because they owned the studio which had backed the picture and the company which would distribute it, so had complete control. They asked Joe who he would choose to write the music, and he said he wanted Michel Legrand. One of the distributors asked if he spoke English – totally irrelevant!

Which studios did you work at mostly?

At Shepperton. It had good facilities and a wonderful man called John Cox in charge of sound. He not only knew about everything, he could also *do* things in sound, and it was a privilege to work with him. He used to mix films himself, such as *The Sound Barrier*, which won an Oscar for sound. All the studios then had so-called directors of recording. Few of them actually *did* anything, but they were credited on all films made at the studio as the Director of Recording. MGM in USA never credited individuals, only Douglas Shearer. When MGM took on staff for their studios at Boreham Wood, after the war, we were told that the same system would apply to sound credits for pictures made there. This was most strongly resisted by all the sound staff and, thanks to the backing of the ACT union, then very strong, the proposal was dropped by the company. Apart from Shepperton I had also worked, with Wilcox, at EMI Studios, Elstree and of course I had worked at MGM Studios in Elstree.

What sort of studio facilities would you have required?

Just recording equipment, but there was often little or no choice in what was supplied. In some cases the equipment supplied was decided by people whose theoretical and technical knowledge may have been brilliant but whose practical experience of film sound recording was minimal. EMI Elstree was the worst. It was bad enough when I had worked there in the '50s on the Wilcox films, much to the annoyance of the studio management and union, who, if Herbert Wilcox had not been so loyal to his staff, would have insisted that EMI personnel were employed on Wilcox films. By the time I worked again on films based at EMI studios, the situation had become even less satisfactory and even more ruled by technical dogma from the office rather than practical experience. The equipment, and some studio staff, supplied for *The Railway Children* and *The Go-Between*, both based at Elstree, were certainly not what I would have chosen, but like any sound recordist who worked there or, for instance, at Pinewood, I was given absolutely no choice. Pinewood was almost as repressive a place to work in as EMI. I never had the misfortune to work for the Rank Organisation who owned it, but people who have worked for Rank at Pinewood have told me it was absolutely stultifying from a sound point of view. It was a dogmatic, bureaucratic studio rule that absolutely all soundtracks for pictures shot on locations must automatically be post-synchronised, so there was no incentive to make any great effort to record good soundtracks on location, because they would almost certainly be replaced by the dead sound of post-synchronisation. I had worked there (against the wishes of the studio management, who resented other than their own employees working at Pinewood) on the American-backed *Sons and Lovers*, and it often appeared as if the permanent staff at the studios actually resented having their way of life interfered with by the making of pictures.

Julie Harris

b. 1921

Costume designer: *Holiday Camp* (1947), *My Brother's Keeper, The Calendar, Quartet, Broken Journey, Good Time Girl* (1948), *Once Upon a Dream* (1949), *Highly Dangerous, Trio, The Clouded Yellow, Another Man's Poison* (1950), *Mr Drake's Duck, Traveller's Joy, Hotel Sahara, Encore* (1951), *Something Money Can't Buy, South of Algiers, Made in Heaven, So Little Time* (1952), *Desperate Moment, *Night Without Stars, Turn the Key Softly, Always a Bride, The Red Beret* (1953), *The Seekers, You Know What Sailors Are* (1954), *Simon and Laura, Value for Money, The Prisoner, Cast a Dark Shadow* (1955), *The March Hare, Reach for the Sky, It's a Wonderful World, House of Secrets* (1956), **The Story of Esther Costello, Seven Thunders, Miracle in Soho* (1957), *The Sheriff of Fractured Jaw, The Gypsy and the Gentleman* (1958), *Whirlpool,* *Sapphire, *Northwest Frontier* (1959), *The Greengage Summer* (1960), *The Swiss Family Robinson, The Rough and the Smooth, The Naked Edge* (1961), *All Night Long, We Joined the Navy, The Fast Lady, The War Lover* (1962), *The Chalk Garden, *Tamahine, Psyche 59* (1963), *A Hard Day's Night, Carry on Cleo* (1964), *Darling, Help!* (1965), *The Whisperers, The Wrong Box, Eye of the Devil* (1966), **Casino Royale, Deadfall* (1967), *Prudence and the Pill, *Decline and Fall* (1968), *Goodbye Mr Chips* (1969), *The Private Life of Sherlock Holmes* (1970), *Follow Me, Frenzy* (1972), *Live and Let Die* (1973), *Rollerball* (1974), *The Slipper and the Rose* (1976), *Candleshoe* (1978), *Dracula, Lost and Found* (1979), *The Great Muppet Caper* (1981)
* Shared credit

B efore the war, Julie Harris did what she describes as 'a (loosely speaking) fashion/commercial course at art school' and had some experience as a 'Court dressmaker'. A useful wartime contact brought her to Gainsborough Studios at the end of the war and since then her credits encapsulate a great deal of British cinema history: from black-and-white Gainsborough dramas like *Good Time Girl*, through the Pinewood-dominated '50s, the swinging '60s (she not only got an Oscar for *Darling* but also dressed the Beatles twice), to the large-scale productions aimed at the international market. She gives a clear sense of the demands and satisfactions of her work – and is wry about some of the great names she had to dress in her long and distinguished career.

Interview date: July 1994

How did you get started in film designing?

When the war came I joined the ATS, and towards the end of my stint in it I met someone who knew someone who worked at Gainsborough Studios. By this time I had decided I would be a costume designer. No question of could I do it, or how. I was lucky enough to get an interview with Maurice Ostrer and was taken on as an assistant to Elizabeth Haffenden at Gainsborough in 1945. I was Elizabeth's assistant for one film only, *The Magic Bow* with Stewart Granger, then Maurice Ostrer sold out to Sydney Box. There was a certain amount of expansion going on in the film industry, and I soon got my own first film, which was *Holiday Camp*. I didn't really know too much about it but I was a quick learner.

Were you under contract to Gainsborough?

I must have had a contract for a year that tided me over when Gainsborough closed its Lime Grove studio. I then went to Pinewood and I think if I hadn't had some kind of a contract with Gainsborough I might have been out of work. As it was, we started on production of *Once Upon a Dream* at Pinewood, where I stayed for a number of years.

What were your facilities like at Pinewood?

There was a very good wardrobe, which even had a bit of stock. You'd never find that today. It had costume stock particularly for things like nurses, maids, other uniforms and character clothes. Today everything has to be made or hired or bought but, in those years at Pinewood for a while, there was some stock as well as ribbons and cottons and needles and things. When people make a film today it's called a 'four-waller': they have to go in and take everything with them, every bit of cotton and every pin. With Gainsborough and at Pinewood, everything was there and you more or less took it for granted, but there are no regular companies making films in Britain today, which is so sad. But, in the late '40s and early '50s, the wardrobe was very good. Things were still rationed then, and we still had to have coupons. You had to apply to the Board of Trade, say how many you wanted and for what, and at the end make a return as to what you had used; but we weren't subject to the same restrictions as other people were.

How important was it to you to keep up with general trends in fashion?

It was very important *then* because fashion was much more regular and recognisable than it is today. It had a definite style, influenced by the Paris collections even quite soon after the war. In 1948 the New Look came in and I put that into a film – with a certain amount of trepidation, because it wasn't instantly accepted everywhere. It took quite a time for skirts to get longer and clothes to get softer, but, during the latter '40s and '50s, fashion was very much influenced by what was 'in' in Paris. It was quite tricky having to second-guess what would be fashionable in a year's time, because a film from start to finish took about nine months; you might do your sketches ten months in advance and, by the time the film came out, fashion had changed. This was much more noticeable in the '60s because then it began to go all over the place. By then skirts were getting much shorter, so that by the time I came to do *Darling* it was noticeably changing. Fashion was still predictable then but it was 'on the move'.

At what stage of a film's development would you usually have become involved?

Not always as early as you'd like, but one had

longer than now. On the early films I would have preliminary discussions with the director and the production designer, primarily. You would also have to refer to the cameraman, sometimes show him samples of colours and fabrics. In the early '50s, with Technicolor, there were lots of problems with blacks and whites: if a man was in a black suit and a white shirt, for instance. There were four shades of Technicolor white and number four was really quite a grubby colour but the contrast between the black and the white was hard for lighting, so you took your whites down quite a bit. I always thought it was a pity because I never thought anything photographed as well as white. Sometimes even in black-and-white photography the cameramen wouldn't have white. The pale blues we had to use instead came out looking pale grey or 'off-white'.

All your 1940s films were in black-and-white and almost all of your '50s films were in colour. Did you have a preference?

I was very pleased when it was to be in colour, although I suppose my most famous film was *Darling*, which was black-and-white. I was very grateful for that because I would not have got an Oscar had it been in colour; it would have come up against *Dr Zhivago*, which won the award for colour. That was the last year in which the Oscars had separate categories for black-and-white and colour. Colour was more exciting: Technicolor could be quite pretty-pretty, but I enjoyed it, rather than thinking only in terms of shades of grey as one had done previously. There were always problems with Technicolor, of course: yellows were difficult as most would turn egg-yellow and not stay a nice clear colour. Blues could be very bright and reds would sometimes 'bleed' a bit, not be quite clear around the edges. Then there was Eastman Colour, which, fortunately, I never had to use, because it had a sort of brown look all the time which I didn't like.

In the first days it was a case of doing the costumes in colour, just making sure they weren't the same colour as the curtains and so on, but latterly you worked very much with the production designer. You do a kind of colour scheme quite often; it's not all left to chance. I've had so many disappointments over the years when you never see a long shot. That is maddening. Clothes you have spent such a lot of time and money on appear in head-and-shoulder shots, are just gone for nothing.

Who were some of the art directors (or production designers) you worked with?

Carmen Dillon, of course, on *Simon and Laura* for Muriel Box. Jean Baker was the editor, so it was four women in key positions. Muriel was quite a feminist in her day. I also worked with Maurice Carter several times. One was *The Seekers*, for which we all went to New Zealand together, up the Wanganui looking for canoes. That was a very rich and rare location.

You did a lot of work with Ken Annakin. Did you both just happen to be at Pinewood together?

Yes, *Holiday Camp* was Ken's first directing picture and it was also my first picture. Then I think he did *Broken Journey*, followed by *Hotel Sahara* and *The Seekers*. He also did some of the segments for *Trio* and *Quartet*. Later on he did comedy things like *The Fast Lady*, then we did the big Disney production of *The Swiss Family Robinson* together. That was all on location on Tobago so it must have been quite an expensive production even for those times. It was only coincidence my doing such a lot of films with Ken Annakin. I don't know that he specifically asked for me, but it's always nice working with the same people because you learn how their thinking goes, and they have confidence in you.

How important were your relations with cameramen?

Oh, quite important. A good relationship was important with everybody, really, because if you had a bad one (and I don't think I had many) it could be very difficult. I'm not sure Ken Adam and I got on all that well, on *Goodbye Mr Chips*. I found him difficult. Once you'd settled your colours and fabrics you didn't have to be constantly asking their opinion, but it was just nice to have a helpful relationship. You might be standing by waiting to change someone's costume and you might want to ask the cameraman how long he would be lighting before they were ready to shoot; you might be tight for time because of a vital alteration – little things like that which could nonetheless be important if you were pushed for time.

What recollections do you have of working with those big American stars who were brought over to England – such as Lauren Bacall and Jayne Mansfield?

Lauren Bacall was very professional – not much sense of period, though. Now, everything period has to be so right that it all gets a bit boring, I think. Most of *Northwest Frontier* she spent in a blouse and skirt, Edwardian style, but she rolled the sleeves up and opened the neck of the shirt so that it looked modern; it could have been anything. I don't think one got much sense of the period from her.

Jayne Mansfield on *The Sheriff of Fractured Jaw* was all right. She had to wear corsets, of course, and by the time you put that figure into corsets it began to get Mae West proportions and not always in a particularly becoming way. She was very pretty, however, chocolate-box pretty; she didn't have a vast sense of humour but she was very pleasant and giggly. She had some quite nice clothes in it, including a wedding dress, but Raoul Walsh decided to cut the dress and she had to wear an ordinary costume. By which time she was pregnant, which caused a slight problem with the shape but was helped by a large bouquet!

How much were you associated with Joan Crawford on *The Story of Esther Costello*? There is also a credit for 'Gowns by Jean Louis'.

She brought all her wardrobe with her, by which time she had gained or lost a bit of weight, so that we were constantly altering things. She was very much surrounded by her own entourage, so I didn't really see much of her. The Jean Louis clothes were typically her, I thought. There was a lot of Pepsi-Cola stuff going on and if you went to see her she was usually on her way to a Pepsi-Cola meeting. I had brief dealings with her and did sketches, which she approved, for a film which was never made. She really was a star in the old, grand tradition.

Did you encounter much of that in the British people you worked with?

No, I suppose Kay Kendall was one of Rank's bigger stars and certainly one of my most favourite people. I did three or four films with Deborah Kerr and she was so nice, a friend as much as any of them can be. You meet constantly for a brief while on a film and then you part again, you know. I loved working with Deborah and I liked her kind of clothes – and the way she wore them. Deborah specifically requested me a couple of times, I do know that.

What about some of the Gainsborough stars like Margaret Lockwood, Jean Kent, Phyllis Calvert, Diana Dors?

I worked with them all, yes. The main one I did with Jean Kent was *Good Time Girl* and she was all right. I'm not sure she didn't ask Sydney [Box] if I could do her clothes, but you never really know. She was to have been in *Holiday Camp* to begin

with and I must have done some sketches which she liked, I suppose.

I worked with Margaret Lockwood first on *Highly Dangerous*. That was all right too; she didn't have to have anything special for it. There wasn't a decent dress in it, really, just a white coat and a couple of frocks.

Diana Dors probably wore her own clothes in *Holiday Camp*. She had quite a lot of clothes for *Value for Money* and I did all her clothes for personal appearances. She was quite fun but her husband was very trying. He would always be there saying, 'Make the neckline lower.' She could probably have gone on to do more serious work had she not got ill. I think her early days hung around her, though, with a lot of tacky publicity. I had to get the mink bikini made for her; it was her own idea and every photographer in Venice at the Film Festival came to see it – and it wasn't even mink, it was rabbit! Those stunts lingered on, however, to her detriment.

Did male stars cause you the same sorts of challenges, or make the same sorts of demands?

No. Sometimes you would have their clothes made, as in the case of David Niven and Roger Moore. Then it was only a question of going to the tailor and choosing fabrics, ensuring the fittings were done and having the shirts made and choosing the ties. It was all administration, really. Roger Moore and Rex Harrison always had handmade shirts and they had their regular people to do that. It was more expensive than buying them, but I suppose in terms of time and shopping it wasn't – and it made them happy!

Were the costumes one of the main ways in which money was spent on a film?

It was not allowed to be a significant expense, about one per cent of the budget for the whole film. From the '60s on, I think people became much more aware that costumes were important but there has always, always been a budget fight except on a Bond picture – or *Casino Royale*, for which they always wanted something 'yesterday' so it was a case of 'Pay anything, just get it.' Those films were huge money-makers anyway, and the costumes were a drop in the ocean compared to what was spent on everything else.

As a rule, would you have contributed to the budget discussions at the outset, or would you be told how much you could spend?

Slightly told, then afterwards you would have to

do your budget and see what the difference was. There was never a question of doing your budget and getting what you asked for, it was always cut down. Doing a budget was one of the first things you had to do, but you couldn't do it properly until you knew how many costumes were required. You had to talk to production about crowd numbers too, because that's where the money goes in period pictures.

Did you design every costume for the crowd scenes in *The Slipper and the Rose*?

Every costume that wasn't real 'crowd', and the only real crowds were in the ballroom. All the special girls and dancers were designed for, but there was a fill-in of stock clothes and even for those one tried to keep an eye out for colour.

Were you around the studios very much once filming began?

Yes, certainly when people were wearing new clothes. If it was interesting, like musicals (which I loved) or the Beatles, I would be there all the time. You had to be there when people were wearing new clothes or when there were crowds to dress, but you also had to be going on with fittings and future requirements, and perhaps not be able to be in the studio when you wanted to be. Things were being made all the time, of course, it wasn't a case of everything being ready at the beginning. You first have to show your designs to the cameraman or the director, and, of course, the actors who will be wearing them. You had schedules for filming but those change, unfortunately. I also supervised the making of costumes and had to go to the fittings. You have to take the sketch to the costumiers, tell them what you want and then you and they and your assistants find the materials.

Were you also required to be on the floor of the studio, ensuring that everything was being worn properly?

Yes, but you usually had good wardrobe staff and a wardrobe supervisor. In latter years I didn't work without an assistant anyway, so if I wasn't there my assistant would be. I remember *not* being there one day during the filming of *Hazard of Hearts* [made for television] when Fiona Fullerton had a riding scene on location. Although she hadn't worn the costume before, my assistant and I had seen it at fittings so often I decided not to go out to the location. When I saw the film, however, the blasted hat was on back to front! No one would have known but me, but I was so cross.

Did it matter much to you who was directing?

It did make a difference. Some had a feeling for clothes and an interest in it, while some others were concerned only with the action. Raoul Walsh was much more concerned with the horses in the background. On *Goodbye Mr Chips* Herb Ross was enormously concerned, and so was Ken Adam, the production designer. Bryan Forbes minds about clothes. Hitchcock was quite interested, I remember, although I did very little on *Frenzy*, other than for Barbara Leigh Hunt. It was a difficult one, though, designing a dress that could be torn up for the murder the way Hitchcock wanted.

Billy Wilder didn't much mind about the clothes for *The Private Lives of Sherlock Holmes*. Genevieve Page was lovely to work with, though. I've never known anyone so fussy, but when she walked on the set, there was no question of her coming on wearing a dressing gown over her costume with a cup of tea in her hand. She would sail on and the costume would look wonderful; then everyone would say, 'What a beautiful costume,' and that was rewarding.

Do you recall how you gave clues to the nationality or temperament, for example, of characters through their clothes?

Yes, for foreigners of one sort or another you would refer to photographs to see what their style of dress would be. For instance, I did *Desperate Moment* with Dirk Bogarde and that was set in Germany. I've forgotten most of it except that Dirk had to be a chimney-sweep and I had to research what German chimney-sweeps wore. They wore top hats, which were quite distinctive. In the late '40s and '50s American suits were very differently cut, too, and you had to try to get that sort of tailoring, which was rather different from ours. We were not long out of wartime and our suits were much more narrowly tailored.

Would you work from a full copy of the screenplay?

Oh yes. You have to do a dress plot, showing how many characters there are, how many changes everybody has, and that is there for Wardrobe to use for continuity. The dress plot is a sort of Bible as to what each character wears in each scene. The continuity is so important, particularly if it involves something that is to be gradually broken down and made to look more tired, such as for *The Swiss Family Robinson*. Films are almost never shot in sequence, of course, so the continuity factor is vital.

Was there one film which stands out in your mind as wholly satisfactory to you?

I suppose *Casino Royale*. Some of it is very bad but there was lots for me and there were some nice things in it, even if they weren't always used to the advantage they might have been. *Darling* was not the happiest of pictures but I am eternally grateful for the Oscar it got me, and I think it wears well. The clothes look right even now. I loved *The Slipper and the Rose*, of course, because it was a musical, and I think *Goodbye Mr Chips* looks pleasing. *Help!* looks characteristically right, too. Character is harder than dressing someone up in the full fig of glamour, but it's not always more rewarding. It's an achievement if you make someone look right in character, like Edith Evans in *The Whisperers*, which was really quite difficult, and therefore very satisfying. However, no one is going to say you are a great designer for having done that. Your reputation as a designer really rests on the success of the film. People tend not to separate out the good elements from an otherwise unsuccessful film unless they are particularly aware of the artistic endeavours.

Sir Rex Harrison

1908–1990

Actor: *The Great Game, School for Scandal* (1930), *Get Your Man, Leave it to Blanche* (1934), *All at Sea* (1935), *Men Are Not Gods* (1936), *Storm in a Teacup, Over the Moon, School for Husbands* (1937), *St Martin's Lane, The Citadel* (1938), *Ten Days in Paris, The Silent Battle* (1939), *Night Train to Munich, Major Barbara* (1940), *Journey Together* (bit), *I Live in Grosvenor Square, Blithe Spirit, The Rake's Progress* (1945), *Anna and the King of Siam* (1946), *The Ghost and Mrs Muir, The Foxes of Harrow* (1947), *Escape, Unfaithfully Yours* (1948), *The Long Dark Hall* (1951), *The Four-Poster* (1952), *The Charm of Life* (narr), *Main Street to Broadway* (guest role) (1953), *King Richard and the Crusaders* (1954), *The Constant Husband* (1955), **This Is London* (narr) (1956), *The Reluctant Debutante* (1958), *Midnight Lace* (1960), *The Happy Thieves* (1961), *Cleopatra* (1963), *My Fair Lady, The Yellow Rolls-Royce* (1964), *The Agony and the Ecstasy, *Flashes Festivals* (guest role) (1965), *The Honey Pot* (1966), *Doctor Dolittle* (1967), *A Flea in Her Ear* (1968), *Staircase* (1969), *The Gentleman Tramp* (guest role) (1975), *The Prince and the Pauper, The Fifth Musketeer* (1977), *Ashanti, Shalimar* (1979), *A Time to Die* (1983)
* Short film.

'**M**y type's becoming obsolete. Can't compete with the international situation. The thirties produced us and the champagne's gone flat and we're going out with the thirties.'[1] This remark by the charming cad who redeems himself in wartime, portrayed by Rex Harrison in Launder and Gilliat's *The Rake's Progress* (1945), must have struck a responsive chord in the actor. His film career often seemed to be foundering, and twenty years after *The Rake's Progress* he would recreate on film his most famous role, Professor Higgins in *My Fair Lady*, another 'obsolete type'.

'Acting is an extraordinarily difficult thing and the easier it looks to the layman, the more difficult it is to do ... I've striven not to appear to be striving for anything,'[2] he wrote at the end of his life. In a way, Harrison scarcely qualifies as a *British* film star, having spent most of his career in (often ill-judged) American films. He is included, though, because he was one of those British actors who did one thing supremely well.

His lean frame, immaculately dinner-jacketed, the eyes narrowed in sexual calculation of the most urbane kind, the throwaway nonchalance with lines, which actually bespoke superb timing: these equipped him to be the purveyor *par excellence* of his generation of a certain kind of boulevard comedy. 'I was lucky enough to see a lot of wonderful actors of that period [early '30s], who were all specializing in comedy.'[3] He rightly sees himself in a line descended from Sir Gerald du Maurier and Ronald Squire. 'They played comedy as if they weren't playing comedy at all . . . I think that was the beginning of my realizing what I would like to do with my career'[4] – and leading him towards Noël Coward's accolade: 'Rex Harrison is the best light comedian in the business after me.'[5]

Cary Grant is his nearest transatlantic counterpart, though Grant often suggested darker, more complex possibilities. Other English actors with whom there are points of contact include Tom Walls, who brought so many of his Aldwych successes to the screen in the '30s, Hugh Williams, Basil Radford and Naunton Wayne, who all had this one special forte. So did Kenneth More, though he was less elegant than the others.

'I went to Hollywood in the first place for what I still think are good reasons. It was a logical step in my career,'[6] Harrison argued in 1950, after two attractive variants there on the Harrison *persona* in *Anna and the King of Siam* and *The Ghost and Mrs Muir*. In other American films, he was a bemused father in the mangled version of *The Reluctant Debutante*, a fine, quizzical Caesar in *Cleopatra*, a miscast Pope in *The Agony and the Ecstasy* ('an altogether horrendous experience for me'[7]), and a triumphant Oscar-winner for *My Fair Lady*.

In 1939, he had said: 'I much prefer to remain in London, dividing my time between stage and screen.'[8] By that time, he'd established his breezy image in such films as *Men Are Not Gods* ('I was foul in that. Of course, I knew nothing about film acting'[9]), *Storm in a Teacup* and *The Citadel*. But it was *The Rake's Progress* which gave him his finest hour in British films: 'Now, at the end of the war, came a film which tried to say something about the irresponsible types I'd been making my living by portraying, and what it said was, the war had killed him off.'[10] It is as finely calibrated a study of the 'type' as is to be found.

He disliked *Blithe Spirit* ('David Lean was ill at ease with comedy and his tension communicated itself to me'[11]) and Herbert Wilcox's *I Live in Grosvenor Square*, after which Hollywood looked more attractive. However, with the exceptions noted, the rest of his career must have been a disappointment to him.

1 Vivian Kenway, played by Rex Harrison in *The Rake's Progress*, 1945.
2 Rex Harrison, *A Damned Serious Business*, Isis, London, 1991, p 1
3 Harrison, p 19
4 Harrison, p 19
5 Rudy Behlmer, 'Rex Harrison', *Films in Review*, December 1965, p 599
6 'Why I left Hollywood', *Picturegoer*, 5 August 1950, p 7
7 Harrison, p 205
8 J Danvers Williams, 'His life is just a bowl of cherries', *Film Weekly*, 8 April 1939, p 10
9 Freda Bruce Lockhart, 'Success comes to Rex Harrison', *Film Weekly*, 25 December 1937, p 11
10 Harrison, p 87
11 Nicholas Wapshott, *Rex Harrison*, Chatto & Windus, London, 1991, p 83

Sir Anthony Havelock-Allan

b. 1905

Producer (except as indicated): *Badger's Green* (1934), *Love at Sea, Murder by Rope, The*

Scarab Murder Case (1936), *Cross My Heart, Cavalier of The Streets, Missing – Believed Married,*

Lancashire Luck, The Fatal Hour, Holiday's End, The Last Curtain, Mr Smith Carries On, Museum Mystery, Night Ride (1937), Incident in Shanghai, Lightning Conductor, A Spot of Bother, This Man is News (1938), The Lambeth Walk, The Silent Battle, Stolen Life (assoc pr), This Man in Paris (1939), *From the Four Corners (& dir) (1941), In Which We Serve (assoc pr) (1942), This Happy Breed (co-pr) (1944), Blithe Spirit (& co-sc), Brief Encounter (co-pr) (1945), Great Expectations (co-pr & co-sc) (1946), Take My Life (1947), Blanche Fury, Oliver Twist (exec pr), The Small Voice (1948), The Interrupted Journey (1949), Never Take No for an Answer (1951), Meet Me Tonight (1952), The Young Lovers (1954), Orders to Kill (1958), The Quare Fellow (1962), An Evening with the Royal Ballet (& co-dir), Othello (co-pr) (1966), The Mikado (co-pr), Up the Junction (co-pr) (1967), Romeo and Juliet (co-pr) (1968), Ryan's Daughter (1970)
* Short film.

The name of Anthony Havelock-Allan is most firmly associated with the critical and commercial triumphs of the Two Cities and Cineguild production companies from 1942 to 1948 – that is, with filming the works of Noël Coward and Charles Dickens, from *In Which We Serve* to *Oliver Twist*, in the major period of prestige in British cinema. However, Havelock-Allan had already produced more than twenty films in the 1930s, chiefly for Paramount-British. If most of these films were 'quota quickies', they also nurtured many talents which would find their place in the story in the ensuing decades. He entered 'A' film production with *This Man is News*, and thereafter was one of the most influential producers in British films. His recollections of the Coward and the Dickens films valuably complement those of other surviving collaborators. He should also be remembered for two films he made starring his then wife Valerie Hobson: the sombre, sensual melodrama, *Blanche Fury*, which looks remarkably fine today, and the tense home-under-siege thriller, *The Small Voice*, which introduced Howard Keel to the screen.
Interview date: June 1990

You started as a filmmaker in the '30s . . .

Yes, British and Dominion Films had a production manager who was making second features – 'quota quickies', really – for them and between 1932 and 1935 he had made fifteen or seventeen of them. Then he died suddenly and a friend asked me if I thought I could do the job. I had been in the industry for two years and, apart from knowing almost every name and face in the casting directory, I really didn't know much about making films. But I did know about the theatre and I did know about the theory of storytelling, as it were, so I said I thought I could do it. They handed it over to me and I made films non-stop for two years, and I'd never had so much fun. It was a splendid opportunity – Rex Harrison and Vivien Leigh made their first films for us, as did Wendy Hiller, George Sanders, Wilfred Hyde-White, Margaret Rutherford, so many of them; and there were many writers doing scripts for us.

After a very busy producing schedule in the '30s, you began the '40s by directing and producing *From the Four Corners*, a documentary. What was it about?

It was a propaganda film, a three-reeler, and it had Leslie Howard, an Australian, a Canadian and a New Zealander. Leslie met them in Trafalgar Square and began to explain what relevance various things in London had to Australia, New Zealand and Canada; he explained the historical significance of various English places and monuments. It was sponsored by the Ministry of Information.

I would like to know anything at all about your involvement with Two Cities and Cineguild, starting from *In Which We Serve*.

Del Giudice was sent off to an internment camp at the beginning of the war, but, for good reason (he was a staunch anti-Fascist), was later released. He found two backers, Major Arthur Sassoon and Colonel Crosfield, and said he wanted to make a big propaganda film and he wanted to approach Noël Coward. I had met Noël, so Del and I went to see him and asked if he would write a story, like, perhaps, his *Cavalcade*. He said he would think about it. Two weeks later he rang to say he had an idea for a big propaganda film. He had dined with Lord Louis Mountbatten, who had told him the story of HMS *Kelly*, the destroyer of which he had been captain. Del got the money for the film, I was to produce, and I suggested that David Lean was the best possible person to act as technical director; he was a great editor with a great storytelling sense on film. Noël said he wanted Ronnie Neame as cameraman, so we all met and Noël agreed to do the script.

Three months later Noël produced a script which would have taken eight to ten hours on the screen; it started some time before the war, in the Caribbean, then went to the China Station before the war, then there were some scenes in the Café de Paris with some socialites – all long before anything happened to do with the war! When we explained that it was too long, Noël told us to take it away and do something with it. We decided simply to tell the story of one ship, the *Kelly* [renamed the *Torrin* in the film], from the laying of its keel to its 'death' off Crete. We came back to Noël with it and he approved our storyline. Mountbatten was involved and he got for us all the help we needed. When we came to discuss who would play the part of the Captain, Noël said *he* would. I didn't think it was very good casting, and Del Giudice told him this; Noël, however, said, 'He's perfectly right, I'm not, but I want to play it and Tony's going to produce it!' So we went on from there and in fact Noël gave an excellent performance, even though he was not anyone's idea of a 'sea dog'. The commissioning speech, the speech to the survivors in Alexandria, all those speeches were almost word-for-word Mountbatten's own speeches.

We then did *This Happy Breed*; we turned the play into a screenplay; where there was new dialogue required, Noël wrote it.

By that time I had come to the conclusion that all of us ought to be getting on to the bandwagon which was just starting; Arthur Rank thought it was fair that directors and producers should have a percentage of any profits their films made, which was a new idea. He was a splendid influence on the business; one has only to think of the films he made possible, and the opportunities he gave to independent producers – Powell and Pressburger, Launder and Gilliat and ourselves – some of whose films were for all time.

***In Which We Serve* offers an interesting reflection on the class situation in Britain at the time. Do you think British cinema has been too middle-class for wide acceptance?**

When you think of it, the few British films that have been international successes operate on that basis. *A Matter of Life and Death* was about the officer class – nobody in Heaven talked with Cockney accents, all the angels were clearly upper-class! The divisions in the Dickens films are absolute, because Dickens wrote in the framework of a class system which was far more marked in his day than in ours. *Brief Encounter* is about a couple of middle-class people and it seems to work everywhere, including America. Noël wrote almost invariably about the upper classes or, if he wrote about the lower classes, always did so from an upper-class point of view.

Funnily, the one thing David Lean would have changed in *Brief Encounter*, had he had the chance, was the comic scenes with Joyce Carey and Stanley Holloway, the 'lower orders'; but Noël was an extremely skilful theatre writer and he knew that the story would have been intolerably sad otherwise. They provided some relief from the central situation, which was building up to be increasingly painful, both for the audience and for the two principals, for whom the audience feels deep sympathy.

After *In Which We Serve*, your next three films were all based on Coward plays or screenplays: *This Happy Breed*, *Blithe Spirit* and *Brief Encounter*. How did this trio come about?

There was still a desire to have some kind of propaganda edge to whatever we made. Noël had written *This Happy Breed*, which had run in London and it was, in a way, a piece of propaganda for the British people, for their stoicism, the humour and so on, so we decided it would make a good film. After *This Happy Breed* Noël gave us a tremendous plum in a play that had run for two or three years in London and New York and had toured all over America – that was *Blithe Spirit*, although David didn't want to do it.

Noël stipulated who was to play in it and because of that we were in a straitjacket on casting; the point of the play is a middle-aged man well into his second marriage, having long ago put away the follies of his youth with his sexy first wife, and suddenly being 'woken up' by her reappearance as a ghost. Rex Harrison was not middle-aged; and Kay Hammond, though a brilliant stage actress, didn't photograph well and also had a very slow delivery, which was difficult in films. When we started shooting scenes with Kay and Rex it became obvious that Constance Cummings [the second wife] looked more attractive to the average man in the street than Kay. This upset the whole play.

The other thing was that Noël didn't want us to 'open it up' too much; in fact we played forty-eight minutes in one room. All in all, the film was a failure. Better casting would have been the man who played it on stage after Noël – Cecil Parker, who was paunchy and in his late forties. Margaret Rutherford was wonderful in it, though, although she drove Noël mad in the theatre because she never gave the same performance two nights running. I saw five other women playing the part, none of whom was in the same street when it came to getting legitimate laughs.

When we finished that we didn't know what to do, because David Lean wasn't keen on directing comedy. Noël suggested there might be something in the *Tonight at 8.30* plays, so we read them all and the only one we could see expanding into a film was 'Still Life'. We decided to have a go at it, so we did a rough script and Noël supplied the new dialogue we needed; it had been a half-hour play and the film was to be an hour and a half, so we needed more visuals and more words. At one stage during *Brief Encounter*, he was actually in India with an entertainment troupe; we managed to get cables through to him saying we needed thirty seconds of dialogue for the scene in the boat and we got a cable back giving us two lines of dialogue and saying, 'This runs forty-eight seconds; if you want to shorten it, take out the following words . . .'!

Then David didn't want to do any more Coward films. He wanted to do *Great Expectations* because he had seen a production of it in the Rudolf Steiner Hall in which Alec Guinness had played Herbert Pocket. He had been very impressed by the book

and the story and by Alec. I still think it is the finest of all Dickens adaptations ever made.

What do you remember of the relative involvement of David Lean, Ronald Neame, Kay Walsh, Cecil McGivern and yourself in the screenplay?

David, Ronald and I wrote the screenplay and the other two provided additional dialogue; the three of us did all the first draft screenplays up to *Oliver Twist*. We would do the draft and then David would do a final shooting script from it; somehow it worked for the three of us to combine in that way. Kay was very good at dialogue too, particularly when we hadn't written enough 'Dickens' dialogue. The same with Cecil, who worked most on a film we didn't eventually make, unfortunately – Margaret Irwin's book *The Gay Galliard* about Bothwell and Mary Queen of Scots. I think we chose well what to use and it worked.

How closely were you involved as co-producer with the art director John Bryan?

He did one lovely job for me on a film that didn't work but looks very beautiful and stands up quite well, *Blanche Fury*. John Bryan was art director on that and also on *Oliver Twist* and *Great Expectations*. He worked closely with all of us – myself, David Lean and Guy Green, the cameraman.

Cineguild's next venture with Dickens was *Oliver Twist* **. . .**

I didn't have much to do with *Oliver Twist* after we did the first script and preliminary casting. By that time I wanted to make *Blanche Fury* and I thought Stewart Granger would make a very good villain rather than a romantic hero; I also wanted to do something with Valerie. The basis to the story and its most exciting aspect is the murder apparently committed by a gypsy woman, prefiguring *Psycho* because in fact it isn't a woman at all. Stewart Granger refused to play it dressed as a woman, even though you would only have seen a flash of him, so it lost that high-point scene. The director, Marc Allegret, made some splendid films before the war but did not have such success afterwards.

We took far too long over *Blanche Fury*, it cost too much money and it didn't 'work', and never attracted any great audience. David and Ronnie didn't like what I was trying to do with *Blanche Fury*, which was along the lines of the very successful costume films from Gainsborough. I wanted to make a serious one with a better story and I thought it would make a lot of money. I found out that what I was making was a 'hard' film, not a 'soft' film which the others were. There was real hatred in it as well as love, and the public didn't want it. Cineguild more or less broke up over that.

I then formed a company called Constellation Films and made a film in Italy, called *Shadow of the Eagle* over here. It looked nice, had beautiful sets, but again I wasn't pleased with it. When I came back to England we made *The Small Voice* with Howard Keel; it got very good notices and was very well received but didn't make much money. Our director was Fergus McDonell, who was an editor for Carol Reed. Carol had suggested I give him a chance to direct. I nursed him through our film and he obviously had talent but he was so highly strung that he could very easily have had a nervous breakdown. He went to Canada afterwards and did well in the documentary field.

In 1952, you made a film loaded with stars – Nigel Patrick, Valerie Hobson, Martita Hunt – *Meet Me Tonight*.

That was just to have something to do, more or less. Noël was rather unkind about that but he made what I think was a valid point: he said that the point of the 'Red Peppers' segment was to spend an evening seeing Noël Coward and Gertie Lawrence *not* playing Noël Coward and Gertie Lawrence, that is the fun; that the moment you do one of these little plays for real, they don't exist. It was directed by Fay Compton's son, Anthony Pelissier, who had many different talents but none of them big enough to make a real impact. Look at *The Rocking Horse Winner* – he certainly had talent but he never got enough chances. He was a difficult man but, then, so was the man who made *Kind Hearts and Coronets*, yet that didn't stop him from being a great director.

There is a director called Daniel Birt who worked for you on *The Interrupted Journey*.

Yes, he was an editor. Constellation Films had a publicity department with a director and an office in Hanover Square; nothing much happened after we made *The Small Voice* and I was getting a bit desperate with £400 or £500 going out every week. Daniel Birt brought *Interrupted Journey* to us himself because he wanted to do it. We knew we could get Valerie and we thought we could get Richard Todd, who had just done very well with *The Hasty Heart*. I didn't think much of the project but if you have a company you have to do something, because the money keeps on going out. It had no success at all, however. Daniel Birt was obviously not going to be a great director; editors can always make films, but only the very talented ones can make good films.

Your last two films of this period were directed by Anthony Asquith – *The Young Lovers* and *Orders to Kill*. How would you rate him among British directors?

Puffin was never quite a great director – perhaps not ruthless enough – but he was a very, very good one. I think if he'd had enough of the right material, such as several *The Importance of Being Earnest*s, it would have made a difference. For *The Young Lovers* I had wanted Mark Robson to direct, Jimmy Stewart to star, and some very good European actress I intended to find. The Rank Organisation said they didn't have the money for an American star and wanted me to use the young American, David Knight. Puffin was the wrong director for it; it should have been made in that stark, realistic style the Americans were so good at, but Rank wanted to use Puffin. I hadn't made a film for some time and was getting lazy, so I agreed to do it as Rank wanted. It was a perfectly good film but it lacked guts; it didn't have that hard edge to it which it needed. It was intended as a blast against McCarthyism, and was written by a noted anti-Fascist, George Tabori.

The next film was a story which Puffin had found, *Orders to Kill*, which again would have been better with a harder, sharper edge to it. It needed to be conceived more harshly. Both the films I did with Puffin were well made, well crafted, but the impact was soft and did not grip a worldwide audience. *Orders to Kill* was a very good story – how hard it is to kill an enemy when you get to know him personally – but the public simply didn't go for it. Puffin had known Lillian Gish in Hollywood in the '20s and loved her, so that's how she came to be in it.

Dame Wendy Hiller

b. 1912

Actor: *Lancashire Luck* (1937), *Pygmalion* (1938), *Major Barbara* (1941), *I Know Where I'm Going* (1945), *To Be a Woman* (voice only) (1951), *An Outcast of the Islands* (1952), *Single-Handed* (1953), *How to Murder a Rich Uncle, Something of Value* (1957), *Separate Tables* (1958), *Sons and Lovers* (1960), *Toys in the Attic* (1963), *A Man for All Seasons* (1966), *David Copperfield* (1969), *Murder on the Orient Express* (1974), *Voyage of the Damned* (1976), *The Cat and The Canary* (1977), *The Elephant Man* (1980), *Making Love* (1982), *Attracta* (1983), *The Lonely Passion of Judith Hearne* (1987), *The Countess Alice* (1992)*

Wendy Hiller has made only twenty films for the cinema in fifty years, yet few actresses have so secure a place in the history of British cinema. This is partly, no doubt, a matter of the marvellously distinctive looks and voice which have made her so instantly recognisable, partly a matter of having been seen in several films of legendary status in British cinema. No one has effaced the impression she made as Eliza Doolittle in Anthony Asquith's film version of *Pygmalion* or in the title role of *Major Barbara* three years later. The third role which so firmly ensconced her in the affections and memories of filmgoers was that of the spoilt, wilful heroine of Michael Powell's Celtic romance, *I Know Where I'm Going*, in which her materialism cracks under the claims of love. But even in less distinguished films she was always memorable: for example, as the girl seduced and abandoned in *Single-Handed*, as Mrs Aylmer in Carol Reed's version of Conrad, *Outcast of the Islands* (which she dislikes), and in the Hollywood-made *Separate Tables*, for which her touchingly restrained playing as the hotel manageress won her an Oscar. Like the greatest stars, she is one of a kind; one can only wish that she had made twice as many films as she has.
Interview date: June 1991

You have had a long and distinguished career in all the acting media: it looks like a brilliantly planned career.

Oh no, I have to contradict you there because, looking back, I can't think how I managed to be so untidy and wayward in the choice of things I did *and* the things I said no to. I suppose I started in films in a way that some people would say (and I think now I agree with them) was really rather bad luck – to have an enormous success on your first big film, which I did with *Pygmalion*. It was wonderful in one way, but in a perfect career I would have put myself into a drama school and acquired a formidable technical armoury, which I never had for either films or the theatre. Even after I had made *Pygmalion*, then *Major Barbara*, then being lucky enough to make *I Know Where I'm Going*, I didn't think of myself as a film actress. I didn't think, oughtn't one go to Hollywood and oughtn't someone get me a long-term contract? I have been very blessed in being in three or four, perhaps five, films that have had a long life and worn well; that is usually because of the director not being mannered in style, so that the film has been acceptable to another generation.

You have had enormous success both in film and on stage. How do you place films in your career?

To take a purely practical attitude, I now find films easier to manage from a domestic point of view. With a play you know when a run is going to start but you never know when it is going to finish. With a film you do have a finishing date and they usually want to get rid of you on that date, because otherwise you'll cost them money. That has its satisfactory side.

One thing I still can't get used to, with films and television, is what I call 'pacing' myself. As a stage actress, if you have a month's rehearsal and, perhaps, two weeks of touring, then you can pace yourself. When I do a film I learn the whole of it, of course, so that I know how I'm going to play the last scene, but it still takes me by surprise if they do the next-to-last scene first.

How did you come to make your first film, *Lancashire Luck*, in 1937?

It was a 'quota quickie', made in a fortnight. My husband [Ronald Gow] had written the script and didn't want me to be in it; he thought it was nepotism. It was directed by Henry Cass, who was a friend of ours, and it was altogether a very friendly and cosy affair. I think I played a working man's daughter who fell in love with the character played by George Galleon, a tall, handsome creature and a dear boy, but I don't think he had a very successful career. George Carney played my father, as he did in *I Know Where I'm Going* – he was Lancashire, as I am.

And then came *Pygmalion*?

GBS had seen me in my husband's play, *Love on the Dole*, at the Garrick Theatre, the first play I did in London. Then I played *St Joan* and *Pygmalion* at the Malvern Festival to celebrate Shaw's eightieth birthday, and he insisted I should play Eliza when the film was to be made by Gabby Pascal. I don't think Gabby wanted me and certainly the backers didn't, not knowing me from a bar of soap. I didn't want a long-term contract and fought against that. I made the film in about eight weeks, with that very much-to-be-admired director Anthony Asquith, and his straightforward classical approach to a classical piece of work is one reason, apart from the Cinderella story, for the film's success. He shared the director's credit with Leslie Howard; I don't mean to denigrate Leslie but, as one who was in practically every day's shooting, I can say with confidence that I wouldn't have known Leslie was co-directing until the day we were shooting the tea-party scene; Leslie suddenly said, 'She can't play it like that, that won't work.' I didn't have the courage to say, 'Well, Mr Howard, I've played it this way with audiences and it brings the house down.' So I rushed to my dressing-room in floods of tears. That dear actor who played my father, Wilfred Lawson, came in, listened to me snuffling, then just said in a very soothing voice, 'Take no bloody notice of them. Play it the way you know,' and walked out! Poor Leslie must have been warned to leave me alone or they'd never get on, because I was so swollen with weeping and it does cost them money! So we got on with it.

Why was Shaw so attracted to Gabriel Pascal?

Well, he was a beguiling creature and GBS and Mrs Shaw, being the kind of people they were, were entranced by this Hungarian. Hollywood people had been after the rights to *Pygmalion* but in Gabby he had someone who said he had been a distributor, and who was stagestruck and starstruck, although he came to grief when he tried to direct. He had enormous charm and he tried to be clever but, unlike Korda, he wasn't a bit clever. He didn't make any money for himself; he was just an old bumbler-on with great charm and a certain appreciation of good acting and of Shaw.

He ran into problems over *Major Barbara*. We didn't have an experienced director on that: we had a charming man who was a stage director, Harold French, who had a great gift for directing light comedies. We spent ten months in the studio at

Denham making the film, and it is a very difficult and broken play anyway. There was a small fighter squadron based there and we used to have a system of spotters. I remember having to spend one night there when the noise was very worrying, wrapping my head in a towel and thinking, 'Ronnie Neame will be so cross if my face is cut in the morning!' As though if my feet were cut off it didn't matter! Ronald Neame was a dear man and he must have been very clever. So was David Lean who edited it – and directed most of it. And we had that darling actor, Robert Newton. He had trouble with his lines after lunch! He was large and rude and outrageous and lovely.

There is a long gap between those two Shaw films and *I Know Where I'm Going*, some five years later.

Well, there was a war on and I had another baby; also I didn't want to go to Hollywood. If you've played in two Shaw films, you're a little bit choosy, and the things they asked me to do were not what I was looking for. Michael Powell did ask me to be in *Colonel Blimp* and I couldn't, because my son was born. Then he offered me something very strange; then finally he came up with *I Know Where I'm Going* and that lovely actor, Roger Livesey, was dangled before my eyes; I was in love with him before I met him! The location work on Mull was heaven – well no, it wasn't really, because the war was still on and it was pretty hard going. Also Roger wasn't there, he was in a play in London; there were his stand-in and I on Mull, mucking about in boats doing the water scenes for about a month or six weeks, though a lot of the storm scenes were actually shot in a studio tank.

Why do you think the film has worn so well?

I'm not sure. It's very unsentimental for its time and has a very modern attitude; she's a tough girl and yet is truly swept off her feet, and that sort of unsentimental romance is still telling. Also it was very adult, the whole approach, that anti-materialistic thing. It was also lovely to look at, I remember those beautiful colours up in the Isles.

One comes across conflicting attitudes to Michael Powell. What is your feeling about him?

I didn't take to him, personally. Emeric Pressburger was charming but Michael Powell was, I would say, rather a strange character. I could never warm to him. We just managed to get on without too much friction and I enjoyed playing with Roger and

the rest of the lovely cast. I'm sure Michael Powell is a very good filmmaker but I have never enjoyed his films; I think *I Know Where I'm Going* is the warmest, most compassionate and likeable of his films and I don't say that just because I was in it. Pressburger, as a European, did very well to capture that legend; the film is very Celtic in its feel and I think Powell owed a great deal to Pressburger in that respect.

I am surprised you didn't film again for six years.

I was bringing up small children and at that time I didn't have very good health. Then I think I went to New York. One film I never did and would have liked to have done was *The Heiress*, which I played in America with Basil Rathbone. It was a great success and Willy Wyler, for about a month off and on, was always reported to be in the audience. However, it had been several years since *I Know Where I'm Going* and people come and go.

What do you recall of working with Carol Reed in *Outcast of the Islands*?

That was very strange. I knew Carol because he had married a very dear friend of mine, Penelope Dudley Ward, who had played in *Major Barbara*. The film was actually two of Conrad's novels put together, it was a bit of a hybrid. My character was originally a full-blooded native, instead of which they turned it into me, from Beaconsfield! My daughter in the film, Annabel Morley, should have been a half-caste, so that the story of *Outcast of the Islands* is *her* story. Carol Reed was not an intellectual, he saw life entirely visually, through little squares, as did David Lean.

You made another adaptation at the end of the decade, *Sons and Lovers*. When filming a literary classic, do you steep yourself in the original work?

No. I knew the Conrad books quite well but there was no point in going back to them when I found myself cast as I was. It can be a confusion, in a way, to go back to the original. I also knew *Sons and Lovers* very well, and that should have been a much better film but again there were major concessions to Hollywood. It was Jack Cardiff's first film as a director; he was a superb cameraman, but I don't know if he was happy with it as the director. All I know is that Trevor Howard and I got on very well together, and just wanted to get our work over with and get home. Poor Dean Stockwell wanted to be analysing and talking about the inner meaning; we would say rather sceptically, 'There's no time for that, let's get on with it.' He was a very hardworking young actor but he was out of his depth, his country and his class. It was unkind to him and unkind to the film.

Did you enjoy making the comedy thriller, *How to Murder a Rich Uncle*?

Well, I *thought* I would because I had played with Nigel Patrick in something and he had said he was going to direct this film. I thought it would be rather larkish, but it turned out not at all so. Nigel Patrick was not as happy as a director as he was as an actor. I never wanted it to be known that I'd been in it. Then, once, I was travelling by train across America, from Hollywood to New York, we drew up at Albuquerque for a couple of hours and on the platform was a large notice saying: "Coming Next Week – *How to Murder a Rich Uncle*'. I thought, I've made Albuquerque and I didn't know whether to be pleased or not!

You filmed that very English play, *Separate Tables*, in America in 1958 ...

We were all English except Burt [Lancaster] and dear Rita Hayworth. She made a jolly good stab at the film, and she was a lovely creature; I have never been large but Rita was so delicately boned she made me feel like a camel! It was, as you suggest, a bizarre idea to transport all that was so English to Hollywood, but it was a very good film. I know I won an Oscar for it, but it was always the best part in the play.

Dame Thora Hird

b. 1913

Actor: *The Black Sheep of Whitehall, Spellbound* (1941), *The Big Blockade, Next of Kin, Went the Day Well?, The Foreman Went to France* (1942), *2000 Women* (1944), *The Courtneys of Curzon Street* (1947), *Corridor of Mirrors, My Brother Jonathan, The Weaker Sex, Portrait from Life, Once a Jolly Swagman, The Blind Goddess* (1948), *Fools Rush In, A Boy, a Girl, and a Bike, Madness of The Heart, Maytime in Mayfair, Boys in Brown, Conspirator* (1949), *The Cure for Love, Once a Sinner, The Magnet* (1950), *The Galloping Major* (1951), *The Frightened Man, Emergency Call, Time Gentlemen Please!, The Lost Hours* (1952), *Personal Affair, The Great Game, Background, Turn the Key Softly, Street Corner, A Day to Remember, The Long Memory* (1953), *Don't Blame The Stork, The Crowded Day, One Good Turn, For Better, For Worse* (1954), *The Quatermass Xperiment, The Love Match, Tiger by the Tail, Simon and Laura* (1955), *Lost, Women Without Men, Sailor Beware, Home and Away* (1956), *The Good Companions, These Dangerous Years* (1957), *The Clean Sweep, Further Up the Creek* (1958), *The Entertainer* (1960), *Over the Odds* (1961), *A Kind of Loving, Term of Trial* (1962), *Bitter Harvest* (1963), *Rattle of a Simple Man* (1964), *Some Will, Some Won't* (1970), *The Nightcomers* (1971), *Consuming Passions* (1987)

Slatterns, careworn drudges, charladies in pinnies, suspicious landladies with a fag hanging from the mouth, mothers kind and mothers monstrous: in her extraordinary career, Thora Hird has utterly mastered the art of screen character acting. She knows exactly how far to go, stopping short of caricature and imbuing even the briefest cameos with an instantly recognisable humanity. The vicious TV-addicted mum in *A Kind of Loving* is perhaps her most fully rounded screen role, but another kind of TV addict in *Simon and Laura* is just as memorable in comic mode. In the class-bound narratives of much British cinema of the '40s and '50s, she was inevitably below stairs, but frequently giving her 'betters' a piece of her mind. This seems to tally with her general approach to life: by her own account, she is not easily awed. Working incessantly in film, theatre and television, she has become one of the best loved of all British players.

Interview date: July 1994

Out of the many films you've made, the performance that stands out for me is the monstrous mother in John Schlesinger's *A Kind of Loving*.

Oh, that did everything for me. Everybody wanted to work for John Schlesinger, a brilliant man. I looked at it like one of the parts I'd played a great many of – I don't mean without care, but two good lines are worth ten pages of rubbish. That part was great because John worked with us. I remember the fuss when it was on in London, because she [June Ritchie] showed a bare back. You would have thought she was doing a full striptease, the way people were going to see it.

I've known a lot of women like that mother. I was a cashier at the Co-op [Co-operative Society] (drapery through one side, meat the other) for ten years and I've played nearly all those customers I used to serve. I'll do some little thing I've remembered, so simple. I've met that fearful harridan in *A Kind of Loving*. I remember when she said, 'You pig!' to her son-in-law Alan Bates, and a couple of moments later she said, 'You . . .' and you could see (I hope) that she was trying to think of something worse than 'pig' to call him.

I've appeared in hundreds of films and television things, and in some cases I literally mean 'appeared' around the door, that was all. *A Kind of Loving* was such a change from the characters I had been doing – it was the second big change, actually. When I was first at Ealing I was never asked to play anyone from Lancashire. Finally, I was asked if I could manage a Northern woman's part and I thought at first it was sarcasm. When I told them I was from Lancashire they were surprised, they hadn't known. The thing about acting in films or television is that

directors always say, 'Just be yourself,' which is quite different from stage acting.

You have had some wonderful parts on television, very recently in *Memento Mori*.

I'm glad you remember that, people were so kind about it. Of course Jack Clayton is one of the greatest directors anyone could ever work with. We used a hospital, now empty, that used to be a convalescent home for naval officers. On my last day he presented me with a very large and expensive bottle of champagne, saying, 'I don't know what I'm going to do without you tomorrow!' Don't forget, you're talking to someone eighty-three years old who was brought up in this business, brought up with obedience to the business. To be on time, to know your words, and, if Mr de Grunwald said, 'You stand on your head to say this line . . .', at least you tried. I always call directors 'Mr de Grunwald' and they know I do it with respect.

How did you get your first film role, and was it in *Spellbound*, as some references have it?

No, it was in *The Black Sheep of Whitehall*. I was in rep at £1 a week, and one week we were doing a play called *As You Are*, and I got the part of the mother-in-law who would pretend her heart was going on her, if she didn't get her own way. One Tuesday night George Formby came to the theatre, because the play had been bought for a film. I was just taking off my paste nose when the theatre manager said, 'Don't bother with that, Mr and Mrs Formby want to meet you.' I nearly dropped dead! There we were under the stage, where the dressing-rooms were, and I can still hear him saying, 'Eee, ye were good!' Then he said they wanted me for the film and I thought, 'This is fairy talk.' Then George

Formby said he would have the studio send over the casting director to see me in the play and then they'd do a film test. This was Cinderella going to the ball!

On the Friday I was cleaning off again when this camel-coated, snap-brimmed hat with a monocle came to the dressing room. He gave me his card and it said 'Gordon Hamilton Gay, Casting Director, Ealing Studios'. So I went to London to be tested and, although I didn't get the part in the film (I wasn't old enough), Michael Balcon and his brother Chandos sent for me to go to the rushes theatre next day. I didn't know what the rushes theatre was, didn't know anything about films then.

For my test Bill Fraser was paid two guineas to say some lines off camera, not to be seen at all on the screen. Basil Dearden directed my test and after nine takes I said, 'I'm very happy in rep at £1 a week. I didn't want to come here, you asked me to come. If I haven't done it right by nine times, you're just being kind.' Anyway, there I was next morning in the rushes theatre and suddenly the clapperboard came on and filled the screen. It said, 'Thora Hird, Test, Take 11'. There was this awful face – eyelashes, Clara Bow lips – saying, ' "I shall go to London" – and bugger you! I'm not going to do it again, you're just being kind.' And that clinched it. They were all laughing so much.

Did you enjoy working at Ealing?

Oh, yes. It was called 'the studio with the family feeling', but it had one restaurant with two doors in it to separate the wheat from the chaff. If you were a star you went in one door. Same food, of course. It was very much stars and small-part players. It was such a small studio (only two stages) that I think there was a bit more of that than usual. At one time Tommy Trinder was working on one floor and I was on the other, doing *Went the Day Well?* with Leslie Banks. We had to do umpteen takes on Leslie one time. He'd get a word wrong and say, 'I'll just do that again,' and they could do that because they were God, you see, and treated so. I was always aware of my position because I wasn't established then. I played an ATS girl with Patricia Hayes. People like us and Esme Cannon and Beatrice Varley would be in almost every film, for a couple of days' work.

You felt there was a real hierarchy of stars and supporting actors, not just at Ealing?

Oh yes, there was. You could have eyelashes put on if you were a star, but if you weren't a star you couldn't. As a non-star, when I was under contract

to J Arthur Rank, I used to take four means of transport to arrive at Denham at six for six-thirty, because in those days, if you were a *bit* player, you were in for six-thirty and made up. They can't do that now because you can't be called in before seven-fifteen.

You must have worked for most of the British studios during your long career. Did it make much difference to you where you worked?

The nearer the studio, the easier it was to get to it. Lime Grove was easy, just a bus ride. I made *2000 Women* there, for Gaumont-British, with Dulcie Gray. We had to wear the most awful shorts, like the British Army used to wear. There was a wonderful cast in that picture and Gaumont-British was a great studio to work for.

Were you under some kind of contract to Gainsborough, or Gaumont-British? Because you did a lot of films for them.

It was just convenient because they were very small parts I had in them. If they paid you £10 a week and you didn't work, it cost them £520 a year. I was under contract initially to Ealing Studios. Then Rank talked to them after I'd done a play at Notting Hill Gate at a little club theatre, and every agent in London went to it. One week they discovered Kenneth More playing there, the next week it was Dirk Bogarde. By one o'clock on the day after the play I was in opened, I had been offered three films and two West End plays. It was a fairy-tale for me then.

My first West End play was at the Vaudeville Theatre, *No Medals* by Esther McCracken. I played in that for two years and I went on later to do the film of the play (*The Weaker Sex*) for Roy [Ward] Baker. I enjoyed that very much. Ursula Jeans was in the film, doing the part that Fay Compton had played on the stage.

You were in several of Lewis Gilbert's early films, *Once a Sinner*, *Emergency Call* and *Time Gentlemen Please*.

Oh, I liked working for Lewis Gilbert – I played an almoner in *Time Gentlemen Please* [with Ivor Barnard]. I also did *Once a Jolly Swagman* in which I played Dirk Bogarde's mum. That was made for Wessex and directed by Jack Lee; he was a love, wore khaki overalls to direct. I made *Turn the Key Softly* for Jack as well, which Kathleen Harrison was in. Kathleen and I were both under contract and it was usually she or I who got the part. Jack Lee wanted me for the bigger part in *Turn the Key Softly*, but Earl St John said no, it was Kathy's turn!

You worked for so many directors . . .

Yes. Herbert Wilcox was great, always giving the cast champagne after work. All these half-bottles would be sitting in ice in Anna's [Neagle] dressing-room while we worked. My daughter, Janette Scott, played Anna's daughter in one film [*The Lady is a Square*] and Herbert rang us up every night at twenty past eight and kept saying, if we didn't want Janette, they'd adopt her. He was a kind man and he knew what the public wanted.

How important were directors to you? Or did you know what you wanted to do and simply go out and do it?

Ah, but with care. I would know how far I could go. I probably wouldn't try some little bit of comedy halfway through a scene on the first run-through, I'd just wait my time and then ask if I may. I'd never be too familiar with them.

You were in a film that made fun of television early on, Muriel Box's *Simon and Laura*.

Oh yes, with Ian Carmichael doing that walk! And Maurice Denham was in it too. I liked Muriel Box; she was very kind. She was working on the next floor again when I was making *The Quatermass Xperiment* for Val Guest. I also worked for her in *Street Corner*, though it was just one appearance, in a police court, but I had more to do in *Rattle of a Simple Man* for her – I was Harry [H] Corbett's mum.

A new kind of British film appeared in the early '60s and you were in three of them. *The Entertainer*, *A Kind of Loving* and *Term of Trial*. How did you react to these?

Like anybody earning a living, I took most of the work that came along. In *The Entertainer*, my husband was played by Tommy Langley from Blackpool, who wasn't an actor and didn't have an Equity card. He was a builder! I was doing a play there for the season and one night Tony Richardson, John Osborne and Joan Plowright came to see me, and Tony said he wanted me to do a cameo in *The Entertainer*. I said that would be very nice, but I didn't think I'd be able to do it because I'd have to have a deadline of three o'clock on the set at Morecambe, so I could get back to Blackpool in time for the theatre. Anyway, they said that was OK. One day I was sitting with Larry Olivier, waiting to do a scene. He said to me, 'What would you do if you didn't trust someone, Thora?' I said, 'Me, or the character I'm playing?' He said, 'Well, we're hoping there'll be a lot of you in Mrs Thingamepush.' So I told him what my mother used to say: 'Him? I wouldn't trust him behind that curtain with his feet showing!' He laughed, and it's in the film.

Term of Trial was made in Ireland, also with Olivier. I don't know why the film was made in Ireland, but it was done at Bray Studios outside Dublin. I liked working with Larry because we got on well, but there were little things about him that annoyed me. For a start, if I had to do complementaries for him (standing off-camera giving him my lines while they took his close-ups), I would have to be in at eight-thirty in the morning for make-up because Larry insisted everyone be in character, even if they weren't on camera. I asked him about it and he told me he couldn't act to the character if he was looking at *me* – *as* me. I told him that everybody thought he could have done the scene without me even being there.

Sir Alfred Hitchcock

1899–1980

Director: *Number Thirteen* (1922), *Always Tell Your Wife* (1923), *The Prude's Fall* (1924), *The*

Pleasure Garden/ Irrgarten der Leidenschaft, *The Blackguard/ Die Prinzessin und der Geiger* (1925),

The Mountain Eagle, The Lodger (1926), The Ring, Easy Virtue, Downhill (1927), The Farmer's Wife, Champagne (1928), The Manxman, Blackmail (1929), Murder, Juno and the Paycock, Elstree Calling (1930), The Skin Game (1931), Rich and Strange, Number Seventeen (1932), Waltzes from Vienna (1933), The Man Who Knew Too Much (1934), The Thirty-Nine Steps (1935), Secret Agent, Sabotage (1936), Young and Innocent (1937), The Lady Vanishes (1938), Jamaica Inn (1939), Rebecca, Foreign Correspondent (1940), Suspicion, Mr and Mrs Smith (1941), Saboteur (1942), Shadow of a Doubt (1943), Lifeboat, Bon Voyage, Aventure Malgache (1944), Spellbound (1945), Notorious (1946), The Paradine Case (1947), Rope (1948), Under Capricorn (1949), Stage Fright (1950), Strangers on a Train (1951), I Confess (1953), Rear Window, Dial M for Murder (1954), To Catch a Thief, The Man Who Knew Too Much (1955), The Wrong Man, The Trouble with Harry (1956), Vertigo (1958), North by Northwest (1959), Psycho (1960), The Birds (1963), Marnie (1964), Torn Curtain (1966), Topaz (1969), Frenzy (1972), Family Plot (1976)

When Michael Balcon, on the matter of turning Woman to Woman from play to film in 1929, asked his 'assistant director', Alfred Hitchcock, if he knew a writer, he said at once, 'Yes, me.' When the art director proved unready to start, Hitchcock said, 'That's all right. I'll be the art director.'[1] Already, it seems, Hitchcock was itching for the kind of comprehensive control that would in later years ensure that 'a Hitchcock film' meant just that.

As early as 1927, he had asserted the director's authority: 'Film directors live with their pictures while they are being made. They are their babies just as much as an author's novel is the offspring of his imagination. And that seems to make it all the more certain that when moving pictures are really artistic they will be created entirely by one man.'[2]

The received wisdom now is that his pre-war British period is mere prentice work, and to some extent Hitchcock has contributed to this view. For example, in the famous extended conversation with François Truffaut, he says of The Man Who Knew Too Much, which he made in England in 1934 and in the US in 1954, 'Let's say that the first version is the work of a talented amateur and the second was made by a professional.'[3] (It's worth noting, however, that five years later, he prefers the earlier one: 'I think it was more spontaneous, it had less logic. Logic is dull: you always lose the bizarre and the spontaneous.'[4] This remark finds an echo in a 1978 remark about Young and Innocent: '"The first thing I throw out is logic," observed Hitchcock at the time.)[5]

He is actually encouraged by Truffaut to undervalue his British period. Certainly Hitchcock found legitimate grounds for complaint about 1930s British cinema. 'British talkies need more variety . . . Why must we always stick to middle-class drawing rooms and our middle-class characters?'[6] he asked in 1934. The following year he maintained that 'most of our English film actresses come from some school of acting or from the stage. It is always their desire to appear a lady and, in doing so, they became cold and lifeless.'[7] And in 1938, 'Again and again I have been prevented from putting on the screen authentic incidents in British life'[8] or 'Failing to get a good script, I've invariably descended or ascended to using my own resources and becoming a crime reporter.'[9]

Against these complaints, however, must be set the films themselves. If they lack the profundity of the great American masterpieces, they nevertheless have their own very considerable pleasures: they are essentially unpretentious, swift-moving, often sharply percipient about limitations in English life, and bountifully resourceful in their use of cinematic strategies. This latter is true from the time of The Lodger (in which he exploited the 'special terror . . . about being tied'[10]) and Blackmail, his and Britain's first talkie, with its famous sequence in which 'the talk goes on and on, becoming a confusion of vague noises to which the girl no longer listens.'[11] The sexual resonances of The Thirty-Nine Steps prefigure much of his later œuvre; The Lady Vanishes is as exhilarating a train-set thriller as was ever made; and Young and Innocent is a charming 'attempt to do a chase story with very young people involved.'[12] The latter boasts one of the most famous tracking shots in history, as the camera, mounted on a crane, crosses a crowded ballroom to end on a drummer's twitching eye.

His later three British films – Stage Fright, Under Capricorn and Frenzy – are, if not wholly successful, full of felicitous touches – and of his determination to 'try and dodge the cliché. [In Frenzy] I have a scene where a girl comes back to her office after lunch to find that her employer has been murdered . . . I just left the camera outside the building, static, until the scream came.'[13]

By the time he got to Hollywood, he says, 'I did get my own way more than most right from the start.'[14] His determination served him well, and he had learned his 'own way' in Britain.

1 Michael Balcon, *A Lifetime of Films*, Hutchinson, London, 1969, p 19
2 *London Evening News*, May 1927 (no further details available)
3 François Truffaut, *Hitchcock*, Simon & Schuster, New York, 1967, p 65
4 *Films Illustrated*, July 1972, p 22
5 John Russell Taylor, *Hitch: The Life and Work of Alfred Hitchcock*, Faber & Faber, London, 1978, p 145
6 *Film Weekly*, 14 December 1934, p 14
7 *Film Weekly*, 10 September 1935, p 10
8 *Film Weekly*, 5 November 1938, p 6
9 *World Film News*, March 1938, p 5
10 *Sight and Sound*, Winter 1955–56, p 158
11 Truffaut, p 47
12 Truffaut, p 81
13 *Films Illustrated*, p 23
14 *Sight and Sound*, Autumn 1966, p 203

Valerie Hobson

b. 1917

Actor: *Eyes of Fate* (1933), *Two Hearts in Waltz Time, The Path of Glory, Badger's Green, Strange Wives, Great Expectations* (US) (1934), *Oh What a Night, Rendezvous at Midnight, Werewolf of London, Bride of Frankenstein, The Mystery of Edwin Drood, Chinatown Squad, The Great Impersonation* (1935), *August Weekend, Tugboat Princess, The Secret of Stamboul, No Escape/No Exit* (1936), *Jump for Glory* (1937), *The Drum, Q Planes, This Man is News* (1938), *This Man in Paris, The Spy in Black, The Silent Battle* (1939), *Contraband* (1940), *Atlantic Ferry* (1941), *Unpublished Story* (1942), *The Adventures of Tartu* (1943), *The Years Between, Great Expectations* (1946), *Blanche Fury* (1947), *The Small Voice* (1948), *Kind Hearts and Coronets, Train of Events, The Interrupted Journey, The Rocking Horse Winner* (1949), *The Card* (1951), *Who Goes There?, Meet Me Tonight, The Voice of Merrill* (1952), *Background, Knave of Hearts* (1954)

Valerie Hobson's early retirement robbed the British cinema of one of its most stylish leading ladies. After a busy apprenticeship in Hollywood in her late 'teens, she returned to England in 1936 and made a rapid ascent to stardom in Korda's *The Drum* and three good-humoured thrillers, *Q Planes, This Man is News* and *This Man in Paris*. These latter two established what has always seemed to me her forte – sophisticated comedy, for which her elegant touch so well suited her. Her finest opportunity in this vein was *Kind Hearts and Coronets*, in which her ladylike poise so brilliantly offsets Joan Greenwood's bitchy opportunism. She was also an enterprising heroine in the adventure films she did for her favourite director Michael Powell, *The Spy in Black* and *Contraband*; is superb as the extravagant, selfish mother in *The Rocking Horse Winner*; and shows real sensuality and intensity in her performance as the eponymous heroine in that underrated melodrama, *Blanche Fury*. In fact, the body of her work stands up very well to the scrutiny of forty years on.

Interview date: July 1990

How did you come to star in *The Drum* after your spell in Hollywood in the '30s?

In America I met Elizabeth Allan, the lovely English star, and her husband, Bill O'Bryen, was a big theatrical agent. I went to see him when I came back to England and almost at once he introduced me to Alexander Korda, who gave me a test. He wanted someone who looked especially English, with a pale English skin, for *The Drum*, because it was to be made in Technicolor. After a great many tests with peculiar make-up, Korda put me under contract. I can't say I really *worked* with Korda because I saw very little of him. He was the producer, however, and it was directed by Zoltan Korda, vivacious and endearing, quite unlike his two brothers. I was very happy making the film; I was still so young and so happy to be back home.

I particularly admire your work in comedy. Do you recall two comedy thrillers called *This Man is News* and *This Man in Paris*, with Barry K Barnes?

I specially remember them because while making them I met and fell in love with my first husband, Anthony Havelock-Allan. *This Man is News* had an extraordinary success; as a nation we hadn't made a high comedy successfully until then. It was a low-priced film, shot very quickly, and made along the lines of the William Powell–Myrna Loy films. When they put it on at the Plaza, there were literally queues around the block to see it. Yes, I liked comedy, which I found more of a challenge than drama, but I suppose I played more drama, mostly costume drama. I felt happiest in high comedy, though it is harder to play on film than on stage because you don't have audience response, and it requires very careful timing. I did two with Alec Guinness, *Kind Hearts and Coronets* and *The Card*, which were, I think, two of the most elegant British comedies made.

I have always thought that the main reason for the success of *Kind Hearts* was that it was played absolutely dead straight, very seriously. It's a matter of being aware that you are playing a funny situation yet playing it so straight that even the tongue-in-the-cheek doesn't show. Robert Hamer, the director, a genius who died sadly young, was a very sophisticated man, and, to play something that requires sophisticated handling, you cannot have a naïve director. In *Kind Hearts and Coronets*, the whole idea of the D'Ascoyne family was so absurd that, if it hadn't been handled with the most delicate gloves, people would have walked out. As it is, I think it is an important film which will stand the test of time. It was very well cast and of course Alec Guinness was miraculous. He doesn't have the obvious greatness of an Olivier; instead he has the most subtle integrity, and is a wonderful film actor, doing the tiniest things to great effect. I think they were very clever to cast two such contrasting types as Joan Greenwood and myself as the women, and Dennis Price was marvellously 'lacy' as the murderer.

What do you remember of *The Card*, directed by Ronald Neame, and *Who Goes There?* for Anthony Kimmins?

The Countess in *The Card* was a charming but dull character, exactly as Arnold Bennett would have seen a woman of that class at that time. The female characters are very well contrasted, again, one so nice and charming, the other [Glynis Johns] so naughty and flirtatious – rather like the Joan Greenwood character in *Kind Hearts and Coronets*. Their both being physically very small women seemed good casting.

Who Goes There? was from a stage play but I hadn't been in it. Nigel Patrick was an actor with an excellent comedy touch, perhaps slightly heavier than others, but always sure. Comedy playing is very much a matter of being a couple, even more so than playing romantic leads; in a comedy you *have* to work well with your opposite number.

To backtrack, was it your two Michael Powell films. *The Spy in Black* and *Contraband*, which firmly established you as a star?

Probably, yes; they were almost the first films we made at the beginning of the war and, if they were successful, then you couldn't help being successful too. But I'm not sure if the film before those two didn't set the seal: under Korda's umbrella, I made *Q Planes*; it had two such rare actors in it, Olivier and Richardson, even though Olivier was nothing like the major star he was to become after *Henry V*. He didn't have a light comedy touch in those days; he was more of a straightforward romantic actor. Ralph Richardson was hardly known in films, but was magnetic.

I hear such diverse views about working with Michael Powell. What is your view of him?

Mick tried so many different things! He was a very clever man, almost a genius, and he *loved* cinematography. Emeric Pressburger and he were like two bookends together, they were so closely associated. I know some people found working with Mick not such a happy experience but he was easily my favourite director of all. Mick was very sharp and energetic, his mind like a brilliant butterfly, flitting all over the place. He was given to fits of tremendous bad temper which one knew perfectly well weren't genuine and would be immediately forgotten. He could be very sarcastic about someone's performance to try and get the best out of them; that usually has the effect of shrivelling one up, but not so with him, because it was not done from unkindness or bad temper. Alas, I only made two pictures for him but we remained close friends until he died.

Connie Veidt was in both those films and you couldn't find an actor to enjoy working with more. He had a riveting screen presence and yet he was not really a great actor; like some American stars who have the right physique and an amazing talent for the camera without being very interested in acting.

To move on to *Great Expectations*, what did you think of the change to a rather upbeat ending?

I don't really have any thoughts about it, I have seen it so often. My only feeling was that anything was now possible for two young people going from the darkness into the light, away from all the nonsense and evil that had gone on over the years. I think the audience felt that way about it too. In 1935 I was too young to play Estella in Hollywood, but I played Estella *and* Molly in David Lean's 1946 film. In Hollywood I think I was more impressed with the sense of being in the film version of a classic; I was closer then to the reading of Dickens.

The enormous attention to detail you find in the Lean version was the chief difference I found between how England approaches the classics and how it was done in America. My only sense of relating to the original was in terms of the Victorian style, and I think this comes out in the film. In this case, at least, I think we had a perfect script – and that's all you can ask of any film whether or not it's an adaptation. You have to assume people haven't read the book. I didn't go back to it much in 1946 but David and Tony worked very closely from it. Things were pulled out of the book and pruned, getting to essentials. We knew we were in a very rare film. In the immediate post-war period there was a feeling of an end and a new beginning – a tremendous feeling of a Renaissance, of a burgeoning of all the talent that had been squashed in by money restraint during the war. We had virtually *carte blanche* as far as money was concerned; I know more about this than I normally would have because I was then married to Tony Havelock-Allan, who was the producer.

What do you remember about David Lean's direction?

I felt he always stressed the intimacy of the story, so that it seemed enormously domestic. But I think he improved as a director of actors; he was a great technician all the time: a great cutter and editor, which is how he started; but not a great director of actors – then. I didn't feel easy working with him though I was very fond of him as a friend. When he would have forty takes for a shot, it wasn't so much for perfection as out of uncertainty, and as often as not he'd print the third or fourth take. He was one of the world's brilliant directors, but a devil on the set. Don't forget I'm speaking of over forty-five years ago! He was a charismatic person and actors were mesmerised by him; but he was lucky that the cast was filled with remarkable actors – as well as Johnny Mills, there were Alec Guinness, Martita Hunt, Francis L Sullivan – all carefully cast by David and Tony. Both director and producer had fallen in love with Dickens and oversaw the smallest detail.

How did you feel about playing Estella?

I think she's a very unsatisfactory character. It's easy to be cast to play someone without a heart but harder to make people feel you're *acting* cold, instead of being just stiff and unresponsive. It's a slight, thinly written part; it's a nice idea in the book – the 'no heart' business – but it's not well developed there either. Jean Simmons's natural vivacity came out strongly and this helped the contrast with the older Estella. When you see Estella 'grown up', you feel this vivacity has been suppressed, and I think this suited my particular style very well.

Whose idea was it for you also to play Molly?

It was David's idea – about a week before we started – because he said that the girl must have looked a bit like her mother – which was clever of him. I don't think I appear on the cast list as Molly, and perhaps few people realise it was me.

I very much liked *Blanche Fury*. Did you?

Tony [Havelock-Allan] had wanted it very much to be a success because it cost a lot of money; it was beautiful to look at, with wonderful interiors. I had just had our son, who was born mentally handicapped, and he meant the film as a sort of 'loving gift', making me back into a leading lady, which was a wonderful idea. The film didn't work completely. You could hardly do better than Guy Green and Geoffrey Unsworth as cameramen and, of course, that is enormously important to an actress – you know, then, that you are looking the best you *can* look. Our leading man was particularly good – Jimmy [Stewart] Granger can do that wonderful, slightly unpleasant edge, you know, the 'attractive man with the sneer'. We also had a very good director in Marc Allegret. I don't know why it wasn't a smash hit and I was sorry for Tony's sake it wasn't.

I have seen and enjoyed all of Fergus McDonell's films, including *The Small Voice*, but he seems simply to have stopped directing.

Unfortunately I don't know where he is or what he's doing. That film is most remembered for the fact that it was the first film for Howard (or Harold, as he was then) Keel. He was over here doing *Oklahoma!* and it was very clever of Tony Havelock-Allan to have spotted him. He was awfully good in the film as the villain with a heart. It's quite an alarming film and rather *à propos* today.

What do you remember of *The Rocking Horse Winner*, playing perhaps your most unsympathetic role?

Yes, it was very unsympathetic but I loved doing it. It was so well written, by both DH Lawrence originally and Anthony Pelissier, who did the screenplay. Tony caught the fact that there are people like Hester, who love their children and are terribly guilt-ridden because they can't manage their affairs. Both Tony Pelissier and I adored children and I remember saying to him that I found the ending intolerable – that is, the original novella's ending; I don't remember any directive from on high, any censorship that required the ending to be softened as it was; I think it finished that way because Tony and I both felt that we had to show Hester as not being made entirely of stone. It's very carefully made and very accurate about a certain class of family.

I haven't seen your last film, René Clément's *Knave of Hearts*, with the famous French star Gérard Philipe? What do you remember about this?

I'm sorry you haven't seen that film because it was elegantly and well made. Gérard Philipe was a very attractive, rather strange man who died shortly after the film was made. I played one of those endlessly accommodating wives who turn a blind eye: I actually got to keep the husband that time, although I don't think he wanted to be kept! It was a charming and very funny film.

What do you regard as the highlights of your film career?

From the point of view of success, I'd choose *Great Expectations* or *Kind Hearts and Coronets*. But the film I enjoyed most, which was the most enormous fun and my first real little success, was *This Man is News*. I did enjoy it. Certainly the most beautiful film I was in was *Blanche Fury*, and it remains my favourite.

Sir Michael Hordern

1911–1995

Actor: *The Girl in the News* (1939), *The Years Between*, *A Girl in a Million*, *Great Expectations*, *School for Secrets* (1946), *Mine Own Executioner* (1947), *Night Beat*, *Portrait from Life*, *The Small*

Voice, Good Time Girl (1948), Train of Events, Passport to Pimlico (1949), The Astonished Heart, Trio, Highly Dangerous (1950), Flesh and Blood, The Magic Box, Tom Brown's Schooldays, Scrooge (1951), The Card, The Story of Robin Hood and his Merrie Men, The Hour of Thirteen (1952), Street Corner, Grand National Night, The Heart of the Matter, Personal Affair (1953), You Know What Sailors Are, Forbidden Cargo, The Beachcomber (1954), The Night My Number Came Up, The Constant Husband, The Dark Avenger, Storm Over the Nile (1955), Alexander the Great, The Man Who Never Was, Pacific Destiny, The Baby and the Battleship, The Spanish Gardener (1956), No Time for Tears, Windom's Way (1957), The Spaniard's Curse, I Was Monty's Double, I Accuse!, Girls at Sea (1958), Sink the Bismarck!, Moment of Danger, The Man in the Moon (1960), El Cid, Macbeth, First Left Past Aden (narr) (1961), The VIPs, Cleopatra, Dr Syn – Alias the Scarecrow (1963), The Yellow Rolls-Royce (1964), The Spy Who Came in from the Cold, Genghis Khan, The Taming of the Shrew, A Funny Thing Happened on the Way to the Forum, The Jokers (1966), How I Won the War, I'll Never Forget What's 'is Name (1967), Where Eagles Dare (1968), The Bed-Sitting Room (1969), Futtock's End, Anne of the Thousand Days, Some Will, Some Won't (1970), Up Pompeii, Girl Stroke Boy, The Pied Piper, The Possession of Joel Delaney, Demons of the Mind (1971), Alice's Adventures in Wonderland, England Made Me (1972), Theatre of Blood, The Mackintosh Man (1973), Juggernaut, Mister Quilp, Royal Flash, Barry Lyndon, Lucky Lady (1975), The Slipper and the Rose (1976), Joseph Andrews (1977), The Medusa Touch, Watership Down (1978), The Wildcats of St Trinian's (1980), Gandhi, The Missionary (1982), Yellowbeard (1983), Lady Jane (1986), Freddie as FRO7 (voice) (1992)

One of the great exemplars of the British screen tradition of character acting, Michael Hordern had an astonishingly prolific career on stage and television as well. Never having been ambitious, as he says, he simply took what came along and, indeed, a great deal *did* come along. He had made over thirty films before 1956, when he at last had a full-scale role worthy of him: that is, in Philip Leacock's *The Spanish Gardener*, as the ambassador fighting for his son's affections. His roles following this were increasingly prominent: he was often in uniform (the captain in *The Baby and the Battleship*, the commander-in-chief in *Sink the Bismarck!*), or officials of various kind (the commissioner in *Pacific Destiny*); and there were several brushes with Shakespeare (Banquo in George Schaefer's *Macbeth*, Baptista in Zeffirelli's *The Taming of the Shrew*). Michael Hordern was one of those actors who made even bad British films worth going to.

Interview date: June 1990

You began in films in 1939 in *The Girl in the News* directed by Carol Reed – which seems like starting at the top!

Yes, I had one line in it, during a court scene. I was the junior counsel and my senior was a very famous actor, Felix Aylmer. I had to come up to him in the foyer of the Old Bailey and say, 'We're on next, sir.' Not a line you could get a great deal into! I then went into the Navy for the duration of the war. I didn't have any contact with films during that time. I came out of the Navy in 1945, having signed my own demobilisation order. I had trouble getting back into the profession. I was very frightened because I hadn't used my voice for over four years. I got terribly nervous and tightened up, so I had a course of voice teaching over a few months, the only actor's instruction I have ever had.

I always thought of films as being in quite a different slot. In the theatre you have to project, not only voice but a whole performance. There is also the learning as you go along; you rehearse a play for perhaps four weeks and then the curtain goes up on the first night and all that you've learned comes out in a progression. With films, you're as likely as not to be doing the last scene first, so you don't get a progression and that can be very tiresome and difficult.

What do you remember, from your early films, of such directors as Anthony Kimmins, Fergus McDonell and Anthony Darnborough?

On the whole, I found them very helpful to me as a young actor starting out in films. There were only two famous directors with whom I just did not get on and who were hopeless at any sort of tactful direction; they were John Huston and Zoltan Korda. Korda (for whom I made *Storm Over the Nile*) was absolutely hateful; he just loved having a whipping boy who was inexperienced. I was ideal for his purpose! As with directors in the theatre or any other medium, I look for those who can use me, lead me and not direct me – someone who can say to himself, 'I see what this chap can do for me, so I'll encourage that,' as opposed to Zoltan Korda, who bullied one. But it was a good time because the whole British film industry was very much alive then, and expanding.

You made *The Heart of the Matter* and seemed to be an ideal interpreter of Graham Greene's work. Did you admire his novels?

Yes, I have enjoyed his novels very much. That particular film was with Trevor Howard. Then I did *England Made Me* some twenty years later, which I loved. They were the only two Greene parts I did but they were both very enjoyable to attack. Greene himself wasn't involved in the filming; I don't think I've ever met him.

You worked with many famous Hollywood names who were imported into British films in the '50s. What do you recall of them?

I remember playing Errol Flynn's father in *The Dark Avenger* and Errol played the Black Prince; Peter Finch was in it too. Errol was a commanding presence – always drunk but pretty commanding at the same time! I don't remember any feeling of resentment among my profession towards the American imports, because I think we were all aware that they were helping to keep our industry going, by ensuring a certain amount of American distribution.

In 1956 you had a batch of three very good and varied parts: *Pacific Destiny*, *The Baby and the Battleship* and *The Spanish Gardener*,

in which you played various officials. Do you recall working on them?**

I had very much enjoyed Arthur Grimble's book *Pacific Destiny*, and what went wrong with that film was the title. *A Pattern of Islands* was such a lovely, evocative title whereas *Pacific Destiny* could have meant anything. We filmed it in Samoa; there were only four English actors in it, Denholm Elliott, Susan Stephen, Gordon Jackson and myself, and we all went to Samoa. It's a very attractive film, directed by Wolf Rilla, not a great director but workmanlike.

The Baby and the Battleship had some marvellous performances; some of it was very funny. Jay Lewis produced and directed it and he was quite a significant figure in those days.

It's an awful shame *The Spanish Gardener* hasn't had a better showing recently. I think what really happened was that Dirk [Bogarde] was a great draw and a star, yet his part didn't really weight the film, so it was thought to be a bit of a disappointment to his fans. I found Philip Leacock a very sympathetic director, particularly with children; I knew him quite well. I was proud of that film and it was certainly my best film part to that date.

What is your approach in preparing for such a role?

I have no great theories about it; just 'learn your lines and don't bump into the furniture'. Never having been ambitious, I never felt I was working under that pressure and so I would take things very calmly. I have always been a quick study and that's a great advantage, particularly in films, where changes are thrown at you at very short notice. I would become very familiar with a script but wouldn't attempt to learn it until I was to use it the next day. In my experience in films, I have almost never rehearsed beyond the immediate coming take; there was almost never any business of sitting around as a whole cast, going through a screenplay.

There were a great many British war films made in the '50s and you were in *I Was Monty's Double* and *Sink the Bismarck!*, to name two. Do you think it was nostalgia prompting them?

Yes, nostalgia seems rather a nice word for it, but I think it was a tremendous slice of most men's lives, men of my age, and there were many good stories to be told and morals to be drawn. *I Was Monty's Double* was an extraordinary story; I don't think we went on any foreign locations – I was the Governor of Gibraltar but I certainly never went there to film. *Sink the Bismarck!* didn't have any location work either, as far as I was concerned. They built a big model of the ship in the huge tank at Pinewood. I have worn the uniform and insignia of every rank and rating in the British Navy except those of midshipman – some of it in anger, as it were, in the war itself – ending up as Commander-in-Chief in *Sink the Bismarck!*

Unlike many British players, you went on working steadily throughout the '60s, almost as though you hadn't observed that the British film industry was in a decline.

So much of my work has been in the other media that the film industry could have died altogether without my noticing, because I would have been busy in theatre and/or television. I wasn't aware of the general situation in the film industry. I did things like *El Cid*, *Cleopatra* and *Genghis Khan*, it's true. I remember *El Cid*, made in Spain with Samuel Bronston. One of the great advantages of film acting in my life has been travelling; for instance, I don't want to go on holidays to the Costa Brava because I spent two or three months there while making *The Spanish Gardener*, which was very pleasant.

I have to say, about working on epics like *El Cid* with its cast of thousands, that it doesn't really exercise your brain very much; you have to be able to ride a horse. I remember being asked by Richard Lester when we were filming *How I Won the War* whether I could ride; I said that I could, but what he hadn't told me was that he wanted me to ride a camel! I had a terrible time with that beast. I think Dick Lester thought actors were expendable. He also had me doing terrible things in a toga during *A Funny Thing Happened on the Way to the Forum*, which was filmed in Spain. I liked Dick Lester very much; we had lots of laughs during filming and work should be fun!

Do you have a favourite film role?

No, I don't have a favourite film or any other role. I get so much pleasure from being ready to take any job and I enjoy them for entirely different reasons. I loved playing that part in *England Made Me* and enjoyed it for the fun, as much as I enjoyed, say, *The Spanish Gardener*. I don't do much picking and choosing of roles – that is done by the people who employ me. What they know is that I am ready to turn my hand to anything.

Trevor Howard

1916–1988

Actor: *The Way Ahead* (1944), *The Way to the Stars, Brief Encounter* (1945), *Green for Danger, I See a Dark Stranger* (1946), *They Made Me a Fugitive, So Well Remembered* (1947), *The Passionate Friends, The Third Man, Golden Salamander* (1949), *Odette, The Clouded Yellow* (1950), *Outcast of the Islands, Lady Godiva Rides Again* (guest cameo) (1951), *The Gift Horse* (1952), *The Heart of the Matter* (1953), *The Lovers of Lisbon, The Stranger's Hand* (1954), *April in Portugal* (short, voice only), *The Cockleshell Heroes* (1955), *Around the World in Eighty Days, Run for the Sun* (1956),

Interpol, Manuela (1957), *The Key, The Roots of Heaven* (1958), *Moment of Danger* (1959), *Sons and Lovers* (1960), *Mutiny on the Bounty, The Lion* (1962), *Man in the Middle* (1963), *Father Goose* (1964), *Operation Crossbow, Von Ryan's Express, The Saboteur: Code Name Morituri, The Liquidator* (1965), *The Poppy is Also a Flower, Triple Cross* (1966), *The Long Duel, Pretty Polly* (1967), *The Charge of the Light Brigade* (1968), *The Battle of Britain, Twinky* (1969), *Ryan's Daughter* (1970), *Catch Me a Spy, Mary Queen of Scots, The Night Visitor, Kidnapped* (1971), *Ludwig, Pope Joan, The*

Offence (1972), Craze, A Doll's House (1973), Persecution, The Count of Monte Cristo, 11 Harrowhouse (1974), Hennessy, Death in the Sun, Conduct Unbecoming, The Bawdy Adventures of Tom Jones (1975), Eliza Fraser, Aces High (1976), Slavers, The Last Remake of Beau Geste (1977), Stevie, Superman (1978), Meteor, The Missionary, Hurricane (1979), The Sea Wolves, Sir Henry at Rawlinson End, The Windwalker (1980), Light Years Away (1981), Gandhi (1982), Sword of the Valiant (1983), Dust (1984), Foreign Body (1985), White Mischief (1987), The Unholy, The Dawning (1988)

'All my performances are good enough to be seen; I'm not ashamed of anything I've done,'[1] said Trevor Howard in 1988. This is a just piece of self-appraisal; the sad thing is that too few of these performances were in films that deserved him. His first three were directed by Carol Reed, Anthony Asquith and David Lean, and you could scarcely get off to a better start in 1940s Britain, but it would prove hard to maintain.

Howard had trained for the stage before the war, but in 1945 he said that 'to play the same role month in month out . . . would drive me mad.'[2] His returns to the stage were sporadic, though twelve years later he allowed that 'an actor in the theatre is much more responsible for what comes over in his performances.'[3] He nevertheless became a film actor *par excellence*, as did Bogarde, Mason and Attenborough.

After two small roles in *The Way Ahead* and *The Way to the Stars*, he starred unforgettably as Alec Harvey in Lean's *Brief Encounter*. Celia Johnson wrote to her husband, '. . . did I tell you the really terrible thing about him is that he is eight years younger than I am.'[4] She worried unnecessarily: her eloquence and his manly decency were wholly convincing in that classic study of middle-class near-adultery.

Lean used him again as the would-be lover of a married woman in *The Passionate Friends* and twenty-odd years later as the priest in *Ryan's Daughter*, but it was Reed who gave him the best chances. He was unerringly right as the pragmatic Major Calloway in *The Third Man*, and as variously doomed sea-going heroes in *Outcast of the Islands*, *The Key* and even in *Mutiny on the Bounty*. In this last, he rose above the hideously troubled production history to give a fine study of shaken authority as Bligh, though he wrote at the time, 'I'm miserable and fed up and sick of everything.'[5]

From the many other films, one can salvage *Manuela* ('every part was a little jewel'[6]) as the sea captain infatuated with a stowaway; *The Charge of the Light Brigade* ('He [Tony Richardson] gave one a free hand and had ideas of gutsy things, strange things'[7]); and *Sons and Lovers*, in which he and Wendy Hiller as the elder Morels strike authentic Lawrentian chords.

For the rest, there may be no bad performances but many bad films. Perhaps he settled into character roles too early: 'I would much rather play a succession of varied parts,'[8] he said as early as 1946. Perhaps Hollywood might have given him more roles to move round in. Perhaps the tiresome roistering image had enough basis in reality to take its toll on the actor. Speculation aside, there is enough there on celluloid to confirm his place very near the top of British screen actors.

1 *Daily Mirror*, 8 June 1988
2 *Picturegoer*, 4 August 1945, p 11
3 In Campbell Dixon (ed), *International Film Annual*, John Calder, London, 1957, p 90
4 Kate Fleming, *Celia Johnson*, Orion Books, London, 1991, p 169
5 Nicholas Wapshott, *The Man Between: A Biography of Carol Reed*, Chatto & Windus, London, 1990, p 313
6 Vivienne Knight, *Trevor Howard: A Gentleman and a Player*, Sphere Books, London, 1988, p 102
7 Knight, p 158
8 *Picturegoer*, 27 April 1946, p 7

Raymond Huntley

1904–1990

Actor: *Can You Hear Me, Mother?* (1935), *Rembrandt, Whom the Gods Love* (1936), *Knight Without Armour, Dinner at the Ritz, Night Train to Munich* (1940), *The Ghost of St Michael's, Freedom Radio, Inspector Hornleigh Goes To It, The Ghost Train, Once a Crook, Pimpernel Smith* (1941), *When*

We Are Married, The New Lot (short) (1943), *The Way Ahead, They Came to a City* (1944), *I See a Dark Stranger, School for Secrets* (1946), *So Evil My Love, Mr Perrin and Mr Traill, It's Hard To Be Good* (1948), *Passport to Pimlico* (1949), *Trio* ('Sanatorium') (1950), *The Long Dark Hall, The House in the Square, Mr Denning Drives North* (1951), *The Last Page* (1952), *Laxdale Hall, Glad Tidings, Meet Mr Lucifer* (1953), *Hobson's Choice, Orders Are Orders, Aunt Clara, The Teckman Mystery* (1954), *The Dam Busters, The Constant Husband, Doctor at Sea, The Prisoner, Geordie* (1955), *The Last Man to Hang, The Green Man* (1956), *Town on Trial, Brothers-In-Law* (1957), *Next to No Time, Room at the Top, Carlton-Browne of the FO, Innocent Meeting, The Mummy, I'm All Right Jack* (1959), *Our Man in Havana, Make Mine Mink, Follow that Horse, Bottoms Up!, Sands of the Desert, A French Mistress, Suspect, The Pure Hell of St Trinian's* (1960), *Only Two Can Play, Waltz of the Toreadors, On the Beat, Crooks Anonymous* (1962), *Nurse on Wheels, The Yellow Teddybears, Father Came Too* (1963), *The Black Torment* (1964), *Rotten to the Core* (1965), *The Great St Trinian's Train Robbery* (1966), *Hostile Witness* (1968), *The Adding Machine* (1969), *Young Winston, That's your Funeral, Symptoms* (1972)

Dora Bryan recalled that, for some time in the 1950s, she and Raymond Huntley shared the same cleaning lady, who used gently to chide the one for not being as busy as the other in any given week. In fact this lady was 'doing' for two of the busiest and most instantly recognisable character actors in British films of the period. Huntley specialised in pompous civil servants, the sort of bank manager who would inevitably turn down your request for a loan, or the supercilious official who would keep his head while others all around were losing theirs ... Occasionally he was given a role that would enable him to do more than merely stamp his authority on brief cameos. When this happened he revealed himself a consummate screen actor, notably in Carol Reed's *The Way Ahead* as the prissy salesman-turned-soldier, as Geraldine Fitzgerald's chilly, mother-dominated husband in Lewis Allen's *So Evil My Love*, as the cruelly insensitive headmaster in Lawrence Huntington's *Mr Perrin and Mr Traill*; and in Harold French's 'Sanatorium' episode in *Trio*, very moving as the embittered husband, dying of tuberculosis. Huntley is a prime example of the sort of character acting that was once the glory of British cinema.
Interview date: October 1989

What do you recall of Alexander Korda, for whom you made *Rembrandt* and *Knight Without Armour* early in your film career?

I was very fond of Korda; he had such taste, which is a rare enough commodity at any time – practically extinct now! I was in a play called *Bees on the Boat Deck*, one of the five Priestley plays I did. I was very fortunate in having a small part which pretty well ran away with the play. Alex saw it and offered me a part in *Rembrandt*. It was a totally different kind of part, in fact, a pretty bad part, and the make-up and wardrobe departments turned me out looking like Bob Donat's handsome young brother! After a day or two, I went to the rushes and heard Alex say, 'No, no, I want for him to be funny, like in *The Boat Deck*!' He was so perplexed that I wasn't being funny. But he had real flair; he built the Denham studios and they were pretty damn fine in every way. There were people whose careers Alex absolutely *made*.

You acquired a particular character image in films quite early on – rather disapproving,

sometimes supercilious or downright mean ...

In the days of Launder and Gilliat and the Boultings, I had the image of the very pompous type, particularly in *Carlton-Browne of the FO* and that sort of thing. I probably have played a wider range of characters in the theatre than on film, where I sometimes felt a bit pigeonholed.

You worked on several occasions with Carol Reed. How did you find him as a director of actors?

He was absolutely marvellous. One trusted him completely, that was the great thing. He was very quiet, had very little to say; one day, all he said was, 'Very good, just do one more. Raymond, make sure you get the laugh *with* you, not *against* you,' and that was it. The part of Mr Davenport in *The Way Ahead* was very challenging, and very strenuous, one of the best I ever had in films. I've never forgotten that assault course! We did it all, no doubles or anything then. The film was made with the co-operation of the Ministry of Information and the War Office, because the co-writers, Eric Ambler and Peter Ustinov, were both in the Army. It was a superb film, and it stands up enormously well, Among so many others, dear old Stanley Holloway was in it. He and I later did *Passport to Pimlico* together.

You made a number of films for two popular filmmaking teams: the Boulting brothers and Launders and Gilliat. What differences did you feel in the films made by each pair?

I don't know that I could point to any great differences and I could easily get mixed up as to which was which. I didn't work much with John Boulting as a director; most of the time it was with Roy. One of the last I made for them was *I'm All Right Jack*; I had just one small scene at the end, as the judge in the courtroom scene. It is amazing that the union tolerated the film at the time. They might just as easily have walked out and pulled the plugs! It was just as critical of the bosses, true, but it certainly didn't pull any punches as far as the unions were concerned; it made the Peter Sellers character look a real bloody fool. There was a studio manager at Denham at one time who I swear came off the floor the first day of production and said, 'Always be prompt, Peter [Ustinov]. A lacksadaisical director means a lacksadaisical picture which jeropardises the whole business'! When Roy Boulting was directing, he and John weren't on the floor together, but they were very sympathetically attuned

to each other's thinking. The Boulting films were more politically slanted than those of Launder and Gilliat; or maybe they took on so many institutions, like the unions and the clergy, and satirised them, because the subject just appealed to them at the time.

Your first performance in a film directed by Launder and Gilliat was in *I See A Dark Stranger*, as an Englishman spying for the Nazis.

I enjoyed making that, and it was such a pleasure to work with Deborah [Kerr]. She taught me a great deal. It took such a long time to set up dolly shots in those days, and Deborah would always say to the cameraman, 'Is there anything I can do to help?' which appealed to me very much. She certainly knew her business, but she was so patient and took everything in her stride, with a laugh. That film was a happy experience: it was 1945 and we hadn't had much good food for quite a while, so when we went on location to Dublin real meat and eggs were a treat!

Then, at Ealing, you made *They Came to a City*, which you'd done on the stage.

Yes, all the company who had played in it at the Globe [now Gielgud] Theatre had parts in the film – Googie Withers, Renee Gadd, AE Matthews, John Clements, and so on. It was quite a popular film, although I didn't think a great deal of it myself. I think it was one of Jack Priestley's lesser plays; I think he owed a great deal to the cast for its success. Ealing was unique, much smaller than the average studio, with a sort of intimate family atmosphere. Mick Balcon had a sort of school of directors, mostly young men gathering experience, to their great benefit, and not taking large salaries. It was very much a 'family concern' of Balcon's. I didn't like Pinewood as much as Ealing or Denham but I did quite a bit there. Denham, Alex's studio, was slightly smaller; the general atmosphere and the happy times one had there distinguish it in my memory from Pinewood. And Denham also had the most marvellous restaurant!

What do you remember of four other directors you worked with only once each: David Lean, Anthony Asquith, Lance Comfort and Lawrence Huntington, on *Hobson's Choice*, *Freedom Radio*, *When We Are Married* and *Mr Perrin and Mr Traill*?

There is some shop in London which sells stills of old films and someone sent me one of *Mr Perrin and Mr Traill* the other day to sign. I hadn't seen or heard anything of it since we made it. That was Lawrence Huntington, a most neglected director; I don't know what became of him but I've never heard of or from him since. As a director I found him very good, not outstanding, but very agreeable and very competent indeed.

When We Are Married was another Priestley play I'd done on the stage and I don't think the film was nearly as good. I remember it was disappointing – probably I missed some of the original cast, which was marvellous. As to Lance Comfort, I don't think he had very much individual impact.

Anthony Asquith's *Freedom Radio* was very early, at the time of the fall of France. I remember the awfulness of the occasion more than the film. I was only just in *Hobson's Choice*, a very small part as Derek Blomfield's disapproving father.

I remember David saying, 'If I had known you were available for something bigger, I should have been only too glad to offer it.' I said, 'There isn't such a thing as a small part in a David Lean production!' I admired him for his taste and style as a director, though he did later develop a terrific leisureliness about production. Personally, I would put Carol Reed ahead of him, because I got more out of Carol – he was probably more of an actor's director than any of the others.

How did British actors feel about the practice of importing Hollywood players in the '50s?

I don't think we resented their presence at all. I think one simply looked for their quality. I worked with Tyrone Power in *The House in the Square* and he was a lovely actor, and Ray Milland was a very interesting case in *So Evil My Love*. He was technically superb, although as an actor I would say he was quite limited, but it calls into question just what film acting is. We did a very long take, something like six minutes, which was a hell of a long take in those days. It was a very tricky thing with Ray and me together. At the end of the first take, all he said was, 'Joe, Number 66 wants tilting.' That's Hollywood know-how. I liked Ray, got on with him very well and, as a technician, there was no beating him. He asked me to do a film a few years later, *Hostile Witness*. I'm afraid the film wasn't up to very much. But I did like *So Evil My Love*: I greatly enjoyed working with Geraldine Fitzgerald and I have very good memories of the director, Lewis Allen, who had been one of Gilbert Miller's stage managers.

I think one of the finest British films was *Room at the Top*. How do you feel about it now?

I was very dissatisfied with my performance in it; I didn't give the part nearly enough punch. The Yorkshire accent is not difficult for me; I did five plays with Priestley, after all. But I think I was inhibited, in that trying not to use the accent too strongly affected my whole performance; I was far too gentle. Laurence Harvey was certainly happening in a big way then! I got on perfectly well with him, but I remember a favourite actress of mine playing a bit part in *Room at the Top* – Annie Leon – once called him a 'rude bugger'! It was a period of change and I wasn't vastly impressed on the whole. One does not always take kindly to change and I preferred my Launder and Gilliat and Boulting brothers times.

Glenda Jackson

b. 1936

Actor: *This Sporting Life* (1963), *The Persecution and Assassination of Jean-Paul Marat as Performed* by the Inmates of the Asylum of Charenton under the Direction of the Marquis De Sade (1966), The

Benefit of the Doubt (1967), Tell Me Lies, Negatives (1968), Women in Love (1969), The Music Lovers, Sunday Bloody Sunday (1971), The Boy Friend, Mary, Queen Of Scots, Triple Echo (1972), A Touch Of Class, Bequest to the Nation (1973), The Maids (1974), Hedda, Il Sorriso del Grande Tentore / The Tempter, The Romantic Englishwoman (1975), The Incredible Sarah, Nasty Habits (1976), The Class of Miss MacMichael, House Calls, Stevie, Lost and Found (1979), Hopscotch, Health (1980), *The Patricia Neal Story (1981), And Nothing But the Truth / Giro City, The Return of the Soldier (1982), Turtle Diary (1985), Beyond Therapy, Business As Usual (1987), Salome's Last Dance (1988), The Rainbow (1989), King of The Wind, Doombeach (1990)

* Made for television, some cinema release.

D espite coming into films just when the British cinema was losing impetus with the withdrawal of American finance in the late '60s, Glenda Jackson went on to have as remarkable a career as anyone has had in this country. The first credit is tantalising: if only she had worked with Lindsay Anderson again (she has only a bit part in *This Sporting Life*): she seems to have needed strong directors at their strongest to do her best work. And how riveting that best work is. Her Gudrun in Ken Russell's *Women in Love* is magisterial: it is now virtually impossible to reread the novel without seeing her before you – mocking, yearning, piercingly intelligent, abrasive. The passion and *com*passion of her playing in John Schlesinger's *Sunday Bloody Sunday*; the luminous evocation of Stevie Smith in Robert Enders' *Stevie*; and the drab, loving wife who effects *The Return of the Soldier* in Alan Bridges' undervalued film: these are enough to establish her dominant position in British cinema in the last twenty-five years. As well, there has been very notable work for the theatre and television. Since 1992, when Glenda Jackson gained her seat as Labour Member for Hampstead and Highgate, Parliament's gain has been acting's loss.

Interview date: June 1994

How did it feel to you starting a film career in the mid '60s? Did you have much sense of an industry?

I don't think there was a British film industry as such when I began to make what I call 'film' films. They were almost exclusively financed by American money; there were really very good tax breaks for foreign filmmakers in this country. I have to say, however, that I was totally unconcerned where the money came from. My interest was in acting in front of a film camera, something which I had never thought would come my way, and I did find it an extremely exciting medium to work for. And of course, I was lucky inasmuch as the second 'film' film I did was with Ken Russell, who was a director of unique genius, I felt, as far as the cinema was concerned.

There has certainly never been anyone so flamboyant in British cinema history.

I don't agree with you on the unique nature of his flamboyant side; I think there had been directors before who were flamboyant. I am thinking particularly of Powell and Pressburger, whose flamboyance came after a particularly harsh time, namely, the war and the enormous austerity that followed. That tended to make it acceptable because there was such relief on the part of people that we could see that kind of colour on the screen. I think where Ken Russell is extraordinary is more in the way in which he dresses the background. It is very often as important to him as the foreground and he picks up on those minute details that really reveal the interior landscape of a human being.

Would you agree that the commercial aspect of filmmaking is crucial if you are to have an industry?

Clearly, at the moment, the bottom line is commercial but that doesn't mean we must always have an inordinate number of noughts after the first figure. I think it is entirely possible to create a film industry with comparatively small budgets. What I think Britain lacks is sheer volume of product. If you go back to what were the golden days of filmmaking, which, I suppose, means Hollywood from the 1930s to the late '50s, when television took hold, and, if you speak to anyone who was working in those Hollywood studio systems then, you hear they made films in fourteen to twenty working days on average (setting aside the difficulties of particular individuals). As soon as you finished one film, you went on to another. I remember Bette Davis telling me she literally went from film to film.

Therefore, what you had was an enormous amount of product and the interest in that product was being fed and fostered. Out of that amount of product, there would also be two or three – or, if you were lucky, four – films that made money. Hence it was possible for the industry to keep itself constantly working. I think it would be entirely possible to recreate a film industry in this country, with limited budgets, where there was a lot of product coming from it. But what it wouldn't carry with it is that great big bandwagon – 'We're spending x million dollars and we've got all these major stars, special effects, etc,' and what is produced in the end is a piece of crap that nobody wants to see.

There isn't a kind of middle-range film-making available now, for young filmmakers to cut their teeth on. Perhaps they do it in television.

Certainly a great many of the younger directors do – and some of the not-so-young. John Schlesinger always says that he learned his craft doing films for television. Ken Russell is the same and Michael Apted also got his start in television. It is more complex than that, however. You do see young filmmakers now, who can take anything up to two years or longer to raise the finance for a film, although they don't approach it that way. They make it with their friends, with borrowed equipment, they do it on weekends, the film is put together and it's a big success. Their difficulty is then their second film, because there is always going to be someone who comes rushing up saying, 'Here is a big pot of money, go out and make a film.' What they then lose immediately is the overall control of their own product. It's very difficult, I think, for them to withstand that and this is why very often the individual voices become subsumed in that great maw of Hollywood, which people still regard as the apogee of making a film.

Is one of the problems with British cinema that British audiences have on the whole preferred Hollywood films?

I don't think we're any different from the rest of the world in that we do, because it has to be acknowledged that, even when we were making a lot of films, they were very parochial. Intensely so. Perhaps we don't want to see our own backyard all the time. Also, there was a wave for too long of what could be regarded as 'realistic' films which missed out on when people actually wanted something more than that. Of course, the distribution system in this country was virtually held by two major companies, Rank and ABPC, and so the opportunities to see films that were not the kinds of films they wanted to show were very limited.

But where you might expect producers to see certain films as having some cultural cachet, you would not expect distributors or exhibitors in the end to care about that, would you?

I understand the point you're making, but if you are actually looking at the economic viability of a cinema or a chain of cinemas, at a time when it is highly competitive because of television and now video, I would have thought yes. Given that cinemas are now so much smaller, I would have thought that you could attempt to explore where the cultural interests lie – whether on a local or regional basis. Nonetheless, in the last decade or so the surprising box-office smashes have always come from what you would regard as a cultural, as opposed to a commercial, base. I don't even mean as culturally different as Peter Greenaway's films; look at the mid-range: *Chariots of Fire*, *My Beautiful Laundrette*, *Four Weddings and a Funeral*, the stuff that Monty Python did. None of those would have been regarded as commercial at the outset.

How do you feel about the ways in which the British Government has sought to intervene in support of the British film industry?

When it was at its best I would regard it as an acknowledgement that there was not only a commercial benefit to the country, but also a social and cultural benefit to be had in supporting a British film industry. What we've seen since those heady days when we had a Labour Government is the imposition of fifteen years of rank, overt commercialisation of everything and the definition of 'quality' is the ability to make money. There has been no support at all for the film industry in this country, and the support that they claim to give it is so minor that it is virtually meaningless.

Just before the General Election, we floated, as a party, the idea that perhaps we could go the way that the French had in their heyday, of private investors giving x amount of money to a pool for the making of British film and not expecting any return on that investment for, say, five years, but that they would get tax breaks for those five years. The profits would then be ploughed back in again, so that you could begin to build up product – and that's what we need, product. It is possible, however, to make a film of quality for a small amount of money and it seems to me that is what has to be changed: the mind-set that says films cost an enormous amount of money and are very risky ventures.

How important do you think a national cinema is as a kind of cultural flagship?

I can only use the example of America. America is viewed internationally through its film product. Now, a great deal of that film product is not a true picture by any means, and there is a danger in that. This is why I am hesitant about saying yes, the cinema should be a British flagship. There is a danger in the image of nationhood that is presented in that way. For instance, British filmmaking over the last decade has been absolutely stuck in this tedious nostalgia for an England that never was – I mean, *another* film with ladies in long skirts and big hats is just dreary. I wouldn't mind if they told the truth about what it was like at that time but they never do. But *American* culture has swept the world. I think Michael Caine put it most succinctly when he said, 'The British make pictures, the Americans make movies.' He said that pictures are static things which you hang on the wall, whereas movies move, and I think there is more than a grain of truth in that.

That is also true of Powell and of Ken Russell. *Women in Love* seems to me the best film ever made from a Lawrence novel. How

do you rate it now, twenty-five years later?

I haven't seen it recently but it was shown not too long ago and people say that it still stands up. I think it probably does because we all clutched Penguin copies of the book to our chests. It was important to do so on that film. The original script was not Ken's, it was by two Americans and it was very long. Films seem to take on a life of their own when they're working and something that seems essential when you first read the script may well, a week after you start shooting, seem utterly irrelevant and you know that you don't need it. Lawrence would spend pages and pages describing the interior life of a character and then the character would say 'Yes' or 'No' as the sole verbal contribution.

So we all clutched those copies of the novel and I did find it helpful. Ken was very open to that; he respected the book and you could go to him and point out bits of it and say wouldn't it be good if we could do this. The idea that he is some kind of dictator on the set is total rubbish; he will listen to absolutely anybody who's got an idea. He will listen, sometimes he will try it out and eventually he will make up his own mind and go the way he wants to do it. There were aspects of my character in *Women in Love* which I found very difficult to get out on a purely verbal level; it seems to me she is the only character in the book to have a sense of the mysterious aspects of life and it's very difficult to show that verbally, so there had to be ways of showing it visually, that sense of the dark mystery of life. It was a marvellous film to be on. It had a big budget, I think, although I didn't get paid very much. I didn't care about that because it was my first real opportunity to work for the film camera and I found that immensely exciting.

What did you make of FR Leavis's reaction when he described it as an obscene undertaking? I wonder if there are any books not susceptible to filming?

I can't really answer that but I think it is probably unlikely. I think one can run into difficulties. You mention Leavis, who is a great Lawrence scholar; I think it is entirely possible to interpret a book for the screen in a way that is absolutely truthful to the creative energy or the interior state of the writer. Ken took what is central to the book, which is life, energy, the sexual directives and imperatives of life, the confusions that come out of that. So it was full of energy. He was not concerned with the niceties – well, he was very concerned that the clothes were right and the look was right, he is very particular about all of that – but the central, pulsing theme of the book is life and that is very much what he was on about.

I thought it was a great performance from Oliver Reed, even though he is not physically Lawrence's idea of Gerald. Did you find it stimulating to work with him as Gerald?

Oliver and I have absolutely nothing to say to each other off-screen. As people, we are chalk and cheese. What I admire in Oliver is his consummate professionalism. It doesn't matter what state he may be in physically, when they say 'Action!' he is ready and that was the aspect of working with him that I liked. I've worked with him a lot and he is an infinitely better actor than he gives himself credit for. He is also a brilliant comic actor and he's never really explored that in himself.

The film caused a lot of censorship ripples at the time. How did you feel about this?

I thought it was daft. It was that sort of breakthrough period when the idea of female nudity was just beginning to be acceptable, but the idea of two men being shown entirely naked was something that people got very worried about, and the idea that the relationship between Oliver's character and Alan Bates's character could have had some kind of sexual emotional overtone was something which people found quite hard to take at the time. One of the sadnesses about that time, when suddenly there was this breakthrough and nudity was used in virtually in every film, was that it was used exclusively in a sexual context. There is something about the vulnerability of the human body which has never been explored in film and it may take another ten years before it can be.

Where was it filmed, mostly?

All over the place. Some was done in the studios, some in Switzerland, but most of the exteriors were done in Derbyshire and some in Cheshire, around Buxton. The studio was Bray, I think, the old Hammer studios.

The next film you did for Ken Russell, *The Music Lovers*, also provoked outrage and I wondered how you feel about the film, or about that kind of controversial response?

I wasn't particularly concerned about the controversial aspects of it. I thought it was absolutely the film he had set out to make. It was a kind of operatic approach to a true story and, although I haven't seen it since we did it, I know a lot of musicians were somewhat outraged by this approach. I don't expect creative geniuses to be perfect people, and I think the way Ken always approaches things is to ask, 'What were they like as real people? What were the real pressures on them? What did they have to deal with and how could they use that to express it creatively?' and I think that film did it.

You also did a cameo for Ken Russell in *The Boy Friend*. Did you enjoy that?

That was my punishment for not doing *The Devils*. He put me in a plaster cast from six o'clock in the morning until eight o'clock at night. It was a straight lift from *42nd Street*.

***Sunday Bloody Sunday* looks and sounds like a really mature and generous film, even twenty years later. How did you get involved in that?**

They simply sent me the script and I leapt at it. I don't think I had ever read a script of that intelligence and I wanted to work with Schlesinger. The other thing which I found most telling about it was that he treated the homosexual relationship in a way that was neither prurient nor supercilious. It is actually said in the film that it is entirely possible for men to love men in the way that other men love women. There was a balance to it, in that it was about unrequited love as much as about sexual acts. It was quite unsensational.

What did you think about the character of the boy? Is he just an opportunist or is there at least some honesty about him?

I never saw him as a villain and I never saw my character or Peter Finch's character as being exploited. It seemed to me to be an entirely mature look at human relationships and I thought that was central to what the film was saying.

Did John Schlesinger seem to you a very sympathetic director of actors?

Oh, very much so. When you meet John he is seemingly so confident and so multi-faceted, so widely and deeply cultured and cultivated; the surprising thing about him is that on the set, he is the most nervous person there. There is a ritual that has to be gone through every morning, whereby he says, 'The rushes are awful. We're making a piece of shit here, why are we doing this?' He talks himself up to the point where he is saying, 'Well, no, it's really rather good, isn't it?' That's the pattern of it and that vulnerability of directors in a working situation was something I hadn't really experienced before.

Did he give you much direction, or do you normally not expect much detailed direction?

No, because really good directors wait to see what you can do. Really good directors always know what they *don't* want, they are very clear about that, and so they can stop you from pursuing a line that is going to be unproductive. They create a climate in which you can work.

I remember some wonderful scenes with Tony Britton, Peggy Ashcroft and others. Did you get a lot of stimulus from working in scenes like that?

I have to be honest with you and say that acting for a film is not like that. The most interesting thing to work for is the camera. The camera is absolutely fascinated by what you are doing; you never have to work for its interest or its attention because it is totally absorbed in what you are doing. That concentration of energy you get on a film set is something that I find enormously helpful, but acting with other actors on a film is very much a jigsaw process. It's wonderful to work with actors of that quality, of course, but that's not really where your central focus is. You obviously work with people and there is that interchange and interplay, but the really interesting thing to work for is the camera.

Your cameraman on *The Maids*, *Hedda* and *Nasty Habits* was the famous Douglas Slocombe. Did it make much difference to you who the cameraman was? Did you become technically knowledgeable about lighting and so on?

No, not at all, I have absolutely no technical abilities. I would have loved to be able to do as I believe Marlene Dietrich and Joan Crawford could do – walk on a set and say, 'The key light is in the wrong place,' and things like that. I can't do that and, in truth, my relationships were with the technicians. If you are lucky enough to have the main female part, you have a fair bit to do with the lead actor, but the people you see and have dealings with most consistently are the technicians around the camera. The director of photography can be wandering around looking at lights and such, so you may not see him much. However, the guy who is actually operating the camera and the focus-puller – those are the people you are working most closely with all the time, and I was always very lucky in having good relationships with them. Even after they have done all the preliminary setting up with stand-ins, you can be standing in front of the camera for a very long time, so it's nice to have someone you can chat to without actually losing your own energy and concentration.

Joseph Losey, who directed *The Romantic Englishwoman*, was famous for long takes and tracking shots. Were you, as an actor, conscious of this technique?

Not with Losey. I remember distinctly a very long shot we did on *Sunday Bloody Sunday*, which was extremely complicated. I was sitting in one of those egg-shaped chairs that revolve; there was a long telephone conversation and the camera tracked all the way around us, a full 180 degrees, and we did that twenty-six times. Every time we did it it was because there was some technical hitch. The BBC were there that day, filming us as we were working; obviously they couldn't film while we were actually shooting, so when John had finally got a satisfactory take, they asked if we wouldn't mind doing it again for them. We did so but it was just going through the motions. However, if John had said, 'Let's do it again,' we would have been able to give it that performance dimension again. So no, it didn't worry me and I had no sense of it on the Losey film.

My overwhelming feeling with *The Romantic Englishwoman* was one of disappointment – with the film and with Losey, because he was someone I had very much wanted to work for. I found him very much anti-female, there was something very misogynistic about him. Of course, he was terribly plagued with asthma, but he loved difficulties, particularly when they came from his stars, because it gave him that sense of being in control.

I hope you have fond memories of *Stevie*, which is one of my favourite '70s films. Were you an admirer of Stevie Smith's work?

Oh yes, I was. Oddly enough, I had met her in the early '60s when the Royal Shakespeare Company used to do programmes of poetry and jazz at the Aldwych and I was roped in to do one of them. I'd never heard of her at the time but I stood in the wings as she was reading 'Not Waving But Drowning'. The next day I rushed out and bought any copies of her work I could find. I remembered that meeting so distinctly and it informed everything about doing the play and then the film.

***Stevie* looks very much like a chamber film, an actor's film.**

Yes. Ideally I would have liked it never to have moved out of that living-room or out of that house, and I still think it was a mistake to have exterior shots. I think it could have worked if it had stayed within the Palmers Green house.

I think one of the most moving moments in

British cinema of that decade is when you say 'I loved my aunt'.

And she was absolutely brilliant, Mona Washbourne.

What can you tell me about the director Robert Enders, who also wrote *The Maids* and produced *Hedda*.

Bob came to filming initially via documentaries and he worked in Hollywood. He cropped up when that fashion for what I think was called American Theatre was around. That's how he became involved and he did *The Maids*. We then formed a production company although I had nothing to do with it other than appearing in the films. Bob tended to make a film out of plays that I'd done. As I said, I would have liked *Stevie* to have been more hermetically sealed but *Hedda* was opened out more and I think it works extremely well.

Was the film of *Giro City* particularly close to your heart, in that you were interested in the ethics of television broadcasting?

Yes, I was, very much so. I think it's a film that lost its bottle. The director, Karl Francis, had worked in television and was passionate about it, but it got softened and I think it was a mistake, in a way. I think it could have been a much stronger film about television but it tended to get stuck on the idea that the only infringement, the only danger, was in what we were not being told about the Irish situation. That is such an emotive subject that it tends to overbalance what you are saying. There are minutiae of what we see via the television screen that I think are as dangerous, but they weren't touched upon.

A film of yours I like very much but which didn't do too well at the box office is *The Return of the Soldier*.

I thought it was an extremely good film. It was made for a very small budget and under great difficulty, yet I think it worked very well and I'm surprised it didn't do better. I thought Alan [Bates] was absolutely marvellous in it.

How important did you think Luciana Arrighi's designs were to its meaning, and to the Ken Russell films?

They clearly are very important because that kind of period detail is vital; she's very good at that. The other thing, which I think is possibly even more important and something I'm dogmatic about, is new clothes. I hate new clothes, I hate clothes that are immaculate and clearly haven't been worn.

Luciana is very good about that, too, and I think everything I wore was the genuine article. I think it's really important (and certainly for a 'realist' film like that) that the people look real. I don't think she did the sets for *The Return of the Soldier* but she did the costumes and the props for the set dressing.

You were back with Ken Russell in the late '80s for *Salome's Last Dance* and *The Rainbow*. Did you feel his approach had changed by then?

Yes, it had. Only Ken would choose to do that play [*Salome's Last Dance*] and set it in a brothel that had really existed and that Oscar Wilde had really attended. That, as framework for it, was just extraordinary, I thought, a visually extraordinary thing to do.

He had desperately wanted to make *The Rainbow* for a long time and I think it simply didn't work. It is not only too quiet; there were mistakes with the casting, too. I think he took the wrong section of the book to concentrate on. To me, the first part of the book is much more interesting, the beginnings of that relationship between the mother and the girl who eventually becomes Gudrun. She is such an interesting character and that whole relationship is so fascinating, that to focus on the girls and Gudrun at that stage is to me a less interesting part of the book.

What motivated your choice of roles in general, such as *Turtle Diary*? Would it be the director, the screenplay, a matter of ideological stance, or what?

Usually the script. It was a combination of things in the case of *Turtle Diary* because a company had been formed, called United British Artists, of which I was one of the founding directors. It was the idea of Richard Johnson, who was in the film. There was Richard, Albert, me, Maggie Smith I think, and John Hurt. The idea was that we would make films and produce plays which could then be turned into television product and sold to America, in essence using people who were as well known on that side of the Atlantic as on this side. *Turtle Diary* was an original screenplay from the Russell Hoban book. I admire him as a writer and I thought the script very good. I think the film could have been better than it was but nonetheless it was a good film.

Many people I've interviewed, including the Socialist peer, Bernard Miles, have told me that the unions were not helpful to British cinema, in their view.

I think again it is a question of balance. If you

speak to people who began their film careers either before the war or in the early '40s, the wages and conditions were abysmal, appalling. Then there began to be more films made and where the unions protected their members was very much within a studio context; also where, indeed, you could have unions saying they would only work until a certain time after which they wanted to be paid overtime. I'm sure there were occasions when that was exploited. Certainly within my experience of working in the film industry, when there were already changes being made and there were more and more directors wanting to work outside of studio context, I have never been in a film where the plugs were pulled on me, where the people refused to work, where there were time-wasting procedures.

There is a marked difference in the way that British and American studios work; for instance, in America they don't have things like tea breaks and breakfast breaks. What they do have, however, is a permanent, continuously stocked food and drink wagon from which people can get food and drink throughout the entire day. It is much more efficient. They also work for as long as the director wants to work and there is no question that they will not be paid for that work; so, although I can accept that there were certain exploitative processes from the unions, I can understand where they came from. It still seems to me that what we've seen in Britain is a shrinking not only of filmmaking but also a diminution of wage scales and conditions of work which have not, I think, been to the benefit of the people working in the industry as a whole. Most people who work in the industry *like* working in it; they like the life and they like what they do. They take pride in it and I think they should be respected and rewarded.

Gordon Jackson

1923–1990

Actor: *The Foreman Went to France* (1942), *Nine Men, Millions Like Us, San Demetrio, London* (1943), *Pink String and Sealing Wax* (1945), *The Captive Heart* (1946), *Against the Wind* (1948), *Eureka Stockade, Floodtide, Stop Press Girl, Whisky Galore!* (1949), *Bitter Springs, Happy-Go-Lovely* (1950), *Lady With a Lamp* (1951), *Castle in the Air* (1952), *Death Goes to School, Meet Mr Lucifer, Malta Story* (1953), *The Love Lottery, The Delavine Affair* (1954), *Passage Home, The Quatermass Xperiment, Windfall* (1955), *Pacific Destiny, Women Without Men, The Baby and the Battleship, Sailor Beware* (1956), *Seven Waves Away, Let's Be Happy, Hell Drivers, The Black Ice, Man in the Shadow* (1957), *Blind Spot, Rockets Galore, Three Crooked Men* (1958), *Yester-* *day's Enemy, The Bridal Path, Blind Date, The Navy Lark, Devil's Bait* (1959), *The Price of Silence, Cone of Silence, Snowball, Tunes of Glory* (1960), *Greyfriars Bobby, Two Wives at One Wedding* (1961), *Mutiny on the Bounty* (1962), *The Great Escape* (1963), *The Long Ships, Daylight Robbery* (1964), *The Ipcress File, Those Magnificent Men in Their Flying Machines* (1965), *Cast a Giant Shadow, The Fighting Prince of Donegal, The Night of the Generals* (1966), *Danger Route* (1967), *The Prime of Miss Jean Brodie, On the Run, Run Wild, Run Free, Hamlet* (1969), *Scrooge* (1970), *Kidnapped, Madame Sin* (1971), *Russian Roulette* (1975), *The Medusa Touch* (1978), *The Shooting Party* (1984), *The Whistle Blower* (1987)

In his nearly fifty-year career in British films, Gordon Jackson played in virtually every film genre, for all the major

companies, and for most of the key directors of the period. He didn't regard himself as ambitious, never thought of himself as a star, assessing himself simply as a 'Scots type'. Not many would agree. He is one of those British character actors who seems never to have given a poor performance, even when he fetched up in wretched films (think of *Stop Press Girl* or *Happy-Go-Lovely*). Taken up by Ealing in 1942, he regarded his time there as the happiest experience of his career. His unaffected freshness and naturalness are very well used in such films as *San Demetrio, London* and the great *Whisky Galore!*, in which his scenes with Jean Cadell as his beady-eyed mother are among the film's funniest. The 1950s did not generally give him opportunities of the same calibre. Suddenly, then, in Ronald Neame's *Tunes of Glory* in 1960, he began a new phase of his career, appearing in international films and other major films including Neame's *The Prime of Miss Jean Brodie*. His roles in *Tunes of Glory* and as Horatio in Tony Richardson's *Hamlet* show him in two affecting studies of friendship and loyalty: perhaps for an actor so universally well liked, by audiences and by his colleagues, such studies were as to the manner born.
Interview date: September 1989

Before you were twenty, you were playing a leading role in *The Foreman Went to France*. How did this come about?

The first film I did was a fairly major role but mostly I had Scots character parts. I was with Ealing Studios for about ten years on a 'peppercorn' contract. They had a little group of people – Mervyn Johns, Freddie Piper, and others – who just played little character parts and they wrote these parts in for them. They weren't stars and they weren't being built up to be stars. It was my happiest time ever, and I was very lucky to serve my apprenticeship at Ealing, a lovely compact little studio. There was a little group of writers, directors, all working together and wishing each other well. People helped each other out, in fact. Sandy Mackendrick, whose first film was *Whisky Galore!*, told me that Charles Crichton had suggested that wonderful sequence of hiding bottles of whisky with singing going on. Michael Balcon had confidence in the people around him and they enjoyed working together. He was shrewd, of course; he was in it to make money as well, but one was never conscious of that at Ealing.

Those Ealing war films, like *San Demetrio, London*, seem different from the general run – was that the documentary influence?

Oh, yes. For instance Harry Watt was there; he was straight from the Film Unit of the GPO and the John Grierson school. Then Balcon brought in Cavalcanti, who had a lot to do with documentary as well as doing *avant garde* films in France. When you think of the films made at Ealing before then – with George Formby, for instance – well, they were what people wanted at the time, then suddenly the war came and there was that switch to documentary and semi-documentary. Take *Nine Men*, which was on a shoestring budget. Harry Watt was happiest when he was just given a camera and a group of actors, although he didn't even want actors, but that's another story! People used to tell him to go into a field and make a film with a bunch of farmers and see how much money he made!

I'd be interested in your recollections of those Ealing directors.

Well, Harry had made very successful documentary films without actors and he thought we were mollycoddled. Sandy Mackendrick wasn't quite sure what *he* was but I'm sure when he worked with someone like Alec Guinness he was conscious of a very professional actor. Those directors weren't prone to say, 'Do it this way . . . do it that way.' I think a good director, once he has got the people he wants for the film, leaves them to do it themselves. But technically, he should know exactly what he wants from a scene from the point of view of setting up the cameras, and the cutting. At Ealing, directors were technically very efficient because they had been through either script-writing departments or cutting rooms, not straight from the theatre.

Robert Hamer was a sad case. I don't remember *Pink String and Sealing Wax* much and I never watch me in reruns. Of course, Bob really came into his own with the great classic, *Kind Hearts and Coronets*. He also shot quite a lot of *San Demetrio, London* because Charles Frend was taken ill half-way through it. But Bob was really much happier with the humorous side. He was a brilliant man and he was never drunk on the set, although I think he had a big problem even then.

To go back to 1943 and *Millions Like Us*, you were starred above Eric Portman and Anne Crawford . . .

That was only because it was the one time in ten years Ealing lent me out – though Launder and Gilliat, at Gainsborough, were rather Ealing in their approach. It was their first film as directors and they told me they had written so many screenplays that they thought they would like to see one through. They supposedly directed together but I think it was mainly Frank [Launder] who said what was to be done.

Did you feel it was really about the classes pulling together?

I think it was rather sending up the idea of the upper class coming together with the working man. It was essentially a 'man-in-the-street' story. The Anne Crawford character was slightly jokey, the rather grand lady working in the factory, whereas Patricia Roc was just the little suburban girl. I found Launder and Gilliat gentle and charming, consider-ing I was an outsider coming in from another studio. They were a bit worried about my love scenes. They said I always held Patricia Roc as if she were a time bomb. Years later I made a film at Ealing called *Against the Wind* with a then-unknown Simone Signoret. Launder and Gilliat told me they were sitting in the Caprice restaurant talking about their film and how hopeless I was at holding Patricia Roc when, just at that moment, probably the sexiest girl in town – Simone – swept in with *me*!

My personal favourite of all the Ealing comedies is *Whisky Galore!* How do you rate it?

As a Scot I thought it was great fun. Sandy Mackendrick got very depressed because it was his first film and we had pretty rotten weather. The schedule was 'If rain, indoors' and we had con-verted a little church hall into a studio, but the weather was so bad we eventually found ourselves sitting there with nothing else to do inside. There are some marvellous exteriors in it, though. And it had some great comic actors. If you look closely you'll see me laughing sometimes when I shouldn't be, especially in scenes with Jean Cadell, who was a marvellous woman. I find comedy terribly difficult, I can't be funny. If I come across that way it is just because of the situation and the script. Jean played my mother again in the sequel, *Rockets Galore*. That was a sort of Rank–Ealing film, it was just at the transition period and I was moved over to Rank from Ealing. The other film I made at Ealing with Jean was *Meet Mr Lucifer* and she played my aunt, but it wasn't up to the Ealing standard. I enjoyed working with Anthony Pelissier on that, but it hadn't a very good script, and he was called in because none of the Ealing directors would touch it. But he made *The Rocking Horse Winner* and that was marvellous.

Throughout the '50s you made about thirty films – were you under a contract?

Again, it was character work, I wasn't as busy as it sounds. After my contract with Ealing ended, I moved over to Rank and I made one or two films at Pinewood. But I was no use to Rank because they only wanted to build 'stars' and I wasn't the type who could be built into romantic leading man. I made rather a turgid film called *Floodtide* at Rank, then a wicked one with Sally Ann Howes called *Stop Press Girl* which, they say, is the worst film ever made. That was about the end of me at Rank and I can understand why! Thereafter I was 'free-lance'. I had contracts for individual films negoti-ated by an agent.

On *Floodtide* I met my wife, Rona [Anderson]. It was made on the Independent Frame system, which was a good idea but was never really given a chance. They wanted to avoid the cost of building huge sets so Independent Frame came up with the idea of going to a restaurant, filming it when it was empty, and throwing up back projection scenes behind the actors, so that we sat on a banquette in front of this beautiful set. The idea failed because there weren't any decent scripts in *front* of it.

I made a lot of second features in the '50s, some of them terrible. In New York once, I was watching Late Night Movie and I said to Rona, 'This is the worst film I have ever seen.' Suddenly a door opened and I walked in! I didn't even know I was in it! In those days they wouldn't send you the whole script; they would send you your scene and you'd play it and go home. I did a second feature for the Danzigers once. I got my script two days in advance, only to find I was to play a Yorkshire boxer. I pointed out I was Scots. Danziger said, 'You can play it in anything but Jewish!'

What about Joseph Losey, with whom you worked on *Blind Date*?

He was a good man, very slick and very American. I've only recently realised how tough he'd been in all that McCarthy business. On the set he seemed to be a very gentle, artistic man. Now, there was a case of temperament on *Blind Date*. I had to lead Hardy Kruger to a table, and Joe said, 'Just catch him by the arm and say, "Over this way, sir."' Came the shot, the camera was turning and I said, 'This way, sir,' and Kruger said, 'Don't touch me!' He was a German actor over here in a leading part and perhaps he thought, 'I'll take it out on this little policeman.' But, being a practical Scot, I immediately turned to the director and said, 'You told me to do it!'

Two of your finest later performances are for Ronald Neame in *Tunes of Glory* and *The Prime of Miss Jean Brodie*. Was he a particularly good director of actors?

He *records* marvellously anything you do; because he has been a stills man and cameraman, he has been through it all. So he knows what angles he wants and all that sort of thing; having cast the film, that's it. I remember Maggie Smith in *The Prime of Miss Jean Brodie* looking worried and saying, 'He never laughs at any of my jokes.' I told her not to worry, that he would be recording her performance beautifully – which he did, and she ended up getting an Oscar.

I did like *Tunes of Glory*. Guinness was wonderful to watch. He is a superbly technical actor. If you go for ten takes, he will be as brilliant in each one, whereas most of us wilt after three or four. At the end of the film he does a long speech, when he breaks. I was standing behind the camera, giving him an eye-line, and, I couldn't help it, a tear started running down my face because he was so moving. Ronald Neame called, 'Cut, print,' but Alec said no, and asked them to take a shot of my reaction. So they turned the camera around, put the lights on and Alec did his all behind the camera for me. I couldn't do a thing as they filmed me. I stood there, as they say in Scotland, like a pound of mince! I'm an emotional actor and it's very dangerous, and I couldn't turn it on for Takes 2 and 3.

In 1969 you did the best Horatio I have ever seen. How did you come to be involved in *Hamlet*? Were you in the original Roundhouse production?

Yes, I was. I'd got it because I had just done *Macbeth* with Alec Guinness and Simone Signoret at the Royal Court. Tony Richardson was directing *Hamlet* and had seen the *Macbeth*, so he asked me to do it. Again, Alec Guinness had got me the part of Banquo in *Macbeth*, which I would never ordinarily have got. I had never thought of doing Shakespeare.

It reminded me of your performance in *Tunes of Glory*. Both roles give a sense of generous friendship which is quite unusual in films.

Without being too humble, because I hate humble actors, I do like supporting great actors. I hate actors who get in the way of great performances. I find it terribly exciting supporting someone like Guinness or Nicol Williamson, who I think is a brilliant actor. I suppose the friendship comes out of that, because I am not combating in any way. I am milking that performance and helping it as much as I can. I think there are a few very special people on whom the gods look down, and the rest of us are there to help them along – or at least not to get in their way.

Pat Jackson

b. 1916

Director: *Big Money (co-dir), *Book Bargain (co-dir) (1936), *Men in Danger (1937), *Happy in the Morning (1938), *The First Days (co-dir) (1939), *Health in War, *Welfare of the Workers (co-dir) (1940), *Ferry Pilot (1941), *The Builders (1942), *Western Approaches (1944), *Patent Ductus Arteriosus (1947), The Shadow on the Wall (1948), Encore ('The Ant and the Grasshopper'), White Corridors (co-sc) (1951), Something Money Can't Buy (1952), The Feminine Touch (1956), The Birth-

day Present (1957), Virgin Island (1958), Snowball (1960), What a Carve Up! (1961), Seven Keys, Don't Talk to Strange Men (1962), Seven Deadly   *Pills (sc), Dead End Creek (Six-part serial, co-sc) (1964)*
* Documentary.

One of the finest flowers of the British documentary movement is the beautiful 1944 film *Western Approaches*. It is also the finest hour of its director, Pat Jackson, and it influenced his feature-film work in giving him a taste for using non-actors. In 1934, Jackson had joined the GPO Film Unit, which had grown out of the Empire Marketing Board in 1933 and was absorbed in the Crown Film Unit in 1940. These organisations were concerned to 'document' aspects of British life on film, and drew consistently on non-professionals, rather than on actors, in the process. Nearly fifty years later, *Western Approaches* still looks remarkable: it is full of marvellous images of ships and men at sea, combining a strong sense of realism with equally strong narrative interest. In the post-war years, Jackson fell victim to unfortunate contracts and to a studio regime he found unsympathetic, and his career lost the momentum he had established in his documentary years. Nevertheless, there are some very attractive entertainments among his later films. *White Corridors* is a rigorously observed and finely acted film of hospital life; 'The Ant and the Grasshopper', in *Encore*, is an elegant anecdote; and *The Birthday Present* is an unexpectedly tough-minded little drama about customs evasion.

Interview date: October 1990

After your 1930s documentary work with the GPO Film Unit, what sort of wartime filmmaking experience did you have?

When war came, the new school of documentary drama, begun with *Night Mail* in 1935, was now established, while the other – Grierson – school of documentary stayed rooted in its exposition, never liberated from the 'illustrated commentary' style. But Harry Watt [co-director and co-writer, with Basil Wright, of *Night Mail*] was writing a history of England by the careful use of the non-actor. Not that the choice of a non-actor can be taken easily: sometimes Harry would test thirty or forty people – just like testing a professional actor – until he found the real thing.

Then the war came, and of enormous help to the GPO Film Unit was *London Can Take It!* being made by the entire unit and having an enormous impact. Harry and Cavalcanti were its originators; they said to us, 'Go out and shoot any little vignettes you can.' This was all put into some sort of shape by Stewart McAllister, a brilliant editor who cut so many of Humphrey Jennings's films. But the thing that really made it tick was that Harry was in a London pub when he heard the voice of the American correspondent, Quentin Reynolds. Harry got talking to him and asked him to do a commentary for the film. Reynolds's voice added an enormous dimension to it. McAllister edited it over three days and nights and it was out in a week. Reynolds took the film back to Washington in his diplomatic pouch, went straight to the White House and showed it to Roosevelt, who was very moved and influenced by it; it made him even more impassioned to pass the Lend-Lease legislation.

We went on after that, getting other bits and pieces from the Ministry of Information, which was still feeling its way in how to use the medium to advance the war effort. Then, slowly, the service films came through. Watt got *Target for Tonight* to make, which had a huge impact because it was the first film of Britain striking back at the enemy. Parallel with that I was doing *Ferry Pilot*. When Harry finished *Target for Tonight*, he left the Crown Film Unit and joined Ealing and did *Nine Men*. I was then given *The Builders* and I was very lucky in that I walked on to a building site and heard the wonderful Cockney voice of a bricklayer, Charlie Fielding. I tested him on the spot and next day started to film him. He never stopped talking as he kept on laying his bricks without even watching what he was doing. No actor could have done that!

The GPO Film Unit was formed in 1933 and in 1940 it became the Crown Film Unit, under the auspices of the Ministry of Information. Our producer, Ian Dalrymple, was a great administrator who knew how to deal with the Civil Service, and he fought for us to be able to get on with the job he knew we could do. We were given more freedom than we ever had before or since.

How did you come to do *Western Approaches*?

Dal called me into his office one day and asked me if I would like to make *Western Approaches*, about the Battle of the Atlantic. The Navy had seen the RAF getting enormous publicity and éclat for *Target for Tonight* and suddenly realised they should be sharing in this. The Commander-in-Chief, Admiral Sir Percy Noble, called his great friend, the naval historian Owen Rutter, and suggested the making of a film on the Navy. Rutter wrote a twelve-page sketch of an idea, went to see the Crown Film Unit, and I agreed to do the film.

I then had to go to see the Admiral, who took me down to the control room. As we went in, a Wren ran up a metal ladder against this enormous map, right into the middle of the Atlantic, and stuck a little red cross there; it signified a ship which had been hit, and the Navy could divert nothing to go to its rescue. The Admiral turned to me and said, 'That is going on constantly; it is a battle of attrition.' That scene became the opening scene of the film.

I had great trouble finding the key ingredient for a story of a navy at war. Then, suddenly I had the thought: what would happen if a U-boat picked up an SOS message from a lifeboat? Then the answer came: it would use the lifeboat as a decoy. Within ten days I had the story treatment and we had our approval. We only needed three ingredients – the lifeboat, the reaction from the U-boat and, sooner or later, a merchant ship which would pick up the signal from the lifeboat. The naval facilities would

be kept to a minimum, yet these were the basic forces in the Battle of the Atlantic, interacting one against the other and creating an ever-increasing situation of suspense. We were to use a three-strip Technicolor camera, which, in those days, was the size of a household refrigerator. Try to put that in a ship's lifeboat with sound, two arc lamps, a microphone and a cast of unknown but carefully tested seamen and see how far you get!

We were five months doing the lifeboat sequences with poor Jack Cardiff being violently ill most of the time! He was a hero on that film and I think he photographed it brilliantly throughout. I was very lucky to have a wonderful bunch of people from so many walks of life, united in the pursuit of a common goal. British Lion distributed it and made a lot of money from it. Then the Ministry of Information, to their eternal shame, sold it to America for £7,000 or so – peanuts. It did very well over there too.

How did you come to do the US film *Shadow on the Wall* after the war?

When I had finished *Western Approaches*, the Ministry of Information didn't know whether it was any good, so their Honorary Adviser, who was at that time Alexander Korda, was called in to look at it. We screened it for him and he offered me a contract. By the time I took the contract up, he had been sacked by Metro [MGM], but they wouldn't release me.

I finally went to Hollywood and wanted to resign within three weeks, because it was quite clear they were never going to use me. Dore Schary, who had been brought in to 'save the studio', asked why I thought I could come over to America and make films, so I suggested they should have thought of that three years earlier. However, I made *Shadow on the Wall*, which Dore didn't like and which, incidentally, was Nancy Davis's [Reagan] first film. The great thing about working in an American studio was that the back-up was so good; if you made a sensible request, it was immediately granted.

Did you feel the '40s and '50s was a good time to be a film director in Britain?

I'm sure it was a boom period. I came back to do *White Corridors*, which we made in five weeks at Pinewood. John Davis then wanted to put me under contract but, after my experiences with MGM, I didn't want to lose my freedom by being under contract and thus losing the right to say no to an unacceptable assignment. Not easy when in receipt of a fat weekly wage.

I liked the story very much. It wasn't originally in the format in which it finished. I saw how I could make it more dramatic, and I rewrote it with Jan Read and built up the boy's story and character. However, when Arthur Rank saw the film he came up to me and said, 'It's a very nice little film indeed, but I don't think the boy ought to die; I think we've got to retake all that.' I couldn't believe this and said, 'If the boy doesn't die, you haven't got a story.' He said, 'I don't know about that, Mr Jackson, but I don't think the little boy should die.' They have no idea, so many of these people who control the industry, though Rank was a charming man.

Were you trying to get a documentary flow to it?

Oh yes. I was lucky because I had a wonderful cast, with the melding of the amateur actor with the professional cast. You may have recognised the hospital porter as the gunner from *Western Approaches*. He was a non-actor who had been magnificent in *Western Approaches*. The matron who read the prayers in the ward and played that wonderful scene with Petula Clark was an amateur whom I'd met in the Hind's Head, Bray. The boy, Brand Inglis, had never acted before. Wonderful performance!

You made another hospital-set film in 1956 – *The Feminine Touch*. Was this pure coincidence?

I went to Ealing and brought them the *Tirpitz* story [about the giant German battleship of World War II], which Mick Balcon loved, and we went into further researches on it; he felt it was a bit too expensive for him so we abandoned it. I hunted around for another subject, and I felt that *The Feminine Touch* could be made into something, so that's how it happened. I didn't really have a choice. But I loved working at Ealing. The film could have been marvellous had I been able to carry out what I wanted to do. It had some good people and one or two nice little scenes, but it wasn't a good film.

Which of your later films are you most pleased with?

The Birthday Present was an honest piece of film making, with a lovely performance from Sylvia Syms. It was a very interesting story and a well-written script by Jack Whittingham. *White Corridors* pleased me most because it most happily melded the documentary method with 'big box-office' and made no compromises to become 'big box office' – and it was made for £110,000! You couldn't even make a ten-second commercial for that nowadays.

Derek Jarman
1942–1994

Director: *Studio Bankside (1970), *Miss Gaby, *A Journey to Avebury (1971), *Garden of Luxor, *Andrew Logan Kisses the Glitterati, *Tarot (1972), *The Art of Mirrors (1973), *The Devils at the Elgin, *Ula's Fête, *Fire Island, *Duggie Fields (1974), *Picnic at Ray's, *Sebastiane Wrap (1975), *Gerald's Film, *Sloane Square, Sebastiane, *Houston (1976), Jubilee (1978), *Broken English, The Tempest (1979), In the Shadow of the Sun (1980), *TG: Psychic Rally in Heaven (1981), *Pirate Tape, *Pont- ormo and Punks at Santa Croce (1982), *Waiting for Waiting For Godot (1983), The Dream Machine, *Imagining October (1984), The Angelic Conversation, Caravaggio (1985), *The Queen is Dead (1986), Aria (one segment), The Last of England (1987), *L'Inspirazione (1988), War Requiem (1989), The Garden (1990), Edward II (1991), Wittgenstein, Blue (1993), Glitterbug (1994)
* Short film.

'Film has brought nothing but sadness into our lives. The moments when the sun came out were brief, and the further we tried to wander from the straight and narrow of British cinema the less we received,'[1] wrote Derek Jarman in his autobiographical mosaic, *Modern Nature*, two years before his death. As a gay activist filmmaker who always rejected the comfort of compromises, he nevertheless achieved a great deal in so uncongenial a climate. 'The whole gay thing is crucial to my films. I have found it very hard to come to terms with the strictures of society over homosexuality ... The anger in my films is totally justified ... I wanted to be a traditional filmmaker, and have a quiet time. But I know what it's like to live under a totalitarian regime.'[2]

The multi-talented Jarman – he was an art student who became a set designer for theatre and films (especially for Ken Russell), as well as a painter, writer, gardener and film director – left behind on his premature death in 1994 a body of work unique in British cinema. *Sebastiane*, his first feature film, set in a Roman military outpost and with dialogue wholly in Latin and the cast mostly nude, 'was made on a very low budget by James Whaley and myself, and James virtually sacrificed his house and there weren't any pressures on us – it wasn't a question of whether we made it in Latin or not, it seemed the best thing to do, and nobody intervened and said, "Do you have an audience for Latin?" ... it's Roman immediately, you know.'[3] It seems that, in a sense, the low budgets could be liberating as well as frustrating.

Of *Jubilee*, his own favourite, he believed, 'It's the most important film made in the seventies – I really do believe this is so. It's a parable about violence and the power of the media.'[4] If this film has more the sense of a collage than of conventional narrative, his next at least draws on a traditional source, Shakespeare's *The Tempest*, though it is by no means a predictable adaptation. (By comparison with Peter Greenaway's version, *Prospero's Books*, however, it looks relatively straightforward!) 'What I wanted to avoid ... was to have a well-known English actor doing his interpretation of Prospero, and to try to get away from that.'[5] In fact Prospero is played by Heathcote Williams, and the film, set in the derelict Stoneleigh Abbey, 'a big eighteenth-century Palladian house with endless empty rooms,'[6] is played as if it were 'a completely enclosed world – all a nightmare in Prospero's mind.'[7] In *The Angelic Conversation*, Jarman 'tried to rehabilitate Shakespeare as a gay writer,'[8] with Judi Dench reading sixteen of the sonnets on the soundtrack to the accompaniment of images 'putting them into a different context.'[9]

In 1992, he wrote, 'I've grown tired of the cinema, the preserve of ambition and folly ...'[10] but fortunately, as well as the films already mentioned, he had by then made several more equally remarkable. They include: *The Garden*, 'a simple domestic drama, a document. No fiction';[11] *Caravaggio*, a study of the Renaissance painter and 'the first film for which I was paid'[12] (by the British Film Institute); *War Requiem*, drawing on Benjamin Britten's music and the words (spoken by Laurence Olivier) of Wilfred Owen's poem, 'Strange Meeting'; *Edward II*, a highly individualistic crossing of Marlowe and modern gay politics; *Wittgenstein*, a biographical study of the Cambridge philosopher; and *Blue*. In the latter, several voices (including those of Jarman regulars, Tilda Swinton and Nigel Terry, as well as Jarman's own) accompany an unchanging blue screen. It is, in part, a meditation on Jarman's own HIV status and on the deaths of friends; and the colour itself is the subject of a chapter of reflections in his book, *Chroma*.

'Shakespeare, the *Sonnets*, *Caravaggio*, Britten's *Requiem*, what more traditional subject matter could a filmmaker take on? And yet I'm still seen by some as a menace,'[13] he claimed. The subject matter may have been traditional; the treatment was not, and that is what makes him a crucial figure in British cinema.

1 Derek Jarman, *Modern Nature* (first published 1991), Vintage, London, 1992, p 212
2 'Derek Jarman' in Jonathan Hacker and David Price, *Take 10: Contemporary British Film Directors*, Oxford University Press, 1991, pp 255–56
3 'Interview with Derek Jarman', *Film Directions*, Vol 2, No 8, 1979, p 15
4 Mark Sutton, 'Renaissance man', *Stills*, April 1986, p 11
5 *Film Directions*, p 14
6 *Film Directions*, p 14
7 Don Macpherson, 'Visions of a nightmare', *Screen International*, March 1979, p 19
8 Sutton, p 11
9 Roy Grundman, 'History and the gay viewfinder: An interview with Derek Jarman', *Cineaste*, Vol xviii, No 4, 1991, p 26
10 Jarman, *Modern Nature*, p 17
11 Jarman, *Modern Nature*, p 131
12 *Take One*, p 253
13 Jarman, *Modern Nature*, p 234

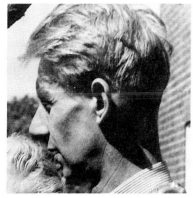

Humphrey Jennings

1907–1950

Director: *Post-Haste, Locomotives* (1934), *Birth of a Robot* (shared credit) (1935), *Penny Journey, Design for Spring, Speaking from America, English Harvest* (1938), *The First Days* (co-dir), *Spare Time, SS Ionian / Her Last Trip* (1939), *Spring Offensive / An Unrecorded Victory, Welfare of the Workers, London Can take It!* (co-dir), *Britain Can Take It!* (co-dir) (1940), *The Heart of Britain, Words for Battle* (& sc) (1941), *Listen to Britain* (co-dir & co- ed) (1942), *Fires Were Started* (& sc), **The Silent Village* (& sc, pr) (1943), **The True Story of Lilli Marlene* (& sc), *The Eighty Days* (& pr) (1944), *A Diary for Timothy* (1945), *A Defeated People* (1946), *The Cumberland Story* (& sc) (1947), *Dim Little Island* (& pr) (1949), *Family Portrait* (& sc) (1950) Unless marked *, all are short and/or documentary films.

'It might reasonably be contended that Humphrey Jennings is the only real poet the British cinema has yet produced,'[1] wrote Lindsay Anderson. Jennings himself never published on the cinema, and only very sparingly on those other arts – music and painting – to which he was also devoted. Since his untimely death at the age of forty-three, while filming in Greece, other people have been willing to speak for him, such as Gavin Lambert, who wrote of his 'passion for cinema.'[2] And the films he left behind speak eloquently of his commitment to Britain, to an unsentimental notion of brotherhood quite devoid of class-consciousness, and to film as an art form uniquely equipped to get to the living heart of our experience.

One of his poems opens in a way which suggests the visual power of his imagination and the juxtaposing of images which contributes so much to the mosaic patterns of his films:

I see London

I see the dome of St Paul's
like the forehead of Darwin

I see London stretching away North and North-East along dockside roads and balloon-haunted allotments

Where the black plumes of the horses precede and the white helmets of the rescue-squad follow . . .[3]

In such short masterworks as *Words for Battle* and *A Diary for Timothy*, the images of land- and town-scape and of all sorts and conditions of men are collated with a poet's eye, and with 'a wisdom of observation'[4] that sets him apart from most of the Griersonian documentarists. Nevertheless, he joined them at the GPO Film Unit in 1936, and much of his work, like theirs, was inspired by social purpose. It was the war which raised his work to new heights. 'I have found people extra helpful and extra charming in war time. They are living in a more heightened existence and are much more prepared to open their arms and fall into someone else's. To that extent . . . they are better film material, and the emotion that they themselves are feeling is part of the emotion that we indeed are always attempting to use and to propagate about life,'[5] he said in a seminar about documentary film in 1943. In this year, he made the unforgettable *Fires Were Started*, a documentary about the fire rescue teams during the war, conveying heroism without heroics, and, without stiff upper lips, it is always truthfully restrained. In the same year, he made *The Silent Village*, in which the Nazi takeover of the Czech village of Lidice is re-imagined in a Welsh rural mining town. Jennings found in the miner's leader 'a Tolstoyan figure',[6] and though, as this remark may suggest, there is some element of idealisation of the village, the passion and humanity of Jennings' vision is movingly clear. He never found subjects to stir him comparably in the post-war world, but the legacy of the war years is priceless.

1 *Film Quarterly*, Winter 1961, p 5
2 *Sight and Sound*, May 1951, p 24
3 Quoted by Kathleen Raine, in 'Writer and artist' in *Humphrey Jennings: A Tribute* (no publication details), p 4
4 Basil Wright's phrase, in Raine, p 9
5 From the Jennings files, BFI Library
6 Quoted in Philip M Taylor (ed.), *Britain and the Cinema in the Second World War*, Macmillan, Basingstoke, 1988, p 71

Rosamund John

b. 1913

Actor: *Secret of the Loch* (1934), *The First of the Few* (1942), *The Gentle Sex, The Lamp Still Burns* (1943), *Tawny Pipit, Soldier, Sailor* (1944), *The Way to the Stars* (1945), *Green for Danger* (1946), *The Upturned Glass, Fame is the Spur, When the Bough Breaks* (1947), *No Place for Jennifer, She Shall Have Murder* (1950), *Never Look Back* (1952), *Street Corner* (1953), *Operation Murder* (1957)

Rosamund John is always being described in the reference books as 'gentle-mannered' and 'pleasant', which seem wan epithets to describe her best screen work. They do less than justice to the crispness and compassion which characterise her most sympathetic roles – for example, as the firm-minded pub-keeping Toddy in *The Way to the Stars* – or to the potential for dangerous repression she suggests in *Green for Danger*. In the latter, her surface gentleness is very cunningly used by actress and director to provide a surprising solution to a murder. As the suffragette wife of the politician who has compromised his ideals, in Roy Boulting's *Fame is the Spur*, she presents a very persuasive study in strength and dedication, and the scenes in the Swiss chalet when she is ill and dying are very moving; so, too, are her scenes of friendship with Douglass Montgomery in *The Way to the Stars*. Rosamund John made only sixteen films and was lucky that half a dozen of them gave her such excellent opportunities. She was also much interested in the politics of the British film industry and remains forthright in her views on it. *Interview date: September 1989*

After your 1934 début, you returned to the screen in 1942 and made three films in a row, all for Leslie Howard. How influential a figure was he in your career?

Oh, he taught me everything I knew about filmmaking. I got on very well with him and luckily he didn't want to get into bed with me, as he did with quite a few people he worked with. I was playing Mrs Mitchell in *First of the Few*. Leslie made me realise that the only thing which matters when you are filming is what you are thinking and feeling, because it will all show in your eyes. Leslie was an actor before he became a director and he saw things from an actor's point of view, but a lot of directors merely looked upon actors as being inconvenient bits of furniture.

The beginning of the film, where he was watching the gulls, was really difficult because, at that time, practically the whole British coastline was covered in barbed wire. We had to go down to Polperro in Cornwall to find a place where there were rocks and gulls and we had a lorry-load of fish to attract the gulls. We tossed the fish around on the rocks and the gulls said, 'So what?' As soon as we packed up to leave for the day, they descended in clouds!

I had done a play [*The Devil's Disciple*] with Robert Donat, who had wanted to make the film but was under contract to MGM. I was up a tree picking cherries at Robert's house one day when a girl I knew in an agency phoned to say Leslie Howard was looking for someone for this film. She had suggested me and I had to go straight away. Leslie said I didn't look like an actress and decided to test me for the part of the wife. I knew nothing about the film but I did the test anyway, and got the part.

I've never forgotten my first appearance on the set. There was this massive crowd for the presenting of the Schneider Trophy, which was won by planes that Mitchell designed before the war, and they had this set with the winning plane – God knows how they got it in the studio – and when I walked on to the set, I could feel a wave of people looking and wondering, 'What the hell has she got?' And I realised there was a lot of antagonism towards a complete newcomer.

The Gentle Sex is officially co-directed by Leslie Howard and Maurice Elvey. What did that mean in practice?

It was directed by Leslie. He was an extraordinary character; I suppose one would call him amoral. He just did what he enjoyed doing. I

remember one day his daughter came on the set and took out a very nice cigarette case. Leslie said, 'Where'd you get that?' 'Don't you recognise it?' she said. 'It's one Merle Oberon gave you. Mummy had the inscription removed and gave it to me.' Leslie just roared with laughter! Leslie's mistress, Violette, died while we were making the film and Leslie was devastated. He asked Maurice Elvey to finish the film. I had never heard of Elvey but everyone in the studio said, 'Oh no, that terrible man!' He was a very pompous little man who had made a lot of indifferent films before the war.

Leslie went off to Lisbon while we were making *The Lamp Still Burns*, and he was shot down on the way back. He was travelling with a man the Germans thought to be Churchill and that is supposedly why they shot the plane down. Leslie had been flying around making speeches in neutral countries like Sweden, and of course Portugal was also neutral.

Was The Gentle Sex made as propaganda for the women's forces?

Partly; they wanted to recruit women for the ATS, and it was originally to have been made by Derrick de Marney, who played a small part in *The First of the Few*. It was about these six girls who join the Army, and I wanted to play the Cockney girl but Derrick said, 'No, you can't, you look all wrong for that,' though I grew up in Cockney London. However, she was played by a girl called Joan Gates, who married a GI and went to live in America, Jean Gillie was the good-time girl, and I was the Scots one. I used to rush off to John Laurie on another set at Denham for help with the dialogue. I think the film *did* work as propaganda, especially in America. Many didn't realise that women were working on gun sites and driving lorries, until they made that film. The Ministry of Information wanted Leslie to do it, which is why he took over from Derrick.

How did you find Maurice Elvey, as the director of The Lamp Still Burns?

I was appalled: he had no idea of what to do or how to do it. The electricians would be shouting, 'Print number three, Maurice!' He was unbelievable. Stewart Granger had been given a contract and he was on the rise although no one had heard of him at that stage. He discovered he was supposed to have a head injury, which would have meant having his hair shaved off and a bandage like a turban. He flatly refused so they had to change it to a broken rib.

Did you feel securely established as a British film star by now?

I don't think so; all I wanted to do was to work. The next thing I did was *Tawny Pipit*, which Bernard Miles made. It was lovely because we went up to the Cotswolds, and it was a charming film about birds, which only the British would care about – making sure the birds could hatch undisturbed in the middle of a war! Rank didn't think they would be able to sell it to America so it was stashed away for a while. When it *was* shown, it was wildly popular, because it was everything that the Americans thought of as being English.

My personal favourite of your films is *The Way to the Stars*. Did you like your role of Toddy?

I loved it. It was written by [Terence] Rattigan, and it was a lovely script. The war ended before the film was finished, so they scrapped a whole lot of wartime stuff we'd done at the beginning and substituted the brilliant idea of the people going back to the aerodrome and seeing all the graffiti on the walls, which linked it all up. They were afraid no one would want to see a film about the war which had just ended. Originally the script was called *Halfpenny Field* because that was the name of a place where they had an airstrip, but they decided nobody in America would be able to pronounce 'Ha'penny' so it had to go.

I can't think of another film in which there is so moving a friendship between a man and a woman as the one between you and Douglass Montgomery . . .

This was a fascinating idea, but they had hell's own job casting it, because every American on this side of the Atlantic was involved in the American armed forces. I was very worried because it was a tricky part to play. Then someone found Douglass, who was actually Canadian. We had made quite a bit of the film by that time. As soon as we started to work, he said he thought it ought to be a love story between our two characters [an English widow and an American airman], when the whole point of the thing was that there *wasn't* a love story! Puffin [Anthony] Asquith – my favourite director – told Douglass we would shoot it at the end, and of course we never did. This relationship got a lot more emphasis when some of the war scenes were cut out.

Reference books describe you as a 'gentle-mannered' English actress, which I think undervalues much of your work.

I think it's the parts I played. In those days we were much more ladylike than they are now. We used to admire French films because in them actresses were allowed to be real; but English films made us unreal because the audience liked being taken out of the reality of the war. I think they cast me as the murderess in *Green for Danger* because no one would ever suspect me! Alastair Sim was wonderful in the film, which was quite a success, which is surprising given the frightful novel from which it came!

Did you think of *Fame is the Spur* as a film of the postwar, Labour Government, England?

No. I never thought about that. I adored it because it was 'costume', and that for an actress is much more satisfying than modern clothes. I was very impressed with Mrs Pethick-Lawrence, the famous suffragette, who told me about her time in prison. I also met Christabel Pankhurst – God, what a bitch she was! The Boultings couldn't wait to get her off the set. I enjoyed that film more than any other. You know how it's said to be based on Ramsay MacDonald; well, the author, Howard Spring, came on the set one day and he said it was based on *any* chap who had feet of clay, and he'd taken bits from various people. I think Roy enjoyed putting over the idea that all these Labour chaps who were supposed to be holier-than-thou in fact had feet of clay.

What do you recall of your work as Actors' Equity representative on the Working Party on Film Production Costs in 1949?

Equity fought to have a representative. Our secretary, a marvellous man called Gordon Sandison, said it was terribly important for actors to be represented. There was a dreadful man on it, then secretary of NATKE [National Association of Theatrical and Kinematograph Employees], who always said he spoke for everyone . . . well, he didn't speak for *anybody*, certainly not actors. So Gordon fought for an Equity representative along with distributors and producers. Harold Wilson was President of the Board of Trade and he agreed to appoint two extra people and asked for a list of names from Equity. I was amazed when I got a letter saying I had been appointed. I met Harold long after that and asked him why he had chosen me. Larry [Olivier] was one of the names on the list but Wilson said he thought that if he had chosen Larry, people would say, 'Oh, you're just having another director, he isn't really there as an actor.' So Harold Wilson said he had appointed me because he had enjoyed my films, and, he said, 'Either you weren't a Communist or you had succeeded in hiding it very well!' because it was the time of McCarthyism in America and if you weren't a staunch Tory you were a goner as a rule!

It was fascinating to be a part of that; actually it was a great advantage being a woman on that Council. All the men around the table were going on about cutting production costs, cutting down wardrobe budgets, and so on. I pointed out that one of the reasons people go to the cinema is to see beautifully dressed women, that the money was not being wasted. The chief function of the Board of Trade's Cinematograph Films Council was to decide what percentage of British films should be shown in each cinema each year – and, presumably, to prosecute those that didn't comply.

What other recollections do you have of your work with Equity?

It was founded by a group of people who realised that hardworking actors needed help in opposing managers who sometimes exploited them. Dame May Whitty donated her dining table to the organisation they set up and the Council still meets around it – but now in Glasgow. The London organisation has outgrown its size. I worked on several committees – like one to establish minimum rates for chorus workers. Then, when TV came on stream in a big way – after World War II – we fought a tough battle with the BBC which wanted to claim that actors were all self-employed and therefore the BBC need not pay their income tax or National Insurance – which would mean they could not claim unemployment benefit. We had to fight to get them paid for performances after the original one too. Whenever we had to go to court, Gerald Gardiner QC – later a Lord Chancellor in a Labour Government [and married to Muriel Box] – represented us.

Dame Celia Johnson

1908–1982

Actor: *A Letter From Home (1941), In Which We Serve, *We Serve (1942), Dear Octopus (1943), This Happy Breed (1944), Brief Encounter (1945), The Astonished Heart (1949), I Believe In You, The Holly and the Ivy (1952), The Captain's Paradise (1953), A Kid for Two Farthings (1955), The Good Companions (1957), The Prime of Miss Jean Brodie (1968)
* short film.

'It's my eyes. It's a great advantage when everything is a blur beyond a certain point,'[1] said Celia Johnson in a rare interview. In her most famous performance, as Laura Jesson in David Lean's *Brief Encounter*, it is those eloquent eyes in close-up that stay with one. If she had made no other film, she would have been assured of her place in British film history. The awful hat, the middle-class wonder at the invasion by passion and, of course, the middle-class rejection of it in favour of other priorities – of affection, of responsibility, of duty – and the way of investing the ordinary with a sense of pain and astonishment: it is a great performance and in the end resists clumsy attempts at analysis. It was the film that converted her to filmmaking: it was 'absolutely non-stop Johnson'[2] as she not only had the leading female role but was the film's narrator as well. After this film, she said, 'And because I was in the studio so much, I got to know something of other people's jobs in film production. It was fascinating.'[3]

After making a wartime short, *A Letter From*

Home, directed by Carol Reed, she asked Noël Coward for the role of the Commander's wife in *In Which We Serve* – and got it after a bizarre-sounding scene in which they recited 'The Walrus and the Carpenter' to each other. 'I enjoyed myself on the set but I wasn't happy with my film-acting technique,'[4] and she was not happy with herself in Lean's *This Happy Breed*: 'I look so awful that even the friend who came with me ... couldn't say anything but that I was meant to look very drab and certainly succeeded.'[5] She is, in fact, very touching as the stoical, limited mother in this version of Coward.

However, though she came to enjoy the 'challenge in trying to act in a little cut-off bit of light' and in later years to 'get a sort of nostalgia for the actual work of filming',[6] her film career was sporadic. She is never less than accomplished and she is sometimes affecting, as in *Dear Octopus*, as the disappointed daughter of the family, or in *The Holly and the Ivy*, as another daughter who seems to be letting life pass her by. As one of Alec Guinness's wives in *The Captain's Paradise*, she is funny enough to make one wish she'd opted more for comedy. It seems not just to have been commitment to the stage that limited her film work,

but the claims of family life seem also to have been rewarding enough to act as a check on ambition. 'For a short while, some years ago,' she said in a 1950s broadcast, 'I was a sort of sub-film star. This was very surprising, and by the time I had got used to it I stopped being one.'[7]

She did indeed, and though she did some memorable television, notably *Staying On*, in which she was reunited with Trevor Howard, her *Brief Encounter* co-star, she made far too few cinema films, so that the respect in which she is held is the more remarkable. Even a film as appalling as *The Astonished Heart* or as dull as *A Kid for Two Farthings* (she's out of her social class and it shows) can scarcely dim the lustre.

1 'Celia Johnson talks frankly to CA Lejeune', *Picturegoer*, 18 August 1945, p 6
2 *Picturegoer*, 18 August 1945
3 John K Newnham, 'Why don't we see more of Celia?', *Picturegoer*, 8 March 1952, p 17
4 Newnham, p 17
5 Kate Fleming, *Celia Johnson: A Biography*, Orion, London, 1991, p 161
6 Fleming, p 205 (from a piece Johnson wrote called 'Film Star Manqué')
7 Fleming, p 204

Margaret Johnston

b. 1918

Actor: *The Prime Minister* (1941), *The Rake's Progress* (1945), *A Man About the House* (1947), *Portrait of Clare* (1950), *The Magic Box* (1951), *The Knave of Hearts* (1954), *Touch and Go* (1955), *Night of the Eagle* (1962), *Girl in the Headlines* (1963), *Life at the Top* (1965), *The Psychopath* (1966), *Sebastian* (1967)

When I asked Margaret Johnston what she thought was the highlight of her film career, she said, 'I don't think I have one, do I?' She gave up acting early to take over the agency made famous by her late husband, Al Parker, a function she fulfils to this day. However, though her career was truncated, it

needs to be stated that there is scarcely a film in which she is less than unusual – and unusually striking. Attractive and elegant, she never became a major star, perhaps because she used to keep hopping back to the stage all the time, perhaps because she was always a character- rather than a personality-based actor. However, she is remembered for a gallery of widely varied roles: for the unillusioned secretary in *The Rake's Progress*; the spinster sister who falls for Latin charm and nearly pays with her life in *A Man About the House*; the careworn second wife of William Friese-Greene in the 1951 film about the early pioneer of kinematography, *The Magic Box*; a bossy executive in a striped suit in René Clément's *The Knave of Hearts*; the neurotic occultist in *Night of the Eagle*; and a bitchy wife in *Life at the Top*. Any one of those would do for a highlight.

Interview date: September 1992

Did your training as a stage actress help you as an actress in films?

I have a theory that if you train as a theatre actress and you automatically go into film, then your instincts take over – you don't have to plan how you do it – and guide you into the medium. I didn't feel that I had to learn a lot of new techniques. I wanted to alternate the two although I probably preferred theatre, as I think most actors do.

How did you come to be in Thorold Dickinson's *The Prime Minister* in 1941? What do you remember of the experience?

Oh gosh, that was the first film I did. There were three sisters, the Prime Minister's children, I think, and they thought I was right to play one of them. For some reason the Blitz was centred on that particular part of London – Twickenham, I think – and it was just unbelievable. It was very sad to go out to the studio after a night's bombing, because every second house was down and we wondered what we would find at the studio. We knew everybody would be grief-stricken because they would have lost people. It's astounding that any films got made at all; but it did have a morale-boosting effect, of course, as any crisis does. Glynis Johns, who was a friend from the theatre, was in it too. I don't think I had any scenes with Gielgud or Fay Compton, but they had such a terrific aura for young people around them, and it was lovely to see them working.

You made no further films until *The Rake's Progress* in 1945. Were you solidly on the stage in those years?

Probably, yes. I went to drama school at the Royal Academy [RADA] for three years also. Jennifer was my first real part, therefore I was very receptive to it. It was a good part and a well-written script, and of course the film has lasted, and Rex Harrison was superb in it. The script was written by the lovely Launder and Gilliat team and it was terrific. There were three excellent women's parts: for myself, Jean Kent and Lilli Palmer. Of course I wanted Lilli's part, just because I was young and stupid, but the best part was the one I played.

The ending, when the rake turns hero, has been criticised. What did you think of it?

I think what they were trying to say was that he was someone who was very happy to risk his life for something that he loved to do. In a funny sort of way, I suppose that is worthwhile. He did contrast very well with Griffith Jones – and I don't know why Griffith didn't have a better career. Rex had this incredible originality of personality and talent; he was a beautiful comedian with a wonderful stage career as well as films, and he had such a light touch.

Your next film, *A Man About the House*, was a gripping melodrama. Do you like melodrama?

It certainly was that. I just thought it was a good part. The character was much older than I was, in her mid-thirties and very spinsterish, which puts the years on too. We did a lot of it on location in Italy. Leslie Arliss, who directed, was fine, and once again it was a good script from a very good novel by Francis Brett Young. You see, if you have the basis right, it doesn't go too wrong.

I'm very interested your next film, *Portrait of Clare*, again from a novel by Francis Brett Young.

I'd forgotten that one, yes, directed by Lance Comfort. It was quite a nice film, except that I played the piano in it! I learned to play the particular section of the piece that was to be used, but when we came to film, they said, 'We're not going to do that bit, we're going to do the next bit,' and I said, 'You're not, you know. I spent three months learning that bit!' They argued with me so I got up and walked off the set – isn't that terrible! But I walked off and wouldn't come back, because I thought it was unfair and wrong. That's the Australian coming out in me! Finally they did my bit anyway. Lance was gentle and nice and good-tempered. He handled that particular situation well; he was big enough to let it happen my way because I had worked so hard on it. He didn't give a lot of direction, although I think he would have if you'd seemed to need or want it.

I had a son in that film, by the first husband, Ronald Howard, and the little boy was Jeremy Spenser. I used to take him and his mother to and from the studio every day. *Portrait of Clare* was quite a graceful film. It has been shown on television a couple of times, so obviously prints still exist. Marjorie Fielding was great in it, such a fine comedienne. Many of the cast were excellent, of course, being highly experienced classical actors who adapted well to the screen.

Unlike most of the huge, all-star cast in *The Magic Box*, you actually had a proper acting role. Did you like that role, as the second Mrs Friese-Greene?

Yes, it was lovely. That was the film they did for the Festival of Britain. The Boulting brothers would get an idea into their heads about who they wanted on a film, and you couldn't change them. Ronald Neame produced it and John Boulting directed. The Boultings were people who would suddenly do wonderful things in their films. They could be very caustic but very funny. I remember *Brighton Rock* with Dickie Attenborough; my husband and I were in the theatre watching it and there is a scene in the hotel where suddenly someone starts paging 'Mr Parker, Mr Al Parker'. Everyone in the business collapsed laughing, because of course Al was Dickie's agent.

Everyone who was anyone was in *The Magic Box*. Who do you remember working with from that all-star cast?

Robert Donat. He was very ill then, fighting for life. He had suffered so much for so many years. But a great actor, and he was very moving in that. They didn't quite know how to do the film, so they decided to do the latter part of his life first because it was too sad and they wanted to end the film on an upbeat note. But it doesn't work that way, people resist that a bit. But there are lovely bits in it – Laurence Olivier as the policeman and Joyce Grenfell as a chorister were great.

***The Knave of Hearts* is a very witty, graceful, rather un-English comedy. Did you admire the French director, René Clément?**

Ah yes, that's one of my favourites. Philipe was such a great comedian and the director was brilliant. Gérard Philipe's life was cut short – he was an angel of a man, too, just wonderful with people. The chauffeur would bring him back at night and he would take the chauffeur in and give him dinner. He couldn't speak English and I couldn't speak French! We both had to learn our lines phonetically. Actually, I got someone from the Berlitz school to come twice a week for three weeks to teach me the French of the script, because I was determined to do that film with Philipe and Clément. But what I didn't know was that my teacher had the equivalent of a Cockney accent in French. I had no idea of this, but René Clément heard it and thought it was marvellous. For all the other French-speaking women in the cast he used Parisian voices, but he used my voice with the Australian accent, which brought the house down when I opened my mouth, especially because I was playing such an arrogant, bossy character!

Gérard Philipe and I did a scene together where he came back drunk at night and I'd been waiting there, furious; when we shot that scene, I threw something at him and he got such a shock he picked up something else and threw it back at me. Clément left the camera running on that whole scene for twenty minutes; we broke up the whole set and he let us! Unfortunately, only bits of it could be used in the film in the end, but that's the sort of director he was, he was wonderful. I can't remember how good his English was, but it worked, obviously. It was a very sophisticated, European film and isn't old-fashioned at all today. Clément was a very adaptable director. For instance, he would find that it was always raining when he came to shoot in London, so he made sure that he never did a shot unless it was raining – he did it on purpose because that's how he saw England.

You made your only Ealing film, *Touch and Go*, in 1955. What do you recollect of Ealing as a place to work?

Oh, very cosy, very relaxing – all the things that actors need. You felt secure because there was someone at the head of it who knew what he was doing – Michael Balcon. The director, Michael Truman, was very gentle, talented, and with good taste. If you knew what you were doing that was fine, he let you get on with it. He would just drop a word or two if he felt certain things should be different. He died rather young.

In that film you all end up not going to Australia, choosing to go on with things just the same.

They wanted to go to Australia but the cat wouldn't let them! Cats are very strange animals, you know. That was a very remarkable cat. It was a nice film, very real.

After that film in 1955, you made no further films until 1962. Did you have more interesting stage offers?

During the late '50s I was at Stratford; I did a season of three plays there – Isabella in *Measure for Measure*, Portia and Desdemona. Then I went down to Chichester where I did Lady Macbeth. After that I began working with the agency because my husband's health was failing.

You made several films in the '60s, including a very good supernatural thriller called *Night of the Eagle*.

Oh, I hated that, even though it was a good part and the film must have been popular because they keep bringing it back. It wasn't the sort of film I enjoyed doing, however. I played a neurotic, dangerous woman with a club foot, who was married to Anthony Nicholls.

I particularly like your scenes in *Life at the Top*. How do you feel about it? Do you think it is a rare example of a sequel that isn't a major let-down?

I did enjoy that. My character was a slut, I remember, who wore terrible, loose, awful suits and had a lot of dogs around her. That film did work. I remember the Canadian, Ted Kotcheff, very well – he was a very good director and it was a film I'd like to see again. They certainly got the top actors in those days.

Your last film was *Sebastian* with Dirk Bogarde, on which Michael Powell was involved as co-producer.

That wasn't good. I did that to make Michael happy. I never liked the script and never wanted to be a part of it, but I realised that he wanted to make a gesture. My heart wasn't in it, however.

When did you begin running your husband's agency?

In 1965. It was a great help having been an actress myself. I still use that all the time, because I can pass on certain things in acting that have been passed on to me in my career by great directors. So you can guide the newcomers to the business. I deal mainly with actors but some directors.

Does an agent actually seek out work for clients, or do you arrange deals when producers come to you?

First of all, an agent sometimes chooses actors and actresses by seeing them in plays and invites them to come and talk; you'll sit down and talk and decide if you will work well together. My husband was extraordinary: he met James Mason at a cocktail party, just saw him across the room and knew he was a star. They had a lifelong relationship, which was quite wonderful. That's really the reason I entered the agency, because my husband's health was failing and I knew it would break his heart if James didn't have proper service. And I knew that James felt I was so close to my husband I would know how to carry on.

There *is* still a film industry but it is a very tough one. Because of the market in America it is very difficult to build stars in this country; the only British stars are built because they eventually go to America and become fundamentally American stars. Also, I don't think the Government understands how much money is needed to make a really good film. Yet it puts money into other things.

John Justin
b. 1917

Actor: *The Thief of Baghdad* (1940), *The Gentle Sex* (1943), *Journey Together* (1945), *Call of the Blood* (1948), *The Angel with the Trumpet* (1950), *The Sound Barrier, Hot Ice* (1952), *Melba, King of the Khyber Rifles* (1953), *The Village, Seagulls over Sorrento, The Teckman Mystery* (1954), *The Man Who Loved Redheads, Untamed, Guilty?* (1955), *Safari, Crime Passionnel* (1956), *Island in the Sun* (1957), *The Spider's Web* (1960), *Le Crime de M. Chardin, Les Hommes Veulent Vivre* (1961), *Candidate for Murder* (1962), **Men in Silence* (voice only) (1964), *Savage Messiah* (1972), *Barcelona Kill / Razzia* (1973), *Lisztomania* (1975), *Valentino* (1977), *The Big Sleep* (1978), *Trenchcoat* (1982)
* Documentary.

John Justin began his film career at the top – as the dashing Prince in Alexander Korda's *The Thief of Baghdad*, in which he was required to be handsome, athletic and romantic. He was placed under contract to Korda, but 1940 was just the wrong time to be twenty-three and on the verge of a film career. He was in the RAF during the war and was released briefly to make two propaganda films – *The Gentle Sex* and *Journey Together*. It was his role in David Lean's *The Sound Barrier* that really launched his screen career and his scenes with Dinah Sheridan brought a needed warmth to the film. Hollywood (20th-Century-Fox) grabbed him in the mid '50s for several CinemaScope epics, but his British films were persistently more attractive, especially Harold French's *The Man Who Loved Redheads*. In the '70s he made three films for Ken Russell: having begun with Korda, and allowing for changes in taste, this must have seemed like watching the flamboyant wheel come full circle.
Interview date: July 1990

How did you come to start in a plum part in *The Thief of Baghdad* in 1940?

I got the part because I had a very good agent at MCA who had come from Hollywood, Harry Ham. One day he told me to go to Denham for a test. I was sick of auditions and was about to give the whole thing up; so I went out to Denham quite relaxed for a change. I went on to the huge stage, which had a boat in the middle of it, in which was a little Indian boy. I put on some kind of costume and got into the boat with this little boy, Sabu; he was very funny and clever and utterly unafraid of all the film people, and this helped me. The two of us sent the whole test up. Normally I would have worked much harder at it but I did it quite casually, and left assuming I had missed out.

Two days later, the front page of one of the newspapers had me on it, with headlines! This whole publicity campaign had started and I had been cast without even knowing about it. Korda had made some very good pictures by then and this was a particularly important one because it was to be in Technicolor, which was rare then, and a lot of the special effects we were to do were very difficult in colour.

How did it come to have three directors' names on the credits – Michael Powell, Tim Whelan and Ludwig Berger?

It was really a Korda film; if it had been the mess it looked like being, then Korda would have been finished, so he might as well get the credit. Korda was technically the producer but he controlled it totally and, effectively, he directed it. Michael was the exterior director, he wasn't on the set. I can't remember Tim Whelan at all. Ludwig Berger was a very successful European director who had just won a prize for his last film, so of course Korda wanted him for *The Thief of Baghdad*.

The day we started shooting, Alex left for Hollywood. We worked for three months and then Alex came back from America, looked at the rushes, and said they were no good. Four days later we started again with a new script. He wanted Berger out but couldn't sack him, so that first day Sabu and I found them both behind the camera. Sabu had a hard enough time with his dialogue but with two directors giving contrary instructions he nearly gave up. Just one example of the two styles – a scene under Berger's direction involved June Duprez, Sabu and me, a donkey, a bale of straw, and a short flight of wet steps. When Alex redid it, it filled the whole of the biggest stage at Denham and included a dozen camels, mules, horses and three elephants, four hundred extras and tons of fruit and vegetables – oh yes, and Sabu and me!

Georges Périnal was lighting it and he was a wonderfully talented man, but also absolutely infuriating. He was the one person to whom Alex didn't dare say anything. He would spend hours on a face and he'd refuse to hurry. Actresses had a bad time with him. He would approach them slowly, eyes narrowed, peering within inches of their faces, and move slowly round them, then, stepping back and throwing his hands in the air, say in despair, 'Aah! Mon Dieu!' and walk away. When he turned, he'd find the girl in tears. I don't think he saw people as *people*, only as objects to be lit perfectly, against great odds, but he did make us look good.

What was your experience of working with Leslie Howard on *The Gentle Sex*?

He was a lovely man, deeply admired by us as a theatre actor, but I didn't know him at all. He was brilliant but nervous. I was only very briefly in *The Gentle Sex* to provide someone's love interest. They borrowed me to do it for the Army, on my Air Force pay, fourteen quid a week!

You made a curious-sounding enterprise called *Call of the Blood* in 1948. Was John Clements particularly keen to do this film, as he both stars in and co-directs it?

And wrecked it too! It was a silly idea. It starred his wife, Kay Hammond, who was a dear lady. We did the whole film in Sicily, which was the only interesting thing about it. It was very rare in those times to do an entire picture on location. All the interiors were actually shot in houses in Sicily, with very low ceilings, and it was quite a trick to get any lighting from the top and not damage the houses at all. It was a terrible Victorian story about a woman doctor; Alex Korda took one look at it and from then on referred to it as *Call of the Bloody*!

Were you working on the stage until you came back to the screen in *The Angel with the Trumpet*?

Yes. I was doing a play with Eileen Herlie called *Thracian Horses*, a mock Greek comedy. It went very well, so Alex came round one night, handed Eileen a blank piece of paper and told her to write her own contract, including salary. Of course, she had no idea of money; not on the scale he dealt with it. What appeared a great gamble, Alex knew was no gamble at all. No agent would have let him get away with it but he'd bypassed the agents. Her first picture under that contract was *Angel with the Trumpet*. Eileen was a fine actress but she wasn't right for the part, and the picture failed. It was the first time I played a role which aged from twenty-two to seventy-five – but not the last.

You did that again in *The Man Who Loved Redheads*, from a Rattigan play, in 1955.

Yes, that was Alex again, as a result of my having played in *The Angel*. Poor Harold French, the director, had a bad time with Alex, who had been starting stories about his direction because the company was too happy! He felt that only unhappy productions make good pictures. Nonetheless it *was* a very harmonious experience, and I loved working with Roly Culver; we both knew our stuff well enough to get the sparks flying a bit. I remember having to embrace Gladys Cooper, who played my wife, and saying to her, 'What a terrific moment in my life, to hold you in my arms!' She was enchanting. The film didn't go down well, though. I suppose if Moira Shearer and I had been huge stars world-wide, people would have come to see it just for that, but neither of us was of that calibre. I liked it, though; there were some wonderful comic actors in it and some very nice moments.

Would you agree that your film career really took off with *The Sound Barrier* in 1952?

Yes, I suppose that made me a real star. David Lean was an extraordinary man who I think hated actors, but he was a *brilliant* editor. The thing about good actors is that they don't act *with* each other but *against* each other, each one working for the best he can get out of himself, and the director is there to see 'fair play', as it were. I remember rehearsing a crucial scene in *The Sound Barrier*, with Nigel Patrick; Nigel was very fast and I kept looking across at David Lean to defend me but he just sat there looking very blank. Finally we paused a moment and David simply said, 'Let me know when you're ready,' and he walked off the set, leaving us to it. We had no direction at all from him: we had the set and the script and we knew the story – that was it. Eventually we sent a message to him that we were ready and he simply said, 'Shoot it.' I loved him though; I don't like too much direction, I prefer simply to be told it's good or it's no good, particularly if I'm going over the top. With that I'm happy, I trust the director absolutely then.

Maybe you remember that sequence where the dive to break the barrier was on. David was at his wits' end to make that dive as long and dramatic as he wanted it to be. On a grey, cloudy day, with the camera tilted, he shot thousands of feet and created one of the most exciting moments in any film. Of course, it's very difficult to explain the idea of breaking the sound barrier. It had only just been done and it was brand-new stuff. Someone said could the pilot push the stick forward, giving the idea that it reversed the controls, so that's what we did. I said the words, 'I'm now going to push the stick forward,' and that was the great moment. It was either right or wrong, his life was at stake.

The relationship between your character and Dinah Sheridan's is important as a foil to the tensions of the other relationships.

Yes, that's the author [Terence Rattigan]. I put a bit in there too and, here again, it shows David Lean as not being a good director of actors. I suddenly knew that, because I had just broken the sound barrier, the laugh at my wife worrying about the children's clothes would really turn into a cry, so I asked David if I could do that and I did. He agreed, but worried in case repeating it might distress me too much! I explained that this was what I did for a living, that I was not really distressed.

Did you feel you were treated differently as a star in your American films from the way you'd been treated in Britain?

You were judged strictly on your salary level, on your billing, whether or not you had a caravan on location, all those things. At first I didn't have a caravan to myself and I mentioned this, not understanding the system, and the next morning there was a caravan for me and everyone apologising. I was working on a quarterly contract, but they had thought it was a year's contract in which case my salary wouldn't have warranted a caravan! In fact I was getting a star's salary although I was a junior star – nothing like Ty Power, who was a very big star.

Korda knew how to pick stars all right, but he didn't know how to groom them. There was nothing like that in England, no organisation at all like that.

Jean Kent

b. 1921

Actor: *The Rocks of Valpre, How's Your Father* (1935), *Hello Fame* (1940), *It's That Man Again, Miss London Ltd, Warn That Man* (1943), *Bees in Paradise, Fanny by Gaslight, 2000 Women, Champagne Charlie, Madonna of the Seven Moons, Soldier, Sailor* (1944), *Waterloo Road, The Rake's Progress, The Wicked Lady* (1945), *Caravan, Carnival, The Magic Bow* (1946), *The Man Within, The Loves of Joanna Godden* (1947), *Good Time Girl, Bond Street, Sleeping Car to Trieste* (1948), *Trottie True* (1949), *The Reluctant Widow, The Woman in Question, Her Favourite Husband* (1950), *The Brown-*

ing Version (1951), *The Lost Hours* (1952), *Before I Wake* (1955), *The Prince and the Showgirl* (1957), *Bonjour Tristesse, Grip of the Strangler* (1958), *Beyond This Place, Please Turn Over* (1959), *Bluebeard's Ten Honeymoons* (1960), *Shout at the Devil* (1976)

When I asked Jean Kent whom she had most admired in American films, she said, without hesitating, 'Claire Trevor.' It seemed a very revealing answer about the kind of parts British films rarely offered women in the 1940s and '50s, or perhaps ever: gutsy, worldly-wise, generous, like the role she'd love to have played and for which Simone Signoret won an Oscar in *Room at the Top*. However, it must be said that she made the most of what came her way. She made her mark as the flashy, determined Lucy in Asquith's *Fanny by Gaslight* and had her best role ever, again for Asquith, as the vicious wife in *The Browning Version*, mining veins of real frustration in Millie Crocker-Harris. After *Fanny*, she became established as Gainsborough's sexy bad girl who usually lost the heroine to more virtuous types, then came into her own with a series of strong starring roles in 1948. As a change of pace, in *Trottie True* she was stylish and charming as the Gaiety Girl who married a duke. In the last three decades she has worked steadily on television and stage but has filmed only once – an absurd waste, to films, of a robust talent.

Interview date: October 1989

Did you feel the role of Lucy in *Fanny by Gaslight* in 1944 was a turning point for you?

Definitely, I was most excited, but I think it was purely accidental that I got the part. Perhaps Ted Black suggested that I be tested. Perhaps he saw the rushes of something else and thought, well, she's blonde too, why don't we test her? But it got me noticed. Perhaps I was just a new face popping up. Certainly, you can't mistake Phyllis [Calvert] and me for each other. *Fanny* was one of the better Gainsborough melodramas. It's a good story, isn't it? And it has marvellous sets and wonderful clothes. There was enormous skill and effort taken over them. Elizabeth Haffenden, who did the clothes, was a magnificent designer.

What sort of director was Anthony Asquith?

Wonderful. The only director who actually introduced members of the cast to each other! He used to wear this blue boiler-suit and sit like a little pixie under the camera. Unless he got under the camera he couldn't actually see what the scene was as it was being shot. He was always encouraging to his actors. You'd rehearse the scene and he'd say, 'I love the way you do so and so . . .' or 'Do you think this?' By the time we'd finished he'd turned the whole thing around as he wanted it, but you'd agree every step of the way. Actors are tender plants – you can't pour acid on them and expect them to flower.

Was it exciting, working for Gainsborough in those highly successful melodramas?

Oh yes. Gainsborough was a very good studio – I mean the Lime Grove one. It's always home to me. The other Gainsborough studio at Islington was closed down; the only film I did there was *Miss London Ltd*. It only had one big stage and one minute stage, whereas Lime Grove had five, two big and three small, and it had a friendly family feeling about it.

You made over twenty films during the remainder of the decade, up till 1950. Were you under contract?

I was under contract to Gaumont-British. They also leased me out to several studios, including

Ealing, where I was never so happy, because there was an edgy atmosphere (though I loved the films I did, *Champagne Charlie* and *The Loves of Joanna Godden*). It was a seven-year contract. I got £5 a day with a guarantee of fifty-two days for the first year, which is approximately £5 a week, so I didn't make a lot of money although I made three films. It ended up after seven years at the magnificent sum of £1,000 a film. After I went into *Caravan*, we tore that contract up.

What do you remember of those early Gainsborough films, *2000 Women* and *Madonna of the Seven Moons*?

I remember those very well. Frank Launder did *2000 Women*, and he was a timid sort of fellow then. I know Phyllis [Calvert] wanted to play my part and I wanted to play hers, but they wouldn't let us change. And I remember Muriel Aked very well, a lovely actress, and she and Flora Robson had some lovely scenes together. And Betty Jardine – oh, the fight we had! We were black and blue. There were no punches pulled in that. I remember we finished filming the fight late one foggy evening, and Frank said, 'Come on, we'll go down to the pub and I'll buy you both a drink,' because we were worn out. He was very pleased with us.

In *Madonna* you had the small, vivid part of Vittoria, Stewart Granger's jealous mistress.

That's right, with the black curly wig. It was rather fun and I enjoyed it very much. It was all done in the studio. In those days the sets were magnificent. They were all wood, done with heavy plaster work. They say it is expensive to build sets, but with the time you waste on location, surely it must be as broad as it is long.

Your 'bad girl' image was confirmed in 1945 with *Waterloo Road*, *The Rake's Progress* and *The Wicked Lady*.

I always said that, if they opened a script and saw 'A girl appears in camiknickers', they used to send for me. But I got good parts. I never wanted to play heroines, they're not my line of country at all. I got the reputation for having sex appeal, and, as you know, no good girl ever has sex appeal. Not in the 1940s anyway. No *good* girl even now.

The doxy you played in *The Wicked Lady* is often omitted from cast lists, yet it's one of the truest things in the film.

I think it's because I wasn't cast for it. Valerie White was cast and she did the first scene: when Margaret [Lockwood] breaks into the room and Mason's in the bed with her, that's Valerie with her

back to the camera. She developed appendicitis, and I was stuffed into a blonde wig and pushed into the part. I got all those splendid close-ups.

What do you feel about *The Magic Bow*?

I had marvellous costumes in that but not a very good part. You expect she [Bianca] is going to do something and she never does. It's a film that went wrong. Originally I believe they wanted Margaret Lockwood to play it. Presumably then it would have been a much better part. I don't know what happened. Bernard Knowles was a very good cameraman but not a director. I made two more with him – *The Man Within* and *The Reluctant Widow* – but we didn't get on very well. I remember a headline about *The Man Within*: 'Miss Kent puts the sex into Sussex' – but I don't remember much else about it.

By 1948 you were virtually solo-starring in *Good Time Girl*, *Bond Street* and *Sleeping Car to Trieste*, all for different companies.

I was being loaned out by the studio. When I signed with Gainsborough, I knew I might be loaned out. At least they did pay you, they were forced to. We used to go halves in what they got for us. I made a lot more money than if I was working for them. I didn't like *Sleeping Car* and didn't get on very well with the director, Paddy Carstairs. You never knew where you were with him. I remember Rona Anderson was in it, her first movie, but apart from that I don't remember enjoying it. I had silly clothes. I wanted to be very French in plain black and a little beret but I had to wear these silly New Look clothes. I was playing a superspy of some kind. But who was I spying for?

I've seen *Good Time Girl* recently and it is impressively hard-hitting. Were you the obvious Gainsborough star to play Gwen Rawlings?

Presumably, yes. Sydney Box had taken over by then. I enjoyed working with David Macdonald, who was a very good director with actors. He was what I call workmanlike. He knew what he wanted. I prefer a director who knows where to put the camera, gets on with the action, says what he wants in that way, and lets me do the acting, and he then can tell me whether it's right or wrong. And David was excellent in that way. In Arthur La Bern's book, the balance of Gwen's character is much better, I think. She's not more sinned against and silly, she's very young, it's true, and rather foolish, but a bit of a bad lot. The father beats her and so forth, but she wasn't quite the wide-eyed little pest she was made out to be in the film. And I thought it was better for being so, because it was the story of the actual girl who *did* get involved with these two men and the taxi murder. She is such a sad character. Her story *is* sad in a way . . .

All I remember about *Bond Street* is that I'd had appendicitis and had to do that fall down the stairs myself after I'd just come out of hospital because the double wouldn't do it. So when I am dragging myself down those stairs, that's real pain!

Did you regard getting *Trottie True* in 1949 as your biggest break to date?

Yes, the three landmarks I would say were *Fanny by Gaslight*, *Good Time Girl* and *Trottie True*. I hoped to do more musicals and more comedy. I adored *Trottie*. It's my favourite film. And Harry Waxman was a marvellous cameraman. They weren't good with the music, though. I had a battle with that. We were scheduled to start, and I hadn't heard a word about the music, so I rang up whoever was the head of Two Cities. Well, I finally managed to get half the music done, and then I had another argument about the first number. It dissolves from the brown-eyed young Trottie [Dilys Laye] to the hazel-eyed big Trottie, which was hysterical. They wanted me to sing something in a schottische. Well, you know what a schottische is [hums] – Carroll Gibbons was doing the music, and he'd written this number, so I said, 'It's a very nice number, but I come from the music halls and I tell you you cannot use a schottische at this point.' So he changed it to 6/8 time.

And another thing – yes, I *did* actually fight on *Trottie*, it's true – I wanted to prevent them, while I was actually singing the number, from cutting away too much, which they used to be very fond of, in British films. The whole point of somebody singing the song is for the audience in the cinema, not the people in the movie. So I had to devise ways to keep moving all the time so they couldn't get the scissors in, particularly during the Marie Lloyd number in the ballroom scene after I'd become the duchess. Oh, I like *Trottie*! I remember that scene when Hugh Sinclair says, 'Will you have a cup of tea?' and I say, 'Oh, many a gal's been caught with a cup of tea. A bottle of champagne, please.' And lovely Philip Stainton, who turns around and says, 'I'm in wool,' and I say, 'Oh, does it tickle?'

Was there much competition for the role of Astra in *The Woman in Question*? It seems like an actress's dream role.

I don't know. I remember Puffin [Asquith] taking me out to lunch at the Savoy Grill, and telling me about the part, and saying, 'I will be quite frank with you; we originally wanted Bette Davis.' And I said, 'I am deeply honoured that you feel I could accomplish something that you really wanted Bette Davis for.' And of course I accepted with alacrity.

It's a little patchy, I think. When I saw it, I was a bit disappointed. It's a *Rashomon* sort of story [Japanese film about four different accounts of a murder]; you're not really supposed to know what she was like. I thought the nearest to what she was really like was probably the character in the John McCallum episode – the good-hearted, lovable, don't-care-very-much sort of girl. This is the point I started from. To do a character which is five different versions of one person is very tricky. It's tricky to get enough difference and for each to be near enough to the others. I thought it was a pity that the Susan Shaw version of the character went over the edge. It wasn't a bit real.

The wife in *The Browning Version* must have been your most unsympathetic role ever. What attracted you to it?

I thought it was a splendid play. I always feel that, even with unsympathetic characters, you should always endeavour to show why you feel that character is like that. With Millie [Crocker-Harris], you can see why she is exasperated with that man, because he *is* an exasperating character. You can see why she has taken a lover and why the lover didn't want it to go anywhere, and why he slipped into that relationship, which he shouldn't have done. You can understand everyone's behaviour, and I think that's how one should create the picture. I think Millie is really fascinating, but I always said she finished my career because, in playing a woman who should have been, say, forty-five when I was only at that time thirty-two or thirty-three, they kept thinking I *was* that age. I swear it finished my career in pictures . . .

There was *The Prince and the Showgirl* with Olivier and Marilyn Monroe.

I'd forgotten that, yes. I was supposed to do a big musical number called 'I'm a little Coconut Girl' and then they ran so far over schedule and budget that it was a question of whether or not they should do the Coronation scene or the musical thing. So they paid me out of the musical scene. I think it was the wrong choice, because who the hell cared about the Abbey scene whereas the musical scene would have given the thing a lift. As for Monroe, offscreen she was just a totally insignificant little blonde, but on camera she was magic.

From 1960, you worked solidly in the theatre for sixteen years. Was this because it offered more interesting opportunities?

Well, to be honest, I have to admit I prefer working in the theatre, but then I think most actors do. Though as I get older, I'd love to make a film, if somebody would only ask me. I have a very good agent, but the trouble is I think I am plagued in a way with this curious costume-picture image from the '40s and '50s.

Was there any role you'd really like to have played?

Yes. I wanted very much to play Alice in *Room at the Top*, and I'd have been very good at it, if I may say so. I was the right age too. They didn't have to bring Simone Signoret to do it. She's a wonderful actress, but it was never meant to be a foreigner. It was this old English thing that only foreigners have sex appeal. They'd forgotten me by that time, you see, they'd forgotten that I was supposed to be the sexy girl in the movies.

Deborah Kerr

b. 1921

Actor: *Major Barbara* (1940), *Love on the Dole, Penn of Pennsylvania, Hatter's Castle* (1941), *The Day Will Dawn* (1942), *The Life and Death of Colonel Blimp* (1943), *Perfect Strangers* (1945), *I See a Dark Stranger* (1946), *Black Narcissus, The Hucksters* (1947), *If Winter Comes* (1948), *Edward My Son, Please Believe Me* (1949), *King Solomon's Mines* (1950), *Quo Vadis?, Thunder in the East* (1951), *The Prisoner of Zenda* (1952), *Julius Caesar, Young Bess, Dream Wife, From Here to Eternity* (1953), *The End of the Affair* (1955), *The King and I, The Proud and Profane, Tea and Sympathy* (1956), *Heaven Knows, Mr Allison, An Affair to Remember* (1957), *Separate Tables, Bonjour Tristesse, The Journey* (1958), *Count Your Blessings, Beloved Infidel* (1959), *The Sundowners, The Grass is Greener* (1960), *The Naked Edge, The Innocents* (1961), *The Chalk Garden* (1963), *The Night of the Iguana* (1964), *Marriage on the Rocks* (1965), *Eye of the Devil* (1966), *Casino Royale* (1967), *Prudence and the Pill* (1968), *The Arrangement* (1969), *The Assam Garden* (1985)

British studios suffered a major loss when Deborah Kerr went to Hollywood in 1947 and became an international star. Nevertheless, before this time she had established herself as one of the most attractive and incisive actresses in British films, and nearly fifty years later her performances still have a remarkable truthfulness to them. She is very affecting as the daughter who marries out of poverty in *Love on the Dole*, understands the melodramatic needs of Lance Comfort's *Hatter's Castle*, differentiates clearly among the three female protagonists of *Colonel Blimp*, suggests the passion suppressed beneath the nun's habit in Powell's *Black Narcissus*, and is entrancing as the anti-British heroine in Launder and Gilliat's *I See a Dark*

Stranger. Hollywood eventually broadened her range, notably in *From Here to Eternity*, and finally gave her a well-deserved honorary Oscar, but the images she created in those earlier British films remain ineradicably fresh. She returned to the big screen in 1985 with a finely astringent performance as a former memsahib adjusting to the Home Counties in *The Assam Garden*.

Interview date: April 1990

Unlike most of the notable British film actresses of the 1940s, you seem to have been pre-eminently a film star rather than a stage star. Was this essentially a matter of preference?

No, it was purely a matter of chance, as these things tend to be.

You made your first film appearance in *Major Barbara*. How did that come about?

Gabriel Pascal saw me on the stage when I was playing with the Oxford Repertory Company, and chose me for the part of Jenny Hill in *Major Barbara*. Gabby was hell to work with, but he did have great taste and flair.

At barely twenty years old, you starred in three films in 1941: *Love on the Dole*, *Penn of Pennsylvania* and *Hatter's Castle*. Was someone looking after your career?

I had a very good agent at the time, John Gliddon, and he got me these roles.

***Penn of Pennsylvania* and *Hatter's Castle* were both directed by Lance Comfort, a director who interests me and who is, I believe, underrated. What do you remember about him?**

I enjoyed working with Lance enormously, and I agree with you that he is very underrated and is scarcely heard of today.

***Hatter's Castle* seems to me an absorbing melodrama. Would you agree with me that British cinema, unlike American, often seemed shy of melodrama?**

Melodrama has never been well portrayed in British cinema. Our producers always seemed shy of it. In *Hatter's Castle*, I must say that working with Robert Newton was a bit nerve-wracking, but despite his faults he was a marvellous actor.

***Love on the Dole* seems an oddly bleak (and very moving) film to be made in wartime. How did you feel about this film's depiction of such lives?**

It was an excellent book and an excellent play, and I think they made a very good movie from it. Strangely enough, it was much more appreciated in America than in Britain.

What do you remember of Harold French's *The Day Will Dawn*?

It was really a propaganda piece, done in the guise of a thriller.

How did you come by the splendid triple role in *Colonel Blimp*? Did you find Michael Powell a sympathetic director of actors?

I'd had a small part in Michael Powell's earlier film, *Contraband*, but it was cut from the final print. Then he chose me for the triple role of the heroine in *Colonel Blimp*. Michael really was a brilliant man of the cinema, and I loved working for him on both *Colonel Blimp* and *Black Narcissus*. Though *Black Narcissus* looks like wonderful location shooting, it was all filmed entirely at Pinewood Studios in England.

The film you did for Alexander Korda. *Perfect Strangers*, is essentially a comedy dealing with a serious subject. Was it stimulating to work with Robert Donat? What sort of director did you find Korda?

Robert Donat was a fine actor, and Korda was both a very clever man and an unexpectedly good director.

One of your most charming '40s films is *I See a Dark Stranger*. What do you recall of the Launder–Gilliat team?

I loved the film. Frank Launder and Sidney Gilliat contributed wonderfully British humour in all their work, and I found working with them a joy.

You went to Hollywood in 1947 – what were some of the major differences you found in filming there?

Oh, the obvious differences. Hollywood has vast studios and dozens of technicians; everything was on a much bigger scale. I appreciated all my Hollywood films, with very few exceptions. They gave me such a wide range of opportunities – romantic dramas, comedies, adventure epics, and so on. I have always wanted to play completely different parts, and I think if you look at my record I *have* played just about everything. Two I did in a row – *An Affair to Remember* and *Separate Tables* – could hardly be more contrasted.

You came back to England for *Edward My Son* in 1949. What attracted you to the role of the wife?

It was an excellent and challenging role for an actress, and of course it was a great thrill to be working with Spencer Tracy. I had admired him greatly for so many years.

Your next British film was Otto Preminger's *Bonjour Tristesse*. I wonder how you found working for him?

Otto was a very clever and witty man, but he was certainly difficult to work with. However, when one met him socially, he was delightful and amusing.

How important do you think stars were in building a film industry?

I think they *were* important, but there are no longer the great studio 'star-makers', which is rather sad. I think I was very lucky to be part of those exciting days.

Who do you regard as the most influential filmmakers in your own career?

I think I can only answer that by saying just about everyone I have ever worked with!

What do you regard as the highlights of your post-'60s career?

The highlight has definitely been a British picture I made in 1984 called *The Assam Garden*, directed by Mary McMurray.

Note:

When preparing this book, I invited Miss Kerr to add to the answers given by letter in 1990 but she wrote: 'I have reread through my answers and I'm afraid I can add nothing more, much as I would like to oblige! Working with Lance Comfort on *Penn of Pennsylvania* and *Hatter's Castle* – and indeed on the other films you particularly mention [the Powell and Launder and Gilliat films] – all took place some fifty years or more ago, and I really cannot recall more than I have already said. It's half a century since I made them and I made many more films after that.' Fortunately for us, the images remain intact.

Sir Alexander Korda

1893–1956

Director: *The Stolen Bride, The Private Life of Helen of Troy* (1927), *Yellow Lily, Night Watch* (1928), *Love and the Devil, The Squall, Her Private Life* (1929), *Lilies of the Field, Women Everywhere, The Princess and the Plumber* (1930), **Service for Ladies* (1932), **Wedding Rehearsal, The Private Life of Henry VIII, *The Girl from Maxim's* (1933), **The Private Life of Don Juan* (1934), **Rembrandt* (1936), **Lady Hamilton* (1941), **Perfect Strangers* (1945), **An Ideal Husband* (1947)
*& (co-)producer.

Producer: *Men of Tomorrow, That Night in London, Strange Evidence, Counsel's Opinion, Cash* (1933), *The Rise of Catherine the Great, The Scarlet Pimpernel* (1934), *Sanders of the River, The Ghost Goes Wild* (1935), *Miss Bracegirdle Does Her Duty* (short), *Things to Come, Moscow Nights, Men Are Not Gods, Forget-Me-Not* (1936), *The Man Who Could Work Miracles, *Fire Over England, I, Claudius* (uncompleted), *Dark Journey, Elephant Boy, Knight Without Armour, The Squeaker, The Return of the Scarlet Pimpernel, Storm in a Teacup* (1937), *The Divorce of Lady X, The Drum, *South Riding, The Challenge* (exec pr), *Prison Without Bars* (exec pr) (1938), *Q Planes* (exec pr), *The Four Feathers, *The Spy in Black, The Lion Has Wings* (1939), *Over the Moon, Twenty-One Days, Conquest of The Air, The Thief of Baghdad* (1940), *Lydia* (1941), *The Jungle Book* (1942), *The Biter Bit* (short) (1943), *Anna Karenina, *The Fallen Idol, Bonnie Prince Charlie* (1948), **The Third Man* (1949), **Gone to Earth* (1950), *The Elusive Pimpernel* (co-pr)

* 'Presenter'.

Only Korda's English-speaking films are listed above.

'It was as if I had won the Derby with an unknown horse,'[1] said Alexander Korda about his success with *The Private Life of Henry VIII*, which gave a new status to British films. He is the one genuine mogul in British film history (Balcon and Rank seem, by comparison, too domestic to be thought of as 'moguls'). He was flamboyant, famously charming and wildly extravagant. 'He is, in fact, a Napoleon of dreams,'[2] wrote a columnist in 1936, chiding him for having announced at least thirty-nine post-*Henry VIII* films of 'which only eight have been made and shown.' 'And what exquisite dreams they are,' the writer concluded, of unfulfilled projects including Donat as Hamlet, Flora Robson as Queen Elizabeth, and Merle Oberon in *The Red Shoes*.

Born in Hungary, where he began his filmmaking career, he had also filmed in Vienna, Berlin, Hollywood and Paris, before he fetched up in Britain to make quota films for Paramount-British in 1931. In the following year, he set up London Films Productions, made two small films before *Henry VIII* took the film world by storm, and, in 1934, began construction of Denham Studios, which he intended to be an English Hollywood.[3] At the time, he told the reviewer CA Lejeune, 'Denham is a marvellous place ... You will admire it far more than any of our pictures ... From the minute we take over Denham, we shall be able to work at full pressure.'[4]

Well, his aspirations wildly outpaced the actuality, but in the 1930s he indisputably did make some of the British films which found world-wide audiences. By now deeply Anglophile, he believed that '... to be really international a film must first of all be truly and intensely national.'[5] He added that 'you cannot convey a proper sense of the English spirit ... unless you go down to the roots,'[6] and that 'stories that dig deep into national roots start with a handicap.'[7] He produced imperial adventures such as *The Drum* and *The Four Feathers* which are still exhilarating today; he brought HG Wells to the screen memorably in *Things to Come*; and he 'presented' that persuasive hymn to English consensualism, *South Riding*.

He is, in fact, more notable as a producer than as a director, but *Rembrandt* is an admirable 'attempt to place on the screen the unbiased life-story of a genius';[8] *Perfect Strangers* is a charming romance of wartime flowering and post-war adjusting; and *An Ideal Husband* has costumes by Cecil Beaton, and Paulette Goddard at least looks ravishingly dangerous as Mrs Cheveley.

But it is as an entrepreneur – as a deal-maker and a star-maker – that he is important in British film history. He foundered somewhat after the war, when the kind of Britishness he had purveyed began to look old-fashioned, though there was a notable deal struck in 1948 with David Selznick. 'I am quite sure that in the deal we have found a pattern for true and fair cooperation between American and British filmmakers,' thus helping British producers to achieve 'a real popularity in the American market.'[9] Certainly, this instigated *The Third Man*, one of the crowning glories of British cinema, and the first two names which appear on its credits are those of Korda and Selznick.

He was legendarily able to charm the birds out of the trees (and money out of the Prudential Assurance Company) and elsewhere in this book the actor Dulcie Gray and producer John Woolf, and others, attest to this. Ralph Richardson claimed, 'Alexander Korda continuously makes people do things against their will but seldom against their interest,'[10] and gave several of his best star performances in Korda-backed films, such as *Things to Come, The Four Feathers*, and *The Sound Barrier*. Olivier, who became a romantic hero for Korda in two films that co-starred him with Vivien Leigh, *Fire Over England* and *Lady Hamilton*, recalled his saying: 'I want you to become a star because it will help make you rich, but even more so because it will help make me rich.'[11] Korda made stars also of Robert Donat, Charles Laughton (though he complained that 'Charles needs a midwife, not a director')[12] and Merle Oberon, whom he married and who became (for a short while) the first Lady Korda.

The Hungarian Jew who, after only modest success elsewhere, came to England in 1931 and made his first film there in 1932, was ten years later knighted, partly perhaps for his wartime services to Churchill, primarily for lifting British cinema out of the provincialism in which he had found it. Though his name does not appear on the credits of most of the London Films productions of the post-war period, he remained very much involved with its fortunes and some of the most famous films of the period – for instance, Olivier's *Richard III* and Lean's *Summer Madness* – and most of the most illustrious filmmaking talents appeared under the London Films logo of Big Ben. 'I am not afraid of spending big money on big pictures,'[13] he had said

in 1937; the following two decades, even allowing for failures, bore out the efficacy of his approach.

1 Michael Korda, *Charmed Lives*, Allen Lane, London, 1980, p 104
2 Leonard Wallace, 'Korda's castles in the air', *Film Weekly*, 7 November 1936, p 43
3 Sarah Street, 'Denham Studios: The Golden Jubilee of Korda's folly', *Sight and Sound*, Spring 1986, p 118
4 Street, p 119
5 Karol Kulik, *Alexander Korda: The Man Who Could Work Miracles* (first published 1975), Virago Books, London, 1990, p 97
6 Kulik, p 97
7 Kulik, p 98
8 J Danvers Williams, 'Korda replies', *Film Weekly*, 7 November 1936, p 43
9 *Kinematograph Weekly*, 20 May 1948, p 7
10 Garry O'Connor, *Ralph Richardson: An Actor's Life*, Limelight Editions, New York, 1985, p 83
11 Thomas Kiernan, *Olivier*, Sidgwick & Jackson, London, 1981, p 112
12 Korda, *Charmed Lives*, p 312
13 'What I am doing at Denham', *Film Weekly*, 10 July 1937, p 11

Walter Lassally

b. 1926

Director of photography (unless otherwise stated): *Smith, Our Friend (1948), *Every Five Minutes (1950), *Forward a Century, *From Plan Into Action (1951), *At Whose Door?, *Festival, *Three Installations, *Wakefield Express (1952), House of Blackmail (ass ed), *The Pleasure Garden, *Strange Stories (cam ass), *Sunday by the Sea, *Thursday's Children (1953), The Passing Stranger, Another Sky (1954), *The Children Upstairs, *Continuous Observation, *Foot and Mouth, *Green and Pleasant Land, *Henry, *A Hundred Thousand Children (1955), *Momma Don't Allow, To Koritsi Me Ta Mavra / A Girl in Black, *Together (1956), *Every Day Except Christmas, To Telefteo Psema / A Matter of Dignity (1957), *George Bernard Shaw,

*We are the Lambeth Boys (1958), *An Enquiry into General Practice (1959), Aliki sto Naftiko / Aliki in the Navy, Beat Girl, Eroica / Our Last Spring, Maddalena (1960), Electra, I Liza kai i Alli / Liza and Her Double, A Taste of Honey (1961), The Loneliness of the Long Distance Runner (1962), Tom Jones (1963), *The Peaches, Psyche '59, Zorba the Greek (1964), Assignment Skybolt (1966), The Day the Fish Came Out (1967), Anikiti Epistoli / Open Letter, Joanna, Oedipus The King, Olimpiada en Mexico (shared credit) (1968), The Adding Machine, Three Into Two Won't Go (1969), Something for Everyone, Twinky (1970), Adventures of a Brown Man in Search of Civilisation, *Can Horses Sing?, Le Mans (race footage – uncr)

(1971), *Savages, To Kill a Clown, Gun Before Butter* (1972), **Bilocation, Happy Mother's Day ... Love George, Malachi's Cove, Visions of Eight* (segment only) (1973), *Après le Vent des Sables, *Carved in Ivory* (1974), *Ansichten eines Clowns / The Clown, Autobiography of a Princess, The Wild Party, Pleasantville* (1975), **Ernst Fuchs, Ivo / Fluchtversuch, The Great Bank Hoax / Shenanigans, Requiem for a Village* (additional photography) (1976), *The Blood of Hussain, Die Frau Gegenüber / The Woman Across the Way* (1977), **How the Myth was Made:* *A Study of Robert Flaherty's* Man of Aran (1978), *Hullabaloo over Georgie and Bonnie's Pictures, Too Far to Go, Something Short of Paradise* (1979), *The Pilot, Der Preis fürs Uberleben* (1980), *Engel aus Eisen / The Iron Angel, Memoirs of a Survivor* (1981), *Tuxedo Warrior* (1982), *Heat and Dust, Private School* (1983), *The Bostonians* (1984), *Indian Summer* (1987), *The Deceivers, The Perfect Murder* (1988), *Fragments of Isabella* (1989), *Ballad of the Sad Café* (1991)

* Documentary or short film.

Walter Lassally won his Oscar for *Zorba the Greek*, though he thought it was 'easier to do' than some of the other films he shot for Michael Cacoyannis. His Greek period comes between two other distinguished collaborations: first, with the Free Cinema directors, Karel Reisz, Tony Richardson and Lindsay Anderson, linking up with them in the late '50s, as they were all on the brink of feature-film making; and, later, with the Merchant–Ivory team, during what some might consider their best years, before they gave themselves over so wholly to 'heritage' filmmaking. He was clearly a major contributor to the New Wave's realist 'look' in such films as *A Taste of Honey* and *The Loneliness of the Long Distance Runner*, and to the vernal freshness of *Tom Jones*. His Ivory films are distinctive and idiosyncratic to look at, especially *Autobiography of a Princess* and *Heat and Dust*, about which, as on his work in general, he is articulate and intelligible to the layman.

Interview date: July 1994

How hard was it for you, as a German refugee, to get started in films after the war?

It was difficult to get studio work because all the ex-servicemen were coming out of the forces after the war and had a right to have their old jobs back with their old employers, so there were only a certain number of available posts. Also, the hierarchy still existed that meant it was very much 'jobs for the boys', and most jobs were filled in that kind of way.

You began as a director of photography on short films in the '50s. How did you come to meet Lindsay Anderson, with whom you did nine or ten short films?

While trying to become a clapper-boy in a big studio, I made two amateur films, the second of which was a 'semi-professional' production called *Saturday Night*. I formed a small film unit with a friend, Derek York, and we embarked on *Saturday Night*, for which he wrote the script and directed and I photographed. It was before magnetic tape and we shot everything mute, without any guide track or any sound whatsoever – just notes of what people were saying. We planned to post-synchronise the whole thing and it just got beyond us. We never got to that point, but the rushes of that material led to my first professional job as director of photography, because a producer called Leon Clore saw the material and thought it good enough to give me a job. So I started professional work on a more or less permanent basis in 1950.

My contact with Lindsay Anderson started when he was co-editing the magazine *Sequence*. They gave us some publicity in the magazine because we were always wanting short ends and gifts of material, having no money to make our film. In return for that magazine space we went around the various British film studios selling copies of *Sequence*.

The whole Free Cinema thing is often misunderstood these days. It was never a movement: it was a phrase coined by Lindsay for a group of films to be shown at the National Film Theatre. Then there was a 'manifesto', a declaration signed by Lindsay, Karel [Reisz], Tony [Richardson], myself, John Fletcher and Lorenza Mazzetti. Lindsay particularly hoped that Free Cinema would have some influence on mainstream British cinema, and of course the influence was nil. Then out of Free Cinema, with other film streams joining it, came the Woodfall company, which was really the key to the New Wave in Britain. *Room at the Top* was a forerunner of that period but the director, Jack Clayton, came from a very different tradition from either the Free Cinema people or John Schlesinger. Even if you take Richardson, Anderson and Reisz as a group, I think their approaches were very different indeed. I felt closest to Lindsay because I think his was the most poetic approach – dangerous word! I think Lindsay's films are the most deeply felt and *This Sporting Life* is a most extraordinary film. It has flaws but there are scenes in that film which have never been equalled for their sheer emotional power in any other British film.

How difficult was the actual business of filming *Every Day Except Christmas* in Covent Garden?

It wasn't very difficult. It was made possible by the recent invention of the first 400 ASA black-and-white negative material, made by Ilford and called HPS. Without that material we could not have made the film, because we used little or no lighting. The key things on that film were a combination of that film stock with hand-held cameras and the willingness to make the choice (which in those days you always had to make) between improvising and hand-holding or getting synchronised sound. The biggest problem – and my fondest memory of that film – was Lindsay wandering around the market in the late preparatory stages, saying, 'This is useless, there's nothing here.'

It may not be generally known, but it was planned as a twenty-minute film and it grew, mainly in the editing, into a forty-minute film, largely due to the generosity of Leon Clore, the producer, and the generous sponsorship of the Ford Motor Company. Ford didn't interfere in any way; they just said rather plaintively, 'If you could just avoid close-ups of the rival companies' motor cars . . .' Karel Reisz was the Films Officer for Ford Motors, which is how the whole thing came about.

Did the Free Cinema films feel very different to you from mainstream British filmmaking in the '50s?

Oh yes, absolutely. If one continues that into the Woodfall years, I think the most significant thing about *Tom Jones* is that we set out very deliberately and consciously to make a period film which would look and feel completely different from the period films of either Britain or Hollywood made before that time. It would be much closer to a documentary or realist approach than those other films – much less studio, much less artificial – and I think we succeeded there.

You shot three films in a row for Tony Richardson, in different styles: *A Taste of Honey*. *The Loneliness of the Long Distance Runner* and *Tom Jones*. Did you work closely in the early stages with him?

Yes, indeed. I see *Loneliness* and *A Taste of Honey* as being more similar than different. The differences of linearity versus flashbacks, etc, were not evident at the script stage. It was certainly true of the three films I made for Tony that they were extensively re-edited; there is an enormous difference between the first cut and the final cut – a really enormous difference. The script for *Loneliness* certainly envisaged flashbacks but the final shape of the film was very much a product of the editing, and that is also true of the other two films. The first two films were in black-and-white, and yet it was the effect of the shooting style of those two upon the shooting style of *Tom Jones* that I see as one of the most significant factors about the production of *Tom Jones*.

The genesis of *A Taste of Honey* was as follows: the script and casting were in place over one year prior to production, but the film could not be financed, because Tony wanted to make *A Taste of Honey* entirely on location and the powers-that-be on the distribution and financing side of the business were not prepared to agree to that. So the film was effectively shelved for a year. Then it was revived because *Saturday Night and Sunday Morning* was such a huge success. Tony was able to use the profits of that film to give a guarantee of cross-collateralisation. The British Lion–Bryanston group, who financed and distributed *A Taste of Honey*, agreed for him to do it in that way, albeit with considerable misgivings, provided he guaranteed that money be available as a sort of reserve. So that was the first decision, to make it all on location.

The second important decision was to use the relatively newly developed high-speed films. *A Taste of Honey* was actually filmed on three different filmstocks, and it was the first time anyone had done that on a mainstream film, as far as I know. Until that time there was only Plus X and what was called Super XX (which was only suitable for emergencies in newsreel work and never considered as an option for feature work). Plus X had a speed of 80 ASA to daylight and was always used for feature filming. The ability to use a much faster film was a major factor on *A Taste of Honey*, and I was responsible for the decision to use three different filmstocks. Not only that, but to link the granularity of the filmstock to the type of setting, so that the first apartment that they live in, being the most slummy, was shot on a very grainy filmstock, which goes hand-in-hand with the art direction. It was known when the set was designed that it would be shot on very grainy film and it would be lit in available-light style. It was lit with very little light and very few lamps, which enabled one to work in relatively small rooms and make them look as though they were not lit. If you compare the interiors of *A Taste of Honey* with those of *Saturday Night and Sunday Morning*, there is an enormous difference, which comes not from the fact that there were different cameramen but from the fact that they were lit in completely different styles and using a different filmstock. Of course the distributors and everybody in the processing labs said, 'You can't do that, we don't advise it . . .' and we said we were going to do it anyway.

Now, of course, the reflected-light technique we used is widely used for photographing colour films because in colour films you don't run into the danger of everything being too flat. You can't be too flat in a colour film, whereas in a black-and-white film, the quality of the image is very dependent on a basic minimum of contrast; once you go below that, you have no image left, it goes muddy. *Tom Jones* was my first major experience of making a colour feature film.

It has a wonderful leafy freshness about it. How was that achieved?

That was partly due to the season: it was shot in high summer. But the key decision, made by Tony, myself, the costume designer and the art director, was that, if the décor and costumes were impecc-

ably in eighteenth-century period, then the photography, the camera style, could be very modern. I think that is the key to the look of that film. It was photographed in much the same way as *A Taste of Honey* and *The Loneliness of the Long Distance Runner*, with a certain amount of hand-held camerawork.

The use of freeze frames was an editing decision which I think we didn't really need, but Tony became very depressed at the end of shooting because he thought none of the jokes worked, so he speeded it up with these tricks. The one thing that Tony never learned, I believe, was that in the editing process there can very easily come a point where a producer needs to get you by the scruff of the neck, remove you from the Moviola and send you somewhere for a holiday. You get too close to the material; you are tempted to rejig it. The first half of *Tom Jones* was very roughly, even violently re-edited because of this fear that it wasn't working, and some of Diane Cilento's best scenes were cut entirely – at least half of them.

You then did several films for the Greek director, Michael Cacoyannis, including *Zorba the Greek*. Does it make much difference to you who the director is?

It matters enormously, there is a huge difference. I often cite the difference in approach between Michael Cacoyannis and Tony Richardson, as opposite extremes of directorial approach. Cacoyannis pre-planned his scenes down to the last detail although he didn't actually make sketches. In other words, his scripts were written in shots, not in scenes, as a sort of notebook for himself. Very fortunately, it turned out that his vision, the way he looked at things, and my way of looking at things were very similar, so that we were in the luxurious situation of him being able to leave the visual, compositional side of things entirely to me and still get exactly what he wanted.

Now, Tony worked in a completely different way. He worked much more closely with the actors and wasn't all that interested in the visual side, apart from the over-all concept. He wasn't interested in individual framings or compositions, or in découpage or blocking; he worked that out with his operator, because on that film we had Desmond Davis as operator. I much prefer to operate myself, if one has enough time, but on the English films I couldn't because the union said you couldn't. So on English and some American films, the director tends to work very closely with his operator, leapfrogging over the DoP in some ways, although the DoP can lend an ear to their discussions. It is not uncommon for the DoP to occupy himself with the lighting while the director and the operator work out the details of the shot – whether to have a tracking shot or to do it in cuts or whatever.

Did you find some actors much easier to photograph than others?

I fully understand that they want to look their best and I consider it an essential part of my work to make them look their best, but even that is fraught with considerable problems! I often say that as a director of photography my work is one-third photography, one-third psychology and one-third meteorology, because people are always asking you when the sun's going to come out and you're supposed to know! I was never a diplomat and I always thought that a professional actor owed it to the rest of the company to behave professionally, and not to make great scenes about how they look.

You have made some people look fabulous. One thinks of Susannah York as one of the imperishable images of the early '60s in *Tom Jones*.

Susannah is a darling, there were never any problems with her. Rita Tushingham was more difficult to light; but she has a very interesting face, which can look very beautiful provided it is lit in a certain way, and I think I managed to achieve that. Julie Christie had no cause for complaint, I think, in the two films I did with her. I did, however, have problems with Vanessa Redgrave on both *The Bostonians* and *Ballad of the Sad Café*; we were ancient sparring partners, so we could go into a sparring match without animosity.

In 1972 you began your association with James Ivory, on *Savages*. How did you respond to him as a director?

Savages is almost my most favourite film. It is highly original; but it was not my first film with James; I shot a documentary with him in 1970, called *Adventures of a Brown Man in Search of Civilisation*, which is a portrait of the Indian writer Chaudhury, made for the BBC. The interesting things about the Merchant–Ivory films were the selection of subjects, the writing, the creation of original scripts, the feeling for atmosphere and decor – I think James is a frustrated art director. He is much more interested in the exact quality of the silverware than in the camera set-up, although he's certainly interested in the actors.

His 1975 film, *Autobiography of a Princess*,

has always seemed like a small masterpiece to me.

It arose out of the fact that they discovered a lot of footage in the vaults of the Maharajah of Jodhpur and wondered how they could present it. The film was written as a framework for the footage. It is actually in three parts: the Kensington footage, which was specially shot; the footage of interviews with other maharajahs in India, once again specially shot but not by me; and the bulk of the stuff that they view on the projector, which was archive material in the vaults of the Maharajah of Jodhpur, who had a personal photographer working for him right through the '30s. James Mason was one of the great actors of the cinema and I'm sorry I didn't have another opportunity to work with him.

On *Heat and Dust*, how did you achieve the markedly different look between the present-day sequences and the period ones?

It's interesting that you differentiate between the modern-day footage and that purportedly from the '20s, because it highlights one of the chief decisions which has to be made before you make a film like that: what difference do you create in the photographic treatment of the two periods? I always tended to be very suspicious of purely technical means – filters and so on – and I managed to persuade James [Ivory] at the beginning that, if he left it to me, I would devise a means of differentiating between the two periods. I wanted to give the 1920s sequence a softness, a pastel quality, which is true of both the colour and the movement; it would be slower, more gentle in every way. The 1980s sequence would have brighter colours, be faster-moving and perhaps have more hand-held shots, but in any event it would be entirely up to me in any particular sequence to do that, and it would also involve a certain amount of luck. When we came to shoot the bungalow sequence with Greta Scacchi, we had a slightly more hazy day than that on which we shot Julie Christie and her partner at the same location, which is turned into the post office in the 1982 sequence. It was sheer luck. Apart from that, in composing a shot for the 1923 sequence, if I saw a strident colour somewhere, some object in the background that wasn't coherent with the over-all image I had in mind for the period, then I would remove it or pan off it or frame it out.

But the change of style is simply a concept at the back of one's mind and, if there is anything that doesn't gel with that concept, then the bells ring. That is the only difference. The whole film was photographed through a fairly strong diffusion filter – both the modern and the 1923 sequence – so there is no difference there. The costumes, the décor, the photography are all of a piece, which is as it should be. I discussed these things mainly with James and to some extent with the set designer, although there is not a lot he could have done because we were adapting palaces and so on. There wouldn't have been the money to repaint huge areas or anything like that.

What would you regard as the most satisfactory achievements of your career?

I would say *Electra*, *Savages* and *Heat and Dust* but I am also very happy with *Zorba the Greek*, *A Taste of Honey* and *Ballad of the Sad Café*; In general I prefer the chamber works.

Philip Leacock

1917–1990

Director: **Out to Play* (1936), **Kew Gardens* (1937), **The Londoners* (1939), **Island People*, **The Story of Wool* (1940), *Riders of the New Forest* (serial) (1946), **Pillar To Post* (1947), *Out of True*, *Life in Her Hands*, **Festival in London* (1951), *The Brave Don't Cry* (1952), *Appointment in London*, *The Kidnappers* (1953), *Escapade* (1955), *The Spanish Gardener* (1956), *High Tide at Noon* (1957), *Innocent Sinners* (1958), *The Rabbit Trap* (1959), *Hand in Hand*, *Let No Man Write My Epitaph*, *Take a Giant Step* (1960), *The War Lover*, *Reach For Glory*, *13 West Street* (1962), *Tamahine* (1963), *Firecreek* (pr only) (1968), *Adam's Woman* (1970), *Baffled* (1971), *Escape of the Birdman* (1972)
* Documentary

One of the unexpected successes – critical and commercial – of the 1950s was a small-scale film set in a Nova Scotian forest, with a cast of grandparents, unconventional lovers and two gravely charming little boys who find and hide a baby in the woods. The film, *The Kidnappers*, established Philip Leacock as a sensitive director of children, an impression he confirmed in other films such as *The Spanish Gardener*, *Escapade* and *Innocent Sinners*. Like many directors of the period, his background was in wartime (and earlier) documentary, and his early fiction films (e.g., *The Brave Don't Cry*) skilfully combine the social and the didactic with the expectations of film storytelling. His first Hollywood film, *The Rabbit Trap*, also exemplifies his major strengths as a filmmaker, and he directed a lot of efficient television there, but his best work is arguably to be found in his British films of the '50s. Leacock's was a gentle talent, at its best in recording the minutiae of everyday life, in rooting well-observed human drama in realistic settings.
Interview date: June 1990

During the war, were you with the Army Kinematograph Unit?

I didn't start off there. I had been in the Army for about a year, doing my training. Carol Reed had been brought into the Army as an instant captain to do a film called *The New Lot*, written by Eric Ambler and Peter Ustinov. I was the sergeant whose job was to show them how to dress properly, etc, and be their liaison with the Army itself. This was a film to show people what the Army was like. Then they really remade it as *The Way Ahead*, a feature film. Later, I was in the AKU for a while; I was commissioned and directed some interesting stuff on training, although some of it was very routine. After the war, I came back and worked for the Crown Film Unit.

How did you come to be assistant director to Lawrence Huntington on *Mr Perrin and Mr Traill*?

Donald Taylor was one of the producers on *Mr Perrin and Mr Traill* and he put my name up to the actual producer [Alexander Galperson]; they just wanted me to do two weeks of background shooting down in Cornwall for the climactic sequence of Marius Goring and David Farrar fighting on a cliff. There was a lot of back-projection material, very technical, and we ended up staying there about two months. Lawrence Huntington was certainly very nice to me, and very helpful in explaining things to me when I was in Cornwall.

Did you feel you were combining the experiences of documentary and feature film-making in your first films as director – *Out of True* and *Life in Her Hands*?

Very much, yes. *Out of True* was written by my wife's father, Montagu Slater. The Government wanted us to make this film as an answer to *The Snake Pit*, because the mental hospitals had been trying for a long time to break down the image of their being 'hell holes'; this film was meant to allay people's fears about them. We shot the whole thing in a mental hospital called Nethern, somewhere in south London.

On *Life in Her Hands* we were trying to capture the reality of the locations and some of the people were actual hospital people. That was all shot on location at a hospital on the outskirts of London, near Barnet. Even the party scene was for real, partly actors and partly nurses.

The Brave Don't Cry was made for Group 3, I think.

Yes. Grierson talked to me about doing a film for Group 3, which had Government finance to help young directors. He told me about a coalmining disaster that had occurred in Ayrshire and gave me some press cuttings of the story; a lot of people had been killed and others trapped. Montagu Slater and I did some research on it and spent a lot of time in Scotland in the actual coalmine.

Montagu particularly felt that we weren't getting the full story, that these guys had been trapped in a situation where they couldn't be got out because the only escape route would have allowed gas to flare up into the mine. They had to get oxygen masks from all over Europe before they had enough to get the rescue equipment in to the trapped men. We had a party to loosen the miners up a bit, because they were wonderful, dour people who didn't say a great deal. Somebody started to blurt out what had really happened: there were about a hundred of them underground and their official leadership had lost the confidence of the men, who couldn't understand why they weren't being got out, and there was a real riot situation where the younger guys took over. It was their energy and anger that really got the British Coal Board to make this huge international effort of getting the gas masks to them.

This gave us a core of conflict which worked well. There is no music in the film, other than when the men sing a song. 'Flow Gently, Sweet Avon' was recorded by a choir which sounded absolutely terrible, so we won and used our original footage. We did some location shooting but very little; it was a very small budget. Group 3 was a wonderful idea; all their films were interesting. It's suggested they were unpopular with the unions but I don't know if that's true.

Was *Appointment in London* your first big-budget film?

Yes. I was lucky to have Aubrey Baring as producer; he was wonderful to me. Also Dirk Bogarde and I got on extremely well. It was a very hardworking picture, with a lot of night shooting; I was incapable of handing over to a second-unit director, out of pride or whatever, so I was working two shifts at one point when we were on location. We got wonderful co-operation for all the planes and so forth.

Would you say that the key element in your reputation as a British director of the '50s was your ability to direct children?

Probably. My feeling is that, especially for younger kids, acting is part of their social life, part of playing. Margaret Thompson, who had done a lot of film work with children, was absolutely wonderful and she worked with the kids more than I did. For *The Kidnappers* she actually found Vincent Winter in Aberdeen, although Jon Whiteley was known, having already done a film. We brought the children in to test for the parts; we did play situations, as we did with the film itself. Vincent couldn't read so he had to be firmly taught lines – he had a memory like a computer. He would do his own lines aloud and then silently mouth everyone else's words! I was lucky to get Jean Anderson for *The Kidnappers* because the brass wanted a bigger name. In the event there was some sort of a conflict just before we were to start shooting; Jean was available so I was able to have her as the grandmother after all.

We filmed the long wide shots of rivers and streams at Glen Affric in Scotland (not Nova Scotia), in the Highlands outside Inverness, and made back-projection plates to use back at the studio. The interiors were all studio stuff. We searched for places to build the cabin, which was stupid of us because, after all, Pinewood *was* called 'Pinewood', so we finally went out to the back of the studios and built it there! It was certainly the film I most enjoyed.

I think *The Spanish Gardener* is one of the finest films of the '50s. What do you recall of it?

Dirk originally turned the picture down; I was so upset, having become good friends after *Appointment in London*. So I suggested we get together and talk it through, and eventually it worked out all right. John Bryan was a very good producer; he had been an art director and was one of the few such who really dominated the visual look of a picture. The look of *Great Expectations* is very much John's work. On *The Spanish Gardener* John was producer but nonetheless he tore practically all of the models to pieces.

Was it the pacifist theme that most interested you about the 1955 film, *Escapade*, again with excellent child actors?

Yes, I liked the irony of it – to be a pacifist you really have to be a fighter. And I liked the children's parts. Donald Ogden Stewart actually wrote the script under a pseudonym because he wasn't allowed to have his name on the credits. I'm sure he wasn't a communist, but the McCarthy mob made it so rough for him he left the US and came over here.

Your three films in 1956, '57 and '58 – The

***Spanish Gardener, High Tide at Noon* and *Innocent Sinners* – are all for Rank. Were you under a contract?**

I had a seven-year contract with Rank, I think. Michael Balcon was the chairman of the board of the Rank film section and they turned *The Kidnappers* down on the script; Balcon said they all liked it but they didn't think there was a possibility of its being successful. We were absolutely devastated.

Some time later I had a phone call on a Saturday morning, asking if I could come in to see Arthur Rank in a couple of hours' time. So, I had a strange interview with this big man with a North Country accent, who said he was about to do something he had never done before, and that was to go against the advice of his board. He said he liked the story and believed I would do a good job of it. Then he said he had one thing to ask me, and my heart sank; but he only asked me if I would bring in 'the name of the Good Lord' – I think that was the phrase he used.

Was there a lot of location work on *High Tide at Noon* and *Innocent Sinners*? Did you favour location work?

Yes, I think most directors do. *High Tide at Noon* was done at Pinewood, but we did some shooting in Nova Scotia with a few of the cast, mainly footage of the boat landing, stuff like that. Then we did two locations in Cornwall; we had great difficulty with getting the boat started and we had one of the local fishermen on the boat in the storm scene and the engine broke down. It was a nasty fifteen minutes while this little boat was drifting nearer to the rocks and we couldn't do a damn thing.

For *Innocent Sinners* we did quite a bit of location work although all the interiors would have been shot on the stage. Flora Robson was in both of those films and she was a lovely woman. I remember she had supreme contempt for 'method' acting; she would say, 'The method I use is *my* method!' She didn't believe you had to 'feel' it; she said her job was to make other people feel it. In one scene she was to be very emotional and crying on the screen; off the set she was knitting while we were getting ready to shoot, and she began to tell a very long and complicated story. In the middle of the story she was called to do her scene, which she did with tears streaming down her face – absolutely genuine. She finished the scene, still with tears everywhere, and she said, '. . . and then . . .', and proceeded to go on with the story!

Sir David Lean

1908–1991

Editor: *The Night Porter* (1930), *These Charming People* (1931), *Insult* (1932), *Money for Speed, Matinee Idol, The Ghost Camera, Tiger Bay, Song of the Plough* (1933), *Dangerous Ground, The Secret of the Loch, Java Head* (uncr) (1934), *Escape Me Never, Turn of the Tide* (1935), *Ball at the Savoy, As You Like It* (1936), *Dreaming Lips, The Wife of General Ling, Dreaming Lips, The Last Adventurers* (1937), *Pygmalion* (1938), *Spies of the Air, French Without Tears* (1939), *Major Barbara* (ass dir, uncr co-dir), *Spy for a Day* (1940), *49th Parallel* (1941), *One of Our Aircraft is Missing* (1942)

Director: *In Which We Serve* (co-dir) (1942), *This Happy Breed* (& co-sc) (1944), *Blithe Spirit, Brief Encounter* (& co-sc) (1945), *Great Expectations* (& co-sc) (1946), *Oliver Twist* (& co-sc), *The Passionate Friends* (1949), *Madeleine* (1950), *The Sound Barrier* (1952), *Hobson's Choice* (1954), *Summer Madness* (1955), *The Bridge on the River Kwai* (1957), *Lawrence of Arabia* (1962), *Doctor Zhivago* (1965), *Ryan's Daughter* (1970), *Tomorrow Is Yours* (short) (1977), *A Passage to India* (1984)

'It was magic to me. If you knew what the London suburbs were like, you will understand – it was very grey, and the movies were a journey into another world.'[1] There could scarcely be a more striking contrast or sense of imaginative journeying than between Croydon in the 1920s and the worlds of, say, *Lawrence of Arabia* or *A Passage to India*, and, more than any other English director, David Lean became associated with the epic, with vast exotic panoramas, with great elemental forces at work. 'I love travelling, going to strange corners of the world,'[2] he said by way, perhaps, of accounting for turning from the intensely British – *English* – films of the first half of his career.

There were losses as well as gains. *The Bridge on the River Kwai*, that study of military obsession, brought his work to a vast international audience in 1957, and it had the sweep and passion of great Hollywood successes, winning seven Oscars and numerous other awards. But the losses were of two kinds. First, there would be only four more films in the remaining thirty years of his life, all of them long in gestation, all of them of epic aspirations, sometimes misplaced. 'The story of *Dr Zhivago* is very simple. A man is married to one woman and in

love with another. The trick is in not having the audience condemn the lovers,'[3] he explained. The trick, it might be added, was to get the audience to keep its mind on these protagonists in over three hours of ravishing spectacle.

The same might be said of *Ryan's Daughter*: 'And we really stuck our chin out because we've made, as it were, an old-fashioned picture ... intentionally over-romantic, so that the girl would have a frightening fall back to earth and realize that her heaven does not indeed exist.'[4] Again, the triangular love story has a hard time maintaining its visibility in three hours of pictorial grandeur. The second kind of loss, then, is that of the human drama. As the films got longer, slower, more lavish and less frequent, for some viewers at least they lost the intense personal intimacy that had characterised the earlier ones.

After a 1930s apprenticeship in 'quota quickies', he became Britain's top editor on such prestige films as *Pygmalion*, and this experience may have led him to believe that 'the good things in movies are the scenes that are made up of cuts.'[5] His directorial career (apart from some uncredited scenes on *Major Barbara*) began with his association with Noël Coward on *In Which We Serve*. Following this success, Lean directed three further Coward-based films: *This Happy Breed* ('It's a small domestic story, but it was highly successful in England. People liked it'[6]); *Blithe Spirit* ('It's awfully hard, high comedy ... it's completely unreal'[7]); and, triumphantly, *Brief Encounter*.

For many people, *Brief Encounter* remains the archetypal British film of the period. 'It's all to do with guilt ... And remember the times, remember the times,' Lean said, referring to a scene that 'contained the horror of discovery, the overlay of guilt, the lot.'[8] But it's not just 'the times' that matter: the idea that a sense of responsibilities to others might inhibit the pursuit of one's own wishes is surely not obsolete. Celia Johnson and Trevor Howard, as the ordinary couple, both married elsewhere, who surprise themselves by falling in love, still evoke a poignant sense of fleeting joys and inevitable pain. However, at the time, Lean wrote: 'As films go, it was inexpensive, but *Brief Encounter* was not a big box-office success ... The greater proportion of filmgoers are under twenty-one mentally or physically; they go to the movies to escape from reality.'[9]

These early films are marked by superb performances and an intimate ambience realised by immaculate art direction and camerawork; so, too, are the two Dickens adaptations – *Great Expectations* and *Oliver Twist*. Lean's approach to adaptation was: 'Choose what you want to do in the novel and do it proud. If necessary, cut characters. Don't keep every character and just take a sniff of each one.'[10] These remain the definitive screen versions of Dickens, illustrating, as they skilfully pick their way through tangled plots and populous casts, Lean's maxim: 'Deal with each scene as if it's the most important in the film. Clarity, clarity. The most important thing of all.'[11]

The next three films starred his then wife, Ann Todd: *The Passionate Friends*, from HG Wells's novel, is a glamorised *Brief Encounter*; *Madeleine*, based on a not-proven murder charge, makes cunning use of Todd's chiselled blonde beauty; and *The Sound Barrier* ushers in the emphasis on distant worlds rather than human problems. Todd wrote later that Lean 'never had much consideration for what actors sometimes have to go through – just a relentless drive for what he wanted from a scene'.[12] Lean himself has said: 'I have an enormous respect for this [the actor's] fear and a lot of my job is to give actors confidence.'[13] If he didn't always succeed, no one can deny that some of the finest performances in British cinema – as early as *Brief Encounter*, as late as Peggy Ashcroft's Oscar-winner in *A Passage to India* – are to be found in his films. His real monument may be in having provided the context for these.

1 'David Lean', *American Film*, March 1990, p 23
2 Quoted in Alain Silver and James Ursini, *David Lean and His Films*, Silman-James Press, Los Angeles, 1992, p 141
3 Stephen Silverman, *David Lean*, André Deutsch, London, 1989, p 153
4 Steven Ross, 'In defence of David Lean', *Take One*, July–August 1972, p 14
5 David Lean, *A Life in Films*, London Weekend Television documentary 1984
6 Silverman, p 51
7 Silverman, p 55
8 Quoted in Vivienne Knight, *Trevor Howard: A Gentleman and a Player*, Sphere Books, London, 1988, p 48
9 David Lean, *'Brief Encounter'* in *The Penguin Film Review*, No 4, Penguin, West Drayton, 1947, p 27
10 *American Film*, p 26
11 Hugh Hudson, 'Dreaming in the light', *Sight and Sound*, December 1991, p 21
12 Ann Todd, *The Eighth Veil*, GP Putnam's Sons, New York, 1981, p 97
13 Ross, p 15
NOTE: Since I wrote this note, Kevin Brownlow's magisterial biography of David Lean has appeared.

Jack Lee

b. 1913

Director: **The Pilot is Safe* (1941). **Ordinary People* (co-dir) (1942), **Close Quarters* (1943), **By Sea and Land* (1944), **The Eighth Plague* (1945), **Children on Trial* (1946), *The Woman in the Hall* (1947), *Once a Jolly Swagman* (1948), *The Wooden Horse* (1950), *South of Algiers* (1952), *Turn the Key Softly* (1953), *A Town Like Alice* (1956), *Robbery Under Arms* (1957), *The Captain's Table* (1958), *The Circle of Deception* (1960)
* Documentary.

Like several other British directors of the period (e.g., Pat Jackson and Philip Leacock), Jack Lee cut his teeth on documentary filmmaking, during and immediately after the war. In fact, *Children on Trial*, a documentary focusing on juvenile delinquency, which Lee both wrote and directed, remains his favourite among his films. The influence of these early filmmaking years is felt in the speedway racing drama, *Once a Jolly Swagman*, which has a very convincing feel for place, both in its use of the New Cross speedway stadium in South London and in its evocation of working-class life. He had a big popular success with his next film, *The Wooden Horse*, based on Eric Williams's bestselling account of his wartime escape, and another with *A Town Like Alice*, this time based on Nevil Shute's wartime bestseller. Lee showed a fresh, light touch for reactivating familiar comic ingredients in *The Captain's Table* but, after one further film in 1960, he retired to live in Australia.
Interview date: October 1990

Did you join the Crown Film Unit in 1940?

Yes, the GPO Film Unit changed its name to the Crown Film Unit in 1940 but it was run by the same people. On the first night of the Blitz, Pat Jackson and I decided, as the bombs were falling like mad at about five o'clock, that we would go out and do some filming that night. We were working at our Blackheath studio and we were mixing the sound-track for a film. We filmed all over the East End that night; I fell into the Thames with the camera clutched to my tummy so it wouldn't be damaged; and that was the start of the famous film called *London Can Take It!* Harry Watt liked what we filmed that first night, and sent us out to do more filming every night over the next week or so. I did about one film a year – it took a lot of time to research and write them as well as make them.

My final film for the Unit was *Children on Trial*, which friends say is my best film. It's about a young thief, a juvenile delinquent; it runs for about seventy-five minutes. I wrote and directed it and invited a famous critic, Richard Winnington, to see a rough-cut one Saturday morning. I thought, if he liked it, he would write a piece about it. He did so, saying it was brilliantly written and directed, which I thought was a bit over the top!

I then went to work with Ian Dalrymple's Wessex Films, one of those semi-independent production companies, like Cineguild, under the Rank umbrella of Independent Producers. Dalrymple was a charming and well-educated man, the shyest man I ever

knew. We made a few films together, unsuccessful ones, and he then set up a company making documentaries under the Marshall Plan. I never worked on any of those because I'd had enough of documentaries by then.

There was one thing about *Woman in the Hall*, my first film for Wessex, which revolted me. It reminded me of when I was a child and my mother would send me out on begging expeditions, because she never had any money. It was a bloody awful novel and a terrible film. It was a rare starring role for Ursula Jeans, and she was a splendid woman. Jean Simmons and that wonderful actor Cecil Parker were also in it, and I learned a lot about comedy delivery and timing from him.

You had a change of pace with your second Wessex film. *Once a Jolly Swagman*. What was your experience of working with Dirk Bogarde?

I liked that. Dirk, even then, was a splendid actor, terrified of motorbikes and rightly so, because he'd had a terrible accident about which I knew nothing at the time, but he was jolly good. I built part of a speedway track in a field to do some night scenes; we stripped a truck down to the chassis and Dirk was strapped on to the back of it, tethered by huge elastic bands which forced him down. We drove round that track all night in the dark and I was as frightened as he was.

A lot of it was shot south of the river, and at the New Cross Speedway, which was a bit small but easy to work in. I enjoyed doing it because it was physical, there was action and I had good actors like Bill Owen and Bonar Colleano, and Patric Doonan, who, sadly, committed suicide when he was quite young. Renee Asherson did her part very well because she wasn't that sort at all. Richard Winnington praised the unsentimental treatment of working-class life, which was uncommon in those days. He was working-class himself, as I was. I co-wrote the screenplay with William Rose; and we would have daily meetings to decide on the next bit.

Did you seek out *The Wooden Horse*, which is one of the great escape stories?

Yes, Ian and I had read it and agreed we should do it. I learned later that Johnny Mills had wanted it too; we bid more than he did for the rights, so we got it and Eric Williams [author] and I did the screenplay. I expect John would have been very good in it also, probably better than Leo Genn, who was very stolid as an actor. Tony Steel was fine to work with – just a physical type, a young chap who could do certain things, though he didn't have much acting to do in this. I enjoyed making it, even though a lot of it went over budget. We had to reshoot certain scenes which weren't good enough. Most of it was made in Germany and I've always enjoyed location work. We had to build a POW camp; there were lots of POW camps still in Germany but they were mostly occupied by displaced persons waiting for their immigration papers for Australia, America, and so forth.

There were many reasons for it going over budget. Firstly there was the weather, but probably a lot of it was my fault, taking too long to shoot and shooting too much stuff. Also there was indecision on my producer's part about the ending; Ian said we should shoot things in two different ways. The ultimate ending was a perfectly reasonable one but I was off the film by then. Ian shot it himself.

Then I was out of work for a year; *The Wooden Horse* was a great success but I didn't get any of the profits and my name didn't bring in any work. Just before the end of that year I was offered *South of Algiers*, which was a piece of old hokum, made almost entirely on location. It was quite fun, but it was all cliché stuff, with goodies and baddies and all those spahis riding around chasing bandits.

Your made three consecutive films for Rank. Were you under contract?

The first one, *A Town Like Alice*, came about because I had met Joe Janni, who liked my work. He was an Italian refugee from Mussolini's fascists,

who came to Britain in 1938, a splendid man. One day Joe said he was sending me a script he'd just received. I read it that evening and phoned him to say we should make it. It was *A Town Like Alice*; the script was written by WP (Bill) Lipscombe. I then read the novel and realised Lipscombe had very cleverly cut the book in two, because in fact it is two stories, the second half being set entirely in Australia. The script made me cry and I knew it would make audiences cry too. When Joe and I put this project to Rank they agreed immediately. I worked on the script with Lipscombe first, then with Richard Mason, an old friend, and we rewrote certain scenes and invented a few others.

Then we did a budget and went to Malaya and Singapore. I soon realised that if we cast the film in the UK, decided on their exact clothing, and filmed their characteristic ways of walking, we could find a second cast in Malaya and, if we were careful, we could work very close to them on location. So I always had a strong feeling that I made the film twice: first in Malaya, because I did a great deal of shooting there; then back at Pinewood, shooting all night with the cast wading through mud. We had to fortify them with brandy to keep them going – they were splendid, those women, both in Malaya and in England. I think Virginia McKenna never looked better than when she was covered in mud! A marvellous actress and woman. Marie Lohr and Nora Nicholson were both quite old when they did the film but they didn't mind the arduous work. They were good parts, with good scenes for all of them, and they were doing work they enjoyed. Only recently I learned from Jean Anderson that Renée Houston hated having to wear those terrible clothes, the rags, but, by God, she was good at it. Peter Finch was cast because of his Australian connection. He had a small part in *The Wooden Horse*. I don't think we ever considered anyone else for the part.

How did you come to do *Robbery Under Arms*, from another Australian novel, again with Finch?

After the success of *A Town Like Alice*, Rank put Joe Janni and me under contract for two years as a team. I wanted to work with Finch again and I was attracted to Australia. I remembered landing in Darwin in the mid '50s when it was almost a one-horse town. It was fascinating for an Englishman, coming out to this extraordinary experience, so I wanted to make another film there.

I made a mistake choosing *Robbery Under Arms*,

a complicated Victorian novel with masses of plots and sub-plots, and too much moralising. However, I went ahead with it and chose the part for Peter Finch, who complained that he was overshadowed by everyone else, and, in a way, he was right. Janni and I weren't happy with the script and would have liked to put it off for another year. But we were under pressure from Rank and we had to go ahead with an inadequate script. There are one or two nice scenes in it but it's too slow and talky.

Though it has a lot of familiar ingredients, your next film, *The Captain's Table*, is very fresh and funny.

I thought I'd like to make a comedy at that point, although I really didn't know anything about comedy. I said, 'All we need are funny scenes, funny lines, actors who can pull faces, and that's it.' Joe got a lot of marvellous people writing for it – Bryan Forbes, Nicholas Phipps and John Whiting – and they wouldn't let me near the script. I liked Nadia Grey very much indeed. She brought a very different quality to the film, living as she did in Paris. Donald Sinden was very good too; it was fairly conventional for him, but I was surprised at just how good he was when I saw it again recently. And we had some good old ham actors in it, like Reginald Beckwith, camping away like mad.

Why did you stop making films after *Circle of Deception* in 1960?

Films gave *me* up, in a sense, in that I wasn't wanted. I lost my confidence and I think I lost my enthusiasm. The whole face of the industry was changing at that time and I remember seeing a newspaper article referring to me as 'the veteran British film director'. I thought, '*Am* I?' I realised new talent had taken over and it was unlikely I would make another film. Although I wasn't happy about it, it was something I had to accept. I'd enjoyed my life as a filmmaker very much indeed.

Mike Leigh

b. 1943

Director and screenwriter: *Bleak Moments* (1971), **Meantime* (1983), *High Hopes* (1989), *Life is Sweet* (1990), *A Sense of History* (short) (1992), *Naked* (1993), *Secrets and Lies* (1996), *Career Girls* (1997)

* Television film, some cinema screenings.

Mike Leigh has said: 'It is perfectly obvious to me that my films are motivated by a love for people. My job is to put characters on the screen the way people are – which is to say warts and all.' Born in Salford (home of *A Taste of Honey*, poetic example of 1960s realism), Leigh has had a curious film career. After *Bleak Moments* in 1971, and through no wish of his own, he made no further cinema features until 1988. His work is set in alienating urban landscapes of modern Britain, of which he takes a harsher view than Ken Loach, though his films are less overtly political than Loach's. Leigh's films are also shot through with odd, barely contained outbursts of anarchic social comedy, and he insists on the importance of this comic element. He also professes to 'remain fervently committed to making films about the unextraordinary lives of ordinary people – and making that interesting and meaningful'. So far, and the opinion is intensified by his most recent film, the masterly *Secrets and Lies*, which won the Palme d'Or at the Cannes Film Festival, he is succeeding triumphantly.

Interview date: June 1996

How important is your background in the theatre to your work as a film director?

It's important from a practical point of view, in the sense that there are essential skills that I learnt in the theatre context and which, I suppose, conform not with what I do but *how* I do things in making films, particularly as regards a way of building stories with actors and working over a sustained period. Also, there is a kind of theatrical element in my films, although I wouldn't want to overstate this, and it's certainly not conscious on my part, but there is a degree of heightening that goes on which may relate to certain aspects of my theatre work.

However, having said all of that, I would stress very strongly that, as a person born in 1943, and thus being somebody who started to go to the pictures from the late 1940s onwards, for me, film at the cinema and filmmaking is absolutely, categorically, my first love and passion and motivating force. So even when at the age of seventeen in 1960 I left school and went to the Royal Academy of Dramatic Art to train as an actor, and then went on to art school and film school in the first half of the 1960s, it was with a view to making films – preposterous fantasy though that was at that stage – that I did so. So that the period of 'working in the theatre', prior to making films, was a period of training and learning about things but also a period of exile, really. Because, you know, there was no access to making films during that period; it was just carrying on doing what was accessible, i.e. theatre, prior to the time when it became possible to start to make movies. And during that period, I went to the London Film School and did actually make some very short, and now forgotten, films. All I really wanted to do was get my hands on a movie camera and get it done.

So I am first and foremost a filmmaker and although it's biographically true that I come out of a theatre background, it's spiritually not the case at all. And the theatre was a kind of journey to be

undertaken of necessity, both educational and practical, on the way to actually fulfil the real ambition, which was to make films.

How did you come to get your first film, *Bleak Moments*, off the ground? And the reference to Memorial Pictures – is that Michael Medwin and Albert Finney's production company?

Absolutely. It was quite straightforward. Basically, we approached them and they gave us the money. It was a period when Albert had come into some money through having gone through a percentage rather than a flat fee for *Tom Jones*. They'd made a couple of films, including Stephen Frears's *Gumshoe*, and they backed this film of mine, for which there was no script and for which I could only describe a stage play that I'd done, also called *Bleak Moments*. And to Albert's and Michael Medwin's eternal, immortal place in wherever it is, they said, 'Yeah, OK, we'll go for it.'

Now, the interesting thing is that this was actually a BFI–Memorial Enterprises and Autumn co-production. Autumn Productions was myself and a guy called Les Blair, who also directs now. The BFI bit is quite interesting historically because in order for it to be an 'official experimental film', in other words to be registered as a BFI experiment, it had to be a BFI film, and being an 'official experiment' meant that you didn't have to pay union rates. So, everybody who worked on the film, no matter what department and including the actors, did it for £20 a week. That was the deal and that's how we got to make the picture for £18,500 – 35 mm, 111 minutes, Eastmancolour and costing peanuts. But the thing was that the minimum amount that the BFI, in their rules, could put into a film was £100 and their contribution to the budget of *Bleak Moments* was £100, which made it possible to make the film.

Did you think of it as being in any way descended from the earlier kinds of British

realism – the documentary movement of the '30s and '40s and then Lindsay Anderson, Karel Reisz and that New Wave realism?

You couldn't help, in some implicit way, but assume yourself to be in that tradition. But I don't see them as an influence, though I see they were in a general way an inspiration. I remember when I was about fifteen or so going to see *Room at the Top*; I had a lot of time for Jack Clayton; I think he was a much underestimated director. And, looking at it again with hindsight, it's a good film but, in a way, it's a bit like a lot of those films were – a bit stagey. But growing up as I did in Salford, and actually going to the pictures in a cinema which was surrounded by grey Lowry landscapes and back-streets, to see a movie where you actually saw that landscape was very resonant and important for me – but as a kind of inspiration rather than as an influence.

But I have to say that, even though *Bleak Moments* was actually adapted from a play (this was the only way of getting it going), I believe very strongly in making films, and did even then, that are originals. So far as I'm aware, not one single one of those [New Wave] films was ever based on an original screenplay. I think all of them, unless there are some I don't know about, were adapted from a novel or a play and there was a certain staginess about them. There were things about them which were exciting and cinematic but more, as I say, as a general thing that was going on that you couldn't help feeling part of, rather than something that I felt as a tradition to which I was in some way connected.

If there is a tradition of English filmmaking of a very specific nature about which I feel a much stronger connection with as an aspect of my films – the humorous aspect – it is with Ealing comedies and, to a lesser extent, with the work of the Boultings. I grew up looking at those films as a kid and as a teenager and they had a way of depicting the world that was comic but still 'realish'. It related to the real world, notwithstanding a certain kind of caricature, and it would be wrong to deny those roots.

I was going to ask: did you grow up enjoying British films and who were some of the key figures you admire?

The thing is, I grew up passionately looking at cinema but, until the 1960s when I went down to London, the only films I saw were Hollywood and British movies. The only two films I remember that had subtitles were the dreaded *Le Ballon Rouge* – it bored me to death then, and it bores me to death now – and of course *Rififi*, which was shown because it had a long sequence where nobody speaks so I suppose they thought it was OK to show it to the audience up there. So therefore everything and anything in British cinema was what I grew up very much being educated by, until I discovered world cinema in the '60s.

You made no more cinema films until 1988: how far was that a matter of choice, how far to do with the state of the British film industry?

It was absolutely, categorically not a matter of choice at all! It was a hundred per cent a matter of the state of the British cinema. It had nothing to do with choice: the notion is ludicrous. I've already described to you how my passion was to make movies and we got to make *Bleak Moments* and it won a couple of international prizes and it was very well received. If you'd said to me then that it would be seventeen years before the next feature film, I don't know what I would have done. It was like saying to me now that my next film would be in 2014. It was a horrible fact but you could *not* make picture films.

The '70s was perhaps the worst decade ever in British cinema.

Totally, it didn't exist. What happened was that those of us who were lucky enough, and plenty weren't, got to carry on making films, very consistently, very industriously and very prolifically between us – *but* all for television. We used to sit around at the BBC, because it was the most liberal and richest place to be. We'd say, Look, we make these films on 16mm, we've put all this time and effort and energy into them, they're shown on television once, maybe twice. The world out there, outside of the UK, doesn't know what we're doing; they don't think we have a cinema; we can't even send them to festivals. Why don't you let us make them on 35mm, give them a theatrical life first, export them overseas, promote them and *then* show them on television? And they said, No, no, you can't do that, it's technically impossible, the unions wouldn't allow it, what's the point of having things on television afterwards, etc. Well, of course, eventually Channel 4 began and that's what they did. And it changed the face of filmmaking possibilities; not exactly overnight, but it did make a serious difference and that's really the start of the revolution.

So, for various reasons, I didn't get to do an actual feature until 1988 and that's the reason why there was such a gap. I did actually make one of the earliest Channel 4 films, which was *Meantime*.

Meantime was shown in a cinema in Melbourne.

It was in Australia. But you see *Meantime* was just a victim of history really. If *Meantime* had happened six months later, it would have been made on 35mm and had a proper theatrical life, whereas it was made on 16mm. But they were still formulating their plans and they hadn't quite got their policy together. We desperately wanted to do it on 35mm but they just had cold feet. Six months later it would have happened. In fact it's a tragedy because the film I think really would have taken off had it had a proper international release. It was never in the cinemas anywhere except Australia. All my television films have been shown at various times in festivals and so on, but never with a proper commercial release like *High Hopes*, or *Meantime* in Australia.

How different is making feature-length films for television from making feature films for the cinema?

Fundamentally it isn't and I have never really considered it much. A film is a film is a film. However, if you were making a film for telly and were on location, you'd look through the camera and you'd discuss with the cameraman. We might say, It's a long shot, and you see him at the end of the street, and maybe, given the size of domestic screens, we should go a bit tighter on him, but that's about as far as it ever went. The only other difference was that you worked quicker and, whilst we worked to very high standards, we did not work to 35mm motion picture standards, but that's to do with the size of the budgets. But in principle a film is a film and every film I've ever made on 16mm has been shown somewhere along the line successfully in a theatrical context and of course conversely movies are seen on little screens all the time. So it was never a consideration for me at all. You made films but you weren't making them for the cinema. It's as easy as that.

Can you give me some sense of how you go about the director's job on the set? How much or what sort of guidance do you give? How much use of improvisation do you make?

Well, all my films evolve out of improvisation and the scripts come out of improvisation, so in a way the answer goes without saying. But I'm a very precise director. If you look at my stuff it's very firmly directed and very clearly directed. On the whole I'm not very excited by improvisation *on camera*: the whole thing has evolved from improvisation; all the joy and delight of that has gone on; and, for me, what it's all about is distilling it down to something that is coherent, ordered, dramatic and cinematic. I don't know quite where to begin answering that question. For me, filmmaking is very much about acting, it's very much about working collaboratively with a cinematographer, it's working in a way where collaboration between cinematographer and designer is very important, between actor and designer, costume designer, make-up designer – all these people.

They say that the atmosphere on my shoots is particularly well organised and very friendly and very relaxed. And that's partly from the time we spend together. On *Secrets and Lies*, we spent five months with the actors preparing it before we ever got around to shooting it, and that means that, with my sort of films, you haven't got actors who are wearing costumes they've only just been given and places they're supposed to be living in but have only just seen, and playing husbands and wives when they've only just met, and not knowing who their characters are and how to play them, and being nervous about technicalities. The actors on my film would say that, because it's come out of an organic process, they are able to deal with the technical requirements of the actual shooting better than actors often are, and that means that the actor serves the camera and the camera serves the acting, and we all pull together and there's a real kind of *esprit de corps*.

All your films have marvellous acting performances and I wondered if that is really perhaps the major interest to you. Some directors seem scarcely interested in the actors.

It is *a* major interest, I'm fascinated by acting, I love actors, I trained as an actor, I am concerned with acting, acting is fascinating and what you can do with acting is very important indeed, but it is not the only interest. I am equally interested by film and film considerations, I went to art school, I trained at a film school, I have a visual background as well, and for me it's all these things coming together. I enjoy the shoot, I enjoy the editing, I enjoy everything to do with sound. I am known as the soundman's friend because I involve myself with wild tracks and I think in terms of sound. I make things happen that help the sound editing, I'm fascinated by editing. To me, it's all part and parcel of the same thing. I hate the misrepresentation that I'm an 'actors' director' but not concerned with other aspects of the film – that's not true at all. And one of the things I love as much as anything is what happens to a film when you start to work with a composer – that's fascinating.

Talking about these other collaborators, you've often used the same editor, Jon Gregory, the same cinematographer, Dick Pope, production designer, Alison Chitty, producer Simon Channing-Williams, and some actors who recur. How important to you is that kind of continuity?

It's terribly important. You progress with people, you move forward, and, obviously, if you have a rapport with somebody you want to work with them again. I mean there are directors, who will remain nameless, who famously always work with a new cinematographer and you wonder why, what's the problem? I've been blessed with three tremendous cinematographers. A guy called Remi Adefarasin, who shot all my BBC films, Roger Pratt, who shot *Meantime* and *High Hopes*, and whom I lost to Terry Gilliam when he came to do *The Fisher King*, and then Dick Pope, and I kind of stopped with him and we really had a great rapport. You know there are people who approach filmmaking just as a kind of nine-to-five thing. For me it's a way of life. Dick and I really do have a rapport, we talk the same language and therefore you see it in what's on the screen, I think.

How far is filmmaking tied into matters of political commitment? Your films are always being seen as commentaries on certain aspects of British life. Is that crucial to you?

It is and it isn't. The primary things that my films are about are not England or Britain. Although obviously when you look at something like *Four Days in July* or *Meantime*, which is partly a film about unemployment, or *High Hopes*, which refers very specifically to Margaret Thatcher, there are aspects of those – certain class things – that are pretty clearly English. Still, if you take *High Hopes* for example, the thing that *High Hopes* is primarily about is how and when and whether to have babies and how to deal with growing old and being an ageing parent or having an ageing parent. I think that – and I hope – what my films are about in essence are just basic things like living and dying and surviving and work and relationships and families and all the rest of it.

As to the political side of what I do, unlike some other filmmakers I don't make films that make overt political statements. I think my films ask more questions than they supply answers. They are reflective, they're emotional, they're intuitive, they're implicitly political rather than explicitly so.

I guess most people think of you as a realist director, but it seems to me you're always pushing the limits of realism by suddenly making us come to terms with anarchic comedy. Like that zany sister in *High Hopes* or the anorexic daughter played by Jane Horrocks in *Life is Sweet*. How do you respond to this idea of the comic pushing away at the edges of realism?

I think that's absolutely accurate. I would have said that too. I think in different films I pitch it at different levels. *Meantime* doesn't quite have that comic pitch at the comic thing although you've got a guy that comes around at one point and talks about windows and anthills. He's the same actor, Peter Wight, who plays the security guard in *Naked* and I think it's interesting because there's a slight relationship between those two characters.

That long dialogue David Thewlis and Peter Wight have together in *Naked* is very daring. It's as though you just suddenly got fascinated by the discussion, and decided to let it have its head.

It's interesting you should say that. That scene is a very good illustration of how I would have only been able to get that action and that dialogue going on by the way we did it, which is to say by rehearsing physically at night in that empty building. Because only when I can *see* the event in the location, in other words in visual terms, am I able to organise the writing of it. So although you say it's just letting the argument have its head, what is going on cinematically and visually is integral to how it works; it's not just a whole lot of talking.

Not many films dare to assume their audience will accept a long discussion of a serious nature.

No, that's right. And, as a matter of fact, when we were editing it there was some doubt from some of the people backing it: you know, 'You ought to abbreviate this because you'll lose the audience,' and I said, 'Look, people are not thick.' I mean, if it loses the audience at this stage then the film is a turkey. It's never been an issue: people never question that scene and I think it doesn't lose the audiences. I think it's just too interesting. It's about things that ordinary people suddenly recognise as being about them; we are talking about *you* and *me*, about this whole thing of the serious prospect of, say, having laser tattoos instead of credit cards. It's going to happen in our lifetime.

With *Secrets and Lies* you seem to me to be adopting almost a minimalist attitude to certain aspects of film practice and I don't know how conscious this is. There is a breath-taking scene between Brenda Blethyn and Marianne Jean-Baptiste when they go to the café and I think it's very daring of a director, and shows great faith in the actors, to leave the camera on them for an extremely long time.

Nine minutes. Well, you see, I appreciate the spirit in which you say it and in that sense I take it as a kind of compliment. However, I've argued with people about that technique, for example in Carl Dreyer's *Gertrud* where the camera hardly ever moves and it becomes a kind of affectation, although I think it's a very strong film in many ways. But it's so relentless, so unyielding, that it seems to impose itself on the action. If I did that, then I think it would be unhealthy. The camerawork in *Secrets and Lies* and the cutting are very varied and all kinds of different devices are used: the camera sometimes moves around and sometimes it doesn't. It depends on the scene and the moment and the dynamics and the context within the film. There are two scenes in *Secrets and Lies* where the camera is pretty static: one is that, and the other one is in the barbecue scene towards the end. Well, there you can see there's a huge amount of choreography, it's very precisely worked out, and I wanted that to happen for different reasons, because there I felt there were so many things on the go. There's the food and the comings and the goings and there's the mounting tension and the threat of what's going to happen when they find out about Hortense and there's the general kind of physical nervousness of Cynthia and so on. In each sequence you use the camera or the cutting or whatever according to its needs. If it is appropriate to let it happen and to be absolutely static, then that would only make sense to me within the broader context of varied ways of using shooting and editing.

So, I'm slightly hesitant to allow the notion that it is minimalistic to take too much of a hold, it's just how that scene is shot. In the end it's a function of what's going on. To be honest about it, there is a trick in the scene which not everybody seems to have spotted, but the fact of the matter is that it is supposed to be a Saturday evening and it's near Holborn station and they go off in that direction, which, to be literal about it, must be somewhere in the direction of Covent Garden. Now, where on a summer evening on a Saturday would you find such a quiet, empty café? It's nonsense really, so there is a heightening poetic licence involved there and in that sense it's a minimalistic choice.

It's not often you see films that seem to show such trust in the actors, deciding where the camera's going to be and letting them get on with it.

And the fact is, with actors like that you can do it. You don't have to wade in there and shoot every which way to cover them. One of the great screen performances, we cannot deny, is Marilyn Monroe's in *Some Like it Hot*, but we know she couldn't remember half a word, and the whole thing was a mess. But by some means, they managed to film every bit and stick it together and you'd never know. When you've got actors who are at the other end of the spectrum, who really are doing the business like they [Blethyn and Jean-Baptiste] do, goodness, you're free to do that.

And in the barbecue scene, it's almost a theatrical way of arranging people. I loved the stillness of that. Then, once the barbecue's over and they've gone inside and the beans have been spilt, then the shooting fragments. I wondered if that was intentional?

That's why I did it, because I knew that was going to happen. Once you get inside, you're going to have to shoot everybody's individual shot and really investigate the scene in the most detailed way with a great deal of editing.

What can you tell me about Thin Man Films and your association with Simon Channing-Williams, with Film Four and British Screen?

Simon and I formed Thin Man Films: we first met when he was the first AD [Assistant Director] on a film I made for the BBC called *Grown-Ups*. He came in as co-producer for Portman Productions on *High Hopes* and after that we decided to form our own company exclusively to make my films. We formed Thin Man Films, which is named after our respective corpulent shapes, his particularly, and our first film was *Life is Sweet*. We also made *Naked* and *Secrets and Lies* and a short film called *A Sense of History* – and it's the only film I've made which isn't actually written by me but by Jim

Broadbent, the actor who plays the only character in it apart from the narrator. It's just a kind of comic, smooth documentary about an earl walking around his estate.

And we've done a number of other things, like a famous trailer for the London Film Festival and a number of commercials. The relationship with Channel 4 is very good, it goes back to *Meantime*;

and Channel 4 have actually been involved in every single one of my feature films, finally including *Secrets and Lies*. It was exclusively CiBy2000 in Paris but Channel 4 bought all the British rights, for theatrical and television screenings. And they've backed another film I'm just finishing which doesn't have a title yet. British Screen have also been very supportive, especially on *Naked*.

Vivien Leigh

1913–1967

Actor: *Things Are Looking Up, The Village Squire, Gentleman's Agreement, Look Up and Laugh* (1935), *Fire Over England, Dark Journey, Storm in a Teacup* (1937), *A Yank at Oxford, St Martin's Lane* (1938), *Gone With the Wind* (1939), *Twenty-One Days,* *Waterloo Bridge* (1940), *Lady Hamilton* (1941), *Caesar and Cleopatra* (1945), *Anna Karenina* (1948), *A Streetcar Named Desire* (1952), *The Deep Blue Sea* (1955), *The Roman Spring of Mrs Stone* (1961), *Ship of Fools* (1965)

'Alex was like a father to us – we went to see him with every little problem we had. We usually left convinced that he had solved it – or that we'd got our own way.'[1] So said Vivien Leigh of Alexander Korda.

Like Merle Oberon and Margaret Leighton, also exquisite beauties, Vivien Leigh owed her start to the Korda star-building processes; but it cannot be said that British cinema made anything like proper use of her. Korda, who undoubtedly had an eye for stars and a talent for soothing their anxieties, was also unreliable in building them up, often keeping them waiting years to showcase them, and then sometimes not choosing wisely. Films such as *Storm in a Teacup* and *Twenty-One Days* are adequate entertainments but hardly star-makers.

Vivien Leigh was one of the most famous women of her time, a household name indeed, but she was never primarily or even seriously famous as a star of British films. Having said, 'I couldn't possibly play a Southern belle. The accent!,'[2] Leigh became an Oscar-winning world star in Hollywood as Scarlett O'Hara, and gained a further Oscar there a dozen

years later for *A Streetcar Named Desire* (after playing Blanche on the stage in London, she said, 'Knowing her so well helped enormously when we made the film.'[3]) But she was never given anything comparable to do in Britain. Pre-war, she had given evidence of a pleasing minor talent in *Fire Over England* (with her future husband, Laurence Olivier), in two films for Victor Saville, *Dark Journey* and *Storm in a Teacup*, in *St Martin's Lane*, and – with a lively display as a minx – in *A Yank at Oxford*. Post-war, she was cast beyond her capacities – or at least beyond those of her directors – in two major failures, *Caesar and Cleopatra* (for Gabriel Pascal) and *Anna Karenina* (for Julien Duvivier), in both of which she was out-performed by her senior male co-stars, Claude Rains and Ralph Richardson respectively. Kieron Moore, who played Vronsky in *Anna Karenina*, recalled: 'She wanted to show the hard, driving nature of Anna's obsession,'[4] but that was not Duvivier's intention. She made only two further British films: *The Deep Blue Sea*, a Korda production dominated by Kenneth More's one perfect screen role as her younger, ex-

RAF lover, and *The Roman Spring of Mrs Stone*, in which she is poignant as a middle-aged woman grasping again at the chance of a younger lover. She seems to have wanted, above all, a stage career to compare with Olivier's. This eluded her, as did major British film stardom, though no doubt her two American Oscars offered compensation.

1 John Cottrell, *Laurence Olivier*, Weidenfeld & Nicolson, London, 1975, p 112
2 Quoted in Thomas Kiernan, *Olivier*, Sidgwick & Jackson, London, p 156
3 Maud Miller, 'Upsets over *Cleopatra*', *Picturegoer*, 16 February 1952, p 17
4 Quoted in Anne Edwards, *Vivien Leigh*, Methuen, London, 1987, p 253

Margaret Leighton

1922–1976

Actor: *Bonnie Prince Charlie, The Winslow Boy* (1948), *Under Capricorn* (1949), *The Astonished Heart, The Elusive Pimpernel* (1950), *Calling Bulldog Drummond* (1951), *Home at Seven, The Holly and the Ivy* (1952), *The Good Die Young, Carrington VC, The Teckman Mystery* (1954), *The Constant Husband* (1955), *The Passionate Stranger* (1957), *The Sound and the Fury* (1959), *The Waltz of the Toreadors* (1962), *The Third Secret* (1963), *The Best Man* (1964), *The Loved One* (1965), *Seven Women* (1966), *The Madwoman of Chaillot* (1969), *The Go-Between* (1970), *Bequest to the Nation, From Beyond the Grave* (1973), *Galileo* (1974), *Great Expectations* (1975), *Trial By Combat* (1976)

'I'd decided to storm in and see him – have it out with him and put up my own ideas . . . But there he would be in his office smiling, happy to see me . . . and all my set speeches of protest would be forgotten.'[1] So Margaret Leighton described her dealings with Alexander Korda, who launched her career, but – as in the case of Vivien Leigh – cannot be said to have followed up his initial awareness of a striking talent and beauty.

Margaret Leighton never became as famous as she ought to have. She had beauty, elegance, wit and intelligence, which all but disqualified her for a star career in the war heroics of '50s British cinema. 'Are they wasting Maggie Leighton?' fearlessly demanded a *Picturegoer* columnist (actually Bryan Forbes, using a pseudonym)[2] in the early '50s. Korda put her into his expensive flop, *Bonnie Prince Charlie*, for which she, as Flora MacDonald, received encouraging notices. Stage-trained, she said at the time: 'The strict limitation of movement and positioning dictated by camera angles was something I found quite disconcerting . . . This was something that affected me much more than shooting out of sequence.'[3]

She played with warmth and feeling as the expelled cadet's sister, Kate, in Asquith's *The Winslow Boy*; was effectively neurotic as Ralph Richardson's daughter in *The Holly and the Ivy* and as David Niven's wife in *Carrington VC*, again for Asquith; seethed superlatively as Julie Christie's mother in Losey's *The Go-Between*; and made the most of some waspish moments – and a great last line – as Lady Melbourne in *Lady Caroline Lamb*. Her Hollywood films, *The Best Man* and *The Sound and the Fury*, gave her arguably better opportunities than she ever had in Britain, but it should be on record that, whatever the material, *she* was never less than stylish and affecting. A columnist noted in 1950 that 'she still lacked the straightforward, emotional appeal that makes a film star, as opposed to a first-rate actress.'[4] The first part of that statement was perhaps true; but her acting skills are not in doubt. She herself wrote: 'I've made terrible mistakes in accepting some roles and turning down others, but some good is bound to come of doing, rather than not doing, any role.'[5]

She made the most of what came her way, but it was rarely what she deserved, and she died too soon, after a harrowing illness. 'The great and marvellous Margaret Leighton – tragically dead, adorable woman – suffering terribly from arthritis, played baseball in her costume at lunchtime.'[6] These are Joseph Losey's words and they offer a fitting epitaph for a fine actress and a brave woman.

1 Karol Kulik, *Alexander Korda*, Virgin Books, London, 1990, p 165
2 Interview with Bryan Forbes, October 1989
3 Leonard Wallace, 'Another Margaret comes to town', *Picturegoer*, 9 October 1948, p 11
4 Duncan Blair, 'What's next for Margaret Leighton?', *Picturegoer*, 18 November 1950, p 13
5 'Margaret Leighton' in Lillian Ross and Helen Ross (eds), *The Player: A Profile of an Art*, Limelight Editions, New York, 1984, p 393
6 Joseph Losey, 'Dialogue on film', *American Film*, November 1980, p 54

Russell Lloyd

b. 1916

Editor: *The Squeaker* (1937), *Over the Moon, So This Is London* (1939), *School for Secrets* (1946), *A Man about the House* (1947), *Anna Karenina* (& 2nd-unit dir) (1948), *The Last Days of Dolwyn* (& co-dir) (1949), *Treasure Island* (2nd-unit dir) (1950), *I'll Get You For This* (1951), *Decameron Nights, Saturday Island* (1952), *The Sea Shall Not Have Them* (1954), *Moby Dick, Star of India* (1956), *Jhansi Ki Rani, Heaven Knows, Mr Allison* (1957), *The Roots of Heaven, The Naked Earth, Count Five and Die* (1958), *Whirlpool* (1959), *The Unforgiven* (1960), *The Queen's Guards* (uncr) (1961), *The Happy Thieves* (uncr), *The Lion* (1962), *Bitter Harvest, The Wild Affair* (1963), *Of Human Bondage* (1964), *Return from the Ashes* (1965), *Ninety Degrees in the Shade, After the Fox* (1966), *Reflections in a Golden Eye, Casino Royale* (shared credit) (1967), *Sinful Davy, A Walk with Love and Death* (1969), *The Kremlin Letter* (1970), *The Last Run, Christa* (1972), *The Mackintosh Man, Love and Pain and the Whole Damn Thing* (1973), *The Man Who Would Be King, The Amorous Milkman, In Celebration* (1975), *Caligula* (uncr) (1979), *Tristan and Isolt, The Fiendish Plot of Dr Fu Manchu, The Lady Vanishes* (1980), *The Link* (1983), *Where is Parsifal?* (1984), *Absolute Beginners, Turnaround* (1986), *Ette Rubicon* (1987), *Foxtrot* (1988), *The Dive* (1989)

Editing seems to be one way to stay in films for a long time. In the early 1930s, Russell Lloyd began at Korda's London Films, doing uncredited assistant's work on such famous films as *The Scarlet Pimpernel, Things to Come, Rembrandt, Sanders of the River* and Asquith's *Moscow Nights*, and finally getting credit on *The Squeaker* as a result of combined luck and generosity. Following some wartime documentary experience, he worked as editor, on a couple of occasions (*Anna Karenina*, *Treasure Island*) as second-unit director and once as co-director – on a long-missing oddity called *The Last Days of Dolwyn*. His career as a top-flight editor really took off when he began his long association with the director John Huston on *Moby Dick* and went on to do a further ten films with this often British-based American director. Clearly, Huston's confidence in his editor (there seems to have been a similar trust between Huston and cameraman Oswald Morris) enabled Lloyd to exercise the editor's function with a maximum of creativity – at least enough of the latter to make him satisfied with the cutting room and not to hanker after the director's chair.

Interview date: June 1994

Is *The Squeaker* the first film on which your name appears?

I was the editor, but of course in those days there was usually a supervising editor also. This particular fellow was called Jack Dennis, who died a long time ago. He was a wonderful man but he did like his drink and his socialising. One day William K Howard, the director, called me up and asked me to tell Jack he needed to see a particular sequence cut because they had to break the set down. I couldn't find Jack so I thought there was only one thing to do: I cut the sequence myself and hoped Jack would be back by then. He didn't come back so I called Howard and said, 'Jack's cut the sequence you wanted but he's had to dash off again' (we were very protective of our bosses in those days). I showed the sequence to him; there were no repercussions and they tore the set down. I told Jack what had happened, and in fact this happened frequently after that, so at the end of the picture Jack went to Bill Hornbeck, who was the boss of the cutting rooms, and said he would like me to have the credit for the film since I'd done most of the cutting, and Bill agreed.

Technically, the editor is the person who does the work of cutting while the supervising editor runs the picture with you when you are showing it to the director and he might make a few suggestions. I've often thought it is a credit I wouldn't want. I've been credited as supervising editor but I've also edited the picture.

Before *The Squeaker*, you had worked for Korda on several films such as *The Scarlet Pimpernel* – in what capacity?

I was just an assistant. In those days there was an editor and one assistant to each film. Nowadays there would certainly be two assistants but then the numbering of the film was done by one person. I started numbering when I first joined London Films. As you know, picture and sound are separate and so you would number Scene 1 as '1000', then the machine would turn over and the numbers would run '1001, 1002,' and so on. You then numbered the sound exactly the same, so that, if you wanted to get synchronisation, you found the sound number such-and-such, put it with the picture with the same number, and that was your sync point. Every shot was numbered in the same way; it had its slate, then its footage from '0' onwards, and that was always a check for sync.

I don't think the Hollywood coding system is as good as ours. In ours we start numbering the rushes at '1' and go until the picture is finished. The American slating system uses the scene number followed by 'A' for the first shot, 'B' for the second shot, and so on. If they have a lot of film on one sequence they go into 'AA', 'BB', and so forth. The roll is numbered by scene number, I suppose, right the way through the roll regardless of how many shots are there, while ours are numbered per shot. When we come to look for something, I look at the film and it says '12000', so I go to a tin which is labelled '12' and I get '12' out. In America they have to look up a book to see what scene number so-and-so is.

Was there plenty of work for an editor in the '30s? Your credits look busy.

I was with London Films until after *Over the*

Moon. Then I had a slight disagreement with Alex Korda, after which I left and went to Pinewood, starting on a picture made by what was called 20th-Century Productions over here. Then the war came along and I joined the Navy. I was involved with film work twice during the war. First I was brought back from sea to work at Pinewood on a Jack Lee film about submarines for the Crown Film Unit, which was finally called *Close Quarters.* There was some discussion during shooting as to what the title should be, and it was at the time when *In Which We Serve* had just come out. One of the sailors in the cast quipped, 'How about *In Which We Submerge?*' Then, just after D-Day, I was again recalled from sea back to Pinewood, where we made a film about Mulberry Harbour. It was a documentary of about half an hour, commissioned by the Admiralty.

Did some directors make an editor's life easier, or more difficult?

Oh, certainly. The director of one film I know about shot almost a million feet of negative and printed nearly everything. A two-hour film is 10,800 feet long, so you can appreciate the wastage. John Huston, though, was economical from that point of view. He didn't shoot a lot of stuff but it was usually all there when you wanted it. If a director shoots far too much film there are millions of ways you can put it together and it's confusing. Of course you do run rushes before the film gets to the cutting stage and a certain amount of material may be selected then. During the rushes the director may say, 'Use Take 3 and not the others,' but even then you have to bear the other takes in mind, because sometimes there may be one line which is much better in another take.

Would you see the daily rushes in the presence of the director?

Yes, and we would have discussions at that point. He may have another input when you come to run the picture or the sequences, but I have found that it's very often better if the director doesn't see the picture too often when it is being shot and cut.

The editor seems to have enormous control over how the finished film hangs together.

One does, yes, but don't tell the directors that! I think some directors come to see their films too much and, what is worse, they see it on a flatbed machine. They like to run it and control it by running it backwards and forwards. Huston, however, would never, ever come to the cutting room. The first one I did for him was *Moby Dick.* He said to me, 'If I see anything, I don't want to see it on

that stupid little equipment you've got. I want to see it on the screen, like an audience.' I think directors really should see it on the screen and preferably when the film is complete. One should really think of one's first impression because, as I would say to directors, 'You have to be clear about everything because the audience haven't read the script; they haven't seen the rushes; they will see it maybe once, and they have to understand everything the first time, so let's make it simple.' I think a lot of pictures nowadays are hard to follow.

When does the actual process of editing get under way?

You see the rushes after the first day's shooting and they are numbered. As soon as that's done you start cutting. The whole unit can watch the rushes if they want to. Some people don't like the actors being there and some actors don't like to see the rushes, but everybody concerned, from the director and producer down to the clapper-boy, can see them if they are so inclined.

What would an editor's typical day be like?

The first thing is to synchronise the soundtrack and the picture for the rushes, which the assistant would do. Then it's a matter of when the director wants to see rushes. It might be at lunchtime, or it might not be until the evening because he can't just leave the floor during shooting. You don't really cut anything until the whole sequence is shot and it might not be finished on the first day so you don't do anything. There is really no such thing as a typical editor's day; it's not like an assembly line. On days when I had nothing to do I would probably go on the set; it wasn't really necessary for me to be on the set, although it was quite interesting to see what they were doing. Again, I don't like to see things too much before I cut, nor do I follow the script. In fact, I say that I'm not cutting the script, I'm cutting the film, which may be a little different in many ways. The script gives an order, certainly, but that doesn't stop you from moving scenes around if necessary.

Would you consult the director in making such a decision?

With some directors you would have to, while others – like John – never minded if I changed sequences around and re-ordered them. If he saw it and said nothing, then I knew he approved. That gave me a lot of freedom and, at the same time, if John didn't like it he'd say so; then you knew that your judgement had perhaps been wrong. He was seeing it fresh and wasn't expecting it, so he had a different perspective. It was an area where I could exercise some creativity.

Some films have a separate credit for a 'sound editor', but I take it that you edited both sound and image?

Before the war we had an editor and an assistant; there was no such thing as a sound editor on the pictures I did because we did it ourselves. After the war, however, the sound editors arrived and we have had some very good ones. What they do is to make all the effects – the birds chirping, buses passing and all of that. Also, if an actor has to be re-voiced or post-synched, they will fit that to the picture. They don't actually have anything to do with the cutting of the picture, though. In the early days you had one dialogue track and maybe a second one if there was some post-sync. You had usually one music track, seldom two unless they were segueing or something like that. We were on optical track in those days, remember. Then we might have perhaps three effects tracks. Now it is nothing to have seven dialogue tracks and copious music and effects tracks, and everything is made as easy as possible for the dubbing mixers, they have control of everything. We didn't have those facilities in the early days and I really admired sound mixers then; if they made a mistake when they came to do a track it meant a thousand feet of optical track out the window. They had to equalise the dialogues as they went along, because they only had one dialogue track and they didn't have footage counters as they do now; so it was a matter of sitting near the mixer and saying, 'There's a bicycle bell coming up shortly on Track 2.' Now they have a footage ticker so they know exactly when they are coming to something like that.

Did you have any dealings with the continuity person?

She is very important because she makes some cuts easy where they might be difficult with a bad continuity girl. It's a very tricky job, and we have some very good continuity girls. With multi-camera shooting (of which I don't altogether approve), certain problems don't arise because they have various cameras all shooting at the same time, so that people naturally do the same thing for each camera but from different angles. With single-camera shooting, however, the continuity is very important. If the character has a pipe in his mouth in one place and then you try to cut to his close-up, and you suddenly find he hasn't got the pipe in his mouth, the footage is unusable.

Angela Allen was continuity girl on a lot of John Huston's pictures and she was very good. She had great thoughts about the pictures. I also worked with Pamela Davis and she is also very good.

Would you have had much to do with the actors?

Not a lot, really, except of course with *Treasure Island*, and *The Last Days of Dolwyn*, which I was co-directing, as Emlyn [Williams] was also playing in the picture. In fact, Richard Burton [making his début in *Dolwyn*] always introduced me to people as 'my first director'. It was interesting to have contact with the actors – and such notable ones. Edith Evans was lovely. She said to me one day, 'Russ, you know I had my hair done and the little girl said to me, "Sit down, Edith," and really, I think she should not address me so at the first time of our meeting.' I have always addressed directors as 'Mr' for a few days until I ask if I can call them by their first name for simplicity's sake. I think it's only polite.

When did you first work with John Huston?

I was approached for *Moby Dick* but they said there was another editor (Ralph Kemplin) who had done pictures for John and who might be available. I was told to start, even if it was only to be for a short time. They told me to cut a sequence and I refused, saying I wouldn't cut anything until I had met John. I volunteered to go down to Milford Haven, where John was on location; we had long discussions, then he finally said, 'Let's get started,' so I did.

We were on *Moby Dick* for a long time, over a year I think. John couldn't stay in England after shooting finished (for tax reasons, I believe) and he went to France. There was still a lot of model stuff to be done and John could never come to England during the post-production period, so we had to oversee the music and we were responsible for the mixing or the dubbing. Once things were done, we'd take them to Paris for John to see.

John had a method of shooting, which I liked, so that his work kind of slotted together. He would do an opening shot, usually of some distinction, then maybe you'd go into favouring shots over one shoulder and then the other, and then you'd have close-ups for the same thing. There was always enough but not too much, so that part was easy. But when you went from the favouring shot to the close-up, he would never want you to go back to the favouring shot. He said that the whole thing should build so that, mechanically, you also got closer, to build up the emotion you were building up. John's shots were all well designed; he didn't just do a lot of shots and hope they would come together in the cutting room.

He also had a long-term collaboration with Oswald Morris as cameraman. Did the practices of certain cameramen make life easy for you?

With John at least, he would set up the shot and Ossie just had to light it. Angela would make observations if she thought it was going to create difficulties in the cutting room, but John was organised. From that point of view he laid out what the shot was and Ossie lit it. It didn't make a great deal of difference to me, however, who the cameraman was, but it was good to see everything well lit.

What do you recall about *Of Human Bondage*, which had a tortured production history, I believe?

Yes, it was started by Hank Hathaway and we got on very well. One day at Ardmore in Ireland, I went on to the set and found Hank going around saying goodbye to everyone. I don't know whether he'd decided to leave or what, but I know he couldn't get on with Kim Novak. Some time later, I was still on the picture when Hank phoned me asking if I was free. I told him no, that I was still working on *On Human Bondage* and he said, 'What? On that load of crap?'

It was an interesting picture for me, however. It was decided after shooting had finished that we were really missing a scene of Laurence Harvey taking Kim Novak back to her home and she swings around the lamp-post. I said to give me a week and I'd see what I could do. I got all the spares of this one scene that had been shot, and I cut it entirely differently. I got lines and words from all sorts of places and fitted them to the faces, making an entirely new scene with new dialogue.

The picture went on for years and years and eventually I was put on to help with the editing of *A Wild Affair*. The two films overlapped, in fact. That also happened with *Cleopatra* when it was being filmed at Pinewood and directed by Rouben Mamoulian. Rouben did a few days of shooting and I think I had about fifteen minutes of cut stuff when it went back to America. Had the unit gone to Italy I'd have stayed on. During all the delays that happened, I was put to work on *The Queen's Guards* for Michael Powell. I moved back and forth between the two for a while but I don't think I'm credited on *The Queen's Guards*.

You edited *In Celebration* for Lindsay Anderson. Was that a difficult film to cut?

It was quite interesting. I liked Lindsay and the only thing I would say against him is that he did live in the cutting room. I don't mind if that is what the director wants to do, but I really think he should make his suggestions and then look at the film in the theatre.

Ken Loach

b. 1936

Director: *Poor Cow* (1967), *Kes* (1970), *Family Life* (1971), *Black Jack* (1979), *The Gamekeeper* (1980), *Looks and Smiles* (1981), *Singing the Blues in The Rain* (1986), *Hidden Agenda* (1990), *Riff-Raff* (1992), *Raining Stones* (1993), *Ladybird, Ladybird* (1994), *Land and Freedom* (1995), *Carla's Song* (1996)

For thirty years, Ken Loach has been making films about working-class life. He has done so without ideological compromise, which is remarkable enough in a cinema so often – and often justly – accused of being middle-class. Equally impressive is his refusal of aesthetic compromise. He not merely resists the use of star names to 'sell' his films, but, perhaps even more daringly, resists the lure of conventional narrative structures. A newer director, Mike Leigh, shares this seemingly loose approach; and Antonia Bird, whose *Priest* often led to comparisons with Loach, is really much more mainstream in her storytelling procedures. One of his most recent films, *Land and Freedom*, which looks back (and its structure enjoins such retrospection) on the Spanish Civil War, is in some ways his most ambitious, but it is still intransigently a Loach film. Since the mid '60s, when he tore viewers apart with the excoriating teleplay, *Cathy Come Home*, Loach has seemed a one-off to be cherished in British cinema.

Interview date: October 1995

You seemed to have rationed your film-making very sparingly since your first in 1967. How far is this a matter of choice and how far is it a matter of the sheer difficulty of getting feature films made in Britain in the last three decades?

Well, it's the latter. We had a little flurry at the end of the '60s and early '70s and did three films then. After that, it was impossible to make our kind of cinema films in Britain throughout the '70s because everything had to look to America. So, with Tony Garnett, I worked on about six or seven films, feature-length films, for television. For instance, we made the quartet of films called *Days of Hope* and two films called *The Price of Coal*. It was a total of six ninety-minute films really. We were churning them out but they were just for the BBC. And then in the early '80s I was trying to make documentaries because I hadn't had any luck with feature films. I did about six documentaries, four of which got themselves permanently banned from Channel 4 because there was a kind of dispute over the politics of them. Then Channel 4 were investing in cinema films and I was late to try to tap that source. It was really only in the late '80s, starting with *Hidden Agenda*, that we've been a bit lucky and made about six, I suppose, over the last six or seven years.

The pace seems to have speeded up, as you say, in the last few years. But it seems to me you've quite astonishingly kept making films for nearly thirty years while the bottom keeps dropping out of British cinema ...

Well, you just have to duck and dive between the various channels that are open. You've heard the old saying: 'One door opens, another one slams in your face' – then you find a chink of light somewhere else, and try and make for that. But I've been very lucky: one thing that was very fortunate for us was working with a group of people at Parallax, which is three producers and three directors now. For a long time it was a question of walking around London with a briefcase wondering where you could make the next phone-call as a freelance agent, and that can be quite dispiriting. But in the last five or six years, things have been a lot easier because there has been a base: somewhere to work from and a little structure, and so you can start to plan scripts and work ahead. So the big difference now is that we've got two or three scripts in the pipeline and I am working on a new one at the same time, whereas in the past I was just an individual wandering around the streets with a few papers stuffed in a briefcase.

Could you tell me a few details about when and how Parallax was set up and how it works?

The film that really turned the corner for me was *Hidden Agenda*, which was a film set in Ireland which we did in '88 or '89, and then the one after that was a small film really I did for Channel 4 called *Riff-Raff*. That was with a producer who was working in the company called Parallax but it was actually for someone else.

Was that Sally Hibbin, the producer?

Yes, and then Parallax reformed to include the producer I'd worked with on *Hidden Agenda*, Rebecca O'Brien, and another producer and director, and the thing was reformed as a co-operative and it's functioned ever since – over the last five years or so.

You seem to have quite a lot of continuity among your collaborators. I mean people like Tony Garnett, Sally Hibbin, cameramen Chris Menges and Barry Ackroyd, Stewart Copeland for music, and some actors. How much is that a matter of choice, and is it important to you?

I think it's very important really, particularly with the writers; that element has been very important. Jim Allen and I first worked together in 1967 – God help us! – and other writers like Barry Hines and now a new writer called Paul Laverty have come along. I think it's very important because, when you start to share some sort of common groundwork, you can then build on that. You can start to take the simple things for granted because you share the same outlook and the same way of doing things, and actually you can then be much more adventurous, because you don't have to spend the early part of the work just building the foundation. I guess it's the same as any collaborative enterprise, isn't it? I mean it's a real cliché; it's a team. There's a kind of comforting quality about knowing how people you're with think and work. It's a lot better.

How influenced were you by either the British documentary tradition or by the Free Cinema films of the '50s? I don't associate you with that New Wave cinema of the early '60s?

Well, not consciously. I think when I started with Tony Garnett and the other people at the BBC we felt we were working in opposition to what they'd done, but, looking back, that wasn't the case. We were actually building on what they'd done. You mean the Lindsay Anderson films? We never thought about this Free Cinema at all, but I think what was interesting about Tony Richardson and Lindsay and Karel Reisz and so on was that they used the north of England and the working class as a location for four or five or six years, then they all left. Most of them went to America; only Lindsay stayed here. I think he was a very thoughtful man, a serious and very original man. He and I would always have disputes but that's OK, that's just as it should be; but he was a very stimulating, provocative, original man, I think. But, in general, it seemed it was only a location for them, there was no long-term commitment to really exploring that experience, politically and socially, and trying to develop it and constantly re-evaluate it. It seemed to be a location which went out of fashion. And also the acting style and the camerawork seemed something to move on from. The fact that it had happened when it happened was very important, but it was also important for us to try to build on it. It was very important it was done. But I think, if I dare say it, our aesthetic influences were quite different.

How do you mean, when you speak of aesthetic differences?

Well, it sounds a bit pretentious, but I mean I found the lighting and the camerawork and the acting not what I wanted, and a bit later, the Czech cinema came to us and that seemed to us, just as a way of filmmaking, much more sympathetic and subtle and enigmatic and deep. It seemed to be much more elusive in a way, but elusive in the right way, in that it didn't over-simplify things: it just allowed people to *be*, without pushing them through contrived theatrical performances. And the use of lighting is much more thoughtful and much more original. Particularly with Chris Menges, the cameraman, who'd worked as an assistant for a Czech cameraman, we tried to rethink what we were doing in those terms.

Your first feature film, *Poor Cow*, was produced by Joseph Janni, whom I associate with mainstream filmmaking, and I wondered how this association came about and how it worked.

It came about because he'd seen some films I'd done on television and so he bought the rights to the next book of a writer I'd worked with, called Nell Dunn. He'd produced some of the northern films but I mean he had no concept of what the North was, I mean the people or anything. To him it was a location – it was in fashion, then it was out of fashion.

I think he produced for John Schlesinger.

Yes, yes. For me, he was a very charming man in many ways and very generous but we didn't talk the same language at all. He didn't really know what I was on about and I didn't know what he was on about. We didn't fall out and we got on perfectly OK but it wasn't a fruitful relationship, unlike, say, Tony's and mine. We were both peas out of the same pod so we saw the world in a very similar way.

Did Joseph Janni nevertheless give you more or less a free hand with *Poor Cow*?

Not really. I was too inexperienced. I didn't know what I was doing. The film's a mess really.

Although this film starred well-known '60s actors Terence Stamp and Carol White, who'd been in *Cathy Come Home*, you've usually worked with relatively unknown actors. What have you seen as the advantages of that?

Just a freshness, an originality. Often when people do a big film, or a film for the first time, they bring a sort of innocence to it that they never recapture. But it's always a question of finding the person who's going to make it come alive the best. That's what it's about, you just find the person and you think, 'Well, they're really going to make this story live.'

Has it ever made box-office problems for you, not going with known stars?

Well, I've never been very commercial, so it's never been something I've chased, really; mainly because I don't think I'd be very good at it.

You've sometimes used actors on several occasions: are they people you just feel easy with?

Yes, and also I think they have a depth and a kind of veracity about what they do that means they're not exhausted, and they're not afraid of giving a performance and then that's it. I mean they're really three-dimensional people that you can endlessly find interesting things about.

You had wonderful performances in your last three films – Robert Carlyle in *Riff-Raff*, Bruce Jones in *Raining Stones* Crissie Rock in *Ladybird*. I'm just wondering, what sort of director are you with actors?

You'd have to ask them, I'm afraid! Well, we just go through the story and try and keep it as spontaneous as possible. I just play little tricks on them, take them by surprise, try and live dangerously with them! I think actors get directed *out* of good performances. I don't show them the script now. You used to go to a first reading and people would be very good and just interesting and very simple. And then after two weeks of rehearsal they'd lost it, because they'd thought about it far too much, it was all secondhand, they'd been asked to do things that weren't right, and most directing is directing actors out of good performances into bad ones, I think.

So in the film that you're making now, are you going for new actors again?

Yes, mainly, but Bobby Carlyle is going to be in it.

He was the young man in *Priest*, wasn't he?

Yes, he was.

A lot of the reviews for Antonia Bird's *Priest* have raised your name as a comparison but I thought hers was a passionate melodrama whereas you're much less interested in narrative formalities. I wondered what you thought of this idea.

Well, I don't know, I haven't seen it all so I can't really talk about it and, you know, it's always invidious to talk about another director's work. I think my films tend to be more kaleidoscopic. We've worked very hard on this structure; I think it can still have a narrative drive but have it through a kind of juxtaposition of sequences, rather than just moving from A to B. I couldn't really talk about *Priest* particularly; but I've heard very nice things about her.

Your last three films – *Riff-Raff*, *Raining Stones* and *Ladybird*, *Ladybird* – seem like a trilogy of working lives. They've all been critically successful; have they been commercially so? How do the audiences react to them?

In Europe they have, yes. In Europe they've gone a bomb. One of them ran for a year in Madrid – I think it was *Raining Stones* – and *Riff-Raff* also ran for a long time. They did very well because they're obviously not huge budgets, but they're all well into the black now. That's good because it means you can carry on working.

What's the name of your new film?

After *Land and Freedom*, you mean? The one after that is the one we're just starting, which is set in Nicaragua. We haven't got a title yet.

Margaret Lockwood

1916–1990

Actor: *Lorna Doone* (1934), *The Case of Gabrielle Perry, Some Day, Honours Easy, Man of the Moment, Midshipman Easy* (1935), *Jury's Evidence, The Amateur Gentleman, Beloved Vagabond, Irish for Luck* (1936), *The Street Singer, Who's Your Lady Friend?, Dr Syn, Melody and Romance* (1937), *Owd Bob, Bank Holiday, The Lady Vanishes* (1938), *A Girl Must Live, Susannah of the Mounties, Rulers of the Sea* (1939), *The Stars Look Down, Night Train to Munich, Girl in the News* (1940), *Quiet Wedding* (1941), *Alibi* (1942), *The Man in Grey, Dear Octopus* (1943), *Give Us the Moon, Love Story* (1944), *A Place of One's Own, I'll Be Your Sweetheart, The Wicked Lady* (1945), *Bedelia, Hungry Hill* (1946), *Jassy, The White Unicorn* (1947), *Look Before You Love* (1948), *Cardboard Cavalier, Madness of the Heart* (1949), *Highly Dangerous* (1950), *Trent's Last Case* (1952), *Laughing Anne* (1953), *Trouble in the Glen* (1954), *Cast a Dark Shadow* (1955), *The Slipper and the Rose* (1976)

'For too long I'd been playing novelettish parts – we were never ever given real scripts to read or real people to play, and censorship problems were unbelievable ... then Dirk took me out to lunch and told me about Freda in *Murder Mistaken* ... I was dubious about being able to play such a character, though I liked her honesty ... I'm glad I did it, but am still wondering exactly where it got me.'[1] Margaret Lockwood did well to wonder, because after this part, in the film *Cast a Dark Shadow*, she didn't film again for twenty-one years. At the time, she wrote, 'Now that I am an independent actress under contract to no one I need no longer take parts that don't appeal to me. One that did was in the film version of the stage play called *Murder Mistaken*.'[2] But *Cast a Dark Shadow*, expertly directed by Lewis Gilbert, failed to 'appeal' to Lockwood's fans, and she turned to stage and television for the next two decades. One stresses this film because, as the shrewd barmaid, she had just given the best performance of her career and seemed all set for a new one as a character actress.

After a début at eighteen, in *Lorna Doone*, her 'first really big picture, *Bank Holiday*, with a beautifully written script and a wonderful part for me,'[3] drew on her '30s image of the nice suburban girl, this time with a touch of spice added by her embarking on an illicit weekend with boyfriend Hugh Williams. 'My career up to *Bank Holiday* had been a matter of steady, entirely unsensational progress.'[4] She had the great advantage in this 'realist' breakthrough film of being directed by Carol Reed, for whom she made six other films, most notably *A Girl Must Live*, a sharply observed study of showgirls on the make, and *The Stars Look Down*. Of the latter, she said, 'The part offered to me was that of an unpleasant type of woman ... I found I was thoroughly enjoying playing this new type of character.'[5] As Michael Redgrave's shallow, selfish wife, she did her most incisive work to date, though one should recall her engaging heroine in *The Lady Vanishes* for Hitchcock, of whom she said, 'I found him most disconcerting because, having worked out his film thoroughly in script and sketch form, he rarely spoke to his players when actual shooting was in progress.'[6]

Sadly, apart from Asquith on the charming *Quiet Wedding*, she never had such skilful direction again, though she went on to become Britain's No 1 female star in the mid '40s. The Gainsborough melodrama, *The Man in Grey*, was a huge and unexpected success, giving her a chance to be spectacularly wicked. Beneath the suburban gentility, there seemed a coarser, more interesting Lockwood: 'You silly twit. Stop being a gentleman and finish the bloody scene,'[7] she chided Stewart Granger for not hitting her hard enough. In *The Wicked Lady*, bored with country-house life, she takes to lovers and the life of the road – and audiences adored her. 'At first, as usual, I did not like the thought of playing a villainous role again, but it was such a good one that I knew it would be madness to refuse it,'[8] she wrote, but in 1950 she described it as 'the highpoint of my career'.[9]

Little after gave her much satisfaction. The entertaining wicked-woman thriller, *Bedelia*, was 'not a favourite with me';[10] she got out of *The Magic Bow* by appealing direct to Rank, claiming the part was 'just popping up behind hedges and looking jealous';[11] *Hungry Hill* was a lugubrious trudge through several generations of a tiresome family; and *Cardboard Cavalier*, a slapstick romp as Nell Gwyn, with Sid Field, was a disastrous miscalculation ('I was terribly distressed when I read the press notices of the film'[12]). In the '50s, she floundered through a contract with Herbert Wilcox, who, she said, 'has a natural gift for making an occasion out of anything.'[13] Not, sadly, out of *Trent's Last Case*, which is mildly enjoyable but gives her little to do, or *Laughing Anne* or *Trouble in the Glen*, which are dire.

'The British star who waits for the ideal role . . . will do a lot of waiting,'[14] she said in 1944. By all accounts a true professional, she didn't wait, did what she could with what she got, and went on to fresh fields in theatre and television, returning to the big screen only once, in 1976, to play the cruel stepmother in *The Slipper and the Rose*.

1 Eric Braun, 'The indestructibles', *Films and Filming*, September 1973, p 38
2 Margaret Lockwood, *Lucky Star*, Odhams Press, London, 1955, p 188
3 Lockwood, *Lucky Star*, p 55
4 Margaret Lockwood, 'My life story', *Picturegoer*, 1 April 1950, p 14
5 Margaret Lockwood, 'Nice girl turns bad girl', *Picturegoer*, 8 April 1950, p 11
6 Lockwood, 'My life story', p 15
7 Stewart Granger, *Sparks Fly Upward*, Granada, New York, 1981, p 65
8 Lockwood, *Lucky Star*, p 107
9 Margaret Lockwood, 'To my surprise I am a star', *Picturegoer*, 15 April 1950, p 17
10 Margaret Lockwood, 'Was I difficult?', *Picturegoer*, 22 April 1950, p 14
11 Alan Wood, *Mr Rank*, Hodder & Stoughton, London, 1952, p 198
12 Margaret Lockwood, 'Was I Difficult?', p 15
13 Lockwood, *Lucky Star*, p 160
14 Margaret Lockwood, 'What is a star to do?', *Picturegoer*, 2 September 1944, p 11

Herbert Lom

b. 1917

Actor: *Zena Pod Krizem* (1937), *Mein Kampf – My Crimes* (1940), *The Young Mr Pitt* (1941), *Secret Mission, Tomorrow We Live* (1942), *The Dark Tower* (1943), *Hotel Reserve* (1944), *The Seventh Veil, Night Boat to Dublin* (1945), *Appointment with Crime* (1946), *Dual Alibi* (1947), *Snowbound, Good Time Girl, Portrait from Life, The Brass Monkey / Lucky Mascot* (1948), *The Lost People, The Golden Salamander* (1949), *Night and the City, State Secret, The Black Rose, Cage of Gold* (1950), *Hell Is Sold Out, Two on the Tiles, Mr Denning Drives North, Whispering Smith Hits London* (1951), *The Ringer, The Man Who Watched Trains Go By* (1952), *Rough Shoot, The Love Lottery, The Net, Star of India* (1953), *Beautiful Stranger* (1954), *The Ladykillers* (1955), *War and Peace* (1956), *Fire Down Below, Hell Drivers, Action of the Tiger* (1957), *Chase a Crooked Shadow, I Accuse!, The*

Roots of Heaven, Intent to Kill, No Trees in the Street, Passport to Shame, The Big Fisherman (1958), Northwest Frontier, Third Man on the Mountain (1959), I Aim at the Stars, Spartacus (1960), Mr Topaze, El Cid, Mysterious Island, The Frightened City (1961), The Phantom of the Opera, The Treasure of Silver Lake, Tiara Tahiti (1962), The Horse without a Head (1963), A Shot in the Dark (1964), Return from the Ashes, Uncle Tom's Cabin (1965), Our Man in Marrakesh, Gambit, Die Nibelungen, Whom the Gods Wish to Destroy (1966), Die Nibelungen II, Assignment to Kill, The Karate Killers (1967), The Face of Eve, Villa Rides!, 99 Women (1968), Doppelgänger / Journey to the Far Side of the Sun, Mister Jericho (1969), Count Dracula, Dorian Gray, Hexen Bis Aufs Blut Gequält (1970), Murders in the Rue Morgue (1971), Asylum (1972), Dark Places, Mark of the Devil, Blue Blood, And Now the Screaming Starts (1973), The Return of the Pink Panther, Death in Persepolis, And Then There Were None (1974), The Pink Panther Strikes Again (1976), Charleston (1977), Revenge of the Pink Panther (1978), The Lady Vanishes, The Man with Bogart's Face (1979), Hopscotch (1980), Trail of the Pink Panther (1982), Curse of the Pink Panther, The Dead Zone (1983), Memed My Hawk (1984), King Solomon's Mines (1985), Whoops Apocalypse, Going Bananas (1986), Coast of Skeletons, The Master of Dragonard Hill (1987), River of Death, Death on Safari (1988), The Masque of the Red Death (1990), The Sect, The Pope Must Die (1991), The Son of the Pink Panther (1993)

Though Herbert Lom rightly complains of being stereotyped as 'sinister foreigner' in British cinema, he was also one of its busiest actors throughout the 1940s and '50s. Indeed, after 1960, he scarcely noticed the decline of the British film industry because he was filming all over the world. Despite difficulties of typecasting, he was memorably sympathetic as the psychiatrist in *The Seventh Veil*, a rare romantic hero in *Hell Is Sold Out*, a likeable philanderer in *The Net*, comically menacing in *The Ladykillers*, and a striking presence in such superior melodramas as *Good Time Girl*, *Chase a Crooked Shadow* and *Hell Drivers*. His career took a new turn with the *Pink Panther* films and, sixty-odd years after its start, it is still going strong.
Interview date: June 1991

You settled quickly into British films in the early '40s. How did this come about?

Carol Reed was looking for an unknown to play Napoleon in a film called *The Young Mr Pitt*. He interviewed me and gave me the small part. I got the interview through my agent, Christopher Mann, who was married to a concert pianist called Eileen Joyce whom I later met when she did the actual playing on the soundtrack for Ann Todd in *The Seventh Veil*. I was thrilled to be chosen by Carol Reed and he was certainly a charming man.

After several entertaining films in the early '40s, did you regard your big success in *The Seventh Veil* as a turning point?

Yes, not only in my career, but also in British films. It took psychiatry seriously, in the most popular sense, of course. No girl would have chosen a sadistic man who beat her with a stick while she practised the piano. But the sadist was James Mason and so psychiatry was 'popularised' to suit the star. The psychiatrist I played was of course meant to be years older than I was then, but the make-up people put black lines under my eyes and greyed my hair. I was meant to be presenting a very sympathetic image of psychiatry as a form of treatment. Also I think the romantic use of classical music helped the film's popularity. But, really, it owed everything to Sydney and Muriel Box, who were the creative team behind it all, and of course James Mason was becoming a very big star.

You made four films in 1948. Did you have much choice of roles then?

Not at all; I think I had a three- or four-picture deal with Gainsborough Studios, and that's when I made films like *Snowbound* and *Good Time Girl*. David Macdonald directed them, but I don't remember much about him except that he looked rather like Ronald Colman and that I got on very well with him.

Were you happy with the suave villain image you had at this time?

I was a foreigner and in English eyes all foreigners are villains. I did have one romantic role in a film called *Hell Is Sold Out*, with Mai Zetterling, then a budding star, and directed by a very nice man, Michael Anderson, who went on to do big films. The newspapers often made the comparison with Charles Boyer, and in the early '50s it might have come about, but not in England.

I'd been signed to a seven-year contract with 20th-Century-Fox in Hollywood, when the US refused me an entry visa. No reason was given, which meant it was clearly political – I was judged to be a 'fellow traveller' and was a victim of that anti-Communist fever of the time in the US. My political inclinations were certainly leftish but I had never been a member of the Communist Party. However, I was a Czech and, as my parents were still in Czechoslovakia, I had followed the war news keenly and been intensely interested in the role of the Russians in expelling the Nazis. So I was not as anti-Russian as I might have been, or as Hollywood would have liked. One of life's ironies is that, some years after the war, I wanted to return to Czechoslovakia and was refused a visa by the Communists. Eventually, I was able to get my parents to England.

What do you recall of the three films you made at Ealing in the early '50s – *Cage of Gold*, *The Love Lottery* and *The Ladykillers*?

I don't really remember the first two, except that David Niven played a film star in *The Love Lottery*, but I do remember *The Ladykillers*, which we all enjoyed making. The writer, Bill Rose, told me he had dreamt the story one night and then had written it down the next morning. As for your idea that the gang of criminals, led by Alec Guinness as a mad eccentric, is like a comic cross-section of the English social system at the time, I never thought of that but there could be something in it. And Katie Johnson, I remember, was a very charming old lady, who was brought out of retirement for the part. She had a great success in the film and then, sadly, died very shortly afterwards.

What was your experience of working with some of that steady stream of Hollywood players imported into British films in the '50s?

You need to remember that it was cheap to make films here then and a lot of American companies took advantage of this. When the pound recovered in the late '60s, the Americans pulled out. As for the Americans I played with, I particularly liked Anne Baxter, a beautiful actress and a beautiful woman, with whom I did *Chase a Crooked Shadow*.

Then there was *Rough Shoot* with Joel McCrea and Evelyn Keyes. McCrea did not enjoy being called an actor, but there was an odd mixture of modesty and pride when he'd say, 'I'm not an actor, I'm Joel McCrea!' I remember the director Robert Parrish saying to him, 'When Artur Rubinstein plays the piano, he plays high and low notes, soft and loud notes. He's looking for the right note.' McCrea replied, 'Well, I found the right note a long time ago and I've stuck with it.' Evelyn Keyes was the leading lady; she had once played Scarlett O'Hara's sister in *Gone With the Wind*. I thought she was very attractive, entertaining and intelligent, and was much underused.

Is an American influence at work in a film as tough and vigorous as *Hell Drivers*, which you made for Cy Endfield in 1957?

Yes. I think there's an American influence in matters like dramatic tempo and vigour, and that was a very popular film which often crops up on television. It's exciting and it has a good script and a strong cast, with actors like Stanley Baker and Patrick McGoohan, and Sean Connery in a bit part. It worked very well, but Cy Endfield was a rather unhappy character, who didn't fit too well in English society.

You played Napoleon again for King Vidor in *War and Peace*.

I enjoyed working for King Vidor and doing Napoleon again after all those years. But we had two directors making this huge epic. Mario Soldati was the Italian director and Vidor the American and the two could never agree on anything. I was criticised in the French press for portraying a mean and villainous Napoleon, which is how Tolstoy presents Napoleon. For the French he is always 'The Emperor', and my performance didn't fit their image of him.

Would you choose a film on the basis of its director?

Yes, I would certainly choose a film if it was to be made by a director I respected, but I'd be even more likely to choose one on the basis of the script. When I look back at all the parts I've played, I think I was most often attracted by what I thought they would teach me. The parts I really loved taught me what it was like to be a Harley Street psychiatrist, or a disillusioned emperor, or the victim of a concentration camp, or a lunatic police inspector. I'm attracted to a script that offers me a role which will take me out of my own skin and into other lives.

As for directors, the kind I don't like is the one who comes to me before a take and says, 'Now, Herbert, give me your best.' Often people who've been actors before they become directors are especially good to work with. They know what an actor suffers; they speak his language; they *like* actors. I think of people like Carol Reed or, as you suggest, Harold French [for whom Lom made *Secret Mission* and *The Man Who Watched Trains Go By*], who used to address his cast as 'My darlings'. David Lean was a great director in many ways, but I think he was a little afraid of actors, didn't quite know how to tackle them.

Unlike many British stars of the '40s and

'50s, you went on working steadily throughout the next three decades. Was your involvement in the *Pink Panther* movies a major highlight?

Oh, certainly. I was badly typecast in British films and it needed an American – Blake Edwards – to take me away from endless villainous roles, and into the comedy of the *Pink Panther* films. I loved playing the part of a dithering lunatic of a police inspector. I think people *like* to see the police in trouble; they enjoy seeing Inspector Dreyfus reduced to an utter, twitching wreck.

Has it, in recent years, been increasingly difficult to maintain an interesting career in Britain?

I find it quite impossible to maintain an interesting career in Britain. Mind you, for as long as I can remember British films have been hovering on the brink of death, so perhaps it is not really too different today. Certainly, in recent decades, I have filmed all over the place more often than in Britain.

Joseph Losey

1909–1984

Director: *Pete Rolum and His Cousins* (& sc, pr), *A Child Went Forth* (co-dir, sc, co-pr) *Youth Gets a Break* (& sc) (1941), *A Gun in his Hand* (1945), *The Boy with Green Hair* (1948), *The Dividing Line* (1949), *The Prowler* (1950), *M, The Big Night* (1951), *Stranger on the Prowl* (1952), *The Sleeping Tiger* (1954), *A Man on the Beach* (1955), *The Intimate Stranger* (1956), *Time Without Pity* (1957), *The Gypsy and the Gentleman* (1958), *Blind Date* (1959), *The Criminal* (1960), *The Damned* (1961), *Eve* (1962), *The Servant* (& co-pr) (1963), *King and Country* (& co-pr) (1964), *Modesty Blaise* (1966), *Accident* (& co-pr) (1967), *Boom, Secret Ceremony* (1968), *Figures in a Landscape* (1970), *The Go-Between* (1971), *The Assassination of Trotsky* (1972), *A Doll's House* (& pr) (1973), *Galileo* (& co-adpt) (1974), *The Romantic Englishwoman* (1975), *Mr Klein* (1976), *Les Routes du Sud* (1978), *Don Giovanni* (& co-adpt) (1979), *La Truite* (& co-adpt) (1982), *Steaming* (1984)

* Short film.

'For some reason interviewers are always saying that the experience has left me embittered, and this just is *not* the case,'[1] said Joseph Losey in 1983 about his blacklisting by the House Un-American Activities Committee in the early '50s. 'In a way my being blacklisted was one of the best things that ever happened to me because it forced me to go to Europe to continue my career as a filmmaker. Otherwise I might have stayed on in Hollywood merely making money instead of making pictures I want to make.'[2] However he viewed the blacklist, Losey certainly made most of his best films in Britain, and he became one of the most articulate of all film directors about his work, and one of the most interviewed.

After several socially acute minor films in America, he began his British career under a pseudonym with *The Sleeping Tiger*, 'a piece of sensational melodrama which had no real premise and didn't hang together,'[3] but which brought him together with Dirk Bogarde, with whom he would, a decade later, make several of his finest films. He made several more melodramas in the '50s, including *Time Without Pity*, in which an alcoholic Michael Redgrave fights to save his condemned son's life ('The subject was a phony subject; visually it was exciting'[4]) and, as part of a frustrating Rank contract, *The Gypsy and the Gentleman*. Of the latter, a famously panned film, more interesting as a precursor of *The Servant* than in its own right, he said: 'I had decided that we should make an extravagant melodrama and at the same time try and present something of the feeling of the Regency period . . . Of a period that was cruel and dirty and not just lovely and elegant.'[5]

Following this bitter disappointment, 'John Davis announced he wished to settle my contract,'[6] and, after a year of unemployment, he went on to a decade or more of remarkable achievement. This includes hard-edged thrillers such as *Blind Date* and *The Criminal*, both starring Stanley Baker, one of his key collaborators, of whom he said: '. . . he was a man of great appetites. He did everything excessively, which appealed to me.'[7]

Of Bogarde, he said: 'I certainly can't claim responsibility for his growth; it was intrinsic in him,' but acknowledges that without Bogarde's agreeing to appear in *The Sleeping Tiger* 'my life might have been very different'.[8] He is absolutely right when he adds, 'We have been mutually helpful,'[9] as they went on to make *The Servant*,

King and Country, *Modesty Blaise* and *Accident*. Arguably, no actor–director team had such a run of interesting films in '60s Britain. 'You have the most successful class system in the world,'[10] he told an English interviewer in 1961, and in *The Servant* he vividly showed that system in a state of crumbling desuetude. The theme of class is obliquely crucial to *King and Country*, in which Bogarde's World War I major must defend a deserting private, and in *Accident* it is complexly interwoven with sexuality and the worlds of academe and television. 'I'm constantly amazed by how oblivious people are to the destructive thread through their own and other people's relationships . . . It's a common thread in my pictures.'[11]

He explores this theme as perceptively as anyone in British cinema has ever done, in *Accident* and in *The Go-Between*, of which he said: 'I felt that the most important thing . . . was what became of the boy, what kind of man he became, and why and how he was destroyed.'[12] 'Norfolk helped me a lot . . . The house was there . . . Most of the costumes were genuine . . . Carmen Dillon [designer] is brilliant,' he wrote. This is a wonderful-looking film which chills the blood as it probes the pain beneath the exquisite surfaces.

Perhaps no Englishman would have dared confront – or been so acutely aware of? – the treacheries inherent in the system. Most of the rest of Losey's career took him out of England, though he returned for his last film, *Steaming*; but for a decade he lifted British cinema out of its realist confines to create a dark and dangerous poetry.

1 Chris Peachment, 'Joseph Losey: Boy from the blacklist', *Time Out*, 10–16 November 1983, p 41
2 Gene D Phillips, 'Hollywood exile: An interview with Joseph Losey', *Journal of Popular Film*, Vol v, No 1, 1976, p 34
3 Tom Milne, *Losey on Losey*, Secker & Warburg, London, 1967, p 43
4 Milne, p 44
5 Michel Ciment, *Conversations with Losey*, Methuen, London, 1985, p 151
6 Ciment, p 154
7 Ciment, p 176
8 Milne, p 161
9 Milne, p 162
10 Andrew Sarris (ed.), *Interviews with Directors*, Avon Books, New York, 1967, p 331
11 Adrian Hodges, 'Losey – My one ambition', *Screen International*, 7–14 August 1982, p 3
12 'Joseph Losey: Dialogue on film', *American Film*, November 1980, p 55

Alexander Mackendrick

1912–1993

Director: *Kitchen Waste (1942), *Contraries, *Nero (1943), Whisky Galore! (1949), The Man in the White Suit (& co-sc) (1951), Mandy (1952), The 'Maggie' (1953), The Ladykillers (1955), Sweet Smell of Success (1957), Sammy Going South (1963), A High Wind in Jamaica (1965), Don't Make Waves (1967)
* Short film.

After the box-office failure of his first American film, *Sweet Smell of Success*, made in 1957 and now regarded as a masterpiece, 'I took off as fast as possible for home,' said Alexander Mackendrick. 'The trouble was, there wasn't a home to take off for. At that stage the so-called British industry didn't exist . . . Ealing by that time had collapsed and there was no equivalent.'[1] Mackendrick, the Ealing director most admired by the New Wave of Anderson, Reisz *et al.*, was presumably unable to find a place in the British realist vogue of the late '50s and early '60s.

American-born, of Scottish parents, Mackendrick came to Britain at the age of sixteen and served an apprenticeship on propaganda shorts for the Ministry of Information and then as a screenwriter at Ealing, before being entrusted with the direction of *Whisky Galore!* in 1949. 'It looks like a home movie; it doesn't look as if it was made by a professional at all. And it wasn't,'[2] says Mackendrick with misplaced modesty in Philip Kemp's exemplary study of him, in which he also acknowledges the 'great generosity towards beginners'[3] shown by the Ealing Studios boss, Michael Balcon.

Mackendrick directed only five films for Ealing but they established him as its most impressively astringent filmmaker. Though he deprecates the 'utterly unjustified cult of the director',[4] all his films are distinctly his own, however crucial the input of his gifted collaborators. *Whisky Galore!* is persistently dry, anti-authoritarian in a way that feels for the authority figure ('. . . the most Scottish character . . . is [Captain Waggett] the Englishman . . . the only Calvinist, puritan figure, who's against looting and so on[5])' as much as it enjoys the sabotaging anarchy of the thirsty islanders. Similarly in *The 'Maggie'*, while the Scottish locals are engaging, Mackendrick is equally aware of 'the savagely unfair way he [the American businessman] was treated.'[6]

The other two comedies, *The Man in the White Suit* and *The Ladykillers*, are much less cosy than the 'Ealing comedy' tag conjures up in affectionate recollection. The former satirises capitalism, unionism and scientific idealism and the second makes traditional England look (literally) shaky in the image of Mrs Wilberforce's house. Both offer evidence for Mackendrick's self-styled 'perverted and malicious sense of humour'[7] *and* for the superlative performances he drew from actors. Of the latter, he said, 'You watch what the actor is going to do anyway and then you help him . . . What you're looking for is the instinctive and intuitive impulses of the actor in the character,'[8] claiming that 'casting is nine-tenths of the job'.[9] Just think of the wonderful ensemble in *Whisky Galore!* (including Jean Cadell darkly foreseeing cannibalism), Guinness and Greenwood in *The Man in the White Suit*, Guinness and the whole 'string quintet' in *The Ladykillers* (Peter Sellers, as the wide boy, nearly missed out: 'Frankly, we can't see him with a broken nose and a cauliflower ear'[10] which were needed for the role played by Danny Green) and the sublime Katie Johnson as Mrs Wilberforce.

The non-comedy triumph of the Ealing years is *Mandy*, in which the treatment of a deaf child is skilfully interwoven with a study of precarious family life, on one level a microcosm for a Britain in which growth and inhibition are in painful conflict. 'Children are often better actors than adults because they have a greater capacity for believing completely in a situation at a given moment,'[11] Mackendrick said in 1953. His confidence in this capacity is borne out by little Mandy Miller's performance as the deaf child, as well as those in his last two British films, *Sammy Going South* and *A High Wind in Jamaica*, two flawed films which, nevertheless, still resonate with this tough-minded talent of which British films could have made much more use. Mackendrick spent the last decades of his life teaching film in America.

1 'Do make waves: Sandy', Alexander Mackendrick interviewed by Kate Buford, *Film Comment*, May–June 1994, p 43
2 Philip Kemp, *Lethal Innocence: The Cinema of Alexander Mackendrick*, Methuen, London, 1991, p 20
3 Kemp, p 22
4 Theresa Fitzgerald, 'A conversation with Alexander Mackendrick', *Screen International*, 29 September – 5 October 1990, p 21
5 Kemp, p 25
6 Kemp, p 105
7 'Ealing', *Omnibus*, BBC Television, 5 May 1986
8 *Film Comment*, May–June 1994, p 42
9 Philip Kemp, 'Saving grace', *Sight and Sound*, Summer 1990, p 149
10 Alexander Walker, *Peter Sellers*, Coronet Books, London, 1984, p 94
11 'As I see it', interview in *The Film Teacher*, Spring 1953, p 12

Virginia McKenna

b. 1931

Actor: *The Second Mrs Tanqueray, Father's Doing Fine* (1952), *The Oracle, The Cruel Sea* (1953), *Simba, The Ship that Died of Shame* (1955), *A Town Like Alice* (1956), *The Smallest Show on Earth, The Barretts of Wimpole Street* (1957), *Carve Her Name With Pride, Passionate Summer* (1958), *The Wreck of the Mary Deare* (1959), *Two Living, One Dead* (1961), *Born Free* (1965), *The Lions Are Free* (1967), *Ring of Bright Water, An Elephant Called Slowly* (1969), *Waterloo* (1970), *The Lion at World's End* (1971), *Swallows and Amazons* (1974), *Holocaust 2000, The Disappearance* (1977), *Blood Link* (1982), *Staggered* (1994)

After three forgettable films, Virginia McKenna appeared in *The Cruel Sea* in 1953 and became for the rest of the decade Britain's top female star. Her success in the 1950s is the more striking since the decade was so male-dominated and since the war films in which she established herself were notoriously short of rewarding roles for women. Her role in *The Cruel Sea* was followed by a similarly small but memorable role in the Dearden–Relph film, *The Ship that Died of Shame*. The films for which she is perhaps best remembered are those two accounts of heroic women – *A Town Like Alice* and *Carve Her Name With*

Pride. In these two extremely arduous roles, she subjugated her delicate beauty and apparent fragility to the unglamorised rigours required of her, and scored major successes. Since 1960, she has been most closely associated with her role as Joy Adamson (opposite her late husband, Bill Travers) in *Born Free*, and she and Travers worked together on several films reflecting their interest in and concern for wildlife. She still films occasionally and has done some notable work for television.

Interview date: October 1989

You are one of the very few British film actresses to have become a star in the 1950s. Was there a shortage of good roles for women?

That's traditional, I think. I was lucky because, at the beginning of the '50s, they started to make those wonderful war stories, starting with *The Cruel Sea* and going on to *A Town Like Alice* and *Carve Her Name With Pride*. I just happened to arrive at the right moment and had the kind of very English looks or personality which just fitted into that slot. At the time, Britain was wanting to look back, and to show the courage and struggles people had had to go through was a very pertinent thing.

You became a star in tough roles for women, showing a woman could be just as brave and as enduring as a man. Were you aware of this kind of image being built up?

No, I never thought of it like that. I *do* think there are women who are just as brave as men, though they usually face quite different kinds of problems and challenges. I became very close friends with Odette [Churchill] during the making of *Carve Her Name With Pride*, because she was our technical adviser, and there was living proof of a woman who had suffered enormously – torture, solitary confinement, things which are probably almost impossible for us to imagine coping with. Films hadn't been made about women during war so often; they hadn't had the same opportunity to show other dimensions of their nature until that time. But though they were enormously courageous and tough, I always tried to show where they were vulnerable, to make them whole people.

Were you being carefully groomed, as you might have been in Hollywood?

Oh no. I never went to Rank's Charm School or anything like that. I went into rep for six months in Dundee, then did two plays in London for Ten-nent's, then I did *The Second Mrs Tanqueray*, for Dallas Bower, and other films and television, then back to the theatre. I had a very good agent who put me up for things, some of which I got and some I didn't. I was offered a Hollywood contract but I didn't take it, because I didn't want to be what you've just described – a sort of groomed, Hollywood-type young actress, cast in roles for which I didn't much feel anything.

What sort of contracts were you under?

My only film contract was with Rank; I had to sign it in order to do *A Town Like Alice*. It was for five films; I did that one, *Carve Her Name With Pride* and *The Passionate Summer*. I was pregnant when I did the last one, so that was the end of that for a bit. Then they asked me to do a film I didn't want to do, and when they asked me to do a further film I was having my next child, so I think they gave up on me and released me from my contract. At one time I was leased by Rank to do *The Smallest Show on Earth* and they charged a lot of money for me to do it, although I was only paid my contract money.

***The Cruel Sea* really brought you to public notice. Did you enjoy working at Ealing?**

Oh, I loved it. I didn't have a very big part but, as it was virtually the only woman's part in it, it was much sought after. People always remember that film, and they remember me – I think it was the Wren's hat, which was attractive, and everyone seems to remember that! It was the first time I had really had a screen kiss! I was very nervous and it's quite difficult at first. Later on you learn not to take any notice of the people standing around looking at you. It was Donald Sinden's first film, too, and he was very jolly and nice. My character was very British and a bit 'stiff-upper-lip'.

After a season at the Old Vic, you returned to films in Brian Desmond Hurst's *Simba*.

Why were there so many of these outpost-of-Empire films in the '50s?

Perhaps it was the need for adventure, standing up against other cultures or environment which seemed harsh – pitting ourselves against these other, unknown forces and again emerging as courageous and brave, I suppose. Also it was the beginning of filming in other lands, which has increased as the years have gone by. Africa had its moment, when practically every film you saw seemed to have been shot in Kenya. I got on extremely well with Brian Desmond Hurst and, of course, Dirk Bogarde was the leading man in that film and he was so sensitive and kind and helpful. He was much more experienced than I was and he was very supportive when we were rehearsing. I've never met anyone who *hasn't* liked working with Dirk. He was the top male star in Britain then and he developed into such an incredible character actor.

I think *Simba* was ideologically fairly black-and-white – an unfortunate term! I think it was rather 'we were the victims of this devastatingly cruel group of people who wanted to massacre us all'. In reality many more Africans than British were killed by the Mau Mau. It was just a story of this one family and what happened to them; and I played the daughter. Dirk and I didn't go on location, we did our filming at Pinewood. They did it with doubles. They decided to dress my double in this scarlet dress for the scene when I discovered my parents killed and it seemed all wrong.

You won awards for your next role, as Jean in *A Town Like Alice*. Was this the film that really established your image with filmgoers?

Probably. Again, we never went away, we did it all in the studio! There was a second unit, which did a little bit in Alice Springs and all the jungle stuff. We tramped through the woods at Burnham Beeches in the freezing cold with glycerine sprayed on our faces! It was quite nasty because we were wading through a swamp full of tins and the things people just chuck, and we were falling all over ourselves and absolutely freezing. When we came off, we were quickly wrapped in blankets and given brandy. It was a great success and Peter Finch was superb in it. He was one of the most imaginative and truly creative actors I think we ever had here. I got such a lot from working with him. We would sit and rehearse our scenes quietly together and it was wonderful; there are people who don't like to rehearse at all, but I find it important to rehearse first, and then hope that the first take is the one. Jack

Lee, the director, was a very creative person, very quick, and there was a cast full of marvellous actresses – Marie Lohr, Renée Houston, Jean Anderson and Maureen Swanson. Making the film was a happy experience; I don't think we had anyone who was difficult.

The Smallest Show on Earth was your second film for Basil Dearden, who had also done *The Ship that Died of Shame*. How would you describe him as a director of actors?

He was quite low-key in his advice. He was very helpful but he left you a lot of freedom; I think he liked actors – some directors don't. *The Smallest Show on Earth* was a lightweight sort of comedy. I think that's the film I had the most fun making. What with Margaret Rutherford, Peter Sellers, Bernard Miles, Leslie Phillips – and of course, my husband Bill, although he wasn't my husband then – it was tremendous fun. People were so amusing in their scenes, we only stopped ourselves from laughing with difficulty.

Having starred in several films, what attracted you to the secondary role in *The Barretts of Wimpole Street*?

The leading role had already been cast anyway, to Jennifer Jones, and I think Henrietta is a wonderful part, almost better than Elizabeth Barrett. There is a defiance and grit about Henrietta which I found very interesting – standing up against authority, madly in love and defying everything for that. More interesting than lying on a chaise longue! I enjoyed playing her very much.

In a way, the star system is more evident on an American film. Jennifer sat slightly apart but she was always charming to talk to. If she was a little detached, that was the background of American stars. We don't have a star system in that way.

How did you prepare yourself to play the role of Violette Szabo in *Carve Her Name With Pride*?

I read the book, of course; I went to a gymnasium in London and learned judo and how to shoot a Sten gun; I learned parachute jumping, things I had to learn; and of course I talked to Odette. She told me a lot of stories about prison camp. And I met people who had known Violette in the coding office, including the man who wrote her code poem, and I did quite a lot of research. It's one of the films I'm proudest of – not because of what *I* did, but to have told the story of this extraordinary person who represents so many others whose stories have not been told. The courage of women who work behind enemy lines, the terror they must feel on a day-to-day basis, risking their lives and risking never seeing their families again. It became a real experience for me which affected me very deeply.

Two Living, One Dead is one of the most mysterious films – directed by Anthony Asquith and with well-known stars – and virtually unseen.

We went to Sweden to make it and it was really fascinating. Asquith was a superb director – he looked like a brilliant pixie – and I think it's an excellent picture. But when it was shown to the distributors they said it had no sex and no violence, so they refused to handle it. It was never seen, unless perhaps at two o'clock in the morning on television. Patrick McGoohan was in it and Bill, my husband, and Alf Kjellin and Dorothy Alison. It's about the victims of a robbery in a post office, about the postmaster who is accused of collusion with the robbers and how it ruins his life. It was very well done.

You filmed much less frequently after 1960. Did you find fewer congenial roles or did your interests after Born Free change more to matters to do with wildlife?

I think the main reason was that I started to have a family. I had my first child in 1958, and others in 1960, 1963 and 1967, so it was really my family time. *Born Free*, by the time we had filmed it and come back, took over a year out of the '60s. Playing a real person, who was not only alive then but was there during much of the filming, made it a unique experience; and the relationship that developed between us and the lions sowed the seeds of the work, in our charity, Zoo Check, now renamed the Born Free Foundation.

In 1996, Zoo Check, together with the Great Ape Escape, Orca Alert, Operation Wolf, The Bright Water Appeal and Elefriends, are projects of the Born Free Foundation.

James Mason
1909–1984

Actor: *Late Extra* (1935), *Troubled Waters, Twice Branded, Blind Man's Bluff, Prison Breaker, The Secret of Stamboul, Fire Over England* (1936), *The Mill on the Floss, The High Command, Catch As Catch Can, The Return of the Scarlet Pimpernel* (1937), *I Met a Murderer* (& pr, co-sc) (1939), *This Man is Dangerous, Hatter's Castle* (1941), *The Night Has Eyes, Alibi, Secret Mission, Thunder Rock* (1942), *The Bells Go Down, The Man in Grey, They Met in the Dark, Candlelight in Algeria* (1943), *Fanny by Gaslight, Hotel Reserve* (1944), *A Place of One's Own, They Were Sisters, The Seventh Veil, The Wicked Lady* (1945), *Odd Man Out, The Upturned Glass* (1947), *Caught, Madame Bovary, The Reckless Moment, East Side, West Side* (1949), *One Way Street* (1950), *Pandora and the Flying Dutch-* man, *The Desert Fox* (1951), *Lady Possessed* (& pr, co-sc), *Five Fingers, The Prisoner of Zenda, Face to Face* (1952), *The Man Between, Charade* (& co-sc), *The Story of Three Loves, The Desert Rats, Julius Caesar, Botany Bay* (1953), *Prince Valiant, A Star is Born, 20,000 Leagues Under the Sea* (1954), *Forever Darling, Bigger Than Life* (& pr), *Island in the Sun* (1956), *Cry Terror, The Decks Ran Red* (1958), *North by Northwest, Journey to the Centre of the Earth, A Touch of Larceny* (1959), *The Trials of Oscar Wilde* (1960), *The Marriage-Go-Round, Escape from Zahrain* (1961), *Lolita, Hero's Island, Tiara Tahiti, Torpedo Bay* (1962), *The Fall of the Roman Empire* (1963), *The Pumpkin Eater* (1964), *Lord Jim, Genghis Khan, Les Pianos Mécaniques* (1965), *The Blue Max, Georgy Girl, The Deadly*

Affair (1966), *Stranger in the House* (1967), *Duffy, Mayerling, The London Nobody Knows* (documentary) (1968), *The Age of Consent, The Sea Gull* (1969), *Spring and Port Wine, The Yin and Yang of Mr Go* (1970), *Cold Sweat, Bad Man's River* (1971), *Kill! Kill! Kill!* (1972), *Child's Play, The Last of Sheila, The Mackintosh Man, Frankenstein: The True Story, Trikinia* (1973), *11 Harrowhouse, The Marseille Contract, Kidnap Syndicate* (1974), *Mandingo, Inside Out, Autobiography of a Princess, Great Expectations,* *The Flower in his Mouth, The Schoolmistress and the Devil, La Mano Sinistra Della Legge* (1975), *The Voyage of the Damned, Homage to Chagall* (narr only) (1976), *Cross of Iron, Fear in the City* (1977), *Heaven Can Wait, The Boys from Brazil* (1978), *Murder by Decree, The Passage, Bloodline, The Water Babies, North Sea Hijack* (1980), *A Dangerous Summer, Evil Under the Sun, The Verdict* (1982), *Yellowbeard, Alexandre* (1983), *The Assisi Underground, The Shooting Party* (1984)

'I came to cinematic prominence as a "cruelie" in the early 1940s. I set about Margaret Lockwood with a riding crop in *The Man in Grey* and thrashed the fingers of Ann Todd as a pianist in *The Seventh Veil*. Those parts won the applause of the public and after that I seemed to play a brutal, boorish character in every film I made,'[1] recalled James Mason in 1981. As Everywoman's favourite brute, he also taunted Phyllis Calvert, Jean Kent and (most subtly) Margaretta Scott in *Fanny by Gaslight* (best of the Gainsborough melodramas), drove Dulcie Gray to drink and suicide in *They Were Sisters*, and made Margaret Lockwood his accomplice in highway robbery in *The Wicked Lady*. This batch of vivid melodramas, capitalising on his brooding handsomeness, made him the No 1 male star in Britain.

Of *The Man in Grey*, he wrote: 'There was nothing about it that I could actually bring myself to like, and I had no clue about how I could do anything with a part so monstrously nasty as that of Lord Rohan.'[2] Well, he found a way to huge success, whereas in the attractive rendering of an Osbert Sitwell ghost story, *A Place of One's Own*, he found that his fans 'wanted me to appear only as some heroic young lady-killer; or better still, lady-basher.'[3] This early venture into character playing, as an elderly retired manufacturer, may have displeased his public, but his performance is in fact wholly sympathetic and convincing and anticipates the direction his career would take.

After a major critical success as the dying Irish gunman in Carol Reed's *Odd Man Out* ('the only film I've made that might possibly be called great'[4]), Mason left for Hollywood amid a good deal of adverse publicity. He had earlier signalled this move: 'The war over, I should like to be able to work on stage and screen in any country where there are new influences and I figure I can work well . . . For us to make the occasional pictures in Hollywood prevents our becoming insular . . . and

greatly increases our "name value".'[5] Later, still on the subject, he conceded: 'I brought a lot of bad publicity on myself over the years. When I settled in the United States, London papers attacked me as if I'd insulted England . . . A lot of that was unfair and it did make me irascible.'[6]

His Hollywood career was regarded as a disappointment at the time, by himself as well as by the critics, though a film like Ophuls's *The Reckless Moment* now looks masterly. He returned spasmodically to Britain: for the bizarrely beautiful *Pandora and the Flying Dutchman*; for the Cold War thriller, *The Man Between*, directed by Carol Reed ('one of my super heroes in the film world'[7]); to delineate Humbert Humbert with precision and tact in Kubrick's *Lolita*; compelling as a vindictive cuckold in *The Pumpkin Eater* (in accounting for 'its failure to grip', he said, 'I choose to look in Pinter's direction'[8]); and unforgettably poignant, first, as Cyril Sahib in James Ivory's faultless *Autobiography of a Princess*, and, last of all, as the gentle-mannered aristocrat in *The Shooting Party*.

His starring days were, in truth, in '40s Britain, but he became thereafter one of the world's greatest cinema actors. Too intense for a conventional leading man, he seems in retrospect always to have been cut out for character roles. In 1975 he said, 'I did not quite achieve what I was aiming at or rather I did ultimately achieve it, but it came a different way. Not just by personality and flash, but by persistence and the determination to become a good actor.'[9] That he reached this goal, no one will deny.

1 'Endurance', James Mason in an interview with Iain McAsh, *Films*, November 1981, p 15
2 James Mason, *Before I Forget*, Hamish Hamilton, London, 1981, p 139
3 Mason, *Before I Forget*, p 143
4 *Films*, p 15
5 James Mason, 'I may find myself obliged to migrate', *Picturegoer*, 8 December 1945, p 5
6 Sheridan Morley, *Odd Man Out: James Mason*, Weidenfeld

& Nicolson, London, 1989, p 138

7 Michael Buckley, 'James Mason', *Films in Review*, January/February 1994, p 12

8 Clive Hirschhorn, *The Films of James Mason*, LSP Books,

London, 1975, p 164

9 'James Mason', the Sue Summer star interview, *Screen International*, 13 September 1975, p 21

▼ Doctor in the House *1954*

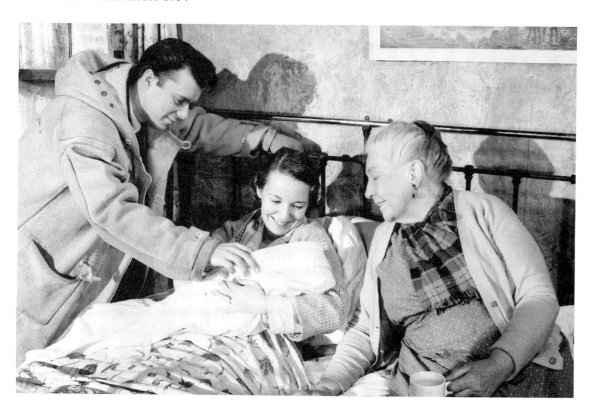

▲ The Dam Busters *1955* ▼ Room at the Top *1959*

▲ Peeping Tom *1960*   ▼ The Brides of Dracula *1960*

▲ Cash on Demand *1961*   ▼ Tom Jones *1963*

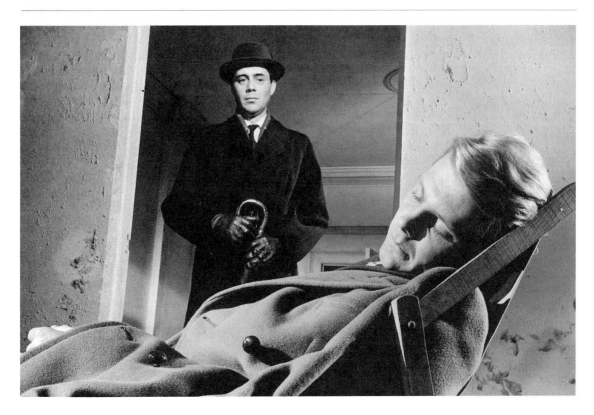

▲ The Servant *1963*   ▼ A Hard Day's Night *1964*

Anna Massey

b. 1937

Actor: *Gideon's Day* (1958), *Peeping Tom* (1960), *Bunny Lake is Missing* (1965), *David Copperfield* (1969), *The Looking-Glass War* (1970), *Frenzy* (1972), *A Doll's House, Vault of Horror* (1973), *A Little Romance* (1979), *Sweet William* (1980), *Five Days One Summer* (1982), *Another Country, The Little Drummer Girl* (1984), *The Chain, The McGuffin* (1985), *Foreign Body* (1986), *Impromptu, Killing Dad* (1989), *Mountains of the Moon* (1990), *Haunted, Angels and Insects* (1995), *The Grotesque* (1996), *Driftwood, Sweet Angel Mine* (1997)

A nna Massey spent most of the first decade of her career on the stage in such successes as *The Reluctant Debutante* and *The Miracle Worker*, emerging to play leading roles for John Ford, Michael Powell and Otto Preminger. She was not alone at the time in finding Powell's *Peeping Tom* a disturbing experience: it is still disturbing, but now also looks like a dark masterwork, and her threatened innocence is a crucial element in the film's impact. It was during those ten years that she might have established herself as an *ingénue* lead in films, but, if she had, there was no guarantee that she would have gone on to be one of the most rewarding character players in film or television. Some of her best opportunities have been in television: as Laura Kennedy in *The Pallisers*, as Mrs Danvers in *Rebecca*, and above all as the novelist heroine of *Hôtel du Lac*. However, she has made the most of some notable screen chances too, especially as the crucially incompetent nursery school superintendent in *Bunny Lake is Missing*, as a compassionate Mrs Linde in Patrick Garland's *A Doll's House*, the featherbrained society mother in *Another Country* and as Nigel Hawthorne's put-upon wife in *The Chain*. She can be very funny or sharply chilling as necessary, but a lovely, wry sympathy is her greatest strength.
Interview date: July 1994

How did you come to be in John Ford's *Gideon's Day*, your first film?

He was my godfather. My father [Raymond Massey] was filming *Hurricane* when I was born. I thought John Ford was wonderful. He was a minimalist on the set insofar as he edited as he shot;

he never shot more than he needed. He didn't give me much detailed direction, even though I was very green at the time.

I'd be interested in your recollections of your 'parents', Jack Hawkins and Anna Lee, in that film.

Both Jack and Anna were completely delightful. They were very kind to the young ones and it was a very happy experience. Everyone got on well; there were no great dramatic stirrings or anything. Everything went smoothly and it was very efficiently choreographed.

Coming from your family background, was there ever any question that you might become anything other than an actor?

It was taken for granted from a very early age. I wanted to be a nanny at one point but very shortly after that, when I was about four, it was just taken for granted. I regret that I never really pursued any other alley, as I perhaps should have done.

Am I right in thinking that instead of doing more film roles after *Gideon's Day*, you then went on the stage with Paul Rogers in TS Eliot's *The Elder Statesman*?

I can't remember the dates but that was my third stage role. The first nine years or so of my career I spent mainly in the theatre. It wasn't a conscious decision; you do what you're offered. Had I been offered a great deal of filming, I think I would probably have done it – but I wasn't. If good stage plays came along at that stage, I did them.

You next starred in what must have been one of the most controversial films ever made in Britain, Michael Powell's *Peeping Tom*. Did Powell seek you out personally for the role of Helen Stephens?

Yes, he did. He was a great friend of my father's, although my father had very little to do with me because I was one year old when my parents split. But my father was in a picture for Michael Powell called *Stairway to Heaven* in America and *A Matter of Life and Death* here, and he became very close friends with Powell and Pressburger. I don't want this to sound as if all my film work was nepotistic in origin, because it wasn't. I may have gone along to read for that film, but I can't remember, it was a long time ago. However, I know I certainly was Michael Powell's first choice for the role.

Did you find the story and the manner of the murder alarming? It caused a furore at the time.

Yes, I did, quite horrendous, even during the actual filming. When it opened it was a complete flop. Dilys Powell has just written a piece about it in the *Sunday Times* in which she now acknowledges it as a masterpiece.

What are your recollections of the actual filming and of Powell's direction?

Powell *did* direct. He gave much more detailed direction than John Ford – mind you, it was a much more complicated scenario, but always, before a long and complicated take (which was presumably incredibly technical in itself), he had to have some sort of row, with a lot of tension going. I remember the camera operator in particular was often the butt of his anger. He was quite complicated and not the most pleasant of men. He could also be very unkind, but he was a very clever man and I must say he wasn't unkind to me. However, I did observe that unkindness to other people – it was as if he needed some sort of stimulus; it always happened just before a take that he would attack, so that you would do the scene with an added adrenalin. It was not always necessary because an actor can provide that without being prodded, but perhaps I didn't read that correctly. Perhaps he perceived that some actors needed it, I don't know.

Why do you think the film provoked such hostility?

Well, it's quite a disturbing film, isn't it? We are talking about 1959 and it is not a very beautiful film to watch, in terms of its content, although it is wonderfully filmed. I've never really been able to watch it objectively; the memories of filming it are still too vivid. And I've never been happy about my own performance.

You had most scenes with Carl Boehm and Maxine Audley. How did you find them to work with?

Oh, they were absolutely delightful. I think Carl is working for the World Health Organisation now. I enjoyed working with them very much, they couldn't have been more charming and we all got along very well. Michael Powell had his own special way of working that was right for him and he achieved some remarkable results.

If Powell had a reputation for being demanding, your next director, Otto Preminger, has given rise to stories of absolute tyranny. What was your experience of working for him on *Bunny Lake is Missing*?

I thought he was a very difficult man. He was very unkind to Keir Dullea, who got most of his wrath. But on the last day I had to be released early because I was doing a matinée of a play. When I went to him to say goodbye, he said to me, 'You are a stage actress, aren't you? So I have to dub your whole part. You shouted, you were raucous, always too loud!' I went to the theatre in tears, of course. But he didn't need to dub my part at all, except for one sentence! He just had to be unkind and disturbing. If it had been true, it wasn't a very nice way to tell me – but it wasn't actually true. I had to dub one sentence and it wasn't because I'd over-pitched it, but because of some technical fault. But I did enjoy the film very much when I saw it.

Did he give you a lot of careful direction?

Not very much, I don't think. Olivier had difficulty learning his lines; in the scene I had with him, we had to do it almost line by line. Preminger was never rude to Olivier, of course, and, to be perfectly fair to him, he was never rude to me while we were shooting, only on that last day when he seemed to want to annihilate me after I'd finished my job.

In general, what did you look for, or hope for, in a director?

The subtleties. A film director knows the size of the shot he wants; it is a more internal way of working than stage acting, so that you need to give them something that comes from within. In the theatre everything comes from within too, but it is a different size, whereas the camera can pick up things that you are almost unaware you are thinking yourself. It is up to a film director to get that moment, and the more you can rehearse for a film, of course, the better.

Has it been a common experience of yours that directors would rehearse?

We didn't rehearse at all on my early films; they rehearse much more now. In the early films, you would get the part and go in and do it on the day, which means that you didn't get all the subtleties of performance. You have to do your homework. But of course you rehearsed a great deal before the takes.

Those first three films had very distinguished scriptwriters – TEB Clarke, Leo Marks and Penelope Mortimer. How much would you be influenced by a screenplay in deciding to do a film?

I just love filming so much, but the director, the writer, the part and the script are all of equal importance in making my decision.

I think *Frenzy* is a very enjoyable film. Was making it a pleasurable experience?

It was so fascinating working with Hitchcock, of course. You don't often get the chance to work with a legend, as he was. Personally, I think the film works much better when it's on television. On the big screen, for me it's too stagey and rather mechanical.

Hitchcock is famously on record for how actors should be treated.

I thought he was extremely helpful. I found him completely and utterly approachable and delightful, full of irony – and a lot of people can't take irony. I do understand, because I'm not a great fan of it myself, but, if you take the fact that he *was* ironic, then he was a very helpful director. You could ask him anything. He was a brilliant technician. He wasn't a brilliant director insofar as knowing how to play a scene, but he would sure tell you if he didn't like it.

Are you aware, on the set of a film like that, how suspense and tension are being built up?

You are with Hitchcock, very much so. You were with Powell, too – for instance, when Carl tried to murder me at the end of *Peeping Tom*, there was a terrific amount of tension which was simply created by the story itself and the way that they filmed it.

You were a very sympathetic Mrs Linde in *A Doll's House*. Was this a part you felt strongly drawn to?

No, not at all, but I was strongly drawn to working in such illustrious company. I didn't think Mrs Linde was a sympathetic character but I'm glad you think I made her so. I loved acting with Denholm Elliott. He taught me more about film acting than anyone I ever knew; he really had film acting down to the finest, finest point.

When you do a film based on a novel or a play, do you find it helpful to go back to the original text?

I didn't in that particular instance because I thought the screenplay was so very powerful. Anyway, you can't go back to the original because it was in Norwegian! Sometimes it is useful to go back to the original; on other occasions it can be confusing if it is at odds with the screenplay.

Do you recall working with the legendary Fred Zinnemann on *Five Days One Summer*?

Oh, I loved that and I thought he was wonderful. He is not the greatest director for actors, but he creates the most wonderful atmosphere. He has a magical personality. We made the film in Pontresina. Sean Connery was charming and couldn't have been more fun.

Did you enjoy the sophisticated comedy of your role in *Another Country*?

Yes, I liked that and I liked working with Marek Kanievska. My part wasn't in the original play although it was talked about. The original play all takes place within that room at the boys' school and the film opens it out. I think it was a really successful film. Plays can be harder to film than novels, it's true, but Julian Mitchell did his own adaptation for that one and it worked wonderfully well, I thought.

The Chain is a sharp and entertaining comedy. How did this part come your way?

I think Jack Gold just asked me to do it. I did enjoy working with Nigel Hawthorne, and Jack Gold was a delightful director to work with, helping one to pitch the comedy truthfully.

Some of your most notable film work has been for television. Do you find the filming procedures much different?

The procedures are different because of subtleties about which the director would know, but from an actor's point of view they are not that different. Film is film, but the difference has to do with the size of the shot, the pace of the film, those sorts of things. The subject has a lot to do with it, too. I mean, if you are going to film something like *Dances with Wolves*, then you do it for the big screen for the panoramic shots.

How do you rate *Hôtel du Lac*, which seems to me one of the best things I've seen on television?

I think it's a charming film, yes. This film means a great deal to me. We filmed it at the Park Hotel, Witznau, near Berne. I had read all of Anita Brookner's novels up to that point and the producer, Sue Birtwhistle, and I wrote to her asking if she would like to write a television film. She wrote back and said, not at all, but that she had a new book which might be suitable and she sent us a copy. I had always been too old to play her heroines up until then, as they were all in their late twenties, but we bought the rights to her new novel on the spot. It went on to win the Booker Prize and it was one of those projects where there were no hiccups at all along the line. Everything fell into place and we had a very good cast.

Have you ever been tempted to work in Hollywood on an extended basis?

Nobody has tempted me but I would be delighted to be tempted! I'd love to do a good film in Hollywood, Czechoslovakia – wherever, you name it.

Muir Mathieson

1911–1975

Music director: *The Private Life of Don Juan* (1934), *The Ghost Goes West, The Scarlet Pimpernel, Sanders of the River* (1935), *Things to Come* (1936), *Wings of the Morning* (1937), *Sixty Glorious Years, The Four Feathers, The Spy in Black* (1939), *The Thief of Baghdad* (1940), *49th Parallel, Love on the Dole* (1941), *They Flew Alone* (1942), *The Demi-Paradise* (1943), *The Way Ahead, Henry V* (1944), *Brief Encounter* (1945), **A Diary for Timothy* (1946), *Odd Man Out* (1947), *Oliver Twist* (1948), *Chris-* *topher Columbus* (1949), *The Wooden Horse* (1950), *The Sound Barrier* (1952), *The Four-Sided Triangle* (1953), *The Sleeping Tiger* (1954), *Cockleshell Heroes* (1955), *Trapeze* (1956), *Night of the Demon* (1957), *Vertigo* (1958), *The Savage Innocents* (1959), *Macbeth* (1960), *Only Two Can Play* (1961), *The L-Shaped Room, Life for Ruth* (1962), *The Running Man* (1963), *Becket, Woman of Straw* (1964), *The High Bright Sun* (1965)
*Documentary

Muir Mathieson's credits run to hundreds of films, so the above is a mere selection of his work. He directed *Instruments of the Orchestra* (short) (1946) and made personal appearances with the London Symphony Orchestra in *The Seventh Veil* (1945) and *A Girl in a Million* (1946).

'The position of the composer writing for films raises a number of interesting questions. There is, of course, the matter of artistic satisfaction. Most composers seem to agree that film music is not irksome or unworthy any more.'[1] That this was so may be attributed largely to the author of that remark – Muir Mathieson, who may well have more credits than anyone else in the history of British cinema. The list above is no more than representative of the range of directors he worked with and the genres he worked in.

Mathieson had firm ideas about the nature and function of a film's music soundtrack. 'Music can help to humanise the subject and widen its appeal ... Music can make the film less intellectual and more emotional ... It can prepare the eye through the ear. It can merge unnoticeably from realistic into pure music. It can shock. It can startle. It can sympathise. It can sweeten.'[2] Staunch advocate as he was of the importance of film music, he was nevertheless clear about its place in the film as a whole: 'As things are now, pictures are designed to be seen only once, and on one viewing the music cannot hope to emerge as a conscious element of the entertainment. In fact, it is not meant to, for the music should be an integral part of the construction.'[3] He confirms this view elsewhere, saying that 'the audience should not normally be conscious of it as a separate entity.'[4]

Apart from his own contribution as music director to an astonishing range of British films, including some of the most famous and distinguished of all, perhaps his greatest legacy is in the way he attracted the foremost British composers of his day to write for films. 'With Arthur Bliss's *Things to Come*, film music established itself in its own right,'[5] he wrote in 1947. By this time, he had secured the composing services of, among others, Richard Addinsell (*Dangerous Moonlight*), William Alwyn (*The Way Ahead*), Arthur Benjamin (*The Scarlet Pimpernel*), Benjamin Britten (who wrote the music for Mathieson's own film, *Instruments of the Orchestra*), Miklos Rozsa (*The Thief of Baghdad*), William Walton (*The First of the Few*) and Vaughan Williams (*49th Parallel*). 'For the composer,' he said in 1949, 'film music is a new outlet which, in many cases, enables him to live by practising his art. The cinema has become the musician's patron as royal courts used to be in the past; when in the last two or three hundred years have composers been able to live by writing music? Now, at last, it is possible.'[6]

He was full-time music director to Korda's London Films from 1935, formed the London Film Symphony Orchestra, was music director to the Crown Film Unit and to the Army and RAF film units, and, post-war, worked for David Lean, Anthony Asquith, Carol Reed, Humphrey Jennings and dozens of others. Though he never wavered in his belief that film music 'must be always approached with an eye to the context as well as its purely musical value',[7] he was also a pioneer of the recording and concert hall performance of film music. He identified two types of film music: 'Firstly, there is the standard music which is merely recorded and used *in* a film, and, secondly, there is the music specially commissioned and written *for* a film: I believe in the latter.'[8] This was fortunate for composers and for British films.

1 Muir Mathieson, 'Developments in film music', *Penguin Film Review*, No 4, West Drayton, 1947, p 43
2 'Muir Mathieson', *Films and Filming*, January 1976, p 45
3 Muir Mathieson, foreword to John Huntley, *British Film Music*, Skelton Robinson, London, 1947, p 7
4 Mathieson, 'Developments in film music', p 44
5 Mathieson, foreword to Huntley, p 7
6 Catherine de la Roche, 'Music, Mathieson, please', *Picturegoer*, 8 October 1949, p 17
7 Mathieson, 'Developments in film music', p 42
8 Mathieson, foreword to Huntley, p 7

Jessie Matthews

1907–1981

Actor: *The Beloved Vagabond* (1923), *This England, Straws in the Wind* (1924), *Out of the Blue* (1931), *There Goes the Bride, The Midshipmaid* (1932), *The Man From Toronto, The Good Companions, Friday the Thirteenth* (1933), *Waltzes from Vienna, Evergreen* (1934), *First a Girl* (1935), *It's Love Again* (1936), *Head Over Heels, Gangway* (1937), *Sailing Along* (1938), *Climbing High* (1939), *Forever and a Day* (1943), **Victory Wedding* (dir only) (1944), *Candles at Nine* (1945), **Life is Nothing without Music, *Making the Grade* (1947), *Tom Thumb* (1958), **A Hundred Years Underground* (1963), *The Hound of the Baskervilles* (1977)

* Short film.

'If I ceased to be a star, all that interest in my home life would evaporate, I believe. Perhaps it is the price one has to pay for being a star,'[1] reflected Jessie Matthews in 1934, very nearly at the peak of her fame. Indeed, she seems to have paid a considerable 'price' for her fame, in unhappy marriages and a perhaps unresolved tension between her humble origins and her international stardom. 'You know,' said Jessie, quietly, 'I used to live near here,'[2] as she stepped from a limousine to visit a children's hospital in Soho, the scene of her early poverty.

One draws attention to this suggestion of a divided life because, unlike her great contemporary Gracie Fields, who stayed resolutely true to her class in her film *persona*, Matthews, on both stage and screen, cultivated an upper-class diction that removed her from hers. Nevertheless, unlike Fields, she *did* become 'Britain's First World Woman Star',[3] as the title of a 1936 article proclaimed. Once she hit her stride in the early '30s, her effortlessly lissom dancing, the distinctive face (wide eyes, tip-tilted nose, pert chin), the sexily exposed figure, the prettily piping singing voice, and her infectious gaiety as an actress, made her *the* British cinema star of the '30s.

Of her first major film, she wrote: 'It was a disaster . . . *Out of the Blue* was adapted from a stage musical and it should never have left the boards.'[4] The next three were better, amiable enough if not memorable; then in 1933 she found the director who would guide her to a fame hitherto unparalleled in British cinema. This was Victor Saville, now valued as a major '30s director, who made five key films with her. She said of the first, a fine, unmannered adaptation of JB Priestley's *The Good Companions*: 'I think I enjoyed making this more than any other film, because there was so much theatrical atmosphere in it. Of course, Victor Saville is a marvellous director to work for, anyhow . . .'[5] In this and her other films for Saville, she had the advantage of well-written screenplays, attractive supporting casts and strong production values, but the emphasis was always firmly on *her* talents. She wrote later: 'I knew that Victor had given me this screen personality that went down so well with the public . . . the little girl from Soho, the waif with the great big eyes, who had become a sex symbol . . . He'd handled this image so well, with enough discretion never to make it vulgar.'[6]

As a result of these films – *Friday the Thirteenth, First a Girl, It's Love Again* and, especially, *Evergreen*, in which she repeated her stage 'dual' role of a singer impersonating her own mother – she became sought after by Hollywood. America dubbed her 'The Dancing Divinity', and she told reporters in 1935, 'I've had several offers to star in American films since the success of *Evergreen* in the US, and I am considering them,'[7] confessing that 'One of my greatest ambitions is to dance with

Fred Astaire.'[8] Sadly, negotiations to bring this about foundered, and her only US appearance was in the 1943 all-star fundraiser, *Forever and a Day*.

When her husband, the charmless Sonnie Hale, began directing her films, their fragile, art deco charms came to seem thin, and even a film with Carol Reed, *Climbing High*, did not arrest the decline, though she described him as 'a completely new breed of director . . . There was no slickness about this young man.'[9] In the post-war world, she was unable to find a niche again, except in the long-running radio soap, *Mrs Dale's Diary*. She did a couple of cameo roles, theatre at home and abroad, and on television was a sparkling Aunt Bessie in *Edward and Mrs Simpson*, which recreated the '30s world she had so entranced.

1 Jessie Matthews, 'Hands off my private life', *Picturegoer*, 10 March 1934, p 13
2 John K Newnham, 'Jessie Matthews – A study in contrasts', *Film Weekly*, 27 February 1937, p 7
3 *Picturegoer Weekly*, 15 August 1936, p 12
4 Jessie Matthews, *Over My Shoulder*, WH Allen, London, 1976, p 117
5 Doris Mackie, 'Jessie Matthews talks about herself', *Film Weekly*, 19 May 1933, p 12
6 Matthews, *Over My Shoulder*, p 147
7 Michael Thornton, *Jessie Matthews*, Hart-Davis, MacGibbon, London, 1974, p 125
8 Jessie Matthews, 'My comeback', *Film Weekly*, 14 June 1935, p 11
9 Nicholas Wapshott, *The Man Between: A Biography of Carol Reed*, Chatto & Windus, London, 1990, p 118

Michael Medwin

b. 1923

Actor: *Piccadilly Incident* (1946), *The Root of All Evil, The Courtneys of Curzon Street, Black Memory, Just William's Luck* (1947), *An Ideal Husband, Call of the Blood, Night Beat, Anna Karenina, My Sister and I, Woman Hater, Another Shore, Look Before You Love, Operation Diamond, William Comes to Town* (1948), *For Them That Trespass, Forbidden, Queen of Spades, Trottie True, Boys in Brown, Children of Chance, Helter Skelter* (1949), *Shadow of the Past, Someone at the Door, Trio, The Lady Craved Excitement* (1950), *Four in a Jeep, The Long Dark Hall* (1951), *Curtain Up, Hindle Wakes, Top Secret, Love's a Luxury, Miss Robin Hood* (1952), *The Oracle, Street Corner, Genevieve, The Intruder, Malta Story, Spaceways* (1953), *Bang! You're Dead, The Green Scarf, The Harassed Hero, Conflict of Wings, The Teckman Mystery* (1954), *Above Us the Waves, Doctor at Sea* (1955), *A Man on the Beach, Charley Moon, A Hill in Korea, Checkpoint, The Man in the Road* (1956), *Doctor at Large, The Steel Bayonet* (1957), *The Duke Wore Jeans, The Wind Cannot Read, I Only Asked!* (1958), *Carry On Nurse, Heart of a Man* (1959), *The Longest Day, Crooks Anonymous* (1962), *It's All Happening, Kali-Lug – Goddess of Vengeance, Kali-Lug – The Mystery of the Indian Tomb* (1963), *Night Must Fall, Rattle of a Simple Man* (1964), *I've Gotta Horse, 24 Hours to Kill* (1965), *The Sandwich Man, A Countess from Hong Kong* (1966), *Scrooge* (1970), *O Lucky Man!* (1973), *Law and Disorder* (1975), *The Sea Wolves* (1980), *Britannia Hospital* (1982), *The Jigsaw Man, Never Say Never Again* (1983), *Paradise Hotel* (1986), *Falcon's Maltester* (1987), *Staggered* (1994)

Producer: *Charlie Bubbles* (1967), *If. . ., Spring and Port Wine* (1968), *Gumshoe* (1971), *Alpha Beta, O Lucky Man!* (1973), *Law and Disorder* (1975)

Michael Medwin has had several careers in British show business, conducting them sometimes concurrently. Over a span of fifty years, he has been one of the most familiar of British cinema's character actors; a stage actor, scoring notable success in the title role in *Alfie*; a television star and producer; and a film producer for whose company several major British films were made. The latter include two by Lindsay Anderson (*If...* and *O Lucky Man!*) and three starring his business partner Albert Finney (*Charlie Bubbles*, *Gumshoe* and *Alpha Beta*). None of these is a conventional film, unlike – it must be said – many of those in which he acted during the '40s and '50s. Nevertheless, working for many important directors, in films major and minor, in the genres that were the staple of British filmmaking in the post-war decades, Medwin stamped a recognisable ease and authority on dozens of roles, making the most of what was offered. He is strikingly effective as the soldier-turned-criminal in Guy Hamilton's excellent *The Intruder* and he is a notably amusing figure in such entertainments as *Genevieve* (as the pregnant father) and *Doctor at Large*. The breadth of his experience makes him a valuable commentator on the fortunes of British cinema.

Interview date: October 1992

As far as I know, your first film was *Piccadilly Incident* in 1946.

No, actually my first in 1946 was *The Root of All Evil*, on which I had one day. John McCallum and Phyllis Calvert were in it and the director was Brock Williams. I got into it because I knew a producer called Harold Huth, who was then with Gainsborough; he gave me this one-day part. I had been in rep in Newcastle at £7 10s a week, after the war, learning my trade. To my amazement I got this part – and I got £7 or £8 a day, which in 1946 was untold riches. *Piccadilly Incident* came just after that, with Herbert Wilcox, who was pleased with me and rather took me up.

You had a much bigger part in his next film, *The Courtneys of Curzon Street*.

Yes. I only had to deliver a telegram to Michael Wilding in *Piccadilly Incident*, but Wilcox must have liked the way I delivered it, because I suddenly became Anna Neagle and Michael Wilding's son, which I think must have done away with typecasting for me!

Herbert was a wonderful man, and absolutely delightful and helpful to work with as a director. He had infectious charm, which is terrific for the artistes and the whole unit. And he was so devoted

to Anna, and in filmmaking that sort of thing spills over. There is a sort of reverberation. He loved Michael Wilding, he brought those two together, and at a time just after a major war, when people wanted some froth and bubble and romance and charm and a bit of escapism. In today's world it is probably a bit of an anachronism, but then it was absolutely right, and he was the major successful producer at that moment.

Between *Piccadilly Incident* and the end of 1950, you seem to have appeared in no fewer than twenty-five films. Was this work easy to come by?

I became 'flavour of the month' as a young character actor. I did a film for Alexander Korda called *Night Beat*, again produced by Harold Huth, who was one of my patrons, and I had a vignette which was effectively unwritten, so there was some extemporary work. I was a Cockney spiv, being arrested in a charge room. Korda was never going to show the film but – and this is how luck works in an actor's life – a film fell out at the Empire; they needed a replacement and *Night Beat* was allowed to go in. It got the most appalling reviews; I didn't have a credit on it, but all the critics said that the only good thing in the film was somebody the producers hadn't even had the decency to give a credit to. A mate of mine was there and told them who I was.

Then, the next time they were reviewing, I had a very small role in Duvivier's *Anna Karenina*, playing an elderly doctor, no longer a spiv; again it was a vignette but I was clearly a character actor and I had the two great reviews, so I was offered a contract by both Rank and Korda, which I didn't sign at that time. Suddenly, I remember very well, in about 1949 I was earning £350 a week, because I was doing films at Worton Hall, Denham, Garden City, Pinewood, and all those studios which have now closed.

Was Korda's flair really that of a producer rather than a director?

I think he was a very great producer, a giant. He loved film, loved it to be right; he was very kind to me and subsequently I did sign a contract with him. I remember very well a marvellous moment: it is always lovely to be accepted, and after I'd done *Night Beat* I was sent down to Shepperton for the Duke of Nonsuch [a Korda invention] in Korda's *An Ideal Husband*; I was with the casting director when Alex Korda was sweeping by and he stopped, saying, 'Oh, you played the spiv. Very good – let him have the Duke!' and swept on. To be accepted so quickly is wonderful; it's a moment of celebration and always will be.

You made three films at this time which interest me: Brian Desmond Hurst's *Trottie True*, Thorold Dickinson's *Queen of Spades* and Montgomery Tully's *Boys in Brown*.

I was the Duke of Maidenhead, I think, in *Trottie True*, a friend of James Donald's. I thought it had a lot of charm. It was about George Edwardes's Gaiety Theatre and there were a lot of 'escorts' or stage-door johnnies. One of them was Roger Moore, as was Christopher Lee, and Patrick Cargill was in it. It is interesting, too, that when I became known as a character actor I played all those Cockney parts for a long time, yet I had started off playing dukes in *Trottie True* and *An Ideal Husband*.

One of the screenplay's authors, Rodney Ackland, started directing *Queen of Spades* before Thorold took over. When Thorold took over I was sent for and he told me it was a rather heavy film and needed something lighter, so I got the part. My first scene was in a theatre box with Edith Evans – who'd recently been made a Dame – in her first major film. I got a few laughs from the unit before the take and I was rather embarrassed, because here I was confronting this great lady of the theatre. However, she took to me, though I was extremely nervous.

Then Thorold built up the part and it kept going throughout the film, so I was delighted. I was in many scenes but at the première I found that most of them had been cut. I met Thorold at the première and he said, 'I made a great mistake, Michael. I put you in to lighten it and I cut it all out, and I should have left it in!', which is not what you want to hear. I knew I had a good character role but it ended up on the cutting-room floor. The art direction was done by the great Oliver Messel; it's in black-and-white and looks simply sensational.

You played a rather nasty piece of work in your next film, *Boys in Brown*.

It was awful. I had seen the play and it was the best comedic part in it. I was very disappointed because it was a part I would have died for; on the stage I would have been terrific in it, but I wasn't at all happy with the way I did it in the film. Montgomery Tully was not the most inspired director and everything on the film was wrong although it was a very good cast. We used Independent Frame in making it.

I hope you can tell me about Group 3, for which you did *Miss Robin Hood* and *The Oracle*.

Group 3 was a worthy experiment. We shot *The Oracle* down in my own country [Dorset] and I enjoyed making it very much. It was a very happy experience. Rather a nice idea. Group 3 was put together by the National Film Finance Corporation, using new directors, new ideas and low budgets. I don't know how it worked out commercially, but, if they'd known that television was going to come along, they probably would have continued it, because they would have had an extremely good library of low-budget films for television showing. John Guillermin, who directed *Miss Robin Hood*, went on to Hollywood and directed some major films. I remember doing a test for that with a young Joan Collins, but she was far too glamorous, too wildly exotic for the part.

Would you agree that Guy Hamilton gave you your best part to date in your next film, *The Intruder* in 1953, which still seems interesting as a critique of post-war Britain?

It was the biggest role I'd had, a leading role. I think I was still under contract to Korda then. The casting director was Bill O'Brien, who was a very senior executive with British Lion. He liked me and was responsible for pushing me into that role. It was one of Guy's first pictures as a director. I enjoyed doing it very much, and I heard later that when certain directors saw the film they took me seriously as an actor, which was nice.

Were you satisfied with the range of parts you were getting in a lot of popular films in the '50s? Were you contracted to Rank from the mid '50s?

I've never been ambitious, I was just happy to work. Being a character actor in a high-risk business can be difficult, so it was always a joy to be employed. I had no Everest to climb. I was contracted to Korda for a couple of years, then British Lion went bankrupt. Most of my other films were with Rank but they were through my agents or through being loaned out by Korda.

You did the title role for Wendy Toye in *The Teckman Mystery*.

She was under contract to Korda and did it for him. I think it was OK but it is hard to remember. Directing in films is not quite the same process as in the theatre, where you have time to talk about the part and how you do it. And directors today work differently; they are technical people who don't necessarily know a lot about directing. In many cases they are directing untrained actors too, and I'm a trained actor, I can change. In that sense it wouldn't have made too much difference who was directing, because I was skilled and could look after myself. There are certain egotistical stars who don't want to be directed, but of course one is always begging (if one wants to be good) for skilled direction from an outside eye; you need it vitally.

Again, I don't remember much about *The Teckman Mystery* other than that Margaret Leighton was in it. She lived in the Albany, that wonderfully *recherché* set of chambers, and she invited me there to lunch. She was absolutely obsessive about her weight – not anorexic, but practically so – and lunch with her was lemon juice and charcoal biscuits, and I'm not quite used to that!

You made a number of films for the successful and enduring director–producer team of Ralph Thomas and Betty Box. What were your impressions of them?

They were terrific to me because they employed me a lot and I went to some very exotic locations with them. I went to Delhi for *The Wind Cannot Read*, to Florence for *Checkpoint*. Ralph and Betty liked me, so I did a lot of films for them. For *Doctor at Sea* we went from Venice to Piraeus in a boat.

They were a very good team. I also did one film for the Gerald Thomas–Peter Rogers team, a vignette in the second *Carry On* film.

After a gap in your film work for about three years, 1959–62, when you were having success on television, you made some films in the '60s with interesting credentials, including Karel Reisz's *Night Must Fall* and Charles Chaplin's *A Countess from Hong Kong*. What are your recollections of working in these?

I was sort of a conventional romantic lead in *Night Must Fall* but rather hopeless, the sort of guy who doesn't get the girl in the Hollywood tradition. I got an offer to do it in a cablegram from Karel when I was working on the *Kali-Lug* films in Italy, and of course I said yes. The film never really quite worked; personally I think it was a melodrama and could only be used as such. Trying to update it, make it psychological, I don't think worked.

I was producing *Charlie Bubbles* for Universal and we were in the same office as Jerry Epstein, who was producing the Chaplin film. He asked me if I'd like to play a vignette in it and invited me down to Pinewood to meet Charlie. At the end of the day I was introduced and it was an audition. It's one thing to be given a part by Chaplin and another thing to audition. I was now a producer and I didn't want to audition – and not get it. I was extremely angry and could have killed Jerry Epstein. Anyway, Charlie was lying on a chaise longue; I was given a script, so I read a few lines and got the role.

The film was the most unrewarding experience, not the fantastic experience of working with a genius that you'd expect. I disliked him enormously. You did exactly what he told you – it was almost done by numbers. He was awful, the atmosphere was terrible; Brando never came out of his caravan; no one was speaking. Chaplin would rehearse with Jerry Epstein and then Brando would come out, by this time totally disenchanted with the whole thing. It was simply the worst atmosphere of any film I've ever been on.

It must have been a relief to get back to producing *Charlie Bubbles*. How did you view the producer's function? Did it give you as much satisfaction as acting?

Sort of. They are such different functions. Being the producer is extremely wearing; there are calls at night . . . and of course it's the director you have to protect. In the end it would become very onerous. But I did it for a long time and met some wonderful people.

Is Memorial your own production company?

Yes, Albert Finney's and mine, but it's wrapped now, although we were talking the other day about finding one more to do. I wish Albert would direct something else, he's absolutely wonderful. *Charlie Bubbles* is a film that will last, it's a film that concerns itself with perennial relationships and problems. It didn't take a lot of money to make, either. He is also a terrific actor. We only did our films with majors, so we never embarked on a film without a distribution contract. At least you know it is going to be shown when you have a distribution guarantee.

Do you think I'm right in regarding the '40s and '50s as a kind of boom period in British cinema?

Yes, I suppose so. Just after the war people were going to cinema and they were going to British films. But once Hollywood found itself we were right back – for instance, Albert Finney, as a young man, wouldn't dream of going to see a British film. He and his generation found all those too-too-British voices so alien to where he came from and he loved American films. But in the '40s and '50s people were happy to see British films and, of course, they were being made in large numbers and we had some stars.

Bernard Miles (Lord Miles)

1907–1991

Actor: *Channel Crossing* (1933), *The Love Test* (1934), *Late Extra, Twelve Good Men, Crown vs Stevens, Midnight at Madame Tussaud's* (1935), **Kew Gardens* (narr) (1937), *The Citadel, The Challenge, 13 Men and a Gun, Convict 99, The Rebel Son* (1938), *Q Planes, The Four Feathers, The Spy in Black, The Lion has Wings, The Stars Look Doing* (1939), *Band Waggon, Pastor Hall, *Dawn Guards, *Sea Cadets, Contraband* (1940), *Freedom Radio, This was Paris, Quiet Wedding, *Home Guard, The Common Touch, The Big Blockade* (1941), *One of Our Aircraft is Missing, The Day Will Dawn, In Which We Serve, The First of the Few, The Goose Steps Out* (1942), *Tunisian Victory* (narr) (1943), *Tawny Pipit* (& dir), **Two Feathers* (1944), *Carnival, Great Expectations* (1946), *Nicholas Nickleby, Fame is the Spur* (1947), *The Guinea Pig* (1948), **Bernard Miles on Gun Dogs* (1949), *Chance of a Lifetime* (& dir) (1950), *The Magic Box* (1951), **River Ships* (narr), *Never Let Me Go* (1953), *Moby Dick, Tiger in the Smoke, The Man Who Knew Too Much, Zarak* (1956), *Fortune is a Woman, The Smallest Show on Earth, St Joan* (1957), *Tom Thumb, *The Vision of William Blake* (narr) (1958), *Sapphire* (1959), **A Flourish of Tubes* (1961), *Heavens Above!* (1963), **The Specialist* (1966), *Baby Love* (1968), *Run Wild, Run Free* (1969)

* Documentary or short film.

Bernard Miles's great strength as an actor was his capacity to suggest simplicity and goodness without weakness. This screen *persona* was established with his performance in *In Which We Serve*, in which he is the incarnation of working-class stoicism, and memorably clinched in his role as Joe Gargery in *Great Expectations*. In 1956 he appeared in two films which made use of and subverted the kindly Miles image: *Tiger in the*

Smoke, an often-chilling thriller, and Hitchcock's remake of *The Man Who Knew Too Much*, in which his benign *persona* makes the revelation of his villainy the more shocking. Perhaps as a result, in later films, such as *Sapphire*, one is led to wonder whether the kindly surface hides slyness or something more dangerous. The two films he directed – *Tawny Pipit* and *Chance of a Lifetime* – evoke him and their period vividly in their visions of cross-class consensual activity.
Interview date: July 1990

You made a great many films during the 1930s. What do you remember of working with people like Michael Powell?

Mickey was lovely; I made *The Love Test* for him when he was doing 'quota quickies'. He was rising through the ranks as I was making my own little way and we did several films together. I enjoyed working with him; he used to come to our home, a little country cottage, and he loved our food! I used to cycle twenty-five miles to the studio each day and twenty-five miles back. I met Del Giudice then too; he was a true genius who had lived an outrageous life. Two Cities was really Del Giudice's creation – he was really responsible for *In Which We Serve*.

What do you remember of this film, which really established you as a film star?

Noël Coward decided he would like to make a naval film, having spent wonderful times with the Mediterranean fleet; Dickie Mountbatten felt it was high time a film was made about the Navy and he hit on the idea of a film about a destroyer; he fed the information to Noël, who did the script. Dickie Mountbatten sold the idea to the King, then he came to see Del Giudice with two Royal Marines in full uniform. It was financed by a great man, the Jewish carpet merchant, Sassoon. When Sassoon sent him the cheque, with one stroke Del Giudice was the only free man in the industry, the only man with £195,000 in his pocket, and he owned *In Which We Serve*. He was a great impresario. Dickie Mountbatten himself suggested me for the part I played – Kath Harrison and I were a real working-class couple.

Did the two films you made for the Boultings, *The Guinea Pig* and *Fame is the Spur*, appeal to your Socialist instincts?

Yes, they did. *Fame is the Spur* was said to be based on Ramsay MacDonald's career. The film didn't do very well; Michael Redgrave wasn't a popular star and it wasn't a sympathetic role, but Rosamund John was wonderful in it.

I also did some of the writing for *The Guinea Pig* with Warren Chetham-Strode – a difficult man who didn't want his play altered. I wrote some lovely things which the Boultings had to force him to accept. Dickie Attenborough was very good in it. He was also wonderful in *In Which We Serve*. His part in that was modelled on a young sailor on the *Kelly*, which was sunk at Crete. He was stationed below decks, loading shells, when he heard dive bombers overhead and ran away.

How did you come to direct *Tawny Pipit* and *Chance of a Lifetime*?

I directed *Tawny Pipit* for Two Cities. Del Giudice was asked by Dickie Mountbatten and others to make a film about the true nature of the British people. Del asked me to think up a story and he would get the money from Arthur Rank. I lived near Julian Huxley, the great biologist; and he suggested that, in the teeth of all the people making war films like *San Demetrio, London*, I should make a film about something which was then happening in the ornithological world. A bird had been sighted in Norfolk which had never been seen in Britain before; and he showed me a picture of the tawny pipit. He put me on to a publican in Norwich, Jim Vincent, who had seen the original nest. Well, he didn't want to show us where it was, so we had to get Julian Huxley to talk to him.

It was a charming film, I think. When the Americans saw it first, they dumped it in a cupboard for two years, but it was finally shown and got the greatest notices. I didn't know anything about filming really; I had a good cameraman and I knew the cutters were good. Charles Saunders was really the cutter but I felt he should be given credit as co-director because he put the whole thing together as a coherent film. We had Rosamund John, Lucy Mannheim, a German refugee and a fine actress, who married Marius Goring, and Jean Gillie, who was absolutely gorgeous; she died a few years later.

Del liked it very much and asked me to do another film for him. By that time I had become a sort of Socialist; I'd met Ernie Bevin, Stafford Cripps, all of whom backed Del Giudice. I was very attracted to the idea of co-operation between management and workers; that was my kind of Socialism. A few years later, I came up with the story for *Chance of a Lifetime*; I got the idea of the one-way plough from the great industrialist, Harry Ferguson, who actually manufactured and sold this implement. The plough is really the star of the film. Basil Radford played the boss of the factory and he was a wonderful actor – he could only do one thing but he did it better than anyone else. Del knew Arthur Rank wouldn't like it, being a rich Methodist Tory; so Del set about winning Stafford Cripps, Bevin and others.

When we arranged the showing, it was seen by half the Labour Party. Anthony Crosland was there, and Sir John Reith too. I stood in the doorway waiting for them to come out and Reith, the head of the BBC, said, 'Great job, you should be proud of it.' Then Crosland came up to me and said, 'Bloody marvellous! And you don't mention the word "Socialism" – you're a clever bugger!' You see, I had a conceit that I could 'speak for England'. Churchill had used that phrase in a speech as Prime Minister and I didn't see why I shouldn't borrow it! So I was impudent enough to make the films 'speak for England'.

Did you enjoy playing Joe Gargery in *Great Expectations*?

I got on very well with David Lean. I fell foul of him once, though, because, when Joe Gargery meets Pip and Herbert in London and is so struck with the importance of the meeting, he is supposed to put his new top hat on the mantelpiece. However, the mantelpiece was very narrow and I realised I couldn't do the shot; I was very shy of David then, so I went on with the first take and of course the hat fell off. David was disappointed because it would have been such a good shot, so I asked if I could do it the way I had the first time, which was to catch the hat each time it fell off the mantelpiece.

Francis L Sullivan as Jaggers was wonderful, a great presence. Martita Hunt [Miss Havisham] was a flamboyant character offscreen as well as on; she had taken Alec Guinness under her wing. All those scenes with the boy [Pip], Tony Wager, were done

in north Kent on the river, near the marsh country. We stayed in Gravesend when we were doing all that stuff.

Why do you think it was such a success?

I think the moralities had changed. Pip is awful, really, because he lets Joe and Magwitch down. John Mills was so good in it, he's such a great technician and a lovely human being. David Lean did a marvellous job with the script, given that he was a non-reader. I didn't steep myself in the book to play the part but I knew my Dickens; I also played Newman Noggs in Cavalcanti's film of *Nicholas Nickleby*, which we made at Ealing.

Cavalcanti was lovely to work with but the crew played bad tricks on him. He had one or two altercations with the electricians at the time when the trade unions were very strong. I was doing a scene one day and there was a book or something lying on the floor of the set; Cav called to Jack Martin, the First Assistant in charge of the shot, and said we had to get rid of it. Jack replied that we couldn't touch it because there were no Props people available and if anyone else touched it there'd be a strike. They had to send a car to Wembley to fetch a Props man to move the thing, while shooting just stopped. I remember Cedric Hardwicke in that; he decided at the outset of his film career that he couldn't play romantic leads, that he would have to specialise as a character actor.

What do you recall of working for John Huston on *Moby Dick* in the mid '50s?

When the sun wasn't shining we would all meet on the deck of the *Pequod* – Huston, Richard Basehart, Greg Peck, Leo Genn and I – and we would play poker until the sun came out and we could start filming again. Greg was usually given 'handsome' parts and he had a lovely light comic touch, but he was marvellous in *Moby Dick*, such a tragic part. He was so modest, an absolutely lovely man. I kept in touch with Huston until he died, too. I was there when Orson Welles did his great preaching scene; he came on to the stage and Huston called for quiet; he told us that he (Huston) would leave the stage. He gave the impression that Welles was such a great actor, we were privileged to have him there. Orson didn't like Huston very much, used to give him orders because he was so used to directing himself. John always spoke softly, but he was a bit cruel and liked to let the actors suffer a bit.

Sarah Miles

b. 1943

Actor: *The Roman Spring of Mrs Stone, Term of Trial* (1962), *Six-Sided Triangle, The Servant* (1963), *The Ceremony* (1964), *Those Magnificent Men in Their Flying Machines, I Was Happy Here* (1965), *Blow Up* (1967), *Ryan's Daughter* (1970), *Lady Caroline Lamb* (1972), *The Hireling, The Man Who Loved Cat Dancing* (1973), *Great Expectations* (1975), *The Sailor Who Fell from Grace with the Sea* (1976), *The Big Sleep* (1978), *Priest of Love* (1980), *Venom* (1981), *Agatha Christie's Ordeal by Innocence, Steaming* (1984), *Hope and Glory, White Mischief* (1987), *The Touch* (1992)

After no more than a walk-on in her first film, Sarah Miles suddenly found herself starring opposite her idol, Sir Laurence Olivier, in *Term of Trial* in 1962. Not just starring opposite, but also seducing him, and doing so with a sensual boldness unthinkable in British cinema before this time. The confrontation of the great acting knight by this sexually dangerous teenager (she was eighteen) seems in retrospect a symptom of the whole disruptive decade. In her next film, *The Servant*, she continued her transgressive course, not merely sleeping with master (James Fox) and servant (Dirk Bogarde), but being instrumental in the confusion of their roles and thereby calling the class system into question. Sex and class were two issues about which '60s British cinema was more honest than it had hitherto been and Sarah Miles's performances in these two films are key contributions to the ongoing dialectic; so is her finely wrought study of a nervously ill woman feeling her way back to health in *The Hireling*. She lost interest in the cinema from time to time, but she enjoyed *The Sailor Who Fell . . .*, which has now acquired a cult following in the US, and in 1987 she suddenly appeared in two vivid character roles, in *Hope and Glory* and *White Mischief*, suggesting she could have a whole new career – if she wants it.
Interview date: July 1994

You got some of the choicest roles going for an actress in Britain in the 1960s. Did it seem like a good time to be starting a film career?

I didn't really think about it – one just gets on with the parts and goes for it. I suppose one didn't think that the '60s was probably going to be the best decade we had in British films. At the time of course, presumably, one didn't make hay while the sun shone because one didn't think the sun was going to go down, as it were.

Was anyone, such as an agent, guiding your career at this time?

I had a wonderful agent called Robin Fox. They just don't make agents like that any more, alas. I went straight from RADA into a West End play directed by John Gielgud, then into rep, and within three months I'd got a plum role opposite Laurence Olivier. Oddly enough, I had been seriously in love with him since I was about eleven and kept his picture under my pillow for many years.

How did you come to get that role opposite your idol in *Term of Trial*?

I think just by being quite cantankerous! I couldn't believe it when Robin Fox told me to go and test for a role opposite Olivier. I was late, having come up from Worthing rep, where I was playing in *The Moon is Blue*, and I had to get back by seven. The queue was enormously long – I've never seen so many blondes in a row in all my life. I decided I would have to queue-barge if I were to have time to test at all. As soon as one girl came out I shot in, and explained that I had to get back to Worthing in time for curtain up. I made a speech about them apparently wanting a blonde and I was the only brunette in the line. They quietened me down and asked me to read a scene, which I did rather badly, I thought.

Had you read James Barlow's novel?

I hadn't at that point, but I did after I'd been offered the part. Reading is a terrible strain on me because of my dyslexia, so I read as little as possible. I think it is probably dangerous to do too much research, because it may conflict with the screenplay. You usually have to hope that the writer of the screenplay has done his research sufficiently, and that the part you are playing is down on the pages of the script as well as it can be.

What was your experience of working with Laurence Olivier?

I think it was because I was staring and so palpably in love that got me the role! I don't think it was any acting ability whatsoever. There was one point in the film when I was feeding him the lines-off for his close-up, and I began giggling. There was hushed silence until the director asked me what on earth that was about. I apologised, and Larry said, 'You were laughing at me, weren't you?' and I said, 'Yes, sir, I'm sorry, I was.' He said we should all

have a tea-break while he spoke to me back in his dressing room. He asked me what had been so funny and I explained that every time his eyebrow went up it was a danger sign of lost lines ahead. He was absolutely riveted at being caught out like this, so he sat down in front of a mirror and we did the scene again. I think from that moment onwards something gelled between us and he had some sort of respect for me, because what I had said was true. I think the film has been very underrated. It is never on television and no one sees it. Critically, Larry didn't come out of the film as well as he deserved, but it was fashionable to slam him at the time.

***The Servant* now seems a landmark film in British cinema. Did it seem, as you were making it, an important film?**

No, not at all, it was just a frolic. I didn't get the impression it would be the way it turned out to be. I knew we were doing stuff in that film that probably hadn't been done before, and I knew I dreaded my parents seeing it. I was right about that because, when they'd seen a preview, they came to my home and said, 'How dare you! The servants will leave!' When it came out a couple of weeks later, my parents had to eat humble pie. They had no idea it was going to be the triumph that it was. I can never bear to see my films twice, but for some reason I saw it again recently. There is some very good stuff in it, the way the camera is so fluid and economical: it just seems to move around, picking up the story with such a delicate grace and economy. I can see now that it is an extraordinary piece of work.

Was Joseph Losey's preference for the long take and the gliding, tracking camera very demanding for an actor?

I find it very challenging and exciting because you have to have all your wits about you. I'd much rather be doing that than 'Cut, close-up, cut,' etc, which is so dreary. Perhaps American actors without a stage background would find it gruelling, because it is hardly ever done today.

Were you very aware of Douglas Slocombe as the cameraman?

I was always very aware of Douglas on a personal level. He is one of the most brilliant cameramen of all, I think. He makes everything look new – he adds a certain something, rather than making it look the same as it is in life. He is adding something without it being false or bland or showbizzy. He adds a dimension that is not arty but somehow just more real. I can't quite explain it.

Were you technically knowledgeable?

I wish I had been because I'd have looked a damn sight better if I were. I once worked with Faye Dunaway [in *Ordeal by Innocence*] and, my God! she had her own lighting man telling them where to put the lights, telling her where to look and so on. I don't know which side of my face is the 'right' one – I'm not saying I'm not vain, it's just that I don't know left from right. I think it is a Hollywood thing. I think it is disgraceful that I don't know these things.

Did Joseph Losey give you a lot of direction? Was it helpful?

Yes, it was in a way. We had different ideas of how to play Vera, alas, and right at the start of the film I had a very clear vision of the girl I was playing, which didn't quite sit with his vision, so we had a set-to over that. I told him there were hundreds of girls out there who could play her as a bimbo, so he should go out and get one of them! He finally let me play it my way. I can honestly say I don't think I've been helped hugely by any director. But I learned an awful lot from Dirk Bogarde on that film. He was a great professional and it was lovely watching him. It's a tough film and they're not nice people at all. It is surprising how it holds your attention, when you're not rooting for one person, as it were.

Blow Up is one of the most influential films of the '60s. How did you respond to Antonioni's direction?

That's a tricky one. There was no script so obviously you had to take it on faith. I suddenly disappear from the film at a certain point because I walked off after he and I locked horns. I think I was within my rights to behave as I did, which was to challenge him as to why he had me in bed making love to a man to whom I hadn't been introduced, and why David Hemmings comes in and finds me making love to another man, and I indicate that he should stay and watch. I found it very embarrassing to be in bed with this man I didn't know; to have to play an extremely vulnerable sex scene. I didn't know whether he was my husband or my lover and I didn't know whose flat I was in, or indeed who David Hemmings was. So I asked if I could have a word with Antonioni and he said, 'Of course, of course – call me Michelangelo.' I asked him these questions and he said, 'It does not matter.' I said, 'Well, if that doesn't matter, nothing matters,' and I packed my bags. Then I heard that he was doing a tennis match without a ball and with painted trees; my curiosity got the better of me and I had to go

and have a peek, but he saw me, so I went up and asked him what the painted trees and no tennis ball were all about. He said, 'Is for the critics.' I took my hat off to that and, having had doubts about the man, I ended up liking him for that one remark! And the scene has driven critics mad ever since! For me, it was a typical example of the Emperor's new clothes, but for most it seems to sum up the '60s.

A much more conventional film was Those Magnificent Men in Their Flying Machines. Was that enjoyable to make?

It was wonderful to make, and never before or again will there be such a fine list of comedians involved. I'm very proud of it and I think it works. It is such a good-natured film, very up and happy, and it makes people feel good. I've never understood myself why I went off with Stuart Whitman instead of James Fox in the end – extraordinary! The US distribution factor seems the most likely explanation.

What do you recall of making Ryan's Daughter? How did you find the location work?

To me, personally, it was hard slog: up at five o'clock on that hill every single day, waiting for the rain to stop. I probably had the toughest time of all because I was always there – if not working, then doing weather cover of some sort for the second unit, and it was enormously hard work. But there were some wonderful bonuses; there were some great characters in it, and having all of these extraordinary egomaniacal people in the little town of Dingle, sitting there waiting for the rain to stop.

Is it true that Stephen Grimes built a whole village for the film?

Oh yes, and it was a real village, not just a set. The pub was a proper pub, the houses were real houses, and at the end we asked the locals if they wanted us to leave it intact. 'Take the fookin' lot down,' they said, 'we're sick of the lot of ye!' We had got most of it down when they came back to us. 'We've had a little meeting and we've decided we want the village after all, so would ye kindly put it back up again. We realise now how valuable it'll be for the tourists.' Sorry, old chap! We did manage to keep the schoolhouse intact, though, and thousands of people trail over it every year to see where *Ryan's Daughter* was made.

Did you feel any notably different approaches to film acting from the major British and American stars?

They all hold their liquor very well! I suppose the

American approach is much subtler but I have my own idea of what was good in the film. The one who went by almost unnoticed was Trevor Howard; if you look at the film again you will see that he is giving a truly remarkable performance.

How did you find working with David Lean?

I think David was a very complex creature, one of the most complex I have had the privilege of knowing. Of course, any kind of greatness is usually coupled with ruthlessness, because in order to get what you want you have to be fairly ruthless toward that end. I think David had a problem with actors, perhaps thinking they were not very intelligent (and he was probably right), but he belittled them a lot and also liked to find their breaking point. I'm not sure whether it is a game he played or whether he did it deliberately, so that once he had broken them he could then get them to do what he wanted. I don't know what his motive was but he certainly wanted to find every actor's breaking point. But you have to remember that I loved and respected the man very deeply, because all he cared about was what was good in that frame and to hell with everything else. People can die or drown, boats can disappear – it doesn't matter as long as he gets what's in that frame. And that's why he is where he is. A tough director automatically goes with the results, I think. Nice men do good work but not great work.

Your next two films could scarcely have been greater contrasts to each other: *Lady Caroline Lamb*, a vast historical piece, and *The Hireling*, almost a chamber film. Did you have a preference for one kind of film over another?

No, I just like a good tale told as well as possible, with some good, shiny, sparkling dialogue that clips along. I don't feel interested in watching films any more. I refuse to be in a 'special effects' movie or in violence, so obviously I don't work very much now.

***Lady Caroline Lamb* was both written and directed by Robert Bolt. Do you think this double role is an advantage?**

I think probably so. I say this warily because often it takes another eye to get the distance, to be able to see it from perhaps a more over-all or 'holistic' point of view. I think Robert did an excellent job anyway, and the film stands up.

Margaret Leighton was surely one of the great actresses of British cinema. How did you find working with her?

She was a very dear friend; we were eerily close from the very start and she was ludicrously like my mother. We had such a rare rapport! When she married Michael Wilding and they were so happy together, both having had such rough lives, I was so pleased. One day in her trailer, she had just been told she had that awful creeping paralysis; she just laughed it off in that knowledgeable, wise, flippant way of hers.

How pleased were you with *The Hireling*?

My brother [director Christopher Miles] and I had tried to get the rights for that much earlier, but Wolf Mankowitz had already got them. I think it almost came off and it was a good stab at Hartley. I like Alan Bridges and I loved Robert Shaw. Coincidentally, we both got offers of scripts from America on the same day. Robert was longing to be an international star, while I was not yearning so much because it meant travel and I didn't want to leave my dogs. Robert received *The Sting* and I received *The Man Who Loved Cat Dancing*. He went on to be an enormous star after that, while I had a tragedy on my tail.

***The Hireling* is a film which approaches the class issue head on.**

Yes, it does, head on. I'm very happy with it; I think we all did the best we could under the circumstances. We all sat around a table and rewrote it on a daily basis. We filmed in Bath on the Royal Crescent, and we also used Paul Getty's home in Sutton Place, Guildford, as my home in the film. Paul was there while we were filming and he used to take me aside each day. 'How many crew members are there?' he would ask. 'About thirty, I suppose.' 'Well, I've got them down to fourteen, the rest are redundant!' he would say. He could see that most people on a film set do absolutely nothing, it's all union stuff. I hadn't even bothered to look at that side of things before.

You were reunited with Joseph Losey after twenty years for his last film, *Steaming*. Did you find any difference in his approach to actors?

No, I think he was much the same. He was very ill at the time and probably not at his best. I feel very sorry about that film because it could have been so good if he had just listened. It could have been a very erotic, sensual film had it been treated properly. The joy for me was meeting Diana Dors for the first time. We were like twin souls meeting and we couldn't understand why we hadn't met before. The media always treated us as sex objects, so I hadn't any idea when I met Diana that she was generous-spirited and such a great raconteur and wit.

You appeared in two excellent, contrasted roles both released in 1987, John Boorman's *Hope and Glory* as a suburban mum, and Michael Radford's *White Mischief* as a dissolute woman in colonial Africa. What do you remember of the two roles?

In each case the director asked me to do the part. *Hope and Glory* had a most elaborate set, the whole thing built somewhere outside London. Some of the houses were real so we could use them as interiors as well as exteriors. I enjoyed very much working with Susan Wooldridge, in fact I enjoyed the whole film. Some of it was filmed in the Thames Valley.

It was nice to have those two films back-to-back.

I went to Africa for *White Mischief*, which was wonderful. I met some people there including Douglas Hamilton, who works with the elephants, and they took me all over in their plane to see the elephants. It was the most extraordinary experience, making that film. They were about to fire Trevor Howard because he didn't know his lines, and I said if they fired him they would have to fire me as well, so I had to come up with a way of saving him and from then on I had to be his nurse, really. I had to make him learn his lines and it was quite heavy duty; I had to be with him all the time. But it was worth it because for me he had always been such a great man; he had innocence, and that has always been my favourite quality.

Hayley Mills

b. 1946

Actor: *Tiger Bay* (1959), *Pollyanna* (1960), *The Parent Trap*, *Whistle Down the Wind* (1961), *In Search of the Castaways* (1962), *Summer Magic*, *The Chalk Garden* (1963), *The Moon Spinners*, *The Truth About Spring* (1964), *Sky West and Crooked*, *That Darn Cat* (1965), *The Daydreamer* (voice only), *The Trouble with Angels*, *The Family Way* (1966), *Pretty Polly*, *Africa – Texas Style!* (1967), *Twisted Nerve* (1968), *Take a Girl Like You* (1969), *Endless Night*, *Mr Forbush and the Penguins* (1971), *Deadly Strangers* (1974), *The Diamond Hunters* (1975), *What Changed Charley Farthing?* (1976), *Appointment with Death* (1988), *After Midnight* (1989), *A Troll in Central Park* (voice) (1993)

For several years, Hayley Mills was the most popular child star in the world; indeed, one of the top box-office draws of any age. In her début film, *Tiger Bay*, she brought a fresh approach to child acting; without any trace of the more usual Hollywood winsomeness, she was irresistibly tough and mischievous, and allowed no recourse to sentimentality. She obviously had a marvellously sensitive director in Lee Thompson and, in this way, she was lucky again in having Bryan Forbes to guide her through the touching North Country fable, *Whistle Down the Wind*. Disney, of course, made her an international household name, but it is doubtful if she ever had more attractive opportunities than in these two and a later British film, Roy Boulting's *The Family Way*, an affecting study of a young marriage beset by family problems. Now a stage actress of versatility and distinction, she could easily have a second film career if some producer would notice how interestingly she has matured.

Interview date: January 1993

Was there ever any question that you might become anything other than an actress? Were your parents [actor John Mills and playwright Mary Hayley Bell] happy for you to follow this career?

I think my parents thought long and hard about it. I don't think they were too concerned about the first film I did, which was *Tiger Bay*, which happened because J Lee Thompson, the director, was a great friend of theirs. He visited my parents at the farm when he was auditioning boys to play opposite Horst Buchholz, the German film star, in his first English-speaking movie. At that point he hadn't managed to find a boy to play the part and I was twelve and a real tomboy – climbing trees and not given to wearing dresses. I think he saw me doing commercials out in the garden, and the idea suddenly occurred to him that the character didn't have to be a boy. So he suggested to my parents that I did a screen test with Horst Buchholz, which I did, and I fell instantly in love with Horst. My father had already agreed to be in the film – I think that's why Lee Thompson had come to lunch, to talk to my father about this part.

What do you recall of Lee Thompson's directing of you?

He was very gentle, very kind, he never made me feel nervous or worried about what I had to do. In a very gentle way he explained what he wanted and said things that I could understand about Gillie and what she was feeling, and he appreciated what I did, which made me feel reassured. I wasn't anxious, but I was a little bit unsure of myself, slightly lost, being involved in the scene on the first day – because it *was* the first day, and the first day was the scene on the ramp at the beginning of the movie. All I had to do was watch some boys fighting with guns, playing Cowboys and Indians, and stare at them through the railings. It was outside, there were other kids there and there was so much to take in, so much going on. My parents were there and it was reassuring and very normal to have my father in the

film also, because I'd been on so many film sets with him. The only difference now was that the camera was pointing at me. I had to have a fight with one of the oldest boys because he snatched a packet of sausages from me; I remember finding it terribly difficult to pound this boy on the chest. I can see now that I was inhibited in doing that because it *was* the first day; if we'd shot that scene a week later I wouldn't have had any trouble at all! I was well into it by that time. When you start acting young, it is an extension of your own imaginative games.

It was a stunning success. Were you aware of all the fuss about the film, the enormous amount of publicity?

It was extremely lucky for me that it was such a beautifully made film and beautifully acted by everybody. It was a story that captured people's imaginations; it turned into a love story between this tough girl and this Polish seaman who has killed his girlfriend (played by Yvonne Mitchell). Gillie observes the murder, which is an accidental *crime passionnel*, through the letterbox and she is a bit concerned about the murder, but much more concerned about the fact that he has then hidden the gun, which she wants. It is her entrée into the world of the kids on the ramp; she is going to be a bigshot there. It's a marvellous story. It was shot in Cardiff, the location stuff was actually shot in Tiger Bay. The exteriors we shot at Talybont-on-Usk – marvellous name. There was a bit of studio work at Beaconsfield Studios – not working now.

You did at least one film a year throughout the '60s. Were you happy about this? Did you ever feel you were missing out on other teenage pleasures?

I was very happy about it. It was a slow build and there wasn't a lot of manipulation on anybody's part. After *Tiger Bay*, which was very well received, I just went back to boarding school and forgot about it. Nothing happened, no more interest or offers for a year, and I didn't even think about it. Then Walt

Disney's wife happened to see *Tiger Bay* and called Walt to tell him she thought she might have found the girl who could play Pollyanna, which he was casting at that time in the States. Disney called the Rank Organisation to ask if they would release a copy of the film for him to see and they refused!

One would have thought Rank would see it as a great opportunity to build you up.

The British never thought like that. There's never really been an industry as such, with a collective consciousness of 'build this person, find projects and films for this person'. It's all been a bit arbitrary and undynamic. I was never under contract to Rank, of course.

It seems as if becoming a star in British films happened almost accidentally.

Yes, that may be one of the reasons British films had such a hard time abroad. It wasn't their mentality. They thought more in terms of stories and directors; casting was a secondary thing. The star system was a totally Hollywood concept. British films were squeezed out of the major circuits and had to make do with art-house showings. Actors *had* to go to America. But I think British films have always remained at their best when they have focused on subjects that were true to Britain, or, if you like, that were personal.

How did you find working for the Disney organisation?

I was very well looked after by them, like a cherished daughter. I wasn't used, abused or manipulated until the very end, when I wanted to play a very different kind of role and that wasn't possible within the confines of the Disney philosophy or my contract. I'm sure you've heard that, before a film went on the floor, they drew up storyboards and you had to shoot according to the shots. I felt I was expected to make the face the artist had drawn on the storyboard! I remember being on location in Greece and the director, Jimmy Neilson, wanted to change something in the script – actually at the behest of one of the actors in *The Moon Spinners* – and shooting came to a grinding halt for a couple of days because he had to get through to Walt Disney in Hollywood for permission.

Did you feel a contrast in coming back to Britain for *Whistle Down the Wind*?

Oh, it was wonderful, I loved it. It was like *Tiger Bay* all over again. It was black-and-white; the entire thing, except for a very few sequences, was shot on location. It was cold, wet, and it was real. We practically lived on that farm, in a little caravan, which we had to get to by leaping from one duckboard to another to avoid the mud. I did my schoolwork in the caravan, we ate lunch in the caravan, drank hot soup out of polystyrene cups there while we waited to work. All the films I've made in Britain have been remarkable for the cold! It is very hard to act well when you're absolutely rigid with cold. Certainly it adds a kind of realism!

On the first day, the seven-year-old boy, Alan Barnes, in a cap and wellies, walks onto the set and he sees all these chairs in a row – the director's chair (Bryan Forbes), Richard Attenborough, Alan Bates, Hayley Mills – and he goes, 'Ee! Alan Bates? They've spelt me name wrong!' Years later, when they got me for the *This Is Your Life* programme, when I was twenty-five, they brought on Alan Barnes and Diane Holgate, who'd played my sister. Alan still had exactly the same face but he's now six feet tall, very thin, and he was at that time a fitter in a factory. Diane was working in a bank, just about to get married. They were both perfectly happy with their lives and had absolutely no regrets about not having gone on to Hollywood and become movie stars.

Although it is Bryan Forbes's first film, it is still perhaps his most attractive.

He was marvellous, wonderful with the kids and with me. He worked *with* you, he didn't stand back and just give orders which you found it difficult to implement. He was your friend, he spoke your language and worked with you. One scene was terribly difficult for me to do – where Bernard Lee suddenly realises there is a man in the barn because Charlie spills the beans. He gets his gun and drags Kathy out of the house; she is screaming and yelling, trying to stop him. I wasn't sure how to do that and I was worried about the scene. Bryan just instinctively knew what to say and how to help me get into the right emotional frame of mind.

The other time he was very wise and clever was in the playground scene, where the boy (Roy Holder) denies Jesus three times. Kathy steps forward and says, 'I *have* seen Jesus.' Then the boy has to strike me across the face, which is extremely difficult to do, and of course I didn't want to get my nose broken or anything. The scene wasn't working at all, so for the close-up Bryan said, 'I'll do it, because all we need is the hand.' In the close-up he really hit me and I couldn't cry, because Kathy wouldn't have cried, so I had to hold it back but as soon as they stopped filming I burst into tears!

Some of your other Disney films which came

after this are technically British – such as *In Search of the Castaways* and *The Moon Spinners*. Was there any difference between Disney's British operation and the American one, or were they mostly done on location anyway?

Unfortunately they weren't done mostly on location. I was hoping that *The Castaways* would be, but it wasn't, we did the entire thing at Pinewood. It was set in Patagonia, but we never got there! It was all sodium vapour and The Tank, special effects – horrible. The only interesting thing was that the sets for *Cleopatra* were up at the time so we had a good time playing around there. Robert Stevenson was the director – very gentle and sensitive, like Lee Thompson. Obviously it seemed more like an English movie because we were in an English studio with an English crew and not surrounded by the big Disney organisation. English dressing-rooms and English canteen. There is a cosiness about the English industry because there isn't the money. I loved Pinewood, which had a marvellous feeling of activity and different movies going on; you could go and visit people on their sets. When I was making *Whistle Down the Wind*, my father was doing *Tunes of Glory* on one stage and my sister Juliet was working with Betty Box on another, doing *No, My Darling Daughter*, so we were all there. I adore Pinewood, and after Pinewood I like Shepperton.

You went on location for *The Moon Spinners*, you said. Do you recall Pola Negri in that?

Yes, we went to Crete. I was very impressed with Pola Negri. She was terribly kind to me. She was very grand and was playing this eccentric millionairess living on a yacht, and she had a tame cheetah. She insisted that the fur coat she wore had to be real sable and the jewels had to be real diamonds. So everywhere she went, she was followed by two very nervous-looking security men as she trailed the sable coat in the dust of the sound stage. She would come into the studio very early in the mornings, muffled up in a cape and a big hat and big black glasses, and disappear into the make-up room. Two hours later she would come out, revealed in all her splendour. I think James Neilson really gave her – within the confines of what was needed – great respect.

Do you like a lot of guidance from your director?

In my experience, most actors, if they respect the director, really like guidance if it is useful. I've worked with directors who are really not good with actors, though very good technically, very good with the editing. With them you're on your own and, once you know you're on your own, that's fine. It's when you're still trying to sort out whether you are on your own or not that the situation is difficult.

Ronald Neame seems to be a director who got wonderful performances from actors. You had your most complex part to date for him in *The Chalk Garden*.

Yes, that was a difficult time for me too. I was moving out of childhood and developing into another kind of actress, because I was developing into a woman. It was new territory and I wasn't so sure of myself. He is very clever at casting the right people and he is an extraordinarily nice man.

Was working with Edith Evans a formidable experience?

She was the sort of person you were naturally respectful to, but loved her because she had enormous warmth and humour. On the morning of my sixteenth birthday, during *The Chalk Garden*, she was sitting in the make-up chair and I was sitting in the chair beside her. She suddenly gave me a little parcel and in it was an opal ring, and she said, 'That was given to me on my sixteenth birthday by somebody I loved very much.' I was thrilled, I thanked her and gave her a hug. She said, 'At work, I am Dame Edith. But when I'm at home I'm just an old trout!'

One of my favourites is your next film, *The Family Way*. How do you feel about it?

I have great affection for *The Family Way*. It was a wonderful part for me – it was like going back to the beginning, working with my father, who was so lovely as Ezra. And Marjorie Rhodes was great, and darling Avril Angers as my mum. It was a darling film, I absolutely adored it.

You made several films with Hywel Bennett after that. Did you enjoy, as an actress, having a recurring co-star relationship?

Yes, it was really nice. He is godfather to my eldest son. We haven't kept very close, unfortunately, although we liked each other and got on very well. I wasn't really enjoying acting, but I did enjoy making that film. We did it at Shepperton and we also went up to Lancashire and shot the exteriors at Bolton. Perhaps if I hadn't fallen madly in love with Roy Boulting I might well have given it up. Roy is a wonderful director with actors, one of the best I've ever worked with. He has great presence on the set and is a natural leader. He has the knack of giving you the key to a scene in a very few words.

The other two films you did with Hywel Bennett were *Twisted Nerve*, directed by Roy, and *Endless Night*, directed by Sidney Gilliat. Do you like that sort of thriller?

I liked *Twisted Nerve*, a more interesting story, I think. Roy wrote it with his friend Leo Marks, who did the *Peeping Tom* screenplay and is psychologically orientated. It's a sort of psychological thriller,

and Hywel was a sort of psychopath who has no emotions, no feelings of guilt or remorse. I wish I could have played his part, that's the only thing! *Endless Night* was an Agatha Christie type of thing, but fun. My last cinema film was also Agatha Christie, *Appointment with Death*, but I'm hardly in it and I never quite knew what I was supposed to be!

Sir John Mills

b. 1908

Actor: *Words and Music, The Midshipmaid* (1932), *Britannia of Billingsgate, The Ghost Camera* (1933), *The River Wolves, A Political Party, The Lash, Those Were the Days, Blind Justice, Doctor's Orders* (1934), *Royal Cavalcade, Forever England / Brown on Resolution, Car of Dreams, Charing Cross Road* (1935), *First Offence, Tudor Rose* (1936), *OHMS, The Green Cockatoo* (1937), *Goodbye Mr Chips* (1939), *Old Bill and Son, *All Hands* (1940), *Cottage to Let, The Black Sheep of Whitehall* (1941), *The Big Blockade, The Young Mr Pitt, In Which We Serve* (1942), *We Dive at Dawn* (1943), *This Happy Breed, *Victory Wedding, Waterloo Road* (1944), *The Way to the Stars, *The Sky's the Limit, *Total War in Britain* (narr) (1945), **Land of Promise* (voice only), *Great Expectations* (1946), *So Well Remembered, The October Man* (1947), *Scott of the Antarctic* (1948), *The History of Mr Polly* (& pr), *The Rocking Horse Winner* (& pr), **Friend of the Family* (narr), **The Flying Skyscraper* (narr) (1949), *Morning Departure* (1950), *Mr Denning Drives North* (1951), *The Gentle Gunman, The Long Memory* (1952), *Hobson's Choice, The Colditz Story* (1954), *The End of the Affair, Above Us the Waves, Escapade* (1955), *It's Great To Be Young, War and Peace, The Baby and the Battleship, Around the World in Eighty Days, Town on Trial!, The Vicious Circle* (1956), *Dunkirk, Ice-Cold in Alex, I Was Monty's Double* (1958), *Tiger Bay, Summer of the 17th Doll* (1959), *Tunes of Glory* (1960), *The Swiss Family Robinson, The Singer Not the Song, Flame in the Streets* (1961), *The Valiant, Tiara Tahiti* (1962), *The Chalk Garden* (1963), *The Truth About Spring* (1964), *Operation Crossbow, King Rat* (1965), *The Wrong Box, The Family Way* (1966), *Chuka, Africa – Texas Style!* (1967), *Lady Hamilton, A Black Veil for Lisa, Oh! What a Lovely War* (1968), *Run Wild, Run Free, Adam's Woman* (1969), *Ryan's Daughter* (1970), *Dulcima* (1971), *Young Winston, Lady Caroline Lamb* (1972), *Oklahoma Crude* (1973), *The 'Human' Factor, A Choice of Weapons* (1976), *The Devil's Advocate* (1977), *The Big Sleep, The Thirty-Nine Steps* (1978), *Zulu Dawn, Quatermass* (1979), *Gandhi* (1982), *Sahara* (1984), *Who's That Girl?* (1987), *Deadly Advice* (1994), *The Grotesque* (1995), *Hamlet* (1996)

Producer: *The History of Mr Polly, The Rocking Horse Winner* (1949), *Sky West and Crooked* (& dir) (1966)

* Documentary or short film.

A star of British films for over sixty years, John Mills has had one of the longest careers in all British cinema, not to mention on stage and in television. He has made almost one hundred films for the screen, and the range is as impressive as the number. During the '40s he was much associated with 'brave servicemen' roles, but, even in these, there is a surprising range: he is as convincing below decks in *In Which We Serve* as when playing the RAF officer in *The Way to the Stars*; and he is a persuasive villain in *Cottage to Let*. His graceful and intelligent playing as Pip holds together the episodes of *Great Expectations*, in which a cast of superb grotesques does its appointed turns. He is a different kind of upwardly mobile hero in *Hobson's Choice*, in which his quietly dogged Willie Mossop is a match for the pyrotechnics of Charles Laughton, and gave one of his finest performances as the neurotic officer in *Tunes of Glory*. He filmed regularly throughout the next two decades, winning an Oscar for his role in *Ryan's Daughter* in 1970. In 1949 he produced two films – *The History of Mr Polly* and *The Rocking Horse Winner* – which, unsuccessful in their day, now hold up very well.

Interview date: July 1990

You made nearly twenty films during the 1930s, many of which, I imagine, were 'quota quickies'. What was your experience of making them?

I didn't realise I had made so many then. I was learning during those pictures, putting the money in the bank and also gaining great experience. What they taught me was to rely on myself, because you couldn't really rely on a director or anyone else then, you just had to deliver the goods. That has stood me in good stead. Terrible films, most of them – I remember one was called *The Lash*, an absolute shocker. We used to shoot them at Twickenham and we'd have two shoots on at once – a day shoot and a night shoot. So if you went in at seven-thirty in the morning for the day shoot, you walked in to the most unbelievable atmosphere: make-up, orange peel, cigar ends and all sorts of other peculiar smells. You would use the studio in which other people had been working all night – shift work, it was, and about seven days per film.

It was the '40s which established you as a major star. You worked several times with Anthony Asquith. How did you find him as a director?

Wonderful, very sympathetic and totally charming. He loved actors, loved movies. I made a film called *The Way to the Stars* with him; one very hot day we were doing the famous John Pudney poem ['For Johnny']. Puffin [Asquith] said he wanted to do the whole thing in one long tracking shot with no cut, so I started off with Take 1 and it seemed to go all right. I had tears in my eyes. I got to the end of it but nobody said 'Cut', so I waited; then I looked around and there was Puffin, cross-legged like a little Buddha, sitting underneath the camera fast asleep! When he woke up he said, 'Wonderful! Print it.' My first film for him was *Cottage to Let* and I needed it badly because I'd just come out of the Army and was very hard up. Any job would have done but I loved playing the villain. I was remembered from before the war as a hero and I was attacked by the fans for 'letting down the country' and all that stuff. It had a very good cast – Alastair Sim, George Cole, and so on.

Your next Asquith film, *We Dive at Dawn*, was made at Gainsborough, as was *Waterloo Road*. What do you recall of it as a studio to work at?

It was a nice little studio. I remember *Waterloo Road* very well because that was Sidney Gilliat's first picture. The great fight with Stewart Granger was interesting. When I saw Sidney's script it had the hero and the villain not meeting until the very end of the movie, running parallel to one another throughout the film; they were to meet at the very end and I (the hero) was to knock him out and that was to be it. I told Sidney that people would expect a major fight. Well, Granger and I rehearsed for ten days; he was a very good boxer and I'd done quite a lot too, so it was a really good fight. I think it was a damn good movie, almost all of it made in Gainsborough's Islington studio, except the bit where I'm running across live railway lines!

How do you feel about your third Asquith film, *The Way to the Stars*, one of my personal favourites?

I saw it recently on television and it's like watching a piece of history now. I don't like watching my films because I'm much too critical of them, but I thought this one had great reality. It was very nostalgic and helped very much by being in black-and-white. At the time we hoped it would help Anglo-American relations. I talked a lot about that to Terry Rattigan [screenwriter] and to Tolly de Grunwald, who produced it, and we felt we had something there which might be considered important later on. The main thing during the making of it was, 'Is it entertaining?' and that's always been my yardstick. I don't like speaking from the pulpit; if you have a message it should be packaged in a chocolate wrapper. I think *The Way to the Stars* is an entertaining movie *and* very much a movie for peacetime.

You made *The Young Mr Pitt* for Carol Reed in 1942. Did you feel it was really a film about 1940s England as much as an historical film?

I didn't think about that aspect of the film, all I was worried about was my wig and the coat! I went into that at the last moment because Carol hadn't got anyone for it; I hadn't been long out of the Army and I needed the job. Carol suddenly cast me as Wilberforce and there were no clothes; I was fitted out on the morning I played the scene in the House of Commons. Carol was one of the best directors I ever worked with. He had an uncanny sense of the right moment and spotted anything that was slightly untrue; he loved actors and was a good actor himself.

How did you come to be involved in *In Which We Serve*?

Noël Coward wrote the part of Shorty Blake for me because he knew I needed the work. I owe him so much. There were some terrific scenes, such as the one with Bernard Miles and the telegram, and

the scenes with Kay Walsh – all that stuff was handled beautifully. Kay's great strength is her reality. I did *This Happy Breed* with her too. You can hardly believe she is acting; when the cameras turned over she just *did* it. And of course there was the fun of working with David Lean for the first time; essentially, he directed the picture even though he and Noël are credited as co-directors. Part of Noël's genius was that he could judge when to leave it to someone else, as he did with David. He knew David was a brilliant technician and of course Carol Reed had suggested David to direct, so he just left the whole thing to David (including the direction of Noël's own performance) and they got on like a house on fire.

David has a reputation for not liking actors and not getting on with them, but I can't join that club. We started together with *In Which We Serve* and went on to make four or five other pictures together. The thing about David Lean is this: I don't care if I wait a year, I know that the set-up for each shot is going to be the best set-up I could possibly have. I waited a year for him in Ireland [*Ryan's Daughter*] and it was well worth it – I got an Oscar out of it! David is the best editor in the world, bar none. He is also a great story teller and anyone who can do the script of *Great Expectations*, take a book of that length and do such a masterful job of making a script which keeps the story – well! I firmly believe you must cut any scene that doesn't promote either the character or the story. You have to be ruthless, and David's films have always held their storyline.

In Which We Serve was a very arduous film to make, physically, with lots of time spent in cold water in the tank. We were in that tank for nearly two weeks and it was absolutely filthy by the time we finished.

Did you feel *Great Expectations* was something special at the time?

Yes, I did – at least I thought so halfway through when we were shooting the river scenes with the paddle-steamer; when I saw those rushes I thought they were sensational, and I loved the script. I felt the film was going to be a very big success but what I didn't know was that it would turn out to be David's best picture, in spite of the bigger films later on.

I remember David saying he wanted me to play a part which could be seen as a coat-hanger for the other great characters. He said he needed someone with a lot of drive for Pip, otherwise the whole thing would collapse. You couldn't have that picture succeed on the other characters, *they* had to succeed, in a way, on Pip. Where I think David was so clever was to use that voice-over commentary I did because that enabled us to cover chunks of the story in a couple of lines. Pip avoided the coat-hanger effect and avoided being too much smothered by the others. In other words, Pip emerged as a good leading man's role.

I loved playing with all those great grotesque characters; they were themselves such wonderful characters to act with – Francis L Sullivan, for instance, as Jaggers. And there has never been a better Miss Havisham than Martita Hunt, ever. If I remember any scene particularly it is the one in which she caught fire. It was very difficult to stage because we only had one take; the long table which David had set up for the wedding feast, with the cake and the mice and cobwebs, had taken Props two days to do; luckily they got it in one take. The business of her seeming to be on fire was done with padding soaked in methylated spirits on top of everything. It was a brilliantly shot scene. It could have been very dangerous but not if you had, as we did, very good Props and Special Effects people.

What do you think of the rather upbeat ending of *Great Expectations* where you and Valerie Hobson run down the path together?

I remember David wanted a happier ending. I liked it because there had been so much tragedy and heartbreak throughout the story and it was nice to send them off feeling it was all right in the end. It could have been a touch of post-war optimism also – I know David didn't want people to go out feeling sad.

Do you remember Anthony Wager, who played the young Pip?

Yes, I worked with him quite a bit and he was very good. We did a couple of things like getting him to do hand movements which I did later on, so that we'd seem like the same character.

You seem to have worked for a number of different companies throughout the '40s and '50s. What kinds of contracts did you have?

For about twelve years I was under contract to Rank, to act, direct and produce; the other ones were just one-off picture deals. It was a very enjoyable way to work: often I'd be two weeks into a film before I'd signed a deal. You'd say you liked it, shake hands and start shooting! Now it's endless lawyers, agents, and contracts. It was a very happy time to make movies then.

Did producing add greatly to your worries on *The History of Mr Polly* and *The Rocking Horse Winner*?

I don't think I worried enough! I wasn't a very good producer because I was always dying to get on the floor and I didn't really like the office work. However, I wanted to make those two movies and people were shying away from them because they weren't run-of-the-mill. Now I'm rather proud of them. At the time, *Mr Polly* didn't succeed because I was then a blue-eyed hero and the audiences hated seeing me as a little, wizened chap with smarmed hair and a moustache, being a henpecked husband. But I wanted to do it, and I thought *The Rocking Horse Winner* was a wonderful story, so I also wanted to do that. I'm not ashamed of doing either of them, but they weren't hits with the public. Anthony Pelissier [director] was a great friend of mine and very talented; I gave him his start with those two films.

A nice thing about it all was that, when I said I wanted to do the film, they didn't oversee us, didn't come to see it until the cut version was available. Rank was a very nice, honest man who didn't know anything about movies. He came to my dressing-room during *Great Expectations* and said he would like me to sign a contract; he didn't want to go through an agent, just for me to take a pencil and write my own deal. I couldn't believe it! I called my agent and we wrote a deal together; we didn't ask for the earth, but it was a wonderful deal and almost immediately he allowed me to make those two seemingly non-commercial films. I was *very* fond of Arthur Rank.

What drew you to *Scott of the Antarctic*?

I had been a schoolboy admirer of Scott; when I heard Mickey Balcon was doing it I rang him up and asked to play the part of Scott. It was one of the best experiences of my whole career. I think the whole unit got carried away with the Scott story, partly because we shot it in continuity. We shot in hair-raising conditions, at the top of the Finse Glacier for instance, and at one stage the cameraman was sent home with very bad frostbite. The location work had such reality and we actually *did* it all, some of it quite dangerous. The continuity aspect of it was important emotionally – and also from the point of view of our beards!

You did several films in the '50s for Roy Ward Baker, a director I admire. What do you recall of *The October Man, Morning Departure* and – one I haven't seen – *The Singer Not the Song*?

The October Man was Roy's first film. I've worked with quite a few first-time directors. Yes, he was a very intelligent, very nice man and it was a good, tense little picture. *Morning Departure* was rather good too, I think. It was the story of the *Truculent*, the ship which went down just before we were due to start shooting the movie. We thought we couldn't make it then, so we sent the script to the Admiralty, who said to go ahead because it was uplifting rather than depressing. So we made it and I received about twenty-five letters from the relatives of the boys lost on the *Truculent*, saying how glad they were we had made the film.

But *The Singer Not the Song* – you haven't seen it? Oh, you haven't lived! That was one that went wrong. I had better be careful what I say. It was to have originally been played with me and Brando. When Brando finally turned it down, Dirk, who was under contract to Rank at the time, was asked to play it and he agreed. But he wasn't happy with the film, nor was Roy. You couldn't have two more different people than Bogarde and Brando, chalk and cheese.

What do you remember of working with Charles Laughton in *Hobson's Choice*?

Charles was a unique, enormously gifted actor, capable of doing the most exciting things suddenly. I always admired him very much, ever since seeing him in *Henry VIII*. He was a weird one, talking in rather a high-falutin' way when we were rehearsing; I loved working with him, although David Lean was rather in awe of him, because he was the first international star David had worked with. And Willie Mossop was a wonderful part for me – he was an unglamorous chap, but he was a hero, you see. It was the performance I have enjoyed most.

You made a lot of war films in the 1950s. Why do you think, a decade after the war, British films were so preoccupied with it?

I suspect because people saw the war as rather heroic, exciting and romantic; we were still going through a certain degree of austerity. *Ice-Cold in Alex* was a tremendously exciting picture to make and Lee Thompson was a wonderful director; he could make a scene out of nothing. For instance, the minefield sequence was two lines in the script, yet it took four days to shoot and was one of the best sequences in the film; most of it was put in on the spur of the moment by Lee Thompson. It was 110 degrees in the shade, I remember. I was so disappointed in my love scene with Sylvia Syms because up to then I had made love to virtually nothing but submarines and destroyers and this was my big chance, and most of it was cut! A good actress, Sylvia.

Would you agree that *Tunes of Glory* gave you one of the best parts of your career?

It did, definitely. That was what attracted me to the film – a super script. It was a toss-up to begin with, which part Alec [Guinness] would play and which I would do; I was originally intended to play Jock but I preferred the part I did in the end, though it was frightfully difficult. I've been asked a hundred times how I did the quivering eye bit – and I'll never tell you, either! I had been produced and photographed by Ronnie Neame but this was the first time he had directed me, and he said to me, 'I'll tell you one thing to make you feel confident: if you manage to produce a moment of magic, I promise to be in the right place to get it.' You can't ask more than that.

One thing I'm rather proud of is pulling out all the stops when I blew my top in the ballroom scene. I told Ronnie I would rather not rehearse that scene and that I would try to get it on Take 1. I'm a great believer in Take 1 in films; I think it's rather like a first night – it's very fresh and warm and you can get the best. So we did Take 1, with about a hundred extras on the floor, and it seemed to work all right. Although the sound man wanted another take I refused to do it, feeling that I'd rather have raucous screaming sound and keep the performance I had given the first time. It was a performance I would have given in Wyndham's Theatre, I hadn't geared it down at all.

Kenneth More

1914–1982

Actor: *Windmill Revels, Carry on, London, Not Wanted on Voyage* (uncr) (1936), *School for Secrets* (1946), *Scott of the Antarctic* (1948), *For Them That Trespass, Man on the Run, Now Barabbas Was a Robber, Stop Press Girl* (1949), *Morning Departure, Chance of a Lifetime, The Clouded Yellow, The Franchise Affair* (1950), *No Highway, The Galloping Major* (uncr), *Appointment with Venus* (1951), *Brandy for the Parson, The Yellow Balloon* (1952), *Never Let Me Go, Genevieve, Our Girl Friday* (1953), *Doctor in the House* (1954), *Raising a Riot, The Deep Blue Sea* (1955), *Reach for the Sky* (1956), *The Admirable Crichton* (1957), *A Night to Remember, Next To No Time, The Sheriff of Fractured Jaw, *Design for Living, The Thirty-Nine Steps* (1958), *North West Frontier* (1959), *Sink the Bismarck!,* *Man in the Moon, *Island of Surprise* (narr) (1960), *The Greengage Summer* (1961), *Some People, The Longest Day, We Joined the Navy* (1962), *The Comedy Man* (1963), *The Mercenaries* (1967), *Fraulein Doktor* (1968), *Oh! What a Lovely War, Battle of Britain* (1969), *Scrooge* (1970), *Concorde – The 24-hour World* (narr), *Look, No Hands* (narr), *Walking Wounded* (narr) (1973), *The Blind Shall Read* (1975), *The Slipper and the Rose* (1976), *Viaje al Centro de la Tierra / Where Time Began, Leopard in the Snow* (1977), *The Silent Witness* (narr), *So Much to Offer* (narr) (1978), *The Spaceman and King Arthur* (1979), *The Delessi Affair* (1981)

* Short film.

'The chief executives at Pinewood had seen *Genevieve* and decided it was terrible. Some argued that they should have realised this from the beginning because the film had always been a gamble, with the four chief characters played by actors who were virtually unknown outside of London ... all those associated with it were made to feel they must take a major share of the blame for what seemed bound to be a failure.'[1] More had already appeared in twenty films, including uncredited bits in the 1930s and '40s, before establishing himself indelibly in *Genevieve*, which, as he says, 'was nearly rejected, but which has become a classic and one of the greatest successes ever made in a British studio'.[2] As Ambrose, the vintage-car-driving Lothario, he established one of his two key *personae*: the raffish, rumpled womaniser, who is, perhaps, no real match for a strong woman.

This element of his screen image reaches its most complete realisation in *The Deep Blue Sea*. Here, he plays an ex-RAF playboy type, adrift in the post-war world and caught in an emotional attachment with an older woman who finally sends him away. He had made a success of this role on the stage but said, 'This was in every way a disappointing film for me ... I think there was a great deal of miscasting, particularly Vivien Leigh. All the intimacy and tenseness of the play was lost.'[3] There is something in what he says about the film as a whole, but his own performance is immaculate.

This film combines both the womanising streak (which informed his British Film Academy Award performance in *Doctor in the House*) with the other crucial More characteristic. This is the 'piece-of-cake' jauntiness and/or teeth-gritting determination he brought to the service types he played in such popular films as *Appointment with Venus*, *Sink the Bismarck!* and, above all, *Reach for the Sky*. (Like many British leading men of the '50s, such as John Gregson, John Mills and Jack Hawkins, he spent much of the decade in uniform.) Asked in 1954 if there was a role he hankered for, he said, 'Yes, but Richard Burton's got it all sewn up. It's Douglas Bader in *Reach for the Sky*. But there I go with my head in the clouds again.'[4] The qualities he brought to the role, which finally came his way, helped make him a major box-office draw in the latter half of the '50s.

Though he did become stereotyped, and though his career petered out in 'cameo' roles, there is also evidence of his willingness to try riskier enterprises. Of *A Night to Remember*, he wrote: 'Although the *Titanic* would obviously be the star, I felt a part of this ship and agreed to play the part of Second Officer Lightoller'[5] because he was 'intrigued' by the story. His favourite role was as a down-at-heel repertory actor in the undervalued *The Comedy Man*, and, asked to play a devious romantic role in *The Greengage Summer*, for which he felt unsuited, he said, 'I went on a diet, for this was a film I dearly wanted to make.'[6]

Elsewhere, he claimed that 'if I'd listened to all the warnings I was given . . . I wouldn't have made *Doctor in the House*, *Reach for the Sky*, *The Admirable Crichton* and *A Night to Remember* . . . Alex Korda thought it was too risky for a man with two good legs to play a legless hero . . . [and] I was told nobody would accept me as an Edwardian butler.'[7] Well, they were wrong. In 1980, he said, 'Making films then was a pastime; today it's much more of a business.'[8] For More, and for nearly ten years, it may have been a pastime, but it was also a highly successful business.

1 Kenneth More, *More or Less*, Hodder & Stoughton, London, 1978, p 159
2 More, *More or Less*, p 161
3 Quoted in David Shipman, *The Great Movie Stars: The International Years*, Angus & Robertson, London, 1972, p 372
4 Dick Vosburgh, 'Any MORE questions?', *Picturegoer*, 2 October 1954, p 28
5 More, *More or Less*, p 171
6 More, *More or Less*, p 180
7 'To blazes with the "experts" ', *Picturegoer*, 20 September 1958, p 8
8 Iain F McAsh, 'A Tale of Two Actors', *Films Illustrated*, December 1980, p 116

Diana Morgan

1910–1996

Screenwriter: *Ships With Wings* (1941), *The Foreman Went to France*, **Go to Blazes*, *Went the Day Well?* (1942), *Halfway House*, *Fiddlers Three* (1944), *Pink String and Sealing Wax* (1945), *Poet's Pub*, *A Run For Your Money* (1949), *Dance Hall* (1950), *Let's Be Happy* (1957), *Hand in Hand* (1960)
* Short film.

Though Diana Morgan's career as a screenwriter is almost wholly an Ealing affair, one should remember that she was also a successful author of plays and revues, often in collaboration with her husband Robert MacDermot and sometimes acting in them herself. She also wrote for television and radio, but she is now very firmly associated with Ealing and remembered as one of very few women writers in British films. She worked with most of the famous Ealing alumni, but seems to have had particularly enjoyable working partnerships with Robert Hamer and Alexander Mackendrick, who no doubt responded to her wit and sharpness. At Ealing, she wrote – almost always in collaboration – comedies, war films, melodrama and fantasy, winning a reputation for her professionalism in that male-dominated studio. Away from Ealing she wrote the charming *Hand in Hand*, about friendship between a little Jewish girl and a Catholic boy, and won several awards for her work.

Interview date: October 1992

Was it harder for women to get established as screenwriters?

I suppose it was. I was the only one they ever had at Ealing. At intervals they used to say, 'Don't you think we ought to get a nice, fresh mind?' and then they'd say, 'We'll put up with the stale one we've got.' So I stayed. Ealing was a very male studio; they didn't like actors very much and didn't like actresses at all. So many of their films are male-dominated. I was called in originally in 1940 to put the love interest into a dreadful film called *Ships With Wings*. When I arrived I met my fellow writer, Patrick Kirwan, who said, 'I'm sorry, duckie, I'm doing the love interest – you're doing the naval battle scenes!' So I got a naval adviser and I did it, while Patrick Kirwan wrote the stuff for Ann Todd and Jane Baxter.

How valuable was your theatrical background, as actress and writer, when you came to write for the screen?

I think, in an odd way, that having been an actress helped, because you were able to write better parts for people. Especially since Cavalcanti had joined Ealing, it had become very documentary- as well as male-dominated. It wasn't really very different writing for the screen as opposed to the stage.

The public has a perception of Ealing as a cosy kind of place, whereas in fact you seem a diverse group of people.

Oh yes, very. But we worked well together. I loved all the people, all the very different characters, although they were often difficult: I don't know why it was, but we had the same kind of minds, in a curious way. I'd known Robert Hamer at Cambridge; Charlie Frend, Charlie Crichton and various others were at Oxford, and Angus MacPhail was a most remarkable man with a lovely wit. He taught me a lot. I'd never written for the screen before, and anything I wanted to know Angus taught me. He'd been around in the 1930s with Hitchcock. He was responsible for that wonderful ending in the music hall in the original *The Thirty-Nine Steps*. Angus wasn't a very good writer but he had great ideas. He could do dialogue for Will Hay but he couldn't do it for ordinary people.

The success of Ealing seems to have depended partly on people being sufficiently like-minded to be able to get on together.

Yes. I think we were a rather highbrow lot in many ways, and we were very snobbish about other studios, like Gainsborough, for instance: 'Dreadful, corny stuff!' I've enjoyed seeing those Gainsborough films in later years, but we weren't allowed to do anything like that.

I suppose they were rather sexy films in a way, and Ealing would have been opposed to that.

Oh no, we weren't allowed to do anything like that! And yet most of the boys off-screen had the most fantastic sex lives! But never in the studio, because of Michael Balcon. He wanted them to be family films, and he was very strict. It was an extraordinary approach in a way, but Mick was wonderful, we loved him. And he kept in touch for years after. The place did have an atmosphere. When I first went there I expected a great big studio, lots of buildings and tough people. Instead I found a little house with a garden behind it with beehives, and little huts around the house. No huge sound stages, only two rather small ones. It was during the war, so we had to have an enormous amount of back projection and we couldn't do anything after nightfall.

It seems to have been very egalitarian amongst writers and directors, with everyone prepared to pitch in with a point of view.

Yes. We used to have terrific arguments. I had one with Sandy Mackendrick when we were writing *Dance Hall*; we had Donald Houston standing on the roof, gazing down, thinking of suicide. I kept asking how the audience would know. Sandy said, 'Oh, everyone knows,' and this went on all morning, all through lunch and all afternoon. At half-past five Sandy burst out laughing and said, 'The bitch is right, you *don't* know!' So we went over to the Red Lion, where we all drank much too much. Of course we never drank anything at the studio. It was a terrible tragedy that Robert Hamer was later destroyed by drink. He really was a genius. He was a great friend of my husband's and mine, and we had written things together at Cambridge, before we went to Ealing. A wonderful man.

On your Ealing films you were always a collaborator on the screen credits.

Yes, and some films I wrote for were never credited. Originally I wasn't credited for *The Foreman Went to France.*

Leslie Arliss gets a writing credit for that: he seems an unlikely person to find in that company.

Yes, he didn't last very long. He wasn't an Ealing man at all, much more into the Gainsborough 'bodice-rippers'. I don't know why he was at Ealing but he was only there for that film.

There were five of you writing on that film. How was it done?

There was originally a story by Priestley and John Dighton, and Angus MacPhail worked on it with Leslie Arliss. I don't know why Roger Macdougall worked on it, or why I did for that matter, but we did. I suppose we were brought in for dialogue or something, I can't remember. It's an excellent film. There is another film I wrote that I'd love to see again, called *Hand in Hand*, which wasn't done at Ealing.

I read you'd won fourteen awards for that screenplay.

I think there were eight. It was my last work for the cinema and it was a very nice film directed by Philip Leacock, who was awfully good with children. It is about a Jewish child and a Catholic child; the man who played the priest is dead now but he was an excellent actor – John Gregson. Kathleen Byron was in it too; I worked with her later on *Emergency Ward Ten.* She was in the first script I wrote for it and she played an alcoholic. She was awfully good.

To take you back to Ealing, you worked several times with both Angus MacPhail and John Dighton. Did you have especially good working relationships with them?

Angus I knew very well but John was a very reserved sort of man; a nice, quiet, retiring man. Angus, Charlie Crichton, Robert Hamer and I had lunch together every day; we decided that if we were to lunch together for a long time we'd get bored with each other, so we played very strange, intellectual word games. Angus was a wit, very erudite, very well read and wonderful company. He drank too much, that was his downfall.

You worked with almost the full range of Ealing directors, including Cavalcanti. I'd be interested in your recollections of them.

When Cavalcanti came in he altered the whole basis of Ealing films, because of his documentary background. You were either a Cav person or you were a MacPhail person at Ealing. I was more of a MacPhail person whereas Robert Hamer was a great Cav boy. When I say people were either Cavalcanti people or not, I mean they were influenced by him or not. His documentary style was very different from the Grierson style. Ealing was a commercial filmmaker when I first went there, whereas Cav was much more a documentary filmmaker and the two merged to make an 'Ealing film'.

So Ealing films became fiction in more realistic settings?

Yes. Mick [Balcon] was wonderful; if one of the boys went to him and said, 'I want to write a film about so-and-so,' Mick would say, 'All right, go ahead and do it.' If he liked the idea, he would let them go ahead and make it. I think Cavalcanti was really the 'great spirit' behind Ealing films. Hamer and the others used to go to the French Club and see a lot of him outside. I never did because I had a husband and a child, so I went home.

Cavalcanti's *Went the Day Well?* is a fascinating film. How did you and your co-authors Dighton and MacPhail work together?

I think Angus and John had been at it before I came in and I did all I could to make better parts for the actors. Neither of them knew much about writing parts for actors – Angus wrote terrible parts. He gave Elizabeth Allen the line, 'From tomorrow we'll be sharing the same milk bottle.' I told him it was the worst line that had ever been written for any film, so any time he got difficult with us, we would just chant that line at him! We never let anybody get away with anything, we were very tough with each other, but we never alienated each other. It was wonderful to know that we could argue and criticise without its ending up in a feud.

Did you have any direct dealings with

Graham Greene?

No, we never met him and we never read the story, which Greene called *The Lieutenant Died Last* and which appeared in some magazine [*Collier's*]. Cav had read it and liked the idea; all we knew was that we had to write a story around an English village taken over by German paratroopers. So we did, working under the title *They Came in Khaki*. Cav didn't have any input to the screenplay. The film was done in a village in the Cotswolds. We were told it was full of very nice little virgins and we were not to shock them by fast film ways. When we got there, they shocked us! They were up to all kinds of things and Balcon's boys and girls never did anything like that.

The director for whom I find it hard to identify a personal style is Charles Frend.

He didn't really direct *San Demetrio, London*, almost all of that was directed by Robert Hamer, but he didn't get a credit. Charlie Frend was credit-hungry. He also got a credit on a film which I wrote nearly all of, called *A Run For Your Money*. I got a credit for 'additional dialogue' and he got the credit for the screenplay. He was the one person there that I never really had much contact with. He was very English, a very strange man. You thought he was very calm and collected but he was much more neurotic. Robert Hamer, Angus MacPhail, Charlie Crichton and I were all one lot, you know, but Charlie Frend was to one side, as it were. I think he was a very good, competent director though I didn't think the film about Scott [*Scott of the Antarctic*] was an Ealing film at all. I think he lacked heart – even the sort of high intellectual, purist heart the other boys had. But I did very much enjoy doing *A Run For Your Money* for him – being Welsh and having a wicked sense of humour helped!

What are your recollections of *Halfway House* and those Ealing stalwarts Basil Dearden, Michael Relph and Sidney Cole?

Sid I liked very much, he was very nice to work with. Basil was an interesting man; I think he was a good director although not very distinguished. He always had a bit of a complex at Ealing because he felt he wasn't as intellectual as everyone else. I can't think why he felt that way, but he did. He had been brought up in the theatre and hadn't been to university like everyone else, and he felt that. Michael Balcon did like to gather university people around him.

Halfway House, **like all those films for which Michael Relph was art director, looks wonderful. Was his great contribution really as an art director?**

Yes, he was very good indeed as an art director. *Halfway House* was done on location in Somerset. I don't know how they managed to do a film like *San Demetrio, London*, though, in that tiny studio and all indoors. They didn't go on location at all.

You wrote *Halfway House* with TEB Clarke and Angus MacPhail?

Yes. TEB Clarke was a very funny man, very witty. *Halfway House* was one of his earliest credits. It came from a play called *The Peaceful Inn*. I don't think we had any idea of a 'message' in writing films; I loved working in films and loved working at Ealing, but I don't think I ever had a 'message'. I think it was Beatrice Lillie who said, 'If it's a play with a message, I won't dress.'

Harry Watt seemed like an unlikely director to do *Fiddlers Three*.

He gave up halfway through, Robert Hamer did most of it. Harry also got a credit as co-author but he wasn't. Hamer and I did it all. Harry wanted to do a comedy and he wanted to do a musical, so Mick let him, but he gave up very soon and Hamer took over as he did on *San Demetrio, London*. The three fiddlers were Diana Decker, Tommy Trinder and Sonnie Hale. Ealing had had a big success earlier with *Sailors Three*; they had Trinder and Diana Decker, and Sonnie Hale was more or less on hand, so it happened. Trinder had a big reputation as a radio comedian as well as being at Ealing.

I'd be interested to hear anything about the great Robert Hamer and, for instance, *Pink String and Sealing Wax*.

He used to get terrific passions, obsessions for people, and of course he also used to drink too much. I knew his family well and he used to go back to Wales and stay with his aunts and uncles, who'd dry him out. You can see from his films he was just awfully good at directing women – no other Ealing films give such parts to women. He was the only one who liked women, really. Then there were all those sexual jokes in *Kind Hearts and Coronets*, which Mick never cottoned on to. They wouldn't be there if he had! Nobody has ever given Dennis Price enough credit, I don't think; he was marvellous in that film.

On your last Ealing film. *Dance Hall*, you had Charles Crichton as director. What do you remember of working with him?

He was bliss, lovely to work with – a lovely, funny man and very understanding. The dance hall wasn't really a different world to me, because my husband was with the BBC and he was on what was called the 'Slush Committee', which meant we had to go to a lot of dance halls and take notes on people like Geraldo.

Did you work with Alexander Mackendrick on *Dance Hall*?

Yes. I worked mostly with Sandy rather than with EVH Emmett, who was also associate producer. I loved working with Sandy, he was so difficult in a nice way, a lovely Scottish, metaphysical way.

Do you agree with my view that the '40s and '50s was really the key period of British cinema, the heyday?

It was the last fling, I think. Ealing was so exciting and there was an industry, there was continuity. I don't know why British films never did better in America, but even the Ealing films, though much loved in America, were only loved in the art houses. I know the British actors would love to have been stars, but there wasn't much chance of being stars. How could you be a star at Ealing? Nobody wrote 'star' parts. They were more group films, rather like Ealing itself, which was a group place.

Oswald Morris

b. 1915

Camera operator: *I Met a Murderer* (1939), *Green for Danger* (1946), *Captain Boycott* (1947), *Oliver Twist, Blanche Fury* (1948), *The Passionate Friends* (1949)

Director of photography: *Golden Salamander, Cairo Road* (1950), *The Adventurers, Circle of Danger* (1951), *Saturday Island, The Card, So Little Time* (1952), *South of Algiers, Moulin Rouge, Indiscretion of an American Wife, Beat the Devil* (1953), *Knave of Hearts, Beau Brummell* (1954), *The Man Who Never Was, Moby Dick* (1956), *Heaven Knows, Mr Allison* (1957), *A Farewell to Arms, The Key, The Roots of Heaven* (1958), *Look Back in Anger, Our Man in Havana* (1959), *The Entertainer* (1960), *The Guns of Navarone* (1961), *Satan Never Sleeps,* *Lolita, Term of Trial* (1962), *Come Fly With Me, The Ceremony* (1963), *Of Human Bondage, The Pumpkin Eater* (1964), *Mr Moses, The Battle of the Villa Fiorita, The Hill* (1965), *The Spy Who Came in from the Cold, Life at the Top, Stop the World I Want to Get Off* (1966), *The Taming of the Shrew* (1967), *The Winter's Tale, Reflections in a Golden Eye, Great Catherine, Oliver!* (1968), *Goodbye Mr Chips* (1969), *Fragment of Fear, Scrooge* (1970), *Fiddler on the Roof, Lady Caroline Lamb* (1971), *Sleuth* (1972), *The Man With The Golden Gun, The Odessa File* (1973), *The Man Who Would Be King* (1975), *The Seven-Per-Cent Solution* (1976), *Equus* (1977), *The Wiz* (1978), *Just Tell Me What You Want* (1980), *The Great Muppet Caper* (1981), *The Dark Crystal* (1982), *John Huston* (1988)

Ossie Morris is so articulate about his craft, and his memory of his fifty-year career is so clear, that it goes much against the editorial grain to have had to cut any of his reminiscences. His detailed account of the filming of *Moulin Rouge* is representative of the several similar ones regretfully curtailed here. It is apparent, from talking to directors, actors and others, how much his contribution has been valued. He won his Oscar for the American *Fiddler on the Roof*, but his work on widely varied British and Anglo-American productions (especially his association with John Huston) made him one of the world's most sought-after cameramen. He was a byword for finding solutions to technical problems and for his insight into the whole process of filmmaking.

Interview date: October 1992

Unlike many British directors of photography, you did not go on to be a director. Did you ever want to direct?

I can answer that very simply. I simply did not want to direct movies because I find it very difficult to handle actors and actresses and it took me a long time during my early stages of lighting to resolve that. You have to handle them in the end, of course, because the more confidence they have in you the easier they are to deal with. Also, with one or two exceptions, I don't think any cinematographer has really made it as a top-line director.

After much perseverance, you worked on a lot of films between 1936 and 1939.

Yes, during '36 to '39 I was trained with the 'quota quickies', that's my background, and I progressed from clapper-boy to camera assistant to camera operator, but not to cameraman. I didn't become a cameraman till after the war, because of that interruption.

Am I right in thinking that your first film, after wartime service in the RAF, was as camera operator on *Green for Danger*?

Yes, *Green for Danger*, and then I went on to *Captain Boycott* – these were Launder and Gilliat films. My contract was with Independent Producers, comprising Individual Pictures, Cineguild (Lean, Neame and Havelock-Allan); and The Archers (Michael Powell and Emeric Pressburger). Ian Dalrymple [Wessex] came in later.

What was it like to be assistant to cameramen such as Wilkie Cooper and Guy Green?

There's a big difference between them. Wilkie was a very experienced cameraman, who worked throughout the war, as indeed Guy did, but I think Wilkie got his break earlier than Guy. Wilkie was very fast, very commercial, and, if I may say so now, not very artistic. Art wasn't of the essence in those days; it was to get the films done as quickly as possible. But Guy was an artist, and I'm very proud to have been able to work with him; in fact, I

modelled my first picture on *The Passionate Friends*, which is the last picture on which I operated for Guy.

How do you mean, 'modelled'?

Well Guy's lighting is basically very simple and, in turn, is based on Ronnie Neame; we're a family which starts with Ronnie, goes on to Guy and then to me, and then younger people have copied me – people I've trained. Ronnie developed this system, in which he believed it would be possible to light a group of actors evenly with one light, and that had never been done before. The lights in those days were so inefficient that if you put one light on to a wall it would be as bright as blazes in the middle and would fall off very quickly at the edges. Ronnie felt that that was an inefficient lamp, and, if he could get the lamp developed so that the light was even, he could use one light, against using two or three, and that would save time. Ronnie developed this system of one key light, a little back light, and a soft fill light, basically three units, and if he could develop that further he'd use less light and therefore go faster.

Now, Wilkie didn't work this system. Wilkie was brilliant at lighting very quickly with masses of lights, which I could never understand. He used what we call kicker lights. This sort of light you see on German movies where it kicks three-quarter back under the jawline. You see a lot of it on television. Ronnie, Guy and I hated that sort of thing – look at any of my films and you won't see those kicker lights at all. I think it's a complicated idea and not very flattering to a lady. Wilkie could do it and make it look acceptable.

Was *Blanche Fury* your first experience of Technicolor?

I was thrown in on *Blanche Fury* with Guy as a result of an accident to another operator, Ernie Steward. He was operating on the camera and with a breakaway set. They were tracking in with a crane through this set. They were going in through a door, so they couldn't pull the set away to let the camera through until the sides of the door were out of the shot. The equipment was very primitive in those days – I'm talking about just after the war – and what happened was that they were late in pulling the set away and the blimp hit the top of the set. Technicolor blimps were huge and it broke the whole blimp off the crane; it crashed to the floor, which put the crane out of balance because the weights at the back were totally wrong and it shot Ernie out like a catapult. He went over and over and crashed. Luckily, he wasn't killed! He broke some fingers and was stunned. But the film had to go on. I'd finished *Oliver Twist* and was still under contract. So I was put straight on to *Blanche Fury* the next day.

How did you come to graduate from camera operator to director of photography on *Golden Salamander*?

I'd been operating for about three years, this would be 1948/49, when suddenly Ronnie Neame said, 'How would you like to photograph my next film?' I said, 'Marvellous,' then to my horror I found that most of the film was to be shot on location in Tunisia, of all places. Very difficult to get to during 1948/49, and even more difficult to communicate with because the telephone system was non-existent. I found also that we weren't going to see any of our material while on location. Now, on my first film in charge, if I couldn't see my first day's work the next day, it was going to frighten the life out of me, because I wouldn't know whether I'd over-exposed or under-exposed, or whatever. All I was told by Ronnie was that John Bryan, a brilliant designer, who was responsible for designs on *Blanche Fury*, *Great Expectations* and *Oliver Twist*, was going to look at them and he'd cable or try telephoning every day. And that's how I started. I don't like location shooting. I would have been much happier in the studio. It's obviously much harder to control the lighting on location.

You worked several times with former cameraman-turned-director, your mentor Ronald Neame. Did you notice any differences in working with a director who had been a great cameraman before he turned director?

Oh yes, it does make a big difference. Let me give you a perfect comparison. I worked with Frank Launder and Sidney Gilliat, who were writers who, when they direct, listen to their dialogue. They don't look at what they're seeing, they listen to their dialogue and watch actors' movements. In fact, there's a great story that goes around – Sidney

Gilliat went in to see the rushes one day with Wilkie Cooper, came out at the end and said, 'Wilkie, I thought they were fine, but they were a bit dark, weren't they?' So Wilkie said, 'Yes, Sidney, you have your dark glasses on.' Now with Ronnie, it's totally different. Ronnie sees the set and works the action into the set and that's the difference between visual directors and dialogue directors.

Perhaps your most famous collaboration, certainly around this period, was with John Huston. How did this come about, and what did you value in this working friendship?

Well, how it came about – I did eight films with Huston. The story of how I photographed *Moulin Rouge* is really almost like a fairy-tale. I had just finished a film for Max Setton, *So Little Time*, with Marius Goring and Maria Schell, and out of the blue I received a phone message asking if I would go and see John Huston. Now, he'd finished *African Queen* and I knew he was about to start *Moulin Rouge* and I knew he had a cameraman, Otto Heller, assigned to do it. So I phoned Ronnie, because I was very close to him, and he said, 'Well, honestly, there must be something strange going on between Huston and Otto Heller.' I had to go to Claridges and I went to his room, and there was the great man sitting at a desk. He called me in and asked if I knew anything about Toulouse-Lautrec's paintings. Well, I didn't, so I said, 'I'm afraid not.' 'Do you know anything about the other French Impressionists?' I said, 'Yes, I know a little about them.' He went on scribbling and we chatted for a while. I went home and I said to my wife, 'I think that was a disaster.'

Anyway, a few days later, I got a message asking if I would go and see John Woolf [producer]. I rang Ronnie again, and he said, 'Well, you've got the film. When you go there, you've got to up your money a lot because you're only getting the minimum. Now, he'll know you only get £40 a week and he's going to try and get you for that. But you ask for £100 a week and stick to it, you'll get it.' So I went to see John Woolf and he said, 'John Huston wants you to photograph *Moulin Rouge* for him.' He said, 'Would you like to do it?' 'Oh yes, please.' 'What money do you want?' '£100 a week.' '£100 a week! You're only getting £40 a week at the moment,' which of course they always knew. I said, 'Yes, but I think I deserve more than that.' 'But you've never photographed a big colour film before.' I said, 'I know, but I think it's worth £100 a week.' 'Oh all right.' So I got the £100 a week and I started on the film. I saw Huston again and found out afterwards that Otto Heller had made some tests with Huston and he didn't like the results, and he didn't like Otto Heller's rather flippant way of approaching the subject.

Huston said to me, 'Os, kid, I want this film to look as though Toulouse-Lautrec directed it. I want you to go down to the museum at Albi, south of France, and look at all his paintings. I want you to take a second camera crew down there and get them to photograph all the paintings for montages.' So down we went to Albi and I took Cyril Knowles, whom I knew very well; he was a very good second-unit cameraman who would do exactly what was wanted. I saw the paintings, came back and had another meeting with Huston. He said, 'Now, what are you thinking?' 'Well, John, we've got to do a lot of things about this Technicolor system because it's not right for the Lautrec paintings.' He said, 'Well, what do you suggest?' I said that I'd like to do a few tests to show to him. He said, 'OK, fine.'

So I had little bits of about six of the sets built. They were all designed by a Frenchman called Vertès, a great impersonator of Lautrec style. He did all the hand drawings which are supposed to be Joe [José] Ferrer in the film. I did lots of these tests and one thing I was determined about was to kill the colour, because in those days Technicolor was so garish. I had Huston on my side, so I had a lot of punch, because by then *African Queen* had come out and it was a tremendous success, and he could do no wrong. If Huston wanted £500,000 for something, John Woolf would find it.

So I did these tests and put a lot of fog/smoke in the sets and fog filters on the camera. We saw these tests, and I said, 'What do you think?' He said, 'I think you're on the right lines, kid.' So we carried on testing and we were going to start filming in Paris, up in Montmartre, big night locations with this high key light. We had to place all the arcs, and many other lights, ahead of time, and the last series of tests that we'd made were brought over to Paris for Huston and me to look at in a cinema on the afternoon before we were due to start the film that night. A whole gaggle of Technicolor people came over; Huston didn't know them but *I* knew them all. I thought this was very odd. All the top echelon were there. Anyway, we ran the tests, and they sat in the front of the balcony and Huston and I sat a little way back. Huston said to me at the end, 'Well, what do you think, kid?' 'Well, I think they're great, John, I think they're just right.' 'So do I. That's what we'll do.'

Just as we were leaving, somebody from the Technicolor group said, 'Mr Huston, Ossie Morris, we cannot accept any responsibility for what you are doing to our system. We implore you to change your approach and go back to the true Technicolor style. You're destroying line, outline, you're destroying colour, destroying separation, and that is not acceptable to the House of Technicolor.' They implored us to change it. So Huston said to me, 'Os, what do you think, kid?' and I said, 'Well, John, I think it's fine, I think we're right,' and he said, 'So do I.' So he said, 'Gentlemen, thank you very much – and fuck you,' and walked out of the cinema and we started the film.

Shortly after that, we both had letters from Technicolor, saying they could not accept what we were doing. They covered themselves by letter to Huston and myself, and we carried on making the film and it got very, very exciting. We did the most extraordinary things. I mean, we filled the stages with thick smoke at eight in the morning, because three-strip Technicolor could cut through mist and fog, and we had to keep the stages very hot to keep it going, feeding in mist and fog all day. The electricians went on strike, they insisted on extra money, and then it was argued that their health was being ruined by all this smoke Ossie Morris was putting up in the gantry. The doctors were summoned and said, 'All they need is extra milk,' so they gave them a lot of milk to drink, and I asked for the stage to be kept closed at lunchtime so that it didn't destroy the smoke, but in the end the unions won the day. 'Those stages have got to be opened at lunchtime, you cannot persecute the electricians like this.' We carried on right through to the end and I think we achieved some wonderful effects. When it was visually successful, Huston and I each received letters from Technicolor saying how proud they were to have been associated with such a marvellous breakthrough in colour design, etc, etc.

Was there a lot of daunting location work on Huston's *Moby Dick*?

Oh yes. Daunting location work. The classic excuse is we ran out of weather. We had large-scale sections of whale in the sea, the mid section, nose section or tail section. These were enormous; it took so long to get these things organised and the actors had to be in the water for hours. Greg Peck couldn't stay in the water any longer, because it was getting too cold around these shores, so after finishing all work in the studio, in the middle of December we flew down to the Canary Islands to Las Palmas, and we finished the film down there because it was warmer. Greg could stay in the water there for six or eight hours, but he couldn't sustain that in the UK in September.

Have you been able to choose ever since which side of the Atlantic you wanted to work at?

Yes. I have been a freelance all my life. I never was under contract to a studio. After I finished *Golden Salamander*, the studio said, 'You can come back under your contract, but you'd have to go back to operating because there's nothing more for you.' I said I didn't want to do that and I took a chance.

Would you have used an agent?

I didn't use an agent at first, I used what is known as a film solicitor. There were certain solicitors who specialised in one-off contracts for films, and Ronnie gave me the name of somebody to go to, a man called Clive Nicholas. I stayed with him for a while and then he formed London Management with Dennis Van Thal – it's now a huge organisation with the Grade family. Clive Nicholas fell out with Dennis later and I stayed with London Management from then on. But a lot of people used to approach me. I never dealt with the financial side at all. If I had a clash of two people wanting me, which seldom happened, London Management would sort it out.

Did you notice differences between Hollywood methods and those of British studios when you started working for American companies?

Yes. First of all, I was never allowed to work in Hollywood. I worked in New York, but the unions in California would never allow any foreign cameramen. They would allow designers, editors, directors, but not cameramen. They were very powerful unions – they still are.

So you had trouble really with the unions in the two countries?

Yes. But in America they work a different system really. In America the gaffer, that's the chief electrician, roughs in all the lighting. The cameraman has his own gaffer who knows the cameraman's ways, and the gaffer roughs it in while the cameraman is with the operator working out the set-up, the movement of the camera. In England, I work differently. I'd get an operator like Freddie Francis or Arthur Ibbetson, who knew my ways, and I could leave them with the director to work out roughly the set-up, having asked them where they were going to cover, while I did the lighting. So we worked slightly differently in England. British ways were more interesting – it's a bit dull just hanging around to get the set-up, it's more exciting setting the lighting.

What do you recall of your involvement with those British New Wave films? You worked for Tony Richardson, now sadly dead, on a couple of very influential films, *Look Back in Anger* and *The Entertainer*. Did you feel that you needed a different visual style for those films?

Oh yes, I did. First of all, before that I'd photographed a film for René Clément, *Knave of Hearts*. Now that was the big breakthrough into what I call that new style. He had a very unorthodox way of making movies and I learnt a lot from him, and it was as a result of that that Tony Richardson asked me to photograph *Look Back in Anger*, and then *The Entertainer*. With Clément, sets could be built in the studio, but you were never to take any walls or ceilings off. That was René Clément's ruling. You had to live with the difficulties of the environment, otherwise it was bogus. Now you may think – and *I* thought – that's making life very difficult, as it was, but because you have to overcome those difficulties you gained a sort of a realism which you normally wouldn't have. It's not comfortable working in a room which is only the size of a soapbox and you've got to get several actors in it, and a camera; they have to record sound too; you're required to light it, so straight away you're in a totally different ball-game. Your whole approach is different.

I'm fascinated you think *Knave of Hearts* led you on to being the cameraman for things like *Look Back in Anger*.

Oh it did, definitely. I only captured the picture because Tony Richardson saw *Knave of Hearts*; he said, 'You know I've never directed a film, and I'd like you to photograph my film.' That's how it started.

And on those Woodfall films, did you work very closely with Richardson, with Osborne, on the design?

Not John Osborne. Tony did not value John Osborne's contribution to the filmmaking of it; he did not value John Osborne being on the set; in fact, John Osborne wasn't *allowed* on the set. He respected John's contributions to writing but John's film ideas he rather ridiculed.

I remember the seedy look of *The Entertainer*. Were those two films both shot in

actual places, the way you'd done *Knave of Hearts*?

Most of it was, not all of it. The composite sets, if we go back to *Look Back in Anger*, that's the rooms, the flat where they lived and so on, were built in the studio. Tony felt that, because he'd never been in a film studio before, the limitations of having the four walls was too great, and I think he was right. He was very good, very bright, was Tony. He picked it up very quickly, but he needed the walls to come out. However, we kept everything very claustrophobic. It was the same with *The Entertainer*; we did a lot of that in theatres, a terrible theatre at Morecambe, where Olivier does these awful numbers, and there's only about six or eight people in the audience. That was done up there; the scenes on the buses, the open-top buses and all that sort of thing were done there, but again the apartment scenes were created in the studio. *The Entertainer* was filmed at Shepperton and *Look Back in Anger* at Elstree.

Are you, as director of photography, usually involved in preliminary discussions?

Always. If you don't do that, you're at a terrible disadvantage. If they want you to be able to go fast, to prepare in advance, to contribute something, even if they don't want to hear your views, you've got to be in at the beginning to know what's going on. Otherwise you can't prepare efficiently.

Have you found some directors easier in this respect than others, some with whom you were able to get a sense earlier on of what they wanted?

Towards the end, or rather halfway through my career, I hooked myself with good directors and I only made one mistake, who shall be nameless in fairness to him, but all the others were good directors. You can categorise directors very easily. There's director A who's a brilliant technician, brilliant with actors and knows the business inside out. David Lean of course, Ronnie Neame, Carol Reed, were all brilliant with script, brilliant with editing, brilliant with actors, quite good on the visuals but, if something has got to go, Carol would let the visuals go, if he was in a corner. He's the most cunning director I've ever worked with. Carol was like Hitchcock. Carol said yes to everything anybody said. Two people could go up to him with totally conflicting ideas and he'd say yes to both of them, which created utter confusion, which was what he wanted. He pulled the strings to the puppets, and we were all puppets, and he had them

in his hands. Hitchcock always treated actors like that. So did David Lean. David would never stay in a hotel with actors.

Then you get director B who's brilliant with script, like Joe Mankiewicz, brilliant with actors, handling actors, but hopeless in getting set-ups.

Then you get directors like Sidney Lumet, who's very efficient all the way down the line, knows where he wants the camera, and is very, very fast.

What do you recall about filming *Equus* for him? It seems a very difficult play to turn into a film.

I saw the play when I knew I was about to do the film, and I thought it was marvellous. But the film was a terrible disappointment. The first argument with Sidney was whether we would use real horses, or stylised horses as they did in the play. You know, those men with horse-shaped chromium heads. It was agreed that we'd never get away with that on film; it had to be real horses. And therefore it had to be real locations. He gathered a wonderful cast together, and they did all these long sections of dialogue. Richard Burton had acted the play in New York. We waited for Richard to finish something else, and did two or three weeks without him. Everything was done to make it work and yet it just didn't click.

There's a scene where the boy has finished worshipping the horse and the camera seems just to do a long, long track and ends up in Burton's office. How did you do that?

We go off onto blackness. We filmed on the night location – the boy's in the field in Toronto at night – and he does the worshipping business there, and then we ran off him onto black and match the movement off the black in the office, and come onto Richard. Then we just joined the two together. It's quite simply done. Just a slow pan of the boy onto blackness, and then we pick that up again in the studio. The secret – the camera movement has to be the same speed!

What sort of visual effect were you and Carol Reed after in *Oliver!*?

I think I can fairly say that he left the visuals entirely to me. All he would say was, 'I want a Dickensian look about it,' and left that to me. Musicals aren't real anyway, so you try to get away from reality because if you don't people get confused. A musical isn't real – people don't go along the street singing – and yet you don't want it to look like a pantomime.

Do you remember a shot of St Paul's,

similar in lighting and composition to one in David Lean's film? Did you have this in mind?

No, the set was designed with St Paul's in the back of the Fagin's Kitchen set and in one sequence it is bathed in a sort of pinky light (I think Fagin is going out at sunset to the Three Cripples pub to meet Sikes, who has been out on the job with the boy). I don't remember linking it with *Oliver Twist* at all. Of course I only operated on *Oliver Twist* and one was in colour and one was black-and-white. I think all they intended was that St Paul's *is* London, so they decided to put it in the background. You'd have to ask John Box, the designer, about that – or John Bryan in the original.

What about the filming of Onna White's dance sequences – were they logistically difficult?

There was great friction between Carol and Onna White, and between Carol and the legendary Johnny Green – particularly Johnny Green, the music director. There were times when I wondered why Carol ever took the film on, because he hated the music; he was only interested in Fagin and the boys. Whenever we started a musical number with the boys, with Onna White or Johnny Green there, Carol became just bloody-minded. Yet the music is part of it. I think it was because he thought they knew more about that part of it than he did, as he knew little about choreography or music and what you could do, so he proceeded to make Johnny Green's work almost impossible. I mean, he decimated the score as we went along and Johnny had to keep altering it. Carol wanted to add little bits and pieces of business with the boys all the time, which naturally required extra music score.

Dame Anna Neagle

1904–1986

Actor: *Should a Doctor Tell?, The Chinese Bungalow* (1931), *Goodnight, Vienna* (1932), *The Flag Lieutenant, The Little Damozel, Bitter Sweet* (1933), *The Queen's Affair* (1934), *Nell Gwyn* (1935), *Peg of Old Drury, Limelight* (1936), *The Three Maxims, London Melody, Victoria the Great* (1937), *Sixty Glorious Years* (1938), *Nurse Edith Cavell* (1939), *Irene* (1940), *No, No, Nanette, Sunny* (1941), *They Flew Alone* (1942), *Forever and a Day, Yellow Canary* (1943), *I Live in Grosvenor Square* (1945), *Piccadilly Incident* (1946), *The Courtneys of Curzon Street* (1947), *Spring in Park Lane* (1948), *Elizabeth of Ladymead, Maytime in Mayfair* (1949), *Odette* (1950), *The Lady with a Lamp* (1951), *Derby Day* (1952), *Lilacs in the Spring* (1955), *King's Rhapsody, My Teenage Daughter* (1956), *No Time for Tears* (1957), *The Man Who Wouldn't Talk* (1958), *The Lady is a Square* (1959)

Producer: *These Dangerous Years* (1957), *Wonderful Years* (1958), *Heart of a Man* (1959)

'Herbert [Wilcox] and I have always had a marked preference for pleasant films about pleasant people, and these films were light and gay, deliberately designed to give people a lift,'[1] said Anna Neagle in 1967. Two comments on this view are in order. First, the time for such 'pleasant films about pleasant people' was quite past by the time she spoke, washed away by a new wave of social and poetic realism in the early '60s. Second, in fact Wilcox and she did venture into more demanding territory than the remark suggests, notably in *Nurse Edith Cavell* and *Odette*. The days of their ascendancy in British cinema were from the mid '30s to the early '50s: 'They were lovely days, but they are over, and Herbert and I are not looking back,'[2] she said in the same 1967 interview.

Wilcox was undoubtedly the driving force behind her career, her devoted husband as well as her director, and their films together made her a top box-office star in Britain and winner of numerous awards. According to some interviewed for this book, she was actually tougher-minded on her own than she ever was in his presence. She nevertheless insisted, 'I was so fortunate to have someone like Herbert who was so understanding ... I needed people who could encourage me and bring me out, as it were.'[3]

Nell Gwyn established her stardom and the pattern of painstaking research for the historical characters she would undertake: *Peg of Old Drury* (as eighteenth-century actress, Peg Woffington); *Victoria the Great* and *Sixty Glorious Years* (further events in Victoria's reign); *Nurse Edith Cavell* in Hollywood; aviatrix Amy Johnson in *They Flew Alone*; wartime heroine Odette Churchill in *Odette*; and Florence Nightingale in *The Lady with a Lamp*, all directed by Wilcox. In her autobiography, she recalls (in tribute to the make-up man Guy Pearce) how, for *Victoria the Great*, 'It was when I looked in the mirror and saw, not myself, but the old Queen herself, that I began to "get" the character,'[4] and on the sequel she had the advice and recollections of Lady Antrim, lady-in-waiting to Queen Victoria, who 'was full of fascinating anecdotes about this very strong-minded and sometimes unpredictable lady'.[5] Ten years later came *Odette*: 'This was the greatest imaginable experience because I felt so close to it ... Odette was with me at the time, and Peter Churchill. I found this with all my subjects, especially Odette, that the more I was with her and went into the atmosphere, the prison cell, the more the externals fell away.'[6]

Despite this conscientious approach to portraying the famous, it is probably the 'London series' which made her so hugely popular. It began with *I Live in Grosvenor Square*, an exercise in Anglo-American relations in which she plays a duke's daughter. Then came *Piccadilly Incident*, which 'was a staggering success. It was a romantic drama, not a comedy',[7] and which initiated the very successful teaming with Michael Wilding. Prior to engaging him, Wilcox and she had thought, 'He was *all right*, but hardly co-starring material' but, 'since everyone else we wanted was otherwise engaged, we took a chance',[8] and the rest is box-office history, peaking with *Spring in Park Lane*, 'the biggest hit of all ... light, life, gaiety and fun'.[9] Wilding's breezy manner complemented her rather stately style.

By the mid '50s, it was really over. After two unrewarding co-starring ventures with a similarly drifting Errol Flynn (*Lilacs in the Spring* and *King's Rhapsody*), she played in and/or produced a number of films ineptly aimed at a younger audience, several of them starring Frankie Vaughan. Somewhat sadly, she told an interviewer in 1973, 'They are writing very few subjects for the older woman, except on the theme of the mature woman who has an affair with a young man ... but it's not for me.'[10] She went back to the stage, where audiences still welcomed her talents and her brand of non-confronting charm.

1 Alan A Coulson, 'Anna Neagle', *Films in Review*, March 1967, p 159
2 Coulson, p 159
3 Tony Williams, 'Dame Anna Neagle in interview', *Films and Filming*, May 1983, p 20
4 Anna Neagle, *Anna Neagle: An Autobiography* (first published 1974), Futura, London, 1979, p 83
5 Neagle, *Autobiography*, p 96
6 Williams, p 22
7 Williams, p 22
8 Neagle, *Autobiography*, p 140
9 Neagle, *Autobiography*, p 142
10 Eric Braun, 'Images in a chocolate box', *Films and Filming*, November 1973, p 40

Ronald Neame

b. 1911

Cinematographer: *Blackmail* (ass ph) (1929), *Happy* (co-ph) (1933), *Girls Will Be Boys* (1934), *Drake of England* (co-ph), *Honours Easy*, *Invitation to the Waltz* (1935), *A Star Fell From Heaven*, *The Crimes of Stephen Hawke*, *King of the Castle*, *Once in a Million*, *Radio Lover* (1936), *Against the Tide*, *Café Colette*, *Strange Experiment*, *Brief Ecstasy* (co-ph), *The Londonderry Air*, *Catch As Catch Can*, *Feather Your Nest*, *Member of the Jury*, *There Was a Young Man* (1937), *The Ware Case*, *The Gaunt*

Stranger, Who Goes Next?, I See Ice (co-ph), It's in the Air (co-ph), Murder in the Family, Penny Paradise (co-ph), Second Thoughts (1938), Cheer Boys Cheer (co-ph), Young Man's Fancy (co-ph), Come On George (co-ph), The Four Just Men, Let George Do It (co-ph), Let's Be Famous (co-ph), Trouble Brewing (1939), Major Barbara, Return To Yesterday (co-ph) (1940), In Which We Serve (1942), This Happy Breed (1944), Blithe Spirit (1945)

Producer: Brief Encounter (co-pr) (1945), Great Expectations (co-pr, co-sc) (1946), Oliver Twist, The Passionate Friends (1949), The Magic Box (1951)

Director: Take My Life (1947), The Golden Salamander (& co-pr) (1950), The Card (1952), The Million Pound Note (1953), The Man Who Never Was (1956), The Seventh Sin, Windom's Way (1957), The Horse's Mouth (1959), Tunes of Glory (& co-sc) (1960), Escape to Zahrain (& pr) (1961), I Could Go On Singing (1962), The Chalk Garden (1963), Mister Moses (1964), A Man Could Get Killed (co-dir), Gambit (1966), Prudence and the Pill (co-dir) (1968), The Prime of Miss Jean Brodie (1969), Scrooge (1970), The Poseidon Adventure (1972), The Odessa File (1975), Meteor (1979), Hopscotch (1980), First Monday in October (1981), Foreign Body (1986), The Magic Balloon (1990)

Ronald Neame is the most distinguished of those British directors who began their careers as cameramen. Son of actress Ivy Close and a successful photographer, he shot more than thirty films in the 1930s, many of them 'quota quickies', hitting the big-time with *Major Barbara* in 1940. This began his very fruitful collaboration with David Lean, culminating in his co-producing films, such as *Great Expectations*, associated with the period of major prestige of British cinema. His first film as director was the excellent, unpretentious thriller, *Take My Life*, and during the ensuing decades he made a number of first-class entertainments, filming on both sides of the Atlantic. *The Card*, a charming adaptation from Arnold Bennett, is the first of several excellent films Neame made with Alec Guinness, including *The Horse's Mouth*, in which Guinness played anarchic artist Gulley Jimson, and *Tunes of Glory*, with its fine co-starring performances from Guinness and John Mills. Neame also elicited one of Judy Garland's best performances in *I Could Go On Singing* and an Oscar-winning display from Maggie Smith in *The Prime of Miss Jean Brodie*. He is a very sympathetic director of actors and a craftsman of the kind British cinema now badly needs.
Interview date: October 1989

After working on so many 1930s films, how did you come to photograph *Major Barbara* in 1940?

At Ealing I'd worked on a lot of Michael Balcon pictures as a cameraman. My opportunity came when I was phoned by Gabriel Pascal. I'd worked for him on a 'quota quickie' and he wanted me to photograph a test of the star of his new film –

Wendy Hiller. Gabby was away on location on *Major Barbara* and the young editor in charge of directing this test was David Lean. (He really directed *Major Barbara*, though Gabby has the credit.) For the first time I was photographing a really important picture. David and I became close friends, and we then worked together on Michael Powell's *One of Our Aircraft is Missing*.

Around this time a man called Filippo Del Giudice, an Italian who decided that he wanted to put British films on the map, asked Noël Coward if he would make a film about the British war effort. Noël was a bit lukewarm about it. He didn't have anything particularly in mind. Then he was chatting with his friend, Lord Louis Mountbatten, and they got talking about Mountbatten's ship the *Kelly*, which was a destroyer that had been sunk by the Germans in the Mediterranean. Noël suddenly thought, 'I'll make the story of the *Kelly*.' So he got back to Filippo and said, 'I'll make a film for you; I don't know a great deal about directing films. I *want* to direct it, but I must have around me people I admire and who are professional,' and he went to see a lot of films, amongst them *Major Barbara*.

As a result, David Lean joined with me and Tony Havelock-Allan, an executive producer, and we launched into *In Which We Serve*. One evening Noël invited us to his studio to read us the script of this film he had written, and David, Tony and I sat down, with a big roaring fire and a nice large drink.

Noël said, 'I will now read you my story,' and for the next four hours did just that. There were some wonderful things in this story, but we saw that if it was put on the screen in the way it had been written, it would run for four hours. So we said, 'Can we take the screenplay and analyse it a bit?' It was David's idea that we should take the best things from the Coward screenplay and drop the rest, then link them together to make a full story with the shipwrecked crew clinging around a raft in the water, and flashing back to what they were before they found themselves there. So we went back into the lives of Johnny Mills, Bernard Miles, and so on. I think we got a pretty good script out of it and a very good cast, mainly because of Noël's influence.

Again because of Noël's influence, we got enormous support from Lord Mountbatten and the British Navy. However, at the time we had great opposition from officialdom in England, from the Ministry of Information, etc. They said this was a very bad film to make, because it showed a British ship being sunk by the Germans and this was not the kind of film to present when we were hoping to win a war. But Mountbatten, who was very powerful, overcame that opposition.

Now, *In Which We Serve* had a strange history because Del Guidice was one of the pirates – I mean men who were determined to get their film made no matter what they had to do, no matter how many ships they have to sink – and I'm inclined to get Del mixed up with Gabriel Pascal because they were so similar. Anyway, *In Which We Serve* was Del's baby and he gave this party, to which everybody was invited, and announced the commencement of the film we'd been shooting for about ten days at Denham. A bit later, Del came to David and me and Tony and said, 'Don't tell Noël, but I have something terrible to tell you. We have no money. The whole thing was done on credit. The studios have built everything till now without getting any money. Outside of the few salaries that I paid there was nothing. But we have one hope that we might be able to continue. We've shot ten days. David, over this weekend can you cut the first twenty minutes that we shot and get it into some kind of shape that could be shown?' David said, 'Yes, I think I can do that.' He said, 'Well, Sam Smith, who is the head of British Lion film distributors, has promised to come and see the film on Monday. I hope he will like the material and we'll get the guarantee,' and that's exactly what happened.

You went on as a cameraman with *Blithe Spirit*, I think?

After *In Which We Serve*, Noël became very enamoured of our little crew, and he said, 'I have a lot of material, why don't you film some more of it?' and so we made *This Happy Breed*, which is the first film I photographed in colour, using it to make drab rather than bright colours. We wanted to use colour in a new way and I think we did it successfully. Yes, *This Happy Breed* is a key film, and then came *Blithe Spirit*, which was a tremendous challenge for a cameraman, because the ghost lady, played by Kay Hammond, was in a grey tulle dress and completely grey make-up and had to be lit with a green light to create the ghostly illusion. This green light had to follow her everywhere, with the problem of keeping it off the other actors, and it was even more difficult when she walked behind them. However, I think we achieved quite a good result and I must say I think *Blithe Spirit* holds up today, whereas *This Happy Breed* doesn't. And I don't think *In Which We Serve* holds up any longer. Last time I saw it, I felt, well, it's sort of gone.

Some of the upper-class stuff is a bit excruciating, but a lot of the rest isn't. You know, Bernard Miles and co.

Yes, their side of it, the lower deck, stands up. One of our problems was that we had two advisers. We had a lower-deck adviser, an AB (Able-Bodied Seaman) who had been Mountbatten's batman during the time of the *Kelly*. Then we had a lieutenant in charge of the upper-deck routine and behaviour. They regarded themselves as the technical advisers and they never could agree about anything, and sometimes we got into such trouble that we would get on to the Admiralty just to get their opinion.

What were your relations with Rank and Cineguild?

After *Blithe Spirit* we formed Cineguild and Noël was very sarcastic about it. He wanted us to go on making Noël Coward projects and we wanted – Tony and David and I – to form our own little company because we didn't always want to make Coward stuff. Noël was never part of Cineguild, which became part of Independent Producers, which was totally owned by Rank.

Now, Arthur was a wonderful man. He said to us, 'Make me some good films and leave the rest to me.' First of all he sent me to America for six weeks in 1944. He wanted me to look at the American studios and see what we had to do to bring ourselves up-to-date so that we could compete. At that time he was wooing 20th-Century-Fox.

When I came back from America, having loved it, I was convinced I could make a film American audiences would like and accept. I told Arthur I preferred to produce it. I was a good cameraman and I was still very young, but I thought I *could* become a producer. Arthur said, 'I don't see why you shouldn't, so what do you want to do?' I said I would like to ask David Lean if he would consider directing if I produced it, and he said, 'Go ahead, Ronnie. Tell me what you want to make.'

So I asked David if he would direct *Great Expectations*, and I can remember to this day walking around the studios together and David saying, 'You're one of the top cameramen in the country and it's true I've directed, but are you sure this is good idea?' I said, 'In my opinion, David, you're going to be one of the great directors and it would be an honour for me to produce a film if you'd direct it.' The American market liked *Great Expectations* very much, but of course it was still an art-house film, as all ours were. There were several others that were all acclaimed as highly successful films, but we were spending too much money. *Great Expectations* cost only about £375,000 but it was too much for what we were receiving back. We needed a world market and we needed America.

Then Arthur, with his tremendous enthusiasm, began to get the Rank Organisation into financial difficulties [in the late '40s]. Eventually, the Independent Producers – Cineguild, Wessex Films, etc –

were shut down. John Davis, Rank's right-hand man, said we must stop making films for a while, which was not such a silly move because, the moment we stopped making films, this outlay also stopped. Davis was more interested in diversifying the Rank Organisation. He reduced the overdraft in twelve months, but stopped making films and started selling property. A little later he realised that, because Rank owned six hundred theatres, they had to have some product for those theatres, even if it was only to bargain with the Americans in terms of how much they were charging for their films. We needed films, so they formed another company at Pinewood where I worked under an American called Earl St John, who was Executive Producer. We started again as if we were independently there, making pictures for Rank, but under much tighter control.

Cineguild had really broken up after we made *Great Expectations*, *Oliver Twist* and *The Passionate Friends*, which David directed. By that time [1948] David was becoming more and more important as a director and really didn't need a producer. I would have been so overshadowed by David that it was better that we part. However, I'd decided I would like to direct and indeed I had started to direct before Rank collapsed. I directed my first film, *Take My Life*, in 1947. It was a thriller with Tam [Hugh] Williams and Greta Gynt, and Rosalie Crutchley in her first film. Then, after that came *The Golden Salamander* with little Anouk Aimée and Trevor Howard.

Did you film that on location?

Yes, we went to North Africa. I think a film should be made where it *should* be made. Some films should be made in studios; but I think that, if a film fits being shot in North Africa with mud huts, that's where it should be shot.

The next film you directed was *The Card*, in 1952.

The Card with Alec Guinness was the first picture we made when I went back. By that time David had long since left and gone to Korda, but I went back with John Bryan, who was one of the greatest set designers in the world. He did the Dickens films and he also did the sets, although he was producer, on *The Card* and *The Horse's Mouth*. After that we parted company, in a friendly way.

The Card was not Cineguild. It was for British Film Makers and that was the new regime; it was the Rank Organisation under the auspices of John Davis, and made at Pinewood. A man called Robert

Clark was the boss of Elstree Studios, which owned *The Card* but had done nothing with it. They had an option which ran out, and I went to the Arnold Bennett estate and bought it because I thought it was a perfect Guinness part. I sent the book to Guinness and he read it and said, 'Yes, I'll do this one.' We brought in Eric Ambler, who did the screenplay, and it was one of the happiest pictures I have worked on. We had a superb cast – Alec, Valerie Hobson, Glynis Johns, Edward Chapman, Veronica Turleigh . . . they all just fell into place, they all wanted to do it. They all loved the idea of working with Alec and it was a very good script.

Your next two films had American stars, Gregory Peck in *The Million Pound Note* and Clifton Webb in *The Man Who Never Was*. Was this casting a matter of economic strategy?

Not entirely. I think it was John Bryan who, shortly after we finished *The Card*, read a short story by Mark Twain called *The Million Pound Note*, and we got a girl called Jill Craigie [who later directed several films] to come in and write the screenplay. She turned this short story into a full-length film and I think did it very well. We wanted Dinah Sheridan for the female lead but she'd stopped acting by then. We were in desperate straits because we just couldn't find a girl. Greg came in because it's an American part. We owe that to John Davis, because, by now, he had built up a relationship with the people who were running United Artists. They said they would put up the money for Greg Peck, if he would do it. Greg wanted to make a picture in England, he took a liking to the story, and his salary on it was £75,000, which was a very reasonable sum for Greg.

What about *The Man Who Never Was*? It seemed a curious pairing – Clifton Webb and Gloria Grahame.

That was purely 20th Century-Fox. Darryl Zanuck's son-in-law, André Hakim, came over to England to produce a film and he brought this story, a true story. I was what is laughingly known as a 'hot' director at that time, and André asked me if I would direct it. I liked the idea and we got in Nigel Balchin, who knew a lot about that particular aspect of the war because he had been in Intelligence himself, and so we got rather a good script. This went back to Zanuck, who said, 'Well, this is fine but I've got to have names and I have Clifton Webb under long-term contract, and I suggest that he could play a British officer and get away with it.'

Well, he *was* a name and I took a liking to him, and Gloria Grahame was, I guess, another of Zanuck's suggestions. I don't know whether the character was originally American, but it wasn't being dishonest to use an American in that part and we cast her as a useful second name. I thought she was very good, but she got bad reviews for it. That again was a very happy film and it was very interesting going to Spain where 'the man who never was' was buried under the name of the naval officer.

Your next film. *The Seventh Sin* for MGM, was I think your first strictly American film.

I was given the opportunity of directing a film in Hollywood and I jumped at it without really considering whether it was any good or not. It was a dreadful script, based on a Somerset Maugham novel, and it was a desperately unhappy venture. In fact, it became quite clear, once I started shooting in the studio, that it was going to be disastrous for me because the management of the studio was just changing, and I became very insecure indeed. Anybody else can show insecurity, but not the director, and I knew I would never be able to finish the picture. I had never been in such a state in all my life. Eventually Vincente Minnelli finished the film; he didn't want a credit on it; neither did I, but I had to take it.

The reason I am telling you this story is to show that there are some wonderful things that can happen, as well as the bad. When I got home that night, convinced that my career was at an end, the phone rang. A voice said, 'This is George Cukor. I am phoning because I imagine you're feeling pretty low this evening, aren't you?' and I said, 'That's putting it mildly.' He said, 'Well, the reason I am phoning is I want to tell you that it is not going to make any difference to your career. It will not do any damage at all, and you must not worry about it. I speak with authority because I was the director who was thrown off *Gone With the Wind*.'

Did you go back to England to make *Windom's Way* after that?

Immediately after that, John Bryan, who had been my partner, rang and said, 'I read in *Variety* that you left the picture. How about coming back and making *Windom's Way*?' He was going to produce it, with Peter Finch. It was not a successful picture, I'm afraid. I think it fell between two stools, neither politically profound nor exciting enough as an action film. John just liked the book very much and I would have directed anything in order to get back to the studios again. John and I had a wonderful relationship together. We were going to start another picture many years later and he, though he was a producer, agreed to come back and do the sets – and then he had a stroke and died.

Did you work with James Kennaway on the screenplay for *Tunes of Glory*?

Yes, we did the screenplay together. I firmly believe that the best director, theoretically, is the writer-director because then you have one man who both creates the material and directs it, but that's not always practical, because sometimes a writer is not a good director and vice versa. So the next best thing is to have a director and a writer who work so closely together that they are like one man and that's the way I work with writers.

***Tunes of Glory* seems like a film that would make a good stage play ...**

Yes, and funnily enough, I was asked, by an American called Doolittle, who has a theatre in Los Angeles, if I would turn it into a play and direct it. I would have liked to, but I am afraid of the theatre. I am scared of going into television, too, because I'm convinced that they'd fire me after the fourth day for being two days behind schedule! *The Horse's Mouth* and *Tunes of Glory* were both financed by a man whose name I've forgotten. He was a partner of Alexander Korda and he inherited London Films' contracts when Korda died. One of the contracts was a three-picture deal with Alec Guinness, who still had two to do for (I think) £12,000 each.

Did *Tunes of Glory* and *The Horse's Mouth* do well in America?

They did very well, in terms of kudos. People in America today always say, 'I loved your film *Tunes of Glory*.' Everybody saw *Tunes of Glory* but they saw it on television, and this raises another point which is interesting about this particular period. Arthur Rank did everything on God's earth to try to get British films on to the American market and he failed. Then on American television they just didn't have enough material to fill the hours on air. They were frantic for material and among the cheap, easy material they could lay their hands on were old British films. And so British films became understood and appreciated by Americans through television, and what Arthur tried so hard to do for so many years happened automatically.

What would you see as the major strengths and weaknesses of British cinema of the period we have been talking about?

There was too much emphasis placed on 'this is a *British* film' and I think the most guilty person there was Michael Balcon, who was very parochial in his thinking, though he made some lovely films. I think that, at one time, he wanted a title at the end of each film, 'This is a British film', and the last thing Americans wanted was British films. When I was making *Tunes of Glory* it didn't concern me in the least whether it was successful in America because it was a wholly British scene. Now before I make a film my first thinking is, 'Will this be for a mass American audience?' and we fall between two stools. We are trying in England, except that there's practically no industry anyway now, to make films that will appeal to the world market and we can't. We don't know how to do it.

Nanette Newman

b. 1934

Actor: *Hear We Come Gathering* (1945), *Personal Affair* (1953), *Triple Blackmail* ('Broken Honeymoon') (1955), *Faces in the Dark, The League of Gentlemen* (1960), *The Rebel, Pit of Darkness, House of Mystery* (1961), *The Painted Smile, Twice Round the Daffodils, The L-Shaped Room, The Wrong Arm of the Law* (1962), *Seance on a Wet Afternoon, Of Human Bondage* (1964),

The Whisperers, The Wrong Box (1966), Deadfall (1967), Captain Nemo and the Underwater City, Oh! What a Lovely War, The Madwoman of Chaillot (1969), The Raging Moon (1970), The Love Ban (1972), Man at the Top (1973), The Stepford Wives (1974), International Velvet (1978), Restless Natives (cameo) (1985), The Mystery of Edwin Drood (1993)

Nanette Newman might easily have made a career as a great beauty, of a serenely gentle kind that did not grow on trees in the 1960s. However, she worked at being an actress and when the role gave her half a chance she could be touching (as in her best part, in *The Raging Moon*), or charmingly romantic (as in *The Wrong Box*) or convincingly distraught (as in *Seance on a Wet Afternoon*). She came from showbusiness parents, and was in two films as a child, before doing time in 'B' films of the early '60s, including Vernon Sewell's properly chilling *House of Mystery*. That her film career has been somewhat sporadic is no doubt explained by the value she placed on a stable personal life (she is married to Bryan Forbes and has often appeared in his films), but she has also enjoyed success on television, especially in *Jessie* (1980), and as a writer of children's books. She is, though, such a gift to the cameras that one hopes she has not seriously retired.

Interview date: July 1994

After a couple of childhood appearances, you did a few 'B' pictures. Did they feel notably different from the 'A' pictures you went on to?

I think they did, inasmuch as you were aware that they were shot very quickly and not a lot of attention was paid to them, not a lot of publicity. You got paid less and got less good treatment. They filled the bill alongside the feature films. There were certain actors and actresses who probably made quite a good living just doing that type of movie. It kept them in work. I think there was a feeling of being a 'jobbing actor' which today you wouldn't find.

A superior 'B' film is Vernon Sewell's *House of Mystery*.

I remember that, yes. He made no waves, people got paid, and it was an area in which certain directors made a good living. Making 'B' pictures wasn't very demanding and, if they weren't ambitious, they settled for that, I guess. Actors, I know, look back at things and say, 'God! That was appalling!' and yet, at the time, you go into it thinking, 'I shall make something of this.' It's an actor's eternal optimism. About *House of Mystery*, I think at that time people loved mystery stories, which were popular before the vogue for horror films.

Your first film connected with Bryan was *The League of Gentlemen*. Did being the producer/director/screenwriter's wife create any difficulties for you, like coming home to the person you had been working with at the studio?

No, I've always enjoyed working with Bryan because he's very much an actor's director. It is something that you either love and enjoy doing, or you hate it – there's no in-between. The only thing you have to be very aware of is that you must never have any special treatment and never make the actors you are working with feel that you have an 'in', because that could be very worrying. So you have the worst calls and so on. Other than that, it's very nice because you have a kind of shorthand with your husband, which is very useful on a film as it speeds everything up. I never quite believe those people who say that, when they go home of an evening, they never discuss anything to do with the film they're working on. Your work is always something you would talk about at home.

In *The League of Gentlemen* I had only a spit and a cough, a tiny little part, so I wasn't there for long. It's an interesting film which stands up quite well, although the last time we saw it we thought it creaked a little. I think it's an interesting subject because it was so much a part of that period, the feeling of your usefulness being over. Combining that with a thriller worked well, I think. When you look back at British films, I think we made very good films of certain types (war films, comedies) and they were very, very British. They epitomised everything that went on in our country. The sad thing is that when we started to try and home in on the American market, to Americanise everything, we lost our individuality. Looking back on English films, we seemed to have a character and a purpose that was very, very English.

You were in some striking films in the early '60s – *The L-Shaped Room*, *The Wrong Arm of the Law* and *Seance on a Wet Afternoon*.

I liked doing *The Wrong Arm of the Law* because I was thrilled to be working with Peter Sellers. It was very exciting and, when you work with comics, like Sellers and Lionel Jeffries, it's wonderful to see how inventive they are. I had a tiny part in *The L-Shaped Room*, because I just wanted to work with Bryan. I'd just had my first daughter and I really didn't have the drive then; I wanted to work because I enjoyed it, but I didn't want to leave my children or be away from Bryan, so I just worked in order to fit in with my life. Really dedicated actresses don't do that, so I think that I drifted along doing whatever came my way. At the end of your career, as I am now, perhaps you suffer for that, although I don't consider I suffer because it was my own decision and I don't regret it. You may not have a great background of work to look back on but you have a happier life.

I think Bryan got the best performances ever out of Cicely Courtneidge.

Yes, I think she was very good in *The L-Shaped Room* in which she was playing a character who was very near to herself, an old vaudeville actress. I think her earlier films were very much playing to the gallery and very 'over the top', but then that was the style in that period. Her whole personality was effervescent and dynamic and she perhaps thought she had to do that on the screen.

You had a good part in *Seance on a Wet Afternoon* as the distraught mother.

Yes, I really liked that. Kim Stanley was extraordinary, to say the least. She was a totally enchanting woman but obviously had a drinking problem, and she was also a Method actress. She posed certain problems, for Bryan and Dickie [Attenborough] – not in a nasty, difficult way, but just out of wanting to be good. I think she was a brilliant actress, but she was a very bizarre woman and it was a great tragedy, I think, that her career in films suffered because of this. She wasn't a conventional 'leading lady' at all. *Seance* was one of Bryan's most individual films and produced one of Dickie's best performances too. It had a claustrophobic quality and John Barry, whom Bryan used a lot, made an enormous contribution with his superb music.

What do you remember of the troubled production of *Of Human Bondage*?

Bryan took over directing that for a while, until they found Ken Hughes to take over. Everyone was horrid to Kim Novak, yet I think she was extraordinarily nice and better than anybody gave her credit for. The first director, Henry Hathaway, was a monstrous man and really, really nasty to her. He had curious obsessions. I remember going for a costume fitting, and he said, 'I want you to be dressed like a boy.' I was playing a sweet young girl! Lunatic things he wanted! Then of course, when it changed, I was dressed in a much more feminine way. In the end the notices weren't very good, yet it is a wonderful subject.

I have never managed to see *The Whisperers* and I'd like to know what your experience was of working with Dame Edith Evans.

That was immensely thrilling. I had one scene with her where I had to come in clutching a black baby (my character was living with a black man). Bryan found her amazing to work with; she was no trouble. She took direction very well and she adored Bryan. She had a sad, lonely life. She just dedicated her whole life to acting.

You responded very well to Gerry Turpin's Technicolor camera in *The Wrong Box*. How important was the cameraman to you? Did you become technically knowledgeable?

No, I didn't. I was very aware of the fact that Gerry was a superb lighting man – some men are wonderful at lighting women. I knew I was being very well lit and that one would look one's best, which is always very pleasant. In those days you could take more time, so he could be intricate in the way that he lit. *The Wrong Box* is a pleasure to look at – the set design, the lighting, the costume designs by Julie Harris (which I thought were beautiful), everything was at its best.

We had the best time on that film; we were shooting in the Royal Crescent at Bath, and all I can remember is laughing, because it was a very entertaining cast to be working with. Ralphie Richardson used to live and die by the sausages each day, always waiting for the food to arrive at lunchtime. Michael Caine was always talking about *Alfie*, which he had just made, and he was on the verge of becoming very big. I think it was Peter Cook and Dudley Moore's first film, so they were very excited to be doing it. Tony Hancock was in it as well and I thought he was marvellous. And of course there was Willie [Wilfred] Lawson, who was totally bizarre.

A terrible thing happened on that film. There was one scene where Michael and I were on the hearse, going to the funeral. It was just a tracking shot so they set up this shot and Michael knows as much about horses as I do (which is negligible). We were sitting there and the camera was in front of us, going away. Suddenly the horses bolted, they just went mad, and people were screaming to me to jump. I couldn't, because I was in a period corset, with those long skirts and everything. So I just screamed and thought we were going to be killed, because those carriages are very high up. To his credit, Michael managed by some means to calm the horses down and get the hearse to stop. In the film you only see the bit where we're going along rather sedately, but we would both have been thrown and probably killed if he hadn't kept his head.

His great strength seems to me to be in making it look all so easy, as if he's doing nothing.

I think that's very true. His whole personality is very laid-back, with a sort of Cockney practicality, and I think he approaches filmmaking in a very straightforward way. He's not a complex person and I think he is a very good actor. He's nice to work with, uncomplicated and easygoing. Michael was a rougher version of Cary Grant, that the English could take to. I think it was very interesting, too, that he made an equal success in America, and he and Sean Connery are two among the very few who have done so. I suppose, really, having done something as positive as *Alfie*, a bit of that has remained with him whatever else he's done. I think it's true of people like Cary Grant and Kate Hepburn, too, that they basically played themselves – and they did it so brilliantly, with little variations that made you feel you were watching a different character. They realised the value of being a movie

star as distinct from being an actor – even though some of them were both.

***The Madwoman of Chaillot* has an extraordinary gathering of people.**

Yes, that was an amazing cast. I remember sitting in the make-up room in the Victorine Studios where it was shot, and I looked down and saw Charles Boyer, Danny Kaye, Giulietta Masina, Edith Evans, Yul Brynner – everybody all in a row, because you don't go individually into hair and make-up as in England, it's done in one long room. I thought, 'My God! This is really making a movie!' I was very thrilled, again, because Kate [Hepburn] had always been an idol of mine and she's such an extraordinary woman in real life as well.

The film wasn't a success, though. Bryan took over from John Huston at very short notice and I think he wishes now that he'd had more time. He had to be approved of by Kate and everything was already set up. He recast the two young people because they were French and couldn't speak any English, so Richard Chamberlain and I were brought in; but he didn't have the time to alter the fundamental structure of the film. I think Bryan would wish in retrospect that he had shot Kate as she was, in real life, and taken away all that fey kind of whimsy, but he didn't have the luxury of doing that.

When you came to play the paraplegic Jill Matthews in *The Raging Moon*, did you do a lot of research?

Yes, Malcolm McDowell and I went to Stoke Mandeville hospital and met with a lot of people. We learned how they got into bed and how they used the wheelchair and the things they could do. We had two young technical advisers on the film, both paraplegics, who eventually got married, which was a happy ending. To go to Stoke Mandeville and see all those young people with far worse disabilities than the characters we played in the film was very sobering. They had amazing spirit in the way they overcame their disabilities. That was a marvellous film to me, firstly because I think it was the best part I'd ever had. Everybody took a cut in salary, it was done on a very small budget and we were just a little group of people in a house. It had a wonderful feeling: shots would be grabbed, you worked in what you arrived in (there were no costumes), and you had a feeling of everybody pulling together, wanting the film to be good. I have a very special feeling for that film. A lot of people felt that it should have ended on a happy note. But you see, that is what happens to a lot of those characters in real life and I think the point of the film was to say that people always have to go on.

Were you at all apprehensive about doing a follow-up to the famous *National Velvet*?

Well yes, I was. They had offered it to Elizabeth Taylor and I think she should have played it, because that would have given it a kind of intrigue. But she didn't want to do it, she was married at the time to the politician John Warner. I think it was a shame in a way, because it would have been much more interesting – even though I'm glad I did it and I enjoyed it. We shot a lot of it in Mothercombe in Devon, which is where Bryan and I did a television film called *Jessie*, a wonderful period thing. It's beautiful countryside. Not a week goes by that I don't get a letter from someone about it. It was meant to be an emotional, sentimental movie, a success story, the kind of family film that you don't hear much about nowadays.

How did *The Mystery of Edwin Drood* come about?

That came about through a group of people who were trying to revitalise the British film industry. They had no money and everybody did it for nothing. I haven't seen the film, but they asked a lot of English actors if they would be in it and not take a salary up front; they just wanted a British film with British cast, British locations. That was the plan, but I gather it was disastrous. They couldn't get distribution and so it didn't do the trick, which is sad. Everyone signed a contract to say that they'd be paid if the film were ever sold and made any money, but I think I might be a hundred and two before I see any!

Leslie Norman

1911–1993

Editor: *The Price of Things* (1930), *Potiphar's Wife, Men Like These* (1931), *Lucky Girl, Maid of the Mountains* (1932), *Timbuctoo, Facing the Music, I Spy* (1933), *Red Wagon, Over the Garden Wall* (1934), *Blossom Time, The Old Curiosity Shop, Mimi, Heart's Desire* (1935), *Perfect Crime* (1937), *Everything Happens to Me* (1938), *They Drive By Night, Hoots Mon* (1939), *The Overlanders* (sup ed) (1946), *Nicholas Nickleby, Frieda* (1947), *Eureka Stockade* (& assoc pr) (1948)

Producer: *A Run For Your Money* (1949), *Bitter Springs* (assoc pr) (1950), *Where No Vultures Fly* (& co-auth) (1951), *Mandy* (1952), *The Cruel Sea* (1953), *West of Zanzibar* (1954)

Director: *Too Dangerous To Live* (co-dir) (1939), *The Night My Number Came Up* (1955), *X the Unknown* (1956), *The Shiralee* (1957), *Dunkirk* (1958), *The Long and the Short and the Tall* (1960), *Spare the Rod, Summer of the 17th Doll* (1961), *Mix Me a Person* (1962), *The Lost Continent* (uncr) (1968)

Leslie Norman served a long apprenticeship while awaiting his chance to direct. When it finally came, he showed himself adroit in extracting the maximum suspense from a strikingly original thriller, *The Night My Number Came Up*, in

1955. By this time, however, Ealing, which he had served well as editor and producer, was entering its last days. His reference to Balcon's intellectual snobbery adds an astringent note to the often cosy recollections of the studio on the green. He had edited for several prolific and long-forgotten directors of the 1930s and, post-war, he had been much associated with Ealing's Australian venture. *Dunkirk*, a qualified success, is in many ways an archetypal Ealing film: a study in cross-class consensualism; an enterprise which honours the group rather than the individual; and a war film which plays down heroics.

Interview date: October 1992

There are some interesting names threading their way through your 1930s credits. Any recollections of producer Walter Mycroft? directors Paul Stein, Arthur Woods, Roy William Neill? comedian Max Miller? an actress called Molly Lamont? And Richard Tauber in the Paul Stein films?

Walter Mycroft was a script editor for BIP. He was hunchbacked, unfortunately, and I think he resented people being straight-backed and this showed in his attitude sometimes, but he was a very nice chap and a bloody good story editor. He didn't do any directing in my time at BIP.

Arthur Woods was killed in the war but I made one picture with him. I edited *They Drive By Night* and directed some of the exteriors. That was a good picture, with Emlyn Williams. It was quite 'gutsy' about the working class and criminal life. He was a very fine young director and it was a great loss to the film industry when he went. I also edited *Timbuctoo* for him; unfortunately it was a very big flop.

You don't hear much about Paul Stein now but he was big in those days. He directed *Red Wagon*, he did two films with Richard Tauber – *Blossom Time* and *Heart's Desire*. Diana Napier, who was in a lot of his films, married Richard Tauber. Paul Stein did quite a few '30s musicals but actually I always felt he was lost once he got away from two or three people; he couldn't handle big crowds.

Molly Lamont I remember from *Lucky Girl*; she was great fun and a great beauty. She went on to Hollywood and became a very good character actress.

Max Miller I worked with a lot. He was very popular. A funny man – he would be as tight as a drum over spending fourpence, yet he would endow

beds in hospitals all over Brighton. He was noted for his rather 'blue' comedies.

Sometimes in your career you were credited as Editor, sometimes as Supervising Editor.

I was supervising editor on only one film, an Australian film called *The Overlanders* which Harry Watt directed. Ted Hunter was the editor and when they got back they weren't very satisfied with what he'd done, so they asked me to take it over. I actually ripped it all apart and started over again. But I thought this could ruin Ted Hunter's career so I suggested they credit him as editor and I would take the title of supervising editor. I think that editing is the *only* background for directing, apart from lighting. The greatest example is David Lean, a brilliant editor and a brilliant director.

How did your post-war involvement with Ealing come about?

During my last weeks in uniform I went to Ealing to see some old pals of mine – Hal Mason, Charlie Frend and Sid Cole. I was longing to get back and do some films. When I visited Ealing, Hal Mason was the production manager, who really ran things, and he said they could get me out of uniform; that they had a film I could do something with, to help sort it out. That was *The Overlanders*.

You were then involved in the three Australian-set films: *The Overlanders* as supervising editor: *Eureka Stockade* as both editor and associate producer; and *Bitter Springs* as associate producer. What were your impressions of Australia as a place to make films in those days?

I thought it was great. We had terrific co-operation from the technicians – I found so much keenness. They really wanted to know, because there was no film business there then. Of those three films, *The Overlanders* was without doubt the most successful. I was on location for *Eureka Stockade*; and for *Bitter Springs* I went out there because they were in trouble. I went out as a sort of hatchet man. It was a shame, but that film was awkward, a bit stiff and staid. When we went out to make *Eureka Stockade*, *ad valorem* duty was in force and that held us up for nearly six months, because of the question of whether it would be a British picture or a foreign picture. If it was a British picture we could get it into the country duty-free, so it was a question of taking so many artistes out from England to make it a British subject. Most of the cast were Australian but by the time the picture came out, the *ad valorem* duty had been abolished anyway.

Ealing set up an Australian company to shoot in Australia, under a fellow called 'Bungy' [Eric] Williams. He was a Welshman, sent out by Balcon to run Ealing Pictures in Australia.

What were your impressions of Harry Watt as the director of those first two Australian films?

I loved Harry. He'd find a story that none of us would see. He found *The Overlanders* by reading a release from the Ministry of Agriculture in Australia, talking about their beef and what they would do if they were invaded by Japan, shipping the beef away from places where they might be attacked. Harry was a great socialist, which is why he wanted to make *Eureka Stockade*. Working with him was exciting. He hated actors, though, couldn't get on with them.

What was your contribution to the screenplay of *Where No Vultures Fly*, for which you are credited with co-authorship, along with Ralph Smart and William Lipscomb?

It worked the way it does in most films: Bill Lipscomb wrote the script based on Harry Watt's ideas, then Ralph Smart came in and added a bit. The script was turned down generally, so I went in and added my bit, which made them accept it. It was a great success, with a Royal Command Performance. I was in Africa during the shooting, as associate producer (which, in Ealing credits, really means producer). Michael Balcon never had anything to do with the actual making of films but he always retained the title of producer. He was very mean with credits.

Did the position of producer (or associate producer) vary much when you worked with different directors?

Yes, always. Alexander Mackendrick would never take a story as it was; he always wanted to go

'around the back'. He was a very, very cluey young man and he would never take the obvious. He wanted to know what caused this or that. What was a particular character? How was he made up? He wanted to know. For instance, I found the story for *Mandy*, from about the first two hundred pages of a book. I took it to Mick and said I wanted to make it; he said it would be a flop, 'too bloody miserable'. I said what about *Johnny Belinda*, which had practically the same emotions. [American film, 1948, with deaf-and-dumb heroine.] He said that was a flop and I said, 'Don't be daft, it was great – and it won an Oscar.' He finally came around and said OK, who would I want to direct? I said the only person to do it would be Sandy Mackendrick. I wouldn't want to do it because I'd make it too sentimental, but Sandy was what it needed.

At the time there was criticism of the Phyllis Calvert–Terence Morgan marriage, but now that seems to be one of the most interesting aspects of the film. How did you feel about that?

I was all for it. That was one of Sandy's ideas. Another of his ideas was the mother and father having the same relationship as the son and daughter-in-law. A nice outcome of *Mandy* for me was this: I went out to Africa to make *West of Zanzibar*, and when I arrived America had sent out a new ambassador. Because we were filming in Nairobi at the time, Harry Watt and I were invited to visit. We were being introduced when a woman came flying across the room, put her arms around me and kissed me on both cheeks. I said, 'That's very nice. What's it for?' And she said, 'They told me you made *Mandy*. Thank you. I have a child who was born deaf and we never knew what to do with her until we saw your film.'

Did you feel you'd had a long wait before you got to direct your first film?

Yes, and I know why. I had a council-school education, hadn't been to university and Mick Balcon was a real academic snob – anyone who had a degree *must* be good, he thought. So that slowed me down.

Your first film as director. *The Night My Number Came Up*, is a terrific thriller. How did you come to do it?

The original story came from a magazine short story I found and thought it would be a good film story. I wanted to do the screenplay myself; I don't think RC Sherriff added anything to it. Anyway, I wrote a synopsis and sent it to Mick. He agreed for me to do it but wouldn't let me write the screenplay. We shot some of it in Hong Kong, some at an English airport which has now gone. I chose the cast myself. I'd seen Alexander Knox in *Wilson* and had always admired him, as a great actor. I'd also always admired Michael Redgrave. And Denholm Elliott, Michael Hordern – what better actors could you get? Ursula Jeans was the weak link. The Cockney actor who played the engineer, Victor Maddern, was excellent. I was pretty pleased with it and it got very good reviews.

Your next film was not for Ealing but for Hammer, *X the Unknown*. How did you come to do this?

They asked Mick if they could use me. I suppose they'd seen *The Night My Number Came Up*. It was a sort of science-fiction film. I hated working at Hammer, though, because I never got on with Anthony Hinds. We had Eddie Chapman in the cast, who had a distinct squint in one eye, and Leo McKern, who has only one eye – and I had to play a scene with them looking at each other. I said, 'For Christ's sake, look at each other!' and they said, 'We are!'

You were back in Australia in 1957 for *The Shiralee*. Had you been taken with D'Arcy Niland's book?

Yes, that's right. I read it, loved it and sent it over to Mick. Mick roasted me, said it was full of foul language and how dare I? I said that wouldn't be in the film, so he said all right and to get him a script. I went away and wrote the script and showed it to Mick. He claimed it was a different story, so we called in Neil Patterson to rewrite. He only rewrote one scene but it was enough to appease Mick. I suffered a lot from Mick.

Peter Finch was not an Ealing regular. Did you particularly seek him out and did you enjoy working with him?

He was marvellous. He told Trader Faulkner [his biographer] that it was the best film he'd ever worked on. It was great working with him. Of course he was not a Balcon sort of character at all – too wild a lifestyle. The little girl, Dana Wilson, I found in the most peculiar way. When we got out to Australia I spoke to the press and said I didn't care what the kid looked like, she could have a tooth missing and it wouldn't worry me. After that we had people trying to take kids' teeth out! Anyway, I went to a school to look at the kids, watching them dance and so on. I looked over my shoulder and there was a little kid preening in front of a mirror,

and I said, 'That's her.' So we took her back and tested her and she was marvellous. Most of it was shot in Australia, all over the place but mostly outback New South Wales.

***Dunkirk* is the last Ealing film and is like a lot of Ealing films in that it doesn't really focus on one star. It's really a group effort.**

So was Dunkirk. To my mind Ealing was one of the best production houses ever, anywhere. I think Mick Balcon had one great asset – he knew how to pick people. Every time you made a feature you would show it to all the other producers and directors – all of them – and ask for their comments. And people were absolutely frank with each other. I take my hat off to Mick because he stage-managed that, really.

Dunkirk was bloody difficult to make from a logistics point of view. Yet it was made for £400,000 and came in under budget. At one time I was standing up and talking to thirty-eight different sections of people, directing them all on walkie-talkies. I had the troops for three days, that was all, rain or shine. As you say, it was by no means an 'epic' – rather small-scale. I always felt that there were 300,000 stories in *Dunkirk*, because there were 300,000 men involved. But my idea for the film was to pick out a few of them.

It's not a conventional '50s war film from the class viewpoint; it makes clear this was a national effort.

I was the council schoolboy who became a major in the war, and that had a lot to do with the way I felt about Dunkirk. I didn't think that Dunkirk was a defeat; I always thought it was a very gallant effort but not a victory.

Was it your experience of having worked in Australia before that led you to the making of *Summer of the 17th Doll*?

Yes, and I wanted to keep it Australian, but unfortunately the Americans said they couldn't understand the Australian accent and I had to cut out all the Australianisms. That picture broke my heart. Of course, it was criticised for not being 'Australian' enough, as it should have been. At one stage Burt Lancaster was going to play the lead but he turned it down and Ernie Borgnine took over. He was great to work with, a nice bloke.

John Dighton did the screenplay, and he is noted for very English successes, isn't he?

Yes, but don't underestimate John. What buggered him up – and me – was cutting out the Australianness and giving it a more upbeat ending.

It is one of the best plays I have ever seen, but I can't say I'm happy with the film.

Did you see the Royal Court's production of *The Long and the Short and the Tall* before you filmed it?

No, never. But I tell you what happened – they made me have Laurence Harvey and I wanted Peter O'Toole, but he wasn't a name then. It was made after Ealing had packed up, although it was still for Michael Balcon Productions. Hal Mason was the producer and he was the most underrated man. He started off as an extra and then became a stuntman, but he was badly damaged as a stuntman, so he took up production, first as an assistant director and then as a production manager. There is no finer man in the business than Hal Mason.

Were you pleased with Laurence Harvey in the end?

No. He and Richard Harris let the film down, Richard Harris because he resented Laurence Harvey, despised him – and they didn't get on with Richard Todd. I was very pleased with my side of the film in the end. It was all made in a studio, we never set foot outside for a month. I asked to go on location, but a jungle's pretty claustrophobic for sure.

Do you think that British cinema ever developed a strong studio system?

Yes – at Ealing. And Hammer was very, very successful in its own way. I think a strong studio system makes an industry, because of the continuity it allows.

Merle Oberon

1911–1979

Actor: *Alf's Button* (1930), *Fascination* (1931), *For the Love of Mike, Ebb Tide, Aren't We All?, Wedding Rehearsal, Men of Tomorrow* (1932), *The Private Life of Henry VIII* (1933), *The Battle, The Broken Melody, The Private Life of Don Juan* (1934), *The Scarlet Pimpernel, Folies Bergère, The Dark Angel* (1935), *These Three, Beloved Enemy* (1936), *I, Claudius* (unfinished), *Over the Moon* (1937), *The Divorce of Lady X, The Cowboy and the Lady* (1938), *Wuthering Heights, The Lion Has Wings* (1939), *'Til We Meet Again* (1940), *That Uncertain Feeling, Affectionately Yours, Lydia* (1941), *Forever and a Day, Stage Door Canteen, First Comes Courage* (1943), *The Lodger, Dark Waters* (1944), *A Song to Remember, This Love of Ours* (1945), *A Night in Paradise, Temptation* (1946), *Night Song* (1947), *Berlin Express* (1948), *Pardon My French* (1951), *24 Hours in a Woman's Life* (1952), *Todo Es Posible En Granada, Désirée, Deep in my Heart* (1954), *The Price of Fear* (1956), *Of Love and Desire* (1963), **The Epic That Never Was* (doc), *The Oscar* (1966), *The Other World of Winston Churchill* (doc), *Hotel* (1967), *Interval* (1973)
*some theatrical release

'I couldn't dance or sing or write or paint. The only possible opening seemed to be in some line in which I could use my face. This was, in fact, no better than a hundred other faces, but it did possess a fortunately photogenic quality.'[1] It did indeed: Merle Oberon's face, that is. For several decades one of the world's most beautiful women, Oberon was surely being a little disingenuous in 1973 when she said, 'I have never liked my looks.

Being in London in the '30s where all the beauties were blonde and blue-eyed . . . I stood out, you know, with this strange face.'[2]

One stresses the fabulous beauty, with its almond eyes, high, curved forehead, olive skin and black hair, because, in truth, she was a limited actress. One of Alexander Korda's 'young ladies', and for a time his wife, she was never really given very exciting chances in British films. Korda kept highlighting her 'exotic' quality (she was in fact of Anglo-Indian parentage) and 'she had to go to Hollywood to have the artificial trappings of glamour removed,'[3] wrote a columnist in 1937. She became a big star of the '30s on both sides of the Atlantic, particularly for her Hollywood work in *These Three*, *Dark Angel* and *Wuthering Heights*.

In Britain, she had her first sizeable part in Korda's *Wedding Rehearsal*: 'I looked gauche and my voice was quite uncontrolled,'[4] she claimed. Korda then cast her as Anne Boleyn in *The Private Life of Henry VIII*: 'I was thrilled. I thought, here I've got the big part and then Alex gave me the script – I had these two pages.'[5] Small though it was, she played it touchingly and was very thoroughly noticed, but it was followed by more exotic roles in *The Battle*, *The Broken Melody* and *The Private Life of Don Juan* ('a beautiful picture – I mean the settings and the costumes'[6]). Even Lady Blakeney in *The Scarlet Pimpernel* is made exquisitely artificial: 'Leslie Howard was a great help and marvellous to me on the picture'[7] – actually, not really *enough* help.

Back in England after her Hollywood success, her motor accident brought to a halt the troubled production of *I, Claudius*, with Charles Laughton as Claudius and Merle as Messalina. In the surviving footage, she *looks* superb, and perhaps director Joseph Von Sternberg might have done for her what he'd done for Dietrich. Oberon said in *The Epic That Never Was*, the BBC documentary on the ill-starred production: 'If the film had been going absolutely wonderfully . . . and I had been in that taxi and gone through that windscreen, even though

I had shot all that stuff, I know that they would have replaced me.'[8]

Whatever the reason, until 1952 Merle Oberon made only three more films in England – two pallid romantic comedies, *Over the Moon* and *The Divorce of Lady X*, and the propaganda film, *The Lion Has Wings*, in which she is given very embarrassing, patriotic things to say. She returned for the picturesque but stodgy *24 Hours in a Woman's Life*, which she describes as 'unfortunate, because Victor Saville didn't turn out to be a good director in that.'[9]

I met her only once, in 1970, and her off-screen manner was much warmer than her screen *persona* might have led one to suspect. Ambitiously, I suggested she ask George Cukor to direct her as Madame de Vionnet in a version of Henry James's *The Ambassadors*, believing that her best performance, as the cast-off Josephine in *Désirée*, suggested a more characterful career as an actress. Perhaps her undimmed, legendary beauty prevented such a development.

1 J Danvers Williams, 'Merle Oberon traces her steps to stardom', *Film Weekly*, 20 May 1939, p 7
2 John Calendo, 'Merle Oberon is not a Hindu', *Andy Warhol's Interview*, July 1973, p 30
3 Freda Bruce Lockhart, 'Merle finds herself', *Film Weekly*, 6 February 1937, p 7
4 Danvers Williams, p 8
5 Al Kilgore and Roi Frumkes, 'Merle Oberon: an interview', *Films in Review*, February 1982, p 85
6 Kilgore and Frumkes, p 80
7 Kilgore and Frumkes, p 80
8 Quoted in Karol Kulik, *Alexander Korda* (first published 1975), Virgin Books, New York, 1990, p 197
9 Kilgore and Frumkes, p 92

Laurence Olivier (Lord Olivier)

1907–1989

Actor: *Too Many Crooks, The Temporary Widow, Friends and Lovers, Potiphar's Wife, The Yellow Ticket* (1931), *Westward Passage* (1932), *No Funny Business, Perfect Understanding* (1933), *Moscow Nights* (1935), *As You Like It, Fire Over England* (1936), *Twenty-One Days* (1937), *The Divorce of Lady X, Q Planes* (1938), *Wuthering Heights* (1939), *Rebecca, Conquest of the Air, Pride and Prejudice*

(1940), *Words for Battle (voice only), Lady Hamilton, 49th Parallel (1941), The Demi-Paradise, *The Volunteer, *Malta GC (narr only) (1943), This Happy Breed (uncr narr) (1944), Henry V (& dir, pr, uncr co-adpt), *Fighting Pilgrims (narr only) (1945), Hamlet (& dir, uncr co-adpt) (1948), *A Gift of Life (narr), *Many Neighbours (narr) (1949), The Magic Box, Carrie (1951), A Queen is Crowned (narr), The Beggar's Opera, *The Drawings of Leonardo da Vinci (narr) (1953), Richard III (& dir, pr, uncr co-adpt) (1955), The Prince and the Showgirl (& dir, pr) (1957), The Devil's Disciple (1959), The Entertainer, Spartacus (1960), The Power and the Glory, Term of Trial (1961), Bunny Lake is Missing, Othello (1965), Khartoum (1966), Romeo and Juliet (voice only), The Shoes of the Fisherman, The Dance of Death (1968), Oh! What a Lovely War, Battle of Britain (1969), David Copperfield, Three Sisters (& dir) (1970), Nicholas and Alexandra, *Tree of Life (narr) (1971), Lady Caroline Lamb, Sleuth (1972), The Rehearsal (1974), Love Among the Ruins, The Gentleman Tramp (voice only) (1975), The Seven-Per-Cent Solution, Marathon Man (1976), A Bridge Too Far (1977), The Betsy, The Boys From Brazil (1978), A Little Romance, Dracula (1979), The Jazz Singer, Inchon (1980), Clash of the Titans (1981), Wagner (1982), The Jigsaw Man (1983), Wild Geese II (1985), War Requiem (1988)

* Short film.

'**K**orda gave me opportunities which I took only disdainfully because I still despised the medium,'[1] Olivier said of his early approach to filming. His British films of the 1930s, a poor lot, included No Funny Business, co-starring his first wife Jill Esmond: 'the cameras liked her,'[2] he said watching it years later and acknowledging his own woodenness. It was while playing Heathcliff in William Wyler's Wuthering Heights in Hollywood that '. . . gradually I came to see that film was a different medium and that if one treated it as such, and tried to learn it, humbly, and with an open mind, one could work in it. I saw that it could use the best that was going.'[3]

By common consent the most distinguished theatre actor of the century, Olivier also left a memorable legacy on the screen. In British films, his huge contribution was in showing how Shakespeare might be filmed without betraying the Bard or undervaluing what the cinema could do. He believed that 'if you are going to cut a Shakespearian play . . . there is only one thing to do – leave out scenes. If you cut the lines down merely to keep all the characters in, you end up with a mass of short ends.'[4] In his beautiful Henry V, for instance, the three English traitors are cut from the early scenes (in the interests, no doubt, of wartime morale as well), and from his Hamlet, which he describes as 'an essay'[5] on the play, Rosencrantz and Guildenstern, among others, are excised.

These are adventurous films cinematically. For Henry V, he recalled the designer–art director team of Paul Sherriff and Carmen Dillon from Asquith's The Demi-Paradise ('amusing to do, Russian accent and all'[6]) and recruited Roger Furse as costume designer: 'We agreed that they . . . should all put their heads together and do lots of sketches, colour sketches, no matter how rough, but maybe with one indicative detailed element . . . I had meantime remembered my Très Riches Heures du Duc de Berri and they gorged their eyes [on illustrations of these].'[7] And, so, much of the film's look was struck. On Hamlet, he chose 'black-and-white for it rather than colour, to achieve depth of focus, a more majestic, more poetic image, in keeping with the stature of the verse.'[8]

When it came to Richard III, 'I took Richard's misshapen body and his sardonic smile, but I wanted to convince the audience of the mind behind the mask. A demonic mind, a witty mind . . . Everything about the way I shot the opening soliloquy fills me with pleasure . . . from the main idea of having Richard speak direct to the camera.'[9]

Apart from the Shakespearian roles, Olivier's most accomplished screen performances are probably in such Hollywood films as Wuthering Heights, Rebecca, Pride and Prejudice, Spartacus and Wyler's Carrie. His only non-Shakespeare film as a director, The Prince and the Showgirl, was neither a happy production nor a sparkling film: Marilyn Monroe emerges with some charm though Olivier recalled that 'half the time her head was so full of the rigmarole of "method", her natural talent was suppressed.'[10] However, there is still plenty of choice work in the British films. He brought his stage triumph as John Osborne's Archie Rice to the screen in The Entertainer, and, after ten years of cameos while working to establish the National Theatre, he returned to star in the film version of Sleuth, deciding that '. . . it was about time I played a leading role again. It is awfully nice, all these cameos that come along, but after you've done about six of them, there is a whole generation of people who think you're a small-part actor.'[11]

Though he again played many cameo roles, often in poor films, in his last ten years, when he was dogged by ill-health, no one was ever in much danger of thinking of him as a small-part actor.

1 Laurence Olivier, 'The Entertainer', *American Film*, November 1986, p 28
2 Tarquin Olivier, *My Father Laurence Olivier*, Headline Books, London, 1992, p 50
3 DeWitt Bodeen, 'Laurence Olivier: The man and his films', *Films in Review*, December 1979, p 584
4 Donald Spoto, *Laurence Olivier: A Biography*, Harper Collins, 1991, p 216
5 Spoto, p 178
6 Laurence Olivier, *Confessions of an Actor*, Coronet, London, 1982, p 131
7 Olivier, *Confessions*, pp 132–3
8 Olivier, *Confessions*, p 161
9 Olivier, 'The Entertainer', p 29
10 Olivier, 'The Entertainer', p 30
11 Robert L Daniels, *Laurence Olivier: Theater and Cinema*, Tantivy Press, London, 1980, p 217

Peter O'Toole

b. 1932

Actor: *The Savage Innocents, Kidnapped, The Day They Robbed the Bank of England* (1960), *Lawrence of Arabia* (1962), *Becket* (1964), *What's New, Pussycat?, Lord Jim, The Sandpiper* (voice only) (1965), *The Bible, How to Steal a Million, Night of the Generals* (1966), *Casino Royale* (1967), *The Lion in Winter, Great Catherine* (1968), *Goodbye Mr Chips, Country Dance* (1969), *Murphy's Law* (1970), *Under Milk Wood* (1971), *The Ruling Class, Man of La Mancha* (1972), *Rosebud, Man Friday* (1975), *Foxtrot* (1976), *Power Play* (1978), *Zulu Dawn, Caligula* (1979), *The Stunt Man* (1980), *My Favorite Year* (1982), *Supergirl* (1984), *Creator* (1985), *Club Paradise* (1986), *The Last Emperor* (1987), *High Spirits* (1988), *In una Notte di Chiaro di Luna, As Long As It's Love* (1989), *Wings of Fame, The Nutcracker Prince* (voice only) (1990), *King Ralph, Isabelle Eberhardt* (1991), *Worlds Apart, Rebecca's Daughters* (1992), *The Seventh Coin* (1993), *Phantoms, Illumination* (1997)

'That's what show business is – getting the moment.'[1] For Peter O'Toole, the moment came in David Lean's *Lawrence of Arabia* and lasted for over three hours – or, to use a different measuring criterion, for over three decades. Nothing he has done since, and that includes some notable work in British and other films, has been able to eclipse the poetic image he struck as this visionary zealot who has exercised such a hold on the twentieth-century imagination.

O'Toole himself pays full – and fulsome – tribute to Lean as the one great influence on his career. 'If there's any influence, it's through the pores and it would be David Lean. I was two years and three months with David, and it was as though he'd given me a course in how to be a director . . . I learnt more from David than from anybody else in theatre or cinema.'[2] He acquired then the habit of 'saturating' himself in a part, of following up the research initiated by the screenplay's author, even subjecting himself to learning to ride a camel to play Lawrence: 'There's no bridle, just a little stick to tap its nose with. When the camel gets up, back legs first, you feel as though you're going to be flung for yards, so you grab the front pommel for all you're worth . . .'[3]

The saturation process was also put to work on the two versions of Henry II, in *Becket* and *The Lion in Winter*, two intelligent, rather literary costume pieces: 'It was marvellous because they were somehow extensions of each other ... unless I'd played Anouilh's Henry, I couldn't have played Jimmy Goldman's Henry [opposite Katharine Hepburn's Eleanor of Aquitaine] the way I did. 'Cause the sense of the loss of Becket filled everything I did in the other play [sic].[4] His charisma and his technical command are at their most magnetic in these films, in which he plays *against* his potent co-stars, Burton and Hepburn, with a controlled intensity he would not always show in later years.

His career is largely international, like that of so many British actors of his generation, but there are several further roles to be savoured among his British films. His aristocrats (and he was not to the manner/manor born, as his autobiography[5] indicates) in *Country Dance* and *The Ruling Class* are finely honed studies of obsession in high places; and even *High Spirits* ('Well, comedy is great fun, if it works,'[6] he said of it hopefully) still shows a zany comic talent to be reckoned with, as a ghost-raising Irish castle-owner. Of the rest of his British films, only *Goodbye Mr Chips* needs mentioning. He doesn't efface Robert Donat in the role, but he is

endearing. 'I'm a hoofer *manqué*, actually,' he said of it, 'but every time I've been in a musical it's been disastrous.'[7] Too severe on *Chips*, and, though there have been plenty of other disasters, the ravaged glamour can still touch the heart, as the English tutor's final moments in China do in *The Last Emperor*. For O'Toole 'getting the moment' is still an option. 'It's the thing that keeps one going after all these years of clanking around.'[8]

1 Brian Case, 'Cut and dried' (interview with Peter O'Toole), *Time Out*, 7 December 1988, p 21
2 Joseph McBride, 'O'Toole ascending', *Film Comment*, March–April 1981, p 50
3 Howard Kent, *Single Bed for Three: A Lawrence of Arabia Notebook*, Hutchinson, London, 1963, p 21
4 Lewis Archibald, 'Peter O'Toole: A man who dreams impossible dreams', *Show*, January 1973, p 30
5 Peter O'Toole, *Loitering with Intent*, Macmillan, London, 1992
6 Case, p 19
7 McBride, p 51
8 McBride, p 21

Bill Owen

b. 1914

Actor: *Song of the People, The Way to the Stars, Perfect Strangers* (1945), *School for Secrets, Daybreak* (1946), *Dancing with Crime, When the Bough Breaks, Easy Money* (1947), *Trouble in the Air, My Brother's Keeper, The Weaker Sex, Once a Jolly Swagman* (1948), *Trottie True, Diamond City, The Girl Who Couldn't Quite* (1949), *Hotel Sahara* (1951), *The Story of Robin Hood and His Merrie Men, There Was a Young Lady* (1952), *The Square Ring, A Day to Remember, Thought to Kill* (1953), *The Rainbow Jacket* (1954), *The Ship that Died of Shame* (1955), *Not So Dusty* (1956), *Davy* (1957), *Carve Her Name With Pride, Carry On Sergeant* (1958), *Carry On Nurse, The Shakedown* (1959), *The Hellfire Club, On the Fiddle, Carry On Regardless* (1961), *Carry On Cabby* (1963), *The Secret of Blood Island* (1964), *Georgy Girl, The Fighting Prince of Donegal* (1966), *Headline Hunters* (1968), *Mischief* (1969), *Kadoyng* (1972), *O Lucky Man!* (1973), *In Celebration* (1974), *Smurfs and the Magic Flute* (1975), *The Comeback* (1977), *Laughterhouse* (1984), *The Handmaid's Tale* (1990)
* Documentary.

Bill Owen came to notice in his first feature film, Anthony Asquith's *The Way to the Stars*, as a cheerful sergeant. As he says, he never got to play a rank higher than sergeant and most of his characters were called Fred or Alf. Within the middle-class limitations of British cinema, Owen had a very busy career, bringing effortless credibility and authority to such roles as the Australian speedway driver down on his luck in *Once a Jolly Swagman*, and as Jean Kent's music hall partner in *Trottie True* (he could sing and dance, too). He had a good run of films at Ealing, where he credits the Basil Dearden–Michael Relph combination with understanding and using his talents, but his best opportunity came in 1974 when he played the father in *In Celebration*, directed by Lindsay Anderson, for whom he has worked several times on the stage. He has done notable work in the theatre, including *As You Like It* with Katharine Hepburn and as Albert Finney's father in *Luther*, and in television he appeared for twenty-odd years in the hugely popular series, *Last of the Summer Wine*.

Interview date: November 1990

Before the war, you'd been an entertainments manager at Warner's holiday camp and worked for the left-wing Unity Theatre. Did you have any film involvement then?

Through my work at the Unity Theatre, whose members included HG Wells, O'Casey and Paul Robeson, I had been involved, before the war, with the Crown Film Unit and done documentaries, so I had tasted filmmaking quite early on. I appeared for odd moments in documentary films, as a worker in a line, for instance. The Crown Unit used to come to the Unity quite often to cast people for film work. During the war, I served with the Royal Pioneer Corps, where I reached the rank of Second Lieutenant. I was released in 1943 and went straight back to Unity. There I was discovered, in a revue, by David Henley of the Myron Selznick agency, and he offered to take me on. My first job through them was a part in *The Way to the Stars*, which was a good film to start with. It was one of those performances that I would give over and over in many films. Anybody who knew his business used to jump from one film to another in those days. The industry was enormous.

British cinema then seems to have been primarily middle-class. When you were in *The Way to the Stars*, were you aware you were playing 'the working-class character'?

Of course. I think I played one of the few characters of that type in the film. I was a sergeant and I never played anything higher. Apart from the two extraordinary characters I played in the stage musicals, *The Threepenny Opera* and *The Mikado*, and even with the breadth of my range, my roles are in the main all working-class. That was my compartment in those days.

Is it true your name was changed because Rowbotham wasn't actorish enough?

It was after I signed my Rank film contract with Sydney Box that the American distributor said that the name Bill Rowbotham (my real name, with which I had scored quite well both on stage and in films) could have 'an adverse marketable effect'. After a great deal of pressure I agreed to use two of my Christian names and became Bill Owen. I did several films under that Rank contract including *When the Bough Breaks*, *Easy Money* and *Once a Jolly Swagman*.

When the Bough Breaks was not a good piece of casting. If ever there was a film I shouldn't have been launched in, it was that. I played the leading role with a very beautiful and popular actress called Patricia Roc. Then I went to America for about a year for *As You Like It*, with Katharine Hepburn. When I returned I don't think my contract was renewed. I didn't do much of anything then, except some good work at the Unity.

Do you remember the gloomy-sounding

melodrama, *Daybreak*, directed by Compton Bennett, and the thriller, *Dancing with Crime*?

The part I had in *Dancing with Crime* was perfect for me – a sharp young spiv, a real Cagney character. I was shot in the first reel and the critics took note. The next time such a part, in which I could really exploit my character, occurred was with Basil Dearden, who filmed the play I'd done, *The Square Ring*. This way I could have been made into a name at the box office, but such films weren't being made. I remember very little about *Daybreak*, other than the care taken by Eric Portman to put me at my ease.

Did you enjoy your song-and-dance role in *Trottie True*?

This was the kind of role I could play. I was part of a knockabout vaudeville act, the other members being Hattie Jacques and Jean Kent. Jean provided the glamour and I, as the little working-class comic, was hopelessly in love with her. But with a name like Joe Jugg, what chance did I stand? It should have been a real musical, of course . . .

What about Jack Lee, who directed you in *Once a Jolly Swagman*?

I liked him and it wasn't a bad part either. I played an Australian has-been dirt-track star, on the skids and drinking a lot.

What do you recall of Ken Annakin's comedy, *Hotel Sahara*?

The story is set in the midst of the Sahara desert and was made entirely in a studio at Pinewood! Ken Annakin concentrated on his actors, and what an excellent team he had. I think it is one of the best films he ever made and I had the impression he felt very comfortable directing it.

Do you think I over-stress the director's function?

I must admit to preferring to work with a director who concerns himself more with what his actors are doing in front of the camera than with the effect of the angle at which he is photographing them. I remember Silvio Narizzano, the young Canadian director who did *Georgy Girl* – I remember his sharpness and how he cared about the actors and their roles. I remember being in at least one of those Pinewood films that used the experimental technique of Independent Frame. I was in one starring Michael Redgrave and written and directed by Noël Coward, called *The Astonished Heart*, and I know Michael and I had a ball on my one scene. Then I picked up the paper a few days later to read that Michael had walked off the film. I got a phone-call

to come back to the studio; Noël Coward had taken over; he'd written it, he was acting in it, and now directing it! I reshot my scene with Noël in half a day; it had taken nearly a week with Michael. I went to see the film and I wasn't in it at all; Noël had cut the whole scene.

Did you have a contract with Ealing when you went there to make *The Square Ring* in 1953?

I didn't have a contract there. Working at Ealing was like working in a family atmosphere, a very compact studio which, under the guiding hand of Michael Balcon, had at this time become one of the most prestigious production companies in the country. The four films in which I appeared, all made by Michael Relph and Basil Dearden, gave me leading roles and fitted me like a glove – the lightweight boxer in *The Square Ring*, the warned-off jockey in *The Rainbow Jacket*, the member of the music hall act in *Davy* and the bos'n in *The Ship that Died of Shame*. Basil was the only person who seemed concerned to find the right 'lane' for me to travel in.

***The Ship that Died of Shame* now looks like a key film of its times. Did you feel the ship's story was a sort of metaphor for post-war England?**

You may be right about the ship being a metaphor but I don't remember much about it, except the extreme discomfort of filming at sea. Above all was the feeling of security that came with the making of those films: here were a couple of filmmakers [Dearden and producer Michael Relph] who seemed to understand what I was about.

Did you feel you were getting a satisfying range of roles in the '50s?

I certainly knew and felt I was capable of better things, but then what actor doesn't?

How did you get involved in the *Carry On* films at the end of the decade?

I only did about four, I think. I was certainly in the most important one, which was *Carry On Nurse*. I think the reason I was dropped might have been that the people in the regular company were more suited; people like Kenneth Williams were such definite types.

You filmed less often in the '60s and early '70s. Were there fewer congenial film roles on offer or did you find more interesting opportunities on stage?

I suppose I was symptomatic of a fading industry which is now almost non-existent in this country. I wasn't being offered parts because films weren't being made. I think if I'd been a young actor at the Royal Court Theatre then, things would have been entirely different. I did work at the Royal Court but as a much older actor. And, although I say it myself, I was able to do so many things: I was able to sing, dance, do a music-hall act, anything, so that my spectrum was very wide. Whether I did them well or not is another thing, of course, but the fact is that I could do them. I did some interesting things in the theatre during that time.

What do you regard as your most satisfying film work in the post-50s period?

Oh, the one major film I made, Lindsay Anderson's film version of *In Celebration* by David Storey. Lindsay first directed it as a play at the Royal Court, with the same cast. It was a milestone for me because I was virtually finished in the profession until Lindsay came along, picked me up, and dusted me off.

Muriel Pavlow

b. 1921

Actor: *Sing As We Go* (1934), *Romance in Flanders* (1937), *Quiet Wedding* (1940), *Night Boat to Dublin* (1946), *The Shop at Sly Corner* (1947), *Out of True* (1951), *It Started in Paradise* (1952), *The Net, The Malta Story* (1953), *Doctor in the House, Conflict of Wings* (1954), *Simon and Laura* (1955), *Eyewitness, Reach for the Sky* (1956), *Tiger in the Smoke, Doctor at Large* (1957), *Rooney* (1958), *Whirlpool* (1959), *Murder She Said* (1962)

M uriel Pavlow belongs so firmly to British cinema of the 1950s that one is startled to find that she has been in films since the 1930s, starting as a child with a bit role in a Gracie Fields film. Because she was always acting on the stage, her screen career seems to start several times: first with Asquith's immaculate version of *Quiet Wedding*; second, opposite the legendary roisterer, Robert Newton, in *Night Boat to Dublin*; and third, when her run really begins, in the early 1950s. If she was never asked to do anything wildly at odds with her established *persona*, she appeared in a wider range of roles and genres than might be supposed. Her normality and responsiveness to those around her are easy to undervalue when in fact they are very important to the balance of such comedies as *Doctor in the House* and *Simon and Laura*. She was also an attractive heroine in such thrillers as *Eyewitness* and *Tiger in the Smoke* and in war films such as her own personal favourites, *The Malta Story* and *Reach for the Sky*. Following 1960, she (and her late husband, Derek Farr) worked a great deal on the stage and in television, recently in the delectable *Memento Mori*.

Interview date: July 1990

Do you think of yourself as primarily a stage star who made some films or a film star who often worked on stage?

I think of myself as a stage actress because I began in the theatre when I was fourteen. It wasn't until the beginning of the 1950s that I suddenly got a little run of films. I never considered myself a 'film star'; I just suddenly got an extraordinary run of exciting things to do.

Had you played the part of Miranda in *Quiet Wedding* **on the stage?**

No, Glynis Johns had played it on the stage and I think she was unavailable, so the part fell to me. That was how I first met Derek [Farr], who was starring in it with Margaret Lockwood. I saw it recently and it's typical of English comedies of the time. I remember working with Anthony Asquith as a director; he was a charming, slightly 'pixie' character, so gentle in his direction, yet he knew exactly what he wanted from his actors and usually got it.

Six years later you returned to the screen as leading lady to Robert Newton in *Night Boat to Dublin*. **Was this a daunting experience?**

I was extraordinarily naïve. This was around 1945 and I must have been the only person working in the British film industry who didn't realise that Robert Newton had a drink problem! One morning I was called for eight o'clock as usual and there was a long pause while I waited in my dressing-room. Only much later did I realise poor Bob had been in no fit condition to work when he arrived at the studio that morning. I remember him as being very charming but I just didn't realise the problem was there. Everyone treated him as if he were made of eggshells, so as not to upset him in any way, but in his best roles he was sheer magnetism on the screen.

What do you remember of Lawrence Huntington as a director?

I remember him well because *Night Boat* was my first film role of any importance. I was very lucky to have him directing me then; he wasn't a brilliant director but he knew his job and was very workmanlike, very professional, with a good understanding of actors. He just rather faded away, I'm afraid; he was a dear man.

The only other film you made in the '40s was *The Shop at Sly Corner*, **based on the stage play.**

What I remember about that film was that I fell in love during the making of it. I was having costume fittings and still didn't know who was to be my leading man; one day the producer's wife came up to me and announced that it was to be Derek Farr. The first scene we had was the one where she comes in, sees him, throws herself into his arms and kisses him – and that did it! We announced our engagement in September 1946, and married in January 1947.

I saw the film on television a few weeks ago, and I was amazed at how well it stood up. The set-up of some of the scenes was a little mannered, which perhaps came from its having been a stage play. It had a very good cast, including Oscar Homolka. He would always upstage me and I gave up after the first day's work! I knew that if I tried to fight this experienced actor on that score I would come off the worse; and I just enjoyed working with him after that. He was a 'cuddly bear' sort of man but he had a very penetrating glance, nothing escaped him. George King, the director, was very easygoing, but with his eye on the budget.

You made at least one film a year throughout the '50s. Was this a good time to be getting a film career going?

Well, I met Lawrence Huntington again when I had just done the first of my 1950s films; he asked what I was doing and I told him, saying that the studio felt this film would be good for me. 'Ah, my dear,' he said, 'I'm afraid it's too late!' He said that the film business was going downhill. But to me, making films during the '50s was super and I have always been glad that my turn came then; it was the last carefree period of British filmmaking.

What do you recall of making a film for the director Philip Leacock, a semi-documentary called *Out of True*?

It was about mental breakdowns and we filmed it in a mental hospital south of London; it was very interesting and, for me, very worthwhile because from that I got *It Started in Paradise*, which started my whole run. There were a lot of 'backstage' problems on *It Started in Paradise*. It was about the world of *haute couture* and they engaged a nice young woman who had produced some fine designs but had no experience of dressing films. It became apparent about a third of the way through that what she was doing was a disaster; so another designer was brought in to finish off the film, and from then on we all began to look rather smarter. The story was fairly 'Peg's Paper'; still, it was a very lucky film for me. Compton Bennett had considerable success directing in Hollywood, but in this one he didn't whip us along as he should have done.

You then did *The Net*, again directed by Anthony Asquith.

Yes, it wasn't my best part but it had a bit of bite and it was nice to be part of the leading quartet with James Donald, Phyllis Calvert and Herbert Lom, also the young actor Patric Doonan. We were all sitting around the lunch table one day, laughing about the progress or otherwise of our careers; someone asked if we were to be players of whom people would say, 'Whatever became of so-and-so?' and poor Patric, about a year later, committed suicide. That lunchtime conversation haunted me after that.

What do you remember of working with Brian Desmond Hurst on *The Malta Story*?

Oh, I thought he was very talented and I liked his direction but he was inclined to get a bit bored with a project; towards the end of the film you could see his interest was waning. The whole cast went to Malta for the exteriors and night shootings, and the studio work was done at Pinewood. It remains a highlight for me, even though it wasn't a successful film, because of the experience of working with Alec Guinness. I played a Maltese girl who became Alec's girlfriend; it was a moving part and I loved playing it.

I suppose *Doctor in the House* was your most commercially successful film. Was it fun to make?

Oh yes, it was fantastic; it was my first experience of being in a genuine hit. And making it – oh, we had such fun! And that marvellous director of comedy, Ralph Thomas, was so easygoing and relaxed. For instance, I had to say a very long medical word when I was giving Dirk directions on how to reach a certain department; Ralph said to me, 'Don't worry, darling, you won't get it first time but it's all right, we've plenty of time.' Later one of the 'sparks' came up with a great bouquet of flowers for me because I did manage it in one take! If you're surrounded by people like Dirk, Kenneth More, Donald Sinden, Donald Houston, and so on, it can't fail to be fun. It was the first of that series and it was the best, I think. When I first read the script I laughed, and said to Derek how lucky I was to be in this lovely comedy but we had no idea it would take off in the way it did.

Then Dirk did *Doctor at Sea* with Brigitte Bardot, followed by *Doctor at Large* with me in it again (and Derek playing a Harley Street smoothie); that was fun too, but it didn't have the freshness of the first one, which has all the right ingredients: the balance of casting was right and, as we say, the soufflé rose. Of course, Nicholas Phipps, who did the screenplay, was one of the great comedy writers of the '50s, a very witty man.

Do you remember making *Conflict of Wings* for Group 3?

Yes, we made it all on the Norfolk Broads, just a few interiors at Beaconsfield. I had to drive one of those little power boats and it went quite well. That was a happy film too. John Eldredge, the director, had a background in documentary films, and his career was hampered by bad health; I doubt if he made any more films after that.

Your co-star, John Gregson, starred with you again four years later in *Rooney*. Did you feel you worked well together?

Yes, I think we did. He, too, was very easygoing and relaxed and, if your co-star is relaxed, then you are too. It was a sweet 'Cinderella' story, really. It was directed by George Pollock, who was a first assistant for many years. He then directed some minor films and finally began to be given the big films, including the Miss Marples with Margaret Rutherford. Barry Fitzgerald was in *Rooney*, and he was an old darling. We were all very protective of him, because he really was very old at that stage. We worried that we might be tiring him or whatever, but he was fine.

How did you find working with a woman director – Muriel Box – on *Simon and Laura* and *Eyewitness*?

She was a fine director and a charming woman with great knowledge of filmmaking, and we got on very well, but I think I respond better to a male director. Somehow I am more stimulated to bring out the best by a male director. *Simon and Laura* was a Rank film; I wasn't under contract then, but I could have been described at that time as 'the flavour of the month'. I only went under contract for the last two films I made for Rank; it was supposed to be three films but I foolishly turned down one called *The Gypsy and the Gentleman* – foolishly because, although it was a rubbishy film, it was directed by Joseph Losey. I do think Kay Kendall and Peter Finch were delightfully cast in *Simon and Laura* and Ian Carmichael was *very* good too.

As for *Eyewitness*, I can't remember much about it except that I started off with a good scene with Michael Craig, from which I stormed out, witnessed the hold-up which Donald Sinden was carrying out, was then promptly knocked down by a bus and spent the rest of the film in a hospital bed looking like a cross between an advertisement for Elizabeth Arden and a nun! I just lay there, in the worst-guarded hospital of all time!

How did you come to play Thelma in *Reach for the Sky*?

I really fought for the part as Douglas Bader's wife. In 1954 I read the book; I phoned my agent and told him that if ever a film was to be made of the book, I wanted to play Thelma. About a year later, I met Danny Angel [producer] and Lewis Gilbert [director] and asked them to let me test. Lewis was rather keen that I should play Brace, the nurse, but I couldn't see it. So I tested and got the part of Thelma. I attended a Royal Première of the film at the Cannon Theatre in Shaftesbury Avenue about two weeks ago; it was to tie in with the fiftieth anniversary of the Battle of Britain. For the first time since around 1957 I saw it again on the big screen and it was a marvellous print. I suddenly felt rather proud to have been associated with it.

Your next film seems to me a genuinely scary thriller, *Tiger in the Smoke*. Had you read Margery Allingham's novel?

Yes, I was a great fan of Margery Allingham. I was delighted when I got the part but the film didn't quite come off, unfortunately. I didn't think Tony Wright was sinister enough and I would like to have seen him and Donald Sinden reverse their roles. Tony had too much charm for the villain; he was too relaxed almost.

Do you hope to film again?

Yes, but I'm realistic about my chances. I'm lucky to be able to look back on *The Malta Story*, *Reach for the Sky* and *Doctor in the House* – three wonderful films in which to be involved.

Nova Pilbeam

b. 1919

Actor: *Little Friend, The Man Who Knew Too Much* (1934), *Tudor Rose* (1936), *Young and Innocent* (1937), *Cheer Boys Cheer* (1939), *Pastor Hall* (1940), *Spring Meeting, Banana Ridge* (1941), *Next of Kin* (1942), *Yellow Canary* (1943), **Out of Chaos, *Man of Science* (1944), *This Man is Mine* (1946), *Green Fingers* (1947), *The Three Weird Sisters, Counterblast* (1948)
* Documentaries.

Lady Jane Grey was nine days a queen but her name resonates through British history with an insistent sweetness and innocence at odds with the brevity of her place in the story. It is tempting to see a parallel with the actress who played her unforgettably in the 1936 film, *Tudor Rose*: that is, Nova Pilbeam, whose name echoes through British cinema history with an insistence at odds with her comparatively few films. During the 1930s she was undoubtedly Britain's most celebrated child and teenage star, holding her own in such formidable adult company as Matheson Lang in *Little Friend* (in which she is very affecting as the daughter of divorcing parents), Leslie Banks and Peter Lorre in Hitchcock's original *The Man Who Knew Too Much*; and Cedric Hardwicke and Sybil Thorndike in *Tudor Rose*. If her nine feature films of the '40s never gave her such opportunities again, she was never less than charming and intelligent, and *The Three Weird Sisters* is a genuine curiosity. She particularly relished her bitchy role in *Green Fingers* in 1947, but a year later she vanished from British films. However, her name, her beauty and her talent remain in the annals and the memory.

Interview date: June 1990

Though you made most of your films in the '40s, I'd like to ask you about several of your '30s films. Did Hitchcock cast you as the kidnapped daughter in *The Man Who Knew Too Much* **on the basis of seeing you in** *Little Friend***?**

I don't know, but it was for Gaumont-British, to whom I went under contract after *Little Friend*. I assume they would have done the casting. It was a very long contract – six or seven years, which was pretty outrageous. It prevented me from being in the theatre as much as I would have liked.

What are your recollections of *The Man Who Knew Too Much***?**

A lot of it was set in Switzerland; I don't know if the others went on location but I certainly didn't. My part was all made at Gaumont-British. I've heard people who worked with Hitch say it was not the most exhilarating experience, and, though I was only about fifteen, I felt something of that. Hitch had everything in his head before he went near the set; therefore one was rather moved around and manipulated but, having said that, I liked him very much. For instance, in *Young and Innocent* there was a dog both Hitch and I adored; there came a time when we had finished the sequences with the dog and he was supposed to go back. We were both so upset that Hitch decided to write him another sequence, and we kept him for another five or six days!

Did you enjoy making *Young and Innocent* **for him?**

Very much. We did a lot in the country and I enjoyed that. My first husband [Penrose Tennyson] was Hitchcock's assistant director and he was on that film too. I think it was quite the sunniest film I was involved with. We didn't use doubles; if you remember that scene in the mine, I did that and it was my husband-to-be, Pen's, hand holding me up

as I dangled there. I was terrified! Now, Hitch had this quirky sense of humour and he made it go on and on, so that I thought my arm would come out of its socket. My daughter had never seen the film until it came to a little cinema in Camden Town recently and she insisted on seeing it. I hate to watch my films but I took a large sip of gin beforehand and we went.

What amazed me was that, firstly, the cinema was full and, secondly, it was full of young people. I would have thought *Young and Innocent* was a very dated film – yet they seemed to find it fascinating. I don't remember the details of how that great tracking shot at the end was done, but I know it went on and on and everyone had to know exactly when to move – it was done like a military manoeuvre. I think Hitchcock's early films were lovely – things like *The Thirty-Nine Steps* and *The Lady Vanishes*. He was a wonderful director and he was charming, though he had a really wicked wit.

You were the star of *Tudor Rose* **at the age of sixteen. Did it seem a big responsibility?**

I must have been very excited at the time; it was certainly a wonderful part. I had known about Lady Jane Grey and thought the script was extremely good. I was very overpowered by the names in the cast list – Cedric Hardwicke, Sybil Thorndike, all those great people; I felt very supported by them but I was also scared, as you can imagine. Robert Stevenson [director] was very supportive of me and I liked him very much. He was married to Anna Lee, who was so beautiful! Oh, and I do remember John Mills, who was very young also, and we both rather held each other up! Martita Hunt played my mother in the film and she was as great an eccentric off the screen as she was on it. She was a highly intelligent and witty woman.

I can remember doing the close-up for the final scene in the Tower, when the cannon goes off, meaning Jane had been beheaded. In order to make the noise of the cannon they used a gong, and I can recall having the great desire to have hysterics, it seemed such an extraordinary noise to make! I haven't seen the remake [*Lady Jane*] but I read some reviews which suggested she was played as a much more headstrong character; I would have found it very difficult to play it that way because, as a young girl brought up in Tudor times, I'm sure she would have done as she was told.

You made two films in 1941 directed by Walter Mycroft, *Spring Meeting* and *Banana Ridge*. Do you remember him?

He did quite a number of films but he isn't much heard about for some reason. He was a rather unobtrusive director, but I do remember *Spring Meeting* with Michael Wilding; that was lovely. It had been a famous play and quite amusing. I think *Banana Ridge* must have been based on a stage farce; that was with Alfred Drayton and Robertson Hare. They were very funny as comedians but, like most comedians, they weren't at all funny off the set. Hare and Drayton were such a physical contrast to each other – and in every other way too. Alfred Drayton was rather an obsessive, dogmatic character, whereas Robertson Hare was very gentle and charming. And Isabel Jeans was in it too: she had tremendous style. I have memories of her being wonderfully dressed, very chic.

What you remember of the Ealing film, *Next of Kin*?

We went on location for that, somewhere in the south-west. It had a very interesting director, Thorold Dickinson. It was intended as a propaganda film, but it went a little beyond that and was a good film in its own right. I imagine it was through the Ministry of Information but it was Mickey Balcon's studio and I think Thorold was under contract to Mickey. I did several films at Ealing and I was very fond of Ealing and of Mickey.

My husband Pen was also under contract to him. We had plans to work together in the future but he was killed in the war two years after we were married. I think *Next of Kin* stands up well and even during the making of it I thought it was a very interesting film. And Thorold was a very warm person. I liked someone who gave me room to move but at the same time would be open to discussion.

Do you recall *Pastor Hall*, made before the war but, because of its anti-German sentiments, not released until 1940?

I have little recollection of it, other than the cast,

which included Wilfred Lawson, and that it was directed by Roy Boulting, who is a very interesting, intelligent man. I did think it was an interesting script and very prophetic.

You played Anna Neagle's sister in *Yellow Canary*. Did you enjoy working with the Wilcoxes?

They were lovely to work with, Anna and Herbert. I didn't spend much time with them because I only had a couple of scenes with Anna, including a breakfast scene with Marjorie Fielding as our mother. Anna and I did look rather alike, I think; we could both see the resemblance. Again, this was pretty much a propaganda film.

You are listed in one reference as having made two films in 1944, *Out of Chaos* and *Man of Science*, which I haven't been able to trace. Were they documentaries?

Man of Science could have been a short film about Faraday. I don't recall the other one.

The film I do remember and very much enjoyed doing, utterly unlike anything I had done before, was called *Green Fingers*. I don't think it was a particularly good film but I simply loved playing in it. I played a bitch, coming between Robert Beatty and Carol Raye, and that was fun. I suppose the film was fairly controversial in its day, being about osteopathy, which was not recognised then.

These films all have very strong casts ...

I do think England has always had the most wonderful reservoir of character actors and that is still true, although perhaps we were never very good at making stars. I suppose you could say I was made into a star in the '30s, but not by Hollywood standards. After I made *Tudor Rose*, nothing happened for something like eighteen months. I longed to do something in the theatre but I wasn't allowed. Then Hitchcock wanted me to go to Hollywood to test for *Rebecca* but my name meant nothing over there. *Tudor Rose* played at the Roxy in New York but beyond that I think it only showed in the art houses. I don't know if I would have been allowed to go – I suppose Selznick would have had the last word on it.

Your last two films represent a complete break in that they were both crime films.

Yes, one of them was very interesting. It was called *Three Weird Sisters*, a sort of Gothic horror job, and it had a script by Dylan Thomas. They found it difficult to get him to finish a scene, because by then he was well on to the bottle! It didn't work but it was an interesting film. Mary

Merrall was in that, as were Nancy Price and Mary Clare, and they were formidable! Daniel Birt, the director, and I got on very well, and he was very amusing. We did some of it in a Welsh mining district. Time draws a veil over the making of it – nobody got on with anybody, except Dan in the middle, who was lovely and made it all possible for everyone! He was a highly intelligent man with wide interests.

The second of those crime films was *Counterblast*. What do you remember of it?

That was Robert Beatty again, yes – we'd been

together in *Spring Meeting* – and Mervyn Johns and Margaretta Scott, who was lovely. It was something about laboratories and rats in cages, that's all I remember. I've obviously blocked it out!

In the '40s, were you able to choose your roles?

In the '40s what I really wanted to do was the theatre and I did do quite a bit. The films I made were mostly not very good and I didn't particularly like the business of filming. My first husband was in the profession and, had he not been killed, I suspect I might have stayed in it.

Eric Portman

1903–1969

Actor: *The Girl from Maxim's* (1933), *Maria Marten, Abdul the Damned, Old Roses, Hyde Park Corner* (1935), *The Cardinal, The Crimes of Stephen Hawke, Hearts of Humility* (1936), *The Prince and the Pauper, Moonlight Sonata* (1937), *49th Parallel* (1941), *One of Our Aircraft is Missing, Uncensored, Squadron Leader X* (1942), *We Dive at Dawn, Escape to Danger, Millions Like Us* (1943), *A Canterbury Tale* (1944), **The Air Plan* (narr only), *Great Day* (1945), *Wanted for Murder, Men of Two Worlds* (1946), *Dear Murderer, The Mark of Cain, Corridor of Mirrors* (1947), *Daybreak* (made in 1946), *The Blind Goddess* (1948), *The Spider and the Fly* (1949), *Cairo Road* (1950), *The Magic Box, His Excellency, *Painter and Poet* (narr only) (1951), *South of Algiers* (1952), *The Colditz Story* (1954), *The Deep Blue Sea* (1955), *Child in the House* (1956), *The Good Companions* (1957), *The Naked Edge* (1961), *The Man Who Finally Died* (1962), *West 11* (1963), *The Bedford Incident* (1965), *The Spy with a Cold Nose, The Whisperers* (1966), *Deadfall* (1967), *Assignment to Kill* (1968) * Short film.

'We're certainly off on a big job. I wonder if it will be successful,'[1] Eric Portman is reported to have said as Michael Powell's company left England to film *49th Parallel* in 1940. The answer, from Portman's point of view, was that it was resoundingly successful: he more than held his own with his famous co-stars (Laurence Olivier, Raymond Massey, Leslie Howard, Anton Walbrook) and it launched him into a very busy film career in the decade that followed. Despite a string of impressive starring roles, though, in 1949 *Picturegoer* was still puzzled by him: 'He remains one of the problem figures of British pictures, regularly doing work of distinction in them, never quite belonging to them.'[2]

He crossed swords with Powell on *49th Parallel*: 'Michael, are you completely mad? You're going to drown us all,' and 'You bastard, you'll kill us all for your damned movie,'[3] Powell, in his autobiography, records him saying, but he went on to do superb work for the famously difficult director in *A Canterbury Tale*, as the JP who pours glue in girls' hair. After several minor films in the '30s, including an unhappy stint in Hollywood ('You can say in your paper that I walked out on Hollywood,' he told the *Hollywood Reporter*[4]), he had diversely effective roles throughout the '40s. He starred for Powell as the businessman-turned-pilot in *One of Our Aircraft is Missing*; was very touching as the embittered ex-World War I Captain in Lance Comfort's *Great Day*; mined the darker potential of his *persona* in Lawrence Huntington's *Wanted for Murder* as a father-obsessed strangler; played the District Commissioner in conflict with a Tanganyikan witch-doctor in Thorold Dickinson's *Men of Two Worlds*; and was interestingly paired with Ann Todd (as hangman and faithless wife) in Compton Bennett's gloomy *Daybreak*.

He valued 'this range of characters that prevents one from becoming stale and mannered,'[5] but it means that one remembers him less as a star in the Granger/Mason mould than as an actor. His frequent interviews with *Picturegoer* suggest that, having trained for the stage, he had thought seriously about screen acting. He believed that, on screen, 'once you achieve that power of thinking yourself into a part, you can convince audiences by your thoughts, even if you are not the conventional physical type for the role.'[6] Four years later he opined that 'both camera and soundtrack are ruthless in revealing weaknesses, but . . . they enable the actor who has mastered the technique of his work to be seen and heard at his best.'[7]

His best was on display in Robert Hamer's *The Spider and the Fly*, in which he and Guy Rolfe fight a tense and sophisticated battle of wits ('a strange friendship based on mutual respect develops,'[8] he told a reporter); and for Hamer again, in *His Excellency*, he was the blunt trades union leader who takes on the local establishment of the colony he is sent to govern. There were good character roles in the '50s: the imprisoned Colonel in *The Colditz Story*; the deregistered doctor in *The Deep Blue Sea*; and, nearer his Yorkshire roots, Jess Oakroyd in the remake of *The Good Companions*. In the last decade of his life he worked for Huston in *Freud* and twice for Bryan Forbes, in *The Whisperers* and *Deadfall*. Co-starring with Edith Evans in the former, as her no-good husband, he asked Forbes, 'Do you think, dear boy, you could somehow insert an extra line which would indicate she married a much younger man?'[9] whereas she had wanted a line that suggested she had married beneath her.

If Portman is not much remembered now, that should be remedied: his work holds up remarkably well.

1 MW, 'Prescription for Portman', *Picturegoer*, 9 June 1945, p 11
2 L Wallace, '*The Spider and the Fly*', *Picturegoer*, 17 December 1949, p 16
3 Michael Powell, *A Life in Movies*, Heinemann, London, 1986, p 373
4 Quoted in Bernard Slydel, 'The Portman puzzle', *Picturegoer*, 16 February 1952, p 10
5 Bruce Woodhouse, 'Eric Portman, the star who likes to take chances', *Picturegoer*, 17 August 1946, p 11
6 GY, 'Who is he? An interview with Eric Portman', *Picturegoer*, 11 July 1942, p 7
7 Woodhouse, p 11
8 'Round the British studios', *Picture Show*, 20 August 1949, p 11
9 Bryan Forbes, *Ned's Girl*, Elm Tree Books, London, 1977, p 250

Sally Potter

b. 1949

Director: *Thriller* (1979), *The Gold Diggers* (1984), *The London Story* (1986), *Orlando* (& adapt) (1993), *The Tango Lesson* (1997)

As British cinema celebrates its centenary, it is heartening to think that a talent as original and intelligent as Sally Potter's is there to help shape its future. *Orlando*, one of the most ravishing-looking films of recent years, is a highly individual reworking in cinematic terms of Virginia Woolf's 1929 novel, made relevant to film audiences over sixty years later. It is her first clearly mainstream success, though it has not made compromises in achieving that sort of status. All her films are impelled by both a rigorous feminism *and* a clear and affectionate grasp of cinema history and narrative practice. *The Gold Diggers*, in particular, offers a lively critique of popular Hollywood genres reslanted to a feminist perspective, and, backed by the British Film Institute, is also remarkable in having been made entirely by women. It will be very interesting to watch the shape of a career practised by one who is so articulate about what she is doing.

Interview date: February 1996

An American writer once talked about film in terms of 'convergence among the arts'. To what extent do you think of film as a sort of wonderful 'mongrel' art form, drawing on all others?

Well, Lenin called it the greatest twentieth-century form and I find it a paradoxical form that has continued to enchant me – and it's paradoxical because its actual matter is a bunch of old plastic in a tin can but the only way you can see it is to project it through light. Then, you can't touch it, you can't taste it and you can't smell it; it's metaphysical. So it has this peculiar mixture of something very crude and, well, plastic, in the first instance, which becomes something quite magical; it appears to represent reality but it does not; it's only visible in the dark, yet its essence is light. The paradoxes go on and on, it's like a kind of riddle. I think, rather than a mongrel, it is its own kind of thoroughbred. It *is* a convergence, it is a love affair between all the arts, each of which is interdependent on the others. Maybe 'mongrel' *is* better because a mongrel is the result of a long chain of different species, isn't it, and maybe that's exactly what the cinema is.

What can you tell me about how you came to make your first film, *Thriller*? I mean both in terms of backing and of its aesthetic origins in *La Bohème*?

There wasn't much backing. We started with a bunch of friends and some old secondhand stock. I think the total budget was three or four thousand pounds. It really came out of my dance and performance-art background mixed with the background I already had in independent cinema, the half dozen or so teeny little films I'd already made. What I was doing, I suppose, was looking at where so-called high art meets popular art, hence where *La Bohème* meets *Psycho*, where opera meets cinema, and trying to find some way of both decoding the lush romanticism of it and going with it at the same time, so it was a kind of passionate austerity that led to it. It was made in a house in which I was squatting at the time with people who were also my friends. I was the crew – there was no other crew – and there was one light available. So it was a film born out of economic necessity and a kind of aesthetic austerity mixed with musical passion about the things it laughed at.

Were the film's feminist politics a crucial starting point for you as well?

Not so much a starting point, more a kind of immersion of self into what was then a burgeoning movement, almost an ecstatic movement, I think, of a feeling of possible liberation – not just for women but for everyone, because it was a new way of thinking politically. That is, to identify the ways in which one as an individual is less than one could be in every sense, and then finding out it's not a personal problem but a general social one that has no basis in a deeper level of reality. It was about identifying and claiming an identity as a woman and then moving on from that position with a kind of fervour.

However, what I always thought then (and still think now) is that films don't work best as illustrations of political messages. In other words, the politics of the film have to be deeply embedded in its imagery, in its life, in such a way that it can be digested and felt by people in a natural way. I think it's really a matter of how conscious you decide to be about what you're saying and then how consciously or not people read the messages that are there. But feminism was an important and fresh movement at that time and only later became a movement that, in many people's eyes, had become a stereotype of itself.

Your first feature, *The Gold Diggers*, seems to combine feminist interests with a critical affection for old movie conventions. How fair a summary would you say that is?

Pretty fair! I think there was, as in *Thriller* in a way, a love of and a respect for what had gone before. It's as if *The Gold Diggers* is occupying a terrain (and I use the word advisedly) where people have trodden before. It's almost like visiting a memory of cinema through the film itself. I think, however, that *The Gold Diggers* has a more didactic political message and is the weaker for it, although, interestingly enough, many people couldn't understand what the political message was; they just knew there was one!

People in general do tend to resist didacticism, don't they?

Yes, they don't like to be told how to have an experience, and film *is* an experience. But that film was also about pushing certain things to the limit. It was a film to test memory, to test black-and-white, to test what it was like having an all-female crew, to test what happened if you put a film star in with unknowns. It was a kind of pushing the boat out and seeing whether it would sink or not – and there is an image of that in the film itself.

So you were consciously wanting to make audiences think again about those narrative traditions that they take for granted?

Yes, because that's what I was in the middle of doing and I found that gripping, exciting and thrilling. I wanted to understand, What is storytelling? Why do things go a-b-c-d and not a-b-d-z-p-q, what's the difference, and why? Do the structures of stories we take for granted, whether they be love stories or adventure stories, tell us other stories that we're not even conscious of? In other words, how innocent is storytelling?

That is a pretty sophisticated intention, isn't it: to be asking that of audiences?

Yes, but you see, from a background in performance art, and theatre, and music improvising, what I had learnt and discovered is that audiences are infinitely more sophisticated than the material they watch, on the whole. If you can take people with you on a journey of passionate exploration of whatever you're interested in, generally people will leap at the chance and go with you. But you have to be very skilled in the way that you do it. When you are on stage as a live performer, you can adjust your timing and you can make things digestible; you make them pleasurable – I hate to use the word 'entertaining' but that is really the word. It's a live situation. Film is much more unwieldy in that you're doing and making something way in advance of when it will be seen, with no opportunity to have the dress rehearsal and then the real thing. The dress rehearsal *is* the real thing. You get one shot at it and that's it. You can transform it, to a degree, in the cutting room but you can't change what you've shot. I hadn't really learnt that before. I learned about the function of the script being the dress rehearsal for the film through making *The Gold Diggers*.

How difficult was it to set the film up as an all-female production enterprise?

Not difficult at all because after I'd made *Thriller*, which had been well received, the British Film Institute were very open to the idea. It was difficult from another point of view, which is that there were not women in many of the technical grades in the film industry, so a lot of them were trained up for the job, or trained up *on* the job, which made it tense and difficult for many and extremely challenging. It was a first at the time, although it's now commonplace.

How important was Julie Christie's name and reputation to the project, and how did she become involved in it anyway?

She became involved basically because I called her up and asked if she'd like to do it. I had met her before and that was the origin of it. It wasn't set up around her name, because it was a British Film Institute-funded thing. Strangely, I think it confused people at the time. Again, it's more common now for a big-name person to go into a relatively low-budget film but at that time it wasn't. It was like bringing two impenetrable worlds into collision with each other, which was very exciting. I learned a lot from that and Julie was a wonderful person to work with – with that incredible blend of professionalism and ease and hardworking and the many other things that she is. She became an integral part of the whole concept of the film because the idea was to find somebody who had such an iconic face and presence – well, her, in fact. She *is* a cinematic presence. She has an extraordinary, intuitive understanding of the camera and how it works, and the light loves to fall over her face. And she has a knowledge of a certain kind of stillness that attracts the camera and attracts the gaze of the audience.

To come now to *Orlando*, what in the first place drew you to Virginia Woolf's novel? I think it's a very daring choice to film.

I'd been attracted to it since I was a teenager. It had been in my mind even when I'd done live performances and so on, particularly the use of the elements in the book, ice especially, but the whole feeling for the elements of earth and ice and air and wind and water, and the fact that those elements go on beyond the human lifespan, that they contain it and nurture it, and the context in which we live.

Almost immediately after I finished *The Gold Diggers*, I wrote a treatment for *Orlando*. I then tried to get it funded, completely without success. Everybody said it was a film that couldn't be made, shouldn't be made, it was far too difficult and would be terribly expensive and so on. So, not discouraged in a final way but temporarily discouraged, I put it aside and worked on other things. I found, however, that it kept coming back to haunt me, if you like; it was like something that I had to do, in a sense. I was never daunted by the size of it, or the challenges of it; I was impassioned by that – seriously, not daunted. It was other people who were daunted. Of course, it was a massive challenge, in technical, writing, design, lighting, conceptual and casting terms – a challenge of the first order, and the challenge of getting people to finance it was probably the greatest of all.

What exactly were some of its main challenges to a filmmaker and to you, not merely as the director but as the adaptor as well?

How to create credibility with somebody who is clearly living for four hundred years. How can one believe that? Because in the book you can take those kinds of things on the chin, it can just be a convention in writing. But cinema is much more literal. If you see someone whose hair suddenly changes, you think 'Oh, they're wearing a wig,' whereas if the writer describes that their hair changes, you think 'Oh yes, it has changed.' So it was hard to overcome the credibility factor. And

how to make the central character lovable? And how to create a cohesion of look and feel with something that was going to span four centuries, how to give a kind of flow to that? The other thing was the fact that the other characters come and go while there is only one character who lives for the whole duration. One is used, in stories, to there being a dynamic of relationship that makes for some kind of continuity, but in *Orlando* people just come and go like flies. That was a challenge, both as an adaptor and as a filmmaker.

In adapting a famous novel, how important did the issue of fidelity to the original seem to you?

Faithful to the spirit and ruthlessly unfaithful to the form wherever necessary, just in the same way I would be to an idea of my own. You have to be prepared to throw away the things you love but that don't work. It would have been no service, indeed there never is any service to any writer, including Virginia Woolf, to be slavishly faithful to the matter of the book because a film is not a book. I'm stating the obvious, but she was concerned with literature and making something work in terms of literature, that was her passion. The only way to be faithful to the spirit of her literature was to think in terms of cinema. Having said that, though, there were many things in the book which it would not only have been a disservice to change, it would have been silly to change, because they were the reason for doing the book in the first place. The fact that the character changed sex, for instance: some people tried to persuade me to change, or tried to persuade me to cast a man and a woman, you know, two people in the same role. There were many other examples which seemed to me to be the great magic of the book. So I think it's a curious mixture, actually, of fidelity and ruthlessness.

Were there any ways in which you felt you were actually commenting on the novel, as distinct from simply transposing it to another medium?

Probably where I differentiated, where I really did change things, but it's only a comment on the novel for people who know the novel. I was keen to make it work as a film for people who had never heard of the novel and would never read it, as much as for people for whom the book was a trusted old friend. For example, the scenes that in the book are set in Constantinople and have a rather exoticised feel, I changed to an unnamed place in Central Asia and also changed the relationships of the characters and the events there, to bring up the issue of the English as colonialists rather than just accepting it as part of the background flavour, which Virginia Woolf did.

And I suppose bringing it up to date is a kind of commentary in itself.

Yes, it is, and it's therefore slightly more self-knowing or self-ironic, perhaps. Although Virginia Woolf was very self-ironic, she came from a different period, a different time and class. And I think she was besotted by the English upper class in a way that I'm not. So it's a slightly different view of that. I wanted to find the core of all that, that one could love, but not be so much in love with all its finery, you know?

Could you say why you decided to bring it up to date?

At the very end, you mean? Because that's exactly what she did. She took it up to the very moment when she put down her pen as she finished writing the last page. In other words, she took it into her present moment, so to be faithful to that I brought it up into my present moment. And I think that – given that the whole narrative is about coming out of the past into the present and how do we finally arrive in the present out of our personal histories and our national histories – it had to be brought into the present. It's not an archaic period piece, not at all.

It is a brilliantly cast film. How much control did you have over that?

Total control, but I worked with a wonderful casting director called Irene Lamb. The three people that I was absolutely sure I wanted from the very beginning were Tilda Swinton, Quentin Crisp and Heathcote Williams, and the rest of the cast kind of fell into place around that trio. Casting, I think, is one of the great alchemical secrets, really.

How did you work with Tilda Swinton? Did you have a lot of rehearsal or give a lot of interpretive direction, for instance?

We had the paradoxical opportunity of being able to rehearse for about four years, on and off, because that's how long it took to raise the money. This length of time was both a curse and a gift. One of the ways it was a gift was that I was able to work really intensively with Tilda over a long period of time. And that took many forms. It took the form of her reading the script aloud to me at different draft stages; it took the form of us watching all the films of Greta Garbo and many other films in which there were women playing men – film research, if you like; then tests with video; then endless discussions about the look of hair and so on; then I took thousands of photographs of her, including some in costumes and different settings to develop the look of the film. I think what this did was that, by the time we came to shoot, we had an amazing rapport and trust, so that in a very crowded shooting schedule we could go a long way fast. The interpretive work was really done through studying the script together and talking about everything: all the ideas, all the scenes, what was happening with the character and why, what were the changes and what were the key change points. You know, the usual ways one analyses a script but usually doesn't have the time to go into it so deeply.

What was your experience of working with the legendary Quentin Crisp?

Nothing short of delight from beginning to end. He was a stalwart trouper in an incredibly heavy and cumbersome frock, shooting through the night and in cold conditions. He was droll, he was himself, he was co-operative and charming – he was a hero.

I guess this film has been a breakthrough to major commercial distribution. What can you tell me about the setting up of this multi-national production?

That's all thanks to Christopher Sheppard, the producer, who really hand-carved a co-production out of incredibly resistant forces, and one that finally worked extremely well. It created an enormous amount of paperwork for him and an enormous amount of jetting about and convincing people and getting co-production agreements drawn up and all the rest. But finally, I think it can be a great strength to have a co-production because as a director you have, paradoxically, greater artistic freedom since there is no one source of finance who can control you. It probably gives the producer that kind of freedom as well, and I think that there is a great benefit, if you can make it work to your advantage, in having an international crew. The atmosphere and co-operation between people of different backgrounds and cultures and languages, when it works well, is really exciting. It opens everybody's eyes to each other's reality, culture, language – there's a kind of buzz, the buzz of co-operation.

The whole thing seems like an absolutely international enterprise as well as being intensely English, too.

Yes. A film has to be itself. There is no such

thing as an 'international film'; I mean, film is an international medium, but the film has to tell its own story in its own way and, if that is about one house on one block in one city in one country, then that is what it is. You can't start peppering it up with apparently international references, or you end up with nothing. But I think the process of making a film is another matter. For example, I found on *Orlando* having Dutch designers gave a very different perspective on the look of the film than, say, an English person, to whom the references were more obvious, might have given.

You also had a great Russian cameraman, Alexei Rodionov. How crucial was he to the success of the whole operation?

I think each person was crucial in their own way. We were shooting in Russia, all the ice scenes which were very important sequences, and that was part of the reasoning. But also I was very intrigued and interested to work with somebody from such a different tradition of cinema – and the Russian cinema is such a wonderful tradition. Somebody who hadn't worked in advertisements, for example, who hadn't done commercials, who had a completely different set of criteria, a different kind of eye, a different history and different way of looking. He was used to much longer schedules (his previous film had taken a year to shoot, whereas *Orlando* was ten weeks), so you can imagine the shock to his system. He didn't move like greased lightning at the beginning, it has to be said, but he brought something else to the whole film which is, finally, astonishingly beautiful.

Who are some of the British filmmakers you have admired or perhaps been influenced by?

Michael Powell and Emeric Pressburger; Carol Reed for *The Third Man*, which is one of the great works; Lindsay Anderson. They are the ones that first spring to mind.

What about Peter Greenaway or Derek Jarman?

Derek Jarman because he was a friend and I think one of the greatest possible human examples of how to work against adversity. His actual films influenced me less but his way of working and his person, his being, his attitude, his state of mind influenced everybody that he was near. Peter Greenaway would probably claim similar roots of influence – like Powell and Pressburger – as did Derek. I would say he was less of a direct influence, even though I worked with the designer with whom he had worked many times.

As to Lindsay Anderson, I think *This Sporting Life* is one of the great British films. It came out of a period of black-and-white British filmmaking with a high political sensibility, it used wonderful actors that were in many other ways ground-breaking. I also have to mention the Ealing comedies, films like *The Man in the White Suit* by Alexander Mackendrick, and Alexander Korda as a producer. All that period of British filmmaking is part of my roots. I think of it with affection, love, respect and, in some cases, adoration!

Dilys Powell
1901–1995

Film critic

'Highwaymen, doxies, poisoned cordials, Tyburn hangings with song, dance and huzzah – the hoary, the tedious and the disagreeable are married with an infelicity rare even in costume.'[1] Thus did Dilys Powell write in the *Sunday Times* about the popular Gainsborough melodrama, *The Wicked Lady*, in November 1945. I do not know whether she ever revised her opinion of such 'cheaply romantic pieces',[2] as she later designated these films, but it would not be surprising. However exacting she was, she was also flexible and receptive to changes.

She became the film critic of the *Sunday Times* in 1939, remained in this position until 1976, when she at once began writing about films on television for it, and continued to do so until she died, serving as film critic for *Punch* as well for several years. Her agenda was unpretentious but sound: 'I did want to entertain and amuse my readers ... But I hope I always thought I was being serious. Not only serious but truthful ... I really think I have always wanted to explain why I thought *this* film was good.'[3]

No one rivalled her longevity as a critic. During the '40s and '50s, CA Lejeune, at the *Observer*, was the other of the 'Sunday ladies', and many others, in a country which has to this day a high standard of film reviewing, have come and gone. One thinks of Graham Greene in the 1930s, of Richard Winnington's eloquent asperities during the decade 1943–53, of Kenneth Tynan, briefly, and Penelope Gilliat in the 1960s, and Alexander Walker, perhaps the longest-serving of the current reviewers. She not only lasted longer but has worn better than anyone. Whereas Lejeune seemed witty at the time, her pieces, read today, are curiously insubstantial, as if she did not really take the cinema seriously, as Dilys Powell always did. She contrives always to give a palpable sense of what is *there* in the film, not just what *she* thought of it. To read her collected criticism is to feel oneself in the presence of a 'civilised mind',[4] it is also possible to read straight through in a way that would not be true of many reviewers, and what emerges is a shrewdly appraising sense of the growth of an art form.

Her long life overlaps almost the entire history of the cinema, and no other British critic could match her overview of its developments. Never a slave to fashionable trends, she welcomed innovation and was keenly aware of its onset. As to British cinema, she was in no doubt that the war changed everything. 'It took a war to make the British look at themselves and find themselves interesting,'[5] she claimed, and she developed this notion in a long essay in 1948. In terms of treatment, she credited the influence of the documentary filmmakers: 'Their work was alive; it had its roots in contemporary society.'[6] A decade later, she praised a new realist impulse at work in *Room at the Top*: 'Nothing over-emphasised, everything given value; the detail closely woven to form a comment on the narrative theme.'[7] In fact, in relation to this film, she recognised its importance over-all as a breakthrough in the torpor of late-1950s British cinema: 'After months when one had begun, against all one's instincts, to think that the best hope lay in coproduction ... suddenly a film which succeeds by being native', she wrote, going on to praise it for the way in which 'subtlety ... is married with an emotional directness not often found in a British film. The love scenes are quite unlike the usual dormitory charade; a quarrel has the savageness of people who are still in love.'[8]

It was not, of course, only British films that she wrote about. Nor, in spite of her blind spot about Gainsborough, was there anything offensively mandarin in her approach. She loved the film masterpieces from every filmmaking country; and she loved great work in the popular genres: Westerns, thrillers and musicals. She could also distil boredom or distaste in a terse but rancourless sentence: of a 1971 disaster, she wrote: 'I emerged from *Myra Breckinridge* pining for a long evening with Norma Shearer.'[9]

Dilys Powell was admired by – and encouraged – the *Sequence* generation of filmmakers (Anderson, Reisz, etc); she was in fact an object of respect to her fellow critics and to filmmakers alike. She exercised influence on British film culture also as one of the founders of the London Film Festival, as a governor of the British Film Institute and as a director of the Independent Television Authority.

Dirk Bogarde's obituary for her is aptly entitled, 'Nobody's opinion was as important as hers.' She told him: 'I don't want to know how films are made. That's not my job. I only want to know if it has involved me and who has done so and why ... Just let me be enthralled.'[10] Hers was an unbeatable combination: a passion for cinema, the judgement to recognise what is valuable, and the verbal precision to articulate this.

1 Dilys Powell, '*The Wicked Lady*' (1945), reprinted in George Perry (ed.), *The Golden Screen*, Pavilion Books, London, 1989, p 54
2 'Films since 1939', *Since 1939*, Readers Union/British Council, London, 1948, p 91
3 Preface to Christopher Cook (ed.), *The Dilys Powell Film Reader*, Oxford University Press, 1992, p xi
4 Lindsay Anderson, 'Film's fairest fan', the *Guardian*,

5 June 1995, p 11
5 'Films since 1939', p 83
6 'Films since 1939', p 65
7 Cook, p 20

8 Cook, p 21
9 Cook, p 206
10 'Dilys: a lifetime's love for the cinema', the *Sunday Times*, 4 June 1995, p 2

Michael Powell

1905–1990

Director: *Two Crowded Hours* (1931), *My Friend the King, Rynox* (& co-sc), *The Rasp, The Star Reporter, Hotel Splendide, COD, His Lordship* (1932), *Born Lucky* (1933), *The Fire Raisers, The Night of the Party, Red Ensign, Something Always Happens* (1934), *The Girl in the Crowd, Lazybones, The Love Test, The Phantom Light, The Price of a Song, Someday* (1935), *Her Last Affaire, The Brown Wallet, Crown vs Stevens, The Man Behind the Mask* (1936), *The Edge of the World* (1937), **The Spy in Black, The Lion Has Wings* (co-dir) (1939), **Contraband* (& co-sc), *The Thief of Baghdad* (co-dir) (1940), *An Airman's Letter to his Mother* (short), **49th Parallel* (1941), **One of Our Aircraft is Missing* (1942), *The Silver Fleet* (pr only), **The Life and Death of Colonel Blimp, *The Volunteer* (short) (1943), **A Canterbury Tale* (1944), **I Know Where I'm Going* (1945), **A Matter of Life and Death* (1946), **Black Narcissus, The End of the River* (pr only) (1947), **The Red Shoes* (1948), **The Small Back Room* (1949), **Gone to Earth* (1950), **The Elusive Pimpernel, *The Tales of Hoffmann* (1951), **The Sorcerer's Apprentice* (short), **Oh Rosalinda!* (1955), **The Battle of the River Plate* (1956), **Ill Met By Moonlight* (1957), *Luna de Miel / Honeymoon* (& co-sc) (1959), *Peeping Tom* (1960), *The Queen's Guards* (1961), *Bluebeard's Castle* (1964), *They're a Weird Mob* (1966), *Sebastian* (pr only) (1967), *Age of Consent* (1969), *The Boy Who Turned Yellow* (1972), *Return to the Edge of the World* (1978)
* In association with Emeric Pressburger as screenwriter and/or producer.

'I was at last going to make the film that I myself wanted to make: all the others had been chosen for me and I had to try to make entertainment out of them,'[1] wrote Michael Powell of *The Edge of the World*, his 1937 breakthrough film. After a six-year apprenticeship in 'quota quickies' (some of them recently re-appraised), he found in this romantic melodrama, set on a Scottish island, 'a turning point of my life in art, and I found it impossible to return to the world of cheap thrillers.'[2]

'My life in art' is a key phrase. The *art* of the movies was what Powell saw himself, romantically, as practising, and, however difficult he was to work with, as many testify, he created perhaps the most strikingly original *œuvre* of any British director. 'I'm difficult to categorise. I never want to make the same sort of subject twice,'[3] he claimed, and this is borne out by the films which followed the two stylish wartime thrillers, *The Spy in Black* and *Contraband*.

There is indeed an astonishing diversity of riches. *49th Parallel* is a picaresque Nazi-hunt shot through with philosophical musings: 'That was really the start of wartime films, the proper start.'[4] And for Powell, as for many other commentators, 'The real start of British films . . . came with the war.'[5] *One of Our Aircraft is Missing* is a story of wartime escape and the Dutch resistance; and *The Life and Death of Colonel Blimp* ambitiously explores the *rapprochement* of youth and age (and the nature of friendship and loyalty) touched on in the preceding film, but this time '. . . we had consciously set out to make a big epic because we didn't think we could tell the three episodes of Blimp's life in much less than two hours and a half.'[6] *A Canterbury Tale* is a beautiful meditation on Englishness and also the recurring opposition of materialism and idealism: 'At the time nobody thought that *A Canterbury Tale* worked, but I must say that it contained some of my favourite sequences.'[7] *I Know Where I'm Going* rehearses the theme of materialism versus idealism in terms of romance and Celtic legend, and celebrates the idiosyncratic beauty of Wendy Hiller and Pamela Brown; *A Matter of Life and Death* wonders deliriously about post-war relations in settings which weave us in and out of real and dream worlds; *Black Narcissus*, 'the most erotic film I've ever made,'[8] dramatises the clash of flesh and spirit in a wind-racked Himalayan convent; and so the list goes on, to include the films explicitly converging on the other art forms of the ballet (*The Red Shoes*) and opera (*The Tales of Hoffmann*).

Throughout this period of great achievement, his collaborator was the Hungarian, Emeric Pressburger. 'Anyone who thinks they can make films alone needs their head examined,'[9] said Powell, and on all these films he and Pressburger share the director/producer/writer credit, though Powell is always the director. In his two vast volumes of autobiography, he has told us more perhaps than any other director about how his films were made. In answer to the criticisms of the veracity of his recollections, one might in his defence quote him as saying, 'I distrust documentary. Always have. I have no interest in what people tell me is the truth. I'd rather make up my own truth.'[10]

When the collaboration finished in the late '50s, Powell went on to make *Peeping Tom*, the most notorious film in British cinema history. Though Powell himself insisted that it was 'a very tender film, a very nice one,'[11] this study of deviant sexuality and murder, now regarded as a masterpiece by many, destroyed his career at the time. His genius awaited another generation of filmmakers for full recognition.

Powell is the great romantic of British cinema. In 1950, he wrote, in answer to adverse critical response to *The Elusive Pimpernel* and *Gone to Earth,* 'Beauty, truth and the heart of England, I believe in these three things . . . And they are in the two films which we made.'[12] This kind of instinctive response is at the heart of all his great films. Even when they are flawed, they remain the films of a man with a passion for what cinema could do.

1 Michael Powell, *A Life in Movies*, Heinemann, London, 1986, p 251
2 Powell, *A Life*, p 259
3 Saskia Baron, 'The Archers at eighty', *Cinema Papers*, July 1986, p 13
4 David Badden, 'Powell and Pressburger: The war years', *Sight and Sound*, Winter 1978/79, p 9
5 Badden, p 8
6 Badden, p 11
7 In Ian Christie (ed.), *Powell, Pressburger and Others*, BFI, London, 1978, p 33
8 Powell, *A Life*, p 584
9 Baron, p 13
10 Quoted in John Russell Taylor, 'Michael Powell: Myths and supermen', *Sight and Sound*, Autumn 1970, p 227
11 Quoted in David Thomson, 'Mark of the Red Death', *Sight and Sound*, Autumn 1980, p 258
12 'Mr Powell replies', *Picturegoer*, 30 December 1950, p 12

Sir David Puttnam

b. 1941

Producer or executive producer: *Melody* (1970), *The Pied Piper* (1972), *The Last Days of Man on Earth, Mahler, Swastika, That'll Be the Day,* *The Double-Headed Eagle* (1973), *Brother, Can You Spare a Dime?, Stardust* (1974), *James Dean – The First American Teenager, Lisztomania* (1975), *Bugsy*

Malone (1976), *The Duellists* (1977), *Midnight Express* (1978), *Foxes* (1980), *Chariots of Fire* (1981), *Experience Preferred but Not Essential, P'Tang Yang, Kipperbang, Secrets* (1982), *Arthur's Hallowed Ground, Local Hero, Red Monarch, Those Glory Glory Days* (1983), *Cal, Forever Young, The Killing Fields, Winter Flight* (1984), *Defence of the Realm, The Frog Prince, Mr Love* (1985), *Knights and Emeralds, The Mission* (1986), *Memphis Belle* (1990), *Meeting Venus* (1991), *Being Human, The Confessional* (1994)

'I try to make films about morally accountable individuals, trying to hold true to their beliefs against the mindless violence of ideological genocide or religious fanatics,'[1] said David Puttnam in 1988. In the same lecture, he further elaborated his view of filmmaking: 'I find that view of entertainment, that it is an alternative to the engagement of the mind, the worst kind of evasion, posing what is, in reality, a false choice,' and he rejects élitism, 'because it is the élitist who tends to sneer at the idea of entertainment, as though entertainment and serious engagement of the mind are opposing forces.'[2] Puttnam, that is, is a man who *thinks* about what he is doing in the film industry: he accepts that it *is* an industry, that it must market itself skilfully, and that it is a craft first, art second – and not always. 'I don't think cinema is, of itself, an artistic pursuit . . . I think a film in hindsight can have been a work of art. On odd occasions. Whilst it's being manufactured, and it *is* manufactured, it is a craft. Now, I happen to have the highest respect for craft.'[3]

Since Korda, Balcon and Rank, in their respective ways, Puttnam, from a more modest social background than any of them, is the nearest approach to a mogul in British cinema. In the '70s and early '80s, almost single-handedly it seemed, he worked as producer/entrepreneur to raise the level of British films. 'It would be encouraging to see a few more noble failures instigated by British producers,'[4] he urged in 1984, insisting that 'our films have to be much, much better if they are to sustain world attention.'[5] By then, he'd won an Oscar for *Chariots of Fire* and his standing was secure enough to allow him to make such pronouncements – and to be listened to.

He began as a photographers' agent in the late '60s, and worked his way into production in the '70s, achieving real success with the pop musicals, *That'll Be the Day* and *Stardust*. 'That'll Be the Day established me as a producer, because the film worked and, more importantly, the entire marketing approach worked.'[6] Elsewhere, he stressed, 'I'm a marketing man who happens to produce films, rather than a film producer who markets his own films.'[7] His approach was always realistic in terms of what was commercially viable, as well as being morally responsible. Such *succès d'estime* as *The Killing Fields* and *The Mission* were obviously made with a strong sense of the human values involved, and the former, particularly, was also a solid box-office performer.

Puttnam was very often the conduit for new directors: think of Alan Parker (who wrote *Melody*, aka *S.W.A.L.K.*) on *Bugsy Malone* and *Midnight Express* (about the violence of which Puttnam later had moral misgivings); Ridley Scott's auspicious debut, *The Duellists*, in regard to which Puttnam noted 'the dangerous and extraordinary quality of mindless violence, which is something I encountered a lot of as a kid';[8] Roland Joffe on *The Killing Fields* and *The Mission*; and Bill Forsyth on *Local Hero* (a latter-day breath of Ealing), and, in the US, *Housekeeping*.

Since the demise of Goldcrest, of which he was a director,[9] and since his unhappy stint in Hollywood, where he tried to run Columbia on brave new lines,[10] Puttnam has located himself in Britain. In 1981, he had said: 'I simply feel more secure with British subjects and I think there are lots worth playing.'[11] Let's hope his sense of 'responsibility to British cinema'[12] will find the outlet it deserves in the later 1990s.

1 Edited version of *Financial Times* Arts Lecture, 30 November 1988, in *Sight and Sound*, Winter 1988/89, p 89
2 *Financial Times* Arts Lecture
3 John Walker, *The Once and Future Film*, Methuen, London, 1985, p 119
4 'British Cinema: Life before death on television', *Sight and Sound*, Spring 1984, p 117
5 'British Cinema', p 118
6 'David Puttnam' (interviewed by Peter Beilby and Scott Murray), *Cinema Papers*, February–March 1980, p 12
7 Walker, p 118
8 Walker, p 121
9 For the story of Puttnam's involvement with Goldcrest, see Jake Eberts and Terry Holt's *My Indecision is Final: The*

Rise and Fall of Goldcrest Films, Faber and Faber, London, 1990
10 See Andrew Yule's *Fast Fade: David Puttnam, Columbia Pictures, and the Battle for Hollywood*, Delacorte Press, 1988
11 'Journals', *Film Comment*, September–October 1981, p 9
12 'Journals', p 9

J Arthur Rank (Lord Rank)

1888–1972

'**M**y one desire is to improve the quality of British films and to give them a chance in world markets,'[1] Arthur Rank once told an interviewer. It is a very characteristic remark in the way that it so simply expressed aims which were enormously complex. Another duality at work in this giant figure of British film history is that he wanted films not merely to be profitable but also to do good. His most recent biographer rightly speaks of 'two competing narratives'[2] at work in the story of Rank, the Methodist millionaire.

As everyone must know, Rank, son of a prosperous Yorkshire flour-miller, entered films so as to spread Christian teaching. Finding the quality of religious films to be poor, in 1935 he produced his own film, prophetically entitled *Turn of the Tide*. It was critically well received but poorly distributed. Rank realised that you couldn't do good with a film if people didn't see it, and he began the process of carving out a comprehensive film empire. By 1948, he could say: 'We have laid the foundations of an industry by providing the practical means of survival – the vital facilities of production, distribution and a proper flow of equipment.'[3]

In the intervening years, Rank had been very busy. He had acquired a controlling interest in General Film Distributors; he established Pinewood Studios as a production centre in 1936, transferring activities to Denham during the war; and, in 1941, after the death of its owner, Oscar Deutsch, he acquired the Odeon cinema chain. And, while building this tripartite bulwark of production, distribution and exhibition facilities, he never lost the conviction 'that I was being led by God'.[4]

A further duality at work in Rank is that, though he wanted British films to be good, to be valued in the world, he was very ignorant about the medium, and, indeed, about cultural production of any kind. '. . . the trouble really was that I didn't know anything about producing films. I only took it on because there was nobody else to do the job,'[5] he confessed simply but not, it seems, disingenuously. What is incontrovertible is that under his leadership some remarkable filmmaking talents were allowed to flourish. In the latter half of the 1940s, he provided a financial umbrella for a group of companies known as Independent Producers and they provided him with some of the best British films: Cineguild (David Lean, Anthony Havelock-Allan, Ronald Neame) made *Great Expectations* and *Brief Encounter*; The Archers (Powell and Pressburger) made *A Matter of Life and Death* and *Black Narcissus*; Individual Pictures (Launder and Gilliat) offered *The Rake's Progress* and *The Happiest Days of Your Life*; and Olivier made *Henry V* and *Hamlet* for Two Cities. By several accounts, Rank offered these producers ideal working conditions: he signed the cheques and let them get on with the creative work.

Rank was also ready to experiment and, if none of his experiments delivered the goods as Independent Producers did, the effort is worth recording and the fault may lie essentially in the execution. The Independent Frame technique, hated by actors who were required to perform in front of photographed backgrounds, was an attempt to cut production costs. The Children's Film Foundation grew from Rank's question, 'Why not show some films that would do them [children] good?'[6] The film magazine series, *This Modern Age*, was a British riposte to *The March of Time* (US), and he also backed the work of animator David Hand. In an attempt to build stars, he established a 'Company of Youth' (cruelly dubbed 'the Charm School'), which produced Diana Dors, Christopher Lee and several others who went on to have respectable careers. At Highbury Studios, he consciously initiated a programme of 'B' film production to showcase these young talents. With the exception of Terence Fisher's cautionary tale, *To the Public Danger*, they are inept films; but they are also curiously different from the run-of-the-mill British supporting feature.

Apart from these brave but doomed ventures, Rank never ceased in his pursuit of world-wide (meaning essentially US) distribution for British films. 'The Americans are tough, but so am I, and I have learnt quite a lot about the ways and the methods of the trade,'[7] he said. Elsewhere, he argued, 'It is all very well to talk of being able to make good pictures without bothering about American or world markets, but in all honesty the continued existence of British film production depends on overseas trade.'[8] Though he told a reporter in 1945, 'I do not want to get into America if I have to be half American to do it,'[9] he made all possible efforts to secure US distribution for British

films, but never really succeeded beyond the art-house circuits.

Rank ran into enormous financial problems by 1950, for reasons too complex to rehearse here. This was the cue for John Davis, his right-hand man (hatchet-man, as many would say), to embark on a series of Draconian cuts, which made Davis hugely unpopular even as they achieved some of their purpose. There had been major disasters (e.g., *London Town*); perhaps the prestige producers were getting too leisurely; the *ad valorem* duty imposed on American films had fatally backfired; and expensive initiatives had failed. The Rank Organisation diversified in the '50s, but nothing can diminish the role in British film history of this plain-spoken millionaire with a vision.

1 Peter Noble, 'Miller who became the biggest force in UK film industry', *Screen International*, 13 April 1985, p 24
2 Geoffrey Macnab, *J Arthur Rank and the British Film Industry*, Routledge, London, 1993, p 32
3 *The Times*, 25 January 1948, p 4
4 Alan Wood, *Mr Rank: A Study of J Arthur Rank and British Films*, Hodder & Stoughton, London, 1952, p 68
5 Wood, p 124
6 Wood, p 173
7 Wood, p 218
8 Macnab, p 48
9 *Kinematograph Weekly*, 11 January 1945, p 35

Sir Michael Redgrave

1908–1985

Actor: *The Lady Vanishes, Climbing High* (1938), *Stolen Life, A Window in London* (1939), *The Stars Look Down* (1940), *Kipps, Atlantic Ferry, Jeannie* (1941), *The Big Blockade, Thunder Rock* (1942), *The Way to the Stars, Dead of Night* (1945), *The Captive Heart, The Years Between* (1946), *The Man Within, Fame is the Spur* (1947), *Mourning Becomes Electra, The Secret Beyond the Door* (1948), *The Browning Version* (1950), *The Magic Box, *Winter Garden* (voice only) (1951), *The Importance of

Being Earnest* (1952), *The Green Scarf, The Sea Shall Not Have Them* (1954), *The Night My Number Came Up, The Dam Busters, Oh Rosalinda!, Confidential Report* (1955), *1984, *Kings and Queens* (voice only) (1956), *The Happy Road, Time Without Pity* (1957), *Law and Disorder, Behind the Mask, The Immortal Land* (voice only), *The Quiet American* (1958), *The Wreck of the 'Mary Deare', Shake Hands with the Devil* (1959), *No, My Darling Daughter, May Wedding* (voice only) (1960), *The

Innocents (1961), *The Loneliness of the Long Distance Runner* (1962), *Young Cassidy, The Hill, The Heroes of Telemark* (1965), *Assignment K* (1967), *Oh! What a Lovely War, Battle of Britain, Goodbye*

Mr Chips, Connecting Rooms, David Copperfield (1969), *Goodbye Gemini, The Go-Between, Nicholas and Alexandra, The Last Target* (1971)
* Short film.

'I didn't think I'd be any good in films ... I couldn't imagine myself on the screen. Besides, there were such exciting things to do in the theatre, so much to learn,'[1] recalled Michael Redgrave in 1946, adding, 'I never lost touch with the stage and I never shall. But – make no mistake – I love film.' He went on to make more than fifty films, without ever losing the commitment to the stage – and without ever becoming a major film 'star'. It may be that his appeal was too strongly cerebral, rather than directly emotional, for easy stardom.

He began with Hitchcock's legendary *The Lady Vanishes*, in which he did seem like attractive star material, even though he didn't much enjoy the experience. 'What I did discover that first morning was the want of that quality essential to good acting on the stage: the rapport between artists who have worked together for at least as long as the rehearsal period ... I respected her [Margaret Lockwood's] professionalism, as I respected Hitchcock's, yet secretly saw little to praise in it.'[2]

He co-starred with Lockwood again in *The Stars Look Down*, directed by Carol Reed, whom he described as 'one of those dedicated beings, the artist who is completely absorbed by his dream. He eats, drinks and sleeps cinema.'[3] He made two other films for Reed, *Climbing High* and *Kipps*, and found him 'the gentlest of directors ... Yet underneath that gentle touch was an iron will which eleven times out of twelve would have its own way.'[4] Claiming that 'I have learned most of what I know about films through my directors,'[5] he made three strikingly different films for Anthony Asquith: *The Way to the Stars, The Browning Version, The Importance of Being Earnest*, certainly three of the key films of Redgrave's career. Of *The Browning Version*, in which he excelled as the disappointed schoolmaster, he praised Terence Rattigan's script as 'a marvel of its kind. There are scripts now and then where every line seems so right that you do not have to learn them. It is enough to repeat the words a few times for every line to fall into place.'[6]

Redgrave is more articulate than many about his craft as an actor, and especially about film–theatre differences: '... to this day [1958] I find on occasion the inflexibility of the cinema, which

demands, for example, that if you have sat down on a certain word of a sentence you should sit down on precisely the same word in another take or from another angle, can produce a wooden effect.'[7] He believed that 'the *best* plays and films have a deeper undercurrent, an implicit commentary on the conditions in which the people live, their ideas and ideals,' citing the example of *Kipps*: 'Kipps's adventures are sometimes comical, sometimes sad. The interesting point is that most of them are brought about by his mistaken efforts to "get out of his class".'[8]

His last years were clouded by Parkinson's disease, and this 'period remains a grey expanse ... but numerous films came along, some very good, like *The Go-Between*.'[9] If he had been more of a star and less of an actor, he might not have suggested so poignantly in that film the elderly man whose whole life has been emotionally stunted by childhood trauma. 'The basic will of an actor must be, quite simply, to act: not to think, not to feel ... *but to act*.'[10] And that is what he memorably did in *The Go-Between* and many others. There have now been four generations of acting Redgraves: his parents (Roy Redgrave and Margaret Scudamore) were actors, as are all his children (Vanessa, Corin and Lynn) by actress-wife Rachel Kempson, and several of his grandchildren (Joely and Natasha Richardson, Gemma Redgrave). It is as impressive a dynasty as is to be found in British cinema or theatre.

1 John K Newnham, 'Michael Redgrave: They knew what they wanted', *Picturegoer*, 16 March 1946, pp 6–7
2 Michael Redgrave, *In My Mind's Eye: An Autobiography*, Weidenfeld & Nicolson, London, 1983, p 123
3 Michael Redgrave, *Mask or Face*, Heinemann, London, 1958, p 136
4 Redgrave, *In My Mind's Eye*, p 143
5 Redgrave, *In My Mind's Eye*, p 124
6 Redgrave, *In My Mind's Eye*, p 196
7 Redgrave, *Mask or Face*, p 130
8 Hubert Cole, 'Carol Reed and Michael Redgrave discuss "the stuff to give them"', *Picturegoer and Film Weekly*, 5 October 1940, p 8
9 Redgrave, *In My Mind's Eye*, p 230
10 Catherine de la Roche, 'Master of his destiny: An interview with Michael Redgrave', *Films and Filming*, December 1955, p 11

Vanessa Redgrave

b. 1937

Actor: *Behind the Mask* (1958), *The Circus at Clopton* (narr only) (1961), *Morgan – A Suitable Case for Treatment, A Man For All Seasons* (1966), *Blow-Up, *Tonite Let's All Make Love in London, Red and Blue, The Sailor from Gibraltar, Camelot* (1967), *The Charge of the Light Brigade* (1968), *Isadora, A Quiet Place in the Country, Oh! What a Lovely War, The Sea Gull* (1969), *Drop Out!, The Body, La Vacanza* (1970), *The Devils, The Trojan Women, Mary Queen of Scots* (1971), *Murder on the Orient Express* (1974), *Out of Season* (1975), *The Seven-Per-Cent Solution* (1976), *Julia, The Palestinians* (1977), *Agatha, Bear Island* (1978), *Yanks* (1979), *The Bostonians* (1984), *Steaming, Wetherby* (1985), *Prick Up Your Ears, Comrades* (1987), *Consuming Passions* (1988), *Diceria dell'Untore, Stalin's Funeral* (1990), *Ballad of the Sad Café* (1991), *Howards End* (1992), *Little Odessa, Great Moments in Aviation* (1994), *A Month by the Lake, The Wind in the Willows* (1995), *Mission Impossible, Looking for Richard* (1996), *Wilde, Mrs Dalloway, Smilla's Sense of Snow* (1997), *Deep Impact, Tea with Mussolini* (1998)
*documentary

After making her film début in 1958, playing her father's daughter in *Behind the Mask*, Vanessa Redgrave made no further film for eight years. When she returned it was to co-star with David Warner in Karel Reisz's *Morgan – A Suitable Case for Treatment*, one of the major critical successes of the new British cinema of the 1960s. Already established as a notable theatre actor, she was now clearly a potent new talent in British films, and in the ensuing decade she confirmed this impression in a series of demanding and diverse roles. These included several for her then husband Tony Richardson (among them, *The Charge of the Light Brigade*), the title role in Karel Reisz's *Isadora*, and two for Sidney Lumet (*The Sea Gull* and *Murder on the Orient Express*), and for nearly thirty years she has sustained a dominant position in a changing and uncertain industry. Her 1992 performance in James Ivory's *Howards End*, as Mrs Wilcox, a woman tired and ill and blossoming briefly in a new friendship, is as finely moving as anything in her formidable repertoire.
Interview date: February 1996

How did you become involved in *Behind the Mask*, your first film, in which you played your father's on-screen daughter?

My father suggested me to the director, Brian Desmond Hurst, and I did a screen test for the producers, Sergei Nolbandov and John Somlo. The test was a nightmare: in spite of the cameraman being helpful, and people trying to put me at my ease, I still felt ungainly and frozen with fear.

How did you enjoy the actual filming experience?

I didn't enjoy it because that was the bad old days of British cinema, when a woman was expected to be either an English rose or a blonde bombshell and I fitted neither category. I mean, certainly there were some good films made then, and a few wonderful films, but that wasn't one of them.

Some actors have spoken with affection of the flamboyant director Brian Desmond Hurst.

Well, I knew him as a director and liked him as a director. There's no way I would call him flamboyant – that's somebody else's view.

I wonder if it seemed a quite different generation of British filmmaking when you made *Morgan* eight years later, in 1966.

Well, obviously. I mean, it was a completely new period of filmmakers.

What do you recall of *Morgan*? What brought you back to the screen for that film?

Karel Reisz asked me to play the part. He saw me at a party and he had certainly seen me on the stage. I'd done quite a lot of theatre by then. It was a wonderful experience. Karel Reisz is an extraordinary director, as has been proved by his films, and I found him wonderful to work with. I was very excited by his understanding of film: the moment is all important, and the film is really 'made' in the editing.

It seems light years away, in my recollection, from the kind of 'studio' film years of, say, *Behind the Mask* and so on.

Well, the entire film climate had completely changed. You have to know British cinema to know why that had happened.

Yes, a new kind of realism, I suppose, in the early '60s. But *Morgan* isn't essentially a realist film, would you say?

I don't know that one would call any of them realist films. They weren't all realist films but they had a new subject. *The Loneliness of the Long Distance Runner*, which was one of Tony Richardson's very, very best films; Karel Reisz's own film, *Saturday Night and Sunday Morning*, which Tony produced; I mean, they were also very poetic films. And also *Look Back in Anger*, Tony Richardson's first film, was also a very poetic film, I think.

Speaking of difference, Antonioni's *Blow-Up* seems even more different. How disconcerting was it, if at all, to act in a film with so little conventional concern for plotting or character?

Yes, it was different. It was very modern, it wasn't trapped in the past or past conventions. It was a modern film. For Antonioni, the camera angles, the colours and compositions told the story; dialogue was of secondary importance. He had a very subtle ear for the sounds of nature, like that of leaves rustling.

It always interests me to know how actors making the film are aware of these things at the time.

I think, usually, some of us are unaware and we learn in the course of making the film. Antonioni, for instance, was a legend already for his films. You know, we're not uneducated people; and we try to educate ourselves – that is to say, if we're *not* educated. But the landmark filmmakers in France, Italy and America and Russia had made their mark much, much earlier on. By the time that we were at last making modern films in Britain, thanks to these filmmakers – some of them British, some American, some Italian and French – we were part of the world again. We all learned a lot and by the time Antonioni did *Blow-Up*, he'd already done the most extraordinary films.

I've written about things like this in my book [*Vanessa Redgrave: An Autobiography*] because I know these kinds of questions are of considerable interest to people who love film. That was one of the reasons why I wrote it, so that people would know.

One is lucky enough, sometimes, to be offered extraordinary stories written by extraordinary people and directed by extraordinary directors, and I've been lucky that I've had chances like that to work with Fred Zinnemann and Karel Reisz and Antonioni and Tony Richardson.

Tony Richardson's *The Charge of the Light Brigade* was to me one of the most exciting films of the 1960s.

It is a masterpiece of all time. I think it's one of the best films ever made about the British Empire and about the horror of war.

What do you recall about the filming of it? Where was it made?

A lot of it was made in Turkey and the rest of it was made in England. It wasn't possible at the time for them to get the permissions necessary to shoot in the Crimea, which, if you remember, is one of the places that the story is set in and where it actually happened.

Why do you think permission was turned down?

I've no idea. I know it was to do with all the questions that came up in this period – to get permission to film you had to deal with authorities, governments and bureaucracies in the Soviet Union. But I don't think that's the main issue. The main issue is the film itself.

I am interested in the perception you have of screen stardom . . .

That's for gossip columns. That's nothing to do with British cinema.

Oh, I'm interested in the notion of stardom in the British cinema because it seems to me very different . . .

Well, in what sense, in what relation and in what context?

. . . in how far Britain went about the building of stars in ways comparable with Hollywood, because British cinema has always been in competition – commercially, anyway – with Hollywood . . .

I don't think it has, really. I certainly wasn't a star who was built up! I don't know why you're using these words because they have nothing to do with Britain or with cinema.

I suppose it is a perception that people would have of you.

If one's interested in film, one isn't following perceptions people have in the newspapers about stars. I mean, there were a few stars that were built – Diana Dors was one – but essentially it wasn't run like that except for a very brief period. And some pretty wonderful people worked in that time and they went straight to America, because that was the place where films were made.

You were in a couple of films that were very much star-laden enterprises, like for instance *Murder on the Orient Express*, which I think is charming, and *Oh! What a Lovely War*. I am trying to find out what you think about this notion of stardom and how important it was.

I find these questions very difficult to answer because they're not really about filmmaking. They were extraordinary actors and they were assembled and chosen, I think, in a very right way. I can't say anything different from that. They were very different subjects and one can't sort of lump them together, exactly.

Did you relish your particular role, as Sylvia Pankhurst, in *Oh! What a Lovely War*? Was it exciting to do?

Yes, it was, and I loved it. It was a very important story and Dickie Attenborough is a terrific director.

What do you mean when you say that someone is a terrific director? Do you look for assistance in the way of interpretive direction?

Well, filmmaking isn't only about what kind of direction the director gives the actor. It's about how he handles the scene; it's about how he works with his lighting cameraman; the camera set-ups that he chooses; the editor he works with; how he responds to the story – and the actor is a part of that.

In considering the thirty-odd directors I've talked to, I am interested in the difference they see in their job. To take, say, Sidney Lumet and Richard Attenborough, or Karel Reisz: are there any obvious differences about how they wanted you to approach your work?

Well, all directors are different. Sidney Lumet gives a lot of direction to his actors, he's very specific. For instance, when we did *The Sea Gull*, which I don't suppose you've ever seen . . .

I have . . .

. . . but you referred to *Murder on the Orient Express*.

Yes. I've seen them both and I am aware that they came out within a few years of each other.

Well, we literally rehearsed for two weeks before we filmed and it was an eight-week schedule. Sidney gave wonderful and particular direction to all of us – James Mason and Simone Signoret and myself and David Warner and the other actors – very, very specific, because in part that was based on the play and was to a certain extent a film of the play, although set by a real lake and not filmed theatre. It's a very, very beautiful film. He gives a lot of direction to actors. I can't just give a run-down of all kinds of superficial differences. The thing about a film director is not how he directs the actors, it's how he directs the film.

You spoke of rehearsal for *The Sea Gull*. Was Karel Reisz a director who liked rehearsal? You worked for him on *Isadora* as well as the earlier film, *Morgan*.

We didn't rehearse except in the case of *Isadora*

for the dances, but Karel gives wonderful direction during the shooting, very specific also. But we didn't have rehearsals. It depends how they're taken, you know, they mean different things to different directors. We rehearsed a little with Fred Zinnemann when we did *Julia* but his main direction of us was during the shooting.

Karel Reisz was worried about industrial aspects of *Isadora*. He said there was trouble over the distribution/exhibition and that this to some extent affected his shaping of the film. It seems to me a wonderful role for an actress and I wondered what you thought about it.

The role and the film are different things. Karel did his own cut and this was shown on American television three years ago. I prefer his own cut, I think it's wonderful. It's longer than the original film. If you are interested in that subject, you would be interested to see the difference between his cut and the cut which was distributed, which is rather vital for directors, as you know. It's really worth it to see what the difference is, because it has now become the custom – certainly in America – to show directors' final cuts as opposed to the first-release cuts. Some remarkable films have been shown with the director's cut and it's very important to see them.

I wonder if you recall *Out of Season*, a strange and absorbing little film ...

Yes, I do recall that. I haven't seen it for a long, long, long time. I don't remember it so distinctly. I remember Cliff Robertson – I liked working with him very much and the director, Alan Bridges, is a very interesting British director.

Throughout your career you have been photographed by some great cameramen. How much does it concern you who is DoP?

The making of any film, whether I'm in it or not, concerns me as to how it's made. It's a wonderful creative and technical process and the director of photography is not just a technician. He's an artist.

Some actors have told me that they never became knowledgeable about the technicalities of filmmaking. Others said it was enormously important to them. That is the kind of distinction I am making.

The distinction I'm making is that it's not a question of whether it's important to me, or to him or to her, it's important to the film.

Yanks **seems to me very attractive and I wondered what experience you had of the director, John Schlesinger, who's always**

seemed to me to be a very sympathetic director of actors, and the actor Richard Gere, both of whose work I have admired.**

John Schlesinger is a superb director. I love working with him. I loved that film, too. Any John Schlesinger film is quite unlike any other. I mean, he is a great filmmaker. I think one would call him an *auteur*. His films really do have wonderful acting performances. He is really very, very good at directing actors, and the subject itself was also very interesting.

In the recreation of that little wartime town, how much of it was a studio film and how much was location work?

All the work that I did was on location. How much of it was studio work, I can't tell you – perhaps a little bit. Keighley, up north in Yorkshire, was one of the towns but there were lots of different locations. One of them was Lamberhurst in Kent.

In spite of crises in the British film industry, you went on working in some of the most interesting British films of the last decade, such as *Steaming*, *Prick Up Your Ears*, *Comrades* and *Howards End*. Has it seemed to you difficult to come by these roles?

I would think it would be fairly clear to you, from what you've just said, that I have been lucky to do such wonderful roles in wonderful films. I would say Maggie Smith also has done that kind of work; Eileen Atkins has done that kind of work.

Those are all very notable films in one way or another. How did you respond to Joseph Losey's direction in *Steaming*? I gather he liked to use long takes and long tracking shots, for instance, rather than lots of cuts. Is that the kind of thing that you, as an actress, enjoy?

The longest tracking shot I've been involved in was devised by Vittorio Storaro when we did *Agatha* and that was brilliant. I don't remember long tracking shots in *Steaming*, though I expect there were some. But after all, a tracking shot is chosen by the director and the cinematographer on the basis of the particular film and the choices they have made as to how the camera will move. For the camera set-ups any great director makes their choices, not always permanently but subject to the film and the story.

That kind of technical difference from film to film – is that something that makes a real impact on you as an actress?

Well, we obviously come from very different viewpoints. I come from the viewpoint that the entire and concerning interest is as to all the components, the creative components and departments and individual skills and artistry that go into the making of a film. If I am a part of a particular sequence, the way that the cinematographer and the director have decided to convey what a particular scene is about, through the camera set-ups they've chosen, is extraordinarily absorbing.

A film that appealed to me enormously was *Comrades*, which in Australia disappeared after about a week. Is this a film of which you have fond recollections?

I thought it was a wonderful film and I thought Douglas was an incredible director. I loved working with him and I loved my tiny part in it – and I loved

the story too. Not all good films are commercially successful, but they live and endure.

The last film in which I've seen you is James Ivory's *Howards End*. I think Mrs Wilcox is one of the great achievements among your roles.

I loved the role but if we're talking about the making of a film and one's part in it, the character isn't just a creation of the actor; it's the creation of the man who wrote the story, the screenwriter, the director, the choices that were made to introduce such a person, such a character, and the understanding of the fundamental significance of a character to the whole story. It's when you get into particulars like that, that you become aware of how any writer, actress, director, cinematographer functions.

Sir Carol Reed

1906–1976

Director: *It Happened In Paris* (co-dir) (1935), *Midshipman Easy, Laburnum Grove* (1936), *Talk of the Devil, Who's Your Lady Friend?* (1937), *Bank Holiday, Penny Paradise* (1938), *Climbing High, A Girl Must Live* (1939), *The Stars Look Down, Night Train to Munich* (1940), *The Girl in the News, A Letter from Home* (short), *Kipps* (1941), *The Young Mr Pitt* (1942), *The New Lot* (short) (1943), *The Way Ahead* (1944), *The True Glory* (documentary) (1945), **Odd Man Out* (1947), *The Fallen Idol* (& co-pr) (1948), **The Third Man* (1949), **Outcast of the Islands* (1951), **The Man Between* (1953), *A Kid for Two Farthings* (1955), *Trapeze* (1956), *The Key* (1958), **Our Man in Havana* (1960), *Mutiny on the Bounty* (completed by Lewis Milestone), **The Running Man* (1963), **The Agony and the Ecstasy* (1965), **Oliver!* (1968), *The Last Warrior* (1971), *Follow Me* (1972)
* Also produced.

'Making a film is like going down a mine for eight weeks,'[1] Carol Reed told James Mason, who saw in him a 'total commitment' he had seen in no other director. Everyone agrees that Reed saw life wholly in terms of film and this seems to have been a mixed blessing to him. 'Making a picture is all about work and worry and fear and panic,'[2] he said in 1950 – and the traumatic remake of *Mutiny on the Bounty* was still over a decade away.

He seems to have had little interest in the world except as a source of stories. 'The first duty of a film is to tell a good story. If the story is handled properly, its serious implications will be expressed so that they do not interfere with the human interest of the story itself but actually add to it. I hope that is what we have managed in *The Stars Look Down*.'[3] Of this same film, Reed said, 'I simply took the novel by Cronin. I didn't feel particularly about his subject, the nationalisation of the mines. One could just as easily make a picture on the opposite side.'[4]

For ten years Reed made some of the most distinguished and varied films ever made in Britain, and in them 'the human interest of the story' is always uppermost, and *does* bear the serious implications of each film's theme. After working for Edgar Wallace in the theatre, where he learned to be sensitive to actors, he made a dozen or so films as actor or assistant director before getting his first solo directing job, *Midshipman Easy*, in 1935. Of his 1930s films, he said, 'You were handed a script and told you had to shoot so many scenes a day . . . If you didn't make up your lost time, you were likely to be taken off the picture.'[5] In *Bank Holiday* (1938), he united several fictional plots with a concern for realism of place and behaviour. This combination asserted itself again in *The Stars Look Down* and *Kipps*, and above all in his wartime masterpiece, *The Way Ahead*, in which a bunch of raw recruits is moulded into a fighting unit.

The great period of his ascendancy (and that of British films) was in the years after the war, when he made *Odd Man Out*, *The Fallen Idol* and *The Third Man* in succession. About the first, he 'liked the theme of someone who had done something wrong for the right reasons,'[6] and made from it a film of a romantic intensity perhaps still unequalled in British cinema. On the other two masterworks, he collaborated congenially with Graham Greene, who always felt he had been best served in the cinema by Reed. 'I think it is the director's job . . . to convey faithfully what the author had in mind,' said Reed. 'Unless you have worked with the author in the first place you cannot convey to the actors what he had in mind . . .'[7] *The Fallen Idol* is the apotheosis of his use of children as a focus for innocence betrayed; and *The Third Man* is surely one of the most seductive films ever made. Part of its appeal is visual as it captures war-ravaged Vienna 'with a wide-angle lens that distorted the buildings and emphasised wet cobblestones';[8] and part is in the haunting zither music of Anton Karas.

From 1950 on, he never quite achieved such success. While filming *Outcast of the Islands*, he described Conrad's original as 'a darn good story',[9] perhaps indicating a limited grasp; of *The Key*, he said, 'When we were nearly done I was persuaded that too much rode on the success of this picture to be risked on a downbeat ending';[10] and his last film version of a Greene story, *Our Man in Havana*, is a pale shadow of the '40s triumphs. As early as 1952, he had said, 'Sometime in the future I'd like to make a musical.'[11] Seventeen years later, he directed *Oliver!*, but discovered 'that in a big musical the man who directs it is far more dependent on other people than in a straight film.'[12]

Alec Guinness was dismayed when Reed told him, on *Our Man in Havana*, 'We don't want any of your character acting. Play it straight,'[13] but many actors did some of their most memorable screen work for him. Think of Mason in *Odd Man Out*, Ralph Richardson in *The Fallen Idol*, Trevor Howard in *The Third Man*, or Margaret Lockwood and the other girls on the theatrical make in *A Girl Must Live*. Even Orson Welles didn't create smiling, lethal Harry Lime on his own.

1 James Mason, *Before I Forget*, Hamish Hamilton, London, 1981, p 238
2 Stephen Watts, 'The fourth man . . . Carol Reed', *Picturegoer*, 4 March 1950, p 7
3 Hubert Cole, 'Carol Reed and Michael Redgrave discuss "the stuff to give them" ', *Picturegoer and Film Weekly*, 5 October 1940, p 8
4 Nicholas Wapshott, *The Man Between: A Biography of Carol Reed*, Chatto & Windus, London, 1990, p 124
5 Hilton Tims, *Once a Wicked Lady* (first published 1989), Clio Press, Oxford 1992, p 91
6 Wapshott, p 179
7 Wapshott, p 196
8 Wapshott, p 228
9 Bernard Slydel, 'Carol Reed tells how I made the *Outcast*', *Picturegoer*, 23 February 1952, p 12
10 Wapshott, p 291
11 Slydel, p 12
12 Wapshott, p 332
13 Alec Guinness, *Blessings in Disguise*, Fontana/Collins, Glasgow, 1986, p 288

Karel Reisz

b. 1926

Director: *Momma Don't Allow (co-dir) (1956), *Every Day Except Christmas (pr) (1957), We Are the Lambeth Boys (1958), Saturday Night and Sunday Morning (1960), This Sporting Life (pr) (1963), Night Must Fall (1964), Morgan – A Suitable Case for Treatment (1966), Isadora (1969), The Gambler (1974), Dog Soldiers / Who'll Stop The Rain? (1978), The French Lieutenant's Woman (1981), Sweet Dreams (1985), Everybody Wins (1990)
* Short film.

Karel Reisz has had a wide-ranging involvement in British cinema. He worked on the short-lived but provocative journal, *Sequence*; he edited *The Technique of Film Editing* (1953), a ground-breaking text on film editing, drawing on key sequences from major British films; along with Lindsay Anderson and Tony Richardson, he was responsible for the Free Cinema programmes of the later '50s, programmes that breathed new social and aesthetic life into British cinema; and, like his colleagues, he went on to make feature films which changed the face of British cinema in the '60s. In fact, it could be said that it was the huge commercial success of his first feature, *Saturday Night and Sunday Morning*, which enabled a whole batch of social-realist films to follow in its train. Not that these films are really as homogeneous as that sounds: Reisz's films have a more coolly observant edge than, say, Richardson's: but they did all bring new impulses into British cinema when it needed them. Reisz's films, whether American or British, are characterised by fine performances and a rejection of anodyne conclusions to complex situations.
Interview date: October 1992

How did you come to be associated with the influential journal, *Sequence*?

I met Lindsay Anderson on a Green Line bus to Aston Clinton, where the British Film Institute had its archive in those days. I was going to look at some film for my editing book and he was there, oh, probably, to see some early Ford picture . . . yes, it was *The Iron Horse*. We had to take turns on an ancient Editola. The magazine he was editing, *Sequence*, was in its seventh or eighth issue at that time. I had started writing about films a bit, and he asked me to contribute, which I did. I co-edited the last few issues with him. *Sequence*, incidentally, had been started at Oxford by a group of undergraduates – Lindsay, Gavin Lambert, Penelope Houston and Peter Ericsson. By the time I got involved, Peter had left the field altogether and Gavin was editing *Sight and Sound*.

What sorts of values did *Sequence* seem, to you, to stand for?

Principally, the director's cinema. Most of the issues were built around a long central article about an individual director – Ford, Carné, early Hitchcock, Disney, and so on. Much of the emphasis was on American cinema. This was a time when most literate writing on the cinema was pretty patronising about Hollywood. Russian and German silent films and French cinema were the canon of 'serious' film criticism. *Sequence* concentrated on the movies we enjoyed at the Odeon – musicals, Disney, Ford, Preston Sturges, and so on.

***Sequence* was not kind to British cinema, on the whole, was it?**

You have to remember that British films were heavily dominated by country-house comedies, patriotic war epics and period melodramas. They were not concerned with contemporary British life – the changing realities were largely ignored. You have to remember, too, that this was the time of Italian neo-realism, which engaged passionately with contemporary life. There was nothing remotely equivalent in British cinema. I don't think it would be right to say that we were not kind to British films. We greatly admired Humphrey Jennings and wrote well about the films of people like Sandy Mackendrick and Robert Hamer. We certainly liked Reed. Our line on Powell – it's so long ago – was probably to prefer the very English films; I mean *I Know Where I'm Going*, *A Canterbury Tale* and later *The Small Black Room*. You have to see all this in the context of the big British production companies attempting large-scale 'mid-Atlantic' work to compete with Hollywood. The British cinema seemed to us out of touch with what was going on, and stiflingly class-bound: it was due for a radical shake-up.

Do you think this class issue accounts for why British cinema didn't, in the '40s and '50s, easily grab an international audience as Hollywood did?

Perhaps. But it was only part of it. The general level of filmmaking was very provincial and airless.

How did you come to do your famous text on film editing?

The British Film Academy advertised for someone to collate the views of distinguished British editors and directors, to produce a textbook on film editing. I got the job. It was to be a straightforward factual kind of book, not critical, more like a primer of film editing. And this we did. The book is built around an analysis of sequences from actual films (not only British). It doesn't aspire to any sort of theory of montage. For me, the job was a gift from God. I'd never been near a cutting room when I started writing it, but I wanted to *make* films. I spent a happy year analysing in detail sequences from finished films with the help of their makers. The book is still in print after forty-five years and twenty-five editions, because it is unpretentious and because it's the only book on the subject.

When you came to make your Free Cinema films in the mid '50s, did it seem that mainstream British cinema had little to offer you?

Quite. There didn't seem any point in going on with all those pictures about country houses with comic servants or stiff-upper-lip officers and Cockney conscripts. A lot was happening in the ten years after the war. We'd had a Labour Government and an Education Act and a lot was changing in people's lives. To take a simple practical example, the young actors who were going through RADA were not the same sort of people who had come before the war. People like Albert Finney, Tom Courtenay and Richard Harris would simply not have got to drama school pre-war. And of course the writers – novelists and playwrights – were taking note of the changes. The cinema *followed*. We felt our pictures should reflect more of what was in the air.

How would you summarise the goals of Free Cinema?

Oh no, I can't go through all that again! There was a manifesto at the time and a lot of public debate. And it's all very well – too well – documented. I suppose the main issue was independence for the director – independence from the big battalions of Pinewood and Elstree, and the demands for 'international' filmmaking.

Films like *We Are the Lambeth Boys*, *Momma Don't Allow* and *Every Day Except Christmas* focus on a class of people British cinema had not taken seriously.

Yes, the films give screen time to people and events that had not been seen on the screen. In *We Are the Lambeth Boys*, I felt it was worthwhile to have a five-minute sequence of the boys horsing around in the yard, knocking a cricket ball around in the nets. I thought it was interesting. We wanted to start from observation of the contemporary world. The traditional idea of documentary – of using factual footage to illustrate argument – seemed to us to be as wrong-headed as the reliance of the feature industry on the theatre.

Did you feel your first feature film, *Saturday Night and Sunday Morning*, was a natural extension of your Free Cinema work?

Absolutely. *Saturday Night and Sunday Morning* is a sort of companion film to *We Are the Lambeth Boys*, an extension of it. There are certain things you simply can't do with documentary, like getting inside character. I had been a teacher in a secondary modern school in London for a few years, and was therefore very much in contact with the young people in the clubs and the schools. The three films, *Momma Don't Allow*, *We Are the Lambeth Boys* and *Saturday Night and Sunday Morning*, were underpinned by my schoolteaching experience.

Arthur Seaton is not just a figure of the times, but also an enduringly heroic figure because he will not knuckle under.

Yes, that's right, but there is a tension between Alan's [Sillitoe] book and my film. I think in Alan's book Arthur is more simply a hero, a spokesman – Alan's heart goes with him. The film has that element, but it also sees him as part of his landscape and tries to see him as a product of the way he has to make a living. In other words, it sees the victim side of his predicament. When I looked at it later, I saw that this is the difference between someone who has done it from within – that is to say, Alan – and somebody who's been a schoolteacher. But I don't say this apologetically. The ending, for instance, is only in the movie.

You mean when Shirley Ann Field says something like, 'You shouldn't throw stones,' and he says, 'There'll be a lot more thrown'?

The bit I liked best about that sequence is the way her high heels kept getting stuck in the muddy ground. I like the way she walks on those heels, determined but wobbly. The film doesn't really suggest that she and Arthur Seaton have much of a chance, but it wishes them well.

Was Albert Finney your first choice for Arthur?

Absolutely. Albert had a small part in *The Entertainer* [film], a tiny part, which came just before *Saturday Night and Sunday Morning*. I got credit for discovering a great star but everybody in the business knew that Albert and Peter O'Toole (who had already worked at Stratford or in the West End) were two great young actors coming up.

And Rachel Roberts, a great actress, but I can't believe she would have been a star ten years before.

Rachel was never really a star in the conventional sense; she was a leading lady in *our* movies, and that's about it. I suppose the actress that you would have to compare her with was Anna Magnani – she was *that* kind of figure. Except, of course, that the Italian cinema found work for Magnani for many years to come. The British cinema never knew how to use Rachel in later years.

How closely did you work with your director of photography. Freddie Francis?

He held my hand. He was experienced and I wasn't. He was very important. Freddie is one of those cameramen who, when he's not directing, doesn't *want* to direct. He really wants to know what you want and, if he can't give it to you, he'll say so, but he'll bend over backwards to try. Freddie's made half a dozen films with first-time directors; he has a very strong, generous, avuncular side which was tremendously helpful. Also he is absolutely *for* the movie. When we were doing that long fairground sequence in *Saturday Night and Sunday Morning*, we did it in two days – a lot of it on the run, like a newsreel. Freddie knew that if he didn't compromise with the lighting, we wouldn't get it; so he just winged it.

The fairground sequence contrasts with the plain style of the rest.

It's also the place where the story comes to a head, where, ironically, among the merry-go-rounds, reality catches up with Arthur.

Could you tell me briefly about the Woodfall set-up and its connection with Bryanston or British Lion?

Woodfall was Tony Richardson's production company. Bryanston was an association of financiers and film producers, among them Mick Balcon (Sir Michael Balcon) and Maxwell Setton. British Lion was the distribution company and Bryanston had a contract to deliver so many films to British Lion every year. Well, Bryanston hung out their shingle and said, 'Anybody who wants to, come and make films for us.' Tony Richardson (who *was* Woodfall really) answered their call. Tony went to them and got money for three films and they were very successful, so there was no reason why they shouldn't give him more. They were good people to work for because they were filmmakers; they gave you the money and told you to come back with the movie. And while the films were successful – and those films *did* make a lot of money – there was no reason to disturb it.

Later on things got a bit more difficult. They were financiers who had a distribution arrangement with British Lion. *Saturday Night . . .* was a very big success all over the world. In America, of course, we were only in the art houses. We were banned by the Legion of Decency, so it didn't go on to the big circuits.

What in particular did you aim at in your remake of *Night Must Fall*? Did you, in 1964, want a kind of psychological updating?

I don't know really what we thought. What happened was that Albert and I formed a company. Albert at that time had an Australian girlfriend, Zoë Caldwell, who said, 'Why don't you fellows make a film about Ned Kelly?' We asked David Storey to write a script and we went to Australia to look for locations. It took us about fourteen months to prepare it. But David Storey's script was very good, very dark. When we delivered it to Columbia, who had commissioned it, I remember Mike Frankovitch said, 'I've commissioned a Western and you're giving me *Macbeth*. I'm not making this. Goodbye.'

It so happened that MGM offered us a remake of the Emlyn Williams thriller, *Night Must Fall*, and we took it on. Ten weeks later we were on the floor. It was a film made on the rebound. About a week before we started shooting, I said to Albert, 'We could make a very good movie out of this subject, if only Danny didn't have to be a murderer.' It ended up rather uncomfortably between a matinée thriller and a character study.

Albert Finney was very striking and Mona Washbourne, a wonderful actress, was more interesting than Dame May Whitty in the old film version.

Mona was a *great* character actress: she had a way of playing middle-class women with irony but no condescension – her last scene is the best thing in the film. The film had good things in it, some scary moments.

Between these two you produced Lindsay's first feature film, *This Sporting Life*. What, as producer, was your involvement?

After *Saturday Night . . .* I was offered a lot of pictures. One of the projects I was offered was to adapt David Storey's novel, *This Sporting Life*, which I knew Lindsay was very keen to direct. I said to the money people, 'I'll produce it if Lindsay directs it.' The finished film is absolutely Lindsay's: I hope I gave him a sympathetic atmosphere to work in, but from any creative point of view it's Lindsay's film . . . and of course David Storey's.

Though those films all exhibit a new social realism, they're really very different in tone, aren't they?

Yes, completely different. *This Sporting Life* was shot in stylised black-and-white and its manner is heightened, Expressionistic. And the acting style owes nothing to regional naturalism at all, it is theatrical. It is perhaps for that reason that reactions to the film were so widely polarised. There are people who do not want to accept Richard Harris's bravura acting. He has the courage to do the big stuff and his high voltage can sometimes short-circuit the material he's given, but I thought he was very fine in *This Sporting Life*.

Did you ever came across this comment about *Morgan* from the American critic John Simon: 'It's the first underground movie made above ground'?

No, I haven't. But he wasn't the only one to say something of that kind. We were very lucky to get money for the film at all. It was a very strange period of British filmmaking then. The Bryanston people had gone out of business and British Lion had been sold to six producing units. One of these units was Tony Richardson's and mine, and we had an agreement that each group could make its own films. When we put *Morgan* on the table, the other five groups all said, 'Please don't! This is an experimental highbrow picture!' I thought it was a comedy – about serious things. And I hoped there were enough pratfalls for it to work with the popular audience. And it worked very well. There's a rather unhappy strand of continuity in it, where we used accelerated motion, which I regretted later. But I thought Vanessa [Redgrave] was wonderful and so was David [Warner]. And Irene Handl: she had that gift of being both a foot off the ground *and* real. And I think David Mercer wrote well for the cinema. He was quite uninterested in realistic story-telling; he jumped around recklessly between fantasy and reality; comment and description all jumbled; it was a time when anything seemed possible.

Did you see Morgan as a descendant of Jimmy Porter and Arthur Seaton?

I don't think so. It was sometimes bracketed with 'swinging London' and Dick Lester and all that. I don't see that at all, because I think *Morgan* has a certain substance; it's not pure *jeu d'esprit*, which is what the Beatles films and the swinging London thing were. *Morgan* was a one-off. It had a very curious history. The script was brought to my attention by David Storey, who was a friend of Mercer's. David Mercer had written a one-hour television play about a man in dialogue with his psychoanalyst. Out of these dialogues he kept jumping into the stories he recounted on the couch. I said to David Mercer, 'Let's do this, but let's drop the analyst altogether; let's just do this thing in the present tense.' And using some of the fantasies (or 'free associations' the character had presented to the analyst in the television script), we evolved a continuity.

Oscar Lewenstein, one of the Woodfall producers, had wanted to produce a film of three episodes: I was to do one, Lindsay was to do one, and Tony Richardson was to do a third. Mine turned out to be *Morgan*; when we delivered the script, it was really too long for a three-episode film. We decided it should be a film on its own, and we broke away and did it. The three-episode film was later made: Lindsay made *The White Bus*, Tony made *Red and Blue*, a dance film with Vanessa, and the third item was a film Peter Brook directed, with Zero Mostel travelling from Heathrow airport into London. It was a very highbrow little concoction, though I thought Lindsay's was very good.

Morgan isn't highbrow really; it's zany and odd, and almost surrealist sometimes.

Yes, and it's about something quite serious. It's about a god that failed. It was about a man who had all those Marxist images on his nursery walls, and the images were failing him. I'm Czech and I was disillusioned with Marxism early on. But a lot of the left-wing people objected to *Morgan* in England, because it was going over to 'the other side'.

You've been very sparing in the matter of feature films. Was this a matter of choice?

There's no real reason for it. I'm lazy. I don't find the process very enjoyable. I think it is very hard to make a film. And I have sometimes had to abandon projects because I felt I couldn't cast them. My films tend to be portrait films, that revolve around a central character. There is a sense of tension and ambiguity between the *persona* of the specific actor cast in the central role and the part he plays. This is often the subject of my films. So when I haven't been able to cast a central role ideally, I've sometimes abandoned the project.

Which is the case with *Isadora* ...

Australia was the one country in which it was well received. It was a pretty good disaster, *Isadora*. I loved making it ... but things went horribly wrong with the distribution over the editing. Let's talk about something else!

How did your first American film, *The Gambler*, come about?

My American agent sent me a script by an unknown writer called James Toback. It was a kind of documentary about gambling. I really liked the dialogue, but I said to the writer, 'Let's not make a documentary about gambling, let's dramatise it through the story of a passionate gambler,' and we invented a kind of 'Hero of our Time', a sort of Byronic loser, to put through this story. It ended up being a rather harsh vision. But Paramount were amazingly loyal about it.

I would have thought *The French Lieutenant's Woman* was a very difficult novel to adapt and I wondered how pleased you were with Harold Pinter's device.

There were half a dozen script attempts to adapt the novel for the cinema which never reached the screen. The book presents some difficult formal problems. On the purely narrative level it is a modern novel about Victorian characters. But Fowles keeps interposing other elements – discussions of Victorian and modern times; and speculations about the nature of fiction itself. He keeps taking time out from the narrative to wonder about the meaning of the story. When you examine this complicated scheme, you find that there are jumps in the narrative which are not explained. There is a huge leap about halfway through the book when the central character is suddenly transformed from the outcast existence·she had led in the country to a self-possessed and calmly functioning member of a sophisticated artist's family in London. There are a couple of other leaps of the same kind and it is simply impossible to tell the story in a straight linear way. You need another element which grasps the nettle for the audience and shares with it the idea that they are being presented with a fiction. The device we arrived at – the film within the film – solves that problem on a formal level. Whether it succeeds in making the two strands of continuity illuminate each other, isn't for me to judge.

Was it your intention – and Freddie Francis's work again – to have a quite different look about the Victorian from the modern scenes?

Yes. Completely different: the modern scenes are shot with a lot of 'bounced' light; the Victorian scenes are much more directionally lit, harder-edged, with the unambiguous outlines of Victorian painting.

Finally, what do you think of that very unkind remark of François Truffaut's about 'a certain incompatibility between the words "British" and "cinema" '?

Oh, he was just teasing. Actually, I seem to remember that he said it in connection with the idea that English culture was primarily a literary one. I think it would be a bit pointless – certainly a bit humourless – to mount a defence.

Michael Relph

b. 1915

Designer or art director: *Everything Happens To Me* (co-des), *Many Tanks, Mr Atkins* (co-des), *Mr Satan* (co-des) (1938), *They Drive by Night* (co-des) (1939), *The Bells Go Down* (1943), *Halfway House, They Came to a City, Champagne Charlie* (1944), *Dead of Night* (1945), *Nicholas Nickleby* (1946)

Producer or associate producer: *The Captive Heart* (& art dir) (1946), *Frieda* (1947), *Saraband for Dead Lovers* (& art dir) (1948), *Kind Hearts and Coronets, Train of Events* (1949), *The Blue Lamp, Cage of Gold* (1950), *Pool of London* (1951), *I Believe In You* (& co-sc), *The Gentle Gunman* (1952), *The Square Ring* (1953), *The Rainbow Jacket* (1954), *Out of The Clouds* (& co-sc) (1955), *The Ship that Died of Shame* (& co-sc) (1955), *Who Done It?* (1956), *The Smallest Show on Earth, Davy* (dir) (1957), *Rockets Galore* (dir), *Violent Playground* (1958), *Sapphire, Desert Mice* (co-pr) (1959), *The League of Gentlemen, Man in the Moon* (& co-sc) (1960), *The Secret Partner, Victim* (1961), *All Night Long* (& des), *Life for Ruth* (1962), *The Mind Benders, A Place to Go* (& co-sc), *Woman of Straw* (& co-sc) (1963), *Masquerade* (& co-sc) (1964), *The Assassination Bureau* (& co-sc) (1969), *The Man Who Haunted Himself* (& co-sc) (1970), *Scum* (co-exec pr) (1979), *An Unsuitable Job for a Woman* (co-exec pr) (1981), *Heavenly Pursuits* (1985), *The Torrents of Spring* (Production Consultant) (1988)

Michael Relph's career of more than fifty years as producer, director, screenwriter and art director has given him a very comprehensive grasp of British cinema. He began as an assistant art director at Gaumont-British and became a notable set designer and art director at Ealing on such handsome films as *Dead of Night*, *Nicholas Nickleby* and *Saraband for Dead Lovers*. The central and most enduring element of his career was his long partnership with the director Basil Dearden, in which their capacities fruitfully complemented each other. Relph has an unpretentious approach to filmmaking: he and Dearden, he says, loved making films and weren't prepared to wait around for the ideal project to turn up. Nevertheless, they made a large number of impressive films – often films which contrived to *say* something within their genre frameworks, including such titles as *The Blue Lamp*, *The Ship that Died of Shame*, *Sapphire*, *Victim* and *The League of Gentlemen*. Those five films reflect a good deal of post-war British life and attitudes, and they are all very accomplished entertainments.

Interview date: October 1989

Yours is one of the longest and most varied careers in British cinema. Were you always wanting to direct or produce, and moving consciously towards this?

No, not until I went to Ealing as art director. I had actually started as an apprentice with Michael Balcon at Gaumont-British Studios and he was a friend of my family, so there was a spot of nepotism involved. After a brief episode as art director at Warner Brothers, I was very pleased to end up at Ealing, because Balcon had a reputation for promoting people from the ranks, as it were, and this encouraged me towards producing. We were turned into director–producer teams and, though Mick had the final word on everything, the origination and development of projects was up to those teams. The directors got their credits whereas the producers didn't because of the conflict with Balcon's own credit. Eventually, although our function didn't change in any way – I suppose Mick just got a little older and more secure – he allowed the credits to read 'A Michael Balcon Production' (full screen), 'Produced by Michael Relph' (or whoever – also full screen).

In the mid '40s you were set designer and art director on three Ealing films directed by Alberto Cavalcanti – *Champagne Charlie*, *Dead of Night* and *Nicholas Nickleby*. What are your recollections of that period, and of Cavalcanti?

Balcon was searching for some more realistic roots to put down because of the war situation. He brought Cavalcanti and Harry Watt over from the Crown Film Unit and Cavalcanti, particularly, became the sort of *éminence grise* of the studio and had tremendous influence with Balcon. Cavalcanti was very anxious, first of all, to get more documentary realism into our filmmaking, and he also played power politics with everybody. My ultimate partner, Basil Dearden, had been there before Balcon's time and I had worked (as art director) with Basil, who was directing a film called *Halfway House*, which Cavalcanti produced, and he thought I was a good influence on Basil, that I was able to direct his amazing technical skills into the right channels. So

Cavalcanti suggested to Balcon that he should team Basil and myself, and I think it was a very good arrangement. Basil was a very easy person to work with and I was able to convey any creative ideas I had through him. We complemented each other, I think, and also we loved making films. I made all my Ealing films with him, except for *Kind Hearts and Coronets*, directed by Robert Hamer. Some people at Ealing were inclined to make a film every three years or so, waiting for the perfect subject for their reputations. But we had a big staff working there and we had to keep the studio going. Basil and I were always stepping in with some subject or other. It mightn't have been the one subject in the world we really wanted to make, but it kept the studio working.

How did you divide the co-producing activities?

It was always a problem really because the system was a bit unfair as far as I was concerned. Being an equal partner with Basil in all our projects, I wasn't getting the same sort of credit, so he very generously agreed to share. We took various forms of credit, rather as Powell and Pressburger did. We might, for instance, take a joint credit as 'Produced, directed and designed by . . .' even though, of course, I did all the designing and he did all the directing but, because we were jointly responsible for the production, it conveyed more of the partnership.

You are sometimes credited as co-director on *The Gentle Gunman*, *The Square Ring*, *Out of the Clouds* and *The Ship that Died of Shame*, and for some of these films you also co-produced and co-wrote.

It was all part of the attempt to get an expression for the very close creative partnership we had, which wasn't really reflected by pigeonholing our activities. It was generous of Dearden, because the director's credit is sacrosanct anyway, but I think the joint credits really reflected the fact that we had a joint creative responsibility for the films. When we were doing a film, we would usually both be on the studio floor together. I use the simile that the director is like a tactical commander and the producer is more of a strategic commander. In other words, the producer stands a little further back from it, thereby keeping a better perspective.

I didn't go down on to the floor and intervene between director and actors, but I spent a good deal of time there, albeit in a behind-the-scenes, low-key position. If I saw something in the way a scene was being mapped out that I thought was wrong or to which I thought I could contribute, I would speak to Basil on the quiet and he would either agree or not, as the case may be. But I was very careful not to intervene publicly, so that he had total control of the studio floor, which is very important for a director. Basil agreed to my directing occasionally – *Davy*, *Rockets Galore* – but it always boiled down to my getting the subjects on which he wasn't particularly keen. And I am not really temperamentally cut out to be a director. A director has to have a tremendous amount of patience and the ability to take detailed pains, and I find it very difficult to do that. I get impatient, start to cut corners, and I am much more at home being a producer.

Would you say there are continuing themes and interests running through the films you either directed or produced?

There were certain things, in the sense that we felt it wasn't worthwhile unless the film had something to say other than just tell an entertaining story. So we were always looking for themes that had some social significance, and a lot of our films have that element. It was a conscious policy of tackling important social issues in the framework of an entertainment film. If you get too serious about it, it limits your audience, so we tried to wrap it up in an entertaining form, as an exciting thriller or whatever. *Sapphire*, for instance, was a taut thriller about something very topical: it looks dated now because of the changes in race relations since then, but it was a good film at the time. It was very successful in America. We had a writer team of Janet Green and John McCormack, who wrote both *Sapphire* and *Victim*; she was a very clever thriller writer and a playwright and novelist. We had a very close partnership with them and they turned out some good scripts for us.

I Believe in You, a film we made at Ealing, was much more episodic. It was essentially a comedy, written by Sewell Stokes, a 'gent' whose spare-time hobby was working as a probation officer, and the story was autobiographical. The nub of the comedy arose out of the fact that the central character was a

bit of a fish out of water, but it was also a very moving little film. I really enjoyed it, although it didn't have a very high voltage. My father [George Relph] played in it, as the ageing probation officer, with Cecil Parker and Celia Johnson. It was also Joan Collins's first film.

Did you see *The Ship that Died of Shame* as a critique of British post-war society as well as a thriller?

Yes, we did. The ship, in a sense, represented what people had done with the country they had inherited after the war. It was a sort of allegory, and it's probably better than one thought at the time. It came from a short story by Nicholas Monserrat and we were immediately attracted to it. The film emerged during a newspaper strike and so we didn't see any proper reviews of it – that was the only way we could ever tell whether our films were any good, because we never saw any returns.

Was there a good creative atmosphere at Ealing in the '40s?

Oh, it was marvellous because we didn't have to think about what I consider the more boring aspects of production such as distribution and financing. One had to be practical and keep to budgets and schedules, but one didn't have to go into the marketplace and raise the money, so in a way it was almost like working for the BBC. We really did sit around discussing projects, usually in the pub of an evening; that was the way most of the script conferences went on.

I am very interested in your film, *Saraband for Dead Lovers*, which I have not been able to see.

It was a magnificent-looking film, but it wasn't a success at the time. We were trying to get away from the Gainsborough-type romantic costume picture, which was totally unreal, and to do a serious historical epic. I think the public probably wasn't ready for it and also it ended up being a bit heavy. It certainly had a very good cast – Stewart Granger, Joan Greenwood, Flora Robson and Françoise Rosay. I was very pleased to get an Oscar nomination for the set design – there were only two of us nominated: Cedric Gibbons of MGM and myself, and unfortunately he won! It was Ealing's first colour film, shot on three-strip Technicolor, and was very expensive for those days.

When did you finish at Ealing?

More or less when Ealing finished; the studio had been sold and we moved over to the MGM studio at Elstree, where we were never very happy. I think the whole seam of Ealing films had rather run out by that time. I directed one film called *Davy*, with Harry Secombe, which wasn't very good. It was written by Bill Rose, who had written some of the big Ealing films such as *The Ladykillers*, but *Davy* wasn't one of his best. He had another subject, on which we had always been very keen, and which for some reason Balcon wouldn't do. That was *The Smallest Show on Earth*, about a couple inheriting a run-down cinema. I thought it would make an enchanting film, so, given that we could see the end of Ealing coming, we took the umbrella, as it were, of doing it for Frank Launder and Sidney Gilliat's company.

Did you in 1958 set up your own company to make *Rockets Galore*?

No, that was for Rank. We made *The Smallest Show on Earth* and were then given a contract with Rank at Pinewood and we made *Violent Playground* and then *Rockets Galore*, which wasn't a great success. It was rather a silly thing to do – to make a sequel to *Whisky Galore!* We were with Rank for quite a long time and made some successful films such as *Sapphire*, and then we formed a company with Dickie Attenborough, Bryan Forbes and Jack Hawkins – Allied Filmmakers – which was a sort of mock distribution company, funded by Rank. It was quite a nice arrangement in fact, but it all fell apart because everyone wanted to go their own ways. However, we made some very successful films for it, such as *Victim* and the first one, *The League of Gentlemen*.

Rank did the actual physical work of distribution but Allied had a small override on the commission. It was the only way anyone could make any money out of films. Everybody was trying to be independent and have the necessary freedom, and one way of channelling money into production (which Rank and other distribution companies tried) was this strategy of forming groups of independent producers. If a film was financed by Rank, then we used Rank studios, distribution, labs and so on – it was, to all intents and purposes, a Rank picture and probably made at Pinewood, where we worked for about fifteen years. When we worked for British Lion we shot at Shepperton, and when we made *The Mind Benders* for Anglo-Amalgamated we had to work at Elstree. In other words, the people who put up the money dictated which studios you used.

***Victim* was surely a very courageous film to make in 1961.**

I was rather surprised that Dirk [Bogarde] agreed to do it. He was famous as a matinée idol and one didn't think he would take the risk of playing a part which suggested homosexuality. I think he was very courageous to do it and so was Rank to allow us to make it at that time, because Dirk was one of their biggest assets. It was a tremendous challenge to any actor but in fact it did Dirk's career a lot of good; it was a very wise step for him but at that time it could very well not have been. And it was good for us too.

How did you view the New Wave of social-realist filmmaking that came in with *Room at the Top* at the end of the '50s?

We welcomed it tremendously because that was what we had been trying to do, although by that time we were a bit old-fashioned, really. We made one film in that sort of mould which came at the end of the cycle and it was very unsuccessful. It was called *A Place To Go*, with Rita Tushingham and Mike Sarne. Looking at it now, it doesn't look so different from all those other 'kitchen sink' type films but it came too late. Those films made everyone feel that filmmakers were really dealing with life as it was.

The '40s and '50s seem to me to constitute a boom period in British cinema history. Would you agree?

I do think so. It was certainly the best time to be working in the industry. It produced much more benign working conditions, to my mind. But, of course, that coincided with the big mass audiences, which then fell away, and it has become constantly more of a struggle. The real difficulty here is that we are now quite unprotected by any sort of legislation and we just have to compete, in a totally unequal struggle, with the American product. They make films costing $30 million or $40 million and we have to compete with little films costing maybe $3 million. We can't do that and I think it is making our films very parochial, the fact that we have to make do with shoestring budgets. Certainly the British market is no longer strong enough to support films which don't penetrate the American market, so it is the crucial factor in every case.

What is your attitude to the way that the Government and its instrumentalities have, over the decades, intervened in the British film industry?

Well, they have always tried to redress the imbalance between us and the American industry, and I think Harold Wilson's measures went a long way towards helping the industry to survive. I mean the National Film Finance Corporation and the Eady levy. But his Government did want to see the survival of the industry. Now, whether it is because they don't like the sort of subjects that are being made, or whether it is simply an ideological refusal to interfere in the market, I don't know. The Conservative Party appears to have no interest in films at all or, if there is any interest, I think it is an antagonistic one.

Can you tell me about the Eady levy, introduced in 1950, and how it helped British producers?

The Eady levy was a very clever scheme to try to redress the balance between British and American films in the cinemas, and the Americans were really very generous in agreeing to go along with it. What would happen was that they would skim off a small percentage from the takings of all films – mostly American; that percentage would go straight into the Eady fund and would then be divided – monthly or quarterly – between all the British films then on release. It was quite a complicated formula, the amount of distribution depending on how well the films had performed, so there was a premium on box-office success. I thought it a very good device to encourage the making of popular films. If you had a very successful British film you could make quite a lot of money from the Eady fund. The exhibitors, however, managed to convince this Government that this was unfair on them, that they were in desperate straits and so on. In fact it hasn't proved to be true at all, in that the exhibitors have now gone from strength to strength.

How would you respond to criticisms that British cinema has been too literary, too class-bound and too tied to the theatre?

I think they are perfectly true. Of course, the country is class-bound and, insofar as British film reflects life in this country, then class is sure to come into it as an element. Ealing films were very middle-class, really; it was a middle-class business at that time.

As for being too literary, obviously we have a great literary tradition which seeks some sort of expression. Another thing is that to be utterly physical on the scale of *Indiana Jones* requires an enormous amount of money. So, if you are going to rely on physical excitement you are making very expensive films. Perhaps this has forced British filmmakers back into the literary mould, trying to find interesting subjects which don't require enormous costs.

I think that, while British acting has benefited from the contact with the theatre, it definitely worked against the cinema in the '30s and '40s. The upper- or middle-class stage acting then looked ridiculous on film, when you consider the realism that people like Cagney were bringing to the cinema at that time. My father was a distinguished stage actor and he always said that British stage acting was an absolute killer as far as film was concerned. British stage acting in the '30s and '40s was almost totally middle-class and it was just not transferable to the screen. And it was, I think, a great disadvantage that the theatre and the film industry were situated in such close proximity to each other. It was good for actors but a great obstacle to the film industry; it meant that we were using people from a very narrow spectrum. All those new regional people who came in with the 'kitchen sink' era were revolutionary, a real shot in the arm.

Sir Ralph Richardson

1902–1983

Actor: *The Ghoul, Friday the Thirteenth* (1933), *Java Head, The Return of Bulldog Drummond, The King of Paris* (1934), *Bulldog Jack* (1935), *Things to Come* (1936), *The Man Who Could Work Miracles, Thunder in the City* (1937), *South Riding, The Divorce of Lady X, The Citadel* (1938), *Q Planes,*

The Four Feathers, The Lion Has Wings (1939), Health for the Nation (short), On the Night of the Fire (1940), The Day Will Dawn (1942), The Silver Fleet (1943), The Volunteer (short) (1944), School for Secrets (1946), Anna Karenina, The Fallen Idol (1948), The Heiress (1949), Outcast of the Islands (1951), Home at Seven (& dir), The Sound Barrier, The Holly and the Ivy (1952), Richard III (1955), Smiley, The Passionate Stranger (1956), Our Man on Havana (1959), Oscar Wilde, Exodus (1960), The 300 Spartans, Long Day's Journey Into Night (1962), Woman of Straw (1964), Dr Zhivago (1965), The Wrong Box, Chimes at Midnight (voice only), Khartoum (1966), The Midas Run, The Bed-Sitting Room, Oh! What a Lovely War, The Looking-Glass War, Battle of Britain, David Copperfield (1969), Eagle in a Cage, Who Slew Auntie Roo? (1971), Tales from the Crypt, Lady Caroline Lamb, Alice's Adventures in Wonderland (1972), A Doll's House, O Lucky Man!, Frankenstein: The True Story (1973), Rollerball (1975), Time Bandits (1980), Dragonslayer (1981), Invitation to a Wedding, Greystoke (1984)

'You have to swing on a chandelier and bellow to make an entrance in the theatre. But the film set is so intimate that you can speak in your natural voice, and make an entrance merely by raising your eyebrows,'[1] said the newly knighted Richardson in 1947. He did, indeed, in his own disarmingly eccentric way, create a gallery of subtly delineated film portraits, claiming, two decades later: 'I think films are a marvellous medium, and are to the stage what engravings are to painting . . . the cinema teaches you the details of craftsmanship.'[2] One sees this sort of detail at work in one of his less notable films, The Holly and the Ivy, where he invests an unconsciously selfish country vicar with a dozen little touches that establish habits of thought and behaviour, as in the way he automatically allows – expects – his daughter to help him on with coat and muffler.

His whole career, like those of so many of his colleagues, is dominated by the stage: 'I don't honestly think I should be very happy if I devoted myself entirely to films,' he said; and, like theirs, his film career looks at once prolific and random. For two decades he could say, 'My film career had always been in the hands of Korda . . . I had always appeared in Korda films. I had no other contacts in the film business; and when he died I was out of the swim.'[3] In 1936, he scored a notable success for Korda with Things to Come as the amoral 'Boss', explaining: 'I start with a rough sketch, and then keep on doing different ones until I'm satisfied that I have created a suitable character . . . I tried all sorts of things. It was like a charade. The blustering fellow you saw in the pictures resulted, and I made my final sketch on those lines.'[4] He preferred his performance as a 'peppery old colonel' (he was thirty-five) in The Man Who Could Work Miracles ('I think my character work in this film is definitely promising'[5]). He is finely restrained and passionate as the troubled Carne in South Riding, but suggests the wrong social class in On the Night of the Fire, though he 'considered it my most exciting screen role to date' and felt that 'Every day, working with people like [cameraman] Gunther Krampf and [director] Brian Desmond Hurst, I seem to learn something new.'[6]

There are three great roles in the late '40s: he is a wonderfully subtle, knuckle-cracking Karenin in Anna Karenina, the best thing in a misconceived film; he mines the butler's character in The Fallen Idol for pathos, dignity and humour; and is a chilling patriarchal figure in The Heiress, in Hollywood. After Korda died in 1956, Richardson's career drifts into cameo roles, that graveyard of the English acting knights, occasionally making an impression powerful enough, as in Long Day's Journey Into Night or as the hero's grandfather in Greystoke, to make us wish he'd taken films more seriously. Perhaps he needed another Korda, 'original and helpful to one's problems'.[7] 'I don't mind how small the part is so long as it is interesting,'[8] he said, and some of the cameos were so – for example, Sir Edward Carson in Oscar Wilde or George III in Lady Caroline Lamb. But he was a great original, mysterious and un-nailable, and one wanted him to do on the screen the sort of full-length roles he did on the stage.

1 Brenda Cross, 'Sir Ralph Richardson', Picturegoer, 18 January 1947, p 6
2 Alan A Coulson, 'Ralph Richardson', Films in Review, October 1969, p 457
3 Coulson, p 467
4 John K Newnham, 'He's different every time', Film Weekly, 13 February 1937, p 10
5 Horace Richards, '"The Boss" speaks', Film Weekly, 13 June 1936, p 28
6 Film Weekly, 22 July 1939, p 13
7 Garry O'Connor, Ralph Richardson: An Actor's Life, Limelight Editions, New York, 1985, p 82
8 Coulson, p 467

Tony Richardson

1928–1994

Director: *Momma Don't Allow* (doc, co-dir) (1955), *Look Back in Anger* (1959), *The Entertainer* (1960), *Sanctuary, A Taste of Honey* (pr, co-sc) (1961), *The Loneliness of the Long Distance Runner* (pr) (1962), *Tom Jones* (pr) (1963), *The Loved One, Mademoiselle* (1965), *The Sailor from Gibraltar* (co-sc), *Red and Blue, The Charge of the Light Brigade* (1968), *Laughter in the Dark, Hamlet* (1969), *Ned Kelly* (co-sc) (1970), *A Delicate Balance, Dead Cert* (1973), *Joseph Andrews* (co-sc) (1977), *Death In Canaan* (1978), *The Border* (1982), *Hotel New Hampshire* (sc) (1984), *Turning a Blind Eye* (doc) (1985), *Blue Sky* (1990)

'I should certainly like British films to be different from what many have been in the past. ... It is absolutely vital to get into British films the same sort of impact and sense of life that, what you can loosely call the Angry Young Man cult, has had in the theatre and literary worlds. It is a desperate need.'[1] Tony Richardson, in 1959, seems here to be speaking for an important generation of British filmmakers, including Karel Reisz, Lindsay Anderson and John Schlesinger. All progressed to feature films via critically regarded documentaries; all got some of that 'angry young' feeling, born in other media, into the cinema; and all, to varying degrees, answered 'a desperate need'.

Richardson's first features were adaptations of two stage successes, *Look Back in Anger* and *The Entertainer*, both written by John Osborne, with whom Richardson formed the influential Woodfall Films company. Richardson found that *The Entertainer* was much more difficult to translate to the screen than *Look Back* ... 'Film is a totally realistic medium and Archie Rice [protagonist of *The Entertainer*] can only be a failed vaudevillian . . .'[2] He cannot, Richardson perceptively suggests, be successfully created by a director who has 'gone all out for metaphor' at the expense of the reality. It is at least arguable that neither of these films, groundbreaking though they were at the time, stands up as well today as the three British adaptations which followed: *A Taste of Honey*, *The Loneliness of the Long Distance Runner* and *Tom Jones*.

All three are characterised by striking location work (brilliantly captured by cameraman Walter Lassally), and Richardson expressed a preference for the kind of realism he felt could only be obtained in this way. 'It was my decision to do *A Taste of Honey* independent of a studio because I think you get an authenticity that you can never get in a studio ... I wanted to force a much rougher style on the film, and to force myself to shoot in, I hope, a freer way.'[3] Later, he added, '. . . the reason I like working on location is that you go off like gypsies, a band of travellers, focusing all your efforts and indeed all your life on making that film, for the period of shooting.'[4] One stresses this now because, along with the introduction of fresh new acting faces (Rita Tushingham in *Honey*, Tom Courtenay in *Loneliness*), these films are now memorable for the evocation of aspects of British life largely neglected by mainstream British filmmaking. *Tom Jones* was the great commercial success of his career: 'The sixties were starting to swing and *Tom Jones* became part of the "revolution". The movie went on to success after success beyond our financial dreams.'[5] Hollywood beckoned again, though he claimed, after his unhappy experiences while filming *Sanctuary* there, that 'I'm thrilled I went there because I know that I never want to make a film in Hollywood again.'[6] For the rest of his career he worked often in America, without major success, though the American-made *A Delicate Balance* is an intelligent, beautifully acted adaptation of Edward Albee's play. Back in England, he made the controversial *The Charge of the Light Brigade* ('We wanted to do something different, to concentrate on the charge itself . . . It was to be a film about the ironies of war'[7]); a brilliant screen version of his Roundhouse theatre production of *Hamlet*, 'using only close-ups and letting the performances and the words carry the whole thing.'[8]; the mysteriously unseen *Dead Cert*, based on a Dick Francis novel; and the undervalued return to Henry Fielding with *Joseph Andrews*.

In a 1955 essay he differentiated between 'the creators' who transform their material 'into an artistic whole' and 'the interpreters who have translated their material professionally into cinematic terms but have not transformed it.'[9] In his very uneven career, Richardson was, at less than his best, an indifferent 'interpreter'; at his best, he deserved the label of 'creator'.

1 'The Man Behind an Angry-Young-Man', *Films and Filming*, February 1959, Vol 5, No 5, p 9
2 *Long Distance Runner: A Memoir*, Faber and Faber, London, 1993, p 108
3 'The Two Worlds of Cinema', *Films and Filming*, June 1961, Vol 7, No 9, p 41
4 'Within the Cocoon: an interview with Gordon Gow', *Films and Filming*, June 1977, Vol 23, No 9, p 14
5 *Long Distance Runner*, p 175
6 'The Two Worlds of Cinema', p 7
7 *Long Distance Runner*, p 193
8 'Within the Cocoon', p 16
9 'The Metteur en Scène', *Sight and Sound*, Oct/Dec 1954, p 62

Nicolas Roeg

b. 1928

Director of photography: *Information Received* (1961), *Doctor Crippen* (1962), *The Caretaker, Nothing but the Best, The Masque of the Red Death, Just For You* (1963), *The System, Every Day's a Holiday* (1964), *Victim Five* (1965), *Fahrenheit 451, A Funny Thing Happened on the Way to the Forum* (1966), *Far from the Madding Crowd, Petulia* (1967)

Director: *Performance* (co-dir) (1970), *Walkabout, *Glastonbury Fayre* (1971), *Don't Look Now* (1973), *The Man Who Fell To Earth* (1976), *Bad Timing* (1980), *Eureka* (1982), *Insignificance* (1985), *Castaway, Aria* (dir one segment) (1987), *Track 29* (1988), *The Witches* (1990), *Cold Heaven* (1992), *Hotel Paradise* (1995), *Two Deaths* (1996)
* Documentary.

It may not seem that Nicolas Roeg and Peter Greenaway have much in common, but they share at least two characteristics: both are clearly distrustful of linear narrative structures; and both have contrived to go on working in spite of their apparent disregard for the dictates of popular filmmaking. Roeg began conventionally enough – how else? – in British cinema of the

'50s, mostly as camera operator, sometimes as co-writer. Then, in the '60s, he was director of photography on some very high-profile films for 'hot' directors (John Schlesinger, Richard Lester, Clive Donner), before finally taking his chance as director. Many of his films, from the puzzling, absorbing *Performance* on, have explored questions of identity, life patterns and choices, and the intricacies of relationship. He is an intellectual director who is also able to move and disturb his audiences.

Interview date: July 1994

In the forty years since you began your career in films, have you seen a major decline in the feasibility of a British cinema?

There is no British cinema in terms of that phrase. Americans speak of 'the film business' and American studios are run as businesses – big businesses. Their subsidiary companies make tapes and machines and so on. But there is no film business in Britain in that sense. The idea of having a British film business would be wonderful, but the 'film business' has never caught the imagination here. Since the demise of Rank and the studio system, they are all independent filmmakers. You don't have a 'business' unless *business* is involved; that is the cold fact of the matter.

Your first screen credit was as Second Assistant Director in the MGM-British film, *The Miniver Story* [a 1950 sequel to *Mrs Miniver*]. How did this come about?

I was Second Assistant Cameraman, actually. I'd been in the cutting room before that and I wanted to get into studio work. MGM had a studio over here in those days (at Boreham Wood) and I answered an advertisement for a job there. (In those days most people went into cinema because they lived near the studio – it was their 'local factory', as it were.) I was interviewed by Freddie Young and started in the loading room.

Before you began directing you held many positions, sometimes as camera operator, sometimes director of photography, sometimes second-unit director and sometimes even co-author of the screenplay.

The structure of things has changed so much with the coming of television. I wanted to work in films because I enjoyed watching them, although I didn't come from a film background and in fact knew nothing about them. I didn't have what is popularly known as a 'driving ambition' to get on, I just enjoyed being there. So my diverse jobs included

the cutting room, translating French films into English, the post-sync department, which was interesting – I suppose my apprenticeship was rather like going to a film school today, except that we got more tea and more hands-on experience, more opportunity to see people making films for their living. I was taken with the industry and in many ways that creates less fear in people to whom you offer thoughts and ideas.

You were director of photography on several distinguished and diverse films, including Clive Donner's *Nothing but the Best*, Richard Lester's *A Funny Thing Happened . . .* and *Petulia*, and John Schlesinger's *Far from the Madding Crowd*. How different did you find the demands made on you by different directors, in this role?

They all had their different qualities but most of all they were not only my directors, they were also friends. They weren't at their peak at the time – coming up to it – and they all had their different qualities. It was easy for me as the cameraman because I enjoyed their friendship and I wanted to do as well as I could for their films. I wasn't only thinking of my life as a cameraman because a lot of that came later, in commercials with dazzling photography and pyrotechnics, which are not necessarily the best thing for a movie. I remember when I was a young camera assistant I worked with an old American cameraman called Joe Ruttenberg, who said to me, 'Never forget you're dealing with a movie, not trying to get your photograph in the Royal Society of Photography.' That was a wonderful tip and I guess that's what got me totally involved in trying to get what the director wanted.

Those directors all had great taste. I suppose Richard Lester was the one with the most knowledge but, even then, until you've actually done the job, that knowledge is always semi-superficial: it goes on taste more than on how to express it. That is why being friends with those directors was helpful to me, giving me terms of reference we could talk about.

Your first film as director is *Performance*, which still seems to me a very unsettling film. How did this project come your way? How did the co-director credit shared with Donald Cammell work in practice?

It was good timing, a coming together of events. I'd known Donald some years before: he was a painter and writer and he became a rather fashionable man-about-town in terms of his friends, mixing with people in the emerging rock scene. He and Mick Jagger became friendly. Donald had already written a film for James Coburn, called *Duffy*, and he was a fine screenwriter. Anyway, we were friendly – a most unlikely combination. He and Sandy Lieberson, the producer, raised the money on a treatment that Donald had written on an idea for a film about a rock star. He picked up our old friendship again and it became a unique partnership, fifty-fifty involvement all the way. In private we would push and tease each other to extremes in order to make the project work. It was never finished in the proper way, as a script.

Warner Brothers were very excited about the idea of a film with Mick Jagger (I think they thought they were getting some sort of *Summer Holiday*!) and it came as a great shock to their system. In any case, the film developed day by day, in a way which could never happen today except perhaps on a film with a very small budget. It was a risky business with a major studio. Donald and I became totally absorbed with the film and it is difficult to say where the divisions came between us. The question has been asked for years: 'How did it happen, how did it come about?' and sometimes you can't quite put your finger on the exact thing, especially with something so amorphous as that was. We didn't have any jealousy of each other; for that brief period in time we had no other agenda except the film, both of us supporting its idea and its thoughts.

It was a role very different from anything James Fox had done before. Did you feel he and Jagger complemented each other in an interesting way?

Yes, that also developed on the set as things were progressing during the shooting. James's father sent a message by chauffeur while we were in the middle of a scene; I never saw the letter but James intimated that his father didn't want him to go on with it, had heard terrible things about it. But James was also involved by that time. I don't know whether we were a happy band but we were certainly a band – not even in it for gain, just for the film.

There was a clash of life-styles between the gangster and the rock star, but there is a different kind of life-style clash in *Walkabout*, your next film. Is this a theme that particularly interests you, of people being plunged into unusual settings?

I think that what people think of as a usual setting is always a fragile idea. We are constantly surprised at what life is. We see breakdowns in society and think it will all stabilise itself again eventually – from Bosnia to Rwanda to Haiti. What comes first, identity or society? Obviously identity comes first, so when an established society breaks down we say things like, 'It wasn't like that in our day.' I think I always somehow, subconsciously, sense that nothing is what it seems.

***Walkabout* was originally a children's book and yet your film is very much not a children's film. What first drew you to the story?**

I liked the setting; I liked the idea of being lost – of being lost in life. I have always felt that the plot is just the shell of a life that is inhabited by the players, and what is there is the story. The plot is inhabited by people; I never believed in the transference of a book or story from one medium to another, never felt it was important to be so faithful to the actual written description of what is happening. I was caught by the idea of two children lost in a desert. Children are lost people anyway, trying to search for themselves; they are trying to grow up and become people. Adults generally put responsibilities of behaviour on them that they don't even understand and they feel they are lost and alone because they don't have enough information yet.

I found the ending very moving, the tremendous sense of loss the young girl sustains. Is that what you meant by the washed-out look of the final sequence back in Sydney?

Exactly that. She has been trying all her life to get away and she finds herself back in the same place that her parents were.

Your son played the part of the little boy, didn't he?

Yes, he did. He was only six and I don't think he

knew it was a movie. It became life for him. We were travelling in the desert, putting up tents and taking advantage of seizing the moment and incorporating it in the film. When we first arrived, the script was very short, only about forty pages, and David Jennings (the production manager) thought it was a documentary. It was a clean, bare, naked script. Edward Bond was a fine playwright and, when I approached him to do a script for me, he said he was interested in writing a play about 'a journey – just that, a journey. Our first draft was only about eighteen pages long but it was perfect, because I don't like a lot of descriptive writing in a script. That is like setting the scene before it has happened.

What I think of as your mosaic approach to narrative seems to get underway with *Don't Look Now*: do you think of this as an accurate description? Does it give a truer sense of human experience than a linear narrative?

The cinema is a curiously conservative medium. You refer to a mosaic form of narrative: in its early days the cinema was searching for a visual drama and very early films are quite loose in their use of narrative. In literature, you drift into someone's mind in one chapter, then you drift somewhere else, and that is quite acceptable. But in film, even today, anything away from the 'mid-shot, long-shot, close-up', any breaking of that grammatical canon is thought of as extraordinary. It is still so conservative because, after all, there is a great deal of money involved. I am answering your question but my mind might be ahead of it on to something else. What better way is there than film to show that? Scientifically nothing is linear, so why should it be in artistic terms?

On a more specific level, were you happy with the famous and, for its time, rather daring love scene in that film, between Christie and Sutherland?

I didn't consciously set out to make it that way. It came out of the fact that their performances were so wonderful. I gradually realised as we were shooting that, in reality, they were a young married couple with children and that in every scene they were rowing or something, and they were two rather grumpy people. But in their private time they would have moments of intimacy. They are dressing to go out and she is lying on the bed looking at a magazine. 'Look at this,' she says to him. He flops on the bed beside her and looks at the magazine,

stroking her back as he does so. By that you know they are a married couple and they are in love. Sexual intimacy is part of love and marriage, closeness and oneness, and it was very innocently shot. The scene stemmed from their performances and because the moment was right. I pondered about putting the scene in or leaving it out, but whenever I ran the film without that scene there was obviously something it didn't have. Once you knew that they were in love, it had a different dimension. It is sexy but it is not prurient.

Your next film, *The Man Who Fell To Earth*, recalls *Performance* in having a stranger entering an alien environment, and using a singing star of the time. Do you think you get special value out of using such cult figures as Jagger and David Bowie as points of narrative focus?

As far as *Performance* goes, who better to play a rock'n'roller than a rock'n'roller? I had first thought of using someone else as the alien, Michael Crichton, with whom I was quite friendly. He is unusual, not only in that he is nearly seven feet tall; he is also an extraordinarily clever haematologist as well as being a writer and a filmmaker. Then I saw a documentary called *Cracked Actor* and I liked the idea of David Bowie, who changed his performance *persona* with every concert. He was androgynous, almost role-playing, and he didn't stick to one set musical form. That attracted me in itself as being an alien form of behaviour. We talked about it in New York and he liked the idea as well. I could see no one else in the part.

I gather there were serious distribution problems with *Eureka*.

Yes, there were. It came at the wrong time. You remember the old story from the Greeks about the man who was given everything he desired and became lost in hope. The film came at the beginning of the '80s, the time of Thatcher and Reagan, and the idea of material things being completely valueless, a plot where a man has all the material things he could possibly need and has an empty soul, came at the wrong time. That was not the sort of message that was currently happening in people's minds. Also, the head of MGM had given the go-ahead for it but was ousted while we were shooting, so the film was transfered to United Artists and the heart, the enthusiasm, went out of it.

For me, *Bad Timing* is the most moving of all of your films. How do you rate it?

It was just the *right* timing for me to make it. I

think it was Verlaine who said, 'I write stories and then let them happen to me,' which I think is wonderful. Yale [Udoff, screenwriter] and I worked very hard on it and we knew what we were going to do in terms of who the people were. But you can't write every shot – that happens with the release script, when the film is put on to Moviola and the continuity girl writes down every shot. The script is only one part of a film. I shoot a lot of stuff. With *Bad Timing*, I got back from Vienna and found that the set had been dressed. I love set dressing because to me it is part of the person. So I went out and bought books and things, to be part of the life of Helena, and re-dressed the set.

The police investigator, played by Harvey Keitel, is almost like a psychoanalyst, in the way that he strips away layers of confusion and deceit trying to get to the truth.

Well, he is, yes. The truth – what is that? Something you tell to the police? Perhaps. Originally the name of the character was Schwab or something. I went to dinner with an Austrian painter called Roman Scheidel and his gallery owner, whose name was Netusil. Roman, having read the script, said to me that the police character should be called Netusil. He said, 'It is an odd Bohemian name, very difficult to translate. It means a man who knows everything about something – except one little thing. It is like Monsieur Netusil here – he knows everything about painting except one little thing – and I know that!' I decided I must use that name.

I am interested in a general way in how much direction you give to actors.

It varies a lot. I am not of the theatre and I couldn't possibly direct technique, but I like to encourage actors to understand my reasons for wanting them to play the character in the first place. Secondly, I want to excite their desire to be the person I see that character as. Not through technique, because I'm wary of technique – I couldn't possibly manipulate it and I'm frightened of it when I see it, because it sometimes stands out very clearly and brings a false note for me. I tell the actors stories about the persons they are playing. Then I like to feel that they gradually become that person.

Did having star names like Gary Busey, Theresa Russell and Tony Curtis help overcome any distribution difficulties with *Insignificance*?

Not really. They are more star names now than they were then, of course, except for Tony, who at that time was past his 'sell by' date. They helped, of course, but at a different level. It wasn't all that popular in commercial terms. It had its life, went to Cannes, but it's very difficult to assess how popular it would be without major distribution. It's all a matter of timing, catching the imagination. The test of a film is if it lives, not its immediate success.

The most recent of your films I have seen, which I think is entirely charming, is *The Witches*. What drew you to the Roald Dahl story?

He is a very truthful writer. He is a most interesting writer – for children, or when you read him for yourself. How many children's books would have an opening where the child loses both his parents in a car crash? A child understands truth; it's deceit and cover-up that they can't cope with. We had no money for lots of special effects so most of it was done by the cameraman, using some of the oldest tricks in the book.

What made you think of using Mai Zetterling, who hadn't made a film for years?

Oh, a lovely woman. She died last year. I was looking at actresses of that age and Mai had had an extraordinary life – she was a great beauty, had made many movies. The grandmother in the film had had a full life and people who have are, on the whole, more compassionate because they have fulfilment. Casting is everything.

Would you say that the nature and demands of sexual passion are a recurring interest in your films and are not a recurring interest in British films in general?

Sex is like eating, isn't it? The world couldn't exist without it, though you wouldn't think so from a lot of British films; but I can't think in terms of Britishness, as I said at the beginning.

Peter Rogers

b. 1916

Screenwriter: *Dear Murderer* (co-sc), *Holiday Camp* (co-sc), *When the Bough Breaks* (co-sc) (1947), *Here Come the Huggetts* (co-sc) (1948), *The Dog and the Diamonds* (co-sc) (1953), *The Gay Dog, Up To His Neck* (co-sc) (1954)

Producer or associate producer: *It's Not Cricket, Don't Ever Leave Me, Marry Me* (1949), *Appointment with Venus* (1951), *Venetian Bird* (1952), *You Know What Sailors Are* (& sc) (1954), *Circus Friends* (& sc), *To Dorothy a Son* (& sc) (1956), *The Passionate Stranger, The Vicious Circle, After the Ball, Cat Girl, The Tommy Steele Story* (exec pr), *Time Lock* (& sc) (1957), *The Solitary Child, The Duke Wore Jeans, Carry On Sergeant, Chain of Events* (1958), *Please Turn Over, Carry On Nurse, Carry On Teacher* (1959), *Carry On Constable* (1960), *Carry On Regardless, Raising the Wind* (1961), *Twice Round the Daffodils, Carry On Cruising, The Iron Maiden* (1962), *Nurse on Wheels, Carry On Cabby, Carry On Jack* (1963), *Carry On Spying, Carry On Cleo* (1964), *Carry On Cowboy, The Big Job* (1965), *Carry On Screaming, Don't Lose Your Head* (1966), *Follow That Camel, Carry On Doctor* (1967), *Carry On Up the Khyber* (1968), *Carry On Camping, Carry On Again Doctor* (1969), *Carry On Up the Jungle, Carry On Loving, Carry On Henry* (1970), *Assault, Carry On At Your Convenience, Quest for Love, Revenge* (1971), *All Coppers Are, Carry On Abroad, Carry On Matron* (1972), *Bless This House, Carry On Girls* (1973), *Carry On Dick, Carry On Behind* (1974), *Carry On England* (1976), *Carry On Emmanuelle, That's Carry On* (1978), *Carry On Columbus* (1992)

Peter Rogers's name is now so inextricably linked to the *Carry On* series, which began its astoundingly successful life in 1958, that it is easy to forget that his career began a good twenty years earlier. In fact, he began by working on Rank's religious films in the '30s and after the war resumed his film career as script assistant to Muriel Box at Gainsborough, where Sydney Box had taken charge in 1946. He was also involved as associate producer on several lesser Gainsborough films, including the very funny *It's Not Cricket*, and maintained both writing and producing functions on a variety of films, mostly comedies, and often directed by Gerald Thomas, in the '50s. The major turning point came with the box-office triumph of *Carry On Sergeant* in 1958. For twenty years, he and director Gerald Thomas turned out *Carry On*s at the rate of at least one a year, making the series the longest-lived in screen history. The producer's hand is seen in the continuity of personnel, in the strict adherence to budgets and schedules without any appear-

ance of skimping in production values, and in gauging just what aspects of public life audiences would find funny. The *Carry On* films have been taken up by scholars, but the box-office receipts are a surer guide to their place in British film history.
Interview date: October 1992

Is it true that you began working on J Arthur Rank's religious film scripts?

Yes. I was in fact involved with *Turn of the Tide* and *The Great Mr Handel*, both directed by Norman Walker. I went to Rank from the BBC. I was writing radio plays at the time and he asked me to join them and gave me a scriptwriting contract for his religious films, which were very interesting actually. He was still making religious films in the early '40s. Norman Walker was the 'W' of GHW Productions, a company which I bought years later. GHW was made up of Dr Benjamin Gregory, who was a clergyman, a Colonel Hake, who was in charge of J Arthur's estate, and Norman Walker, who was the director, and they called it GHW Productions.

Rank seems to have been in earnest about the capacity of films to do good.

He wanted to 'spread the word', as he called it, and he thought the best way was through the medium of the cinema, which in those days had such vast audiences. He instituted a five-minute programme called *Thought for the Week*, which I used to write for. He had an old silent actor [and former stage matinée idol] called Stewart Rome as Doctor Goodfellow, leaning over a farm-gate talking to the audience, telling them they should all be good boys and girls. Now one Sunday night – they used to show *Thought for the Week* between the feature and second feature – at eight-thirty they started throwing things at the screen, at Stewart Rome. So, J Arthur decided that wasn't a good thing any more. I suppose he really didn't understand the film industry sufficiently. Some of the film companies lying idle he bought. He even built cinemas in America to try to break into the American market, but of course you can't break into the American market.

Why can't you?

Because they are only interested in making money out of their own pictures. If you've got American finance for a picture they will show it over there. Why should they spend money on prints of a British picture? They don't want to know. They

pretend they don't understand the language, which is rubbish. Of course they understand it. Why would they have artistes like Rex Harrison and David Niven otherwise? They don't *want* and they don't *need* British films. Through Hollywood, they had an international monopoly. Whereas British audiences have always wanted American films, British films have rarely succeeded in America. Americans bought British films and put them in the bottom drawer of their desks and never showed them. Like the famous *Gaslight* case.

Muriel Box's autobiography says you were engaged as her assistant editor at Gainsborough.

Yes. She was scenario editor in the script department at Gainsborough Studios at Shepherd's Bush, from '45 or '46, when Sydney Box took over from the Ostrers. My job was to sift through scripts that had been submitted, and to work on scripts.

Is *Dear Murderer*, on which your name appears as co-author of the screenplay with Sydney and Muriel Box, your first credit?

No, I had a scriptwriting credit first of all on *Holiday Camp*. What happened was that, after Rank's religious films folded, I went to Fleet Street, and in my capacity as a Fleet Street journalist I met Sydney, who immediately asked me if I had any ideas for a film called *Holiday Camp*, which I did, so I sent him some and he took me on as a scriptwriter and that's how I met Betty [Box, Rogers's wife].

There are six names sharing the credits on *Holiday Camp*: Godfrey Winn, you ...

Yes, I know. The reason for that was that the idea was Godfrey Winn's. The screenplay and most of the stories were by me but Mabel Constanduros and one or two other people had little ideas. Sydney was always on the side of writers and always gave writers credit, even if they just had two lines in the script. It was my idea to introduce the Dennis Price character, based on the Heath murders. The only bit that Mabel Constanduros contributed was the scene between Jack Warner and Kathleen Harrison on the cliffs.

Why do you think the Huggett films caught on in such a big way?

The same way that the *Carry On*s caught on – you've got ordinary people doing amusing things. Kathleen Harrison and Jack Warner were called 'Huggett' from *Holiday Camp*. Then the *Daily Mirror* came along with the idea that we should make a series called *The Huggetts*. And we did. I worked on all the *Huggett* films, as a scriptwriter.

Would you say that giving people what they want is crucial to success in filmmaking?

It's like shopkeeping. People used to say, 'Why don't you make different films, maybe something important or significant?' But, if I'm running a sweet shop and kids came in for Liquorice Allsorts, I'm not going to try to persuade them to have Turkish Delight if they don't like it. I'd be out of business. If you don't please the audience, they won't please you. They'll be very faithful as long as you give them what they want, and I think familiarity breeds affection. That's what they've been like with the *Carry On* films.

How did you come across *Sylvester*, the Edward Hyams novel that you wrote and co-produced as *You Know What Sailors Are*?

It came my way by chance, and I met Hyams; I went out of my way to meet him. I produced it actually, Julian Wintle didn't produce it. What happened was that he was under contract to Rank and hadn't made a picture for some time, and they asked if I would mind if it was made as a Julian Wintle Production because it would have solved his contract. Not very fair really, because I'd written and produced the film and he never came anywhere near it. But Rank gave people all the chances in the world.

And what about when John Davis became Rank's right-hand man?

He became the right-hand man because someone had to stop J Arthur from being so generous. He didn't want to say no. He got himself into a lot of financial difficulties. When John Davis, as the new accountant, came in and said I think you should do this or that, he eventually got things going. But the cuts he made certainly weren't popular.

How do you account for your extremely long and successful working career with Gerald Thomas? Did you complement each other?

Oh yes. We were friends long before we started making pictures together. You see Betty and Ralph liked making pictures in foreign locations. Ralph used to leave his wife, Joy Thomas, behind, and Betty used to leave me behind, her husband. So Gerald Thomas, being their editor, used to take Joy out to dinner and look after her, and then they invited me to join them. One day I said to Gerald, 'Why don't we make a film together?' Gerald wanted to be a director but of course his brother wouldn't have made him a director, or helped him had he been a director, because it would have looked a suspicious relationship.

So I said to Betty one day, 'I think you're going to lose your editor because I want a director.' There were several editors here at the time that I was thinking of, but I thought to myself, because I'm very friendly with Gerald, let's set up together. I gave Gerald a contract. So I wrote one or two children's films and he directed those; then John Woolf came along with *Time Lock*. Gerald directed that, which is a very good £21,000 picture, a little gem, and after that John Woolf said, 'I think he can direct the Francis Durbridge thing' that we did with John Mills. That was *The Vicious Circle*, and so we got going. I never wanted to direct. Writing and producing is my major input. I did a lot of rewriting on the *Carry On*s, of course.

What was John Woolf's connection then with Beaconsfield?

He had no connection with Beaconsfield. John and Jimmy Woolf were brothers and had Romulus Films, and as distributors they often bought subjects they wanted made, so they came to us. So we were then employed by them to make the film.

There's a film called *After the Ball* that interests me.

Oh yes, that was another one for the Woolfs. Jimmy wanted that made because he wanted a vehicle for Larry Harvey – and Pat Kirkwood. It was a biography of Vesta Tilley, the music hall star. Pat Kirkwood wasn't easy to work with. I wouldn't have worked with her again.

***Please Turn Over* has some very good scenes. Were you pleased with that?**

Yes, that was among the comedies that we made for Anglo-Amalgamated, which were non-*Carry On* comedies but which were being called *Carry On*s because they had the same people – Joan Sims, Leslie Phillips, and so on. It had some others though, like Jean Kent, for instance, and Lionel Jeffries. And Ted Ray and June Jago, who I liked very much, and who was very good. It's based on a play called *Book of the Month* by Basil Thomas, a cousin of Gerald and Ralph. Poor bugger, I think he suicided soon after that, I don't know why.

How did the *Carry On* series come about? One book credits you with 'conceiving' the idea.

I don't know how it came about. I just thought of it. Way back almost in the silent days there was a film, called *Carry on, London*, I think. I mean, 'carry on' is a phrase that is commonly used. We didn't invent the phrase but, certainly, after one or two of them, we had almost exclusive rights to the expression. And the English have always said, 'What a carry on!'

Was *Carry On Sergeant* an immediate big box-office hit?

Oh lord, overnight. I don't like to analyse why. Audiences liked it and that was that. I remember being interviewed by the BBC on one occasion about this and, in the first five minutes of the interview, the man said, 'What do you think is the reason for the success of the *Carry On*s?' and I said, 'I've no idea.' So he stopped the interview and said, 'There's no point in going on, is there?' I said, 'Quite honestly I do not believe in analysing things, so leave it alone. If I start being complicated about why people go to the cinema, people are going to hear this and say, "My God, is that why I go? I don't think I'll go again." '

There's a clear-cut quality to the characters that is very attractive.

Yes, it works the other way too, by casting some of these people *against* type. Like Sid James, as the Viceroy of India, writing to Queen Victoria, 'Dear Vicki'. I sat next to Princess Margaret, when we were running that on one occasion, and she said, 'I don't like that, Peter, I don't think he should do that.'

You very quickly established a kind of repertory company of actors. Was that the intention?

The idea was that we must not have a star, no one artiste to get above another. We never put one above the title. The star of these pictures is the expression 'Carry On'. *That* is the star, that is what they go to see, they don't care who's in it as long as they know that's the title of the film they're going to see. No one was allowed to be a star. If anyone tried to do it, they were certainly put down, because they were all on the floor together. They were friends. They used to say it was like going back to school. They all had a great rapport with each other. It's a group effort . . .

Were there people queuing up to be in the *Carry On*s?

A lot of them, yes. A lot of people wanted to be in them. And some who would never have wanted to be in them, who probably hated the things. I sometimes wonder if we did our artistes a very good turn because they were so typecast as *Carry On* artistes that, to appear in other films as other characters, they wouldn't have been accepted at all. They were typed and they couldn't get out of it. Really we were hoist with our own petard. I couldn't get up anything else. I wanted to make other pictures but producers said, 'Oh no, Peter, don't do that, let someone else.'

Who was chiefly responsible for generating each new *Carry On*? Did you have a great team?

No, it wasn't like that. We had over the whole series, I think, only three script writers: Talbot Rothwell started, and then there were Norman Hudis and David Freeman. We had Rothwell, mostly, until he died. I would think of the titles in the bath, and as a writer I was taught that the title should indicate the theme of the work. So I'd ring up Tolly and say 'Carry on something', and from that he would work out an idea, come and talk to us about it, then go back and write the script. Our script conferences lasted about five minutes. It was always at the back of my mind and Gerald's that, once the script came in, I would take it home and work on it. I didn't take credit for it but I worked on it.

Did you feel that that kind of continuity was really very important? Not just you and Gerald Thomas but Norman Hudis, Talbot Rothwell and Dave Freeman?

I think so, but there were times of course when Tolly Rothwell's scripts began to be a repeat of the last one. We wore him out, I think. He only left because he died. Dave Freeman's done the most recent one, *Carry On Columbus*.

Can you tell, from looking at a *Carry On* film, whose screenplay it is?

Oh yes. Hudis had heart. I used to say to Norman Hudis, 'I want a Chaplin script,' but Tolly couldn't or didn't write with heart at all; he was against that. He used to write the crazy gags, you see, and his marvellous one-liners and his names for people and so on.

Alfred Roome was the editor on fourteen of the *Carry On*s. Did you and Gerald Thomas work closely with him in the editing process?

Oh yes. He'd been in the business so long. But no editor can actually know the film as Gerald and I wanted without our going over it. Gerald and I used to sit in the theatre and watch and I would squeeze his arm if I thought something was wrong. I would never say anything in front of the editor if I wanted a cut or something. I'd wait until afterwards. Gerald would never tell the editor what he wanted done. As a director, he has never lost his love of any aspect of filming; he's happiest in the cutting room.

With actors, does he more or less let them get on with their stuff?

With the sort of schedule and budget that we had, you can't be a performance director; you can't spend all the morning getting a performance out of an artiste on one-liners. The *Carry On* people knew what to do in front of the camera. It's only moving about with direction. It wasn't 'How can I say "shut the door" until I know what I've had for breakfast?' and so on.

Among the other collaborators is music director, Bruce Montgomery . . .

He was Edmund Crispin, the detective story writer. He wrote a screenplay for us called *Raising the Wind*, about music students. He said it was a complete copy of *Doctor in the House*, of course, with them all living in digs somewhere together. It was a funny film, I thought. Bruce Montgomery did the music too. They start with a good blast, and a large orchestra for the credit titles, then you can have flutes and whatever, if you've had your curtain-raising music.

Until *Don't Lose Your Head*, which is presumably a *Carry On* film in all but name, your films have been distributed by Anglo-Amalgamated?

That's right. Anglo-Amalgamated were Nat Cohen and Stuart Levy. They used to buy films from America, second features and so on, but they didn't do a production until the *Carry On* sagas. But of course they were released through ABC distribu-tion. If a distributor hasn't got cinemas he's got no outlet. There were two big circuits then – Rank and ABC. We changed to Rank distribution in 1963 because Anglo didn't want it any more. They wanted big things like *Far from the Madding Crowd*. I think they got a bit of culture up their backside.

The *Carry On* series is the longest in film history. Is this a mixture of production efficiency and the tapping of a peculiarly British sense of humour?

They were economical pictures but they were always very well monitored. We paid top rates for everybody, cameraman, art director, the lot, nothing cheap about it. Economical yes, because you're dealing with other people's money, but nothing cheap. We didn't go on location, we made use of the Pinewood grounds and faked our places, but that's the job. Oh, there were little bits of location shooting in snow to fake the Khyber Pass, but other people would have taken the whole unit to India. We had a card from a man who had been in the Khyber Pass, and he said, 'I recognise this.' When we did *Follow That Camel* (they're all *Carry On*s, as you know), we built a fort at Camber Sands. India's a desert and we had a camel that couldn't walk on sand.

And you got Phil Silvers in for that.

Yes. The distributors again said, 'Let's have an American in it and see if we can break in.' And it was a very great mistake. I knew it'd stick out like a sore thumb, but I did it. And it *did* stick out like a sore thumb.

Did the *Carry On* films ever go over budget or were you always on schedule?

Oh never, another day another penny, they were all under budget, and they all made money in great sums.

Alfred Roome

b. 1907

Editor/cutter: *Blackmail* (ass cam op) (1929), *Thark, Leap Year* (1932), *Blarney Stone, London on a Night Like This* (1933), *A Cup of Kindness* (1934), *Foreign Affairs, Stormy Weather* (1935), *The Man Who Changed His Mind, Pot Luck* (1936), *Dr Syn, Said O'Reilly to McNab, Good Morning Boys, Oh, Mr Porter* (1937), *The Lady Vanishes, Old Bones of the River, Owd Bob, Alf's Button Afloat, Bank Holiday* (1938), *Ask a Policeman, Shipyard Sally, Where's The Fire?, Frozen Limits* (1939), *Band Waggon, *Channel Incident, Inspector Hornleigh Goes To It, *A Letter from Home* (1940), *Kipps, *Mr Proudfoot

Shows a Light, Once a Crook (1941), *Young Mr Pitt, Partners in Crime, King Arthur was a Gentleman* (1942), *Miss London Ltd, Millions Like Us* (1943), *Bees in Paradise, Give Us the Moon, Waterloo Road* (1944), *I'll Be Your Sweetheart* (1945), *The Magic Bow* (1946), *The Man Within, Holiday Camp* (1947), *Broken Journey, My Brother's Keeper* (dir), *It's Not Cricket* (co-dir), †*Helter Skelter* (1948), †*Boys in Brown,* †*The Bad Lord Byron, Once Upon A Dream,* †*A Boy, a Girl and a Bike,* †*Marry Me,* †*Don't Ever Leave Me,* †*Christopher Columbus,* †*Traveller's Joy,* †*Helter Skelter,* †*The Lost People,* †*Diamond City* (1949), †*The Astonished Heart, Highly Dangerous, Trio* (1950), *Hotel Sahara, Encore* (1951), *The Planter's Wife, Penny Princess* (1952), *Top of the Form, Always a Bride* (1953), *You Know What Sailors Are, Up to his Neck* (1954), *A Woman for Joe* (1955), *The Black Tent* (1956), *Across the Bridge* (1957), *A Tale of Two Cities, The Big Money, Nor the Moon by Night* (1958), *The Thirty-Nine Steps, Upstairs and Downstairs* (1959), *Doctor in Love* (1960), *No, My Darling Daughter, No Love for Johnnie* (1961), *A Pair of Briefs, The Wild and the Willing* (1962), *Doctor in Distress, The Informers, Hot Enough for June* (1963), *The High Bright Sun* (1965), *Doctor in Clover, Deadlier than the Male* (1966), *Follow that Camel, Carry On Doctor* (1967), *Carry On Up the Khyber* (1968), *Carry On Camping, Carry On Again Doctor* (1969), *Carry On Loving, Carry On Up the Jungle* (1970), *Carry On Henry, Carry On At Your Convenience* (1971), *Carry On Matron, Carry On Abroad* (1972), *Bless This House, Carry On Girls* (1973), *Carry On Dick* (1974), *Carry On Behind* (1975)

* Short film.

†Associate producer (see interview for use of term).

A lfred Roome's remarkable list of credits reads like an inventory of popular British film history. He edited for Hitchcock and Herbert Wilcox in the '30s, was Gainsborough's resident editor through most of the '40s, worked with such proficient suppliers of entertainment in various genres as Ken Annakin and Ralph Thomas at Pinewood in the '50s, and finished his career cutting the capers of the *Carry On* gang. Happiest as a back-room boy, and obviously much in demand in this capacity, he nevertheless directed two of Gainsborough's more successful late '40s pieces: *It's Not Cricket*, a lunatic farce, contains some of the funniest moments in a British film; and *My Brother's Keeper*, anticipating Stanley Kramer's *The Defiant Ones* by a decade, humanely records the flight of a first offender (George Cole) and an embittered old lag (Jack Warner!) handcuffed together. Both these films have sequences good enough to make one wish Roome had been less self-effacing in his approach to his career.

Interview date: October 1992

How did you get started as an editor at Gaumont-British in 1934?

It was before that. I actually started in the Property Department at Elstree in 1927 in the silent days. Herbert Wilcox had just started at Elstree then. Then I went into the cutting room, which I'd always wanted; then on to the camera and into editing gradually. I arrived at Shepherd's Bush, Lime Grove, with Gaumont-British in 1933, and the first film I ever cut was called *Thark*, for Tom Walls and Ralph Lynn. I had a title on that, as Editor. Those films were really filmed stage farces which had come from the Aldwych Theatre. I used to have a lot of trouble in the beginning in making dear old Tom Walls understand how you could do it. The cast was usually about eight people and he tended to get them in a half-circle like they do on the stage. Ben Travers used to come into the cutting room with me and see how films were made, so that he could write his stories film-wise.

What was your experience of editing *The Lady Vanishes*?

That was very interesting. Hitchcock shot his stuff so well that it scarcely needed editing. It went together so that it only needed some final trimming up here and there. I'd worked with him earlier, as a boy at Elstree on the camera. *The Lady Vanishes* was made by Gainsborough, over at Islington. All the model train stuff was done in a disused garage, and we got some train footage in the south of France. That was nearly a disaster, because a cameraman doing the shot alongside the train was a bit careless. We had checked the amount of clearance when two trains passed each other, but when the second train went past, which was what we wanted, his head missed it by about two inches! Hitchcock always liked pulling people's legs, and during the running of the rough cut he would sleep and snore; yet the moment the lights came up he would give detailed notes to his secretary as to what he wanted – he hadn't been asleep at all. I was on *Blackmail*, his first sound picture; he shot that in small pieces, just as we always did in silent films. He wasn't a bit scared of sound, while all the other directors were frozen stiff. Carol Reed was also very easy to edit, not quite as easy as Hitch, but he knew exactly what he wanted when he came on to the floor. He was very nice, never shouted or got excited and was very conciliatory if you couldn't get something done in time, but I still did not know him.

What do you remember of the Ministry of Information films you did – *Channel Incident, Mr Proudfoot Shows a Light*?

They were just shorts. I was lucky because I was thirty-two when the war started and at that age you weren't called up immediately, and, as far as studio personnel went, if the studio guaranteed you were going to do so many propaganda films a year, you got exemption from call-up. So we did these shorts in between films. Gainsborough made the pictures for the Ministry. They were distributed as support films.

Did it make much difference to you, as an editor, who shot the film?

No, generally I don't think the cameramen would have any influence at all on how easy or otherwise my job was. It was the director, because he is the one who selects the shots and how he is going to do them. There were a lot of directors who would shoot masses of stuff and you'd have to put it together.

After *Millions Like Us*, you did several films for Val Guest . . .

I helped Val a great deal on his first two or three films, I was on the floor a lot helping him to set up his cameras to get the shots he wanted (because he was a writer). Then there was *Give Us the Moon* with Vic Oliver and a very young Jean Simmons. That one had an interesting scene between Margaret Lockwood and the little girl, at a café table, and this little girl – Jean – acted Margaret Lockwood clean off the screen! That was also directed by Val Guest, as was *I'll Be Your Sweetheart*, with Margaret Lockwood, Michael Rennie and Vic Oliver. That was interesting because that was the first real musical I'd ever been on – the first one Gainsborough tried, and the last! It was actually an interesting story, about the days when songwriters used to write very good songs and didn't get any money; a pirate would just copy them and sell them off.

What else did you do at Gainsborough at this period?

There was *The Magic Bow* about Paganini, with Menuhin involved. It was directed by the ex-cameraman Bernard Knowles and was one of the most difficult films I've ever had to cut. I evolved a system whereby I'd number every foot of film on the roll, from the first note to the last; then I'd get the sheet music and identify the music all the way through with these numbers. On the floor, Stewart Granger could only do little bits and it was very difficult, with classical music, to find out the bit you wanted. David McCallum (father of the actor David McCallum) was first violinist with the London Symphony (I think it was), and he was Granger's coach; he would point out on the music the bit they wanted to do, and I could say to the projectionist who was running the track to give me, say, 80 feet to 130 feet. It was a brute of a picture to cut, though. There was one famous shot up the violin: it had Stewart Granger in close-up with the violin under his chin; he held his hands behind him while Dave McCallum used the bow and somebody else was doing the fingering! I got caught out on that film because it was so bad, the critics had time to notice details. They also quite rightly pointed out that at least the Pope could have tapped his foot in time with the music! After *The Magic Bow* I did *The Man Within*, my first colour film; I think that was the first one with Sydney Box as producer. Next was *Holiday Camp*, directed by Ken Annakin, who had done some documentaries with Sydney, who asked me to be on the floor as much as possible to give Ken a hand, as he'd never done a feature before. He actually didn't need much sorting out, because he was naturally a film man.

You directed only two films. Was there a reason for that?

I'm really a back-room boy by nature, I'm not too keen on dealing with the foibles of actors. Sydney persuaded me to do those two. After I'd done *It's Not Cricket*, he sent for me and explained that there was a hell of a mess in the cutting room and would I mind going back and sorting them out? I agreed, but asked what my title would be; I didn't want to go back to editing and become a laughing-stock, to have people think I'd made a right mess of directing. He said, 'Anything you like,' so I became an 'associate producer' – which meant nothing at all! I actually recut *The Bad Lord Byron*, which was so bad the first time. It wasn't the editor's fault; the director, David MacDonald, had just let it run, pages of stuff without any cuts. I did all sorts of tricks with it – bits of Byron's poetry, travel shots – but it was an unsaveable film.

It's Not Cricket **is very funny.**

It's a slapstick action thing, really, almost a children's picture. What I'd do now is cut out all the terrible, boring romance stuff with Susan Shaw; there was a lot of other chat that should have gone too, but other than that, it's not too bad. Basil Radford and Naunton Wayne play two very dud English officers who decide to run a detective agency. The first job they have to do is to track down a stolen diamond and they find it hidden inside a cricket ball which is eventually played in a match. It had dear old Maurice Denham as a German spy; he asked me how he should do it and I told him, 'Just do it over the top!' We managed to doll the sets and clothes up quite nicely, so that it looked quite expensive.

On the two films you directed, Roy Rich is sometimes listed as co-director, sometimes as dialogue director. What exactly was his function?

On *My Brother's Keeper* he was what was called a dialogue director. I had told Sydney I would direct it but that I had trouble dealing with actors, so Sydney said Roy Rich, who had come from the BBC and wanted to learn about filmmaking, would act as dialogue director and handle the artistes if I had trouble with them. On the next picture, *It's Not Cricket*, Roy asked if he could be co-director and we said yes. Those two films were both made in 1948. Then I went down to sort out the jam in the cutting room.

My Brother's Keeper **stands up very well.**

Yes, but we collided with a big Ealing film, *It Always Rains on Sunday*. Both were about escaped convicts and the Ealing one was considered a better film at the time. I was very satisfied with Jack Warner and George Cole, they were very good. Jack Warner was such a nice man and he thoroughly enjoyed playing a nasty thug instead of light comedy. There is one scene where he goes across a railway line in front of a train; Sydney Box nearly had kittens when he saw the rushes because, he said, 'You might have killed him!' In fact I had angled the camera so that he was much further away from the train than he looked to be. It was a very good cast, all of whom were under contract and for use by the studio. David Tomlinson played a reporter who talked too much; that's the part I would like to have cut out. Raymond Lovell played a newspaper proprietor and I based the character on Lord Northcliffe, having been brought up on him by my father.

Towards the end of his regime, Sydney Box said to me, 'What is the matter with our films?' I said there was too much talk, too many words. Sydney and Muriel made their name writing short plays for schools, so they were always very good with words – but too many of them.

What were some of those films on which you had 'Associate Producer' credit?

There was a whole lot there . . . *Helter Skelter*, that was for Ralph Thomas – terrible, you couldn't do anything with that; *Traveller's Joy*, also for Ralph, with Googie Withers, that wasn't bad. Then *Diamond City* with David Farrar; David MacDonald did that one, all done at Denham Studios. I was rushing around then because I was supervising stuff at Shepherd's Bush, Pinewood and Denham. There was also a terrible one which I'm not sure has ever been shown, *The Lost People*. Why I say it was terrible is that we shot for ages, then it stopped and started again and got terribly boring. I think it was directed by Bernard Knowles, but it actually had two or three directors who came and went. That was in 1949.

Boys in Brown was the first one for which we moved out to Pinewood. That again was a near-disaster, because the Independent Frame technique supposedly meant the end of having to use sets, and Rank paid enormous sums of money for the very intricate equipment. It was all completely wasted because it tied you down too much. You had to sit in an office and work out exactly what you were going to do and you couldn't move an inch from that afterwards. The actors would be filmed on a bare stage; sometimes the frames would be in position behind them, sometimes not.

In 1950 we started a new deal, because by this time we were feeling the beginnings of television, and the box-office was dropping off. So nearly all the contracts the studios could get rid of, they did, and I lost my contract at that time and became an 'independent labourer'. The first film I did then was *Trio*, the first three Somerset Maugham stories – still a Gainsborough film and made at Pinewood. Two of the three parts were directed by Ken Annakin and one by Harold French. They were very nice pictures to work on. The first one was set in the Scottish sanatorium where the inmates hated each other – Finlay Currie and John Laurie. That was one of the pictures I put together that I don't think I ever altered right to the end; that had never happened before. It went together so beautifully. That was also one of the first pictures on which we had the travelling matte, which is widely used now – that is, you have the actors playing against a blue screen and the laboratory double-prints with the external scenery behind.

You then worked on some adventure films at Pinewood ...

Yes. It was interesting to work on because it meant splicing together the studio stuff with the location footage, as I did, except on *Nor the Moon by Night*. I used to have to try to get Ken Annakin on the phone in the Serengeti Game Park; I'd get as far as Johannesburg, then the line would go dead. I'd need to talk to him urgently. You have to be very careful with location scenes if you're near a river, because otherwise the river suddenly changes direction and flows the other way! Sometimes matching studio and location footage can be a problem with colour but the laboratory very often sorts that out.

You obviously enjoyed working with Ken Annakin.

Yes, he and I used to have marvellous arguments but we got on very well. I did *Across the Bridge* for him in 1957, which should have been better than it was – pretty good, even so. We had a lot of trouble at the editing stage because masses of stuff had to be cut out. Rod Steiger got the bit between his teeth

in the scenes where he was thrown out of his home town and wandered through the streets looking for shelter. Earl St John didn't like it and I said we could cut it out, but Ken didn't want it cut.

Is the next one *A Tale of Two Cities*?

Yes, that's the first one I did with Betty Box. Betty and Ralph Thomas were an enormously successful team, first because they could turn out pictures on schedule and therefore within budget. Also, at the time, they did seem to tap into what the public wanted. Actually, if you look at their films today, they run very well on television; they were not too big. I knew what Ralph liked and they knew what I could do or make a muck of. Betty could be pretty tough sometimes if she didn't like something, but, once you explained why you had done it, she was very reasonable and also very efficient. I enjoyed working with her.

In 1967 Betty rang me up, to say there would be a bit of a gap but that Peter Rogers was looking for someone to help with their *Carry On* films. They'd had trouble with the editing and she asked me if I'd have a go. I started on *Follow That Camel*, for which Phil Silvers was brought in because Sid James had been ill, and that didn't help matters much. I enjoyed working with Peter and Gerald Thomas, they were both very nice people and amusing to work with. I did that whole series of *Carry On* films; *Carry On Henry* was interesting because we used all the costumes from one of the big Tudor pictures that was on at the time – I think Keith Michell's *Henry VIII and His Six Wives*. Peter Rogers was very good at doing a deal! He also used all the *Cleopatra* sets for *Carry On Cleo*, and for *Carry On Up the Khyber* we used a lot of the big stuff, the palace and the castle, from *Chitty Chitty Bang Bang*. I used to have the same team of assistants most of the time and we'd carry all the stock, paper, rubber bands, pencils and paper clips through to the next picture – that saved a few pence. The last one I did was *Carry On Behind* in 1975 and it was the last one which did any good.

Do you see any period of your working life as a highlight?

It seems to have broken itself up into sections, hasn't it? I think I liked the latter end best because I'd got the editing side down so that it had become easy and I could go at a hell of a lick.

501

▲ Goldfinger *1964*   ▼ If . . . *1968*

▲ Carry On Camping *1969*   ▼ Women in Love *1969*

▲ Sunday Bloody Sunday *1971*　▼ The Go-Between *1971*

▲ Chariots of Fire *1981*   ▼ Gandhi *1982*

Ken Russell

b. 1927

Director (cinema features only): *French Dressing* (1964), *Billion Dollar Brain* (1967), *Women in Love* (1969), *The Music Lovers* (1970), *The Devils, The Boyfriend* (1971), *Savage Messiah* (1972), *Mahler* (1974), *Tommy, Lisztomania* (1975), *Valentino* (1977), *Altered States* (1980), *Crimes of Passion* (1984), *Gothic, Aria* (co-dir) (1987), *The Lair of the White Worm, Salome's Last Dance* (1988), *The Rainbow* (1989), *Whore* (1991), *Die Unersättliche Mrs Kirsch* (short) (1993), *Erotic Tales* (co-dir) (1994), *URI, Mindbender* (1995)
Actor: *The Russia House* (1991)

'There are certain points in every film I do, where I deliberately want to shock people into awareness,'[1] said Ken Russell in 1970; '. . . to turn everything upside down will make everyone, including myself, look at a situation from a different point of view and gain fresh perspectives.' His career has spanned almost three decades of more or less 'shocking' and productive output since then. It is easy to invoke the *enfant terrible* label for Russell, but two things restrain one. First, his kind of flamboyant daring has not been so common in British cinema that it can be quickly dismissed as vulgar eruption: that is, it may just be a matter of energy and originality. Second, if actors as distinguished as Glenda Jackson and Dorothy Tutin find him a stimulating director (see elsewhere in this book), then he needs to be taken seriously. His films are full of acting treats, perhaps because 'I only work with people who understand what I am trying to do . . .'[2] Certainly Oliver Reed, for example, has never matched elsewhere the work he has done for Russell.

He claims, '. . . my education proper began at the age of thirty-two with Huw Wheldon [television producer, who edited and presented *Monitor*, 1957–64]. And I stammered and stuttered my way through twenty documentaries with him.'[3] Before making his first feature film in 1964, *French Dressing* ('a very unhappy film as far as I was concerned'[4] – though some of it is very funny), he had made a name for his television documentaries

on the lives of composers and of Isadora Duncan. He carried this interest into feature films with *The Music Lovers*: 'I followed the practice that I had established in my television biographies of great artists by making a definite connection between the man's life and his work,' claiming that all the music in the film is 'there to reflect some aspect of Tchaikowsky's life and personality.'[5]

He has worked much more in America than in Britain since the late 1970s, though it is at least arguable that the British films are the most vivid and interesting. Is there anyone else like him in British cinema? 'I don't particularly like English films though, and I've seen very few I care for, but naturally one can't help being influenced by them.'[6] There are some points of contact with Jarman and Greenaway, and he has some of Michael Powell's passion for the arts and some of his prodigality in stylistic matters. His feeling for artists is intense and he saw Gaudier-Brzeska's life (the subject of *Savage Messiah*) as 'a good example to show that art, which is simply exploiting to the full one's natural gifts, is really bloody hard work, misery, momentary defeat and taking a lot of bloody stick – and giving it.'[7]

His films derived from DH Lawrence suggest that some of the iconoclasm has gone out of Russell since he made *Women in Love* in 1969. That is a film of great beauty – and great daring, not so much because of its famous nude wrestling match as because of the amount of Lawrentian dialectic it includes. He found 'a lot of the book seemed pretentious and repetitive,'[8] but he and scriptwriter Larry Kramer have dared to tax audience intelligence by offering lengthy dialogue on matters of heart and mind. Twenty years later, *The Rainbow* is, by comparison, pallid and lacking the passion of the earlier film, and *Lady Chatterley's Lover*, made for television, is some distance from the solemn, sensual celebration of the novel. Russell's work is always in danger of aesthetic overkill, but rarely of dullness.

1 'Shock treatment: Ken Russell talks to Gordon Gow', *Films and Filming*, July 1970, p 8
2 Gene D Phillips, *Ken Russell*, Twayne Publishers, Boston, 1979, p 83
3 Ken Russell, *A British Picture*, William Heinemann, London, 1989, p 22
4 Russell, *A British Picture*, p 146
5 Phillips, p 93
6 '*Savage Messiah*: Ken Russell talks to Peter Buckley', *Films and Filming*, October 1972, p 15
7 Russell, *A British Picture*, p 220
8 Russell, *A British Picture*, p 175

Dame Margaret Rutherford

1892–1972

Dusty Ermine, Talk of the Devil (1936), Beauty and the Barge, Catch As Catch Can, Big Fella, Missing, Believed Married (1937), Quiet Wedding (1941), The Yellow Canary, The Demi-Paradise (1943), English Without Tears (1944), Blithe Spirit (1945), While the Sun Shines, Meet Me at Dawn (1947), Miranda (1948), Passport to Pimlico (1949), The Happiest Days of Your Life, Her Favourite Husband (1950), The Magic Box (1951), Curtain Up, The Importance of Being Earnest, Castle in the Air (1952), Miss Robin Hood, Innocents in Paris, Trouble in Store (1953), The Runaway Bus, Aunt Clara, Mad About Men (1954), An Alligator Named Daisy (1956), The Smallest Show on Earth, Just My Luck (1957), I'm All Right Jack (1959), On the Double (1961), Murder She Said (1962), The Mouse on the Moon, The VIPs, Murder at the Gallop (1963), Murder Most Foul, Murder Ahoy (1964), The Alphabet Murders (1965), A Countess from Hong Kong, Chimes at Midnight (1967), Arabella (1969)

'I never intended to play for laughs. I am always surprised that the audience thinks me funny at all,'[1] Margaret Rutherford insisted. Elsewhere, she is quoted as saying: 'I have been told I was a natural clown . . . I can never think of myself in that way. I play each role as I see it and always try to give it a new interpretation.'[2] Whatever her own views on the matter, audiences agreed for several decades in finding her one of the funniest women in the movies, a unique eccentric.

After an unhappy childhood, she began acting at thirty-three and kept at it for over forty years. Though, like most British actresses, she trained for the stage, she came to enjoy film work: 'I found it lonely work on the set, but the need to be precise, to remember that minute changes of experience would be visible to everyone and not merely to the front row appealed to me.'[3]

From the accounts of various directors, she seems to have been quite unconscious of how funny she was, with her bulky body swathed in tweeds and beads, her chins wobbling, her eyes darting, and her mouth pursed in rebuke or in nonsense uttered with great solemnity. Her earliest famous film role is that of the medium, Madame Arcati, 'deafened with birdsong' as she cycles to conduct the crucial seance in David Lean's *Blithe Spirit* ('though we all got tired of it before the end'[4] because of its protracted schedule). There is also a choice batch for Anthony Asquith and she told his biographer of the 'friendship and admiration and gratitude for all that "Puffin" has done for me', crediting to his sympathetic understanding her 'grand entrance as Queen in the village pageant in *The Demi-Paradise* . . . that was entirely due to him.'[5] Of Miss Prism, which she played first on the stage, then in Asquith's film of *The Importance of Being Earnest*, she said: 'I still felt that I had not yet met my testing part. And here it was; the incomparable Miss Prism . . .'[6] The film preserves an interpretation as definitive in its way as Edith Evans's Lady Bracknell.

Though she continued to act on the stage, she claimed, 'I don't approve of long runs in the theatre. I like a nice change of routine.'[7] And though she is, of course, always instantly recognisable, she still rang the changes on comedy and pathos in several dozen films. She cowed Alastair Sim's headmaster in the splendid farce, *The Happiest Days of Your Life*; she was an ecstatically dotty mermaid's nurse in *Miranda* and its sequel, *Mad About Men*; she was a ladylike shoplifter in Norman Wisdom's first starring film, *Trouble in Store* ('. . . there was a real warmth and understanding between us'[8]); and she

pronounced Pimlico's sovereign status with incontestable scholarly authority in *Passport to Pimlico*.

In the early '60s, she overcame her distaste for murder – 'not the sort of thing I can get close to'[9] – and won a new legion of fans as Miss Marple (though Joan Hickson's incarnation is nearer to Agatha Christie). Her gift for pathos vied with her comic gifts to win her an Oscar as the Duchess of Brighton in Asquith's *The VIPs*, though she originally turned down the part because 'There were just one or two gags and nothing very amusing in it . . . It was not really a character part.'[10] Then, very near the end of her life, she was unforgettably moving as Mistress Quickly telling of the death of Falstaff in Orson Welles's elegiac *Chimes at Midnight*.

1 *Margaret Rutherford: An Autobiography* as told to Gwen Robyns, W H Allen, London, 1972, p 47
2 Jerry Vermilye, 'Margaret Rutherford', *Films in Review*, August/September 1990, pp 390–1
3 John Roberts, 'Margaret Rutherford: beloved character actress', *Classic Images*, August 1993, p 40
4 Dawn Langley Simmons, *Margaret Rutherford: A Blithe Spirit*, McGraw-Hill, New York, 1983, p 69
5 RJ Minney, *Puffin Asquith*, Leslie Frewin, London, 1973, p 138
6 Simmons, p 47
7 Angela Best, 'Dowager duchess of laughs', *Picturegoer*, 20 November 1954, p 17
8 Simmons, p 95
9 *Films in Review*, October 1990, p 459
10 Minney, p 204

Victor Saville

1897–1979

Director: *The Arcadians* (& pr), *The Glad Eye* (co-dir), *Tesha* (1927), *Kitty, Woman to Woman, Me and the Boys* (1929), *The W Plan, A Warm Corner, The Sport of Kings* (1930), *Sunshine Susie, Michael and Mary* (1931), *Hindle Wakes, The Faithful Heart, Love on Wheels* (1932), *The Good Companions, I Was a Spy, Friday the 13th* (1933), *Evergreen, Evensong, The Iron Duke* (1934), *Me and Marl-* borough, *The Dictator* (1935), *First a Girl, It's Love Again* (1936), *Storm in a Teacup, Dark Journey* (1937), *South Riding* (& pr) (1938), *Forever and a Day* (co-dir) (1943), *Tonight and Every Night* (& pr) (1945), *The Green Years* (1946), *Green Dolphin Street, If Winter Comes* (1947), *Conspirator* (1949), *Kim* (1950), *Calling Bulldog Drummond* (1951), *24 Hours of a Woman's Life* (1952), *The Long Wait*

(1954), *The Silver Chalice* (1955)

Producer: *Woman to Woman* (co-pr), *The White Shadow* (co-pr) (1923), *The Prude's Fall* (co-pr) (1924), *Mademoiselle from Armentières* (1926), *Hindle Wakes, Roses of Picardy, The Glad Eye, The Flight Commander* (co-pr) (1927), *Action for Slander* (1937), *The Citadel* (1938), *Goodbye Mr Chips* (1939), *Earl of Chicago, Bitter Sweet, The Mortal Storm* (uncr) (1940), *Smilin' Through, A Woman's Face, Dr Jekyll and Mr Hyde* (1941), *The Chocolate Soldier, White Cargo, Keeper of the Flame* (1942), *Above Suspicion, Forever and a Day* (1943), *I, the Jury* (1953) *Kiss Me Deadly* (1955), *The Greengage Summer* (1961), *Mix Me a Person* (co-pr) (1962)

'I hope I shall not personally direct many more films. I have never considered myself highly as a director . . . my one ambition has always been to become a producer.'[1] So said Victor Saville with twenty-seven feature films behind him as a director, including some of the most successful British films of the 1930s. He was interviewed a good deal in the decade and was articulate on many matters pertinent to British cinema, and the nature of his concern does tend to mark him out rather as a producer than a director with a very personal style.

He had entered the industry (in distribution) in 1916, met up with Michael Balcon in the '20s as a producer, left him and returned in the '30s at Gaumont-British, where he made a string of very attractively English entertainments. He remade two of the silent films he had produced and/or directed, *Woman to Woman* and *Hindle Wakes*, which stands up very well, especially in Belle Crystal's fresh portrayal of a strong-minded working girl. But, above all, I should choose to represent him, at his warmly sympathetic best, as a director, with *The Good Companions* and *South Riding*. Of the former, he wrote: 'The part of the story before the joining up of the characters . . . is, in essence, comprised of three revolts against circumstances . . . Then they form a triangle – with the uniting element, the concert party, in the middle and so parallel cases of the revolts are unfolded quickly and the characters brought together.'[2] It made an international star of Jessie Matthews, whom he had to cajole into the part of Susie Deans, urging her to 'Let me make a test . . . to prove that you *will* photograph and also how great you will be as Susie.'[3] He went on to direct her in five more films, including her greatest hit, *Evergreen*. Of *South Riding*, based on Winifred Holtby's fine novel of provincial life and local government, he said nearly forty years later, 'I saw it again recently and was very moved by it . . . I think it's my best film. I feel it emotionally; they're real people, except in one scene in which the comedy is overplayed.'[4]

In the late 1930s, he joined MGM as a producer and oversaw the two MGM-British triumphs, *The Citadel* and *Goodbye Mr Chips*, insisting that 'We are not going to attempt to make "American" pictures in England. All the subjects scheduled for production here are those which call for English settings.'[5] In the event, he went to Hollywood for ten years, where he produced some prestige films for MGM and improbably made three Mickey Spillane thrillers for United Artists in the '50s, returning at intervals to Britain to direct three indifferent films – *Conspirator, Calling Bulldog Drummond* and *24 Hours of a Woman's Life*. His real contribution to the history of British cinema is in his pre-war period, when he was a major figure of the domestic industry, his films giving evidence of his belief that 'we are slowly learning how to make English subjects interesting – how to turn events in the daily life of our nation into interesting motion-pictures.'[6] Though insisting that 'I dislike anything revolutionary', he also believed that 'an experiment in filmmaking, if it is to mark an epoch, must be bold, terrific, in the grand scale.'[7] He was outspoken about stars, about film acting, and about the importance of 'an original idea strong enough really to rouse the interest and emotions of the public.'[8] That is exactly what his best films of the '30s impressively do, and they couldn't be more indigenous.

1 J Danvers Williams, 'Victor Saville talks about his plans for British films', *Film Weekly*, 16 October 1937, p 14
2 Stephen Watts, 'Victor Saville talks about telling 120,000 words in 90 minutes', *Film Weekly*, 18 November 1932, p 12
3 Michael Thornton, *Jessie Matthews: A Biography*, Hart Davis, MacGibbon, London, 1974, p 99
4 'Interview with Victor Saville', *Victor Saville*, National Film Archive, BFI, London, 1972, p 12
5 John K Newnham, 'Victor Saville: working for Leo', *Film Weekly*, 19 March 1938, p 14
6 Danvers Williams, p 14
7 Victor Saville, 'What I should like to see in 1935', *Picturegoer Weekly*, 26 January 1935, p 38
8 Victor Saville, 'My ideal film', *Picturegoer Weekly*, 9 December 1933 p 12

John Schlesinger

b. 1926

Director: *Horror (1946), Black Legend (1948), The Starfish (1950), *Sunday in the Park (1956), *Terminus (1961), A Kind of Loving (1962), Billy Liar (1963), Darling (& co-auth) (1965), Far from the Madding Crowd (1967), Midnight Cowboy (1969), Sunday Bloody Sunday (1971), Vision of Eight ('The Longest' section) (1972), The Day of the Locust (1974), Marathon Man (1976), Yanks (1978), Honky Tonk Freeway (1981), The Falcon and the Snowman (1985), The Believers (1987), Madame Sousatzka (1988), Pacific Heights (1990), The Innocent (1992), Cold Comfort Farm (1994), Eye for an Eye (1995)
* Short film or documentary.

Of all those directors who brought new impulses into British cinema in the early 1960s, John Schlesinger has been the most prolific. His work has included the cinema, television, the stage and the opera; he has acted as well as directed; and he has worked as much in America as in Britain. Despite this latter, he remains very much a British director, and, with the notable exception of *Midnight Cowboy*'s critical and commercial success, his most attractive and interesting work has been British. His contributions to the new realism of the '60s are the humanely felt *A Kind of Loving*, and *Billy Liar*, which mixes witty fantasy with the realism. His films are all notable for their fine acting performances, from actors like Julie Christie, Alan Bates and Glenda Jackson, all of whom have done arguably their best work for him. And it's not just the stars; his films are generously cast even in minor roles: think of Tony Britton's redundant executive in *Sunday Bloody Sunday*, that compassionate triangular love story, which remains one of the most eloquent British films.
Interview date: July 1994

Did you enjoy your early acting experiences, because you always seemed to me a very sympathetic director of actors?

I think what it did was to make me sympathetic to the problems of having to get out there and do something in front of that nasty bit of glass – the camera lens – and having to play a high emotional scene at eight-thirty in the morning, which must be very difficult. I understood the problems of confidence and also the problems of being shoved into the middle of something without having been able to work up to it because we were shooting the end of the story first. The whole business of locating an actor emotionally, locating very precisely where he is at a moment in time, was something that I was and am good at. I suppose I have a natural sympathy towards actors although they madden me very often. They can behave like spoilt brats, but by and large I would never take the attitude that a lot of directors more famous than I have taken: that they are puppets, or cattle.

Of those filmmakers who came to prominence in the early '60s, you have been the most prolific over a long period. How difficult in these decades has it been to sustain a director's career?

Very. It's got more difficult now because there isn't the freedom we had. Films are more expensive to make – and to sell – and therefore people want to hedge their bets with stars who, they think, will put bottoms on seats. I think the energy level and the desire for the fight are difficult to sustain. I mean, I'm still working but not with any great ease. I made *A Kind of Loving* when you could be happy to be paid £4,000 to do a picture and you could do it for £180,000 and still get eleven weeks to shoot it – *and* make the money back in our own country. That's how I started and that was comparatively simple. So was *Billy Liar*. The funding came from an independent company within the UK, which wasn't relying on American money for backing. It wasn't until I made *Darling* that I ran into my first set of trouble with the difficulties of getting it set up, with the people from the Film Finance Corporation giving me a sort of viva examination almost. Then you started to have to deal with stupidity: 'The main character in the script is so unsympathetic. Why should we care about an anti-hero?' I mean, they cannot see beyond the ends of their noses, those money men on some board or other.

How important was *Terminus* in getting your feature-film career moving?

When I was working for *Monitor* (which was an arts magazine programme) there was a wonderful barn-storming Italian scratch opera company coming to play at the Drury Lane Theatre, and I did a little portrait of this company. As a result of that, Joe Janni (an Italian producer who worked under contract for the Rank Organisation and who had made *A Town Like Alice*) sent me a message asking me to go and see him. He liked the film I had made of the opera company for its atmosphere and use of detail, and he said 'I'd like to discover you.' He had also seen *Terminus* and an entire programme of *Monitor* which I'd made, called *The Class*, which we screened at the National Film Theatre. He had a commercials company at the time and I made a few commercials for him; then he offered me *A Kind of Loving*.

I notice Edgar Anstey's name is on *Terminus* as producer. How important was his influence?

Quite important. He had a considerable documentary background although he was then head of British Transport Films. He'd seen some of my films for *Monitor* and asked me to come and make a film for them. I suggested a 'Day in the Life of . . .' kind of thing, which became *Terminus*. It did get quite a lot of attention. I remember the critics here in England being quite snide about it, particularly after it had won the Golden Lion at Venice, but I'm used to that from British film critics.

***A Kind of Loving* still seems to me the most warmly human of those regionally-set films that came out in a block at that time. What drew you to Stan Barstow's novel in the first place?**

The atmosphere and subject matter in those days were set rather by the Royal Court Theatre – by *Look Back in Anger*, by John Osborne, by the presence of Woodfall – and so when I read *A Kind of Loving* I thought it a particularly human story which I could tell well. I sent a card to Joe Janni saying I loved the novel and would he please give me a chance to do it. What he gave me the chance to do first, was a test of Tom Courtenay in *Billy Liar*; I knew the test was really for me as much as for Tom Courtenay. Is he any good with actors? was always the question mark when I was doing second-unit work.

In *A Kind of Loving*, did you see Vic Brown as a victim of constrained circumstances?

I don't think he was a rebellious character. He was the sort one could readily identify with – an ordinary 'boy next door'. A decent guy. It was about love in a general sense; it had no particular political axe to grind, and I think it was a film about human difficulties and the illusions of love, and the compromise that he felt he finally had to make. It is a film about compromise, which is what many of my films are about.

It was also the first of a number of films you made with Alan Bates. Has this been a particularly sympathetic working relationship?

Yes, I love working with him. We've done four films together, I think, and I wish we could do more. He is great fun and a good friend; it is one of my few actor friendships that has really endured, because working with actors is rather like a shipboard romance – you are all thrown together very closely for a short time, swear undying loyalty and love, then you're jolly glad when the thing's over. But Alan and Julie Christie and a few more have become good friends.

What became of the excellent June Ritchie, who seems to me absolutely dead right in that film?

I think she opted for marriage and children. She came back to do a musical at Drury Lane, then she went to America with Alan doing an Osborne play. She was one of many actresses brought in by the casting director – Miriam Brickman, a great casting director from the Royal Court. They all screamed in horror when she came to work with me because I was considered an outsider by that group, even though I'd been at Oxford with several of them. They rather looked down their noses at me. I remember Lindsay Anderson saying once, 'You've got to set your sights higher than television.' I felt resented, quite frankly.

Were you pleased with Thora Hird's monstrous mum, stopping short of caricature?

Yes, loved her! We had a unit that was so bloody suburban in the way they viewed the film. I remember being on location in Burnley, for the scene where they go into a chemist shop to buy contraceptives; we had a very good and experienced continuity girl who sulked behind the counter in the chemist's, and when I asked what was wrong she said, 'You're ruining your beautiful film with this vulgar sequence.' When Alan had to be sick, I had a deputation (including the continuity girl and the cameraman) saying, 'Must you ruin the film? Must he be sick in the room? Why can't he go outside?' But it was a very, very happy film. I remember us all being so thrilled with it, and with the situation we found ourselves in after the press show, when people genuinely liked it.

We made a lot of it in Oldham, Burnley and Manchester, and some of it at Shepperton Studios. That was my first experience of working in a studio, and I started then to get into the studio way of making films. You can control the lighting and the sound there. I eventually liked working in a studio although I resisted it for some time. Most of the films I've done have been partly made in a studio, with the exception of *Far from the Madding Crowd*.

Did *Billy Liar* have quite a lot of regional location work?

Oh yes. We had to go back and reshoot a lot of it because Julie Christie wasn't cast originally in the role; we had cast someone else who got ill, so we went back to our tests and decided we'd been mad not to cast Julie in the first place. That shot of her swinging down the street was a compilation of stuff we'd done in London, Bradford, Manchester – all over the place. It's a wonderful entrance and it was a very famous sequence for her.

Did you work very closely with Willis Hall and Keith Waterhouse on the screenplay?

Yes, but later I began to have closer associations with writers. We did all work closely on *Billy Liar* and certainly Joe Janni was very good at the script stage. He was absolutely insistent on long, detailed, sometimes exhausting re-examinations of the script at all times and I was certainly in on those discussions. Joe was quite ruthless in that, if the authors hadn't licked it, he would get in someone else. He was a very creative producer – not very interested in *selling* a movie, but wonderful at the script stage and the casting. We made six films together and I loved working with him. It was wonderful to have that sort of support from a producer. To be on one's own is very lonely and I don't like having to deal with all the financial worries of a film as well as trying to do the creative side of things.

Billy Liar, **although a regional film, has a totally different feeling from *A Kind of Loving*. Did you feel this?**

Yes, well, we decided to do it in CinemaScope so that we could have those little 'bubble' thoughts, the fantasies. I've always been interested in fantasy and it was fun to do. It was a lovely cast too. Ethel Griffies had played the grandmother in the play; I saw her in it and tried to persuade her to come back to England from America, where she lived. She was reluctant but she came. I think Mona Washbourne had also done the play – she was a wonderful actress. Most of the others were brought in by the casting director.

I don't think we felt the film worked quite as well as *A Kind of Loving* when we saw it; I remember that we screened the cut as soon as we'd finished shooting, for the authors, the producer and myself. I thought, 'Oh dear, what do we do? It's not working.' My agent, Richard Gregson, was at that screening too, and he said it was neither fish nor fowl. Now, I won't look at a cut until I've had at least a couple of weeks off. The film wasn't a commercial success but I don't think it is because of a 'downbeat' ending. I don't think it is a downbeat ending at all, because Billy stayed with his fantasy. He funked going to London, missed his opportunity with the girl and with life and everything else, but he still had his fantasy and he returned in triumph to his house, marching along with that invisible army. I thought that was wonderful.

Darling is very much a film of its time, but on seeing it again lately I thought it held up very well. How do you feel about it now?

Darling is probably one of my least favourite films, heaped with honours though it was. I thought it was too pleased with itself. We thought we were very smart boys. Freddie Raphael [writer] *is* smart and a bit of an intellectual snob; we had a run-in on that film and he refused to come back to work until much later. I think it's a dated film, it's of its time, and I think for it to be given the New York Critics' Award was ludicrous. The British critics, who were very unpleasant about it, were probably right, although I think they were probably influenced by its American success. They are a very nasty lot. But it's far too pleased with itself. It's something to do with the script, something to do with the way we shot it; they're not very deep people, rather effete. I don't know what to say about it. All I can say is that when it's being shown on television I leave the room.

The whole thing came about because a journalist, Godfrey Winn, who had been in the opening sequence of *Billy Liar* doing the radio programme *Housewives' Choice*, had lunch with me one day and said he had an idea for a subject. He told me a story about a girl who had been kept by a syndicate of showbiz and business people; they all had access to her, bought her a flat and she was their mistress. She finally threw herself off a balcony. I thought this was an interesting, nice-nasty subject. Then Freddie Raphael said we didn't need to follow Godfrey Winn's idea and he was perfectly capable of writing something totally out of his imagination. Joe said it had no basis in reality and he introduced us to a woman he knew who had been married several times. We spent time with her, went to openings of galleries and so forth with her and she was very entertaining.

Freddie wrote the film around her, in particular a lovely sequence in which Diana and her gay photographer boyfriend burgled her own house. It was a brilliant and funny sequence. At that moment, however, the real person we'd been following about (with a rather unwilling Freddie, to begin with, until he began to see the point) wanted to divorce her stockbroker husband and she issued an injunction on the film, because she'd told us too much. So we had to change the whole thing and were never able to use that brilliant sequence which had been one of the best things in the script.

Again with Janni and Raphael you did *Far from the Madding Crowd*. What attracted you to filming Hardy?

We were sitting around the mixing theatre, waiting for reels to be changed or something, on *Darling*. Jim Clark was the editor – a very fine editor and a very good friend who has saved my bacon many times since. We were wondering what we'd do next, something with Julie in it, and Jim said, 'What about a Hardy?' I hadn't read any Hardy but someone suggested *Far from the Madding Crowd*, so I took a copy with me when I went to America on an intense publicity tour for *Darling*. I realised it was a wonderful book and we all agreed to do it.

It didn't happen very quickly, of course. Alan Bates wanted to do Sergeant Troy, but I realised that his great inner quality would be wonderful for Gabriel Oak. Finally, he agreed to play it and we cast Terry Stamp for Troy. I think the casting of Alan as Gabriel worked wonderfully well. I felt that Peter Finch was right for Boldwood and he was wonderful; he was going through a very bad emotional patch at the time and he wasn't a happy man. He was much happier and more secure when we came to do *Sunday Bloody Sunday*.

How important was Nicolas Roeg's camera work to what is a fabulous-looking film?

Oh, very, and one mustn't forget Richard Mac-Donald, who had been Losey's designer for many years. That was my first experience (of three) of working with Richard, who taught me everything I know about colour, the use of muted colour, how to ration the use of primary colours like red. He was a wonderful man and a great artist – I learned a great deal from him.

Your American career got off to a spectacular start with *Midnight Cowboy*. How does a British director come to be making such an American film?

Midnight Cowboy was something that had never been done before – and never since, really. It was very daring stuff. It was all brought back to me forcibly this year with its twenty-fifth anniversary celebrations and re-release. It was way ahead of its time. We made it in New York, Florida and Texas and we had trouble on it. It wasn't a very happy film – but then, *Darling* hadn't been happy either: the electricians had gone on strike and been very difficult. I hated a lot of the technicians on the New

York crew of *Midnight Cowboy*, but Dustin Hoffman and Jon Voight were wonderful to work with and I loved the experience of working with American actors, who were freewheeling in a way that I hadn't found to quite the same extent in England. We are more reserved and kind of held-in. It was a huge success, fantastic.

Sunday Bloody Sunday seems to me one of the handful of best British films ever made. How do you rate it?

Very highly. It's the most personal of all my films. I'm an openly gay director – I can now much more easily say this – and I'd had a relationship with a much younger man that was funny and enjoyable. It didn't last for that long, two years, but we're still great friends and at the end of it, I thought, 'There's a film in there.' I went to Joe, who knew about the relationship, and he thought it a good idea. Penelope Gilliatt had asked me to do a rather well-written script of hers after I did *Billy Liar*. She was a critic with the *Observer* and I don't like critics; I think it's impossible to have a friendship with a critic. While we were editing *Far from the Madding Crowd*, I spent days with Penelope, talking very freely about each other's personal lives. Out of this came the film and the only thing I think is missing from it is enough humour.

However, Penelope wrote a script which wasn't entirely right, but the final scene – talking directly to the camera – was in the first draft and made me want to persevere with the screenplay. Penelope never wrote another script that got done. I never forgave her for having the printer put on the back of the published script, 'Miss Gilliatt first thought of this screenplay on a train in Switzerland, on her way to see Vladimir Nabokov.' How's that for intellectual pretension (and a lie)?

Such wonderful writing, though, it's a pity she was such a sad woman. We didn't like each other very much – she was an intellectual snob and I resented that. There was a kind of tension between us but I think that, perhaps, out of that tension came a very good film.

How important is the factor of Daniel's Jewishness to the film?

Very important, because it was personal to me. I'm Jewish, I belong to a synagogue although I don't like the Jewish social pressures. I've been to that kind of bar mitzvah where I'm faced with that business of cousins asking when I'm going to get married because otherwise I'll be very lonely and all

that shit, and I've always wanted to use it. We hadn't originally planned to have a bar mitzvah scene, but Joe Janni and I went to a ceremony and found it so moving and powerful that we decided we had to put it in the film. The Chief Rabbi at the time had turned down one request to use an Orthodox synagogue because of the content of the film. I found a renegade rabbi who still had a lot of Orthodoxy in his congregation; he said he thought the film was a wonderful idea and we should use his synagogue and they'd all be in it, and they were.

Many people have been very unsympathetic towards the young man. How sympathetic did you want him to be?

I would have liked him to be funnier, more amusing. I think I cast the wrong person. Murray Head came in and entranced us all at the audition by wearing a cowboy hat and carrying a guitar. We thought he would be good. Peter Finch was wonderful and Murray is what he is. He was good, but if I'd had my druthers I'd have cast someone else, someone funnier who would have made them laugh so the audience could see why people were attracted to him.

You didn't make another film in Britain until *Yanks* in 1978. It seems an odd film to find being made in Britain in 1978. How did it come about?

It came about because, while I was making *Marathon Man* in America, Colin Welland visited the set and he told me that he wanted to write a screenplay about the Americans in Britain just before D-Day. It was an idea that immediately made me both very nostalgic and keen to go home to England to make another film; I hadn't done one there since *Sunday Bloody Sunday*. And Paramount, at first, seemed very keen to develop the project, which it did. They passed on it eventually, and we had quite a long struggle setting it up because no English company seemed to be interested in the idea. I wanted to make it because, having spent quite a lot of time in America, I have great affection for it. Also, I just liked the idea of doing a film about the two cultures and the encounter and the clash, and the affection between the two, as well as the unpopularity. Certainly the Yanks, when they were in Britain during the war (I remember them here), came in for a good deal of criticism and I think there was envy as well. I wanted to take a very affectionate look at that period. I wasn't interested in just recreating the period; I wanted an evaluation of what both countries were about, and stood for, at that time, and the encounter and love affair between a young American and this rather protected girl from a prejudiced household – certainly from a very prejudiced mother. I enjoyed making the film very much.

I would rate Richard Gere's contribution to the film very highly; I thought he was extraordinarily good and sensitive about it and I liked working with him a lot. He was very keen and very careful about it. He was critical of the script; at a certain stage we had to bring in Walter Bernstein – the American writer – to write the American side of the story. I didn't think that Colin, and certainly not I, were really capable of doing that quite as fully as we would have liked to have done.

How important was Richard Rodney Bennett's contribution?

His contribution was extremely valuable. I'd done four things with him – three films and a play – I think it's a most beautiful score for *Yanks*, as it was for *Far from the Madding Crowd*. Before that he had composed the score for *Billy Liar*. His keen ear and sensibilities were very much in tune with both *Yanks* and *Far from the Madding Crowd* and I thought that his score was a particularly notable one.

By and large, I think I make quite a lot of contribution to the actual musical score, in that I am highly musical. I can read a score and certainly hear when something seems too thickly or thinly orchestrated, or when some other instrument, perhaps, should take over, rather than the one that the music has been scored for. I am either a bane or – I hope – a help to composers, which many directors aren't.

For many people, *An Englishman Abroad* remains one of the best television films. Whose idea was it?

Coral Browne told me this story [about her meeting with the defector Guy Burgess in Moscow in 1958] and asked if I thought I could make a film from it, and I was immediately attracted to the idea. Alan Bennett and I know each other quite well and Coral had told him the story. I thought his script was one of the best and wittiest screenplays I'd ever come across. I love Alan Bennett's work and he's great to work with; his ear for dialogue is absolutely extraordinary. You cannot fiddle about with Alan Bennett's dialogue, any more than you can with Pinter's. There were certain things we did alter, and certain things that I hope I helped to visualise, because dialogue is not the only thing that you need to look after in film, as we all know. We had to do it on a shoestring. I've always been keen to come home to England to work. Television is at least a way of getting something on a screen, albeit a small one, though it is never very satisfactory because it has such little shelf life. To a certain extent we were doing the film for Coral. It was her story, she was a sick woman and we had to look after her, so her state of mind and state of health were always of graver concern to us all than the actual problems of the film, which really made it a more special task.

Has the variety of film and television work been satisfying to you?

Of course, I'd rather be making films for the big screen but things have changed since I started. To make individualist films has become really difficult. It's easier to make films for television; at least it *was*; there was a much larger demand for it than perhaps there is now. The fact that people don't watch television and regard it with the same importance as they do a film is something that has always irked me.

Is there a film you regard as a personal highlight?

I don't know if I can answer that very clearly. My first film, *A Kind of Loving*, which did have a success, was my break, as it were, into the cinema. *Midnight Cowboy* was my first American film and that brought me a great deal of success. I'm not sure if it's my favourite film but it made quite a lot of money, which inevitably allowed me to make my most personal film, which was *Sunday Bloody Sunday*, and that is the film that is dear to me. I have a soft spot for *Madame Sousatzka*, which was a film about a music student, a musical film in the true sense of the word and, because music is so important in my life, that was an important, pleasurable film to make. I suppose those have been my highlights.

Margaretta Scott

b. 1912

Actor: *The Private Life of Don Juan, Dirty Work* (1934), *Peg of Old Drury* (1935), *Conquest of the Air, Things to Come* (1936), *Action for Slander, Return of the Scarlet Pimpernel* (1937), *Girl in the News* (1940), *Quiet Wedding, Atlantic Ferry* (1941), *Sabotage at Sea* (1942), *Fanny by Gaslight* (1944), *The Man from Morocco* (1945), *Mrs Fitzherbert* (1947), *The Idol of Paris, The First Gentleman, Counterblast, Calling Paul Temple, The Story of Shirley Yorke* (1948), *Landfall* (1949), *Where's Charley?* (1952), *The Last Man to Hang, Town on Trial* (1956), *The Scamp* (1957), *A Woman Possessed* (1958), *An Honourable Murder* (1960), *Crescendo* (1969), *Percy* (1970)

One of the pleasures of British television in the last decade or so has been the glimpses it gives of British players no longer active in cinema films. Margaretta Scott, regularly seen as the benevolent upper-class Mrs Pumphrey in *All Creatures Great and Small*, has appeared in television since its early days at the Alexandra Palace, but, regrettably, in no feature film since 1970. That she has forgotten many of the films she made can be explained partly by the fact that too many of them were indeed unworthy of her and partly because the stage was always her first love. However, she does remember – and was memorable in – those films which gave her real opportunities: *Things to Come, Quiet Wedding, Fanny by Gaslight* and *The Man from Morocco*. Her striking, dark beauty and sure sense of style made her a vivid presence in these films. As Alicia in *Fanny by Gaslight*, lovelessly married to Stuart Lindsell's gentle politician and conducting an affair with the sadistic rake played by James Mason, she created a potent figure of cold-hearted, humanly believable selfishness; and she was a gracious heroine when Anton Walbrook offered her the chance in *The Man from Morocco*.
Interview date: June 1990

Among your '30s films, *Things to Come* particularly interests me. Did you feel then that this was a landmark film?

Not as much as it became. It was a great adventure but I was a bit young to really enjoy all the people I met; and I never got to know Korda well. It was also the first time I worked with wonderful Ralph Richardson, and Raymond Massey. You know, I am shown on the cast list of *Things to Come* as playing both Roxanne and

Rowena but Rowena was cut. I was going to be in the future sequences (in the white outfits) as Raymond Massey's wife. I had been Ralph's 'moll' in the earlier sequences, and it was to be Raymond's and my daughter (Pearl Argyle) who was to be sent to the moon. I played quite a few scenes for it but they were never used – I think it was a question of time, not because we were so bad!

The film was all done at Denham and the huge open lot which we used for the City Square was for years afterwards known as that. I remember William Cameron Menzies, the director, very well; he was a delightful person to be with and frightfully good. I think Menzies and Korda worked very much as a team and the back-up people were terrific. Korda's brother Vincent did the art direction, and he was responsible for the design of the sets. The music was by Arthur Bliss, and Georges Périnal, of course, was the cameraman. I didn't have much to compare with then, but Georges really was wonderful at photographing women. Some of the costumes were designed by the Marchioness of Queensberry and I remember she designed the most elaborate costume for me as the future woman, Rowena. Korda didn't like it when I went on the set to show it to him; he chose a very simple white costume from one of the extras for me instead. Korda certainly had an eye for talent because so many of the cast became very big names afterwards.

What I find remarkable about the film is that we actually made it about five years before the war, yet all those scenes of London under the Blitz and so on were so nearly right, very prophetic.

You made three films in a row for London Films – *Things to Come*, *Action for Slander* and *Return of the Scarlet Pimpernel*. Did you have a contract with Korda?

I was under contract although I don't recall for how long. I suppose I was under contract to London Films but Korda *was* the studio, which was at Denham. All those people in *Action for Slander* – Ronald Squire, Ann Todd and Clive Brook – were really theatre actors; the reason those films were so good was that the people in them had a grounding in the theatre. It was based on an actual country-house weekend when someone, I think, had been accused of cheating at cards.

Return of the Scarlet Pimpernel *stars Barry K Barnes, a largely forgotten actor.*

Because I was under a Korda contract I did tests with the other actors, one of whom being tested for the part of Sir Peter Blakeney was Rex Harrison. He didn't get it though; Barry K Barnes did. You couldn't get two people more unalike. It wasn't a very good film, it was so overshadowed by the original with Leslie Howard. Also, it was made by a rather tough German director, Hans Schwartz, who was a bit of a bully; I remember him telling me to cry in a scene and shouting at me and I went very uptight, not a tear in sight.

***Quiet Wedding* still seems a charming film. What do you recollect of it?**

That was Anthony Asquith's film; we did that during the war. I had been in the play, although not in London. When the war came I wanted to go overseas with ENSA and I toured North Africa in *Quiet Wedding* with most of the original cast. In fact I did the play after I did the film, in the same role of Marcia. There were some wonderful people in the film, including Athene Seyler; it really was a happy company.

I remember there was a bomb warning while we were on the set making the film; a friend, a colonel in the Army, had come round to watch the film being made and I remember him commanding loudly, 'On the floor, down everyone!' I was wearing this beautiful nightie and was only crouching on the floor; I wouldn't dream of lying on the floor in it. It was very sad because one of the crew, a young electrician, was hit by a piece of shrapnel – fatally. The film was a huge success. We made it at Shepperton and it was produced by Paul Soskin, a very elegant, beautifully turned-out man.

***Fanny by Gaslight* is the film I most associate you with in the '40s. How did you come to play Alicia, which I think is the most stylish performance in those Gainsborough melodramas?**

Oh, that was lovely, made for Gainsborough at Shepherd's Bush. I can't remember how I got the part but I wasn't under contract. I know I wasn't tested for it. The only contract I ever had was with Korda. We had beautiful sets and costumes, and Arthur Crabtree, the cameraman, lit us beautifully. I liked that part very much; she was rather a bad lot, but humanly so. And of course Anthony Asquith, always known as Puffin, was the most wonderful director. He was very gentle; he would ask you to do something and you might say, 'I don't think I can do that,' and he would say, 'I'm so sorry, but I'm afraid you must.' He was quite firm but with such charm.

Fanny had a wonderful cast; I think that when there is a director whom everybody loves they all want to be in it. Asquith always wore trousers that were a bit too short, sort of cut-down dungarees; I remember him having a party with the crew. He was rather precious and one would have thought the lads mightn't have gone to the party, but they adored him. As a director he was very sympathetic. Really, I liked all my directors except the German one, who was a bully.

The Man from Morocco was a slightly curious project for 1945 in the way it goes back to the International Brigade in 1939.

The Man from Morocco was a great experience for me because it was Anton Walbrook himself who asked me to do it – or persuaded the powers-that-be to invite me to do it. We played together in the theatre in *Watch on the Rhine*, and Anton told me about this film he wanted me to do. They made a test for it and he took infinite care over the test; he got Stanley Hall, the make-up artist, to stay the night in my flat in order to make me up early. Then I went overseas with *Quiet Wedding* and had to leave the tour about a fortnight early in order to start the film. I got back on the day I had promised, sad to be leaving my chums behind, and Anton came to lunch looking very grey in the face; he said 'Peggy, I'm sorry, it's not going to happen.' I think he told me they wanted someone else in the part. Naturally I was shattered, between the disappointment and having left what I was enjoying.

Then, about a week later Anton came to lunch again, much more upbeat and saying, 'Peggy, you are doing it!' I think he really held out for me to play the part and it was a lovely experience. I know Anton was very keen on the project but as to whether it was his idea or Mutz Greenbaum's [Max Greene, director] I can't tell you. I am sure Anton would have given advice to Max about directing and Max would have given advice to whoever was photographing it. I do remember that Anton always insisted on being shot from his right profile, which was also the side I needed to be photographed, so there was a great deal of over-the-shoulder acting! The film wasn't a huge success but I certainly enjoyed it.

What do you recall of The Idol of Paris, which seems to have caused a scandal at the time, partly because of the two whip-cracking heroines, Christine Norden and Beryl Baxter?

I can remember I was playing the Empress Eugenie (with Kenneth Kent), and I was making a tremendous exit when the door handle came off in my hand! I have completely forgotten the duel with whips. I can remember Christine Norden, but not Beryl Baxter, and I recall the director, Leslie Arliss, as being very nice.

You made five films in 1948 after your long run on the stage in The Hasty Heart, including two directed by Maclean Rogers and starring Dinah Sheridan – Calling Paul Temple and The Story of Shirley Yorke ...

Oh yes, she is a wonderful lady. My husband [John Wooldridge] wrote a film called *Appointment in London* about the Bomber Command; he wrote a lovely part for me as a WAAF officer but Susi [Susan Wooldridge] decided to arrive and they couldn't very well have a pregnant WAAF officer! So Dinah did the part most beautifully. John wrote the music for it, because he was a film composer as well. Those two Maclean Rogers films were made very quickly; I don't remember anything of them.

Do you recall Where's Charley?, the musical version of Charley's Aunt?

I know I enjoyed it very much indeed, that was with Ray Bolger, wasn't it? Ray was delightful. I can remember him dancing and being great fun but, apart from that, I can't recall anything about it – or about those others I did in the '50s, *Town on Trial*, *Landfall*, etc.

Did you feel that there weren't many congenial roles in films for women after the end of the '50s?

I think I just wasn't asked. I don't remember turning any down but I have been very busy with television since the early Alexandra Palace days, which were often quite exciting. One's theatre experience backed one up, because it went out live and, if you made any boo-boos, you had to get out of them. There was one memorable time when we were doing *The Merchant of Venice* with me playing Portia; there was a splendid black actor playing the Prince of Morocco, which was memorable in itself, because he was the first black British actor to play in Shakespeare (sadly I can't remember his name). The scene came where the Prince of Morocco meets Portia and he fluffed a line, then fell in a dead faint at my feet, so that I was left saying 'Help, ho! The Prince!' and so on. There were always surprises.

Peter Graham Scott

b. 1923

Director: *CEMA (1942), *This Modern Age (series), *Sudan Dispute (1947), Panic at Madame Tussaud's (1949), Sing Along With Me (1952), Escape Route (co-dir) (1953), Hideout (1956), Account Rendered, The Big Chance (& sc) (1957), Breakout (1958), The Headless Ghost, Devil's Bait (1959), Let's Get Married, The Big Day (1960), The Pot Carriers, Captain Clegg, Bitter Harvest (1962), The Cracksman, Father Came Too (1963), Mr Ten Per Cent (1967), Subterfuge (1968), The Promise (pr only) (1969), The Magnificent Six and a Half (1971)

Editor: Brighton Rock (1947), The Perfect Woman, Landfall (1949), Shadow of the Eagle (1950), Never Take No For An Answer (1951), *Beneath The Seven Seas (1952), The Large Rope (1953), River Beat, *Under the Caribbean (1954)

* Documentary or short film.

Not surprisingly, Peter Graham Scott's chief interest and satisfaction is with his award-winning television achievements, which included such popular series as *The Avengers*, *Danger Man* and *The Onedin Line* and very notable dramas such as *The Last Enemy* and *The Four Seasons of Rosie Carr*. Too young to establish himself in films before the war, he showed real tenacity in making his way in the post-war cinema, full of young men coming back from the services. After cutting his teeth on documentary, with his friend Ken Annakin, his tenacity paid off with some editing assignments for, among others, the Boultings and Anthony Havelock-Allan, and then, throughout the '50s, he directed a steady stream of second features. Most of these are neatly plotted thrillers, serviceably acted and fast-moving, but at least two of them are among the best 'B' films ever made in Britain. They are *Devil's Bait* and *The Big Day*: neither is a conventional thriller, the former tracing the path of poison from a bakery, the latter centred on the tussle for promotion in a small company. Both are marked by excellent acting and an impressive concern for the minutiae of everyday life at lower-middle-class levels. Both showed Scott as a director to be watched; he found the chances he needed in television.

Interview date: August 1995

What was your first work in films?

I trained as an actor at the Italia Conti School, and, after a few London stage appearances in Shakespeare, I was cast as a page-boy in the film *Young and Innocent*, directed by Alfred Hitchcock. I didn't know who this fat Cockney was, but with great authority he was lining up a complicated crane movement which started on a high wide shot of dancers in a hotel with a band playing 'No One Can Like the Drummer Can', then he tracked right in and down (physically, because in those days they didn't have zoom lenses) into a close-up of the eye of the drummer, as it started to twitch, revealing his guilt as the murderer. They took all day on this shot, and I thought, 'Directing is *the* job,' rather than an actor standing around done up as a pageboy, waiting just to say, 'You're wanted on the telephone, sir.'

Having decided to be a film director, I went back to school. War broke out in 1939 – and the certainty of being called up for the services at eighteen spoiled my chance of three leisurely years at university.

After some wartime documentary experience and then war service, you got going again quite quickly . . .

I joined Greenpark Productions and edited a number of documentaries directed by Ken Annakin, then a beginner like me. I also contacted Roy and John Boulting and Anthony Havelock-Allan, hoping one day to edit one of their features. After three months in Africa, directing a documentary on the Sudan, I came back to find a message from the Boultings to say they were now going to start a new feature by Graham Greene. As their regular editor (on *Fame is the Spur*) hadn't finished, would I like to edit *Brighton Rock*? Would I?! I was twenty-three by now and this was my first feature film – and it has since become a classic, although we didn't realise it at the time. I also directed a second feature called *Panic at Madame Tussaud's* for a friend – some friend! – which we had to do at night in ten days between about six o'clock and eleven – it was a load of rubbish. I then went back to Associated British, producers of *Brighton Rock*, to edit Nevil Shute's *Landfall* for Ken Annakin. Then Anthony Havelock-Allan suddenly remembered me and I did two pictures with him in Italy: *Shadow of the Eagle* and Paul Gallico's *Never Take No For An Answer*.

Then I decided to go to the BBC and have a chance to direct things I could write myself. I'd been getting £75 a week as an editor, which was big money in those days. The BBC paid £15! However, I thought it was a good gamble and I was lucky to sell a script to keep afloat. I stayed at the BBC for two years and ITV for a further eight, doing all the things I wanted to do, like *The Last Enemy*, the classic war book by Richard Hillary. I also got offers for small films. That's how I came to direct three films for John Temple-Smith.

What do you recall of making those supporting films?

Usually it was the triumph of ingenuity. The first one I did with John Temple-Smith was *The Hideout*. We met because when ITV-Rediffusion started in 1955 we actually made some TV films at Shepperton, including *A Call on a Widow*, with Jean Kent and Michael Craig. That one we shot in four days, after rehearsing it for two weeks, incredible! John happened to visit the studio and thought I had energy! And I was cheap! The essence of shooting fast is that you have to rehearse – there's no other way, because you can't just come on the floor and start shooting. I used to steal time for rehearsing, at night and so on. With people like Donald Pleasence and Gordon Jackson, you would be given terrific co-operation because they wanted to be good too. We were working a five-and-a-half-day week then. We'd start at eight-thirty, finishing at six-twenty on two days and five-fifty on three days, then at one on Saturdays. The unions ruled in those days; you'd be right in the middle of a take at five-fifty and ask politely, 'May we have the quarter?' which meant they'd have half an hour's overtime; in fact you'd probably just do your take, they'd be away by five to six but they'd get the extra overtime to six-twenty, at double time.

So there was enough in the kitty for that sort of thing?

Oh yes. Take John Temple-Smith with *The Hideout*, for instance. It wasn't a very good script at first but we'd worked on it, and it moved. I asked him where we'd get all the sets we needed. John knew of a film being made at Shepperton with Peggy Mount and they had a very handsome modern flat set; the rest we improvised from old studio stock. The fur warehouse, for instance, was just the studio and we hung the bare walls with furs – no set at all. The posh bar we got from another film. All those wonderful sets were there at Shepperton and just patched up, painted and reused. But it was fast work – as director, you just flew. I used to write a shot-list for each day, which was the only way to work. I knew I had to do, say, thirty shots and I knew what they were; then I used to put a timeline down so that if I hadn't got to Shot 10 by eleven o'clock, I knew I was in trouble and I'd probably have to amalgamate about three shots to catch up.

How much, roughly, was the budget for a supporting film?

John Temple-Smith was a master of low cost. In 1956, he made two (one with another director) at Shepperton for £12,000 each – I don't know how. John had a deal with Rank: £15,000 cash for each film, so he made £3,000 on each. (A fortune in those days!) He'd pay the actors practically nothing – a star like Dermot Walsh might get £500 for three weeks, Rona Anderson about £300, Sam Kydd maybe £100. The second film I did for John, in 1957, was *Account Rendered*, from a novel by Barbara S Harper, who'd helped me with the TV script of *The Last Enemy*.

It's an unusual supporting feature because it's propelled by (a) a woman and (b) the notion of sexual passion. Ursula Howells' character was having an affair with a man played by John Van Eyssen.

Oh, that's who it was. He was a dull actor but Ursula was very good. There was another woman in it, called Mary Jones. When I was at Lime Grove in 1953 she used to come in to play barmaids and housewives. I always thought that everything she did on the screen was very well judged, but she was under-exploited. In *Account Rendered*, she has a big part with an emotional climax, and falls out of a window in the end. We were doing the film at Southall Studio, a really clapped-out dump, although John managed to get some reasonable sets from somewhere (they certainly weren't new); we had to have a large staircase and couldn't afford a balustrade, so we had to have just wide stairs with flats either side.

John then asked if I had a story I wanted to make. I said yes, I had one about a travel agent grabbing a chance to travel, and he asked me if I could make it happen on these sets. I supposed so, and that became *The Big Chance*. I wrote the script over a weekend because I thought, 'I can do it – anybody can do anything.' We were originally going to have Pete Murray, who had played Richard Hillary brilliantly in *The Last Enemy*; he suddenly got the mumps so we cast William Russell (television's Sir Lancelot). He is good in the film although he has a rather high, soft voice. His wife was played by Penelope Bartley, the then wife of Leslie Phillips.

It's another of those British films in which the man has his fling with someone provocative [Adrienne Corri, here], but goes home to his nice, safe, dull wife.

I think there was that morality factor in those days. Now there isn't, unfortunately.

I'm interested in the producers on these films. You mentioned John Temple-Smith, who worked a lot in association with Francis Edge.

That's right. They were co-producers. John was a curious man, very intellectual and well educated, yet he had this gift for begging and borrowing. He wanted to be a top producer and I think he'd packed Francis Edge off by the time he did his major productions.

You then had Julian Wintle and Leslie Parkyn on *Breakout* ...

It's a pity you haven't seen *Breakout*. Billie Whitelaw had a small part, and Lee Patterson was good in the lead. I remember it was freezing in January [1958]. We'd made the barracks in Aldershot look like a prison. It was getting dark but I said we needed to get a particular scene to avoid coming back. Lee said, 'OK, Pete, you know what you're doing,' and did it in one take. Estelle Brody was in it too; she was one of those people who still turned up in all sorts of bits. Another gutsy actress of that type was Jane Hylton, with whom I had a huge success on television in *The Four Seasons of Rosie Carr*.

You made two of the best British 'B' films – *Devil's Bait* and *The Big Day*. They are gripping pieces and I'd like to know how pleased you were with them.

They were all right at the time. My agent said he'd get me seven or eight television films for Lew Grade, a couple of second features and even a feature for Irving Allen. He got all of those films for me, including one called *Let's Get Married* with Anthony Newley and Anne Aubrey, which was not a good film – not my script and not my scene. Of the two for Julian Wintle, I remember *Devil's Bait* was written by Peter Johnston and Diana Watson. I worked with them on the script to make it much tighter, less verbose, and also we gave the policeman, played by Gordon Jackson, much more character. Similarly the two girls who go off on a picnic, and one of whom is poisoned, had no depth at all in the original script.

It is one of the few British films of that period that deals seriously and unpatronisingly with ordinary lives.

Ah well, only by casting Geoffrey Keen as the baker. Julian wanted to have Leslie Dwyer or some comic. I think it was Geoffrey and Jane Hylton who made it real. Poor Jane died very young. I let them have Timothy Bateson as a camp dentist but that was the only bit of overt comedy I allowed. I liked Julian Wintle very much. Indeed, he was a dear and good friend, but he could sometimes be swayed by some flash agent promoting a dull actor. His partner, Leslie Parkyn, was just a businessman; Julian was the creative one. But they were both obsessed with running that studio, Beaconsfield, profitably for their company, Independent Artists; they had all the overheads to think of. I never wanted to make 'studio' films in the first place. I always wanted to work on location, but that was more expensive in those days, because equipment was so heavy then.

Then John Temple-Smith turned up with the script of *Doctor Syn* as made in 1936 with George Arliss. We'd signed Peter Cushing and Oliver Reed when all of a sudden Disney announced they had bought the rights to the *novel* of *Doctor Syn* and we realised we'd only bought the rights to the Gaumont-British *script* of *Doctor Syn*. But we had acquired it in good faith, so Disney said, 'Call it something else,' and we called it *Captain Clegg*. We made it in five weeks and it's one of the best films I ever made. I got leave from Rediffusion in my last year with them to do that one. I'd also done a play on television called *The Pot Carriers* which Associated British decided to enhance as a feature film. They asked me to direct it and I believe it is also one of my best.

Did you write *The Big Day*?

No, it was written by Bill MacIlwraith but I worked with him quite a lot. A very neat script emerged, another three-weeker. I wanted Donald Pleasence for the lead, and Andrée Melly – neither particularly glamorous, but wonderfully true performers. Julian fought hard for a 'star', like Donald Sinden. But I won that battle for realism. Colin Gordon, too, is an actor I love working with, he's so good. It was a strong cast – Harry H Corbett, William Franklyn, Susan Shaw, etc. I was still directing about six plays a year on television, so I knew lots of actors I could ring up and say, 'Come

on, it's a film, only three weeks and 300 quid, but . . .' Julian gave in and I cast everybody, right down to the small parts.

Do you recall Jack Greenwood, the producer on *The Headless Ghost*?

Back in 1958, he was a production manager. The real input came from a sharp American producer called Herman Cohen – whom I liked – but he was officially not allowed to work in Britain, so Jack Greenwood was credited as producer. That's one film we don't talk about, really. I hated the script but my agent talked me into it.

What was the studio at Merton Park like to work in?

Terrible! That's where we made *Sing Along With Me* as well. Merton Park was a small house and in the garden was an old bus garage with great pillars up the middle, so all your sets had to be hinged to fit around the pillars! Then they built another stage that was long and narrow to fit with the shape of the bit of ground, and that too had no soundproofing so if an aircraft went over . . . It was really hideous. *Headless Ghost* had a very small budget, but we did use Allerton Castle and real locations, and Clive Revill was a big plus.

It seems to me that the critics on the whole ignored these supporting features and that must have been very discouraging.

The only reason to make them was for the experience. You didn't get the chance of a press show at a decent hour. Yet all the good-class working American directors like Eddie Dmytryk started out on second features.

You suggested earlier there was a hierarchy in British films whereby television directors were not regarded highly.

Yes, and I quote. I was halfway through directing *Bitter Harvest* when Julian introduced me to John Davis, then head of the great Rank Organisation. He asked me what I'd done before. I mentioned that I'd won various awards for *The Last Enemy* and another one for *The Quare Fellow* and so on. Davis looked puzzled. 'What are they?' I replied they were major television dramas, enjoyed by millions of viewers. He frowned and said, 'Oh well, we won't hold that against you.'

Francis Searle

b. 1909

Director: *War Without End (1936), *Citizen's Advice Bureau, *Sam Pepys Joins the Navy, *Hospital Nurse, *Arrowman, *Coal Front (1941), *They Keep the Wheels Turning, *An English Oilfield (1942), *First Aid on the Spot (1943), *Student Nurse (1945), Girl in a Million (1946), Things Happen at Night (1948), Celia (& sc), The Man in Black (& auth) (1949), The Rossiter Case (& sc), The Lady Craved Excitement (& sc), Someone at the Door (1950), A Case for PC 49, Cloudburst (& sc) (1951), Love's a Luxury, Double Identity (& co-sc), Never Look Back (& sc), Whispering Smith Hits London (1952), Murder at 3 am, Wheel of Fate (& pr) (1953), Profile, Final Appointment (pr), A Yank in Ermine (assoc pr) (1954), One Way Out (& co-pr), Stolen Assignment (pr) (1955), The Gelignite Gang (1956), Day of Grace (& pr, co-sc), Kill Me Tomorrow (pr) (1957), Murder at Site 3 (& production company), *Music With Max Jaffa, The Diplomatic Corpse (pr) (1958), The Trouble with Eve (& co-sc) (1959), Ticket to Paradise (& pr) (1960), Freedom to Die, Dead Men's Evidence (& co-pr), Emergency (& pr), Gaolbreak (co-pr), Night of the Prowler (1962), The Marked One (1963), *Miss MacTaggart Won't Lie Down (& pr) (1966), Talk of the Devil (& pr) (1967), *Gold Is Where You Find It (& pr) (1968), *Hole Lot of Trouble (& pr), *The Pale-Faced Girl (& pr) (1969), *It All Goes To Show (& auth) (1970), *A Couple of Beauties (& pr) (1971)
* Short film.

It was directors like Francis Searle who worked to keep the double-bill programme filled during the twenty years following the end of World War II. Almost invariably, the required genre was the thriller, though Searle would have preferred light comedy, like his first feature film, *Girl in a Million*, which gave Joan Greenwood her starring début, and he came back to comedy at the end of his career with a series of short films. Two points of special interest in Searle's career are his association with Sir James Carreras and the early days of Hammer before it settled into its profitable horror cycle at the end of the '50s, and the importation of American stars to give lift to British 'B' films and to improve the chance of their distribution in the US. Robert Preston in *Cloudburst* may well be the first of this kind in postwar Britain; and Searle particularly enjoyed working with Pat O'Brien in *Kill Me Tomorrow*. As well, he gets interesting work from Hy Hazell in *Celia* and from Eddie Byrne in *One Way Out*, one of those films which show that small budgets can achieve good standards of production.
Interview date: August 1995

After getting started on shorts in the '30s, what was the nature of your filmmaking involvement during the war?

At that time I was with Gaumont-British Screen Services and Gaumont-British Instruction for seven years, making mostly commercials. Came the war, those firms were either shut down or, as we had a pretty good reputation, we were put on the reserved list and seconded to the Army, Navy and Air Force for training films. Then, in conjunction with the Ministry of Information, we made films like *Citizen's Advice Bureau*, *Sam Pepys Joins the Navy*, *Hospital Nurse*, and so on. It was marvellous training, because you had to direct on your feet without detailed scripts. You'd find out roughly what was wanted, and off you went and made it!

The only one I've been able to see was *An English Oilfield* and it was clear and interesting. What sort of audience did you have in mind?

That was sponsored by the Anglo-Iranian Company as part of the war effort. We were producing quite a lot of oil up in the Midlands and this was saving an enormous amount of tanker tonnage with imported oil. It was around 1942, when we were losing an enormous tonnage during a big submarine offensive. I thought it was quite well made. It was slotted in wherever a cinema would take it, as part of the war effort.

How did you get your chance to make your first feature film, *Girl in a Million*?

That was whilst I was still at Gaumont-British; the general production standard had gone up and it was after I'd made *Student Nurse*, which went on at the Dominion, where Sydney Box saw it. At that time he was riding high on *The Seventh Veil*. I got a call asking if I'd come and see him, and he offered me a directorial assignment – which scared the pants off me! It was a major film, you know – stars and all that jazz! I think we were all a bit nervous to start with but Joan Greenwood came across nicely enough – I think they all did. It was quite a nice picture with a neat story which goes way, way back.

Sydney took a chance on young directors. He'd come from roughly the same stables not so long previously. He and his wife Muriel had done a lot of documentary work. He wasn't like some producers looking over your shoulder the whole time – that's bloody terrible. He only came on the set if there was something a bit difficult. I remember the rather delicate scene with Joan and Tam [Hugh] Williams lying in a haystack; it was just after her character

had got her voice back and was trying out all the biggest words she could think of; he came down for that because that was going to be a climactic scene and could quite easily have turned into something a bit comic. But it didn't, it was charming. *Girl in a Million* was made at Riverside, then Sydney went over to Gainsborough almost immediately after. The art director on that film, Jim Carter, became a producer and he, with Alf Shipman who owned the studios, came along with *Poltergeist*, retitled *Things Happen at Night*.

What was your experience of working with those famous actors of farce, Alfred Drayton, Robertson Hare and Gordon Harker, on that?

It was adapted from a play by Jack Legh Clows, and it was real fun because there was so much creative stuff necessary. I'd let them have a go first, chat around it and let them try it for size. They were very funny men. We had a near-disaster on the film because we'd started shooting on the big ballroom scene (at Twickenham Studios) and we were on a very tight schedule. Then Alfred had a heart attack and I hadn't finished the big sequence, with crowd scenes and all that. We had to do a rewrite and try to get around it, because the actual sequence was sawing Gordon Harker in half, with the bits going everywhere. In the end Alfred had to go to hospital and he was off the film, but that wasn't until I'd finished all the other stuff. We brought him back from the hospital, laid him on the ground and just took a shot of him gawping at the sawing in half of Gordon, looking astonished and falling in a faint. That was the best we could do. It could have been a hell of an insurance claim!

That was made at Twickenham and *Girl in a Million* at Riverside. What were those studios like?

Alf Shipman ran three studios. He was quite big in distribution and he owned Twickenham, Riverside and Southall. Riverside was originally Jack Buchanan's, of course. The facilities were fairly good, much the same as all studios. The technical side wasn't anything like as advanced as it is today, of course, but we got all the back-up we needed, particularly on sound. Our lighting was a bit primitive – bloody great arcs and all this sort of thing – but we got away with it.

As a director, did you give your actors a lot of close guidance?

I didn't direct from the chair. I found that sitting around and chatting about a thing, in terms of interpretation, worked better. If you've done your casting carefully, it should not be necessary to give a lot of direction to actors. In any event, most of the subjects weren't deep in meaning; they didn't need great analysis. So you would choose people you thought could do the job. Once they knew the style the director was going to take and that he wasn't going to be temperamental, you got on well and the results were good.

Did you feel this was a good time, in the '40s and '50s, to be running a screen career in Britain?

Yes, with reservations. There was always the problem of our films getting distribution, not to mention a cloud in the sky called television. The pace didn't worry us because we loved it – making three or four pictures a year, writing one, editing one, shooting another – and it all worked once the juices were going. And you knew there was an audience. So one wasn't conscious of the pace at which one was forced to go. When I joined Jim Carreras, for example, at the beginning of Exclusive Films Ltd (before it was Hammer), they'd seen my stuff and, as they were on the up, wanting to do better, I was invited to join them. That was my first experience of shooting in houses rather than in a studio, and that was a real problem to me – no floating walls and staircases here. We coped, but it was a real challenge.

Did they put you under contract?

No, they didn't, though I was there for three years. In any case, there was a gentlemen's understanding and it wasn't until the horror films got going, which I couldn't take to, that the pace slowed for me. When we went from Cookham Dean to Bray, I actually lived at the studio because it was one of those enormous old E-shaped buildings with two wings. I had one of the wings, which also became the stages. Jolly convenient! That was part of the fun too. When the scripts came I had to rewrite them with the foreknowledge of what was available, so every room and door and staircase and closet was used. They went on using that house at Bray for some time, although they eventually started building stages. It's now quite imposing and a very efficient complex.

Is the difference between 'co-feature' and 'second feature' a matter of length, budget or the billing?

It would have been a bit of all those. A co-feature would have a bigger concept, a bigger budget (not much bigger!), be more ambitious and in all probability have a star of some sort, usually one from America – not current stars exactly, but first-ranking. People like Richard Carlson, Robert Preston, George Brent, and the like. That would be part of the deal: that America would provide the lead artiste and we would provide the movie in exchange for distribution territories. Having an American star was the bankable part. That meant our films would be released in America and theirs here. That's what Jim Carreras used to do and they were called Eastern and Western territories.

There seems to have been a very productive industry of co-feature and supporting feature films in Britain, in the '50s particularly. How fast were they made?

Four weeks would be top, a five-day week going into a Saturday if necessary. The front office frowned upon going over schedule; that really brought on the pain!

What was the average cost of these films?

This will give you a shock, when you think of present-day budgets. The second features were done for about £15,000 or £16,000, of which the artistes would be the main item. Co-features were more expensive, upwards of £20,000. Stamp money these days! They would have had more expensive actors who would stay at the Savoy and that sort of thing.

And for these films you would just be paid a flat fee? There was no chance of getting a higher percentage?

No, there were no percentages in those days for directors. We would just get a flat fee. The distributors would have a sort of agreed arrangement with the circuit. You see, every picture had to go on the circuit; if it didn't, it was damn nearly a loss. So what went on then, I wouldn't know. That's where Jim Carreras was so good: he was a brilliant salesman and well in with ABC, so most if not all of his pictures were distributed by ABC. Exclusive Films was formed ages ago by Jim Carreras's father, Enrico, whom I knew and did a bit of business with when I was at Screen Services. I would have five or ten thousand feet of film shot, say, in Malta and I'd buy it and make a short travel film in my spare time. There weren't so many distributors around in those days, of course. There were the big boys like Rank but they wouldn't look at you. There were Eros, Butchers, Renown and Exclusive, and quite a few more. Then when the Eady levy came in, they all became producers! Because they were asked to guarantee distribution and the money went to them first. Renown, for instance, made the famous *Miss Blandish* and I did one for them, with Terry Fisher directing and starring Pat O'Brien, called *Kill Me Tomorrow*. That was great, working with a great Hollywood old-timer. He was remarkable, a great professional and absolutely word-perfect in his lines. The leading lady was the Canadian actress, Lois Maxwell; that wasn't such a success but it wasn't my casting.

Tommy Steele was also in it briefly. One night Terry Fisher and I went to Al Burnett's, a nightclub in Swallow Street, and this young fellow came on and sang rock'n'roll numbers – terrific! We had to cast a scene with a jukebox and we decided to use him live. Much better. That was his film début. The number of times I've seen and heard and read about his early career, never once has it been mentioned that *Kill Me Tomorrow* was his very first picture.

I'd be very interested to hear about the other studios where you worked.

I worked at Twickenham, Riverside, Southall, the old MGM studios, Shepperton quite a bit, Bray (Ardmore in Ireland), Bray (UK), Pinewood, Bushey, Mancunian. Shepperton was my favourite. It was nicely situated, had its own little pub called the Britannia; its facilities were good and I liked the boss man, Andy [Adrian] Worker. I did several films at Twickenham, which was quite good, and I also did a few for Douglas Fairbanks at British National at Elstree. The old MGM studio at Boreham Wood was super and I also worked at Merton Park with Jean Simmons, who I cast in a short picture. Mary Field and Bruce Woolf were the bosses at GBI. Mary Field did children's films and she had a film she offered to me [*Sports Day*, 1945]. Aida Foster, who was a big agent for juveniles, set up an audition and Jean, aged about fourteen, came on as bright as a button; she had learned the part and that was it. I didn't bother looking at any of the others. Later, I introduced her to a big agent, who said, 'Yes, very nice, but not for us.' He's never forgotten or forgiven himself!

I'd also be interested to hear about some of the production companies you've worked for. What about ACT Films?

It was set up to make second features and to provide work during slack periods for any technicians who were out of work, as long as they were prepared to accept minimum rates. If you were out of work ACT would know, of course, and they approached me to produce. I had produced before and had a reasonable track record, so I did three or four films for them. I produced a couple with Terry Fisher directing, *Final Appointment* and *Stolen Assignment*. Later I produced Montgomery Tully's *The Diplomatic Corpse*. That was a near-disaster. We had cast Ursula Howells; then, at the very last moment, she was taken sick and couldn't appear. I then had to find another artiste quickly. We finished up with Susan Shaw and she was all right.

***One Way Out* had a rather unusual story, with Eddie Byrne as the policeman on the point of retirement, whose daughter gets caught up with criminals.**

It was done at Bray. That was down as being produced by John Temple-Smith. I was asked to direct but Temple-Smith was taken ill with appendicitis, poor chap, and never appeared, so I had to produce as well, which, as it was at Bray, was OK. It was made for a company called Major and distributed by Rank. Eddie Byrne was a lovely actor, and a great character. He was quite a lot younger than the character he played in that film.

Did you use location work much, particularly in films like *The Gelignite Gang* and *One Way Out*?

We used to think location work could be a time-waster and a money-loser. Apart from everything else, one had to have a guarantor of completion; the guarantors would go through your script and want to know how and where you planned to do it. If there was any doubt, you wouldn't get your guarantee of completion and if you didn't get that, you didn't get your money and you didn't get your distribution. In *The Gelignite Gang* that was an actual street, yes. I think I shot from the balcony of the block of flats. Obviously I had to go out sometimes; you'd do it as near to the studio as possible, so that the studio was a standby if the weather was bad.

Do you remember *Wheel of Fate*, with Bryan Forbes?

Yes, that was the picture on which he met his wife. I was scared stiff during that location. It was a night shoot and it was raining. The danger of falling over the lines in the dark was nerve-wracking. It was made at Riverside and the man in the wheelchair who's wheeled across is me! They couldn't find anyone to do it, so I thought I'd get into the film – do a 'Hitchcock'!

Certain names recur throughout your career and I'd like to hear any recollections you may have of Anthony Hinds, for instance.

Oh, Tony Hinds, the boss man at Exclusive and Hammer, was a very clever bloke, and I was working with him right from the word Go. Then of course he went on to Hammer and fame and glory with all the horror films. He was very good to work with. I hardly ever saw him (which was very good!), but he did become – and rightly so – quite a celebrity.

What about the writer Brock Williams?

Brock was a lovely chap, an ex-Warner Brothers man and a very good writer. He did *Ticket to Paradise* and *The Trouble with Eve* with Hy Hazell. That was one of the reasons that Hammer took me on – having had a bit of a track record with two or three features behind me. When it comes to artistes they always want to know who's directing, so it was easier to get up-and-coming names.

Most of your second features are crime films. Does this reflect your taste, or market demand?

No, it's not my taste at all. It was the market, because comedy is so much more difficult, and particularly with the low-budget support feature. But I enjoyed making them; after all, they were still movies and I loved making movies.

Peter Sellers

1925–1980

Actor: *Penny Points to Paradise, London Entertains, *Let's Go Crazy (1951), Down Among the Z Men (1952), Super Secret Service (1953), Orders Are Orders (1954), John and Julie, The Ladykillers, *The Case of the Mukkinese Battlehorn, The Man Who Never Was (voice only) (1955), The Smallest Show on Earth, *Dearth of a Salesman, Cold Comfort, *Insomnia Is Good For You (1957), The Naked Truth, Up the Creek, Tom Thumb, Carlton-Browne of the FO (1958), The Mouse That Roared, I'm All Right Jack (1959), Battle of the Sexes, Two Way Stretch, The Running, Jumping, and Standing Still Film (& pr) (1960), Never Let Go, The Millionairess, The Road to Hong Kong, Mr Topaz (& dir) (1961), Only Two Can Play, Waltz of the Toreadors, Lolita (1962), Dock Brief, Heavens Above!, The Wrong Arm of the Law, The Pink Panther (1963), Dr Strangelove, or* How I Learned to Stop Worrying and Love the Bomb, The World of Henry Orient, A Shot in the Dark (1964), What's New Pussycat? (1965), The Wrong Box, After the Fox (1966), Casino Royale, The Bobo, Woman Times Seven (1967), The Party, I Love You, Alice B Toklas (1968), The Magic Christian (1969), Hoffmann, There's a Girl in My Soup, A Day at the Beach, *Simon, Simon (1971), Where Does It Hurt?, Alice's Adventures in Wonderland (1972), The Blockhouse, The Optimists of Nine Elms, Soft Beds, Hard Battles (1973), Ghost in the Noonday Sun, The Great McGonagall, The Return of the Pink Panther (1974), Murder by Death, The Pink Panther Strikes Again (1976), Being There, The Prisoner of Zenda (1979), The Fiendish Plot of Dr Fu Manchu (1980), Trail of the Pink Panther (1982)*
* Short film.

'I have no personality of my own. I reached my present position by working hard and not following Socrates' advice – know thyself ... To me, I am a complete stranger,'[1] Peter Sellers claimed, and this sort of remark became a commonplace from him. Elsewhere, he extended this idea: 'In myself, I have nothing to offer as a personality but as soon as I can get into some character I'm away. I use characters to protect myself, as a shield – like getting into a hut and saying "nobody can see me now".'[2] There is an obvious echo of Alec Guinness in this, an impression reinforced by the fact that both played multiple roles in films, and both made much use of physical disguise. But, in terms of technique, they seem to have been opposites: where Guinness worked from the inside out to create a character, Sellers would say, 'I can't do anything from within myself. I have to project.'[3]

Sellers was already known to radio fans before he began in films and *The Goon Show* is no doubt a major influence on his style and, indeed, on the development of British comedy. 'I start with the voice. Once I have the voice, I find that I do what the character should do, so I no longer have to think about it. My approach is the opposite of Method acting.'[4] On the subject of voices, one has only to recall the malapropistic flatness of the union official, Kite, wistfully imagining Russia 'with all them cornfields and ballee in the evenings' in *I'm All Right Jack* or the RAF captain in *Dr Strangelove* or the general in *Waltz of the Toreadors*, drawing on Major Bloodnok of the Goons, to realise how crucial voice is to one's memories of Sellers.

He called *The Millionairess* (another memorable voice as the Indian doctor) 'my first really big international film',[5] and in many ways that seems unfortunate. His British films from *The Ladykillers* on, and including *I'm All Right Jack*, *Heavens Above!*, *Carlton-Browne of the FO*, the very funny *Only Two Can Play* and *The Naked Truth*, all showcase a flexible, often inspired comic talent, that depended on good writing and a very English ambience. After *The Wrong Arm of the Law*, he decided to do no more 'little English pictures'.[6] From now on the vocal gymnastics and the love of disguise were to be at the service of international films, some of which are among the worst films of their several decades.

Whether it was just bad judgement, or the effects of a chaotic private life, his film career looks increasingly wayward. There are the two successes for Kubrick, as the chameleon Quilty in *Lolita* and in the triple role of *Dr Strangelove*: 'I enjoyed working for Kubrick . . . the prime example of the bright, probing talent who will always say, "I think we should do it this way, but does anyone have any suggestions?" '[7] And, of course, there is the bumbling Inspector Clouseau, protagonist of several decreasingly funny farces. Of his first appearance, in *The Pink Panther*, Sellers decided, 'I'll play Clouseau with great dignity, because he thinks of himself as one of the world's best detectives.'[8] It was a huge box-office hit, but virtually nothing else in these 'international' years, apart from Chance the gardener in *Being There*, in America, seems to have made the break with Britishness worthwhile.

1 David Ansen, 'Peter Sellers' in Elisabeth Weis (ed.), *The Movie Star*, Viking, New York, 1981, p 352
2 Quoted in Michael Starr, *Peter Sellers: A Film History*, Robert Hale, London, 1991, p vii
3 Ansen, p 355
4 David Castell, 'The last masquerade of Peter Sellers', *Films Illustrated*, September 1980, p 469
5 Starr, p 57
6 Alexander Walker, *Peter Sellers: The Authorised Biography*, Coronet, London, 1981, p 156
7 Starr, p 74
8 Walker, p 158

Vernon Sewell

b. 1903

Director: *Kissing Cup's Race* (cam ass) (1930), **The Medium* (1934), **Facts and Figures*, **Men Against the Sea* (1935), **A Test for Love* (1937), **Breakers Ahead*, *The Edge of the World* (pr ass) (1938), *The Spy in Black* (some sequences), *The Lion Has Wings* (bomber sequence) (1939), *The Silver Fleet* (& co-sc) (1943), *The World Owes Me a Living* (& co-sc), *Latin Quarter* (& co-sc) (1945), *The Ghosts of Berkeley Square* (1947), *Uneasy Terms* (1948), *Jack of Diamonds* (1949), *Trek to*

Mashomba (1950), *The Dark Light* (& sc), *Black Widow* (1951), *Ghost Ship* (& pr, sc), *The Crimson Pirate* (2nd-unit dir) (1952), *Counterspy, The Floating Dutchman* (& sc) (1953), *Dangerous Voyage, The Radio Cab Murder* (& sc) (1954), *Where There's a Will* (1955), *Soho Incident, Home and Away* (& sc), *Johnny You're Wanted* (& sc) (1956), *Rogue's Yarn* (& sc) (1957), *Battle of the VI* (& co-pr) (1958), *Wrong Number* (1959), *Urge to Kill* (1960), *House of Mystery* (& sc), *The Winds of Change, The Man in the Back Seat* (1961), *Strongroom* (1962), *A Matter of Choice* (& co-auth), *Strictly for the Birds* (1963), *Some May Live* (1967), *The Bloodbeast Terror, Curse of the Crimson Altar* (1968), *Burke and Hare* (1971)

* Short film.

In Vernon Sewell's letters to me, he was very modest about his film career. When I finally met him on his ninety-first birthday for the first interview he had ever given, he was articulate about his work in various capacities in the '30s, his association with Michael Powell, his offbeat '40s films (including the long-missed Guignol, *Latin Quarter*, and the charming comedy-fantasy, *The Ghosts of Berkeley Square*), about *Battle of the VI*, which he regards as his most important film, and his steady output of supporting films in the '50s and '60s. Several of these starred his steam yacht, the *Gelert*: his owning the yacht enabled him to make the films; making the films enabled him to maintain the yacht. He is one of those unsung British directors who did some excellent work in unpretentious corners of the film industry. Anyone who has seen his notable 1962 co-feature, *Strongroom*, will know to what suspenseful purposes a limited budget could be put. He also made a genuinely unusual supernatural thriller, *House of Mystery*, in which the strangeness is generated more by performances than by special effects.
Interview date: July 1994

You started as camera operator on Castleton Knight's *Kissing Cup's Race* in 1930 and from the mid-'30s you had an important association with Michael Powell.

With a friend, I had set up a little studio to do film tests, and I had been experimenting with foreground models. No one could ever get them to match until I found a way of doing it. Mickey Powell, whom I met at Nettlefold's [Nettlefold Studio, Walton], was making quota films with Jerry Jackson and I showed him this method I had developed. He was amazed and said, 'We could make a whole bloody film in here!' So I found a story called *The Medium*, which had been a Grand Guignol film called *L'Angoisse*. Mickey wrote the script and I directed the picture, all in models.

Mickey wanted me to come in as a technical assistant on *The Edge of the World*, which we were to make on the island of St Kilda. The budget was infinitesimal and the owner of the island wanted £500 to let us use it. We didn't have that money so we found another island, which was serviced by a little rowing boat. But we had to find a ship to take all the gear out. I found a boat in Sunderland, originally a gunboat of about four hundred tons. It had been bought by the Sunderland Pilot Authority as a pilot vessel but they found it too expensive to run so it was for sale. It was ideal for us and we bought it for £600. Without that boat we couldn't have made the film, but the studio were so impressed at having a boat that it was on. The film put Mickey on the map. Korda liked the film and gave Mickey a job.

How did you come to direct your first big film, *The Silver Fleet*?

Mickey had made a film called *One of Our Aircraft is Missing*, a propaganda film for the Dutch Air Force. They then wanted him to go to Surabaya in the Dutch East Indies and make a film on the Dutch Navy. He didn't want to do it, so he suggested me as the best person for the job. So, I was transferred to the Dutch Navy, whose offices were at Marble Arch with that big Dutch firm, CNA. No sooner had I got there than the [Japanese] invaded Surabaya and the whole thing was off! They said they had gone to all that trouble to get me into their Navy, so could I think of something else to do? I found out that, just before the Germans arrived in Holland, a Dutch submarine was nearly completed and they towed it to England right under the Germans' noses. So I wrote the basic story of *The Silver Fleet*. After the première, I had offers of long-term contracts as a director from all the major concerns, but I had to go back to the Navy.

When I finally came out of the Navy, there was still a bit of credit about *The Silver Fleet* around, and I immediately got a job with Del Giudice, who wanted me to make a film about the Atlantic Fleet, the 'liberty ships'. The script was written by a man who knew absolutely nothing about the sea. I thought it was rubbish and didn't want to attempt it. *The Silver Fleet* was very much a popular success and I had great fun working on it with Ralph Richardson. I liked him very much. Kathleen Byron was in it too, and she actually wrote to me to say how glad she was that she'd started her film career with a sympathetic director. I never saw Mickey during the making of the film because he was off making *Colonel Blimp*. He saw the rushes but I never had to do a retake.

You filmed very steadily from the end of the war right through the '50s. How easy was it to keep up that sort of steady pace?

I always finished my films on budget and on time and I really did only the films I wanted to. When I came out of the Navy I was offered a contract by the Ostrers at Gaumont for £10,000 a year, which was a lot of money then. They had signed the contract but I hadn't. They wanted me to do *Madonna of the Seven Moons* but I said it wasn't my type of movie, and that, if it was a condition that I make it, I wouldn't sign the contract at all. They insisted, so I went to British National Studio (run by Louis Jackson) for £2,500 a year, and I had a great deal of fun. Louis Jackson was my producer on *The World Owes Me a Living*, *Latin Quarter* and also the Peter Cheyney movie [*Uneasy Terms*].

Latin Quarter was a big financial success and I followed it with *The Ghosts of Berkeley Square*, a picture I loved. It had a wonderful cast, with all the big stage stars, and it was a lovely picture. But you had to know a bit about English history to under-stand it. You had to know there was a Boer War and certain basic facts, but people didn't. It got quite good critical acclaim but it was a commercial flop. I had great fun with Robert Morley and Felix Aylmer, of course. Bob kept wanting to change the script – and in fact he did contribute some of the funny stuff – but I wouldn't let him do too much; he kept wanting to cut Felix out of it because Felix acted him off the screen. It had been quite a popular novel at the time, written by Caryl Brahms and SJ Simon.

One sequence went wrong at the beginning. It involved Martita Hunt, whom I would always visit in her dressing-room each morning with a bunch of flowers. She said she was delighted to be in one of my films and would do anything I wanted her to, that she was there for me 'to mould'. Anyway, in one scene the ghost was to materialise and throw bottles at her and frighten her. We had done all the preliminary stuff and were about to shoot the scene when she came to me and said, 'I'm afraid I can't allow anything to be thrown at me. I can't have my dignity demeaned.' We finally agreed that the bottle shouldn't be thrown at her until she had gone through an arch and it wouldn't actually hit her. The script called for an enormous plaster pot to be dropped by the props men after she had gone under the arch. Well, just as she walked under the arch the bottle came whizzing past her nose. She had enough momentum to keep going through the arch, then she turned to have a go at me about the bottle and down came this bloody great plaster pot, which only missed her by a few inches!

The Ghosts of Berkeley Square had a lot of trick photography, as you know. Now, travelling mattes had just started and I had seen a lot of them. A travelling matte means a dupe, and the dupe always advertises its arrival. Ernie Palmer [cameraman] said to me, 'Let's do it in the camera.' I knew that would put the shooting schedule up enormously, because I had triple-split mattes and the camera mounted on a concrete base, but of course the results were fantastic. Those ghost effects in *The Ghosts of Berkeley Square* were excellent and all done 'in the camera'. Ernie Palmer was very much like me, he was a mechanic.

How did your association with Derrick de Marney on *Latin Quarter* come about?

He looked the part. I didn't know him beforehand but we got on quite well. He had Associate Producer credit. Louis Jackson, who was head producer and head of the studio, had very little to do with the actual films. Derrick wasn't involved in the concept of the story at all; we discussed it together, as I did with all actors. He didn't like Beresford Egan at all. He had a part in *The Silver Fleet* and, when we came to cast the part in *Latin Quarter*, we couldn't find a classical actor. I thought of Beresford Egan and we tested him, against everyone's will. After the test there was no question that he had the part. But Derrick didn't like him and nor did Joan Greenwood, because he was a rather sinister man (and he had a sinister part in the film – he was the character exactly). He was a difficult, awkward man and he put everyone off. Mickey Powell gave him a job on one or two things but he never got much other work.

British National didn't have contract people. I chose the cast, which is where de Marney came in as associate producer. He had a lot to do with the casting and he knew Joan Greenwood from *The Gentle Sex* with Leslie Howard. We also had a very good art director. A lot of people said to me, 'I see you were very influenced by Monet,' which was nonsense, as I'd hardly heard of him.

What about your cameraman on *Latin Quarter*, Gunther Krampf?

Wonderful! Every single still or frame of his picture you could hang up on a wall. He and I got on extremely well, because, having been on the camera, I could appreciate what he was doing. He used to take an hour to light a set with fifty or a hundred lamps. But if you changed your ideas, then he had to relight the whole set. When he left us he went to ABPC and he told me he was so unhappy; they said he took too long to do everything and that he was 'difficult'. He was the most wonderful cameraman I ever worked with.

You made a lot of co-features during the '50s. What sort of budget would you have had for those?

Dangerous Voyage was a bit more expensive than most of them, but they were all well under £50,000. The shooting schedule for co-features was usually about a month. When the London press came out, some of the co-features I made were switched. For example, *Strongroom* was a very good movie. When it opened in the West End, it was originally the support, but after the good press it was switched to first. It was offered four weeks' run in the West End by Columbia, but the deal fell through, though we ended up with two weeks.

I also worked with Eros, for whom I'd made a very charming film called *Where There's a Will*. Delderfield [the playwright RF Delderfield] and I wrote the script together and it had a wonderful

cast. It is the only film I've seen where the audience applauded in the middle of the movie – and it happened both in the country and in London. It had to do with a farmer who died intestate and a lot of nieces and nephews wanted to inherit the farm. There was a scene where the Minister of Agriculture had come down and made a lot of speeches about the great progress in agriculture; an old farmhand said, 'Well, when I first come to work for the old maister, I got thirty bob a week and the cottage I lived in free, all sorts of things. Now what have I got? Don't you talk about progress to me, Mister!' and the audiences applauded.

I am impressed with what you achieve in your films on such limited budgets. *Ghost Ship*, *The Floating Dutchman* and *Dangerous Voyage* were all made for Merton Park. What was it like to work there?

Those three films were mostly made on my steam yacht, which was a wonderful prop, and it would have cost a lot of money to hire a yacht of that size. I only kept it going because I was able to push it into movies. In the end people used to say, 'Vernon! Your yacht again!' Some of the studio work was done at Merton Park. When [WH] Williams was there it was all right but when he got the sack and someone called Sloane took over, I decided I couldn't work with him so I didn't make any more films for Merton Park.

William Williams produced those three films you mentioned. There is an unbelievable story behind *Dangerous Voyage*. When I worked with Eros I had a good free hand with them. They had bought a dreadful motorcar racing story and had engaged William Lundigan to play in it. I said, sorry, I wasn't going to make the picture no matter who they had for it. They asked me what I would do because Lundigan was arriving in two weeks. I said I had another idea and there was a part in it for him. Then I said I had a story and Sidney Buchman (blacklisted and working anonymously) asked to read it. He said it was a very good story and he agreed to write the script. But Lundigan was never told of the switch. He arrived on the yacht one night, with all kinds of luggage; he said, 'What the bloody hell am I doing here on a yacht? I'm supposed to be doing a film about motorcar racing!' I said, 'You're not, you know!' He wanted to go ashore and I told him he'd have to swim, because I'd already put to sea (the steam yacht made no noise, you see). So he couldn't go back. Anyway, we had a long talk and a few drinks, and he was happy with the new story. It was quite a funny movie in the end, and the script was very good.

What did you really value in a producer?

For them to leave me alone – to make the deal, fix up the money and let me get on with making the film. What usually happened was that a budget and a schedule would be shown to me and I would agree or disagree to direct the film. If I agreed, I kept to it – which very few directors ever did. Because of that I was rarely troubled by producers, since they knew I would bring the film in on time and on budget. I did a lot with Julian Wintle and Leslie Parkyn at Independent and they left me alone. One I did for them was actually a remake of *The Medium*. It was called *House of Mystery* and I wrote it as well. The ending was sensational – the audience was absolutely stunned at the ending. Jane Hylton was a very good actress who should have got more work.

In the '60s you made a number of horror films. Did you have a special interest in this kind of film? There was Boris Karloff in *Curse of the Crimson Altar* and Peter Cushing in *The Bloodbeast Terror*.

I thought they were fun, very funny. The one with Karloff was based on a book by a famous American author, [HP] Lovecraft, called *Tales of the Witches' Room*. I read it and decided I would like to make it. They already had Boris Karloff for it but suddenly discovered they couldn't get insurance for him so he would have to be dropped. So we recast it with Christopher Lee. A week before the film started, the studio decided they had to have Karloff because they had to pay him, whether he died or not! So the whole script was rewritten a week before the start. Christopher Lee played the baddie and Karloff was written in as an extra character in a wheelchair, the goodie! They told me I had to have a naked woman in it somewhere, so I just showed a woman getting out of bed and that was it. I thought the whole genre was funny and I enjoyed doing those films.

People always like the story of *Burke and Hare*, the grave-robbers.

Ah, now that was very, very sad. It was my last picture and it should have been a very good movie. In the end it was recut, putting back scenes which I had cut out, with awful pop music, and the whole thing was a disaster, I never got a penny out of it. After that I decided not to make any more movies. I was in my seventies, then, so I decided to pack up and go yachting!

Moira Shearer

b. 1926

Actor: *The Red Shoes* (1948), *The Tales of Hoffmann* (1951), *The Story of Three Loves* (1953), *The Man Who Loved Redheads* (1955), *Peeping Tom* (1960), *Black Tights / Un, Deux, Trois, Quatre* (1961)

Though Moira Shearer quite properly identifies the plot of *The Red Shoes* as having something of the novelette about it, and though she finds its picture of the ballet world false, there is no denying that her appearance in it ensured her a high place in the British star hierarchy. She is remembered with a tenacity and affection denied to many whose careers were more prolific

and varied. She made two more films for Michael Powell who, by most accounts, was not an actor's dream: *The Tales of Hoffmann* offers a kaleidoscope of colour and image and gives Moira Shearer a chance to show her artistry as a ballerina, whereas *Peeping Tom*, in which she does a banal little dance before being murdered, seems almost like a comic parody of the role that made her famous. Her own favourite part is that of the various redheaded heroines of Harold French's charming *The Man Who Loved Redheads*; it makes one wish she had developed the talent she showed there for romantic comedy.
Interview date: July 1994

Did you avoid the fate of Victoria Page, heroine of *The Red Shoes*, by retiring from the screen and stage in favour of domestic life?

The whole story of Victoria Page is such nonsense from the point of view of any real person, that I can't answer that question realistically. You have to take that film with a huge tin of salt, because there was never a ballet company anywhere which was like that. I'm sure no dancer of any generation ever had this supposedly appalling problem – ending in suicide, if you please – between real life and the ballet. No, leaving the ballet was entirely my own wish. My training was in the Russian style and my subsequent career was with a very English company, which was rather constricting. I was a leading ballerina with the Sadler's Wells (now Royal) Ballet for twelve years and, by the early '50s, had also been given a taste of straight acting. I realised that this interested me much more than the narrowness and self-absorption of a classical dancer's life. And I was now married, with the first of my four children, and I greatly valued normal family life.

Did you admire particularly any of the dancers in films at the time?

Oh, Fred Astaire, yes. His dancing was of a totally different style, of course, but I think he was probably the best dancer I've ever seen in my life. He was unique. It was wonderful to see a man with such grace and elegance as well as absolute facility. Among his dancing partners I admired Eleanor Powell. She hadn't Fred's grace, but her technique was wonderful; she was so expert, such a strong presence, and she matched him better than any of the others.

Had you been nursing any ambition to appear in films when *The Red Shoes* came along?

Far from it, and I held out against that film for a whole year. The director Michael Powell was extremely put out by my continued refusal. It never occurred to him that a young girl wouldn't be overwhelmed by his offer. But I didn't like the story or the script, which seemed a typical woman's magazine view of the theatre, and I also realised he knew very little about the ballet. Also, at that time, 1946, I had just started to dance the ballerina roles in the big classics and the last thing I wanted to do was to interrupt this difficult work with a sugary movie. Powell bombarded me for weeks in 1946 and I remember thinking, 'I have to get rid of this man.' However, he finally got the message and went off in a huff, saying to me, 'I am now going around the world to find the perfect girl for this part.'

He came back a year later; presumably he hadn't found his perfect girl, though he had now engaged Léonide Massine and Robert Helpmann, both of whom I knew well, as dancer-actors and to arrange the choreography. Powell went on and on at me and I think he must have bombarded Ninette de Valois because she called me to her office and amazed me by saying, 'For God's sake, child, do this film and get it off your chest – *and* ours, because I can't stand that man bothering us any longer!' I asked one question, 'If I do it, can I come straight back to Covent Garden when the film is complete?' and her answer was, 'Yes, of course you can.' And I did – but not happily. There was a lot of jealousy and bad feeling. I'm afraid I was very naïve. Helpmann told me later that the only reason de Valois wanted me to make the film was to give advance publicity in America for the first coast-to-coast tour of her company in 1949. Which, of course, is what happened.

Was Powell someone you admired and respected in British films?

I had seen his films and, yes, I did admire his cinematic expertise, which is exactly what I still feel today. His films were never my favourites because there was always something cold and rather pretentious about them, but they were certainly never dull. There is a lack of humanity in them all – but then, *he* was lacking in warmth and humanity. He was technically very imaginative and original, but he was also extremely egocentric, unlike his collaborator, Emeric Pressburger, a delightful Hungarian whom we all liked very much. Emeric wrote the scripts for their films – unfortunately a glossy, melodramatic one for *The Red Shoes* – but that was the way of most films of the '30s and '40s.

Was it in fact your first acting role?

Yes, it was. I enjoyed acting but I would have liked it a lot more if I could have been directed by someone of kindness and understanding. Powell was very difficult with actors. He didn't give any of us detailed direction and, perhaps it's unkind to say this, I don't think he could. He didn't seem at all interested in the performances of actors; his main concentration was the camera itself, the experiments with colour, tricks, effects – all the things at which he was brilliant. But he was uneasy with actors and was known as a bully, especially with women. Each day he would pick on someone, always someone in no position to stand up to him, and simply go on and on with cruel sarcasm until the victim was a wreck and quite unable to function properly.

And I'd like to mention the two vast volumes of autobiography that he completed at the end of his life. The kindest view of them is that his mind had gone in old age. But, knowing him, I think the welter of lies about so many people and past situations was quite deliberate. I particularly disliked the way he wrote of his dead wife, Frankie – it was disgraceful and almost certainly untrue.

You were playing opposite two very experienced performers in Anton Walbrook and Marius Goring. Were they supportive and helpful to you?

They were complete opposites. Anton was grand in the old 'star' manner. He wore dark glasses, had a special caravan where he ate lunch alone and never mixed with the rest of the cast. There was virtually no rehearsal, he simply appeared for his shots, speaking only to Powell. I'd never come across anyone like this before. Marius was completely different, charming and very jolly. I became fond of

him immediately but, even so, I never felt I could ask for any particular guidance. I don't quite know why, but perhaps because of the strained, uncomfortable atmosphere of the filming, though we also had a lot of fun, usually when Powell was away from the set. Technical crews in film studios are wonderful, so friendly and supportive and in a way they take the place of an audience and one performs for them.

The sets for *The Red Shoes* still look fabulous nearly fifty years later. What do you recall of them, or the great designer Hein Heckroth?

I liked him very much personally, although I wasn't absolutely wild about his designs. I suppose it was their Germanic quality, which I found rather crude and garish. Perhaps because I was brought up with early editions of Grimm and Andersen fairytales and their much more delicate illustrations. I preferred his designs for *The Tales of Hoffmann*; his Germanic tendency was right for that. And I particularly liked my frilly pantalettes for the doll, Olympia!

Presumably you had almost unlimited space in which to dance, compared with a stage.

No, the sections we danced on were never as large as the Covent Garden stage. Our great difficulty was dancing on concrete; there were floorcloths, sometimes quite slippery, but underneath always the concrete. It is death to the calf muscles. And there were other hazards, mainly the long waiting while cameras, lights, playbacks, etc, were organised. Eventually they would be ready and expect us to leap instantly into the air, but we were now cold and had to limber up yet again. No – filming ballet is not easy.

The camerawork is wonderful and I wondered how aware you were of the camera? Were you required to be technically aware?

No, not technically, but the camera was placed where an audience would be so we naturally performed 'out front'. If by 'technically aware' you mean did we know how the camera would record what we were doing, no – we had no idea of this. And like everyone brought up in the theatre, I missed a live audience very much. I missed, too, the pleasure of performing a role from beginning to end, building it up without interruption. You can improve, polish, change, but it is *your* work and you stand or fall by it. Filming is quite different because so many people have a hand in the finished product. Far more footage of the *Red Shoes* ballet was filmed than was ever seen publicly, and it was cut and edited to suit the technicalities. From several takes of a sequence, one would be much better from the dancing point of view, another for the lighting or camera angle. Always the latter was chosen, which was miserable for us.

Had you worked with any of those dancers before – Robert Helpmann, Léonide Massine or Ludmilla Tcherina?

I had worked with Helpmann and Massine many times and also several of the *corps de ballet* dancers, but I'd never met Ludmilla before. However, with all the hard work, everyone gets on to a very happy, colleague-y basis straight away, everyone trying to do their best despite the difficulties. I think we all felt the same disappointment when we saw the finished film. It was simply the view that someone right outside the profession would have of a Russian ballet company.

What do you remember of the film's reception?

It was received with great excitement. I discovered only recently that Rank and John Davis tried to stop the film half-way through, having seen the rushes. They thought it was going to be a total disaster at the box office and it had cost a fortune already, so they decided to close it down one Saturday. Luckily, Alexander Korda stepped in with the necessary backing and shooting continued on the Monday. Then it became a huge box-office success, and is still shown almost fifty years later.

Did the success of *The Red Shoes* make possible three years later the filming of *The Tales of Hoffmann*, a more daring film commercially?

Yes. It *was* more daring but also rather clumsily put together. A complete opera is too much for the commercial cinema and Powell put all the action into the first third of his film and was then left with long static stretches almost to the end. For a man with such a gift for cinematic effect it seemed very odd. Amusingly, he made it for Alex Korda, who was terribly bored by the result.

What do you remember about dancing the Doll role? Was Michael Powell helpful to you there?

No, he simply arranged the shots and where the camera would be. This was purely dance – it was Frederick Ashton's choreography and, in a way, he became the director, watching (just as in the theatre) to see if it was as he wanted it and asking for another take if necessary. It was very enjoyable –

we had to hit a few marks for the lighting and there was a certain amount of stopping and starting for technical reasons, but working with Fred was such a pleasure and relief.

What are your recollections of Pamela Brown?

She was a charming, funny woman. Sadly, I didn't see her often as she was only on the set on certain days, but I admired her acting very much. I was exceedingly sorry that her part as Niklaus in *Hoffmann* was cut down until it was hardly there.

When you came back to England from making your one Hollywood film. *The Story of Three Loves*, you made one of my favourite 1950s British films, *The Man Who Loved Redheads*. What recollections have you of it?

I loved it. Harold French directed, delightfully and easily, but had a little difficulty with his producer, Alex Korda, who announced he would redirect a certain sequence himself. And he did – Korda, of course, began his career as a director in Hungary. But poor Harold French, I've often wondered how he felt about it. But he was soon back with us again. It was a charming play by Terence Rattigan, originally called *Who is Sylvia?* and we had a marvellous cast, full of the best British character actors (Roland Culver, Harry Andrews, Denholm Elliott, and so on). I played several parts and wished I'd had more experience before tackling it. Timing is everything – a few years later I could have played those parts so much better, but it was the film I most enjoyed doing.

Your last film appearance for Michael Powell was his notorious *Peeping Tom*.

Yes, I did that out of kindness of heart. Michael Powell arrived on my doorstep in 1959, with an ashen face and a large script under his arm. Could I help him? A small part – it would only take four days – the actress he had cast, Natasha Parry, had flown off to New York. At least, would I read the script? So I did, and thought it quite interesting, stupidly forgetting his sadistic streak. It *was* only four days in the studio and I saw nothing else of the filming, so the finished article was quite a shock.

Was it horrifying to do?

No, it wasn't. There was such an air of unreality and artificiality on the set and, as I've already said, Michael Powell was hardly the man to release emotion in his actors. I thought the critics were absolutely right about it. I am only sorry that, recently, those violent boys, Scorsese and Coppola, have tried to make it into a cult film. It is deeply depressing.

Was he utterly unprepared for the response to the film?

I imagine he was, though I didn't see him again for a number of years. I think he probably loved the publicity and would have been contemptuous of anyone who didn't understand what he always called his 'art'.

The only film of yours I've never seen is *Black Tights*.

It was a French film of four of Roland Petit's ballets and, alas, there were drastic cuts. I had to get back into practice after six years and it was really difficult. I danced Roxane in Roland's *Cyrano de Bergerac*; he's a most gifted choreographer and this was the single ballet of the four which was genuinely romantic. Typically, the producers and distributors decided it would bore the public, who would want only the more jazzy, modern works, so it was cut to ribbons. I was terribly upset when I saw the travesty of the final film.

Everyone will want to know why you never made another film.

The simple answer would be that I had never been offered further films, but, in fact, the offers continued for years, including unlikely ones like *El Cid* with Charlton Heston. But I've always found my marriage and my children infinitely more important than any career, so no great decision had to be made.

Dinah Sheridan

b. 1920

Actor: *I Give My Heart* (1935), *As You Like It* (as dancer), *Irish and Proud of It* (1936), *Landslide, Father Steps Out, Behind Your Back* (1937), *Merely Mr Hawkins* (1938), *Full Speed Ahead* (1939), *Salute John Citizen* (1942), *Get Cracking* (1943), *29 Acacia Avenue, For You Alone, Murder in Reverse* (1945), *The Hills of Donegal* (1947), *Calling Paul Temple* (1948), *Dark Secret, The Story of Shirley Yorke, The Huggetts Abroad* (1949), *No Trace, Paul Temple's Triumph, Blackout* (1950), *Where No Vultures Fly* (1951), *The Sound Barrier* (1952), *Appointment in London, The Story of Gilbert & Sullivan, Genevieve* (1953), *The Railway Children* (1971), *The Mirror Crack'd* (1980), *Adam and Evil* (1997)

Watching Dinah Sheridan in television's *Don't Wait Up* in 1990, it was hard to believe that nearly forty years had passed since *Genevieve* appeared. She seems scarcely changed: she has the same graceful touch with comedy and the same wry charm, and she treats the men around her with the same good-humoured exasperation. The other surprising thing is that the continuing affection she has inspired in film-goers is based on such a small number of films as a top star. After fifteen years of taking whatever came along – including George Formby, the *Paul Temple* films and the *Huggetts* – she finally found major British stardom in Ealing's African adventure, *Where No Vultures Fly* in 1951. Two years later, after the success of

Genevieve, she remarried and retired from the screen until 1971. When she did return as Mother in Lionel Jeffries's fond adaptation of *The Railway Children*, it was enough to make you weep for what British films had been missing. In the early 1950s, she was perhaps the most attractive female star in British films; all these years later one hopes she will not be allowed to retire again.

Interview date: September 1989

After eight films in the '30s, you began your '40s career with *Salute John Citizen* and *Get Cracking*. How did you come to be involved in these?

When war broke out we were all conscripted. I was Chief Ambulance Driver for Welwyn Garden City, and I also became secretary to the local Surveyor and Sanitary Inspector. Then suddenly, when I had been doing this for about two years, I got a call to go and see George Formby, for *Get Cracking*. I walked into the office at Denham and there was no Formby, no director; only Mrs Formby sitting behind a desk. She looked at me and asked immediately if I was married; I said, 'Yes,' and she asked, 'How long?' I said, 'Three months,' and she said, 'You'll do.' And if I was on call, she was also on call! She would not let George go anywhere near the leading lady. From a comedy point of view I learned a lot. But I felt so sorry for George! Everyone seemed to work with him at some stage, and they always said that if you played opposite George Formby you went on to better things.

Salute John Citizen *was an 'A' film directed by Maurice Elvey. Were there clear distinctions between 'A' and 'B' productions?*

In a way perhaps, because you went to a different studio and there was a different set-up. When I married Jimmy Hanley he had been invalided out of the Army, and he got a Rank contract. In films like *Salute John Citizen* and *29 Acacia Avenue*, we were being cast as a team – until I started having the children while Jimmy went on filming. But if I was offered a job I had to take it. A fan in eastern USA recently sent me copies of those two films: I thought *Salute John Citizen* was very dated and not much more than a propaganda war effort, whereas *Acacia Avenue* stood up pretty well.

Did you feel that directors like Montgomery Tully and Maclean Rogers were helpful to you?

Oh yes. I was very happy making *Murder in Reverse* with Montgomery Tully – to look at, you would say he was a bank-teller, but on the set he suddenly came to life. Maclean Rogers was a good 'B' picture director; he churned them out. I did a lot of 'B' pictures: for Mac at Butchers Films of course, and elsewhere. I worked for Mac later in *Dark Secret* and also *The Story of Shirley Yorke*, which was better than most. I was very lucky to get that, and it gave me my first meaty romantic lead. It was written by AR Rawlinson, our ex-Attorney-General's father.

What was your experience of Denis and Mabel Constanduros in relation to *29 Acacia Avenue* and *The Huggetts Abroad*?

I never met Denis or Mabel Constanduros, who wrote the play, *Acacia Avenue*. We did a lot of the interiors for that at Riverside Studios, Hammersmith. During indoor filming one of the lights fell off the gantry and everything was chaos. That was the result of the first V-2, which dropped in Chiswick nearby, so you can date it from that. Henry Cass, who directed it, was a dedicated Moral Rearmament enthusiast, desperately trying to convert everyone.

What about Ken Annakin, director of *The Huggetts Abroad*?

Now there was a good director; a nice, inventive man who, one realised, deserved to go further. The *Huggett* films started with *Holiday Camp* and my son, aged one, was in it with his father. Jack Warner and Kathleen Harrison were a wonderful couple and the *Holiday Camp* family was so successful that they became 'The Huggetts' and were very cleverly whipped up by the Constanduros team and others. I replaced Jane Hylton in the third of them. Jane was ill and Jimmy rang me from Islington Studios to tell me I was starting work the next day. It meant quick arrangements for two small children, and my hair had to be lopped off considerably.

Your years as a top star occurred in the early '50s, starting with *Where No Vultures*

Fly.

Suddenly my career took off, in 1949. I was flown out to Africa, which wasn't easy, of course, with two very small children and having home troubles. However, suitable arrangements were made, and that was really the beginning for me. It was the Royal Film of 1951 and it led to four films I made in 1952 – *The Sound Barrier*, *The Story of Gilbert & Sullivan*, *Appointment in London* and finally *Genevieve*.

While *Genevieve* was waiting to come out, I married the man who was at that time the Managing Director [John Davis] of the Rank Organisation, and agreed to give up my career. It was only subsequently, when I went to Hollywood, that I learnt of some of the roles I'd missed as a result, in big films like *The Court Jester* and *The Million Pound Note*. But there's no point looking back and feeling bitter; I'd made my choice.

How did you come to be in *Vultures*?

I wish I knew! A sudden offer on the telephone; I made arrangements for my children and flew over to Kenya within two weeks – with misgivings. But I had had no other offer – it had to be accepted, and its proving such a popular film was the turn of fortunes I needed. When I went to try on the clothes, the wardrobe mistress said, 'Oh, you're not the same size as the other lady, are you?' I asked what other lady, and she implied someone had dropped out or was fired – I still don't know who it was; that's why the whole thing was so rushed.

What was your experience of working with Harry Watt?

Harry was a large bear of a man who should have been tied to a tree and not allowed to come to civilisation. He made very good films, but his idea of filming was that, if he got a good shot of you dying and a jolly good shot of the blood, he'd change the script. I loved being in Africa, even though it was under terribly primitive conditions; I was ready for a total change and it did me good. After four months Michael Balcon sent out Hal Mason, his Production Manager, to ask us to stay an extra two months because they had got a better picture than they expected. They wanted some more good shots with animals.

I think it was the first film not to disguise the animals with back projection; we were actually with them. For instance, there was a scene with a rhino charging the truck we were in; off we went to look for a rhino that would like to charge. We found one sitting under a yellow thorn bush, very tired and hot

and not wanting to be disturbed. The white hunter driving the truck stopped, got out, made rhino-mating noises, and the rhino began to think it was worth getting up! He finally charged; the truck was parked at right angles to him. The white hunter got back into the truck and tried to start it but it stalled. Fortunately the rhino must have realised we were an immovable object and he planted his feet and literally braked before hitting us, but spraying us with dust all the same. By now he was really mad. We did that sequence four more times; the animal was right beside me as we accelerated away, and I could have touched him. But all Harry wanted to know was had they got the shots, not were we all right!

You followed *Where No Vultures Fly* with *The Sound Barrier*. Did you feel it was a good role for you, even though a secondary one?

It was wonderful, because apart from the leading lady, Ann Todd, I was the only other female and I was thrilled to get it. I went to see David Lean and Bill O'Bryen [in charge of production for London Films], and they offered me the part. It was a marvellous part but I have to tell you that a lot of me ended up on the cutting-room floor. I didn't mind being secondary to Ann Todd; what I wanted was to be directed by David Lean, who was wonderful with actors; he somehow brought the best out in you. He praised and criticised at the right time.

Were you in a position to choose roles by then?

No, I don't think I was ever in that position. I had two children to support. *The Story of Gilbert & Sullivan* came along and I was sent to Shepperton to audition for Mrs D'Oyly Carte. Eileen Herlie got the part but they rang to ask if I would play Sullivan's girlfriend instead. I was much happier in that role, though it was quite small. The film was a big popular success. During the making Maurice Evans asked me if I would go to New York and do a play – *Dial M For Murder* – with him but I couldn't because of the children. Then I went on to play opposite Dirk Bogarde in *Appointment in London*, which was marvellous. He's a terribly nice man and a brilliant film actor. I felt it an honour to work with him; it was a well-written, stirring account of wartime flying and I was proud to be in it. While doing that, I had three scripts poked through the letterbox. One was a fairly ordinary 'B' picture about a racecourse, to star Nigel Patrick [*Grand National Night*]; one was about women police

[*Street Corner*]. Both could have been mine by saying yes. The third, which was not mine by any means, was *Genevieve*. I quickly said no to the racetrack and the policewomen, and the next week went to a restaurant called the Vendôme, to meet Henry Cornelius, producer-director of *Genevieve*. I squeezed into a window seat, but when finally Henry Cornelius came in he said in a loud voice, 'I see you're sitting with your back to the light because you know you're too old for this part.' Not a charming start, but that sort of thing went on all the way through. He was not a character I'd have enjoyed working for again. After I had this near-fatal lunch with Henry Cornelius, Bill Rose [screen-writer] came in and we had a few glasses of wine. I must have relaxed and been funny because I was offered the role.

Before the lunch, I'd talked to Dirk when we were out on location somewhere near Shepperton Studios; I told him about the three scripts and he told me to take *Genevieve* if I got it. He had turned it down because he didn't want to do comedy again. They didn't want Kenneth More, they wanted Guy Middleton; they wanted Dirk instead of John Gregson, Claire Bloom instead of me and I can't remember who they wanted instead of Kay Kendall. But we got on so well together and it worked. Ninety per cent of the credit must go to Bill Rose, a wonderful writer.

What lured you back to do *The Railway Children* in 1970?

Lionel Jeffries. He phoned and asked if I had read it or seen it on television. I had read it years ago. He asked me to meet him for lunch. I had my fingers crossed under the table the whole time, hoping he would make a firm offer. We were already on the set when Lionel confessed he·had also had his fingers crossed, hoping I would agree to do it! We had lunch and discussed the film but there was no definite offer made at the time. From *Genevieve* to *The Railway Children* was eighteen years – and another nine years to *The Mirror Crack'd*. We made the film in Yorkshire and it was the most wonderful, joyous time I ever had in making a film. Lionel was an excellent director for actors, being such a very good actor himself.

Do you think British cinema was ever able to compete satisfactorily with American films?

No, because we don't have the money here to make big things. Britain has never really gone in for making stars, whereas look at America, with Bette Davis, Hepburn and so on – they made stars and they had the money to do it. In Britain it's all very genteel, unsophisticated, and made on a shoestring. It always seems as if British cinema hasn't had enough money to tie its stars down, so they go off and work somewhere else.

Alastair Sim

1900–1976

Actor: *The Riverside Murder, The Private Secretary, Late Extra, A Fire Has Been Arranged* (1935), *Troubled Waters, Wedding Group, Keep Your Seats Please, The Big Noise, The Man in the Mirror, Strange Experiment* (1936), *Clothes and the Woman, Gangway, A Romance in Flanders, Sailing Along, Melody and Romance* (1937), *The Squeaker, Alf's Button Afloat, The Terror, This Man is News* (1938), *Inspector Hornleigh, Climbing High, This Man in Paris, Inspector Hornleigh On Holiday* (1939), *The Mysterious Mr Davis, Law and Disorder* (1940), *Inspector Hornleigh Goes To It, Cottage To Let, Her Father's Daughter* (short) (1941), *Let the People Sing* (1942), *Waterloo Road* (1945), *Green for Danger, Hue and Cry, Captain Boycott* (1947), *London Belongs to Me* (1948), *The Happiest Days of Your Life, Stage Fright* (1950), *Laughter in Paradise, Lady Godiva Rides Again, Scrooge* (1951), *Folly To Be*

Wise (1952), *Innocents in Paris* (1953), *An Inspector Calls*, *The Belles of St Trinian's* (1954), *Escapade*, *Geordie* (1955), *The Green Man* (1957), *Blue Murder at St Trinian's* (1954), *The Doctor's Dilemma*,

Left Right and Centre (1959), *School for Scoundrels*, *The Millionairess* (1960), *The Ruling Class* (1972), *Royal Flash* (1975), *Escape from the Dark* (1976)

'**A**s I passed imperceptibly from a beautiful child to a strong and handsome lad, I wanted more than anything else in the world to be, of all things, a hypnotist. I practised on gentle dogs . . .'[1] With such remarks, and there were very few of them, or of any other kind, did Alastair Sim keep interviewers at bay. 'His dislike of self-analysis'[2] and the fact that he was 'always resolutely publicity-shy'[3] are well known.

'I stand or fall in my profession by the public's judgement of my performances. No amount of publicity can dampen a good one or gloss over a bad one,'[4] he rightly but irrelevantly claimed. 'Irrelevant' in the sense that, once having caught the public fancy in the early '40s, he could thereafter do no wrong in its eyes. Like Margaret Rutherford, his great co-star in *The Happiest Days of Your Life*, he was a one-off, creating a gallery of memorable eccentrics.

He came to the London stage in 1930, after an apt-enough stint as an elocution lecturer, and entered films in 1935. In a rare interview, he said: 'At first I was not sure if I liked films. The sequences are so disconnected and mechanical I thought I should have difficulty "getting into the skin" of the characters. But I soon found that the care, precision and concentrated energy that attends the photographing of each scene conspires to pitch one into the right frame of mind.'[5]

He had some success in two series at the end of the decade: the *Inspector Hornleigh* films with Gordon Harker and the two *This Man* films with Valerie Hobson and Barry K Barnes. However, it was such roles as the 'shilling doctor' in *Waterloo Road*, the deceptively vague Inspector Cockrill in the hospital thriller, *Green for Danger*, the dithering headmaster in the popular farce, *The Happiest Days of Your Life* (all for Launder and Gilliat), and the bizarre creator of a boys' comic strip in the seminal Ealing comedy, *Hue and Cry*, that won him the character stardom which he retained until the end of his life.

There are several performances in more serious vein – the title roles in Brian Desmond Hurst's *Scrooge* and Guy Hamilton's *An Inspector Calls*; the headmaster in Philip Leacock's *Escapade* – but, in serious roles, it always seemed as if he might suddenly undermine the whole enterprise with some sly flight of fancy.

1 Charles Hamblett, 'Mr Sim has a secret', *Picturegoer*, 2 December 1950, p 13
2 Hamblett, p 13
3 David McGillivray, 'Alastair Sim', *Focus on Film*, Summer 1972, p 10
4 McGillivray, p 10
5 Sam Heppner, 'Alastair Sim is the name', *Film Weekly*, 21 March 1936, p 29

Jean Simmons

b. 1929

Actor: *Give Us the Moon, Mr Emmanuel* (billed as 'Gene Simmons'), *Kiss the Bride Goodbye, Meet Sexton Blake* (1944), *Sports Day* (short), *The Way to the Stars* (1945), *Caesar and Cleopatra, Great Expectations* (1946), *The Woman in the Hall, Hungry Hill, Uncle Silas, Black Narcissus* (1947), *Hamlet, The Blue Lagoon* (1948), *Adam and Evelyne* (1949), *Trio, So Long at the Fair, Cage of Gold, The Clouded*

Yellow (1950), Angel Face, Androcles and the Lion (1952), Young Bess, Beautiful but Dangerous, The Robe, Affair with a Stranger, The Actress (1953), The Egyptian, Désirée, A Bullet is Waiting (1954), Guys and Dolls, Footsteps in the Fog (1955), Hilda Crane (1956), Until They Sail, This Could Be the Night (1957), Home Before Dark, The Big Country (1958), This Earth is Mine (1959), Spartacus, Elmer Gantry (1960), The Grass is Greener (1961), All the Way Home (1963), Mister Buddwing, Life at the Top (1965), Rough Night in Jericho, Divorce American Style (1967), Heidi (1968), The Happy Ending (1969), Say Hello to Yesterday (1970), Mr Sycamore (1975), Dominique (1978), December Flower (1984), The Dawning, Going Undercover (1988), How to Make an American Quilt (1996)

'Let him go, let him tarry,' sang Jean Simmons at a crowded RAF dance in one of the imperishably affecting moments of 1940s British cinema, in Asquith's *The Way to the Stars*. If she had done no more she would have earned a footnote in this history; the sad thing is that British cinema did let her go, could not find the means to make her tarry when her husband Stewart Granger took off for Hollywood in 1950. It probably has to be allowed that, if there is a new-minted freshness about her early career in Britain, it is Hollywood that made her a star. There is a portrait shot of her in a 1953 *Picturegoer* in which, in the best sense of the term, she has the gloss of stardom, bearing out the accompanying report on her first Hollywood film, *Angel Face*: 'Jean carries the film with the confident ability one usually credits to those older, established stars who can weather the bad, the worse and the indifferent pictures with popularity and reputation unscathed.'[1]

Before that, she had been acting in Britain since *Give Us the Moon*, on which 'Because of the labour laws they needed someone who looked like a twelve-year-old but actually was older [she was fifteen]. I played the brat sister of Margaret Lockwood.'[2] She was put under contract to Rank and rushed into a dozen films, not all of them well chosen, but she always made a vivid impression, never more so than as the young Estella in Lean's *Great Expectations* and, in Powell's *Black Narcissus*, as the sexy Indian girl who distracts Sabu from serious study. Nevertheless, a columnist asked 'Are they being fair to Jean Simmons?'[3] when in 1947 she was chosen to play Ophelia in Olivier's *Hamlet*, without adequate 'preparation'. Later, she herself said, 'I had never seen *Hamlet* on the stage ... I'm sure he [Olivier] didn't think I'd given the best Shakespearian reading he'd ever heard. He's a patient man, however, and he sat down and explained to me his conception of what Ophelia really is ...'[4]

There are other British performances that deserve mention: heroines in various kinds of peril, in that neglected piece of film gothic, *Uncle Silas*, in *So Long at the Fair*, the underrated Ealing melodrama, *Cage of Gold*, in which her distraught young wife is a persuasive site for a clash of values, and the nifty thriller, *The Clouded Yellow*, and one charming comedy role in *Adam and Evelyne*. Then came America. 'If he shakes your hand, it's as good as a contract,'[5] she told Rank's first biographer, enthusing that 'Mr Rank is such a *homely* man.'[6] However, she was not pleased to discover in Hollywood 'that without even telling me, Mr Rank and Gabriel Pascal [she had a tiny role in *Caesar and Cleopatra*] had sold me to RKO.'[7] She eventually got good roles in Hollywood, and returned only rarely to England to act: for example, in the lamentable *Say Hello to Yesterday*, in which she seemed demeaned by the role and the film. In later years, she has appeared on television, once, bizarrely, and with an odd poignancy not wholly to do with the role, as Miss Havisham in a mini-series version of *Great Expectations*.

1 Margaret Hinxman, 'Simmons is a natural', *Picturegoer*, 17 January 1953, p 10
2 Alvin H Marill, 'Jean Simmons', *Films in Review*, February 1972, p 71
3 Wilson D'Arne, 'Are they being fair to Jean Simmons?', *Picturegoer*, 2 August 1947, p 5
4 *Films in Review*, February 1972, p 72 (quoting a *Saturday Evening Post* article of 1965)
5 Alan Wood, *Mr Rank: A Study of J Arthur Rank and British Films*, Hodder & Stoughton, London, 1952, p 40
6 Wood, p 197
7 WH Mooring, 'So much waiting about, says Jean Simmons', *Picturegoer*, 1 March 1952, p 10

Sir Donald Sinden

b. 1923

Actor: *Portrait from Life* (1948), *The Cruel Sea* (1952), *A Day to Remember, Mogambo, You Know What Sailors Are* (1953), *Doctor in the House, The Beachcomber, Mad About Men, Simba* (1954), *Above Us the Waves, An Alligator Named Daisy, Josephine and Men* (1955), *The Black Tent, Eyewitness, Tiger in the Smoke, Doctor at Large* (1956), *Rockets Galore, The Captain's Table* (1958), *Operation Bullshine* (1959), *Your Money Or Your Wife, The Siege of Sidney Street* (1960), *Twice Round the Daffodils, Mix Me a Person* (1962), *Decline and Fall* (1968), *Villain* (1971), *Rentadick, Father Dear Father* (1972), *The National Health, The Day of the Jackal* (1973), *Island at the Top of the World* (1974), *That Lucky Touch* (1975), *The Children* (1990), *Balto* (voice only) (1995)

Donald Sinden was a star in *The Cruel Sea* (virtually his first film) and remained so in the twenty-two films he made in the decade that followed. In his own opinion, he never again had such a good role as that of Lockhart, Jack Hawkins's second-in-command, in *The Cruel Sea*, but, during his years with Rank, he was kept very busy, making three or four films a year. His screen *personae* were usually those of dependable young officers or of irrepressible ladykillers. If Lockhart initiated the former strain, it was his medical student Benskin in *Doctor in the House* which launched the latter. Just once he was allowed to be a dangerous thug (in *Eyewitness*), and, on the other side of the law, he played the aristocratic detective Campion in *Tiger in the Smoke*. In the '50s, he worked five times with director Ralph Thomas in popular entertainments which established Sinden as a reliable Pinewood star. He has built a substantial stage reputation in classical roles; his inimitable voice and comic timing have enlivened several television series; and he is the author of two entertaining volumes of autobiography.
Interview date: September 1989

Did you feel the '50s was a good time to come into films in Britain?

No, not at all. It was just the wrong time. Just before my time the large studios had their own stables of actors under contract – there was the Charm School for the Rank Organisation, ABPC had their own contract players, MGM-British had their lot – and they all tried to copy the Hollywood pattern. Of course, they just couldn't do it. Rank still had a large stable of actors – the largest they had in any one year, when I was there, was fifty-one under contract. One fondly imagined that Rank was looking after one's interests; not at all, they were looking after themselves. So, when a script arrived on my table, I thought, 'They in their wisdom have chosen me, of all people, to be in this film!' It really meant that six other actors had turned it down already. They didn't 'build' stars the way the Hollywood studios did. English actors are always first and foremost theatre actors and 'films' used to be considered what you did for the money, while your 'art' was in the theatre.

How secure did the British film industry feel to you in the '50s?

Secure? We were seeing the rundown at that time. Each year heads would roll. One of the most hideous experiences each year was the Rank Organisation Christmas Dinner, given at the Dorchester or wherever, for contract artistes, directors and producers. J Arthur Rank didn't involve himself in the actual business of making films; but this dinner was his celebration. You knew as soon as you arrived how you stood. The Managing Director was at one end of a large table and the nearer you were to him, the more 'in' you were. If you were at the other end of the table you weren't going to last another year! I spent eight years halfway up the table, which was a safe place to be! Mine was a seven-year contract, renewable on their part (never on mine), and I did eight years because in the middle of it I did a play which ran for a year. My contract bought me two houses – one in London and one in the country, so I can't grumble. I would have to work a long time in the theatre to do that.

You began at Ealing with *The Cruel Sea* but spent most of the decade at Pinewood. Were there significant working differences between the two?

Not really. We worked with the same directors, the same cameramen. At Pinewood they were making sixteen feature films a year in my time, something happening on every stage, so it was a bit more of a 'factory' than Ealing was. I think more particular care went into each individual film at Ealing, but Rank distributed Ealing films as well, which was how my contract came about. When Ealing cast me for *The Cruel Sea*, it was distributed by Rank and my contract with Ealing contained a clause that Rank had the right to put me under contract if they wanted to, and they did. It was all the same organisation with different pockets. At Pinewood, I was under contract to Rank and I had the right to

turn a script down, although they didn't like it if you did. If you turned two down, what a pity, because your contract wouldn't be renewed next year! So you went along with it. Then, for individual producers working under the Rank banner – say, Betty Box or Joe Janni – we were cheaper than having an actor from outside. If they used a contract artiste for a film, they paid the other 'pocket' half that actor's annual salary, and that was cheaper than any other actor because there was no daily or monthly rate or even a picture rate.

You started as a star and never had to serve an apprenticeship, did you?

No, but I don't think I ever had another film as good as *The Cruel Sea*. We were very well looked after but we worked for our living. Being contract artistes, every Saturday throughout the summer months we were sent off to do 'public appearances', such as opening garden fêtes. Every week there would be a film première, which we were expected to attend: the Rank Organisation would send a Rolls-Royce to the door, pick us up in our dinner jackets or evening dresses, and whisk us off to the cinema, where the floodlights would be on and the movie cameras working. In that way, Rank gave me a valuable name, which I wouldn't have got otherwise.

The names which recur most commonly throughout your '50s films are Betty Box and Ralph Thomas. How influential do you regard them in your career?

My third film was *A Day to Remember*, which, until recently, no one had a copy of. That was for Betty and Ralph. I got on very well with them and so they found lots of things for me. I worked more for Betty than for any other single producer. In those days the producer and director were part of a team, and they tended to cast jointly. The director would do the work on the floor and the producer would do the office work. Of course, the film industry is a director's medium whereas the theatre is an actor's medium. Ralph had a great sense of humour and an ability to get on very well with his cast. There was a great enjoyment in being on the set with him, for, say, *Doctor in the House*, every day. You looked forward to going in each morning. We were always encouraged to enjoy ourselves – I mean to find enjoyment in our work.

There was a real sense of camaraderie?

Oh yes. We all knew each other and would go to each others' sets and have lunch together at the restaurant. That restaurant was great fun, not a hierarchical thing at all. When American actors came over we could not understand their hierarchy at all. An exception was Anne Baxter, who was very un-American in that she joined in with everyone else when she came over here to do *Mix Me a Person*. Our salaries were laughable compared with the Americans'. When we came to London in 1953 for the studio work on *Mogambo* Clark Gable received £750 a week apart from his salary – I don't know what that was – as his living expenses. I was being paid £50 a week in total! However you look at it, there is a discrepancy there!

Were you satisfied with the range of roles you got in the '50s?

It was a stable. Dirk Bogarde was the most successful member of that stable: I was inclined to get the 'Bogarde parts' that Dirk didn't want. He was able to do the more dramatic stuff which I would dearly love to have done, such as *A Tale of Two Cities*. Kenneth More had done the Douglas Bader film, *Reach for the Sky*, so he was getting that sort of thing.

Then there was the *Doctor in the House* sort of character which, if you like, I invented – the chap after all the girls – and I grew a moustache for it. Suddenly, all they wanted was for me to wear a moustache and be funny, in every film, which was frustrating. Brian Desmond Hurst [director] and Peter de Sarigny [producer] had got a marvellous script about the Mau Mau and they had gone out to Kenya shooting miles of footage, *not having cast the film*. The title was *Simba*. I was doing a film called *Josephine and Men* and the producer wanted my hair highlit with blond for it; I came into the restaurant one day and Peter de Sarigny saw me. 'Good God! Would you have that done all over?' he said. 'Of course,' I said, so I had my hair dyed blond all over and played the part. But previously they had never thought of the possibility of me dyeing my hair. All I was expected to be was a dark-haired young actor after the girls.

What do you remember of working with Roy Ward Baker, director of *Tiger in the Smoke*?

Margery Allingham wrote it and I believe she was rather disappointed in the film. On the whole, I prefer to be left alone by a director, because, whichever way you look at it, all actors work on some form of Stanislavsky method of getting themselves into a character. So you have an initial discussion with the director as to what sort of character you are going to be playing. Working with

John Ford, for instance, you found he was not at all interested in actors.

What do you recall of *The Captain's Table* for Jack Lee?

Jack now lives in Australia; he is the brother of Laurie Lee. *The Captain's Table* was very light and funny, yes. In the Pinewood restaurant one day, Joe Janni, the producer, told me about this terrific script which meant three months' location work cruising around the Greek islands. I said, 'Count me in!' I didn't even want to read it! Then, three weeks before shooting was to start, Joe phoned to let me know the budget wouldn't stretch to the Greek islands and we would be cruising around the Channel Islands instead. Ten days before shooting started I went for a costume fitting and the wardrobe man told me they were doing it at Tilbury Docks! So we spent three months on this bloody liner, tied up at the docks! We would shoot out to sea on one side, then, when they wanted the reverse shots, they turned the liner around.

You worked with Basil Dearden and Michael Relph on *Rockets Galore*. How clear-cut were their functions as producer and director?

They always worked as a team. Michael Relph didn't direct, though, did he? [He is credited as co-director with Dearden on several films and as solo director on two.] They were always there on location or wherever we were, but the producer looked after contracts, budgets and so on. *Whisky Galore!* was based on a true story, whereas *Rockets Galore*, not so good, was on the same location but based on an invented story.

I'm amazed at the richness of the casts in British films of that time – Raymond Huntley, Dora Bryan, Maurice Denham, etc – often in tiny roles.

Yes, England has produced marvellous character actors over the years but very few romantic leading men, of which the Americans have many. Our strength has always been in the character actor field, the difficulty always being to find two people to play the leads and bring the customers in.

Did you enjoy working with Fred Zinnemann in *The Day of the Jackal*?

Yes indeed, Fred was wonderful. Why am I blossoming more about Fred as a director than about any of the others you mentioned? Because he loved actors and knew a great deal about the theatre, which a lot of film people do not. Before we started shooting *The Cruel Sea* I had lunch with the director, Charles Frend, and I started analysing my character. Charlie looked at me goggle-eyed. He said, 'We've not cast you for the villain. Just play yourself!' I said, 'What *is* myself? I'm an actor – all I do is play other people!' Now *Fred* and I would have little chats, with him saying, 'Too theatrical, too theatrical.' He would cut it down to nothing, and it's true, the best screen acting *is* doing nothing. The camera does fall in love, as people say. It's not a matter of acting ability at all.

Hugh Stewart

b. 1910

Editor (incomplete): *The Man Who Knew Too Much* (1934), *Dark Journey, Storm in a Teacup, Action for Slander* (1937), *South Riding, St Martin's Lane, Q Planes* (1938), *The Spy in Black* (1939), *49th Parallel* (ass. ed.) (1941)

Producer: **Tunisian Victory* (1944), *Trottie True* (1949), *Night Without Stars* (1951), *The Long Memory* (1953), *Up To His Neck* (1954), *Man of the Moment* (1955), *Up in the World* (1956), *Just My Luck* (1957), *Innocent Sinners, The Square Peg* (1958), *Follow a Star* (1959), *Make Mine Mink, The Bulldog Breed* (1960), *In the Doghouse* (1961), *On the Beat* (1962), *A Stitch in Time* (1963), *The Intelligence Men, The Early Bird* (1965), *That Riviera Touch* (1966), *The Magnificent Two* (1967)
*Documentary film

Before becoming a producer in the post-war British cinema, Hugh Stewart acquired a great deal of experience in the cutting rooms of Gaumont-British and Denham, working for the top directors of the day. That is to say, he edited for Victor Saville, Alfred Hitchcock and Michael Powell. After war service, during which he co-produced the famous documentary, *Tunisian Victory*, he embarked on his career as a producer with the charming musical, *Trottie True*, setting up his own company, Europa, under the Rank Organisation. An admirer of the great American silent comedians, he eventually became the regular producer of ten very successful Norman Wisdom films and of the three attempts to launch the television comedians, Morecambe and Wise, on the big screen.
Interview date: October 1992

How did you regard the function of a producer?

It varies from time to time. I like to think that I was the kind of producer who basically was creative, because I'd learnt about how to make films. I wasn't someone who just happened to have some money and had come in from the outside. I attached great importance to an instinct for story, and I think the producer has to be responsible for the script. I worked very closely with my writers at all times. If you have a good story to start with, you can make a good script or a bad script; if you make a good script, then you make a good film or a lousy film, depending on the director; but you can certainly never make a good picture out of a bad idea.

You would also expect to be in control of the financial side?

Yes, I would. The reason I was quite pleased to be a Rank producer, working through the Rank Organisation, is that basically they had competent financial people. My understanding of the money side is to say that this particular set or this particular scene is not worth spending the money on from a story point of view. I prided myself on being able to shoot what was in the picture; I have no use for the kind of person who shoots five hours of film and throws out three of them. I think it is grossly unprofessional from everyone's point of view, both artistically and practically.

You either edited or co-edited some of the important films of the '30s.

Yes, I had been assistant editor to Ian Dalrymple on Victor Saville's *Evergreen*, with Jessie Matthews, which I still think is one of the best British musicals ever made. Victor liked me, so when it came to doing something with Korda he asked me to come along as his editor. They were under the banner of London Films and Korda's top editor was a wonderful man called William Hornbeck and it's his credits that appear on everything. I *did* cut a picture but it was a contractual arrangement that Hornbeck's name was to be on everything. I'm not denigrating him but I did do the job.

You had done *The Man Who Knew Too Much* for Hitchcock at Gaumont British in 1934. Did his technique make it easier for an editor?

The unjust thing about it, which applies to any business, is that you make your name and get your jobs on the films that are good, the ones that are workshopped. You *learn* your job on the ones that you have to rescue somehow. So cutting for Hitchcock got me my jobs, but in fact they were so well shot that, as long as I was competent, Hitch was pleased with the way it came out. On the first day, he came on the set, put the script down on the table and said, 'Right, another one in the bag.' To him it was already set, already done: he wanted to indicate that the script was *it*.

What were your impressions of Michael Powell, for whom you worked on *The Spy in Black* and *49th Parallel*?

What happened on *The Spy in Black* was that Michael, who was very autocratic, was up against the producer Irving Asher, who was also quite a tough character. When the last shot was in the bag, Irving refused to let him come into the studio. Mickey knew me and he wrote me a twenty-three-page letter in his own hand; it was on lined foolscap. He said, 'I have complete confidence in you, so would you please bear these things in mind?' I found in fact that there were several missing shots. There was a sequence at the beginning of Conrad Veidt's U-boat going through a minefield, which had been insufficiently covered, and I somehow got some material for that and one or two other special perspective shots.

Were you attached to the Army Film Unit when you co-directed *Tunisian Victory* with Roy Boulting?

That's right. I was also co-producer, if you like, with Frank Capra from America. Roy was back at Pinewood and he and James Hodson were the writing–directing team. I was in Africa and didn't come back until the work was well underway. We were sitting in the theatre dubbing when we were told that Capra was coming to the Grosvenor tomorrow and would like to see how far we had got. Luckily we had got as far as dubbing. I thought it very important that the American public, who had been very much concerned with their own thing, should realise that Britain was in a war.

You worked for Two Cities during the '40s . . .

For Two Cities the first film I produced was *Trottie True*. After the end of the war, Korda asked me to go back with him at MGM. Needless to say he quarrelled with MGM, so I found myself in the impossible position of working for an American company which was not producing, and Alex was in total chaos, though I did in fact work as his associate producer on *An Ideal Husband*. I shot some second-unit material for MGM. Alex wanted me to work with him on *Bonnie Prince Charlie*, but unfortunately I got jaundice. While I was recuperating I read *Trottie True* and liked it so much I bought it. MGM didn't want to do it so I took it to Two Cities and they agreed to do it. In effect I set myself up as a producer for that. I saw it recently and Jean Kent is very good: she had great punch, a very good character.

What do you recall of the director, Brian Desmond Hurst? Did you choose him?

Yes, I did. There were various people considered – Harold French was one – but Brian was the man. A very able fellow with a maverick Irish sense of humour. There again, I was in an unfortunate situation because I was under contract to Metro and I became the victim of a contract war between MGM and Two Cities. I was really 'hired out' by Two Cities from MGM to produce this film, which was in fact *my* film. I had planned it and paid for the copyright. Once the film was about five weeks underway, Two Cities told me I could go back to MGM, which was a shock to me. In fact I stayed on the film because, when it came to the music and the dubbing and cutting at the end, I had to be in on it. It was very mortifying for me.

It has been said that British cinema has been bedevilled by the British class system. *Trottie True* **seems to address this issue.**

I was interested in that. My father was Scots-Northern Irish and my mother was Scots-born in New Zealand, and I detested the class system. The nice thing about the film business was that it didn't matter who you were as long as you did your job properly. When I went into the Army it was like going back a hundred years. It changed a lot in the '60s, of course, but not really enough. The upper class in Britain is still intact – smaller and more beleaguered, admittedly.

Did you choose your next film, *Night Without Stars*?

Yes, and the company I made it for, Europa, was my company. Quite frankly I didn't want David Farrar, I wanted David Niven. This is a story about a man going blind, who is resentful of this but, because of his essential charm, he never lets you know this. Maurice Teynac, who was a leading actor in the film and well known in the Paris theatre, said, 'David is good with the men but he is no good with the girls.' He was terrified of the love scenes with Nadia Gray. Oh, he was a good actor but I wanted Niven, but the Rank Organisation said, 'Niven is finished.' In 1949! Anthony Pelissier, who directed it, had enormous talent. He was an extremely able man, intuitively clever, a man of great taste but there was something . . . I'm sure it was difficult being Fay Compton's son.

As producer of these films, and of *The Long Memory*, **I imagine you exerted a lot of control over casting.**

I wanted John McCallum to do this film, because

I knew his face would express the terrible anguish in his instinctive knowledge that his wife was lying.

What was your experience of Robert Hamer as director?

Robert at this stage was an alcoholic, it was terrible. The film was a mediocre success and I think Hamer made it as good as it could be. At his best he was brilliant. What he liked doing was something like *Kind Hearts and Coronets*, which was extremely stylish, something for an élite audience. John Davis wanted all producers to be independent, so the Rank Organisation made a deal with Europa Films (my own company) to hire my services, hence every film I made was made through Europa. It was always 'The Rank Organisation presents . . .' on the credits but it was called 'Hugh Stewart Productions', I always got that. John Davis was a very tough character but I got on very well with him. I never tried to bluff him or toady to him.

Between 1954 and 1965 you made ten films starring Norman Wisdom. How did you become involved in these?

I'd always adored the Laurel and Hardy, Keystone Cops comedy, and Harold Lloyd. I didn't realise it until a certain time, but instinctively it had always been my ambition to get back to making films with a minimum of dialogue. I made a film for Ronald Shiner, a Cockney, who was quite fun although not very distinguished. Rank wanted to do another comedy and asked me if I'd do it. *Up To His Neck* did very well and that gave Earl St John the idea, so, when he got Norman Wisdom in the first place, he gave it to Paddy Carstairs and put in as producer-in-charge a very nice guy called Maurice Cowan. They had great success with the first film but Paddy didn't get on with Maurice. Then Maurice wrote *One Good Turn*, and Norman said he wouldn't work with Maurice again, so they asked me to do it, and it worked.

Norman Wisdom was a great popular success because he represents a very special kind of indomitable spirit that says, 'I'm as good as you lot, I have a bath every Saturday.' It's childish but he does represent something uncrushable. The central gift he had was being a particular kind of clown; there's no good in comparing him with anybody else. He's Norman Wisdom and nobody else. He wasn't really a funny man offscreen but he had a tremendous impetus and drive.

The first thing I had to do was convince him that the thing was OK; he'd start off deeply suspicious. He was very insecure. He'd done everything on his own, he'd started from scratch; all his achievements were entirely his own effort, and he needed a lot of convincing. He would never believe that anybody was really on his side. All Norman's films were directed by either Bob Asher or Paddy Carstairs. Paddy had a sort of instinct (he was the son of Nelson Keys) and there was a thing between them. Paddy was fairly casual in his attitude; he did a multitude of things with the greatest of ease and he was a little too easy. He did things purely on instinct with not a lot of finesse. Bob, on the other hand, was a brooding, Jewish talent, terrified of lots of things. He was a mass of inhibitions. Very good for comedy! He understood Norman, and Norman liked him.

You see Jack Davies as the best of the Wisdom writers ...

Yes, the happiest times in my film life were working with Jack. We would meet and discuss ideas during the mornings and then again the next day, fresh but remembering what we had talked about. The story would firm up in Jack's mind, and at the end of two or three weeks he would have the main story structure and principal characters set. We would then show it to Norman. My main problem then was to curb Norman's enthusiasm and keep the script to the right length. He was a great contributor and learned with every script, so that eventually he would work with Jack very closely. Bob would only like to come in when the script was basically set and ready for development. The four of us would bring the script to the final shooting stage, and Bob would do any detailed writing he wanted for the actual shooting. The work was intense, but once we had decided what we wanted it did not take long to deliver the finished script.

Which of the Wisdom comedies do you feel most satisfied with?

The first colossal hit I ever had was *The Square Peg*. It broke through in the outside world, particularly in the Soviet Union. This was the film in which he played a dual role. In *On the Beat* he also played a double role, but it was even more than that, because he had to be Norman the dummy impersonating the gangster and also play the poofy hairdresser. We had a lot of fun with that one. Those two and *A Stitch in Time* were the best, I think. All of his films made money, though, and what's more they had to do jolly well for the Rank Organisation to admit they'd made money.

The series came to an end with *Early Bird* in 1965. You also produced *Innocent Sinners* in 1958. What drew you to that?

I loved the story. It was a book by Rumer Godden called *An Episode of Sparrows* and the studio wouldn't have a project with a title like that. We settled for *Innocent Sinners*. It was the one film I made that got universally good notices, it got prizes, and yet it died a death – the biggest disaster I ever had. As far as I was concerned the principal thing was the children. The critics, like Paul Dehn, went overboard for it: it really got under their skin. Philip Leacock directed – I was very pleased with him. Neil Paterson wrote the script, which was very difficult because Rumer Godden's story was very gossamer, and I was trying to get some bones in it. She hated what Neil did.

Why was it so hard for British films in America?

I remember seeing Louis B Mayer at MGM on one occasion during the war. He said, 'Don't let Mr Rank think he can shake his Union Jack at me!' They didn't want to encourage distribution of British films because they had their own industry to look after. What they would do would be to take British talent and absorb it over there, so you got Rex Harrison becoming an American star. There may be many explanations, one of which could have to do with accents. But for instance, take Morecambe and Wise. They were an enormous success when they came out on television and the Americans living over here loved them as much as we did. But when they were shown in America, it didn't work.

You produced three of their films. *The Intelligence Men*, *The Riviera Touch* and *The Magnificent Two*. Why did they never quite click on screen?

In fact the films were successful, but I think they are primarily television people. Their whole technique, together with their writers', was based on really codding other things like *The Count of Monte Cristo*. They were sketch artistes and my job on the films was really to turn a series of sketches into a ninety-minute film. I adored making them and they've all done well, but they didn't get the critical acclaim we all hope for.

Sylvia Syms
b. 1934

Actor: *My Teenage Daughter* (1956), *No Time for Tears, Woman in a Dressing Gown, The Birthday Present* (1957), *The Moonraker, Ice Cold in Alex, Bachelor of Hearts* (1958), *No Trees in the Street, Ferry to Hong Kong, Expresso Bongo* (1959), *Conspiracy of Hearts, The Virgins of Rome, The World of Suzie Wong* (1960), *Flame in the Streets, Victim* (1961), *The Quare Fellow, The Punch and Judy Man* (1962), *The World Ten Times Over* (1963), *East of Sudan* (1964), *Operation Crossbow, The Big Job* (1965), *Danger Route* (1967), *Hostile Witness, The Desperadoes* (1968), *Run Wild Run Free* (1969), *Asylum* (1972), *The Tamarind Seed* (1974), *Give Us Tomorrow* (1978), *There Goes the Bride* (1979), *There Goes Tomorrow* (1980), *Absolute Beginners* (1986), *A Chorus of Disapproval* (1988), *Shirley Valentine* (1989), *Shining Through* (1992), *Dirty Weekend* (1993), *Staggered* (1994), *Food of Love* (1997)

From the first, Sylvia Syms had starring roles: she was never one of that unhappy species, the British film starlet, and nowadays when she plays even a quite small role, such as the headmistress in *Shirley Valentine*, she invests it with a star's authority. She has in fact become a very striking character actress, on stage and television, as well as on the screen. As she says, she was lucky – in the male-dominated cinema of the '50s particularly – to get a series of strong women's roles. After being launched by the Wilcoxes in *My Teenage Daughter* and *No Time for Tears*, she worked for several of the most interesting directors then working in British cinema, including Roy Ward Baker, Basil Dearden and Pat Jackson. Above all, she was associated with J Lee Thompson, for whom she had three of her best roles: as the 'other woman' in *Woman in a Dressing Gown*, as the army nurse in the excellent war film, *Ice Cold in Alex*, and in the film version of Ted Willis's play *No Trees in the Street*. In a different vein, she was a charming heroine in David MacDonald's swashbuckler, *The Moonraker*, and caught the satirical, acrid mood of Val Guest's *Expresso Bongo*.
Interview date: July 1991

You must have been almost the last star created in the 1950s.

I certainly wasn't 'created' in the way of people nursing my career or guiding me nicely. The only person who nursed me was Herbert Wilcox, who saw me in a television play, interviewed me and gave me the leading part in a film called *My Teenage Daughter* opposite his wife, Anna Neagle. However, I did a very stupid thing. I had been seen in a television play by a charming man called Robert Lennard, who discovered lots of people, and he offered me a contract with ABPC [Associated British Pictures Corporation]. The idea that anybody would pay me £30 a week to work was beyond my wildest dreams! I did another television play then with the Lyons family, and Ben Lyon warned me not to sign any British contracts, that he wanted me to meet some people from 20th-Century-Fox. However, I was frightened by the idea of going away from home, so I signed my ABPC contract. The film with Herbert Wilcox came out and I was an overnight sensation, as they say, and I had saddled myself with a seven-year contract, the options on which were all on ABPC's side. I did my first four starring roles for £30 a week – films like *Ice Cold in Alex*, *No Trees in the Street* – and I genuinely thought they were being kind to me because they gave me these big parts.

What do you remember of playing Anna Neagle's rebellious daughter in *My Teenage Daughter*?

I was so crashingly ignorant. I was very young and Anna and Herbert cosseted me and spoiled me. They made the part bigger as we went along but I was unaware of what they were doing for me, because I had no criterion against which to measure it. When the film was ready, I remember Anna saying I would have equal billing above the title, but I had no idea what they were giving me. Their generosity was incredible. They didn't pay me much but it was more than I was paid for films subsequently. I had a car every day and my meals served in my room at Shepperton, so that I could rest during lunchtimes.

Anna Neagle also starred in your next film, *No Time for Tears*. What do you think was the essence of her enduring popularity?

People just liked her. I can't say that I have often seen her do great performances, although when I was very young I adored her in a film about Nell Gwyn. When she did *Odette*, people believed it. If you played a war hero on the screen today as they really were, nobody would believe you, because they really did believe in behaving impeccably. They didn't use bad language when they were being tortured by the Gestapo!

***Woman in a Dressing Gown* was the first of your three films for J Lee Thompson. Did you**

enjoy working with him?

Yes, he's a strange man, lives in Hollywood now, but he was a good director. I think one of the clever things about Lee and Ted Willis is that they got the right people for the right parts in *Woman in a Dressing Gown*. It was important that my part be played as a respectable girl who inadvertently falls in love. When I was playing the part, hero-worshipping Anthony Quayle as I did, it seemed to me absurd that any wife could behave as Yvonne Mitchell's character did in the film. The part was very close to me, because one of my problems was that, as well as being a gifted actress, I thought it was my bounden duty to be a gifted housewife – to the detriment of my work, because I was always in conflict. So I lived the part.

What do you think about *Conspiracy of Hearts*, which you made for the Ralph Thomas –Betty Box team?

Conspiracy of Hearts was one of my happiest films. I've never worked with a producer who got the small things so right as Betty did. We filmed at Certosa near Florence, although the interiors were done at Pinewood. It was based on a true incident and was really very moving, and it seemed more so when we were making it because Yvonne was Jewish. It was quite successful and I actually won an award for it, a huge eagle, for being the most popular actress in Spain. Ralph gave me a part later in *The Big Job*, which was a very funny film. I think Barbara Windsor must have been busy, so they talked me into playing the tarty sort of role I wasn't often allowed to do.

Pat Jackson told me that *The Birthday Present* is the only one of his later films he is pleased with. What do you remember of it?

I had worked with Tony Britton before on stage, and he was a very 'hot property' at the time, having just played Romeo opposite Virginia McKenna on television. I very much liked Pat Jackson; he is a very nice, gentle man. I was still working for ABPC so I was literally going from one studio to the other. I was making three or four pictures a year. I was initially under a seven-year contract which went on for ten years; I wasn't happy with it but I had poor advice and knew nothing. For the last three years they did pay me a decent salary and they loaned me the money to buy my house, which I paid back within one year just by doing loan-outs.

How much choice did you have about your roles?

None – I just did what I was told. Sometimes I

would fight for something, such as *Expresso Bongo*. That was rather well done and was a happy picture too, because Larry Harvey was delightful. I had just had major abdominal surgery and I can't tell you how carefully he looked after me; he would even check my make-up before a close-up, because he knew how casual I was about those things. He was adorable and so was Cliff Richard. I think the film was ahead of its time because it was such a sharp and witty send-up of the pop scene.

Ice Cold in Alex, The Moonraker and Bachelor of Hearts all came out in 1958. What do you remember of making the very successful Ice Cold in Alex?

It was very arduous. We filmed it in the Libyan desert and there was another film being made there at the same time, which had the most wonderful facilities compared to ours. We were in a hotel in Tripoli for a while and used to travel to the location each day, moved by the British Army. The men were under canvas and the women were in stone sheds inside a ruined Italian fort. It was very difficult and for me, being so young, it would have been impossible without the men in the cast being like Dutch uncles to me. We didn't have time to do much 'acting' – we were cranking the engine and driving that thing in the most appalling conditions, so that we just *became* those people. We were either very hot or very cold; when the winds blew at night it was bitterly cold. As for those love scenes, I don't recall them as being particularly daring but they certainly caused a lot of trouble at the time! I think they had to cut one close-up of what looked like an exposed bosom. In fact, all John did was to undo some buttons and I know I still had a bra on.

I enjoyed The Moonraker . . .

Yes, for its time it's quite sweet, isn't it? I think that, compared with some of the costume dramas coming out of Hollywood at that time, at least we looked right for the period. I had correct hair styling, covered with the modest lace cap, and the costumes were authentic. I liked working with George Baker, who was also a contract player: they only saw him as a tall leading man who could 'swashbuckle', whereas he has subsequently proved what a great character actor he is. And, of course, Max Greene always made me look beautiful.

I remember *Bachelor of Hearts* more clearly because that was done on location in Cambridge, which surely beats the Libyan desert. Hardy Kruger was adorable, a very nice man. It was a most enjoyable, funny film to be on, and Geoff Unsworth, the cameraman, made me look stunning, too.

You certainly had the best cameramen, including Christopher Challis, who photographed you in Flame in the Streets. What do you recall of that film?

It was quite controversial in its day [1958], dealing as it did with race relations. Certainly there hadn't been another British film made with anyone as black as Johnny Sekka, who was blue-black. He was from Senegal. I had the greatest respect for the director, Roy Baker. I've always considered him an underrated director. He was marvellous with that subject and I loved working with him. He was tough on the set but I thought he was very sensitive. All his films are entertaining, and he really had class.

What are your recollections of doing Victim, the first commercial film to deal openly with homosexuality?

I have very strong recollections of it. Dirk's book [*Snakes and Ladders*, 1978] is very honest about it; he says that they offered my part to a lot of people, but nobody was interested in playing the wife. I certainly wasn't the first choice. I remember reading the script and I was five months pregnant at the time. I was very involved in politics then and I thought this was an important film to do. Someone asked me later how a woman could be in love and go to bed with someone and then find out he was a homosexual. But in those days women of a certain class were very innocent. The wife's knowledge of sex would be limited; she may have had her suspicions but I think it was perfectly possible for her to love Dirk's character and have a reasonably happy marriage. Well, they managed to set the schedule so that I was able to do all my scenes within three weeks.

I remember very little about performances as a rule because you live the part at the time and then you put it aside. But I do remember there was one scene when I felt that, if that situation had happened to me, I would have been much less inhibited in my response. I remember actually having to talk myself into being the judge's daughter who would not be able to be uninhibited. When I first saw the film I was very worried about that scene – that scene in which she says, 'Well, you obviously wanted it.' I was worried that I had not brought out the big guns. Only later could I appreciate that I was actually being truthful to the character – that woman could only react in a certain way, still being terribly polite, so that the pain had to be shown through the fact that she *can't* scream and yell. I wanted to scream but, if she had been able to do that, then she wouldn't have been the person he married. And Dirk brought to his part the enormous restraint of somebody who had lived his life knowing something about himself which he refused to acknowledge was true. My part wasn't very long (it only took the three weeks), but I always remember *Victim* for how Dirk worked, when it wasn't his close-up, to help me with my reactions.

What lured you back to the big screen again in the late '80s in *A Chorus of Disapproval* and *Shirley Valentine*?

The answer is simply that nobody asked me before. There was plenty of stage and television work and I've never been out of work for longer than six months in thirty-five years. I've never earned a lot of money even with all those films I did; it's a case of doing whatever you're asked to do. I've turned down some films. I did take my clothes off in *The Tamarind Seed*, but I knew how it was being shot, so that was fine; but there was a time in the '70s when we were all asked to take our clothes off for almost everything. I had young children and I turned down several films. However, I've been lucky enough to find interesting work to do over the years, and I often think of that wonderful song of Sondheim's when I feel a failure (which I often do): it's called 'I'm Still Here'.

Desmond Tester

b. 1919

Actor: *Midshipman Easy, Late Extra* (1935), *Tudor Rose, Sabotage, Beloved Vagabond* (1936), *Non-Stop New York* (1937), *The Drum* (1938), *The Stars Look Down, An Englishman's Home* (1939), *The Turners of Prospect Road* (1947), *Barry Mckenzie Holds His Own* (1974), *Save the Lady* (1981), *The Wild Duck* (1984)

When Desmond Tester registered as a conscientious objector at the start of World War II, he virtually brought his screen career to an end. He speaks frankly, too, about the difficulties facing a child star who wants to continue in the profession as an adult. For five years, in the latter half of the 1930s, he was the chief male child actor in British films and won a succession of choice roles. Today, the best remembered of these is probably the boy given a bomb to carry on a bus in Hitchcock's *Sabotage*, but he did memorable work in several others: he is the sickly boy king, Edward VI, in Robert Stevenson's *Tudor Rose*, very amusing as the musical prodigy in Stevenson's neat thriller, *Non-Stop New York*, the Cockney drummer boy in Zoltan Korda's *The Drum*, and touching as the doomed footballing young miner in Carol Reed's *The Stars Look Down*. In all of these, working for four of the top directors of the period, he is surrounded by some of the choicest acting talent of the decade but his own professionalism ensures that he is not overshadowed by this. He has lived in Australia for the last forty years, and has done a good deal of theatre and television work (including a long-running programme for children) and appeared in several films.

Interview date: July 1996

Did you come from a family which was involved in films or the theatre?

No, but my sister went to Euphan McLaren's Ballet School and Euphan McLaren saw me and asked how old was I – I was twelve – and would I like a job at Christmas. But of course. So I was sent to see Nancy Price, who was running the Duchess Theatre at the time, and she was putting on *The Merry Wives of Windsor*. Plainly I was not trained, but I got the job and played Robin, page to Falstaff. I got good notices for the tiny part so the rot set in.

How did you actually get into your first film?

The very first film was a commercial for Stork margarine in which one sang the 'G is hard in Margarine'. This was directed by Anthony Asquith, at Islington Studios, and Gordon Harker played the lead. I was playing at His Majesty's in a play called *Hervey House*, and I made a bet with Gertrude Lawrence, who was playing the lead, that I wouldn't get into *Midshipman Easy* because I'd always failed tests. But I got the job and that was my first proper film and Carol Reed's first directorship. I'll come back to him because I got to know him better when I worked with him later.

What do you recall of Robert Stevenson, for whom you made two films?

Robert Stevenson – I remember him well. He had thin fair hair and a wide forehead and prominent teeth. He was a very nice man and the easiest to work with so far. I've been in the business for years and have definite opinions re producers of plays and directors of films. Then I was a hard-working, serious actor, punctual and attentive, because, as I've always said, the BBC brought me up and you had to be spot-on with them. I was their favourite choice of boys in those days and I was a pro, but I was not a *dedicated* actor. I believed in working and was very conscious of all that went on on the floor. Some people go into this business and it is their life – but it wasn't ever for me, wasn't going to be my life. It was a job where I earned my money. I was a bit envious of boys who could go to RADA and the

Central School, I knew nothing of the background of the theatre.

When you came to be making these films did you feel the absence of that theatrical training?

Because I'd been a stage actor, Robert Stevenson had to pull me back to the more intimate style of film performance. I was happy to work as he suggested. I loved the costumes, but I don't remember the sets you admired on *Tudor Rose*. I never noticed them. I did not like how my role of Edward VI was written; childish I thought it, having read my history. I got on well with my fellow actors, and the atmosphere on the floor was always very good with Stevenson. I liked working with Nova [Pilbeam, as Lady Jane Grey] but we never saw each other outside the studio. [Sir Cedric] Hardwicke I didn't like; maybe it was the part he played [the calculating Warwick], but dear old Felix Aylmer was a man I could talk to.

Did Stevenson go in for much rehearsal?

No, I don't remember rehearsals. I think one took each scene as it came along. And not having the continuity of the whole story was slightly upsetting to me as a stage actor who was used to going through a play daily, or through each whole scene, not each take.

Did you have to continue schooling while filming?

I'd officially left school at fourteen but went to classes in language and commerce and typing at Pitman's, because I knew it was a fact that child actors rarely succeeded later. Also by now I was becoming increasingly left-wing and I was interested in religion too. All the things that an intelligent but uneducated teenager should concern himself with while he's enjoying himself.

You made *Tudor Rose* at Islington?

Yes. The studio was just a dump in Islington. Islington and Lime Grove [the two Gainsborough studios] were not interesting as they were not purpose-built like Denham, where several films were being made at once. I remember watching

Coral Browne behaving madly on the set of *We're Going to be Rich*, a Gracie Fields picture about a gold rush that Monty Banks directed. Coral had a boyfriend called Shepherd, a play producer, and she used to say, 'Shepherd is my lord, I shall not want.'

It was during work on *Non-Stop New York* that I got to know Robert Stevenson and his wife, Anna Lee, better. I liked Anna; she was a nice person and I guess she was popular at that time. I actually used to call on them down on the South Bank, where they lived in a very old white house right by the Thames.

***Non-Stop New York* is very well made, modest, unpretentious, fast, and with an excellent cast.**

I enjoyed working on it and having to learn to play the violin, that phrase I think was from Mozart, and 'Sweet Sue' on the alto sax. I knew all the cast, I'd worked with many of them before, like Jerry Verno and others. Robert Stevenson was no problem to work with as Kurt Bernhardt [on *Beloved Vagabond*] had been.

Do you remember anything about that set-up in the plane? Was it very confined?

Well yes, in a sense. What they always do, and did then, is take a wall out so they can have a shot at it the other way and put the wall back in again. If I were to watch that film carefully I could almost say, because of camera angles, which part of the plane they'd removed. When you shoot in a very confined area, like a railway carriage, you have to do it like that.

We all thought the plane was fairly ridiculous but a lovely invention! Actually, I recently saw a photograph of a design for a transatlantic aeroplane at that time. It was not dissimilar to the model that they built at the studio and which I saw them making. The Short Sunderlands and those Empire Airways flying boats looked very much the same . . . just smaller, and of course there was no balcony to smooch on! That killed us with laughter!

My favourite line in the film was in answer to Athene Seyler asking why that man had patted me on the head and I replied, 'He was wiping his hands.' I love that joke and I've told it ever since. It had a very witty script actually. Friends who saw it recently said it was great fun. I liked Athene Seyler – I hadn't worked with her before. I knew some of them because I'd been in the business and I wasn't treated as a child because I was a serious actor. Everybody (except, once, Elisabeth Bergner) treated me like an ordinary person.

Were you under contract at the time?

Yes, I had a three- or four-year contract with Gaumont but they broke it in the beginning of '39, when they got out of all their contracts because they saw the war coming. But mine was a four-year contract, as mean as could be. Harold Huth was the sort of front man for them. I had no decent agent working for me, and I'm sure I could say this honestly about other people, that the studios did not look after their people; they just used them, Jessie Matthews or whoever. They didn't take any care of what my education might be over and above coming to the studio. Young people needed looking after by a good agent – the way Al Parker looked after James Mason. He directed that early film of mine, *Late Extra* with James, and later he became an agent. Anyhow, what idiots they were, because if I'd been looked after properly I'd have been worth a lot more money to them. Although it was my first film contract and it was great to have it and to know what sort of money you'd get, looking back on it I feel it could have been a hell of a lot better.

How did you find Hitchcock to work with on *Sabotage*?

I did enjoy working for him because he was funny and he had an easy manner. I liked the way he would send you up and work a practical joke on you. Lovely practical jokes he used to work – he was famous for them. However, I have no very great opinion of *Sabotage*. I think it's a very obvious, almost a silly film. As for the famous bomb scene [Tester's character carries a bomb in a London bus], I was indignant that Hitch put an old lady and a puppy in the scene for sympathy rather than leaving it all to me. I thought it was so obvious. I was jealous too, of course. There was no way one could express one's views, I was only a boy, but I was a believer in real drama as distinct from rigged thrills and suspense. I was a year or two older than everything I ever played, but I believe children are serious actors and not objects. I ran a kid's show later [*Channel Ninepins* on Australian television] and the reason for my success was that I treated kids like people. Well, it was funny to have my teeth brushed in that scene in *Sabotage*, but the tooth-brushing scene and whittling a stick and one or two other things were an adult's view of how a child reacts and in my view were not true. One could not enjoy Sylvia Sidney because she always went straight to her caravan after each scene.

You got some very choice parts in the '30s.

Oh yes, I was number one boy, you see. If anybody else got a part I would be livid. If it was a decent part, as a rule I bloody got it. I was very lucky.

What about playing the drummer boy in Zoltan Korda's *The Drum*?

Cockney drummer boy. It was a good part. I had nothing to say to Sabu because he was really almost childish – well, of course, why shouldn't he be? He was almost entirely uneducated, a year or two younger than I. I was always made out to be a great friend of his because it looked so good in publicity but in actual fact we had nothing to say to each other. You know, they'd stick him on a motorbike and me on the pillion when he couldn't even ride a bike.

Did you do a lot of location work for *The Drum*?

Yes, we went right up into the hills in mid-Wales where they made what they called 'matte' shots. The lower part of the picture on the screen would be mid-Wales mountains and the rest would be genuine Himalayas, because they'd sent a unit there to shoot stuff, and they had to burn the heather to get the colours to match right. I loved going on location. On *Midshipman Easy* we went to Portland Bill, near Weymouth, to make some of the stuff where they had to have the actual sea. I think there's a naval depot nearby.

None of the cast went to India for *The Drum*?

No. The crew went to India at some time prior, to make some background stuff. I remember a lot about the location of making *The Drum*; the wife of the chap who invented Technicolor was on location with us – Natalie Kalmus. All got up and beautiful she was.

What about Raymond Massey? Do you have recollections of him?

Yes, yes. He had that arrogance about him in the parts he often played, and of course he was playing Prince Ghul. He would say to [Zoltan] Korda, 'Oh Zolly, I feel that the Prince at this time would be more something or other,' and Zolly would say, 'No, I want you to play it down a bit,' and it blew up one day when Zolly said to Massey, 'You are my dog! I am not your dog! You do what I tell you!'

What about Carol Reed and *The Stars Look Down*?

I was making *The Stars Look Down* and *An Englishman's Home* at the same time; even on the same *day* I'd drive from Denham to Twickenham. Few things could be worse for an actor. The whole business gets out of proportion to its importance in life and the performer's importance becomes unreal too. The upshot was I couldn't concentrate on either film properly at the time and I was at that time thought to be a bit too big for my boots. The result was I could not work for Reed properly. I did not like his style on the floor. He always seemed worried and I fluffed my lines terribly and got more uptight every time. Of course if you fluff your lines, you do tend to get worse and worse. It was a lack of concentration due to this very fact that I was in both pictures at the same time. No one was rude to me about it.

We finished *The Stars Look Down* on the very last day of peace. And then the bloody war started and I'd registered as a conscientious objector in June, the very first call-up before the war. Now whether that influenced my post-war career or whether I had just lost the charm and ability that I apparently had as a youth, I don't know.

Did you do much location shooting on *The Stars Look Down* or was it just second-unit shooting on location?

A lot of *The Stars Look Down* was shot in Workington in Cumberland, where we went to do some of the exteriors of pitheads and football fields and that sort of stuff. Some of the pithead scenes were shot at Twickenham mixed in with real bits from location. I do remember I played football and skidded about on the football ground up on location in Cumberland. We were filthy and cold. Where I was entombed in the mine in the final scene was shot in the studio.

Even the streets and houses, which I think were studio-made, have a very realistic look. Do you recall them?

Yes, I do. There were 'fronts' for the streets, including the butcher's shop. There were those terrible sorts of houses they had at that period. I was conscious of that social thing at the time, the whole business of exploited work, at the pits and else-where.

That film reunited you with Nancy Price after a decade.

Yes indeed. I always had a great admiration for her and she felt that she had started me, as she had. She was a great lady and a fierce one. One knew that. All my scenes were with her or [Michael] Redgrave and George Carney and the little boy in the mine.

Do you think Carol Reed was interested at all in the labour issues in the film?

I have no idea, I wouldn't know because I didn't

talk to him otherwise. It was only very, very occasionally that one had any chat with the directors; maybe the stars did, but you see I was only a very young fellow and my views were not adult views, although I took myself seriously enough to become a conscientious objector. It was in November that I was called to my tribunal and it was front-page news and I had enormous publicity and an enormous fan mail. I had a big anti-fan mail as well as a praising fan mail. I did agricultural work: I ploughed Richmond Park and I started off as a cowman but I got milkman's dermatitis and had to give up and became a tractor driver.

You came back to films in *The Turners of Prospect Road* in 1947.

You see after the war I didn't know to what extent I was no longer the attractive boy or whether people just thought Desmond was a fake. I'd leave that as an open question. *The Turners of Prospect Road* was a pretty piddling picture, though it had a good cast, you know, Wilfred Lawson and Jeanne de Casalis. That's the only British picture I made after the war. I toured a lot for the Arts Council after the war in Shakespeare and Shaw and so on, but I had no luck with London theatre. I was in several shows but they always folded, and then I was offered the part in the Australian production of *Sailor Beware!* that Gordon Jackson played in London. It gave me a chance of coming to Australia and I've been here ever since.

Ralph Thomas

b. 1915

Director: *Once Upon a Dream, Helter Skelter, Traveller's Joy* (1949), *The Clouded Yellow* (1950), *Appointment with Venus* (1951), *The Venetian Bird* (1952), *The Dog and the Diamonds, A Day to Remember* (1953), *Doctor in the House, Mad About Men* (1954), *Doctor at Sea, Above Us the Waves* (1955), *The Iron Petticoat, Checkpoint* (1956), *Doctor at Large, Campbell's Kingdom* (1957), *A Tale of Two Cities, The Wind Cannot Read* (1958), *The Thirty-Nine Steps, Upstairs and Downstairs* (1959), *Conspiracy of Hearts, Doctor in Love* (1960), *No Love for Johnnie, No, My Darling Daughter* (1961), *A Pair of Briefs, The Wild and the Willing* (1962), *Doctor in Distress, Hot Enough for June* (1963), *The High Bright Sun* (1964), *Doctor in Clover* (1965), *Deadlier Than the Male* (1966), *Nobody Runs Forever, Some Girls Do* (1968), *Doctor in Trouble, Percy* (1970), *The Quest for Love* (1971), *It's A 2'6" Above the Ground World / The Love Ban* (1972), *Percy's Progress* (1974), *A Nightingale Sang in Berkeley Square* (1979)

Ralph Thomas is entirely unpretentious about his film-directing career. The facts are that he is perhaps the most representative British director of the 1950s; that he was enormously prolific; and that several of his films are a good deal more accomplished than his modest self-appraisal suggests. Representative: he made war films, series comedies (the *Doctor* films), literary adaptations and exotically-set romantic adventures, all staples of '50s British cinema. Prolific: he made nearly twenty films in the decade, two films a year from 1953 to 1963, mostly in collaboration with producer Betty Box. Accom-

plished: *Doctor in the House* remains one of the most beguiling entertainments of the '50s, in which high good humour is mixed with enough basis in reality to keep it coherent and credible; and *No Love for Johnnie*, is an unusually sharp, cynical look at a corrupt politician. He is the kind of director on whom film industries are – or, at least, *were* – based: that is to say he wanted to tell, on film, stories that audiences would want to watch, and he was able to gratify himself as well with the occasional more personal project. His brother was the director Gerald Thomas (of *Carry On* fame) and he is the father of producer Jeremy Thomas.
Interview date: June 1990

You were an assistant editor in the '30s and a maker of trailers in the '40s. What kind of training did this provide for someone who wanted to direct?

Making trailers in particular was enormously useful because, having been in the cutting rooms for quite a while, I had learned a lot of the technique of how the varying directors whose pictures I had worked on operated. Also, it teaches one a great deal of discipline about brevity in story-telling.

Looking back, the late '40s and early '50s seem like a boom period in British cinema history. How did it feel then?

Enormously exciting and invigorating. We knew that we were not always doing very creative work, but that there was a chance to gain experience, and that this wasn't going to last. My boss was Sydney Box. You were quite likely to finish shooting on Friday, plan to go into the cutting rooms on Monday to look over your stuff and get your cut ready, then go for a drink, and you'd be given another script and be told, 'The sets are standing and you start on Monday – this is the cast'! It wasn't necessarily good and we didn't get a lot of money, but it was regular!

How did you come to direct *Helter Skelter*, which is quite unlike mainstream British comedy?

Again, it was one of those 'Friday night pictures'. I didn't particularly want to make comedies, but I said I'd enormously admired a crazy American picture called *Hellzapoppin!* We cast it well and enjoyed making it, although I never quite understood the storyline. Funnily enough, it has become a sort of cult picture in odd places. One of the scenes caused a great deal of embarrassment to produce; it

required the heating to go wrong, for the air conditioning in the hotel foyer not to work, and the reception desk had to shiver and shake a little. So we got the special effects men to make a mould of what the desk would be. They filled it with aspic until it seemed firm and then they painted it to look like a real desk. If you blew a wind machine on it it would shake and look rather splendid. So we switched on the fan and didn't realise that by this time the fan was heated; the heat started to melt the jelly, so that instead of just shaking, it literally shrank and melted and the whole of the floor was covered with this jelly. People's feet were stuck in it; we couldn't track the camera; it was an hilarious scene.

Would you say you were a very representative British film director of the '50s, in the kinds of films you made, the people you worked with and the sort of success you had?

I was a sort of journeyman picture-maker and I was generally happy to make anything I felt to be halfway respectable. So my volume of work was enormous; I had a lot of energy and made all kinds of pictures. If you make all kinds, you score a hit sometimes. I made thrillers, comedies, love stories, war stories, one or two adventure things. Some filmmakers have a lot of talent and genius for it; others simply have a lot of energy and I'm afraid I belong in the latter category! There were lots of us then doing a great deal of work. With hindsight, some of it was more respectable than we probably thought at the time.

You made many films with Betty Box as producer. How did this association come about?

She's a smashing producer, a very bright woman,

and she had very good story taste. I started working with her when I made a trailer for a picture called *Miranda*, about a mermaid. It was a rather funny trailer and it obviously helped to sell the picture. Anyway, I then met Betty and we had ideas in common. I didn't see her again until there was a slump and they had to shut down Shepherd's Bush Studios, where I was working. I then went to Pinewood to do *The Clouded Yellow*, and she came over and produced that with me. After that we made twenty-odd pictures together and we remained great friends. Betty mortgaged her house to keep *The Clouded Yellow* afloat until the financial problems in our business sorted themselves out. It was a brave thing for her to do and she didn't tell me until the picture was finished. I'm rather proud of that film: Jean Simmons was lovely in it, so was Trevor Howard: it was a very good movie. And Sonia Dresdel was very good value for money; they don't make them like her any more – wonderful bravura.

I also associate you closely with Dirk Bogarde. How would you describe that working relationship?

Dirk was a very serious and splendid young actor and a wonderful-looking fellow. When we made *Doctor in the House* we decided we didn't want to use actors who were professional funny men. We would cast the best actors we could get, actors we'd have cast if it was going to be a straight dramatic story about medicine. So we cast Dirk, Kenneth More, Kay Kendall, people who were bright, 'hot' and good. Not one of them ever did anything because they wanted to make it *funny*. They played it within a very strict, tight limit of believability. Dirk was able to do that, he got away with it and it stopped him from being just another bright, good-looking leading man and made him a star. We worked together for, I suppose, ten or twelve years and then he moved on to become a more continental actor. He did several, though not all, of the *Doctor* films; he played Sydney Carton in *A Tale of Two Cities* – he was marvellous in it and it's become a sort of school classic all around the world; he was very good in a romantic picture we shot in India, called *The Wind Cannot Read*, as a rather tortured young officer. He was splendid in another mad comedy called *Hot Enough for June*, which was based on a very good book called *The Night of Wenceslas* by Lionel Davidson. It was a sort of send-up of the early James Bond pictures. Dirk did that totally differently and very well. He was a pleasure to work with because he always produced

more than you asked of him. He is a great contributor. Like others, he could be difficult; the only way you could persuade him that what he wanted to do was wrong was to let him do it – the terrible thing was that it very often proved him to be, in fact, right!

***Doctor in the House* is your first major commercial success, isn't it?**

Yes. It was a ridiculously big success and, in a way, it doesn't really do your career any good to have such a big success early on. I remember the night it opened, at the British Film Awards; it brought the house down. It was a very cool, professional audience who had gone there to be seen, to get awards and to watch other people get awards, and they were not an ideal audience but they absolutely loved it. We knew then that it had worked. It opened to the public the next day and we went down to watch the huge crowds queuing in Leicester Square to see it. We went to a party that night and the Chief Executive of the Rank Organisation said, 'I feel sorry for you, Ralph. You've made a picture which is going to be a classic, it's going to be enormously successful commercially. You've got a piece of it and it's going to make you reasonably well off, and it's going to start you off with a totally new career. You're a bit too young and not really ready for it yet.' I thought he was a silly old buffer. But he was quite right; you can easily get thrown off course because you get offered all sorts of things which you don't really want to do and shouldn't do. You become easily flattered because you like this first taste of fame.

Why was it such a huge success?

It was about something which, until that time, had been treated with about as much reverence as you would treat your confessor. People used to hold medicine in great awe. There had been *Dr Kildare* things in which 'young doctor saves lives in hospital'. In our film, people liked and identified with the funny situations they had seen happen or which had happened to themselves as patients, doctors or nurses. It had an enormously wide common appeal – much wider than we understood when we were making it. It was first shown in 1954 and it is still being shown all around the world and producing revenue after all these years.

I recall a very touching scene with an actress called Maureen Pryor.

Yes, she was an exceptional actress. An ordinary little woman, she had this gift of instant emotion. She could say a word which didn't actually mean much, look at the camera and make you cry. She had enormous vulnerability, she was very special. We used her several times [she is very touching as a woman who fears she has cancer in *Doctor at Large*] and she always delivered this sort of thing.

How would you compare it with the Ealing films at the start of the decade and the *Carry On* films at the other end of the decade?

It was less quaint and more realistic than the Ealing films, which I adored, but it didn't have any sort of whimsy at all. You laugh because you are involved in and amused at the situations, rather than at big pay-off gags. The *Carry On* series, which my brother directed, were immensely funny farces constructed to have as many laughs as possible within their ninety minutes of screen time. They were not stories; they used comedians, and were like seaside picture postcards or old variety turns. *Doctor in the House* was between the two, because it was a realistic picture which set a new trend in this sort of comedy, and I'm very proud of it.

You were under contract to Rank, so how much control did you have over making films?

After *Doctor in the House* we had quite a lot of control. We had promised to make another *Doctor* and, as long as the thing we wanted to make had a reasonable budget and was not too idiotic, they would let us do it. There was a huge, cosy operation which served you well if you served them well. I think Rank probably felt Betty and I had served them well; we had three long-term contracts with them, and we liked it because the contracts gave us the same crew. We were allowed to have our own cameraman, art director, production designer, assistant director and production accountant – the five key people. They were on our payroll for the whole year every year, and that was ideal. We probably got a little less in fees through that arrangement but we got a great deal of comfort and a very nice atmosphere. A long-term contract generally meant a certain number of pictures over so many years. If such an operation existed now, we would have a continuity of programming that would enable more people to get chances.

British films of the '50s are sometimes criticised for their preoccupation with wartime themes. Is this a fair criticism?

Yes it is, and it's perfectly natural too. One of the reasons is that, though it sounds rather callous, there is no place to find drama – or comedy – more easily than in a wartime situation. Also, most of the people involved had been much affected by the war; they were still living under wartime conditions several years after the war had finished, because of rationing and shortages; and it seemed that one became slightly obsessed with war films. I made a war picture well into the '50s called *Above Us the Waves*, which was made because William Mac-Quitty, who produced it, was very involved with the Navy and he loved submariners. He had read a book by two young journalists about the sinking of the *Tirpitz* and thought it was very exciting. I thought it was too, and I suppose there was an element of nostalgia about it even though I had been a soldier, not a sailor. So we made it. There were some wonderful stories about the war around, and there still are.

There was also *Appointment with Venus*, a comedy totally about war in which the main protagonist, apart from David Niven and Glynis Johns, was a cow. We actually had about twelve plain-coloured cows which we used to paint with this particular patch on the side. That was a sod because we shot mainly on location on Sark and Guernsey and every time it rained, which it did regularly, the colours would run, and you would think the cow was milking itself because drops of paint were falling on the grass. It was a difficult picture but it was fun.

Another war film was *The Wind Cannot Read*, which I made in India. It was a wonderful book which David Lean had once been going to film, and he gave the script to Betty and me to read. We were about to go off to shoot *Campbell's Kingdom* on location, and Betty rang John Davis from London Airport; she told him what *The Wind Cannot Read* was about and the numbers involved. He very bravely told her that, unless he cabled her in Cortina to the contrary, we could make the picture in India. I think he agreed to it because he trusted David Lean's judgement that it was a splendid book. It was a real three-handkerchief picture, which I thoroughly enjoyed making, and Dirk was very good in it.

We made another war picture, in the late '50s, called *Conspiracy of Hearts*, which was in black-and-white; it was also a very moving, very different picture. It had mainly women in it, all playing nuns. It was very successful in America. Barney Balaban, the head of Paramount at that time, happened to be in London and came to the première; he loved the picture and, at the after-show party at the Dorchester, told John Davis he wanted to buy it. Davis protested that none of his salespeople were there but

Barney insisted he wanted to buy it then and there, and he paid the largest amount Rank had received for a picture until then. You see, few Americans other than servicemen had seen anything of the war and also America has large Catholic and Jewish populations; so the prospect of Catholic nuns saving the lives of little Jewish children had a very large, inbuilt audience.

What of *No Love for Johnnie*?

We made that because we wanted to make it very much. We all loved it – Betty, myself, Peter Finch. Peter got an award in Berlin for it. It got great notices although it was never a commercial success, didn't even pay for itself. The Rank Organisation threw a surprise party for Betty and me after it was finished, and Harold Wilson was there and said he recognised a lot of things in the picture as being absolutely true. It very much reflected the politics of the day. The plain fact is that people were not very interested in the politics of the day. The ending was very cynical but you couldn't *not* be cynical about the story it told. The man was an opportunist, doing the least possible in the House of Commons. The film was very heavily censored because at that time they didn't believe that 'love in the afternoon' by an MP who should have been voting in the House was possible. It's happened rather a lot since!

Betty Box said she wished she'd chosen to make *A Tale of Two Cities* in colour.

Yes, and that was really my fault. I had seen a French picture called *Casque d'Or*, set in France at almost the same period, and it looked so marvellous in black-and-white and made a great impression on me. I argued that if we wanted to keep the flavour of Dickens's book, with a vague feeling of documentary about it, we ought to make it in black-and-white. We fought for that and I'm very sorry we won the battle. It would have been much more successful in colour, with much more exposure on television. The Russians thought it was the definitive work on Dickens! It was one of Dirk's best pictures, I think.

It was a well-cast picture: Cecil Parker, Stephen Murray, Athene Seyler, and Duncan Lamont was a terrific Defarge – it was full of people who knew how to play that sort of piece. Christopher Lee's straight performance as the Marquis was very good, very contained. We were talking about Maureen Pryor before; there was a marvellous girl in *A Tale of Two Cities*, the one who went to her death in the tumbril with Dirk, Marie Versini, who had this quality of saying two lines, looking at the camera, and making you want to cry. The screenplay was written by TEB Clarke, who wrote most of the best Ealing pictures.

It wasn't all drama, though. One of the funniest experiences we had was when Dirk's manager, Tony Forwood, was snoozing in Dirk's new Rolls-Royce in a side street whilst we were shooting. He was woken up by a loud bang, and came to Dirk in fear and trembling, saying, 'Dirk, something terrible has happened to the car and I'm afraid the door and the wing are irreparable. One of the tumbrils ran wild and it ran into us!' We had great trouble helping them to fill in their insurance claim. I mean, how do you say that your Rolls was damaged by a tumbril drawn by a white horse?!

Ann Todd

1909–1993

Actor: *Keepers of Youth, These Charming People, The Ghost Train* (1931), *The Water Gypsies* (1932), *The Return of Bulldog Drummond* (1934), *Things to Come* (1936), *Action for Slander, The Squeaker* (1937), *South Riding* (1938), *Poison Pen* (1939), *Danny Boy, Ships with Wings* (1941), *Perfect Strangers, The Seventh Veil* (1945), *Gaiety George* (1946), *Daybreak, So Evil My Love, The Paradine Case* (1947), *The Passionate Friends, Madeleine* (1949), *The Sound Barrier* (1952), *The Green Scarf* (1954),

Time Without Pity (1957), The Taste of Fear (1961), Son of Captain Blood (1962), *Thunder in Heaven (1964), 90 Degrees in the Shade (1965), *Thunder of the Gods (1966), *Thunder of the Kings (1967), The Fiend (1971), The Human Factor (1979), The McGuffin (1985)

* Documentary (directed by Ann Todd).

Although she had made thirteen previous films, it was Ann Todd's role in *The Seventh Veil* that made her a household name. She played the suicidal Francesca, and she and James Mason, aided by a skilful script from producers Muriel and Sydney Box, made one of the most popular entertainments of the entire '40s. Ann Todd was perhaps best served by those roles in which her fragile blonde beauty seemed to be concealing passions and ambiguities at odds with the exquisite surface. Hence, she is remarkably effective as Ralph Richardson's demented wife in *South Riding*; as the missionary's widow caught up in a tangle of crime and newly-wakened sensuality in Lewis Allen's superb melodrama, *So Evil My Love*; and as the duplicitous *Madeleine* (one of three films directed by her then husband David Lean). Her Hollywood experience with Hitchcock in *The Paradine Case* looms large in her recollections of her career and one sees why he was drawn to use her. She has directed, written and appeared in several very individual travel documentaries, and is the author of an autobiography entitled *The Eighth Veil*.

Interview date: June 1990

Alexander Korda's *Things to Come* is one of the most ambitious British films of the '30s. What do you recall of it?

I don't remember very much about it because I was very young and didn't have a large part. I can remember having to be gassed, and they tied me to a post and floated in a lot of smoke, which was intended to represent the attack. It was so real, and I was so nervous and over-acting that I actually passed out. Korda said, 'Well, leave her there and keep filming.' My second husband Nigel [Tangye] got an award for it; he did an incredible job on the aviation sequences. When I saw it on TV, I thought it was a *wonderful* film and Raymond Massey was marvellous in it. Although the film was meant to be science fiction, it was an uncanny portent of what was to come. Korda was a marvellous man – not just a great name, but a great man as well. He was a wonderful teacher. He said to me, 'I don't want you to *act*. I want you to *be*,' which I had never heard said before.

How was the scene of riding the horse up the stairs done in *South Riding*?

I did actually do it. I don't ride so it was very alarming. (I had more riding problems years later in *Madeleine* in a scene with Norman Wooland.) The noise of the horse's hooves on the stairs frightened it even more than me. I played the demented wife by remembering Alex's words about 'being', instead of acting. It was something in *me* which Korda could just find, to draw out the performance. I was terribly disappointed and angry when Alex decided not to film *Lottie Dundas* with me in the part I'd played on the stage. He said I wasn't ready to play a murderess on the screen yet, and I said, 'I could kill *you* now!'

There was a long gap, while you were on the stage, until Korda's *Perfect Strangers* in 1945. What was your experience of playing with Robert Donat?

I loved him. He suffered a lot from ill-health – he had to have screens all around him so that he wouldn't see anybody because of his nerves – but he was so sympathetic to work with. There was a real sense of hierarchy of stars then, and I was grateful to him – the studios were still rather awesome to me, though it helped to have Korda directing.

Georges Périnal photographed you superbly in it ...

I hadn't realised it was him on that film. He did photograph me beautifully, it's true, but it's really only a few shots of me in nurse's uniform with Bob. I saw it last year and thought it looked so touched up and glossy.

Would you say that *The Seventh Veil* was the film which made you a top star?

Yes, it was the turning point of my life, as I say in my book [*The Eighth Veil*]. It had magic and it gave me magic. I don't remember 'acting' the part, but of course I fell in love with James [Mason], which helped. Directors are now the most important people involved, but in those days it was the stars who were important, and the way Sydney Box [producer] put us together was magical, the chemistry was there. It wasn't a startling script, but James and I always used to play the looks between the words. I went to the Royal College of Music to learn the Grieg Concerto and the Rachmaninoff for the film, though not actually playing myself, of course. Herbert Lom was marvellous in it too; I'm such an admirer of his. And when I saw the film last year at the British Film Institute, I must say I was thrilled with it, and with me in it! People still remember me as Francesca, and that makes me happy.

I did it later on the stage, with Leo Genn, but it wasn't anything like as successful. I honestly think the success of *The Seventh Veil* came from our personalities and they *were* exciting; it's something you get from inside which you convey to an audience. The great directors know it. I remember Hitchcock telling me he didn't want me to rehearse [on *The Paradine Case*]: he wanted just what I could bring to it when I did it for the first time.

Your next film, *Gaiety George*, sounds a rather limp follow-up to your great success.

No, it wasn't. I was really quite pleased about that; I loved the character, for which I changed from being a tart at the beginning, wearing fishnet stockings as a 'Gaiety Girl', to eventually marrying into the aristocracy, as Lady Someone, aged fifty or sixty.

You made two striking melodramas in 1947, *Daybreak* and *So Evil My Love*.

Nigel, my husband, wrote the theme song for *Daybreak*, which was set on a barge, I think. Eric Portman was in it, as my husband, but I don't recall much about it. I do remember Geraldine Fitzgerald as the alcoholic wife in *So Evil My Love* and she was *lovely* to work with, a great actress I thought. Ray Milland was very much the star! Hal Wallis, the producer, certainly had style; it's extremely important in films. I loved the beginning of that film, *So Evil My Love*, when I was on the boat coming back to England; it always reminds me of Garbo at the end of *Queen Christina*.

Did you get the Hollywood offer to play Gregory Peck's wife in *The Paradine Case* on the basis of *The Seventh Veil*?

Oh yes, it came very quickly after the first night. Hitchcock took me out to dinner and explained that I was to play the poor little girl whose husband had left her for another woman [Valli], but that he wanted me to be the most exciting person in the film. If he hadn't said that I would never have thought of playing it that way. I know people say that, for Hitch, actors were just part of the furniture, but Grace Kelly, Ingrid Bergman and I loved him and loved working for him. He would say, 'Relax, girl, relax! You can't act if you're not relaxed!'

Your next two films were both directed by David Lean for Cineguild, *The Passionate Friends* and *Madeleine*. Where were they filmed?

They were mostly shot at Pinewood. I loved *Madeleine*; David was never happy about it but I think he did it quite beautifully. It didn't seem to me to matter that people knew about the 'Not proven' verdict. Guy Green was the cameraman and he was marvellous. A good cameraman goes into *you*, and the part you're playing. If he sees you do something in rehearsal which brings a certain expression into your eyes, for instance, he will go to the director and says he's seen something which should be brought out, maybe a camera angle needs changing or something. He and the designer, John Bryan, worked *very* closely with David on *Madeleine*; they were round at the house every day for breakfast, talking and planning. David liked to have every detail right under his thumb. He was the first director I'd worked with in this country to have that sort of presence, to be the master on his set. People ask me now whether it was difficult for me as his wife working with him, and I say, 'Of course it was. Having a genius around *is* difficult. Perhaps you haven't had one!'

He directed you in three films in a row, the third being *The Sound Barrier*. How do you

feel about that now?

I think it was marvellous. I was so proud and excited to see it shown at a National Film Theatre 'do' recently. David did one of the first sort of *cinéma vérité* things when he shot me in the cinema watching the film when my husband [played by Nigel Patrick] was killed. The cameras were all hidden and nobody realised all the bright lights were actually film lights. I had to queue to get my ticket for the film and I got a message telling me to hurry because they were getting into trouble outside. I tried to push forward and a woman in the queue snapped, 'Wait your turn!' and she knocked me in the stomach; I was wearing a 'pregnant' cage under my coat. The woman was alarmed and said, 'Oh I'm so sorry – I've killed it!' I just had to say, 'No no, it's quite all right.' It was a film full of chilling moments, but there were a lot of very human bits too, when I would react as I thought a woman under strain would do, with lots of aggression.

David liked to rehearse a lot, which Hitchcock of course didn't. I wouldn't say I like to get a lot of direction from a director, but I like the director to *know me*.

In 1954 you worked with a now largely for forgotten director, George More O'Ferrall, in *The Green Scarf*.

Oh, I loved him. We were students together at the Central School, where he was studying direction. He didn't have a lot of strength but he was a most sensitive director. I had been very ill before making *The Green Scarf* and someone told me afterwards that, before I came down from my dressing-room, George explained to everyone that, to help me get through, everything on the set had to be just so, very quiet. But I didn't really like the film very much. I had to learn how deaf-and-dumb people speak for it, as I recall.

Three years later you worked with Joseph Losey on *Town Without Pity*, his first English film under his own name, after being blacklisted in Hollywood.

Yes, I enjoyed working with him very much, although a lot of people found him difficult. I don't think artistes bothered much about that blacklisting stuff – except in Hollywood, of course. People would say, 'You worked for Joe Losey! Did you have a terrible time?' And I'd say, 'No, of course not.' *Town Without Pity* was one of Alec Mc-Cowen's first films and almost certainly the first for Leo McKern. Joe Losey brought Leo to my house and told him to stand up and play a scene with me. It was very embarrassing for both of us; I've never had another director do that.

What do you remember of Seth Holt's *The Taste of Fear*? It was a genuinely scary thriller, I thought.

I thought it was a terrible film. I didn't like my part and I found Susan Strasberg impossible to work with, all that 'Method' stuff. Insofar as it worked it was due to the director, Seth Holt; the story was very silly but he kept it going, he made it exciting so that you forget the body couldn't possibly be lifted out of the swimming pool and so on. It felt very stagey to do, though, and it was one of the few films I didn't like doing at all. However, it was very popular.

Do you have a favourite role in films?

I think I'd have to say *The Seventh Veil* – it has never left me and never been allowed to. It made me a 'star', though it's a label I can't stand, and that status didn't give me any more freedom to do parts I wanted, to pick and choose.

Richard Todd

b. 1919

Actor: *For Them That Trespass* (1948), *The Hasty Heart, The Interrupted Journey* (1949), *Stage Fright, Portrait of Clare* (1950), *Flesh and Blood, Lightning Strikes Twice, The Story of Robin Hood* (1951), *24 Hours of a Woman's Life, The Venetian Bird,* **The Elstree Story* (1952), *The Sword and the Rose, Rob Roy – The Highland Rogue* (1953), *The Bed* (1954), *A Man Called Peter, The Virgin Queen, The Dam Busters* (1955), *D-Day the 6th of June* (1956), *Saint Joan, Yangtse Incident* (1957), *Chase a Crooked Shadow, The Naked Earth, Intent to Kill, Danger Within* (1958), *Never Let Go* (1960), *Don't Bother to Knock, The Long and the Short and the Tall, The Hellions* (1961), *The Boys, The Longest Day* (1962), *The Very Edge, Death Drums Along the River* (1963), *Coast of Skeletons* (1964), *Operation Cross-*

bow, *Battle of the Villa Fiorita* (1965), *The Love-Ins* (1967), *Subterfuge, The Last of the Long-Haired Boys* (1968), *Dorian Gray* (1970), *Asylum, The Aquarian* (1972), *No 1 of the Secret Service, The Big Sleep* (1977), *Home Before Midnight* (1979), *House of the Long Shadows* (1983), *Incident at Victoria Falls* (1991)
*Documentary film.

Richard Todd became a major British film star with his second film, *The Hasty Heart*, and his performance as the stocky, touchy Scot remains one of those with which he is most closely associated. Hitchcock had the wit to use him as a killer in *Stage Fright*, though for the rest of the '50s he was usually cast in heroic and/or romantic roles. Of these latter, perhaps the most notable were as Guy Gibson in *The Dam Busters*, one of the best of the decade's many war films, and as the Rev. Peter Marshall in *A Man Called Peter*, made during his second spell in Hollywood. He brought a very convincing no-nonsense sincerity to both these roles and, indeed, this sturdy believability – in or out of uniform – was his distinguishing feature. As one who values a well-prepared production, he particularly enjoyed his three costume romps for Disney – *Robin Hood*, *The Sword and the Rose* and *Rob Roy*. In recent years he has been much preoccupied with the stage, but he continued into the 1980s to bring authority to supporting roles in the occasional film.
Interview date: June 1991

Suddenly, at thirty, you became a major British film star in *The Hasty Heart*, your second film. How did this happen?

I didn't want to go back into the theatre after being in the Army but I agreed to do one play for Dundee Rep – and stayed eighteen months, when Robert Lennard, my agent for a short time before the war, rang me to say he had the ideal part for me and would I come to London to test for it. So I did a screen test for a film called *For Them That Trespass*, directed by Cavalcanti, and was given the leading role. As a result I got a contract with Associated British Pictures [ABPC], one of the two big production companies in Britain at that time. The contract was for seven years – peanuts to begin with, but I thought I was damn lucky to get a contract at all. My first film didn't light any fires, but Cavalcanti taught me a great deal about techniques to overcome my faults and, really, the rudiments of screen acting.

On the last day of the film there was a reception at Elstree Studios for Jack Warner Jr and Vincent Sherman, who were in England to make *The Hasty Heart*. Sherman caught sight of me while he was talking to Robert Clark, who was the executive director of productions, and said I was just the kind of guy he wanted for the Scot in *The Hasty Heart*. Clark said I was one of their contract players, so Sherman said he wanted me to test. I did two scenes and a few days later I was called to Bob Lennard's office and told I had the part.

What was your experience of starring with Patricia Neal and the future President of the United States?

They were wonderful. At that time they were both established and I was totally unknown, having done one film which hadn't even been screened yet. I did get the impression that Ronnie Reagan was sizing me up a bit at the beginning, but I think his misgivings faded when he saw I could handle the part all right; he was extremely nice and helpful. The film was all shot in the studio; most of the action takes place inside the hospital hut, the only exterior scenes being those of the sandy compound outside. It is also largely interior in that it is about Lachlan McLachlan coming to terms with other people. I had seen boys in the war in much the same state and I knew what he was feeling. I got a great deal of direction from Vincent Sherman, who was most helpful. If you were doing a very emotional scene and you saw tears running down his face, you knew you were doing all right! It was a huge popular success and it made me an international artiste straight away.

What were your views on the British star-building system?

There wasn't really one, not anything like they had in America. I was extremely lucky because I was more or less the white-haired boy at ABPC and they actually bought subjects for me and got behind me in terms of publicity. Then, when I went to do my first film in America, ABPC went to quite a deal of expense to see that my new bride and I went in style. But I was lucky; that was not normal here.

In 1950, you worked for Hitchcock in *Stage Fright* – was it a daring move for a newly established star to play the murderer?

I don't think so; it was a terrific surprise and a feather in my cap to have Hitchcock wanting me. It was my fifth film, I think, but only a couple of the earlier ones had come out – *The Hasty Heart* hadn't even been released at that stage. It came out while we were shooting *Stage Fright* and Hitchcock's attitude to me changed overnight! He was a strange man, not a lot of help to his actors. He didn't rehearse you, he just gave his first assistant a diagram of what he wanted, and then he would go off to his office. Once we had rehearsed together and worked out our moves, he would come down to have a look at it, say if it was OK or not, and then shoot it. I think he took the view that you only hire people who know what they are doing. However, he said I had expressive eyes and spent a lot of time doing shots on me where only the eyes were lit, because they tell the story.

What was your experience of working with the legendary Marlene Dietrich?

Wonderful, we got on tremendously well together. She was, again, a great professional. What a cast that was! Dietrich, Jane Wyman, Michael Wilding, Sybil Thorndike, Alastair Sim, Kay Walsh, Joyce Grenfell – little parts, some of them, but brilliantly done.

You made *24 Hours of a Woman's Life* for Victor Saville almost at the end of his career.

Yes, we shot a lot of that in Monte Carlo. It was very enjoyable to make although I don't think it was a great picture. Saville was all right and Merle Oberon was another of those highly professional people. So was Anne Baxter, with whom I played in

Chase a Crooked Shadow. I had to drive a sports car very fast round a mountain ledge in the south of Spain. It was pretty dicey, because the balance of the car had been changed considerably by having cameras bolted to it on scaffolding. I had a couple of really nasty moments driving it, it was very dangerous, but Anne never turned a hair. That's what I admired about her. She was also a very intelligent actress.

What sorts of differences did you find between British and American directors and stars, either here or in Hollywood?

I found everything in Hollywood to be so well geared and professional compared with the rather haphazard, happy-go-lucky way things were done in England. At Elstree, the ABPC studios, the so-called 'star dressing rooms' were very spartan and I once said to the studio boss, Robert Clark, that visiting American stars would expect a good deal better than that. In America you had a whole bungalow to yourself: you were really pampered. English productions were often good, but they were nothing like so organised as the Americans'. The best-organised films I ever did here were for Disney – *Robin Hood*, *The Sword and the Rose* and *Rob Roy*. For each of those, before we went into production, I (as the star), the director, producer, scriptwriter and cameraman all had conferences. As we went through each shot, a sketch artist would sketch exactly what each angle was to be, so that when the set designer started building the sets there was never an inch of wood or whatever wasted. I could look through my copies of the sketch artist's drawings for a particular scene and know exactly where I was to come into close-up, where I would be in a medium or a long shot. Not only were they extremely efficient, they were also extremely nice to work with. Walt himself wasn't too much in evidence during the making of the films, although he came over to visit us a number of times and he actually became a great friend of mine.

You worked several times for Michael Anderson . . .

I did *Yangtse Incident*, *The Dam Busters* and *Chase a Crooked Shadow* for him – all good films, and Michael was, to me, a supremely authoritative, quiet, collected director who knew exactly what he wanted and what he could get out of his actors. He only had to give me a little quiet guidance, and we worked together very well. When I was first told he was to direct *The Dam Busters*, I thought it was typical ABPC cheeseparing instead of getting an expensive, well-known director. Michael had made only small films before that, having previously been the best first assistant director in the business. But I had dinner with him one night and was totally won over by him; he knew what he was doing and was a delight to work with.

The British cinema of the '50s seems to have been dominated by war films. Why do you think this was so?

Well, America has cowboys and Indians and we don't. The only action films that we make with any sort of reality to them are war films. I suppose there is an element of nostalgia for 'our finest hour' in it as well. I do think *The Dam Busters* is the best military war picture ever made. I never met Guy Gibson, but I got to know as much as I could about him. We spent about two years researching and preparing the picture and I spent a lot of time with his father, his widow and Micky Martin, who served with him. I also spent time with Barnes Wallis [the inventor], who was a fascinating man. They got the technical details about the bomb itself from him, although some of that had to be cheated a bit because it was still secret.

The crucial thing about the preparation was the model work on the dams because, if you didn't have dams bursting realistically, you didn't have a film. So all the model work was done first and, when that was OK'd, we started shooting the film. We had to have five Lancasters rebuilt for us as well. There were terrible floods in the Ruhr valley that year, so we sent a plane over and shot a lot of film there. Mickey Anderson deliberately made it in black-and-white, for two reasons: one was that we could use a lot of stock shots in black-and-white of the original bombs being tested. Also, he felt that colour would prettify it too much and I think he was right. Erwin Hillier was the cameraman on it and it was very well photographed.

We had one RAF officer, who was actually the station commander on the airfield at Scampton at that time, and he was with us as technical adviser. I also had with me an RAF flying instructor who sat in the fuselage with me and taught me the movements I should go through. The aircraft in the studio was mounted on a pedestal with a ball-and-socket mechanism that could be electrically activated, so

that it banked, climbed and dived.

You made a good war film called *Danger Within* with director Don Chaffey.

Don was very workmanlike. It was a true story and a very gripping picture. It was filmed on the heath in Surrey, where they constructed a complete prison camp. The opening was inspirational on Don's part. It opened with a full-scale battle in the desert, stock shots taken from actual war footage; the titles rolled over this huge battle and, when they finished, the camera came in to a body lying in the sand, face down. You naturally think this is one of the casualties of the battle. The camera dwells on the body for a few moments and suddenly its right hand comes around and scratches its backside. Then the camera pulls away and you see it is just one of the prisoners-of-war snoozing in the compound. It was a wonderful shot.

Your last film of this period sounds rather bizarre – *Never Let Go* with Peter Sellers and Adam Faith.

Ah yes, that was a good film. It also had Elizabeth Sellars and Carol White, who was very good. I loved doing it because it was a character part for me, playing a scruffy little salesman whose car had been stolen. Sellers played the head of the gang of crooks.

Which of your films are you particularly pleased with?

Certain films are much better than others, but, when you look back, you recall enjoying one because you had a good part in it or because you made a lot of money out of it, because it was an exciting location or it brought a lot of kudos. The one film I *loathed* making was *The Long and the Short and the Tall*; I didn't enjoy working with Laurence Harvey, but I won't go into that because the poor chap's dead. I took it for granted they'd cast Peter O'Toole, who was marvellous in the part on the stage, but they said no, they wanted a 'name'. To my delight, before we had finished the film David Lean had cast him for *Lawrence of Arabia*.

In my memory the outstanding films I've done are *The Hasty Heart, Robin Hood, Rob Roy, The Dam Busters, A Man Called Peter, Never Let Go, Chase a Crooked Shadow, Yangste Incident* and *The Virgin Queen*.

Bill Travers

1922–1994

Actor: *Conspirator* (1949), *Trio, The Wooden Horse* (1950), *The Browning Version* (1951), *Hindle Wakes, It Started in Paradise, The Planter's Wife* (1952), *Mantrap, Street of Shadows, Counterspy, The Square Ring* (1953), *Romeo and Juliet* (1954), *Geordie, Footsteps in the Fog* (1955), *Bhowani Junction* (1956), *The Barretts of Wimpole Street, The Seventh Sin, The Smallest Show on Earth* (1957), *The Passionate Summer* (1958), *The Bridal Path* (1959), *Gorgo* (1961), *Two Living, One Dead, The Green Helmet, Invasion Quartet* (1961), *Born Free* (1965), *Duel at Diablo* (1966), *A Midsummer Night's Dream* (1968), *Ring of Bright Water, An Elephant Called Slowly, Boulevard du Rhum / Rum Runner* (1970), *The Belstone Fox* (1973), *Christian the Lion* (1977)

The key films in Bill Travers's career are *Geordie* (1955) and *Born Free* (1965). *Geordie* established him as a popular British leading man, after a dozen small roles in the preceding five years. There is a strong element of wish-fulfilment about its theme, and this, together with Launder and Gilliat's good-natured screenplay, helped to make it a strong box-office favourite, both in Britain and America. As a result, Travers won starring roles in three MGM films – *Bhowani Junction, The Barretts of Wimpole Street* (made in England) and *The Seventh Sin*. After several bouts of transatlantic work and a stint with the Royal Shakespeare Company, Travers and his wife, Virginia McKenna, made the hugely successful *Born Free*. This launched a career as a filmmaker with a particular interest in the way animals are treated in captivity (*Ring of Bright Water* also treats this theme), and provided him with another opportunity for the convincingly natural, good-humoured playing that was his forte.

Interview date: February 1991

After war service and then some theatre work, you had small roles in ten or eleven films between 1949 and 1953. What do you recall of making any of these?

I remember doing bits in *The Wooden Horse*, mainly vaulting over the bloody thing; then quite a nice part – Benvolio – in *Romeo and Juliet* for Castellani, a good director. That was a good step forward and I learned quite a lot doing it. I joined the company in Venice; they had lovely, specially woven clothes of the period, and we used to dress up in these seventeenth-century clothes, then wander through the streets to make-up, where they had wonderful Italian artists doing everyone's make-up.

Then we would get into a gondola and go down the canals. The tourists would see us dressed in these beautiful clothes, on our way to the set, and would wave to us and we would carry the part off as best we could.

The turning point in your career seems to be 1955, with the title role in *Geordie*. How did you come by this?

I was about to take a part at Windsor Rep when I was offered a test for *Geordie*. I did nine tests altogether, some with people who were going to play the other parts, but I think Launder and Gilliat, who had scripted and sunk a lot of money into *Geordie*, had great difficulty persuading the distributors that they could play an unknown in the title role. I had to train at Joe Bloom's gym in Cambridge Circus, eat a lot of red meat, and do exercises to build up my muscles, so that I could actually throw the Scottish hammer and, hopefully, the Olympic hammer a reasonable distance, because they wanted to make the thing as real as possible. I think my arms grew if my chest didn't, as the pull of the Olympic hammer increased with each spin round.

Why do you think the film was so popular?

I think Launder and Gilliat were good scriptwriters, producers and directors. They let you get on with it; they had great patience and, if you weren't happy with it, they let you have another shot. They listened to what you had to say and so they were good from the actors' point of view. Also, they certainly knew how to write and edit. *Geordie* has a good theme – 'local boy makes good' sort of thing; it was a bit jingoistic about the Scottish, but the Scottish people are very popular, particularly in America, and are spread out all over the world, and people liked to see a Scotsman doing well. I signed a personal contract with Launder and Gilliat on making the film.

Were your next three films – *Bhowani Junction*, *The Barretts of Wimpole Street* and *The Seventh Sin* – part of an MGM contract? Did you find differences in working for a Hollywood company?

I got an MGM contract after making *Bhowani Junction*. I made *Footsteps in the Fog* first, with Stewart Granger and Jean Simmons, which gave me a different kind of part to do, and I guess that was important; it also got my name around, which was useful. I was interested to get the part in *Bhowani Junction* because the book had been written by my brigade major in the Chindits, John Masters, who

wrote many bestsellers. Also, being in the Gurkhas for some time, I could speak Gurkhali and of course Urdu; I had seen quite a lot of India in the six years I was in the East, and I knew how it was for the Anglo-Indians or Eurasians who were working on the railways. I have always had great admiration for Anglo-Indians: a lot of them were very brave indeed. So I knew a little about the character of Patrick, how vulnerable he was, and I also could do a fairly reasonable 'chi-chi' or Anglo-Indian accent. There was a lot of location work, all done near Lahore.

George Cukor was a wonderful director, who really knew how to get people to act. He didn't look through a camera very much. Freddie Young, who did the lighting, got on with it while George was rehearsing. There was all the difference in the world working for a Hollywood company. You were in with the 'big boys' instead of 'Uncle Frank and Uncle Sidney', as Launder and Gilliat were known. You had lots of 'Heads of Department' and you had to adapt to the treatment, to people photographing you all the time, and people talking about careers much more than what the part was like.

The Barretts of Wimpole Street was a remake and occasionally the director [Sidney Franklin] would call me 'Freddie' (because Fredric March had played it before) and he really only wanted to repeat the earlier film. Jennifer Jones was OK but she didn't like rehearsing and, since all my experience had been on the stage, I relied totally on rehearsing a scene before we played it.

Your other 1957 release, *The Smallest Show on Earth*, is a very British, rather Ealing-like film. Do you enjoy playing comedy?

That was Bill Rose's script; Frank Launder showed it to me and said he hardly had to rewrite anything at all. Rose was an American, yet he had a wonderful understanding of the British. *The Smallest Show on Earth* was a most enjoyable film to make. I found that going on the set with Peter Sellers (it was his first film) was magical – he had such a great sense of humour. Margaret Rutherford was quite wonderful to act with – I mean, you didn't know when she was acting or not. So was Bernard Miles. They were just great people to work with.

I did enjoy playing comedy, yes, it was fun, but it wasn't always that easy. We had quite a small budget for films in England and, because there was no guarantee they were going to be sold into the big markets of the world, you had to make them cheaply enough to recover the majority of their costs in this country. So there was quite a lot of pressure to get on with the job. I recall watching other people working and thinking, 'He's doing that, so what will I do next; where will they cut in this next scene; how am I going to manage my props?' Douggie Slocombe, who lit *The Smallest Show on Earth*, was always lighting as we were rehearsing; he was a marvellous lighting cameraman. There wasn't really much wasted time, and that's how we 'got on'. Also the director cut as he directed; he wouldn't take a scene further than where he knew he was going to cut.

Were producers keen to promote you and your wife as a team in films like *The Passionate Summer*, directed by Rudolph Cartier, an important figure in British television?

I suppose producers thought that, as we were both currently popular, if they offered us parts together, we would be more keen to do it. Neither of us cared very much for *The Passionate Summer*; Cartier was already an important person in television – that was how he got *The Passionate Summer* – but I'm not sure that he translated well to the big screen. He did a lot of rehearsal, and I'd begun by this time to shed the idea of doing a tremendous amount of rehearsal, which had been my security in the earlier days. I wanted by then to make things more natural and I found that Cartier was bound by what had happened at rehearsal. I think it needed something much more impressionistic than Cartier's direction. It needed to be made like a French film. I think it was as a result of that film we became less than favourites with the Rank Organisation.

Was *The Bridal Path* conceived as a follow-up to *Geordie*?

Frank Launder rang me up and said he'd got another film; he sent me the book and then I received the script. Yes, *Geordie* had made Launder and Gilliat quite a lot of money, I guess, so I think they saw *The Bridal Path* as a follow-up. I don't think it had quite the dimensions of *Geordie* and it wasn't such a success, but it was always fun working with Launder and Gilliat and I liked them tremendously as people. I remember driving around Scotland with Frank looking for locations. Sometimes we'd shoot a bit along the way; I had some of my kit in the back of the car, so every now and then I'd get into my gear and run up and down the mountains while they filmed me. We would do that if it was particularly beautiful, if the lighting was wonderful (as it often is in Scotland) and you just had to grab it while you could.

What light can you shed on *Two Living, One Dead*, one of the most 'missing' films of all time?

It was made by myself and Carl Moseby. The story had been suggested to me by Frank Launder. I read it and tried to get the film rights because I thought it would make an interesting film about what happened to people after a crime. I found out that Moseby, a Norwegian, had also tried to get an option. Someone engineered it so that we met his agent and we decided to go into it together. My wife and I were to play in it and we had several meetings but it didn't work out, in spite of the fact that 'Puffin' [Anthony] Asquith was the director – a wonderful director – and Teddy Baird was the producer. One of the problems was also that Carl Moseby, we discovered much too late, was unfortunately an alcoholic and desperately ill, and we were left with too many financial uncertainties.

How did you come to make *Born Free* in 1964–65, after a gap of several years away from films?

In 1962, when I was at Stratford, Tom McGowan (the original director of *Born Free*) told me about this property he had, called *Born Free*, although he hadn't got the money for it or got it set up. He was trying to find out if anyone would be daft enough to take on the part. So, after a play I did in America folded, I got in touch with my agent to ask what had happened to *Born Free*. I was amazed to get a telegram back saying yes, they were going ahead and Carl Foreman was waiting to meet us when we got back. We went to see Paul Radin and Sam Jaffe, the two producers, at the Mayfair Hotel in London. By that time we'd read the book. We thought it sounded like an amazing challenge although we didn't know how we would do it. Anyway, it is part of both Ginny's and my make-up to welcome a certain amount of risk or danger. *Born Free* was directly responsible for my later work, because of the experience of working with the lions: I went on to make my first documentary afterwards on what happened to the *Born Free* lions; the film is called *The Lions Are Free*.

You worked again for director James Hill in *The Belstone Fox* ...

He helped me to edit *The Lions Are Free*, and we formed a partnership and went on to make several more films together. He asked me if I would like to play a character part in *The Belstone Fox*, knowing how much I liked character parts, and it was an opportunity I really enjoyed – particularly working with Eric Porter. I had played Macduff in his *Macbeth* in 1962 and it was nice to be working with him again.

Linden Travers

b. 1914

Actor: *Children of the Fog* (1935), *Wednesday's Luck* (1936), *Double Alibi, Against the Tide, Brief Ecstasy, The Last Adventurers* (1937), *Bank Holiday, Almost a Honeymoon, The Terror, The Lady Vanishes* (1938), *Inspector Hornleigh on Holiday, The Stars Look Down* (1939), *The Ghost Train, The Seventh Survivor, South American George* (1941), *The Missing Millions* (1942), *Beware of Pity* (1946), *Jassy, The Master of Bankdam* (1947), *No Orchids For Miss Blandish, Quartet* ('The Colonel's Lady') (1948), *Christopher Columbus, The Bad Lord Byron, Don't Ever Leave Me* (1949), *The Schemer* (short) (1955)

Watching Hitchcock's *The Lady Vanishes*, you can't imagine why Michael Redgrave doesn't simply ditch Margaret Lockwood, push Cecil Parker out of the way and make off with the latter's disenchanted inamorata, Linden Travers. She is – simply – gorgeous and a film industry less bedevilled by gentility would have made her a great star. Graham Greene, no less, detected in her, in *Brief Ecstasy*, a refreshing sensuality, and ten years later she is far more exciting than the eponymous heroine deserves in *No Orchids for Miss Blandish*. Not that *No Orchids* is more or less fun than many like it: the point is that the 'many' were usually American. The outrage that followed it (Dr Edith Summerskill warning the Married Women's Association against it) has tended to obscure its main virtue, which is Linden Travers's performance. She is elegantly knowing as Cecil Parker's mistress (again) in *Quartet*, and provides almost the only real leaven in the lumpish Columbus and Byron disasters. Linden Travers (sister of the late Bill) has had a long and happy retirement from the screen, but British movies have missed her.

Interview dates: November 1992 and July 1994

In 1937, after several minor films, you made *Brief Ecstasy*, which Graham Greene praised for a much bolder approach to sexuality than was usual in British films.

I think it was. It was quite subtle because in those days you couldn't do anything like you can do today. It was about this young girl marrying an older man, a professor, and having a young lover, or *seeming* to have a young lover – it wasn't confirmed exactly. It was directed by a French director called Edmond Gréville, who had that little subtle touch of sexuality. One wasn't quite aware of it, at least I don't think I was. I was young and wasn't really very clued up, but I think the way he photographed and directed it gave a sort of sexy touch to it, for the time. Paul Lukas was the elderly husband, and Hugh Williams was the young lover. It was made at Ealing Studios, you know. It's only in my older years, seeing the film again, that I realised that it was much more sensual, perhaps, than one would have thought at the time.

Two of your 1938 releases both have top directors, Carol Reed in *Bank Holiday* and Hitchcock in *The Lady Vanishes*. How did you respond to them?

Carol Reed was brilliant. I think one was a bit in awe of him; he seemed to be a very English, rather grand gentlemen at times. I only had a small part and I did what I was told.

Now, Hitchcock was a different cup of tea. I was devoted to him. He made a test first, though I think he'd already decided on me. You see, he was a very subtle man. He said to me, 'Can you speak with your mouth closed?' And I thought, 'I know what he means, he doesn't want big mouthing.' He asked me a few questions and I answered them with my mouth closed. Of course, I made an absolute fool of myself, but I think he enjoyed it. He liked to make you uncomfortable but, anyway, I got the part and I was delighted. He had this thing about wanting to make you wriggle a bit.

How did you find the star of that film, Margaret Lockwood, with whom you did several other films?

We got on. She was a very practical actress – very down-to-earth, very efficient, very professional and very good. Of course, she was the star of the thing and she seemed to get her way. I don't think I had a lot to do with her except we talked together, and, of course, all of us had lunch together very often. I was mostly with Cecil Parker, who was playing my partner on an illicit weekend. And Dame May Whitty was lovely. She was seventy-two at the time, and she said to me, 'I've just got a contract to go to Hollywood, it's on account of my voluptuous lips.'

Was it all done in the studio?

Yes. They must have done some exteriors in Austria or somewhere like that for when the train stops, but otherwise it was all in the studios. Hitchcock really enjoyed himself. I go on about him because I liked him so much. He was the sort of director who, with a long shot, miles away from the camera, with all of us in it, would suddenly say, 'Miss Travers, would you cross your right leg over your left, instead of your left over your right.' Nobody could even see it, but he would pick on something just to maintain control.

You played either Cecil Parker's wife or his mistress in three films: *The Lady Vanishes*, *The Stars Look Down* and *Quartet*. Did you enjoy this partnership?

Very much. He, again, was a very professional man. He wasn't the sort of person who made passes or anything. He was a very serious, dedicated actor. Once I asked him, 'How do you manage all this? Do you have flights of the imagination? How do you approach parts?' He said, 'I'm the dullest man on our street.' He was just a serious actor.

You usually looked as if you knew more than he did, except as Mrs Todhunter, when you were rather nervous about the whole situation.

Well, you see the affair was breaking up. I remember I said, because he ordered two rooms, 'You weren't so fussy in Paris last year.' 'Then, the exhibition was at its height,' he said. He was a very polished actor, wonderful. He had a broken neck, from the war I think, and used to hold his head a little to one side. I had a restaurant scene with him in *The Stars Look Down* when Emlyn Williams came and sat at the table, and I was eating oysters. I think I was having an affair with Emlyn on the side. I always seemed to be doing that. It's amazing, I don't know why it was, because I wasn't really very sophisticated myself.

You never got to play home-loving girls. To go back for a second to Carol Reed: were *Bank Holiday* and *The Stars Look Down* made partly on location?

I had a very little part in *Bank Holiday*. What I did was all in the studio. I didn't go to Hastings, where some of it was shot. And *The Stars Look Down* was all done in the studio. I think Carol was the most brilliant director, but I never got to know him very well. Occasionally, my husband and I would meet with him and his wife, Penelope Dudley Ward, who was wonderful, and talk. He was quite detached. I think he was always thinking about cinema.

What do you recall of working with George Formby, who was a huge star in the '30s?

I seemed to have jumped out of being mistresses into playing with the comics – Tommy Trinder, Arthur Askey and then George Formby. That was *South American George*. Beryl, his wife, controlled him. She was his manager. And she wasn't inclined to encourage any girls hanging around who were attractive. I wouldn't have been interested in George, anyway, though he was nice to work with and very professional. She looked after him all the time; she and I eventually became good friends and she helped me a lot with my clothes. She was very good for him, and I think she realised that she'd put him, or helped to put him, where he was and didn't feel somebody younger and prettier than she was should get hold of him. I think she was very sensible. In his time, he was terribly funny and he played his ukulele so well. It was a case of the ordinary person winning the race, you know. People like seeing the underdog succeed; they think, well, I might win.

Why did you make no films between 1942 and 1946, when *Beware of Pity* was released?

I was doing *No Orchids for Miss Blandish* on the stage for a year. I did it for two months in Blackpool, I think it was. This was during the war. And then we came to London and it ran for nearly a year – about ten months. Then I think I did *Quality Street* and was on the stage for a couple of years or a bit more. Then I started again in films.

What do you recall about *Beware of Pity*, perhaps Maurice Elvey's best film?

He was a tricky one, Maurice Elvey. I don't know what other people said about him, but I don't care anyway. He was sarcastic to the crew, though not to me specially. And I had rather a dull part. I was the companion of Lilli Palmer, so I was just sitting around a lot of the time. I *wanted* to be in it, though, because it was a big prestige production. Lilli was brilliant. She knew how to light herself, she knew how to write the script, she knew everything. Oh, and there was Ernest Thesiger, who used to do a little bit of stitching. We used to have tea together, and travel in the bus sometimes or share a taxi, and I found him very cosy and chatty. He seemed dreadfully old, of course.

Beware of Pity is a superb-looking film. Do you remember the sets at all?

Yes, they were lovely, very elegant. Alex Vetchinsky did them. And didn't Cecil Beaton do the costumes? There were beautiful clothes and very handsome sets.

You were back at Gainsborough for *Jassy* in 1947. Did you find that it had changed much?

No. Sydney Box was the kingpin. It all seemed to be more or less the same. It was my first colour film, but the make-up man dealt with that. I can hardly remember *Jassy*, now. I played Basil Sidney's wife, and I was having a fling in the summerhouse with Bryan Coleman. I remember doing this kissing scene with Bryan. It's difficult to do a kiss, because it has to *look* all right as well as *feel* all right. It's difficult to do it without noses getting in the way of each other. I remember saying to Bernard Knowles after this kiss, 'Is that enough? Is that all right?' and he said, 'What else can you *do*?'

What do you remember of playing yet another scheming type, Clara (wife of Stephen Murray) in *The Master of Bankdam*?

Goodness, you are taking me back! I enjoyed that. I had to start at age twenty-one, which I wasn't at the time, and go up to about fifty. It was a case of clogs-to-clogs in three generations. Clara, the part I played, was really a bitch. I wanted to be made up to look like an older Bette Davis, but Walter Forde [director] wanted a softer image. It was his last film, I think. It was a good story and I can remember being very fascinated by it. And I liked Walter Forde and his wife, Cully. I seemed to get on quite well with the directors *and* their wives!

You had contrasting releases in 1948 – the prestigious, literary, *Quartet* and the then-scandalous *No Orchids for Miss Blandish*. What do you remember about the charming 'Colonel's Lady' story in the former?

That was with Cecil Parker again. I liked working with Ken Annakin and I enjoyed the whole thing. I remember one annoying thing. I had done this scene in a very nice white négligé when Cecil Parker arrives at the flat and talks to and puts his hand on me. Then they said there couldn't be any négligé. I was totally covered up, it was like a dressing gown. It wasn't even a low neck, but they said no, it couldn't be, so I had to put on a black evening dress which I wore in a subsequent scene. People must have thought I only had one dress, one black evening dress, and nothing else. We'd done this scene and it had been very good, and better, I think, in the négligé. I looked a bit more like a mistress. The censor thought he shouldn't have arrived when she wasn't dressed, but she was a sort of high-class, ladylike, knowing mistress. This man wanted somebody who knew how to behave and wasn't ringing up the wife all the time. And the wife was beautifully played by Nora Swinburne. We all met Somerset Maugham at a big dinner. They were very popular, those Maugham films, because he always had good stories.

Now, *No Orchids for Miss Blandish* **...**

Were you going to say, 'What on earth made you want to do that'?! I was offered the leading part, and I had done the play, which had a successful run with Robert Newton as a draw.

What interests me is why the film caused such an outrage.

Well, the kiss lasted forty-nine seconds! I've got a cutting about it. Someone asked a question in the House. In those days, they had other things to write about instead of gossip about MPs. So there was a parliamentary question ... Forty-nine seconds is not such a long time for a kiss, really, is it? Also, we had somebody like Slim Grissom [Jack La Rue], who was a leading man but was on the bad side. Jack La Rue was very nice to work with. The silly part about that forty-nine seconds is that he had only just arrived in England, I hardly knew the man and there we were locked in the embrace that caused such a stir. He was very American; I didn't have a lot to do with him, but he was very pleasant – they all were in this film.

The director [St John Clowes] became ill halfway through and then somebody else – Oswald Mitchell – took over. I didn't think it was particularly good, but it had some quite good bits about it. The scenes between Lily Molnar as the mother and Jack La Rue are very good, though I think it was better in the play. Mary Clare, who was a big woman, played the mother, and, of course, Robert Newton was out-rageous, and people came to see it because of him. He put more into it than Jack La Rue, who behaved, though, more like a tough American. I think we were lucky to have him to give it a bit of balance. I think it did quite well. It had all that publicity, and it's a good title, you see.

I can't think of another English actress, except possibly Googie Withers, who could have done that. It's almost the only sexy heroine in British films in that period.

Oh, that is nice of you to say so. Having done the play, you know, I suppose made it easier. I haven't got a copy of it but it has been shown on television in the afternoon, without causing a stir any more. At the time, it was not accepted as OK for her to go and live with him. But it didn't show anything like they do these days, like taking off all your clothes and everything. The only thing he did was put his hand down my front, when we went outside, into the woods ... outside Reigate, in the Home Counties!

What was your experience of those two enormously expensive Gainsborough releases in 1949, *Christopher Columbus* **and** *The Bad Lord Byron***?**

They were both directed by David MacDonald, who was one of my favourite directors. I think they both lost a lot of money, and they cost more than usual, but I never knew much about that side of things. I enjoyed playing Beatriz de Peranza in *Columbus*. When I was in the Canary Islands on holiday, I remember saying to a receptionist at the hotel, 'I played a part once when I was banished from the Spanish Court on account of misbehaviour, and I became the Governor of the Canary Islands,' which was true. She was sent away, you see, because she was seducing King Ferdinand. Anyway, I told this receptionist, who wasn't the least impressed!!

What do you remember of making *The Bad Lord Byron***?**

That was with Dennis Price as Byron. I was playing his half-sister, with whom he had an affair in real life. Naturally those suggestions of incest weren't in the film. She had a child by him in real life. I thought it was a pretty interesting thing to do, though I think it needed a wilder type than Dennis Price for Byron. It wasn't very good but I enjoyed it; I really enjoyed *working*. I was never terribly nervous, because I never carried the whole film on my shoulders.

▲ The Draughtsman's Contract *1982*   ▼ Dreamchild *1985*

▲ Distant Voices, Still Lives *1988*   ▼ A Fish Called Wanda *1988*

▲ Howards End *1992*   ▼ Four Weddings and a Funeral *1994*

▲ Secrets and Lies *1996* ▼ The English Patient *1997*

Rita Tushingham

b. 1942

Actor: *A Taste of Honey* (1961), *The Leather Boys, A Place to Go, The Girl with Green Eyes* (1963), *Doctor Zhivago, The Knack ... and How To Get It* (1965), *The Trap* (1966), *Smashing Time* (1967), *Diamonds for Breakfast* (1968), *The Bed-Sitting Room, The Guru* (1969), *Straight On Till Morning, Where Do You Go From Here?* (incomplete) (1972), *Instant Coffee* (1974), *Rachel's Man* (1975), *The 'Human' Factor, Ragazzo di Borghese* (1976), *Slaughter Day / The Situation, Gran Bollito/Black Journal* (1977), *Mysteries, Sotto Choc* (1978), *Spaghetti House* (1982), *Flying / Dream to Believe, A Judgement in Stone* (1986), *Single Room* (incomplete) (1987), *Resurrected* (1989), *Hard Days, Hard Nights* (1990), *A Csalas Gyonyore, Paper Marriage* (1992), *Desert Lunch, The Gospel According to Harry* (1993), *An Awfully Big Adventure* (1994), *The Boy from Mercury* (1997)

The camera loved Rita Tushingham's eloquent wide-eyed face from the moment she appeared as Jo in Tony Richardson's *A Taste of Honey*, her award-winning début in 1961. The yearning for affection, the suppressed poetry, the zany humour: all these were poignantly caught in this exceptional first role. Throughout the '60s, there were more opportunities to capitalise on these endearing qualities in British films in the then-fashionable realist mode as well as in those with a surreal edge to them. The British cinema as an entity was crumbling in the '70s, but she went on to make over twenty further films – in Israel, Canada, and all over Europe, resurfacing in British films in the mid-'90s. She has negotiated the moves from teenager to leading lady to character roles with impressive resilience.

Interview date: August 1995

How did you come to be cast in *A Taste of Honey*?

When I was at Liverpool Rep, I read in the entertainment column in a newspaper that John Osborne and Tony Richardson were looking for an unknown actress to play Jo in *A Taste of Honey*. So I wrote and sent a photograph to John Osborne's agent, which he sent on to the Woodfall Films office. They wrote to me and I went to an audition and improvisation; then I did a film test and so did a lot of actresses, mostly from London and the south, I think; then they looked at another group of girls from the north. Then there were more tests – and I got the role.

Looking back, do you feel that you actually started at the top with this role?

I wasn't thinking about that because you don't know what you're doing when you're young and inexperienced; it was a lovely role to play; I had wonderful people around me and it was fun. Only afterwards, when it came out, did you realise what was involved, because you were going all over the place doing interviews, going to festivals and so on, and you realised that the *next* one was going to be important. When you look back, it was an incredibly rich time and one wonders why things like that happen. We say the '60s were so good; we'd just come out of the '50s and we'd had the war, so it must have seemed fantastic.

Those films looked so realistic at the time. Did you feel, at the time, that these films were opening up the cinema?

They did open up cinema because women's roles had been rather more restrained; they weren't the force of the film as much, perhaps, as these were, especially young women. There would always be the woman and the man, but the man would always shoulder the responsibilities – well, in many films. And suddenly here was youth coming into it, regardless of whether they were responsible or irresponsible, and their lives were being shown and people were wanting to see it. It was opening it up to the younger market of film.

So it was really a shift in youth, gender and class.

Yes, I think it was, and it all came at once, not just in film but in theatre as well – and in such a way that often it wasn't liked because it wasn't the norm, it wasn't Terence Rattigan and it wasn't something that people felt comfortable with because it peeled away a lot of layers. In England in the '60s we still had this ridiculous class system – we still have it – and people were saying 'Who would be interested in seeing what people do in their kitchens?' and suddenly yes, people *did* want to see it and were quite shocked at times. It broke down a lot of barriers in a sense, I think. Before this, these people wouldn't have been acceptable unless they were caricatured – and these people were *not* caricatures. Suddenly it was 'This is it. We can create, we can think, we can write, we can paint, we can do all those things' – as Jo could, in fact.

Yes, that was an interesting touch in Jo. I'd be interested to know anything you recall about filming *A Taste of Honey*.

We started shooting on my nineteenth birthday. Since I'd never made a film before, filming on location didn't seem to me difficult at all. I was weaned on locations and it was just great, because you'd have all the people around; it was shot in Manchester and they were very friendly. We went to Blackpool and Dora Bryan and I had to go on this rollercoaster – which I'll never do again in my life, because it was the most frightening thing in the world – and you remember things like that. It was a wonderful time for me, with great memories.

Paul Danquah, who played the sailor, is one of my closest friends and still visits me. He's in Morocco now. Dora I occasionally see and I love. She is so lovely, and what a talent! Why isn't she a Dame? And to work with, she was just *there* for you. I was very lucky because she was such a very *normal* person. I love acting but I couldn't bear to be 'actressy' and I like to have people as friends after the professional relationship ends. Dora played a lot of caricatures before that, of course, then she suddenly did this and she was brilliant, I thought; she was so touching. No one could have done it as well as she. And Murray Melvyn and Sir Robert Stephens – you know, marvellous people. It was like I was working with an intimate family group, which a film so often is, and it was great. I couldn't have been luckier. And of course Tony Richardson, whom I adored.

Did he give you a lot of close direction?

He was one of those people who knew what he wanted but he'd let you work at it and then maybe he'd say this or that, but he'd let you discover it, all of us. That was what was very useful, but you knew that he was there, guiding you in a very subtle way – but obviously guiding you in a very good way, because the film came out so well.

What do you recall of the critical and audience response to this film?

They seemed to like it. It was a huge success at the time, because one was being given awards all over the place, you know. It was probably good that it happened to me while I was young. If it happened now, I'd have to wonder how long it's going to go on for. And it didn't. I was terribly naïve. It was great that people liked it, but, I suppose, being surrounded by people from Woodfall who were doing other films and people who were also doing successful work, it made you suppose that's how it always is – until it stops being like that, which was when the film industry started to peter out.

In the next few years you had a run of very good roles. How did you get these roles? Did you have a contract with Woodfall?

I had a contract with Woodfall when I did *A Taste of Honey*. Carlo Ponti wanted me to have a contract with him but I never did sign one. That was later. But there were a lot of scripts at the beginning, a lot of them about pregnant teenagers, as you can imagine. Even then they didn't have the imagination, but they were better roles.

Did you have a good agent?

I didn't have an agent when I got the film, but I got an agent after that when I was doing theatre and film. My agent was Olive Harding. She was Peter Finch's agent as well. An agent can say 'There's this fantastic script, you must read it,' and perhaps it is never offered to you, but they may suggest you. Sometimes scripts will come and they'll say, 'We want you to do this.' A script will come and they'll ask you what you think about it but not necessarily say they want you for it. So it's a mixture. I think if people send you something you should always meet them and chat about it, because you might be completely wrong. People have very different ideas about you. So they might think you're not right for this but you'd be absolutely right for something else.

Did your second film, *The Leather Boys*, seem controversial at the time, with its homosexual subplot?

I suppose it was quite controversial, but with Sidney Furie we improvised quite a lot on that. I didn't really think it was controversial, although it couldn't have happened five years earlier. It was held up for a year, before they released it. I think they were a bit worried about it because of its content. These days it would really be quite tame but ... I mean, *A Taste of Honey* was also not shown in certain countries. I don't know how many screen kisses there had been between a black man and a white woman; I should think this must have been one of the first.

You then worked for the famous Ealing team of Basil Dearden and Michael Relph on *A Place to Go*. I'd be interested in any recollections of that film or of Mike Sarne.

Yes, this was quite a different film for Basil Dearden. I got on with him very well indeed. Dearden and Relph were completely different from Tony Richardson, of course, but they were very competent, knew what they were doing and I enjoyed working with them. I got on OK with Mike Sarne. He'd done that pop record, 'Come Outside', and so he was sort of a name. I don't know what became of him.

Your next one, *The Girl with Green Eyes*, is charming. What did you think of it?

I loved doing that. Lynn Redgrave and I are very close friends and Peter Finch was one of the best actors I've ever met. He was so natural, he was easy, you could laugh, you could do a scene and you'd have fun. And Desmond Davis, the operator on *A Taste of Honey*, was the director on that. He was a very gentle man, and a lovely director. It's a nice film. We did it in Wicklow and Dublin.

In the 1960s you did realistic films on the one hand, and on the other, poetic, almost surrealistic films. Were you pleased with the range of things you were getting?

Yes, and also I don't think I was overly ambitious. I also had family – the children, so I had a mixture of things going on in my life. I was generally pleased with the roles I was getting but there were certain things I didn't want to do. There were some things I turned down that maybe I should've done, but I don't think you should look back. Sometimes they do tend to typecast you and think you can only do one thing. I'd love to have done period film and I've never done it. I think the earliest would be about 1938–1940; I've never done anything earlier than that. I've worked with James Ivory but the film I did for him, *The Guru*, wasn't one of his period ones. Isn't that typical! I mean, in *Zhivago* everyone had lovely costumes but I was in a boilersuit and Wellingtons!

You were very touching in *Zhivago*. Were you pleased with it?

I loved doing it and, for me, being directed by David Lean was fantastic. He really made you concentrate and, when you're younger, that's not so easy. He made you think and he made you think for a reason, obviously. We were working in Spain, in Madrid and on the Portuguese border. My scenes were at the beginning and end of the film but they did them all in one block. It took about five or six weeks. That was quite slow filmmaking, yes. It wasn't so much elaborate camera set-ups; I think it was that they'd do something and, if David didn't like the set, it would be removed and another one put up – that sort of thing. I very much enjoyed working with Alec Guinness, who has a fantastic sense of humour.

***The Knack* and *The Bed-Sitting Room* are what I meant by non-realist films.**

I think the marvellous thing about them is that if you play them for reality it's even funnier. You have to believe the situation you're in and, if you believe it, then you're perfectly normal. This is how this character behaves, so it's perfectly normal to that character.

So that if it appears to an audience as having a kind of surrealist edge, that is in a sense the way the director has put it all together.

Yes, but you as the actor have to *be* it – and this is one of the things that Richard Lester is very good with. He knows exactly what he wants in comedy. He has such a quick mind. He's editing as he goes along, so he just takes what he's going to use, in a sense. He doesn't let you overdo it but he lets you go a little bit further. You feel very, very safe in his hands. He wants it to be real but to be very funny in the way he shoots it and the way you are. There's always a great feeling on the set with him.

How did you find working with the Merchant–Ivory team on *The Guru*?

Oh, I loved it. Ismail is always trying to save every penny but why not? He was good at that and I admire them very much for what they've done. Ruth [Prawer Jhabvala] I liked very much and James I worked very well with; he's very serious but he's got a good sense of humour. We made the film in Bombay, Bikaner and Benares.

Were filming conditions different there?

The only thing that was different was that you'd arrive at eight o'clock and the Indians wouldn't come in until nine-thirty. That used to drive me mad because I thought I'd get into bad habits. I mean, when you're called for eight, you come in at eight. But you get used to going with their rhythm, which is completely different from ours. It's warmer and so they work at a slower pace. I loved them, loved India.

Since 1970 you have filmed all over the place. Was this a matter of preference?

It just so happened that the things I was asked to do and chose to do were all over the place. For instance, I did six films in Italy, which I loved doing. And *Rachel's Man* in Israel with Mickey Rooney – a real legend. It's not an easy business to keep going in, you know. You get to a certain age and there aren't so many roles – especially for women, it's true.

Was *Resurrected* about the Falklands?

Yes, with Tom Bell, myself and David Thewlis, who is one of our best. It was directed by Paul Greengrass. It was based on a true story, about a man who has amnesia and is missing for seventy days. It's a very good film with a very good director. I loved working with Tom, of course, and David is wonderful. He'll be a very big star and it will be great if he stays with British films. He is brilliant in Mike Leigh's *Naked*.

What can you tell me about *An Awfully Big Adventure*?

That was a film for Mike Newell, whom I enjoyed working with, and it had Alan Rickman, who is terrific, and also Hugh Grant, who had a very different role and I think was very good in it. I had scenes mostly with Alun Armstrong, who is a brilliant actor. It's written by Beryl Bainbridge, about a young girl who wants to work at the Liverpool Playhouse. She lives with us and I'm her aunt. A lot of my scenes went, unfortunately.

You're now making a film in Ireland?

Yes, it's called *The Boy from Mercury* and it will be released in 1997. The director is Martin Duffy and he wrote the script, and Tom Courtenay is in it.

Dorothy Tutin

b. 1930

Actor: *The Importance of Being Earnest* (1952), *The Beggar's Opera* (1953), *A Tale of Two Cities* (1958), *Cromwell* (1970), *Savage Messiah* (1972), *The Shooting Party* (1984), *Great Moments in Aviation*, *The Great Kadinsky* (1994), *Indian Summer* (1996)

Y̶ou can't help wondering what agents and/or casting directors are up to when you realise that a talent and face as distinctively attractive as Dorothy Tutin's should have been used in no more than seven films in forty years. She was of course always busy on the stage, in classical and modern roles, and did some remarkable television, but the cinema, which would have given her major exposure, neglected her. She made the most auspicious debut as Cecily in Asquith's *The Import-ance of Being Earnest*, striking exactly the right blend of ingenuousness and knowingness, more than holding her own with that dazzling cast; despite her misgivings, her Lucie Manette is much more incisive than any of the Rank young ladies of the time was likely to have been; she is very touching as Queen Henrietta in Ken Hughes's underrated *Cromwell*; she responded well to Ken Russell on *The Savage Messiah* . . . So why isn't there more? Perhaps Mike Newell will find a way to use her as he has so often done with vintage actresses.

Interview date: July 1994

You seem to have rationed yourself very austerely in the making of cinema films. Was this a matter of choice?

No, it wasn't – I would have loved to be in more films but I didn't exactly have 'the face of the moment' when I was young. I never had a very photogenic face. I remember a lighting man saying to me, 'How can I light that nose?' and I never quite got over that. I was very lucky, though, to have the opportunity of being in a few good films – *The Importance of Being Earnest* when I was twenty-one, and then *The Beggar's Opera* and *A Tale of Two Cities*. After that I went to the Royal Shakespeare Company in Stratford and so I was out of the running. I don't remember turning anything down except *I Am a Camera*; I didn't like the script after having been in the play. Then there was a new wave of young actors and actresses coming on, and I'd done too much classical work, I think, for people to think of me as Cockney, North Country or whatever. I would have loved to have had a go at any of those things; however, I wasn't a part of that new wave so nobody asked me.

How difficult was the transition to film from stage work? Did you have to learn a lot of new techniques?

Oh yes, it's completely different. Filming was very nerve-wracking to begin with, on *The Import-ance of Being Earnest*, but because it was played in a very theatrical way I didn't find it that difficult. I

didn't think about the camera. I wish I could say I had become knowledgeable about cinema tech-nique. I can't bear the sight of myself on the screen or the sound of myself. The whole thing was a total shock to me, because I thought I would look different; I was playing Cecily and I thought my face would look as I imagined hers would be. I think people who are very good on the screen know their face and are at home with it, and can use it as an instrument.

How did you get the part of Cecily?

I was playing Princess Katherine in *Henry V* and Michael Redgrave, who was going to be in the film, saw me and recommended me to Anthony Asquith. Asquith came to see me perform, then he asked me to read in his office. Then he asked me to do a test, which was terrible – or it felt terrible. But Asquith was so sweet, and gave me another test. I went back and did another scene, and this time he told me I had the part. I wish I'd been more mature, to understand how lucky I was to be working with him and how prepared he was, how skilfully he had thought the film out. We did the whole play in sequence, which is very rare in filming, and it was wonderful for a stage-trained actress. But I thought filming went on forever and what appalled me was that we did the Diary Scene on the first day of filming – we did four minutes' filming and he said that was it. I said I couldn't bear the pace and couldn't I please do it again? I was taken to one side by the producer (Teddy Baird), who asked did I realise how much it cost to do a retake – something like £200 a minute – so I shut up after that! Because I was so young I felt I needed amazing direction all the time. I think 'Puffin' was very skilful and simply let me play it the way I did, but it worried me.

This is a famously handsome-looking production and I wondered what you remember of either Carmen Dillon's sets or Beatrice Dawson's costumes.

I thought they were wonderful. I got to know Carmen quite well during the film and I thought she was brilliant; the sets were superbly designed and I thought the costumes were wonderful. They were very over-the-top, of course, and very uncomfortable because both Joan [Greenwood] and I had to wear corsets, and one couldn't make up one's mind to eat with the corsets on, or take them off and eat in comfort, then have the agony of putting them back on again! The whole house and garden was a fantastically beautiful set. I totally believed I was in the country, apart from the smell of the set which you never get rid of. I thought Carmen's work was wonderful, as was the business of starting the whole film off in the theatre. It was a perfect way of announcing that this was a film of a play, and not to expect anything too realistic. It was a masterpiece of artificiality and 'Puffin' wasn't pretending that it was anything else.

It was a fabulous cast, of course. What recollections do you have of working with Edith Evans and Margaret Rutherford?

Oh, Margaret Rutherford was perfection. To be on the set when she was doing that scene with her handbag was such a privilege. She did it in two takes, both of which were wonderful, and I was practically in tears. Everyone on the film was very kind to me, except that I didn't have such a happy relationship with Edith. It was just one of those tragic things that happen when you're young. I did get to know her later and I adored her. I also adored working with Joan Greenwood, who, to me, was the definitive Gwendolen. I loved doing the garden scene with her, and we were greatly helped by having Merriman the butler with us. That was Puffin's idea, that it would be like a tennis match with him as the umpire scoring each point.

The following year you did *The Beggar's Opera* for producers Laurence Olivier and Herbert Wilcox. Was it a part you knew?

No, not at all. I was absolutely thrilled to be asked to do it. I had to audition and do a film test, before which I had about an hour to learn one of Polly's speeches. Then they had the problem of matching our voices to singers: we had to sing with our own voices anyway, even though the recorded voices weren't to be ours.

What was it like to be co-starring with Olivier at this very young age?

It was wonderful, although a very strange experience: the filming went on for about six months, I don't know why. Daphne [Anderson] and I were never bored because when we weren't filming, we were practising our dubbed singing. I had Adele Leigh's voice, which I thought was absolutely magical, and I wanted to make sure people thought that voice was coming from me. Larry had a lovely natural baritone, you know, but he was trained by an Italian tenor. I think if he had used his natural voice, which was so good, and maybe if we had all used less operatic voices to sing, it would have sounded better.

When I first met Peter [director Peter Brook] and we talked about his plans for the film, he said he was going to do it in a very Hogarthian manner, we would all be sweaty and rough and dirty, and I thought that sounded wonderful. You wouldn't have people worrying about powdering your face and all that nonsense that goes on. Then I found to my horror that we were put into picture-book costumes, clean as a whistle and made up to look pretty.

Five years later you played Lucie Manette in *A Tale of Two Cities* for two wholly cinema-trained people – Ralph Thomas and Betty Box. Did this make any difference to you?

No, not really. I didn't think I was right for the part: it needed to be a blonde, beautiful girl like Virginia McKenna. I knew the novel well, so I was never going to turn it down, I just never felt I was quite right visually. I think Dirk really got me the part and I think he was wrong, although I enjoyed the filming in France until I got ill, and I did enjoy working with Dirk, who was extremely nice. But I felt the whole film was a bit slow, lacking energy. I did think it was a good idea to film it in black-and-white, so I'm surprised that Dirk, Ralph and Betty all thought it should have been filmed in colour. It was done in Pinewood and then in Bourges in France, where it rained a great deal, I think.

You made no further films until *Cromwell* in 1970. How did this happen?

I don't think I was asked. I find that agents aren't particularly imaginative, nor are people in casting, so unless somebody specifically asks for you, you tend not to be offered a lot of parts. I don't know how *Cromwell* came about. It was a very grand production, I remember that great staircase that was built wherever we did it – Pinewood, possibly. The costumes were designed by an Italian and they were very, very heavy and completely authentic. I didn't have a very big part and I regretted it rather.

The relationship between you as Queen Henrietta and Alec Guinness is very movingly done.

There was one scene which we never did and I kept on asking Ken Hughes when we were going to do it. It took place in a carriage and it was just one moment that really defined that relationship. We never came to do it and I asked Ken at the final party to do it and let me pay for it, because I felt it was important. But if, as you say, the relationship works then maybe he was right and we didn't need the scene after all.

I found Queen Henrietta fascinating as a woman – I had to read about her because she really isn't written up very much in the script. But Ken was meticulous about the historical accuracy and perspective of the film and he really knew his stuff. I thought it was a good script and of course Ken was able to use a transcript of the trial scene, which is wonderful, it's famous. That business about the Divine Right of Kings and Parliament suddenly having the strength and courage to say no. It was extraordinarily dramatic and beautifully incorporated, I thought.

Was working for Ken Russell on *Savage Messiah* different from your other filmmaking experience?

Yes, absolutely. For the first time I felt really part of filmmaking as opposed to being an actress playing a part. It was an interesting script and I loved the woman that I played – kind of mad, a very interesting character; I also fell in love with Gaudier-Brzeska. I met Ken for tea one day to discuss the script and he told me the story in a wonderfully vivid and exciting way. Then he showed me a portrait of Gaudier-Brzeska, I looked at it and almost fell in love with that face. It was very tough, very arduous, but I learned more about filming than I did in any of the other films I'd done. Ken refused to let me wear any make-up, which, in a way, was awful but he was adamant and he was quite right.

Sophie was a very embarrassing woman, very peculiar; in the film she sings two songs and I offered to write them because I would then know that I could sing them. Ken said I could and let me go ahead. When we came to do one of the scenes, the Vortex scene with everything going at funny angles, I thought we would have rehearsed it first but Ken said no, just do it. I asked for a brandy and then went into the scene – and it worked, because I was embarrassed as well as embarrassing; I went completely scarlet and came out in a sweat. It's all in the film and it really does look quite extraordinary. I knew at the time it was rather a good thing.

A lot of it was done in long scenes because Ken rarely did over-the-shoulder shots – what was filmed was what he got, it was organic. A long shot was a long shot, he never did a cutaway. We did twenty-eight takes of a tracking shot in a market – my feet were killing me and I'd say, 'Ken, can't you cut away to a cabbage or something?' 'No, no,' he said, 'this is a *long* shot.' The interesting part was not always knowing how Ken was going to shoot something or what he wanted of me. I would be doing a scene and he would suddenly tell me to do this or do that, and I just loved that. He was very careful about some things being prepared but he liked to be spontaneous about others, and I found that joyful. I hoped that my film career might just be starting again!

I very much liked *The Shooting Party*. Were you familiar with the Isabel Colgate novel?

Yes, I was. It's a terrifically good story. There were many difficulties on the film, including all the leading actors being injured in an accident with the runaway cart. Paul Scofield couldn't continue on the film because he broke his leg; Edward Fox had ribs broken; Robert Hardy had a badly injured knee and ribs; the Egyptian actor [Aharon Ipalé] hurt his knee. It was a shocking accident and it held up filming for two weeks while everyone recovered. James Mason came in to replace Paul and he played it so beautifully. I thought it was a wonderful performance and he was lovely to work with. He was a very fine man and a great screen actor, so intelligent about film and filmmaking.

It seems to be a film which really addresses the matter of class, and calls to account the difficulties that class might make.

Absolutely. It also uses class as an example of the inevitability of confrontation if you are going to divide people into certain levels. It is almost a microcosm of Europe in that sense, the actual going out to shoot.

What have you done most recently?

A film called *Great Moments in Aviation* which was shot as a film but may be shown on television. That was for Beeban Kidron. It's a lovely script by Jeanette Winterson and with a lovely cast. Vanessa Redgrave and I played two lesbian missionaries. I don't know why it has that title because it isn't a series of episodes at all.

Sir Peter Ustinov

b. 1921

Actor: *Hullo Fame, Mein Kampf – My Crimes, Let the People Sing* (dialogue dir) (1940), *One of Our Aircraft is Missing, The Goose Steps Out* (1942), *The New Lot* (& co-sc) (1943), *The Way Ahead* (& co-sc), *Carnival* (co-sc) (1944), *School for Secrets* (dir, sc, co-pr), *Vice Versa* (& dir, sc, co-pr) (1946), *Private Angelo* (& co-dir, pr) (1949), *Odette* (1950), *Hotel Sahara, The Magic Box, Quo Vadis?* (1951), *Beau Brummell, The Egyptian* (1954), *We're No Angels, The Wanderers, Lola Montes* (1955), *Les Espions, The Man Who Wagged His Tail* (1957), *Adventures of Mr Wonderbird* (voice only) (1959), *Spartacus, The Sundowners* (1960), *Romanoff and Juliet* (& dir, pr, sc) (1961), *Billy Budd* (& dir, co-sc, co-pr) (1962), *John Goldfarb, Please Come Home, *The Peaches* (narr), *Topkapi* (1964), *Lady L* (dir, sc) (1965), *The Comedians, Blackbeard's Ghost* (1967), *Hot Millions* (1968), *Viva Max!* (1970), *Hammersmith is Out* (dir), *Big Mack and Poor Clare* (1972), *Robin Hood* (voice only) (1973), *One of Our Dinosaurs is Missing* (1975), *Logan's Run, Treasure of Matecumbe* (1976), *Double Murders, Taxi Mauve / Purple Taxi, The Last Remake of Beau Geste* (1977), *Death on the Nile, Tarka the Otter* (voice only) (1978), *Ashanti* (1979), *Charlie Chan and the Curse of the Dragon Queen* (1980), *The Great Muppet Caper* (1981), *Evil Under the Sun* (1982), *Memed my Hawk, Grendel, Grendel, Grendel* (voice only) (1983), *Appointment with Death* (1988), *La Révolution Française* (1989), *C'era un Castello con 40 cani* (1990), *Lorenzo's Oil* (1993), *The Phoenix and the Carpet* (1994), *Stiff Upper Lip* (1997)

* Documentary or short film.

Writer, producer, director, actor: Peter Ustinov has carried out all these functions in British films, as well as finding new audiences all over the world for his television performances, his plays and one-man stage shows, his novels and autobiography. So diversely talented as he is, it must be said that British cinema has never made the most of him. Indeed, both his Oscars were for American films, *Spartacus* and *Topkapi*, and his Emmy was for US television. However, when barely twenty he was already giving notable character performances in such films as *One of Our Aircraft is Missing* and *The Way Ahead* (which he also co-authored) and he gives a lovely comic performance as the Protean innkeeper in *Hotel Sahara*. The films he directed are an idiosyncratic bunch: in the '40s he made three off-beat comedies, *School for Secrets*, *Vice Versa* and *Private Angelo* (in which he also starred), full of sly humours; while his personal favourite is *Billy Budd*, a fine version of Herman Melville's novella. In recent years he has played a very engaging Poirot in several Agatha Christie films, establishing yet another hold on the popular imagination.

Interview dates: June 1982 and August 1990

Which do you generally find more satisfying: acting, producing, writing or directing?

I think acting is intrinsically easier than writing. It is a sort of tactical excitement; it does not give you the strategic pleasure of writing something which is accepted. I have never regarded myself as a professional director, in the sense that I know how to deal with actors, I know what I want, but I do not have a very developed visual sense in the case of moving pictures. You always betray where you came from: anybody who sets out to be a film director must start somewhere else. He is either an assistant or a writer or a cutter. I suppose my path has been a more literary one and therefore, in the last analysis, I trust a verbal imagination more than a visual one. So, I have never really thought of myself as a professional director who is waiting for material. *Billy Budd* is probably my most successful and certainly my favourite film as a director and it was extremely rigorous because they were asking me, 'Where are we going now?' They were asking me as the skipper as much as the director. Also, the visual imagination was automatically stunted by the narrow possibilities which were imposed by the fact that we were on the ship.

I therefore feel that probably I have more to contribute as an actor because I am a type of which there are not a tremendous number about. I do not work terribly consistently because people have a conventional sense of casting. Poirot has been very helpful to me because it has found me a niche, but I would hate to spend the rest of my time doing nothing but Poirot.

Were you given leave from the Army to make *One of Our Aircraft is Missing*?

No, I wasn't in yet, I did that in 1941. It was directed by Michael Powell, who was a very disturbing kind of director, because he would stare at you and never say anything. I got to know him much better when he was very old and he had plans to do *The Tempest* as a film and wanted me to play Caliban. He was much more approachable then, and

I suspect his earlier manner was a strange shyness, and certainly [Emeric] Pressburger was more approachable. Powell when young was rather metallic and obscure, even up to a point cruel, which I don't think he was by nature; I thought that everything he said needed translation. I felt he didn't really understand actors well but, at the same time, knew what he wanted. When he was young he was frightfully like a sarcastic schoolmaster, and that was near enough to my own schooldays to worry me.

How did your collaboration with Eric Ambler work on *The Way Ahead*?

It began as a training film. We were all sent to Scotland and that's where we first met. Carol Reed applied for me and I joined him in Troon, in very strange circumstances. Carol had automatically been made a captain, Ambler was still a lieutenant and David Niven was a colonel; I was the only private there. We had a make-up man from Ealing who was a lieutenant but he was well over 60, a technical man with an almost sexual respect for pay parades; I had to go off with him in a truck to a disused hotel, in order to have a pay parade all by myself. He would go into a room while I waited outside; then he would shout, 'I'm ready now!', like children playing hide-and-seek, and I would then go in, sign for my pay and take it out to the corridor; then we would drive back together while he told me nostagically about other pay parades in the south.

We were brought there to make a film describing in detail the technique of landing on enemy beaches by commandos. Then came Dieppe and it was such a shambles that the whole procedure had to be re-examined and we realised whatever we did would be out of date by the time the film came out. So the whole project was abandoned and we were threatened with being returned to our own units. I then had the idea, simply because I was closer to that situation than anyone else, that there should be a film shown to new recruits as they came into the Army to show that, however inhuman it seemed, the

Army was still an organisation made up of human beings. So we did a forty-minute training film called *The New Lot*, based on the idea of a group of new recruits, who got to know each other while they learned the techniques of discipline and so on. Eventually they went to see a commercial film (a mock one) on their day off, in which Robert Donat, being extremely funny, led a charge in the 1914 war and was silhouetted on the skyline; and they all roared so much with laughter they were asked to leave the cinema. They realised how stupid that film was and that they were now different, they were trained.

From that forty-minute film, which was very highly approved of by the Army Council, we were then asked by Two Cities films to do a commercial film on the same basis, but on a much larger scale and starring David Niven. I was put on reserve for a while because I couldn't deal with generals, being still a private, and I came out of the Army for about eight months and did *The Way Ahead*. We had the bright idea of putting at the end, instead of 'The End', 'The Beginning'. It came out on the day of the invasion of Normandy and was sensational. I was very upset at having to play a Moroccan, because they thought I didn't look English enough to play an Englishman, but at least I was out of the Army and able to travel to North Africa. Then I had to go back into the Army again, still as a private; the first thing that happened was I was marched four miles to Dover Castle to see *The New Lot* – because I was a new recruit!

How, at twenty-five, did you come to be directing Ralph Richardson and Richard Attenborough in *School for Secrets*?

At twenty-five I thought they had left it rather late to ask me! *School for Secrets* was the idea of Del Giudice, a man who was a kind of Sancho Panza to J Arthur Rank's Don Quixote. They didn't get on terribly well and I knew it couldn't last, but at one time he was tremendously important. It was he who gave me that chance, although I did *School for Secrets*, which was a big success, for the Air Ministry really. They wanted to have something about radar which was on the same lines as *In Which We Serve* or *The Way Ahead*. I did all my research in uniform at RAF stations, often getting rooms which were reserved for visiting air marshals and having WAC corporals clean my shoes, and I was dressed as a private.

You mentioned the actors ... I knew Dickie Attenborough very well because my first play had

been done at the Arts Theatre just after he had made a great hit there in *Awake and Sing*. So we were great buddies at that time. Raymond Huntley had been in a play with my then wife; he was a wonderful kind of sourpuss. He was also in *The New Lot*, playing a private, and he was very funny in it. I was always very fond of him. Ralph Richardson I was a little scared of; he was like a gigantic Pyrenean puppy who would put his paws on your shoulders and lick your face. I thought he was overdoing things a bit while I was directing him, but it turned out to be just him and he had always been acceptable.

Were you under contract to Two Cities at this time?

The contract with Two Cities was verbal: we had an agreement with each other which was valid while Del Giudice lasted. He left following a terrible row. It's never gone on record but I remember that Rank was trying to do a deal with the Americans and it attracted a whole lot of American executives who would have awakened anybody's suspicion. I was sitting at a huge banquet given by Rank for these sleazy people at the Dorchester Hotel and, as Rank got up to speak, Frank Launder turned to me and said, 'Is this the face that lunched a thousand shits?'

What do you think is the enduring appeal of the story of your second film, *Vice Versa*, recently remade? Were you happy with the way your version turned out?

I am surprised at how well it has stood up. All I know is that when I watched it again recently, at one point I couldn't remember what came next but I said to myself, 'If I were writing this today, the next line would be so-and-so,' and strangely enough it was. My favourite author at the time was Linklater and it had his kind of quality, I thought. I was amazed at how convincing Anthony Newley was as someone with an old mind inside him; I thought he was rather better than Roger Livesey who somewhat overdid the infantile side. The business of the boy changing into the man without any apparent cuts involved a lot of split-screen stuff and you had to be very careful that everything matched.

What attracted you to the Linklater novel, *Private Angelo*?

Because I wanted to do a film absolutely in the countryside and, in that sense, I was ahead of everybody. I wanted to do an *affected* film, one without any incidental music; the music was all supplied by the village band from that particular Tuscan village, Trequanda, near Siena. It was all made on location. The British unions insisted we put a toilet there because of the low standard of local sanitary engineering; we built a toilet in the village, which was unveiled by the priest, who prayed to God to 'render our work fecund'. We used everything local except one or two English actors, including Marjorie Rhodes and James Robertson Justice. Maria Denis was a local girl we discovered; as far as I know she never filmed again.

Did Michael Anderson essentially direct you?

He's an old friend of mine and we've always got each other out of difficulties. I was in Michael Todd's office when [John] Farrow called to say he couldn't do *Around the World in 80 Days*, which was really a conspiracy by the other film companies, who did everything they could to bitch Michael Todd. I myself had a strange contract with 20th-Century-Fox that pre-empted me from playing Detective Fixit in the film. Michael didn't know what to do, so I suggested he try Mickey Anderson, and he ultimately did the film. Years later, I had a kind of crisis and didn't know what I was going to do next, when Mickey called up and asked me to play that old man in *Logan's Run*.

Your next two films offered you very solid character roles. What do you recall of working with Herbert Wilcox and Anna Neagle in *Odette*?

Herbert was a very endearing character, with his inability to pronounce his 'r's. He was like a guardian to her: I talked to her after he died and I found her to have much more spirit than she displayed under his aegis, however good for her he was in other ways. I thought *Odette* was a good, functional film of the period, although I find it difficult to judge any film about the war because it always has the same kinds of biases in it. God knows, it's difficult today, but in those days it was damn near impossible, because we had all got used to certain conditioned reflexes. At one point I even satirised the kind of scene that would happen between Dickie Attenborough and Jack Hawkins in a naval film, where Jack would say, 'That will be all, Bellamy,' and Dickie would say, 'Yes, thank you, sir.' Then he'd go to the door, turn, and say, 'And sir . . .', 'Yes?', 'Nothing, sir.'

In your next film, *Hotel Sahara*, you had the chance to work with a different approach to the problems of war.

Yes, that's what attracted me to it. I felt that war mystique needed a bit of debunking and ventilating.

That was my one romantic triumph in films in that I ended up with Yvonne de Carlo – apart from one other with Maggie Smith, in *Hot Millions*, but that was a more mature relationship! Yvonne had the reputation, through the press, of being the most beautiful woman in the world. She was a very simple girl who certainly didn't behave as if she were the most beautiful girl in the world. She was absolutely charming, very professional, and even rather giggly. She was very relaxed, and entered into the spirit of whatever was going on.

Why didn't you direct more films, because the three you directed in the 1940s showed a quirky talent that British films could have used?

I'm never very much in vogue, I think that's the trouble. Now people may rediscover those films and I'm happy if they do, but I felt the British film industry was barking up the wrong tree. They were trying to get advice from the US – or from Americans – on how to break into the American market. This meant they got hold of some very third-rate American advisers to tell us how to do it, like how to develop mid-Atlantic accents so we could be understood. I opposed the tendency of trying to enter the American market with an amorphous, hybrid product. Then, for some reason, my career as an actor developed very quickly. I was asked to do *Quo Vadis?* and suddenly there was no looking back in that line.

What do you recall of making spectacular films such as *Quo Vadis?*, *The Egyptian* and *Spartacus* in America?

I think the Americans are the only people who can do ancient Roman films for the simple reason they are *like* the ancient Romans. If you go into the Chase National Bank to get a loan you are taken into a room with columns of Gorgonzola and, in the middle of all this, a furled flag and an eagle behind him, his feet on the table, the bank manager is saying, 'Why don't we go home and continue this conversation by the atrium and kick this idea around?' It is the mixture of extreme relaxation and formality and majesty which Americans do terribly well. Michael Curtiz really didn't know what he was talking about most of the time. With *The Egyptian*, I felt that I was on the set of a provincial company of *Aida* and the music hadn't arrived yet, so we were rehearsing the text. In fact, one day I came on the set and found him shooting on my stand-in by mistake.

Back in England you made *Beau Brummell*.

Did you relish the role of the Prince Regent?

I rather enjoyed the role, yes, it's a lovely period. Liz Taylor was very agreeable and Rosemary Harris, with whom I had a lot to do in the film, was excellent as Mrs Fitzherbert. The Royal Family was supposedly outraged by the film because it showed the Queen's great-great-grandfather trying to strangle her great-grandfather.

From 1954 you seem to have made no further British films during the decade. Am I right to regard the '40s and '50s as a key period in the British film industry?

Yes, but I would say this: the British film industry can never really be regarded as a consistent industry. It has a sudden blossoming of wonderful things and then they die again as they are absorbed by the Americans.

Twenty-odd years later you made several films (for large and small screens) based on Agatha Christie's novels ...

I think the first one [*Murder on the Orient Express* starring Albert Finney] was very good, and surprising because it was a 'retro' sort of thing. But I don't think the formula can go on working forever: it will become merely a camp thing. *Death on the Nile* had Egypt; the next one, *Evil Under the Sun*, only had Majorca; and Israel, where one of them [*Appointment with Death*] is set, is a country full of holes and is not very visually exciting. I think those all-star casts were helpful, but if you make it a habit it just becomes stale.

Dermot Walsh

b. 1924

Actor: *Bedelia* (1946), *Hungry Hill, Jassy* (1947), *The Mark of Cain, To the Public Danger, My Sister and I* (1948), *Third Time Lucky, Torment* (1949), *The Frightened Man, Ghost Ship* (1952), *Counterspy, The Blue Parrot, The Straw Man, The Floating Dutchman* (1953), *The Night of the Full Moon* (1954), *Bond of Fear, Hideout* (1956), *At the Stroke of Nine* (1957), *Woman of Mystery, Sea Fury, Chain of Events, Sea of Sand* (1958), *The Bandit of Zhobe,* *The Crowning Touch, Crash Drive, The Witness, Make Mine a Million* (1959), *The Flesh and the Fiends, The Challenge, The Clock Struck Three, The Tell-Tale Heart* (1960), *The Trunk, Breaking Point, Shoot to Kill, Tarnished Heroes, Out of the Shadows* (1961), *Emergency* (1962), *The Cool Mikado, Echo of Diana, The Switch* (1963), *Infamous Conduct* (1966), *Dr Frankenstein* (1973), *The Wicked Lady* (1983)

When Michael Winner cast Dermot Walsh in a small role in his 1983 remake of the 1945 box-office success, *The Wicked Lady*, this may have been the result of a long-standing friendship. It also recalls the earlier period when Walsh, signed on the strength of his work at the Gate Theatre, Dublin, was one of the Rank Organisation's promising young leading men, in such films as *Hungry Hill* and *Jassy*. Some bad luck over an Ealing film in 1949 may have cost Walsh an extended career in

'A' features, but he maintained his leading man status on the stage for forty years. As well, he made many better-than-average supporting films for director Vernon Sewell, for Robert Baker and Monty Berman's Tempean operation (*The Frightened Man* is a good example) and for the legendary Danzigers, for whom he also made a successful television series, *Richard the Lionheart*. He became one of those reliable actors who could stamp a certain conviction and authority on 'B' films and he is candid about the making of these often unjustly neglected programme-fillers, some of which stand up surprisingly well.
Interview date: August 1995

How did you come to make your first film?

In 1945 the Rank Organisation in England, who were the major motion-picture-producing company over here, wanted to make some pictures about Ireland. They had bought Daphne du Maurier's novel *Hungry Hill* and FL Green's novel *Odd Man Out*, and there were other movies with Irish backgrounds in the pipeline as well, like *Captain Boycott*. In anticipation of this production, which would get rolling in 1946, their talent scouts came to Dublin in '45 and interviewed actors all over the place. I was playing at the Gate; they saw me in that production and interviewed me, then I heard no more from them. Then, when I was in England a little later, an agent whom I'd previously contacted from Dublin sent me for an interview at Ealing Studios, where Lance Comfort was making *Bedelia*, and Lance engaged me to play a tiny part as a chauffeur in that.

How did you come to get the part of Wild Johnny in *Hungry Hill*? Did it seem like a great start for you?

I wasn't aware at that time how important it was. It was produced by an American called Bill Sistrom and directed by a flamboyant Irishman called Brian Desmond Hurst. Brian wanted another Irish actor called Seamus Locke but Sistrom wanted me, and they had a bit of a barney over that. After I made an exhaustive test, Sistrom called in all the girls from the front office, sat them down and ran the test. The girls got me the part!

What was Brian Desmond Hurst like, as a director, on *Hungry Hill*?

Well, I couldn't judge because it was only my second movie, but he was helpful to me, though. He kept saying, 'Stop acting!', which was extraordinarily helpful because of course the fundamental difference between theatre acting and cinema acting is projection. Brian was really saying, 'Stop projecting.' Sistrom also gave me a very good piece of advice. He said that in theatre an actor can play a most moving scene while thinking of his laundry list, but if you do that in a cinema close-up, what will photograph is 'laundry list'.

Hungry Hill was made for Two Cities, a Rank-owned company, Where was it filmed?

Most of it was done in the studio although some location work was done in Ireland; however, when I had outside shots to do, the location was reconstructed on the set. We did a lot of that in those days. We were only shooting about forty seconds a day because we were going to twenty takes and they'd spend two hours lighting a close-up of Margaret Lockwood. Desmond Dickinson was the cameraman, a very good portrait cameraman. That film took around five months to make. Every shot was composed, they'd spend hours trying to get it as beautiful and as dramatically effective as possible.

You have a good scene at the end with an aged Margaret Lockwood in a gambling place somewhere in London, and I think you're drunk.

Yes, I was nearly always drunk throughout that movie. He was a wild boy, a philandering sort of chap who seduces Siobhan McKenna. I was enormously impressed with Maggie Lockwood and had tremendous respect for her. She was wonderful to work with because she was totally professional, a supreme craftswoman as far as cinema technique was concerned. She never delayed, never threw tantrums and she always got it right.

I like your next film with her – *Jassy*, for Gainsborough.

The BFI have made a wonderful new print of it, enhanced the colour and everything, and they invited me down to see it recently. They had a job finding actors from it who were still alive, but they managed to rake up Maurice Denham and myself and we trotted off to see it. Maurice, of course, is indestructible.

Did *Hungry Hill* and *Jassy* seem as lavish in the making as they appear on the screen?

Oh gosh, yes. I had about twelve or fourteen costumes for *Hungry Hill* which were designed and handmade for me on Savile Row. I happened to be in the production office one day when they were settling accounts and I discovered that the cost of my costumes was about three times what I had been paid as an actor on the film.

Do you remember working with Dennis Price, who was in both of those films with you?

I remember Dennis particularly well because he was very kind to me and became a good friend of mine at that time. He was a lovely man, Dennis, but an unfortunate, poor fellow, with a very tragic life. He played my father in *Hungry Hill* but for *Jassy* they offered the part of my father to Peter Graves, who turned it down on the grounds that playing father to a twenty-one-year-old boy would make him look too old. So poor old Dennis was trundled out. He did about four or five pictures a year at that time, never stopped, and the pressure on him was enormous.

Your next film with Brian Desmond Hurst, *The Mark of Cain*, again for Two Cities, wasn't well received at the time, but is a good melodrama. What did you think of it?

I haven't seen it since the 1940s but I remember a great deal about the making of it. The sets were by Vetchinsky and Eric Portman was the leading man and he had casting control – although not for the leading lady's part, which was played by Sally Gray, who was one of the most beautiful women in the business and had a lovely voice. (She was also a very nice person.) A lot of actors 'up-classed' their voices because class was tremendously important in Britain at that time. There were two young men in the movie and Brian wanted me to play the better of the two parts, Patrick Holt to play the other part. Eric had to pass me, and, when I was taken to meet him, he looked at me, straight in the face, and I just knew in that instant that this guy wasn't going to have me playing the lead! And so it turned out; they gave Patrick Holt the main part and me the other.

One of the most striking things about the film is the massive, oppressive Victorian sets.

Yes, they were huge, powerful sets. Vetchinsky, of course, was very highly thought of and he had a remarkable career in cinema.

The next thing you did was the best of those supporting films, which Rank made in 1948: *To the Public Danger*. I'd be very interested in anything you recall of it.

I remember quite a bit about it, actually. To start with, it was taken from an excellent radio play by Patrick Hamilton, who was a brilliant writer, and he wrote it from the heart, because a friend of his had been killed in a motor-car accident by a drunken driver. He was a supreme craftsman so we had a perfect script. Secondly, we had a potentially brilliant director in Terry Fisher, who was starting at that time and went on to do all the Hammer things. I was an established first feature, above-the-title name at that time; my co-actors were Susan Shaw, a little blonde Cockney kid who was a waif, who had a tremendous quality on screen. And the comic was Roy Plomley, who created *Desert Island Discs*. The three of us got on awfully well together. An exciting thing for me as a young man at the time was that I got to drive a brand-new Bentley!

They were trying to achieve several things at this time. First, because of the shortage of dollars, Britain restricted imports that were not totally necessary and this included Hollywood films; Rank was a socialist and we had a socialist Government, and Rank said that he could fill the gap and supply the movies. Now, they knew the international movie thing was dependent on the star system. They knew the popularity of people like Maggie Lockwood and James Mason and they wanted stars, so they started looking for people who were photogenic and they found quite a few, like Constance Smith. Rank gathered together these people and they came to be called 'the Charm School', with a woman called Molly Terraine in charge of them and Helen Goss working on them for voice. At Highbury they decided to make movies to give these kids some experience in acting to the camera, and they stiffened it with people like myself to carry the movies. So that's what Highbury was about; it was set up to give experience to young players. The aim was to work them up into the position of carrying the shows. The atmosphere at Highbury was much more relaxed, less intense than in the big studios. That was probably my first experience of shooting more than a minute a day.

The whole thing was doomed to failure in the end, however. What happened was that, when the

Government stopped the import of American movies, Rank rushed into production with a new process by which you could make movies quickly. It was called Independent Frame and actors hated it. Also, there is only a limited amount of talent available anywhere at any one time and we just didn't have sufficient creative writing talent to turn out movies to compete with the Americans. By the time Rank's movies were ready for release, about a year later, the Government had lifted the embargo on American movies. The Americans flooded the market with the best movies they'd made during the past couple of years, so of course the Rank movies were just laughed off the screen.

But Rank was a great trier, wasn't he?

He was, yes. I think management was a fault with the British movie industry. We had terrific cameramen, terrific editors, some of the directors were quite brilliant – but there's a hell of a difference between an American producer and a British producer, or there was in those days. The fundamental objective of business is profitability, even if the business you're in is an artistic business like ours, albeit an industrialised art: it has to be, otherwise the whole thing collapses. I don't think they bore that in mind enough.

Did you feel that you were being carefully built up, groomed, by the Rank Organisation?

I had a very high opinion of myself at the time. It never crossed my mind that a career needed management in the way the Americans would choose to put an actor into this or that kind of a part and build them up gradually. The British industry didn't do that; you were just cast as 'the young man', regardless of whether the subject was right or wrong. I wasn't aware of being built up, and for Rank I only made *Hungry Hill*, *Jassy*, *The Mark of Cain*, *To the Public Danger* and *My Sister and I*, and *Third Time Lucky* (on rent-out to Anglo-Amalgamated and an Italian producer called Mario Zampi). I was finished with Rank by the end of *My Sister and I* so I actually did very few movies under contract.

You made an early John Guillermin film, *Torment*, and then there is a gap of a few years. Did you go back on the stage then?

I think *Torment* was renamed *The Paper Gallows* [in USA]. A number of things happened on it. An electrician fell asleep up on the rail and fell twenty feet down onto the floor, but Guillermin wouldn't hold up production, he just went on shooting. On another occasion, I fired a blank at John Bentley and

they hadn't stopped up the front of the muzzle, so that Bentley's face was speckled with gunpowder! Luckily it didn't hit his eye and it was far enough away not to damage him, but it could have blown his eye out or his face off. I never saw John Guillermin again. It's a funny thing about the movies: if you work with someone who is just starting and, in effect, you're doing them a favour by being in their film, they never want to know you afterwards. They don't like people who 'knew them when'. However, directing is a very responsible job, so I suppose you can make allowances for them.

But to answer your question: my Rank contract really ended in 1949 but I had extended it because, during the course of it, I kept taking time out to work in the theatre and that time was added to the end of my contract. So in fact my contract went through to April 1950. After the Guillermin film in 1949 I did the Malvern Festival that year, and I also got married that year to my first wife, an actress called Hazel Court. At the end of 1949, I went to Ealing to make a movie for Charlie Crichton. It was called *Dance Hall* and it had Natasha Parry, Gordon Parry's daughter, as the leading lady. I was to a play a character who had to dominate the first three scenes in the movie; the scene was a dance hall full of people, and this spivvy character had to come in and dominate all these other young people.

Crichton set up the first shot of the dance floor, then he panned on to the crowd standing around watching the dancers. They had chosen very good extras – tall, good-looking people – and you see these people all smiling and beating time; then you see this little figure trying to push his way through them to come to the front, which was me! The next scene they shot was a three-hander and I had to dominate that as well, so Charlie put me downstage left in a chair, in profile. Now of course, you can't dominate from downstage left. There was a third scene which was equally inept from the point of view of presenting me as a dominant character, so I was taken off the movie. They replaced me with Bonar Colleano and reshot it, making it possible for him to dominate in ways that hadn't been available to me. So I did feel very cross about that. In effect, you see, they'd ruined my career in first features.

Is that why you did such a lot of co-features in the '50s?

Yes. Around 1951, I was approached to do a second feature called *Ghost Ship*, directed by Vernon Sewell. Vernon owned a huge private yacht called the *Gelert* which he'd used to help out in the evacuation of Dunkirk. It was moored somewhere on the south coast, near Brighton. He wanted to get her scraped, which meant she would have to go into dry dock, so he wrote a story and set it on the yacht. He took the classic story of the *Marie Celeste* and called it *Ghost Ship*. So he hired his own ship for his own story; got her scraped and repainted, which he worked into the action, and made this movie, which turned out rather well. Vernon was quite a clever director and a very nice man.

You made several films with him, including *Counterspy*. It's a quite strange part for you: a quite meek, suburban sort of accountant.

Yes, there was a theatre attitude prevailing that said you ought to be able to play anything, which is not really correct for cinema. In cinema you should find out what you do best, like Arnold Schwarzenegger, and just do it all the time.

You also made *The Floating Dutchman* for Sewell, in which Sidney Tafler was running a nightclub. Do you remember it?

I remember working with Mary Germaine, who was a lovely-looking girl, and I remember Sidney trying to bugger me up by playing with a handkerchief all the time. You can control the editing, you see, if you control movements. In those days they wouldn't cut on a movement, so if you were playing with a handkerchief you could manage to keep the camera on you for as long as possible! Sidney was brilliant, I thought, in *It Always Rains on Sunday*. But that's all I remember about *The Floating Dutchman*. In 1953 I did about five second features and a couple of tours as well.

Were you aware of major production differences between these co-features and the 'A' films you had made?

Speed was the principal thing. Some actors are very aware of the context in which they're working – the set, the costumes, the props, and so on. All my work is from the text, really, and dressed up by the other things, whereas some actors see those things as important. It's just different ways of working. I was surprised when you spoke of the plushiness of the sets on *The Mark of Cain*; I had to be reminded of that because it was not important to me at the time of making the film. The settings on the 'B' pictures were never relevant to me, they didn't affect me one way or the other. It was what I was doing, what I was thinking and my playing to camera. But certainly there was a difference because we were making those pictures for about £5,000 and shooting sixty minutes in ten or fifteen days. They

would deliberately write the scripts with long dialogue scenes: once the cameras are set up for a long dialogue scene you can get two or three minutes in the can. They cut down on tracking as much as possible and used much more static camera or panning from a static position. The minute you start tracking there are so many things that have to coincide, that you can run to a great number of takes to get it right.

What do you remember about the studios where these 'B' films were made?

They were little studios like Southall, Walton-on-Thames and Merton Park, which were intimate and friendly from the off-stage point of view. They had all the facilities you needed for what you were doing and I quite enjoyed them, actually.

What do you recall of working for the legendary Danziger brothers or at Merton Park?

The Danzigers were a much bigger thing in my life. I started making second features for them and they were quite good: they used to pinch stories and reshape them into good plots! They were Americans, Coney Island operators, and mystery always surrounded Harry and Eddie Danziger because they were well off: they had a huge hotel in Monte Carlo, you know, and a Mayfair hotel. They lived on Park Lane and one of them, I think it was Harry, had a collection of Impressionists on the walls. I mean, they were real entrepreneurs. There are aspects of cinema that are very like circus, you know. Whether they loved movies or not, I don't know. It might well have been a commodity to them. They were never at the studio; they just handed it over to other people to get on with it. I don't know how much control they exercised.

I remember one film I made for them, called *Tarnished Heroes*. They took the story of *The Dirty Dozen* and reshaped it to the Second World War. I played a commanding officer who was given twelve chaps, who'd been sent to the glasshouse for some misdemeanour, to do some suicidal mission. I enjoyed making that and it turned out well, and, once I started working for them, they kept using me. They did an Edgar Allan Poe story, *The Tell-Tale Heart*, which I did with Adrienne Corri and Laurence Payne, an interesting actor who never really had a good career.

The Danzigers then decided to do a series on Richard the Lionheart and commissioned thirty-nine scripts, which were delivered, and they cast me as Richard. I worked at the Danziger studios at Elstree for seven months; we did thirty-nine episodes in twenty-six weeks, I think it was. I was in every set-up except the reverses; and I thoroughly enjoyed it. It had a huge success here. We were shooting six or seven minutes a day, and on one take. That's the other thing, you see: on big movies you can go to as many takes as you need to get it right, whereas we had to get it in one. If it went to two takes there was a real problem.

One movie I made for them there was called, I think, *Crash Drive*, about a racing motorist who has an accident in which his mind is more affected than his body. His mind is affected so that he can't walk; he's convinced he has lost the use of his legs. In one scene, the doctor is explaining this to the driver's wife and he's supposed to say, 'Mrs Smith, I have bad news. Your husband has no legs – I don't mean literally, I mean metaphorically.' Instead of that, the actor playing the doctor said, 'Mrs Smith, your husband has no legs – I don't mean metaphorically, I mean literally' – and they printed it! It's in the final print. The movie goes on and, of course, eventually I get up out of the wheelchair and walk! That was the speed at which we worked.

For Lance Comfort, you did *At the Stroke of Nine*, which has never come my way. I think Patricia Dainton and Stephen Murray were in it.

I've forgotten that, I'm afraid. But Lance was one of the very few gentlemen in the business. He was kind, generous, efficient and professional. So far as I remember, he would only direct you if you were doing something wrong. He'd slow you down or speed you up, perhaps, but I don't remember him giving direction in matters of interpretation. I didn't do anything very deep for him that would require a great deal of interpretation. Mostly on 'B' pictures the lines are sheer commonsense; it's a straightforward interpretation of fact, it's not nuances. There isn't time anyway. I also remember working with Lance's son, John, who was production manager on a film I did in Spain with Victor Mature.

You made several films for John Gilling with the Baker & Berman outfit, Tempean Films.

Bob and Monty are exceptions to the rule I quoted earlier about people forgetting you when they move on in their careers. They didn't. I did several second features for them and then, when they did their first big feature, *Sea of Sand*, they gave me a small part in it, which was jolly nice of them.

Bob and Monty were enormously efficient technically. They knew the technical side of the business backwards and they were really nice to work with. They were efficient, professional and got on with it and no nonsense. All the times that I worked with them, Monty Berman was on camera as well. I was in the position of being a booking name. The public call them star names but you can't talk about 'stars' in 'B' pictures. The rest of the casting was then done by a casting director, who would use people whom she knew and whose work she knew.

Kay Walsh

b. 1914

Actor: *How's Chances?*, *Get Your Man* (1934), *The Luck of the Irish*, *Smith's Wives* (1935), *All That Glitters*, *If I Were Rich*, *The Secret of Stamboul* (1936), *Keep Fit*, *The Last Adventurers* (1937), *I See Ice*, *Meet Mr Penny* (1938), *The Mind of Mr Reeder*, *All at Sea*, *Sons of the Sea*, *The Missing People*, *The Middle Watch*, *The Chinese Bungalow* (1939), *The Second Mrs Bush* (1940), *In Which We Serve* (1942), *This Happy Breed* (1944), *Vice Versa*, *The October Man* (1947), *Oliver Twist* (1948), *Last Holiday*, *Stage Fright*, *The Magnet* (1950), *The Magic Box*, *Encore* ('Winter Cruise') (1951), *Hun-*

ted, *Meet Me Tonight* (1952), *Young Bess, Gilbert Harding Speaking Of Murder* (1953), *The Rainbow Jacket, Lease of Life* (1954), *Cast a Dark Shadow* (1956), *Now and Forever* (1956), *The Horse's Mouth* (1958), *Tunes of Glory* (1960), *Greyfriars Bobby* (1961), *Lunch Hour* (1962), *80,000 Suspects,* *Dr Syn – Alias The Scarecrow* (1963), *Circus World, The Beauty Jungle, Bikini Paradise* (1964), *A Study in Terror, He Who Rides a Tiger* (1965), *The Witches* (1966), *A Taste of Excitement, Connecting Rooms* (1969), *The Virgin and The Gypsy, Scrooge* (1970), *The Ruling Class* (1971), *Night Crossing* (1982)

After a busy apprenticeship during the 1930s, in which she twice co-starred with George Formby, as well as working with other, now forgotten comics, Kay Walsh suddenly in 1942 found real scope for her warmth and naturalness as an actress in *In Which We Serve*, for Noël Coward and David Lean. In the next Lean–Coward collaboration, *This Happy Breed*, she brought sympathetic understanding to the role of Queenie, the discontented daughter of the family who kicks over the traces. Though she greatly dislikes her performance as Nancy in *Oliver Twist*, many have found it very affecting. Perhaps she moved too soon into character roles after that, but what a gallery of these she created – the sly housekeeper in Hitchcock's *Stage Fright*, the garrulous spinster in *Encore*, the frustrated vicar's wife in *Lease of Life*, and the shrewd and worldly Charlotte in *Cast a Dark Shadow*, to name but four. Wit, precision, and a capacity for making ordinariness significant were among her many strengths.

Interview date: June 1991

You began as a dancer, I think. Did you come from a theatrical background?

No, but I'd always danced. I can't remember a time when I didn't dance. The first memory of a public performance was darting into Church Street, Chelsea, and dancing to a barrel organ, aged three.

Do you remember any of those '30s films with special affection or interest?

I remember all those films of the '30s with affection and fear. Affection because of the warm-hearted old pros Sandy Powell, Will Fyffe, Ernie Lotinga. Fear, because of having broken out of the chorus at a time of appalling unemployment and presenting myself as an actress; I had had no training and dreaded being rumbled.

Later in the '30s you made two films with George Formby, *Keep Fit* and *I See Ice*. You described George Formby's films as 'the aristocracy' by comparison with these other films. Did you have experience of the formidable Mrs Formby?

The Formby films at Ealing were high-flying compared with the 'fit up' DIY quickies. But then Ealing Studio was a well established concern – Monty Banks, Gracie Fields, JB Priestley, Basil Dean with his wife Victoria Hopper brought comedies and classics to the screen with skill and first-class technicians. I remember particularly Jack Kitchen, a film editor who simply made those Formby films move. I didn't find Beryl Formby formidable. She and George had been a professional team together for many years and I could understand that she felt rejected with these little blondes cavorting around her George and his ukulele. For me it was tough being under contract to Ealing for a year. I was happy when it came to an end, but Basil Dean persisted in thinking me talented – he had seen me in a play starring Victoria Hopper. He tested me and I was given a contract for a year – I was glad of the 'shoe leather'. My flatmate David Lean was still unemployed and we walked everywhere.

You did a lot of films during the '30s: did you have a good agent at this time?

No, I didn't have an agent. Agents are big business and I had nothing to sell. I'd spent desperate months, years, knocking on doors; they didn't always open.

Would you agree that the turning point in your career, the film which put you into the big time, was *In Which We Serve*?

Yes, I would say that *In Which We Serve* was a turning point, but it didn't put me – as you say – 'into the big time'. I was never in the big time, and I don't remember ever wanting to *be* in the big time. I enjoyed working, just working.

What do you think of the way the film represented class distinctions in Britain at the time?

I don't agree that it represented class distinction in Britain in 1942. Professional naval officers were there to give technical advice to the actors, director and the producers, and they needed it. There were representatives from the upper deck and the lower deck and that is the structure of the British Navy. I can't imagine going to sea in a ship without it.

***This Happy Breed*, your next film, was again a Coward film, in 1944. I thought your part was very significant for the way you are dissatisfied with being stuck in that class and wanting something more.**

I never got over the wonder of working with Noël Coward. My part in *This Happy Breed* was a gift from him to me and to my then husband David Lean. I played Queenie Gibbons. The only difference between Queenie and me was that I would never have given in, never have gone back home.

I'm interested to ask you about the credit on *Great Expectations* which says 'written by David Lean, Ronald Neame, Anthony Havelock-Allan, with additional dialogue by Kay Walsh and Cecil McGivern'. How much can you remember about that?

I remember everything about *Great Expectations*, especially the loss of 'Trabb's Boy' – and so many other jewels that had to go to fit in with standard film lengths. During my life with David Lean, I had worked closely on scripts with him – the silent opening of *Oliver Twist*, the end of *Great Expectations* – and much besides. As an actress I was delighted to be given a screenwriter's credit.

You didn't make another film appearance

until 1947 when you did *Vice Versa* with Peter Ustinov. How do you remember that experience, playing an easygoing lady opposite Roger Livesey?

I went to the first day's rushes on *Vice Versa* and saw two wonderful wicked characters burst out on the screen – James Robertson Justice – his first major film, and Anthony Newley, aged fifteen, another first. I telephoned David at Pinewood, where he was preparing *Oliver Twist* and doing dreadful things in the make-up room to Alfie Bass's face [to test him for the Dodger]. I said, 'I've got your Dodger.'

What do you recall of a film for Roy [Ward] Baker called *The October Man*, playing the good-hearted Molly who gets murdered?

Another original face and voice burst forth in *The October Man* – Joan Greenwood, tiny Joan, we called her 'Half Pint', a true original.

I enjoyed Catherine Lacey's unpatronising performance as the landlady, too.

I could never believe that the silent woman I would pick up at 6am for our Denham call was the powerhouse of acting, Catherine Lacey. From a frivolous character in JM Barrie's *The Admirable Crichton* to Schiller's *Mary Stuart* to the agony of *The Trojan Women*, an actress to remember.

How much choice did you have about those many character parts in the '50s? I am thinking particularly of the *Stage Fright* role, the very sympathetic housekeeper in Henry Cass's film *Last Holiday* with Alec Guinness, and the wonderful part in *Encore*.

Hitchcock gave me a good part in his not very good film *Stage Fright*. By now I had met such giants that I gave up thinking I was dreaming. Watching Marlene Dietrich tuck into the steak and kidney pudding in the canteen was something! I had worked with some marvellous actors and the most lovable was Ted Ray, with whom I did the 'Red Peppers' segment in *Meet Me Tonight*. I would have loved to have gone on the halls with him. Directors I have enjoyed most are not always the best known – such as Don Sharp, I believe a one-time actor and an Australian. Basil Dearden, Lewis Gilbert, Val Guest – these are directors who have made me feel at the end of a difficult day that I was not in the wrong box.

Sir Herbert Wilcox

1892–1977

Director-producer: *The Wonderful Story, *Flames of Passion (1922), *Paddy the Next Best Thing, Chu Chin Chow (1923), Southern Love / A Woman's Secret, Decameron Nights / Decameron Nachte (1924), The Only Way, Nell Gwyn (& sc), London (1926), Tiptoes (& sc), Mumsie, Madame Pompadour, *The Luck of the Navy (co-pr) (1927), Dawn (1928), The Woman in White, The Bondman (1929), Rookery Nook, The Loves of Robert Burns, Wolves (1930), The Speckled Band, Plunder, Carnival, The Chance of a Night Time (co-dir) (1931), *Thark, *The Flag Lieutenant, *Say It With Music, *The Love Contract, The Blue Danube, Money Means Nothing (co-dir), Goodnight Vienna (1932), Yes Mr Brown, *Sorrell and Son, The Little Damozel, The King's Cup, Bitter Sweet (1933), The Queen's Affair (1934), Nell Gwyn, *Brewster's Millions, Peg of Old Drury, *Escape Me Never (1935), The Three Maxims, This'll Make You Whistle, Limelight (1936), *The Gang Show, *The Frog, *The Rat, *Sunset in Vienna, *Our Fighting Navy, Victoria the Great, London Melody (1937), Sixty Glorious Years, *Blondes for Danger (1938), Nurse Edith Cavell (1939), No, No, Nanette, Irene (1940), Sunny (1941), They Flew Alone (1942), The Yellow Canary, Forever and a Day (co-dir, co-pr) (1943), I Live in Grosvenor Square (1945), Piccadilly Incident (1946), The Courtneys of Curzon Street (1947), Spring in Park Lane, Elizabeth of Ladymead (1948), Maytime in Mayfair (1949), Odette (1950), *Into The Blue (co-pr), The Lady with a Lamp (1951), Derby Day (1952), Trent's Last Case, Laughing Anne, *The Beggar's Opera (co-pr) (1953), Trouble in the Glen, Lilacs in the Spring (1954), King's Rhapsody (1955), *Yangtse Incident, My Teenage Daughter (1956), These Dangerous Years (dir only), The Man Who Wouldn't Talk (1957), Wonderful Things (dir only), The Lady is a Square (1958), *The Navy Lark, The Heart of a Man (dir only) (1959)

* Producer only.

'With my Army gratuity of £117 and anything else my brother and I could raise between us we opened our own film distribution agency. That was my début in the industry.'[1] So Herbert Wilcox described his 1919 entry into the film world, adding, 'Selling films gave me the idea of what the public wanted. I naturally became keen to embody that experience in pictures of my own.' Any account of Wilcox's career should probably start with reference to his skill in 'selling films', since that is what he pre-eminently did during several decades. Until his grasp of public taste faltered in the 1950s, he had a run of box-office successes perhaps unparalleled in British film history.

'The simple problem that faces British productions today is that costs have gone up and the box office has gone down,'[2] he announced firmly at the height of the *ad valorem* duty crisis in late 1947. 'You must know that the goods you are turning out are aimed at the market for which you are designing them.' He was better placed than most to know what the public wanted. In the '30s he had brought the Aldwych farces to the screen with considerable domestic success, and was cunning enough to keep one eye on critical respectability. For instance, he wrote that 'One spot of prestige in a spate of popular box-office successes was *Escape Me Never*, which introduced Elizabeth Bergner to British films.'[3]

In 1932 occurred the meeting which would change his whole career and his life. He had gone to the Hippodrome for a meeting with Jack Buchanan and 'Jack was on the stage and to while away the time I watched the show. Thus I set eyes on Anna Neagle.'[4] He seems to have adored her for the rest of his life, by the accounts of all who worked with them, even of those who felt she was potentially a better actress than his direction, proficient rather than inspired, allowed her to appear. He saw in her '... simply and solely charm, a single word expressing a complex mixture of kindness, tenderness, and the habit of behaving naturally in all circumstances.'[5] Through the '30s, he guided her through roles modern and historical, achieving major successes with *Nell Gwyn*, *Peg of Old Drury* and especially *Victoria the Great*. 'Above all, it was to be an intimate study of the great Queen: not so much about the history of her reign as about the woman behind the history,'[6] he wrote, going on to talk about the thoroughness of the research into settings and costumes.

There was a stint in Hollywood in the early years of the war, after which the Wilcoxes embarked on their phenomenally popular 'London Series'. The first was *I Live in Grosvenor Square*, starring Neagle with Rex Harrison, who was unavailable for the follow-up, *Piccadilly Incident*, thus paving the way for Michael Wilding to carve out his niche in British film history. 'In his very first scene with Anna, everything about him – his naturalness, his repose, his figure, and most of all, his smile – shouted out loud that here was a new star.'[7] Wilcox was right again and for several years the Wilding –Neagle team dominated British box offices and popular awards. Inevitably the 'London Series' ran out of steam, but *Spring in Park Lane*, in its gossamer world of lavish white mansions and butlers who prove to be aristocrats in disguise, is really the 1948 apogee of a whole strain of 1930s filmmaking which would be gone forever within a few years. Wilcox, Neagle and Wilding gave austerity-weary audiences exactly what they wanted. The films were romantic tosh, a brutal critic might say, but they are not without charm and skill.

Wilcox continued to steer his wife through representations of Great Women of History – Victoria was followed by Edith Cavell, the aviatrix Amy Johnson, the wartime heroine, Odette Churchill ('I would like to be remembered as the man who made *Odette*'),[8] and Florence Nightingale. However, in the '50s he lost his way: *The Beggar's Opera* was 'a chronic headache'[9] because of conflict with the director Peter Brook; his suggestion of Errol Flynn for *Lilacs in the Spring* (an idea which came to him on finding Flynn holidaying in Rome while the Wilcoxes were there too)[10] proved less than successful, though, undaunted by the failure of the Neagle–Flynn chemistry, he went on to star them again in *King's Rhapsody*. Then there was the doomed attempt, beginning with *These Dangerous Years*, to make a film star of pop singer Frankie Vaughan: 'I will direct, but this is your idea, so you will produce,'[11] he told Anna. Wilcox was finally forced into bankruptcy in 1964 and the filmmaking and film-going world had changed irrevocably, but as a purveyor of popular entertainment for nearly three decades he remains an important figure in British film history.

1 JD, '16 years of British films – An interview with Herbert Wilcox', *Picturegoer Weekly*, 18 January 1936, p 39
2 Herbert Wilcox, 'These must go if we are to step up production', *Kinematograph Weekly*, 18 December 1947, p 19
3 Herbert Wilcox, *Twenty-five Thousand Sunsets: The Autobiography of Herbert Wilcox*, The Bodley Head, London, 1967, p 93
4 Herbert Wilcox, 'The secret of Anna Neagle', *Picturegoer Weekly*, 16 July 1932, p 7
5 Wilcox, 'The secret of Anna Neagle', p 7
6 Herbert Wilcox, 'How we made *Victoria*', *Film Weekly*, 25 December 1937, p 20
7 Wilcox, *Twenty-five Thousand Sunsets*, p 144
8 Wilcox, *Twenty-five Thousand Sunsets*, p 183
9 Wilcox, *Twenty-five Thousand Sunsets*, p 163
10 Anna Neagle, *Anna Neagle: An Autobiography* (first published 1974), Futura, Aylesbury, 1979, p 173
11 Neagle, p 176

Michael Winner

b. 1935

Director: **The Square* (& sc, pr), **This is Belgium* (assoc pr), *Man With a Gun* (sc), **The Clock Strikes Eight* (1958), **Floating Fortress* (assoc pr), **Danger: Women at Work* (& sc), **Swiss Holiday* (& sc) (1959), *Climb up the Wall* (& co-sc), *Shoot to Kill* (& sc), **Pony Tale* (& sc), *Young Entry* (& sc,

pr) (1960), *Old Mac*, **Haunted England*, *Some Like It Cool*, *Out of the Shadow* (& sc, assoc pr), *Girls, Girls, Girls, It's Magic* (& sc) (1961), **Behave Yourself*, *Play It Cool* (1962), *The Cool Mikado* (& co-sc), *West II* (1963), *The System* (1964), *You Must Be Joking!* (& auth) (1965), *The Jokers* (& auth) (1966), *I'll Never Forget What's 'is Name* (& pr) (1967), *Hannibal Brooks* (& co-auth, pr), *The Games* (1969), *Lawman* (& pr) (1970), *The Nightcomers* (& pr), *Chato's Land* (& pr) (1971), *The Mechanic, Scorpio* (1972), *The Stone Killer* (& pr) (1973), *Death Wish* (& co-pr) (1974), *Won Ton Ton, the Dog Who Saved Hollywood* (& co-pr) (1975), *The Sentinel* (& co-pr, co-sc) (1977), *The Big Sleep* (& sc, co-pr) (1978), *Firepower* (1979), *Death Wish 2* (1981), *The Wicked Lady* (& co-sc) (1983), *Scream For Help* (& pr) (1984), *Death Wish 3* (1985), *Appointment with Death* (& pr) (1987), *A Chorus of Disapproval* (& co-sc) (1988), *Bullseye!* (& pr, co-auth) (1989), *Dirty Weekend* (& pr, sc) (1992), *Decadence* (actor only) (1994)
* Short film.

The image of tenacious teenage reporter bluffing his way into the film studios and sustaining a syndicated column based on his interviews with the famous appropriately foreshadows the filmmaking career of Michael Winner. He is a phenomenon in that, for over thirty years, he has averaged at least one film a year, some made in the US, most in Britain, almost all aimed firmly at a large popular audience. He believes in the power of star names, and has worked with many of them, and he is trenchant in his views on the inadequacies of the British industry, on its incapacity to support enterprise and to capitalise on one-off successes. Winner made a series of successful youth-oriented films in the '60s; these took him to Hollywood, where he hit pay dirt with *Death Wish*. Clearly attracted to literary sources, he has not been afraid, between box-office hits, to undertake more risky undertakings, like *The Nightcomers*, prequel to the Henry James ghost story, *The Turn of the Screw*, or Alan Ayckbourn's black comedy, *A Chorus of Disapproval*. *Interview date: June 1994*

You have been an outspoken critic of the British film industry. Why do you think it has been so difficult for Britain to sustain a steady output of films?

A Fish Called Wanda and *Four Weddings and a Funeral* are probably the only two British films in the last ten years to have made a profit. *Clockwise* could not get shown in one cinema in Chicago, and John Cleese said that was ridiculous, that he wanted to make a film that would be widely shown. He'd spent a lot of time making *Clockwise*, which he didn't produce or direct, but he said he wanted to create a film that would be seen. So the reasons that the British industry went into the toilet and never got out of it, other than quality-wise, are still here, in my view. I don't see any change in the thinking of the people.

What would you say to Lindsay Anderson's criticism that British cinema has always been a middle-class affair?

I think this is largely what I'm saying as well. I think that it has been for the middle-class intellectual, it has never been for the larger public. For example, one of the biggest hit films in the last five years has been *Robin Hood – Prince of Thieves*. Can you imagine the British making *Robin Hood*? It's their own subject, their own history, but can you imagine an Englishman saying, 'I think there is a lot of money to be made in *Robin Hood*'? But Hollywood looked at British history, saw the potential and did it. I don't think there has been any successful film operation in this country since Nat Cohen and Stuart Levy closed down Amalgamated in the mid- or late '60s, and since Colonel James

Carreras closed Hammer – well, he didn't close it but he passed it on to his son, who ruined it. Those were the last two successful little operations that I saw, and they were twenty years ago. It's always one-offs. What really is so ridiculous is that we get a one-off like *Four Weddings and a Funeral* and everyone says that the British film industry has revived. It hasn't revived, you've simply had one picture in ten years that has made a profit. There is no industry there to capitalise on it; it's a freak film.

Your films obviously haven't been set up to appeal to some kind of rarefied audience.

Well, some of my *British* films have. I have been guilty of the same disease, but I have at least known that when I've been doing it. If I made *A Chorus of Disapproval* with Anthony Hopkins and Jeremy Irons, which I loved, I know that's not going to be a big international film. The difference is that, in between, I've done an enormous number of highly commercial pictures that are shown all over the world to this day on peak-time television.

You have made a lot of films abroad. How much easier, more efficient, is it to make films in the US than in Britain?

The Americans are more efficient, there's no question. The technicians are better at it. Although we have very good technicians here, almost any crew over there is good whereas here there are maybe two or three good crews. I had three enormous critical successes in the '60s – *The System*, *I'll Never Forget What's 'is Name* and *The Jokers*. The *New York Times* praised all three like they were the Coming of Christ, and *The Jokers* made a profit, which was a miracle. So then I got asked to Hollywood to do a lot of pictures – and I went because, for a kid who'd been brought up watching Hollywood pictures, it was an exciting thing to do. I now prefer life in Europe, and I'm not prepared to spend so much time in Hollywood, even though I know that will affect my career poorly.

How true are those stories of union problems in Britain?

The union problems used to be horrific, certainly until about five years ago, and occasionally they still are. Strangely enough, it's not because of the unions, because the union rules were pretty fair; it was union members, creating their own rules as they went along. People let them get away with this. It is very weak management. The union membership basically did catch-as-catch-can. They were absolutely terrible. I wouldn't put up with it on my crews, but even I had to fight them from time to time. Now, with the great recent slump, they've all become far more reasonable but they all talk too much about the catering – they're mollycoddled compared to the Americans, that's for sure.

How important do you think a healthy studio system is to an industry?

Not at all. I don't think a healthy studio system means anything today, because, for the last ten years, studios have been empty, losing a fortune, closing down, and not many films today are made in studios. When I came into the industry as a writer in around 1952, we had an enormous number of studios. There was MGM at Elstree (gone), Denham Studios (gone), Nettlefold Studios – we had dozens of them, but they slowly petered out because of lack of use. Today people make films in the real places; a very limited number of films need studios.

How important are stars, and how good has Britain been at building them?

Stars are vitally important, but what has happened in Britain is that when we've created bankable stars, they have immediately had better offers from Hollywood and gone there – Sean Connery, Daniel Day Lewis, or whoever. So we have created stars but the English then couldn't afford them any more. The Americans say that, on the whole, the world likes to see American-speaking pictures, so we'll put them in American-speaking pictures. I'm afraid that has meant that the talent – both actors and directors – has gone to America, where there is more opportunity and more money, and you can't blame them. I did it myself. We discovered a few stars in the early '60s – Connery, Caine, Christie – and then there was a very long gap until we got any more. That's in the last five years, really, so you're talking about from 1963 to nearly 1990 before we suddenly threw up some good stock – Irons, Hopkins, Hoskins, Day Lewis, Hugh Grant. Whether they have the longevity of a Sean Connery remains to be seen.

One reference book says you were a film critic and entertainment columnist at sixteen. Is that true?

Actually I was fourteen when I had my own film column in a syndicate of thirty newspapers. I was never paid for it. It happened because an old boy of my school published film books and I asked him if he would send me some. His name was Paul Hamlyn, a very famous publisher. He sent me the books free and I then phoned up the studios and said I was writing a book for him (which I wasn't!). I went around the studios until eventually they complained to him and said, 'Who is this fraud? Stop him.' I had been on a film set with John Howard Davies (the original Oliver in *Oliver Twist*), so I took an article about him to my local paper and it was printed three days later; thus I became a regular columnist. They never paid me for it but it gave me access to everybody and everything.

When I came down from Cambridge, I wrote some scripts, dabbling in journalism only when I couldn't get enough work in cinema. In those days, the mid-'50s, there were three thirty-minute documentaries playing the circuits every week and that was where you trained. We made those short films for the cinemas, with proper 35mm cameras, sometimes in VistaVision, and that was my training. It was in the early '60s that suddenly the French New Wave showed people that you could have young directors. We then started making films with pop stars like Cliff Richard and Billy Fury, and those the older directors said were 'temporary phenomena'. They used to call them 'messenger boys' and refuse to make films with them. So they [the producers] turned to the younger people like myself, Dick Lester, Peter Yates, and we made these pop films.

You made a number of what I take to be co-features or 'B' pictures.

Yes, because they were very popular in those days, when film-goers wanted what was called a programme. You had the main film, a 'B' picture which was only an hour long, and a twenty- or thirty-minute short. This was the time of the Eady system, whereby the cinemas paid a levy per seat into a communal pot to encourage British films. The second-feature films and the shorts got double or treble Eady, so they were very commercially viable, because they not only got their rental from the cinemas, but they also got a bigger share of the Eady fund and they were an industry – a wonderful training ground.

The first film I wrote, while I was still at Cambridge, was *Man with a Gun*, starring Lee Patterson. I directed a lot of 'B' pictures and a lot of half-hour documentaries and comedy shorts. I even made a nudist film, called *Some Like It Cool*, which made its money back in two weeks at one cinema. Terrible film, of course, but it helped me get my first feature film, *Play It Cool* with Billy Fury. The 'B' films were deliberately made as such; they were not failed 'A' films. The nudist film was an oddity, but my first 'A' film was *Play It Cool*.

Was anyone helping your career at this time? Were you under a contract?

No, I think the only person who helped me at the very beginning was Lewis Gilbert. He and Lord Brabourne, a very distinguished British producer, invested in a short film because they thought I was very good, and they took me around to introduce me to people, so they were a great help. It wasn't then until the great success of *The System* (called *The Girl-Getters* in America), which got rave reviews, that a number of American companies vied for my services. I had, first, a contract with Universal and then one with United Artists.

Four of your films, *The System*, *The Jokers*, *I'll Never Forget What's 'is Name* and *Hannibal Brooks*, starred Oliver Reed. To what do you attribute the success of this working relationship?

I met Oliver Reed and wanted to use him in a film called *West 2*, but the producer said that he was a 'B'-picture actor. So anyway, when I had a say in the matter I chose Oliver Reed for *The System* and used him several times after that, because, when I used him in *The System*, the film got unbelievable rave reviews in America. So Universal Pictures, who were then willing to make *The Jokers*, were quite happy to have the star of that great critical and box-office success. They approved *What's 'is Name* in three days, which is unheard of. Oliver and I were by then quite friendly, and when United Artists came to make *Hannibal Brooks* they thought he was fine. I like him very much, he's a very kind and decent person.

Did this feel like a good time to be getting a director's career going in Britain?

There's no question that in around 1965, after the big success of three films – the Bond films, the Beatles' films and *Tom Jones* – the Americans suddenly thought England was a goldmine and they opened up offices and poured a lot of money in. Four years later they closed the offices down again and left, because they'd lost a fortune. So to start your career, as I did in 1962, training through the '50s in short films, and then to hit the 1965 golden period was a very good position to be in. My timing was not bad! *The System* was one of the last films made for Bryanston and, when it got those rave reviews in America, it helped me to cash in on this golden period. When that period died, I had already turned to American films by accident, through commissioning the Western *Lawman*, and this took me through the late '60s and most of the '70s doing American action films.

How and when did you come to set up Scimitar Films, which seems to have had a long life as a production company?

'Scimitar' was the name of an English jet plane on an aircraft carrier in one of the first films I made about the Navy. We formed the company in around 1957 and it had its name on quite a few significant films. *The Jokers* was the first of them. From 1963, really, until today – but massively from 1963 to 1983 – I don't think any single British operation matched what I did, and I say that with no modesty. During that twenty years and even since, we employed Brando, Bronson, Sophia Loren, Faye Dunaway, Jack Palance, Robert Mitchum – an enormous number of major stars again and again. I don't think that any individual person has had that track record.

You made *The Games* for 20th-Century-Fox, as I understand, not for Scimitar?

Well, sometimes you used your own company and they financed your company – you made the film for a distributor through your own company. *The Games* was made directly by Fox, but I had exactly the same control as if it had been for my own company. It came from a good popular novel; it wasn't a great piece of writing. It was the pet project of Darryl Zanuck, the head of 20th-Century-Fox, who loved the Olympic Games. They are now very popular but I remember Ryan O'Neal saying to me in 1969, 'You know, Michael, the Olympic Games on television are free and they're 106 in the ratings!' Nobody cared about them and there we were, making a 5.5-million-dollar film about them! So it was never likely to be a vastly popular subject but it was great fun to make. It was about five people on their way to the Olympic Games and what they did in the marathon. It was an old 20th-Century-Fox kind of film, like *Three Coins in the Fountain*, about a group of people.

Apart from *The Nightcomers*, your next seven films are all either made in America or for American companies. You adapted very quickly and happily to Hollywood as a place to work?

Yes I did, because I think that my whole style of filmmaking was very polished and very snazzy. My films were very energetic, very robust, and I edited them all myself in a very pacy American way. They were very un-British in that sense.

Whose idea was it to make *The Nightcomers*?

The Nightcomers was a wonderful film, I think.

There was a brilliant writer here called Michael Hastings, who told me he'd written a film. It seemed a bit odd when I read it, as if someone had cut it. He said his agent had cut it down because it was too long. I told him to give me the cut pages and I'd decide on what should be cut, and we bought the script like that. I had nothing to do with its creation whatever and I wish it could happen again. Eventually we got Brando and it was going to be Vanessa Redgrave, but she was filming in Italy and the film ran over, so at the last minute we had to recast it with Stephanie Beacham, who'd had a small part in *The Games*. It just came to me out of the blue and it was a very lucky day that I got *The Nightcomers*.

How did you enjoy working with Brando?

He was the most professional, the most excellent, the most understanding and, above all else, the most humorous and witty person to be with. Everyone says to me, 'Michael, you've been lucky. Brando was wonderful with you; Bronson was wonderful with you; but with Faye Dunaway you've met your match!' Faye Dunaway was *wonderful* with me, marvellous! I don't go in to these people shaking. I go in thinking, until they harm me, they are wonderful people. Marlon always said something about me which I consider very complimentary. He said to other people, 'Michael Winner is the only man who doesn't speak to me as he thinks I wish to be spoken to.' And I think this means you get on well.

Did you have difficulty directing the children, especially in the sexual scenes?

Well, the sexual scenes were changed a bit. They were very good. I liked the children, directed them rather well, I think, and Marlon was very helpful. There appeared to be sexual activity with the children but in fact there was nothing.

I thought Thora Hird was great as the housekeeper.

Oh, brilliant. For me to go into an old house and suddenly there are Thora Hird and Marlon Brando acting together, I mean, it was absolutely magical. You couldn't have two more different people in the world! And they were both excellent; Thora is a terrific actress.

You wrote, produced and directed the remake of *The Big Sleep*, so presumably this was very much a personal choice.

Elliot Kastner, the producer, said he wanted to do *The Big Sleep* and we did it; I had never read Raymond Chandler and *The Big Sleep* is one film I would make differently if I were to make it again –

not that I didn't like it. I was so riveted by Chandler, I found it such incredible writing. It was poetic, epigrammatic, and I fell totally in love with this writing, so I didn't want to disturb it with too much trickery in the photography or too much atmosphere. A couple of the American critics did say it was the most faithful Chandler ever, and marvellous, but I was snowed under by the writing and, in a way, I think I was a little reticent in imposing too much cinematic style upon it.

When you came to do another remake, *The Wicked Lady* a few years later, what drew you to that?

The Wicked Lady was a film that had deeply affected me in my youth – a great piece of entertainment. It was one of the very few times the British tried to entertain and succeeded. I had a script done by Edna O'Brien but it hadn't worked. Then I met Faye Dunaway at an airport and she told me she was desperate to do a film in England. So I went back to the original script and rewrote it myself. Although I used the original script, which was very good, I didn't actually work with Arliss or any of the other three original writers. I sent it to Faye and that's how it got made. We also had Gielgud, Alan Bates and Joan Hickson in it – a good cast. It was always a very camp film, very kitsch, which I loved. It was fairly overt about the love scenes; we made it deliberately almost like Victorian kitsch, which had a lot of nudity and lasciviousness. We unashamedly made it like that.

My favourite among your films is *A Chorus of Disapproval*. How closely did you work with the author, Alan Ayckbourn?

We worked very closely. He wrote the script with me; he rewrote the script; he approved the script; he showed me the locations around Scarborough; he had casting approval, although not in the contract. If he didn't like an artist that I liked, we just went on until we found one we both liked. It didn't worry me at all and we ended up with a fabulous cast. Sylvia Syms is also in my new film, *Dirty Weekend*, and she's brilliant. She is a great character actress, like one of the old-time character players. For *A Chorus of Disapproval* I got Jeremy Irons and Anthony Hopkins just before they got 'big' – they weren't all that big then. Of course, you couldn't make it today. It was a film about a group of amateur actors in Scarborough – it's not a subject matter the young public are going to rush to see, and I knew they wouldn't. Also, it is a very bleak, hard, bitter piece and I think we showed that. In fact, we gave it a slightly happier ending, because we had Jeremy Irons singing and dancing on the platform, as if he is going on to have fun again, and that was a more upbeat ending than the play.

We did OK, it was a very low-budget film and I took no salary. Nor did I take any salary on *The Nightcomers* or *Dirty Weekend*, because they were films I particularly wanted to make. Most of my films I'm rather pleased with, however conceited that may seem, and, in spite of the English critics, none of them am I deeply depressed about.

Norman Wisdom

b. 1917

Actor: *A Date with a Dream* (1948), *Trouble in Store* (1953), *One Good Turn* (1954), *Man of the Moment* (1955), *Up in the World* (1956), *Just My Luck* (1957), *The Square Peg* (1958), *Follow a Star* (1959), *There Was a Crooked Man*, *The Bulldog Breed* (1960), *The Girl on the Boat* (1961), *On the Beat* (1962), *A Stitch in Time* (1963), *The Early Bird* (1965), *The Sandwich Man*, *Press for Time* (1966), *The Night They Raided Minsky's* (1968), *What's Good for the Goose* (1969), *Double X* (1992), *Adam and Evil* (1997)

Whether or not he was your cup of tea, there was no denying Norman Wisdom's enormous popularity. For over a decade, his name above a film's title was a guarantee of its commercial success, and his own explanation of this phenomenon is as good as any. His *persona* – cheerful little bloke in clothes just too small for him, up against the smooth and corrupt but exposing them in the end, longing for the seemingly unattainable girl and finally winning her – seemed in some ways like a latter-day George Formby. However, he had a talent for pathos which is not part of the Formby image. His films always had the advantage of strong casts, which enabled Norman (his character was always called Norman, in a blurring of man and performer) to seem as if he were inhabiting an actual world rather than doing a series of turns.
Interview date: June 1994

You were one of the great phenomena of British films in the '50s and '60s. What do you think were some of the reasons for your enormous popularity?

I think that everybody makes mistakes in this life; when you see someone else make a mistake you can either laugh or cry. No matter where you come from or what language you speak, slipping on a banana skin is a laugh anywhere in the world. If you slip and people laugh, and then they see that you're on the floor and you've hurt yourself, they don't laugh, they cry. Pathos, in my opinion, is just as important as getting laughs all the time. I think it gives plausibility. Quite often people have referred to my work as slapstick, but it's not. I think everything has to be plausible, and slapstick isn't. You can be a little bit over the top here and there, yes, but it has to be plausible. I was the little bloke that people laughed at and laughed with.

How did you come to get the lead in *Trouble in Store*?

I was appearing at the Prince of Wales Theatre in London, topping the bill in *Paris to Piccadilly*, and the Rank Organisation came round to Billy Marsh, my agent, and asked if I would be interested in doing a film and would I sign a contract? Billy said yes and then asked me. Of course I said, 'Cor, would I? Not 'arf!' It so happens that ABPC films were after me at the time as well, although I didn't know it then. The Rank Organisation signed me on a seven-year contract. Normally they would give you a screen test first, especially if you weren't known in film, but they signed me on first and then

tested me. I remember I did my test with a young lady called Petula Clark and it was directed by Ronald Neame. I had to say to Petula, 'Your eyes are as light as gossamer,' and I thought, 'Can this be a test for a comic?' It was an absolute failure and they paid me off for the first film, whatever it was.

When it came around to the second film the following year, Rank had obviously decided they didn't want to have to pay me off every year, so they gave me a film written by Jill Craigie, called *Trouble in Store*. When they told Jill I was doing the film, she didn't want her name on it. I don't know the full story but I do know she had written the original script. The Rank Organisation and all the producers were frightened out of their lives putting me into the film, because they didn't know whether it was going to work or not. They had a sneak preview of the film when it was finished, at the Odeon in Camden Town. I remember standing in the foyer before the film started, and John Davis and Earl St John passed me, saying, 'Good luck, Mr Wisdom.' I was terribly nervous. When the film started I didn't watch it, I watched the audience's faces and they were screaming with laughter. Then I stood in the same spot in the foyer as everyone came out, and they were all saying, 'Oh darling, you were wonderful!' It's called the bullshit of show business.

That was the first of six films in a row you did for the director John Paddy Carstairs. Why do you think this was such a successful partnership?

Because he was a damn' good director and we

got on very well together. Then the time came that he didn't direct any more of my films because he wanted to go on to other things. On nearly all those films for Carstairs, the floor manager was a bloke called Bob Asher and he directed the next few films, starting in 1959. Hugh Stewart came to me on the next film and asked me if I fancied anyone in particular to direct it. I said I thought Bob could do it, because he had been directing some of the shots for crowd scenes in the Carstairs films, and I thought he had done it well. Bob was a smashing bloke, too. So they let him direct the next film and it worked.

By this time, were you and your films so well established that it didn't make much difference who directed?

I suppose so, but I always felt that as long as you have someone who's efficient, and you also have fun together, then you do your work to the best of your ability. There was very little difference in the films in the end, whether Paddy Carstairs or Bob Asher directed them.

There were several other directors for whom you did one film each: Stuart Burge, William Friedkin and Robert Hartford Davies.

Hartford Davies wasn't the director, he was the producer. Oh, he did direct *The Sandwich Man* but I only did a cameo part in that. He produced *Press for Time*, though, which Bob Asher directed, and he also produced *What's Good for the Goose* for Menahem Golem. Golem has done brilliantly in America, but as a director I reckon he was a ——! He wouldn't let me do anything my way, he kept telling me how and I think that spoilt it. I like to suggest doing various things, but he insisted on doing everything absolutely his way.

You don't like a lot of detailed direction?

I don't mind it, but I do like to have my own opinion on a way to do something as well, and then we come to an agreement. With Bob Asher and Paddy Carstairs, it worked altogether. When I was doing *The Square Peg* with Paddy Carstairs, the writer Jack Davies had suggested I play the part of the German general rather than have another actor play it. Paddy Carstairs said no, it was a part for a straight actor. Then Hugh Stewart said he thought it was a good idea for me to play the General and Paddy Carstairs had to agree. He was annoyed about it and when we did the rehearsals for that part, he just went back to his desk and took no notice. But as we proceeded through the rehearsal, he came towards us, obviously with more interest. When

we'd finished the rehearsal he did the shot, and when the shot was finished he came over and kissed me on the cheek. That was it. He said, 'From now on, we talk, Norman.'

Did you have a favourite director?

Yes, it would be a choice between Paddy Carstairs and Bob Asher. William Friedkin was very good but I wasn't a star in *The Night They Raided Minsky's*; the stars were Jason Robards and Britt Ekland. Even so, I was nominated for Best Actor for that film.

How did you suddenly come to do an American film?

I had been over there doing *Walking Happy*, a musical version of *Hobson's Choice*, and it was a very successful show. William Friedkin came around to my dressing-room one night and said he'd like me to do a part in the film he was making and would I come along to meet Norman Lear, the producer. I went to the studios and met Norman Lear, who apologised but he thought I wouldn't be right for the part. I asked him why and he said it was because I was English, whereas the film was about American burlesque. I know this sounds ridiculous, but I said that burlesque was a type of variety and I used to do that in England. I pointed out that Stan Laurel and Chaplin had done variety and burlesque, and he looked at me and said, 'You've got the job.' No tests or anything, because they had seen some of my films. I enjoyed making the film very much.

Ten of your films were produced by Hugh Stewart and I wondered what sort of dealings you would have had with him, as producer.

We got on very well and I still see him now and again. We were on first-name terms on the set back then, and he came on the set quite regularly. He wasn't just a money man.

Another man who produced a couple of your films was John Bryan, who had been a great art director in British films. What was he like as a producer?

I remember John well. He was a bit strict as a producer. Not with money – I never have any problems about money, I leave that to my agent. I remember one incident where I left the set for a short while. I had a terrible headache or something, so I went to the dressing-room to sit down. I was away longer than the few minutes I'd said I would be, about quarter of an hour, and John came in and gave me a real telling-off. I just said I was sorry and went back on the set. He wasn't quite so jovial as Hugh Stewart, but still an efficient man.

How involved were you in the writing of scripts for your films? Did you work with writers like Jack Davies and Henry Blyth?

Yes, Jack Davies and Henry Blyth used to write the format of the storyline, then Jack used to come to my flat in London and we'd talk it through. He'd be laughing because I'd make suggestions here and there. By the time we did our third or fourth film together, he would do the storyline and then ask me to write the script, so I did, sometimes with a friend of mine called Eddie Leslie. He was a good pal of mine, I'd worked with him in pantomime and I got him into films because he was a good writer. We used to write films together and I used to write the songs as well.

You were usually surrounded by quite strong casts, often famous British character actors. Did you have a say in the casting?

Not really, no. I suppose here and there I might have had a bit of influence, like getting Eddie Leslie in, but they knew he was good. They just chose Edward Chapman automatically for Mr Grimsdale [a recurring character]; he was almost part of the story in the first place. And Jerry Desmonde was also part of the team. He had worked with Sid Field.

Do you ever think of yourself as a sort of successor to Sid Field?

Sid Field starred in shows at the Prince of Wales Theatre for about three or four years on the trot. When I went to the Prince of Wales to do my show, *Paris to Piccadilly*, on the opening night I received a telegram which I've still got in my study and I'm very proud of it. It says, 'If anyone can take his place, we think it's you. Love, Sid Field Family.' He was dead by then, of course.

It seems to me that having real actors around you might make you feel more a part of a story, rather than just doing a comic turn.

Sort of, but I suppose the most important thing was that I would say to myself, 'Fancy having this lot working with me, isn't it lovely!' It made me feel that they'd be proud to be working with me as well.

Your female leads were often promising young actresses of the period. What recollections do you have of working with Lana Morris, Maureen Swanson, Jill Dixon, Honor Blackman, Susannah York – all strikingly different from each other?

Yes, and all absolutely wonderful! Some went on to bigger careers than others; Susannah York was

absolutely lovely, and Lana Morris was a sweet lady. If you've got good mates there, it makes it easy to work. Maureen Swanson married into the aristocracy – she's a duchess or something.

Nearly all the characters you played were actually called Norman. Whose idea was this?

It was just acceptable from the start. I was known stage-wise as Norman and by that time I'd done television as well, so they thought they'd stick to the same name. It gave a sort of continuity to the films. I never forget when I was doing a show in Tehran, before the trouble. I was walking along a street and a crowd of students on the other side of the road spotted me. They were all shouting, 'Mister Norrman! Oh, Mister Norrman!' My films are shown all over and they knew me. They didn't go all that well in America at the time, but in the past few years they've come along quite well – at three o'clock in the morning, admittedly, but they show them and I get quite a bit of fan mail from America.

How much freedom did you have do to other work while you were under contract to the Rank Organisation?

I was quite free to do stage work, my agent would have seen to that. Once I had done a film I was free to do anything I liked. My contract was for a film a year for seven years. Once the contract was up I don't think they worried about it time-wise, and I just continued working for them from then on, film by film.

You several times played dual roles, such as in *The Square Peg*. Whose idea was this?

Jack Davies suggested the dual role in *The Square Peg* and I just looked upon it as having fun in another way. I wasn't looking to broaden my range, didn't think of it like that at all. I'd established the fact that I could do almost anything and Jack Davies had great faith in me, so he used to just put in a double role and they accepted it. The same went for *A Stitch in Time*, the one set in the hospital where I played a nurse.

You've been perfectly happy, then, to be a comedian and not hankered for strong dramatic roles?

Yes I have, here and there. I did a thing called *Going Gently*, for instance. It's a television film for Stephen Frears, produced by Innes Lloyd; who wrote to me and asked if I'd be interested in doing it. I asked him to send me the script and I decided I'd love to do it. It is about a patient dying of cancer in hospital. I talked to Hugh Stewart about it and he suggested we have lunch with Stephen Frears;

during the lunch Stephen pointed out that there weren't any laughs in the film. He just said, 'We'll talk in the office after lunch.' So we went to the office and he said, 'Norman, I don't want any laughs,' I said, 'Well, why did you call me? Why mess me about like this? I can earn my living anywhere, I don't have to be messed about by the likes of you and I won't stand for it!' He said, 'Now, Norman, just keep calm.' Then I looked at him and said, 'Well, how's that for acting?' Then he laughed and said OK.

We never had any problems. I remember the first scene, where I was lying in bed dying of cancer and saying, 'Why me? I don't smoke, I hardly ever drink, I've behaved myself. Why has God picked on me?' Stephen called 'Cut!' and came over to me. He just ruffled my hair, nothing else, and that was good enough for me. And the wonderful Fulton Mackay, who died recently, was in *Going Gently* and so was the queen of them all, Judi Dench. She is an absolute angel.

Do you have a favourite among your films?

No, not an absolute favourite. *A Stitch in Time* is one, *On the Beat* is another and so is *Trouble in Store*. Then there is *The Bulldog Breed*, the one in the Navy. You can get the videos in Woolworths, you know, the lot – about twelve or thirteen anyway. I think it's great, even though I don't get a ha'penny out of it. They're seeing my films, I'm still known and I still get plenty of offers of work, so it's fine by me.

Do you want to film again on the big screen?

Yes, I've got a film that I'd love to do. It's a short story by JB Priestley, called 'Tober and the Tulpa', and I have an option on the rights. It's about an elderly man who's never had many friends; he would love to have a lady friend and he finds a way, through Chinese mythology, of creating what is called a tulpa, a woman he and everyone else can see even though she is a fantasy; he can sit in his little room off the Edgeware Road and say 'tulpa' and she is there; he can carress and kiss her until he hears the landlady coming; then he says 'away' and she's gone. Gradually he finds it more difficult to get rid of her because she likes it, then he can't get rid of her at all. I named my character Adam Tober and, because she is evil, I have called the film *Adam and Evil*. I've adapted it for film and I've been talking about it for two or three years now – that's what they do in films nowadays, talk about it! It would make a smashing film but it's hard to get a project off the ground these days.

Adam and Evil *went into production in early 1996.*

Googie Withers
b. 1917

and John McCallum
b. 1917

Googie Withers, actor: *The Girl in the Crowd, The Love Test* (1934), *Windfall, Her Last Affaire, All at Sea, Dark World* (1935), *Crown vs Stevens, King of Hearts, She Knew What She Wanted, Accused, Crime Over London* (1936), *Pearls Bring Tears, Paradise for Two* (1937), *Paid in Error, If I Were Boss, Kate Plus Ten, Strange Boarders, Convict 99,*

The Lady Vanishes, You're the Doctor (1938), *Murder in Soho, Trouble Brewing, The Gang's All Here, She Couldn't Say No* (1939), *Bulldog Sees It Through, Busman's Honeymoon* (1940), *Jeannie* (1941), *Back Room Boy, One of Our Aircraft is Missing, The Silver Fleet* (1942), *On Approval, They Came to a City* (1944), *Dead of Night, Pink String* and Sealing Wax (1945), The Loves of Joanna Godden, It Always Rains on Sunday (1947), Miranda (1948), Once Upon a Dream, Traveller's Joy (1949), Night and the City (1950), White Corridors, The Magic Box (1951), Derby Day (1952), Devil on Horseback (1954), Port of Escape (1956), Nickel Queen (1971), Country Life (1994), Shine (1996)

John McCallum, actor: *South West Pacific, *Joe Came Back, A Son is Born, *Australia is Like This (1946), *Bush Christmas, The Root of All Evil, The Loves of Joanna Godden, It Always Rains on

Sunday (1947), The Calendar, Miranda (1948), A Boy, a Girl and a Bike, Traveller's Joy (1949), The Woman in Question (1950), Valley of the Eagles, The Magic Box, Lady Godiva Rides Again (1951), Derby Day, Trent's Last Case (1952), The Long Memory, Melba (1953), Devil on Horseback, Trouble in the Glen (1954), Port of Escape, Smiley, *Three in One (1956) * Commentary only.

Producer: They're a Weird Mob (1966), Nickel Queen (& dir) (1971), Attack Force Z (1978), The Highest Honour (1981)

There was nobody like Googie Withers in 1940s British cinema. Throughout the 1930s, she learnt her trade in 'quota quickies', several directed by Michael Powell, who subsequently gave her her first big chances in *One of Our Aircraft is Missing* and *The Silver Fleet*. After holding her own against the formidable competition of Beatrice Lillie and Clive Brook in the delectable *On Approval* in 1944, she embarked on her great period with Ealing, and this is where her individuality is most potently seen. Whether she is seducing Gordon Jackson in *Pink String and Sealing Wax* or proving a match for several men (including husband-to-be McCallum) in *The Loves of Joanna Godden* or jeopardising her marriage to help an ex-lover (McCallum again) in *It Always Rains on Sunday*, there is a marvellously confronting sensuality about her, a brazenness and authority that rivet the attention.

When John McCallum came to England in 1947, after brief experience of filmmaking in Australia, he quickly found himself in leading roles opposite Phyllis Calvert and Googie Withers. His best films are also the Ealing-made ones – *The Loves of Joanna Godden* and especially *It Always Rains on Sunday*. (The quality of Ealing and director Robert Hamer can be judged by comparing the latter with the McCallum–Withers episode in Herbert Wilcox's *Derby Day:* it is not that they perform less well but that the whole enterprise lacks the Ealing point and rigour.) McCallum had other successes as a tormented detective in *The Long Memory* (Hamer again) and as a romantic leading man in *The Woman in Question* with Jean Kent and in the entertaining satire, *Lady Godiva Rides Again*.
Interview date: March 1990

Miss Withers, during the 1930s you were on stage seven times and made twenty-four films. Did this reflect your preference at the time?

GW: My preference was for where the money and the work were and, naturally, my agent [Picot Schooling] was pushing me like mad for films because you get great exposure from them. It was very good training for me. In those days they made 'quickie' films in three weeks. My first was an early Michael Powell film, called *The Girl in the Crowd*, and Mickey, however great a director he was, was not a very easy man to work for. He used to say terrible things and upset people badly. I got on very well because I'm pretty tough – and was, even at that age. I can only say that he became a good friend of mine, because when Michael came up against someone he found he could not bully he respected them. I think he admired my acting talent; and I would say that he was the man who really started my career, giving me my first job in *The Girl in the Crowd*, and the film that really set me off, *One of Our Aircraft is Missing*. He told me that he had a wonderful script and that, because I was half Dutch and could speak Dutch, I would be perfect casting in the part. 'But,' he said, 'the producers are terribly against you playing it because they say you have only played opposite comics like Will Hay.' They wouldn't take me seriously for the part, which had no comedy in it at all. I asked Mickey if he thought I could do the part, and he said he was *quite* sure I could. He remembered me in *Her Last Affaire*, when I had to play a serious bit, and realised I could play drama, and he believed I would be very good in *One of Our Aircraft is Missing*.

I read the script and told him I would give anything to do it, because it would give me a jump into major films instead of little quickie comedies. So he persuaded the producers to let me do it. I think that *One of Our Aircraft is Missing* and *The Silver Fleet* were the two most 'understandable' films he made; they were true stories. Godfrey Tearle was one of the people Michael was rude to, and Godfrey said nothing – he was *very* dignified, but I used to get very angry with Michael if he said anything I didn't like. He was very meticulous about what he wanted – from actors as well as everyone else. He used to *say* exactly what he wanted, but I sometimes used to wonder how much he knew about acting. Mickey produced *The Silver Fleet* but Vernon Sewell directed. Mickey was there all the time; we saw all the rushes together.

I remember Ralph Richardson on that film – he was truly an adorable man, kind and funny and witty. He used to think up the most extraordinary things: for instance, he had to say goodbye to me in the morning, knowing he would never see me again but pretending he would be home that evening; and he said, 'I think it would be rather nice, Googie, if I brushed your hair.' I said, 'What!? I've just had my hair done and what on earth will I look like after ten takes, with you pulling it about?' 'Oh, just a

thought,' he said. The hair-brushing was in the film, eventually.

One of your great strengths was that on screen you never looked like a stage actress.

GW: That is probably because I had no proper theatre training except as a dancer. After I had made some films I started doing a play here and there. So probably I was bringing a film performance to the theatre, and just made it louder and funnier!

Did you feel you had a long apprenticeship throughout the '30s?

GW: I've never really had to go after anything; I've just been offered things I've wanted to do. I didn't have any of that '30s studio grooming. Like many actresses, I did a film with George Formby at Ealing – *Trouble Brewing*. That was a saga because his wife, Beryl, was a terribly jealous woman and she used to organise every moment of his life. He wasn't allowed to speak to anybody, especially not a pretty young leading lady, apart from saying our lines in the script. And of course he always insisted on *having* pretty young leading ladies because it was good box office. Beryl always sat on the set, and there was always the kiss at the end, to which *Beryl* said 'Cut!' – not the director, because he might have let it go on two seconds longer! But he was awfully clever, very funny. I learned technique from comics like him and Will Hay, who is pretty much forgotten these days, but was wonderful. He was a very academic man, a comic by accident, I think.

No sooner had you established yourself as a star in the two Powell films, than you vanished for a year. Was this to do the Priestley play, *They Came to a City*?

GW: Yes, for two years actually. I was thrilled to be asked to do it because I was known as a film star in those days and, when Binkie Beaumont (who ran HM Tennent) suggested me for the part, I suppose it was because I was a name. That was when I very nearly *changed* my name, because Binkie was horrified about putting my name up in lights. He tried to persuade me to change it before we opened in London; but finally I decided I couldn't bear to and told him I wouldn't and pointed out that he had already signed the contract with me. He insisted nobody would be interested in someone called 'Googie' playing Lady Macbeth or whatever, and I pointed out that someone called Ginger Rogers appeared to be doing rather well despite her name. So, I did the play for two years and also did a film of it for Ealing. It was totally uncommercial. I don't know who Ealing imagined would be interested in it. We were all pleased because they were giving us a percentage of the profits but, of course, there were none!

How did you come to make *On Approval*? There's no other British film like it!

GW: A lot of funny things happened with that. We started off with Brian Desmond Hurst as director and Clive Brook didn't see eye-to-eye with him at all. They had some awful rows. Anyway, the film was finished and put on the shelf. Then a few months later my agent told me that Clive was putting up his own money because he believed it would be a money-spinner and he wanted to cut a lot of it, redirect it and spend three weeks reshooting. I imagine he was responsible for that spoken prologue. So it was eventually released, got fabulous notices and went to America. It was extraordinary casting; I mean, Bea Lillie was bizarre, she really was! She was hopeless to work *with* because she was too used to working on her own. She really was a marvellous performer, so funny, but she had to be a one-woman act.

Now follows what I see as the great period of your screen career – your time at Ealing. How was it as a place to work?

GW: It was lovely – and they had the most wonderful directors. Charlie Frend, Charlie Crichton, Sandy Mackendrick, they were all such dear people and such fun. And Robert Hamer, if he had been alive today, would have wiped Mickey Powell and all those other directors off the map. I did *Pink String and Sealing Wax, Dead of Night* and *It Always Rains on Sunday* with him. He threw his life away with drink. He was very sympathetic to work with; he knew what you wanted to do. He was not an actor but he understood actors, the way actors wanted to work, and he would give you your head and be patient. And that's what you want as an actress; you do it a few times, improving as you do so, and if he's worth his salt he then knows where he can push you.

John McCallum, you came into British films around 1947. Was it a good time to be launching a career?

JM: It was an extraordinary period. I was here [Australia] with Gladys Moncrieff in a musical comedy and they wanted me to go to New Zealand. I read in the paper one day that my old friend Trevor Howard had been an enormous success in a film called *Brief Encounter*, so I thought, 'If old Trevor can do this, why can't I? Better than going to

New Zealand.' I'd had some small film experience in Australia, so I packed my trunk and went to England. I had an agent in England from before the war, who suggested the part of a lawyer in *The Root of All Evil*. There was a shortage of actors then, and I got the part. The director, Brock Williams, asked me to test for a part in another film and I got the lead – I was staggered!

You worked with director Ralph Smart on *A Boy, a Girl and a Bike* in England. What do you remember of him?

JM: I remember the film with affection and it had a lovely location in the Yorkshire Dales. A lot of the cast (Diana Dors, Honor Blackman, Barry Letts) were only in it for three or four days and there was a great pool of available talent then. Ralph became a good friend and he was a very funny man. He was fun to work with for a start; he didn't know much about acting, but he knew his camera. Of all the directors we have worked with, there are very few who are good with cameras *and* good with actors.

Is the cameraman almost as important as the director to an actor?

GW: It is for women. The first thing you ask is who's on the camera and who's lighting it.

JM: Also, a lot of lighting cameramen actually direct the film, because many directors don't know much about camera. In fact, quite often a cameraman will go on to be a director. Mutz Greenbaum [aka Max Greene] used to say to Herbert Wilcox, 'You'd be better to do it this way, Herbert', and he would change the whole set-up. Greenbaum really directed most of Wilcox's films, I can tell you.

Did you feel you were being groomed as a leading man, given a star-building treatment?

JM: Not really. They did that with young starlets in their Charm School (Diana Dors was in that) but they didn't say much to the men. You just went from one film to another; you were supposed to know your job. I think Rank central office did have some eye on promoting, and also according to my contract you could be farmed out for a profit. I made one or two outside films from which they got some money.

GW: We never came across J Arthur Rank much. He didn't really care for actors very much, I don't think. He just put his money where he thought it would make the most back for him. He had an interest in films but he didn't have much interest in us. We were making money for him but we never saw him.

How do you compare the two studios you

worked at in the '40s – Gainsborough and Ealing?

GW: Ealing was miles ahead of Gainsborough as a place to work. Gainsborough's Islington studios were abominable. To get there you had to drive through slums. When you arrived, there was this awful old building and the dressing-rooms were dreadful. The make-up room was a box and the canteen food was uneatable. But Ealing was a little bit countrified, just off the Ealing Common, and it was a house whose gardens had been made into studios.

JM: It had a family atmosphere; if they liked you, you were there forever. The directors were under contract so they were guaranteed a yearly salary – although it was a pittance. Michael Balcon paid them very little.

GW: He paid us *all* very little! But at the same time, it was a fascinating place to go because there were some extraordinarily clever people there. There was Robert Hamer, of course; and then there was Diana Morgan and Bobbie MacDermot, her husband; Monja Danischewsky, Michael Relph, Sidney Cole, Charles Frend, Angus MacPhail, and so on. They were extremely intelligent, very high-brow, and at lunchtime in the canteen they used to play the most extraordinary word games. And then there was always the evening at the pub over the way; they all went and most of them got very, very drunk. I had done five films there by then so John and I were very 'in'.

Mind you, there was something of the headmaster in Michael Balcon; we almost leapt to attention when he came in. He was a funny fellow, very sweet with us, but he was also a moralist – didn't like any hanky-panky, yet he had all these men around him getting terribly tight all over the place! I think he knew how brilliant they were so he let them have their fun. Every single morning at ten-thirty sharp he walked on to the set as the producer. Filming stopped, then we stood there while he watched a scene or two; we would all say, 'Good morning, Michael,' then he would go off again with a retinue of men behind him.

Your image in the '40s was extraordinary: nobody else was as bold as you were, bold, sensual and brazen.

GW: I wasn't aware of it; something to do with my own personality, I suppose. I was very comfortable in *Pink String and Sealing Wax*; I loved those meaty parts. I didn't want, and never played, the genteel parts, the English-rose type. Maybe it has

something to do with the fact that I'm not altogether English, because my mother was a mixture of Dutch, French and German. It never occurred to me that I had that image, though. Robert Hamer used to try very hard to get around the rule at the time that you had to have one foot on the floor in a scene with a couple on a bed. Although in *It Always Rains on Sunday*, I was in bed with Edward Chapman (my husband in the film), reading the Sunday papers, we were almost fully dressed, with the covers pulled up. Sex was very understated in films then, and your imagination took over, whereas now . . . I think it was *much* better when it was left to your imagination.

You were both in *It Always Rains on Sunday*. Were you very taken with that film then?

GW: It's always in retrospect that one sees how good they were. The thing that struck me then was that Bob said, 'I want to do this out in the streets where it all happens,' so there was very little studio work. I think this was the first film to be made like that.

JM: Because *It Always Rains on Sunday* is a group film, we didn't really know what was going on with the others: marvellous character actors who each contributed their own little stories. There were about four plots going on – but we didn't see them in the making. Bob was a perfectionist: he took five weeks to shoot that end sequence in the railway yard. We took awful risks – going under moving trains and running on top of them, things like that. The same lighting man, Douglas Slocombe, did all those films – *It Always Rains on Sunday*, *Pink String and Sealing Wax* and lots of other Ealing films of the period, and he has won an Oscar since. He didn't interfere in the direction as much as Max Greene did but, by God, he was good.

To jump a couple of years, what do you think of *Derby Day*, in which you seemed to be doing a kind of watered-down rerun of *It Always Rains on Sunday*?

GW: It was one of those fill-in things. John was under contract to Herbert Wilcox, who thought it would be rather fun if I came along and played in the film with him. I don't think we were keen on it then, and I hate it when I see it now.

JM: It was papered together compared with the other film and, of course, there is a vast difference between directors, between dear old Herbert and Robert Hamer! Herbert was a dear sweet man but . . .

GW: He used to break every day at twelve o'clock for a glass of champagne! I ask you!

JM: He would do nothing in the mornings, just sort of work it out with Mutz; then came the champagne, and by the end of the day you had five minutes in the can and it was terrible stuff. But he was a showman: he had a nose for what subject to make. Also he was a very congenial man and could get immediately on side with the big American stars and persuade them to do things against their better judgement! Rank was going downhill, not making many films, and Herbert kept going, he was a real terrier. Herbert was tied up with RKO and they eventually took him over. He set up his own independent production company but went bust in the end.

He did two films with Orson Welles around this time. How directable was Welles?

JM: Absolutely not. Orson took over entirely. At one point Herbert pointed to an empty sound stage, telling Orson to go over there and work out what he wanted to do while he, Wilcox, carried on without him. Welles had great presence and he was wonderful in *Trent's Last Case*. A very selfish actor for all that; he was very difficult for other actors to work with. I worked with him again on *Trouble in the Glen* and we got on very well, but he was one of those actors you act *against*, not with. I played Victor McLaglen's son and we were gypsies. We had a great time – it was a dreadful film, though.

Joanna Godden was a charming film. Were you attracted to it at the time?

GW: It was lovely, we adored working on it. It was the most beautiful location, though unfortunately bad weather. But that meant we were there for three months instead of about three weeks, in the Romney Marshes. We were living in the most beautiful house, which belonged to a family who couldn't afford to keep it going; so they turned it into a sort of hotel taking twelve paying guests. They had, would you believe it, a cook and a butler called Neat and Tidy! It was an interesting film which really predated the feminist movement. Even now when I am in that part of the world, elderly people often come up to me and say they were extras in the film. Once again Douglas Slocombe did the lighting on that – beautiful black-and-white photography. It was the only time I worked with Charles Frend, but we got on with him terribly well. He didn't spend much time with actors on their performances. He had been an editor, I believe, before he turned to directing.

You did that batch of three comedies at Gainsborough, including *Miranda, Traveller's

Joy and Once Upon a Dream. Had the studio changed much now that Sydney Box was running it?

GW: No, it hadn't changed much.

JM: Sydney became a good friend of ours. He was very fair, full of ideas, and he brought a lot of properties with him. He had a great success with *The Seventh Veil*. He did a lot of work with Ralph Smart; they used to do radio scripts together.

GW: Sydney's sister Betty Box produced *Miranda*. And *Once Upon a Dream* was quite extraordinary because Ralph Thomas was auditioned by *me*. Sydney told me he wanted Ralph to direct it but that first I was to do a scene with him and, if I liked him, they would give him the job! Since then, of course, he has become a very well-known director. When we went to work at Pinewood there wasn't really a head there. They were studios that were let out to various companies who worked there. Earl St John was there in charge of the studios, but no one was really there as head.

I want to ask about a Pinewood film, *White Corridors*.

GW: I adored that. I was determined to look as if I could hold a stethoscope and take someone's pulse, as if I was a surgeon. I went into Richmond Hospital every day for a month to watch people at work; I was taught how to give injections, watched operations, and that sort of thing. We had a surgeon on the set with us the whole time, to make quite sure that what we did was correct. I really loved that part, because it took place in a real kind of hospital. The film was largely made in the studio but we did do some work at Richmond Hospital, mainly exteriors.

Your nearest brush with Hollywood was making *Night and the City* for Fox. I'd have expected you to be drawn to the *films noirs* being made then.

The reason I didn't go to Hollywood was that I was married with a child in England. I liked working with Richard Widmark and with Jules Dassin, who was an amazing director. We worked all through the night in the slums in this film. Dassin was very good with actors but of course the original version was slashed and he wrote me long letters full of four-letter words about the censors who had cut so much of the film. Gene Tierney was a very nice girl – poor thing later became seriously ill. There was none of that 'big-American-stars' act with her or Widmark.

I was married to Francis L Sullivan in the film,

and that was rather an unpleasant experience, principally because I'm a bit squeamish and he was very fat, and he also sweated a lot. I had to put my arms around him and cuddle his head. He was an unhealthy man and all that sort of thing rather revolted me, but he was so dear that one could never let him know how one felt. Most of the men who played those Soho parts were the real thing; they had been picked out by Jules and they were ponces, racketeers, very dangerous men most of them – but they just loved being in the film!

Did you feel that British films were running out of steam in the '50s?

JM: Yes, they were. Rank had pulled out; they were losing money and they weren't making very many films – down from a hundred or so a year to about fifty or sixty.

GW: And people were either going to America or into television, or back to the theatre as we did. We simply found the theatre more congenial and we wanted to come back to Australia.

Sir John Woolf
b. 1913

Producer: *Pandora and the Flying Dutchman* (1951), *The African Queen* (1952), *Moulin Rouge, Innocents in Paris, Beat the Devil* (1953), *Carrington VC, The Good Die Young* (1954), *The Bespoke Overcoat, I Am a Camera* (1955), *Dry Rot, Sailor Beware!, Three Men in a Boat* (1956), *The Story of Esther Costello* (1957), *The Silent Enemy* (1958), *Room at the Top* (1959) *Term of Trial, The L-Shaped Room* (1962), *Life at the Top* (1965), **Oliver!* (1968), **Day of the Jackal* (1973), **The Odessa File* (1974)

* As sole producer; all other films produced with brother James Woolf, for Romulus or Remus Productions.

It is always more difficult to obtain accurate credits for, and information about, producers than it is for directors or stars, perhaps because the producer's function is less clear-cut. It is even more difficult when the producers' names are subsumed in a production company's name as the Woolf brothers' names were in Romulus and, later, Remus Films. Their distinctive contribution was to produce films genuinely international in appeal, but films which also brought credit to the British film industry. While they also made smaller, more parochially British films such as *Sailor Beware!*, their name – or that of Romulus – was really made with their first three Anglo-American productions, especially *The African Queen*, and with *Room at the Top*, the film which ushered in a new realist strain in British cinema.

Interview date: June 1990

How did Romulus Films begin?

When I returned from the war at the end of 1945 I went back as joint managing director of General Film Distributors, which had become a subsidiary of the Rank Organisation. I didn't really enjoy being a small cog in a large wheel, so in 1948 with my brother's [James] help I started Romulus Films (a production company) and Independent Film Distributors, financing a programme of British films. Independent started by putting up seventy per cent of the cost of a number of films, most of which weren't very successful. In fact I started off as badly as my father [CM Woolf] had with General Film Distributors.

My brother and I then decided to go into production ourselves, and that's how Romulus started. I sent my brother to America at the time of the Un-American Activities Committee, when a number of directors and artistes wanted to leave America because they were being questioned by McCarthy and Co. He went to California to look for interesting proposals to bring to England; the first one he found was *Pandora and the Flying Dutchman*, which was to be directed by Albert Lewin, who was having trouble with the UAC. He used to be a director for MGM, which was going to make *Pandora*, but they cancelled it because of the political problems. So we brought Lewin to England to make the film with James Mason and Ava Gardner. That's what started us off with Anglo-American productions because British films were then very parochial – the best were the Ealing films and even they didn't sell in America.

Pandora wasn't all that successful, although it covered its costs eventually. It was a rather turgid film but we didn't have much experience as film producers then. Lewin was actually the producer but it was made through Romulus Films and to that extent we were in charge of production. It was too long and I couldn't get Lewin to agree to cut it, but in many ways it was a brilliant film – for instance, that night bullfighting scene was superbly shot and the opening shot, through the bell, had a very poetic quality. It was shot at Tossa del Mar, on the coast near Barcelona.

What was your experience of working with John Huston?

The book, *The African Queen*, was owned by Warner Brothers, who had bought it for Bette Davis. At the time we became interested in it, John Huston thought he was going to be able to get Humphrey Bogart and Katharine Hepburn. Sam Spiegel was involved in it but his company didn't have the finance, so we undertook the finance, other than the American contribution. We signed Bogart, Hepburn, Huston and Spiegel, and Huston made the film magnificently, reliably, in time and under budget. As far as I was concerned it was a very harmonious production, but Spiegel and Huston fell out because Sam was always short of money. When the unit was in Africa at the beginning of the film, Sam was supposed to have paid Huston and Bogart out of the American budget, but the money hadn't arrived and I think Huston got very fed up. In the end I had to give the guarantee of completion to the American bankers (Heller and Company) myself. So I took a huge risk with *The African Queen*, but fortunately it was an enormous success.

Alexander Korda, who had been an old friend of my father's, warned me against a film 'about two old people going up and down a river in Africa, with a director whose last film was a disaster'. If it had failed it would probably have been the end of Romulus, but it was the only film we ever made, apart from *Room at the Top*, which didn't get one single adverse criticism. Bogart won his one and only Oscar for his magnificent performance, and Hepburn was also nominated. After he finished *The African Queen*, Huston didn't particularly want to go back to America and naturally we wanted to keep him in England. We had just read *Moulin Rouge* by Pierre la Mure and thought it would be a wonderful follow-up to *The African Queen*. I gave it to Huston to read but he didn't want to do it. We nagged him until eventually he asked who we envisaged as Toulouse-Lautrec. We told him we thought José Ferrer would be perfect. Huston said that if we could get Ferrer he would think about it again. Ferrer loved the idea, so then Huston agreed to do the picture. The rest of the cast was gathered from all over. We were friendly with Zsa Zsa Gabor and she very much wanted to play the part of Jeanne Avril. Her singing was of course dubbed.

The film was not all plain sailing. We were shooting it in Technicolor, through gauzes and smoke to get that hazy effect, and after a month the Technicolor people met Huston, Ossie Morris, our cameraman, and me and said it was a disgrace, not the sort of thing they wanted to put their name to. Elliott Elisofon was advising Huston and Morris on the use of colour because in those days Technicolor was very chocolate-boxy. It was a big international success, though it didn't get as good reviews as those for *The African Queen*, but it won seven nominations and three Oscars, including colour photography!

What drew you to *Beat the Devil*?

Huston still wanted to stay in England and he gave me a book called *Beat the Devil*, written by an Irishman named Claude Cockburn. I didn't like it but John said he'd directed *Moulin Rouge* at my insistence, and in return I should back his judgement on *Beat the Devil* – it would be another *Maltese Falcon*. So I interested an Italian friend of mine, Robert Haggiag, in making the film as an Anglo-Italian production and it had a wonderful cast – Humphrey Bogart, Jennifer Jones, Robert Morley, Peter Lorre and Gina Lollobrigida – but it never had a proper script. It was being rewritten every day as we were shooting. It taught me a lesson and I would never do that again. It was quite an amusing film and has in fact become a cult film in America. But at the time it was a disaster and, as Executive Producer, I was rather ashamed of it.

Just after that period, by which time we were well established, we were going to make *I Am a Camera* and the director Henry Cornelius and producer Monja Danischewsky wanted to do it on location in Berlin, rightly, because it was based on Christopher Isherwood's Berlin stories. At that time there was a freeze and we couldn't get any currency for overseas location work, so I went to see Alex Korda, who was very pleased with the success of *Moulin Rouge*. He had a German film distribution company and I had given him *Moulin Rouge* to distribute there. I thought he would provide us with the Deutschmarks we needed. He had left British Lion by that time, and I had visions of his sitting in his office with nothing to do, being delighted to be back in association with us. Instead, when I walked in to his offices, he had with him Laurence Olivier, Carol Reed, David Lean and his brother Zoltan Korda. I asked what he was doing and he said he was making four films – one with each of them! By the time I left I had forgotten all about having gone there to get marks to make *I Am a Camera* in Berlin; instead I found I was his partner and had put up half the money for his four films – more money than I had available! It was not far short of £1 million, which in 1953 was a very considerable sum. However, Lloyds Bank backed my judgement, as they always had done. The films were *Richard III*, *A Kid for Two Farthings*, *Summer Madness* and *Storm Over the Nile*. Fortunately all four films were successful.

You then made several smaller, more

'English' films ...

There were two or three comedies, *Sailor Beware!*, which was a big success, and *Dry Rot*. I had seen the play, *Sailor Beware!*, at the Connaught Theatre in Worthing with a marvellous, funny actress, Peggy Mount, who of course also starred in the film. We also made *Innocents in Paris*, with a very good cast (Margaret Rutherford, Alastair Sim, Larry Harvey and Claire Bloom). I remember flying over to Paris with the cast and Margaret Rutherford was sitting next to me. She saw the Eiffel Tower through the window and, with all her chins wobbling said, 'Oooh, lattice work!' Then there was *Three Men in a Boat* which we made at Henley – disastrous location, it never stopped raining. It was a funny film but it wasn't successful except in England and in Paris, where it ran for nine months on the Champs Elysées.

***Room at the Top* was a change of pace after these ...**

It was the first film on which my brother and I put our own names as producers. I was watching *Panorama* on television and Woodrow Wyatt was interviewing a group of housewives in Bradford about a book their local librarian had written; it was called *Room at the Top* and the librarian was, of course, John Braine. They made the book sound quite sensational. I told my brother about it and we got hold of the proofs from the publishers. It obviously had two marvellous parts: for Laurence Harvey and Heather Sears, whom we had used in *The Story of Esther Costello* with Joan Crawford, and who were both under contract to us. We acquired the film rights the next day for, I think, £5,000. Jack Clayton, our Production Executive, who had always wanted to direct, had made a success of directing a short film I had given him, *The Bespoke Overcoat* (Oscar for Best Short Film), so we offered him *Room at the Top* to direct, having already cast it with Larry Harvey and Simone Signoret. (We'd tried to get Vivien Leigh but she wasn't free.) Simone was marvellous and won an Oscar; Larry was also nominated.

Did it seem to you at the time to be a breakthrough for British cinema?

I don't know if we realised that when we were making it, but we had turned the film over to the censor and it came back with a red slip – which meant they were turning it down. The only certificate they would give it was an 'X' certificate and at that time the 'X' certificate had just replaced the 'H' (for Horror) certificate. So I rushed over to see the Chief Censor [John Trevelyan] and said I couldn't possibly accept an 'X' certificate; the Rank Organisation had announced they wouldn't play any 'X' films, so it would be a disaster. But he said it was exactly the film they wanted to establish the 'X' certificate and that it was a brilliant film. So we decided to try it out on an audience and we had to find somewhere where 'X' certificate films were shown. We chose the Bruce Grove Cinema in Tottenham, because they were showing *Dracula* and *Frankenstein*, two 'H' films which had become 'X' films. The audience booed at the showing and poor Jack Clayton was in tears, this being his first feature film. The audience was annoyed that they had come to see *Frankenstein* and been fobbed off with social realism. Rank wouldn't play 'X' films; ABC wouldn't touch it unless they could see what happened after it opened. So I opened it at the Plaza in central London and it got rave reviews, on the strength of which ABC agreed to book it. We had had nothing like those reviews since *The African Queen*, and it was a great success all over the world.

Was *Oliver!* a very ambitious film for a British studio at the time?

Yes, it was. There'd been no comparably lavish British musical. Lewis Gilbert was to have directed it, but he had to withdraw because he had a contract with Paramount which required him to do a film in Japan, so I was without a director four or five weeks before we were due to start shooting. I suddenly thought of Carol Reed, because of that marvellous film he made with the little boy, *The Fallen Idol*. I signed him, albeit having some difficulty with Columbia over it. I brought over Johnny Green, the celebrated music director, and Onna White, the well-known Canadian choreographer, to supervise the musical numbers. It was a wonderful film to make, as I had a very happy association with Johnny and Onna, as well as with Carol, and the film won six Oscars, including those for Best Film and Best Director. It was also a huge box-office success.

I later produced *The Day of the Jackal* and *The Odessa File*, after which, before retiring in 1988, I produced over a hundred *Tales of the Unexpected* for Anglia Television.

Michael York

b. 1942

Actor: *The Taming of the Shrew* (1966), *Smashing Time, *Confessions of a Loving Couple, Accident, *Red and Blue* (1967), *The Guru, Romeo and Juliet, The Strange Affair* (1968), *Justine, Alfred the Great* (1969), *Something for Everyone* (1970), *Zeppelin, La Poudre D'Escampette / Touch and Go* (1971), *Cabaret, England Made Me, Lost Horizon* (1972), *The Three Musketeers* (1973), *Murder on the Orient Express, The Four Musketeers* (1974), *Great Expectations, Conduct Unbecoming* (1975), *Seven Nights in Japan, Logan's Run* (1976), *The Island of Dr Moreau, The Last Remake of Beau Geste* (1977), *The Riddle of The Sands, Fedora* (1978), *Final Assignment, The White Lions* (1980), *Success is the Best Revenge, Au Nom de Tous les Miens* (1983), *Dawn / (L'Aube)* (1985), *Phantom of Death, Lethal Obsession* (1987), *Midnight Cop* (1988), *The Return of the Musketeers* (1989), *Eline Vere, The Wanderer* (1991), *The Long Shadow, The Wide Sargasso Sea, Rochade* (1992), *Discretion Assured, The Shadow of a Kiss* (1993), *Gospa, Not of this Earth* (1995), *Dark Planet* (1996), *Austin Powers, Goodbye America, The Long Way Home* (1997)
* Short film.

As he says, Michael York could not have known that the British film industry was heading for a major collapse just as he came into it in the mid-'60s. He was therefore very fortunate to get the run of striking roles which established him quickly as a new leading man to be reckoned with. His work in such varied films as *Accident* and *Romeo and Juliet* also indicated that he was not to be a conventional juvenile lead: there is a suggestion of real pain in the former and of fiery sensuality in the latter, in which his Tybalt is very memorable. And whether by chance or design, his career continued to take unexpected turns. He worked for Merchant–Ivory long before it was fashionable to do so, in *The Guru*; he was a properly bemused young policeman in David Greene's sour and stylish study of corruption, *The Strange Affair*; he gave one of his most perceptive performances as Graham Greene's young drifter in Peter Duffell's neglected *England Made Me*; and, in the *Musketeer* films and *Murder on the Orient Express*, he entered with zest into the fun and charm of their all-star pleasures. A willingness to chance his arm has continued to mark his film work, which has increasingly removed him from the flagging scene of British cinema.

Interview date: July 1995

How did you come to be involved in Franco Zeffirelli's very popular film version of *The Taming of the Shrew*?

I had worked with him in his production of *Much Ado* at the National Theatre in London. A year later he asked me to audition for his film of *The Shrew*. It was to be the real thing, a filmed test in Rome.

How did you react to the idea of filmed Shakespeare? Were you worried about cuts and changes to the text?

I was so thrilled to be in a movie that no question even crossed my mind about the viability of filming Shakespeare. Certainly one of my favourite films had been Laurence Olivier's *Henry V*, so I knew that it did work on screen and it worked wonderfully.

What was your experience of working with the Burtons, then possibly the most famous film stars in the world?

Obviously I realised that, as Burton and Taylor were not only the film's stars but also its producers, their contribution was going to be significant. Indeed there were certain scenes of mine that were filmed as playing Lucentio that were cut and edited out of it, and the focus was very much on Petruchio and Katharina, as it is in the play. The subplots necessarily had to be trimmed. I think this was more practicality – a question of time – rather than any pulling of rank by the stars, and working with them was a delight. I didn't come into contact with them very much: I was there on the fringe: but they were very supportive and helpful and the whole thing was an enjoyable experience. What was also interesting was to see that even seasoned professionals, like Burton and Taylor, could experience a certain kind of nervousness and that was very reassuring. I started the film first – I shot for two weeks knowing I was the first in the film, and not knowing much about film technique, and then the others followed. It was a baptism of fire, but a terrific one; it was a lovely experience, and I was very lucky to start in such a prestigious way.

The following year you made a very strong impact again for Zeffirelli in *Romeo and Juliet*. How did you feel about playing Tybalt, who seems to me one of the most striking characters in the play?

What happened was this: when I was asked to be in *Romeo and Juliet* I was already engaged to do a film for Paramount, *The Strange Affair*, but *Romeo and Juliet* was also for Paramount. And Zeffirelli said to me, 'Listen, I'm sure I can persuade them to let you come to Rome.' Originally he was going to offer me Paris and then decided on Tybalt. He said,

'It's really not going to take very long, a couple of weeks,' and of course I was there three months. But, luckily, as it was for Paramount, the start date of *The Strange Affair* was put back so I was able to have my cake and eat it too, which has always been my ambition in life!

Zeffirelli said he wanted Tybalt to be this golden boy in every sense, in the way he dressed and so on, in his confidence, in his popularity. He did everything well, a true Renaissance dandy. Even the costumes made him look wonderful, those bright oranges and purples and reds and that wonderful kind of hat. It was a great physical portrait and I owe Zeffirelli a lot. I liked also the fact that the affair which is implicit between him and Lady Capulet is very much there in this film. I think it works without distorting the balance of the play or the integrity of the writer. It's very Italian and Natasha Parry's outburst of emotion on hearing of Tybalt's death feels very right, light years away from English *sang froid*. It was very much a physical film: in all those fights, which are necessarily restricted on stage, and terrifying as they can be there, we were given free scope while filming on location up in Pienza. Leonard Whiting, John McEnery, everyone involved, really trained in swordsmanship, so that we could protect ourselves and respond to any changes, such as when Zeffirelli changed the location in which we had been expecting to film. So it has a wonderful *cinéma vérité* effect; there was a verisimilitude in the acting, as if we were really fighting for our lives.

You came by a succession of interesting parts – did you rely on a good agent to get these for you, or were you under any sort of contract?

The thing was, I became a film actor with that label around my neck and I was suddenly available for a whole lot of roles that were in the offing and I did have a wonderful agent at the time. I think it was a time when agenting was a much more pleasurable pursuit than it is today, when agents seem to be in the business of power-broking and the last thing that seems to interest them is to represent actors. I was the new face and I knew that I had to consolidate this image. As a film actor, I had so much to learn and I felt it was important to seize upon these opportunities. The whole film medium was so exciting, I felt as though I belonged there. It seemed to me the medium of our time, it was the accepted way to tell a story, tremendously powerful and also, of course, international.

I should also add that careers go up and down,

they look pretty much like a pendulum swing, and you're in and out of favour. I mean, if you are in this business for 'the run of the show', and we all hope we are, you know there's no retirement, no cut-off. If we hope to drop in harness, then I think it's unreasonable to expect to be on the crest of the wave the entire time.

***Accident* is one of the most riveting British films in the later '60s.**

I'm glad you thought so. Apparently some casting agent had noted my work at the National Theatre, particularly in *Trelawny of the 'Wells'*, where I played the juvenile lead, and when Joe Losey was casting *Accident* and was looking for the juve lead my name was put up. It was a question of me flying to the south of France for the day, where Losey was presenting *Modesty Blaise* at the Cannes Film Festival. It was at Cannes that I met him and Dirk Bogarde and it was a very significant encounter. Joe told me about the film, and I suppose that was a sort of audition because later he asked me to be in it. I was thrilled because it presented such a contrast to the classical costume drama – *The Shrew* – that I was filming. This was very modern, a Harold Pinter script and, as director, someone who I admired enormously for the extraordinary work he'd done within the framework of the British film industry.

Did his practice of using long takes and long tracking shots make unusual demands on actors?

I was still learning the language of the cinema, so I wasn't aware that these practices were anything unusual. This was all new to me and I plunged in. I can't tell you what a happy summer that was, I was in my element. I had just returned from location in Rome, where I had my own apartment, and I was feeling very, very fortunate. And here I was back, not just working in England but working in Oxford, where I had been a student just a few years before. In fact I borrowed some stuff from my college for the film.

Your co-stars included two of the most dominant actors in British films at the time – or indeed any time: Dirk Bogarde and Stanley Baker. How did you find working with them?

I'd been a great admirer of Dirk Bogarde's work for a long time. He was a major movie star, but, particularly with films like *Victim*, he broke his own particular mould and took risks. Certainly this was true of the films that he made with Joe Losey – *The Servant* and *King and Country*, even the trial and error ones like *Modesty Blaise*. Stanley Baker, I got to know less well. He was more reserved. Dirk Bogarde took me under his wing, we became friends, and I think he taught me a lot. He was my tutor in the film but he was also a kind of unofficial tutor in terms of film behaviour and technique, often by example, and his friendship extended beyond the film set and I valued this encouragement and, I suppose, affirmation. I'm only sorry I didn't work with Joseph Losey again.

The Strange Affair **is indeed a strange affair, but a compelling study of corruption. How did you react to doing something so off-beat?**

One's never quite certain how a film will turn out. This one started with a lot going for it. David Greene was a very interesting director and it was a hard-hitting contemporary story, but I think the emphasis on the sexuality of the case was overdone. I think it got carried away with a kind of '60s obsession, this liberated fixation with certain sexual freedoms. I think if it had been more contained it would have been more interesting but I'd like to see the movie again. I've never actually thought ahead – maybe I should – about whether the image or the film itself might be possibly damaging.

Did you have anyone guiding you in the early days of your career, in the way the old Hollywood studios guided their budding stars?

I think the basic guiding thing is that you have to establish certain gut instincts which you rely on and it takes time to establish these, often by trial and error. But, although I came in on the tail end of the studio system, and I was under contract to both Columbia and Paramount, I was never put through their kind of schooling, their factory process where they turned out movie stars, thank God! I've always relished the fact that I've been totally freelance and done whatever I've wanted to do and also borne the responsibility of what I've done myself.

You made a batch of American films around the start of the '70s – *Justine, Cabaret* **and** *Lost Horizon.* **What kinds of differences in working procedures did you notice? What were your views on the famous Hollywood professionalism?**

I didn't very much enjoy working in Hollywood on *Justine.* I loved being in the town but the work itself wasn't very enjoyable. I much preferred the location work – maybe that's significant – when the film was in Tunisia and was being directed by Joe Strick. I didn't particularly get on with George Cukor, and he was under all kinds of pressures. But of course the language of film is the same: it's just

spoken with a different accent. It was a thrill to be on the lot and it's always a thrill. I mean driving into a big studio one has a little *frisson.*

About *Cabaret***: what would you say to the idea that, though Sally is such a vivid character, Brian Roberts is really the protagonist?**

Well yes, I am a camera; you're absolutely right, he's the still, quiet centre of the film and I was lucky that Hugh Wheeler [credited as 'research consultant'] was able to expand my role and flesh it out and that we had this rehearsal time at the beginning of the film when the musical numbers were being rehearsed, where this could be done. And I think also that Sally is such a strong character that she has to be counterbalanced and that seemed to work out well. I also thought the connection between the musical numbers and the story was remarkable, because they commented on it.

Sandwiched between these big-scale films is a relatively small-scale British film, *England Made Me***, one of my favourites among your films.**

Oh I'm so glad, it's one of *my* favourites. This is one that very nearly got away. I'd just been making *Cabaret* and it seemed to me that I would be repeating myself by doing this; you know, another young man in Nazi Germany, and I very nearly turned it down. There was something about it that appealed – maybe the fact that one of my very favourite actors, Peter Finch, was going to be involved, or that it was Graham Greene or that we were going to shoot it in Yugoslavia, which is a place I'd never been to. All of these elements, plus the fact that I was free and because I had a philosophy of just doing things rather than not doing them. I mean, if it was halfway decent as this was ... The script was only half-written, so in a sense it was a gamble, but I've always liked gambling. Peter Duffell and I enjoyed working together and got each other's confidence, and he allowed me to put back certain scenes which I got straight from the book and I helped rewrite the script. I loved his resourcefulness, and I loved, after being on a big studio picture, working on something which had a certain freewheeling style.

I'm delighted to say that Graham Greene was of the opinion that this was one of the more successful adaptations of his work. He liked it very much and I think it enshrines a great performance from the late lamented Sir Michael Hordern as Minty, one of my favourite characters, and so is Anthony Farrant too, the drifter, the ne'er-do-well, the fake, living off his charm. It was Brian Roberts stretched in a more interesting way, Brian Roberts without the kind of moral backbone.

By the time you were making the *Musketeers* films and *Murder on the Orient Express*, it is harder to be sure if we are talking about British or American films. How important to a country are its film images of itself? Or does the whole idea of a national cinema simply not seem central any more?

That's a very good question. I think a national cinema is absolutely vital. It's the PR front on the country, it's how we access information about the country in the most convenient and obvious way. It does seem to me a native industry is absolutely essential. I think it has to provide that window of opportunity, that kind of insight, that kind of contribution to a United Nations of visual images. When I was working in the early '60s there was very much a British industry: the films by Losey, for example, even though he was an American, were part of a tradition that had been carried over. A lot of films, of course, were heavily subsidised by Americans and it always has been a place full of remarkable craftsmen where films are made well for other markets. But it's our authentic voice, and, as everything is being homogenised, it's even more essential that this unique voice be heard.

Orient Express **seems almost like a musical or a revue in which everyone gets a chance to do his or her turn.**

The fun part of doing this film was the cast: to be associated with so many legendary, luminous people in a film which was actually rather boring to make, because it was all made in a studio, sitting in a train. The compensation was of course this glorious collection of people and lunch on the *Orient Express* set became the high spot of the day. It was a kind of famous Algonquin Round Table where people would drop by, and I suppose it did set a sort of trend. It was certainly a pleasure to make.

I'd be very interested in any recollections of making *Great Expectations*.

This started out as a musical. But what we found when we started putting it together was the songs interrupted the kind of narrative flow of the piece. I was singing things like 'I have great expectations', all very nice, but Dickens is too entertaining in himself. He doesn't need this kind of extra comment and it just held up the whole action. I suppose it was a kind of cosy version of Dickens, unlike that other

way of tackling Dickens that Christine Edzard has made her own.

I loved the chance of working with James Mason. He's an actor with whom I shared a certain kind of temperament and I admired his work so much. It was a great treat to have the chance to work with a legendary actor.

In the same year you did *Conduct Unbecoming*, which I thought was a very workmanlike version of a sturdy play. Where did you do most of your filming?

Yes – workmanlike, it was a sort of miracle actually. It had been intended for a large screen version and it never got made; this version was all shot in the studio and very quickly. It was done so efficiently that all the lighting was done in one certain direction and scene after scene was shot in that direction and very, very efficiently and very fast. And then a second unit was sent to Pakistan to pick up some exterior footage, which was meshed in to the studio footage. It plays very well but then most courtroom dramas do. Again, it was a very good role with a very starry cast and it introduced me to the director Michael Anderson. We got on enormously well and that's why, I think, when I found myself in Hollywood at the same time that he was casting *Logan's Run*, we renewed our association.

How important is the director to you? What do you expect of a film director? Do you like to be given lots of detailed direction?

Well, I just mentioned my relationship with Michael Anderson and I think that exemplifies the ideal kind of working relationship, where not much is said. It's more that you tune into each other and often anticipate each other's needs and it's not a question of someone standing over you cracking the whip. I've had that in working with George Cukor, and loathing the experience and just being so disappointed that I was working with one of the truly great Hollywood legends and hating it and being made to do thirty takes of something humiliatingly simple. I think the great directors for me are the ones that can catalyse talent, encourage it, create an atmosphere of space where people feel safe and at home and can do more than deliver the obvious.

You've made films which the critics have praised highly (*Accident*) and some which they have not been kind to (*Lost Horizon*): what is your own personal approach to reviews?

The thing about a film is that it's timeless, so when a critic appraises a film when it comes out it's of the moment. I think one's got to learn that some things take time to mature. Take the example of Billy Wilder's *Fedora*; when it first came out it was dismissed or damned with faint praise, and then, recently, I was in London when it was being shown on the BBC and the *Radio Times* wrote about it in terms of 'masterpiece'. The reverse process happens too. Some films elaborately praised when they first come out fall by the wayside. The only critics that I really despise are those who have composed their jokes before they come in and use the review to trot them out, and it's all too easy and so unfair.

Susannah York

b. 1942

Actor: *Tunes of Glory, There Was a Crooked Man* (1960), *The Greengage Summer* (1961), *Freud – The Secret Passion* (1962), *Tom Jones* (1963), *The Seventh Dawn, *Scene Nun, Take One* (1964), *Scruggs, Sands of the Kalahari* (1965), *Kaleidoscope, A Man for All Seasons* (1966), *Sebastian* (1967), *Duffy, The Killing of Sister George* (1968), *Lock Up Your Daughters!, Oh! What a Lovely War, Battle of Britain, They Shoot Horses, Don't They?, Country Dance* (1969), *Jane Eyre* (1970), *Zee and Co, Happy Birthday, Wanda June* (1971), *Images* (1972), *Gold, The Maids* (1974), *Conduct Unbecoming, That Lucky Touch* (1975), *Sky Riders, Eliza Fraser* (1976), *The Shout, Long Shot, The Silent Partner, Superman* (1978), *The Golden Gate Murders, Alice* (1979), *The Awakening, Superman 2, Loophole, Falling in Love Again* (1980), *Yellowbeard* (1983), *The Land of Faraway* (1987), *American Roulette, Just Ask for Diamond, A Summer Story* (1988), *Bluebeard, Bluebeard / Barbebleu, Barbebleu, Melancholia* (1989) *A Handful of Time / En Haandfull Tid, Fate* (1990), *Illusions* (1992), *Pretty Princess* (1993)
* Short film.

Interview date: June 1994

The diversity of Susannah York's credits – on stage and television as well as screen – offers evidence of her determination to be taken seriously as an actress. She was undoubtedly in the tradition of the blonde, blue-eyed English rose and her Sophie Western in *Tom Jones* is perhaps the visual apogee of the type. But she had a good deal more going for her than her remarkable beauty. As early as *The Greengage Summer*, she had shown a capacity for suggesting the tensions beneath the lovely surface; her tough-minded baby cunning in *The Killing of Sister George* is not overshadowed by the flamboyance of Coral Browne and Beryl Reid; she is a very touching Margaret Roper in *A Man for All Seasons*, and is sensuously enigmatic in *Conduct Unbecoming* and, in a different way, in *Images*; and she responds convincingly to the physical rigours of *The Seventh Dawn* and *The Sands of the Kalahari*. The range of the achievement is impressive.

You were less than twenty when you suddenly appeared in your first leading role in a film, with Alec Guinness in *Tunes of Glory*. How did this come about?

I was just very lucky. I was at RADA and playing Nora in *A Doll's House* when a wonderful agent – Al Parker – saw me; and he thought I was the bee's knees. He was quite an old man by the time I met him, but he still personally managed Trevor Howard, James Mason and Hardy Kruger. They were his 'babies' and I was added. I wouldn't attribute that early success solely to having a good agent; it was luck which *got* me a very good agent. And you can have all the luck in the world without talent, so I have to think that I also had talent. I was also photogenic – I don't mean with a still camera, I was too mobile. Al always used to say, 'Susie, you got mental projection.' If the camera picks up on your thinking, on what's happening to you inside, that's what Al called 'mental projection'.

How knowledgeable were you about the camera?

Oh, not at all; I'd been trained at RADA specifically for the theatre and only that. Film or television wasn't really a consideration; you understood you'd pick that up as you went along, and, anyway, it wasn't *important*, it wasn't 'proper acting'. But about the camera, if you knock at the door and no one's at home, it shows less in the theatre, but the camera is more searching. There has always been a big deal made about the differences in acting for the camera and for the theatre but, for me, as an actress, there isn't that much difference. I think someone has to be at home all the time. I think a listenable-to voice is as important on film as it is in the theatre, though the level of projection has to vary.

I suppose I was fairly arrogant in one way, although I don't think I was vain, but I used to think that films were for pretty people and, since I was going to be an actress, that didn't concern me. I didn't take films very seriously at all. It used to upset me greatly when people would talk about the way I looked as opposed to the performances I had given – and that's what people generally did. So I didn't worry about what the cameraman was doing. What used to matter to me terribly, however, was the camera operator, because he was my audience in a way; that was my human presence and human warmth and I used to play to that.

Was it awe-inspiring suddenly being there with Alec Guinness and John Mills on *Tunes

of Glory, with Ronald Neame as the director?**

I felt blessed and lucky but I somehow thought that life was like that. I remember having come straight out of RADA and playing *Cinderella* with a little provincial repertory theatre, when I was called to London for a film test. Most unusually, the test was with Alec Guinness, because they usually have another actor standing in. All I was worried about was getting it done and getting back in time for my rehearsals for *Cinderella* at two o'clock, in Derby. It was only on the train coming back that I thought, 'That was Alec Guinness!' I had a couple of very good scenes with him, although most of my scenes were with John Fraser.

I hardly ever watch anything I've done but *Duffy* came up on television a few months ago and I watched it. I sat there saying, 'What's she doing . . .?' – 'she', you see, nothing to do with me – and writhing with embarrassment at this silly actress. Some months later I switched on accidentally to *Tunes of Glory* and thought, 'Oh yes, that's me.' I recognised me.

Do *Duffy* and *Kaleidoscope* seem to you absolutely products of their period and not to have lasted?

Yes, although I think *Kaleidoscope* was a rather good story which just didn't quite work. It was an amusing script but I never could quite get hold of the character. And Segolene even less, in *Duffy*. That was a disaster as far as I was concerned, I simply couldn't get hold of the character at all. She was supposed to be 'cool' and I hadn't a notion what 'cool' meant. It was an unstructured performance and it frightened me like anything. As you say, it was a film of its period but it was also one of the worst of its period.

You had a demanding role in *Freud – The Secret Passion*. What recollections do you have of the director John Huston, star Montgomery Clift, or the sad Larry Parks?

I thought it was sad Montgomery Clift, why sad Larry Parks? – oh, the McCarthy trials, yes. I didn't know much about Larry's past at the time, although, as I understand it now, he named other people at the McCarthy trial and that's what figures with me. I don't say 'sad Larry Parks', because I think I felt about him that he was someone who would name his friends. Thank God one didn't go through that time or who knows how one might have behaved, but you are very judgemental as a young person. I just didn't feel the kind of respect for him that I felt for Montgomery Clift.

Unfortunately, John Huston worked by the 'divide-and-rule' method. Shooting took six months and within weeks I knew that I simply had to take sides. So there was Susan Kohner and Larry Parks on one side, Montgomery Clift and me on another, and there was Huston, who had taken so against Monty and what he was doing. I knew Monty was drinking but I didn't know about his drug habit – I didn't know anything about drugs at all. Atrocious things were happening; the film was supposed to take three months but lasted six, and a lot of that was because scenes were constantly being rewritten. It was a most extraordinary time in my life. I used to work late at night with Monty because he needed a lot of support. I was very young and didn't really understand all that, but I thought it was wonderful to be working with someone I thought such a fantastic actor with an enormous eye for truth. He had such keenness but, of course, he was struggling with his health. I didn't understand just how much he was struggling. And of course John Huston was rewriting scenes and the prose was becoming increasingly 'purple'.

I think Marilyn Monroe was originally mooted for the part I played, but it came after *The Misfits* and she was out of favour with Huston. It went through various other casting ideas until John Huston came to me on the basis of *Greengage Summer*; I don't know why, because, though I loved it, I didn't think that was a totally successful film. I always felt that Dirk Bogarde was the person for the Kenneth More role. It needed someone with a touch of dark mystery and Dirk would have been perfect.

Would you agree that *Tom Jones* was the film which really established you as an international star?

I suppose so, yes. I'd actually turned it down three times because I really wanted to do some theatre. I had made up my mind to say no once and for all at a lunch I cooked for Tony Richardson, after three or four wooing lunches from him and Vanessa Redgrave. I did all the classic things – salt instead of sugar, burnt the meringues – and, in the midst of all my apologies, I accepted.

How much fun was the actual doing of it?

The locations were wonderful, of course – Dorset, London, Somerset. The country ones in particular were, with lovely summer days. I remember riding in the Dorset hills with Diane Cilento, or having caravan lunches with Albert Finney. There were wonderful memories and times but I don't know that it was such a happy film. Albie wasn't

always very happy. I don't think we knew – I certainly didn't – how good it was going to be. It was brilliantly edited, of course, and the music brought it together and synthesised it.

How did you find Tony Richardson as a director?

He was a bit like Huston in that he never really tried to direct you, he just left you out there. I think they had a lot in common, in that they *chose* wonderfully well. Tony chose wonderful actors, the cream of actors; a wonderful writer in Henry Fielding and the book was superbly adapted by John Osborne; the music; the costume designer Jocelyn Herbert – every element was superbly put together.

Do you like to receive a lot of direction or do you prefer to be allowed to get on with the job yourself?

I think directors generally cast people they like for the role and then give you support if you need it, if there's something you are afraid you can't do and you need courage to go ahead with it. I must say, John Huston did do that, as did Tony.

My favourite director of all time was Robert Altman, for whom I made *Images*. He is so generous and so brave; he will take all the responsibility, but at the same time he gives you all the encouragement you need. You just feel totally trusted and so you respond completely open-heartedly. When I first read the script I said I didn't know what this woman was and I was very reluctant to do the film because of this. He told me that is the way he writes, and that when he gets to know the actor he starts to draw from them. When he came to this Greek island where I was holidaying, to persuade me to do the part, he said, 'You don't just lie in the sun all day, do you?' and I said no, I was trying to write a children's book. So he said, 'Fine, then we'll make her a children's writer!' He asked to see some of the book so I showed him a few pages of the first draft, and he said, 'Right, yes. We'll use it.' I think most actors love to be demanded of, without being told necessarily what to do. Bob Altman is inventive, funny, bold, unjudgemental; he just lets you swim as far as you want, until you get out of line, then he draws you gently back.

You did a couple of exotic adventure films in the '60s: *The Seventh Dawn* for Lewis Gilbert and *The Sands of the Kalahari* for Cy Endfield. How physically demanding were these?

They probably were demanding. I think I'm quite

a physical person, so it never worried me being hot or having to walk a long way. I remember there was a storm scene which was pretty cold and wet in *The Sands of the Kalahari*, which we actually filmed on the edge of the Kalahari desert in south-west Africa. We'd dry off and then go out to get cold and wet again for another shot. *The Seventh Dawn* was filmed in Malaysia. I didn't get very involved with any of the cast – William Holden, Capucine – on that film, didn't really get to know any of them, except Tetsura Tamba, the Japanese actor, who was huge fun.

You were immensely busy all through the '60s. Did it seem like a good time for a young actress to be establishing a career?

Oh yes, it was. I never really had to worry about where my next part was coming from. I just seemed to keep falling on my feet and being very lucky. There were one or two things I would have liked to have done that didn't come my way. I was offered two or three contracts, but I think the time of the studios and production companies had just about gone by. It pretty much depended on you liking what you were next offered.

A Man for All Seasons **was a major prestigious success. Fred Zinnemann has a reputation for being immensely painstaking. Was this your experience of him?**

Yes, he was enormously particular and in a quite different way from Tony Richardson, who had to have the very best in everything – the best locations, the best costumier – but in another way was quite slapdash, because once he'd got all these elements together he would sort of throw them up in the air to see how they'd land. Fred chose the best too, but was always working out how everything would land and planning everything in the most careful manner. I admired him immensely, but found working with him as an actor rather difficult. I was so aware of what he wanted that somehow it stopped me from doing all *I* wanted. I'd liked to have felt freer. On the other hand, I'm not sure that that's what was required – and in any case he always drew wonderful work from his actors. He's a splendid man. And I absolutely adored Wendy Hiller, who has become a good friend of mine. She's a wonderful woman and actress and she was extraordinarily moving in that part [Sir Thomas More's wife]. She is highly intelligent and sensitive, yet she created a quite stupid though totally sensate character.

What was Orson Welles like to work with at that stage?

I didn't have any scenes with him. Robert Shaw, though, was huge fun to work with. He had such panache, such gaiety and such outrageous charm – he was a glorious Henry. A totally golden, charismatic actor.

Where was it shot?

I can't remember exactly where we did the riverside filming but it was on the Thames. It was mostly shot on location. I like studio work but I also love working on location. I've had very happy days at both Pinewood and Shepperton, and I have lovely memories of Pinewood being so sunlit, and of lunches there on my first film, *Tunes of Glory*, particularly with James Kennaway, who'd written it.

What did you think of Britain's capacity for building up stars? Were you conscious of the notion of 'the film star'?

Yes, I was conscious of it but I was also rather trying to knock down that image all the time. I hated that appellation, I was an actor. I did not want to have an image, be seen as the blue-eyed, golden-haired *ingénue*. Being a 'star' seemed to lock you into an image and I was always frightened of that because I knew I would disappoint people. I knew I wasn't going to be like that and I didn't want them to get the wrong end of the stick early on. So I was always trying to do different things like *Freud* or *Greengage Summer* or *Tom Jones*. I went on to do such films as *The Killing of Sister George* and *They Shoot Horses, Don't They?* because I didn't want to be branded. It has its disadvantages, of course, because in a way people like to be able to identify actors in a particular kind of role, and it's as if they 'own' you in some way. But I don't want to be owned. I suppose that has given me the reputation of being rebellious sometimes.

The Killing of Sister George **was a scandalous success at the time. Did you feel you were taking a great risk playing that part?**

I suppose I did, yes. I must say I thought quite a lot about whether or not I should do it. I had seen the play on its first night in Bath, before it came to the West End, and the play had not really resolved itself at that point. And of course I was very nervous about being seen naked. It was the thought of having to partially undress that worried me much more than playing a lesbian, though other people worried about that aspect on my behalf. I always thought the play was about a marriage in its death pangs, which might have been resuscitable except for the advent of Mercy Hastings.

Played by the devastating Coral Browne, who always seemed to me larger than life ...

Yes, she was. Actually, Beryl Reid was *plumper* than life, and Coral was *taller* than life, and being with them was very funny. They were chalk and cheese but they both rather liked me so I was kind of the jam in the sandwich. I got on well with each individually, but they loathed each other. Robert Aldrich was a wonderful and very generous director. He was hugely endearing, bigger than life, much bigger, himself. A bit like his films.

What do you remember of working in those big all-star films, *Battle of Britain* and *Oh! What a Lovely War*?

They were very flash-in-the-pan for me. For *Oh! What a Lovely War* I did one day's work with Dirk Bogarde and we just enjoyed our day. I did it because I wanted to work with Dirk again; I'd enjoyed doing *Sebastian* with him a few years earlier. *The Battle of Britain* was written by my friend James Kennaway, who had also written *Tunes of Glory* and *Country Dance*, so I wanted to do it for that reason.

You had a very diverse mixture of roles in the '70s and '80s: the *Superman* films, the stage adaptations *Conduct Unbecoming* and *The Maids*, the Australian adventure *Eliza Fraser*, and the bizarre version of Robert Graves's *The Shout*.

I don't know that I was always happy with the finished results but I've never done anything that I haven't got something out of. *The Shout* is a very strange piece of work and I don't think I can explain it. It is visually arresting but I certainly wasn't always very clear about what I was doing. I read the Robert Graves original but I can't remember much about it other than it is a very good short story and very evocative.

The *Superman* films were just a lot of fun. One didn't take them very seriously. The draw as far as I was concerned was Marlon Brando, and the people were all very enjoyable to work with. There's not a lot I can say about what went into the performance. I suppose it's good to be seen in a film that is going to be very popular and it's quite flattering to be chosen as the mother of Superman! The special effects were fabulous and you were very aware of all that going on – tramping over polystyrene and so on.

Are there one or two films you think of as highlights in your career?

If you mean 'best', I can't say what is best, but a highlight for me personally in the sense of what I got out of it and how much I enjoyed it would be *Country Dance* with Peter O'Toole. I learned such a lot from so many of the films I did, but I suppose *The Killing of Sister George* and *Images* are favourites.

Frederick A [Freddie] Young

b. 1902

Director of photography: *The Flag Lieutenant (1926), The Somme (documentary) (1927), *Victory (1928), *The 'W' Plan, On Approval, Canaries Sometimes Sing (1930), The Speckled Band, The Chance of a Night Time, *Almost a Divorce, Up for the Cup, Plunder, *Carnival, Tons of Money, Mischief (1931), The Blue Danube, Goodnight Vienna, A Night Like This, The Mayor's Nest, Thark, The Love Contract, Leap Year, It's a King (1932), Just My Luck, The King's Cup, Yes Mr Brown, The Little Damozel, Up for the Derby, Night of the Garter, Summer Lightning, Bitter Sweet, That's a*

Good Girl, Trouble (1933), The Queen's Affair, Girls Please!, Nell Gwyn, The King of Paris (1934), Peg of Old Drury, Escape Me Never (1935), When Knights Were Bold, Two's Company, The Three Maxims (1936), Victoria the Great, The Rat, Sunset in Vienna (1937), Sixty Glorious Years (1938), Goodbye Mr Chips, Nurse Edith Cavell (1939), Contraband, Busman's Honeymoon (1940), 49th Parallel, They Flew Alone, Young Mr Pitt (1941), *Caesar and Cleopatra (& 2nd-unit dir) (1945), Bedelia (1946), So Well Remembered, While I Live (1947), Edward My Son, Escape, The Winslow Boy (1948), Conspirator (1949), Treasure Island (1950), Calling Bulldog Drummond (1951), Ivanhoe, Time Bomb (1952), The Knights of the Round Table, *Mogambo (1953), Betrayed, Invitation to the Dance (1954), Beyond Mombasa, Bedevilled (1955), Bhowani Junction, *Lust for Life, The Barretts of Wimpole Street (1956), I Accuse!, Island in the Sun, The Little Hut (1957), Indiscreet, Inn of the Sixth Happiness, Gideon's Day (1958), Solomon and Sheba, The Wreck of the Mary Deare (1959), Macbeth, Hand in Hand (1961), Lawrence of Arabia (1962), Lord Jim (1964), Doctor Zhivago (1965), The Deadly Affair (1966), You Only Live Twice (1967), Sinful Davy (1968), Battle of Britain (1969), Ryan's Daughter (1970), Nicholas and Alexandra (1971), The Asphyx, Luther (1973), The Tamarind Seed (1974), Permission to Kill (1975), The Blue Bird (1976), Stevie (1978), Blood Line (1979), Richard's Things, Rough Cut (1980), Invitation to the Wedding, Sword of the Valiant – The Legend of Gawain and the Green Knight (1983), Arthur's Hallowed Ground (dir – for TV, some cinema screenings) (1984)
* Shared credit.

Freddie Young, one of the most distinguished cameramen ever, began as a lab assistant at Shepherd's Bush studios in 1917. He directed a film called *Arthur's Hallowed Ground*, for David Puttnam's 'First Love' series on Channel 4, in 1984. It is therefore at least arguable that he has had the longest career of anyone working in British cinema. The range of work is extraordinary too: in the '30s, he was trying to make Tom Walls's stiffly theatrical film versions of Aldwych farces a little more cinematically fluid; he worked for all the big names in British cinema, including Reed, Powell, Asquith and most notably Lean, for whose *Lawrence of Arabia*, *Dr Zhivago* and *Ryan's Daughter* he won Oscars, as well as nominations for *Ivanhoe* and *Nicholas and Alexandra*; he did his best to salvage *Caesar and Cleopatra*, worked with major visiting American directors (Cukor, Minnelli, Mankiewicz and Ford) and was indeed under contract to MGM-British for many years, prior to which he had been contracted to Herbert Wilcox. In all sorts of ways, his career offers a microcosmic history of British cinema.
Interview date: September 1992

Starting in 1917, you must have had one of the longest careers in the history of British cinema. Were you with Gaumont then throughout the '20s?

Yes, but I wasn't under contract; you were paid by the week. I was there from 1917 to '27, and at the end of ten years a director named MA Weatherell came to me and said, 'Freddie, I'd like you to photograph my next picture.'

Was that *Victory*?

That was *Victory*, yes. So I gave a week's notice to the boss, Colonel Bromhead, and I remember he said, 'Freddie, you're a young fool because this is the biggest studio in England and you'll be crawling back for another job here.' I said, 'No, it's time I made a break, and, you know, I've been offered £20 a week,' which floored him. So I did this film *Victory*, which is about the battle of Somme and which we made on the Salisbury Plain.

A little later, Herbert Wilcox offered me a contract at Elstree, and I stayed with him for ten years. In those days, we used to do a film every six weeks. There were no unions, we worked long hours, but I enjoyed it. I was very enthusiastic in those days, didn't mind how long I worked, and at the end of ten years my contract needed renewing and Herbert said, 'Freddie, we're going to Hollywood next.' I said, 'They won't let me work in Hollywood,' and he said, 'Oh yes they will, I've got a contract with the RKO studios and there won't be any trouble at all.' So I went off with Herbert and Anna Neagle to Hollywood to do *Nurse Edith Cavell*. Of course, when we got there they said, 'Oh no, you can't work here,' and there was endless trouble about getting me a work visa. Finally I started working at RKO, and we shot *Nurse Cavell* in about six weeks, I suppose.

By then the war was imminent, and I said to Herbert, 'I want to go back to England quickly,' so he said, 'No, Fred, don't be a fool, you go down to Malibu and have a nice holiday and we'll be doing another film shortly.' But I refused and I went back on the *Normandie*, which was practically empty. There was no one going back to England in those days; they were all coming out. I was told I was too old for the Army – I was nearly forty, I suppose; so instead I went to Canada and shot *49th Parallel*. We were in Canada for four months.

How did you feel about working with Michael Powell on this and *Contraband*?

I found him all right, but he was a bit of a taskmaster. He prided himself on his physique, you know. I remember in Canada on *49th Parallel*, we had to do a shot on Baffin Island, which was a rocky island where nobody but Eskimos lived. We had to do a shot on the rocks of the submarine down below where the aeroplanes bomb it and sink it. We went up these rocks carrying heavy cameras and equipment. Mickey Powell had on mountain boots with spikes, and he went bounding ahead, and every time we got up to where he was he'd disappear and he'd gone up another height, so by this time we were worn out when we got to a certain height. Finally, I'd say, 'Look, Mick, you come down here. This is high enough.' So we stared at each other for a long time and he finally came down and we shot it from where I wanted to. This is what happens sometimes: directors get so enthusiastic about something but it all depends on which lens you use, not on how high you are.

I thought it was a very good film. It was really a propaganda film designed to bring America into the war to show them how they could be attacked through Hudson Bay. The next thing was a film with Carol Reed, at the old Gaumont studio, which is now rebuilt.

Was this *Young Mr Pitt*?

Yes. Then after that came Thorold Dickinson, who had made a propaganda film called *Next of Kin*, which was very well liked, and he asked me to go in with him as chief cameraman, with the rank of Captain. Thorold went in as a Major and the cameraman was a Sergeant and the operator was a Corporal, the focus-puller was a Lance-Corporal. I was three years making these training films. I had a year at a place where they made films to show the Army how to use new tactics for fighting the Germans, called the School of Infantry, at Barnard Castle in County Durham. We worked long days on the moors with tanks and machine-guns and Bren guns.

Eventually I was invalided out of the Army because I'd got very ill, and I'd no sooner been out of the Army than MGM signed me up and I was with them for the next fifteen years. In 1937, Herbert Wilcox had lent me to them for *Goodbye Mr Chips* with Robert Donat, which was a big success.

I thought *Caesar and Cleopatra* was your first post-war film.

That's right. I think I must have been lent by MGM to do it. That was with Gabriel Pascal. He was a real fraud, you know, who didn't know anything about film directing. The film had been started by Bobby Krasker, who fell ill after he'd been on it for about three weeks, and asked me to take over. I'd just come out the Army, as I told you, and we were working at the old Denham Studios with Vivien Leigh and Claude Rains, and so on. I remember Claude Rains saying to me, 'Freddie, I'm in a very difficult position, you know; I'm here on a tax-free basis, and I've got to be out in twelve weeks. Please do your damnedest to get me out by then.' So I got him out with one day to spare. He sent me a gold Dunhill lighter from New York as a gesture of thanks.

Anyway, at the end of shooting, having to tell Gabby what to do all the time, because he didn't know what film direction was about at all, I then had to go to Egypt and do the second unit. He insisted on having a second unit in Egypt. So I went out, though of course the war was still on, and I had about one thousand Egyptian troops dressed up as Roman soldiers. I was directing because they wouldn't allow Gabby out, because he was an enemy alien, so I had to direct all the second-unit stuff. One day, I had a telegram from Tom White, who was a production manager, to say, 'I'm awfully sorry, Freddie, but Gabby's got leave to go out for twenty-four hours.'

A few days later I was on the top of a mound in the desert directing a scene where a lot of untrained young Egyptian soldiers had to gallop round on horseback dressed as Romans. I suddenly saw an entourage arriving across the desert on white horses and one of them, of course, was Gabby, in a red fez, a white suit and sandals, and with a gold-topped cane. He came striding up this little hill to me. I knew it was going to be trouble. Gabby said, 'What are those men doing there?' I explained to him what was going on, and he said, 'This is no good, Freddie.' I said, 'Look, Gabby, if you want to take over . . .' and I handed him the microphone, but he said, 'No no no, Freddie.' In the next shot some of these chaps came galloping around and fell off their horses, and Gabby said, 'You are a lot of Jews, bloody awful Jews. I am an officer in the Hungarian Hussars,' and a whistle blew and I said, 'Now you've done it, Gabby, you ruined the whole thing.'

You mean that, among all his other problems, Pascal was an anti-Semite as well?

Yes. He was such a show-off, you know; it was probably a lot of lies about being a Hungarian officer. I got on a jeep and dashed off after the column, and I got to the head of the column, where a Captain Zacky was leading them. I pleaded with them and finally they let me into the Officers' Mess, where I said, 'You can't do this. J Arthur Rank's put £1 million into this film and you just can't do this.' So I was told that if I got rid of Gabby they would continue. I reported this to Gabby, who was going anyway, and after he went we carried on. Gabby was indefatigable, but he was finished in England because of *Caesar and Cleopatra.*

You must have noticed a difference when you came to work for a batch of American directors in the 1940s: Edward Dmytryk, George Cukor, Joseph Mankiewicz. What do you remember of any of those?

Oh yes, they were very efficient. I've great memories of them. I remember working for Joseph Mankiewicz on *Escape*, with Rex Harrison. He was a nice chap, Mankiewicz. I worked with a lot of the best-known Hollywood directors and all the actors

like Clark Gable and Cary Grant and Spencer Tracy. They all came over and I made films with them. One of the films I did with Spencer Tracy was *Edward My Son*, which I thought was very good. George Cukor directed that. We were doing long takes in those days, a thousand feet in one take, on a crane where it moved around the whole sequence. Bits of set had to slide away for the crane to go through and all that sort of thing. George would shoot everything ten times whether or not he was satisfied.

How much advice would you give on matters of, say, camera distance, or angle or movement?

Some directors don't know anything about the camera at all; some always want to look through the camera, and some never look through the camera at all. They just talk to the actors.

Who are some that don't care about the camera?

George Cukor never looked through the camera, neither did John Ford. But David Lean always wanted to look through the camera, and in a way that's fine because they're very interested in that side of it. On the other hand, as a general rule, it's the cameraman who decides where the camera's going to be and which lens you're going to use and so on – that's the general rule. It varies with different directors. The cameraman has to get on with every director he works with.

What do you remember about working with Vincente Minnelli on *Lust for Life*?

It was a very enjoyable experience because we went to all the places where Van Gogh painted. We shot in Belgium, France, Holland, all the actual places that he worked at. We reconstructed all the paintings as exactly as we could. It was very difficult but very enjoyable. I'm a painter myself and I really enjoyed getting into these paintings, getting the photography to look exactly like the paintings.

Minnelli always seemed to me very much a visual director.

Minnelli was a very interesting director, but all directors, as I've said before, have their idiosyncrasies and their pet foibles. I'll tell you a particular instance. We were doing a shot with Kirk Douglas as Van Gogh sitting in the foreground painting this scene of the wheat field with the crows flying around his head. Well, MGM bought this wheat field from the farmer and the wheat was just about ready to cut, so they had to buy the whole field and then with the bulldozer we ploughed a road through the wheat field just like it was in the painting. And there was to be a big cherry tree, in the foreground. They got this cherry tree, which must have weighed two or three tons. So they had to dig a big hole, and with a crane they lowered this enormous tree into it, then they put the earth around the roots and stamped it down, and they put piano wire from the branches, and tied it off in every direction. We set it up and it was right by the painting.

So Vincente got to the camera and he said, 'Oh no, no good, we've got to move the cherry tree three feet to the left.' I said, 'Vincente, that's completely absurd. All we've got to do is to move the camera a couple of inches to the right and it's the same thing.' 'No no no, it's got to be moved.' So I said, 'Well, it's a very difficult thing, you won't get the shot today.' He insisted on it anyway. So they dug the tree up again and broke a lot of the branches. That's what I mean when I say a director should keep his nose out of the cameraman's field. The cameraman knows much more than he does about composition and what the lenses are doing and so on. George Cukor would not have done that because he wouldn't have looked through the camera. But I had a lot of fun on that film. Years later, after Vincente had died, Liza Minnelli told me that *Lust for Life* was her father's favourite film.

You had a very famous Oscar-winning association with David Lean. Did those vast, spectacular films – *Lawrence, Dr Zhivago, Ryan's Daughter* – pose particular problems?

David Lean used to edit some of my early films with Herbert Wilcox, so I knew him as an editor, and then, because I'd been under contract for fifteen years with MGM, I never worked with him again. Finally, when I left MGM in 1959, I thought, Oh my God, for the first time in my life I'm out of work. One day Sam Spiegel rang me up and said, 'David Lean would like you to photograph *Lawrence of Arabia*.' So I said, 'OK, it's on.' I went out to Jordan and met David; he'd been doing a recce out there, and I joined him by car and horseback over all the locations he'd seen. Then he said he wanted to do it in 70mm, so when I left him I had to go to Hollywood to get a 70mm Cannon lens and all the equipment. When I was leaving, David said, 'Freddie, one thing I'd like to get is a mirage, I don't know how the hell we'll do it, but I want you to think about it.'

So I went off to Hollywood, to Panavision, and met Robert Gottschalk, who was the boss there. He invented the Panavision camera. I was going through all the camera equipment, choosing the lenses and dollies and so on, when, one day, on a bench I saw a long lens, and I said, 'What lens is that, Bob?' and he said . . . I think it was 430 long-focus . . . I said, 'Well, put that in my equipment.' I suddenly had an idea the way to get a mirage effectively is to do it with a long-focus lens, because a mirage is always a long way away from you, and by putting a long-focus lens on you got a close-up of it. So when I got back to start the film in Jordan, I said to David, 'I've got the lens to do the mirage scene. It's a long-focus lens so it will get you a close-up.' He was very intrigued and, when we got to the mirage sequence, we put this lens on and we sent Omar Sharif a long way away in the desert until he was an absolute pin-point. Then David said to him, 'Just ride straight towards the camera.' In the foreground, we had Peter O'Toole and an Arab [played by Zia Mohyeddin] and they were by this well, and, while they were pulling up some water on a long rope from the well, they suddenly became aware of this little dot coming towards them, coming right through this mirage. They were fascinated watching it, because it sort of comes right through waves of water and peculiar streaks, and the Arab got very nervous because he knew he'd been drinking water out of a well that didn't belong to his tribe, and they're not allowed to do that. So as he got closer you saw . . . and you began to *hear* the footsteps of the camel, thump, thump, thump, thump, on the sand. It became very, very fascinating from the way David cut it, and he was a very good editor, remember, he kept cutting backwards and forwards to this image coming towards you through the mirage, with Peter O'Toole and the Arab in the foreground, and the menace got stronger and stronger and stronger, very dramatic. Eventually the Arab loses his nerve and rushes to his camel to get the revolver which Lawrence had given him the day before, and, as he took the revolver from the holster of the camel, Omar Sharif shot him with a rifle and killed him. In the end this sequence fascinated everybody who saw it, because they'd never seen a mirage in colour, photographed with a long-focus lens on 70mm film. It was a very, very exciting shot and one of the things I suppose I got an Oscar for.

I understand from some actors that David Lean liked to do things over and over again.

No, no, absolutely wrong! David's shots were very economical once he started shooting because he only shot what he wanted to use in the film. He was unlike Americans in the early MGM days, they always wanted what they call coverage – every sort of shot, long shot, medium shot, close shot, over the shoulders, big heads and all different angles, so that when they edited it they could cut it around whatever way they wanted. John Ford was like Lean; he shot very economically and he only printed a shot that he wanted so that there was no room for anybody to mess about with the film afterwards. They would rehearse and then they would shoot; they wouldn't keep going over and over and over again. Once you've done Take 1 and got through it all right, it's usually the best take, because everybody is fresh. Usually we got the scene in one or two, or three takes at the most.

And the long periods that it took Lean to make his films presumably were partly because they were shot all over the world?

That's right. But I've tried to explain to people, if you've got two hundred and fifty Bedouins on camels, they don't speak English, and they've only come to do the film because King Hussein asked them to come as a favour to him, it can get complex. Just compare shooting a film like *Lawrence* to shooting a scene in the studio with a couple of trained actors; *then*, you could do ten minutes a day comfortably. What the public don't understand is why David Lean would take so long to do a film like *Zhivago*: we shot most of it in Spain, and we had to have snow scenes and summer scenes and autumn scenes and all that had to be arranged.

Was it all fake, the snow for instance?

We shot that house in the snow at a place called Soria and it was about four hours north of Madrid by car and it was reputed to be the coldest place in Spain. When we went there to do it, it had been snowing but you could still see the furrows in the field. So there happened to be a marble factory nearby and we got hundreds of tonnes of marble dust, like you'd have sawdust from a carpenters' mill, and we covered acres of field with marble dust on top of the snow. We covered bushes and we sprayed trees white with white paint and covered bushes with white tarpaulins, so you could see vast distances of nothing but white snow. Then in the autumn we always carried around lorry loads of autumn leaves and when we did an autumn scene we'd blow the autumn leaves around with wind machines. All these things . . . it's slightly different from doing a scene in a television studio with actors!

It's a long way from, say, *Edward My Son* to waiting twelve months on the Irish coast for *Ryan's Daughter*.

That storm sequence we did was a real storm, and it took months to do that. We used to have to do a two-hour journey by car to get to that bit of coast. It was the nearest point to America, where storms come straight across the Atlantic. We'd have a warning the night before there was going to be a storm and we'd dash off and, when we'd get there, we'd set up the cameras. We had to chain the cameras to the rocks because of the wind. It was quite dangerous but nevertheless the storm would rage perhaps for two hours and then quieten off and disappear. So then we'd have to go off, get on with some other part of the film and wait for the next storm warning, and that went on for months.

I guess you've worked at all the British studios. Do some seem to you to be better for working at than others?

Oh yes. MGM was a fine studio. It was built and never used; then, during the war, they stacked sugar in it, I think, and after the war MGM bought it, spent £1 million raising the roof another fifteen feet and putting in air conditioning and so on. But MGM never used it to its full advantage.

Afterword
British Cinema into the Second Century

It is possible to discern in the *types* of films now being made in Britain, if not in the production circumstances – ie, the studio system – from which they emerge, some parallels with the booming situation of fifty years ago. That point of prestige, perhaps the highest ever enjoyed by British cinema, derived largely from two (sometimes interwoven) strands of filmmaking: the literary adaptation and socially responsible realism. Certainly in hindsight, the governing creative impulses seem to have been towards the literature-based respectability of, say, *Henry V*, *Great Expectations* and *The Fallen Idol*, and the realist observation of people, place and period in such films as *It Always Rains on Sunday* and *The Blue Lamp*, the two impulses conjoined, as it were, in *Brighton Rock* or *The Third Man*. To one side of these influential trends lay the Powell and Pressburger enterprise, whose output was more idiosyncratic, romantic and painterly, and there was of course a prolific vein of popular genre filmmaking as well, from studios like Gainsborough and Hammer.

Fifty years on, filmmakers are no longer supported and/or constricted by a studio system: there are no contemporary equivalents for Rank, ABPC, Korda or Ealing, and Goldcrest has famously come and gone. Further, audiences have become much smaller and more capricious. However, it can be argued that something of the production patterns sketched in the paragraph above is once again visible. The dictates of social realism clearly shape the work of Mike Leigh (whose latest, *Secrets and Lies*, has won the Palme d'Or at the 1996 Cannes Film Festival), Jim Sheridan (*In the Name of the Father*, 1993), Antonia Bird (*Priest*, 1995), Angela Pope (*Hollow Reed*, 1996), and – filming more frequently than before – Ken Loach. The literary strand has been taken up by, above all, Kenneth Branagh, whose 'great desire' in filming *Henry V* in 1989 'was to make it look like a film of today, to take the curse of medievalism off it, so that the *Batman* audiences could conceivably be persuaded to see it.'[1] His all-star *Hamlet* was released in early 1997. As well as being a major interpreter of

literary texts, he also has the panache of a genuine entrepreneur, which may be just what British cinema needs. There are other diectors new to film with an interest in the filming of literary works: for example, Nicholas Hytner (*The Madness of King George*, 1995), Philip Haas (*Angels and Insects*, 1996), Christopher Hampton (*Carrington*, 1995; *The Secret Agent*, 1996), Michael Winterbottom (*Jude*, 1996, though his earlier success, *Butterfly Kiss*, 1995, owes nothing to the literary tradition), Iain Softley (*Wings of the Dove*, 1997) and Trevor Nunn (*Twelfth Night*, 1996) and writer-actor Emma Thompson won an Oscar for her screenplay for *Sense and Sensibility* (1996). The Merchant–Ivory team can scarcely be thought of as British, but their oeuvre has often been derived from English literature and set in an endlessly picturesque England of the past. Following the success of the Jane Austen craze, we may well be due for a sustained onslaught on the 'great tradition'.

The more maverick talents, who, in some respects, recall Powell and Pressburger, include Terence Davies, Sally Potter (whose most famous film, *Orlando*, is of course a daring adaptation of Virginia Woolf's novel) and Peter Greenaway, all of whom have found considerable 'art-house' favour. Davies has claimed, 'Well, I don't feel part of a British tradition, because I don't think there is one. I think every once in a while we produce films *in spite of* our lack of film tradition, like Powell and Pressburger or the Ealing comedies or Nic Roeg's *Bad Timing*.'[2] Besotted with American movies as Davies is, it is ironic that his first American-set film, *The Neon Bible*, was much less well-received, as if his touch were less sure away from his home ground.

It is perhaps Mike Newell, director of one of the most commercially successful of all British films, *Four Weddings and a Funeral* (1994), who has his finger most firmly on the popular pulse. Rejecting comparisons with other contemporary British directors he says: 'Where it leaves you is that you are mainstream – which somehow gives you a guilty feeling. I suppose that's where I am at.'[3] Someone's got to be there if cinema is to remain popular, and Newell has shown himself adept at navigating its currents. His latest film, *Donnie Brasco*, was, however, made in America with Al Pacino and Johnny Depp as stars, and Newell is a director who once claimed, 'I'm not happy in America . . . I don't understand the town, as it were.'[4]

Of others working behind the camera, there are those who strike chords in attentive filmgoers without their actually being household names. Stephen Poliakoff, who divides his time among theatre, television and the screen, directed and wrote the striking melodrama, *Close My Eyes* (1992), which treated incest with unprurient passion. Scottish Danny Boyle's blackly comic *Shallow Grave* (1995) and the hugely popular critical success, *Trainspotting* (1996), suggest a director with a distinctive tone of voice and visual flair. Playwright David Hare directed and wrote the screen version of his enigmatic *Wetherby* (1985) and several other films which just failed to take off; and Anthony Minghella is the writer-director of *Truly, Madly, Deeply*, 1991, and of the much-praised, American-made *The English Patient*, 1997. David Jones (*Betrayal*, 1984; 84 *Charing Cross Road*, 1987), Tim Sullivan (*Jack and Sarah*, 1995), Beeban Kidron (*Antonia and Jane*, 1992), Hettie MacDonald (*Beautiful Thing*, 1996) and Nancy Meckler (*Sister My Sister*, 1995) have all made at least one attractive British film, among other work for television and/or in the US.

There are others, too, who have filmed sporadically in Britain – Mike Figgis, Stephen Frears, Terry Gilliam, Bill Forsyth, Michael Apted and Alan Parker – and senior figures, such as Richard Attenborough, John Schlesinger and Karel Reisz, from whom further British output is still a possibility. And directors are not all it takes to maintain a British cinema: imaginative producers, writers with a feeling as much for the cinema as for the distinctively national idiom, all those other collaborators whom this book celebrates, are, of course, crucial to the process. (British cinema is also about a lot of 'industry' matters outside the scope of this note.) One thinks here of writers such as Alan Bennett (*A Private Function*, 1984; *The Madness of King George*, 1995), Harold Pinter, who has adapted his own plays as well as writing brilliant scripts for Joseph Losey and others since the 1960s, and Richard Curtis, who scored a major success with his script for *Four Weddings and a Funeral*. And there are producers such as Simon Relph and Mark Shivas who appear dedicated to the proposition of a British cinema. Currently, there is an encouraging burst of independent filmmaking, backed by a whole range of finance sources, from the BBC and Channel Four to the French firm CiBy 2000.

In terms of financial prospects, one inevitably thinks of star names: Branagh, Thompson, Hugh Grant, Miranda Richardson, Tilda Swinton, Alan Rickman, Richard E Grant, Natasha Richardson, Kate Beckinsale, Imogen Stubbs, Saskia Reeves, Tim Roth, Linus Roache, Michael Maloney, Tara Fitzgerald, Ewan McGregor, Nicholas Farrell, Helena Bonham Carter, Kate Winslet and Kristin Scott Thomas. There are enough of these at various stages of stellar ascent to be going on with. Whether they will remain predominantly British stars is anyone's guess. Emma Thompson, to take a key example, has recently made *Primary Colors* in America, for director Mike Nichols with Jack Nicholson as her co-star. At the time of winning her Oscar for *Howard's End* (1992), she claimed that she didn't want to go to Hollywood: 'You don't need smarmy British people wandering in saying, "Employ us, too, please." I want to work on the stage and on television in my own country.'[5] If she still means that, and if she includes film in her plans, she is perhaps the surest bet for a female British screen star for the next decade. Miranda Richardson, another major contender, said in the same year, 'If Hollywood wants to seduce me, it will . . .'[6] With her appearances in Robert Altman's *Kansas City* (1996) and her co-starring role opposite Jack Nicholson in *The Evening Star*, the seduction seems to have taken place. Among the men, Hugh Grant, playing a 'series of repressed Englishmen,'[7] established himself as potentially the best romantic comedy lead in the English-speaking world in *Four Weddings*, but it doesn't seem very likely that British cinema could hold his obvious star quality for very long.

The problem with writing about British actors is that, as soon as they show convincing star potential, they are almost inevitably whisked off to Hollywood. Who, now, can confidently think of Anthony Hopkins, Daniel Day-Lewis or Jeremy Irons as stars of *British* cinema? As names, they have become too big to find a regular place in the British industry. Even John Cleese, who, on the strength of the Monty Python films and TV's *Fawlty Towers*, might have seemed invincibly British, has had what looks like a random career in British films. Since his triumphant success with *A Fish Called Wanda* (1988), he, like Irons or Hopkins, or like Alan

Rickman, is at least as likely to be making American as British films. Others, like Maggie Smith, Michael Gambon, Ian Holm and Helen Mirren are as often busy on stage or television as on the cinema screen – or making American films. Brilliant as she is, Mirren is surely, since the *Prime Suspect* television series, better known for her work on the small rather than the large screen. Perhaps there will never be again British film stars in the way that Dirk Bogarde and Margaret Lockwood once were.

As well as the stars who may sparkle briefly over Britain before the apparently inevitable transatlantic journey, there is that wonderful continuing strength of British character players, including Prunella Scales, Alun Armstrong, Fiona Shaw, Tom Wilkinson, Nigel Hawthorne, Imelda Staunton, Hugh Laurie, Richard Briers, Alison Steadman and Elizabeth Spriggs. Among such names are to be found the obvious successors to the imperishable likes of Dora Bryan, Maurice Denham and Thora Hird. Often with strong theatrical backgrounds or television successes to their credit, such actors have long constituted one of the incontrovertible pleasures of British films. Recently savouring Kenneth Griffiths, a fixture in British cinema since the 1940s, as an irascible guest in *Four Weddings and a Funeral* and Elizabeth Spriggs as the cheerfully vulgar Mrs Jennings in *Sense and Sensibility*, one realises happily that this tradition at least lingers on.

As we enter the second century of British cinema, if there is not exactly a thriving film industry here, there are at least films being made in Britain that are again among the most attractive and intelligent from anywhere in the world. A production centre which throws up such divergent entertainments as *Trainspotting*, *Sense and Sensibility*, *Secrets and Lies*, *Richard III*, *An Awfully Big Adventure* and *Priest* within a year may be in a state of crisis, as one is constantly being told, but it is hard to see this as terminal.

As this is an 'autobiography', let us conclude with extracts from my interview (February 1997) with director ANTHONY MINGHELLA whose film, *The English Patient*, has just won nine Oscars. Made all over the place, with American money and producer, with a British director and predominantly British cast, it raises the issue of what actually constitutes a British film – or filmmaker.

Do you look forward to working in England again or do you regard yourself as settled in America? Or is that no longer a relevant question to a filmmaker?

I'm not settled in America, I never have been. I've never lived in America except to work. My home is in London and I want to think of it in that way, although if you were to count up the days I've been in London in the '90s they wouldn't add up to very many. That's something I want to rectify if I can. I feel very excited about the fact that, at this particular point in history, Britain is full of marvellous actors, marvellous technicians and crews; there are more cinematographers than you can count. You can cast a film in Britain now which can speak to the entire world and that's certainly been the case with *The English Patient* which, as you said, is populated by some really gifted British actors who also are beginning to have international as well as national appeal.

Who do you think are some of the major prospects for the continuity of British cinema who are around now? What sort of names would leap to your mind?

Well I think that the Danny Boyle-Andrew McDonald team [of *Trainspotting* fame] is a very significant force. I think that Ken Branagh enjoys a less good press in Britain than he deserves. His energy and his belief are two things which are not cherished in Britain and they ought to be. I think his ambition – and his achievement – has been one of the prime inspiring factors for a lot of British filmmakers in the last few years and I have enormous regard for what he is trying to do and for his images. I think he will play a great part in what happens in the film industry in the next ten or twenty years. I think that Emma Thompson is a remarkable force too – she has a personal modesty and a professional ambition which I think are also inspiring. I'm also happy that Mike Leigh is now getting such recognition because, for me as a young writer, he was a great inspiration and a source of joy. I think it's also important to take note of companies like Working Title in Britain who have done a great deal to give opportunities to British filmmakers and to insist that British filmmaking be taken seriously – as far as I'm concerned I think that in Ralph Fiennes and Daniel Day-Lewis and Liam Neeson, you have three of the best actors in the world.

How long can they be thought of as British actors?

Well, I think what you'll find, as far as Ralph is concerned, is that he constantly punctuates his film work with theatre work. He is as attached to his career in the theatre as he is to his career ininternational cinema. You're right to say that the boundaries are rather irrelevant to the moment, although having said that, I wouldn't be at all surprised to see a lot of British filmmakers making films in Britain. There is no reason why the British film industry now can't become a force to be reckoned with. It uses the same language as American film and that means that there is no natural impediment to its speaking to the entire world. For a time, in the '70s and '80s, the only way you could get material in front of a film camera was to write for television, which is what happened to me. For me, the journey has been one of trying to find a way of opening my shoulders as a filmmaker and to do that I had to go to an American producer and get American financing. I think there is every opportunity now for that and I think you can look at Branagh's films and see how he's done the same. I think that all of us can bring that information and experience back to the British Isles and make films of a reasonable scale in Britain, and I mean really interesting cinema too.

All these Oscar nominations are going to bring you and this film into enormous prominence. That surely might have a valuable flow-on?

Oh, I think so. The film doesn't get any better because it's got twelve Oscar nominations, but it is manifest that what directors need to attract money is some power and this film will give me a little bit more power than I had before to preserve and insist on my own voice – good or bad. Any predictions I might make about British cinema are just meditations on what might happen – except to say that, at the moment, I think the well is very full with talent.

1 'Two Kings', *Film Comment*, November–December 1989, p 6
2 Harlan Kennedy, 'Familiar Haunts: Terence Davies' *Distant Voices, Still Lives*', *Film Comment*, September–October 1988, p 17
3 *Films and Filming*, February 1989, p 26
4 'Oriental Strangers: Mike Newell in Conversation with Adrian Sibley', *Films and Filming*, February 1989, p 26
5 Rachel Abramowitz, 'The Americanization of Emma', *Premiere*, April 1992, p 110
6 Mark Salisbury, 'Miranda Richardson: The Best-Kept Secret in the Movies', *Empire*, November 1992, p 56
7 Cyndi Stivers, 'Hugh Romance', *Premiere*, May 1994, p 78

Suggestions for Further Reading

Armes, Roy. *A Critical History of British Cinema*, London, Secker & Warburg, 1978

Barr, Charles. *All Our Yesterdays: 90 Years of British Cinema*, London, BFI Publishing, 1986

Ealing Studios (new revised edition), London, Studio Vista, 1993

Curran, James and Porter, Vincent (eds). *British Film History*, London, Weidenfeld & Nicolson, 1983

Dixon, Wheeler Winston (ed). *Re-Viewing British Cinema 1900–1992*, Albany, State University of New York Press, 1994

Durgnat, Raymond. *A Mirror for England: British Movies from Austerity to Affluence*, London, Faber and Faber, 1970

Eberts, Jake & Ilott, Terry. *My Indecision is Final: The Rise and Fall of Goldcrest Films*, London, Faber and Faber, 1990

Harper, Sue. *Picturing the Past: The Rise and Fall of the British Costume Film*, London, BFI Publishing, 1994

Higson, Andrew. *Waving the Flag: Constructing a National Cinema in Britain*, Oxford, Clarendon Press, 1995

Landy, Marcia. *British Genres: Cinema and Society 1930–1960*, Princeton, Princeton University Press, 1991

Murphy, Robert. *Realism and Tinsel: Cinema and Society in Britain 1939–1948*, London, Routledge, 1989

Sixties British Cinema, London, BFI Publishing, 1992

Perry, George, *The Great British Picture Show*, London, Pavilion, 1985

Petrie, Duncan. *The British Cinematographers*, London, BFI Publishing, 1996

Richards, Jeffrey. *The Age of Innocence: Cinema and Society in Britain 1930–1939*, London, Routledge & Kegan Paul, 1984

Richards, Jeffrey and Aldgate, Anthony. *The Best of British: Cinema and Society 1930–1970*, Oxford, Basil Blackwell, 1983

Taylor, John Russell and Kobal, John. *Portraits of the British Cinema*, London, Aurum Press, 1985

Vermilye, Jerry. *The Great British Films*, Secaucus, NJ, Citadel, 1978

Walker, Alexander. *Hollywood, England: The British Film Industry in the Sixties*, London, Michael Joseph, 1974

National Heroes: British Cinema in the Seventies and Eighties, London, Harrap, 1985

Warren, Patricia. *The British Cinema in Pictures: The British Film Collection*, London, BT Batsford, 1993

Journals

The following is a list of the main journals and trade publications quoted from in the career sketches in the book. Exact references are given in the endnotes. Non-British journals are indicated.

The American Cinematographer (USA)
American Film (USA)
Cinema Papers (Australia)
The Cine-Technician
Classic Images (USA)
Empire
Film Comment (USA)
Film Dope
Film Quarterly (USA)
Film Weekly
Films
Films and Filming
Films Illustrated
Films in Review (USA)
Focus on Film
The Historical Journal of Film, Radio and Television Interview (USA)
Kinematograph Weekly
Monthly Film Bulletin
Penguin Film Review
Picturegoer

Picture Show

Premiere

Quarterly Review of Film Studies

Screen International

Sight and Sound

Stills

Take One (Canada)

Time Out

Variety (USA)

Title Changes

Britain	America
The Admiral Crichton	Paradise Lagoon
Albert R.N.	Break for Freedom
The Amorous Prawn	The Playgirl and the War Minister
Appointment with Venus	Island Rescue
Atlantic Ferry	Sons of the Sea
Background	Edge of Divorce
Bank Holiday	Three on a Weekend
Barnacle Bill	All at Sea
The Battle of the River Plate	Pursuit of the Graf Spee
Battle of the VI	Missiles from Hell
Beat Girl	Wild for Kicks
Before I Wake	Shadow of Fear
Beyond This Place	Web of Evidence/PO Box 303
Blind Date	Chance Meeting
Brighton Rock	Young Scarface
Britannia Mews	The Forbidden Street
Captain Clegg	Night Creatures
The Card	The Promoter
Carlton-Browne of the FO	Man in a Cocked Hat
Carrington VC	Court Martial
A Choice of Weapons	Trial by Combat
Cone of Silence	Trouble in the Sky
Confidential Report	Mr Arkadin
Conflict of Wings	Fuss Over Feathers
Contraband	Blackout
Cosh Boy	The Slasher
Cottage to Let	Bombsight Stolen
Country Dance	Brotherly Love
The Courtneys of Curzon Street	The Courtney Affair
Danger Within	Breakout
The Dark Avenger	The Warriors
The Day Will Dawn	The Avengers
Dear Octopus	The Randolph Family
The Demi-Paradise	Adventure for Two
Derby Day	Four Against Fate
The Devil Rides Out	The Devil's Bride
The Drum	Drums

Britain	America
The Elusive Pimpernel	The Fighting Pimpernel
English Without Tears	Her Man Gilbey
Family Life	Wednesday's Child
Fanny by Gaslight	Man of Evil
Father Brown	The Detective
The First of the Few	Spitfire
The Flesh and the Fiends	Mania
The Foreman Went to France	Somewhere in France
Fortune is a Woman	She Played with Fire
49th Parallel	The Invaders
Freedom Radio	A Voice in the Night
Gaiety George	Showtime
Gaslight	Angel Street
Geordie	Wee Geordie
Gideon's Day	Gideon of Scotland Yard
The Gift Horse	Glory at Sea
Girl in the Headlines	The Model Murder Case
Gone to Earth	The Wild Heart
Grand National Night	Wicked Wife
The Guinea Pig	The Outsider
Happy Ever After	Tonight's the Night
The Happy Family	Mr Lord Says No
Her Favourite Husband	The Taming of Dorothy
The High Bright Sun	McGuire Go Home
Highly Dangerous	Time Running Out
Hot Enough for June	Agent 8 3/4
House of Secrets	Triple Deception
Hunted	The Stranger in Between
I Live in Grosvenor Square	A Yank in London
I See a Dark Stranger	The Adventuress
Ice Cold in Alex	Desert Attack
I'll Get You for This	Lucky Nick Cain
Ill Met by Moonlight	Night Ambush
Isadora	The Loves of Isadora

Original	Changed
The Kidnappers	The Little Kidnappers
Knave of Hearts	Lover Boy
Lady Godiva Rides Again	Beauty Queen
The Last Days of Dolwyn	Woman of Dolwyn
The Late Edwina Black	Obsessed
Latin Quarter	Frenzy
Laxdale Hall	Scotch on the Rocks
Life for Ruth	Walk in the Shadow
Light up the Sky	Skywatch
Lilacs in the Spring	Let's Make Up
London Belongs to Me	Dulcimer Street
London Town	My Heart Goes Crazy
The Long, the Short and the Tall	Jungle Fighters
Love Story	A Lady Surrenders
The 'Maggie'	High and Dry
The Man Who Watched Trains Go By	Paris Express
The Man Within	The Smugglers
Mandy	The Crash of Silence
Manuela	Stowaway Girl
A Matter of Life and Death	Stairway to Heaven
Men of Two Worlds	Witch Doctor
Midshipman Easy	Men of the Sea
The Million Pound Note	Man with a Million
Morning Departure	Operation Disaster
My Teenage Daughter	Teenage Bad Girl
The Naked Truth	Your Past is Showing
The Net	Project M7
The Night Has Eyes	Terror House
Night of the Eagle	Burn Witch Burn
Nobody Lives Forever	The High Commissioner
Nor the Moon by Night	Elephant Gun
Northwest Frontier	Flame over India
Odd Man Out	Gang War
Once a Jolly Swagman	Maniacs on Wheels
The Passionate Friends	One Woman's Story
The Passionate Stranger	A Novel Affair
Penn of Pennsylvania	The Courageous Mr Penn
Perfect Strangers	Vacation from Marriage
Pimpernel Smith	Mister V
The Planter's Wife	Outpost in Malaya
Pretty Polly	A Matter of Innocence
Q Planes	Clouds over Europe
Quartermass and the Pit	Five Million Years to Earth
The Quatermass Xperiment	The Creeping Unknown
Quatermass II	Enemy from Space
The Raging Moon	Long Ago Tomorrow
The Rake's Progress	Notorious Gentleman
Rockets Galore	Mad Little Island
The Romantic Age	Naughty Arlette
Rough Shoot	Shoot First
Sailor Beware	Panic in the Parlor
St Martin's Lane	The Sidewalks of London
Saraband for Dead Lovers	Saraband
Sea of Sand	Desert Patrol
Seagulls over Sorrento	Crest of the Wave
The Seekers	Land of Fury
Seven Waves Away	Abandon Ship
The Ship That Died of Shame	P.T. Raiders
The Shop at Sly Corner	The Code of Scotland Yard
The Siege of Pinchgut	Four Desperate Men
Singlehanded	Sailor of the King
Sixty Glorious Years	Queen of Destiny
Sky West and Crooked	Gypsy Girl
The Small Back Room	Hour of Glory
The Smallest Show on Earth	Big Time Operators
The Small Voice	Hideout
Soft Beds, Hard Battles	Undercover Hero

The Sound Barrier	Breaking the Sound Barrier
South of Algiers	The Golden Mask
The Spy in Black	U-Boat 29
The Squeaker	Murder on Diamond Row
The Story of Esther Costello	The Golden Virgin
Street Corner	Both Sides of the Law
Summer of the Seventeenth Doll	Season of Passion
The Tall Headlines	The Frightened Bride
Taste of Fear	Scream of Fear
Tell England	The Battle of Gallipoli
These Dangerous Years	Dangerous Youth
They Flew Alone	Wings and the Woman
They Made Me a Fugitive	I Became a Criminal
Tom Brown's Schooldays	Adventures at Rugby
Top Secret	Mr Potts Goes to Moscow
A Town Like Alice	The Rape of Malaya
The Trials of Oscar Wilde	The Man with the Green Carnation
Trottie True	The Gay Lady
Tudor Rose	Nine Days a Queen
24 Hours in a Woman's Life	Affair in Monte Carlo
Uncle Silas	The Inheritance
Venetian Bird	The Assassin
The Voice of Merrill	Murder Will Out
Waterfront	Waterfront Women
The Way Ahead	Immortal Battalion
The Way to the Stars	Johnny in the Clouds
The Weak and the Wicked	Young and Willing
Went the Day Well?	48 Hours
Where No Vultures Fly	Ivory Hunter
Whisky Galore	Tight Little Island
White Cradle Inn	High Fury
The White Unicorn	Bad Sister
Who Goes There?	The Conqueror Worm
The Woman in Question	Five Angles on Murder
Women of Twilight	Twilight Women
The Woman with No Name	Her Panelled Door
Yangtse Incident	Battle Hell
Yield to the Night	Blonde Sinner
Young and Innocent	The Girl Was Young
The Young Lovers	Chance Meeting
Zee and Co	X, Y and Zee

Index